THE BOOK OF PRESIDENTS

THE BOOK OF
PRESIDENTS

BY TIM TAYLOR

ARNO PRESS

A NEW YORK TIMES COMPANY

New York • 1972

Library of Congress Cataloging in Publication Data

Taylor, Tim, 1920–
    The book of presidents.

    "The Constitution": p.
    1. Presidents—United States—Biography.
I. United States. Constitution. 1972. II. Title.
E176.1.T226   973′.099 [B]   74-164708
ISBN 0-405-00226-2

Published in the United States by Arno Press

Manufactured in the United States of America

To Lynne,

with all my love

INTRODUCTION

When the Bibliography Division of the Library of Congress first published its selected list of biographies of the Presidents of the United States in 1926, it consisted of a mere 75 entries. Admittedly, there had been many more than 75 books published prior to 1926 about the Presidents, but the bibliographer wisely chose to ignore the considerable number of campaign biographies, memoirs of White House gardeners, and other inconsequential treatments of presidential data.

The literature on the Presidency and the 36 men who have held that office has proliferated at an ever-increasing rate since 1926. Since the beginning of the New Deal, no year has passed without the addition of several dozen volumes to the shelves of presidential lore in our libraries' history divisions, and the years marking the quadrennial contests for the highest of offices have always brought forth a spate of specialized books on the Presidents and the Presidency. Just as the office of the Presidency has grown, so has the literature on the office and the men who have occupied it. The Library of Congress's current selected list of references on the subject, Donald H. Mugridge's remarkable compilation, contains more than fifteen hundred titles, and yet it barely scratches the surface of available material.

My intention in *The Book of Presidents* was to compile the most comprehensive collection of presidential lore in a single volume. This is not to say that it contains all of the available information on any or all of the Presidents. Rather, it is one author's selection of presidential fact from the vast library that now exists. Although many people have offered suggestions and advice, I alone am responsible for any mistakes of commission or omission in the book.

The Book of Presidents is a chronology. Separate chapters are devoted to each of the 37 Presidents of the United States. Each chapter is divided into five major sections, beginning with biographical data and followed by sections concerning the EARLY YEARS of the future President, his significant public achievements prior to election (NATIONAL PROMINENCE), his presidential ADMINISTRATION or administrations, and the period, if any, following his term of office (THE FORMER PRESIDENT). Each chapter also includes sub-sections concerning elections, conventions (post-1832), inaugurations or oath-taking ceremonies, the Vice President, the Cabinet, and the Supreme Court.

A STATISTICAL SUMMARY, in which all major statistics are grouped alphabetically by subject for quick reference, is included in the Appendix.

The research for this book was done over a period of 28 years. To gather the information, literally tens of thousands of sources were examined, including public documents, newspapers and periodicals, letters, biographies, collective biographies, memoirs of presidents, and books written by or for presidents' relatives, associates, contemporaries, friends, and enemies. Much of this book was researched in the Library of Congress, the National Archives, the Frederick Lewis Allen Room of the New York Public Library, *The New York Times* library and morgue, and numerous historical society and presidential libraries.

Since *The Book of Presidents* was conceived for the general reader, rather than the scholar or specialist, I have omitted footnotes and bibliography.

All acknowledgements are necessarily inadequate. Several hundreds of individuals have been of assistance over the years, commencing with Stephen R. Early, Franklin D. Roosevelt's press secretary, who did not know in 1944 that his kindness to a young reporter led to the original entries in my earliest file on the Presidents and the Presidency. Press officers of virtually every governmental agency were helpful, as well as scores of elected and appointed officials of the executive, legislative, and judicial branches of the federal government. I feel duty bound to single out Francis R. Valeo, Secretary of the U. S. Senate, who has answered query after query after query over the years.

Invaluable assistance was rendered by my resourceful associates, Diane Moeller and Marc Woodward, both of whom devoted so much time and effort over several years to *The Book of Presidents*. My editor at Arno Press, Nancy Lincoln, who guided the book from manuscript to type, deserves a special word of appreciation.

A wife who can coexist with a husband who spends years cluttering up the house with hundreds of files and thousands of pages of notes and manuscript deserves the riches of the earth, and this is the due of my wife, Lynne Rogers, who never complained (well, hardly ever) at the many sacrifices I asked her to make during the writing of this book. But, more importantly, I must acknowledge the positive contributions of my wife. Her criticism and suggestions were vitally important to the final form of this book. I am a very lucky man.

Tim Taylor

New York City
June 7, 1972

All entries in *The Book of Presidents* are based on information available as of January 1, 1972.

CONTENTS

THE BOOK OF PRESIDENTS

First President

GEORGE WASHINGTON

Full name: George Washington
- He was the first of 17 presidents who did not have middle initials or middle names.

Date of birth: Feb. 22, 1732 (Feb. 11, 1731/1732 O.S.)
- He was the first of three presidents who were born in February.
- He was the first of four presidents who were born before the Gregorian (new style) calendar replaced the Julian (old style) calendar in England and the British colonies, 1752.

Place of birth: Family estate on south bank of Potomac River, near mouth of Popes Creek, later known as Wakefield, Westmoreland County, Va.
- He was the first of two presidents who were born in Westmoreland County. The other was Monroe.
- He was the first of eight presidents who were born in Virginia.
- His birthplace was destroyed by fire, probably on Christmas Day, Dec. 25, 1779.
- The house site and the family burial ground were donated to the United States by the heirs and the State of Virginia, 1882. The Wakefield National Memorial Association was organized to recover and restore

the birthplace grounds, 1923. The estate again became the property of the United States as the George Washington Birthplace National Monument, Jan. 23, 1930.
- Congress authorized the erection of a house at Wakefield to resemble the birthplace as much as possible. Since no records indicating the appearance of the original house exist, the design was based on those of surviving houses of the period. Therefore, the eight-room mansion, constructed in 1931–1932, is not a copy of the birthplace, but represents a Virginia plantation house of the eighteenth century.
- The estate, enlarged by the Wakefield Association with the aid of John D. Rockefeller, Jr., consists of 393.68 acres. Administered by the National Park Service, it is open to the public daily, 9 A.M. to 5 P.M., extended hours during the summer season. Admission: $1 per car (50 cents per person in buses), June 14 to Labor Day. No charge for educational groups with reservations.

Family lineage: English
- He was the first of 12 presidents who were of English ancestry.

Religious denomination: Episcopalian
- He was the first of nine presidents who

1

were Episcopalians.
College: None
• He was the first of nine presidents who did not attend college.
• He was the first of 15 presidents who were not graduated from college.
• In 1749, he was given an appointment as surveyor by the College of William and Mary. This was equivalent to a degree in engineering.

PARENTS AND SIBLINGS

Father's name: Augustine Washington
Date of birth: probably 1694
Place of birth: Westmoreland County, Va.
Occupations: Farmer, planter
Date of death: Apr. 12, 1743
• George was 11 years, 49 days old when his father died.
Place of death: Ferry Farm, King George County, Va.
Age at death: about 49 years

Father's first wife: Jane Butler Washington
• Her name was Jenny, but it was changed to Jane by stipulation in her father's will.
Date of birth: Dec. 24, 1699
Place of birth: Westmoreland County, Va.
Children: 4; 3 sons, 1 daughter
• Butler was born in 1716; Lawrence in 1718; Augustine in 1719 or 1720; and Jane in 1722. Butler died in infancy.
• Washington was the first of six presidents who had half brothers or half sisters.
Date of death: Nov. 24, 1729
Place of death: probably Popes Creek, Westmoreland County, Va.
Age at death: 29 years, 335 days

Mother's name: Mary Ball Washington
Date of birth: probably during winter of 1708–1709
Place of birth: Lancaster County, Va.
Date of marriage: Mar. 6, 1731
• Washington was the first of five presidents whose mothers were second wives.
Children: 6; 4 sons, 2 daughters
• George was born in 1732; Betty in 1733; Samuel in 1734; John Augustine in 1736; Charles in 1738; and Mildred in 1739. Mildred died in infancy.
• George was his mother's eldest child.
• He was his father's fifth child.
• He was the first of five presidents who came from families of ten children.

Date of death: Aug. 25, 1789
• Washington was the first of ten presidents whose mothers lived to see their sons' inauguration or oath-taking days. Mrs. Washington did not attend the ceremony.
Place of death: Fredericksburg, Va.
Age at death: about 81 years

MARRIAGE

Date of marriage: Jan. 6, 1759
Place of marriage: New Kent County, Va.
• Washington was the first of four presidents who were married in Virginia.
Age at marriage: 26 years, 318 days
• He was the first of 27 presidents who married in their twenties.
Years married: 40 years, 342 days

Wife's name: Martha Dandridge Custis Washington
• Washington was the first of six presidents who married widows. In 1749, she had married Daniel Parke Custis, who died in 1757.
• She was the first of 33 first ladies.
• She was the first of 40 wives of presidents.

Note: All first ladies are wives of presidents, but seven wives of presidents were not first ladies.

Date of birth: June 21, 1731
• She was the first of four first ladies who were born in June.
• She was the first of five wives of presidents who were born in June.
Place of birth: New Kent County, Va.
• She was the first of three first ladies who were born in Virginia.
• She was the first of six wives of presidents who were born in Virginia.
Wife's mother: Frances Jones Dandridge
Wife's father: John Dandridge, planter
Age at marriage: 27 years, 199 days
• She was the first of 26 first ladies who married in their twenties.
• She was the first of 30 wives of presidents who married in their twenties.
Years older than husband: 246 days
• She was the first of six first ladies who were older than their husbands.
• She was the first of six wives of presidents who were older than their husbands.
Children: None
• Washington was the first of six presidents who were childless.

•His wife had had four children by her first husband, two of whom died in infancy. The children who lived were John Parke Custis and Martha Parke Custis.

•He was the first of three presidents who had stepchildren.

•In 1781, the two youngest of his stepson's four children, Eleanor (Nelly) Parke Custis and George Washington Parke Custis, moved to Mount Vernon. The latter's daughter, Mary, married Robert E. Lee, 1831.

Years she survived her husband: 2 years, 159 days

•She was the first of 21 first ladies who survived their husbands.

•She was the first of 23 wives of presidents who survived their husbands.

Date of death: May 22, 1802

Place of death: Mount Vernon, Va.

•She was the first of three first ladies who died in Virginia.

•She was the second of four wives of presidents who died in Virginia. Martha Jefferson had died in 1782.

Age at death: 70 years, 335 days

•She had celebrated her 70th birthday, June 21, 1801.

•She was the first of 16 first ladies who lived to be 70.

•She was the first of 17 wives of presidents who lived to be 70.

Place of burial: Mount Vernon, Va.

•She was the first of six first ladies who were buried in Virginia.

•She was the second of seven wives of presidents who were buried in Virginia.

EARLY YEARS

Mar. 11–Apr. 13, 1748, accompanied surveying party that charted western estate of Lord Fairfax, beyond Blue Ridge Mountains

May 5, 1749, received license as surveyor from College of William and Mary, Williamsburg, Va.

•Washington was the first of three presidents who were surveyors.

July 20, 1749, appointed official surveyor of newly formed Culpeper County, Va.

•This was his first public office.

•He purchased much land during the three years that he worked as a professional surveyor. He had bought or inherited nearly five thousand acres by the time he was 21.

Sept. 28, 1751–Jan. 28, 1752, accompanied his half brother, Lawrence, to Barbados, British West Indies

•This was his first and only sea voyage, his only visit to foreign soil. While in Barbados, Nov. 3 to Dec. 21, he contracted smallpox.

Nov. 4, 1752, initiated into fraternal order of Free and Accepted Masons, Fredericksburg, Va.

•He was the first of 13 presidents who were Masons.

Nov. 6, 1752, appointed district adjutant of Virginia by Governor Robert Dinwiddie

•This was Washington's first military appointment. He was one of four adjutants; his rank was major.

Feb. 22, 1753, his 21st birthday

•This was the first year that his birthday fell

on the 22nd, the Gregorian calendar having been accepted in 1752. Privately, he continued to celebrate his birthday on the 11th.

Aug. 4, 1753, degree of Master Mason conferred by Fredericksburg Lodge No. 4, Fredericksburg, Va.

Oct. 31, 1753–Jan. 16, 1754, delivered English ultimatum to French

•As representative of Governor Dinwiddie, he journeyed to northwestern Pennsylvania and delivered an order to withdraw to the French commandant of Fort Le-Boeuf, now Waterford. He returned to Virginia with information that the French would fight to hold the Ohio valley.

•His account of the mission, *The Journal of Major George Washington*, was published shortly after his return to Virginia. This was his only book.

•He was the first of 21 presidents who wrote books that were published during their lifetimes.

Mar. 15, 1754, commissioned lieutenant colonel of Virginia regiment

Apr. 2, 1754, commanded small force of militia dispatched to build forts and defend outposts

•This was his first military command.

May 28, 1754, defeated small French scouting party

•This was his first military victory, insignificant as it was.

May 30–June 3, 1754, built Fort Necessity at

Great Meadows, east of present Union-town, Pa.

June 4, 1754, surrendered Fort Necessity to superior force of French and Indians
• This was his first military defeat.

Nov. 5, 1754, resigned his colonelcy
• Governor Dinwiddie ordered the regiment divided into companies. When Washington was offered the reduced rank of captain, he resigned.

Dec. 17, 1754, acquired Mount Vernon
• He rented the estate from Colonel George Lee and Mrs. Lee. The latter was the former Anne (or Nancy) Fairfax Washington, widow of Washington's half brother, Lawrence. The agreement ran for the term of Mrs. Lee's life interest in the estate. The rent ranged from £80 to £175 annually, dependent on the price of tobacco.
• Washington was the first of nine presidents who owned slaves.

May 10, 1755, appointed aide-de-camp to Major General Edward Braddock
• He joined the staff of Braddock—commander of all British forces in America—as a volunteer without rank.

July 9, 1755, had two horses shot from under him, four bullets pierce his uniform during ambush of Braddock's army
• Braddock was mortally wounded during the ambuscade by the French and Indians, on the Monongahela River near Turtle Creek, Pa. A total of 63 officers and 914 men of the British force of 1,459 were killed or wounded.

Aug. 13, 1755, appointed colonel and commander-in-chief of Virginia regiment

Feb. 4, 1756, set out for Boston, Mass., from Winchester, Va.
• His right to command a military contingent had been challenged by Captain John Dagworthy of Maryland, who held a royal commission. Governor William Shirley of Massachusetts, who was senior to the governors of Virginia and Maryland, decreed that Washington should command, Mar. 5.
• This was his first trip to Philadelphia, New York City and New England. He returned to Virginia, Apr. 2.

July 24, 1758, elected to Virginia assembly, House of Burgesses
• This was his entry into politics.

Nov. 14, 1758, given command of brigade for expedition against Fort Duquesne
• The brigade arrived at the burned and abandoned French fort, Nov. 27. The English named the rebuilt post Fort Pitt.

Dec. 5, 1758, resigned his commission

Jan. 6, 1759, married Martha Dandridge Custis, New Kent County, Va.

Feb. 22, 1759, assumed his seat in House of Burgesses, Williamsburg, Va.
• He was originally a member from Frederick County, later represented Fairfax County, served until 1774.
• George Mercer, a fellow member, described him as "straight as an Indian, measuring six feet two inches in his stockings and weighing 175 pounds. . . ." He probably weighed better than 200 pounds.
• He was the first of 14 presidents who were six feet tall or taller.
• The others were Jefferson, Monroe, Jackson, Tyler, Buchanan, Lincoln, Garfield, Arthur, Taft, Harding, Franklin D. Roosevelt, Kennedy, and Lyndon B. Johnson.

Apr. 6 or 7, 1759, arrived with his wife and her two children, Mount Vernon
• The children were John (Jackie) Parke Custis, who was four years old, and Martha (Patsy) Parke Custis, two.

Mar. 14, 1761, inherited Mount Vernon
• He inherited the estate at the death of Mrs. George Lee, according to the terms of his half brother's will.
• Mount Vernon, off state highway 235, is maintained by the Mount Vernon Ladies' Association. Open to the public daily, 9 A.M. to 5 P.M., Mar. 1 to Oct. 1, and 9 A.M. to 4 P.M., Oct. 1 to Mar. 1. Admission: adults, $1.25; children and student and youth groups, grades 1 through 12, 50 cents; student and youth groups, grades 1 through 6, Sept. 1 to Mar. 1, free.

May 16, 1769, introduced nonimportation resolutions
• The resolutions, framed by George Mason, were adopted unanimously by the House of Burgesses. They stated that Virginians could be taxed only by Virginians and condemned the British threat to ship Americans charged with a crime to England for trial.

Oct. 5–Dec. 1, 1770, made exploratory trip to junction of Ohio and Great Kanawha Rivers

1770–1772, secured more than twenty thousand acres of western lands, extended his holdings of Virginia property to more than twelve thousand acres

May 20, 1772, sat for first portrait

•This portrait was painted by Charles Willson Peale.

June 5, 1772, began operating ferry

•He took title to the ferry, as well as its Virginia anchorage and a fishery, when the owner, Captain John Posey, was unable to repay a long-overdue loan. He operated the ferry, which crossed the Potomac to Maryland, until 1790.

May 10, 1773, departed for New York City

•He attended a testimonial dinner for General Thomas Gage in New York City, May 27. He and the British commander had served together under Braddock. He returned to Virginia, June 8.

June 19, 1773, his stepdaughter, Patsy Custis, died

Feb. 3, 1774, attended wedding of his stepson, John Parke Custis, and Eleanor Calvert, Mount Airy, Md.

Aug. 1, 1774, attended first Virginia provincial convention, Williamsburg

Aug. 5, 1774, chosen as one of seven Virginia delegates to First Continental Congress

Sept. 5–Oct. 26, 1774, attended First Continental Congress, Philadelphia, Pa.

•He was the first of five presidents who were members of the Continental congresses.

May 10–June 23, 1775, attended Second Continental Congress, Philadelphia, Pa.

•He had departed from Mount Vernon, May 4. He was not to return to his home for more than six years.

June 16, 1775, accepted commission as commanding general of Continental Army

•He was the first soldier of the American military forces.

•He was the first American general.

•He was the first of 12 presidents who were generals.

THE REVOLUTION

1775

July 3, took command of Continental Army, Cambridge, Mass.

•Washington was the first of three presidents who served in the Revolutionary War.

•He was the first of 21 presidents who served in the military during wartime.

Sept. 2, commissioned first naval officer, Captain Nicholas Broughton of Marblehead, Mass.

Oct. 13, authorized Colonel John Glover of Massachusetts to arm fishing vessels

•The first American naval force was not ready for sea duty until Oct. 29. Congress adopted rules for the regulation of the navy, Nov. 28.

Nov. 5, first town named in his honor

•The town of Forks of Tar River, N.C., became the first community to take his name.

•In addition to the national capital and the state of Washington, there are presently 31 counties and 17 communities named in his honor.

1776

Jan. 1, raised flag of United Colonies, Cambridge, Mass.

•This was the first time that the flag was raised officially in the colonies. It had 13 alternate red and white stripes, and the canton contained the crosses of St. George and St. Andrew.

Mar. 4–5, occupied and fortified Dorchester Heights, Mass.

•Since the heights commanded Boston, the occupation forced General William Howe to evacuate the city, Mar. 17.

Mar. 20, entered Boston with main body of army

Mar. 25, was awarded Congressional Medal, then highest award, for capture of Boston

Mar. 27, shifted army from Boston to New York City

Apr. 3, received honorary degree of Doctor of Laws, Harvard College, Cambridge, Mass.

•This was the first of his five honorary degrees.

•He received similar degrees from Yale in 1781; the University of Pennsylvania in 1783; Washington College of Chestertown, Md., in 1789; and Brown University in 1790.

Apr. 4–13, journeyed to New York City

•His first headquarters in New York City was on Pearl Street.

May 23–June 5, conferred with Congress, Philadelphia, Pa.

June 27, Thomas Hickey hanged, New York City
• Hickey, a member of Washington's personal bodyguard, was hanged before a crowd of twenty thousand people. Hickey had been convicted of conspiring to kill or capture Washington.
July 9, ordered Declaration of Independence read to army, New York City
July 12, refused to accept letter from Admiral Richard Howe
• The letter from the British naval commander was addressed to George Washington, Esq., and gave details of the king's offer of pardon to those colonists who withdrew from rebellion.
Aug. 27, Battle of Long Island
• A superior force of British and Hessian troops fell on the unprotected American left flank at Jamaica Pass, inflicted nearly 1,500 casualties, including 300 killed. British and Hessian losses were about 375. The fleeing Americans retreated to Brooklyn Heights. Admiral Howe failed to follow up his advantage and, inexplicably, pulled back his troops.
Aug. 29–30, withdrew army to Manhattan
Sept. 12, decided to evacuate New York City
Sept. 16, repulsed British attack below Harlem Heights
Oct. 21–28, withdrew army northward to White Plains, N.Y.
• A rearguard of twelve hundred was left at Fort Washington, near present West 183rd Street and Fort Washington Avenue, New York City.
Oct. 28, Battle of White Plains
• The Americans were forced to retreat once more, but again the British failed to follow up their advantage. American losses were about 150 killed and wounded; British and Hessian losses slightly more than 300.
Oct. 31–Nov. 1, withdrew army to North Castle heights
Nov. 14–15, inspected Fort Washington
• He crossed the Hudson from Fort Lee, N.J. and returned to New Jersey during the night.
Nov. 16, Fort Washington captured
• The garrison had been reinforced by nearly 1,600 troops during the previous week. About 50 Americans were killed and 250 wounded during the assault by 8,000 British and Hessians. About 2,800, including the wounded, were captured when the fort fell. The enemy lost about 450 killed and wounded.
• The British had been presented with the plans of Fort Washington by Ensign William Demont (or Dement) of the 5th Pennsylvania battalion, who had deserted, Nov. 3.
Nov. 20–Dec. 8, retreated across New Jersey into Pennsylvania
Dec. 25–26, Battle of Trenton
• Crossing the Delaware River at night, the Americans won their first major victory. More than nine hundred prisoners were taken and valuable military supplies were captured during the surprise attack. The Americans returned to the south bank of the Delaware, Dec. 27.
Dec. 30–31, again crossed Delaware, reoccupied abandoned Trenton

1777

Jan. 3, Battle of Princeton
• Nearly 8,000 British troops were prepared to destroy the American army in Trenton, but the colonials slipped around the left flank at night and attacked Princeton, inflicted about 275 casualties at a cost of 40 killed or wounded.
Jan. 6, established winter headquarters, Morristown, N.J.
Jan. 25, commanded all who supported British to take oath of allegiance to United States within 30 days or withdraw behind British lines
May 1, appointed Alexander Hamilton as aide-de-camp
May 29–July 3, maintained headquarters at Middlebrook, N.J.
Aug. 1, conferred with members of Second Continental Congress, Philadelphia
Aug. 24, marched army through Philadelphia
Sept. 11, Battle of Brandywine Creek
• The British outmaneuvered the Americans, fell on their right rear, and inflicted more than 1,200 casualties in the battle north of Chad's Ford, now Chadds Ford. The British lost about 575 killed and wounded.
• The enemy occupied Philadelphia, Sept. 26. Congress had fled to Lancaster, Pa., Sept. 19, and moved on to York, Pa., Sept. 30.

Oct. 4, Battle of Germantown
• The Americans lost about one thousand men in this audacious, though ill-advised attack on British headquarters. A heavy fog aided the attackers in the early stages, but added to the confusion at the height of the encounter. The Americans fled in panic. However, morale was high after the colonials regrouped since they mistakenly believed that they had come close to victory.
Nov. 5, informed of major victory at Saratoga, N.Y.
• More than fifty-seven hundred British and Hessian troops under General John Burgoyne laid down their arms, Oct. 17.
Nov. 9, wrote General Thomas Conway
• By inference, he asked for an explanation of a letter in which Conway was alleged to have written: "Heaven has been determined to save your country; or a weak General and bad Councellors would have ruined it."
• A plan to replace the commander-in-chief, led by Samuel ("Sam") Adams and other New England leaders, has come to be known as the "Conway Cabal." Conway was a minor player in the scheme, if, in fact, he held any role whatsoever.
Nov. 23, informed Congress that British controlled Delaware River, had firm possession of Philadelphia
Nov. 30, decided on Valley Forge, Pa., as winter quarters
Dec. 19, established headquarters at Valley Forge

1778

Feb. 23, welcomed von Steuben, Valley Forge
• Baron Friedrich Wilhelm Augustus von Steuben, who was appointed inspector-general with the rank of major general, May 5, organized and disciplined the amateur army.
May 6, announced to army that France had become ally of U.S.
• The commercial and military treaty with France, which was signed, Feb. 6, was ratified by Congress, May 4.
• This was the only treaty of alliance made by the U.S. prior to the North Atlantic Treaty Organization (NATO) agreement, which was signed in 1949.

June 19, broke camp at Valley Forge
• The British had evacuated Philadelphia, June 18, and set out toward New York City with the Americans in pursuit.
June 28, Battle of Monmouth, N.J.
• Disorder and confusion marked this encounter, fought in 100 degree heat. Major General Charles Lee's order to retreat was countermanded by Washington. Losses were about equal for both sides, slightly more than 350 killed or wounded. In addition, about 600 enemy troops, including about 450 Hessians, deserted. The British slipped away after midnight, retreated to Sandy Hook, June 30, and reached New York City, July 5.
• Monmouth was the last major confrontation in the North.
July 4–Aug. 12, court-martial of General Lee
• Lee, who was found guilty of disobedience of orders, misbehavior before the enemy, and disrespect to the commander-in-chief, was suspended from command for one year.
July 20, moved army to White Plains, N.Y.
Sept. 16, moved army to Fredericksburg, N.Y.
Nov. 28, set out for winter headquarters, Middlebrook, N.J.
• He stationed nine brigades of the army west of the Hudson River, seven of the nine at Middlebrook. He stationed five brigades east of the river, three at Danbury, Conn., and two at Fishkill, N.Y.
• He arrived at Middlebrook, Dec. 11.
Dec. 22, arrived for conferences with Congress, Philadelphia

1779

Jan. 15, suggested defensive campaign to Congress
• His plan was adopted.
Feb. 5, returned to Middlebrook headquarters
Mar. 3, Battle of Briar Creek, Ga.
• When Savannah fell, Dec. 29, 1778, followed by Augusta, Jan. 29, all Georgia was under the control of the British.
• This attempt to retake Augusta cost more than 350 men at Briar Creek.
May 31, ordered expedition against Indians of Six Nations

• The frontier settlements of New York and Pennsylvania had been terrorized for more than a year. The expedition, led by General John Sullivan and General James Clinton, defeated a force of fifteen hundred Tories and Indians at Newtown, near present Elmira, N.Y., Aug. 29.

June 2–7, shifted army to Smith's Clove, N.Y.

• He positioned the army between the enemy and West Point, which had become vulnerable, June 1, when the British captured Stony Point on the west bank and Verplanck's Point on the east bank of the Hudson.

June 21, established headquarters at New Windsor, N.Y.

• New Windsor was six miles above West Point on the Hudson.

July 4, granted general pardon on Independence Day to all American soldiers under sentence of death

July 14, ordered General Anthony Wayne to attack Stony Point, if feasible

• "Mad Anthony" Wayne's corps of light infantry took Stony Point, July 15–16, killed or wounded 100, and captured the remainder of the garrison of about 625 men. After destroying the works and removing 12 cannon and substantial stores, the Americans evacuated the post, July 18.

July 21, established headquarters at West Point

• He remained at West Point until Nov. 28, where he supervised the construction of strong defenses at the fort.

Aug. 28, reported successful raid on Paulus Hook to Congress

• Paulus Hook, now in Jersey City, N.J., was attacked, Aug. 19, by troops under Captain Henry ("Light-horse Harry") Lee. More than 150 prisoners were taken during the surprise raid.

Oct. 21, reported imminent evacuation of Newport, R.I., to Congress

• The British, who had occupied Rhode Island for almost three years, evacuated Newport, Oct. 25.

Nov. 1, reported British evacuation of Stony Point and Verplanck's Point to Congress

Dec. 1, established winter quarters at Morristown, N.J.

Note: The earliest known application of the phrase, "Father of His Country," appeared in a German almanac, the *Nord America-*

nische Kalender for 1779, published at Lancaster, Pa. The phrase used was *"Des Landes Vater."*

1780

Jan. 14, ordered raid on British post, Staten Island

• A detachment of twenty-five hundred under Major General Lord Stirling (William Alexander, who claimed the earldom of Stirling) crossed the ice from Elizabethtown, N.J., in five hundred sleighs, Jan. 14–15. The raid was unsuccessful since the enemy had received prior knowledge of the plan.

Jan. 23, first town incorporated with his name

• The community, Washington, Ga., is now a city, the county seat of Wilkes County.

May 10, received commission as lieutenant general and vice admiral of France

• The commission, brought to Morristown by the Marquis de Lafayette, insured Washington's authority as commander of the united forces of the U.S. and France.

June 1, informed of surrender of Charleston, S.C.

• The British had captured Charleston, May 12.

June 7, retreated to Short Hills, southeast of Morristown

• The British had landed at Elizabethtown Point from Staten Island during the night of June 6.

June 21, moved army to North River

• The British advanced from Elizabethtown, burned Springfield, N.J., then retired to the coast and crossed back to Staten Island.

June 27, moved army to Ramapo, N.J.

July 1, established headquarters at Preakness, N.J.

July 14, informed Congress of arrival of French fleet off Newport, R.I.

• The fleet had arrived, July 10. It consisted of eight ships of the line, two frigates, and two "bombs" (bomb-galliots) and carried five thousand French troops.

Aug. 1, moved army to King's Ferry, N.Y.

• An attack on New York City was planned when it was learned that the British had sailed in transports to the east, with Newport as their objective. When the British turned back, the plan was cancelled, and the army was ordered back to New Jersey.

Aug. 8, established headquarters at Tappan, N.J.

Aug. 23, moved army south to Teaneck, N.J.

•His headquarters were in present Englewood.

Sept. 4, moved army to base near Hackensack, N.J.

Sept. 5, learned of defeat near Camden, S.C.

•Lieutenant General Charles Cornwallis soundly defeated the southern army under General Horatio Gates, Aug. 16.

Sept. 18, departed for Connecticut conference with French leaders, Lieutenant General Rochambeau and Admiral Ternay

Sept. 20, ordered army back to Tappan, N.J.

Sept. 21–22, conferred with Rochambeau and Ternay, Hartford, Conn.

•While no definite plan of operations was decided upon, amicable relations were established.

Sept. 25, informed of desertion of General Benedict Arnold

•Washington arrived at Robinson House, Arnold's headquarters below West Point on the east side of the Hudson, about one hour after the traitor had departed.

Sept. 28, summoned board of officers to try Major John Andre as spy

•The board of 14 general officers found Andre guilty and sentenced him to death. The British officer was hanged at Tappan, Oct. 2.

Oct. 7, moved army to Paramus, N.J.

•He reestablished headquarters at Preakness, Oct. 8, and remained until Nov. 27.

Nov. 5, informed of victory at King's Mountain, S.C.

•The Battle of King's Mountain was a major victory over the British and supporting Tories by Virginia and Carolina mountain men, Oct. 7.

Nov. 27, detached troops to winter quarters

•The army was quartered near Morristown, N. J.; in Orange County, N. Y.; in the vicinity of Albany; and in the West Point area.

Dec. 6, established winter headquarters, New Windsor, N.Y.

1781

Jan. 3, informed of mutiny of Pennsylvania line

•About thirteen hundred Pennsylvania troops mutinied near Morristown and marched off toward Philadelphia to present their grievances to state officials, Jan. 1. An agreement satisfactory to the defectors and their superiors was reached at Trenton, Jan. 11.

Jan. 23, ordered New England troops to put down mutiny of New Jersey line

•New Jersey troops mutinied at Pompton, N.J., Jan. 20. Two leaders of the revolt were executed; order was restored.

Feb. 12, his birthday celebrated, Newport, R.I.

•This was the first public recognition of his birthday. The ceremonies (held on the 12th since the 11th was a Sunday) consisted of a parade of American and French troops, the firing of a salute, and the suspension of further labors for the day.

Feb. 17, informed Congress of victory at Cowpens, S.C.

•American forces under General Daniel Morgan defeated a British army at Cowpens, Jan. 17.

Mar. 2, departed from New Windsor for Newport conference with Rochambeau

•Washington arrived at Newport, Mar. 6, remained until Mar. 13, and returned to New Windsor, Mar. 20.

Mar. 5, informed that Congress had ratified Articles of Confederation

•Delayed since 1777, the articles were ratified, Mar. 1.

•Congress adopted a new title, "The United States in Congress Assembled," Mar. 2.

Apr. 4, informed of Battle of Guilford Court House, N.C.

•Outnumbered by more than two-to-one, the British were victorious, Mar. 15, but at a price of more than one-quarter of Cornwallis's nineteen hundred officers and men. General Nathaniel Greene forced the enemy to abandon the Carolinas and retreat to Virginia.

Apr. 24, received honorary degree of Doctor of Laws from Yale College

•This was the second of his five honorary degrees.

Apr. 30, chastized Lund Washington for saving Mount Vernon

•Lund Washington, the general's third cousin and manager of his estate, had supplied the British with provisions rather than see Mount Vernon burned to the ground. Washington wrote his overseer:

It would have been a less painful circumstance to me to have heard, that in consequence of your non-compliance with their request, they had burnt my house and laid the plantation in ruins. You ought to have considered yourself as my representative, and should have reflected on the bad example of communicating with the enemy, and making a voluntary offer of refreshments to them with a view to prevent a conflagration.

May 5, arranged to have his war papers recorded
•He appointed Colonel Richard Varick to superintend the recording of his papers.
May 21–22, conferred with Rochambeau, Wethersfield, Conn.
•A French and American operation against New York City was agreed upon, as well as an alternate plan "to extend our views to the Southward as circumstances and a naval superiority might render more necessary and eligible."
June 15, congratulated southern army under General Greene on successes in South Carolina
•The British had been forced to evacuate Camden and surrender Orangeburg, Fort Motte, and Fort Granby, May 10–15.
June 25, joined army at Peekskill encampment
July 7, with Rochambeau, reviewed combined French and American armies
•The junction of the allied forces occurred at Phillipsburg, N.Y., near Dobbs Ferry, July 6.
Aug. 14, abandoned plan to attack New York City, decided on southern campaign
•He received word that the French fleet had sailed from the West Indies for Chesapeake Bay and would be available from about Sept. 1 to Oct. 15.
Aug. 20–25, French and American armies crossed Hudson River
Aug. 30, with Rochambeau, arrived in Philadelphia, Pa.
Sept. 5, departed from Philadelphia for Head of Elk, Md.
•En route, at Chester, Pa., Sept. 5, he learned that the French fleet had reached Chesapeake Bay.
Sept. 9, arrived at Mount Vernon
•This was his first visit to his home in more

than six years. He remained until Sept. 12.
Sept. 14, arrived at Williamsburg, Va.
•He and Rochambeau conferred with Admiral François De Grasse aboard flagship, *Ville de Paris.*
•The French fleet of 28 ships of the line, plus transports carrying three thousand troops, had arrived off Yorktown, Va., Aug. 30, and moved out to sea to battle the British fleet. When De Grasse was joined by Admiral Louis Barras's squadron from Newport, Sept. 9, the outgunned British fleet sailed off for New York.
Sept. 14–24, combined armies moved from Head of Elk to Williamsburg in French transports
Sept. 25–26, allied armies assembled, Williamsburg
•His command numbered more than 17,-300, including 7,800 French troops. Cornwallis was badly outmanned, having only 9,750 men at Yorktown.
Sept. 28–29, Yorktown encircled
Sept. 30, learned Cornwallis had given up his outworks
Oct. 1–6, brought up siege guns
Oct. 6, congratulated General Greene on Eutaw Springs "victory"
•Greene had surprised the British forces at Eutaw Springs, S.C., Sept. 8. The Americans suffered more than five hundred casualties but inflicted heavier losses on the enemy. While Greene technically lost the battle, the weakened British were forced to withdraw to Charleston.
Oct. 6–7, advanced to within six hundred to eight hundred yards of most of British inner defense line
•A two-thousand-yard-long first parallel (entrenchment) was constructed during the night.
Oct. 10, full artillery bombardment began
•The battery of 52 guns, mostly French, nearly silenced the British cannon.
Oct. 11, ordered construction of second parallel
•The construction, roughly halfway between the first parallel and the enemy, was completed Oct. 14, except for ground commanded by British redoubts 9 and 10.
Oct. 14, witnessed assaults on redoubts
•The French captured redoubt 9, and an American unit commanded by Colonel Alexander Hamilton overran redoubt 10. Fatigue parties completed the second parallel that night.

Oct. 16, British counterattack repulsed
• When the early morning counterattack failed, Cornwallis realized that his position was desperate. A last-ditch attempt to break through the French-American line by crossing the York River at night was unsuccessful when a violent storm scattered the British boats.

Oct. 17, received proposal from Cornwallis of 24-hour truce for meeting of commissioners

Oct. 18, surrender terms settled at meeting of commissioners, Moore House, Yorktown

Oct. 19, British army surrendered
• Cornwallis, who pleaded illness, assigned his second in command, Brigadier General Charles O'Hara of the British Guards, to lead the surrender march. When O'Hara offered Cornwallis's sword to Washington, the American commander indicated that it should be accepted by his second in command, Major General Benjamin Lincoln.
• Casualties at Yorktown: British and Hessian, about 150 killed, 320 wounded, and 70 missing; French, about 60 killed, 190 wounded; American, about 25 killed, slightly more than 100 wounded.
• The Revolution had ended.

1781

Oct. 24, his communique regarding British surrender read to Congress, Philadelphia, Pa.

Nov. 5, departed from Yorktown
• Later that day, he learned of the death of John Parke Custis, who died at Eltham, New Kent County, Va. Custis, the only son of Martha Washington, was the father of the two Custis children raised by the Washingtons.

Nov. 12, visited his mother, Fredericksburg, Va.

Nov. 13, arrived at Mount Vernon
• He remained at his estate until Nov. 20.

Nov. 26, arrived at Philadelphia
• He received the congratulations of Congress, Nov. 28.

Dec. 30, presented with two stands of colors taken at Yorktown
• The presentation was made by the secretary of war, Benjamin Lincoln, in the name of Congress.

1782

Jan. 22, circulated letter to state governors in which he urged sums requisitioned by Congress be paid

Jan. 31, circulated second letter to state governors in which he urged completion of troop quotas as requested by Congress

Feb. 8, issued proclamation in which he offered pardons to all deserters who returned to army by June 1

Mar. 22, departed from Philadelphia for Newburgh, N.Y.
• He established headquarters at Newburgh, Mar. 31.

June 15, Washington College chartered, Chestertown, Md.
• This was the first college named in his honor. Degrees were awarded beginning in 1783. Washington College is the tenth oldest college in the U.S.
• Harvard was chartered in 1642; William and Mary in 1693; Yale in 1701; Princeton in 1746; Columbia in 1754; Pennsylvania in 1755; Brown in 1764; Rutgers in 1766; Dartmouth in 1769; and Washington in 1782.

June 24–July 2, visited posts in upper New York State
• He visited Albany, June 26; Saratoga Springs, June 29; Schenectady, June 30; returned to Newburgh, July 2.

July 15, conferred with Rochambeau, Philadelphia

Aug. 7, instituted Badge of Military Merit
• The "Purple Heart" was awarded to only a few Revolutionary War soldiers.

Aug. 18, informed of evacuation of Savannah, Ga.
• The British had occupied Savannah from Dec. 29, 1778, to July 11.

Sept. 1, moved army to Verplanck's Point, N.Y.

Sept. 16, first use of Great Seal of United States
• The Great Seal, which had been adopted by Congress, June 20, was used on a document that granted him the authority to consult with the British regarding prisoner exchange.

Sept. 19, junction of French and American armies, near Verplanck's Point
• The French had departed from Williamsburg, Va., June 23.

Oct. 22, French army departed for Boston, Mass.

Oct. 26, ordered army into winter quarters
• The army departed from Verplanck's Point, Oct. 26; crossed the Hudson to West Point, Oct. 27; arrived at New Windsor. N.Y. and winter quarters to the west, Oct. 28.
Oct. 28, established headquarters, Newburgh, N.Y.
Dec. 7–14, visited by Rochambeau, Newburgh
• This was the last meeting of the American and French commanders. Rochambeau sailed for France from Annapolis, Md., Jan. 11, 1783.
Dec. 24, French army sailed from Boston, Mass.
• The French forces had been under Washington's command for nearly two and a half years.

1783

Jan. 23, informed of evacuation of Charleston, S.C.
• The British had occupied Charleston from May 12, 1780 to Dec. 14, 1782.
Mar. 11, issued order that forbade rump meeting of disgruntled officers, Newburgh, N.Y.
• An anonymous call for a meeting of officers to discuss grievances about back pay, unpaid food and clothing accounts, and pensions had been circulated, Mar. 10.
Mar. 15, addressed authorized meeting of officers, Newburgh
• A second anonymous address had been circulated, Mar. 12, in which it was implied that the commander-in-chief was party to the complaints. At this meeting, which he ordered, he criticized the unsigned documents and appealed for reason. After he departed, the officers unanimously expressed confidence in the Congress and repudiated the "infamous propositions" in the second address.
• The anonymously-issued documents, which have come to be known as the Newburgh Addresses, were written by John Armstrong, who later served in the Senate, as ambassador to France, and as secretary of war under Madison.
Mar. 30, received communication from Congress that announced general treaty of peace had been signed
• Lafayette had notified Congress that the

treaty had been signed in Paris, Jan. 20. This communique arrived in Philadelphia, Mar. 23.
Apr. 18, ordered proclamation of Congress regarding cessation of hostilities published
• The proclamation was posted at the door of the New Building, Newburgh, at noon, Apr. 19.
May 6, conferred with British commander-in-chief, Sir Guy Carleton, Dobbs Ferry, N.Y.
May 8, received by Carleton with military honors aboard British sloop
• The first complimentary salute (17-gun) by Great Britain in honor of an officer of the U.S. was fired at Washington's departure.
June 8, circulated letter to state governors in which he urged stronger union of states
• This was the last official communication he issued as commander-in-chief.
June 19, elected president-general of Society of the Cincinnati, Newburgh
• The society had been formed by officers of the army, May 13. He served in this office until his death.
July 4, received honorary degree of Doctor of Laws from University of Pennsylvania
• This was the third of his five honorary degrees.
July 18, departed for tour of upper New York State
• He visited Albany, Saratoga Springs, Fort Edward, Ticonderoga, Crown Point, Schenectady, and Fort Schuyler. He traveled about 750 miles in 19 days, returning to Newburgh, Aug. 5.
Aug. 17, issued last order as commander-in-chief
• He appointed Major General Henry Knox in his place while he reported to Congress at Princeton, N.J. Congress sat at Princeton, June to November.
Aug. 18, departed from Newburgh for Princeton
• He was officially praised and congratulated on his military successes by Congress, Aug. 26.
Nov. 2, issued farewell address to army, Rocky Hill, N.J.
Nov. 3, army disbanded by general order of Congress
• The order, proclaimed Oct. 18, disbanded all but a small force that was stationed at West Point.
Nov. 25, took possession of New York City
• The British had evacuated the city at noon.

•He established headquarters at Fraunces'
Tavern, at Broad and Pearl Streets.
Dec. 4, took leave of his officers, Fraunces'
Tavern
•He said:
> With a heart full of love and grati-
> tude I now take leave of you. I most
> devoutly wish that your latter days
> may be as prosperous and happy as
> your former ones have been glori-
> ous and honorable.

Dec. 8–15, visited Philadelphia
Dec. 19, arrived at Annapolis, Md.
Dec. 23, resigned his commission as commander-in-chief, Annapolis
•He delivered his commission to the president of Congress and thus became a private citizen for the first time since June,
1775. He had served as commanding general for more than eight years and six
months.
•Congress sat at Annapolis in November
and December.
Dec. 24, departed for Mount Vernon
•He arrived at his estate the same day.

1784–1789

Jan, 1, 1784, acknowledged receipt of his
war papers
•He had received the 37 volumes of his Revolutionary War papers from Colonel Richard Varick.
May 4–18, 1784, attended first general
meeting of Society of the Cincinnati, Philadelphia
Sept. 1–Oct. 4, 1784, visited his western
lands
May 17, 1785, elected president of Potomac
Company, Alexandria, Va.
•The company was organized to link the
upper waters of the Ohio River with the
Potomac and other Virginia rivers. The
first corporate navigational improvement
for public use was achieved with the construction of a short canal and locks around
the Great Falls of the Potomac.
Dec. 5, 1785, received jackass from Charles
III, King of Spain
•The exportation of fullblooded jacks was
against Spanish law at the time. He named
the Spanish jack, *Royal Gift*. Later, he received a Maltese jack and two jennets from
Lafayette. He named the second jack,
Knight of Malta.

1785–1786, worked as his own plantation
manager
•Shortly after he returned to Mount Vernon, he divided his 4,500-acre estate into
five units—the mansion house farm and
four plantations, which were known as the
Union farm, Dogue Run farm, Muddy Hole
farm and the River farm. When at home,
he visited each farm each weekday, a tour
of about 15 miles.
Dec. 5, 1786, appointed one of seven Virginia delegates to proposed convention of
states
•He first declined the appointment but
later consented to go to Philadelphia.
Mar. 2–3, 1787, visited by "Parson" Weems
•The Reverend Mr. Mason Locke Weems
wrote and published the most widely read
biography of Washington. The first of the
more than 80 editions appeared in 1800.
Originally an 80-page pamphlet entitled,
*The Life and Memorable Actions of
George Washington*, it was amplified by
Weems until, in its seventh edition, it contained 228 pages. The hatchet and cherry
tree and cabbage-seed stories first ap-
peared in the fifth edition (1806), along
with other Weemsiana.
May 9, 1787, departed from Mount Vernon
for Philadelphia
•He arrived, May 13.
May 25, 1787, unanimously elected presi-
dent of federal convention, Philadelphia
•The convention had been scheduled to be-
gin on May 14, but a quorum was not ob-
tained until May 25.
July 31, 1787, visited Valley Forge, Pa.
•The convention adjourned from July 26 to
Aug. 6.
September, 1787, charter granted to Wash-
ington Academy, Washington, Pa.
•The academy became Washington College
in 1806, and Washington and Jefferson Col-
lege in 1865.
Sept. 17, 1787, signed Constitution
•He addressed the convention for the first
and only time on this last day of the session.
•He was the first of two presidents who
signed the Constitution. The other was
Madison.
• *See* Constitution, pages 637–645.
Sept. 18, 1787, departed from Philadelphia
for Mount Vernon
•He arrived, Sept. 22.
Dec. 7, 1787, Delaware ratified Constitu-
tion

• Delaware was the first state to ratify the Constitution.

• Pennsylvania ratified, Dec. 12; New Jersey, Dec. 18; Georgia, Jan. 2, 1788; Connecticut, Jan. 9; Massachusetts, Feb. 6; Maryland, Apr. 28; South Carolina, May 23; and New Hampshire, June 21.

• New Hampshire was the ninth and decisive state to ratify the Constitution.

• See Constitution, Article VII, page 642.

Jan. 18, 1788, elected chancellor of College of William and Mary, Williamsburg, Va.

• He accepted the office of chancellor, Apr. 30.

• He was the first of two presidents who were chancellors of William and Mary. The other was Tyler.

June 26, 1788, Virginia ratified Constitution

July 26, 1788, New York ratified Constitution

Jan. 7, 1789, cast vote for presidential elector from his district, Alexandria, Va.

• Virginia was one of three states whose presidential electors were chosen by popular vote. The others were Maryland and Pennsylvania.

• See Constitution, Article II, Section I, pages 639–640.

Feb. 2, 1789, cast vote for congressman from his district

• See Constitution, Article I, pages 637–639.

Feb. 4, 1789, presidential electors cast ballots, New York City

• See Election of 1789, below.

Mar. 4–6, 1789, borrowed £600 to discharge debts, pay costs of trip to New York City, "if I go thither"

Mar. 7–9, 1789, visited his mother, Fredericksburg, Va.

• This was his last visit with his mother, who died, Aug. 25.

Apr. 1, 1789, first quorum of House of Representatives, New York City

• The first meeting, Mar. 4, had lacked a quorum. Deliberations began, Apr. 8.

Apr. 6, 1789, first quorum of Senate; first session of 1st Congress

• Ballots cast by presidential electors were officially counted.

• Washington and Adams were officially declared elected.

• The administration controlled both the Senate and the House of Representatives. The Senate (26 members) consisted of 17 members of the administration and nine opponents. The House (64 members) consisted of 38 members of the administration and 26 opponents.

Apr. 14, 1789, officially notified of election by Secretary of Congress Charles Thomson

Apr. 16, 1789, departed from Mount Vernon for New York City

Apr. 21, 1789, Adams inaugurated as vice president

Apr. 23, 1789, arrived in New York City

• Washington was escorted to the first presidential mansion, which was located on Cherry Street, at the corner of Queen Street, east of present Franklin Square.

ELECTION OF 1789

• Ten states sent electors to the capital, New York City, Feb. 4. North Carolina and Rhode Island had not yet ratified the Constitution; New York had not yet chosen presidential electors.

• The electors from five states, Connecticut, Delaware, Georgia, New Jersey, and South Carolina had been appointed by their state legislatures, while those representing Maryland, Pennsylvania, and Virginia had been elected by popular vote. In Massachusetts and New Hampshire the electors were selected by popular vote and the legislatures.

• George Washington of Virginia received 69 of the 138 electoral votes from ten states, the largest number possible since each elector voted for two persons (Connecticut, 7; Delaware, 3; Georgia, 5; Maryland, 6; Massachusetts, 10; New Hampshire, 5; New Jersey, 6; South Carolina, 7; Pennsylvania, 10; Virginia, 10).

• He was the first of two presidents who received the electoral votes of all the states. The other was Monroe.

• John Adams of Massachusetts received 34 votes and was elected vice president (Connecticut, 5; Massachusetts, 10; New Hampshire, 5; New Jersey, 1; Pennsylvania, 8; Virginia, 5).

• The remaining 35 votes were divided among ten candidates. John Jay of New York received nine votes (Delaware, 3; New Jersey, 5; Virginia, 1); Robert Hanson Harrison of Maryland, six votes (Maryland, 6); John Rutledge of South Carolina, six (South Carolina, 6); John Hancock of Massachusetts, four (Pennsylvania, 2; South Carolina, 1; Virginia, 1); George Clinton of

New York, three (Virginia, 3); Samuel Huntington of Connecticut, two (Connecticut, 2); John Milton of Georgia, two (Georgia, 2); James Armstrong of Georgia, one (Georgia, 1); Edward Telfair of Georgia, one (Georgia, 1); and Benjamin Lincoln of Georgia, one (Georgia, 1).

THE PRESIDENT (1st)

Term of office: Apr. 30, 1789, to Mar. 4, 1797 (7 years, 308 days)
- Washington was the only president who was unanimously elected.
- He was the first of 12 presidents who were elected to second terms.
- He was the only president who was unanimously reelected.
- He was the first of 16 presidents who served more than one term.
- He was the first of nine presidents who served two terms.

State represented: Virginia
- He was the first of four presidents who comprised the Virginia Regime.
- Four of the first five presidents were from Virginia and thus were referred to as the "Virginia Regime."
- He was the first of five presidents who represented Virginia.

Political party: Federalist
- He was the first of two presidents who were Federalists. The other was John Adams.

Congresses: 1st, 2nd, 3rd, 4th

Administrations: 1st, 2nd
Age at inauguration: 57 years, 67 days
Inauguration day: Thursday, Apr. 30, 1789
- He took the oath of office on the balcony of the Senate chamber, Federal Hall, New York City. The oath was administered by Robert R. Livingston, chancellor of the State of New York.
- He was the first of three presidents who took the oath of office in the Senate chamber.
- This was the first of five inaugural ceremonies in the Senate chamber (albeit the balcony).
- He was the first president who was inaugurated outdoors.
- He was the first of two presidents who took the oath of office in New York City. The other was Arthur.
- He was the first of seven presidents who took the oath of office from an official other than a justice of the Supreme Court.
- He delivered the first inaugural address in the Senate chamber. The address contained 1,428 words.

THE 1st ADMINISTRATION

1789

May 1, received Vice President Adams, federal and state officers, foreign ministers
May 7, attended first inaugural ball
- The ball was held in the Assembly Room on lower Broadway.
May 11, his title debated in House of Representatives
- A lengthy wrangle developed over Washington's formal title. The simple title designated by the Constitution prevailed, President of the United States of America.
May 11, attended theater
- He and his guests saw a production of Sheridan's *The School for Scandal*, at the John Street Theatre. He was a frequent theatergoer.
May 27, escorted his wife from Elizabethtown Point, N.J., to New York City
- They were conducted across the bay from Elizabethtown in the presidential barge, rowed by 13 pilots. A welcoming committee met them at the landing, Peck's Slip.
June 1, signed first act of Congress
- This act prescribed the oaths of allegiance to be taken by members of Congress, all officers of the federal government, and all state officials.
June 24, received honorary degree of Doctor of Laws from Washington College, Chestertown, Md.
- He was one of the first trustees and benefactors of the college.
- This was the fourth of his five honorary degrees.
July 4, signed act placing duty on imports
July 27, signed act establishing department

of foreign affairs
•The name of the first executive department was changed to the department of
state, Sept. 15.
Aug. 7, signed act giving president power to
remove any officer of government except
member of judiciary
Aug. 7, signed act establishing department
of war
Sept. 2, signed act establishing department
of treasury
Sept. 11, first secretary of treasury, Alexander Hamilton, took oath of office
Sept. 11, signed act establishing executive
department and judicial salaries
•The president was to receive $25,000 an-
nually; the vice president, $5,000; the chief
justice of the U.S., $4,000; associate justices
of the Supreme Court, $3,500; the secre-
taries of state and treasury, $3,500; and the
secretary of war, $3,000.
Sept. 12, first secretary of war, Henry Knox,
took oath of office
Sept. 22, signed act that temporarily established post office, created office of postmaster general under secretary of treasury
Sept. 24, signed Judiciary Act of 1789
•The judiciary act provided for a six-mem-
ber Supreme Court, a chief justice of the
U.S. and five associate justices.
•The act also established the office of attorney general, whose salary was to be $1,500
annually.
•He appointed John Jay as the first chief
justice of the U.S.; John Rutledge, William
Cushing, James Wilson, John Blair, and
Robert Hanson Harrison as associate jus-
tices. All were confirmed, Sept. 26, but
Harrison declined to serve.
•Washington was the first of 14 presidents
who appointed chief justices.
•He was the first of four presidents who ap-
pointed associate justices who declined to
serve.
•Harrison was the first of seven appointees,
confirmed by the Senate, who declined to
serve.
Sept. 26, appointed first secretary of state,
Thomas Jefferson
•Jefferson did not take office until Mar. 22,
1790. In the interim, John Jay served as
department head.
Sept. 26, appointed first attorney general,
Edmund Jennings Randolph
•Randolph did not take office until Feb. 2,
1790.

Sept. 26, first postmaster general, Samuel
Osgood, took oath of office
Sept. 28, 12 proposed amendments to Con-
stitution submitted to states for ratification
Sept. 29, signed first appropriation act
•A total of $639,000 was appropriated to
defray expenses of the civil list, the war
department, outstanding warrants, and
veterans' pensions during 1789.
Sept. 29, first session of 1st Congress ad-
journed
Oct. 3, issued proclamation that established
Thanksgiving Day in the U.S.
•The first Thanksgiving Day was Thursday,
Nov. 26.
Oct. 15–Nov. 13, toured New England states
•This was the first presidential tour and also
the first time he had departed from the
capital. Accompanied by his aide-de-camp,
his private secretary, and six servants, he
visited Connecticut, Massachusetts, and
New Hampshire.
Nov. 21, North Carolina ratified Constitu-
tion
Dec. 29, Fort Washington completed, Cin-
cinnati, Ohio

1790

Jan. 7, second session of 1st Congress
Jan. 8, delivered his first annual address to
Congress
•This was the first State of the Union ad-
dress or message.
Feb. 1, first session of Supreme Court
•Only three justices attended this session,
held in the Royal Exchange Building. The
five justices who had accepted appoint-
ments were present when the Court was
formally organized, Feb. 2.
Feb. 9, appointed James Iredell as associate
justice
•Iredell, who was confirmed by the Senate,
Feb. 10, was the seventh of Washington's
13 appointments to the Court. This ap-
pointment completed the first Supreme
Court.
Feb. 22, first reception on occasion of his
birthday
Feb. 23, moved to Broadway from Cherry
Street
•The second presidential mansion, the Ma-
comb mansion, was located at what is now
39 Broadway.
Mar. 1, signed act that provided for first

federal census

Mar. 22, first secretary of state, Thomas Jefferson, took oath of office

Mar. 25, attended consecration of Trinity Church, New York City

• The original building, constructed in 1696 and enlarged in 1737, was destroyed in the great fire of Sept. 21, 1776. The new building was erected on the same site in 1788. During the ceremony, Washington sat in a canopied pew set apart for the President of the United States.

Apr. 10, signed first patent act

May 7, conferred with senators regarding foreign service bill

• This was the first instance in which he overtly attempted to influence legislation. He consulted with Senator Charles Carroll of Maryland and Senator Ralph Izard of South Carolina, asking them to exert their efforts in the Senate to reverse the House of Representatives vote to reduce the foreign service appropriation.

May 29, Rhode Island ratified Constitution

• Rhode Island was the last of the 13 original colonies to enter the Union.

May 31, signed first copyright act

July 16, signed act establishing temporary and permanent seats of government

• This act provided that the federal city was to be established in a district on the Potomac, not to exceed ten miles square; that the capital was to be Philadelphia, Pa., from the first Monday in December, 1790, to the first Monday in December, 1800.

Aug. 2, first census announced

• The official population was 3,929,214, which included 697,697 slaves and 59,557 free Negroes.

Aug. 5, assumption board of commissioners created

• The government had assumed the debts incurred by the states during the Revolution, estimated at $21,500,000, which brought the national debt to more than $70,000,000.

Aug. 12, second session of 1st Congress adjourned

• The 1st Congress was the only Congress that met in New York City.

Aug. 15, departed for Rhode Island

• He arrived in the new state, Aug. 17; returned to New York City, Aug. 22.

Aug. 30–Sept. 2, moved from New York City to Philadelphia

• As president, he had resided in New York

City for one year, 122 days.

Sept. 1, received honorary degree of Doctor of Laws from Brown University

• This was the last of his five honorary degrees.

Sept. 6, departed for Mount Vernon

• He arrived at Mount Vernon, Sept. 11; departed for Philadelphia, Nov. 22.

• This was his first visit to his home as president.

Nov. 27, returned to Philadelphia

• He went directly to the third presidential mansion at 190 High, or Market, Street. High Street was commonly called Market Street, but the name was not changed officially until 1853.

Dec. 6, third session of 1st Congress

• This was the first session of Congress that met in Philadelphia.

Dec. 8, delivered his second State of the Union address to Congress

1791

Jan. 1, initiated custom of New Year's Day reception

• The New Year's Day social event was revived by Jefferson; there is no evidence that the custom prevailed during the administration of John Adams. The annual reception was suspended in 1934 by Franklin D. Roosevelt, who found it too difficult to stand on the receiving line.

Jan. 10, Vermont ratified Constitution

Jan. 24, issued federal district proclamation

• He directed the commissioners, who had been appointed July 16, 1790, to lay out four lines to determine the exact location of the ten-mile-square district.

Feb. 18, signed act providing for admission of Vermont as state as of Mar. 4

Feb. 25, signed act granting charter to Bank of United States

Mar. 2, signed first internal revenue act

Mar. 3, signed act providing for defense of frontiers

Mar. 3, third session of 1st Congress adjourned

Mar. 4, appointed Arthur St. Clair as major general and commanding officer of expedition against Indians

Mar. 4, Vermont admitted as 14th state

• Vermont was the first of three states admitted during his term of office.

Mar. 5, accepted resignation of Associate

Justice Rutledge
Mar. 30, issued proclamation delineating boundaries of federal district
Mar. 31–Apr. 7, visited Mount Vernon
Apr. 7–June 12, toured southern states
•He traveled south from Mount Vernon through Virginia, North Carolina, South Carolina, and Georgia. When he returned to Mount Vernon, he had traveled 1,887 miles.
May 24, simultaneously offered Supreme Court justiceship to two men
•In a unique letter, he offered to appoint either Charles Cotesworth Pinckney or Edward Rutledge, both of South Carolina. Washington asked them to decide which would accept the seat; both declined.
•John Rutledge, whose resignation had created the vacancy, Mar. 5, was the brother of Edward Rutledge.
June 12–27, remained at Mount Vernon
June 29, visited Georgetown, federal district
•He announced the locations he had selected for the presidential mansion and the legislative and executive department buildings.
July 6, returned to Philadelphia
Sept. 15, departed for Mount Vernon
•He returned to the capital, Oct. 21.
Oct. 24, first session of 2nd Congress
•The administration maintained control of both the Senate and the House of Representatives. The Senate (29 members) consisted of 16 Federalists and 13 Democratic-Republicans. The House (70 members) consisted of 37 Federalists and 33 Democratic-Republicans.
Oct. 25, delivered his third State of the Union address to Congress
Oct. 31, appointed Thomas Johnson as associate justice
•He had first appointed Johnson, Aug. 5, but withdrew the appointment, Aug. 15.
•Johnson, who was confirmed by the Senate, Nov. 7, was the eighth of Washington's 13 appointments to the Supreme Court.
Nov. 11, received first minister from Great Britain, George Hammond
Nov. 26, first cabinet meeting
•While he had consulted executive department officials individually as early as October, 1789, this was his first recorded meeting with the three secretaries and the attorney general. Foreign and military affairs were discussed. The word, "cabi-net," did not come into vogue until 1793.
Dec. 8, received account of defeat of St. Clair by Ohio Indians
•Major General Arthur St. Clair, governor of the Northwest Territory, was surprised and defeated by the Miami chief, Little Turtle, on the Wabash, Nov. 4. About six hundred regulars and militia were killed or wounded.
Dec. 15, ten of 12 proposed amendments to Constitution declared ratified
•These ten amendments are known as the Bill of Rights.
• See Constitution, 1st–10th Amendments, page 642.

1792

Feb. 20, signed act detailing provisions for permanent post office
Mar. 1, signed presidential succession act
•This act provided that in case of the removal, death, resignation, or disability of the president and the vice president, the president pro tempore of the Senate would succeed and the speaker of the House would be next in the line of succession.
Mar. 23, received Indian chiefs of Six Nations
•Red Jacket, the Seneca chief who had led his tribe against the Americans during the Revolution, was presented with a silver medal.
•This was the first presidential presentation of its kind.
Apr. 2, signed act establishing mint
Apr. 5, vetoed apportionment bill
•The House of Representatives voted to sustain his veto, Apr. 6. The vote was 28 to sustain, 33 to override the veto, which was eight less than the necessary two-thirds to nullify his veto.
•This was the first of his two vetoes.

Note: For an explanation of the veto power, *see* Constitution, Article I, Section 7, page 638.

May 8, first session of 2nd Congress adjourned
May 10, departed for Mount Vernon
•He returned to Philadelphia, June 1.
June 1, Kentucky ratified Constitution, admitted as 15th state
•Kentucky was the second of three states admitted during his term of office.

July 18, departed for Mount Vernon

Aug. 23 and 26, attempted to reconcile Jefferson and Hamilton

•In letters to the secretary of state, Aug. 23, and the secretary of treasury, Aug. 26, Washington tried to arbitrate their political differences but was unsuccessful.

Sept. 15, issued proclamation warning citizens not to resist excise tax

•There had been incidents in protest of the tax in central North Carolina and western Pennsylvania.

Oct. 13, returned to Philadelphia

•During his first administration, he had spent 322 days away from the capital cities, New York City and Philadelphia. He had toured New England and the southern states, visited Rhode Island, and traveled to Mount Vernon five times.

Oct. 13, cornerstone of presidential mansion laid, federal district

•He did not attend the ceremony, despite legend.

Nov. 5, second session of 2nd Congress

Nov. 6, delivered his fourth State of the Union address to Congress

Dec. 5, presidential electors cast ballots

• See Election of 1792, below.

ELECTION OF 1792

•The electors had been chosen in the 15 states on various dates in early November. The electors from nine states, Connecticut, Delaware, Georgia, New Jersey, New York, North Carolina, Rhode Island, South Carolina, and Vermont had been appointed by their state legislatures, while those representing Kentucky, Maryland, New Hampshire, Pennsylvania, and Virginia had been elected by popular vote. In Massachusetts, the electors were selected by popular vote and the legislature.

•When the electoral votes were tabulated by Congress, Feb. 13, 1793, George Washington of Virginia received 132 of the 264 electoral votes cast from the 15 states, the largest number possible since each elector voted for two persons (Connecticut, 9; Delaware, 3; Georgia, 4; Kentucky, 4; Maryland, 8; Massachusetts, 16; New Hampshire, 6; New Jersey, 7; New York, 12; North Carolina, 12; Pennsylvania, 15; Rhode Island, 4; South Carolina, 8; Vermont, 3; Virginia, 21). Three of the original 135 electors failed to cast their ballots.

•John Adams of Massachusetts received 77 votes and was elected vice president (Connecticut, 9; Delaware, 3; Maryland, 8; Massachusetts, 16; New Hampshire, 6; New Jersey, 7; Pennsylvania, 14; Rhode Island, 4; South Carolina, 7; Vermont, 3).

•The remaining 55 votes were divided among three candidates. George Clinton of New York received 50 votes (Georgia, 4; New York, 12; North Carolina, 12; Pennsylvania, 1; Virginia, 21); Thomas Jefferson of Virginia, four (Kentucky, 4); and Aaron Burr of New York, one (South Carolina, 1).

1793

Feb. 13, electoral votes tabulated by Congress

•Washington and Adams were officially declared elected.

Feb. 15, officially notified of reelection by joint committee of Congress

Mar. 2, second session of 2nd Congress adjourned

THE 2nd ADMINISTRATION

1793

Mar. 4, his second inauguration day

•Washington took the oath of office, administered by Associate Justice William Cushing, in the Senate chamber, Federal Hall, Philadelphia.

•He was the only president who took the oath of office from an associate justice of the Supreme Court.

•This was the second of five inaugural ceremonies in the Senate chamber.

•He was the first of two presidents who were inaugurated in Philadelphia. The other was John Adams.

•He was the only president who was inaugurated in two cities—New York City and Philadelphia.

•He delivered his second inaugural address in the Senate chamber. This was the short-

• *See* Constitution, 11th Amendment, page 643.

Mar. 3, second session of 3rd Congress adjourned

Mar. 7, received details of Jay's Treaty

• The treaty, which adjusted difficulties brought on by violations of the Treaty of Paris in 1793, had been signed in London by Jay and Baron Glenville, Nov. 19, 1794.

Mar. 8, submitted treaty to special session of Senate

Apr. 14, departed for Mount Vernon

• He returned to Philadelphia, May 2.

June 24, Jay's Treaty conditionally ratified by Senate

June 29, accepted resignation of Chief Justice Jay

July 1, appointed John Rutledge as chief justice

• He was the first of three presidents who appointed more than one chief justice.

• Rutledge—the second of Washington's four appointments of chief justices and the tenth of his 13 appointments to the Supreme Court—took the oath of office, Aug. 12, and presided at the term then beginning. When the Senate convened, Dec. 15, the appointment was rejected, 14–10.

• This was the first senatorial refusal of confirmation of a presidential appointment to the Court.

• Washington was the first of three presidents who nominated chief justices not confirmed by the Senate.

• He was the first of 15 presidents who nominated justices not confirmed by the Senate.

• Rutledge was the first of four nominees for chief justice who were not confirmed by the Senate.

• Rutledge was the first of 25 men nominated to the Supreme Court who were not confirmed by the Senate.

July 10, issued proclamation pardoning insurrectionists

• This proclamation, which was not published until Aug. 6, granted full pardon to those involved in the Whisky Rebellion who gave assurance of submission to the law.

July 15, departed for Mount Vernon

• He conferred with the federal district commissioners, July 20.

• He returned to Philadelphia, Aug. 11.

Aug. 12, conferred with cabinet regarding Jay's Treaty

Aug. 18, signed Jay's Treaty

Aug. 19, summoned Randolph for explanation of French dispatch

• The dispatch, dated Oct. 31, 1794, was one of a packet of communiques from Fauchet, which had been captured by the British and given by the British minister to Secretary of Treasury Wolcott. The contents inferred that the secretary of state was susceptible to a French bribe. When handed the intercepted dispatch by the president, Randolph asked for time to write his version of the matter. Instead, he resigned.

Aug. 20, received and accepted Randolph's resignation

Aug. 23, Attorney General Bradford died

• Bradford, who succumbed to yellow fever, was the first member of the cabinet who died in office.

Sept. 8, departed for Mount Vernon

• Washington conferred with the federal district commissioners in Georgetown, Oct. 13.

• He returned to Philadelphia, Oct. 20.

Dec. 7, first session of 4th Congress

• The administration maintained control of the Senate and regained control of the House of Representatives. The Senate (32 members) consisted of 19 Federalists and 13 Democratic-Republicans. The House (106 members) consisted of 54 Federalists and 52 Democratic-Republicans.

Dec. 8, delivered his seventh State of the Union address to Congress

• "This was the first time he had ever entered the walls of Congress without a full assurance of meeting a welcome from every heart," wrote Federalist pamphleteer William Cobbett *(Peter Porcupine).*

Dec. 10, his third secretary of state, Timothy Pickering, and his third attorney general, Charles Lee, took oaths of office

• Pickering resigned as secretary of war.

1796

Jan. 26, accepted resignation of Associate Justice Blair, effective, Jan. 27.

Jan. 26, appointed William Cushing as chief justice

• Cushing, the 11th of Washington's 13 appointments to the Supreme Court, was confirmed by the Senate, Jan. 27. He declined to serve, Feb. 2, and chose instead to continue as an associate justice.

•Washington was the first of two presidents who appointed chief justices who declined to serve. The other was John Adams.

•Cushing was the second of seven appointees, confirmed by the Senate, who declined to serve.

Jan. 26, appointed Samuel Chase as associate justice

•Chase, the 12th of Washington's 13 appointments to the Supreme Court, was confirmed by the Senate, Jan. 27.

•Washington appointed more associate justices than any other president—nine. He and Franklin D. Roosevelt appointed an equal number of associate justices who served on the Court—eight.

Jan. 27, his third secretary of war, James McHenry, took oath of office

•McHenry was the last of Washington's 11 cabinet appointments.

Feb. 29, issued proclamation calling Jay's Treaty law of land

•The treaty had been ratified in London, Oct. 28, 1795.

Mar. 3, appointed Oliver Ellsworth as chief justice

•Ellsworth, who was confirmed by the Senate, Mar. 4, was the last of Washington's four appointments of chief justices and the last of his 13 appointments to the Supreme Court.

•Ellsworth was the last of 11 justices appointed by Washington who served on the Supreme Court.

•Washington was the only president who appointed more than one chief justice who served on the Supreme Court.

•He was the only president who appointed four chief justices.

Mar. 30, refused to release Jay's Treaty papers to House of Representatives

•Debate in the House, which had begun, Mar. 2, culminated in a resolution requesting the president to release treaty instructions, correspondence, and documents, Mar. 24. The members of the cabinet unanimously advised the president to refuse; Chief Justice Ellsworth said the House had no constitutional right to the papers. House debate continued until Apr. 29, when the assigned committee approved writing the necessary laws to carry out the treaty.

•Washington had resisted the principle that the assent of the House was necessary to the validity of the treaty with Great Brit-

ain. This assertion of his executive perogative set an important precedent.

June 1, first session of 4th Congress adjourned

June 1, Tennessee admitted as 16th state

•Tennessee was the last of three states admitted during his term of office.

June 13, departed for Mount Vernon

•He visited the federal district on June 18 and on Aug. 18. He returned to Philadelphia, Aug. 21.

Aug. 22, recalled James Monroe, minister to France

Sept. 17, issued his Farewell Address

•The address, which was never delivered as a speech, was published in the *American Daily Advertiser*, Philadelphia, Sept. 19.

Sept. 19, departed for Mount Vernon

•He returned to Philadelphia, Oct. 31.

•During his second administration, he had spent 295 days away from the capital. He had supervised the Whisky Rebellion military expedition and had traveled to Mount Vernon nine times.

Dec. 5, second session of 4th Congress

Dec. 7, presidential electors cast ballots

• *See* Election of 1796, pages 31–32.

Dec. 7, delivered his eighth and last State of the Union address to Congress

1797

Feb. 28, vetoed bill to reduce cavalry contingent of army

•The House of Representatives voted to sustain his veto, Mar. 1. The vote was 55 to sustain, 36 to override the veto.

•This was the second of his two vetoes.

•He was the first of three presidents who exercised the regular veto power, but did not employ the pocket veto.

•He was the first of 11 presidents who never had a veto overridden.

Mar. 3, labeled published letters as forgeries

•In a letter to Secretary of State Pickering, he said he had not seen or heard of the seven letters until they were published. Purportedly written by him in June and July, 1776, and taken by the British from one of his servants at Fort Lee, N.J., in November, 1776, the spurious documents were published in London, 1777; reprinted in New York City, 1778, and Philadelphia, 1795. In 1796, they were republished in London and New York City. The latter event brought forth the disavowal.

Mar. 3, second session of 4th Congress adjourned

THE FORMER PRESIDENT

Mar. 4, 1797, attended inauguration of John Adams
•Washington's age upon leaving office was 65 years, 10 days.
Mar. 9, 1797, departed from Philadelphia
•He arranged to take most of his public papers with him, which set a precedent. During the winter of 1797–1798, he began their arrangement but never completed the task.
Mar. 15, 1797, arrived at Mount Vernon
•He was the first of six presidents who were farmers, planters, or ranchers after their terms of office.
Jan. 19, 1798, Washington Academy established, Lexington, Va.
•The college, previously known as Liberty Hall Academy, was renamed following a gift from Washington. It became Washington College, Jan. 2, 1813, and Washington and Lee University, Feb. 4, 1871.
July 2, 1798, nominated as lieutenant general and commander-in-chief of armies by Adams
•He was confirmed by the Senate, July 3; Adams signed his commission, July 4.
•He was the only president who served as commander-in-chief after his term of office.
July 13, 1798, accepted commission
Nov. 5, 1798, departed for Philadelphia
•He arrived in the capital, Nov. 10.
Dec. 8, 1798, attended joint session of Congress
•On this occasion, Adams delivered his second State of the Union address.
Dec. 14, 1798, departed from Philadelphia
•This was Washington's last visit to the capital.
•He returned to Mount Vernon, Dec. 19.
Jan. 6, 1799, with Mrs. Washington, celebrated 40th wedding anniversary
Feb. 22, 1799, attended wedding of Eleanor (Nelly) Parke Custis, to Lawrence Lewis, Mount Vernon
July 9, 1799, executed his last will and testament
•The 29-page will and 13-page addenda were written entirely by hand.
Dec. 12, 1799, complained of sore throat

•He had ridden his normal circuit of his farms that morning, when it had hailed and snowed.
Dec. 13, 1799, made last diary entry
•The diary notes were the last words he wrote.
•His last words were said to have been, " 'Tis well."

DEATH

Date of death: Dec. 14, 1799
Place of death: Mount Vernon, Va.
•Washington was the first of four presidents who died in Virginia.
Age of death: 67 years, 295 days
•He lived two years, 285 days, after the completion of his term of office.
Cause of death: Pneumonia
Place of burial: Mount Vernon, Va.
•He was the first of seven presidents who were buried in Virginia.

THE VICE PRESIDENT (1st)

Full name: John Adams
• *See* also pages 26–39.
•He was the first of two vice presidents who were born in Massachusetts. The other was Gerry.
•He was the first of three vice presidents who were Unitarians.
•He was the first of seven vice presidents who were elected to second terms.
•He was the first of five vice presidents who served two terms. Since he did not assume office until Apr. 21, 1789, he served 47 days less than eight full years.
•He was the first of four vice presidents who served for more than seven years.
•Washington and Adams were the first of 41 president-vice president teams.
•They were the first of five president-vice president teams who were reelected.
•Adams was the first of four vice presidents who represented Massachusetts.
•He was the only vice president who was a Federalist.

• He was the first of two vice presidents who died in Massachusetts. The other was Coolidge.
• He was the second of three vice presidents who died on the Fourth of July.
• He was the first of two vice presidents who were buried in Massachusetts. The other was Wilson.

THE CABINET

State: Thomas Jefferson of Virginia, Mar. 22, 1790, to Dec. 31, 1793
• Edmund Jennings Randolph of Virginia, Jan. 2, 1794, to Aug. 19, 1795
• Timothy Pickering of Massachusetts, Dec. 10, 1795, to May 12, 1800
Treasury: Alexander Hamilton of New York, Sept. 11, 1789, to Jan. 31, 1795
• Oliver Wolcott of Connecticut, Feb. 3, 1795, to Dec. 31, 1800
War: Henry Knox of Massachusetts, Sept. 12, 1789, to Dec. 31, 1794
• Timothy Pickering of Massachusetts, Jan. 2, 1795, to Dec. 10, 1795
• James McHenry of Maryland, Jan. 27, 1796, to May 13, 1800
Attorney General: Edmund Jennings Randolph of Virginia, Sept. 26, 1789, to Jan. 2, 1794
• William Bradford of Pennsylvania, Jan. 27, 1794, to Aug. 23, 1795
• Charles Lee of Virginia, Dec. 10, 1795, to Feb. 18, 1801

THE SUPREME COURT

Chief Justices: John Jay of New York, appointed, Sept. 24, 1789; confirmed, Sept. 26, 1789; resigned, June 29, 1795
• John Rutledge of South Carolina, appointed, July 1, 1795; presided at August term; rejected by Senate, Dec. 15, 1795
• William Cushing of Massachusetts, appointed, Jan. 26, 1796; confirmed, Jan. 27, 1796; declined to serve
• Oliver Ellsworth of Connecticut, appointed, Mar. 3, 1796; confirmed, Mar. 4, 1796
Associate Justices: John Rutledge of South Carolina, appointed, Sept. 24, 1789; confirmed, Sept. 26, 1789; resigned, Mar. 5, 1791
• William Cushing of Massachusetts, appointed, Sept. 24, 1789; confirmed, Sept. 26, 1789
• Robert Hanson Harrison of Maryland, appointed, Sept. 24, 1789; confirmed, Sept. 26, 1789; declined to serve
• James Wilson of Pennsylvania, appointed, Sept. 24, 1789; confirmed, Sept. 26, 1789
• John Blair of Virginia, appointed, Sept. 24, 1789; confirmed, Sept. 26, 1789; resigned, Jan. 27, 1796
• James Iredell of North Carolina, appointed, Feb 9, 1790; confirmed, Feb. 10, 1790
• Thomas Johnson of Maryland, appointed, Aug. 5, 1791; withdrawn, Aug. 15, 1791; appointed, Oct. 31, 1791; confirmed, Nov. 7, 1791; resigned, Mar. 4, 1793
• William Paterson of New Jersey, appointed, Feb. 27, 1793; withdrawn, Feb. 28, 1793; appointed, Mar. 4, 1793; confirmed, Mar. 4, 1793
• Samuel Chase of Maryland, appointed, Jan. 26, 1796; confirmed, Jan. 27, 1796

Second President

JOHN ADAMS

Full name: John Adams
- He was the first of two presidents named Adams. He and John Quincy Adams were father and son, the only presidents so closely related.
- He was the first of five presidents named John.
- He was the first of eight presidents who had the same full names as their fathers.
- He was the second of 17 presidents who did not have middle initials or middle names.

Date of birth: Oct. 30, 1735 (Oct. 19, 1734/1735 O.S.)
- He was the first of five presidents who were born in October.
- He was the second of four presidents who were born before the Gregorian (new style) calendar replaced the Julian (old style) calendar in England and the British colonies, 1752.

Place of birth: Braintree, now Quincy, Mass.
- His birthplace, 133 Franklin Street, maintained by the city of Quincy, is open to the public daily except Mondays, Apr. 19 to Sept. 30. Admission: adults, 50 cents; children under 16, free. The fee to visit the birthplace and the adjacent birthplace of his son, John Quincy Adams, is 75 cents.
- He was the first of two presidents who were born in Braintree. The other was John Quincy Adams.
- He was the first of three presidents who were born in Massachusetts.

Family lineage: English
- He was the second of 12 presidents who were of English ancestry.

Religious denomination: Unitarian
- He was the first of four presidents who were Unitarians.

College: Harvard College, Cambridge, Mass.
- He was the first of 27 presidents who attended college.

Date of graduation: July 16, 1755, Bachelor of Arts
- He was the first of five presidents who were graduated from Harvard.
- He was the first of 21 presidents who were graduated from college.

PARENTS AND SIBLINGS

Father's name: John Adams
Date of birth: Jan. 28, 1691

Place of birth: Braintree, now Quincy, Mass.
Occupations: Farmer, shoemaker
Date of death: May 25, 1761
Place of death: Braintree, now Quincy, Mass.
Age at death: 70 years, 117 days

Mother's name: Susanna Boylston Adams
Date of birth: Mar. 5, 1699
Place of birth: Brookline, Mass.
Date of marriage: Oct. 31, 1734
Children: 3 sons
•John was born in 1735, Peter Boylston in 1738, and Elihu in 1741.
•Adams was the first of five presidents who came from families of three children.
•He was the first of eight presidents who were the eldest children in their families.
•He was the first of five presidents who had male siblings only.
Date of death: Apr. 17, 1797
•Adams was the second of ten presidents whose mothers lived to see their sons' inauguration or oath-taking days. Mrs. Adams did not attend the ceremony.
Place of death: Braintree, now Quincy, Mass.
Age at death: 98 years, 43 days
•Susanna Adams was the mother of a president who lived to the most advanced age.

MARRIAGE

Date of marriage: Oct. 25, 1764
Place of marriage: Weymouth, Mass.
•Adams was the first of two presidents who were married in Massachusetts. The other was Theodore Roosevelt.
Age at marriage: 28 years, 361 days
•He was the second of 27 presidents who married in their twenties.
Years married: 54 years, 3 days
•He was the president who was married for the longest time.

Wife's name: Abigail Smith Adams
•She was the second of 33 first ladies.
•She was the second of 40 wives of presidents.
Date of birth: Nov. 23, 1744

•She was the first of three first ladies who were born in November.
•She was the first of three wives of presidents who were born in November.
Place of birth: Weymouth, Mass.
•She was the only first lady who was born in Massachusetts.
•She was the first of two wives of presidents who were born in Massachusetts. The other was Alice Roosevelt.
Wife's mother: Elizabeth Quincy Smith
Wife's father: William Smith, Congregational minister
•Adams was the first of five presidents who married the daughters of clergymen.
Age at marriage: 19 years, 337 days
•She was the first of four first ladies who were married in their teens.
•She was the first of five wives of presidents who were married in their teens.
Years younger than husband: 9 years, 24 days
Children: 5; 3 sons, 2 daughters
•Abigail was born on July 14, 1765; John Quincy on July 11, 1767; Susanna on Dec. 23, 1768; Charles on May 29, 1770; and Thomas Boylston on Sept. 15, 1772. Susanna died Feb. 4, 1770.
•Adams was the first of three presidents who had five children.
•He was the first of 19 presidents who had both male and female children.
•He was the first of 30 presidents who had children.
Date of death: Oct. 28, 1818
Place of death: Braintree, now Quincy, Mass.
•She was the first of three first ladies who died in Massachusetts.
•She was the first of three wives of presidents who died in Massachusetts.
Age at death: 73 years, 339 days
Place of burial: Braintree, now Quincy, Mass.
•She was the first of two first ladies who were buried in Massachusetts. The other was Louisa Adams.
•She was the first of three wives of presidents who were buried in Massachusetts.
Years he survived his wife: 7 years, 249 days
•Adams was the first of 14 presidents who survived their wives.

EARLY YEARS

1741–1749, attended primary and Latin schools, Braintree, Mass.

1750–1751, tutored by Joseph Marsh, Braintree

November, 1751, entered Harvard College, Cambridge, Mass.

July 16, 1755, was graduated from Harvard College

August, 1755, taught school, Worcester, Mass.

•Adams was a schoolmaster for slightly more than three years.

•He was the first of seven presidents who taught school.

Aug. 21, 1756, began studying law with James Putnam, Worcester

•Adams was the first of 26 presidents who studied law.

October, 1758, returned to Braintree

Nov. 6, 1758, admitted to Massachusetts bar, Boston

•He was the first of 23 presidents who were lawyers.

May 25, 1761, his father died

1761, elected surveyor of highways, Braintree

•He had no surveying experience, but all male members of the community capable of contributing were expected to perform some civic duty.

•This was his first public office.

•He was the second of three presidents who were surveyors.

November, 1761, sworn in as barrister before superior court, Boston

1764, elected selectman and overseer of poor, Braintree

Oct. 25, 1764, married Abigail Smith, Weymouth, Mass.

•They were married in the Weymouth meeting house by her father.

July 14, 1765, his first daughter born

•The girl was named Abigail Adams. She was called Nabby.

1765, published his "A Dissertation on Canon and Feudal Law," Boston

•The essay originally appeared as four unsigned articles in the Boston *Gazette*. It was reprinted in the London *Chronicle* under the title, "The True Sentiments of America."

September, 1765, drafted set of instructions regarding Stamp Act for Braintree town meeting

•The instructions for the Braintree representative to the general court in October were published in the *Massachusetts Gazette and Boston News Letter*, and served as a model for the instructions to delegates from many towns. His instructions declared the Stamp Act unconstitutional, and also attacked the admiralty court, which tried offenders without jury.

1766, interpreted English constitution from patriot point of view, Boston *Gazette*

•He adopted *Clarendon* as his pen name. The Earl of Clarendon had been a moderate leader and historian of the English Civil War, 1642–1646.

Mar. 3, 1766, elected selectman, Braintree

July 11, 1767, his first son born

•The boy was named John Quincy Adams.

January, 1768, moved to Boston

•His first residence in Boston, on Brattle Square, was known locally as "the White House."

1768, declined appointment as advocate general of admiralty court

1768–1769, successfully defended John Hancock

•Hancock, owner of the sloop, *Liberty*, was charged with smuggling a cargo of wine to avoid paying duty. If convicted, Hancock would have forfeited the ship and been fined three times the cargo value, £10,000. The case dragged on for months by design of the crown attorneys before the charge was withdrawn.

Dec. 23, 1768, his second daughter born

•The girl, who was named Susanna Adams, died in infancy, Feb. 4, 1770.

May 29, 1770, his second son born

•The boy was named Charles Adams.

Sept. 7, 1770, successfully defended Captain Thomas Preston

•Captain Preston was the British officer of the guard involved in what has come to be known as the Boston Massacre. Three members of the mob had been killed, and two others had been mortally wounded, Mar. 5, when fired upon by British soldiers after provocation. The trial was delayed six months to allow tempers to cool. Preston was acquitted. Three weeks later, Adams served as counsel for the eight members of Preston's squad who also faced murder charges. Six were acquitted; two were found guilty of manslaughter. The latter two pleaded "benefit of clergy," read from Scriptures, were branded on the thumbs, and released.

Apr. 13, 1771, moved back to Braintree
•He commuted to his Boston law office.

Sept. 15, 1772, his third son born
•The boy was named Thomas Boylston Adams.

October, 1772, again moved to Boston
1773, elected to general assembly

•He was appointed to the governor's council, but was rejected by Governor Thomas Hutchinson for the "very conspicuous part" he had taken "in opposition."

June, 1774, elected one of five Massachusetts delegates to First Continental Congress, Philadelphia, Pa.

Aug, 10, 1774, departed Braintree for Philadelphia

NATIONAL PROMINENCE

Sept. 5, 1774, attended opening session of First Continental Congress
•He and his cousin, Sam Adams, were appointed as the Massachusetts members of the committee for stating rights and grievances.
•Adams was the second of five presidents who were members of the Continental congresses.

Oct. 26, 1774, departed for Braintree after adjournment of First Continental Congress

Jan. 23–Apr. 17, 1775, published 12 letters defending patriot position, Boston *Gazette*
•The letters, signed *Novanglus* (New England), were in reply to a series of 17 letters espousing the British cause, which had been signed *Massachusettenis*. Adams believed that *Massachusettensis* was his friend, Jonathan Sewall. He was mistaken. His Tory opponent was another friend and colleague, attorney Daniel Leonard of Taunton, Mass.

Apr. 22, 1775, rode over route followed by British troops, Cambridge to Concord
•The battles of Lexington and Concord, the opening skirmishes of the Revolution, had occurred, Oct. 19. Only the arrival of reinforcements had saved the British column, which retreated to Charlestown. Before the day had ended, 73 British soldiers had been killed and about 200 had been wounded or were missing. About 90 of the 4,000 Americans had been killed, wounded, or were missing.

Apr. 25, 1775, set off for Second Continental Congress, Philadelphia

May 10, 1775, attended opening session of Second Continental Congress

June 14, 1775, proposed George Washington as commander of army
•Washington was nominated and elected

unanimously as commanding general, and Congress adopted the army at Cambridge, June 15.

August, 1775, returned to Braintree
•In his absence, he had been elected as chief justice of the Massachusetts superior court. The court did not sit.

September, 1775, returned to Philadelphia
October–November, 1775, served on naval committee
•He framed the regulations and the commissions for privateers, which were approved, Nov. 28. However, little action was taken by Congress during the next months. The fitting out of armed vessels was not authorized until March, 1776.

January, 1776, his pamphlet, *Thoughts on Government*, published

June 11, 1776, appointed member of five-man committee to frame Declaration of Independence

June 11, 1776, appointed to committee "to prepare a plan of treaties to be proposed to foreign powers"

June 12, 1776, appointed chairman of board of war and ordnance
•In effect, he was named secretary of war.

Aug. 2, 1776, signed Declaration of Independence
•He was the first of two presidents who signed the Declaration. The other was Jefferson.

Sept. 11, 1776, appointed member of committee sent to confer with Admiral Richard Howe, Staten Island, N.Y.
•Admiral Howe had proposed an informal peace conference after the battle of Long Island. Adams, Benjamin Franklin, and Edward Rutledge met with Howe at British headquarters on Staten Island. The meeting was a failure since Howe would not receive the trio as members of Con-

gress, and they, in turn, refused to confer as "private gentlemen."

Sept. 29, 1776, appointed to committee to consider establishment of military academy
• He had suggested a military academy as a means of creating a professional army.

Feb. 17, 1778, sailed for France
• He had been appointed by Congress in December, 1777, as third minister to France, replacing Silas Deane.

Mar. 29, 1778, landed in Bordeaux
• He arrived in Paris, Apr. 5; he presented his credentials to Count de Vergennes, the French foreign minister, a few days later.

May 8, 1778, received by King Louis XVI, Versailles

June 18, 1779, sailed for U.S.
• He arrived in Boston, Aug. 2.

August, 1779, elected as representative of Braintree to Massachusetts constitutional convention
• He was a member of the committee of 30 appointed to draft the state constitution, Sept. 4. He was appointed to a committee of three, and, in turn, was designated by the subcommittee to write the draft. The Massachusetts constitution of 1780 was his handiwork; the only major changes from his draft were the articles on religious freedom and the power of the legislature to override the executive veto by a two-thirds vote.

Sept. 27, 1779, appointed minister plenipotentiary to negotiate treaties of peace and commerce with Great Britain

Nov. 14, 1779, sailed for France

Dec. 8, 1779, arrived at El Ferrol, Spain
• The *Sensible*, the French frigate that carried Adams to Europe, sprang a leak during a storm, and the captain decided to put into the Spanish port for safety.

Feb. 9, 1780, arrived in Paris
• He crossed the Pyrenees Mountains from Spain to France.

July 27, 1780, set out for Holland

Sept. 17, 1780, informed of his appointment as interim congressional representative to Holland

Feb. 25, 1781, received commission as minister plenipotentiary of Congress to The Netherlands

August–October, 1781, stricken by severe fever
• Early in his illness, he was in coma for five days.

December, 1781, received revocation of his commission to make treaty of commerce with Great Britain

Apr. 19, 1782, presented his credentials to Prince of Orange, The Hague
• Adams was the first of two presidents who served as ministers to The Netherlands. The other was John Quincy Adams.
• He was the first of seven presidents who served as diplomats.

July, 1782, negotiated Dutch loan of five million guilders ($2,000,000)

Oct. 7, 1782, signed treaty of amity and commerce with The Netherlands

Oct. 26, 1782, arrived in Paris to join conversations with British
• Shortly after his arrival, he was informed of the April, 1781, instructions from Congress to the peace commissioners; they were ordered "ultimately to govern yourselves by the advice and opinion of the French ministry." He considered resigning; instead, the instructions were ignored.

Jan. 20, 1783, with Benjamin Franklin, signed preliminary articles of peace and armistice with Great Britain, Versailles

Sept. 3, 1783, with Franklin and John Jay, signed peace treaty with Great Britain, Paris

Sept. 5, 1783, informed of appointment with Franklin and Jay to negotiate commercial treaty with Great Britain

Oct. 20, 1783, departed for London

Nov. 8, 1783, sent for his wife
• "Come to Europe with Nabby [his daughter, Abigail] as soon as possible," he wrote, adding, "I cannot be happy nor tolerable without you."

December, 1783, departed for Amsterdam
• American credit was on the verge of collapse. He negotiated a new loan with Dutch bankers at the "enormously avaricious" terms of six percent interest.

July, 1784, informed of appointment with Franklin and Jefferson to negotiate commercial treaties with all European powers

Aug. 7, 1784, joined wife in London
• His wife and daughter had arrived in England in July.

Aug. 8, 1784, departed for Paris, with wife and daughter, to confer with Franklin and Jefferson

Feb. 24, 1785, elected by Congress as first minister plenipotentiary to Court of St. James's
• Informed of his appointment in late April,

he returned to London, May 25.

June 1, 1785, presented credentials to King George III

• He was the first of four presidents who served as ministers to Great Britain.

1786, wrote first volume of his *A Defence of the Constitutions of Government of the United States of America*

• The three-volume work was published in London by C. Dilly, 1787–1788. Volume I was published in Philadelphia, 1787, and in Boston, 1788, but the entire work was not published in the U.S. until 1797.

• He was the second of 21 presidents who wrote books that were published during their lifetimes.

September, 1787, purchased farm in Quincy from Leonard Vassall Borland

Apr. 28, 1788, sailed for U.S.

• He arrived in Boston, June 7. He had been in Europe for more than ten years.

• Upon his arrival, he was informed that he had been elected to the Continental Congress as a delegate from Massachusetts.

Feb. 4, 1789, elected vice president

• He received 34 of the 138 votes cast by presidential electors in New York City, second only to Washington. No other candidate received more than nine votes.

• His 34 votes were cast by electors from six states (Connecticut, 5; Massachusetts, 10; New Hampshire, 5; New Jersey, 1; Pennsylvania, 8; Virginia, 5).

• *See* Election of 1789, pages 14–15.

Mar. 5, 1789, received unofficial confirmation of election

Apr. 6, 1789, electoral vote tabulated by Congress

• He was officially declared elected as vice president.

Apr. 13, 1789, departed for New York City

Apr. 21, 1789, inaugurated as vice president

Dec. 5, 1792, presidential electors cast ballots

• He received 77 votes from the electors of ten of the 15 states (Connecticut, 9; Delaware, 3; Maryland, 8; Massachusetts, 16; New Hampshire, 6; New Jersey, 7; Pennsylvania, 14; Rhode Island, 4; South Carolina, 7; Vermont, 3).

Feb. 13, 1793, electoral vote tabulated by Congress

• He was officially declared reelected as vice president.

Apr. 17, 1794, his vote defeated bill in Senate to suspend all commercial relations

with Great Britain

Dec. 7, 1796, presidential electors cast ballots

• *See* Election of 1796, below.

Feb. 8, 1797, electoral vote tabulated by Congress

• Adams and Jefferson were officially declared elected.

• This was the only time that the president and the vice president represented different political parties.

• Adams was the first president who, as presiding officer of the Senate, announced his own election.

ELECTION OF 1796

• By informal agreement, the Federalists had nominated John Adams of Massachusetts and Thomas Pinckney of South Carolina. The Democratic-Republican candidates were Thomas Jefferson of Virginia and Aaron Burr of New York.

• The electors from eight states, Connecticut, Delaware, New Jersey, New York, Rhode Island, South Carolina, Tennessee, and Vermont had been appointed by their state legislatures, while those representing Georgia, Kentucky, Maryland, North Carolina, Pennsylvania, and Virginia had been elected by popular vote. In Massachusetts and New Hampshire the electors were selected by popular vote and the legislatures.

• When the electoral votes were tabulated by Congress, Feb. 8, 1797, John Adams of Massachusetts received 71 of the 276 electoral votes from the 16 states (Connecticut, 9; Delaware, 3; Maryland, 7; Massachusetts, 16; New Hampshire, 6; New Jersey, 7; New York, 12; North Carolina, 1; Pennsylvania, 1; Rhode Island, 4; Vermont, 4; Virginia, 1).

• Thomas Jefferson of Virginia received 68 votes and was elected vice president (Georgia, 4; Kentucky, 4; Maryland, 4; North Carolina, 11; Pennsylvania, 14; South Carolina, 8; Tennessee, 3; Virginia, 20).

• The remaining 137 votes were divided among 11 candidates. Thomas Pinckney of South Carolina received 59 votes (Connecticut, 4; Delaware, 3; Maryland, 4; Massachusetts, 13; New Jersey, 7; New York, 12; North Carolina, 1; Pennsylvania, 1;

South Carolina, 8; Vermont, 4; Virginia, 1); Aaron Burr of New York, 30 (Kentucky, 4; Maryland, 3; North Carolina, 6; Pennsylvania, 13; Tennessee, 3; Virginia, 1); Samuel Adams of Massachusetts, 15 (Virginia, 15); Oliver Ellsworth of Connecticut, 11 (Massachusetts, 1; New Hampshire, 6; Rhode Island, 4); George Clinton of New York, seven (Georgia, 4; Virginia, 3); John Jay of New York, five (Connecticut, 5);

James Iredell of North Carolina, three (North Carolina, 3); John Henry of Maryland, two (Maryland, 2); Samuel Johnston of North Carolina, two (Massachusetts, 2); and Charles Cotesworth Pinckney of South Carolina, one (North Carolina, 1). Two electors, one from Virginia and the other from North Carolina, obstinately voted for George Washington of Virginia, who was not a candidate.

THE PRESIDENT (2nd)

Term of office: Mar. 4, 1797 to Mar. 4, 1801 (4 years)
- Adams was the first of 12 presidents who had served as vice presidents.
- He was the first of three presidents who took office upon the completion of their vice-presidential terms.
- He was the first of two presidents who had previously served as vice president for two terms. The other was Nixon.
- He was the first of 19 presidents who served one term or less than one term.
- He was the first of ten presidents who served for four years.

State represented: Massachusetts
- He was the first of four presidents who represented Massachusetts.

Political party: Federalist
- He was the second of two presidents who were Federalists. The other was Washington.

Congresses: 5th, 6th
Administration: 3rd
Age at inauguration: 61 years, 125 days
Inauguration day: Saturday, Mar. 4, 1797
- Adams took the oath of office, administered by Chief Justice Oliver Ellsworth, in the chamber of the House of Representatives, Federal Hall, Philadelphia, Pa.
- Adams was the first president to whom the oath was administered by the Chief Justice of the U.S.
- He was the first of five presidents who took the oath of office in the House chamber.
- This was the first of six inaugural ceremonies in the House chamber.
- He was the second of two presidents who took the oath of office in Philadelphia. The other was Washington.

THE 3rd ADMINISTRATION

1797

Mar. 4, retained Washington's cabinet
Mar. 25, called special session of Congress, May 15, to consider French-American relations
- Relations with France had been steadily deteriorating since the Genet affair.
- *See* page 20.
May 8, escorted wife to capital
- Adams met the first lady about 20 miles west of New York City. They arrived in Philadelphia, May 9.
May 10, attended launching of first major U.S. naval vessel, *United States*
May 15, first session of 5th Congress
- This was the first special session.

- The administration controlled both the Senate and the House of Representatives. The Senate (32 members) consisted of 20 Federalists and 12 Democratic-Republicans. The House (106 members) consisted of 58 Federalists and 48 Democratic-Republicans.
May 16, delivered first war message to Congress
- He did not ask for a formal declaration of war. He recommended the arming of merchant vessels, the enlargement of the naval force, and the reorganization of the militia.
- This was the first of seven war messages.
May 31, appointed commissioners to secure treaty of commerce and amity with France

•The commissioners confirmed by the Senate were Charles Cotesworth Pinckney, John Marshall, and Francis Dana. Elbridge Gerry replaced Dana, who was in poor health.

June 1, appointed his son, John Quincy, as minister plenipotentiary to Prussia

June 12, sent special message to Congress recommending legislation to form Mississippi Territory

June 14, signed act prohibiting exportation of arms

June 24, authorized to raise eighty thousand militia for three months

July 10, first session of 5th Congress adjourned

July 19, departed for Quincy

•This was the first time he departed from the capital, except to escort his wife to Philadelphia. He arrived at his Massachusetts home, Aug. 5.

Nov. 13, second session of 5th Congress

Nov. 15, returned to Philadelphia

•He and Mrs. Adams, who had set out for the capital from Quincy at the end of September, stopped off in New York City until word was received that Philadelphia was free from yellow fever.

Nov. 22, delivered his first State of the Union address to Congress

•His address was based primarily on a draft prepared by Secretary of State Pickering. Although moderate in tone, it was denounced by the Republicans as tantamount to a declaration of war on France.

1798

Jan. 8, declared 11th Amendment to Constitution ratified

• *See* Constitution, page 643.

Feb. 22, refused to attend Washington's Birthday celebration

•He disapproved of the annual celebrations, considered them a form of deification.

Mar. 4, received dispatches from commission to France

Mar. 12, nominated his son, John Quincy, as commissioner to negotiate new treaty of commerce and amity with Sweden

Mar. 19, sent special message to Congress reporting failure of negotiations with France

•He reiterated the recommendations he had made in his "war message" to the special session and issued an executive order that authorized the arming of merchant vessels.

Apr. 3, submitted dispatches from commission to France to House of Representatives, as requested

•The Republicans, hoping to embarrass the administration, had called for the publication of the dispatches but reversed their position once they had read the correspondence, which revealed what has come to be called the "XYZ affair." The Senate, however, ordered fifty thousand copies printed and distributed throughout the country.

•The dispatches detailed the difficulties encountered by the commission. Three unofficial agents of the French foreign minister, Tallyrand, who were identified in the published version as X, Y, and Z (their names were Hottinguer, Bellamy, and Hauteval), had asked for a sizable "loan" to France, a $250,000 "gratuity" for Tallyrand, and what would have amounted to an apology for the criticism of France in the presidential address to Congress of May 16, 1797.

Apr. 7, signed act that established Mississippi Territory

May 2, attended New Theater, Philadelphia

•The mood of the times had prompted Joseph Hopkinson to add lyrics to "The President's March." Sung nightly by Gilbert Fox at the New Theater, the hymn became known by the first two words of the lyrics, "Hail Columbia."

•This was the first occasion on which the patriotic lyrics were sung in the presence of the president. Mrs. Adams had attended Fox's first performance, incognito, Apr. 25.

May 3, signed act that established navy department

May 21, appointed first secretary of navy, Benjamin Stoddert

•Stoddert took office, June 18.

June 18, received John Marshall, who had returned from France

•Adams had been prepared to ask Congress for a declaration of war, but changed his mind upon hearing Marshall's report that the French believed they could bully the Americans but would be more reasonable if convinced that the U.S. position was supported by a majority of the people.

•"Millions for defense, but not a cent for tribute!", a toast proposed •hat evening at a Philadelphia banquet for Marshall, became a rallying cry. The toast was offered by Robert Goodhoe Harper, Federalist congressman from South Carolina—not by Charles Cotesworth Pinckney, as legend has it.

June 18, signed amended naturalization act
•This act changed the period of residence required for full citizenship from five to 14 years.
•This was the first of four acts that came to be known as the Alien and Sedition Acts.

June 25, authorized by alien act to deport all aliens regarded as dangerous to public peace and safety
•This was the second of the Alien and Sedition Acts. It expired in 1800 and was not renewed.

July 2, nominated Washington as lieutenant general and commander-in-chief of armies
July 4, signed Washington's commission
July 6, authorized to arrest, imprison, or banish enemy aliens in time of war
•This was the third of the Alien and Sedition Acts. It was never applied, but many French aliens left the country after its enactment.

July 7, treaty with France abrogated by Congress
•This was the only treaty of alliance made by the U.S. that was repealed.

July 9 and July 14, signed direct federal property tax acts
July 14, signed sedition act
•This act provided fines and imprisonment of citizens or aliens who entered into combinations to oppose execution of national laws, foment insurrection, or to write, publish, or utter false or malicious statements about the chief executive, the legislature, or the government.
•This was the fourth and last of the Alien and Sedition Acts.
•Enforcement of the act resulted in the prosecution of 25 and the conviction of ten Republican editors and printers.

July 16, second session of 5th Congress adjourned
July 20, departed for Quincy
Aug. 28, Associate Justice Wilson died
Sept. 29, appointed Bushrod Washington as associate justice
•Washington, who was confirmed by the Senate, Dec. 20, was the first of Adams's four appointments to the Supreme Court.

•Washington was a nephew of the first president.
Nov. 25, returned to Philadelphia
Dec. 3, third session of 5th Congress
Dec. 8, delivered his second State of the Union address to Congress

1799

Feb. 5, issued proclamation that ordered insurgents in eastern Pennsylvania to disperse
•The rioters, led by John Fries of Bucks County, liberated several prisoners arrested by U.S. marshals and "arrested" the federal agents. Fries and his several hundred followers opposed the direct property tax acts of 1798. Fries was convicted of high treason and was sentenced to be hanged.

Feb. 18, nominated William Vans Murray as commissioner to France
Feb. 25, nominated Patrick Henry and Oliver Ellsworth as commissioners, with Murray, to negotiate with French
•Henry declined to serve for reasons of health and was replaced by William Richardson Davie. Henry died in June.

Mar. 3, third session of 5th Congress adjourned
Mar. 5, departed for Quincy
Oct. 5, departed from Quincy for Philadelphia
Oct. 16, met with Commissioners Ellsworth and Davie, Trenton, N.J.
•Adams ordered them to sail for France by Nov. 1.

Oct. 20, Associate Justice Iredell died
Oct. 20, appointed Alfred Moore as associate justice
•Moore, who was confirmed by the Senate, Dec. 10, was the second of Adams's four appointments to the Supreme Court.

Oct. 25, with Mrs. Adams, celebrated 35th wedding anniversary
Dec. 2, first session of 6th Congress
•The administration maintained control of both the Senate and the House of Representatives. The Senate (32 members) consisted of 19 Federalists and 13 Democratic-Republicans. The House (106 members) consisted of 64 Federalists and 42 Democratic-Republicans.

Dec. 3, delivered his third State of the Union address to Congress

Dec. 14, publicly announced death of George Washington

• With the death of Washington, Adams became the first of four presidents who served for periods when no former president was living.

1800

Feb. 25, sent Prussian treaty, negotiated by John Quincy Adams, to Senate

Apr. 4, signed first federal bankruptcy act

May 6, accepted resignation of Secretary of War McHenry, effective, May 13

May 7, signed act that established Indiana Territory

• The territory, which included Indiana, Illinois, and Wisconsin, as well as parts of Minnesota and Michigan, had been part of the Northwest Territory.

May 10, requested resignation of Secretary of State Pickering

• When Pickering refused to resign, Adams dismissed him, effective, May 12.

May 13, appointed his second secretary of war, Samuel Dexter

May 14, first session of 6th Congress adjourned

• This was the last session of Congress that met in Philadelphia.

May 20, issued general amnesty freeing John Fries and others

May 20, departed on inspection trip of Washington, D.C.

• He found the public buildings "in a much greater forwardness" than he expected. The executive mansion would be ready for occupancy in the fall, and one wing of the Capitol was nearing completion.

• He also visited Mrs. Washington at Mount Vernon.

June 6, appointed his second secretary of state, John Marshall

July 5, arrived in Quincy

Sept. 30, Chief Justice Ellsworth resigned

Nov. 1, took up residence in White House

• The White House was the fourth executive mansion.

Nov. 1, received resignation of Secretary of Treasury Wolcott

• Wolcott's resignation became effective, Dec. 31.

Nov. 2, wrote first letter from White House

• In this letter to his wife, he wrote: "I pray Heaven to bestow the best of blessings on this house and all that shall hereafter inhabit it. May none but wise and honest men ever rule under this roof."

• This fitting passage was inscribed on the mantel in the State Dining Room of the White House by order of Franklin D. Roosevelt.

Nov. 17, second session of 6th Congress

• This was the first session of Congress that met in Washington, D.C.

Nov. 22, delivered his fourth and last State of the Union address to Congress

• He was the last outgoing president who delivered his State of the Union message in person until Lyndon B. Johnson did in 1969.

Nov. 30, his son, Charles, died

• Charles Adams was the first of five children of presidents who died during their fathers' terms of office.

Dec. 3, presidential electors cast ballots

• *See* Election of 1800, pages 44–45.

Dec. 15, sent special message to Senate proposing convention with France

• Since neither the Americans nor the French desired to continue the undeclared war, but could not agree on matters discussed, a "convention" was agreed upon instead of a treaty.

Dec. 16, learned that South Carolina had voted Republican

• This signalled defeat, since Jefferson then led by one electoral vote with only Georgia and Tennessee, both Republican states, unreported.

Dec. 18, appointed John Jay as chief justice

• Jay, who was confirmed by the Senate, Dec. 19, was the third of Adams's four appointments to the Supreme Court. Jay declined to serve, Jan. 2, 1801.

• Jay was the third of seven appointees, confirmed by the Senate, who declined to serve.

• Adams was the second of two presidents who appointed chief justices who declined to serve. The other was Washington.

Dec. 23, learned that Georgia and Tennessee had voted Republican

Note: The official population, according to the second census, was 5,310,458, which included 894,452 slaves and 104,335 free Negroes.

1801

Jan. 1, his second secretary of treasury, Samuel Dexter, took oath of office
• Dexter continued to serve as secretary of war until Jan. 31.
Jan. 20, appointed John Marshall as chief justice
• Marshall, who was confirmed by the Senate, Jan. 27, was the last of Adams's four appointments to the Supreme Court.
• Adams was the second of three presidents who appointed more than one chief justice.
• He was the second of 14 presidents who appointed chief justices.
Feb. 11, electoral votes tabulated by Congress
• *See* Election of 1800, pages 44–45.
• Jefferson and Burr each received 73 electoral votes. Adams received 65 electoral votes.
• He was the first of seven presidents who were defeated when they sought reelection.
Feb. 13, signed Judiciary Act of 1801

• This act reduced the Supreme Court to five members. It established 16 circuit courts, and added a considerable number of marshals, attorneys, and clerks.
• This act enabled him to make the so-called "midnight appointments." He is supposed to have remained up until midnight on or after, Mar. 3, signing commissions of Federalist appointees to various judicial positions. While he had made several dozen appointments during the last two weeks of his term, he only signed the commissions of three judges appointed for the District of Columbia (including William Cranch, his wife's nephew) on Mar. 3. However, his Republican opponents labeled all of his appointments under the judiciary act as "midnight appointments."
Feb. 18, accepted resignation of Attorney General Lee
Mar. 3, second session of 6th Congress adjourned

Note: He was the first of seven presidents who did not exercise the veto.

THE FORMER PRESIDENT

Mar. 4, 1801, did not attend inauguration of Jefferson
• Adams's age upon leaving office was 65 years, 125 days.
• He departed from the capital early in the morning and headed for Quincy.
• He was the first of four presidents who did not attend the inaugurations of their successors.
March, 1801, returned to Quincy
• He busied himself in the routines of his farm, Stony Field. The farm was also known as Peacefield and Montizello.
• The original farmhouse on the property, built in 1731, was enlarged during his term of office. Additional alterations were made on the "Old House," as it was called, by his son, John Quincy Adams, in 1836; by his grandson, Charles Francis Adams, 1869–1873; and by his great-grandson, Brooks Adams, in 1906. Brooks Adams, who died in 1927, was the last of the family to occupy the property. The Adams Mansion was designated a national historic site, Dec. 9, 1946, after the property had been given to the federal government by the Adams

Memorial Society. The name was changed to the Adams National Historic Site, Nov. 26, 1952. It contains 4.77 acres and includes the house, stables, gardens, and a stone library, a separate building containing books that belonged to John Adams and John Quincy Adams.
• Administered by the National Park Service, the Adams National Historic Site is located at 135 Adams Street, Quincy. It is open to the public daily, 9 A.M. to 5 P.M., Apr. 19 to Nov. 10. Admission: adults, 50 cents; educational groups with reservations and children under 16, free.
Sept. 9, 1801, wrote to friend, "If I were to go over my life again, I would be a shoemaker rather than an American statesman."
1804, began autobiography
• In addition to working on his autobiography, he engaged in voluminous correspondence.
Oct. 30, 1805, celebrated his 70th birthday
• He was the first of 16 presidents who lived to be 70.
1805, his *Discourses on Davila* published by

Russell and Cutler, Boston
- Written in 1790, when he was vice president, the *Discourses* appeared as a series of essays in John Fenno's Federalist newspaper, the *Gazette of the United States*. Enrico Caterino Davila had written a history of the civil wars of France, published in 1630. Adams compared the civil wars and the French Revolution, making the point that the revolution would fail if a balanced government was not formed. Attacked as a monarchist and worse by anti-Federalists, he discontinued the essay series on the advice of Fenno.
- When they were published 15 years later by Russell and Cutler, the byline read, "By an American Citizen."

Oct. 30, 1810, celebrated his 75th birthday
- He was the first of ten presidents who lived to be 75.

1810, *Correspondence of the Late President Adams* published by Everett and Monroe, Boston
- This book consisted of 63 letters written to the Boston *Patriot*, Apr. 10, 1809, to Feb. 10, 1810, in which he defended his administration—particularly his actions in 1799, when he had dispatched the mission to France against the advice of his cabinet.
- The use of the phrase, "Late President," in the title, meant president lately in office.

December, 1811–January, 1812, renewed correspondence with Jefferson
- The reconciliation had been arranged by their mutual friend, Dr. Benjamin Rush. At Rush's insistence, Adams had written to Jefferson a few days after Christmas. He also sent two volumes of the writings of his son, John Quincy, "two pieces of homespun lately produced in this quarter by one who was honored in his youth by some of your attention and much of your kindness."
- Jefferson replied, Jan. 21, saying that Adams's letter had reminded him of the times when "laboring always at same oar . . . we rode through the storm with heart and hand, and made a happy port." Jefferson added that he looked forward to another letter, "like mine, full of egotisms," with details of "your health, your habits, occupations, and enjoyments."
- Their correspondence continued until shortly before their deaths.

Aug. 13, 1813, his daughter, Abigail, died
Oct. 25, 1814, with Mrs. Adams, celebrated

50th wedding anniversary
- He was the first of four presidents who celebrated their golden wedding anniversaries.

Nov. 23, 1814, Mrs. Adams's 70th birthday
- She was the second of 16 first ladies who lived to be 70.
- She was the second of 17 wives of presidents who lived to be 70.

Oct. 19, 1815, his first great-grandchild born on his 80th birthday
- Oct. 19 was his birthday according to the Julian calendar.
- John Peter de Wint, the father of the child, Caroline Elizabeth de Wint, also had been born on Oct. 19. "Tell her," Adams wrote the new father, "that her great-grandfather is but a little older than her, only eighty years, and that is but a span; but that although life is short, yet it is a very precious blessing, and every moment of it ought to be employed and improved to the best advantage."

Oct. 30, 1815, celebrated his 80th birthday
- He was the first of six presidents who lived to be 80.

Oct. 28, 1818, his wife died

1819, *Novanglus and Massachusettensis* essays published by Hews and Goss, Boston
- The *Massachusetts Gazette* had published 17 letters in defense of the British cause, Dec. 12, 1774, to Apr. 3, 1775. In reply, he had written 12 letters that were published under the pseudonym, *Novanglus*, in the Boston *Gazette*.
- When Adams wrote the preface for this edition, he still believed that *Massachusettensis* was his friend, Jonathan Sewall.

Fall, 1820, visited ancestral home of his mother, Brookline, Mass.
- He had not visited the old Boylston estate since childhood.

Oct. 30, 1820, celebrated his 85th birthday
- He was the first of four presidents who lived to be 85.

November-December, 1820, attended state constitutional convention, Boston
- He had been elected a member of the convention as representative of Quincy, "the purest honor of my life."
- He spoke against universal suffrage, and favored a small property tax, but was outvoted.

December, 1820, contracted a fever
- He was confined to his bed for nearly two months.

6666

May, 1821, defended proposed changes in state constitution, Quincy town meeting
•The amendments to the constitution were approved.
Aug. 14, 1821, reviewed U.S. Military Academy corps of cadets, Quincy
•The two hundred West Point cadets went through close-order and extended-order drill in the field across from his home, while he watched from the porch. Afterwards, he spoke to them on their duties and obligations as future military leaders of the U.S. A cold buffet was served in the courtyard. The afternoon ended with a concert by the cadet band.
•This was his last public appearance.
1823, *Correspondence Between the Hon. John Adams and the late William Cunningham, Esq.* published by E. M. Cunningham, Boston
•He had pledged Cunningham not to publish the letters—written between 1803 and 1812—during his lifetime. When Cunningham committed suicide in 1823, his son, a Jacksonian, published the correspondence in an effort to discredit John Quincy Adams.
•Some of the letters were strongly anti-Jefferson, but their publication did not cause another breach. "It would be strange indeed if, at our years, we were to go an age back to hunt up imaginary or forgotten facts to disturb the repose of affections so sweetening to the evening of our lives," wrote Jefferson to Adams, Oct. 23.
Fall, 1824, visited by Lafayette, Quincy
Mar. 4, 1825, his son, John Quincy Adams, took oath as president, Washington, D.C.
•He did not attend the inauguration.
Oct. 30, 1825, celebrated his 90th birthday
•He was the first of two presidents who lived to be 90. The other was Hoover.
Winter, 1825, his portrait painted by Gilbert Stuart, Quincy
June, 1826, reluctantly declined to participate in 50th anniversary celebration of Independence Day, Boston

DEATH

Date of death: July 4, 1826
•Adams was the second of three presidents who died on the Fourth of July. He and Jefferson died on the same day; Jefferson died several hours earlier.

Place of death: Quincy, Mass.
•He was the first of two presidents who died in Massachusetts. The other was Coolidge.
Age at death: 90 years, 247 days
•He was the president who lived to the most advanced age.
•He lived 136 days longer than Hoover.
•He lived 25 years, 122 days, after the completion of his term.
Cause of death: Debility
Place of burial: Quincy, Mass.
•He was the first of two presidents who were buried in Massachusetts. The other was his son, John Quincy Adams, who was also buried in Quincy.

THE VICE PRESIDENT (2nd)

Full name: Thomas Jefferson
• *See also* pages 40–52.
•He was the first of two vice presidents who were born in Virginia. The other was Tyler.
•He was the first of two vice presidents who were of no specific religious denomination. The other was Andrew Johnson.
•He was the first of two vice presidents who attended the College of William and Mary. The other was Tyler.
•He was the first of four vice presidents who served in the cabinet.
•He was the first of 14 vice presidents who served as state governors.
•He was the first of 17 vice presidents who served four-year terms.
•Adams and Jefferson were the second of 41 president-vice president teams.
•He was the first of two vice presidents who represented Virginia. The other was Tyler.
•He was the first of six vice presidents who were Democratic-Republicans.
•He was the first of three vice presidents who died in Virginia.
•He was the first of three vice presidents who died on the Fourth of July.
•He was the first of two vice presidents who were buried in Virginia. The other was Tyler.

THE CABINET

State: Timothy Pickering of Massachusetts, Dec. 10, 1795, to May 12, 1800
•John Marshall of Virginia, June 6, 1800, to

Feb. 4, 1801
Treasury: Oliver Wolcott of Connecticut,
Feb. 3, 1795, to Dec. 31, 1800
•Samuel Dexter of Massachusetts, Jan. 1,
1801, to May 13, 1801
War: James McHenry of Maryland, Jan. 27,
1796, to May 13, 1800
•Samuel Dexter of Massachusetts, May 13,
1800, to Jan. 31, 1801
Attorney General: Charles Lee of Virginia,
Dec. 10, 1795, to Feb. 18, 1801
Navy: Benjamin Stoddert of Maryland, June
18, 1798, to Mar. 31, 1801

THE SUPREME COURT

Chief Justices: John Jay of New York, appointed, Dec. 18, 1800; confirmed, Dec.
19, 1800; declined to serve, Jan. 2, 1801
•John Marshall of Virginia, appointed, Jan.
20, 1801; confirmed, Jan. 27, 1801
Associate Justices: Bushrod Washington of
Virginia, appointed, Sept. 29, 1798; confirmed, Dec. 20, 1798
•Alfred Moore of North Carolina, appointed, Oct. 20, 1799; confirmed, Dec. 10,
1799

Third President

THOMAS JEFFERSON

Full name: Thomas Jefferson
• He was the first of two presidents named Thomas. The other was Wilson.
• He was the third of 17 presidents who did not have middle initials or middle names.
Date of birth: Apr. 13, 1743 (Apr. 2, 1742/1743 O.S.)
• He was the first of four presidents who were born in April.
• He was the third of four presidents who were born before the Gregorian (new style) calendar replaced the Julian (old style) calendar in England and the British colonies, 1752.
Place of birth: Shadwell estate, Goochland County, now Albemarle County, Va.
• His birthplace was destroyed by fire in 1770.
• He was the second of eight presidents who were born in Virginia.
Family lineage: Welsh-Scottish-Irish
• He was the only president who was of Welsh-Scottish-Irish ancestry.
Religious denomination: None
• He was the first of three presidents who were of no specific denomination.
College: College of William and Mary, Williamsburg, Va.

• He was the first of three presidents who attended William and Mary.
• He was the second of 27 presidents who attended college.
• He was the first of six presidents who attended but were not graduated from college.
• He was the second of 15 presidents who were not graduated from college.

PARENTS AND SIBLINGS

Father's name: Peter Jefferson
Date of birth: Feb. 29, 1708
• Jefferson's father was the only parent of a president who was born on this day.
Place of birth: probably Osborne's, on James River, Chesterfield County, Va.
Occupations: Planter, surveyor
• His father also was sheriff, magistrate, and a member of the House of Burgesses.
Date of death: Aug. 17, 1757
• Thomas was 14 years, 126 days old when his father died
Place of death: probably Shadwell estate, Goochland County, now Albermarle County, Va.

Age at death: 49 years, 170 days

Mother's name: Jane Randolph Jefferson
Date of birth: probably February, 1720
Place of birth: London, England
• His mother was the first of eight parents of presidents who were born abroad.
• His mother was the first of four mothers of presidents who were born abroad.
Date of marriage: 1738 or 1739
Children: 10; 6 daughters, 4 sons
• Jane was born in 1740; Mary in 1741; Thomas in 1743; Elizabeth in 1744; Martha in 1746; Peter Field in 1748; a son in 1750; Lucy in 1752; and Anna Scott and Randolph in 1755. Peter Field died when six weeks old; the unnamed son died on his day of birth.
• Jefferson was the first of five presidents who were third children.
• He was the second of five presidents who came from families of ten children.
• He was the only president who had twin siblings.
Date of death: Mar. 31, 1776
Place of death: Monticello, near Charlottesville, Va.
Age at death: about 56 years

MARRIAGE

Date of marriage: Jan. 1, 1772
• Jefferson was the first of two presidents who were married on New Year's Day. The other was Polk.
Place of marriage: The Forest (her father's home), Charles City County, Va.
• He was the second of four presidents who were married in Virginia.
Age at marriage: 28 years, 263 days
• He was the third of 27 presidents who were married in their twenties.
Years married: 10 years, 248 days

Wife's name: Martha Wayles Skelton Jefferson
• Jefferson was the second of six presidents who married widows. On Nov. 20, 1766, she had married Bathurst Skelton, who died, Sept. 30, 1768.
• She was the third of 40 wives of presidents.
Date of birth: Oct. 30, 1748

• She was the first of six wives of presidents who were born in October.
Place of birth: Charles City County, Va.
• She was the second of six wives of presidents who were born in Virginia.
Wife's mother: Martha Eppes Wayles
Wife's father: John Wayles, planter and attorney
• Wayles was the first of four fathers-in-law of presidents who were attorneys.
Age at marriage: 23 years, 63 days
• She was the second of 30 wives of presidents who were married in their twenties.
Years younger than husband: 5 years, 200 days
Children: 6; 5 daughters, 1 son
• Martha was born on Sept. 27, 1772; Jane Randolph on Apr. 3, 1774; a son on May 28, 1777; Mary on Aug. 1, 1778; a daughter on Nov. 3, 1780; and Lucy Elizabeth on May 8, 1782. Only Martha and Mary reached maturity. Four of the children, including his only son, died in infancy; Mary died on Apr. 17, 1804, at the age of 25.
• Jefferson was the first of four presidents who had six children.
• He was the second of 19 presidents who had both male and female children.
• He was the second of 30 presidents who had children.
• His wife had borne one son, John Skelton, by her first husband. The child, who was born Nov. 7, 1767, died in infancy, June 10, 1771.
Date of death: Sept. 6, 1782
• She was the first of five wives of presidents who died prior to their husbands' inaugurations.
• She was the first of seven wives of presidents who were not first ladies.
Place of death: Monticello, near Charlottesville, Va.
• She was the first of four wives of presidents who died in Virginia.
Age at death: 33 years, 311 days
Place of burial: Monticello, near Charlottesville, Va.
• She was the first of seven wives of presidents who were buried in Virginia.
Years he survived his wife: 43 years, 301 days
• Jefferson was the second of 14 presidents who survived their wives.

EARLY YEARS

Aug. 17, 1757, his father died
•Jefferson inherited an estate of one thousand acres.
•He was the second of nine presidents who owned slaves.
Mar. 25, 1760, enrolled at College of William and Mary, Williamsburg, Va.
•He attended college until Apr. 25, 1762; he left without a degree.
1762, studied law under George Wythe, Williamsburg
•Jefferson was the second of 26 presidents who studied law.
Apr. 13, 1764, assumed management of estate
•He was appointed to two of his father's offices, justice of the peace and vestryman.
Apr. 5, 1767, admitted to bar of Virginia, Williamsburg
•He was the second of 23 presidents who were lawyers.
May 11, 1769, elected to House of Burgesses
•He was reelected annually six times, serving until 1775.
1769, building at Monticello began
1770, Shadwell burned
•He moved to Monticello, Nov. 26.
Jan. 1, 1772, married Martha Wayles Skelton, Charles City County, Va.
•He took his wife to their honeymoon cottage at Monticello a few days later.
•Monticello, three miles from Charlottesville on state highways 20 and 53, is maintained by the Thomas Jefferson Memorial Foundation, Inc. It is open to the public daily, 8 A.M. to 5 P.M., Mar. 1 to Oct. 31,

and 9 A.M. to 4:30 P.M., Nov. 1 to Feb. 28. Admission: adults, $1.50; children under 12, 50 cents; student groups of 15 or more, 50 cents.
Sept. 27, 1772, his first daughter born
•The girl was named Martha Washington Jefferson.
1773, John Wayles died
•His father-in-law left an estate of 40,000 acres and 135 slaves. This legacy doubled Jefferson's estate.
1774, elected to first Virginia provincial convention
•Due to illness, Jefferson did not attend the convention in Williamsburg, which met, Aug. 1. However, he prepared a draft of instructions for the Virginia delegation to the First Continental Congress. The draft, considered quite radical, was not accepted by the convention. Published in pamphlet form, *A Summary View of the Rights of British America* was reprinted in England that same year.
Apr. 3, 1774, his second daughter born
•The girl, who was named Jane Randolph Jefferson, died in infancy, September, 1775.
Mar. 25, 1775, selected as alternate delegate to Second Continental Congress
June 20, 1775, took seat in Second Continental Congress, Philadelphia, Pa.
•He replaced Peyton Randolph.
•He was the third of five presidents who served in the Continental congresses.
Mar. 31, 1776, his mother died

NATIONAL PROMINENCE

June 11, 1776, appointed member of five-man committee to prepare Declaration of Independence
•He was chosen by his fellow committeemen to write the first draft. Others on the committee were Benjamin Franklin, John Adams, Robert Livingston, and Roger Sherman.
July 2–4, 1776, Declaration of Independence debates
•The Declaration underwent many revisions before being approved, July 4.
Aug. 2, 1776, signed Declaration of Independence

•He was the second of two presidents who signed the Declaration. The other was John Adams.
Sept. 2, 1776, resigned from Continental Congress
Oct. 7, 1776, again elected to House of Burgesses
Oct. 8, 1776, notified of election as commissioner to France
•He had been elected by Congress to represent the U.S. in Paris, along with Benjamin Franklin and Silas Deane. He declined the appointment, Oct. 11.
May 28, 1777, his only son born

•The boy, name unknown, died in infancy, June 14.

Aug. 1, 1778, his third daughter born
•The girl was named Mary Jefferson.

January, 1779, elected governor of Virginia
•He was elected by the legislature to succeed Patrick Henry, who was serving a third term.

June 1, 1779, took office as governor
•He was the first of three presidents who served as governors of Virginia.
•He was the first of 13 presidents who served as state governors.

1779, instrumental in moving state capital to Richmond

1779, founded first professorship of law in America, College of William and Mary

1780, reelected governor

Nov. 3, 1780, his fourth daughter born
•The girl, name unknown, died in infancy, Apr. 15, 1781.

Jan. 4, 1781, forced to flee Richmond
•A marauding expedition, led by Benedict Arnold, sailed into Chesapeake Bay, Dec. 31, 1780. Arnold and his nine hundred men held Richmond for 23 hours, Jan. 5–6.
•Four times during the spring of 1781, the governor and the legislature were obliged to quit the capital because of the approach or the threat of the British.

1781, declined renomination for governor
•He was of the opinion that the civil and military powers should be combined. He supported the commander of the state militia, General Thomas Nelson, who was elected.

1781, again elected to House of Burgesses

May 8, 1782, his fifth daughter born
•The girl, who was named Lucy Elizabeth Jefferson, died in infancy, Nov. 17, 1785.

Sept. 6, 1782, his wife died

Nov. 13, 1782, notified of appointment as commissioner to France
•He was to assist Benjamin Franklin and John Adams in negotiating for peace. The ship on which he was to sail was icebound in Chesapeake Bay until March, 1783. His orders were cancelled, Apr. 1.

June 6, 1783, elected to Congress
•He took his seat in Annapolis, Md., in November. As chairman of the currency committee, he was instrumental in establishing the decimal system. He proposed the system of dollars and cents; he was unsuccessful in his attempts to apply the decimal system to all measures.

May 7, 1784, elected as commissioner to France for third time
•His orders were to join Franklin and John Adams in negotiating commercial treaties with European nations.

July 5, 1784, sailed from Boston, Mass.
•He arrived in Paris, Aug. 6. He was to remain in Europe until 1789.

May 2, 1785, notified of his appointment as minister to France
•His commission as successor to Franklin was for three years from Mar. 10, 1785.
•He was the first of two presidents who served as ministers to France. The other was Monroe.
•He was the second of seven presidents who served as diplomats.

1785, his first book, *Notes on the State of Virginia,* privately printed, Paris
•The first public edition of his book was published in London by J. Stockdale, 1787. The first American edition was published in Philadelphia by Prichard and Hall, 1788.
•He was the third of 21 presidents who wrote books that were published during their lifetimes.

March–April, 1786, visited England

1786, his act for freedom of religion passed by Virginia legislature

Mar. 3–June 10, 1787, journeyed from Paris to southern France and northern Italy

Mar. 3–Apr. 23, 1788, visited Amsterdam, The Netherlands, and Strasbourg, France

July 1789, declined invitation to assist French constitutional committee

Oct. 22, 1789, sailed for U.S.
•He had been granted a six months' leave of absence. He landed in Norfolk, Va., Nov. 23.

Dec. 15, 1789, wrote Washington regarding cabinet appointment
•When Jefferson returned to the U.S., he received a letter from Washington, dated Oct. 13, informing him that he had been appointed secretary of state, Sept. 26. In his reply, Jefferson expressed his desire to return to France and then to retire from public life.

Feb. 14, 1790, accepted office of secretary of state
•Shortly after he arrived at Monticello, Dec. 23, 1789, Jefferson received a second letter from Washington, dated Nov. 30, which urged his acceptance of the cabinet post. He acquiesced.

Feb. 23, 1790, attended marriage of his

daughter, Martha, to Thomas Mann Randolph

Mar. 1, 1790, departed from Monticello for New York City

•He arrived in the capital, Mar. 21.

Mar. 22, 1790, took office as secretary of state

•He was the first of six presidents who served as secretary of state.

•He was the first of eight presidents who served in the cabinet.

Aug. 23, 1792, Washington letter regarding feud with Hamilton

•The differences between the secretary of state and the secretary of treasury had become acute. Washington tried to reconcile the two cabinet members but was unsuccessful.

July 31, 1793, submitted his resignation as secretary of state

•His resignation became effective, Dec. 31.

September, 1794, declined appointment as special envoy to Spain

Apr. 24, 1796, wrote Mazzei letter

•This letter to Philip Mazzei, an Italian-born Jeffersonian, severed Jefferson's relations with Washington when it was published in 1797. An indiscreet attack on Washington and the Federalists, it was first published in Florence, Italy, Jan. 1, 1797, and was republished in England, May 14, 1797.

Feb. 8, 1797, elected vice president

•He received 68 votes from the electors of eight of the 16 states (Georgia, 4; Kentucky, 4; Maryland, 4; North Carolina, 11; Pennsylvania, 14; South Carolina, 8; Tennessee, 3; Virginia, 20).

• *See* Election of 1796, pages 31–32.

Mar. 4, 1797, inaugurated as vice president, Philadelphia

1797, elected president of American Philosophical Society

•He served until 1815.

1798, drafted Kentucky Resolutions

•Introduced in the Kentucky legislature by W. C. Nicholas, the resolutions expressed Jefferson's belief that the Alien and Sedition Acts were unconstitutional. He was persuaded to draft the resolutions by Madison and Nicholas, who remained silent about the identity of the author for some time.

•The Kentucky and the Virginia resolves (Madison drafted the latter) asserted that the federal judiciary was not the only arbiter of constitutionality. After several northern states repudiated the resolves, a second set of Kentucky Resolutions added that "a nullification . . . is the rightful remedy."

Dec. 3, 1800, presidential electors cast ballots

• *See* Election of 1800, below.

Feb. 11–17, 1801, electoral votes tabulated by Congress

•Jefferson and Burr were officially declared elected.

•The difficulties of this election led to the adoption of the 12th Amendment to the Constitution.

• *See* Constitution, page 643.

Feb. 27, 1801, published his *Manual of Parliamentary Practice*

•This code still substantially governs U.S. deliberative bodies and was the forerunner of the Senate and the House of Representatives manuals.

ELECTION OF 1800

•Thomas Jefferson of Virginia and Aaron Burr of New York had been nominated by the Democratic-Republicans in opposition to the Federalist candidates, John Adams of Massachusetts and Charles Cotesworth Pinckney of South Carolina.

•The electors from 11 states, Connecticut, Delaware, Georgia, Massachusetts, New Hampshire, New Jersey, New York, Pennsylvania, South Carolina, Tennessee, and Vermont had been appointed by their state legislatures, while those representing Kentucky, Maryland, North Carolina, Rhode Island, and Virginia had been selected by popular vote.

•When the electoral votes were tabulated by Congress, Feb. 11, 1801, Jefferson and Burr each received 73 of the 276 electoral votes from the 16 states, the only instance of an electoral vote tie. Jefferson and Burr received identical votes from nine states (Georgia, 4; Kentucky, 4; Maryland, 5; New York, 12; North Carolina, 8; Pennsylvania, 8; South Carolina, 8; Tennessee, 3; Virginia, 21).

•The remaining 130 electoral votes were divided between three candidates. John Adams of Massachusetts received 65 votes (Connecticut, 9; Delaware, 3; Maryland, 5; Massachusetts, 16; New Hampshire, 6;

New Jersey, 7; North Carolina, 4; Pennsylvania, 7; Rhode Island, 4; Vermont, 4); Charles Cotesworth Pinckney of South Carolina, 64 (Connecticut, 9; Delaware, 3; Maryland, 5; Massachusetts, 16; New Hampshire, 6; New Jersey, 7; North Carolina, 4; Pennsylvania, 7; Rhode Island, 3; Vermont, 4); and John Jay of New York, one (Rhode Island, 1). One Maryland elector did not cast his vote.
•The Jefferson-Burr tie vote necessitated an election in the House of Representatives, to be decided on the basis of one vote for each state.
•Jefferson received the votes of eight states

on the first ballot, Feb. 11. Six states voted for Burr; the votes of two states were null because delegations were evenly divided. Since neither candidate had a majority of the 16 states, further balloting was required.
•Jefferson was elected president on the 36th ballot, Feb. 17, by the votes of ten states. Burr received the votes of four states and was elected vice president. The votes of two states were null.
•This was the first of two elections decided by the House of Representatives. The other was the Election of 1824.
• *See* pages 82–83.

THE PRESIDENT (3rd)

Term of office: Mar. 4, 1801, to Mar. 4, 1809 (8 years)
•He was the second of 12 presidents who had served as vice presidents.
•He was the second of three presidents who took office upon the completion of their vice-presidential terms.
•He was the second of 12 presidents who were elected to second terms.
•He was the second of 16 presidents who served more than one term.
•He was the only president who served two terms after the completion of his vice-presidential term.
•He was the second of nine presidents who served two terms.
•He was the first of eight presidents who served for eight years.
State represented: Virginia
•He was the second of four presidents who comprised the Virginia Regime.
•He was the second of five presidents who represented Virginia.

Political party: Democratic-Republican
•He was the first of four presidents who were Democratic-Republicans.
Congresses: 7th, 8th, 9th, 10th
Administrations: 4th, 5th
Age at inauguration: 57 years, 325 days
Inauguration day: Wednesday, Mar. 4, 1801
•Jefferson took the oath of office, administered by Chief Justice John Marshall, in the Senate chamber of the Capitol, Washington, D. C. Only the north wing of the Capitol had been completed; it then accommodated both houses of Congress.
•This was the first of nine inaugurations at which Marshall officiated.
•Jefferson was the second of three presidents who took the oath in the Senate chamber.
•This was the third of five inaugural ceremonies held in the Senate chamber.
•Jefferson was the first president who took the oath of office in Washington, D. C.

THE 4th ADMINISTRATION

1801

Mar. 5, appointed his only secretary of state, James Madison; his first attorney general, Levi Lincoln; and his only secretary of war, Henry Dearborn
•Madison took office, May 2.
Mar. 19, moved into White House
May 6, Secretary of Treasury Dexter resigned, effective, May 13

May 6, appointed his second secretary of treasury, Albert Gallatin
•Gallatin took office, May 14.
May 14, Pasha of Tripoli increased tribute demands, declared war on U.S.
•Jefferson had followed the policy of Washington and Adams of paying annual tribute —as did the major European countries— to the Barbary States: Tripoli, Algiers, Morocco, and Tunis. His answer to the

Tripolitan pasha, Yusuf Karamanli, was to dispatch a squadron of American naval vessels to the Mediterranean, May 20.

July 4, reviewed Marine Corps, White House
• This was the first presidential review of military forces at the executive mansion.

July 4, held public reception, White House
• He shook hands with more than one hundred guests. During public receptions held by Washington and Adams, guests had bowed when presented to the president.

July 14, appointed his only secretary of navy, Robert Smith
• Smith took office, July 27.

Dec. 7, first session of 7th Congress
• The administration controlled both the Senate and the House of Representatives. The Senate (32 members) consisted of 18 Democratic-Republicans and 14 Federalists. The House (105 members) consisted of 69 Democratic-Republicans and 36 Federalists.

Dec. 8, sent his first State of the Union message to Congress
• He was the first president to write his State of the Union message, rather than deliver it orally. He also announced that no reply was expected. This custom prevailed until 1913, when Wilson chose to address Congress in person.

1802

Jan. 15, charter issued to Jefferson College, Canonsburg, Pa.
• In 1865, the college was combined with Washington College, renamed Washington and Jefferson. It is now located at Washington, Pa.

Mar. 8, Judiciary Act of 1801 repealed
• He had suggested revision of the judiciary system in his first State of the Union message.

Mar. 16, signed act that established U. S. Military Academy
• This act also reduced the army to the peacetime strength of 1796—one regiment of artillery and two regiments of infantry.

Apr. 14, naturalization act of 1798 repealed
• This act changed the period of residence required for full citizenship from 14 to five years, and reestablished the provisions of the naturalization act of 1795.

Apr. 29, signed Judiciary Act of 1802
• The Supreme Court was restored to six justices. Six circuit courts, each headed by a Supreme Court justice, were established.

Apr. 30, signed first enabling act
• This act authorized the inhabitants of the eastern division of the Northwest Territory to hold a constitutional convention, the first step toward statehood for Ohio.

May 3, Washington, D.C., incorporated as city
• It was established that the mayor was to be appointed by the president.

May 3, first session of 7th Congress adjourned

Dec. 6, second session of 7th Congress

Dec. 15, sent his second State of the Union message to Congress

1803

Jan. 12, James Monroe confirmed as his special envoy to France
• Jefferson's instructions to Monroe were to negotiate for the purchase of New Orleans and West Florida.

Jan. 18, sent special message to Congress in which he proposed exploration expedition to western ocean
• When Congress approved the plan, he named Meriwether Lewis to head the expedition. Lewis selected William Clark as his associate in command.

Feb. 24, *Marbury v. Madison*
• Jefferson had ordered Madison to withhold the commission of William Marbury, who had been appointed justice of the peace by Adams in 1801. (Marbury's commission had been one of Adams's "midnight appointments."). The Supreme Court dismissed Marbury's suit, stating that the Court lacked jurisdiction and in the process declared a section of the Judiciary Act of 1789 unconstitutional.
• This was the first time that the Court held an act of Congress invalid. The Court did not again invalidate an act of Congress until the *Dred Scott* decision of 1857.
• More importantly, *Marbury v. Madison* was a precedent-setting decision, which authorized all federal courts to review the constitutionality of legislation.

Mar. 1, Ohio admitted as 17th state
• Ohio was the only state admitted during his term of office.

Mar. 3, authorized to call eighty thousand militia and build arsenals in West
Mar. 3, second session of 7th Congress adjourned
May 2, treaty with France transferring Louisiana to U.S. signed
• The treaty, antedated, Apr. 30, was signed by Robert Livingston, minister to France, and Monroe; they had exceeded their original instructions to purchase New Orleans and West Florida.
• The area of the U.S. was more than doubled by the purchase of Louisiana. The price was about $15,000,000. The territory consisted of what are now the states of Missouri, Nebraska, Iowa, Arkansas, North Dakota, and South Dakota, most of Louisiana, Kansas, Minnesota, Montana, and Wyoming, and parts of Colorado and Oklahoma.
June 30, gave instructions to Lewis and Clark
Oct. 17, first session of 8th Congress
• The administration maintained control of both the Senate and the House of Representatives. The Senate (34 members) consisted of 25 Democratic-Republicans and nine Federalists. The House (141 members) consisted of 102 Democratic-Republicans and 39 Federalists.
Oct 17, sent his third State of the Union message to Congress
Oct. 20, Senate ratified treaty with France, 24–7
Oct. 30, authorized to take possession of Louisiana
Dec. 20, William C.C. Claiborne, governor of Mississippi Territory, took formal possession of Louisiana for U.S.

1804

Feb. 25, nominated by Democratic-Republicans for president
• *See* Election of 1804, page 48.
Mar. 5, accepted resignation of Associate Justice Moore
Mar. 22, appointed William Johnson as associate justice
• Johnson, who was confirmed by the Senate, Mar. 24, was the first of Jefferson's three appointments to the Supreme Court.
Mar. 27, first session of 8th Congress adjourned

Apr. 17, his daughter, Mary died
• Mary Jefferson was the second of five children of presidents who died during their fathers' terms of office.
May 14, Lewis and Clark expedition began ascent of Missouri River
July 11, Alexander Hamilton fatally shot by Vice President Burr in duel, Weehawken, N.J.
• Hamilton died, July 12.
Sept. 25, 12th Amendment to Constitution ratified
• This amendment provided that voters shall "name in their ballots the person voted for as President and in distinct ballots the person voted for as Vice President." This amendment was a direct result of the Election of 1800, when Jefferson and Burr received the same number of electoral votes. The tie vote had necessitated an election in the House of Representatives.
• *See* Election of 1800, pages 44–45.
• *See* Constitution, page 643.
Nov. 4, second session of 8th Congress
Nov. 8, sent his fourth State of the Union message, to Congress
Nov. 13, election day
• *See* Election of 1804, page 48.
Dec. 5, presidential electors cast ballots
• *See* Election of 1804, page 48.

1805

Jan. 11, signed act which established Territory of Michigan, effective, July 1
Feb. 13, electoral votes tabulated by Congress
• Jefferson and Clinton were officially declared elected.
Mar. 1, Associate Justice Samuel Chase acquitted
• Chase, an ardent Federalist, had been impeached for his conduct during the trials of John Fries and James Thompson Callender. The failure to convict Chase brought to an end the Jeffersonian attacks on Federalist judges.
• Chase was the only Supreme Court justice impeached.
Mar. 2, issued executive order for 25 gunboats for port and harbor protection
Mar. 3, second session of 8th Congress adjourned
Mar. 3, Attorney General Lincoln resigned

ELECTION OF 1804

- Thomas Jefferson of Virginia was nominated for president and George Clinton of New York was nominated for vice president by a caucus of Democratic-Republican members of Congress, Feb. 25. This was the first congressional caucus to nominate party candidates for president and vice president.
- Leaders of the Federalist party had informally agreed upon Charles Cotesworth Pinckney of South Carolina as the candidate for president and Rufus King of New York as the candidate for vice president.
- The electors from 11 states, Kentucky, Maryland, Massachusetts, New Hampshire, New Jersey, North Carolina, Ohio, Pennsylvania, Rhode Island, Tennessee, and Virginia, had been selected by popular vote, while those representing Connecticut, Delaware, Georgia, New York, South Carolina, and Vermont had been appointed by their state legislatures.

- This was the first time that a majority of the states had selected their electors by popular vote.
- Jefferson and Clinton received 162 of the 176 electoral votes from the 17 states. Pinckney and King received 14 electoral votes.
- Jefferson and Clinton received the electoral votes of 15 states (Georgia, 6; Kentucky, 8; Maryland, 9 of 11 votes; Massachusetts, 19; New Hampshire, 7; New Jersey, 8; New York, 19; North Carolina, 14; Ohio, 3; Pennsylvania, 20; Rhode Island, 4; South Carolina, 10; Tennessee, 5; Vermont, 6; Virginia, 24).
- Pinckney and King received the electoral votes of two states (Connecticut, 9; Delaware, 3). The Federalist candidates also received the votes of two Maryland electors.
- This was the first election in which electoral votes were cast under the provisions of the 12th Amendment of the Constitution.
- *See* Constitution, page 643.

THE 5th ADMINISTRATION

1805

Mar. 4, his second inauguration day
- Jefferson took the oath of office, administered by Chief Justice John Marshall, in the Senate chamber of the Capitol, as he had in 1801.
- This was the second of nine inaugurations at which Marshall officiated.
- This was the fourth of five inaugural ceremonies in the Senate chamber.
- Jefferson's age at his second inauguration was 61 years, 325 days. He was the first of 21 presidents who were younger than their vice presidents. He was three years, 261 days younger than Clinton.
June 4, peace treaty with Tripoli signed
- American forces had seized Derna, the principal city of Tripoli, Apr. 26. An effective blockade brought the war to an end. The treaty designated that the U.S. was free to sail the Mediterranean and that Tripoli relinquished its claim for tribute. However, U.S. payment of annual tribute to the other Barbary States continued until 1815 and 1816.
Aug. 7, appointed his second attorney gen-

eral, John Breckenridge
Nov. 12, his plan of reopening negotiations for purchase of Florida adopted by cabinet
Nov. 15, Lewis and Clark arrived at mouth of Columbia River
- Part of the U.S. claim to Oregon was based on this accomplishment.
Dec. 2, first session of 9th Congress
- The administration maintained control of both the Senate and the House of Representatives. The Senate (34 members) consisted of 27 Democratic-Republicans and seven Federalists. The House (141 members) consisted of 116 Democratic-Republicans and 25 Federalists.
Dec. 3, sent his fifth State of the Union message to Congress

1806

Jan. 17, James Madison Randolph born in White House
- Jefferson's grandson, the son of Thomas Mann Randolph and Martha Jefferson Randolph, was the first child born in the White House.

Apr. 21, first session of 9th Congress adjourned

May 17, appointed James Monroe and William Pinkney as commissioners extraordinary to negotiate treaty with Great Britain

Sept. 9, Associate Justice Paterson died

Nov. 10, appointed Henry Brockholst Livingston as associate justice.

•Livingston, who was confirmed by the Senate, Dec. 17, was the second of Jefferson's three appointments to the Supreme Court.

Nov. 26, issued proclamation that warned persons not to conspire against Spain

•He ordered the arrest of those concerned in military expeditions into Spanish territory. He referred to the Burr expedition.

Dec. 1, second session of 9th Congress

Dec. 2, sent his sixth State of the Union message to Congress

Dec. 14, Attorney General Breckenridge died

1807

Jan. 20, appointed his third attorney general, Caesar Rodney

Feb. 24, signed judiciary act increasing Supreme Court from six to seven members

Feb. 28, appointed Thomas Todd as associate justice

•Todd, who was confirmed by the Senate, Mar. 3, was the last of Jefferson's three appointments to the Supreme Court.

Mar. 2, signed act that prohibited the importation of slaves as of Jan. 1, 1808

Mar. 3, second session of 9th Congress adjourned

Mar. 5, received treaty negotiated by Monroe and Pinkney with Great Britain

•Since there was no provision in the treaty —signed Dec. 3, 1806—regarding impressment of seamen or seizure of American vessels, he refused to submit it to the Senate.

June 20, refused to appear as witness at treason trial of Aaron Burr

•Burr was acquitted Sept. 1.

July 2, issued proclamation that required all British warships to leave American waters

Oct. 26, first session of 10th Congress

•The administration maintained control of both the Senate and the House of Representatives. The Senate (34 members) consisted of 28 Democratic-Republicans and six Federalists. The House (142 members) consisted of 118 Democratic-Republicans and 24 Federalists.

Oct. 27, sent his seventh State of the Union message to Congress

Dec. 22, signed embargo act that prohibited commerce with Great Britain and France

•This was the first embargo act.

1808

Jan. 9, signed second embargo act

•This act, more stringent than the act of Dec. 22, 1807, was popularly called the "O grab me act," which is "embargo" spelled backwards.

Mar. 1, Embargo Act of 1807 repealed

Mar. 12, embargo modified; authorized to permit vessels to transport American property home from foreign ports

Apr. 25, first session of 10th Congress adjourned

Nov. 7, second session of 10th Congress

Nov. 8, sent his eighth and last State of the Union message to Congress

Dec. 7, 1808, presidential electors cast ballots

•See Election of 1808, page 57.

1809

Jan. 9, signed enforcement act, which supplemented embargo, increased powers of collectors in making seizure of vessels

•This act also authorized the president to employ the militia and navy to enforce the regulations.

Feb. 3, Territory of Illinois established

Mar. 1, signed Non-Intercourse Act

•This act repealed the embargo, which was to go into effect, Mar. 15, reopened trade with all nations except Great Britain and France, and authorized resumption of trade with the British and French when they ceased neutrality violations.

Mar. 3, second session of 10th Congress adjourned

Note: He was the second of seven presidents who did not exercise the veto.

THE FORMER PRESIDENT

Mar. 4, 1809, attended inauguration of Madison
•Jefferson's age upon leaving office was 65 years, 325 days.
•He retired to Monticello, where he lived the rest of his life. He actively supervised the running of the estate, entertained a constant stream of guests, and carried on extensive correspondence.
•He was the second of six presidents who were farmers, planters, or ranchers after their terms of office.
Apr. 13, 1813, celebrated his 70th birthday
•He was the second of 16 presidents who lived to be 70.
Jan. 26, 1815, Congress authorized purchase of his library
•The library, consisting of nearly sixty-five hundred volumes, formed the basis for a new Library of Congress. The original had been burned by the British in 1814. He received $23,950 for the books, which required ten wagons for transportation to the capital. With typical thoroughness, he specified the form of packing, loading, and shipping the books. He also supplied, at the request of the librarian of Congress, a system of classification for cataloguing, which was adopted with only minor changes.
1817, drafted bill for establishment of University of Virginia
•The bill, which called for the establishment of public elementary schools as well as the university, was introduced in the state legislature by his friend, Joseph C. Cabell.
Apr. 13, 1818, celebrated his 75th birthday
•He was the second of ten presidents who lived to be 75.
1819, University of Virginia chartered
•He designed the buildings, supervised their construction, laid out the curriculum, and chose the faculty. The university opened in March, 1825, with 40 students in the first class.
•He served as rector until his death.
Apr. 13, 1823, celebrated his 80th birthday
•He was the second of six presidents who lived to be 80.
1826, saved from bankruptcy by gift of $16,-500 from friends

•He had been financially embarrassed for most of his retirement as a result of his openhanded hospitality and such gestures as cosigning notes for friends. He was on the verge of losing Monticello when he received this timely gift. Mayor Philip Hone of New York City raised $8,500, an additional $5,000 came from Philadelphia, and $3,000 arrived from Baltimore.

DEATH

Date of death: July 4, 1826
•Jefferson was the first of three presidents who died on the Fourth of July. He and John Adams died on the same day; Adams died several hours later.
Place of death: Monticello, near Charlottesville, Va.
•He was the second of four presidents who died in Virginia.
Age at death: 83 years, 82 days
•He lived 17 years, 122 days, after the completion of his term.
Cause of death: Diarrhea
Place of burial: Monticello, near Charlottesville, Va.
•He was the second of seven presidents who were buried in Virginia.

THE VICE PRESIDENTS
(3rd and 4th)

Note: Jefferson was the first of seven presidents who had two vice presidents.

Full name: Aaron Burr (3rd)
Date of birth: Feb. 6, 1756
Place of birth: Newark, N.J.
•He was the first of two vice presidents who were born in New Jersey. The other was Hobart.
Religious denomination: Presbyterian
•He was the first of 11 vice presidents who were Presbyterians.
College: College of New Jersey, now Princeton University, Princeton, N.J.
Date of graduation: 1772
Occupation: Lawyer

•He served in the Continental army, rose to the rank of lieutenant colonel, resigned because of ill health, 1775–1779; admitted to the bar in New York, 1782; practiced law, 1783–1789; New York state attorney general, 1789–1791; represented New York in Senate, 1791–1797; built political machine, using the Tammany Society, which insured victory for the Democratic-Republican faction in the 1800 presidential election.

•He was the first of 17 vice presidents who served in the Senate before their terms of office.

Term of office: Mar. 4, 1801, to Mar. 4, 1805 (4 years)

•He was the second of 17 vice presidents who served four-year terms.

•Jefferson and Burr were the third of 41 president-vice president teams.

Age at inauguration: 45 years, 26 days

State represented: New York

•He was the first of ten vice presidents who represented New York.

•He was the first of 13 vice presidents who represented states that were not their native states.

Political party: Democratic-Republican

•He was the second of six vice presidents who were Democratic-Republicans.

Occupation after term: Lawyer

Date of death: Sept. 14, 1836

Place of death: Staten Island, N.Y.

•He was the first of two vice presidents who died in Staten Island. The other was Tompkins.

•He was the first of nine vice presidents who died in New York.

Age at death: 80 years, 221 days

Place of burial: Princeton, N.J.

•He was the first of two vice presidents who were buried in New Jersey. The other was Hobart.

Full name: George Clinton (4th)

Date of birth: July 26, 1739

Place of birth: Little Britain (now Ulster County), N.Y.

•He was the first of eight vice presidents who were born in New York.

Religious denomination: Presbyterian

•He was the second of 11 vice presidents who were Presbyterians.

Occupation: Lawyer

•He was a brigadier general in the Continental army; a delegate from New York to the Second Continental Congress, 1775; elected as first governor of New York, served six successive terms, 1777–1795; wrote the seven *Cato* letters, in which he opposed the ratification of the Constitution, published in the New York *Journal*, 1787; received three electoral votes for the vice presidency, 1789; defeated for vice presidency by John Adams, 77–50, 1792; declined to stand for reelection as governor, 1795; received seven electoral votes for vice presidency, 1796; served seventh term as governor, 1801–1804.

•He was the second of 14 vice presidents who served as state governors.

Term of office: Mar. 4, 1805, to Apr. 20, 1812 (7 years, 47 days)

•He was the second of four vice presidents who served more than seven years.

Note: Clinton also served as vice president under Madison. *See* page 64.

•Jefferson and Clinton were the fourth of 41 president-vice president teams.

Age at inauguration: 65 years, 221 days

State represented: New York

•He was the second of ten vice presidents who represented New York.

Political party: Democratic-Republican

•He was the third of six vice presidents who were Democratic-Republicans.

THE CABINET

State: James Madison of Virginia, May 2, 1801, to Mar. 3, 1809

Treasury: Samuel Dexter of Massachusetts, Jan. 1, 1801, to May 13, 1801

•Abraham Alfonse Albert Gallatin of Pennsylvania, May 14, 1801, to Feb. 8, 1814

War: Henry Dearborn of Maine, Mar. 5, 1801, to Mar. 7, 1809

Attorney General: Levi Lincoln of Massachusetts, Mar. 5, 1801, to Mar. 3, 1805

•John Breckenridge of Kentucky, Aug. 7, 1805, to Dec. 14, 1806

•Caesar Augustus Rodney of Delaware, Jan. 20, 1807, to Dec. 11, 1811

Navy: Robert Smith of Maryland, July 27, 1801, to Mar. 7, 1809

THE SUPREME COURT

Associate Justices: William Johnson of South Carolina, appointed, Mar. 22, 1804; confirmed, Mar. 24, 1804

• Henry Brockholst Livingston of New York, appointed, Nov. 10, 1806; confirmed, Dec. 17, 1806
• Thomas Todd of Kentucky, appointed, Feb. 28, 1807; confirmed, Mar. 3, 1807

Fourth President

JAMES MADISON

Full name: James Madison
• He was the first of five presidents named James.
• He was the second of eight presidents who had the same full names as their fathers.
• He was the fourth of 17 presidents who did not have middle initials or middle names.
Date of birth: Mar. 16, 1751 (Mar. 5, 1750/1751 O.S.)
• He was the first of four presidents born in March.
• He was the last of four presidents who were born before the Gregorian (new style) calendar replaced the Julian (old style) calendar in England and the British colonies, 1752.
Place of birth: Port Conway, King George County, Va.
• He was the third of eight presidents who were born in Virginia.
Family lineage: English
• He was the third of 12 presidents who were of English ancestry.
• He and Zachary Taylor were second cousins.
Religious denomination: Episcopalian
• He was the second of nine presidents who were Episcopalians.

College: College of New Jersey, now Princeton University, Princeton, N.J.
• He was the first of three presidents who attended Princeton.
• He was the third of 27 presidents who attended college.
Date of graduation: Sept. 25, 1771, Bachelor of Arts
• He was the first of two presidents who were graduated from Princeton. The other was Wilson.
• He was the second of 21 presidents who were graduated from college.

PARENTS AND SIBLINGS

Father's name: James Madison
Date of birth: Mar. 27, 1723
Place of birth: probably Orange County, Va.
Occupations: Planter and farmer
• Madison's father also was lieutenant of Orange County.
Date of Death: Feb. 27, 1801
Place of death: Montpelier estate, Orange County, Va.
Age at death: 77 years, 337 days

Mother's name: Eleanor Rose Conway Madison

Date of birth: Jan. 9, 1731

Place of birth: Caroline County, Va.

Date of marriage: Sept. 15, 1749

Children: 10; 5 sons, 5 daughters

- James was born in 1751; Francis in 1753; Ambrose in 1755; Catlett in 1758; Nelly Conway in 1760; William in 1762; Sarah in 1764; Elizabeth in 1768; Reuben in 1771; and Frances Taylor in 1774. Catlett died in 1758; Elizabeth and Reuben in 1775.
- Madison was the third of five presidents who came from families of ten children.
- He was the second of eight presidents who were the eldest children in their families.

Date of death: Feb. 11, 1829

- Madison was the third of ten presidents whose mothers lived to see their sons' inauguration or oath-taking days. Mrs. Madison did not attend the ceremony.

Place of death: Montpelier estate, Orange County, Va.

Age at death: 98 years, 33 days

MARRIAGE

Date of marriage: Sept. 15, 1794

Place of marriage: Harewood estate, near Charles Town, then Frederick County, Va., now Jefferson County, W. Va.

- He was the third of four presidents who were married in Virginia.

Age at marriage: 43 years, 183 days

- He was the first of two presidents who were married in their forties. The other was Cleveland.

Years married: 41 years, 287 days

Wife's name: Dorothea Payne Todd Madison

- She was called Dolley.
- Madison was the third of six presidents who married widows. Her first husband, John Todd, had died in 1793.
- She was the third of 33 first ladies.
- She was the fourth of 40 wives of presidents.

Date of birth: May 20, 1768

- She was the first of three first ladies who were born in May.
- She was the first of three wives of presi-

dents who were born in May.

Place of birth: near Greensboro, N.C.

- She was the only first lady or wife of a president who was born in North Carolina.

Wife's mother: Mary Coles Payne

Wife's father: John Payne, farmer and planter

Age at marriage: 26 years, 118 days

- She was the second of 26 first ladies who were married in their twenties.
- She was the third of 30 wives of presidents who were married in their twenties.

Years younger than husband: 17 years, 65 days

Children: None

- Madison was the second of six presidents who were childless.
- Mrs. Madison had had two children by her first husband; one died in infancy.
- Madison was the second of three presidents who had stepchildren.

Years she survived her husband: 13 years, 14 days

- She was the second of 21 first ladies who survived their husbands.
- She was the second of 23 wives of presidents who survived their husbands.

Date of death: July 12, 1849

Place of death: Washington, D.C.

- She was the first of nine first ladies who died in Washington.
- She was the first of nine wives of presidents who died in Washington.

Age at death: 81 years, 53 days

- She had celebrated her 80th birthday, May 20, 1848.
- She was the third of 16 first ladies who lived to be 70.
- She was the third of 17 wives of presidents who lived to be 70.
- She was the first of 14 first ladies who lived to be 75.
- She was the first of 15 wives of presidents who lived to be 75.
- She was the first of nine first ladies who lived to be 80.
- She was the first of ten wives of presidents who lived to be 80.

Place of burial: Montpelier estate, Orange County, Va.

- She was the second of six first ladies who were buried in Virginia.
- She was the third of seven wives of presidents who were buried in Virginia.

EARLY YEARS

June, 1762, entered school conducted by Donald Robertson, Innes plantation, King and Queen County, Va.
• Madison attended the Robertson school for five years.
1768–1769, tutored at home by Reverend Thomas Martin
September, 1769, entered College of New Jersey, now Princeton University, Princeton, N.J.
Sept. 25, 1771, was graduated from College of New Jersey
• He remained at the college for more than six months after graduation, studying Hebrew and ethics. He departed for home in April, 1772.
Dec. 22, 1774, elected to committee of safety, Orange County, Va.
• His father was chairman of the 11-man committee.
Oct. 2, 1775, commissioned as colonel of Orange County militia
• He participated in drills and marches, saw no active duty.
Apr. 25, 1776, elected to Virginia convention, Williamsburg
• The convention met, May 6. He served on the committee formed to draft a state constitution. The constitution was adopted, June 29; the convention adjourned, July 5.
Oct. 7, 1776, elected to first House of Delegates, lower house of state assembly
Apr. 24, 1777, defeated for reelection to House of Delegates
• He refused to solicit votes or furnish rum or punch for the voters, as was the current custom.
Nov. 12, 1777, elected member of governor's council of state
• He took his seat Jan. 14, 1778. He served on the eight-man council, under Governor Patrick Henry and Governor Thomas Jefferson, until 1779.
Dec. 14, 1779, elected to Second Continental Congress
• He was the youngest member of the Continental Congress.
• He took his seat, Mar. 20, 1780; he served until Oct. 25, 1783.
• He was the fourth of five presidents who served in the Continental congresses.
1784, again elected to House of Delegates
• He led the opposition to a bill to impose a state tax "for the support of teachers of the Christian religion," which was defeated in 1785. His religious freedom act abolished the state religious test.
• He served until 1786.
1784–1786, read law intermittently
• He had given the law some thought after he was graduated from college. He continued his "course of reading," he explained in a letter to Edmund Randolph, July 26, 1785, but was "far from being determined ever to make a professional use of it." Also, he felt his weak voice and shortcomings as an orator detrimental to a law career.
Sept. 11, 1786, attended Annapolis convention
• The legislature of Maryland called for a convention of state representatives to consider the problems of interstate commerce. Only five states sent delegates (Virginia, Delaware, Pennsylvania, New Jersey, and New York); action was deferred. However, a second convention was recommended, to be held in Philadelphia the following May, to deal with the regulation of commerce, but also "other important matters."
1786, again elected to Second Continental Congress
February, 1787, took seat in Continental Congress, New York City
• He and Alexander Hamilton were the leaders of the bloc that convinced the congress to call a convention similar to the one recommended at Annapolis. The Philadelphia convention was sanctioned "for the sole and express purpose of revising the Articles of Confederation." The title of Constitutional Convention came later.
May 3, 1787, arrived in Philadelphia
• The convention, which was scheduled to open, May 14, lacked a quorum until May 25.

NATIONAL PROMINENCE

May 25–Sept. 17, 1787, attended Constitutional Convention
- His role in the debates that led to the final version of the Constitution cannot be exaggerated. He wrote the Virginia Plan, which favored representation based on population. The opposing theory, the New Jersey Plan, held to the theory of one vote to one state. After both plans had been incorporated and it was decided that a two-chambered legislature (an upper house based on equal representation and a lower house elected according to population) should prevail, it was his compromise that solved the congressional apportionment problem. His suggestion that five slaves be counted as three individuals won both northern and southern support. This and other contributions—like his suggestion that a proper proportion of the legislature should be allowed to overrule the executive veto, which led to the two-thirds rule—earned him the name, "Father of the Constitution."
- The convention was held behind closed doors, which was not unusual at the time. His copious notes, which comprise the largest part of our knowledge of the proceedings, were purchased for $30,000 by act of Congress in 1837, and were published in three volumes in 1840.

Sept. 17, 1787, signed Constitution
- He was the second of two presidents who signed the Constitution. The other was Washington.
- *See* Constitution, pages 637–645.

Oct. 27, 1787, first of Federalist essays published in New York *Independent Journal*
- The 85 essays urging adoption of the Constitution, which have come to be known as the *Federalist Papers*, were written by Madison, Hamilton, and John Jay. From Oct. 27, 1787, to Apr. 2, 1788, 77 of the essays appeared in New York newspapers over the signature, *Publius*. At least 24 of the essays—and possibly 29—were written by Madison. His first contribution, No. 10, appeared in the New York *Daily Advertiser*, Nov. 22, 1787.
- The first complete edition of the 85 essays was published in two volumes in New York City by J. and A. McLean, 1788.
- Madison was the fourth of 21 presidents who wrote books (in this instance, as a collaborator) that were published during their lifetimes.

March, 1788, elected to Virginia convention to consider ratification of Constitution
- The convention met, June 2. Madison led the fight for ratification, was supported by Marshall, Wythe, Randolph, and Henry Lee, and was opposed by Henry, Mason, Monroe, Tyler, and Harrison. Virginia was the tenth state to ratify, June 26, by the narrow margin of 89–79.

October, 1788, defeated for election to Senate
- Henry took the extreme step of stating that Madison was the one man who should not be elected to the Senate. Henry nominated Richard Henry Lee and William Grayson, both of whom were elected.

Feb. 2, 1789, elected to House of Representatives
- Henry had attempted to deprive him of a seat in the lower house also. Henry supported Monroe.
- Madison was the first of 17 presidents who served in the House of Representatives.

Apr. 6, 1789, took seat in House of Representatives
- He served in the 1st, 2nd, 3rd, and 4th Congresses.
- He was the first of 17 presidents who were elected to the House of Representatives.

Sept. 28, 1789, 12 proposed amendments to Constitution submitted to states for ratification
- He was a leading advocate of the 12 amendments, ten of which were declared ratified, Dec. 15, 1791 (the Bill of Rights).
- *See* Constitution, 1st–10th Amendments, page 642.

Sept. 15, 1794, married Dorothea Payne Todd, near Charles Town, then Frederick County, Va., now Jefferson County, W. Va.

1798, drafted Virginia Resolutions
- Adopted by the Virginia legislature, Dec. 24, the resolves maintained that the Alien and Sedition Acts were unconstitutional.

Apr. 24, 1799, again elected to House of Delegates

Mar. 5, 1801, appointed secretary of state by Jefferson

May 2, 1801, took office as secretary of state
- He was the second of six presidents who served as secretaries of state.

• He was the second of eight presidents who served in the cabinet.

Jan. 17, 1806, James Madison Randolph born

• Madison's namesake, the grandson of Jefferson, was the first child born in the White House.

1806, wrote *An Examination of the British Doctrine, which Subjects to Capture a Neutral Trade, Not Open in Time of Peace*

• This 204-page paper was reprinted several times during the next two years, including a London edition. John Randolph sneeringly classified it as the secretary of state's "shilling paper hurled against eight hundred ships of war."

Dec. 7, 1808, presidential electors cast ballots

• *See* Election of 1808, below.

Feb. 8, 1809, electoral votes tabulated by Congress

• Madison and Clinton were officially declared elected.

Mar. 3, 1809, resigned as secretary of state

ELECTION OF 1808

• James Madison of Virginia was nominated for president and George Clinton of New York was nominated for vice president by a congressional caucus of Democratic-Republicans, Jan. 23, after Jefferson refused to run for a third term.

• The Federalists again nominated Charles Cotesworth Pinckney of South Carolina for president and Rufus King of New York for vice president.

• The electors from ten states, Kentucky, Maryland, New Hampshire, New Jersey, North Carolina, Ohio, Pennsylvania, Rhode Island, Tennessee, and Virginia, had been selected by popular vote, while those representing Connecticut, Delaware, Georgia, Massachusetts, New York, South Carolina, and Vermont had been appointed by their state legislatures.

• Madison received 122 of the 176 electoral votes from the 17 states. Pinckney received 47 electoral votes and Clinton received six. One elector from Kentucky was absent.

• Madison received the electoral votes of 12 states (Georgia, 6; Kentucky, 7 of 8 votes; Maryland, 9 of 11 votes; New Jersey, 8; New York, 13 of 19 votes; North Carolina, 11 of 14 votes; Ohio, 3; Pennsylvania, 20; South Carolina, 10; Tennessee, 5; Vermont, 6; Virginia, 24).

• Pinckney received the electoral votes of five states (Connecticut, 9; Delaware, 3; Massachusetts, 19; New Hampshire, 7; Rhode Island, 4). He also received the votes of two Maryland and three North Carolina electors.

• Clinton, a vice-presidential candidate, received the votes of six New York electors for president.

• Clinton received 113 electoral votes and was elected vice president (Georgia, 6; Kentucky, 7 of 8 votes; Maryland, 9 of 11 votes; New Jersey, 8; New York, 13 of 19 votes; North Carolina, 11 of 14 votes; Pennsylvania, 20; South Carolina, 10; Tennessee, 5; Virginia, 24).

• King received 47 votes (Connecticut, 9; Delaware, 3; New Hampshire, 7; Massachusetts, 19; Rhode Island, 4). King also received the votes of three North Carolina and two Maryland electors.

• John Langdon of New Hampshire received nine votes (Ohio, 3; Vermont, 6).

• James Monroe of Virginia received the votes of three New York electors.

• Madison, not technically a vice-presidential nominee, received the votes of three New York electors.

THE PRESIDENT (4th)

Term of office: Mar. 4, 1809, to Mar. 4, 1817 (8 years)

• Madison was the third of 12 presidents who were elected to second terms.

• He was the third of 16 presidents who served more than one term.

• He was the third of nine presidents who served two terms.

• He was the second of eight presidents who served for eight years.

State represented: Virginia

• He was the first of four presidents who succeeded presidents who represented the same state.

• He was the third of the four presidents who comprised the Virginia Regime.

•He was the third of five presidents who represented Virginia.

Political party: Democratic-Republican

•He was the second of four presidents who were Democratic-Republicans.

Congresses: 11th, 12th, 13th, 14th

Administrations: 6th, 7th

Age at inauguration: 57 years, 353 days

•He was the second of 21 presidents who were younger than their vice presidents. Madison was 11 years, 233 days younger than Clinton.

Inauguration day: Saturday, Mar. 4, 1809

•Madison took the oath of office, administered by Chief Justice John Marshall, in the chamber of the House of Representatives in the Capitol.

•This was the third of nine inaugurations at which Marshall officiated.

•He was the second of five presidents who took the oath in the House chamber.

•This was the second of six oath-taking ceremonies in the House chamber.

THE 6th ADMINISTRATION

1809

Mar. 6, appointed his first secretary of state, Robert Smith; his first secretary of war, William Eustis; and his first secretary of navy, Paul Hamilton

•He retained Jefferson's secretary of treasury, Albert Gallatin, and attorney general, Caesar Rodney.

•Eustis took office, Mar. 7; Hamilton, May 15.

Apr. 19, issued proclamation terminating Non-Intercourse Act, renewing trade with Great Britain

May 22, first session of 11th Congress

•The administration controlled both the Senate and the House of Representatives. The Senate (34 members) consisted of 28 Democratic-Republicans and six Federalists. The House (142 members) consisted of 94 Democratic-Republicans and 48 Federalists.

June 27, appointed John Quincy Adams as minister to Russia

June 28, issued proclamation legalizing trade with Great Britain

June 28, first session of 11th Congress adjourned

Aug. 9, issued proclamation renewing Non-Intercourse Act against Great Britain

Nov. 27, second session of 11th Congress

Nov. 29, sent his first State of the Union message to Congress

1810

May 1, signed act that banned British and French armed vessels from U.S. waters

May 1, second session of 11th Congress adjourned

Sept. 13, Associate Justice Cushing died

Oct. 27, issued proclamation on taking possession of West Florida from Mississippi to Perdido Rivers as part of Louisiana Purchase

Dec. 3, third session of 11th Congress

Dec. 5, sent his second State of the Union message to Congress

Note: The official population, according to the third census, was 7,239,903, which included 1,191,364 slaves and 186,746 free Negroes.

1811

Jan. 2, appointed Levi Lincoln as associate justice

•Lincoln, who was confirmed by the Senate, Jan. 3, was the first of Madison's five appointments to the Supreme Court. Lincoln declined to serve, Jan. 5.

•Madison was the second of four presidents who appointed associate justices who declined to serve.

•Lincoln was the fourth of seven appointees, confirmed by the Senate, who declined to serve.

Jan. 15, authorized by Congress in secret session to take possession of East Florida as well as West Florida if local authorities consented or foreign power attempted to occupy

Feb. 4, appointed Alexander Wolcott as associate justice

•Wolcott, the second of Madison's five appointments to the Supreme Court, was rejected by the Senate, Feb. 13.

•Madison was the second of 15 presidents who nominated justices not confirmed by

the Senate.
- Wolcott was the second of 25 men nominated to the Supreme Court who were not confirmed by the Senate.

Feb. 21, appointed John Quincy Adams as associate justice
- Adams, who was confirmed by the Senate, Feb. 22, was the third of Madison's five appointments to the Supreme Court. Adams declined to serve, April 5.
- Adams was the fifth of seven appointees, confirmed by the Senate, who declined to serve.

Feb. 21, vetoed bill to incorporate Alexandria, Va. church
- This was the first of his seven vetoes.

Feb. 28, vetoed land grant bill for Mississippi church
- This was the second of his seven votes.

Mar. 3, third session of 11th Congress adjourned

Apr. 1, accepted resignation of Secretary of State Smith

Apr. 2, appointed his second secretary of state, James Monroe
- Monroe took office, Apr. 6.

June 19, Associate Justice Chase died

Nov. 4, first session of 12th Congress
- The administration maintained control of both the Senate and the House of Representatives. The Senate (36 members) consisted of 30 Democratic-Republicans and six Federalists. The House (144 members) consisted of 108 Democratic-Republicans and 36 Federalists.

Nov. 5, sent his third State of the Union message to Congress

Nov. 15, appointed Joseph Story and Gabriel Duval as associate justices
- Story and Duval, who were confirmed by the Senate, Nov. 18, were the fourth and last of Madison's five appointments to the Supreme Court.
- Story, who was 32 years old, was the youngest member of the Supreme Court.

Dec. 5, Attorney General Rodney resigned, effective, Dec. 11

Dec. 11, appointed his second attorney general, William Pinkney

1812

Feb. 10, paid political adventurer, John Henry, $50,000 for papers that purported to show disaffection of New England states
- The documents implied that the British

government had attempted to alienate the northeastern states.

Mar. 9, laid before Congress papers purchased from John Henry

Mar. 29, attended first wedding in White House
- Mrs. Lucy Payne Washington was married to Associate Justice Thomas Todd of the Supreme Court. Mrs. Washington was a sister of Mrs. Madison; she was the widow of George Steptoe Washington.

Apr. 3, vetoed bill regulating trials in district courts
- This was the third of his seven vetoes.

Apr. 10, authorized to call on states and territories for respective quotas of 100,000 militia for six months' service

Apr. 20, Vice President Clinton died, Washington, D.C.

Apr. 30, Louisiana admitted as 18th state
- Louisiana was the first of two states admitted during Madison's term of office.

May 18, renominated by Democratic-Republicans for president
- He was renominated unanimously under the promise of a declaration of war against England.

June 1, sent war message to Congress
- His message cited four grounds for war: impressment of American seamen; violation of American neutral rights and territorial waters; blockade of American ports; and British refusal to revoke the Orders in Council.
- This was the second of seven war messages.

June 4, House of Representatives supported declaration of war, 79–49

June 18, Senate supported declaration of war, 19–13

June 19, issued proclamation of declaration of war

July 6, first session of 12th Congress adjourned

July 26, authorized U.S. chargé in London, Jonathan Russell, to propose suspension of hostilities if Great Britain would agree to discontinue impressments and blockades

Oct. 27, replied to British offer of armistice that condition must be suspension of impressment

Nov. 2, second session of 12th Congress

Nov. 4, sent his fourth State of the Union message to Congress

Nov. 6, House of Representatives received memorandum of disapproval of naturalization bill
- This bill had been passed during the first

session of the 12th Congress. It was techni-
cally vetoed at the end of the session, when
Madison refused to sign it.
• This was the fourth of his seven vetoes, the
first of his two pocket vetoes.
• This was the first presidential pocket veto.

Note: If a bill passed by Congress is presented to the president for approval within
ten days (Sundays excepted) of the close of
a session, and the president fails to sign and
return it, the bill does not become a law.
This is a pocket veto.

Dec. 2, presidential electors cast ballots.
• *See* Election of 1812, below.
Dec. 31, accepted resignation of Secretary
of Navy Hamilton

1813

Jan. 1, accepted resignation of Secretary of
War Eustis, effective, Jan. 13
• Madison appointed Secretary of State
Monroe as secretary of war ad interim.
Monroe served until Feb. 5.
Jan. 12, appointed his second secretary of
navy, William Jones
• Jones took office, Jan. 19.
Jan. 13, appointed his second secretary of
war, John Armstrong
• Armstrong took office, Feb. 5.
Jan. 29, authorized to raise 20 regiments of
regular troops for one year's service
Feb. 10, electoral votes tabulated by Con-
gress
• Madison and Gerry were officially declared
elected.
Feb. 24, laid before Congress British proclamation and circular letter from governor
of Bermuda
• The letter cited a British Order in Council
on colonial trade with instructions to
colonial governors to show special privileges to the New England states.
Mar. 3, second session of 12th Congress adjourned

ELECTION OF 1812

• James Madison of Virginia was nominated
for president and John Langdon of New
Hampshire was nominated for vice president by a caucus of Democratic-Republican members of Congress, May 18. Lang-

don declined the nomination. Elbridge
Gerry of Massachusetts was nominated for
vice president at a second party caucus.
• An antiadministration faction of the Democratic-Republican party nominated De
Witt Clinton of New York for president and
Charles Jared Ingersoll of Pennsylvania
for vice president, in New York City, May
29.
• Leaders of the Federalist party met in New
York City in September. They did not officially endorse Clinton, but their failure to
nominate a candidate made Clinton the *de
facto* Federalist candidate for president.
• The electors from nine states, Kentucky,
Maryland, Massachusetts, New Hampshire, Ohio, Pennsylvania, Rhode Island,
Tennessee, and Virginia, had been selected by popular vote, while those representing Connecticut, Delaware, Georgia,
Louisiana, New York, New Jersey, North
Carolina, South Carolina, and Vermont
had been appointed by their state legislatures.
• Madison received 128 of the 217 electoral
votes from the 18 states. Clinton received
89 electoral votes. There was one vacancy
in the electoral college; the official total of
electors was 218.
• Madison received the electoral votes of 11
states (Georgia, 8; Kentucky, 12; Louisiana,
3; Maryland, 6 of 11 votes; North Carolina,
15; Ohio, 7; Pennsylvania, 25; South Carolina, 11; Tennessee, 8; Vermont, 8; Virginia, 25).
• Clinton received the electoral votes of
seven states (Connecticut, 9, Delaware, 4;
Massachusetts, 22; New Hampshire, 8;
New Jersey, 8; New York, 29; Rhode Island,
4). He also received the votes of five Maryland electors.
• Gerry received 131 electoral votes and was
elected vice president (Georgia, 8; Kentucky, 12; Louisiana, 3; Maryland, 6 of 11
votes; North Carolina, 15; Ohio, 7; Pennsylvania, 25; South Carolina, 11; Tennessee, 8;
Vermont, 8; Virginia, 25).
• Gerry also received the votes of one New
Hampshire and two Massachusetts elec-
tors.
• Ingersoll received 86 votes (Connecticut,
9; Delaware, 4; Massachusetts, 20 of 22
votes; New Hampshire, 7 of 8 votes; New
Jersey, 8; New York, 29; Rhode Island, 4).
• Ingersoll also received the votes of five
Maryland electors.

THE 7th ADMINISTRATION

1813

Mar. 4, his second inauguration day
•Madison took the oath of office, administered by Chief Justice John Marshall, in the chamber of the House of Representatives in the Capitol, as he had in 1809.
•This was the fourth of nine inaugurations at which Marshall officiated.
•This was the third of six-oath-taking ceremonies in the House chamber.
•Madison's age at his second inauguration was 61 years, 353 days.
•He was the third of 21 presidents who were younger than their vice presidents. Madison was six years, 242 days younger than Gerry.
•He was the first of two presidents who were younger than both of their vice presidents. The other was Cleveland.
May 9, dispatched Albert Gallatin and James A. Bayard as peace commissioners to discuss offer to mediate by Alexander I of Russia
•Gallatin and Bayard arrived in St. Petersburg, July 21, but the British had declined mediation, July 5.
May 24, first session of 13th Congress
•The administration maintained control of both the Senate and the House of Representatives. The Senate (36 members) consisted of 27 Democratic-Republicans and nine Federalists. The House (180 members) consisted of 112 Democratic-Republicans and 68 Federalists.
Aug. 2, first session of 13th Congress adjourned
Nov. 4, British offered to negotiate for peace directly with U.S.
•This communique was received at Washington, Jan. 3, 1814.
Dec. 6, second session of 13th Congress
Dec. 7, sent his fifth State of the Union message to Congress
Dec. 9, sent special message to Congress in which he recommended embargo to prohibit trading with enemy
•New York and New England merchants had been supplying the British with beef, flour, and other staples.
Dec. 17, signed embargo act
•This act was modified Jan. 25, 1814.

1814

Jan. 3, ordered court-martial of General Hull for surrender of Detroit
•Brigadier General William Hull had surrendered Detroit to the British without firing a shot, Aug. 16, 1812.
Jan. 18, his nominees as peace commissioners confirmed by Senate
•The commissioners were John Quincy Adams, James A. Bayard, Henry Clay, and Jonathan Russell. The Senate confirmed the fifth commissioner, Albert Gallatin, Feb. 8. The meeting place decided upon was Ghent, Belgium, Aug. 8.
Feb. 2, sent report of secretary of war to House of Representatives
•This report explained the failure of the army on the northern frontier.
Feb. 8, accepted resignation of Secretary of Treasury Gallatin
Feb. 9, appointed his second secretary of treasury, George W. Campbell
Feb. 10, accepted resignation of Attorney General Pinkney
Feb. 10, appointed his third attorney general, Richard Rush
Mar. 26, General Hull sentenced to death for cowardice and neglect of duty
•The sentence was first approved, then remitted because of Hull's commendatory Revolutionary War record.
Mar. 31, sent special message to Congress in which he recommended repeal of embargo and nonimportation acts
•The repeal bill was passed by the House of Representatives, Apr. 7, and the Senate, Apr. 12.
Apr. 14, signed act repealing embargo and nonimportation acts
Apr. 18, second session of 13th Congress adjourned
Aug. 8, American and British peace commissions met, Ghent, Belgium
Aug. 24–25, White House, Capitol, and all government buildings except Patent Office burned by British
•Madison and his cabinet fled to Virginia.
•He was the first of five presidents who visited war zones while in office.
•The British burned Washington in retaliation for the burning of York (Toronto), Ontario, Canada. York was the capital of Up-

per Canada; the governor's residence and the assembly houses had been destroyed by U.S. forces, Apr. 27, 1813.

Aug. 27, returned to Washington, D.C.

•He and Mrs. Madison resided at Octagon House while the president's mansion was being repaired.

Sept. 3, Secretary of War Armstrong resigned

•Madison again appointed James Monroe as secretary of war ad interim.

Sept. 19, third session of 13th Congress

•This session was held in the Patent Office, the only major government building spared by the British.

Sept. 20, sent his sixth State of the Union message to Congress

Sept. 27, appointed his third secretary of war, James Monroe

Oct. 5, accepted resignation of Secretary of Treasury Campbell

Oct. 6, appointed his third secretary of treasury, Alexander J. Dallas

Nov. 23, Vice President Gerry died, Washington, D.C.

Dec. 1, accepted resignation of Secretary of Navy Jones

Dec. 19, appointed his third secretary of navy, Benjamin W. Crowninshield

•Crowninshield took office, Jan. 16, 1815.

Dec. 24, peace treaty signed by American and British commissioners, Ghent, Belgium

•The treaty provided for the release of prisoners and the restoration of conquered territory. Provisions were made for a commission to establish the U. S.-Canadian northeastern boundary. However, the treaty did little to solve the problems that caused the war. The maritime differences —impressment of U. S. seamen, the rights of neutral commerce, and the fisheries question—were ignored.

1815

Jan. 8, Battle of New Orleans

Jan. 30, vetoed bill to incorporate Bank of U.S.

•This was the fifth of his seven vetoes.

Feb. 11, peace treaty arrived aboard British warship, *H.M.S. Favorite*, New York City

Feb. 15, peace treaty unanimously ratified by Senate

Feb. 17, issued proclamation ending War of 1812

Feb. 28, reappointed James Monroe as secretary of state

•Monroe took office, Mar. 1, and resigned as secretary of war, effective, Mar. 2.

Mar. 3, third session of 13th Congress adjourned

Mar. 14, appointed Secretary of Treasury Dallas as secretary of war ad interim

June 30, treaty signed by Dey of Algiers

•The Dey agreed to release all American prisoners and renounced molestation of American commerce and tribute.

•This treaty was concluded, July 3.

July 3, commercial convention with Great Britain admitted American commerce to East Indies

Aug. 1, appointed his fourth secretary of war, William H. Crawford

Dec. 4, first session of 14th Congress

•The administration maintained control of both the Senate and the House of Representatives. The Senate (36 members) consisted of 25 Democratic-Republicans and 11 Federalists. The House (182 members) consisted of 117 Democratic-Republicans and 65 Federalists.

Dec. 5, sent his seventh State of the Union message to Congress

•He recommended a federal network of roads and canals.

1816

Apr. 30, first session of 14th Congress adjourned

Apr. 30, vetoed free importation of Bible stereotype plates bill

•This was the sixth of his seven vetoes, the second of his two pocket vetoes.

Oct. 21, accepted resignation of Secretary of Treasury Dallas

Oct. 22, appointed his fourth secretary of treasury, William H. Crawford

•Crawford resigned as secretary of war.

•Crawford was the last of Madison's 14 cabinet appointments.

Dec. 2, second session of 14th Congress

Dec. 3, sent his eighth and last State of the Union message to Congress

•He suggested that the establishment of a national bank merited "consideration."

Dec. 4, 1816, presidential electors cast ballots

• *See* Election of 1816, page 70.
Dec. 11, Indiana admitted as 19th state
• Indiana was the second of two states admitted during his term of office.

1817

Feb. 6, authorized by Congress to employ John Trumbull to paint four Revolutionary War scenes for Capitol
• The paintings are *The Declaration of Independence, Surrender of Burgoyne at Saratoga, Surrender of Cornwallis,* and

The Resignation of Washington at Annapolis.
Mar. 3, second session of 14th Congress adjourned
Mar. 3, signed act that established Alabama Territory
Mar. 3, vetoed internal improvements bill for federally subsidized highway and canal system
• This was the last of his seven vetoes.
• This was his last official act.

Note: He was the second of 11 presidents who never had a veto overridden.

THE FORMER PRESIDENT

Mar. 4, 1817, attended inauguration of Monroe
• Madison's age upon leaving office was 64 years, 310 days.
April, 1817, departed Washington for Montpelier estate
• He lived on the four-thousand-acre estate for the remainder of his life. Periodically, he exchanged visits with Jefferson, who lived about 30 miles away.
• He was the third of six presidents who were farmers, planters, or ranchers after their terms of office.
• Montpelier is privately owned and not open to the public.
May 12, 1818, addressed Agricultural Society of Albemarle
• He was president of the society.
• This speech was published as a 31-page pamphlet in 1818 by Shepherd and Pollard, Richmond, Va.
Mar. 16, 1821, celebrated his 70th birthday
• He was the third of 16 presidents who lived to be 70.
1821, began book on Constitutional Convention
• Aided by his wife, he labored on his *Notes on the Federal Convention,* until his death. Congress bought the notes and other private papers for $30,000 in 1837. On Mrs. Madison's 80th birthday, May 20, 1848, Congress bought the remainder of his private papers for $25,000.
November, 1824, visited for several days by Lafayette
Mar. 16, 1826, celebrated his 75th birthday
• He was the third of ten presidents who lived to be 75.

1826, succeeded Jefferson as member of board of rectors, University of Virginia
Feb. 11, 1829, his mother died
• Mrs. Madison was 98 years old.
Mar. 16, 1831, celebrated his 80th birthday
• He was the third of six presidents who lived to be 80.
1834, served as delegate to Virginia constitutional convention
• He nominated Monroe for president of the convention
1834, sold several slaves
• He had experienced financial difficulties for years.
• He owned more than one hundred slaves at Montpelier.
• He was the third of nine presidents who owned slaves.
• For a number of years, he was president of the American Colonization Society and favored the gradual purchase and deportation of female slaves.
Mar. 16, 1836, celebrated his 85th birthday
• He was the second of four presidents who lived to be 85.

DEATH

Date of death: June 28, 1836
Place of death: Montpelier estate, Orange County, Va.
• Madison was the third of four presidents who died in Virginia.
Age at death: 85 years, 104 days
• He lived 19 years, 116 days, after the completion of his term.
Cause of death: Debility

Place of burial: Montpelier estate, Orange County, Va.
- He was the third of seven presidents who were buried in Virginia.

THE VICE PRESIDENTS
(4th and 5th)

Note: Madison was the second of seven presidents who had two vice presidents.

Full name: George Clinton (5th)
- He was the first of two vice presidents who served under two presidents. The other was Calhoun.
- *See also* page 51.
- He was the second of seven vice presidents who were elected to second terms.
- Madison and Clinton were the fifth of 41 president-vice president teams.

Age at second inauguration: 69 years, 221 days

Date of death: Apr. 20, 1812 (died in office)
- He was the only vice president who died during his second term.
- He was the first of seven vice presidents who died in office.

Place of death: Washington, D.C.
- He was the first of six vice presidents who died in Washington.

Age at death: 72 years, 269 days

Place of burial: Kingston, N.Y.
- He was the first of nine vice presidents who were buried in New York.

Full name: Elbridge Gerry (5th)
- The word, "gerrymander," which means to divide a voting district in such a manner as to give an unfair advantage to one political party, derives from his name + salamander—which was the shape of a district divided by the legislature during Gerry's term as governor of Massachusetts.

Date of birth: July 17, 1744

Place of birth: Marblehead, Mass.
- He was the second of two vice presidents who were born in Massachusetts. The other was John Adams.

Religious denomination: Episcopalian
- He was the first of eight vice presidents who were Episcopalians.
- Madison and Gerry were both Episcopalians. They were the first of seven president-vice president teams of the same religious denomination.

College: Harvard College, Cambridge, Mass.

Date of graduation: 1762

Occupations: Shipping tradesman, privateer
- He was elected to the Massachusetts general court, 1772; a member of the provincial congresses and the committee of safety, 1774–1776; a delegate to the Second Continental Congress, 1776–1780 and 1783–1785; signed the Declaration of Independence and the Articles of Confederation; served in the House of Representatives, 1789–1793; was appointed a member of the mission to France by President Adams, 1797; served as governor of Massachusetts, 1810–1812.
- He was the first of 21 vice presidents who served in the House of Representatives before their terms of office.
- He was the third of 14 vice presidents who served as state governors.

Term of office: Mar. 4, 1813, to Nov. 23, 1814 (1 year, 264 days)
- Gerry was the first of 14 vice presidents who served less than one term.
- Madison and Gerry were the sixth of 41 president-vice president teams.

Age at inauguration: 68 years, 230 days

State represented: Massachusetts
- He was the second of four vice presidents who represented Massachusetts.

Political party: Democratic-Republican
- He was the fourth of six vice presidents who were Democratic-Republicans.

Date of death: Nov. 23, 1814 (died in office)
- He was the first of six vice presidents who died before completing their first terms.
- He was the second of seven vice presidents who died in office.
- Madison was the only president whose two vice presidents died in office.

Place of death: Washington, D.C.
- He was the second of six vice presidents who died in Washington.

Age at death: 70 years, 129 days

Place of burial: Washington, D.C.
- He was the only vice president who was buried in Washington.

THE CABINET

State: Robert Smith of Maryland, Mar. 6, 1809 to Apr. 1, 1811
- James Monroe of Virginia, Apr. 6, 1811, to

Sept. 30, 1814 and Mar. 1, 1815, to Mar. 3, 1817

Treasury: Abraham Alfonse Albert Gallatin of Pennsylvania, May 14, 1801, to Feb. 8, 1814

• George Washington Campbell of Tennessee, Feb. 9, 1814, to Oct. 5, 1814

• Alexander James Dallas of Pennsylvania, Oct. 6, 1814, to Oct. 21, 1816

• William Harris Crawford of Georgia, Oct. 22, 1816, to Mar. 6, 1825

War: William Eustis of Massachusetts, Mar. 7, 1809, to Jan. 13, 1813

• John Armstrong of New York, Jan. 13, 1813, to Sept. 3, 1814

• James Monroe of Virginia, Sept. 27, 1814, to Mar. 2, 1815

• William Harris Crawford of Georgia, Aug. 1, 1815, to Oct. 22, 1816

Attorney General: Caesar Augustus Rodney of Delaware, Jan. 20, 1807, to Dec. 11, 1811

• William Pinkney of Maryland, Dec. 11, 1811, to Feb. 10, 1814

• Richard Rush of Pennsylvania, Feb. 10, 1814, to Nov. 13, 1817

Navy: Paul Hamilton of South Carolina, May 15, 1809, to Dec. 31, 1812

• William Jones of Pennsylvania, Jan. 19, 1813, to Dec. 1, 1814

• Benjamin Williams Crowninshield of Massachusetts, Jan. 16, 1815, to Sept. 30, 1818

THE SUPREME COURT

Associate Justices: Levi Lincoln of Massachusetts, appointed, Jan. 2, 1811; confirmed, Jan. 3, 1811; declined to serve

• Alexander Wolcott of Connecticut, appointed, Feb. 4, 1811; rejected by Senate, Feb. 13, 1811

• John Quincy Adams of Massachusetts, appointed, Feb. 21, 1811; confirmed, Feb. 22, 1811; declined to serve

• Joseph Story of Massachusetts, appointed, Nov. 15, 1811; confirmed, Nov. 18, 1811

• Gabriel Duval of Maryland, appointed, Nov. 15, 1811; confirmed, Nov. 18, 1811

Fifth President

JAMES MONROE

Full name: James Monroe
- He was the first of two presidents who shared the initials of a previous president (Madison). The other was Andrew Johnson.
- He was the second of five presidents named James.
- He was the fifth of 17 presidents who did not have middle initials of middle names.

Date of birth: Apr. 28, 1758
- He was the second of four presidents who were born in April.

Place of birth: Westmoreland County, Va.
- He was the second of two presidents who were born in Westmoreland County. The other was Washington.
- He was the fourth of eight presidents who were born in Virginia.

Family lineage: Scottish-Welsh
- He was the only president who was of Scottish-Welsh ancestry.

Religious denomination: Episcopalian
- He was the third of nine presidents who were Episcopalians.

College: College of William and Mary, Williamsburg, Va.
- He was the second of three presidents who attended William and Mary.
- He was the fourth of 27 presidents who attended college.
- He was the second of six presidents who attended but were not graduated from college.
- He was the third of 15 presidents who were not graduated from college.

Father's name: Spence Monroe
Date of birth: *Unknown*
Place of birth: *Unknown*
Occupations: Farmer, circuit judge
Date of death: 1774
- James was about 16 years old when his father died.

Place of death: Westmoreland County, Va.
Age at death: *Unknown*

Mother's name: Elizabeth Jones Monroe
Date of birth: *Unknown*
Place of birth: probably King George County, Va.
Date of marriage: 1752
Children: 5; 4 sons, 1 daughter
- Elizabeth was born in 1754; James in 1758; Spence in 17—; Andrew in 17—; and Jo-

seph Jones in 1764.
• Monroe was the first of seven presidents who came from families of five children.
• He was the first of ten presidents who were second children.
Date of death: *Unknown*
Place of death: *Unknown*
Age at death: *Unknown*

MARRIAGE

Date of marriage: Feb. 15, 1786
Place of marriage: New York, N.Y.
• Monroe was the first of five presidents who were married in New York City.
• He was the first of seven presidents who were married in New York.
Age at marriage: 27 years, 293 days
• He was the fourth of 27 presidents who were married in their twenties.
Years married: 44 years, 220 days

Wife's name: Elizabeth Kortright Monroe
• She was the fourth of 33 first ladies.
• She was the fifth of 40 wives of presidents.
Date of birth: June 30, 1768
• She was the second of four first ladies who were born in June.
• She was the second of five wives of presidents who were born in June.
Place of birth: New York, N.Y.
• She was the first of two first ladies who were born in New York City. The other was Eleanor Roosevelt.
• She was the first of two wives of presidents who were born in New York City.
• She was the first of six first ladies who were born in New York.
• She was the first of seven wives of presidents who were born in New York.

Wife's mother: Hannah Aspinwall Kortright
Wife's father: Lawrence Kortright, merchant
• Kortright, who had achieved the rank of captain as a British army officer, was one of the founders of the New York Chamber of Commerce in 1770.
Age at marriage: 17 years, 231 days
• She was the second of four first ladies who married in their teens.
• She was the second of five wives of presidents who were married in their teens.
Years younger than husband: 10 years, 63 days
Children: 3; 2 daughters, 1 son
• Eliza Kortright was born in 1787; a son in May, 1799; and Maria Hester in 1803. The boy, name unknown, died in infancy.
• Monroe was the first of seven presidents who had three children.
• He was the third of 19 presidents who had both male and female children.
• He was the third of 30 presidents who had children.
Date of death: Sept. 23, 1830
Place of death: Oak Hill, Va.
• She was the second of three first ladies who died in Virginia.
• She was the third of four wives of presidents who died in Virginia.
Age at death: 62 years, 85 days
Place of burial: Richmond, Va.
• She was originally buried at Oak Hill. In 1903, she was reinterred at Richmond.
• She was the third of six first ladies who were buried in Virginia.
• She was the fourth of seven wives of presidents who were buried in Virginia.
Years he survived his wife: 284 days
• Monroe was the third of 14 presidents who survived their wives.

EARLY YEARS

June 20, 1774, entered College of William and Mary, Williamsburg, Va.
Sept. 28, 1775, commissioned second lieutenant, Third Virginia Regiment
November, 1775, initiated into fraternal order of Free and Accepted Masons, Lodge No. 6, Williamsburg, Va.
• Monroe was the second of 13 presidents who were Masons.
Mar. 25, 1776, quit college to join army as first lieutenant

Sept. 15, 1776, joined Washington's forces, New York City
• He was the second of three presidents who served in the Revolutionary War.
• He was the second of 21 presidents who served in the military during wartime.
Oct. 28, 1776, fought in Battle of White Plains
Dec. 25–26, 1776, wounded in Battle of Trenton
• He was the first of four presidents who

were wounded or injured in action.
•He was promoted to the rank of captain after Trenton.
August, 1777, joined staff of General Lord Stirling as volunteer aide
Sept. 11, 1777, fought in Battle of Brandywine Creek
Oct. 4, 1777, fought in Battle of Germantown
Nov. 20, 1777, promoted to rank of major
•He was appointed aide-de-camp to General Lord Stirling.
June 28, 1778, fought in Battle of Monmouth
Dec. 20, 1778, resigned from army
•He and other young officers were retired inasmuch as there were not sufficient troops to command. He returned to Virginia and applied for a rank in the state line. He was unsuccessful.
May, 1779, visited Washington's headquarters, Middlebrook, N.J.
•He hoped to raise a corps in Virginia and

sought the support of Washington and General Lord Stirling. Both wrote glowing letters of recommendation.
•He returned to Virginia, but his plan to recruit a corps and join the southern campaign never materialized.
1779, began law studies under Jefferson, Williamsburg
•Monroe was the third of 26 presidents who studied law.
June, 1780, appointed military commissioner by Governor Jefferson with rank of lieutenant colonel
•As commissioner from Virginia to the southern army, Monroe's duties were to report about conditions and prospects in the southern theater of military operations.
1782, elected to Virginia assembly from King George County
•He was also elected by the assembly to the executive council.

NATIONAL PROMINENCE

June, 1783, elected to Fourth Congress of Confederation
•Monroe's term of office began, Nov. 3. Twice reelected, he served until 1786, attending sessions in Annapolis, Trenton, and New York City.
•He was the last of five presidents who served in the Continental congresses.
Feb. 15, 1786, married Elizabeth Kortright, New York City
October, 1786, admitted to bar, courts of appeal and chancery, Fredericksburg, Va.
•He was the third of 23 presidents who were lawyers.
•In 1928, descendents of Monroe acquired the brick building at 908 Charles Street, in which he had begun the practice of law. In 1947, the building and its contents, including the Louis XVI furniture the Monroes used in the White House, were given to the James Monroe Memorial Foundation. A library wing was added in 1962, and, in 1964, the museum-library was given by the foundation to the Commonwealth of Virginia. It is now a division of the University of Virginia. It is open to the public daily except Christmas, 9 A.M. to 5 P.M. Admission: adults, 75 cents; children of elementary and high school age, 35 cents. Groups

of eight or more: adults, 50 cents; children, 25 cents.
April, 1787, admitted to general court, Fredericksburg, Va.
Dec. 5, 1787, his first daughter born
•The girl was named Eliza Kortright Monroe.
June 2, 1788, member of Virginia convention to ratify Constitution
November, 1790, elected to Senate
•He was the first of 16 presidents who were elected to the Senate.
Dec. 6, 1790, took seat in Senate, Philadelphia
•He served in the 1st, 2nd, and 3rd congresses, 1790 to 1794.
•He was the first of 15 presidents who served in the Senate.
1791, member of commission for revising laws of Virginia
May 27, 1794, nominated by Washington as minister to France
•Monroe was confirmed by the Senate, May 28.
Aug. 2, 1794, arrived in Paris
•He was received by the national convention of France, Aug. 15.
•He was the second of two presidents who served as ministers to France. The other

was Jefferson.
• He was the third of seven presidents who served as diplomats.
Nov. 4, 1794, effected release of Thomas Paine from Luxembourg prison, Paris
• Paine, who was born in England, was imprisoned on the technical charge of being a national of a country at war with France, Dec. 28, 1793. The pamphleteer, who had been made a French citizen by the Assembly and elected to the national convention in 1792, had incurred the wrath of Robespierre when he opposed the execution of Louis XVI. Upon his release, Paine lived at the Monroe home.
Aug. 22, 1796, recalled as minister to France
• He did not receive the letter of recall from Washington's secretary of state, Timothy Pickering, until November.
Dec. 30, 1796, took formal leave of his diplomatic post
• He delayed his departure to avoid a winter sea voyage; he sailed for the U.S. in the spring.
December, 1797, wrote *A View of the Conduct of the Executive in the Foreign Affairs of the United States*
• This highly critical examination of Washington's foreign policy was Monroe's only book.
• He was the fifth of 21 presidents who wrote books that were published during their lifetimes.
1798, moved to Ash Lawn, Charlotteville, Va.
• He was the fourth of nine presidents who owned slaves.
• Ash Lawn, his home until 1820, now is privately owned. It is open to the public daily.
Dec. 5, 1799, elected governor of Virginia
• He was reelected twice, serving until 1802.
• He was the second of three presidents who served as governors of Virginia.
• He was the second of 13 presidents who served as state governors.
May, 1799, his only son born
• The infant, name unknown, died, Sept. 28, 1800.

Note: The child's gravestone bears the initials "J.S.M." probably for James Spence Monroe.

1803, his second daughter born
• The girl was named Maria Hester Monroe.
Jan. 11, 1803, nominated by Jefferson as en-

voy extraordinary and minister plenipotentiary to France and Spain
• He was confirmed by the Senate, Jan. 12.
Apr. 12, 1803, arrived in Paris
Apr. 18, 1803, commissioned minister to Great Britain
Apr. 30, 1803, signed treaty with France transferring Louisiana to U.S.
• The treaty was signed by Monroe and Robert Livingston, minister to France, May 2, but antedated Apr. 30.
July 12, 1803, arrived in London
• He was the second of five presidents who served as ministers to Great Britain.
1804, negotiated with Spain
• His mission to Madrid, to seek a mutually satisfactory agreement regarding Florida, was unsuccessful.
• He was the only president who served as minister to Spain.
May 21, 1805, departed Spanish court, returned to England
May 17, 1806, appointed by Jefferson as commissioner extraordinary to negotiate treaty with Great Britain
• Monroe and William Pinkney violated their instructions and signed a treaty, Dec. 3, which contained no provision regarding impressment of seamen or the seizure of American vessels.
• Jefferson, who received the treaty, Mar. 5, 1807, refused to submit it for ratification by the Senate.
Oct. 29, 1807, departed from London
• He arrived in the United States in December.
1808, unsuccessful candidate for president
1810, reelected to Virginia assembly
January—March, 1811, served as governor of Virginia
Apr. 2, 1811, appointed as secretary of state by Madison
• He took office, Apr. 6. He served to Sept. 30, 1814.
• He was the third of six presidents who served as secretary of state.
• He was the third of eight presidents who served in the cabinet.
Jan. 1, 1813, appointed as secretary of war ad interim by Madison
• He served to Feb. 5. He also served as secretary of war ad interim, Sept. 3 to Sept. 27, 1814.
Sept. 27, 1814, appointed as secretary of war by Madison
• Monroe served to Mar. 2, 1815. During this

period—from Oct. 1, 1814, to Feb. 28, 1815—he also served as secretary of state ad interim.

• He was the only president who held two cabinet posts.

• He was the first of two presidents who served as secretary of war. The other was Taft.

Feb. 28, 1815, reappointed as secretary of state by Madison

• He took office, Mar. 1. He served to Mar. 3, 1817.

• He was the only president who served as secretary of state on two occasions.

Mar. 4, 1816, nominated by Democratic-Republicans for president

Dec. 4, 1816, presidential electors cast ballots

• See Election of 1816, below.

Feb. 12, 1817, electoral votes tabulated by Congress

• Monroe and Tompkins were officially declared elected.

ELECTION OF 1816

• James Monroe of Virginia was Madison's choice as successor, but a group of "young Turks" vigorously supported William Harris Crawford of Georgia. Monroe defeated Crawford in the caucus of Democratic-Republican members of Congress, 65–54, Mar. 4. Daniel D. Tompkins of New York was nominated for vice president by the Democratic-Republicans.

• The Federalist party, in disrepute after the Hartford Convention of 1814–1815, did not nominate candidates but supported Rufus King of New York for president. Support was divided among several vice-presidential candidates.

• The Hartford convention was a meeting of 26 Federalist representatives from Massachusetts, Rhode Island and Connecticut

that convened, Dec. 15, 1814. A report attacking Madison's administration and its conduct of the War of 1812 had been issued on Jan. 5, 1815.

• The electors from ten states, Kentucky, Maryland, New Hampshire, New Jersey, North Carolina, Ohio, Pennsylvania, Rhode Island, Tennessee, and Virginia, had been selected by popular vote, while those representing Connecticut, Delaware, Georgia, Indiana, Louisiana, Massachusetts, New York, South Carolina, and Vermont had been appointed by their state legislatures.

• Monroe and Tompkins received 183 of the 217 electoral votes from 19 states. There were four vacancies in the electoral college when three Federalists from Maryland and one Federalist from Delaware failed to vote; the total number of electors was 221.

• King received 34 electoral votes.

• Monroe and Tompkins received the electoral votes of 16 states (Georgia, 8; Indiana, 3; Kentucky, 12; Louisiana, 3; Maryland, 8 of 11 votes; New Hampshire, 8; New Jersey, 8; New York, 29; North Carolina, 15; Ohio, 8; Pennsylvania, 25; Rhode Island, 4; South Carolina, 11; Tennessee, 8; Vermont, 8; Virginia, 25).

• King received the electoral votes of three states (Connecticut, 9; Delaware, 3 of 4 votes; Massachusetts, 22).

• The Federalist vice-presidential candidates received 34 electoral votes.

• John Eager Howard of Maryland received the votes of the 22 Massachusetts electors.

• James Ross of Pennsylvania received the votes of five Connecticut electors.

• John Marshall of Virginia received the votes of four Connecticut electors.

• Robert Goodloe Harper of Maryland received the votes of three Delaware electors.

THE PRESIDENT (5th)

Term of office: Mar. 4, 1817, to Mar. 4, 1825 (8 years)

• Monroe was the fourth of 12 presidents who were elected to second terms.

• He was the fourth of 16 presidents who served more than one term.

• He was the fourth of nine presidents who

served two terms.

• He was the third of eight presidents who served for eight years.

State represented: Virginia

• He was the second of four presidents who succeeded presidents who represented the same state.

• He was the third president in succession who represented Virginia.

• He was the last of four presidents who comprised the Virginia Regime.

• He was the fourth of five presidents who represented Virginia.

Political party: Democratic-Republican

• He was the third of four presidents who were Democratic-Republicans.

Congresses: 15th, 16th, 17th, 18th

Administrations: 8th, 9th

Age at inauguration: 58 years, 310 days

Inauguration day: Tuesday, Mar. 4, 1817

• Monroe took the oath of office, administered by Chief Justice John Marshall, on a platform constructed on the east portico of the Capitol. The choice of location came as the result of a dispute between members of the Senate and the House of Representatives over the allotment of seats for the ceremony.

• This was the fifth of nine inaugurations at which Marshall officiated.

• He was the first president who took the oath of office on the east portico of the Capitol.

THE 8th ADMINISTRATION

1817

Mar. 5, appointed his only secretary of state, John Quincy Adams

• Adams took office, Sept. 22.

• Monroe retained Madison's secretary of treasury, attorney general, and secretary of navy.

Apr. 29, Rush-Bagot agreement signed

• An outgrowth of the Treaty of Ghent, this agreement called for Anglo-American disarmament on the Great Lakes.

• The arrangement was the culmination of an exchange of notes between Charles Bagot, the British minister to the U.S., and acting Secretary of State Richard Rush. The groundwork had been laid by Monroe and the British foreign minister, Lord Castlereagh.

May 5, departed on eastern tour

• His official tour of duty of the eastern seaboard was turned into a personal triumph by the enthusiastic reception he received, especially in New England. He traveled as far west as Detroit before returning to Washington, D.C., in September.

July 12, Benjamin Russell of Boston *Columbian Centinel* coined phrase, "Era of Good Feelings"

• The catchall phrase was widely used to describe the Monroe administrations. The decline of the Federalist party and the lack of formal political opposition gave rise to the use of the epithet. In actuality, the phrase held little meaning.

Oct. 8, appointed his only secretary of war, John C. Calhoun

• Calhoun took office, Dec. 10.

Nov. 13, accepted resignation of Attorney General Rush

Nov. 13, appointed his second attorney general, William Wirt

Nov. 20, first Seminole War began

Dec. 1, first session of 15th Congress

• The administration controlled both the Senate and the House of Representatives. The Senate (44 members) consisted of 34 Democratic-Republicans and ten Federalists. The House (183 members) consisted of 141 Democratic-Republicans and 42 Federalists.

Dec. 2, sent his first State of the Union message to Congress

Dec. 10, Mississippi admitted as 20th state

• Mississippi was the first of five states admitted during his term of office.

Dec. 26, assigned General Andrew Jackson to command of troops against Seminole Indians

1818

January, received "Rhea letter" from General Jackson

• "Let it be signified to me through any channel (say Mr. J. Rhea) that the possession of the Floridas would be desirable to the United States and in sixty days it will be accomplished," wrote Jackson, Jan. 6.

• Monroe did not reply; Jackson chose to regard the official silence as tacit approval.

• John Rhea was a Democratic-Republican congressman from Tennessee.

Apr. 4, signed flag act

• The flag was established as having 13 horizontal red and white stripes and a white star for each state in a blue field.

Apr. 18, ordered ports closed to British vessels from British colonial ports in West Indies

• This order was in retaliation to a British decree closing West Indian ports to American vessels.

Apr. 20, first session of 15th Congress adjourned

Apr. 28, issued proclamation that detailed Rush-Bagot agreement

• The Senate had ratified the agreement, Apr. 16.

May 24, first Seminole War ended

• The capture of Pensacola by General Jackson ended the campaign and brought all of East Florida under U.S. military control.

Aug. 9, his representative, Captain James Biddle, formally claimed Astoria as U.S. territory

• The trading post of Astoria in northwest Oregon near the mouth of the Columbia River had been founded by John Jacob Astor in 1811 and was taken by the British in 1813.

Sept. 30, accepted resignation of Secretary of Navy Crowninshield

Oct. 6, Astoria restored to U.S. by British

Oct. 20, Convention of 1818, sequel to Treaty of Ghent, signed in London

• American fishing rights along Newfoundland and Labrador coasts were recognized; the boundary between the U.S. and Canada was established from Lake of the Woods in northern Minnesota to the Rocky Mountains along the 49th parallel.

Nov. 9, appointed his second secretary of navy, Smith Thompson

• Thompson took office, Jan. 1, 1819.

Nov. 16, second session of 15th Congress

Nov. 16, sent his second State of the Union message to Congress

Dec. 3, Illinois admitted as 21st state

• Illinois was the second of five states admitted during his term of office.

1819

Feb. 25, approved Adams-Onis Treaty with Spain

• The treaty, which provided that Spain renounce all claims to West Florida and cede East Florida to the U.S., had been signed by Secretary of State John Quincy Adams

and Luis de Onis, the Spanish minister, Feb. 22.

Mar. 2, Arkansas Territory set off from Missouri Territory

Mar. 2, signed first immigration act

Mar. 3, authorized to take possession of East and West Florida, establish temporary government

Mar. 3, authorized to return illegally imported slaves to Africa

Mar. 3, second session of 15th Congress adjourned

Dec. 6, first session of 16th Congress

• The administration maintained control of both the Senate and the House of Representatives. The Senate (42 members) consisted of 35 Democratic-Republicans and seven Federalists. The House (183 members) consisted of 156 Democratic-Republicans and 27 Federalists.

Dec. 7, sent his third State of the Union message to Congress

Dec. 14, Alabama admitted as 22nd state

• Alabama was the third of five states admitted during his term of office.

Note: The Panic of 1819, the first of nine U.S. depressions, was initiated by a contraction of credit by the mismanaged Second Bank of the U.S., which followed wide speculation in western lands and overextension in manufacturing investments. Western and southern states felt the effects most severely.

1820

Mar. 3, Missouri Compromise

• With the admission of Alabama in 1819, the 22 states were evenly divided, 11 free and 11 slave. A bill to admit Missouri as a slave state, introduced in the House of Representatives, threatened to upset the balance and made the slavery question a matter of national controversy.

• Representative James Tallmadge of New York attached an amendment to the House bill that prohibited the further importation of slaves to Missouri and provided for the emancipation of children of Missouri slaves at the age of 25. The bill passed the House, but was defeated in the Senate.

• A bill to detach Maine from Massachusetts was passed by the House in January. It became obvious to both factions that pairing Maine with Missouri would preserve the balance. An amendment to the paired statehood bills, introduced by Senator Jesse Burgess Thomas of Illinois, proved to contain the acceptable compromise. The Thomas amendment prohibited slavery north of latitude 36° 30'—the southern boundary of Missouri—except for the area of the proposed state.

• The decisive votes were cast by northern Republican defectors who feared a Federalist revival. Both the North and the South welcomed the compromise. It offered the South its immediate objective, maintenance of balance. To the North, it seemed to lay the question of further extension of slavery to rest.

Mar. 9, attended wedding of his daughter, Maria Hester, to Samuel Lawrence Gouverneur, White House

• This was the first of eight White House weddings of daughters of presidents.

• This was the first of nine White House weddings of children of presidents.

Mar. 15, Maine admitted as 23rd state

• Maine was the fourth of five states admitted during his term of office.

May 15, signed slave trade act

• This act provided the death penalty for Americans convicted of engagement in the importation of slaves and declared slave trading to be piracy.

May 15, first session of 16th Congress adjourned

Nov. 13, second session of 16th Congress

Nov. 14, sent his fourth State of the Union message to Congress

Dec. 6, presidential electors cast ballots

• *See* Election of 1820, below.

Note: The official population, according to the fourth census, was 9,638,191, which included 1,538,125 slaves and 233,504 free Negroes.

1821

Feb. 14, electoral votes tabulated by Congress

• Monroe and Tompkins were officially declared elected.

Mar. 3, second session of 16th Congress adjourned

ELECTION OF 1820

• James Monroe of Virginia and Daniel D. Tompkins of New York had become the *de facto* candidates for reelection when a sparsely attended caucus of Democratic-Republican members of Congress in April failed to make nominations.

• The electors from 15 states, Connecticut, Illinois, Kentucky, Maine, Maryland, Massachusetts, Mississippi, New Hampshire, New Jersey, North Carolina, Ohio, Pennsylvania, Rhode Island, Tennessee, and Virginia, had been selected by popular vote, while those representing Alabama, Delaware, Georgia, Indiana, Louisiana, Missouri, New York, South Carolina, and Vermont had been appointed by their state legislatures.

• Monroe received 231 of the 232 electoral votes from the 24 states. John Quincy Adams of Massachusetts received one electoral vote. There were three vacancies in the electoral college because of deaths of electors from Mississippi, Pennsylvania, and Tennessee; the official total of electors was 235.

• Monroe received the electoral votes of all 24 states (Alabama, 3; Connecticut, 9; Delaware, 4; Georgia, 8; Illinois, 3; Indiana, 3; Kentucky, 12; Louisiana, 3; Maine, 9; Maryland, 11; Massachusetts, 15; Mississippi, 2 of 3 votes; Missouri, 3; New Hampshire 7 of 8 votes; New Jersey, 8; New York, 29; North Carolina, 15; Ohio, 8; Pennsylvania, 24 of 25 votes; Rhode Island, 4; South Carolina, 11; Tennessee, 7 of 8 votes; Vermont, 8; Virginia, 25).

• Monroe was the second of two presidents who received the electoral votes of all the states. The other was Washington.

• John Quincy Adams received the vote of William Plumer of New Hampshire.

• Tompkins received 218 electoral votes and was elected vice president (Alabama, 3; Connecticut, 9; Georgia, 8; Illinois, 3; Indiana, 3; Kentucky, 12; Louisiana, 3; Maine, 9; Maryland, 10 of 11 votes; Mississippi, 2 of 3 votes; Missouri, 3; New Hampshire, 7 of 8 votes; New Jersey, 8; New York, 29; North Carolina, 15; Ohio, 8;

Pennsylvania, 24 of 25 votes; Rhode Island, 4; South Carolina, 11; Tennessee, 7 of 8 votes; Vermont, 8; Virginia, 25).
• Tompkins also received the votes of seven Massachusetts electors.
• Richard Stockton of New Jersey received eight votes (Massachusetts, 8 of 15 votes).

• Daniel Rodney of Delaware received the votes of the four Delaware electors.
• Robert Goodloe Harper of Maryland received the vote of one Maryland elector.
• Richard Rush of Pennsylvania received the vote of one New Hampshire elector.

THE 9th ADMINISTRATION

1821

Mar. 5, his second inauguration day
• Monroe took the oath of office, administered by Chief Justice John Marshall, in the Hall of Representatives of the Capitol. The ceremony was held indoors because of rain and snow.
• This was the sixth of nine inaugurations at which Marshall officiated.
• He was the third of five presidents who took the oath of office in the House of Representatives chamber.
• This was the fourth of six oath-taking ceremonies in the House chamber.
• He was the first of five presidents who postponed their oath-taking ceremonies to Monday because Mar. 4 fell on Sunday.
Apr. 5, appointed General Jackson as military governor of Florida
Aug. 10, Missouri admitted as 24th state
• Missouri was the last of five states admitted during his term of office.
Dec. 3, first session of 17th Congress
• The administration maintained control of both the Senate and the House of Representatives. The Senate (48 members) consisted of 44 Democratic-Republicans and four Federalists. The House (183 members) consisted of 158 Democratic-Republicans and 25 Federalists.
Dec. 3, sent his fifth State of the Union message to Congress

1822

Mar. 8, sent special message to Congress proposing recognition of independent republics of Central and South America
• The countries concerned were the United Provinces of La Plata (dominated by Argentina), Brazil, Chile, Colombia, Mexico, Peru, and the Federation of Central American States.

Mar. 30, signed act establishing Territory of Florida
May 4, signed act that provided for diplomatic missions to independent republics of Central and South America
May 4, vetoed Cumberland Road appropriation bill
• He submitted his objection to national appropriations for internal improvements. This was his only veto.
• He was the second of three presidents who exercised the regular veto power but did not employ the pocket veto.
• He was the third of 11 presidents who never had a veto overridden.
May 6, authorized to appoint superintendent of Indian affairs
May 8, first session of 17th Congress adjourned
Dec. 2, second session of 17th Congress
Dec. 3, sent his sixth State of the Union message to Congress

1823

Jan. 27–28, appointed first ministers to Argentina, Chile, and Mexico
Mar. 3, second session of 17th Congress adjourned
Mar. 18, Associate Justice Livingston died
Aug. 31, accepted resignation of Secretary of Navy Thompson
Sept. 1, appointed Smith Thompson as associate justice
• Thompson, who was confirmed by the Senate, Dec. 19, was Monroe's only appointment to the Supreme Court.
Sept. 16, appointed his third secretary of navy, Samuel L. Southard
• Southard was the last of his eight cabinet appointments.
Dec. 1, first session of 18th Congress
• The administration maintained control of both the Senate and the House of Repre-

sentatives. The Senate (48 members) consisted of 44 Democratic-Republicans and four Federalists. The House (213 members) consisted of 187 Democratic-Republicans and 26 Federalists.
•This was the last Congress in which the Federalist party was represented.
Dec. 2, sent his seventh State of the Union message to Congress, which included Monroe Doctrine
•The Monroe Doctrine, while received enthusiastically by Americans, was virtually ignored by the Europeans. The portion of the message that outlined the doctrine, based on John Quincy Adams's principle, virtually in Adams's phraseology, read:

> In the wars of the European powers in matters relating to themselves we have never taken any part, nor does it comport with our policy so to do. It is only when our rights are invaded or seriously menaced that we resent injuries or make preparation for our defence. With the movements in this hemisphere we are, of necessity, more immediately connected, and by causes which must be obvious to all enlightened and impartial observers. The political system of the allied powers is essentially different in this respect from that of America. This difference proceeds from that which exists in their respective governments. And to the defence of our own, which has been achieved by the loss of so much blood and treasure, and matured by the wisdom of their most enlightened citizens, and under which we have enjoyed unexampled felicity, this whole nation is devoted. We owe it, therefore, to

> candor, and to the amicable relations existing between the United States and those powers, to declare that we should consider any attempt on their part to extend their system to any portion of this hemisphere as dangerous to our peace and safety. With the existing colonies or dependencies of any European power we have not interfered, and shall not interfere. But with the governments who have declared their independence, and maintained it, and whose independence we have, on great consideration and on just principles, acknowledged, we could not view any interposition for the purpose of oppressing them, or controlling in any other manner their destiny, by any European power, in any other light than as the manifestation of an unfriendly disposition toward the United States.

1824

Apr. 30, authorized to initiate surveys for roads and canals of national import ince
May 27, first session of 18th Congress adjourned
Nov. 29, election day
• *See* Election of 1824, pages 82–83.
Dec. 6, second session of 18th Congress
Dec. 7, sent his eighth and last State of the Union message to Congress

1825

Mar. 3, second session of 18th Congress adjourned

THE FORMER PRESIDENT

Mar. 4, 1825, attended inauguration of John Quincy Adams
•Monroe's age upon leaving office was 66 years, 310 days.
•About three weeks later, he departed Washington for his new home, Oak Hill. He had prevailed upon Jefferson to design his mansion, which was built by James Hoban, on land in Loudoun County, Va., that

he had inherited from his father-in-law in 1806. Completed in 1823, Oak Hill was furnished with the better pieces from Ash Lawn and his personal belongings from the White House.
•He personally planted the oaks that gave the estate its name, one from each state of the Union. The young trees had been furnished by congressmen from the in-

dividual states.

1825, petitioned Congress for reimbursement of expenses in public service
• Congress ultimately authorized payment of $30,000 to cover various expenses and interest.

Aug. 7–9, 1825, entertained Lafayette and President John Quincy Adams, Oak Hill

1826, served on board of regents, University of Virginia

Apr. 28, 1828, celebrated his 70th birthday
• He was the fourth of 16 presidents who lived to be 70.

1829, served as delegate to Virginia constitutional convention
• He was elected president of the convention, after having been nominated by Madison.

Sept. 23, 1830, his wife died

Nov. 26, 1830, made his last public appearance
• He presided at a meeting in Tammany Hall, New York City, to celebrate the overthrow of Charles X of France and the establishment of the Second French Republic.

1831, sold Oak Hill
• His last years were characterized by financial difficulties. In 1825, he had been forced to sell his 3,500-acre estate, Ash Lawn. After disposing of Oak Hill, he moved to New York City, where he lived with his daughter, Maria, and her husband, Samuel L. Gouverneur.

DEATH

Date of death: July 4, 1831
• Monroe was the last of three presidents who died on the Fourth of July.

Place of death: New York, N.Y.
• He was the first of three presidents who died in New York City.
• He was the first of eight presidents who died in New York.

Age at death: 73 years, 67 days
• He lived six years, 122 days, after the completion of his term.

Cause of death: Debility

Place of burial: Richmond, Va.
• He was the fourth of seven presidents who were buried in Virginia.

THE VICE PRESIDENT (6th)

Full name: Daniel D. Tompkins

Date of birth: June 21, 1774

Place of birth: Fox Meadows, now Scarsdale, N.Y.
• He was the second of eight vice presidents who were born in New York.

Religious denomination: Presbyterian
• He was the third of 11 vice presidents who were Presbyterians.

College: Columbia College, New York, N.Y.

Date of graduation: 1795

Occupation: Lawyer
• He was admitted to the bar, New York City, 1797; elected to the House of Representatives, 1804; resigned almost immediately to accept appointment as justice of the New York supreme court; served as governor of New York, 1807–1817.
• He was the second of 21 vice presidents who served in the House of Representatives before their terms of office.
• He was the fourth of 14 vice presidents who served as state governors.

Term of office: Mar. 4, 1817, to Mar. 4, 1825 (8 years)
• He was the third of seven vice presidents who were elected to second terms.
• He was the second of five vice presidents who served two terms.
• He was the first of three vice presidents who served eight years.
• Monroe and Tompkins were the seventh of 41 president-vice president teams.
• They were the second of five president-vice president teams who were reelected.

Age at inauguration: 42 years, 256 days

State represented: New York
• He was the third of ten vice presidents who represented New York.

Political party: Democratic-Republican
• He was the fifth of six vice presidents who were Democratic-Republicans.

Occupation after term: Lawyer

Date of death: June 11, 1825

Place of death: Tompkinsville, Staten Island, N.Y.
• He was the second of two vice presidents who died in Staten Island. The other was Burr.
• He was the second of nine vice presidents who died in New York.

Age at death: 50 years, 355 days

Place of burial: New York, N.Y.

•He was the only vice president who was buried in New York City.

•He was the second of nine vice presidents who were buried in New York.

THE CABINET

State: John Quincy Adams of Massachusetts, Sept. 22, 1817, to Mar. 3, 1825

Treasury: William Harris Crawford of Georgia, Oct. 22, 1816, to Mar. 6, 1825

War: John Caldwell Calhoun of South Carolina, Oct. 8, 1817, to Mar. 7, 1825

Attorney General: Richard Rush of Pennsylvania, Feb. 10, 1814, to Nov. 13, 1817

•William Wirt of Virginia, Nov. 13, 1817, to Mar. 3, 1829

Navy: Benjamin Williams Crowninshield of Massachusetts, Jan. 16, 1815, to Sept. 30, 1818

•Smith Thompson of New York, Jan. 1, 1819, to Aug. 31, 1823

•Samuel Lewis Southard of New Jersey, Sept. 16, 1823, to Mar. 3, 1829

THE SUPREME COURT

Associate Justice: Smith Thompson of New York, appointed, Sept. 1, 1823; confirmed, Dec. 19, 1823

Sixth President

JOHN QUINCY ADAMS

Full name: John Quincy Adams
- He was the first of four presidents who had the same surname as a previous president. He and John Adams were son and father, the only presidents so closely related.
- He was the first of 19 presidents who had middle initials or middle names.
- He was the second of five presidents named John.

Date of birth: July 11, 1767
- He was the first of two presidents who were born in July. The other was Coolidge.

Place of birth: Braintree, now Quincy, Mass.
- His birthplace, 141 Franklin Street, is open to the public daily except Mondays, Apr. 19 to Sept. 30. Admission: adults, 50 cents; children under 16, free. The fee to visit the birthplace and the adjacent birthplace of his father, John Adams, is 75 cents.
- He was the second of two presidents who were born in Braintree. The other was his father.
- He was the second of three presidents who were born in Massachusetts.

Family lineage: English
- He was the fourth of 12 presidents who were of English ancestry.

Religious denomination: Unitarian

- He was the second of four presidents who were Unitarians.

College: Harvard College, Cambridge, Mass.
- He was the fifth of 27 presidents who attended college.

Date of graduation: July 18, 1787, Bachelor of Arts
- He was the second of five presidents who were graduated from Harvard.
- He was the third of 21 presidents who were graduated from college.

PARENTS AND SIBLINGS

Father's name: John Adams
- *See* pages 26–39.
- John Quincy Adams was the only president whose father had been president.
- He was the first of two presidents whose fathers had signed the Declaration of Independence. The other was William Henry Harrison.
- He was the first of three presidents whose fathers were ministers plenipotentiary or ambassadors.
- He was the first of six presidents whose

fathers lived to see their sons' inauguration or oath-taking days. John Adams did not attend the ceremony.

Mother's name: Abigail Smith Adams
• *See* page 27.
• Adams was the second of ten presidents who were second children.
• He was the second of seven presidents who came from families of five children.

MARRIAGE

Date of marriage: July 26, 1797
Place of marriage: London, England
• Adams was the first of two presidents who were married abroad. The other was Theodore Roosevelt (second marriage).
• He was the first of two presidents who were married in London.
Age at marriage: 30 years, 15 days
• He was the first of six presidents who were married in their thirties.
Years married: 50 years, 212 days

Wife's name: Louisa Catherine Johnson Adams
• She was the fifth of 33 first ladies.
• She was the sixth of 40 wives of presidents.
Date of birth: Feb. 12, 1775
• She was the first of two first ladies who were born in February. The other was Bess Truman.
• She was the first of two wives of presidents who were born in February.
Place of birth: London, England
• She was the only first lady or wife of a president who was born outside the U.S.
Wife's mother: Catherine Nuth Johnson
Wife's father: Joshua Johnson, merchant and diplomat
• Johnson was U.S. consul, stationed in London, at the time of the marriage of his daughter.
• Johnson was the only father-in-law of a president who was a diplomat.
Age at marriage: 22 years, 164 days
• She was the third of 26 first ladies who were married in their twenties.
• She was the fourth of 30 wives of presidents who were married in their twenties.
Years younger than husband: 7 years, 216 days

Children: 4; 3 sons, 1 daughter
• George Washington was born on Apr. 12, 1801; John on July 4, 1803; Charles Francis on Aug. 18, 1807; and Louisa Catherine on Aug. 12, 1811. Louisa Catherine died in infancy.
• Adams's two older sons were the only children of a president who were named for previous presidents.
• His second son was the only child of a president who was born on Independence Day. Coincidentally, President John Adams, for whom the boy was named, died on July 4.
• John Quincy Adams was the first of three presidents who had children who were born abroad. His eldest son was born in Berlin, Prussia, and his daughter was born in St. Petersburg, Russia.
• He was the first of four presidents who had four children.
• He was the fourth of 19 presidents who had both male and female children.
• He was the fourth of 30 presidents who had children.
Years she survived her husband: 4 years, 81 days
• She was the third of 21 first ladies who survived their husbands.
• She was the third of 23 wives of presidents who survived their husbands.
Date of death: May 15, 1852
Place of death: Washington, D.C.
• She was the second of nine first ladies who died in Washington.
• She was the second of nine wives of presidents who died in Washington.
Age at death: 77 years, 93 days
• She had celebrated her 75th birthday, Feb. 12, 1850.
• She was the fourth of 16 first ladies who lived to be 70.
• She was the fourth of 17 wives of presidents who lived to be 70.
• She was the second of 14 first ladies who lived to be 75.
• She was the second of 15 wives of presidents who lived to be 75.
Place of burial: Quincy, Mass.
• She was the second of two first ladies who were buried in Massachusetts. The other was Abigail Adams.
• She was the second of three wives of presidents who were buried in Massachusetts.

EARLY YEARS

Feb. 17, 1778, accompanied his father to France
• Adams's first formal schooling was at a school near Paris.
June, 1779, returned to U.S.
December, 1779, made his second trip to France
• He attended a school in Paris for six months.
August, 1780, accompanied father to Holland
• He studied at the Latin School in Amsterdam, then entered the University of Leyden.
July 7, 1781, traveled from Amsterdam to St. Petersburg, Russia
• He accompanied his father's secretary of legation, Francis Dana—who had been appointed minister to Russia—as private secretary.
Aug. 29, 1781, arrived at St. Petersburg
• Dana was never officially received by the Russians.
October, 1782, left St. Petersburg, traveled alone through Sweden, Denmark, northern Germany, and France
April, 1783, arrived at father's home in The Hague
May, 1785, sailed for U.S.
July, 1785, arrived at Braintree
• After some preliminary study, he entered Harvard College as a junior in the winter

of 1785–1786.
July 18, 1787, graduated from Harvard College, Cambridge, Mass.
• He was the first of three presidents who were members of Phi Beta Kappa elected as undergraduates.
• He was the first of 11 presidents who were members of Phi Beta Kappa.
1787–1790, studied law with Theophilus Parsons of Newburyport, Mass.
• He was the fourth of 26 presidents who studied law.
July 15, 1790, admitted to the bar, Boston Mass.
• He opened offices in Boston, but his practice was minuscule.
• He was the fourth of 23 presidents who were lawyers.
June–July, 1791, published 11 articles in Boston *Columbian Centinel*
• The letters, which appeared under the pseudonym, *Publicola*, criticized certain positions taken by Thomas Paine in *The Rights of Man*. In England, the articles were attributed to his father.
December, 1793, published series of articles criticizing conduct of Minister Genet
• The articles, which were refused by the Boston newspapers, appeared in Noah Webster's New York City paper, the *Minerva*, under the pseudonym, *Columbus*.

NATIONAL PROMINENCE

May 29, 1794, appointed minister to The Netherlands by Washington
• Adams was confirmed by the Senate, May 30.
Sept. 17, 1794, sailed for Holland
Oct. 31, 1794, arrived at The Hague
• He was the second of two presidents who served as ministers to The Netherlands. The other was John Adams.
• He was the fourth of seven presidents who served as diplomats.
1796, appointed minister to Portugal by Washington
• Adams asked to remain at The Hague until his successor was appointed. He never presented his credentials in Lisbon.
Mar. 4, 1797, his father inaugurated
June, 1797, left Holland for England

• Upon his arrival in London, he learned that he had been appointed minister to Prussia by his father.
July 26, 1797, married Louisa Catherine Johnson, London
Fall, 1797, presented credentials as minister to Prussia, Berlin
• He was the only president who served as minister to Prussia.
1799, negotiated treaty of amity and commerce with Prussia
• During his residence in Berlin, he learned German and translated *Oberon*, by Christoph Martin Wieland. He finished his translation, which was not published, shortly after the appearance of a translation by William Sotheby. Wieland is said to have adjudged the Sotheby as the more poetic

but not the more faithful of the two translations.

1800–1801, journeyed through Silesia

•His "Letters from Silesia" were published in the Philadelphia *Portfolio*. The account of his tour of Silesia was published in London by J. Budd, 1804.

Apr. 12, 1801, his first son born, Berlin

•The boy was named George Washington Adams.

September, 1801, returned to U.S.

•He resumed the practice of law, Boston.

1801, appointed to Massachusetts senate

1802, defeated for House of Representatives

•He ran for the Boston seat in Congress but was defeated by William Eustis by 59 votes.

July 4, 1803, his second son born

•The boy was named John Adams.

1803, elected to Senate

•He ran against Timothy Pickering and was appointed by the state legislature.

•He was the third of 16 presidents who were elected to the Senate.

Oct. 17, 1803, took seat in Senate

•He was the third of 15 presidents who served in the Senate.

1806, appointed Boylston Professor of Oratory and Rhetoric, Harvard College

•His lecture schedule was arranged so as not to interfere with his duties in the Senate. He served until 1809.

•Two volumes of his lectures were published by Hilliard and Metcalf, Cambridge, 1810.

•He was the sixth of 21 presidents who wrote books that were published during their lifetimes.

Aug. 18, 1807, his third son was born

•The boy was named Charles Francis Adams.

December, 1807, supported Jefferson embargo act

•He served on the committee that reported the bill and vigorously supported the measure. His stand on the embargo cost him his Senate seat.

June, 1808, his successor in Senate appointed by Massachusetts legislature

•His term of office extended to Mar. 4, 1809. The early appointment of James Lloyd was intended and accepted as an insult.

June 8, 1808, resigned from Senate

July, 1808, declined Democratic-Republican nomination for House of Representatives

Mar. 6, 1809, appointed minister to Russia by Madison

•He sailed for Russia, Aug. 5.

•He was the first of two presidents who served as ministers to Russia. The other was Buchanan.

Feb. 21, 1811, appointed as associate justice by Madison

•He was confirmed by the Senate, Feb. 22, but declined to serve, Apr. 5.

Aug. 12, 1811, his only daughter born

•The girl, who was named Louisa Catherine, died in infancy, 1812.

Sept. 21, 1812, received offer of Alexander I to act as mediator between U.S. and Great Britain

•The British spurned the Russian offer before the arrival in St. Petersburg of the U.S. peace commissioners, Albert Gallatin and James A. Bayard, July 21, 1813.

January, 1814, appointed member of five-man peace commission to negotiate directly with British

Aug. 8, 1814, peace talks began, Ghent, Belgium

•The other U.S. commissioners were Gallatin, Bayard, Henry Clay, and Jonathan Russell; the British representatives were Lord Gambier, Dr. William Adams, and Henry Goulburn.

Dec. 24, 1814, Treaty of Ghent signed

Mar. 20, 1815, witnessed return of Napoleon from Elba, Paris

May 26, 1815, arrived in London

•He, Clay, and Gallatin had been appointed commissioners to negotiate a new commercial treaty with Great Britain. Upon his arrival in London, he was informed of his appointment as minister to the Court of St. James's.

•He was the third of five presidents who served as ministers to Great Britain.

July 13, 1815, new commercial treaty with Great Britain signed by Adams, Clay, and Gallatin

Mar. 5, 1817, appointed as secretary of state by Monroe

June 15, 1817, departed for U.S.

Aug. 5, 1817, arrived in New York City

•He had been in Europe for eight years.

Sept. 22, 1817, took office as secretary of state

•He was the fourth of six presidents who served as secretaries of state.

•He was the fourth of eight presidents who served in the cabinet.

Oct. 28, 1818, his mother died

Feb. 22, 1819, signed Adams-Onis Treaty with Spain

•He and the Spanish minister, Luis de Onis, signed the treaty, which provided that Spain renounce all claims to West Florida and cede East Florida to the U.S. The U.S. assumed the claims of American citizens against Spain up to $5,000,000 and renounced any claim to Texas. The western boundary between Louisiana and Mexico was established by the treaty, which became effective with the exchange of ratifications, Feb. 22, 1821.

Dec. 6, 1820, received only electoral vote not cast for Monroe

•William Plumer of New Hampshire was the only elector who did not vote to reelect Monroe.

• *See* Election of 1820, pages 73–74.

Dec. 2, 1823, his hemispheric principle, as embodied in the Monroe Doctrine, submitted as part of Monroe's seventh annual message to Congress

• *See* page 75.

Feb. 15, 1824, nominated for president by eastern faction of Republican party, Boston

Nov. 9, 1824, election day

•This was the first election in which the popular vote was tabulated.

• *See* Election of 1824, below.

Dec. 1, 1824, presidential electors cast ballots

• *See* Election of 1824, below.

Jan. 8, 1825, his support urged by Clay

Feb. 9, 1825, elected as president by House of Representatives

•This was the second of two elections decided by the House of Representatives.

• *See* Election of 1800, pages 44–45.

•Adams and Calhoun were officially declared elected.

ELECTION OF 1824

•There were five candidates for president. All were Republicans, but party affiliation had given way to sectionalism. Secretary of War John C. Calhoun of South Carolina, supported by the Deep South, had announced his candidacy in 1821, but ultimately withdrew to become a vice-presidential candidate. The Tennessee legislature had nominated Andrew Jackson

of Tennessee, July 20, 1822. Jackson drew support from all sections, but particularly the West. The Kentucky legislature had nominated Henry Clay of Kentucky, Nov. 18, 1822. Clay support also came from the West. The last of the congressional caucuses, attended by only 66 of the 216 eligible members, had nominated Secretary of Treasury William H. Crawford of Georgia, Feb. 14. Crawford had suffered a paralytic stroke about five months earlier; the question of his health practically eliminated him as a serious contender. John Quincy Adams of Massachusetts had been nominated by an eastern faction in Boston, Feb. 15.

•The electors from 18 states, Alabama, Connecticut, Illinois, Indiana, Kentucky, Maine, Maryland, Massachusetts, Mississippi, Missouri, New Hampshire, New Jersey, North Carolina, Ohio, Pennsylvania, Rhode Island, Tennessee, and Virginia, had been selected by popular vote, while those representing Delaware, Georgia, Louisiana, New York, South Carolina, and Vermont had been appointed by their state legislatures.

Election day, Tuesday, Nov. 9, 1824

Popular vote: 361,120

  Adams, 114,023

  Jackson, 152,901

  Clay, 47,217

  Crawford, 46,979

•Adams was the first of 15 presidents who were elected without receiving a majority of the popular vote.

Electoral vote: 261, 24 states

  •Jackson, 99, 11 states

  (Alabama, 5; Illinois, 2 of 3 votes; Indiana, 5; Louisiana, 3 of 5 votes; Maryland, 7 of 11 votes; Mississippi, 3; New Jersey, 8; North Carolina, 15; Pennsylvania, 28; South Carolina, 11; Tennessee, 11)

•Jackson also received the vote of one New York elector.

  • Adams, 84, seven states

  (Connecticut, 8; Maine, 9; Massachusetts, 15; New Hampshire, 8; New York, 26 of 36 votes; Rhode Island, 4; Vermont, 7)

•Adams also received the votes of one Delaware, one Illinois, two Louisiana, and three Maryland electors.

  • Crawford, 41, three states

  (Georgia, 9; Delaware, 2 of 3 votes; Virginia, 24)

•Crawford also received the votes of one Maryland and five New York electors.
  • Clay, 37, three states
    (Kentucky, 14; Missouri, 3; Ohio, 16)
•Clay also received the votes of four New York electors.
•No candidate received a majority of the 261 electoral votes from the 24 states. The election was submitted to the House of Representatives, by provision of the 12th Amendment to the Constitution.
• See Constitution, page 643.
•Clay was eliminated as a presidential candidate, inasmuch as the 12th Amendment to the Constitution provides that only the three candidates who have received the highest number of electoral votes are to be considered by the House of Representatives.
•The election was decided by the House of Representatives on the basis of one vote per state, Feb. 9, 1825. John Quincy Adams received the votes of 13 states, one more than the majority required. Jackson received the votes of seven states and Crawford received the votes of four states.
•Calhoun, who had run on both the Adams and the Jackson tickets, received 182 electoral votes and was elected vice president

(Alabama, 5; Illinois, 3; Indiana, 5; Louisiana, 5; Maryland, 10 of 11 votes; Maine, 9; Massachusetts, 15; Mississippi, 3; New Hampshire, 7 of 8 votes; New Jersey, 8; New York, 29 of 36 votes; North Carolina, 15; Pennsylvania, 28; Rhode Island, 3 of 4 votes; South Carolina, 11; Tennessee, 11; Vermont, 7).
•Calhoun also received the votes of one Delaware and seven Kentucky electors.
•Nathan Sanford of New York received 30 votes (Ohio, 16). He also received the votes of seven Kentucky and seven New York electors.
•Nathaniel Macon of North Carolina received the votes of the 24 Virginia electors.
•Andrew Jackson, not technically a vice-presidential nominee, received 13 votes (Connecticut, 8; Missouri, 3). He also received the votes of one Maryland and one New Hampshire elector.
•Martin Van Buren of New York received the votes of the nine Georgia electors.
•Henry Clay, not technically a vice-presidential nominee, received the votes of two Delaware electors.
•One Rhode Island elector failed to vote for vice president.

THE PRESIDENT (6th)

Term of office: Mar. 4, 1825, to Mar. 4, 1829 (4 years)
•John Quincy Adams was the second of 19 presidents who served one term or less than one term.
•He was the second of ten presidents who served for four years.
State represented: Massachusetts
•He was the second of four presidents who represented Massachusetts.
Political party: Democratic-Republican
•He was the last of four presidents who were Democratic-Republicans.
Congresses: 19th, 20th

Administration: 10th
Age at inauguration: 57 years, 236 days
Inauguration day: Friday, Mar. 4, 1825
•Adams took the oath of office, administered by Chief Justice John Marshall, in the Hall of Representatives of the Capitol.
•This was the seventh of nine inaugurations at which Marshall officiated.
•Adams was the fourth of five presidents who took the oath of office in the House of Representatives chamber.
•This was the fifth of six oath-taking ceremonies in the House chamber.

THE 10th ADMINISTRATION

1825

Mar. 7, appointed his only secretary of state, Henry Clay; his only secretary of treasury, Richard Rush; and his first secretary of war,

James Barbour
•Adams retained Monroe's attorney general and secretary of navy.
•Clay took office, Mar. 9.
Mar. 8, appointed first minister to Mexico,

Joel Roberts Poinsett
•Poinsett developed and introduced to this country the Mexican flowering plant that now bears his name, the poinsettia.
Sept. 6, hosted celebration of Lafayette's 68th birthday, White House
•The Revolutionary War hero was concluding a 14-month tour of the U.S. Lafayette sailed home to France, Sept. 7.
Dec. 5, first session of 19th Congress
•The administration controlled both the Senate and the House of Representatives. The Senate (46 members) consisted of 26 administration supporters and 20 opponents, Jacksonians. The House (202 members) consisted of 105 administration supporters and 97 Jacksonians.
Dec. 6, sent his first State of the Union message to Congress
•He announced acceptance of an invitation to send delegates to the Pan-American Congress in Panama, which had been called by Simon Bolivar of Venezuela.
Dec. 26, nominated Richard C. Anderson and John Sergeant as envoys to Pan-American Congress

1826

Feb. 7, Associate Justice Todd died
Mar. 3, castigated by John Randolph
•During the Senate debate regarding participation in the Pan-American Congress, Randolph referred to the president and Henry Clay as "the Puritan and the blackleg." The Virginian suggested that a "corrupt bargain" had been made in 1824, that the post of secretary of state had been offered in exchange for Clay's support.
•Randolph's speech (in which he also had alluded to the fact that Clay was a high-stakes gambler) led to a duel, Apr. 8. Neither Clay nor Randolph was harmed.
Mar. 14, envoys to Pan-American Congress confirmed
•Debate regarding the appropriation for expenses of the delegates delayed the departure of Anderson and Sergeant. Martin Van Buren and John Calhoun led the opposition to participation; southern opposition developed due to Negro leadership of some of the republics involved. Anderson died en route to Panama, and Sergeant was in Mexico when the congress adjourned—a failure because of the nonpar-

ticipation of the U.S.
Apr. 11, appointed Robert Trimble as associate justice
•Trimble, who was confirmed by the Senate, May 9, was the first of Adams's two appointments to the Supreme Court.
May 22, first session of 19th Congress adjourned
July 4, 50th Independence Day
•His father and Thomas Jefferson died only hours apart.
Dec. 4, second session of 19th Congress
Dec. 5, sent his second State of Union message to Congress

1827

Mar. 2, signed act that raised salary of postmaster general to level of executive department heads
Mar. 3, second session of 19th Congress adjourned
Mar. 15, instructed Poinsett to offer $1,500,000 to establish boundary line with Mexico
•He suggested the substitution of the Rio Grande and Colorado rivers as the boundary, instead of the Sabine River, as provided for in the Adams-Onis Treaty of 1819. The offer was rejected by Mexico.
Dec. 3, first session of 20th Congress
•The administration lost control of both the Senate and the House of Representatives. The Senate (48 members) consisted of 28 Jacksonians and 20 administration supporters. The House (213 members) consisted of 119 Jacksonians and 94 administration supporters.
•This was the first time that an administration lost control of both the Senate and the House two years after its election.
Dec. 4, sent his third State of the Union message to Congress

1828

Jan. 12, treaty with Mexico fixed boundary line as designated in Adams-Onis Treaty of 1819
•This agreement did not go into effect until Apr. 5, 1832.
Feb. 25, attended wedding of Mary Catherine Hellen and his son, John Adams, White House
•This was the only White House wedding of

a son of a president.
• This was the second of nine White House weddings of children of presidents.

May 19, signed tariff act
• The excessively high protective tariff provided by this act was considered unjust by the South, where it was known as the "Tariff of Abominations."

May 23, accepted resignation of Secretary of War Barbour

May 26, appointed his second secretary of war, Peter B. Porter
• Porter, who took office, June 21, was the last of Adams's six cabinet appointments.
• This was the only change in his cabinet.

May 26, first session of 20th Congress adjourned

July 4, broke ground for Chesapeake and Ohio canal

Aug. 25, Associate Justice Trimble died

Nov. 11, election day
• *See* Election of 1828, page 95.

Dec. 1, second session of 20th Congress

Dec. 2, sent his fourth and last State of the Union message to Congress

Dec. 3, presidential electors cast ballots
• Jackson received 178 electoral votes; Adams received 83.
• *See* page 95.

Dec. 17, appointed John J. Crittenden as associate justice
• Crittenden was the second of Adams's two appointments to the Supreme Court. This appointment was postponed, Feb. 12, 1829.
• He was the third of 15 presidents who nominated justices not confirmed by the Senate.
• Crittenden was the third of 25 men nominated to the Supreme Court who were not confirmed by the Senate.

1829

Feb. 11, electoral vote tabulated by Congress
• Jackson and Calhoun were officially declared elected.
• Adams was the second of seven presidents who were defeated when they sought reelection.

Mar. 3, second session of 20th Congress adjourned

Mar. 3, moved from White House to temporary residence on Meridian Hill, suburb of Washington

Note: Adams was the third of seven presidents who did not exercise the veto.

THE FORMER PRESIDENT

Mar. 4, 1829, did not attend Jackson inauguration
• Adams was the second of four presidents who did not attend the inaugurations of their successors.
• His age upon leaving office was 61 years, 236 days.

Apr. 30, 1829, his son reported missing
• George Washington Adams fell overboard from a steamer bound for New York City from Providence, R.I. His body was found on City Island, off the east coast of the Bronx, in June. Whether Adams's son committed suicide was never established.

June, 1829, returned to Quincy, Mass.

1830, received delegation who offered support if he were to run for Congress
• When he was asked if he considered it beneath his dignity to run for a House of Representatives seat, he replied that he had no scruples about serving the public in any meritorious capacity. He agreed to run but refused to campaign and stated that he would not be held accountable to any party or faction.

Nov. 1, 1830, elected to House of Representatives
• He was elected as an Anti-Mason.
• He was the only president elected to the House after his term of office.
• He was the first of two presidents who were elected to Congress after their terms of office. Andrew Johnson was elected to the Senate, 1875.
• He was the seventh of 17 presidents who were elected to the House of Representatives.
• He was the fourth of 11 presidents who were elected to both the Senate and the House of Representatives.

Dec. 5, 1831, took seat in House of Representatives
• He represented the district of Plymouth, Mass., in nine congresses. He first served in

the 22nd Congress; he was a member of the 30th Congress when he died.

- He was the only president who served in the House after his term of office.
- He was the seventh of 17 presidents who served in the House of Representatives.
- He was the fourth of ten presidents who served in both the Senate and the House of Representatives.

1831, his eulogy to Monroe published, Boston, Mass.

- The 100-page eulogy was published by the Boston city printer, J.H. Eastburn. When he had delivered the eulogy during memorial services held in Boston following the death of Monroe on July 4, he spoke for 90 minutes but delivered little more than half of his prepared speech, due to excessive heat and humidity.

1832, his book of poetry published, Boston, Mass.

- The 108-page work, published by Carter, Hendee, in four cantos, was entitled *Dermot MacMorrogh, or, The Conquest of Ireland; an Historical Tale of the Twelfth Century.*
- He was the only president who was a published poet.

1833, objected to Harvard College conferring honorary degree on Jackson

- Years later he wrote:
  I would not be present to see my darling Harvard disgrace herself by conferring a Doctor's degree upon a barbarian and savage who could scarcely spell his own name.

1833, defeated as Anti-Masonic candidate for governor

Dec. 31, 1834, delivered eulogy to Lafayette

- Lafayette had died in France, May 20. The eulogy was delivered at the request of both houses of Congress.
- The 96-page tribute was published by D. Green, Washington, D.C., 1835.

May 26, 1836, voted against House of Representatives resolution on slavery

- This resolution, the first "gag rule," provided that "all petitions, memorials, resolutions, or papers relating in any way or to any extent whatsoever to the subject of slavery or the abolition of slavery, shall, without being either printed or referred, be laid upon the table; and that no further action whatever shall be had thereon." When his name was called, he rose and

declared: "I hold the resolution to be a direct violation of the Constitution of the United States, the rules of this House, and the rights of my constituents." The resolution was adopted, 117–68.

- He fought the continuation of the gag rule for years. Almost singlehandedly he campaigned to secure the right of petition; the gag rule was repealed in 1844.

1836, defeated as candidate for Senate

- He had been selected for the Senate seat by the state senate but was defeated in the lower house because of a speech in favor of reprisals against the French.

1836, his eulogy to Madison published, Boston, Mass.

- The 90-page eulogy was published by the Boston city printer, J. H. Eastburn. He had delivered the eulogy at memorial services in Boston following the death of Madison on June 28, at the request of the mayor, aldermen, and common council of the city.

1836–1843, opposed annexation and admission of Texas

- He opposed all attempts to add Texas to the Union because of the slavery issue.

July 11, 1837, celebrated his 70th birthday

- He was the fifth of 16 presidents who lived to be 70.

Feb. 24 and Mar. 1, 1841, argued *Amistad* case before Supreme Court

- A group of slaves being transported aboard the Spanish ship, *Amistad,* had mutinied. The ship was captured off Montauk Point, L.I., Aug. 29, 1839. The Supreme Court sustained the lower courts and freed his clients, the slave mutineers. Mar. 9.

Jan. 21, 1842, presented petition to Congress from citizens of Haverhill, Mass., which asked peaceful dissolution of Union

- A resolution of censure was presented, Jan. 25. During the debates, which extended to Feb. 7, he asked the clerk of the House of Representatives to read the paragraph of the Declaration of Independence which recognizes the right of the people "to alter or to abolish" any form of government when their inalienable rights are threatened.
- The resolution of censure was tabled. The House voted to refuse to receive the Haverhill petition, Feb. 7.

Apr. 14, 1842, reiterated his antislavery principle

- During a House debate on the question of

war with Great Britain and Mexico, he said:

> Whether the war be civil, servile, or foreign, I lay this down as the law of nations: I say that the military authority takes for the time the place of all municipal institutions, slavery among the rest. Under that state of things, so far from its being true that the states where slavery exists have the exclusive management of the subject, not only the President of the United States, but the commander of the army unquestionably has power to order the universal emancipation of the slaves.

July 11, 1842, celebrated his 75th birthday
•He was the fourth of ten presidents who lived to be 75.

Nov. 10, 1843, delivered oration at laying of cornerstone of astronomical observatory, Mount Adams, near Cincinnati, Ohio.
•This was the first observatory established in the U.S.

Dec. 3, 1844, succeeded in repealing "gag rule"
•His motion to rescind the gag rule, which prohibited the presentation of abolition petitions, passed, 108–88.

May 11, 1846, voted against war with Mexico

Aug. 10, 1846, Smithsonian Institution established by act of Congress
•He led the ten-year fight for acceptance of the endowment of James Smithson and was instrumental in securing the favorable vote. Smithson, the illegitimate son of the first Duke of Northumberland, had died in 1829, and had bequeathed his estate to a nephew. The will provided that if the nephew died without heirs—which he did in 1835–the estate was to be given to the U.S. government "to found at Washington, under the name of the Smithsonian Institution, an establishment for the increase and diffusion of knowledge among men." In 1835, the estate was valued at $508,000.

Nov. 19, 1846, suffered first stroke
•He sustained a shock of paralysis and was incapacitated for weeks. He never fully recovered from the effects.

July 11, 1847, celebrated his 80th birthday
•He was the fourth of six presidents who

lived to be 80.

July 26, 1847, with Mrs. Adams, celebrated 50th wedding anniversary
•He was the second of four presidents who celebrated their golden wedding anniversaries.

Feb. 21, 1848, suffered second stroke, collapsed in House of Representatives
•He was carried from his seat to the Speaker's Room, where he lay until his death, two days later.

DEATH

Date of death: Feb. 23, 1848
Place of death: Washington, D.C.
•John Quincy Adams was the first of seven presidents who died in Washington.
Age of death: 80 years, 227 days
•He lived 18 years, 356 days, after the completion of his term.
Cause of death: Paralysis
Place of burial: Quincy, Mass.
•He was the second of two presidents who were buried in Massachusetts. The other was his father, John Adams, who also was buried in Quincy.

THE VICE PRESIDENT (7th)

Full name: John Caldwell Calhoun
Date of birth: Mar. 18, 1782
•He was the first vice president who was not a British subject at birth.
Place of birth: near Calhoun Mills, Abbeville district, S.C.
•He was the only vice president who was born in South Carolina.
Religious denomination: Presbyterian
•He was the fourth of 11 vice presidents who were Presbyterians.
College: Yale College, New Haven, Conn.
Date of graduation: 1804
•He studied law under Tapping Reeve, Litchfield, Conn.
Occupation: Lawyer
•He was elected to the South Carolina legislature, 1808; was a member of the House of Representatives, 1811–1817; was acting chairman of the House committee on foreign affairs and a leader of the "war hawks" prior to and during the War of 1812; was secretary of war under President Monroe, 1817–1825; as secretary, established offices

of surgeon-general and quartermaster-general.

•He was the fourth of 21 vice presidents who served in the House of Representatives.

•He was the second of four vice presidents who served in the cabinet.

Term of office: Mar. 4, 1825, to Dec. 28, 1832 (7 years, 299 days)

•He was the third of four vice presidents who served more than seven years.

Note: Calhoun also served as vice president under Jackson. *See* page 103.

•Adams and Calhoun were the eighth of 41 president-vice president teams.

Age at inauguration: 42 years, 351 days

State represented: South Carolina

•He was the only vice president who represented South Carolina.

Political party: Democratic-Republican

•He was the last of six vice presidents who were Democratic-Republicans.

THE CABINET

State: Henry Clay of Kentucky, Mar. 9, 1825, to Mar. 3, 1829

Treasury: Richard Rush of Pennsylvania, Mar. 7, 1825, to Mar. 5, 1829

War: James Barbour of Virginia, Mar. 7, 1825, to May 23, 1828

•Peter Buell Porter of New York, May 26, 1828, to Mar. 9, 1829

Attorney General: William Wirt of Virginia, Nov. 13, 1817, to Mar. 3, 1829

Navy: Samuel Lewis Southard of New Jersey, Sept. 16, 1823, to Mar. 3, 1829

THE SUPREME COURT

Associate Justices: Robert Trimble of Kentucky, appointed, Apr. 11, 1826; confirmed, May 9, 1826

•John Jordan Crittenden of Kentucky, appointed, Dec. 17, 1828; postponed, Feb. 12, 1829

Seventh President

ANDREW JACKSON

Full name: Andrew Jackson
- He was the first of two presidents named Andrew. The other was Johnson.
- He was the third of eight presidents who had the same full names as their fathers.
- He was the sixth of 17 presidents who did not have middle initials or middle names.

Date of birth: Mar. 15, 1767
- He was the second of four presidents who were born in March.

Place of birth: Waxhaw, S.C.
- He was the only president who was born in South Carolina.
- He was the first of seven presidents who were born in log cabins.

Family lineage: Scottish-Irish
- He was the first of four presidents who were of Scottish-Irish ancestry.

Religious denomination: Presbyterian
- He was the first of six presidents who were Presbyterians.

College: None
- He was the second of nine presidents who did not attend college.
- He was the fourth of 15 presidents who were not graduated from college.

Note: Jackson's father and mother were the second and third of eight parents of presidents who were born abroad.

Father's name: Andrew Jackson
Date of birth: *Unknown*
Place of birth: Ireland
- His father was the first of four fathers of presidents who were born abroad.

Occupation: Farmer
Date of death: early March, 1767
- Jackson's father died less than two weeks before his birth.
- He was the first of two presidents who were born after their fathers' deaths. The other was Hayes.

Place of death: Waxhaw, S.C.
Age at death: *Unknown*

Mother's name: Elizabeth Hutchinson Jackson
Date of birth: *Unknown*
Place of birth: Ireland
- His mother was the second of four mothers of presidents who were born abroad.

Children: 3 sons

•Hugh was born in 1762 or 1763; Robert in 1764 or 1765; and Andrew in 1767.

•Jackson was the second of five presidents who came from families of three children.

•He was the second of five presidents who were third children.

•He was the second of five presidents who had male siblings only.

Date of death: November, 1781

•Andrew was 14 years, eight months old, when his mother died.

•He was the first of two presidents who were orphans. The other was Hoover.

Place of death: Charleston, S.C.

Age at death: *Unknown*

MARRIAGE

Date of marriage (first ceremony): probably August, 1791

Place of marriage: Natchez, Miss.

•Jackson was the only president who was married in Mississippi.

Age at marriage: 24 years and about 5 months

•He was the fifth of 27 presidents who were married in their twenties.

Years married: 37 years and about 4 months.

Date of marriage (second ceremony): Jan. 17, 1794

Place of marriage: Nashville, Tenn.

•He was the first of three presidents who were married in Tennessee.

Age at marriage: 26 years, 308 days

Wife's name: Rachel Donelson Robards Jackson

•She had married Lewis Robards in 1785. She married Jackson in 1791, believing that her first marriage had been legally terminated the previous year, when in actuality the legislature of Virginia had only granted her first husband the right to sue for divorce. After a proper divorce decree

was issued, she remarried Jackson in 1794.

•He was the first of two presidents who married divorcees. The other was Harding.

•She was the seventh of 40 wives of presidents.

Date of birth: June, 1767

•She was the third of five wives of presidents who were born in June.

Place of birth: Brunswick County, now Halifax County, Va.

•She was the third of six wives of presidents who were born in Virginia.

Wife's mother: Rachel Stockley Donelson

Wife's father: John Donelson, surveyor

Age at marriage (first ceremony): 24 years and about 2 months

•She was the fifth of 30 wives of presidents who were married in their twenties.

Age at marriage (second ceremony): 26 years and about 7 months

Years younger than husband: about 90 days

Children: None

•Jackson was the third of six presidents who were childless.

Date of death: Dec. 22, 1828

•She was the only wife of a president who died after his election, but before his inauguration.

•She was the second of five wives of presidents who died prior to their husbands' inaugurations.

•She was the second of seven wives of presidents who were not first ladies.

Place of death: Nashville, Tenn.

•She was the first of three wives of presidents who died in Tennessee.

Age at death: 61 years and about 6 months

Place of burial: Nashville, Tenn.

•She was the first of three wives of presidents who were buried in Tennessee.

Years he survived his wife: 16 years, 168 days

•Jackson was the fourth of 14 presidents who survived their wives.

EARLY YEARS

July, 1780, joined army as mounted orderly or messenger

•Jackson was the last of three presidents who served in the Revolutionary War.

•He was the third of 21 presidents who served in the military during wartime.

Aug. 6, 1780, present at Battle of Hanging

Rock, S.C.

•A small band of partisans commanded by Thomas Sumter defeated a British regiment.

Apr. 10, 1781, taken as prisoner of war

•Along with his brother, Robert, he was taken prisoner at the home of a cousin,

Thomas Crawford. When he refused to clean a British officer's boots, Jackson was slashed with a sword, suffering a gash on the head and a wound to the bone of his left hand.

•He was the second of four presidents who were wounded or injured during wartime.

Apr. 25, 1781, released by British

•He and Robert contracted smallpox while in custody. Both were released on the plea of their mother. Robert died, Apr. 27.

•His oldest brother, Hugh, had died in 1779 after the Battle of Stone Ferry.

November, 1781, his mother died

•After her death, Jackson lived with two uncles.

March, 1783, collected legacy, Charleston, S.C.

•His paternal grandfather, Hugh Jackson, had died in Carrickfergus, Northern Ireland. Andrew's legacy amounted to £300 to £400, which he quickly disposed of over the gaming tables and at the races.

December, 1784, began study of law in office of Spruce Macay, Salisbury, N.C.

•He was the fifth of 26 presidents who studied law.

1786—1787, continued study of law with Colonel John Stokes, Salisbury

Sept. 26, 1787, examined by judges for admission to bar, Wadesboro, N.C.

•He was admitted to the bar in November at Salisbury, began his practice in Johnsonville, N.C.

•He was the fifth of 23 presidents who were lawyers.

Aug. 12, 1788; fought duel with Colonel Waightsill Avery, Jonesboro, N.C.

•Both shot in the air deliberately.

Oct. 26, 1788, arrived in Nashville, now Tennessee

•Nashville then was the seat of justice for the western district of North Carolina.

November, 1788, appointed prosecuting attorney for western district

August, 1791, married Rachel Donelson Robards, Natchez, Miss.

Jan. 17, 1794, second marriage ceremony, Nashville

January–February, 1796, delegate from Davidson County to convention to draft constitution for state of Tennessee, Knoxville

•Tennessee was admitted as a state, June 1.

NATIONAL PROMINENCE

1796, elected without opposition to House of Representatives

•Jackson was the second of 17 presidents who were elected to the House.

Dec. 5, 1796, took his seat in House, Philadelphia

•He was the first member of the House who represented Tennessee.

•He was the second of 17 presidents who served in the House.

1797, voted against White House furniture appropriation

•The bill under consideration was for a $14,-000 appropriation to purchase furniture for the executive mansion.

Mar. 3, 1797, his House term ended

•He declined to seek reelection.

1797, elected to Senate

•He was selected by the legislature to fill the vacancy created when Senator William Blount was expelled.

•He was the second of 16 presidents who were elected to the Senate.

•He was the first of 11 presidents who were elected to both the House of Representa-

tives and the Senate.

May, 1797, challenged Governor John Sevier and Judge John McNairy to duels

•Allusions to Jackson's ambitions brought about the situations. Neither duel was fought, since both Sevier and McNairy apologized.

Nov. 20, 1797, took his seat in Senate, Philadelphia

•He was the second of 15 presidents who served in the Senate.

•He was the first of ten presidents who served in both the House of Representatives and the Senate.

April, 1798, resigned from Senate

June, 1798, challenged Senator William Cocke to duel

•Friends of both parties prevented the encounter.

October, 1798, appointed judge of Tennessee superior court

1800, joined Masonic lodge, Nashville, Tenn.

•He was the third of 13 presidents who were Masons.

1802, elected major general of militia
- Jackson and Sevier each received 17 votes when the field officers of the militia were polled. The tie was broken by Governor Archibald Roane, who had succeeded Sevier.

July 27, 1803, accused Sevier of involvement in land swindle
- In an article published in the Knoxville *Gazette*, Jackson accused Sevier—who was running for governor against Roane—of participation in certain illegal East Tennessee land deals.
- Sevier, an acknowledged spellbinder, convinced the electorate of his innocence and easily won the election.

Oct. 1, 1803, attacked Sevier on courthouse steps, Knoxville
- Jackson tried to cane Sevier, who had slandered Mrs. Jackson ("I know of no great service you have rendered the country," shouted Sevier, "except take a trip to Natchez with another man's wife!"). They were forcibly separated. Jackson challenged the governor to a duel. When Sevier vacillated, Jackson inserted an advertisement in the *Gazette* which proclaimed the governor "a base coward and poltroon."

Oct. 16, 1803, met Sevier at Southwest Point
- Jackson waited five days, with a companion, at the boundary site. One of Sevier's excuses had been that as governor he could not fight on Tennessee soil, where dueling was illegal. When Sevier appeared, supported by several armed men, a wild scene developed. Both Jackson and Sevier drew pistols, exchanged heated words, then put their arms away. More insults followed. Sevier drew his sword, "which frightened his horse and he ran away with the Governor's pistols." After Jackson drew his pistol and Sevier hid behind a tree, Sevier's son drew on Jackson and Jackson's companion drew on young Sevier. Cooler heads prevailed, and Sevier retired from the field.

July 24, 1804, resigned as judge of superior court

August or September, 1804, moved to The Hermitage
- He had purchased the 625-acre property in 1795.
- He was the fifth of nine presidents who owned slaves.

- The Hermitage, 12 miles east of Nashville on state route 70–N, is owned by the State of Tennessee, maintained by the Ladies' Hermitage Association. It is open to the public daily except Christmas, 9 A.M. to 5 P.M. Admission: adults, $2; children, six to 13, 50 cents. Student groups: high school and college, 50 cents; elementary and junior high school, ten cents.

May. 29, 1805, entertained Aaron Burr
- Burr remained at The Hermitage for five days.

May 30, 1806, killed Charles Dickinson in duel, near Harrison's Mills, Ky.
- Dickinson, too, had made disparaging remarks about Rachel Jackson. The quarrel, however, was complicated by other differences of opinion. Dickinson fired first, the ounce ball hitting Jackson's left breast; Jackson steadied himself, fired, and Dickinson fell. Dickinson died that evening. Jackson carried the Dickinson bullet for the remainder of his life; it was lodged too close to his heart to be removed.

Sept. 24, 1806, met again with Burr
- Jackson accepted Burr's story of invasion of U.S. territory by the Spanish and pledged his and the state militia's support.

Nov. 12, 1806, demanded explanation from Burr
- Jackson had learned from a "Captain Fort," who said he was en route to join Burr, that the former vice president was involved in a conspiracy "to divide the Union" by seizing New Orleans, conquering Mexico, and establishing a separate government west of the Mississippi. Burr replied that he held no views "inimical" to the United States.

Dec. 18, 1806, paid call on Burr, Nashville
- His suspicions were quieted by Burr's vehement denials of wrongdoing. He outfitted Burr with two boats, and Burr departed, Dec. 22.
- Jackson was not aware that Jefferson had issued a proclamation, Nov. 26, warning the citizenry against participation in the Burr expedition and ordering the arrest of the unidentified conspirators. He learned of the Jefferson proclamation a few days after Burr's departure, probably Dec. 27.
- Jackson was accused later by political opponents of having aided Burr's escape from Nashville.

Mar. 30, 1807, summoned as witness in Burr treason trial, Richmond, Va.

• He was not required to take the stand and was released from his subpoena. Burr was acquitted, Sept. 1.

January, 1810, legally adopted nephew of wife

• His foster son was named Andrew Jackson, Jr. (not to be confused with another nephew of Mrs. Jackson's, Andrew Jackson Donelson). The boy, born on Dec. 22, 1809, was the son of Severn Donelson, the brother of Rachel Jackson.

• He was the only president who adopted a child.

June, 1812, offered services of his 2,500-man militia division

• His offer was made immediately after word was received that the U.S. had declared war on Great Britain, June 18. His request for duty was accepted, but no orders to take the field were dispatched.

November, 1812, appointed major general of U.S. Volunteers by Governor William Blount of Tennessee

• Jackson was the first of four presidents who served in the War of 1812.

• He was the only president who served both in the Revolutionary War and the War of 1812.

Jan. 7, 1813, with two thousand volunteers, departed for Natchez, Miss.

• The volunteers were to be mustered into federal service at Natchez, but upon arrival he was ordered by General James Wilkinson to demobilize his troops. He refused, declaring that he would return them to their homes "on my own means and responsibility."

• During the eight-hundred-mile march back to Tennessee, one of the volunteers said: "He's tough." Another added: "Tough as hickory." By the time they had reached Nashville, he was affectionately known as "Old Hickory."

Sept. 4, 1813, shot by Jesse Benton, Nashville

• He had quarreled with Thomas Hart Benton, brother of Jesse. Jackson entered the City Hotel with the intention of horse-whipping Thomas Benton, but was shot from behind by Jesse. In the melee that followed, shots were fired by all three participants. He fell, severely wounded, his left shoulder shattered and a ball embedded in his left arm. He refused to allow amputation of the arm.

Sept. 24, 1813, informed Governor Blount

he would lead volunteer force against Creeks

• The Creeks, led by Red Eagle, had massacred 250 persons at Fort Mims in the Mississippi Territory, now Alabama, Aug. 30. Red Eagle was seven-eighths white but had renounced his given name, William Weatherford.

Oct. 7, 1813, took command of volunteers, Fayetteville, Tenn.

Nov. 9, 1813, defeated Creeks at Talladega, now Alabama

• More than three hundred Creek warriors were slain in this battle.

January, 1814, Tennessee volunteers defeated in three encounters with Creeks

• The volunteers fared badly at Emuckfaw, Jan. 22, and Enotachopco Creek, Jan. 24, and sustained heavy casualties at Calibee Creek, Jan. 27.

Mar. 27, 1814, defeated Creeks and Cherokees at Horseshoe Bend or Tohopeka, now Alabama

• About 850 Indian warriors were killed at a cost of about 50 dead and 150 wounded in this decisive battle of the Creek War.

• News of this engagement brought him national acclaim.

May 22, 1814, offered rank of brigadier general, U.S. Army

• He accepted the commission, June 8.

• He was the second of 12 presidents who were generals.

May 28, 1814, offered rank of major general

• The resignation of William Henry Harrison, May 11, brought about the offer of the higher rank, which Jackson accepted, June 20. He was given command of the Seventh Military District, which included Tennessee, Louisiana, and the Mississippi Territory.

Nov. 2, 1814, departed Pierce's Stockade on Alabama River with three thousand men, marched on Pensacola

• The British had established a base at Pensacola, now Florida, but then in Spanish territory. "As I act without the orders of the government, I deem it important to state to you my reasons," he wrote Secretary of War Monroe, Oct. 26. "The safety of the nation depends upon it."

Nov. 7, 1814, captured Pensacola

• The British fled after blowing up Fort Barancas and thus lost face with their Spanish and Indian allies.

Nov. 22, 1814, departed from Mobile, Mis-

sissippi Territory, for New Orleans, La.
- He was convinced that the British would approach New Orleans through Mobile or land at the mouth of the Pascagoula River, 30 miles to the west.

Dec. 1, 1814, arrived at New Orleans

Dec. 15, 1814, declared martial law in New Orleans

Dec. 23, 1814, fought night battle against British about eight miles from New Orleans
- At two in the afternoon, he learned that the British had landed at Lake Borgne some ten days earlier and were advancing toward New Orleans. His immediate decision to attack was a considerable counter-surprise to the British. The enemy advance was halted. After a night of fighting, he withdrew and fortified positions at the Rodriguez Canal, about five miles from the city.

Jan. 1, 1815, his artillery outgunned the British

Jan. 8, 1815, decisive victory in Battle of New Orleans
- The British force of fifty-three hundred under Major General Sir Edward Pakenham made a frontal assault on American positions and were decimated by artillery and rifle fire. The battle lasted about 30 minutes. More than two thousand British, including Pakenham, were killed or wounded. American casualties numbered only slightly more than twenty in the main assault.
- The greatest American land victory of the war, the battle actually was fought after the official end of hostilities. None of the participants was aware that the Treaty of Ghent had been signed, Dec. 24, 1814.

Jan. 23, 1815, honored during day of thanksgiving, New Orleans
- The day was celebrated with pageants and a *Te Deum* at St. Louis Cathedral.

Mar. 31, 1815, fined $1,000 for contempt of court
- Martial law had been maintained in New Orleans until Mar. 13, when word came of the ratification of the peace treaty. While martial law still prevailed, Jackson had ordered the arrest of a member of the legislature, Louis Louaillier, for writing what he considered a seditious article and had refused to honor a writ of habeas corpus signed by Federal Judge Dominick Hall. Judge Hall found him guilty of contempt.

- In 1844, Congress ordered the fine repaid with interest. He received about $2,700.

Mar. 5, 1817, declined appointment as secretary of war by Monroe

Dec. 26, 1817, assumed command of expedition sent after hostile Indians into Spanish Florida
- He received instructions to pursue the hostiles across the boundary but was warned not to molest Spanish forts.

Jan. 6, 1818, sent "Rhea letter" to Monroe
- *See* page 71.

Apr. 7, 1818, captured St. Marks, Spanish post

Apr. 26–29, 1818, court-martial of Arbuthnot and Ambrister
- Alexander Arbuthnot, a Scotsman who had traded with the Seminoles, had been captured at St. Marks. Robert Christy Ambrister, a lieutenant in the Royal Colonial Marines, blundered into the American camp near the Suwannee River. Arbuthnot was charged with spying, aiding the enemy, and exciting the Indians to war; Ambrister with assuming command of the Indians at war with the U.S. Both were found guilty. Arbuthnot was hanged and Lieutenant Ambrister was shot, Apr. 30.
- The executions caused great excitement in England, but no official action was taken.

May 24, 1818, captured Pensacola
- This ended the First Seminole War.

Dec. 18, 1818, Senate committee appointed to investigate his actions in Florida, including executions of Arbuthnot and Ambrister

Apr. 5, 1821, appointed military governor of Florida by Monroe
- Jackson was the first of two presidents who were military governors. The other was Andrew Johnson.

Oct. 5, 1821, resigned as military governor of Florida

Nov. 28, 1821, capital of Mississippi named Jackson
- This was the first of four state capitals named for presidents.
- It was the only state capital named for a president prior to his election.

July 20, 1822, nominated for president by Tennessee legislature

Jan. 5, 1823, appointed as minister plenipotentiary to Mexico by Monroe
- The appointment was confirmed by the Senate, but Jackson refused the offer by letter to Monroe, Feb. 19.

Oct. 1, 1823, again elected to Senate by Tennessee legislature

Dec. 5, 1823, took seat in Senate

Nov. 2, 1824, election day

•This was the first election in which the popular vote was tabulated.

• See Election of 1824, pages 82–83.

Dec. 1, 1824, presidential electors cast ballots

•Since no candidate received a majority of the 261 electoral votes from the 24 states, the election was submitted to the House of Representatives.

• See Election of 1824, pages 82–83.

Feb. 9, 1825, defeated as candidate for president in House of Representatives

•The election was decided on the basis of one vote per state.

•Jackson received the votes of seven states. John Quincy Adams received the votes of 13 states—one more than the majority required. Crawford received the votes of the remaining four states.

•Jackson was the first of three presidential candidates who received a plurality of the popular vote but were defeated in the electoral college.

Oct. 12, 1825, announced resignation from Senate

•The Tennessee legislature had renominated him for the presidency. He told the assemblymen that their action made it improper for him to continue in the Senate.

Nov. 4, 1828, election day

• See Election of 1828, below.

Dec. 3, 1828, presidential electors cast ballots

• See Election of 1828, below.

Dec. 22, 1828, his wife died

Feb. 11, 1829, electoral votes tabulated by Congress

•Jackson and Calhoun were officially declared elected.

ELECTION OF 1828

•This was the first election in which presidential nominations were made by state legislatures rather than congressional caucuses.

•The Democratic-Republicans were sharply divided. The Tennessee legislature had nominated Andrew Jackson for president in 1825, which began a three-year campaign to oust John Quincy Adams from the presidency. The Jacksonians, who now called themselves Democrats, were opposed by the Adams-Clay faction, which joined with former Federalists to form the National Republican party.

•The electors from 22 states, Alabama, Connecticut, Georgia, Illinois, Indiana, Kentucky, Louisiana, Maine, Maryland, Massachusetts, Mississippi, Missouri, New Hampshire, New Jersey, New York, North Carolina, Ohio, Pennsylvania, Rhode Island, Tennessee, Vermont, and Virginia, had been selected by popular vote, while those representing Delaware and South Carolina had been appointed by their state legislatures.

Election day, Tuesday, Nov. 4, 1828

Popular vote: 1,155,350

 Jackson, 647,276

 Adams, 508,074

Electoral vote: 261, 24 states

•Jackson, 178, 15 states
(Alabama, 5; Georgia, 9; Illinois, 3; Indiana, 5; Kentucky, 14; Louisiana, 5; Mississippi, 3; Missouri, 3; New York, 20 of 36 votes; North Carolina, 15; Ohio, 16; Pennsylvania, 28; South Carolina, 11; Tennessee, 11; Virginia, 24)

•Jackson also received the votes of one Maine and five Maryland electors.

• Adams, 83, nine states
(Connecticut, 8; Delaware, 3; Maine, 8 of 9 votes; Maryland, 6 of 11 votes; Massachusetts, 15; New Hampshire, 8; New Jersey, 8; Rhode Island, 4; Vermont, 7)

•Adams also received the votes of 16 New York electors.

•Calhoun received 171 electoral votes and was elected vice president (Alabama, 5; Illinois, 3; Indiana, 5; Kentucky, 14; Louisiana, 5; Mississippi, 3; Missouri, 3; New York, 20 of 36 votes; North Carolina, 15; Ohio, 16; Pennsylvania, 28; South Carolina, 11; Tennessee, 11; Virginia, 24).

•Calhoun also received the votes of two Georgia, one Maine, and five Maryland electors.

•Richard Rush of Pennsylvania received 83 votes (Connecticut, 8; Delaware, 3; Maine, 8 of 9 votes; Maryland, 6 of 11 votes; Massachusetts, 15; New Hampshire, 8; New Jersey, 8; Rhode Island, 4; Vermont, 7).

•Rush also received the votes of 16 New York electors.

•William Smith of South Carolina received seven votes (Georgia, 7 of 9 votes).

THE PRESIDENT (7th)

Term of office: Mar. 4, 1829, to Mar. 4, 1837 (8 years)
•Jackson was the fifth of 12 presidents who were elected to second terms.
•He was the fifth of 16 presidents who served more than one term.
•He was the fifth of nine presidents who served two terms.
•He was the fourth of eight presidents who served for eight years.
State represented: Tennessee
•He was the first of three presidents who represented Tennessee.
•He was the first of 15 presidents who represented states that were not their native states.
Political party: Democratic
•He was the first of 12 presidents who were Democrats.
Congresses: 21st, 22nd, 23rd, 24th
Administrations: 11th, 12th
Age at inauguration: 61 years, 354 days
Inauguration day: Wednesday, Mar. 4, 1829
•Jackson took the oath of office, administered by Chief Justice John Marshall, on the east portico of the Capitol.
•This was the eighth of nine inaugurations at which Marshall officiated.

THE 11th ADMINISTRATION

1829

Mar. 6, appointed his first secretary of state, Martin Van Buren; his first secretary of treasury, Samuel D. Ingham; his first secretary of war, John H. Eaton; his first attorney general, John M. Berrien; his first secretary of navy, John Branch; and his first postmaster general, William T. Barry
•Eaton, Berrien, and Branch took office, Mar. 9; Van Buren, Mar. 28; and Barry, Apr. 6.
Mar. 6, appointed John McLean as associate justice
•McLean, who was confirmed by the Senate, Mar. 7, was the first of Jackson's eight appointments to the Supreme Court.
Mar. 23, sent message to Creek Indians
•"My white children in Alabama have extended their law over your country," he wrote. "If you remain in it you must be subject to that law. If you move across the Mississippi, you will be subject to your own laws and the care of your father, the President."
Aug. 13–15, instructed Van Buren to renew boundary change proposals with Mexico
•An offer of $5,000,000 to change the boundary, as set by the Adams-Onis treaty of 1819, to the Rio Grande, was made and rejected. Minister Poinsett was recalled at the request of the Mexican government, Oct 16.
Nov. 26, Associate Justice Washington died
Dec. 7, first session of 21st Congress
•The administration controlled both the Senate and the House of Representatives. The Senate (48 members) consisted of 26 Democrats and 22 National Republicans. The House (213 members) consisted of 139 Democrats and 74 National Republicans.
Dec. 8, sent his first State of the Union message to Congress
•He advised an inquiry into the constitutionality of the charter of the Second Bank of the U.S. and proposed distribution of surplus revenue among the states.

Note: He suspended regular meetings of the cabinet shortly after he took office, and chose instead to rely on a small group of unofficial advisors. This lower cabinet was quickly nicknamed the "kitchen cabinet" by his opponents. The group's influence remained strong until after the 1831 reorganization of the official cabinet.
•Among the members of the "kitchen cabinet" were Amos Kendall, William Berkeley Lewis, Isaac Hill, Duff Green, and Jackson's nephew, Andrew Jackson Donelson, who served as his private secretary.

1830

Jan. 4, appointed Henry Baldwin as associate justice
•Baldwin, who was confirmed by the Senate, Jan. 6, was the second of Jackson's eight appointments to the Supreme Court.
Apr. 13, gave "Our Union" toast
•He attended the Jefferson Day dinner in

Washington, which had been organized by Senator Thomas Hart Benton of Missouri and Senator Robert Young Hayne of South Carolina. After 24 toasts, most of which advocated states' rights and the principle of nullification, Jackson offered his toast: "Our Union: It must be preserved."

• Vice President Calhoun responded: "The Union, next to our liberty, most dear. May we always remember that it can only be preserved by distributing equally the benefits and burdens of the Union."

• Jackson agreed, at the request of Senator Hayne, to reword his toast for publication to "Our Federal Union."

May 27, vetoed Maysville Road internal improvements bill

• The bill authorized the subscription of stock by the government for a 60-mile turnpike in Kentucky, from Maysville to Lexington. An attempt to pass the bill over his veto in the House of Representatives was defeated, 96–92, May 28.

• This was the first of his 12 vetoes.

May 29, authorized to open American ports to British vessels when British colonial ports had been opened to American ships

May 30, broke with Calhoun

• When he was informed that the vice president, while secretary of war in 1818, had favored punishing him for his conduct in the Seminole War, Jackson demanded an explanation. Unsatisfied with Calhoun's version of events, he wrote, "Understanding you now, no further communication with you on this subject is necessary."

May 31, vetoed Washington Road internal improvements bill

• This was the second of his 12 vetoes.

May 31, signed extension of Cumberland Road act

• He considered the Cumberland Road project of national character. This was the only sizeable land-route project he approved.

May 31, first session of 21st Congress adjourned

Oct. 5, issued proclamation that trade with British West Indies was open to American vessels

Dec. 6, second session of 21st Congress

Dec. 6, sent his second State of the Union message

Dec. 7, vetoed lighthouse and beacons, canal stock internal improvements bills

• These bills had been passed during the first

session of the 21st Congress.

• These were the third and fourth of his 12 vetoes, the first and second of his seven pocket vetoes.

Dec. 7, Washington *Globe* began publication

• The proadministration newspaper was edited by Francis P. Blair, who perfected the maneuver of planting pro-Jackson stories in smaller, rural papers and then reprinting them in the *Globe* "as an indication of public opinion."

Note: The official population according to the fifth census, was 12,866,020 which included 2,009,043 slaves and 319,599 free Negroes.

1831

Feb. 15, Seminole War correspondence published

• A pamphlet containing the Seminole correspondence was published at Calhoun's direction. This completed the breach between the president and the vice president.

Mar. 2, signed harbor improvement act

• He planned to veto the bill, but it became apparent that a veto would be overridden.

Mar. 3, second session of 21st Congress adjourned

Apr. 7, Secretary of War Eaton resigned

• A social feud had developed when the wives of cabinet members refused to receive Peggy Eaton, who had been a barmaid before she became the second Mrs. Eaton.

• Eaton's resignation became effective, June 18.

Apr. 11, Secretary of State Van Buren resigned

• Van Buren submitted his resignation with the knowledge that it would precipitate a cabinet reorganization.

• Van Buren's resignation became effective, May 23.

Apr. 19, requested resignations of Secretary of Treasury Ingham and Secretary of Navy Branch

• Ingham's resignation became effective, June 30; Branch's resignation became effective, May 12.

May 23, appointed his second secretary of navy, Levi Woodbury

May 24, appointed his second secretary of state, Edward Livingston

June 15, requested resignation of Attorney General Berrien

•The only member of his original cabinet who was retained was Postmaster General Barry.

•Berrien's resignation became effective, July 20.

June 25, appointed Van Buren as minister to Great Britain

•The Senate rejected the Van Buren nomination, Jan. 25, 1832.

July 20, appointed his second attorney general, Roger B. Taney

Aug. 1, appointed his second secretary of war, Lewis Cass

Aug. 8, appointed his second secretary of treasury, Louis McLane

Dec. 5, first session of 22nd Congress

•The administration maintained control of both the Senate and the House of Representatives. The Democrats lost one Senate seat, gained two House seats. The Senate (48 members) consisted of 25 Democrats, 21 National Republicans and two Anti-Masons. The House (213 members) consisted of 141 Democrats, 58 National Republicans and 14 Anti-Masons.

•The Anti-Masonic party was the first "third party." One of the Anti-Masons elected was John Quincy Adams.

Dec. 6, sent his third State of the Union message to Congress

1832

Feb. 15, sent special message to Congress in which he recommended speedy migration of Indians beyond Mississippi River

Apr. 6, Black Hawk War began

May 21, renominated for president, Democratic national convention, Baltimore, Md.

• See Election of 1832, page 99.

July 9, appointed first commissioner of Indian affairs

•This office was part of the war department until 1849.

July 10, vetoed extension of charter of Second Bank of U.S. bill

•This was the fifth of his 12 vetoes.

•An attempt to pass the bill over his veto in the Senate failed, 22–19, July 13.

July 14, signed tariff act

•This act modified the duties imposed in

1828, but was far from satisfactory to the South.

July 16, first session of 22nd Congress adjourned

Aug. 27, Black Hawk War ended

Oct. 29, ordered Charleston, S.C., harbor forts placed on alert by secretary of war

Nov. 6, election day

• See Election of 1832, page 99.

Nov. 6, instructed collector at Charleston to seize vessels which entered port, hold until duties paid

Dec. 3, second session of 22nd Congress

Dec. 4, sent his fourth State of the Union message to Congress

Dec. 5, presidential electors cast ballots

•He received 219 of the 286 electoral votes from the 24 states.

• See Election of 1832, page 99.

Dec. 6, vetoed interest on state claims, rivers and harbors bills

•These bills had been passed during the first session of the 22nd Congress.

•These were the sixth and seventh of his 12 vetoes, the third and fourth of his seven pocket vetoes.

Dec. 10, issued proclamation to people of South Carolina

•On Nov. 27, the South Carolina legislature had passed laws necessary to enforce an ordinance which nullified the tariff acts of 1828 and 1832. The ordinance, adopted by a state convention, Nov. 24, prohibited the collection of duties in the state after Feb. 1, 1833, forbade appeal to the Supreme Court, and asserted that any attempt by the federal government to enforce the tariff acts was cause for secession.

•He characterized nullification as "incompatible with the existence of the Union" and an "impractical absurdity." No state had the right to leave the Union, he added, and no state could refuse to obey federal law. "Disunion by armed force is treason," he said.

Dec. 28, Vice President Calhoun resigned

•Calhoun had been elected to the Senate from South Carolina, Dec. 12.

1833

Jan. 16, sent special message to Congress in which he asked power to enforce collection of tariff by use of military if necessary

Feb. 13, electoral vote tabulated by Congress
•Jackson and Van Buren were officially declared elected.
Mar. 2, signed compromise tariff act
•The compromise tariff, proposed by Henry Clay, provided for gradual reduction of duties above 20 percent until 1842, when all duties would be 20 percent.
Mar. 2, signed act that authorized collection of tariff by use of army and navy if necessary
•This was the so-called "force bill"—the name applied by states' rights adherents.
Mar. 2, second session of 22nd Congress adjourned

ELECTION OF 1832

Anti-Masonic party, convened, Sept. 26, 1831, at Baltimore, Md., nominated William Wirt of Maryland for president, Amos Ellmaker of Pennsylvania for vice president.
•This was the first national nominating convention. It was the first of two Anti-Masonic national conventions.
•This was the only Anti-Masonic convention held in Baltimore; it was the first of 17 major party conventions held in Baltimore.
National Republican party, convened, Dec. 12, 1831, at Baltimore, Md., nominated Henry Clay of Kentucky for president, John Sergeant of Pennsylvania for vice president.
•The National Republican party, in which the Adams-Clay faction of the Democratic-Republican party was joined by the minority group which still considered itself Federalist, was absorbed by the Whig party prior to the 1836 election.
•This was the only National Republican convention; it was the second major party convention held in Baltimore.
Democratic party, convened, May 21, 1832, at Baltimore, Md., nominated Andrew Jackson of Tennessee for president, Martin Van Buren of New York for vice president.
•This was the first Democratic national convention.
•This was the first of nine Democratic conventions held in Baltimore; it was the third

major party convention held in Baltimore.
•The rule that candidates must receive the votes of two-thirds of the delegates was adopted at this convention and remained in effect until 1936.
Independent Democrats nominated John Floyd of Virginia for president, Henry Lee of Massachusetts for vice president.
Election day, Tuesday, Nov. 6, 1832
Popular vote: 1,217,691
    Jackson, 687,502
    Clay, 530,189
Electoral vote: 288, 24 states
  • Jackson, 219, 16 states
    (Alabama, 7; Georgia, 11; Illinois, 5; Indiana, 9; Louisiana, 5; Maine, 10; Mississippi, 4; Missouri, 4; New Hampshire, 7; New Jersey, 8; New York, 42; North Carolina, 15; Ohio, 21; Pennsylvania 30; Tennessee, 15; Virginia, 23)
•Jackson also received the votes of three Maryland electors.
  • Clay, 49, six states
    (Connecticut, 8; Delaware, 3; Kentucky, 15; Maryland, 5 of 10 votes; Massachusetts, 14; Rhode Island, 4)
  • Floyd, 11, one state
    (South Carolina, 11)
  • Wirt, 7, one state
    (Vermont, 7)
•Two electors from Maryland did not cast their votes.
•Martin Van Buren received 189 electoral votes and was elected vice president (Alabama, 7; Georgia, 11; Illinois, 5; Indiana, 9; Louisiana, 5; Maine, 10; Mississippi, 4; Missouri, 4; New Hampshire, 7; New Jersey, 8; New York, 42; North Carolina, 15; Ohio, 21; Tennessee, 15; Virginia, 23).
•Van Buren also received the votes of three Maryland electors.
•John Sergeant of Pennsylvania received 49 votes (Connecticut, 8; Delaware, 3; Kentucky, 15; Maryland, 5 of 8 votes; Massachusetts, 14; Rhode Island, 4).
•William Wilkins of Pennsylvania received the votes of the 30 Pennsylvania electors.
•Henry Lee of Massachuetts received the votes of the 11 South Carolina electors.
•Amos Ellmaker of Pennsylvania received the votes of the seven Vermont electors.
•Two Maryland electors did not cast their votes.

THE 12th ADMINISTRATION

1833

Mar. 4, his second inauguration day
• Jackson took the oath of office, administered by Chief Justice John Marshall, in the Hall of Representatives of the Capitol.
• This was the last of nine inaugurations at which Marshall officiated.
• Jackson was the last of five presidents who took the oath in the House of Representatives chamber.
• This was the last of six oath-taking ceremonies in the House chamber.
Mar. 19, sought opinions of cabinet members on bank issue
• Attorney General Taney favored removal of government funds from the Second Bank of the U.S. and distribution of the funds among state banks, Apr. 3. Secretary of the Treasury McLane opposed removal of government funds from the bank but supported the reorganization of a new national bank, May 20.
May 29, reorganized cabinet
• When McLane continued to oppose his bank policy, Jackson realigned the cabinet. He forced the resignation of Secretary of State Livingston, appointed McLane as his third secretary of state, and appointed William J. Duane as his third secretary of treasury.
June–July, toured eastern states
• He returned to Washington, July 3.
July 10, received Duane letter opposing removal of funds
Sept. 10, submitted Kendall report on availability of state banks to cabinet
• He announced that the government would cease using the Second Bank as a depository, Oct. 1. He was supported by Taney and Woodbury and was opposed by Cass, McLane, and Duane.
Sept. 18, read Taney draft of reasons for removal of funds to cabinet
Sept. 22, requested resignation of Duane
Sept. 23, appointed Roger B. Taney as recess secretary of treasury
• Taney announced that public funds no longer would be deposited in the Second Bank, Sept. 26. About $10,000,000 was withdrawn from the bank and transferred to the Girard Bank of Philadelphia and other state banks. A total of 23 state banks

had been selected as depositories by Dec. 31.
Nov. 15, appointed his third attorney general, Benjamin F. Butler
• Taney had resigned as attorney general, Sept. 24.
Dec. 2, first session of 23rd Congress
• The administration maintained control of the House of Representatives. The Democrats lost five Senate seats, gained six House seats. The Senate (48 members) consisted of 20 Democrats, 20 National Republicans and eight Anti-Masons and others. The House (260 members) consisted of 147 Democrats, 53 Anti-Masons, and 60 others (mostly National Republicans).
• This was the only Congress in which the principal minority party was outnumbered in the House by members of other splinter groups.
Dec. 3, sent his fifth State of the Union message to Congress
• He defended his action in removing public funds from the Second Bank of the U.S. and assumed full responsibility.
Dec. 4, vetoed proceeds of land sales bill
• This bill had been passed during the second session of the 22nd Congress.
• This was the eighth of his 12 vetoes, the fifth of his seven pocket vetoes.
Dec. 11, Senate called for Taney report
• Jackson refused to produce the report that he had read to his cabinet, Sept. 18, on constitutional grounds, commenting:

> I have yet to learn under what consitutional authority that branch of the Legislature has a right to require of me an account of any communication, either verbally or in writing, made to the heads of Departments acting as a Cabinet council.

Dec. 26, resolution of censure introduced in Senate by Henry Clay

1834

Mar. 28, Senate adopted resolution of censure
• The resolution stated that he had assumed authority not conveyed by the Constitu-

tion or laws in ordering the removal of public funds.

Apr. 15, entered formal protest against resolution of censure

• He declared that he had been charged with an offense which called for impeachment but had been denied the opportunity to offer a defense.

May 7, Senate refused to make his protest part of official record

June 23, Senate rejected his nomination of Taney as secretary of treasury, 18–28

• Jackson was the first of five presidents whose nominees to the cabinet were rejected by the Senate.

• Taney was the first of eight nominees to the cabinet who were rejected by the Senate.

June 27, accepted resignation of Secretary of State McLane, effective June 30

June 27, appointed his fourth secretary of state, John Forsyth, and his fourth secretary of treasury, Levi Woodbury

• Forsyth and Woodbury took office, July 1.

June 30, appointed his third secretary of navy, Mahlon Dickerson

• Dickerson took office, July 1.

June 30, signed act establishing department of Indian affairs

• This act also set aside a section in the Arkansas Territory for relocated Indians.

June 30, first session of 23rd Congress adjourned

Aug. 11, Associate Justice Johnson died

Dec. 1, vetoed Wabash River internal improvements bill

• This bill had been passed during the first session of the 23rd Congress.

• This was the ninth of his 12 votes, the sixth of his seven pocket vetoes.

Dec. 1, second session of 23rd Congress

Dec. 1, sent his sixth State of the Union message to Congress

• He announced that the national debt had been eliminated.

• He was the only president who served for a period when the U.S. was free of debt.

Note: The Whig party came into existence in 1834 as an anti-Jackson coalition of members of the National Republican party, southern states' rights proponents, and advocates of Henry Clay's "American System" of protective tariffs and internal improvements.

1835

Jan. 5, accepted resignation of Associate Justice Duval

Jan. 7, appointed James Moore Wayne as associate justice

• Wayne, who was confirmed by the Senate, Jan. 9, was the third of Jackson's eight appointments to the Supreme Court.

Jan. 15, appointed Roger B. Taney as associate justice

• Taney was the fourth of Jackson's eight appointments to the Supreme Court. This appointment was postponed, Mar. 3.

• Jackson was the fourth of 15 presidents who nominated justices not confirmed by the Senate.

• Taney was the fourth of 25 men nominated to the Supreme Court who were not confirmed by the Senate.

Jan. 29, his assassination attempted by Richard Lawrence

• As Jackson was departing from the chamber of the House of Representatives, Lawrence fired two pistols at him from close range; both misfired. Lawrence was seized at the scene and later was committed to an asylum for the insane.

• This was the first of two unsuccessful attempts on the lives of presidents. The other attempt involved Truman in 1950.

• *See* pages 476–477.

Feb. 22, committee appointed by Senate to investigate alleged complicity of Senator Poindexter in assassination attempt

• Senator George Poindexter of Mississippi, an outspoken political enemy of the president, was absolved.

Mar. 3, vetoed compromising claims against Two Sicilies bill

• This was the tenth of his 12 vetoes.

Mar. 3, second session of 23rd Congress adjourned

Apr. 30, accepted resignation of Postmaster General Barry

• He appointed Barry as minister to Spain.

• Barry died, en route to his new post, in Liverpool, England, Aug. 20.

May 1, appointed his second postmaster general, Amos Kendall

• Kendall was the last of Jackson's 19 cabinet appointments

July 6, Chief Justice Marshall died

Dec. 7, first session of 24th Congress

• The administration maintained control of

both the Senate and the House of Representatives. The Democrats gained seven Senate seats, lost two House seats. The Senate (52 members) consisted of 27 Democrats and 25 Whigs. The House (243 members) consisted of 145 Democrats and 98 Whigs.

Dec. 7, sent his seventh State of the Union message to Congress

•He recommended that laws be enacted to prohibit circulation of antislavery documents through the mails.

Dec. 28, appointed Philip Pendleton Barbour as associate justice

•Barbour, who was confirmed by the Senate, Mar. 15, 1836, was the fifth of Jackson's eight appointments to the Supreme Court.

Dec. 28, appointed Roger B. Taney as chief justice

•Taney, who was confirmed by the Senate, Mar. 15, 1836, was the sixth of Jackson's eight appointments to the Supreme Court. His appointment of Taney had been strongly opposed, but the Senate confirmed him, 29–15.

•He was the third of 14 presidents who appointed chief justices.

1836

Jan. 18, sent special message to Congress in which he reviewed relations with France

June 9, vetoed regulations of congressional sessions bill

•This was the 11th of his 12 vetoes.

June 15, Arkansas admitted as 25th state

•Arkansas was the first of two states admitted during his term of office.

June 23, signed surplus revenue act

•This act authorized the distribution among the states of all funds over $5,000,000 in the treasury on the basis of representation in Congress. A total of $28,000,000 was distributed during 1837.

July 2, signed act reorganizing post office department

July 4, first session of 24th Congress adjourned

July 11, issued specie circular

•Land agents were ordered to accept only gold or silver for public land sold after Aug. 15.

Oct. 5, accepted resignation of Secretary of War Cass

Nov. 8, election day

• *See* Election of 1836, pages 107–108.

Dec. 5, second session of 24th Congress

Dec. 5, sent his eighth and last State of the Union message to Congress

1837

Jan. 16, resolution of censure expunged from Senate record

•Largely through the efforts of Senator Benton of Missouri, the resolution of Mar. 28, 1834, was deleted.

Jan. 26, Michigan admitted as 26th state

•Michigan was the second of two states admitted during his term of office.

Feb. 6, submitted list of 46 claims against Mexico dating from 1816 to Congress, recommended reprisals

Mar. 3, recognized Republic of Texas

•The Senate had adopted a resolution to recognize the independence of Texas, 23–19, Mar. 1.

Mar. 3, signed judiciary act that increased membership of Supreme Court from seven to nine justices

Mar. 3, appointed William Smith and John Catron as associate justices

•Both Smith and Catron were confirmed by the Senate, Mar. 8, but Smith declined to serve.

•Smith was the sixth of seven appointees, confirmed by the Senate, who declined to serve.

•Jackson was the third of four presidents who appointed associate justices who declined to serve.

•Only Washington and Franklin D. Roosevelt appointed more members of the Supreme Court. Jackson and Taft appointed the same number of members of the Court, six.

Mar. 3, second session of 24th Congress adjourned

Mar. 3, vetoed funds receivable as U.S. revenue bill

•This bill had been amended to provide for the abrogation of the specie circular.

•This veto message was never sent to Congress but was deposited in the department of state.

•This was the last of his 12 vetoes, the last of his seven pocket vetoes.

•Jackson was the fourth of 11 presidents who never had a veto overridden.

Mar. 4, published his farewell address
•This review of Jackson's two terms was

based on a draft written by Chief Justice
Taney.

THE FORMER PRESIDENT

Mar. 4, 1837, attended inauguration of Van
Buren
•Jackson's age upon leaving office was 69
years, 354 days.
Mar. 6, 1837, departed Washington for Her-
mitage
•He was the fourth of six presidents who
were farmers, planters, or ranchers after
their terms of office.
Mar. 15, 1837, celebrated his 70th birthday
•He was the sixth of 16 presidents who lived
to be 70.
July, 1838, joined Presbyterian Church
•He had long planned to join the church but
delayed while in office to avoid giving the
act a political connotation.
Jan. 8, 1840, participated in 25th anniversary celebration of Battle of New Orleans
September–October, 1840, campaigned for
Van Buren
•Jackson and Polk—who was then governor
of Tennessee—campaigned in support of
the reelection of Van Buren.
Mar. 15, 1842, celebrated his 75th birthday
•He was the fifth of ten presidents who
lived to be 75.
February, 1844, received repayment of fine
levied in 1815
•His conviction for contempt of court was
reversed. The payment, which included
interest for 29 years, amounted to $2,732.-
90. The money was particulary welcome
since he had repeatedly been forced into
debt, partially because of attempts to settle
the tangled monetary affairs of his adopted
son, Andrew Jackson, Jr.
1844, actively supported annexation of
Texas
•He played an important role as intermediary between government officials and Sam
Houston, president of the Republic of
Texas. In April, when Van Buren followed
Clay in publicly opposing the treaty of annexation then before the Senate, Jackson
reluctantly abandoned his support of Van
Buren and endorsed Polk for the Democratic nomination.
May, 1845, sat for last portrait

•Commissioned by King Louis Philippe of
France, it was painted by George P. A.
Healy.

DEATH

Date of death: June 8, 1845
Place of death: Nashville, Tenn.
•He was the first of three presidents who
died in Tennessee.
Age at death: 78 years, 85 days
•He lived eight years, 96 days, after the
completion of his term.
Cause of death: Consumption, dropsy
Place of burial: Nashville, Tenn.
•He was the first of three presidents who
were buried in Tennessee.

THE VICE PRESIDENTS
(7th and 8th)

Note: Jackson was the third of seven presidents who had two vice presidents.

Full name: John Caldwell Calhoun (7th)
•He was the fourth of seven vice presidents
who were elected to second terms.
•He was the second of two vice presidents
who served under two presidents. The
other was Clinton.
• See also pages 87–88.
•Jackson and Calhoun were the ninth of 41
president-vice president teams.
Age at second inauguration: 46 years, 351
days
Political party: Democratic
•He was the first of 16 vice presidents who
were Democrats.
Date of resignation: Dec. 28, 1832
•He was the only vice president who resigned. He served 67 days less than eight
years.
Occupations after term: U.S. Senator, secretary of state
•He represented South Carolina in the Senate, 1833–1844; was secretary of state under President Tyler, 1844–1845; returned
to the Senate, 1845–1850.
•He was the first of six vice presidents who

served in the Senate after their terms of office.
• He was the third of 12 vice presidents who served in both the House of Representatives and the Senate.
• He was the first of two vice presidents who served in the cabinet both before and after their vice-presidential terms. The other was Henry A. Wallace.
Date of death: Mar. 31, 1850
Place of death: Washington, D.C.
• He was the third of six vice presidents who died in Washington.
Age at death: 68 years, 13 days
Place of burial: Charleston, S.C.
• He was the only vice president who was buried in South Carolina.

Full name: Martin Van Buren (8th)
• *See also* pages 105–112.
• He was the third of eight vice presidents who were born in New York.
• He was the first of four vice presidents who were Dutch Reformed.
• He was the fourth of 17 vice presidents who served in the Senate before their terms of office.
• He was the third of four vice presidents who served in the cabinet.
• He was the fifth of 14 vice presidents who served as state governors.
• He was the third of 17 vice presidents who served four-year terms.
• Jackson and Van Buren were the tenth of 41 president-vice president teams.
• He was the fourth of ten vice presidents who represented New York.
• He was the second of 16 vice presidents who were Democrats.
• He was the third of nine vice presidents who died in New York.
• He was the third of nine vice presidents who were buried in New York.

THE CABINET

State: Martin Van Buren of New York, Mar. 28, 1829, to May 23, 1831
• Edward Livingston of Louisiana, May 24, 1831, to May 29, 1833
• Louis McLane of Delaware, May 29, 1833, to June 30, 1834
• John Forsyth of Georgia, July 1, 1834, to Mar. 3, 1841
Treasury: Samuel Dulucenna Ingham of

Pennsylvania, Mar. 6, 1829, to June 20, 1831
• Louis McLane of Delaware, Aug. 8, 1831, to May 28, 1833
• William John Duane of Pennsylvania, May 29, 1833, to Sept. 22, 1833
• Roger Brooke Taney of Maryland, appointed, Sept. 23, 1833; rejected by Senate, June 23, 1834
• Levi Woodbury of New Hampshire, July 1, 1834, to Mar. 3, 1841
War: John Henry Eaton of Tennessee, Mar. 9, 1829, to June 18, 1831
• Lewis Cass of Michigan, Aug. 1, 1831, to Oct. 5, 1836
Attorney General: John McPherson Berrien of Georgia, Mar. 9, 1829, to July 20, 1831
• Roger Brooke Taney of Maryland, July 20, 1831, to Sept. 24, 1833
• Benjamin Franklin Butler of New York, Nov. 15, 1833, to Sept. 1, 1838
Navy: John Branch of North Carolina, Mar. 9, 1829, to May 12, 1831
• Levi Woodbury of New Hampshire, May 23, 1831, to June 30, 1834
• Mahlon Dickerson of New Jersey, July 1, 1834, to June 30, 1838
Postmaster General: William Taylor Barry of Kentucky, Apr. 6, 1829, to Apr. 30, 1835
• Amos Kendall of Kentucky, May 1, 1835, to May 19, 1840

THE SUPREME COURT

Chief Justice: Roger Brooke Taney of Maryland, appointed, Dec. 28, 1835; confirmed, Mar. 15, 1836
Associate Justices: John McLean of Ohio, appointed, Mar. 6, 1829; confirmed, Mar. 7, 1829
• Henry Baldwin of Pennsylvania, appointed, Jan. 4, 1830; confirmed, Jan. 6, 1830
• James Moore Wayne of Georgia, appointed, Jan. 7, 1835; confirmed, Jan. 9, 1835
• Roger Brooke Taney of Maryland, appointed, Jan. 15, 1835; postponed, Mar. 3, 1835
• Philip Pendleton Barbour of Virginia, appointed, Dec. 28, 1835; confirmed, Mar. 15, 1836
• William Smith of Alabama, appointed, Mar. 3, 1837; confirmed, Mar. 8, 1837; declined to serve
• John Catron of Tennessee, appointed, Mar. 3, 1837; confirmed, Mar. 8, 1837

Eighth President

MARTIN VAN BUREN

Full name: Martin Van Buren
•He was the seventh of 17 presidents who did not have middle initials or middle names.
Date of birth: Dec. 5, 1782
•He was the first of three presidents who were born in December.
Place of birth: Kinderhook, N.Y.
•He was the first president who was born in the U.S. All of his predecessors had been British subjects at birth.
•He was the first of four presidents who were born in New York.
Family lineage: Dutch
•He was the only president who was of Dutch ancestry.
Religious denomination: Dutch Reformed
•He was the first of two presidents who were Dutch Reformed. The other was Theodore Roosevelt.
College: None
•He was the third of nine presidents who did not attend college.
•He was the fifth of 15 presidents who were not graduated from college.

PARENTS AND SIBLINGS

Father's name: Abraham Van Buren
Date of birth: Feb. 17, 1737
Place of birth: Kinderhook, N.Y.
Occupations: Farmer, tavern keeper
Date of death: Apr. 5, 1817
Place of death: Kinderhook, N.Y.
Age at death: 80 years, 47 days

Mother's name: Maria Hoes Van Alen Van Buren
Date of birth: Feb. 27, 1737
Place of birth: *Unknown*
Date of marriage: 1776
Children: 5; 3 sons, 2 daughters
•Derike was born in 1777; Hannah in 1780; Martin in 1782; Lawrence in 1786; and Abraham in 1788.
•Martin was his father's third child.
•He was his mother's sixth child. His mother had two sons and a daughter by a previous marriage.
•He was the second of six presidents who had half brothers or half sisters.

105

• He was the third of seven presidents who came from families of five children.
Date of death: Feb. 16, 1818
Place of death: Kinderhook, N.Y.
Age at death: 80 years, 354 days

MARRIAGE

Date of marriage: Feb. 21, 1807
Place of marriage: Catskill, N.Y.
• Van Buren was the second of seven presidents who were married in New York.
Age at marriage: 24 years, 78 days
• He was the sixth of 27 presidents who were married in their twenties.
Years married: 11 years, 349 days

Wife's name: Hannah Hoes Van Buren
• She was the eighth of 40 wives of presidents.
Date of birth: Mar. 8, 1783
• She was the first of five wives of presidents who were born in March.
Place of birth: Kinderhook, N.Y.
• She was the second of seven wives of presidents who were born in New York.
Wife's mother: _____ Hoes
Wife's father: _____ Hoes, farmer
Age at marriage: 23 years, 350 days

• She was the sixth of 30 wives of presidents who were married in their twenties.
Years younger than husband: 93 days
Children: 4 sons
• Abraham was born on Nov. 27, 1807; John on Feb. 18, 1810; Martin on Dec. 20, 1812; and Smith Thompson on Jan. 16, 1817.
• Van Buren was the first of six presidents who had only male children.
• He was the second of four presidents who had four children.
• He was the fifth of 30 presidents who had children.
Date of death: Feb. 5, 1819
Place of death: Albany, N.Y.
• She was the first of eight wives of presidents who died in New York.
Age at death: 35 years, 334 days
• She was the third of five wives of presidents who died prior to their husbands' inaugurations.
• She was the third of seven wives of presidents who were not first ladies.
Place of burial: Kinderhook, N.Y.
• She was the first of seven wives of presidents who were buried in New York.
Years he survived his wife: 43 years, 169 days
• Van Buren was the fifth of 14 presidents who survived their wives.

EARLY YEARS

1796, began study of law in office of Francis Silvester, Kinderhook
• Van Buren was the sixth of 26 presidents who studied law.
1801, completed law studies under William Peter Van Ness, New York City
• Van Ness, who was also from Kinderhook, was Burr's second in the duel with Hamilton.
November, 1803, admitted to bar, New York City
• He returned to Kinderhook shortly after being admitted to the bar and began his practice.
• He was the sixth of 23 presidents who were lawyers.
Feb. 21, 1807, married Hannah Hoes, Catskill, N.Y.
Nov. 27, 1807, his first son born
• The boy was named Abraham Van Buren.
1808, moved to Hudson, N.Y.

March, 1808, appointed surrogate of Columbia County, N.Y.
• He served as surrogate until 1813.
Feb. 18, 1810, his second son born
• The boy was named John Van Buren.
May, 1812, elected to New York state senate
• He served from 1813 to 1820.
Dec. 20, 1812, his third son born
• The boy was named Martin Van Buren.
February, 1815, appointed state attorney general
• He served until July, 1819. He retained his seat in the state senate while he held office as attorney general.
1816, reelected to state senate
Jan. 16, 1817, his fourth son born
• The boy was named Smith Thompson Van Buren.
Apr. 5, 1817, his father died
Feb. 16, 1818, his mother died
Feb. 5, 1819, his wife died

NATIONAL PROMINENCE

Feb. 6, 1821, elected to Senate by legislature
• He was the fourth of 16 presidents who were elected to the Senate.
1821, chosen member of state constitutional convention
Dec. 3, 1821, took seat in Senate
• He was immediately made a member of the judiciary and finance committees.
• He was the fourth of 15 presidents who served in the Senate.
1824, supported William H. Crawford for president
1827, reelected to Senate
1828, supported Jackson for president
1828, elected governor of New York
Dec. 20, 1828, resigned from Senate
Jan. 1, 1829, inaugurated as governor
• He was the first of four presidents who served as governors of New York.
• He was the third of 13 presidents who served as state governors.
Mar. 6, 1829, appointed secretary of state by Jackson
Mar. 12, 1829, resigned as governor
• He had run for governor to secure the state house for his party.
Mar. 28, 1829, took oath as secretary of state
• He was the fifth of six presidents who served as secretaries of state.
• He was the fifth of eight presidents who served in the cabinet.
1830, elected to Phi Beta Kappa, Union College, Schenectady, N.Y.
• He was the first of three presidents who were honorary members of Phi Beta Kappa.
• He was the third of 11 presidents who were members of Phi Beta Kappa.
Apr. 11, 1831, resigned as secretary of state, effective, May 23
June 25, 1831, appointed minister to Great Britain
• He was the fourth of five presidents who served as ministers to Great Britain.
• He was the fifth of seven presidents who served as diplomats.
Aug. 16, 1831, sailed for England
• When he arrived in September, he was met by Washington Irving, whom Van Buren had appointed secretary of the legation two years earlier at the behest of a mutual friend. He and Irving became lifelong friends.

Dec. 7, 1831, his nomination as minister sent to Senate
• Jackson had appointed him after the 21st Congress adjourned; the 22nd Congress convened, Dec. 5.
Jan. 25, 1832, rejected as minister by Senate
• His nomination was rejected by the tie-breaking vote of Vice President Calhoun.
Feb. 15, 1832, notified of rejection
Mar. 5, 1832, received by William IV at Windsor Castle
April–June, 1832, traveled to France, Germany and The Netherlands
May 21, 1832, nominated for vice president
July 5, 1832, arrived in New York City
Nov. 6, 1832, elected vice president
Mar. 4, 1833, inaugurated as vice president
Nov. 8, 1836, election day
• *See* Election of 1836, below.
Dec. 7, 1836, presidential electors cast ballots
• He received 170 of the 294 electoral votes from the 26 states
• *See* Election of 1836, below.
Feb. 8, 1837, electoral votes tabulated by Congress
• Van Buren and Richard Mentor Johnson were officially declared elected.

ELECTION OF 1836

Whig party chose several nominees in state conventions, did not hold a national convention. The party strategy was to divide the electoral vote in such a manner as to throw the election into the House of Representatives.
• Daniel Webster was nominated by a Massachusetts legislative caucus in January, 1835. Hugh Lawson White of Tennessee was nominated by his state's legislature and was supported in Illinois and Alabama. William Henry Harrison of Ohio was nominated at the Pennsylvania state convention, which convened, Dec. 14, 1835, at Harrisburg. Other nominees included Willie Person Mangum of North Carolina and John McLean of Ohio. Associate Justice McLean withdrew in August, 1836.
Democratic party, convened, May 20, 1835 at Baltimore, Md., nominated Martin Van Buren of New York for president, Richard

Mentor Johnson of Kentucky for vice president.
- This was the second Democratic national convention. It was the second Democratic convention in Baltimore; it was the fourth major party convention in Baltimore.

Anti-Masonic party, convened, Dec. 16, 1835, at Harrisburg, Pa., nominated William Henry Harrison of Ohio for president, Francis Granger of New York for vice president.

Election day, Tuesday, Nov. 8, 1836 (in most states)

Popular vote: 1,500,345
    Van Buren, 764,198
    Harrison, 549,508
    White, 145,352
    Webster, 41,287

Electoral vote: 294, 26 states
- Van Buren, 170, 15 states
    (Alabama, 7; Arkansas, 3; Connecticut, 8; Illinois, 5; Louisiana, 5; Maine, 10; Michigan, 3; Mississippi, 4; Missouri, 4;

    New Hampshire, 7; New York, 42; North Carolina, 15; Pennsylvania, 30; Rhode Island, 4; Virginia, 23)
- William Henry Harrison, 73, seven states
    (Delaware, 3; Indiana, 9; Kentucky, 15; Maryland, 10; New Jersey, 8; Ohio, 21; Vermont, 7)
- White, 26, two states
    (Georgia, 11; Tennessee, 15)
- Webster, 14, one state
    (Massachusetts, 14)
- Mangum, 11, one state
    (South Carolina, 11)
- No vice-presidential candidate received a majority of the electoral votes. Richard Mentor Johnson of Kentucky received 147 votes; Francis Granger of New York, 77; John Tyler of Virginia, 47; and William Smith of Alabama, 23.
- For the first and only time, the Senate chose the vice president. Johnson was elected over Granger, 33–16, on Feb. 8, 1837.

THE PRESIDENT (8th)

Term of office: Mar. 4, 1837, to Mar. 4, 1841 (4 years)
- Van Buren was the third of 12 presidents who had served as vice presidents.
- He was the last of three presidents who took office upon the completion of their vice-presidential terms.
- He was the third of 19 presidents who served one term or less than one term.
- He was the first of eight presidents in succession who served one term or less than one term.
- He was the third of ten presidents who served for four years.

State represented: New York
- He was the first of eight presidents who represented New York.

Political party: Democratic
- He was the second of 12 presidents who were Democrats.

Congresses: 25th, 26th

Administration: 13th

Age at inauguration: 54 years, 89 days
- He was the fourth of 21 presidents who were younger than their vice presidents. Van Buren was two years, 49 days younger than Johnson.

Inauguration day: Saturday, Mar. 4, 1837
- Van Buren took the oath of office, administered by Chief Justice Roger B. Taney, on the east portico of the Capitol.
- This was the first of seven inaugurations at which Taney officiated.

THE 13th ADMINISTRATION

1837

Mar. 7, appointed his only secretary of war, Joel R. Poinsett
- Van Buren retained Jackson's secretary of state, secretary of treasury, attorney general, secretary of navy, and postmaster general.

Apr. 22, appointed John McKinley as associate justice
- McKinley, who was confirmed by the Senate, Sept. 25, was the first of Van Buren's two appointments to the Supreme Court.

May 10, Panic of 1837 began
- As early as March, cotton prices had fallen by almost 50 percent. When New York

banks suspended specie payments, May 10, similar action by banks throughout the country followed. The depression lasted for more than six years, particularly affecting the South and West.
• This was the second of nine U.S. depressions.
May 15, called special session of Congress, Sept. 4
Sept. 4, first session of 25th Congress
• The administration ostensibly controlled the Senate and the House of Representatives, but a coalition of Whigs and conservative Democrats held the balance of power in the House. The Democrats gained three Senate seats; the Whigs gained nine House seats. The Senate (52 members) consisted of 30 Democrats, 18 Whigs, and four others. The House (239 members) consisted of 108 Democrats, 107 Whigs, and 24 others.
Sept. 5, sent special message to Congress in which he recommended specie currency
• He sharply criticized the state banks and suggested an investigation be made of the independent treasury or subtreasury plan.
• A bill to establish the subtreasury passed the Senate, Oct. 4, but was tabled by the House, Oct. 14.
Oct. 2, fourth installment of treasury surplus to states suspended
• In accordance with the provisions of the Deposit Act of 1836, installments totaling $28,000,000 had been loaned to the states on Jan. 1, Apr. 1, and July 1. The fourth installment was postponed to January, 1839, but was never paid. The loans, while subject to recall by the secretary of the treasury, were never recalled.
Oct. 16, first session of 25th Congress adjourned
Dec. 4, second session of 25th Congress
Dec. 5, sent his first State of the Union message to Congress

1838

Jan. 5, issued proclamation of neutrality regarding disturbance in Canada
• William Lyon Mackenzie, the Canadian insurgent leader who had attempted to seize the capital, Toronto, in 1837, set up a provisional government on Navy Island in the Niagara River, Dec. 13, 1837. He and his army of several hundred, including many U.S. citizens, were forced to aban-

don Navy Island, Jan. 13. Mackenzie was imprisoned for 18 months by the U.S. for violation of neutrality laws.
June 12, signed act that established Territory of Iowa
June 25, accepted resignation of Secretary of Navy Dickerson, effective, June 30
June 25, appointed his second secretary of navy, James K. Paulding
• Paulding took office, July 1.
July 5, accepted resignation of Attorney General Butler, effective, Sept. 1
July 5, appointed his second attorney general, Felix Grundy
• Grundy took office, Sept. 1.
July 9, second session of 25th Congress adjourned
Nov. 21, issued second proclamation of neutrality regarding Canada
Dec. 3, third session of 25th Congress
Dec. 3, sent his second State of the Union message to Congress

1839

Mar. 3, authorized to send troops to Maine, Aroostook War
• A boundary dispute between New Brunswick, Canada, and Maine, culminated in the so-called "Aroostook War"—a bloodless conflict. Rufus McIntire, the Maine land agent appointed to expel Canadian lumberjacks from the Aroostook region, was arrested by the Canadians, Feb. 12. Maine and New Brunswick called out their militia. When the Nova Scotia legislature voted war appropriations, Congress responded with a $10,000,000 appropriation and authorized a military force of fifty thousand men.
• Van Buren dispatched General Winfield Scott, who arranged a truce between the governor of Maine and the lieutenant governor of New Brunswick. War was averted; the dispute was settled by the Webster-Ashburton Treaty of 1842.
Mar. 3, third session of 25th Congress adjourned
Mar. 5, pocket vetoed joint resolution providing for distribution in part of Madison papers
• This veto message was not sent to Congress but was deposited in the department of state.
• This was his only veto.

•He was the only president who did not exercise the regular veto but did employ the pocket veto.

Dec. 1, accepted resignation of Attorney General Grundy

Dec. 2, first session of 26th Congress

•The administration ostensibly controlled the Senate and the House of Representatives, but a coalition of Whigs and conservative Democrats held the balance of power in both houses. The Whigs gained four Senate seats; the Democrats gained 16 House seats. The Senate (50 members) consisted of 28 Democrats and 22 Whigs. The House (242 members) consisted of 124 Democrats and 118 Whigs.

Dec. 2, sent his third State of the Union message to Congress

Dec. 24, sent special message to Congress in which he again urged adoption of subtreasury plan

1840

Jan. 11, appointed his third attorney general, Henry D. Gilpin

Mar. 31, issued executive order that established ten-hour day for government employees without reduction of pay

May 19, accepted resignation of Postmaster General Kendall

May 19, appointed his second postmaster general, John M. Niles

•Niles was the last of Van Buren's ten cabinet appointments.

July 4, signed independent treasury act

•Subtreasuries were established in New York City, Boston, Philadelphia, Charles-

ton, New Orleans, St. Louis, and Washington, D.C.

•This act was repealed in 1841.

July 21, first session of 26th Congress adjourned

Nov. 10, election

• *See* Election of 1840, page 118.

Dec. 2, presidential electors cast ballots

•Harrison received 234 electoral votes. Van Buren received 60.

• *See* Election of 1840, page 118.

Dec. 5, second session of 26th Congress

Dec. 5, sent his fourth and last State of the Union message to Congress

Note: The official population, according to the sixth census, was 17,069,453, which included 2,487,355 slaves and 386,293 free Negroes.

1841

Feb. 10, electoral votes tabulated by Congress

•Harrison and Tyler were officially declared elected.

•Van Buren was the third of seven presidents who were defeated when they sought reelection.

Feb. 24, Associate Justice Barbour died

Feb. 26, appointed Peter Vivian Daniel as associate justice

•Daniel, who was confirmed by the Senate, Mar. 2, was the second of Van Buren's two appointments to the Supreme Court.

Mar. 3, second session of 26th Congress adjourned

THE FORMER PRESIDENT

Mar. 4, 1841, attended inauguration of William Henry Harrison

•Van Buren's age upon leaving office was 58 years, 89 days.

May, 1841, returned to Kinderhook

•He had purchased a two-hundred-acre farm with a 30-room red brick mansion in Kinderhook during his term in office and renamed the estate, Lindenwald.

•Lindenwald, one and a half miles south of Kinderhook on state route 9 H, is privately owned and is open to the public daily.

1842, made six-month trip down Atlantic

seaboard, west to Nashville, Tenn.

•He conferred with political leaders, including Jackson and Clay, and made a number of speeches during his trip.

Apr. 20, 1844, issued letter in which he opposed annexation of Texas

•His stand on Texas greatly upset southern leaders. Later he issued a qualifying letter in which he said he would support the decision of Congress in the matter.

May 27–30, 1844, unsuccessful candidate for president, Democratic national convention, Baltimore, Md.

•He had a majority on the first ballot, but lacked the necessary two-thirds of the votes. His support declined during subsequent ballots; Polk was nominated on the ninth ballot.

August, 1845, declined appointment as minister to Great Britain

•When consulted by Polk for suggestions for secretaries of the treasury and war, Van Buren asked for the right to name the secretary of state and control all patronage in New York. Polk refused.

June 22, 1848, nominated for president, Barnburners faction, Utica, N.Y.

•The Barnburners were antiadministration Democrats

Aug. 9, 1848, nominated for president, Free-Soil party, Buffalo, N.Y.

•The Free-Soil party consisted of antiadministration Democrats, members of the Liberty party, and antislavery Whigs.

Nov. 7, 1848, election day

•He received 291,263 popular votes but no electoral votes.

• *See* Election of 1848, page 144.

•He was the first of three former presidents who were the presidential candidates of minor parties.

1850, returned to Democratic party

1852, began to write *Inquiry into the Origin and Course of Political Parties in the United States*

•His unfinished manuscript was edited by his sons and was published in New York by Hurd and Houghton, 1867.

1852, supported Pierce

Dec. 5, 1852, celebrated his 70th birthday

•He was the seventh of 16 presidents who lived to be 70.

1853–1855, toured Europe

•He visited England, France, Switzerland, Belgium, Holland, and Italy. He was received by Queen Victoria of Great Britain and Pope Pius IX.

•He was the first of eight former presidents who visited Europe.

•He was the first of three former presidents who met with Popes.

Mar. 19, 1855, his son, Martin, died, Paris

1856, supported Buchanan

Dec. 5, 1857, celebrated his 75th birthday

•He was the sixth of ten presidents who lived to be 75.

1860, supported Douglas

Spring, 1862, treated for various infirmities, New York City

•On his return to Kinderhook, he was confined to his bed.

DEATH

Date of death: July 24, 1862

Place of death: Lindenwald, near Kinderhook, N.Y.

•Van Buren was the second of eight presidents who died in New York.

Age at death: 79 years, 231 days

•He lived 21 years, 142 days, after the completion of his term.

Cause of death: Asthma

Place of burial: Kinderhook, N.Y.

•He was the first of six presidents who were buried in New York.

THE VICE PRESIDENT (9th)

Full name: Richard Mentor Johnson

•He was the first of three vice presidents named Johnson.

Date of birth: Oct. 17, 1780

Place of birth: Beargrass, now Louisville, Ky.

•He was the first of four vice presidents who were born in Kentucky.

Religious denomination: Baptist

•He was the first of two vice presidents who were Baptists. The other was Truman.

College: Transylvania University, Lexington, Ky.

Date of graduation: 1800

Occupation: Lawyer

•He was admitted to the Kentucky bar, 1802; member of the Kentucky legislature, 1804–1807; member of the House of Representatives, 1807–1812; resigned from Congress to command a Kentucky regiment, with rank of colonel, under General William Henry Harrison; severely wounded in battle of Thames River, near Chatham, Ontario, Oct. 5, 1813; usually credited with having killed Tecumseh, chief of the Shawnees, during Battle of Thames; member of the House of Representatives, 1814–1819; member of Senate, 1819–1829; again member of the House of Representatives, 1829–1837.

•He was the third of 21 vice presidents who served in the House of Representatives before their terms of office.

•He was the second of 17 vice presidents

who served in the Senate before their terms of office.

• He was the first of ten vice presidents who served in both the House of Representatives and the Senate before their terms of office.

• He was the first of 12 vice presidents who served in both the House of Representatives and the Senate.

Term of office: Mar. 4, 1837, to Mar. 4, 1841 (4 years)

• He was the fourth of 17 vice presidents who served four-year terms.

• Van Buren and Johnson were the 11th of 41 president-vice president teams.

• Van Buren and Johnson were the first of two president-vice president teams that were defeated when they ran for reelection. The other was Hoover and Curtis.

Age at inauguration: 56 years, 138 days

State represented: Kentucky

• He was the first of three vice presidents who represented Kentucky.

Political party: Democratic

• He was the third of 16 vice presidents who were Democrats.

Occupation after term: state legislator.

• He was a member of the Kentucky legislature, 1841–1842.

Date of death: Nov. 19, 1850

Place of death: Frankfort, Ky.

• He was the first of two vice presidents who died in Kentucky. The other was Breckinridge

Age at death: 70 years, 33 days

Place of burial: Frankfort, Ky.

• He was the first of three vice presidents who were buried in Kentucky.

THE CABINET

State: John Forsyth of Georgia, July 1, 1834, to Mar. 3, 1841

Treasury: Levi Woodbury of New Hampshire, July 1, 1834, to Mar. 3, 1841

War: Joel Roberts Poinsett of South Carolina, Mar. 7, 1837, to Mar. 5, 1841

Attorney General: Benjamin Franklin Butler of New York, Nov. 15, 1833, to Sept. 1, 1838

• Felix Grundy of Tennessee, Sept. 1, 1838, to Dec. 1, 1839

• Henry Dilworth Gilpin of Pennsylvania, Jan. 11, 1840, to Mar. 4, 1841

Navy: Mahlon Dickerson of New Jersey, July 1, 1834, to June 30, 1838

• James Kirke Paulding of New York, July 1, 1838, to Mar. 3, 1841

Postmaster General: Amos Kendall of Kentucky, May 1, 1835, to May 19, 1840

• John Milton Niles of Connecticut, May 19, 1840, to Mar. 3, 1841

THE SUPREME COURT

Associate Justices: John McKinley of Alabama, appointed, Apr. 22, 1837; confirmed, Sept. 25, 1837

• Peter Vivian Daniel of Virginia, appointed, Feb. 26, 1841; confirmed, Mar. 2, 1841

Ninth President

WILLIAM HENRY HARRISON

Full name: William Henry Harrison
- He was the first of two presidents named Harrison. He was Benjamin Harrison's grandfather.
- He was the first of three presidents named William.
- He was the second of 19 presidents who had middle initials or middle names.

Date of birth: Feb. 9, 1773
- He was the second of three presidents who were born in February.

Place of birth: Berkeley plantation, Charles City County, Va.
- His restored birthplace, owned by Malcolm Jamieson, is on state highway 5, halfway between Williamsburg and Richmond. The grounds and the main floor are open to the public daily, 8 A.M. to 5 P.M. Admission: adults, $1.50; children under 12, free.
- He was the only president who was born in the same county as his vice president.
- He was the first of two presidents who were born in Charles City County. The other was Tyler.
- He was the fifth of eight presidents who were born in Virginia.

Family lineage: English

- He was the fifth of 12 presidents who were of English ancestry.

Religious denomination: Episcopalian
- He was the fourth of nine presidents who were Episcopalians.

College: Hampden-Sydney College, Hampden-Sydney, Va.
- He was the only president who went to Hampden-Sydney.
- He was the sixth of 27 presidents who attended college.
- He was the third of six presidents who attended, but were not graduated from college.
- He was the sixth of 15 presidents who were not graduated from college.

PARENTS AND SIBLINGS

Father's name: Benjamin Harrison
- Harrison was the second of two presidents whose fathers had signed the Declaration of Independence. The other was John Quincy Adams.

Date of birth: probably April, 1726

Place of birth: Berkeley plantation, Charles City County, Va.

Occupation: Planter
• Harrison's father was a member of the Virginia House of Burgesses, 1749–1775; was a delegate to the First and Second Continental congresses, 1774–1777; again a member of the House of Burgesses, 1777–1781; and was governor of Virginia, 1781–1784.
• Harrison was the first of three presidents whose fathers had served as state governors.
Date of death: Apr. 24, 1791
• William was 18 years, 74 days old, when his father died.
Place of death: Berkeley plantation, Charles City County, Va.
Age at death: about 65 years

Mother's name: Elizabeth Bassett Harrison
Date of birth: Dec. 13, 1730
Place of birth: Eltham estate, New Kent County, Va.
Date of marriage: 1748
Children: 7; 4 daughters, 3 sons
• Elizabeth was born in 1751; Ann in 1753; Benjamin in 1755; Lucy in 17—; Carter Bassett in 17—; Sarah in 1770; and William Henry in 1773.
• Harrison was the first of two presidents who came from families of seven children. The other was Eisenhower.
• He was the first of two presidents who were seventh children. The other was McKinley.
Date of death: 1792
• William was about 19 years old when his mother died.
Place of death: Berkeley plantation, Charles City County, Va.
Age at death: about 62 years

MARRIAGE

Date of marriage: Nov. 25, 1795
Place of marriage: North Bend, Ohio
• Harrison was the first of seven presidents who were married in Ohio.
Age at marriage: 22 years, 289 days
• He was the seventh of 27 presidents who were married in their twenties.
Years married: 45 years, 130 days

Wife's name: Anna Tuthill Symmes Harrison
• She was the sixth of 33 first ladies.

• She was the ninth of 40 wives of presidents.
Date of birth: July 25, 1775
• She was the first of three first ladies who were born in July.
• She was the first of four wives of presidents who were born in July.
Place of birth: near Morristown, N.J.
• She was the only first lady who was born in New Jersey.
• She was the first of two wives of presidents who were born in New Jersey. The other was Caroline Fillmore.
• She and Mrs. Fillmore were the only wives of presidents who were born in the same New Jersey community.
Wife's mother: Anna Tuthill Symmes
Wife's father: John Cleves Symmes, judge
• Symmes was a former chief justice of the New Jersey supreme court and founder of the Miami settlement in Ohio.
• Symmes was the first of two fathers-in-law of presidents who were judges. The other was the father of Edith Wilson.
Age at marriage: 20 years, 123 days
• She was the fourth of 26 first ladies who were married in their twenties.
• She was the seventh of 30 wives of presidents who were married in their twenties.
Years younger than husband: 2 years, 166 days
Children: 10; 6 sons, 4 daughters
• Elizabeth Bassett was born on Sept. 29, 1796; John Cleves Symmes on Oct. 28, 1798; Lucy Singleton on Sept. 5, 1800; William Henry on Sept. 3, 1802; John Scott on Oct. 4, 1804; Benjamin on May 5, 1806; Mary Symmes on Jan. 22, 1809; Carter Bassett on Oct. 26, 1811; Anna Tuthill on Oct. 28, 1813; and James Findlay on May 15, 1814. James Findlay died in infancy.
• Harrison was the president who had the largest number of children before he was inaugurated.
• He was the only president who had ten children.
• He was the fifth of 19 presidents who had both male and female children.
• He was the sixth of 30 presidents who had children.
Years she survived her husband: 22 years, 327 days
• She was the fourth of 21 first ladies who survived their husbands.
• She was the fourth of 23 wives of presidents who survived their husbands.
Date of death: Feb. 25, 1864

Place of death: North Bend, Ohio
•She was the first of four first ladies who died in Ohio.
•She was the first of four wives of presidents who died in Ohio.
Age at death: 88 years, 215 days
•She had celebrated her 85th birthday, July 25, 1860.
•She was the fifth of 16 first ladies who lived to be 70.
•She was the fifth of 17 wives of presidents who lived to be 70.
•She was the third of 14 first ladies who lived to be 75.
•She was the third of 15 wives of presidents

who lived to be 75.
•She was the second of nine first ladies who lived to be 80.
•She was the second of ten wives of presidents who lived to be 80.
•She was the first of six first ladies who lived to be 85.
•She was the first of seven wives of presidents who lived to be 85.
Place of burial: North Bend, Ohio
•She was the first of five first ladies who were buried in Ohio.
•She was the first of five wives of presidents who were buried in Ohio.

EARLY YEARS

1786, entered Hampden-Sydney College, Hampden-Sydney, Va.
•Harrison remained in college for about a year.
1787–1789, attended academy in Southampton County, Va.
1791, studied medicine under Dr. Benjamin Rush, Philadelphia, Pa.
•His father, who wanted him to be a physician, had served with Rush in the Second Continental Congress.
•He was the only president who studied medicine.
Apr. 24, 1791, his father died
Aug. 16, 1791, entered army
•He received his commission as ensign in the First Regiment of Infantry from President Washington, Philadelphia.
•He was the first of four presidents who were professional soldiers.
November, 1791, joined his regiment, Fort Washington, now Cincinnati, Ohio
June, 1792, promoted to lieutenant
•He was soon appointed aide-de-camp to General Anthony Wayne.
1792, his mother died

December, 1793, participated in expedition that erected Fort Recovery on Wabash River
Aug. 20, 1794, fought in Battle of Fallen Timbers
•Wayne decisively defeated Little Turtle's force of eight hundred Indians on the Maumee River, south of present Toledo, Ohio. The region was called Fallen Timbers because of the large number of downed trees in the vicinity, the result of a tornado.
May, 1795, promoted to captain
•He assumed command of Fort Washington about six months later.
Nov. 25, 1795, eloped with Anna Tuthill Symmes, North Bend, Ohio
Sept. 29, 1796, his first daughter born
•The girl was named Elizabeth Bassett Harrison.
June 1, 1798, resigned his army commission
June 28, 1798, appointed secretary of Northwest Territory by John Adams
Oct. 28, 1798, his first son born
•The boy was named John Cleves Symmes Harrison.

NATIONAL PROMINENCE

September, 1799, elected territorial delegate to Congress
•Harrison was elected by the territorial legislature, which had been formed in February. As territorial delegate, he could present bills and engage in congressional debate, but had no vote. He took his seat in

Philadelphia, in the 6th Congress, Dec. 2.
May 12, 1800, appointed governor of new Indiana Territory by John Adams
Sept 5, 1800, his second daughter born
•The girl was named Lucy Singleton Harrison.
January, 1801, took office as governor of In-

diana Territory, Vincennes
•Reappointed by Jefferson and Madison, Harrison held this office until 1812. He negotiated various treaties with the Indians and was largely responsible for opening the area to settlers from the East.
•He was the only president who served as a territorial governor.
Sept. 3, 1802, his second son born
•The boy was named William Henry Harrison.
1803, built his new home, Grouseland, Vincennes
•Grouseland, 3 West Scott Street, is open daily except Thanksgiving, Christmas and New Year's Day, 9 A.M. to 5 P.M. It is owned and maintained by the Francis Vigo Chapter of the Daughters of the American Revolution. Admission: adults, 50 cents; children under 16, 15 cents.
1804, served briefly as governor of Louisiana Territory
•He was appointed by Jefferson.
Oct. 4, 1804, his third son born
•The boy was named John Scott Harrison.
May 5, 1806, his fourth son born
•The boy was named Benjamin Harrison.
Dec. 6, 1806, founded, with others, what is now Vincennes University Junior College
Jan. 22, 1809, his third daughter born
•The girl was named Mary Symmes Harrison.
Sept. 30, 1809, concluded treaty with several Indian tribes by which U.S. bought three million acres on Wabash and White rivers. This and other treaties were condemned by Tecumseh, chief of the Shawnees, who maintained that the consent of all tribes was necessary to a legal sale.
July, 1810, invited Indian leaders, Tecumseh and his brother, the Prophet, to council, Vincennes
Aug. 12–14, 1810, unsuccessful discussions with Tecumseh
•The Indian chief demanded the return of all lands.
July 27, 1811, met again with Tecumseh, Vincennes
•This conference was also fruitless.
Sept. 26, 1811, departed Vincennes with about nine hundred men to establish military post at junction of Wabash and Tippecanoe rivers
•The actual purpose of the campaign was the destruction of Prophetstown, the Indian capital. Resolutions to this effect had

been voted by the citizens of Vincennes, July 31.
Oct. 28, 1811, completed Fort Harrison, near site of Terre Haute, Ind.
Nov. 6, 1811, arrived at Prophetstown, Tippecanoe Creek
•Unaccountably, Harrison agreed to council with the Prophet on the next day. Tecumseh was not on the scene; he was attempting to win the tribes of the southwest to his proposed confederacy.
Nov. 7, 1811, Battle of Tippecanoe
•Aroused by the Prophet, the Indians attacked shortly before dawn. Although the Americans suffered heavy losses during the all-day battle, they succeeded in beating back the attackers, who finally withdrew. Prophetstown was razed. Harrison and his troops returned to Fort Harrison.
•The battle was considered a great victory and was the origin of his nickname.
June 18, 1812, war was declared against Great Britain
Aug. 25, 1812, commissioned major general of Kentucky militia
Sept. 2, 1812, received commission as brigadier general in U.S. Army
•He withheld official acceptance of the commission, which was dated Aug. 22, since he did not wish to be subordinate to General James Winchester, who had been appointed to the command of the northwestern army. Harrison turned over his detachment of militia to Winchester; en route to his home in Vincennes, he met a messenger with a communication from Secretary of War Eustis appointing him to the chief command in the northwest.
•Harrison was the second of four presidents who served in the War of 1812.
•He was third of 12 presidents who were generals.
•He was the fourth of 21 presidents who served in the military during wartime.
Mar. 2, 1813, promoted to major general
May 9, 1813, withstood seige of Fort Meigs, on Maumee River, opposite present Maumee, Ohio
•A second unsuccessful attempt to take Fort Meigs by a force of five thousand British, Canadians, and Indians was made in July.
•The British commanding officer during both attacks was Colonel Henry Proctor.
Sept. 10, 1813, Battle of Lake Erie
•Harrison was able to take the offensive following Commodore Oliver H. Perry's vic-

tory over the British fleet, which cut Proctor's supply lines.

Sept. 29, 1813, recaptured Detroit

Oct. 5, 1813, Battle of the Thames

• He overtook the retreating Proctor on the banks of the Thames, just east of Thamesville, Ontario, and decisively defeated the British and their Indian allies. Among his forces were four thousand volunteers commanded by Governor Isaac Shelby of Kentucky.

• Tecumseh, who had been commissioned a brigadier general by the British, was killed in this battle, supposedly by Richard Mentor Johnson, who was to become vice president under Van Buren.

Oct. 28, 1813, his fourth daughter born

• The girl was named Anna Tuthill Harrison.

May, 1814, resigned from army

• He was displeased when Secretary of War Armstrong assigned him to the Eighth Military District—which included only western states—where he would see no further active duty.

• When Armstrong issued an order to Harrison's subordinate, Major Holmes, without going through channels, Harrison resigned.

May 15, 1814, his sixth son born

• The boy, who was named James Findlay Harrison, died in infancy.

1814–1815, appointed to several Indian commissions

• These commissions concluded various treaties.

1816, elected to House of Representatives to fill Ohio vacancy

• He was the third of 17 presidents who were elected to the House.

• He served in the 14th and 15th Congresses.

• He was the third of 17 presidents who served in the House of Representatives.

Mar. 24, 1818, received gold medal for victory of the Thames

• Two years earlier, a resolution to strike gold medals for him and Governor Shelby of Kentucky passed the House. Harrison's opponents in the Senate objected, claiming he would not have pursued Proctor had it not been for Shelby and struck his name from the resolution by a vote of 13–11. He received the medal after a laudatory letter from Shelby was read in the Senate.

1819, declined to run for reelection to Congress

1819, selected as member of Ohio state senate

1820, served as Ohio presidential elector

• He voted for Monroe.

1822, unsuccessful candidate for House of Representatives

1824, served as Ohio presidential elector

• He voted for Henry Clay.

1824, elected to Senate

• He served from 1825 to 1828, succeeding Jackson as chairman of the military affairs committee.

• He was the fifth of 16 presidents who were elected to the Senate.

• He was the second of 11 presidents who were elected to both the House of Representatives and the Senate.

• He was the fifth of 15 presidents who served in the Senate.

• He was the second of ten presidents who served in both the House of Representatives and the Senate.

May 19, 1828, appointed first minister to Colombia by John Quincy Adams

Nov. 11, 1828, sailed for Colombia from New York City

• This was the only time he left the U.S. except for forays into Canada during the War of 1812. He disembarked at Maracaibo, Venezuela, Dec. 22; traveled overland to Bogota. He arrived in the Colombian capital, Feb. 5, 1829.

• He was the only president who served as minister to Colombia.

• He was the sixth of seven presidents who served as diplomats.

Mar. 8, 1829, recalled by Jackson

• When Jackson appointed Thomas Patrick Moore of Kentucky to replace him, it was not known in Washington whether Harrison had arrived at his post.

Jan. 9, 1830, sailed for U.S.

• Jackson's orders had been to return immediately, but Harrison's departure from Cartagena, Colombia, was delayed for want of a ship.

1830, retired to his farm, North Bend, Ohio

• He served as clerk of the county court and president of the county agricultural society.

1835, nominated for presidency in several states

• He won the support of Whig and Anti-Masonic delegations in Ohio, Pennsyl-

vania, New York, and other states. At the
Whig state convention in Harrisburg, Pa.,
Dec. 14, he was nominated for president.
He was endorsed by other state conven-
tions, but the Whigs were divided among
four presidential candidates.
Nov. 1, 1836, unsuccessful candidate for
president
• *See* Election of 1836, pages 107–108.
Nov. 10, 1840, election day
• *See* Election of 1840, below.
Dec. 2, 1840, presidential electors cast bal-
lots
•He received 234 of the 294 electoral votes
from 26 states.
• *See* Election of 1840, below.
Feb. 10, 1841, electoral votes tabulated by
Congress
•Harrison and Tyler were officially declared
elected.

ELECTION OF 1840

Whig party, convened, Dec. 4, 1839, at Harrisburg, Pa., nominated William Henry
Harrison of Ohio for president, John Tyler
of Virginia for vice president.
•This was the first Whig national convention. It was the only major party convention held in Harrisburg.
Liberty (abolitionist) party, convened, Apr.
1, 1840, at Albany, N.Y., nominated James
Gillespie Birney of New York for president, Thomas Earle of Pennsylvania for
vice president.
•This was the first Liberty national convention. The founding convention of the Liberty party had been held, Nov. 13, 1839, in
Warsaw, N.Y., when Birney and Francis
Julius Le Moyne of Pennsylvania had been

nominated. Le Moyne declined the vice-
presidential nomination.
•Birney and Earle also declined; however,
the Liberty ticket appeared on the ballot
in several states.
Democratic party, convened, May 5, at Baltimore, Md., nominated Martin Van Buren
of New York for president. The choice of a
vice presidential nominee was left to the
state electors.
•This was the third Democratic national
convention. It was the third Democratic
convention in Baltimore; it was the fifth
major party convention in Baltimore.
Election day, Tuesday, Nov. 10, 1840 (in
most states)
Popular vote: 2,411,187
    Harrison, 1,275,016
    Van Buren, 1,129,102
    Birney, 7,069
Electoral vote: 294, 26 states
• Harrison, 234, 19 states
    (Connecticut, 8; Delaware, 3; Georgia,
    11; Indiana, 9; Kentucky, 15; Louisiana,
    5; Maine, 10; Maryland, 10; Massachu-
    setts, 14; Michigan, 3; Mississippi, 4;
    New Jersey, 8; New York, 42; North
    Carolina, 15; Ohio, 21; Pennsylvania,
    30; Rhode Island, 4; Tennessee, 15;
    Vermont, 7)
• Van Buren, 60, seven states
    (Alabama, 7; Arkansas, 3; Illinois, 5;
    Missouri, 4; New Hampshire, 7; South
    Carolina, 11; Virginia, 23)
•The Democratic electoral votes for vice
president were divided among three can-
didates: Richard Mentor Johnson of Ken-
tucky received 48 votes; Littleton Waller
Tazewell of Virginia, 11 votes; and James
Knox Polk of Tennessee, one vote.

THE PRESIDENT (9th)

Term of office: Mar. 4, 1841, to Apr. 4, 1841
(31 days)
•Harrison served the shortest of presidential terms.
•He was the first of nine presidents who
served less than one term.
•He was the fourth of 19 presidents who
served one term or less than one term.
•He was the second of eight presidents in
succession who served one term or less
than one term.

State represented: Ohio
•He was the first of six presidents who
represented Ohio.
•He was the second of 15 presidents who
represented states that were not their na-
tive states.
Political party: Whig
•He was the first of four presidents who
were Whigs.
Congress: 27th
Administration: 14th

Age at inauguration: 68 years, 23 days
•He was the oldest president at inauguration.
Inauguration day: Thursday, Mar. 4, 1841
•Harrison took the oath of office, administered by Chief Justice Roger B. Taney, on the east portico of the Capitol.
•This was the second of seven inaugurations at which Taney officiated.
•Harrison had ridden to the capitol on horseback during a driving rainstorm, wearing neither hat nor coat. The rain continued throughout the delivery of his inaugural address.
•This was the longest inaugural address. It contained 8,441 words.

THE 14th ADMINISTRATION

1841

Mar. 5, appointed his only secretary of state, Daniel Webster; his only secretary of treasury, Thomas Ewing; his only secretary of war, John Bell; his only attorney general, John J. Crittenden; his only secretary of navy, George E. Badger; and his only postmaster general, Francis Granger
•Webster, Ewing, Badger, and Granger took office, Mar. 6.
Mar. 27, took to his bed with severe chill
•He never fully recovered from the cold he had caught during the inaugural ceremony.

Notes: Harrison was the first of two presidents who did not send or deliver State of the Union messages to Congress. The other was Garfield.
•He was the first of four presidents who made no changes in his cabinet.
•He was the fourth of seven presidents who did not exercise the veto.

DEATH

Date of death: Apr. 4, 1841
•Harrison was the first of five presidents who died before they completed their first terms.
•He was the first of eight presidents who died in office.
Place of death: Washington, D.C.
•He was the first of two presidents who died in the White House. The other was Taylor.
•He was the second of seven presidents who died in Washington.
•He was the first of six presidents to lay in state in the White House.
Age at death: 68 years, 54 days
Cause of death: Pleurisy, pneumonia

•He was the first of four presidents who died of natural causes in office.
Place of burial: North Bend, Ohio
•He was the first of five presidents who were buried in Ohio.

THE VICE PRESIDENT (10th)

Full name: John Tyler
• *See also* pages 121–130.
•He was the second of two vice presidents who were born in Virginia. The other was Jefferson.
•He was the second of eight vice presidents who were Episcopalians.
•Harrison and Tyler were both Episcopalians. They were the second of seven president-vice president teams of the same religious denomination.
•Tyler was the second of two vice presidents who attended the College of William and Mary. The other was Jefferson.
•He was the sixth of 21 vice presidents who served in the House of Representatives before their terms of office.
•He was the fifth of 17 vice presidents who served in the Senate before their terms of office.
•He was the third of ten vice presidents who served in both the House of Representatives and the Senate before their terms of office.
•He was the fourth of 12 vice presidents who served both in the House of Representatives and the Senate.
•He was the sixth of 14 vice presidents who served as state governors.
•He was the vice president who served the second shortest term of office, 33 days.
•He was the second of 14 vice presidents who served less than one term.
•He was the first of seven vice presidents who served less than one year.

•Harrison and Tyler were the 12th of 41 president-vice president teams.
•Tyler was the second of two vice presidents who represented Virginia. The other was Jefferson.
•He was the first of two vice presidents who were Whigs. The other was Fillmore.
•He was the second of three vice presidents who died in Virginia.
•He was the second of two vice presidents who were buried in Virginia. The other was Jefferson.

THE CABINET

State: Daniel Webster of Massachusetts, Mar. 6, 1841, to May 8, 1843
Treasury: Thomas Ewing of Ohio, Mar. 6, 1841, to Sept. 11, 1841
War: John Bell of Tennessee, Mar. 5, 1841, to Sept. 13, 1841
Attorney General: John Jordan Crittenden of Kentucky, Mar. 5, 1841, to Sept. 13, 1841
Navy: George Edmund Badger of North Carolina, Mar. 6, 1841, to Sept. 11, 1841
Postmaster General: Francis Granger of New York, Mar. 6, 1841, to Sept. 13, 1841

THE SUPREME COURT

•Harrison was the first of two presidents who made no appointments to the Court. The other was Taylor.
•He was the first of three presidents who did not name a member of the Court. Andrew Johnson's only nomination was not acted upon by the Senate.

Tenth President

JOHN TYLER

Full name: John Tyler
- He was the third of five presidents who were named John.
- He was the fourth of eight presidents who had the same full names as their fathers.
- He was the eighth of 17 presidents who did not have middle initials or middle names.

Date of birth: Mar. 29, 1790
- He was the third of four presidents who were born in March.

Place of birth: near Greenway, Charles City County, Va.
- He was the second of two presidents who were born in Charles City County. The other was William Henry Harrison.
- He was the only president born in the same county as his predecessor.
- He was the sixth of eight presidents who were born in Virginia.

Family lineage: English
- He was the sixth of 12 presidents who were of English ancestry.

Religious denomination: Episcopalian
- He was the fifth of nine presidents who were Episcopalians.

College: College of William and Mary, Williamsburg, Va.
- He was the last of three presidents who attended William and Mary.
- He was the seventh of 27 presidents who attended college.
- He was fourth of six presidents who attended but were not graduated from college.
- He was the seventh of 15 presidents who were not graduated from college.

PARENTS AND SIBLINGS

Father's name: John Tyler
Date of birth: Feb. 28, 1747
Place of birth: Yarmouth, Va.
Occupation: Lawyer
- Tyler's father held several judicial posts in Virginia; was a member and for a while speaker of the House of Burgesses; was elected governor in 1808, served until January, 1811; was appointed U.S. judge for the district of Virginia, 1811.
- Tyler was the second of three presidents whose fathers had served as state governors.

Date of death: Jan. 6, 1813
Place of death: Greenway, Charles City County, Va.

Age at death: 65 years, 312 days

Mother's name: Mary Marott Armistead Tyler
Date of birth: 1761
Place of birth: probably York County, Va.
Date of marriage: 1776
Children: 8; 5 daughters, 3 sons
•Anne Contesse was born in 1778; Elizabeth Armistead in 1780; Martha Jefferson in 1782; Maria Henry in 1784; Wat Henry in 1788; John in 1790; William in 17—; and Christiana Booth in 1795.
•Tyler was the only president who was a sixth child.
•He was the first of two presidents who came from families of eight children. The other was Harding.
Date of death: Apr. 5, 1797
•John was seven years, seven days old, when his mother died.
Place of death: Greenway, Charles City County, Va.
Age at death: about 36 years

MARRIAGE

Date of first marriage: Mar. 29, 1813
Place of first marriage: Cedar Grove plantation, New Kent County, Va.
•Tyler was the last of four presidents who were married in Virginia.
Age at first marriage: 23 years
•He was the first of two presidents who were married on their birthdays. The other was Theodore Roosevelt.
•He was the eighth of 27 presidents who were married in their twenties.
Years married: 29 years, 165 days

First wife's name: Letitia Christian Tyler
•She was the seventh of 33 first ladies
•She was the tenth of 40 wives of presidents.
Date of birth: Nov. 12, 1790
•She was the second of three first ladies who were born in November.
•She was the second of three wives of presidents who were born in November.
Place of birth: Cedar Grove plantation, New Kent County, Va.
•She was the second of three first ladies who were born in Virginia.
•She was the fourth of six wives of presidents who were born in Virginia.

First's wife's mother: Mary Brown Christian
First wife's father: Robert Christian, planter
Age at marriage: 22 years, 137 days
•She was the fifth of 26 first ladies who were married in their twenties.
•She was the eighth of 30 wives of presidents who were married in their twenties.
Years younger than husband: 228 days
Children: 8; 5 daughters, 3 sons
•Mary was born on Apr. 15, 1815; Robert on Sept. 9, 1816; John on Apr. 27, 1819; Letitia on May 11, 1821; Elizabeth on July 11, 1823; Anne Contesse on Apr. 5, 1825; Alice on Mar. 23, 1827; and Tazewell on Dec. 6, 1830. Anne Contesse died in infancy.
•Tyler was the sixth of 19 presidents who had both male and female children.
•He was the seventh of 30 presidents who had children.
Date of death: Sept. 10, 1842
Place of death: White House, Washington, D.C.
•He was the first of three presidents whose wives died while they were in office.
•She was the first of three first ladies who died in the White House.
•She was the third of nine first ladies who died in Washington.
•She was the third of nine wives of presidents who died in Washington.
Age at death: 51 years, 302 days
Place of burial: Cedar Grove plantation, New Kent County, Va.
•She was the fourth of six first ladies who were buried in Virginia.
•She was the fifth of seven wives of presidents who were buried in Virginia.
Years he survived his first wife: 19 years, 130 days
•Tyler was the sixth of 14 presidents who survived their wives.

Date of second marriage: June 26, 1844
•He was the first of three presidents who were married while in office.
•He was the first of five presidents who remarried.
Place of second marriage: New York, N.Y.
•He was the second of five presidents who were married in New York City.
•He was the third of seven presidents who were married in New York.
Age at second marriage: 54 years, 89 days
•He was the first of three presidents who were married in their fifties.

Years married: 17 years, 206 days

Second wife's name: Julia Gardiner Tyler
•She was the eighth of 33 first ladies.
•She was the 11th of 40 wives of presidents.
Date of birth: May 4, 1820
•She was the second of three first ladies who were born in May.
•She was the second of three wives of presidents who were born in May.
Place of birth: Gardiner's Island, N.Y.
•She was the second of six first ladies who were born in New York.
•She was the third of seven wives of presidents who were born in New York.
Second wife's mother: Juliana McLachlin Gardiner
Second wife's father: David Gardiner, U.S. Senator
•Gardiner was the only father-in-law of a president who was a senator.
Age at marriage: 24 years, 53 days
•She was the second youngest first lady. The youngest was Frances Cleveland.
•She was the sixth of 26 first ladies who were married in their twenties.
•She was the ninth of 30 wives of presidents who were married in their twenties.
Years younger than husband: 30 years, 36 days

Children: 7; 5 sons, 2 daughters
•David Gardiner was born on July 12, 1846; John Alexander on Apr. 7, 1848; Julia on Dec. 25, 1849; Lachlan on Dec. 2, 1851; Lyon Gardiner on Aug. 5, 1853; Robert FitzWalter on Mar. 12, 1856; and Pearl on June 20, 1860.
•Tyler was the president who had the largest number of children, 15. He was the father of eight boys and seven girls.
•He was the first of three presidents who had children by two wives.
Years she survived her husband: 27 years, 173 days
•She was the fifth of 21 first ladies who survived their husbands.
•She was the fifth of 23 wives of presidents who survived their husbands.
Date of death: July 10, 1889
Place of death: Richmond, Va.
•She was the last of three first ladies who died in Virginia.
•She was the last of four wives of presidents who died in Virginia.
Age at death: 69 years, 67 days
Place of burial: Richmond, Va.
•She was the fifth of six first ladies who were buried in Virginia.
•She was the sixth of seven wives of presidents who were buried in Virginia.

EARLY YEARS

Apr. 5, 1797, his mother died
1806, attended College of William and Mary
1807–1809, studied law
•Tyler studied with his father until 1808. After his father was elected governor of Virginia, he continued his studies under Edmund Randolph, who had served as Washington's secretary of state.
•Tyler was the seventh of 26 presidents who studied law.
1809, admitted to bar, Charles City County, Va.
•Although he was below the age required for admission to the bar, he received his license. The examining judge did not ask his age; he was nineteen.
•He was the seventh of 23 presidents who were lawyers.
1811, elected to House of Delegates, lower house of state assembly, from Charles City County

•Tyler took his seat in December. He was reelected annually five times and served until 1815.
Jan. 14, 1812, introduced resolution of censure of state's U.S. senators
•The resolution called for censure of Virginia's two senators, Richard Brent and William B. Giles, for voting in favor of the recharter of the Bank of the U.S. despite contrary instructions from the state legislature. A similar incident occurred when Tyler was a member of the Senate, 1836.
Jan. 6, 1813, his father died
•He was the sixth of nine presidents who owned slaves.
Mar. 29, 1813, married Letitia Christian, Cedar Grove plantation, New Kent County, Va.
April, 1813, appointed captain of militia company
•The company was formed to assist in the

defense of Richmond, then threatened by the British. The unit saw no action. His military service lasted for only about a month.
•He was the third of four presidents who served in the War of 1812.
•He was the fifth of 21 presidents who served in the military during wartime.
1815, elected to council of state

•He resigned from the House of Delegates when he was elevated to the council, an eight-member advisory board to the governor.
Apr. 15, 1815, his first daughter born
•The girl was named Mary Tyler.
Sept. 9, 1816, his first son born
•The boy was named Robert Tyler.

NATIONAL PROMINENCE

November, 1816, elected to fill unexpired term of John Clopton in House of Representatives
•Tyler was the fourth of 17 presidents who were elected to the House.
Dec. 17, 1816, took seat in House
•He served in the 14th, 15th and 16th Congresses.
•He was the fourth of 17 presidents who served in the House.
1817, reelected to House
1819, unopposed for reelection to House
Apr. 27, 1819, his second son born
•The boy was named John Tyler.
Jan. 18, 1821, declined renomination to House
•He published a notice in the Richmond *Enquirer* that he would not seek reelection, giving failing health as his reason.
Mar. 3, 1821, returned to private life
•He retired at the adjournment of the second session of the 16th Congress.
May 11, 1821, his second daughter born
•The girl was named Letitia Tyler.
July 11, 1823, his third daughter born.
•The girl was named Elizabeth Tyler.
1823, again elected to House of Delegates
•He served in the state assembly from December, 1823, to December, 1825
1824, nominated to fill vacancy in Senate
•Littleton W. Tazewell was elected to the unexpired term of the late John Taylor.
1824, opposed removal of William and Mary College from Williamsburg
•There was an attempt to move the college to Richmond.
Apr. 5, 1825, his fourth daughter born
•The girl was named Anne Contesse Tyler. She died in infancy.
Dec. 10, 1825, elected governor of Virginia by legislature
•He was the last of three presidents who served as governors of Virginia.

•He was the fourth of 13 presidents who served as state governors.
July 11, 1826, gave oration at Jefferson funeral services
Dec. 10, 1826, unanimously reelected governor by legislature
Jan. 13, 1827, elected to Senate
•He was the sixth of 16 presidents who were elected to the Senate.
•He was the third of 11 presidents who were elected to both the House of Representatives and the Senate.
Mar. 4, 1827, resigned as governor
Mar. 23, 1827, his fifth daughter born
•The girl was named Alice Tyler.
Dec. 3, 1827, took seat in Senate
•He was the sixth of 15 presidents who served in the Senate.
•He was the third of ten presidents who served in both the House of Representatives and the Senate.
Oct. 5, 1829–Jan. 15, 1830, member of Virginia convention for revising state constitution
•He played no conspicuous role in this convention.
Dec. 6, 1830, his third son born
•The boy was named Tazewell Tyler.
Feb. 15, 1833, reelected to Senate
Feb. 20, 1833, voted against "force bill"
•He was the only senator who voted against the Jackson bill to enforce the revenue laws by the use of the military, if necessary. The vote was 32–1; Calhoun, Clay, and others abstained.
1835, nominated for vice president by states' rights Whigs
Feb. 29, 1836, resigned from Senate
•Instructed by the Virginia legislature to vote for Thomas Hart Benton's resolutions to expunge the vote of censure of President Jackson—a situation which paralleled the case of Giles and Brent in 1812—Tyler

refused. He voted against the Benton resolutions and then resigned.

Nov. 1, 1836, received 47 electoral votes as unsuccessful nominee for vice president
•Since no candidate received a majority, the election was decided in the Senate. Richard Mentor Johnson was elected.

Jan. 10, 1838, elected president of American Colonization Society

1838, again elected to House of Delegates
•He was elected speaker of the house.

Feb. 15, 1839, nominated for Senate

•A deadlock developed; his principal rival was William C. Rives. After a number of indecisive ballots, Feb. 15–Feb. 25, the senatorial election was postponed indefinitely, and the legislature adjourned.

Dec. 4, 1839, nominated for vice president at Whig national convention, Harrisburg, Pa.

1840, "Tippecanoe and Tyler Too" campaign

Nov. 3, 1840, elected vice president

Mar. 4, 1841, inaugurated as vice president

THE PRESIDENT (10th)

Term of office: Apr. 6, 1841, to Mar. 4, 1845 (3 years, 332 days)
•Tyler was the fourth of 12 presidents who had served as vice presidents.
•He was the first of eight presidents who, because of the deaths of their predecessors, did not complete their vice-presidential terms.
•He was the first of four presidents who served only the unexpired terms of their predecessors.
•He was the president who served the longest unexpired term of his predecessor.
•He was the fifth of 19 presidents who served one term or less than one term.
•He was the second of nine presidents who served less than one term.
•He was the third of eight presidents in succession who served one term or less than one term.

State represented: Virginia
•He was the last of five presidents who represented Virginia.

Political party: Whig
•He was the second of four presidents who were Whigs.

Congresses: 27th, 28th

Administration: 14th

Age at taking oath: 51 years, 8 days
•The first vice president who succeeded to the presidency because of the death of his predecessor, Tyler took the oath of office at the Indian Queen Hotel, Washington, D.C., on Tuesday, Apr. 6, 1841. The oath was administered by William Cranch, chief justice of the U.S. Circuit Court of the District of Columbia.
•Tyler was the second of seven presidents who took the oath of office from an official other than a justice of the Supreme Court.
•This was the first of two oath-taking ceremonies at which Cranch officiated. Cranch administered the oath to Fillmore in 1850.
•Tyler was the first of four presidents who did not give inaugural addresses.

THE 14th ADMINISTRATION

1841

May 31, first session of 27th Congress
•The administration controlled both the Senate and the House of Representatives. The Whigs gained six Senate and 15 House seats. The Senate (52 members) consisted of 28 Whigs, 22 Democrats, and two others. The House (241 members) consisted of 133 Whigs, 102 Democrats, and six others.

June 30, signed act for relief of Mrs. William Henry Harrison

•Mrs. Harrison was granted $25,000.
•This was the first pension to a widow of a president.

Aug. 16, vetoed bill to incorporate Fiscal Bank
•This was the first of Tyler's nine vetoes.

Aug. 19, signed second federal bankruptcy act
•This act was repealed in 1846.

Sept. 4, signed distribution-preemption act
•This act authorized settlers to purchase as much as 160 acres of surveyed public lands for $1.25 an acre.

Sept. 9, vetoed second Fiscal Bank incorporation bill
• This was the second of his nine vetoes.
Sept. 11, five members of cabinet resigned
• The cabinet members who resigned were Secretary of Treasury Ewing, Secretary of War Bell, Attorney General Crittenden, Secretary of Navy Badger, and Postmaster General Granger.
• Public statements charging that Tyler had committed himself to support the second Fiscal Bank bill were released by all who resigned except Granger.
Sept. 13, appointed his second secretary of treasury, Walter Forward; his second attorney general, Hugh S. Legare; his second secretary of navy, Abel P. Upshur; and his second postmaster general, Charles A. Wickliffe
• Upshur took office, Oct. 11; Wickliffe, Oct. 13.
Sept. 13, first session of 27th Congress adjourned
Sept. 25, issued proclamation warning against participation in planned armed invasion of Canada
Oct. 12, appointed his second secretary of war, John C. Spencer
Dec. 6, second session of 27th Congress
Dec. 7, sent his first State of the Union message to Congress

1842

Jan. 31, attended wedding of his daughter, Elizabeth, and William Waller, White House
• This was the second of eight White House weddings of daughters of presidents.
• This was the third of nine White House weddings of children of presidents.
June 29, vetoed "little tariff" bill
• This was the third of his nine vetoes.
Aug. 9, vetoed second tariff bill
• This was the fourth of his nine vetoes.
Aug. 20, Webster-Ashburton Treaty ratified
• He had played a prominent part in the negotiations which led to the treaty. This agreement fixed the Maine-Canadian border and allotted the U.S. about seven thousand of the disputed twelve thousand square miles.
Aug. 30, signed tariff act of 1842
• This act did not contain the distribution of public land sales provision that had caused

his vetoes of the two previous tariff bills.
Aug. 31, second session of 27th Congress adjourned
Dec. 5, third session of 27th Congress
Dec. 6, sent his second State of the Union message to Congress
Dec. 14, vetoed proceeds of public land sales, testimony in contested election bills
• These bills had been passed during the second session of the 27th Congress.
• These were the fifth and sixth of Tyler's nine vetoes, the first and second of his three pocket vetoes.
Dec. 18, vetoed payment of Cherokee certificates bill
• This bill had been passed during the second session of the 27th Congress.
• This was the seventh of his nine vetoes, the last of his three pocket vetoes.
Dec. 31, sent special message to Congress of recognition of Hawaiian Islands' independence

1843

Jan. 10, impeachment resolution rejected
• A resolution offered by Representative John M. Botts of Virginia—which asked for Tyler's impeachment for gross usurpation of power and abuse of the power of appointments—was rejected by the House, 127–83.
Mar. 1, accepted resignation of Secretary of Treasury Forward
Mar. 3, appointed his third secretary of treasury, Caleb Cushing
• His appointment of Cushing was rejected by the Senate, Mar. 3.
• Tyler was the second of five presidents whose nominees to the cabinet were rejected by the Senate.
• Cushing was the second of eight nominees to the cabinet who were rejected by the Senate.
Mar. 3, appointed his fourth secretary of treasury, John C. Spencer
• Spencer took office, Mar. 8.
Mar. 3, third session of 27th Congress adjourned
Mar. 8, appointed his third secretary of war, James M. Porter
May 8, accepted resignation of Secretary of State Webster
June 17, attended dedication of Bunker Hill monument, Boston, Mass.

• The monument, which stands on adjacent Breed's Hill, was dedicated on the 68th anniversary of the Battle of Bunker Hill.

June 20, Attorney General Legare died

June 24, appointed Secretary of Navy Upshur as secretary of state ad interim

July 1, appointed his third attorney general, John Nelson

July 23, accepted resignation of Secretary of Navy Upshur

July 24, appointed his second secretary of state, Abel P. Upshur, and his third secretary of navy, David Henshaw

Dec. 4, first session of 28th Congress

• The administration maintained control of the Senate but lost control of the House of Representatives. The Democrats gained three Senate and 40 House seats. The Senate (54 members) consisted of 28 Whigs, 25 Democrats, and one other. The House (222 members) consisted of 142 Democrats, 79 Whigs, and one other.

Dec. 5, sent his third State of the Union message to Congress

Dec. 18, Associate Justice Thompson died

1844

Jan. 9, accepted resignation of Secretary of Treasury Spencer, effective, May 2

Jan. 9, appointed John C. Spencer as associate justice

• Spencer, who was the first of Tyler's five appointments to the Supreme Court, was rejected by the Senate, Jan. 31.

• Tyler was the fifth of 15 presidents who nominated justices not confirmed by the Senate.

• Spencer was the fifth of 25 men nominated to the Supreme Court who were not confirmed by the Senate.

Jan. 15, Secretary of Navy Henshaw rejected by Senate

• Henshaw, a recess appointment, had served in the cabinet since July 24, 1843.

• Henshaw was the third of eight appointees to the cabinet who were rejected by the Senate.

Jan. 30, Secretary of War Porter rejected by Senate

• Porter, a recess appointment, had served in the cabinet since Mar. 8, 1843.

• Porter was the fourth of eight appointees to the cabinet who were rejected by the Senate.

Feb. 15, appointed his fourth secretary of war, William Wilkins, and his fourth secretary of navy, Thomas W. Gilmer

• Gilmer took office, Feb. 19.

Feb. 28, cabinet members and others killed

• He and his cabinet were among the 350 dignitaries who were aboard the steam frigate, *U.S.S. Princeton*, when a bow gun of new design—the "Peacemaker"—exploded. Eight men, including Secretary of State Upshur, Secretary of Navy Gilmer, and David Gardiner, father of Tyler's fiancee, Julia Gardiner, were killed. Tyler was below decks when the gun blew up.

Mar. 6, appointed his third secretary of state, John C. Calhoun

• Calhoun took office, Apr. 1.

Mar. 13, appointed Reuben H. Walworth as associate justice

• This, the second of Tyler's five appointments to the Supreme Court, was postponed, June 15, and then withdrawn, June 17.

• Walworth was the sixth of 25 men nominated to the Supreme Court who were not confirmed by the Senate.

Mar. 14, appointed his fifth secretary of navy, John Y. Mason

• Mason took office, Mar. 26.

Apr. 21, Associate Justice Baldwin died

Apr. 22, submitted Texas annexation treaty to Senate with special message urging ratification

• The Senate rejected the annexation treaty, June 8.

May 2, appointed his fifth secretary of treasury, James S. Green

• His appointment of Green was rejected by the Senate, June 15.

• Green was the fifth of eight nominees to the cabinet who were rejected by the Senate.

May 27, nominated for president by Tyler Democrats, Baltimore, Md.

June 5, appointed Edward King as associate justice

• This, the third of Tyler's five appointments to the Supreme Court, was postponed by the Senate, June 15. He appointed King again, Dec. 4. This appointment was postponed, Jan. 23, 1845, and withdrawn, Feb. 7, 1845.

• King was the seventh of 25 men nominated to the Supreme Court who were not confirmed by the Senate.

June 11, vetoed rivers and harbors bill

•This was the eighth of his nine vetoes.
June 15, appointed his sixth secretary of treasury, George M. Bibb
•Bibb took office, July 4.
•Bibb was the last of Tyler's 17 cabinet appointments.
June 17, first session of 28th Congress adjourned
June 26, married Julia Gardiner, New York City
Aug. 22, withdrew as candidate for reelection
•He was the first of five presidents who sought but were denied renomination.
Nov. 12, election day
• *See* Election of 1844, page 134.
Dec. 2, second session of 28th Congress
Dec. 3, sent his fourth and last State of the Union message to Congress
•He recommended that the Texas annexation treaty be accepted by a joint resolution.

1845

Jan. 23, signed act that established first Tuesday after first Monday in November as election day in future presidential elections
Feb. 4, appointed Samuel Nelson as associate justice
•Nelson, who was the fourth of Tyler's five appointments to the Supreme Court, was confirmed by the Senate, Feb. 14.
•Nelson was his only appointee who served

on the Court.
Feb. 7, appointed John Meredith Read as associate justice
•This, the last of Tyler's five appointments to the Supreme Court, was not acted upon by the Senate.
•Read was the eighth of 25 men nominated to the Supreme Court who were not confirmed by the Senate.
Feb. 20, vetoed revenue cutters and steamers for defense bill
•This bill prohibited payment for naval craft that he had ordered constructed.
•This was the last of his nine vetoes.
Mar. 1, signed joint resolution for annexation of Texas
•The joint resolution, which required only a simple majority in both houses, was passed by the Senate, Feb. 27, and the House of Representatives, Feb. 28. The resolution extended the Missouri Compromise line of 36° 30' to Texas and also provided that the new state was to be admitted without preliminary status as a territory.
•This was the first time that a joint resolution was utilized to approve a treaty or to acquire territory.
Mar. 3, Florida admitted as 27th state
•Florida was the only state admitted during his term of office.
Mar. 3, veto of Feb. 20 overridden
•This was the first time that a presidential veto was overridden.
Mar. 3, second session of 28th Congress adjourned

THE FORMER PRESIDENT

Mar. 4, 1845, attended inauguration of Polk
•Tyler's age upon leaving office was 54 years, 340 days.
Mar. 5, 1845, traveled by coach to Richmond, Va., then by boat to Sherwood Forest
•Sherwood Forest, the twelve-hundred-acre plantation he had purchased while president, was located about three miles from Greenway, his birthplace. He lived there the rest of his life, except for summers at Hampton, Va.
•Sherwood Forest is on state highway 5, 30 miles east of Richmond. A National Historic Landmark, it is still the residence of the Tyler family. The main floor and

grounds are open to the public weekdays.
July 12, 1846, his fourth son born
•The boy was named David Gardiner Tyler.
•He was the first of three former presidents who became fathers.
•He was the former president whose wife gave birth to the largest number of children, seven.
Apr. 7, 1848, his fifth son born
•The boy was named John Alexander Tyler.
June 17, 1848, his first daughter, Mary, died
Dec. 25, 1849, his sixth daughter born
•The girl was named Julia Tyler.
June 1, 1850, his third daughter, Elizabeth, died
Dec. 2, 1851, his sixth son born

•The boy was named Lachlan Tyler.
Aug. 5, 1853, his seventh son born
•The boy was named Lyon Gardiner Tyler.
June 8, 1854, his fifth daughter, Alice, died
Mar. 12, 1856, his eighth son born
•The boy was named Robert FitzWalter Tyler.
1859, appointed chancellor of College of William and Mary, Williamsburg, Va.
•He was named chancellor during the 166th anniversary of the founding of the college. The office had been vacant since the death of Washington.
•He was the second of two presidents who were chancellors of William and Mary. The other was Washington.
Mar. 29, 1860, celebrated his 70th birthday
•He was the eighth of 16 presidents who lived to be 70.
June 20, 1860, his seventh daughter born
•The girl was named Pearl Tyler.
•He was the former president who became a father at the most advanced age. He was 70 years, 83 days old, when his 15th child was born.
Jan. 17, 1861, recommended convention of border states
•His suggestion that representatives of the states meet to devise a plan of adjusting the North-South split—the first step toward a constitutional amendment—was outlined in a letter published in the Richmond *Enquirer*.
•The Virginia legislature enlarged upon his plan and recommended a peace convention of delegates from all states.
Feb. 4, 1861, elected chairman of peace convention, Washington, D.C.
•The peace convention was attended by delegates from 13 northern and seven border states. Several resolutions were submitted to Congress, Feb. 27.
Feb. 28, 1861, recommended secession of Virginia
•Convinced that resolutions adopted by the peace convention would be ignored by Congress, he spoke in favor of Virginia asserting her rights as a sovereign state. He spoke from the steps of the Exchange Hotel, Richmond.
•The Senate rejected the resolutions, 28–7, Mar. 2. The House of Representatives did not vote on the resolutions.
Mar. 1, 1861, took seat in Virginia convention on policy

•In his first speech, he advocated the immediate passing of an ordinance of secession.
May 5, 1861, elected to Provisional Congress of Confederation, Richmond
•He was the only president who held office in the Confederacy.
Fall, 1861, elected to represent his congressional district in permanent Congress of Confederation, Richmond
•He died before he assumed his seat.

DEATH

Date of death: Jan. 18, 1862
Place of death: Richmond, Va.
•Tyler was the last of four presidents who died in Virginia.
Age at death: 71 years, 295 days
•He lived 16 years, 320 days, after the completion of his term.
Cause of death: Bilious fever
Place of burial: Richmond, Va.
•He was the fifth of seven presidents who were buried in Virginia.

THE VICE PRESIDENT

•Tyler was the first of four presidents who did not have vice presidents.

THE CABINET

State: Daniel Webster of Massachusetts, Mar. 6, 1841, to May 8, 1843
•Abel Parker Upshur of Virginia, July 24, 1843, to Feb. 28, 1844
•John Caldwell Calhoun of South Carolina, Apr. 1, 1844, to Mar. 10, 1845
Treasury: Thomas Ewing of Ohio, Mar. 6, 1841, to Sept. 11, 1841
•Walter Forward of Pennsylvania, Sept. 13, 1841, to Mar. 1, 1843
•Caleb Cushing of Massachusetts, appointed, Mar. 3, 1843; rejected by Senate, Mar. 3, 1843
•John Canfield Spencer of New York, Mar. 8, 1843, to May 2, 1844
•James S. Green of Missouri, appointed, May 2, 1844; rejected by Senate, June 15, 1844
•George Mortimer Bibb of Kentucky, July 4, 1844, to Mar. 7, 1845

War: John Bell of Tennessee, Mar. 5, 1841, to Sept. 13, 1841

• John Canfield Spencer of New York, Oct. 12, 1841, to Mar. 3, 1843

• James Madison Porter of Pennsylvania, appointed, Mar. 8, 1843; rejected by Senate, Jan. 30, 1844

• William Wilkins of Pennsylvania, Feb. 14, 1844, to Mar. 4, 1845

Attorney General: John Jordan Crittenden of Kentucky, Mar. 5, 1841, to Sept. 13, 1841

• Hugh Swinton Legare of South Carolina, Sept. 13, 1841, to June 20, 1843

• John Nelson of Maryland, July 1, 1843, to Mar. 3, 1845

Navy: George Edmund Badger of North Carolina, Mar. 6, 1841, to Sept. 11, 1841

• Abel Parker Upshur of Virginia, Oct. 11, 1841, to July 23, 1843

• David Henshaw of Massachusetts, appointed, July 24, 1843; rejected by Senate, Jan. 15, 1844

• Thomas Walker Gilmer of Virginia, Feb. 19, 1844, to Feb. 28, 1844

• John Young Mason of Virginia, Mar. 26, 1844, to Mar. 10, 1845

Postmaster General: Francis Granger of New York, Mar. 6, 1841, to Sept. 13, 1841

• Charles Anderson Wickliffe of Kentucky, Oct. 13, 1841, to Mar. 6, 1845

THE SUPREME COURT

Associate Justices: John Canfield Spencer of New York, appointed, Jan. 9, 1844; rejected by Senate, Jan. 31, 1844

• Reuben Hyde Walworth of New York, appointed, Mar. 13, 1844; postponed, June 15, 1844; withdrawn, June 17, 1844

• Edward King of Pennsylvania, appointed, June 5, 1844; postponed, June 15, 1844; appointed, Dec. 4, 1844; postponed, Jan. 23, 1845; withdrawn, Feb. 7, 1845

• Samuel Nelson of New York, appointed, Feb. 4, 1845; confirmed, Feb. 14, 1845

• John Meredith Read of Pennsylvania, appointed, Feb. 7, 1845; not acted upon by Senate

Eleventh President

JAMES KNOX POLK

Full name: James Knox Polk
•He was the third of five presidents named James.
•He was the third of 19 presidents who had middle initials or middle names.
Date of birth: Nov. 2, 1795
•He and Harding were the only presidents who were born on the same day of the year.
•He was the first of five presidents who were born in November.
Place of birth: Mecklenburg County, N.C.
•He was the first of two presidents who were born in North Carolina. The other was Andrew Johnson.
Family lineage: Scottish-Irish
•He was the second of four presidents who were of Scottish-Irish ancestry.
Religious denomination: Methodist
•He was the first of four presidents who were Methodists.
•He often attended Presbyterian services with his wife although he had noted in his diary, "my own opinions and predilections are in favor of the Methodist Church." He was baptized by a Methodist minister a week before his death.
College: University of North Carolina,

Chapel Hill, N.C.
•He was the only president who went to North Carolina.
•He was the eighth of 27 presidents who attended college.
Date of graduation: June 4, 1818, Bachelor of Arts
•He was the fourth of 21 presidents who were graduated from college.

PARENTS AND SIBLINGS

Father's name: Samuel Polk
Date of birth: July 5, 1772
Place of birth: Tryon, N.C.
Occupations: Farmer and planter, surveyor
Date of death: Nov. 5, 1827
Place of death: Columbia, Maury County, Tenn.
Age at death: 55 years, 123 days

Mother's name: Jane Knox Polk
Date of birth: Nov. 15, 1776
Place of birth: probably Iredell County, N.C.
Date of marriage: Dec. 25, 1794
Children: 10; 6 sons, 4 daughters

•James Knox was born in 1795; Jane Maria in 1798; Lydia Eliza in 1800; Franklin Ezekiel in 1802; Marshall Tate in 1805; John Lee in 1807; Naomi Tate in 1809; Ophelia Clarissa in 1812; William Hawkins in 1815; and Samuel Wilson in 1817.

•Polk was the fourth of five presidents who came from families of ten children.

•He was the third of eight presidents who were eldest children.

Date of death: Jan. 11, 1852

•He was the fourth of ten presidents whose mothers lived to see their sons' inauguration or oath-taking days. Mrs. Polk did not attend the ceremony.

•Polk was the first of three presidents whose mothers survived them.

Place of death: probably Columbia, Maury County, Tenn.

Age at death: 75 years, 57 days

MARRIAGE

Date of marriage: Jan. 1, 1824

•Polk was the second of two presidents who were married on New Year's Day. The other was Jefferson.

Place of marriage: Murfreesboro, Rutherford County, Tenn.

•He was the second of three presidents who were married in Tennessee.

Age at marriage: 28 years, 60 days

•He was the ninth of 27 presidents who were married in their twenties.

Years married: 25 years, 165 days

Wife's name: Sarah Childress Polk

•She was the ninth of 33 first ladies.

•She was the 12th of 40 wives of presidents.

Date of birth: Sept. 4, 1803

•She was the first of two first ladies who were born in September. The other was Margaret Taylor.

•She was the first of two wives of presidents who were born in September.

Place of birth: near Murfreesboro, Rutherford County, Tenn.

•She was the first of two first ladies who were born in Tennessee. The other was Eliza Johnson.

•She was the first of two wives of presidents

who were born in Tennessee.

Wife's mother: Elizabeth Whitsitt Childress

Wife's father: Joel Childress, merchant and farmer

Age at marriage: 20 years, 119 days

•She was the seventh of 26 first ladies who were married in their twenties.

•She was the tenth of 30 wives of presidents who were married in their twenties.

Years younger than husband: 7 years, 306 days

Children: None

•Polk was the fourth of six presidents who were childless.

Years she survived her husband: 42 years, 60 days

•She was the sixth of 21 first ladies who survived their husbands.

•She was the sixth of 23 wives of presidents who survived their husbands.

Date of death: Aug. 14, 1891

Place of death: Nashville, Tenn.

•She was the first of two first ladies who died in Tennessee. The other was Eliza Johnson.

•She was the second of three wives of presidents who died in Tennessee.

Age at death: 87 years, 344 days

•She had celebrated her 85th birthday, Sept. 4, 1888.

•She was the sixth of 16 first ladies who lived to be 70.

•She was the sixth of 17 wives of presidents who lived to be 70.

•She was the fourth of 14 first ladies who lived to be 75.

•She was the fourth of 15 wives of presidents who lived to be 75.

•She was the third of nine first ladies who lived to be 80.

•She was the third of ten wives of presidents who lived to be 80.

•She was the second of six first ladies who lived to be 85.

•She was the second of seven wives of presidents who lived to be 85.

Place of burial: Nashville, Tenn.

•She was the first of two first ladies who were buried in Tennessee. The other was Eliza Johnson.

•She was the second of three wives of presidents who were buried in Tennessee.

EARLY YEARS

1806, with family, moved to valley of Duck River, now Maury County, Tenn.

January, 1816, entered University of North Carolina as sophomore

June 4, 1818, was graduated from University of North Carolina, Chapel Hill, N.C.

•Polk was graduated with first honors in mathematics and the classics, delivered the Latin salutatory.

1819, studied law in office of Felix Grundy, Nashville, Tenn.

•He was the eighth of 26 presidents who studied law.

Sept. 20, 1819, appointed clerk of Tennessee senate, Murfreesboro, Tenn.

•He was reappointed in 1821, and also served as clerk during special sessions in 1820 and 1822. As clerk he received $6 a day during sessions of the legislature, which seldom sat for more than a month;

members of the legislature were paid $4 a day.

June 5, 1820, admitted to bar, Columbia, Tenn.

•He was the eighth of 23 presidents who were lawyers.

Sept. 4, 1820, degree of Master Mason conferred by Columbia Lodge No. 31, Columbia, Tenn.

•He was the fourth of 13 presidents who were Masons.

1823, elected to state house of representatives

•While in the legislature, he renewed his acquaintanceship with Jackson, who was a friend of his father. Polk voted for Jackson for the Senate.

Jan. 1, 1824, married Sarah Childress, Murfreesboro, Tenn.

NATIONAL PROMINENCE

August, 1825, elected to House of Representatives

•Polk was the sixth of 17 presidents who were elected to the House of Representatives.

Dec. 5, 1825, took seat in House

•He served in the House for 14 years, serving in the 19th through the 25th Congresses.

•He was the sixth of 17 presidents who served in the House of Representatives.

Nov. 5, 1827, his father died

•He was the seventh of nine presidents who owned slaves.

Dec. 3, 1827, named member of foreign affairs committee

•He opposed most of the policies of John Quincy Adams.

December, 1832, named member of ways and means committee

•In early 1833, he submitted a meaningful minority report in support of Jackson's contest with the Second Bank of the U.S.

1833, selected as chairman of ways and means committee

•As chairman, Polk was Jackson's strongest supporter.

Dec. 7, 1835, elected speaker of House

•He defeated John Bell of Tennessee, whom

he had opposed unsuccessfully for speaker in June, 1834. As speaker, Polk's down-the-line support of Jackson earned him the nickname, "Young Hickory."

•He was the only president who served as speaker.

Sept. 4, 1837, reelected speaker

•He again defeated Bell.

September, 1838, announced candidacy for governor of Tennessee

•He would have preferred to remain in the House, but the defection of Bell and others called for the strongest candidate to hold the state for the Jacksonian wing of the party.

Mar. 3, 1839, resigned from House of Representatives

•As speaker during five sessions, he had decided more questions of parliamentary law than any of his predecessors.

Apr. 11, 1839, opened his campaign for governor

•His opponent was Newton Cannon, the Democratic incumbent.

Aug. 1, 1839, elected governor of Tennessee

Oct. 14, 1839, inaugurated as governor

•He was the first of two presidents who served as governors of Tennessee. The other was Andrew Johnson.

•He was the fifth of 13 presidents who served as state governors.

1840, nominated for vice president by Tennessee legislature

Feb. 19, 1841, received one electoral vote as vice-presidential candidate

Aug. 5, 1841, defeated for reelection as governor

•His defeat was a foregone conclusion due to the Whig sweep in 1840. However, he lost to James C. Jones by only about three thousand votes.

1843, unsuccessful candidate for governor

•He was defeated again by Jones, whose majority rose to nearly four thousand.

Apr. 22, 1844, declared in favor of annexation of Texas

•As a prospective candidate for vice president, he was asked by a committee of citizens of Cincinnati, Ohio, for his sentiments on the subject of annexation. His unequivocal reply won him much support.

May 29, 1844, nominated for president, Democratic national convention, Baltimore, Md.

•Martin Van Buren had received 146 of the 266 votes on the first ballot but failed to get the two-thirds necessary for nomination; Lewis Cass of Michigan received strong support. Polk received no votes until the eighth ballot and was nominated unanimously on the ninth. For this reason, Polk is considered by some historians as the first "dark horse" candidate for president.

Note: A dark horse is a candidate unexpectedly nominated by his party for high office. This usually occurs when there is a deadlock between two or more formidable candidates.

•In his letter of acceptance, Polk declared that, if elected, he would discharge "the high and solemn duties of the office with the settled purpose of not being a candidate for reelection."

Nov. 12, 1844, election day

• *See* Election of 1844, below.

Dec. 4, 1844, presidential electors cast ballots

•He received 170 of the 275 electoral votes from the 26 states.

• *See* Election of 1844, below.

Feb. 12, 1845, electoral vote tabulated by Congress

•Polk and Dallas were officially declared elected.

ELECTION OF 1844

Liberty (abolitionist) party convened, Aug. 30, 1843, at Buffalo, N.Y., nominated James Gillespie Birney of Michigan for president, Thomas Morris of Ohio for vice president.

•This was the second Liberty national convention. It was the first of two major party conventions in Buffalo.

Whig party, convened, May 1, 1844, at Baltimore, Md., nominated Henry Clay of Kentucky for president, Theodore Frelinghuysen of New Jersey for vice president.

•This was the second Whig national convention. It was the first Whig convention in Baltimore; it was the sixth major party convention in Baltimore.

Democratic party, convened, May 27, at Baltimore, Md., nominated James Knox Polk of Tennessee for president, Silas Wright of New York for vice president.

•Wright declined; the vice presidential nomination went to George Mifflin Dallas of Pennsylvania.

•This was the fourth Democratic national convention. It was the fourth Democratic convention in Baltimore; it was the seventh major party convention in Baltimore.

Tyler Democrats, convened, May 27, at Baltimore, Md., nominated John Tyler of Virginia for president.

•Tyler withdrew, Aug. 20.

Election day, Tuesday, Nov. 12, 1844 (in most states)

Popular vote: 2,698,605

  Polk, 1,337,243

  Clay, 1,299,062

  Birney, 62,300

•Polk was the second of 15 presidents who were elected without receiving a majority of the popular vote.

Electoral vote: 275, 26 states

  • Polk, 170, 15 states

  (Alabama, 9; Arkansas, 3; Georgia, 10; Illinois, 9; Indiana, 12; Louisiana, 6; Maine, 9; Michigan, 5; Mississippi, 6; Missouri, 7; New Hampshire, 6; New York, 36; Pennsylvania, 26; South Carolina, 9; Virginia, 17)

  • Clay, 105, 11 states

  (Connecticut, 6; Delaware, 3; Kentucky, 12; Maryland, 8; Massachusetts, 12; New Jersey, 7; North Carolina, 11; Ohio, 23; Rhode Island, 4; Tennessee, 13; Vermont, 6)

THE PRESIDENT (11th)

Term of office: Mar. 4, 1845, to Mar. 4, 1849 (4 years)
•Polk was the sixth of 19 presidents who served one term or less than one term.
•He was the fourth of eight presidents in succession who served one term or less than one term.
•He was the fourth of ten presidents who served for four years.
State represented: Tennessee
•He was the second of three presidents who represented Tennessee.
•He was the third of 15 presidents who represented states that were not their native states.
Political party: Democratic

•He was the third of 12 presidents who were Democrats.
Congresses: 29th, 30th
Administration: 15th
Age at inauguration: 49 years, 122 days
•He was the fifth of 21 presidents who were younger than their vice presidents. Polk was three years, 115 days younger than Dallas.
Inauguration day: Thursday, Mar. 4, 1845
•Polk took the oath of office, administered by Chief Justice Roger B. Taney, on the east portico of the Capitol.
•This was the third of seven inaugurations at which Taney officiated.

THE 15th ADMINISTRATION

1845

Mar. 6, appointed his only secretary of state, James Buchanan; his only secretary of treasury, Robert J. Walker; his only secretary of war, William L. Marcy; his first attorney general, John Y. Mason; his first secretary of navy, George Bancroft; and his only postmaster general, Cave Johnson
•Walker took office, Mar. 8; Buchanan, Mar. 10; Bancroft, Mar. 11.
Mar. 28, Mexico broke off diplomatic relations with U.S.
•The Mexican minister had formally protested the annexation of Texas, Mar. 6.
June 15, ordered General Zachary Taylor to occupy point "on or near the Rio Grande"
•Taylor was instructed to limit action to the defense of Texas unless war was declared by Mexico.
•The U.S. joint resolution for annexation was approved by the Texas congress, June 23. This ordinance was accepted by the people of the republic in convention at Austin, July 4.
Aug. 30, instructed Buchanan to withdraw Oregon offer
•Great Britain had been asked to accept the 49th parallel—without free navigation of the Columbia River—as the boundary line of Oregon, July 12. The British refused, July 29.
Sept. 10, Associate Justice Story died
Sept. 16, appointed John Slidell as secret

agent to Mexico
•Informed in August that the Mexican government was willing to resume diplomatic relations, Polk appointed Slidell as his representative. Slidell was instructed to offer to buy Upper California and New Mexico if a permanent boundary line of the Rio Grande from its mouth to the 32nd parallel and west to the Pacific could be agreed upon.
Sept. 20, appointed Levi Woodbury as associate justice.
•Woodbury, who was confirmed by the Senate, Jan. 3, 1846, was the first of Polk's three appointments to the Supreme Court.
Oct. 17, informed that Mexico would receive American "commissioner"
•He dispatched Slidell with amended instructions, Nov. 10. Slidell, accredited as envoy extraordinary and minister plenipotentiary, was authorized to purchase California for $25,000,000 and New Mexico for $5,000,000 if the Rio Grande boundary was accepted. Slidell arrived in Mexico City, Dec. 6. President Jose Joaquin Herrera, in the face of hostile public opinion, refused to see Slidell, Dec. 16.
Dec. 1, first session of 29th Congress
•The administration controlled both the Senate and the House of Representatives. The Democrats gained six Senate seats and one House seat. The Senate (56 members) consisted of 31 Democrats and 25 Whigs. The House (226 members) consisted of 143

Democrats, 77 Whigs, and six others.

Dec. 2, sent his first State of the Union message to Congress

• He claimed Oregon for the U.S.

• Most historians claim that his strong position was echoed in the rallying cry, "Fifty-four Forty or Fight!" This slogan has long been accepted as having become popular during the presidential campaign of 1844, although there is no evidence to support this contention. Actually, the most popular expansionist phrase of the day, which, of course, meant the same thing, was "The Whole of Oregon or None!"

• "Fifty-four Forty or Fight!" actually came into general usage in 1846. The original form, it seems, was "Phyfty Phour Phorty or Phyght!" (or "Phifty Phour Phorty or Phight!"), which was some unknown humorist's interpretation of "the four P's," a popular abbreviation of "The Political Principles of President Polk."

Dec. 9, sent special message to Congress in which he announced Texas had accepted terms of admission

Dec. 23, appointed George W. Woodward as associate justice

• Woodward, the second of Polk's three appointments to the Supreme Court, was rejected by the Senate, Jan. 22, 1846.

• Polk was the sixth of 15 presidents who nominated justices not confirmed by the Senate.

• Woodward was the ninth of 25 men nominated to the Supreme Court who were not confirmed by the Senate.

Dec. 27, received British request that offer of 49th parallel as boundary of Oregon be renewed, matter submitted to arbitration

• He refused to renew the proposal.

Dec. 29, Texas admitted as 28th state

• Texas was the first of three states admitted during his term of office.

1846

Jan. 13, on his order, Secretary of War Marcy instructed General Taylor to occupy positions on or near left bank of Rio Grande

• This meant invasion of Mexican territory.

Apr. 21, informed cabinet he would recommend Congress adopt energetic measures against Mexico

Apr. 25, first Mexican-U.S. military clash

• An American reconnaisance party was attacked by a superior Mexican unit. A total of 11 were killed, five wounded, and the other 47 Americans were captured.

Apr. 27, signed joint resolution authorizing him to give notice to Great Britain for termination of joint occupation of Oregon

May 8–9, battles of Palo Alto and Resaca de la Palma

• The Mexicans were defeated decisively in both encounters.

May 11, submitted war message to Congress

• He declared that war existed by virtue of Mexico's presence on American soil.

• This was the third of seven war messages.

May 13, war declared

• He was authorized to call for 50,000 volunteers and voted a $10,000,000 war appropriation. This measure was opposed by 67 Whigs, including Garrett Davis of Kentucky, who said, "It is our own President who began this war."

May 14, formulated military campaign plan in conference with Secretary of War Marcy and General Winfield Scott

May 21, served notice on Great Britain that joint occupation of Oregon was to be terminated

• The Anglo-American agreement required one year's notice of termination by either country.

June 10, laid proposal of Great Britain for settlement of Oregon boundary before Senate

• His submission of the proposed treaty to the Senate for its advice and consent set a precedent. The Senate advised acceptance, June 12, and the treaty was ratified, June 15.

July 9, signed act retroceding 36 square miles of District of Columbia to Virginia

July 30, signed tariff of 1846 act

Aug. 3, vetoed rivers and harbors bill

• This was the first of his three vetoes.

Aug. 3, appointed Robert C. Grier as associate justice

• Grier, who was confirmed by the Senate, Aug. 4, was the last of Polk's three appointments to the Supreme Court.

Aug. 8, vetoed French spoliation claims bill

• This was the second of his three vetoes.

Aug. 10, first session of 29th Congress adjourned

Sept. 9, accepted resignations of Attorney General Mason and Secretary of Navy Bancroft
• Polk appointed Bancroft minister to Great Britain. During Bancroft's 18 months in the cabinet, the secretary had established the U.S. Naval Academy as the Naval School in Annapolis, Md., and furthered the progress of the Naval Observatory.
• Bancroft was the author of the monumental *A History of the United States*, published in ten volumes, 1834–1874.
Sept. 9, appointed his second secretary of navy, John Y. Mason
• Mason took office, Sept. 10.
Sept. 25, surrender of Monterey
Oct. 17, appointed his second attorney general, Nathan Clifford
Dec. 7, second session of 29th Congress
Dec. 8, sent his second State of the Union message to Congress
Dec. 28, Iowa admitted as 29th state
• Iowa was the second of three states admitted during his term of office.

1847

Feb. 23, Battle of Buena Vista
• Zachary Taylor's victory ended the war in northern Mexico.
Mar. 3, second session of 29th Congress adjourned
Mar. 29, Veracruz occupied
Apr. 15, gave instructions to peace commissioner to Mexico, Nicholas P. Trist
• Trist, chief clerk of the state department, met with a Mexican commission headed by former President Herrera, Aug. 27–Sept. 6. Nothing of consequence resulted from the negotiations.
June–July, toured eastern states
• Polk's trip took him as far as Augusta, Me. He returned to Washington, July 7.
Sept. 8, Battle of Molino del Rey
Sept. 13, Battle of Chapultepec
Sept. 14, Mexico City captured
Dec. 6, first session of 30th Congress
• The administration maintained control of the Senate but lost control of the House of Representatives. The Democrats gained five Senate seats; the Whigs gained 38 House seats. The Senate (58 members) consisted of 36 Democrats, 21 Whigs, and one other. The House (227 members) consisted

of 115 Whigs, 108 Democrats, and four others.
Dec. 7, sent his third State of the Union message to Congress
Dec. 15, vetoed Wisconsin Territory internal improvements bill
• This bill had been passed during the second session of the 29th Congress.
• This was the last of his three vetoes, his only pocket veto.
• He was the fifth of 11 presidents who never had a veto overridden.

1848

Feb. 19, received treaty ending war with Mexico
• The treaty had been signed at Guadalupe Hidalgo, near Mexico City, Feb. 2.
Feb. 23, submitted treaty to Senate
• The treaty was ratified by the Senate, Mar. 10; by the Mexican congress, May 25; and ratifications were exchanged, May 30.
Mar. 17, accepted resignation of Attorney General Clifford
• He appointed Clifford as U.S. commissioner to Mexico to arrange terms for the cession of California to the U.S.
May 19, wrote letter in which he reiterated his decision not to seek reelection
May 29, sent special message to Congress urging immediate action on Oregon
May 29, Wisconsin admitted as 30th state
• Wisconsin was the last of three states admitted during his term of office.
• Madison, the capital of Wisconsin, was the third of four state capitals named for presidents. It had been the capital of the Wisconsin Territory since 1836.
June 21, appointed his third attorney general, Isaac Toucey
• This was the last of Polk's nine cabinet appointments.
July 4, proclaimed Mexican treaty in effect
July 4, attended laying of cornerstone, Washington Monument
Aug. 14, signed act establishing Territory of Oregon
Aug. 14, first session of 30th Congress adjourned
Nov. 7, election day
• *See* Election of 1848, page 144.
Dec. 4, second session of 30th Congress

Dec. 5, sent his fourth and last State of the Union message to Congress
•This message included confirmation of the discovery of gold in California.

Note: Gas lighting was installed in the White House in 1848.

1849

Jan. 1, with Mrs. Polk, celebrated silver wedding anniversary, White House
•He was the first of five presidents who celebrated their 25th anniversaries while resi-

dents of the White House.
Mar. 3, signed act establishing Territory of Minnesota
Mar. 3, signed act creating department of interior
•Originally named the home department, the department included the office of the census, the office of Indian affairs, and the general land office.
Mar. 3, second session of 30th Congress adjourned

Note: He was the first of three presidents who did not seek renomination after their first terms.

THE FORMER PRESIDENT

Mar. 4, 1849, attended inauguration of Zachary Taylor
•Polk's age upon leaving office was 53 years, 122 days.
May 4, 1849, departed from Washington
•He toured the South en route to his new home in Nashville.
•He traveled down the Atlantic seaboard and across the Gulf states, then up the Mississippi River. He attended numerous testimonial dinners, parades, and other public festivities in his honor, all of which exhausted him. While aboard a steamer on the Mississippi, he became dangerously ill. A doctor was brought aboard who diagnosed his ailment as a mild case of cholera, but it more likely was a recurrence of the chronic diarrhea that had afflicted him throughout his term of office. He rallied in time to take part in the homecoming ceremonies at Nashville.
•Shortly before he left the White House, he had sold his home in Columbia, Tenn., and bought the Nashville residence of the late Senator Felix Grundy. After a short visit at his mother's home in Columbia, he spent most of his time on the reconstruction of Polk Place, as he called his new home. He enlarged and completely redecorated the house and landscaped the grounds, which covered a full city block.
•The Polk ancestral home in Columbia contains many of the furnishings he used in the White House. It is maintained by the Polk Memorial Association, the Polk Memorial Auxiliary, and a yearly appropriation made by the state of Tennessee. It is

open to the public daily except on Christmas, 9 A.M. to 5 P.M., weekdays, and 1 to 5 P.M., Sundays. Admission: $1.

DEATH

Date of death, June 15, 1849
Place of death: Nashville, Tenn.
•Polk was the second of three presidents who died in Tennessee.
Age at death: 53 years, 225 days
•He lived 103 days after the completion of his term.
•He was the president who lived the shortest period of time after completion of his term.
Cause of death: Diarrhea
Place of burial: Nashville, Tenn.
•He was the second of three presidents who were buried in Tennessee.

THE VICE PRESIDENT (11th)

Full name: George Mifflin Dallas
Date of birth: July 10, 1792
Place of birth: Philadelphia, Pa.
•He was the only vice president who was born in Pennsylvania.
Religious denomination: Presbyterian
•He was the fifth of 11 vice presidents who were Presbyterians.
College: College of New Jersey, now Princeton University, Princeton, N.J.
Date of graduation: 1810
Occupation: Lawyer

•He was admitted to the Pennsylvania bar, 1813; served as secretary to Albert Gallatin during Gallatin's mission to Russia, 1813; mayor of Philadelphia, 1828; U.S. district attorney for eastern Pennsylvania, 1829–1831; member of Senate, 1831–1833; attorney general of Pennsylvania, 1833–1835; minister to Russia, appointed by President Van Buren, 1837–1839; practiced law, 1839–1844.
•He was the sixth of 17 vice presidents who served in the Senate before their terms of office.

Term of office: Mar. 4, 1845, to Mar. 4, 1849 (4 years)
•He was the fifth of 17 vice presidents who served four-year terms.
•Polk and Dallas were the 13th of 41 president-vice president teams.

Age at inauguration: 52 years, 237 days
State represented: Pennsylvania
•He was the only vice president who represented Pennsylvania.
Political party: Democratic
•He was the fourth of 16 vice presidents who were Democrats.
Occupation after term: Diplomat
•He was minister to Great Britain, appointed by President Pierce and reappointed by President Buchanan, 1856–1861. While minister he conducted negotiations that led to the Dallas-Clarendon Convention, which set the basis for the settlement of Central American difficulties.
Date of death: Dec. 31, 1864
Place of death: Philadelphia, Pa.
•He was the only vice president who died in Pennsylvania.

Age at death: 72 years, 174 days
Place of burial: Philadelphia, Pa.
•He was the only vice president who was buried in Pennsylvania.

THE CABINET

State: James Buchanan of Pennsylvania, Mar. 10, 1845, to Mar. 7, 1849
Treasury: Robert John Walker of Mississippi, Mar. 8, 1845, to Mar. 5, 1849
War: William Learned Marcy of New York, Mar. 6, 1845, to Mar. 4, 1849
Attorney General: John Young Mason of Virginia, Mar. 6, 1845, to Sept. 9, 1846
•Nathan Clifford of Maine, Oct. 17, 1846, to Mar. 17, 1848
•Isaac Toucey of Connecticut, June 21, 1848, to Mar. 3, 1849
Navy: George Bancroft of Massachusetts, Mar. 11, 1845, to Sept. 9, 1846
•John Young Mason of Virginia, Sept. 10, 1846, to Mar. 7, 1849
Postmaster General: Cave Johnson of Tennessee, Mar. 6, 1845, to Mar. 5, 1849

THE SUPREME COURT

Associate Justices: Levi Woodbury of New Hampshire, appointed, Sept. 20, 1845; confirmed, Jan. 3, 1846
•George Washington Woodward of Pennsylvania, appointed, Dec. 23, 1845; rejected by Senate, Jan. 22, 1846
•Robert Cooper Grier of Pennsylvania, appointed, Aug. 3, 1846; confirmed, Aug. 4, 1846

Twelfth President

ZACHARY TAYLOR

Full name: Zachary Taylor
- He was the ninth of 17 presidents who did not have middle initials or middle names.

Date of birth: Nov. 24, 1784
- He was the second of five presidents who were born in November.

Place of birth: Montebello, Orange County, Va.
- He was the seventh of eight presidents who were born in Virginia.
- He was the second of seven presidents who were born in log cabins.

Family lineage: English
- He was the seventh of 12 presidents who were of English ancestry.
- He and James Madison were second cousins.

Religious denomination: Episcopalian
- He was the sixth of nine presidents who were Episcopalians.

College: None
- He was the fourth of nine presidents who did not attend college.
- He was the eighth of 15 presidents who were not graduated from college.

PARENTS AND SIBLINGS

Father's name: Richard Taylor
Date of birth: Apr. 3, 1744
Place of birth: Orange County, Va.
Occupations: Farmer, soldier
Date of death: Jan. 19, 1829
Place of death: near Lexington, Ky.
Age at death: 84 years, 291 days

Mother's name: Sarah Dabney Strother Taylor
Date of birth: Dec. 14, 1760
Place of birth: probably Orange County, Va.
Date of marriage: Aug. 20, 1779
Children: 9; 6 sons, 3 daughters
- Hancock was born in 1781; William Dabney Strother in 1782; Zachary in 1784; a son in 17—; George in 1790; Elizabeth Lee in 1792; Joseph Pannill in 1796; Sarah Bailey in 1799; and Emily Richard in 1801. The son whose birthdate is unknown was named either Strother or Richard; he died in infancy.
- Taylor was the first of seven presidents

140

who came from families of nine children.
•He was the third of five presidents who
were third children.
Date of death: Dec. 13, 1822
Place of death: *Unknown*
Age at death: 61 years, 364 days

MARRIAGE

Date of marriage: June 21, 1810
Place of marriage: near Louisville, Ky.
•Taylor was the only president who was
married in Kentucky.
Age at marriage: 25 years, 209 days
•He was the tenth of 27 presidents who
were married in their twenties.
Years married: 40 years, 18 days

Wife's name: Margaret Mackall Smith Tay-
lor
•She was the tenth of 33 first ladies.
•She was the 13th of 40 wives of presidents.
Date of birth: Sept. 21, 1788
•She was the second of two first ladies who
were born in September. The other was
Sarah Polk.
•She was the second of two wives of presi-
dents who were born in September.
Place of birth: Calvert County, Md.
•She was the only first lady or wife of a presi-
dent who was born in Maryland.
Wife's mother: Ann Mackall Smith
Wife's father: Walter Smith, planter
Age at marriage: 21 years, 273 days

•She was the eighth of 26 first ladies who
were married in their twenties.
•She was the 11th of 30 wives of presidents
who were married in their twenties.
Years younger than husband: 3 years, 302
days
Children: 6; 5 daughters, 1 son
•Ann Mackall was born on Apr. 9, 1811;
Sarah Knox on Mar. 6, 1814; Octavia Pannill on Aug. 16, 1816; Margaret Smith on
July 27, 1819; Mary Elizabeth on Apr. 20,
1824; and Richard on Jan. 27, 1826. Oc-
tavia Pannill and Margaret Smith died in
infancy.
•Taylor was the second of four presidents
who had six children.
•He was the seventh of 19 presidents who
had both male and female children.
•He was the eighth of 30 presidents who
had children.
Years she survived her husband: 2 years, 40
days
•She was the seventh of 21 first ladies who
survived their husbands.
•She was the seventh of 23 wives of presi-
dents who survived their husbands.
Date of death: Aug. 18, 1852
Place of death: near Pascagoula, Miss.
•She was the only first lady or wife of a presi-
dent who died in Mississippi.
Age at death: 63 years, 332 days
Place of burial: Louisville, Ky.
•She was the only first lady or wife of a presi-
dent who was buried in Kentucky.

EARLY YEARS

1785, with family, moved to Beargrass
Creek, near Louisville, Ky.
•Taylor's boyhood home, "Springfield,"
5608 Apache Road, Louisville, is privately
owned by Mr. and Mrs. Paul M. Davis. It is
not open to the public. "Springfield" was
designated a National Historic Landmark
in 1962.
May 3, 1808, commissioned first lieutenant,
Seventh Infantry Regiment, U.S. Army
•He was the second of four presidents who
were professional soldiers.
May, 1809, assumed temporary command
of Fort Pickering, now Memphis, Tenn.
June 21, 1810, married Margaret Mackall
Smith, near Louisville, Ky.
November, 1810, promoted to captain

Apr. 9, 1811, his first daughter born
•The girl was named Ann Mackall Taylor.
July 1, 1811, reorganized garrison at Fort
Knox, Vincennes, Indian Territory
•The garrison had become demoralized
when a personal feud led to the shooting of
an officer by the former commandant.
June 18, 1812, war declared
•He was the last of four presidents who
served in the War of 1812.
•He was the sixth of 21 presidents who
served in the military during wartime.
Sept. 4, 1812, successfully defended Fort
Harrison above Vincennes from Indian at-
tack
Oct. 31, 1812, promoted to brevet major for
defense of Fort Harrison

•This was the first brevetcy of any rank awarded by the U.S. Army.

1812–1815, participated in campaigns against British and Indians along frontier from Indiana to Missouri

Mar. 6, 1814, his second daughter born

•The girl was named Sarah Knox Taylor.

January, 1815, notified of promotion to major

•His commission was dated, May 5, 1814.

June 15, 1815, honorably discharged from army

•By an act of Congress, Mar. 3, the army was reduced to ten thousand men. When he was reduced in rank to captain, he resigned and returned to Kentucky.

May 17, 1816, recommissioned as major, U.S. Army

•He was ordered to report to Fort Howard, then under construction at Green Bay, Michigan Territory, now Wisconsin.

Aug. 16, 1816, his third daughter born

•The girl was named Octavia Pannill Taylor.

August or September, 1818, returned to Louisville

•He remained in Kentucky for more than a year, where he supervised the recruiting service.

Apr. 20, 1819, promoted to lieutenant colonel

June 30, 1819, breakfasted with President Monroe and General Jackson, Frankfort, Ky.

July 27, 1819, his fourth daughter born

•The girl was named Margaret Smith Taylor.

February, 1820, moved his family to Louisiana

•He established a home for his family at Bayou Sara before he joined his regiment in Mississippi. The family was stricken with a virulent fever that summer; his two youngest daughters died—Octavia Pannill, July 8, and Margaret Smith, Oct. 22.

November, 1821, established Fort Selden in northwest Louisiana

March, 1822, established Cantonment Jesup in western Louisiana

•Later Fort Jesup, the cantonment was near the Sabine River, then considered the boundary between the U.S. and Spanish Texas.

November, 1822, assigned to command of Cantonment Robertson, near Baton Rouge, La.

Dec. 13, 1822, his mother died

Jan. 27, 1823, purchased three-hundred-acre plantation, Feliciana Parish, La.

•He moved his slaves from Kentucky to Louisiana.

•He was the eighth of nine presidents who owned slaves.

Apr. 20, 1824, his fifth daughter born

•The girl was named Mary Elizabeth Taylor.

Jan. 27, 1826, his only son born

•The boy was named Richard Taylor.

Oct. 3, 1826, reported to Washington, D.C.

•He was appointed a member of the board of officers convened to study the future operations of the militia. He returned to duty with the First Infantry at New Orleans, February, 1827.

May 1, 1828, assigned to command of Fort Snelling, advance post in Northwest Territory, now Minnesota

Jan. 19, 1829, his father died

June, 1829, transferred to Fort Crawford, Prairie du Chien, Michigan Territory, now Wisconsin

•He supervised construction of a new fort.

Mar. 6, 1831, purchased 137 acres, Wilkinson County, Miss.

Apr. 5, 1832, promoted to colonel

May–August, 1832, Black Hawk War

•He served under General Henry Atkinson until after the decisive Battle of the Bad Axe, Aug. 3, when Taylor returned to Fort Crawford. Shortly thereafter, Chief Black Hawk, who had surrendered to a band of Winnebago Indians, was received as a prisoner at the fort.

•He was the first of two presidents who served in the Black Hawk War. The other was Lincoln.

Aug. 5, 1832, assumed command of Fort Crawford

•He served as commanding officer until Nov. 16, 1836.

June 17, 1835, his daughter, Sarah Knox Taylor, married Jefferson Davis, near Lexington, Ky.

•Taylor and his wife opposed the marriage. The young couple had met at Fort Crawford in 1833. Davis, a graduate of West Point, had served as a lieutenant on the staff of his future father-in-law. Stricken with malaria, Sarah died less than three months after her marriage, Sept. 15.

November, 1836, assumed command of Jefferson Barracks, Mo.

May–June, 1837, returned to Fort Crawford
•His brief assignment at Fort Crawford was because of Indian scares.
November, 1837, transferred to Florida during Second Seminole War
Dec. 25, 1837, defeated Seminoles near Lake Okeechobee, Fla.
1838, promoted to brevet brigadier general for defeat of Seminoles
•He was the fourth of 12 presidents who were generals.
May 15,1838, appointed commanding officer of all Florida forces
•He held this command until May 6, 1840.

November, 1838, purchased 163 acres, West Feliciana Parish, La.
May–November, 1840, toured most of eastern U.S.
1841, assumed command of second department of western division of army, Fort Smith, Ark.
December, 1841, sold his Mississippi and Louisiana properties
Apr. 21, 1842, purchased Cypress Grove plantation, Jefferson County, La.
June 17, 1844, assumed command of first department of western division of army, Fort Jesup, La.

NATIONAL PROMINENCE

July 31, 1845, arrived at Corpus Christi, Tex.
•Taylor had been ordered, June 15, to occupy a point "on or near the Rio Grande" and was instructed to limit action to the defense of Texas unless war was declared by Mexico.
Mar. 8, 1846, marched at head of three thousand troops from Corpus Christi
•He had been ordered, Jan. 13, to cross the Rio Grande, but the date of this move was left to his discretion because of weather and terrain.
May 8–9, 1846, battles of Palo Alto and Resaca de la Palma
•He defeated the Mexicans in both encounters.
May 13, 1846, war declared
•He was the first of three presidents who served in the Mexican War.
•He was the only president who served in the military during three wars—the War of 1812, the Black Hawk War, and the Mexican War.
May 18, 1846, occupied Matamoros
June 29, 1846, promoted to major general
•He had been promoted to brevet major general after the battles of Palo Alto and Resaca de la Palma.
Sept. 21–24, 1846, Battle of Monterey
•The Mexicans under General Pedro de Ampudia surrendered, Sept. 25, on condition that they be permitted to retreat with some weapons and not be followed for eight weeks. Taylor's decision to accept the two-month armistice brought him much criticism from Washington.
November, 1846, Polk ordered General

Winfield Scott to Mexico
•Taylor was ordered to turn over four-fifths of his troops and materiel of war to Scott, who was to move against Veracruz and later Mexico City. His small force was to remain on the defensive.
Jan. 22, 1847, his letter to General Edmund P. Gaines published, New York *Morning Express*
•Taylor defended his agreement to the eight-week armistice and criticized the Polk administration.
Feb. 23, 1847, Battle of Buena Vista
•He disobeyed orders to remain on the defensive and took a position at Buena Vista, where he was attacked by 20,000 troops commanded by General Antonio Lopez de Santa Anna. The U.S. forces numbered 5,-000, but only three batteries of artillery, a squadron of dragoons, a mounted company of Texans, and a regiment of Mississippi riflemen had previously been under fire. The superiority of his artillery won the day. At the cost of about 300 killed and 450 wounded, the Americans inflicted 1,800 casualties, including about 500 killed. The Mexicans broke and ran.
March–November, 1847, commanded U.S. forces, northern Mexico
Nov. 8, 1847, departed from Monterey
•He left Mexico for the U.S., Nov. 26.
Nov. 30, 1847, arrived in New Orleans
Dec. 3, 1847, hailed as national hero during elaborate public tribute, New Orleans
Dec. 5, 1847, retired to Baton Rouge
June 7, 1848, nominated for president, Whig national convention, Philadelphia, Pa.

Nov. 7, 1848, election day
• *See* Election of 1848, below.
Dec. 6, 1848, presidential electors cast ballots
• He received 163 of the 290 electoral votes from the 30 states.
• *See* Election of 1848, below.
Feb. 14, 1849, electoral vote tabulated by Congress
• Taylor and Fillmore were officially declared elected.

ELECTION OF 1848

Democratic party, convened, May 22, at Baltimore, Md., nominated Lewis Cass of Michigan for president, William Orlando Butler of Kentucky for vice president.
• This was the fifth Democratic national convention. It was the fifth Democratic convention in Baltimore; it was the eighth major party convention in Baltimore.
Whig party, convened, June 7, at Philadelphia, Pa., nominated Zachary Taylor of Louisiana for president, Millard Fillmore of New York for vice president.
• This was the third Whig convention. It was the first of ten major party conventions in Philadelphia.
Barnburners (antiadministration Democratic faction), convened, June 22, at Utica, N.Y., nominated Martin Van Buren of New York for president, Henry Dodge of Wisconsin for vice president.
Free-Soil (antiadministration Democrats, Liberty party members and antislavery

Whigs) party, convened, Aug. 9, at Buffalo, N.Y., nominated Martin Van Buren of New York for president, Charles Francis Adams of Massachusetts for vice president. John Parker Hale of New Hampshire, who had been nominated for president by the Liberty party in November, 1847, withdrew in favor of Van Buren.
• This was the second and last major party convention in Buffalo.
Election day, Tuesday, Nov. 7, 1848
• This was the first national election held on the same day in all states, in accordance with the act of Jan. 23, 1845.
Popular vote: 2,871,906
    Taylor, 1,360,099
    Cass, 1,220,544
    Van Buren, 291,263
• Taylor was the third of 15 presidents who were elected without receiving a majority of the popular vote.
Electoral vote: 290, 30 states
    • Taylor, 163, 15 states
       (Connecticut, 6; Delaware, 3; Florida, 3; Georgia, 10; Kentucky, 12; Louisiana, 6; Maryland, 8; Massachusetts, 12; New Jersey, 7; New York, 36; North Carolina, 11; Pennsylvania, 26; Rhode Island, 4; Tennessee, 13; Vermont, 6)
    • Cass, 127, 15 states
       (Alabama, 9; Arkansas, 3; Illinois, 9; Indiana, 12; Iowa, 4; Maine, 9; Michigan, 5; Mississippi, 6; Missouri, 7; New Hampshire, 6; Ohio, 23; South Carolina, 9; Texas, 4; Virginia, 17; Wisconsin, 4)

THE PRESIDENT (12th)

Term of office: Mar. 5, 1849, to July 9, 1850 (1 year, 126 days)
• Taylor was the seventh of 19 presidents who served one term or less than one term.
• He was the fifth of eight presidents in succession who served one term or less than one term.
• He was the third of nine presidents who served less than one term.
State represented: Louisiana
• He was the only president who represented Louisiana.
• He was the fourth of 15 presidents who represented states that were not their native states.

Political party: Whig
• He was the third of four presidents who were Whigs.
Congress: 31st
Administration: 16th
Age at inauguration: 64 years, 101 days
Inauguration day, Monday, Mar. 5, 1849
• Taylor took the oath of office, administered by Chief Justice Roger B. Taney, on the east portico of the Capitol.
• This was the fourth of seven inaugurations at which Taney officiated.
• He was the second of five presidents who postponed their oath-taking ceremonies to Monday because Mar. 4 fell on Sunday.

THE 16th ADMINISTRATION

1849

Mar. 7, appointed his only secretary of state, John M. Clayton
•Clayton took office, Mar. 8.
Mar. 8, appointed his only secretary of treasury, William M. Meredith; his only secretary of war, George W. Crawford; his only attorney general, Reverdy Johnson; his only secretary of navy, William B. Preston; his only postmaster general, Jacob Collamer; and his only secretary of interior, Thomas Ewing
•Ewing was the first secretary of interior.
•Taylor was the second of four presidents who made no changes in their cabinets.
Aug. 11, issued proclamation warning citizens against participation in armed expeditions being fitted out against Cuba
•His intervention brought about the collapse of the filibustering expedition led by General Narciso Lopez, a Venezuelan adventurer who was supported by southern annexationists.
Dec. 3, first session of 31st Congress
•The administration did not control either the Senate or the House of Representatives. The Whigs gained four Senate and six House seats. The Senate (62 members) consisted of 35 Democrats, 25 Whigs, and two Free-Soilers. The House (230 members) consisted of 112 Democrats, 109 Whigs, and nine Free-Soilers.
•This was the first of two administrations that did not control Congress upon taking office. The other was the Nixon administration of 1969.
Dec. 4, sent his only State of the Union message to Congress
•He recommended the admission of California and advised Congress to "abstain from the introduction of those exciting topics of sectional character which have hitherto produced painful apprehensions in the public mind."

1850

Apr. 19, Clayton-Bulwer Treaty ratified
•This Anglo-American agreement guaranteed neutrality of an isthmian canal. Both countries pledged not to colonize or otherwise acquire Central American territory.

The treaty, opposed by expansionists, was abrogated by the Hay-Pauncefote Treaty of 1901.
May 19, second Lopez expedition against Cuba failed

Note: Taylor was the fifth of seven presidents who did not exercise the veto.

DEATH

Date of death: July 9, 1850
•Taylor was the second of five presidents who died before they completed their first terms.
•He was the second of eight presidents who died in office.
Place of death: Washington, D.C.
•He was the second of two presidents who died in the White House. The other was William Henry Harrison.
•He was the third of seven presidents who died in Washington.
•He was the second of six presidents who lay in state at the White House.
Age at death: 65 years, 227 days
Cause of death: Coronary thrombosis
•He was the second of four presidents who died of natural causes in office.
Place of burial: Louisville, Ky.
•He was the only president who was buried in Kentucky.

THE VICE PRESIDENT (12th)

Full name: Millard Fillmore
• *See also* pages 147–154.
•He was the last vice president who was born in the eighteenth century.
•He was the fourth of eight vice presidents who were born in New York.
•He was the second of three vice presidents who were Unitarians.
•He was the seventh of 21 vice presidents who served in the House of Representatives before their terms of office.
•He was the third of 14 vice presidents who served less than one term.
•Taylor and Fillmore were the 14th of 41 president-vice president teams.
•Fillmore was the fifth of ten vice presidents who represented New York.

• He was the second of two vice presidents who were Whigs. The other was Tyler.
• He was the fourth of nine vice presidents who died in New York.
• He was the fourth of nine vice presidents who were buried in New York.

THE CABINET

State: John Middleton Clayton of Delaware, Mar. 8, 1849, to July 22, 1850
Treasury: William Morris Meredith of Pennsylvania, Mar. 8, 1849, to July 22, 1850
War: George Walker Crawford of Georgia, Mar. 8, 1849, to July 23, 1850
Attorney General: Reverdy Johnson of Maryland, Mar. 8, 1849, to July 22, 1850
Navy: William Ballard Preston of Virginia, Mar. 8, 1849, to July 22, 1850
Postmaster General: Jacob Collamer of Vermont, Mar. 8, 1849, to July 22, 1850
Interior: Thomas Ewing of Ohio, Mar. 8, 1849, to July 22, 1850

THE SUPREME COURT

• Taylor was the second of two presidents who did not make any appointments to the Court. The other was William Henry Harrison.
• He was the second of three presidents who did not name a member of the Court.

Thirteenth President

MILLARD FILLMORE

Full name: Millard Fillmore
•He was the tenth of 17 presidents who did not have middle initials or middle names.
Date of birth: Jan. 7, 1800
•He was the first of four presidents who were born in January.
•He was the last president who was born in the eighteenth century.
Place of birth: Locke, now Summerhill, Cayuga County, N.Y.
•He was the second of four presidents who were born in New York.
•He was the third of seven presidents who were born in log cabins.
Family lineage: English
•He was the eighth of 12 presidents who were of English ancestry.
Religious denomination: Unitarian
•He was the third of four presidents who were Unitarians.
College: None
•He was the fifth of nine presidents who did not attend college.
•He was the ninth of 15 presidents who were not graduated from college.

Father's name: Nathaniel Fillmore
Date of birth: April 19, 1771
Place of birth: Bennington, Vt.
Occupation: Farmer
Date of death: Mar. 28, 1863
•Fillmore was the second of six presidents whose fathers lived to see their sons' inauguration or oath-taking days. Mr. Fillmore did not attend the ceremony.
Place of death: *Unknown*
Age at death: 91 years, 343 days
•Nathaniel Fillmore was the father of a president who lived to the most advanced age.

Mother's name: Phoebe Millard Fillmore
Date of birth: 1778
Place of birth: Pittsfield, Mass.
Date of marriage: probably 1795
Children: 9; 6 sons, 3 daughters
•Olive Armstrong was born in 1797; Millard in 1800; Cyrus in 1801; Almon Hopkins in 1806; Calvin Turner in 1810; Julia in 1812; Darius Ingraham in 1814; Charles DeWitt

147

in 1817; and Phoebe Maria in 1819.
• Fillmore was the second of seven presi-
dents who came from families of nine chil-
dren.
• He was the third of ten presidents who
were second children.
Date of death: May 2, 1831
Age at death: about 53

Father's second wife: Eunice Love Fillmore
• Fillmore was the first of four presidents
who had stepmothers.
• He was the first of five presidents who had
stepparents.
Date of marriage: 1834
Date of death: *Unknown*

MARRIAGE

Date of first marriage: Feb. 5, 1826
Place of first marriage: Moravia, N.Y.
• Fillmore was the fourth of seven presi-
dents who were married in New York.
Age at first marriage: 26 years, 29 days
• He was the 11th of 27 presidents who were
married in their twenties.
Years married: 27 years, 53 days

First wife's name: Abigail Powers Fillmore
• She was the 11th of 33 first ladies.
• She was the 14th of 40 wives of presidents.
Date of birth: Mar. 13, 1798
• She was the first of four first ladies who
were born in March.
• She was the second of five wives of presi-
dents who were born in March.
Place of birth: Stillwater, N.Y.
• She was the third of six first ladies who
were born in New York.
• She was the fourth of seven wives of presi-
dents who were born in New York.
First wife's mother: Abigail Newland Pow-
ers
First wife's father: Lemuel Powers, Baptist
minister
• Fillmore was the second of five presidents
who married the daughters of clergymen.
Age at marriage: 27 years, 329 days
• She was the ninth of 26 first ladies who
were married in their twenties.
• She was the 12th of 30 wives of presidents
who were married in their twenties.
Years older than husband: 1 year, 300 days
• She was the second of six first ladies who
were older than their husbands.

• She was the second of six wives of presi-
dents who were older than their husbands.
Children: 2; 1 son, 1 daughter
• Millard Powers was born on Apr. 25, 1828;
Mary Abigail on Mar. 27, 1832
• Fillmore was the first of seven presidents
who had two children.
• He was the eighth of 19 presidents who
had both male and female children.
• He was the ninth of 30 presidents who had
children.
Date of death: Mar. 30, 1853
Place of death: Washington, D.C.
• She was the fourth of nine first ladies who
died in Washington.
• She was the fourth of nine wives of presi-
dents who died in Washington.
Age at death: 55 years, 17 days
Place of burial: Buffalo, N.Y.
• She was the first of four first ladies who
were buried in New York.
• She was the second of seven wives of presi-
dents who were buried in New York.
Years he survived his wife: 20 years, 343
days
• Fillmore was the seventh of 14 presidents
who survived their wives.

Date of second marriage: Feb. 10, 1858
• He was the first of two presidents who
remarried after the expiration of their
terms. The other was Benjamin Harrison.
• He was the second of five presidents who
remarried.
Place of second marriage: Albany, N.Y.
• This was his second marriage in New York.
• He was the only president who married
twice in New York.
Age at second marriage: 58 years, 34 days
• He was the second of three presidents who
were married in their fifties.
Years married: 16 years, 26 days

Second wife's name: Caroline Carmichael
McIntosh Fillmore
• Fillmore was the fourth of six presidents
who married widows. She was the widow
of Ezekiel C. McIntosh of Albany, N.Y.
• She was the first of three widows who were
the second wives of presidents.
• She was the fourth of seven wives of presi-
dents who were not first ladies.
• She was the 15th of 40 wives of presidents.
Date of birth: Oct. 21, 1813
• She was the second of six wives of presi-
dents who were born in October.

Place of birth: Morristown, N.J.
•She was the second of two wives of presidents who were born in New Jersey. The other was Anna Harrison.
•She and Mrs. Harrison were the only wives of presidents who were born in the same New Jersey community.
Second wife's mother: Temperance Blachley Carmichael
Second wife's father: Charles Carmichael, merchant
Age at marriage: 44 years, 112 days
•She was the first of two wives of presidents who were married in their forties. The other was Edith Wilson.
Years younger than husband: 13 years, 287 days

Children: None
•Fillmore was the first of two presidents who remarried who had children by their first wives only. The other was Wilson.
Years she survived her husband: 7 years, 156 days
•She was the eighth of 23 wives of presidents who survived their husbands.
Date of death: Aug. 11, 1881
Place of death: Buffalo, N.Y.
•She was the second of eight wives of presidents who died in New York.
Age at death: 67 years, 294 days
Place of burial: Buffalo, N.Y.
•She was the third of seven wives of presidents who were buried in New York.

EARLY YEARS

June, 1814, apprenticed as wool carder and cloth dresser
•Fillmore was treated with great injustice by his first employer.
December, 1814, finished first term as apprentice
•He walked home, a distance of about a hundred miles.
June, 1815, again apprenticed as wool carder and cloth dresser
1818, taught school, Scott, N.Y.
•He was the second of seven presidents who taught school.
1819–1821, studied law, Montville and Moravia, N.Y.
•Since he still had two years of his apprenticeship to serve, he agreed to relinquish his salary for the year and pay $30 for his release. In return for working in his first instructor's law office, he received room and board.
•He also taught school during this time.
•He was the ninth of 26 presidents who studied law.
1821, moved to Aurora, now East Aurora, Erie County, N.Y.
1822, read law, Buffalo, N.Y.
1823, admitted to bar, court of common pleas of Erie County
•He began his practice in Aurora.
•He was the ninth of 23 presidents who were lawyers.
Feb. 5, 1826, married to Abigail Powers, Moravia

1827, admitted as attorney of New York supreme court
Apr. 25, 1828, his only son born
•The boy was named Millard Powers Fillmore.
November, 1828, elected to New York state assembly
•He was elected to represent Erie County as an Anti-Mason and served three one-year terms.
May, 1830, moved to Buffalo
Apr. 26, 1831, his bill to abolish prison terms for debt signed by governor
•The bill, which he drafted with the assistance of John C. Spencer, abolished imprisonment for debt but made fraudulent bankruptcy a crime.
May 2, 1831, his mother died
Mar. 27, 1832, his only daughter born
•The girl was named Mary Abigail Fillmore.
1832, published pamphlet on abolition of religious tests for witnesses
•The 16-page pamphlet—an examination of the question, "Is it right to require any religious test as a qualification to be a witness in a court of justice?"—was published by C. Faxon, Buffalo. The material had been published previously in the form of four letters to the Buffalo *Patriot* in support of a bill that was defeated in the state legislature. Under the pseudonym of *Juridicus*, Fillmore concluded that religious tests for witnesses were wrong.

NATIONAL PROMINENCE

November, 1832, elected to House of Representatives
•Fillmore was the eighth of 17 presidents who were elected to the House.
Dec. 2, 1833, took his seat in House
•He was a member of the 23rd Congress.
•He was the eighth of 17 presidents who served in the House of Representatives.
1834, his father remarried
1834, joined Whig party
1835, retired from active politics, practiced law
•The law firm of Fillmore, Hall and Haven was the most prominent in western New York.
1836, elected again to House of Representatives
•Reelected in 1838 and 1840, he was a member of the 25th, 26th, and 27th congresses.
1841–1843, chairman of ways and means committee
•At the time, the ways and means committee also performed the duties of the committee on appropriations. He was instrumental in passing a resolution requiring departments to accompany estimates of expenses with references to the laws that authorized the expenditures.
•He was an author of the Tariff Act of 1842. He also helped secure passage of the bill that appropriated $30,000 for Samuel F.B. Morse's experimental telegraph line between Washington and Baltimore, Mar. 3, 1843.
1842, declined to run for reelection to House
May, 1844, unsuccessful candidate for vice president, Whig national convention, Baltimore
September, 1844, nominated by acclamation for governor by Whigs
•He hoped to be elected to the Senate, but succumbed to the urgings of Thurlow Weed to stand for governor.
November, 1844, defeated for governorship by Silas Wright
•This was Fillmore's first political defeat.
1846, appointed chancellor of University of Buffalo
•He served as chancellor until 1874.
1847, elected comptroller of New York
Jan. 1, 1848, took office as state comptroller
June 9, 1848, nominated for vice president, Whig national convention, Philadelphia
Nov. 7, 1848, elected vice president
Jan. 1, 1849, resigned as state comptroller, effective, Feb. 20
•In his annual report, he recommended a national bank.
Mar. 5, 1849, inaugurated as vice president

THE PRESIDENT (13th)

Term of office: July 10, 1850, to Mar. 4, 1853 (2 years, 237 days)
•Fillmore was the fifth of 12 presidents who had served as vice presidents.
•He was the second of eight presidents who, because of the death of their predecessors, did not complete their vice-presidential terms.
•He was the second of four presidents who served only the unexpired terms of their predecessors.
•He was the fourth of nine presidents who served less than one term.
•He was the eighth of 19 presidents who served one term or less than one term.
•He was the sixth of eight presidents in succession who served one term or less than one term.
State represented: New York
•He was the second of eight presidents who represented New York.
Political party: Whig
•He was the last of four presidents who were Whig.
Congresses: 31st, 32nd
Administration: 16th
Age at taking oath: 50 years, 184 days
•Fillmore took the oath of office in the Hall of Representatives of the Capitol on Wednesday, July 10, 1850. The oath was administered by William Cranch, chief justice of the U.S. Circuit Court of the District of Columbia.
•He was the third of seven presidents who took the oath of office from an official other than a justice of the Supreme Court.
•This was the second of two oath-taking ceremonies at which Cranch officiated.

Cranch had administered the oath to Tyler in 1841.

•Fillmore was the second of four presidents who did not give inaugural addresses.

THE 16th ADMINISTRATION

1850

July 20–23, Taylor cabinet resigned
July 22, appointed his first secretary of state, Daniel Webster; his only attorney general, John J. Crittenden; and his first secretary of navy, William A. Graham
•Webster took office, July 23; Graham, Aug. 2.
•Crittenden was the only attorney general who served under three presidents; he had also served under William Henry Harrison and Tyler.
•Crittenden was the first of nine executive officers who served in the cabinets of three presidents.
July 23, appointed his only secretary of treasury, Thomas Corwin, and his first postmaster general, Nathan K. Hall
Aug. 15, appointed his only secretary of war, Charles M. Conrad
Sept. 9, California admitted as 31st state
•California was the only state admitted during Fillmore's term of office.
Sept. 9, signed act establishing Territory of New Mexico
Sept. 9, signed act establishing Territory of Utah
Sept. 12, appointed his only secretary of interior, Alexander H. H. Stuart
Sept. 18, signed Fugitive Slave Act
•This act amended the slave act of 1793.
Sept 20, signed act abolishing slave trade in District of Columbia
•This was the fifth of the five acts which later came to be known as the Compromise of 1850. The other acts concerned were those of Sept. 9, which admitted California and established the territories of New Mexico and Utah, and the Fugitive Slave Act of Sept. 18.
Sept. 28, appointed Brigham Young as governor of Utah Territory
Sept. 30, first session of 31st Congress adjourned
Dec. 2, second session of 31st Congress
Dec. 2, sent his first State of the Union message to Congress

Note: The official population, according to the seventh census, was 23,191,876, which included 3,204,313 slaves (all but 262 in the South) and 434,449 free Negroes.

1851

Feb. 5, with Mrs. Fillmore, celebrated silver wedding anniversary, White House
•He was the second of five presidents who celebrated their 25th anniversaries while residents of the White House.
Feb. 18, issued proclamation calling on officers and citizens to recapture Shadrach, fugitive slave
•Resistence to the Fugitive Slave Act was widespread in the North. Many states passed personal liberty laws to circumvent the federal law. Shadrach, who had been arrested in Boston, Feb. 15, was rescued by a mob and spirited to safety in Canada.
Mar. 3, second session of 31st Congress adjourned
•During this session, it was decided that sessions of Congress adjourned at noon on Mar. 4.
Apr. 25, issued proclamation that warned against participation in expeditions against Cuba
•A third filibustering expedition led by General Narciso Lopez sailed from New Orleans, Aug. 3, and landed in Cuba, Aug. 11. The invasion was a failure. Colonel William L. Crittenden of Kentucky and 50 southern volunteers were captured, Aug. 13, and were executed in Havana, Aug. 16. When news of the executions was received in New Orleans, Aug. 21, the Spanish consulate was sacked, and ten stores operated by Spaniards were looted. Congress later voted a $25,000 indemnity for the damages done.
•Lopez and his supporters were defeated by the Spaniards, Aug. 24. Lopez was captured, Aug. 28, and was publicly executed in Havana, Sept. 1. The Spanish had captured 162 members of the expedition, half of whom were Americans. The prisoners were shipped to Spain. The Americans were not released until after the indem-

nity for the incidents in New Orleans had been paid.

July 4, laid cornerstone of extension of Capitol
• This extension was not completed until November, 1867.

Sept. 4, Associate Justice Levi Woodbury died

Sept. 22, appointed Benjamin R. Curtis as associate justice
• Curtis, who was confirmed by the Senate, Dec. 20, was the first of Fillmore's four appointments to the Supreme Court.
• Curtis was his only Court appointee who was confirmed.

Oct. 22, issued proclamation that warned against participation in expeditions against Mexico

Dec. 1, first session of 32nd Congress
• The administration did not control either the Senate or the House of Representatives. The Democrats gained 28 House seats. The Senate (62 members) consisted of 35 Democrats, 24 Whigs, and three Free-Soilers. The House (233 members) consisted of 140 Democrats, 88 Whigs, and five Free-Soilers.

Dec. 2, sent his second State of the Union message to Congress

1852

Mar. 19, signed act for repairs to Library of Congress
• This act appropriated $72,500 for repairs to the library, which had been damaged extensively by fire, Dec. 24, 1851.
• About thirty-five thousand of the fifty-five thousand volumes had been destroyed.

June 17–20, Whig national convention, Baltimore, Md.
• *See* Election of 1852, pages 158–159.
• He was the second of five presidents who sought but were denied renomination.

July 19, Associate Justice McKinley died

July 22, accepted resignation of Secretary of Navy Graham, effective, July 25

July 22, appointed his second secretary of navy, John P. Kennedy
• Kennedy took office, July 26.

Aug. 16, appointed Edward A. Bradford as associate justice
• This appointment was not acted upon by the Senate.

• He was the seventh of 15 presidents who nominated justices not confirmed by the Senate.
• Bradford was the tenth of 25 men nominated to the Supreme Court who were not confirmed by the Senate.

Aug. 31, accepted resignation of Postmaster General Hall

Aug. 31, appointed his second postmaster general, Samuel D. Hubbard
• Hubbard took office, Sept. 14.

Oct. 24, Secretary of State Webster died

Nov. 2, election day
• *See* Election of 1852, pages 158–159.

Nov. 6, appointed his second secretary of state, Edward Everett
• Everett was the last of Fillmore's ten cabinet appointments.

Dec. 6, second session of 32nd Congress

Dec. 6, sent his third and last State of the Union message to Congress

1853

Jan. 10, appointed George E. Badger as associate justice
• This appointment was postponed, Feb. 11.
• Badger was the 11th of 25 men nominated to the Supreme Court who were not confirmed by the Senate.

Feb. 21, signed coinage act
• This act reduced the silver content of all coins except silver dollars and provided for minting of $3 gold pieces.

Feb. 24, appointed William C. Micou as associate justice
• This appointment was not acted upon by the Senate.
• Micou was the 12th of 25 men nominated to the Supreme Court who were not confirmed by the Senate.

Mar. 2, signed act establishing Territory of Washington

Mar. 3, signed act raising salary of vice president from $5,000 to $8,000

Mar. 3, second session of 32nd Congress adjourned

Notes: He was the sixth of seven presidents who did not exercise the veto.
• The first kitchen stove was installed in the White House during the Fillmore administration. A cast-iron stove of "small hotel size," it proved too complicated for the

cook. After inspecting the Patent Office model, the president personally instructed the cook as to the intricacies of the stove's system of drafts.

THE FORMER PRESIDENT

Mar. 4, 1853, attended inauguration of Pierce
•Fillmore's age upon leaving office was 52 years, 101 days.
Mar. 30, 1853, his wife died
April, 1853, returned to Buffalo, N.Y.
Mar. 1-May 20, 1854, toured 11 southern states
May 29-June 15, 1854, with son, toured Midwest
July 26, 1854, his daughter, Mary, died
May 17, 1855, sailed for Europe
•He visited England, France, and Italy. In Rome, he met with Pope Pius IX.
•He was the second of eight former presidents who visited Europe.
•He was the second of three former presidents who met with Popes.
Feb. 22, 1856, nominated for president, American (Know-Nothing) national convention, Philadelphia, Pa.
•He was informed of his nomination in Rome.
May 21, 1856, wrote letter of acceptance
•He accepted the Know-Nothing nomination while in Paris and endorsed the party platform, which called for the exclusion of foreign-born persons from public offices and revision of the naturalization law to require 21 years of residency for citizenship.
June 22, 1856, returned to New York City
Sept. 17, 1856, endorsed by Whig party, Whig national convention, Baltimore, Md.
Nov. 4, 1856, election day
•He received 874,534 popular votes and eight electoral votes.
• *See* Election of 1856, page 168.
•He was the second of three former presidents who were the presidential candidates of minor parties.
Feb. 10, 1858, married Caroline Carmichael McIntosh, Albany, N.Y.
•They honeymooned in Europe, spending most of the winter of 1858–1859 in Paris and Madrid.
1862, elected chairman, Buffalo committee of public defense
May 20, 1862, elected president, Buffalo Historical Society

•He served until 1867.
April, 1865, escorted body of Lincoln, Batavia to Buffalo
1867, elected first president of Buffalo Club
Oct. 13, 1869, presided at commercial convention, Louisville, Ky.
•The convention was attended by 520 delegates from 29 states.
Jan. 7, 1870, celebrated his 70th birthday
•He was the ninth of 16 presidents who lived to be 70.
1870, elected president, Buffalo General Hospital
1870 or 1871, wrote brief autobiography at request of Buffalo Historical Society
•The manuscript was deposited under seal, not to be opened until after his death. It was published along with other documents and letters in the two-volume *Millard Fillmore Papers*, edited for the historical society by Frank H. Severance, 1907. It was believed at the time that the bulk of his papers had been destroyed as ordered by his son's last will and testament. But his papers were found in 1908, and are now on file in 44 volumes in the historical society.
Oct. 1, 1873, delivered his last public address, Third International Exhibition, Buffalo

DEATH

Date of death: Mar. 8, 1874
Place of death: Buffalo, N.Y.
•Fillmore was the third of eight presidents who died in New York.
Age at death: 74 years, 60 days
•He lived 21 years, four days, after the completion of his term.
Cause of death: Debility
Place of burial: Buffalo, N.Y.
•He was the second of six presidents who were buried in New York.

THE VICE PRESIDENT

•Fillmore was the second of four presidents who did not have vice presidents.

THE CABINET

State: Daniel Webster of Massachusetts, July 23, 1850, to Oct. 24, 1852
• Edward Everett of Massachusetts, Nov. 6, 1852, to Mar. 3, 1853
Treasury: Thomas Corwin of Ohio, July 23, 1850 to Mar. 6, 1853
War: Charles Magill Conrad of Louisiana, Aug. 15, 1850, to Mar. 7, 1853
Attorney General: John Jordan Crittenden of Kentucky, July 22, 1850, to Mar. 3, 1853
Navy: William Alexander Graham of North Carolina, Aug. 2, 1850, to July 25, 1852
• John Pendleton Kennedy of Maryland, July 26, 1852, to Mar. 7, 1853
Postmaster General: Nathan Kelsey Hall of New York, July 23, 1850, to Aug. 31, 1852
• Samuel Dickinson Hubbard of Connecticut, Sept. 14, 1852, to Mar. 7, 1853
Interior: Alexander Hugh Holmes Stuart of Virginia, Sept. 12, 1850, to Mar. 7, 1853

THE SUPREME COURT

Associate Justices: Benjamin Robbins Curtis of Massachusetts, appointed, Sept. 22, 1851; confirmed, Dec. 20, 1851
• Edward A. Bradford of Louisiana, appointed, Aug. 16, 1852; not acted upon by Senate
• George Edmund Badger of North Carolina, appointed, Jan. 10, 1853; postponed, Feb. 11, 1853
• William C. Micou of Louisiana, appointed, Feb. 24, 1853; not acted upon by Senate

Fourteenth President

FRANKLIN PIERCE

Full name: Franklin Pierce
- He was the first of two presidents named Franklin. The other was Roosevelt.
- He was the 11th of 17 presidents who did not have middle initials or middle names.

Date of birth: Nov. 23, 1804
- He was the third of five presidents who were born in November.
- He was the first president who was born in the nineteenth century.

Place of birth: Hillsborough, now Hillsboro, N.H.
- He was the only president who was born in New Hampshire.
- He was the fourth of seven presidents who were born in log cabins.

Family lineage: English
- He was the ninth of 12 presidents who were of English ancestry.

Religious denomination: Episcopalian
- He was the seventh of nine presidents who were Episcopalians.

College: Bowdoin College, Brunswick, Me.
- He was the only president who went to Bowdoin.
- He was the ninth of 27 presidents who attended college.

Date of graduation: Sept. 1, 1824, Bachelor of Arts

- He was the fifth of 21 presidents who were graduated from college.

Father's name: Benjamin Pierce
Date of birth: Dec. 25, 1757
Place of birth: Chelmsford, Mass.
Occupations: Farmer, soldier, politician
- Pierce's father fought in the Revolutionary War; was a member of the New Hampshire legislature, 1789–1801; was elected governor of New Hampshire for two terms, 1827–1828 and 1829–1830.
- Pierce was the last of three presidents whose fathers had served as state governors.

Date of death: Apr. 1, 1839
Place of death: Hillsborough, now Hillsboro, N.H.
Age at death: 81 years, 97 days

Father's first wife: Elizabeth Andrews Pierce
Date of birth: 1768
Place of birth: probably Hillsborough, now Hillsboro, N.H.
Date of marriage: May 24, 1787

Children: 1 daughter
•Elizabeth was born in 1788.
•Pierce was the third of six presidents who had half brothers or half sisters.
Date of death: Aug. 13, 1788
Age at death: about 20 years

Mother's name: Anna Kendrick Pierce
Date of birth: 1768
Place of birth: probably Amherst, N.H.
Date of marriage: Feb. 1, 1790
•Pierce was the second of five presidents whose mothers were second wives.
Children: 8; 5 sons, 3 daughters
•Benjamin Kendrick was born in 1790; Nancy in 1792; John Sullivan in 1796; Harriet in 1800; Charles in 1803; Franklin in 1804; Charlotte in 18—; and Henry in 1812. Charlotte died in infancy.
•Franklin was his mother's sixth child.
•He was his father's seventh child.
•He was the third of seven presidents who came from families of nine children.
Date of death: January or February, 1839
Place of death: probably Hillsborough, now Hillsboro, N.H.
Age of death: about 70 years

MARRIAGE

Date of marriage: Nov. 19, 1834
Place of marriage: Amherst, N.H.
•Pierce was the only president who was married in New Hampshire.
Age at marriage: 29 years, 361 days
•He was the 12th of 27 presidents who were married in their twenties.
Years married: 29 years, 13 days

Wife's name: Jane Means Appleton Pierce
•She was the 12th of 33 first ladies.
•She was the 16th of 40 wives of presidents.
Date of birth: Mar. 12, 1806
•She was the second of four first ladies who were born in March.

•She was the third of five wives of presidents who were born in March.
Place of birth: Hampton, N.H.
•She was the only first lady or wife of a president who was born in New Hampshire.
Wife's mother: Elizabeth Appleton
Wife's father: Jesse Appleton, Congregational minister, president of Bowdoin College
•Pierce was the third of five presidents who married daughters of clergymen
Age at marriage: 28 years, 252 days
•She was the tenth of 26 first ladies who were married in their twenties.
•She was the 13th of 30 wives of presidents who were married in their twenties.
Years younger than husband: 1 year, 109 days
Children: 3 sons
•Franklin was born on Feb. 2, 1836; Frank Robert on Aug. 27, 1839; and Benjamin on Apr. 13, 1841. Franklin and Frank Robert died in infancy. Benjamin was killed in a train wreck near Andover, Mass., Jan. 6, 1853.
•Pierce was the first of two presidents whose children died before they attained maturity. The other was McKinley.
•He was the second of seven presidents who had three children.
•He was the second of six presidents who had only male children.
•He was the tenth of 30 presidents who had children.
Date of death: Dec. 2, 1863
Place of death: Andover, Mass.
•She was the second of three first ladies who died in Massachusetts.
•She was the second of three wives of presidents who died in Massachusetts.
Age at death: 57 years, 265 days
Place of burial: Concord, N.H.
•She was the only first lady or wife of a president who was buried in New Hampshire.
Years he survived his wife: 5 years, 310 days
•Pierce was the eighth of 14 presidents who survived their wives.

EARLY YEARS

1818–1820, attended Hancock Academy, Hancock, N.H., and Francestown Academy, Francestown, N.H.
Oct. 4, 1820, entered Bowdoin College, Brunswick, Me.
Sept. 1, 1824, was graduated from Bowdoin College

October, 1824, began to read law with John Burnham, Hillsborough
•Pierce was the tenth of 26 presidents who studied law.
1825, elected to Phi Beta Kappa, Bowdoin College, Brunswick, Me.
•He was the first of five presidents who

were alumni members of Phi Beta Kappa.
- He was the second of 11 presidents who were members of Phi Beta Kappa.

April–November, 1825, read law with Levi Woodbury, Portsmouth, N.H.
- A former associate justice of the New Hampshire supreme court, a former governor of the state, and a former member of the House of Representatives, Woodbury was elected to the Senate in 1825. Woodbury later served as secretary of the navy and secretary of the treasury under Jackson and was appointed to the Supreme Court by Polk.
- Pierce completed his law studies under Edmund Parker in Amherst, N.H.

Sept. 5, 1827, admitted to bar, court of common pleas, Hillsborough
- He began the practice of law in Hillsborough. His father built him an office and

contributed half of the cost of his law library, $50.75.
- Pierce was the tenth of 23 presidents who were lawyers.

1829, elected to state legislature
- Representing Hillsborough, he took his seat in June.

May, 1829, appointed justice of the peace, Hillsborough

July, 1829, traveled to Detroit, Mich.
- He made his first trip to the West to pick up his orphaned nieces, Mary (eight) and Anne (four), whose mother had died.
- His brother and their father, Sullivan Pierce, had died in 1824.

1830, reelected to state legislature

1831, reelected to state legislature
- He was elected speaker of the house.

1832, reelected to state legislature
- He was reelected speaker of the house.

NATIONAL PROMINENCE

1833, elected to House of Representatives
- Pierce was the ninth of 17 presidents who were elected to the House.

Dec. 2, 1833, took seat in House of Representatives
- As a member of the 23rd Congress, he served on the judiciary committee.
- He was the ninth of 17 presidents who served in the House.

Nov. 19, 1834, married Jane Means Appleton, Amherst, N.H.
- His residence from infancy to his marriage, the Franklin Pierce Homestead, is located on state route 31, Hillsboro, and is maintained by the State of New Hampshire, Department of Resources and Economic Development. The house is open to the public daily from June 19 to Labor Day, 9 A.M. to 6 P.M. Admission: 50 cents.

1835, reelected to House of Representatives

Dec. 2, 1835, took seat as member of 24th Congress

Feb. 2, 1836, his first son born
- The boy was named Franklin Pierce.

Feb. 5, 1836, his first son died

1836, elected to Senate
- Pierce was the eighth of 16 presidents who were elected to the Senate.
- He was the sixth of 11 presidents who were elected to both the House of Representatives and the Senate.

Mar. 4, 1837, took seat in Senate

- When he took the oath of office, he was the youngest member of the Senate.
- He was the eighth of 15 presidents who served in the Senate.
- He was the sixth of ten presidents who served in both the House of Representatives and the Senate.

August, 1838, moved to Concord, N.H.

January or February, 1839, his mother died

Apr. 1, 1839, his father died

Aug. 27, 1839, his second son born
- The boy was named Frank Robert Pierce.

Apr. 13, 1841, his third son born
- The boy was named Benjamin Pierce.

Feb. 16, 1842, resigned from Senate, effective, Feb. 28

Feb. 26, 1842, departed from Washington, D.C.
- He returned to Concord, where he resumed the practice of law in March.

Nov. 14, 1843, his second son, Frank Robert, died

1844, appointed U.S. district attorney for New Hampshire by Polk

1845, declined appointment to Senate
- Polk had appointed Senator Levi Woodbury to the Supreme Court, Sept. 20.

1845, declined Democratic nomination for governor

May, 1846, enlisted as private in volunteer company, Concord
- He enlisted immediately after receiving

word that war had been declared on Mexico, May 13.

September, 1846, declined cabinet post as attorney general

• He was offered the position by Polk, Aug. 27. Pierce replied that when he had resigned from the Senate he had done so with the fixed purpose never again to be voluntarily separated from his family for any considerable time, except at the call of his country in time of war.

Feb. 15, 1847, commissioned as colonel of infantry, U.S. Army

• His first assignment was to recruit a regiment from New England.

• He was the second of three presidents who served in the Mexican War.

• He was the seventh of 21 presidents who served in the military during wartime.

Mar. 3, 1847, commissioned as brigadier general

• He was the fifth of 12 presidents who were generals.

May 27, 1847, sailed for Mexico

• He and his command—three companies of the Ninth Regiment—sailed from Newport, R.I.

June 27, 1847, arrived in Mexico

• He and his troops landed in Veracruz where they remained until mid-July due to the difficulty of obtaining mules for transportation.

Aug. 6, 1847, joined General Scott, Puebla de Zaragoza

• Scott's forces started for Mexico City, Aug. 10.

Aug. 19, 1847, injured during Battle of Contreras

• Not wounded, he suffered a painful groin injury when his horse was frightened by artillery. He was thrown forward against the pommel of his saddle when the animal stumbled; he fainted. When he regained consciousness, he found that he had severely wrenched his left knee. His horse had a broken leg. He mounted another horse, hurried after and rejoined his troops.

Aug. 20, 1847, reinjured his knee at Churubusco

• He refused to be taken from the field and chose instead to witness the battle.

Aug. 22–23, 1847, served on armistice commission

• He was appointed to the commission by

General Scott, after Santa Anna requested an armistice.

• The armistice of Tacubaya went into effect, Aug. 24. Negotiations between Polk's peace commissioner, Nicholas P. Trist, and the Mexican commission ended unsatisfactorily, and the armistice ended, Sept. 7.

Sept. 14, 1847, entered captured Mexico City

• He did not take part in the Battle of Chapultepec or the capture of Mexico City. He suffered from an intestinal ailment commonly called "Montezuma's revenge."

Dec. 9, 1847, departed from Mexico City

• He sailed for the U.S., Dec. 28.

Jan. 5, 1848, received hero's welcome, Concord

• Shortly after his return, he was presented with a sword by the state legislature.

1848, resumed law practice

1848, again declined Democratic nomination for governor

1850, elected president of state constitutional convention

1850, supported Compromise of 1850

Apr. 12, 1852, wrote letter in which he stated he would not decline Democratic nomination for president

June 4, 1852, nominated for president, Democratic national convention, Baltimore, Md.

Nov. 2, 1852, election day

• *See* Election of 1852, below.

Dec. 1, 1852, presidential electors cast ballots

• He received 254 of the 296 electoral votes from the 31 states.

• *See* Election of 1852, below.

Jan. 6, 1853, his son, Benjamin, killed in train wreck near Andover, Mass.

Feb. 9, 1853, electoral vote tabulated by Congress

• Pierce and King were officially declared elected.

ELECTION OF 1852

Democratic party, convened, June 1, at Baltimore, Md., nominated Franklin Pierce of New Hampshire for president, William Rufus Devane King of Alabama for vice president.

• This was the sixth Democratic national convention. It was the sixth Democratic convention in Baltimore; it was the ninth major party convention in Baltimore.

Whig party, convened, June 16, at Baltimore, nominated Winfield Scott of New Jersey for president, William Alexander Graham of North Carolina for vice president.

•This was the fourth Whig convention. It was the second Whig convention in Baltimore; it was the tenth major party convention in Baltimore.

Free-Soil party, convened, Aug. 11, at Pittsburgh, Pa., nominated John Parker Hale of New Hampshire for president, George Washington Julian of Indiana for vice president.

Election day, Tuesday, Nov. 2, 1852

Popular vote: 3,157,326

Pierce, 1,601,274
Scott, 1,386,580
Hale, 156,667
others, 12,805

• Pierce, 254, 27 states
(Alabama, 9; Arkansas, 4; California, 4; Connecticut, 6; Delaware, 3; Florida, 3; Georgia, 10; Illinois, 11; Indiana, 13; Iowa, 4; Louisiana, 6; Maine, 8; Maryland, 8; Michigan, 6; Mississippi, 7; Missouri, 9; New Hampshire, 5; New Jersey, 7; New York, 35; North Carolina, 10; Ohio, 23; Pennsylvania, 27; Rhode Island, 4; South Carolina, 8; Texas, 4; Virginia, 15; Wisconsin, 5)

• Scott, 42, four states
(Kentucky, 12; Massachusetts, 13; Tennessee, 12; Vermont, 5)

THE PRESIDENT (14th)

Term of office: Mar. 4, 1853, to Mar. 4, 1857 (4 years)

•Pierce was the ninth of 19 presidents who served one term or less than one term.

•He was the seventh of eight presidents in succession who served one term or less than one term.

•He was the fifth of ten presidents who served for four years.

State represented: New Hampshire

•He was the only president who represented New Hampshire.

Political party: Democratic

•He was the fourth of 12 presidents who were Democrats.

Congresses: 33rd, 34th

Administration: 17th

Age at inauguration: 48 years, 101 days

•He was the sixth of 21 presidents who were

younger than their vice presidents. Pierce was 18 years, 230 days younger than King.

Inauguration day: Friday, Mar. 4, 1853

•Pierce took the oath of office, administered by Chief Justice Roger B. Taney, on the east portico of the Capitol.

•This was the fifth of seven inaugurations at which Taney officiated.

•He was the only president who chose to say, "I do solemnly affirm," instead of "I do solemnly swear," an option provided for in the Constitution.

• *See* Constitution, Article II, Section 1, pages 639–640.

•He was the first of two presidents who gave their inaugural addresses as orations, without consulting notes or manuscript. The other was Cleveland, who delivered both of his inaugural addresses as orations.

THE 17th ADMINISTRATION

1853

Mar. 7, appointed his only secretary of state, William L. Marcy; his only secretary of treasury, James Guthrie; his only secretary of war, Jefferson Davis; his only attorney general, Caleb Cushing; his only secretary of navy, James C. Dobbin; his only postmaster general, James Campbell; and his only secretary of interior, Robert McClelland

•Marcy and Dobbin took office, Mar. 8.

•Pierce was the only president who retained the original members of his cabinet for four years. None of his seven executive department officers resigned or died in office.

•He was the third of four presidents who made no changes in their cabinets.

Mar. 21, appointed John A. Campbell as associate justice

•Campbell, who was confirmed by the Senate, Mar. 25, was Pierce's only appointment to the Supreme Court.

Mar. 24, oath of office administered to Vice President King in Cumbre, Cuba

• King was too ill to make the journey to Washington, D. C., for the inaugural ceremony.

• King was the only vice president who took the oath of office outside the U.S.—an event authorized by a special act of Congress. The oath was administered by William L. Sharkey, U.S. consul at Havana.

• King performed none of the duties of his office. He died, Apr. 18.

July 14, formally opened Crystal Palace Exhibition of Industry of All Nations, New York City

• The first World's Fair held in the U.S., it was patterned after the London Exhibition of 1851. The Crystal Palace, built of cast iron and glass, had the largest dome erected in the country up to that time. The structure was destroyed by fire, Oct. 5, 1858.

Dec. 5, first session of 33rd Congress

• The administration controlled both the Senate and the House of Representatives. The Democrats gained three Senate and 19 House seats. The Senate (62 members) consisted of 38 Democrats, 22 Whigs, and two others. The House (234 members) consisted of 159 Democrats, 71 Whigs, and four others.

Dec. 5, sent his first State of the Union message to Congress

Note: The first central heating system was installed in the White House in 1853.

1854

Jan. 18, issued proclamation that warned against participation in expeditions against Mexico

• William Walker organized a filibustering expedition in California, invaded Mexican territory in Lower California, and proclaimed himself president. After his "republic" collapsed, Walker was tried and acquitted in San Francisco for violation of the neutrality laws.

May 3, vetoed land grants for indigent insane bill

• This was the first of his nine vetoes.

May 30, signed Kansas-Nebraska Act

• This act established the territories of Kansas and Nebraska, and repealed the Missouri Compromise of 1820.

May 31, issued proclamation that warned against participation in expeditions against Cuba

June 2, Anthony Burns, fugitive slave, returned to Norfolk, Va.

• Pierce had ordered Burns, who had been arrested in Boston, Mass., to be returned to Norfolk by a revenue cutter. A sympathy demonstration in Boston necessitated the calling out of thousands of troops and police officers when Burns was escorted to the cutter. Many buildings were draped in black and church bells were tolled. The return of this single fugitive slave cost the government more than $100,000.

June 5, appointed Andrew H. Reeder as governor of Territory of Kansas

Aug. 4, vetoed internal improvements bill

• This was the second of his nine vetoes.

Aug. 7, first session of 33rd Congress adjourned

Aug. 16, directed ministers to Great Britain, France, and Spain to meet and form policy regarding Cuba

• This meeting of James Buchanan, John Young Mason, and Pierre Soule at Ostend, Belgium, Oct. 9, and a subsequent conference at Aix-la-Chapelle, Prussia, now West Germany, resulted in the Ostend Manifesto, which recommended the purchase of Cuba or annexation of the island by armed force.

• Secretary of State Marcy disavowed the manifesto, which caused Soule to resign.

Dec. 4, second session of 33rd Congress

Dec. 4, sent his second State of the Union message to Congress

1855

Feb. 10, signed act that secured rights of citizenship for children of citizens born in foreign countries

Feb. 17, vetoed French spoliation claims bill

• This was the third of his nine vetoes.

Feb. 24, signed act that created first U.S. Court of Claims

• Prior to this act, citizens could submit claims against the government only by means of petition to Congress.

Mar. 3, vetoed subsidy for ocean mails bill

• This was the fourth of his nine vetoes.

Mar. 3, second session of 33rd Congress adjourned

July 28, appointed Wilson Shannon as governor of Kansas Territory

•Governor Reeder, who had been charged with irregularities in the purchase of Indian lands by Secretary of State Marcy, June 11, acknowledged receipt of his notice of removal, Aug. 10.

•Shannon took the oath of office, Sept. 7.

Dec. 3, first session of 34th Congress

•The administration maintained control of the Senate, but lost control of the House of Representatives. The Democrats gained four Senate seats but lost 76 House seats. The Senate (62 members) consisted of 42 Democrats, 15 Republicans, and five others. The House (234 members) consisted of 108 Republicans, 83 Democrats, and 43 others. Most of the minor-party representatives were Know-Nothings—as members of the antiforeigner, anti-Catholic National Council of Native American party were known.

Dec. 3, sent his third State of the Union message to Congress

Dec. 8, issued proclamation warning against participation in expedition against Nicaragua

•William Walker, who had gone to Nicaragua at the invitation of the rebels in June, had taken over the leadership of the rebellion in October. He set up a dictatorship.

1856

Jan. 24, sent special message to Congress regarding Kansas

•This message recognized the proslavery legislature of the Territory of Kansas.

Feb. 11, issued proclamation that warned against unlawful combinations opposing constitutional authorities of Kansas

May 14, received emissary of William Walker

•Pierce's reception of the Nicaraguan representative amounted to recognition of the Walker regime.

May 19, vetoed Mississippi River and St. Clair Flats, Mich., internal improvements bills

•These were the fifth and sixth of his nine vetoes.

•Both of these bills were passed over his veto, the first and second of five internal

improvements vetoes that were overridden.

May 22, vetoed St. Mary's River, Mich., internal improvements bill

•This was the seventh of his nine vetoes.

•This bill was passed over his veto.

June 2–6, Democratic national convention, Cincinnati, Ohio

• *See* Election of 1856, page 168.

•He was the third of five presidents who sought but were denied renomination.

July 1, appointed John W. Geary as governor of Territory of Kansas

Aug. 11, vetoed Des Moines Rapids, Mich., internal improvements bill

•This was the eighth of his nine vetoes.

•This bill was passed over his veto.

Aug. 14, vetoed Patapsco River, Md., internal improvements bill

•This was the last of his nine vetoes.

•This bill was passed over his veto. It was the last of his five vetoes that were overridden.

•He was the first of two presidents who had a majority of their vetoes negated. The other was Andrew Johnson.

•He was the last of three presidents who exercised the regular veto but did not employ the pocket veto.

Aug. 18, first session of 34th Congress adjourned

Aug. 19, called special session of Congress, Aug. 21, to settle Kansas question

Aug. 21, second session of 34th Congress

Aug. 30, second session of 34th Congress adjourned

•No answer to the Kansas problem had been found.

•This was the shortest session of Congress, lasting only ten days.

Nov. 4, election day

• *See* Election of 1856, page 168.

Dec. 1, third session of 34th Congress

Dec. 2, sent his fourth and last State of the Union message to Congress

•His message mainly concerned Kansas, and he reiterated his hostility to the free-state partisans.

1857

Feb. 21, signed act declaring foreign coins no longer legal tender

Mar. 3, signed Tariff Act of 1857

•This act reduced the tariff to about 20 percent—the lowest rate since 1850—and enlarged the free list.

Mar. 3, third session of 34th Congress adjourned

THE FORMER PRESIDENT

Mar. 4, 1857, attended inauguration of Buchanan
• Pierce's age upon leaving office was 53 years, 56 days.
March–May, 1857, resided in home of his former secretary of state, William L. Marcy
May, 1857, delivered address to Ancient and Honorable Artillery Company, Faneuil Hall, Boston, Mass.
• He reiterated his stand for Constitutional fidelity and advised the North not to meddle in the affairs of slave states.
Summer, 1857, with Mrs. Pierce, traveled throughout New England
Winter, 1857, traveled to island of Madeira
1858–1859, traveled to Europe
• He and his wife visited Portugal, Spain, France, Switzerland, Italy, Austria, Germany, Belgium, and England. They spent most of the summer of 1858 at Geneva, Switzerland. While in Italy, he renewed his friendship with his college classmate and campaign biographer, Nathaniel Hawthorne.
• Pierce was the third of eight former presidents who visited Europe.
Fall, 1859, returned to U.S.
• He and his wife returned to Concord after their 18-month stay in Europe.
• His residence at 52 South Main Street, Concord, is privately owned by Mr. and Mrs. John Gravelle. It is open to the public only by application to Mr. Gravelle, Apr. 1 to Dec. 15. Admission: none (voluntary contributions).
Jan 6, 1860, wrote "war in streets" letter to Jefferson Davis
• This letter to his former secretary of war brought Pierce much criticism when it was published in 1861; some northern editors likened him to Benedict Arnold. He had written to Davis:

> Without discussing the question of right, of abstract power to secede, I have never believed that actual disruption of the Union can occur without bloodshed; and if, through the madness of northern Abolitionists, that dire calamity must come, the fighting will not be along Ma-

son and Dixon's line merely. It will be within our own borders, in our own streets, between the two classes of citizens to whom I have referred. Those who defy law and scout constitutional obligations will, if we ever reach the arbitrament of arms, find occupation enough at home.

1860, supported John C. Breckinridge for president
• Pierce took no active part in the campaign but cast his influence against Stephen A. Douglas.
Winter, 1860–1861, visited Nassau, British West Indies
• He and his wife spent five months in Nassau.
Apr. 16, 1861, suggested meeting of five former presidents
• Four days after the attack on Fort Sumter, he urged Martin Van Buren to call the meeting immediately, with the object of avoiding civil war. Van Buren replied that he would not call the conference but would attend. Nothing came of Pierce's suggestion.
• The former presidents who were living at the time were Van Buren, Tyler, Fillmore, Pierce, and Buchanan.
Apr. 21, 1861, addressed Union mass meeting, Concord, N.H.
• He urged the people to sustain the government against the threats of the Confederacy.
February, 1862, wrote letter of condolence to Lincoln after death of son
• William W. Lincoln had died in the White House, Feb. 20. Pierce made mention of his own loss in 1853, when his third son, Benjamin, had died. Both children were 11 years old when they died.
1863, Hawthorne dedicated his last book, Our Old Home, to him
• "If Pierce is so exceedingly unpopular," Hawthorne told his publisher, "there is so much the more need that an old friend should stand by him."
July 4, 1863, addressed Democratic rally
• Continuing his opposition to Lincoln's poli-

cies, Pierce spoke condemningly of the "fearful, fruitless, fatal Civil War." During the rally word spread through the crowd of the victory at Gettyburg.

Dec. 2, 1863, his wife died
• Mrs. Pierce never fully recovered from the shock of losing their third and last son in a train accident in 1853.

May 19, 1864, death of Hawthorne
• He and Hawthorne, who was in ill health, were vacationing together in the White Mountains, at Plymouth, N.H., when the writer died.

1865, joined the Episcopal Church
• After the death of his wife, he had become an alcoholic. When he stopped drinking, he joined the church.

1868, suffered severe illness
• He was on the brink of death, but recovered.

1868, made last speech at annual meeting of Society of the Cincinnati, Baltimore, Md.

DEATH

Date of death: Oct. 8, 1869
Place of death: Concord, N.H.
• Pierce was the only president who died in New Hampshire.
Age at death: 64 years, 319 days
• He lived 12 years, 218 days, after the completion of his term.
Cause of death: Stomach inflammation
Place of burial: Concord, N.H.
• He was the only president who was buried in New Hampshire.

THE VICE PRESIDENT (13th)

Full name: William Rufus Devane King
Date of birth: Apr. 7, 1786
Place of birth: Sampson County, N.C.
• He was the first of two vice presidents who were born in North Carolina. The other was Andrew Johnson.
Religious denomination: Presbyterian
• He was the sixth of 11 vice presidents who were Presbyterians.
College: University of North Carolina, Chapel Hill, N.C.
Date of graduation: 1803
Occupation: Planter
• He was a member of the House of Representatives from North Carolina, 1811–

1816; moved to Alabama, 1818; member of the Senate, representing Alabama, 1820–1844; minister to France, 1844–1846; returned to the Senate, 1848–1852.
• He was the fifth of 21 vice presidents who served in the House of Representatives before their terms of office.
• He was the third of 17 vice presidents who served in the Senate before their terms of office.
• He was the second of ten vice presidents who served both in the House of Representatives and the Senate before their terms of office.
• He was the second of 12 vice presidents who served both in the House of Representatives and the Senate.
Term of office: Mar. 24, 1853, to Apr. 18, 1853 (25 days)
• He was the vice president who served the shortest term.
• He was the fourth of 14 vice presidents who served less than one term.
• He was the second of seven vice presidents who served less than one year.
• Pierce and King were the 15th of 41 president-vice president teams.
Age at oath-taking: 66 years, 351 days
State represented: Alabama
• He was the only vice president who represented Alabama.
• He was the second of 13 vice presidents who represented states that were not their native states.
Political party: Democratic
• He was the fifth of 16 vice presidents who were Democrats.
Date of death: Apr. 18, 1853 (died in office)
• He was the second of six vice presidents who died before completing their first terms.
• He was the third of seven vice presidents who died in office.
Place of death: Cahaba, Dallas County, Ala.
• He was the only vice president who died in Alabama.
Age at death: 67 years, 11 days
Place of burial: Selma, Ala.
• He was the only vice president who was buried in Alabama.

THE CABINET

State: William Learned Marcy of New York,

Mar. 8, 1853, to Mar. 6, 1857

Treasury: James Guthrie of Kentucky, Mar. 7, 1853, to Mar. 6, 1857

War: Jefferson Davis of Mississippi, Mar. 7, 1853, to Mar. 6, 1857

Attorney General: Caleb Cushing of Massachusetts, Mar. 7, 1853, to Mar. 3, 1857

Navy: James Cochran Dobbin of North Carolina, Mar. 8, 1853, to Mar. 6, 1857

Postmaster General: James Campbell of Pennsylvania, Mar. 7, 1853, to Mar. 6, 1857

Interior: Robert McClelland of Michigan, Mar. 7, 1853, to Mar. 6, 1857

THE SUPREME COURT

Associate Justice: John Archibald Campbell of Alabama, appointed, Mar. 21, 1853; confirmed, Mar. 25, 1853

Fifteenth President

JAMES BUCHANAN

Full name: James Buchanan
• He was the fourth of five presidents named James.
• He was the fifth of eight presidents who had the same full names as their fathers.
• He was the 12th of 17 presidents who did not have middle initials or middle names.
Date of birth: Apr. 23, 1791
• He was the third of four presidents who were born in April.
Place of birth: Stony Batter, near Mercersburg, Pa.
• He was the only president who was born in Pennsylvania.
• He was the fifth of seven presidents who were born in log cabins.
• His birthplace was moved from Stony Batter to Fayette Street, Mercersburg, where it became a weaver's shop, in 1850. It was purchased by a group of businessmen in 1925, and moved to Chambersburg, where it was a gift shop and later served as Democratic party headquarters. In 1953, it was bought by Dr. Charles S. Tippetts, headmaster emeritus of Mercersburg Academy, and returned to Mercersburg. The cabin stands on the parking circle of the academy. It is open to the public by application. Admission: free.

Family lineage: Scottish-Irish
• He was the third of four presidents who were of Scottish-Irish ancestry.
Religious denomination: Presbyterian
• He was the second of six presidents who were Presbyterians.
College: Dickinson College, Carlisle, Pa.
• He was the only president who went to Dickinson.
• He was the tenth of 27 presidents who attended college.
Date of graduation: Sept. 27, 1809, Bachelor of Arts
• He was the sixth of 21 presidents who were graduated from college.

PARENTS AND SIBLINGS

Father's name: James Buchanan
Date of birth: 1761
Place of birth: County Donegal, Ireland
• Buchanan's father was the fourth of eight parents of presidents who were born abroad.
• His father was the second of four fathers of presidents who were born abroad.

Occupations: Merchant, farmer
Date of death: June 11, 1821
Place of death: Mercersburg, Pa.
Age at death: about 60 years

Mother's name: Elizabeth Speer Buchanan
Date of birth: 1767
Place of birth: Lancaster County, Pa.
Date of marriage: Apr. 16, 1788
Children: 11, 6 daughters, 5 sons
• Mary was born in 1789; James in 1791; Jane in 1793; Maria in 1795; Sarah in 1798; Elizabeth in 1800; Harriet in 1802; John in 1804; William Speer in 1805; George Washington in 1808; and Edward Young in 1811. Mary, Elizabeth, and John died in infancy.

• Buchanan was the only president who came from a family of 11 children.
• He was the fourth of ten presidents who were second children.
Date of death: May 14, 1833
Place of death: Greensburg, Pa.
Age at death: about 66 years

MARRIAGE

• Buchanan was the only bachelor president.
• He was the first of two presidents who were bachelors at the time of their inaugurations. The other was Cleveland.
• He was the fifth of six presidents who were childless.

EARLY YEARS

1796, with family, moved to Mercersburg, Pa.
1797–1806, attended common schools and Old Stone Academy, Mercersburg
September, 1807, entered Dickinson College, Carlisle, Pa.
• Buchanan entered as a junior. The college then had a three-year course of study (freshman, junior, and senior).
September, 1808, expelled from Dickinson for disorderly conduct
• Dr. John King, pastor of the Presbyterian Church, Mercersburg, and president of the Dickinson board of trustees, interceded on Buchanan's behalf. He was reinstated on the promise of good behavior.
Sept. 27, 1809, was graduated from Dickinson College
• He delivered a commencement oration, "The Utility of Philosophy."
December, 1809, read law with James Hopkins, Lancaster, Pa.
• He was the 11th of 26 presidents who studied law.
Summer, 1812, moved to Elizabethtown, Ky.
• His father was part owner of a 3,600-acre Kentucky tract, the title of which had been challenged. Buchanan spent most of the summer in Elizabethtown, considered settling there, but decided to return to Lancaster.
Nov. 17, 1812, admitted to bar, Lancaster
• He was the 11th of 23 presidents who were lawyers.
Mar. 20, 1813, appointed assistant prosecu-

tor, Lebanon County, Pa.
Aug. 24, 1814, nominated for state assembly as Federalist
Aug. 25, 1814, joined Shippen's Company, Lancaster
• He joined the company—which had no official status in either the militia or the regular army—immediately after word reached Lancaster of the burning of Washington by the British. The company marched to Baltimore and offered their services to Major Charles Sterret Ridgely of the Third Cavalry. Buchanan was one of ten volunteers for a secret mission, which turned out to be a raid to round up horses. When the British withdrew from Baltimore, the company was dismissed and returned home.
October, 1814, elected to state assembly
Feb. 1, 1815, made first formal speech in assembly
• He opposed conscription.
October, 1815, reelected to state assembly
• Local custom dictated that two terms in the assembly was the maximum.
1816, resumed law practice, Lancaster
• He formed a partnership with Molton C. Rogers.
Jan. 24, 1817, degree of Master Mason conferred by Lodge No. 43, Lancaster
• He was the fifth of 13 presidents who were Masons.
Summer, 1819, his engagement to Ann Caroline Coleman announced, Lancaster
• Miss Coleman, the daughter of millionaire

Robert Coleman, broke the engagement in early December, after a lovers' quarrel. While visiting her sister, Margaret, in Philadelphia, she died, Dec. 9. The rumors of suicide were reinforced when Buchanan's request to pay his respects and walk as a mourner was returned unopened by her father.

Aug. 25, 1820, nominated for House of Representatives by Federalists

NATIONAL PROMINENCE

October, 1820, elected to House of Representatives
• Buchanan was the fifth of 17 presidents who were elected to the House.
June 11, 1821, his father died
Dec. 3, 1821, took seat in House of Representatives
• Buchanan was reelected to the House four times, serving in the 17th through the 21st congresses. He was a Federalist until 1828, when he ran as a fusion candidate. He was a leader of the opposition during John Quincy Adams's administration and a strong supporter of Jackson during the 21st Congress.
• He was the fifth of 17 presidents who served in the House.
1831, appointed minister to Russia by Jackson
Apr. 8, 1832, sailed for Russia
• He arrived in St. Petersburg in mid-June.
• He was the second of two presidents who were ministers to Russia. The other was John Quincy Adams.
• He was the last of seven presidents who were diplomats.
Dec. 18, 1832, treaty of commerce with Russia signed
• Negotiations regarding a treaty on maritime rights were unsuccessful.
May 14, 1833, his mother died
Aug. 8, 1833, departed Russia for U.S.
• He visited Paris and London, arriving home in November.
Dec. 6, 1834, elected to Senate by Pennsylvania legislature
• He was the seventh of 16 presidents who were elected to the Senate.
• He was the fifth of 11 presidents who were elected to both the House and the Senate.
Dec. 15, 1834, took seat in Senate
• He was the seventh of 15 presidents who served in the Senate.
• He was the fifth of ten presidents who served in both the House and the Senate.
November, 1836, reelected to Senate for full term

1837, elected chairman of foreign affairs committee
• He defeated Henry Clay for the post.
1839, declined appointment by Van Buren as attorney general
January, 1943, reelected to Senate
April, 1844, declined appointment by Tyler as associate justice
May, 1844, defeated for presidential nomination, Democratic national convention, Baltimore, Md.
Feb. 18, 1845, accepted appointment by Polk as secretary of state
Mar. 10, 1845, took office as secretary of state
• He was the last of six presidents who served as secretary of state.
• He was the sixth of eight presidents who served in the cabinet.
September, 1845, sought associate justiceship
• Through an intermediary, he asked Polk to appoint him to the Supreme Court. But he changed his mind two months later and informed Polk that he could not accept a Court appointment.
1846, negotiated Oregon treaty with Great Britain
May, 1848, defeated for presidential nomination, Democratic national convention, Baltimore, Md.
March, 1849, retired to Wheatland, Lancaster, Pa.
• He had purchased the Marietta Avenue mansion the previous summer from William Meredith for $6,750.
• Wheatland is maintained by the James Buchanan Foundation for the Preservation of Wheatland, assisted by the Junior League of Lancaster. A National Historic Landmark, it is open to the public, 9 A.M. to 5 P.M., weekdays, and 10 A.M. to 5 P.M., Sundays, Mar. 15 to Nov. 30. Admission: adults, $1; groups, 75 cents; children under 12, free.
June, 1852, defeated for presidential nomi-

nation, Democratic national convention, Baltimore, Md.

1853, named first president, board of trustees, Franklin and Marshall College, Lancaster

• Franklin College of Lancaster and Marshall College of Mercersburg had merged.

Apr. 11, 1853, appointed minister to Great Britain by Pierce

Aug. 17, 1853, arrived in London

• He was the last of five presidents who were ministers to Great Britain.

Oct. 9, 1854, conferred with ministers to Spain and France, Ostend, Belgium

• This meeting with Pierre Soule and John Young Mason resulted in the Ostend Manifesto, which recommended the purchase of Cuba or annexation of the island by armed force. The declaration was repudiated by Pierce and Secretary of State Marcy. Buchanan's participation in the Ostend conference raised his stock among southern Democrats, who had been clamoring for the annexation of Cuba as additional slave territory.

April, 1856, returned to U.S.

June 5, 1856, nominated for president, Democratic national convention, Cincinnati, Ohio

Nov. 4, 1856, election day

• *See* Election of 1856, below.

Dec. 3, 1856, presidential electors cast ballots

• He received 174 of the 296 electoral votes from the 31 states.

• *See* Election of 1856, below.

Feb. 11, 1857, electoral vote tabulated by Congress

• Buchanan and Breckinridge were officially declared elected.

ELECTION OF 1856

American (Know-Nothing) party, convened, Feb. 22, at Philadelphia, Pa., nominated Millard Fillmore of New York for president, Andrew Jackson Donelson of Tennessee for vice president.

• This was the second major party convention in Philadelphia.

Democratic party, convened, June 2, at Cincinnati, Ohio, nominated James Buchanan of Pennsylvania for president, John Cabell Breckinridge of Kentucky for vice president.

• This was the seventh Democratic national convention. It was the first Democratic convention in Cincinnati; it was the first of three major party conventions in Cincinnati.

American (antislavery minority group), party, convened, June 2, at New York City, nominated John Charles Fremont of California for president, W. F. Johnston of Pennsylvania for vice president.

• This group, who called themselves "Northern Americans," later endorsed the Republican nominees.

Republican party, convened, June 17, in Philadelphia, Pa., nominated John Charles Fremont of California for president, William Lewis Dayton of New Jersey for vice president.

• This was the first Republican national convention.

• It was the first Republican convention in Philadelphia; it was the third major party convention in Philadelphia.

Whig party, convened, Sept. 17, at Baltimore, Md., endorsed the American nominees, Fillmore and Donelson.

• This was the fifth and last Whig convention. It was the third Whig convention in Baltimore; it was the 11th major party convention in Baltimore.

Election day, Tuesday, Nov. 4, 1856

Popular vote: 4,053,967

   Buchanan, 1,838,169

   Fremont, 1,341,264

   Fillmore, 874,534

• Buchanan was the fourth of 15 presidents who were elected without receiving a majority of the popular vote.

Electoral vote: 296, 31 states

• Buchanan, 174, 19 states

   (Alabama, 9; Arkansas, 4; California, 4; Delaware, 3; Florida, 3; Georgia, 10; Illinois, 11; Indiana, 13; Kentucky, 12; Louisiana, 6; Mississippi, 7; Missouri, 9; New Jersey, 7; North Carolina, 10; Pennsylvania, 27; South Carolina, 8; Tennessee, 12; Texas, 4; Virginia, 15)

• Fremont, 114, 11 states

   (Connecticut, 6; Iowa, 4; Maine, 8; Massachusetts, 13; Michigan, 6; New Hampshire, 5; New York, 35; Ohio, 23; Rhode Island, 4; Vermont, 5; Wisconsin, 5)

• Fillmore, 8, one state

   (Maryland, 8)

THE PRESIDENT (15th)

Term of office: Mar. 4, 1857, to Mar. 4, 1861 (4 years)
• Buchanan was the tenth of 19 presidents who served one term or less than one term.
• He was the last of eight presidents in succession who served one term or less than one term.
• He was the sixth of ten presidents who served for four years.
State represented: Pennsylvania
• He was the only president who represented Pennsylvania.

Political party: Democratic
• He was the fifth of 12 presidents who were Democrats.
Congresses: 35th, 36th
Administration: 18th
Age at inauguration: 65 years, 315 days
Inauguration day: Wednesday, Mar. 4, 1857
• Buchanan took the oath of office, administered by Chief Justice Roger B. Taney, on the east portico of the Capitol.
• This was the sixth of seven inaugurations at which Taney officiated.

THE 18th ADMINISTRATION

1857

Mar. 6, appointed his first secretary of state, Lewis Cass; his first secretary of treasury, Howell Cobb; his first secretary of war, John B. Floyd; his first attorney general, Jeremiah S. Black; his only secretary of navy, Isaac Toucey; his first postmaster general, Aaron V. Brown; and his only secretary of interior, Jacob Thompson
• Cobb and Toucey took office, Mar. 7.
Mar. 6, *Dred Scott v. Sandford* decision
• John F. A. Sanford (whose name is misspelled in the official record) claimed ownership of Scott.
• The Supreme Court ruled that Scott, a slave, was not a citizen and could not sue in the courts for his freedom. It has been established that the president was informed confidentially as to the intention of the Court by Justices Grier and Catron.
Mar. 26, appointed Robert J. Walker as governor of Territory of Kansas
• Governor Geary had resigned, Mar. 4, effective, Mar. 20.
• Walker took office, May 26.
July 11, appointed Alfred Cumming as governor of Territory of Utah
• Buchanan had removed Governor Brigham Young, dispatching an army to suppress an alleged rebellion.
• Governor Cumming proclaimed the territory in rebellion, Nov. 27.
Aug. 24, Panic of 1857 began
• The failure of the New York City branch of the Ohio Life Insurance and Trust Company of Cincinnati began the panic, which

was the third of nine major U.S. depressions. Overspeculation in wheat belt real estate and railroad construction brought on the 18-month financial crisis.
Sept. 30, Associate Justice Curtis resigned
Dec. 7, first session of 35th Congress
• The administration controlled both the Senate and the House of Representatives. The Democrats lost three Senate seats but gained 23 House seats. The Senate (64 members) consisted of 39 Democrats, 20 Republicans, and five others. The House (237 members) consisted of 131 Democrats, 92 Republicans, and 14 others.
Dec. 8, sent his first State of the Union message to Congress
Dec. 9, appointed Nathan Clifford as associate justice
• Clifford, who was confirmed by the Senate, Jan. 12, 1858, was the first of Buchanan's two appointments to the Supreme Court.

1858

Feb. 2, submitted Lecompton constitution to Congress, recommended admission of Kansas as slave state
Apr. 6, issued proclamation that declared Mormon government of Utah in rebellion, offering pardons to all except those who persisted in disloyal resistance
• He sent Colonel Thomas L. Kane, a friend of the Mormons, to mediate. Kane and Governor Cumming met with Brigham Young, June 10. The rebellion ended, June 26. Governor Cumming assumed office in

Salt Lake City, June 30.

May 4, signed English act

•This act provided for a popular vote in Kansas on the Lecompton constitution. The constitution was rejected, Aug. 2; Kansas remained a territory.

May 11, Minnesota admitted as 32nd state

•Minnesota was the first of three states admitted during his term of office.

June 14, first session of 35th Congress adjourned

Aug. 16, exchanged greetings with Queen Victoria of Great Britain by Atlantic cable

•The cable was completed, Aug. 5, but lost its conducting power, Sept. 1. It was not returned to service until 1866.

Dec. 6, second session of 35th Congress

Dec. 6, sent his second State of the Union message to Congress

1859

Jan. 7, vetoed overland mails bill

•This bill had been passed during the first session of the 35th Congress.

•This was the first of his seven vetoes, the first of his three pocket vetoes.

Feb. 14, Oregon admitted as 33rd state

•Oregon was the second of three states admitted during his term of office.

Feb. 24, vetoed land grants for agricultural colleges bill

•This was the second of his seven vetoes.

Mar. 3, second session of 35th Congress adjourned

Mar. 8, Postmaster General Brown died

Mar. 14, appointed his second postmaster general, Joseph Holt

Dec. 5, first session of 36th Congress

•The administration maintained control of the Senate, but lost control of the House of Representatives. The Republicans gained six Senate and 21 House seats. The Senate (66 members) consisted of 38 Democrats, 26 Republicans, and two others. The House (237 members) consisted of 113 Republicans, 101 Democrats, and 23 others.

Dec. 19, sent his third State of the Union message to Congress

•He declared that all lawful means should be employed to suppress the illicit slave trade.

1860

Feb. 1, vetoed St. Clair Flats, Mich., internal improvements bill

•This bill had been passed during the first session of the 35th Congress.

•This was the third of his seven vetoes, the second of his three pocket vetoes.

Feb. 6, vetoed Mississippi River internal improvements bill

•This bill had also been passed during the first session of the 35th Congress.

•This was the fourth of his seven vetoes, the last of his three pocket votes.

Mar. 5, House adopted resolution offered by Representative John Covode of Pennsylvania for committee to investigate Buchanan's conduct

Apr. 17, vetoed relief of A. Edwards and Company bill

•This was the fifth of his seven vetoes.

June 22, vetoed homestead bill

•This was the sixth of his seven vetoes.

June 25, first session of 36th Congress adjourned

June 30, Associate Justice Daniel died

Nov. 6, election day

• *See* Election of 1860, page 181.

Nov. 20, Attorney General Black gave opinion that president could use force in states only to protect public property, to aid civil courts in execution of laws

Dec. 3, second session of 36th Congress

Dec. 3, sent his fourth and last State of the Union message to Congress

•The essence of his message was that the South had no legal right to secede, and the government had no power to prevent secession.

Dec. 8, Secretary of Treasury Cobb resigned

Dec. 12, appointed his second secretary of treasury, Philip F. Thomas

Dec. 12, Secretary of State Cass resigned, effective, Dec. 14

•Cass resigned because Buchanan declined to reinforce Fort Moultrie, S.C.

Dec. 17, Attorney General Black resigned

Dec. 17, appointed his second secretary of state, Jeremiah S. Black

Dec. 20, appointed his second attorney general, Edwin M. Stanton

Dec. 29, Secretary of War Floyd resigned

•Floyd had disagreed with the president about the withdrawal of troops from Fort Moultrie, and his resignation was requested.

• Floyd fled to Virginia after he was indicted by the grand jury of the District of Columbia for involvement in the misuse of $870,000 in Indian trust funds. Floyd was later accused of having transferred excessive quantities of arms from northern to southern arsenals.

• The former secretary of war was commissioned as a Confederate brigadier general, May 23, 1861.

Dec. 30, replied to diplomatic letter of South Carolina commissioners but refused to receive them officially

• South Carolina had passed an ordinance of secession, Dec. 20, and had appointed three commissioners to treat for possession of U.S. property within the state, Dec. 21. The commissioners arrived in Washington and addressed a letter to the president, Dec. 28. Buchanan's letter of reply stated that Fort Sumter would be defended.

• Fort Moultrie, which had been abandoned, Dec. 26, was occupied by South Carolina troops, Dec. 27, and the arsenal at Charleston was seized, Dec. 30.

Note: The official population, according to the eighth census, was 31,443,321, which included 3,953,760 slaves and 448,070 free Negroes.

1861

Jan. 8, Secretary of Interior Thompson resigned

Jan. 14, Secretary of Treasury Thomas resigned

• Thomas, a Confederate sympathizer, had served in the cabinet for only 34 days.

Jan. 15, appointed his third secretary of treasury, John A. Dix

Jan. 18, appointed his second secretary of war, Joseph Holt

• Holt had resigned as postmaster general, Dec. 31, 1860.

Jan. 25, vetoed relief of Hockaday and Legget bill

• This was the last of his seven vetoes.

• He was the sixth of 11 presidents who never had a veto overridden.

Jan. 29, Kansas admitted as 34th state

• Kansas was admitted under the Wyandotte constitution, which prohibited slavery.

• Kansas was the last of three states admitted during his term of office.

Feb. 5, appointed Jeremiah S. Black as associate justice

• Black, the second of Buchanan's two appointments to the Supreme Court, was rejected by the Senate, Feb. 21.

• Buchanan was the eighth of 15 presidents who nominated justices not confirmed by the Senate.

• Black was the 13th of 25 men nominated to the Supreme Court who were not confirmed by the Senate.

Feb. 12, appointed his third postmaster general, Horatio King

• King was the last of Buchanan's 14 cabinet appointments.

Feb. 13, electoral votes tabulated by Congress

• Lincoln and Hamlin were officially declared elected.

• Vice President Breckinridge was the first of three presidential candidates who officially announced the elections of their opponents.

Mar. 1, dismissed General David Twiggs for treachery

• General Twiggs had surrendered U.S. posts and military property in Texas to state troops, Feb. 18.

• Texas had been the seventh state to secede, Feb. 1. The others were: South Carolina, Dec. 20, 1860; Mississippi, Jan. 9; Florida, Jan. 10; Alabama, Jan. 11; Georgia, Jan. 19; and Louisiana, Jan. 26.

Mar. 2, signed act establishing territories of Dakota and Nevada

Mar. 4, second session of 36th Congress adjourned

Note: He was the second of three presidents who did not seek renomination after their first terms.

THE FORMER PRESIDENT

Mar. 4, 1861, attended inauguration of Lincoln

• Buchanan's age upon leaving office was 69 years, 315 days.

Mar. 9, 1861, retired to Wheatland, Lancaster, Pa.

•He was not active in public affairs during his retirement, although he maintained extensive correspondence with friends and associates. He assembled voluminous notes for a planned autobiography, but it was not completed. His will provided that his papers and correspondence were to be given to his friend, William B. Reed, for a projected biography. Reed did not finish the book either. Much of the material appeared in *The Works of James Buchanan*, collected and edited by John Bassett Moore in 12 volumes, published in Philadelphia by Lippincott, 1908–1911.

Apr. 23, 1861, celebrated his 70th birthday
•He was the tenth of 16 presidents who lived to be 70.

Apr. 23, 1866, celebrated his 75th birthday
•He was the seventh of ten presidents who lived to be 75.

1866, his only book, *Mr. Buchanan's Administration on the Eve of the Rebellion*, published by Appleton, New York City
•The book was a vindication of his policies during the final months of his administration. Approximately five thousand copies were sold.
•He was the seventh of 21 presidents who wrote books that were published during their lifetimes.

DEATH

Date of death: June 1, 1868
Place of death: Lancaster, Pa.
•Buchanan was the only president who died in Pennsylvania.
Age at death: 77 years, 39 days
•He lived seven years, 89 days, after the completion of his term.
Cause of death: Rheumatic gout
Place of burial: Lancaster, Pa.
•Buchanan was the only president who was buried in Pennsylvania.

THE VICE PRESIDENT (14th)

Full name: John Cabell Breckinridge
Date of birth: Jan. 21, 1821
Place of birth: near Lexington, Ky.
•He was the second of four vice presidents who were born in Kentucky.
Religious denomination: Presbyterian
•He was the seventh of 11 vice presidents who were Presbyterians.
•Buchanan and Breckinridge were both Presbyterians. They were the third of seven president-vice president teams of the same religious denomination.
College: Centre College, Danville, Ky.
Date of graduation: 1839
•He studied law at Transylvania University, Lexington, Ky.
Occupation: Lawyer
•He practiced law in Lexington, Ky., 1845; was a member of the Kentucky state legislature, 1849–1851; was a member of the House of Representatives, 1851–1855.
•He was the tenth of 21 vice presidents who served in the House of Representatives before their terms of office.
Term of office: Mar. 4, 1857, to Mar. 4, 1861 (4 years)
•He was the sixth of 17 vice presidents who served four-year terms.
•Buchanan and Breckinridge were the 16th of 41 president-vice president teams.
Age at inauguration: 36 years, 42 days
•He was the youngest vice president at inauguration.
State represented: Kentucky
•He was the second of three vice presidents who represented Kentucky.
Political party: Democratic
•He was the sixth of 16 vice presidents who were Democrats.

Note: He was nominated for president by the southern faction of the Democrats in 1860. He received 849,781 popular votes, 72 electoral votes, and carried 11 slave states.
• *See* page 181.

Occupations after term: U.S. Senator, Confederate officer, lawyer
•Elected to the Senate in 1859, he was expelled in 1861 after he accepted appointment as a brigadier general in the Confederate army; fought at Shiloh, Vicksburg, and Baton Rouge; commanded a division of the Army of Tennessee at Chickamauga and Missionary Ridge; promoted to major general, 1862; appointed Confederate secretary of war, 1865; fled to Europe to escape arrest after Lee surrendered; returned to Kentucky, 1868; practiced law, 1869–1875.
•He was the second of six vice presidents who served in the Senate after their terms of office.

•He was the seventh of 12 vice presidents who served both in the House of Representatives and the Senate.

Date of death: May 17, 1875

Place of death: Lexington, Ky.

•He was the second of two vice presidents who died in Kentucky. The other was Richard Mentor Johnson.

Age at death: 54 years, 116 days

Place of burial: Lexington, Ky.

•He was the second of three vice presidents who were buried in Kentucky.

THE CABINET

State: Lewis Cass of Michigan, Mar. 6, 1857, to Dec. 14, 1860

•Jeremiah Sullivan Black of Pennsylvania, Dec. 17, 1860, to Mar. 5, 1861

Treasury: Howell Cobb of Georgia, Mar. 7, 1857, to Dec. 8, 1860

•Philip Francis Thomas of Maryland, Dec. 12, 1860, to Jan. 14, 1861

•John Adams Dix of New York, Jan. 15, 1861, to Mar. 6, 1861

War: John Buchanan Floyd of Virginia, Mar. 6, 1857, to Dec. 29, 1860

•Joseph Holt of Kentucky, Jan. 18, 1861, to Mar. 5, 1861

Attorney General: Jeremiah Sullivan Black of Pennsylvania, Mar. 6, 1857, to Dec. 17, 1860

•Edwin McMasters Stanton of Ohio, Dec. 20, 1860, to Mar. 3, 1861

Navy: Isaac Toucey of Connecticut, Mar. 7, 1857, to Mar. 6, 1861

Postmaster General: Aaron Venable Brown of Tennessee, Mar. 6, 1857, to Mar. 8, 1859

•Joseph Holt of Kentucky, Mar. 14, 1859, to Dec. 31, 1860

•Horatio King of Maine, Feb. 12, 1861, to Mar. 5, 1861

Interior: Jacob Thompson of Mississippi, Mar. 6, 1857, to Jan. 8, 1861

THE SUPREME COURT

Associate Justices: Nathan Clifford of Maine, appointed, Dec. 9, 1857; confirmed, Jan. 12, 1858

•Jeremiah Sullivan Black of Pennsylvania, appointed, Feb. 5, 1861; rejected by Senate, Feb. 21, 1861

Sixteenth President

ABRAHAM LINCOLN

Full name: Abraham Lincoln
• He was the 13th of 17 presidents who did not have middle initials or middle names.
Date of birth: Feb. 12, 1809
• He was the last of three presidents who were born in February.
Place of birth: Sinking Spring farm, near Hodgenville, Hardin County, now Larue County, Ky.
• He was the only president who was born in Kentucky.
• He was the first president who was not born in one of the 13 original states.
• He was the sixth of seven presidents who were born in log cabins.
• His birthplace, three miles south of Hodgenville, on Kentucky state route 61 (U.S. 31 E), has been enclosed in a marble memorial building. It is a National Historic Site maintained by the National Park Service and it is open to the public daily except Christmas, 8 A.M. to 4:45 P.M., Sept. 1 to May 31, and 8 A.M. to 6:45 P.M., June 1 to Aug. 31. Admission is free.
Family lineage: English
• He was the tenth of 12 presidents who were of English ancestry.

Religious denomination: None
• He was the second of three presidents who were of no specific denomination.
College: None
• He was the sixth of nine presidents who did not attend college.
• He was the tenth of 15 presidents who were not graduated from college.

PARENTS AND SIBLINGS

Father's name: Thomas Lincoln
Date of birth: Jan. 6, 1778
Place of birth: Rockingham County, Va.
Occupations: Farmer, carpenter
Date of death: Jan. 17, 1851
Place of death: Coles County, Ill.
Age at death: 73 years, 11 days

Mother's name: Nancy Hanks Lincoln
Date of birth: Feb. 5, 1784
Place of birth: probably Campbell County, Va.
Date of marriage: June 12, 1806
Children: 3; 2 sons, 1 daughter
• Sarah was born in 1807, Abraham in 1809, and a son in 1811 or 1812. The third child,

who was probably named Thomas, died in infancy.

•Lincoln was the third of five presidents who came from families of three children.

•He was the fifth of ten presidents who were second children.

Date of death: Oct. 5, 1818

•Abraham was nine years, 235 days old when his mother died.

Place of death: Spencer County, Ind.

Age at death: 34 years, 242 days

Father's second wife: Sarah Bush Johnston Lincoln

Date of birth: Dec. 12, 1788

Place of birth: probably Hardin County, Ky.

Date of marriage: Dec. 2, 1819

•Abraham was ten years, 293 days old, when his father remarried.

•He was the only president who had a stepmother during his childhood.

•He was the first of two presidents who had stepmothers before they reached maturity. The other was Coolidge.

•He was the second of four presidents who had stepmothers.

•He was the second of five presidents who had stepparents.

Children: None

•She had had three children by her first husband, Daniel Johnston.

•Lincoln was the only president who had stepbrothers or stepsisters.

•He had two stepsisters and one stepbrother; Elizabeth Johnston was born in 1807, Matilda Johnston in 1811, and John D. Johnston in 1814.

Date of death: Apr. 10, 1869

Place of death: probably Charleston, Ill.

Age at death: 80 years, 119 days

MARRIAGE

Date of marriage: Nov. 4, 1842

Place of marriage: Springfield, Ill.

•Lincoln was the only president who was married in Illinois.

Age at marriage: 33 years, 265 days

•He was the second of six presidents who were married in their thirties.

Years married: 22 years, 162 days

Wife's name: Mary Ann Todd Lincoln

•She was the 13th of 33 first ladies.

•She was the 17th of 40 wives of presidents.

Date of birth: Dec. 13, 1818

•She was the first of two first ladies who were born in December. The other was Claudia Johnson.

•She was the first of two wives of presidents who were born in December.

Place of birth: Lexington, Ky.

•She was the only first lady or wife of a president who was born in Kentucky.

Wife's mother: Eliza Parker Todd

Wife's father: Robert Smith Todd, banker

Age at marriage: 23 years, 326 days

•She was the 11th of 26 first ladies who were married in their twenties.

•She was the 14th of 30 wives of presidents who were married in their twenties.

Years younger than husband: 9 years, 304 days

Children: 4 sons

•Robert Todd was born on Aug. 1, 1843; Edward Baker on Mar. 10, 1846; William Wallace on Dec. 21, 1850; and Thomas on Apr. 4, 1853. Only Robert Todd lived to maturity; Edward Baker died in 1850, William Wallace in 1862, and Thomas (Tad) in 1871.

•Lincoln was the third of four presidents who had four children.

•He was the third of six presidents who had only male children.

•He was the 11th of 30 presidents who had children.

Years she survived her husband: 17 years, 92 days

•She was the eighth of 21 first ladies who survived their husbands.

•She was the ninth of 23 wives of presidents who survived their husbands.

Date of death: July 16, 1882

Place of death: Springfield, Ill.

•She was the only first lady or wife of a president who died in Illinois.

Age at death: 63 years, 215 days

Place of burial: Springfield, Ill.

•She was the only first lady or wife of a president who was buried in Illinois.

EARLY YEARS

Spring, 1811, with family, moved to farm, Knob Creek, Ky.
• At Knob Creek, Lincoln was an occasional pupil at the local log schoolhouse.
December, 1816, with family, moved to Indiana
• The Lincoln Boyhood National Memorial is on state route 162, two miles east of Gentryville and four miles south of Dale. The cabin on the farm suggests the one in which he grew to manhood. It is administered by the National Park Service. It is open daily, Apr. 1 to Oct. 31, 7 A.M. to 6 P.M., and Wednesdays through Sundays, Nov. 1 to Mar. 31, 8 A.M. to 5 P.M. Admission is free.
Oct. 5, 1818, his mother died
Dec. 2, 1819, his father remarried
• That winter, partly at the urging of his stepmother, of whom he was genuinely fond, he attended a few weeks of classes taught by Andrew Crawford at a nearby schoolhouse. Two years later he attended classes taught by another itinerant schoolmaster, James Swaney. After a gap of another year, he had a few weeks of instruction from Azel Dorsey. That ended Lincoln's formal education, which he later said totalled less than one year.
1826, worked as helper on James Taylor's ferry
• The ferry crossed the Anderson River in Spencer County, Ind. His pay was 37 cents a day.
Jan. 20, 1828, his sister died
1828, built flatboat, took cargo of produce to New Orleans, La.
• He set out from Troy, Ind. After three months on the Mississippi, he arrived at New Orleans, where he sold the boat and the cargo. He traveled home by steamboat.
Mar. 1, 1830, with family, moved to Illinois
• The Lincolns settled near Decatur, Ill., on the Sangamon River, but remained for only one year. When his family moved on to Coles County, Ill., he stayed behind.
Spring, 1831, made second trip to New Orleans
• Together with his stepbrother, John Johnston, and his mother's cousin, John Hanks, Lincoln had agreed to make the trip to New Orleans for Denton Offutt. When they reached Springfield and discovered

Offutt had no boat, they contracted to build one for wages of $10 a month. It took them a month to build the boat. On the trip downriver, he had his first look at New Salem, where the boat got hung up on a dam for a while. He returned from this trip in late July.
September, 1831, moved to New Salem
• He had been hired as clerk at Offutt's general store at wages of $15 a month plus the use of a room behind the store for his sleeping quarters. After he outwrestled Jack Armstrong, the leader of the Clary's Grove boys, he was accepted into the community.
Winter, 1831–1832, attended meetings of New Salem Debating Society
Spring, 1832, decided to run for state legislature
• He published his platform in the *Sangamo Journal*, Mar. 9.
Apr. 21, 1832, volunteered for military service, Black Hawk War
• Since Offutt's store was closing anyway—it was never a financial success—he joined a group of local volunteers responding to a call from the governor. He was elected captain of his company; he later declared this to be the most satisfying honor of his life.
May 9, 1832, sworn into federal military service
• He was sworn into service near the Rock River where his group had joined a number of others, including a detachment of army regulars commanded by Captain Zachary Taylor. When his original 30-day enlistment ended at Ottawa, Ill., Lincoln reenlisted as a private for 20 days and after that for another 30 days. He spent the last period involved in a futile hunt for Chief Black Hawk in southern Wisconsin.
• He was the second of two presidents who served in the Black Hawk War. The other was Taylor.
• He was the eighth of 21 presidents who served in the military during wartime.
July 10, 1832, mustered out, White Water River; returned to New Salem
• He arrived at New Salem in late July and made a brief campaign for a legislative seat. Six months later, when the army paymaster arrived at Springfield, Lincoln received $125 for his 80 days of military service.

Aug. 6, 1832, defeated as candidate for state legislature
• He ran eighth in a field of 13 candidates. He polled 277 of the 300 votes cast in New Salem. This was the only direct election he ever lost.
1832, bought half interest in general store, New Salem
• In exchange for a promissory note, he acquired the interest of Rowan Herndon in a partnership with William F. Berry.
• The business deteriorated and the partnership was dissolved, March, 1833.
May 7, 1833, appointed postmaster, New Salem
• He held this position until the post office was removed to Petersburg, May 30, 1836. His pay, based on receipts, averaged $55 a year; in addition, he enjoyed franking privileges, exemption from military and jury duty, and received one newspaper each day free of postage.
• He was the first of two presidents who were postmasters. The other was Truman.
• He supplemented his income by rail-splitting, helped out at the local mill, worked as a farm hand, served as local agent for the Springfield newspaper, and acted as clerk at elections.
Fall, 1833, began work as surveyor
• He served for three years as deputy to the county surveyor, John Calhoun. In order to undertake his duties, Lincoln bought a horse, saddle, and bridle for $57.86. When he was unable to pay, he was sued and deprived of his personal possessions, which were bought at auction by friends and returned to him as gifts.
• He was the last of three presidents who were surveyors.
Aug. 4, 1834, elected to state legislature
• About this time he began the study of law, encouraged by John T. Stuart, a Springfield lawyer and Whig politician, who loaned him books. Lincoln had previously considered the study of law after his defeat as candidate for the legislature in 1832, but thought it improbable because of his poor educational background.
• He was the 12th of 26 presidents who studied law.
December, 1834, took seat in legislature, Vandalia, then capital of Illinois
• During this session of the legislature, he first met Stephen A. Douglas.
Aug. 25, 1835, Ann Rutledge died

• There is no documentary proof that he was romantically involved with Miss Rutledge. The legend, usually attributed to William Herndon, was based on a story in the Menard *Axis*, Feb. 15, 1862.
Aug. 1, 1836, reelected to state legislature
Sept. 9, 1836, licensed to practice law
• He tried his first case two days later in Springfield.
• He was the 12th of 23 presidents who were lawyers.
Dec. 5, 1836, served as Whig floor leader, Tenth General Assembly, Vandalia
• During this session he was successful in securing the passage of an act to move the capital to Springfield. Near the end of the session, which lasted three months (then the longest in Illinois history), his name was enrolled by the clerk of the state supreme court, the final requirement for the practice of law.
Apr. 15, 1837, moved from New Salem to Springfield
• He formed a law partnership with John T. Stuart.
Aug. 5, 1838, reelected to state legislature
• His partner, John T. Stuart, opposed Douglas in the congressional election. Douglas won by 36 votes out of a total of 36,495.
December, 1838, legislature met for last time, Vandalia
• During this session Lincoln again served as floor manager. He lost the election for speaker when the Whig vote was split.
July 4, 1839, Springfield proclaimed new capital of Illinois
1840, his engagement to Mary Todd announced
• The engagement was broken late that year. They had planned to be married on New Year's Day, 1841.
Aug. 5, 1840, elected to fourth term in state legislature
• He was ill for three weeks during the session that convened in December, some say because of melancholia over his broken engagement. During his attendance he opposed a Democratic move to pack the state supreme court by increasing the number of justices from four to nine; his opposition failed, the act passed, and Douglas was appointed as one of the new judges.
Spring, 1841, dissolved partnership with John T. Stuart
• Lincoln formed a new firm with Stephen T. Long.

Fall, 1842, challenged to duel by state auditor, James Shields
- The *Sangamo Journal* published a satirical letter about Shields, Aug. 27. Purportedly written by a widow named Rebecca, it actually was written by Lincoln. The newspaper published a second letter in which Rebecca offered her hand in marriage to Shields. When Shields was informed who had perpetrated the hoax, the challenge was made. Since duelling was illegal in Illinois, they met across the Mississippi River from Alton. Their differences were reconciled and the duel did not take place. Not until many years later did Lincoln reveal that the second "Rebecca" letter had been written by Mary Todd and her friend, Julia Jayne.

Nov. 4, 1842, married Mary Todd, Springfield
- The only house he owned is at 430 South Eight Street, Springfield. The Lincolns lived here from 1844 to 1860. In 1887, his son, Robert, gave the family home to the people of Illinois. It is maintained by the State of Illinois Department of Conservation, Division of Parks and Memorials. It is open to the public daily except Thanksgiving, Christmas and New Year's Day, 9 A.M.

to 8 P.M., June 1 to Sept. 30, and 9 A.M. to 5 P.M., Oct. 1 to May 31. Admission: free.

May 1, 1843, defeated for Whig nomination as candidate for House of Representatives
- The other candidates were John J. Hardin and Edward D. Baker. When Hardin was nominated, he successfully moved that Baker be endorsed as the candidate for 1844. Rotation of nomination was not uncommon.

Aug. 1, 1843, his first son born
- The boy was named Robert Todd Lincoln.

Fall, 1844, stumped eastern Illinois and southwestern Indiana for presidential candidate, Henry Clay

December, 1844, dissolved partnership with Stephen T. Long
- Lincoln formed a firm with William H. Herndon, a partnership that remained in effect until Lincoln's death.

Mar. 10, 1846, his second son born
- The boy was named Edward Baker Lincoln. Although Edward T. Baker was his political rival, he was also a close personal friend.

May 1, 1846, nominated for House of Representatives, Whig state convention, Petersburg

NATIONAL PROMINENCE

Aug. 3, 1846, elected to House of Representatives
- Lincoln was the 11th of 17 presidents who were elected to the House.

Aug. 15, 1846, published his only public statement on religious convictions
- Charges that he was "an open scoffer at Christianity" had been circulated during the campaign by Peter Cartwright, a circuit-riding Methodist preacher and his Democratic opponent. Friends persuaded him not to reply until after the election. Published in the *Illinois Gazette*, Lacon, the crux of Lincoln's statement was:

  That I am not a member of any Christian Church, is true; but I have never denied the truth of the Scriptures; and I have never spoken with intentional disrespect of religion in general, or of any denomination of Christians in particular.

Dec. 6, 1847, took seat in House of Representatives
- He served in the 30th Congress. The Mexican War was the principal issue at the first session. Although he voted with the Whigs on a number of resolutions designed to place blame for the war on Polk, he consistently voted in favor of measures to provide supplies for the troops.
- He was the 11th of 17 presidents who served in the House.

June 7–9, 1848, attended Whig national convention, Philadelphia, Pa.
- He supported Zachary Taylor.

August–November, 1848, campaigned for Taylor
- After a series of speeches in Washington and Maryland, he toured Massachusetts in September. On his way home, he conferred with the vice-presidential candidate, Millard Fillmore, and the Whig leader of New York, Thurlow Weed, in Albany. Lincoln addressed a Whig rally in

Chicago, Oct. 6. He stumped the northern part of his district until election day.

Dec. 4, 1848, took seat in House for second session of 30th Congress

• During this session, he voted consistently for legislation to establish free governments in California and New Mexico.

Mar. 10, 1849, filed application for patent

• He sought a patent for "an improved method of lifting vessels over shoals" by means of "adjustable buoyant chambers." The patent was granted in May.

• He was the only president who received a patent.

April, 1849, returned to law practice, Springfield

• He was not a candidate for reelection to the House.

June 21, 1849, failed to win desired appointment as commissioner of general land office, Washington

• This was the only occasion on which he sought appointment to executive office.

Aug. 21, 1849, declined appointment as secretary of Oregon Territory

Sept. 27, 1849, declined appointment as governor of Oregon Territory

Feb. 1, 1850, his son, Edward Baker Lincoln, died

Dec. 21, 1850, his third son born

• The boy was named William Wallace Lincoln.

Jan. 15, 1851, his father died

Apr. 4, 1853, his fourth son born

• The boy was named Thomas Lincoln.

August, 1854, reentered politics, opposed Kansas-Nebraska bill

• Although his avowed purpose was to campaign for the reelection of Representative Richard Yates, who shared his views of the Kansas-Nebraska bill, Lincoln agreed to run again for the state legislature. The Kansas-Nebraska bill had been introduced by Senator Stephen A. Douglas.

Sept. 26, 1854, refuted Douglas speech at Whig rally, Bloomington

Oct. 4, 1854, replied to Douglas speech of day before, Illinois State Fair, Springfield

• Lincoln made essentially the same speech at Peoria, Oct. 16, where it was better reported. It has come to be known as the "Peoria speech."

Nov. 7, 1854, elected to fifth term in state legislature

• He resigned shortly thereafter so as to be eligible for election to the Senate.

Feb. 8, 1855, defeated as candidate for Senate

• Although he had 44 of the necessary 51 votes on the first ballot, he trailed off to 15 votes on the seventh ballot. He then supported Lyman Trumbull, an anti-Nebraska Democrat, in order to prevent the election of Governor Joel A. Matteson, a Douglas supporter. Trumbull was elected.

• Trumbull was married to Julia Jayne, the co-author of the second Rebecca letter that almost precipitated the duel with Shields in 1842. Shields was the incumbent in the Senate seat at issue; Shields's supporters had switched to Matteson earlier in the balloting.

1855–1856, resumed his law practice

• He appeared frequently before the U.S. District Court, Chicago. During this period, he earned the largest fee of his career, $5,000, when he represented the Illinois Central Railroad in a suit that involved the right of McLean County to tax the railroad.

May 29, 1856, spoke at convention of anti-Nebraska groups, Bloomington

• This has come to be known as the "lost speech" because there is no authenticated record of its contents.

• This meeting marked the rebirth of the Republican party in Illinois, although for a time many of its supporters avoided the name.

June 17, 1856, favorite son candidate for vice presidential nomination, first Republican national convention, Philadelphia, Pa.

• He received 110 votes on the first ballot. His supporters swung to William L. Dayton on the next ballot; Dayton was nominated.

July–November, 1856, campaigned for John Charles Fremont, Republican party candidate

• He made more than 50 campaign speeches throughout Illinois.

June 16, 1858, unanimously nominated for Senate, Republican state convention, Springfield

• His acceptance address has come to be known as "The House Divided" speech because of his usage of the biblical quotation, "A house divided against itself cannot stand." He had employed the quotation on other occasions, as early as Mar. 4, 1843, in a Whig committee campaign circular.

• In his address he said:

If we could first know where we are, and whither we are tending, we could then better judge what to do, and how to do it. We are now far into the fifth year, since a policy was initiated, with the avowed object, and confident promise, of putting an end to slavery agitation. Under the operation of that policy, that agitation has not only not ceased, but has constantly augmented. In my opinion, it will not cease, until a crisis shall have been reached, and passed. "A house divided against itself cannot stand."
I believe this government cannot endure, permanently half slave and half free. I do not expect the Union to be dissolved—I do not expect the house to fall—but I do expect it will cease to be divided. It will become all one thing, or all the other. Either the opponents of slavery will arrest the further spread of it, and place it where the public mind shall rest in the belief that it is in course of ultimate extinction; or its advocates will push it forward, till it shall become alike lawful in all the States, old as well as new—North as well as South.

July 24, 1858, challenged Douglas to series of debates
• Douglas, the incumbent, agreed to debate once in each congressional district except Chicago and Springfield, where both had already spoken. Seven communities suggested by Douglas were agreed upon: Ottawa, Freeport, Jonesboro, Charleston, Galesburg, Quincy, and Alton.

Aug. 21–Oct. 15, 1858, Lincoln-Douglas debates
• More verbal joustings than arguments of substance since the positions of both candidates were well known before they began, the seven debates still drew immense crowds and much publicity. Douglas reiterated his doctrine of popular sovereignty. At Freeport, Aug. 27, Lincoln emphasized the point that Douglas's endorsement of the *Dred Scott* decision—which had determined that Congress was not empowered to prohibit slavery in the territories—bound his opponent to all future Supreme Court rulings. In reply, Douglas asserted

that Congress could not dictate to a territory and force passage of laws against its will; this came to be known as the Freeport Doctrine, which cost the Democrat a sizable number of votes in the southern districts of the state. By the last debate in Alton, Lincoln had reduced the argument to the moral question of whether slavery was right or wrong. The debates brought Lincoln to national prominence.

Jan. 5, 1859, defeated as candidate for Senate
• Douglas was elected by the legislature, 54–46.

January, 1859, approached about running for president
• Jesse Fell of Bloomington, a Republican leader, was among the first who urged Lincoln's candidacy.

Apr. 16, 1859, disclaimed fitness for presidency
• In a letter to Thomas J. Pickett, the editor of the Rock Island *Register*, who wished to promote his candidacy, Lincoln wrote: "I must, in candor, say I do not think I am fit for the Presidency."

August, 1859, made Midwest speaking tour
• His first address was made at Council Bluffs, Iowa. He also spoke in Columbus, Dayton, Hamilton, and Cincinnati, Ohio; Indianapolis, Ind.; and Milwaukee, Wis. He refused invitations to speak in literally hundreds of communities.

November–December, 1859, made speaking tour of Kansas
• Kansas was about to be admitted to the Union.

Feb. 27, 1860, spoke at Cooper Institute, now Cooper Union for the Advancement of Science and Art, New York City
• The speech had originally been scheduled for delivery at Henry Ward Beecher's Plymouth Church, Brooklyn. The location was changed after sponsorship was assumed by the Young Men's Central Republican Union of New York City, a group intent on stifling the candidacy of William H. Seward for the presidency. Lincoln shared the platform with Horace Greeley and William Cullen Bryant.

March–April, 1860, made speaking tour of New England
• He spoke in a number of Massachusetts, Rhode Island, and Connecticut communities.

May 10, 1860, endorsed as favorite son candidate for president, Republican state convention, Decatur

May 18, 1860, nominated for president on third ballot, Republican national convention, Chicago, Ill.

October, 1860, began to grow beard

Nov. 6, 1860, election day
• *See* Election of 1860, below.

Dec. 5, 1860, presidential electors cast ballots
•He received 180 of the 303 electoral votes from the 33 states.
• *See* Election of 1860, below.

Feb. 13, 1861, electoral vote tabulated by Congress
•Lincoln and Hamlin were officially declared elected.

ELECTION OF 1860

Democratic party, convened Apr. 23, at Charleston, S.C.; adjourned, May 3, without agreement on nominees after 57 ballots. The Democrats reassembled, June 18, at Baltimore, Md., nominated Stephen Arnold Douglas of Illinois for President, Benjamin Fitzpatrick of Alabama for vice president. Fitzpatrick declined; the national committee nominated Herschel Vespasian Johnson of Georgia for vice president.
•This was the eighth Democratic national convention. It was the seventh Democratic convention in Baltimore; it was the 12th major party convention in Baltimore.

Constitutional Union (Whig and American party remnants) party, convened, May 9, at Baltimore, Md., nominated John Bell of Tennessee for president, Edward Everett of Massachusetts for vice president.
•This was the 13th major party convention in Baltimore.

Republican party, convened, May 16, at Chicago, Ill., nominated Abraham Lincoln of Illinois for president, Hannibal Hamlin of Maine for vice president.
•This was the second Republican national convention. It was the first Republican convention in Chicago; it was the first of 23 major party conventions in Chicago.

Democratic (Southern Democrats) party, convened, June 23, at Baltimore, Md., nominated John Cabell Breckinridge of Kentucky for president, Joseph Lane of Oregon for vice president.
•This was the 14th major party convention in Baltimore.

Election day, Tuesday, Nov. 6, 1860

Popular vote: 4,682,069
    Lincoln, 1,866,452
    Douglas, 1,376,957
    Breckinridge, 849,781
    Bell, 588,879
•Lincoln was the fifth of 15 presidents who were elected without receiving a majority of the popular vote.

Electoral vote: 303, 33 states
• Lincoln, 180, 18 states
    (California, 4; Connecticut, 6; Illinois, 11; Indiana, 13; Iowa, 4; Maine, 8; Massachusetts, 13; Michigan, 6; Minnesota, 4; New Hampshire, 5; New Jersey, 4 of 7 votes; New York, 35; Ohio, 23; Oregon, 3; Pennsylvania, 27; Rhode Island, 4; Vermont, 5; Wisconsin, 5)
• Breckinridge, 72, 11 states
    (Alabama, 9; Arkansas, 4; Delaware, 3; Florida, 3; Georgia, 10; Louisiana, 6; Maryland, 8; Mississippi, 7; North Carolina, 10; South Carolina, 8; Texas, 4)
• Bell, 39, three states
    (Kentucky, 12; Tennessee, 12; Virginia, 15)
• Douglas, 12, one state
    (Missouri, 9)
•Douglas also received the votes of three New Jersey electors.
•Lincoln was the first of four presidents who defeated major opponents representing the same state (Douglas).

THE PRESIDENT (16th)

Term of office: Mar. 4, 1861, to Apr. 15, 1865 (4 years, 42 days)
•Lincoln was the sixth of 12 presidents who were elected to second terms.
•He was the sixth of 16 presidents who served more than one term.

State represented: Illinois
•He was the first of two presidents who represented Illinois. The other was Grant.
•He was the fifth of 15 presidents who represented states that were not their native states.

Political party: Republican
• He was the first of 14 presidents who were Republicans.
Congresses: 37th, 38th, 39th
Administrations: 19th, 20th
Age at inauguration: 52 years, 20 days

Inauguration day: Monday, Mar. 4, 1861
• Lincoln took the oath of office, administered by Chief Justice Roger B. Taney, on the east portico of the Capitol.
• This was the last of seven inaugurations at which Taney officiated.

THE 19th ADMINISTRATION

1861

Mar. 5, appointed his only secretary of state, William H. Seward; his first secretary of treasury, Salmon P. Chase; his first secretary of war, Simon Cameron; his first attorney general, Edward Bates; his only secretary of navy, Gideon Welles; his first postmaster general, Montgomery Blair; and his first secretary of interior, Caleb B. Smith
• Seward took office, Mar. 6; Chase and Welles, Mar. 7.
Mar. 9, held first cabinet meeting
Mar. 15, advised by five members of cabinet against provisioning Fort Sumter

• The written opinions were submitted by all of the cabinet except Chase and Blair.
Apr. 1, received Seward's "Some Thoughts for the President's Consideration"
• Seward suggested a foreign war to unite the country.
Apr. 4, Associate Justice McLean died
Apr. 10, sent emissaries to inform Governor Francis W. Pickens of South Carolina Fort Sumter would be provisioned
• The surrender of Fort Sumter was demanded and refused, Apr. 11; the attack began, Apr. 12; and the fort was surrendered about 7 P.M., Apr. 13. The Civil War had begun.

THE CIVIL WAR

1861

Apr. 15, issued proclamation that declared "insurrection" existed, called on states for seventy-five thousand militia
Apr. 15, ordered special session of Congress, July 4
Apr. 19, issued proclamation ordering blockade of all ports of seceded states
Apr. 27, issued proclamation extending blockade to ports of North Carolina and Virginia
• North Carolina seceded. May 20; Virginia, May 23.
Apr. 29, Associate Justice Campbell resigned
• Campbell was the only southern justice of the Supreme Court who joined the Confederacy. He served as assistant secretary of war of the Confederate states.
May 3, called for forty-two thousand volunteers to increase army by ten regiments, navy by eighteen thousand seamen
May 6, Arkansas seceded
May 10, declared martial law and suspension of writ of habeas corpus on Key West,

Tortugas, and Santa Rosa islands
June 8, Tennessee seceded
• Tennessee became the 11th and last state to join the Confederacy.
June 29, presided at council of war
• The decision was made to advance on Manassas, the Confederate base of operations.
July 4, first session of 37th Congress
• The administration controlled both the Senate and the House of Representatives.
• The Republicans gained five Senate seats but lost five House seats. However, the secession of the southern states had reduced Democratic membership in the Senate by 15 seats and in the House by 59 seats. The Senate (50 members) consisted of 31 Republicans, 11 Democrats, seven others, and one vacancy. The House (178 members) consisted of 106 Republicans, 42 Democrats, 28 others, and two vacancies.
July 4, sent war message to Congress
• This was the fourth of seven war messages.
July 21, first Battle of Bull Run, Manassas Junction, Va.

•This battle resulted in a Confederate victory.

July 29, authorized to call out militia for suppression of rebellion

Aug. 5, signed income tax act

•The first rate of taxation was three percent on incomes in excess of $800.

Aug. 6, signed confiscation act

•This act provided for the emancipation of slaves who were employed against the U.S. in arms or labor.

Aug. 6, Congress approved and legalized all acts, proclamations, and orders of president to army and navy issued since Mar. 4

Aug. 6, first session of 37th Congress adjourned

Aug. 16, issued proclamation forbidding commercial intercourse with seceded states

Oct. 24, received first transcontinental telegram

•The telegram was transmitted from Sacramento, Cal.

Dec. 2, second session of 37th Congress

Dec. 3, sent his first State of the Union message to Congress

1862

Jan. 11, requested and received resignation of Secretary of War Cameron, effective, Jan. 14

•Cameron's methods of placing army contracts had become a national scandal. As a means of removing Cameron from the cabinet, Lincoln appointed the secretary of war as minister to Russia.

Jan. 15, appointed his second secretary of war, Edwin M. Stanton

•Stanton took office, Jan. 20.

Jan. 21, appointed Noah H. Swayne as associate justice

•Swayne, who was confirmed by the Senate, Jan. 24, was the first of Lincoln's five appointments to the Supreme Court.

Jan. 27, issued War Order No. 1

•He directed that an advance of all Union forces should take place, Feb. 22. General George Brinton McClellan, general-in-chief, ignored this order.

Jan. 31, authorized to take possession of railroads and telegraph lines when public safety involved

Feb. 20, his son, William, died

•William Wallace Lincoln was the third of five children of presidents who died during their fathers' terms of office.

•He was the only child of a president who died in the White House.

Feb. 25, signed legal tender act

•This act authorized an issue of $150,000,-000 in U.S. paper currency, "greenbacks."

Mar. 6, sent special message to Congress recommending compensated emancipation of slaves in states that adopted gradual abolition

•His plan for pecuniary assistance to states that instituted gradual abolition was adopted by joint resolution, Apr. 10.

Mar. 11, relieved General McClellan of command of all military departments except Army of Potomac

Apr. 6–7, Battle of Shiloh or Pittsburg Landing, Tenn.

•As a result of this northern victory, the Confederates were forced to evacuate most of Tennessee. Union losses, including 1,754 killed, totalled 13,047; Confederate losses, including 1,723 killed, totalled 10,-694.

Apr. 16, signed act abolishing slavery in District of Columbia

•The average compensation paid by the government was $300.

May 15, department of agriculture established

•The activities of the agricultural division of the patent office were expanded, but the department was not raised to cabinet rank until 1889.

May 19, disavowed proclamation of General David Hunter

•Hunter had issued a proclamation that freed slaves and authorized arming of able-bodied Negroes in his military district, which included Florida, Georgia, and South Carolina.

May 20, signed Homestead Act

•This act offered any adult head of a family 160 acres of surveyed public land after five years of continuous residence and payment of a $26 to $34 fee, or $1.25 per acre after six months' residence.

June 5, authorized to appoint diplomatic representatives to Negro republics, Haiti and Liberia

June 19, signed act prohibiting slavery in territories

June 23, vetoed bank notes in District of Columbia bill

•This was the first of his six vetoes.

July 1, signed act that provided for railroad and telegraph line from Missouri River to Pacific Coast

July 1, signed act that established office of commissioner of internal revenue

July 2, issued proclamation calling for 300,-000 volunteers for three-year service

July 2, vetoed medical offices in army bill

•This was the second of his six vetoes.

July 2, signed Morrill Act

•This act granted each loyal state thirty thousand acres for each senator and representative in Congress for the establishment of agricultural colleges. Sixty-nine land grant colleges were established over the years, more than fifty of which exist today.

July 7, received letter of advice from General McClellan

•General McClellan summarized his ideas as to the general conduct of affairs, repeating many of the complaints he had made in a letter to Secretary of War Stanton, June 28. McClellan had accused Stanton of doing his best "to sacrifice this army."

July 11, appointed Major General Henry Wager Hallack as his military adviser

•Hallack was given the title of general-in-chief.

July 12, Medal of Honor authorized by Congress

July 16, appointed Samuel Freeman Miller as associate justice

•Miller, who was confirmed by the Senate, July 16, was the second of Lincoln's five appointments to the Supreme Court.

July 17, authorized to call up militia between ages of 18 and 45, admit Negroes to the military service, appoint judge-advocate general, and organize army corps at his discretion

July 17, second session of 37th Congress adjourned

July 22, submitted first draft of Emancipation Proclamation to cabinet

•After consultation with the cabinet, he decided to delay issuing the proclamation.

Aug. 4, issued call for 300,000 militia for nine-month service

Aug. 9, Battle of Cedar Mountain, Va.

•This engagement resulted in a Confederate victory. Union losses, including about 300 killed, totalled about 2,350; Confederate losses, including about 230 killed, totalled about 1,300.

Aug. 14, received Negro committee, discussed emigration and colonial proposals regarding Liberia and Central America

Aug. 19, Horace Greeley public letter published

•In the letter, addressed to the president and published in the New York *Tribune* under the title, "Prayer of Twenty Millions," Greeley wrote that "all attempts to put down the rebellion and at the same time uphold its inciting cause are preposterous and futile."

Aug. 22, stated his policies in reply to Greeley

Aug. 29–30, second Battle of Bull Run

•Union troops were forced to retreat to Washington.

Sept. 3, appointed Joseph Holt as first judge-advocate general

Sept. 15, capture of Harper's Ferry, W. Va.

•About 10,700 Union troops and large quantities of equipment were lost to a Confederate army under General Thomas Jonathan ("Stonewall") Jackson.

Sept. 17, Battle of Antietam, Md.

•This was the "bloodiest single day" of the war, resulting in more than 26,000 casualties. Union losses, including about 2,100 killed, totalled about 12,400; Confederate losses, including about 2,700 killed, totalled about 13,700. While virtually a standoff, the battle forced General Robert E. Lee to retreat to Virginia.

•Antietam caused France and Great Britain, about to recognize the Confederacy, to reconsider. It also created the atmosphere desired by the president for issuance of his Emancipation Proclamation.

Sept. 22, issued preliminary Emancipation Proclamation

•The proclamation freed all slaves in the Confederate states as of Jan. 1, 1863.

Sept. 23, asked cabinet to consider subject of acquisition of territory to which Negroes might be deported

Sept. 24, issued proclamation that suspended writ of habeas corpus for persons in rebellion and arrested insurgents, declared them subject to trial by court-martial or military commission

Oct. 17, appointed David Davis as associate justice

•Davis, who was confirmed by the Senate, Dec. 8, was the third of Lincoln's five appointments to the Supreme Court.

Nov. 5, relieved General McClellan

• He appointed General Ambrose Everett Burnside as commanding general, Army of Potomac, Nov. 7.

Dec. 1, third session of 37th Congress

Dec. 1, sent his second State of the Union address to Congress

• He recommended passage of a constitutional amendment that would provide compensation to any state that abolished slavery prior to Jan. 1, 1900. He urged that slaves freed by the war be declared forever free and that loyal slaveowners be compensated.

Dec. 17, refused to accept resignation of Secretary of State Seward

• Seward offered to resign because of Senate opposition to his policies.

Dec. 18, removal of Seward asked by committee of nine senators

Dec. 20, refused to accept resignation of Secretary of Treasury Chase

Dec. 31, contracted for Negro emigration to Haiti

• Bernard Kock agreed to transport five thousand Negroes to Vache Island, Haiti, for a fee of $50 each.

Dec. 31, signed act to admit West Virginia as state, June 20, 1863

Dec. 31, accepted resignation of Secretary of Interior Smith

1863

Jan. 1, issued Emancipation Proclamation

• He declared that all slaves in states still in rebellion were "then, thenceforward, and forever free." In actuality, the proclamation freed no slaves since it exempted all areas under Union military occupation.

Jan. 8, appointed his second secretary of interior, John P. Usher

Jan. 25, relieved General Burnside, appointed General Joseph Hooker as commander of Army of Potomac

Feb. 24, Territory of Arizona established

Feb. 25, signed national banking system act

• This act provided a national currency by requiring national banks to invest one third of their capital in U.S. securities.

• This act also established the office of the comptroller of the currency. The first comptroller, Hugh McCulloch, was appointed, May 9.

Mar. 3, Territory of Idaho established

Mar. 3, signed first Conscription Act

• This act made liable for military service all men between the ages of 20 and 45, but exempted those who furnished substitutes or paid $300. The first drawing was made in Rhode Island, July 7. The New York drawing culminated in four days of rioting in New York City, where nearly one thousand persons were killed or wounded, July 13–16.

Mar. 3, authorized to suspend writ of habeas corpus wherever necessary

Mar. 3, signed Judiciary Act of 1863

• The act increased the number of Supreme Court justices from nine to ten and established a tenth circuit of Oregon and California.

Mar. 3, third session of 37th Congress adjourned

Mar. 3, vetoed amended navy bill

• This was the third of his six vetoes, the first of his four pocket vetoes.

Mar. 6, appointed Stephen J. Field as associate justice

• Field, who was confirmed by the Senate, Mar. 10, was the fourth of Lincoln's five appointments to the Supreme Court.

Mar. 10, issued proclamation regarding desertions

• It was estimated that about 9,000 officers and 280,000 enlisted men were absent from duty in the Union army as of Jan. 1. About ten percent of both armies deserted.

May 2–4, Battle of Chancellorsville, Va.

• This was a costly victory for the Confederacy. Among the 1,665 killed and about 9,000 wounded was General Jackson, who was mortally wounded by his own men, May 2. Jackson died, May 10.

May 22, commuted sentence of Clement L. Vallandigham

• Vallandigham, a former Ohio congressman sympathetic to the South, had been convicted of "treasonable conduct," May 16, and sentenced to close confinement in a fortress for the duration of the war.

• Lincoln directed that Vallandigham be sent "beyond our military lines." The Ohioan was sent to Shelbyville, Tenn., May 25.

June 4, rescinded June 2 order of General Burnside to suppress Chicago *Times*

June 11, Vallandigham nominated for governor of Ohio by Democrats

June 15, issued proclamation calling for 100,000 militia for six-month service to resist invasion of North

• These troops were not used.

June 20, West Virginia admitted as 35th state
•West Virginia was the first of two states admitted during his term of office.

July 1–3, Battle of Gettysburg
•Most military historians consider Gettysburg the turning point of the war. This vital Union victory was won at the cost of more than thirty-one hundred killed and about twenty thousand wounded and missing. Confederate losses were about thirty-nine hundred killed, about twenty-four thousand wounded and missing.

July 4, surrender of Vicksburg
•After a six-week siege, Vicksburg and its garrison of twenty thousand men capitulated. When Port Hudson, La., was captured, July 9, the entire Mississippi Valley was in Union control, and the Confederacy was split.

July 30, issued proclamation of protection of Negro soldiers against retaliation by Confederates

Sept. 15, issued proclamation that declared general suspension of writ of habeas corpus when necessary

Sept. 19–20, Battle of Chickamauga, Ga.
•This Confederate victory endangered Chattanooga, Tenn., the gateway to the East.

Oct. 13, Vallandigham defeated in Ohio by 100,000 majority

Oct. 17, issued call for 300,000 volunteers for three-year service or duration of war

Nov. 19, delivered Gettysburg Address at dedication of battlefield cemetery

Nov. 23–25, Battle of Chattanooga, Tenn.
•After this victory the Union armies were prepared to cross Georgia to the sea, so as to bisect the upper and lower South.

Dec. 7, first session of 38th Congress
•The administration maintained control of both the Senate and the House of Representatives. The Republicans lost eight Senate and three House seats. The Senate (51 members) consisted of 39 Republicans and 12 Democrats. The House (183 members) consisted of 103 Republicans and 80 Democrats.

Dec. 8, sent his third State of the Union message to Congress
•He stated that 100,000 Negroes were in military service, half of whom had borne arms.

Dec. 8, issued proclamation that granted amnesty to all Confederates who would take oath of allegiance to Union

•The offer did not extend to civil and diplomatic officers of the "so-called Confederate government" or to certain others, including military officers of high rank.

1864

Feb. 1, issued call for 500,000 men for three-year service or duration of war
•The second draft was set for Mar. 14.

Feb. 20, Battle of Olustee, Fla.
•This Confederate victory was also called the Battle of Ocean Pond.

Feb. 24, authorized to call for such numbers of men for military service as needed, provision made for draft where quota assigned not filled by volunteers

Mar. 9, commissioned Ulysses S. Grant as lieutenant general
•Lincoln conferred the highest rank in the army—the same rank given George Washington in 1798–on General Grant at the White House.

Mar. 26, issued second amnesty proclamation

May 5–7, Battle of Wilderness, Va.
•With decisive results, this bloody battle cost the Union about 18,000 casualties, including about 2,200 killed, while the Confederates suffered about 7,750 casualties.

May 8–12, battles of Spotsylvania, Va.
•Two engagements at Spotsylvania Court House, called the second and third Battles of the Wilderness, proved indecisive but costly to both sides.

May 18, forged proclamation published
•The fraudulent proclamation, which was dated May 17, and called for 400,000 additional troops, was published in the New York *World*, the New York *Journal of Commerce*, and other Democratic newspapers. Written by Joseph Howard, an itinerant newspaperman and former secretary to the Reverend Henry Ward Beecher, it was released with the aim of raising the price of gold.
•Lincoln ordered the *World* and the *Journal of Commerce*, which had been suppressed for two days by order of Secretary of War Stanton, restored to their editors. Several weeks later he ordered the release of Howard, who had been arrested and imprisoned.

May 26, Territory of Montana established

June 1–3, Battle of Cold Harbor, Va.

•This mismanaged and unsuccessful Union assault cost seven thousand casualties on one day, June 3.

June 7, nominated for president, National Union convention, Baltimore, Md.

June 15–18, Battle of Petersburg, Va.

•After an unsuccessful four-day assault, which cost eight thousand men, Grant dug in for what was to be one of the longest sieges of the war, nine months.

June 27, accepted renomination by letter

June 28, Fugitive Slave Act of 1850 repealed

June 30, Secretary of Treasury Chase resigned

June 30, signed Internal Revenue Act

•This act increased the income tax to five percent on incomes in excess of $600 and less than $5,000, and to ten percent on incomes in excess of $10,000.

July 1, appointed his second secretary of treasury, William P. Fessenden

•Fessenden took office, July 5.

July 2, signed act prohibiting coastal slave trade

July 4, first session of 38th Congress adjourned

July 4, vetoed Wade-Davis Reconstruction bill

•This was the fourth of his six vetoes, the second of his four pocket vetoes.

July 5, issued proclamation suspending writ of habeas corpus, declared martial law in Kentucky

July 8, issued proclamation explaining his refusal to sign Wade-Davis Reconstruction bill

•He explained that he could not be "inflexibly committed to any single plan of restoration."

July 18, issued call for 500,000 men for one, two, or three-year service

•This was the third draft call.

July 18, dispatched Horace Greeley to confer with southern peace commissioners, Niagara Falls, Ontario, Canada

•Lincoln instructed Greeley to inform the Confederate representatives that restoration of the South to the Union and renunciation of slavery were mandatory. These terms were unacceptable to the southerners.

Sept. 2, occupation of Atlanta, Ga.

•General William Tecumseh Sherman had set out from Chattanooga, May 7.

Sept. 23, requested resignation of Postmaster General Blair

Sept. 24, appointed his second postmaster general, William Dennison

Oct. 12, Chief Justice Taney died

Oct. 31, Nevada admitted as 36th state

•Nevada was the second of two states admitted during his term of office.

Nov. 8, election day

• See Election of 1864, page 188.

Nov. 19, issued proclamation that declared ports of Norfolk, Va., Fernandina and Pensacola, Fla., open to commerce

Nov. 24, Attorney General Bates resigned

Dec. 2, appointed his second attorney general, James Speed

Dec. 5, second session of 38th Congress

Dec. 6, sent his fourth and last State of the Union message to Congress

Dec. 6, appointed Salmon P. Chase as chief justice

•Chase, who was confirmed by the Senate, Dec. 6, was the last of Lincoln's five appointments to the Supreme Court.

•He was the fourth of 14 presidents who appointed chief justices.

Dec. 7, presidential electors cast ballots

•He received 212 of the 233 electoral votes from the 25 states. The 80 electoral votes from the 11 states that had seceded were not cast.

• See Election of 1864, page 188.

Dec. 19, called for 300,000 men for military service

•This was the last of the four draft calls.

Dec. 22, capture of Savannah, Ga.

•General Sherman set out from Atlanta, Nov. 14. On the march to the sea, Sherman's army of sixty thousand men cut a 60-mile swath, systematically destroying everything of military value along the 300-mile route.

1865

Jan. 18, expressed willingness to confer with southern peace commissioners

•In a letter to Montgomery Blair, Lincoln stated that he was willing to receive the agents of Jefferson Davis informally.

Feb. 1, 13th Amendment to Constitution submitted to states for ratification

Feb. 3, met with southern peace commissioners

•The informal conference took place

aboard the Union transport, *River Queen*, near Fort Monroe, Hampton Roads, Va. The meeting was a failure since the Confederate commissioners had been instructed to insist on recognition of southern independence.

Feb. 8, electoral votes tabulated by Congress

•Lincoln and Andrew Johnson were officially declared elected.

Feb. 17–18, capture of Columbia and Charleston, S.C.

•General Sherman marched northward, burning a dozen or more South Carolina towns. Columbia, the state capital, was burned, Feb. 17; responsibility for the starting of the fire has never been established. Charleston fell, Feb. 18, after a two-year siege.

Mar. 3, second session of 38th Congress adjourned

Mar. 3, vetoed repeal of section of Reconstruction act and joint resolution concerning certain railroads

•These were the fifth and last of his six vetoes, the third and last of his four pocket vetoes.

Mar. 3, Secretary of Treasury Fessenden resigned

ELECTION OF 1864

Radical Republican party, convened, May 31, at Cleveland, Ohio, nominated John Charles Fremont of California for president, John Cochrane of New York for vice president. Fremont and Cochrane withdrew in favor of Lincoln and Johnson, Sept. 17.

Republican (National Union) party, convened, June 7, at Baltimore, Md., nominated Abraham Lincoln of Illinois for president, Andrew Johnson of Tennessee for vice president.

•This was the third Republican national convention. It was the first Republican convention in Baltimore; it was the 15th major party convention in Baltimore.

Democratic party, convened, Aug. 29, at Chicago, Ill., nominated George Brinton McClellan of New York for president, George Hunt Pendleton of Ohio for vice president.

•This was the ninth Democratic national convention. It was the first Democratic convention in Chicago; it was the second major party convention in Chicago.

Election day, Tuesday, Nov. 8, 1864

Popular vote: 4,166,537

    Lincoln, 2,330,552 (including soldiers' vote, 116,887)

    McClellan, 1,835,985 (including soldiers' vote, 33,748)

Electoral vote: 234, 25 states

  • Lincoln, 212, 22 states
(California, 5; Connecticut, 6; Illinois, 16; Indiana, 13; Iowa, 8; Kansas, 3; Maine, 7; Maryland, 7; Massachusetts, 12; Michigan, 8; Minnesota, 4; Missouri, 11; Nevada, 2 of 3 votes; New Hampshire, 5; New York, 33; Ohio, 21; Oregon, 3; Pennsylvania, 26; Rhode Island, 4; Vermont, 5; West Virginia, 5; Wisconsin, 8)

  • McClellan, 21, three states
(Delaware, 3; Kentucky, 11; New Jersey, 7)

•One Nevada elector died before the election.

  • Votes not cast: 80, 11 states
(Alabama, 8; Arkansas, 5; Florida, 3; Georgia, 9; Louisiana, 7; Mississippi, 7; North Carolina, 9; South Carolina, 6; Tennessee, 10; Texas, 6; Virginia, 10)

THE 20th ADMINISTRATION

1865

Mar. 4, his second inauguration day

•Lincoln took the oath of office, administered by Chief Justice Salmon P. Chase, on the east portico of the Capitol.

•This was the first of three inaugurations at which Chase officiated.

•This was the first of four oath-taking ceremonies at which Chase officiated.

•Lincoln's age at his second inauguration was 56 years, 20 days.

•He was the seventh of 21 presidents who were younger than their vice presidents. Lincoln was four years, 45 days younger than Johnson.

Mar. 7, appointed his third secretary of treasury, Hugh McCulloch

•McCulloch took office, Mar. 9.
•McCulloch was the last of Lincoln's 13 cabinet appointments.
Mar. 11, issued proclamation that ordered all absentees from army and navy to return to duty within 60 days or forfeit rights as citizens
Mar. 25, attack on Fort Steadman, Va.
•General Lee, outnumbered by more than two-to-one, attempted to break through the Union lines but was unsuccessful.
Apr. 1, Battle of Five Forks, Va.
•This was Lee's last assault of the war. He struck at the Union left flank at Five Forks, near Petersburg, but was repelled by troops under General Philip Sheridan.
Apr. 2, evacuation of Petersburg and Richmond
•Union troops occupied Petersburg and Richmond, Apr. 3.
Apr. 4, arrived in Richmond

•He was the second of five presidents who visited war zones while in office.
•He spent the night in the captured capital of the Confederacy.
Apr. 9, surrender at Appomattox Courthouse
•The Civil War had ended.

1865

Apr. 11, gave last public address
•He addressed a large throng in front of the White House, outlining in general terms his thoughts on Reconstruction.
Apr. 11, issued proclamation that closed all southern ports
Apr. 14, held last cabinet meeting

Note: He was the seventh of 11 presidents who never had a veto overridden.

THE ASSASSINATION

Apr. 14, 1865, shot by John Wilkes Booth, Ford's Theater, Washington, D.C.
•On this Good Friday evening, Lincoln attended a performance of the Tom Taylor comedy, *Our American Cousin,* starring Laura Keene. He was shot in the back of the head by Booth, an actor of unstable temperament and proslavery sentiments, who was the organizer of a conspiracy to kill the president, the vice president, and other prominent members of the government.
•Booth had entered the presidential booth in the theater in the absence of the assigned guard, John F. Parker, a policeman with an unsavory record, who was indulging his thirst at a nearby saloon.
•Charles Leale, a doctor who was in the audience, rushed to attend the unconscious president. After removing a blood clot from the wound, Dr. Leale said it was impossible that Lincoln would recover. The president was then carried from the theater to a small boarding house across the street at 516 10th Street. He never regained consciousness.
Apr. 15, 1865, died at 7:22 A.M., William Petersen House, Washington, D.C.
•His family and most members of his cabinet were present when he died. A principal exception was Secretary of State

Seward, who had been wounded by another of the conspirators the previous evening.
•The William Petersen House, administratively titled The House Where Lincoln Died, is a unit of Ford's Theater National Historic Site. It is administered by the National Park Service. The first floor of the three-story red brick building is open to the public daily except Christmas, 9 A.M. to 5 P.M. There is no admission charge.
Apr. 26, 1865, Booth died of gunshot wound on Virginia farm
•Booth had managed to escape through the back door of the theater despite the fact that his left shinbone was broken. (When he had jumped from the presidential box to the stage, the spur on his right boot caught on a decorative flag.) He was joined by David E. Herold, another of the conspirators, and together they hid in swamps and woods in Maryland and Virginia before they found refuge at the farm of Richard H. Garrett, between Port Royal and Bowling Green, Va. While sleeping in a tobacco barn, they were surrounded by a squad of soldiers who had tracked their progress. Herold surrendered on orders; Booth refused, claiming he would never be taken alive. The soldiers set fire to the barn. At this point, Booth suffered a mortal

wound. It is likely that he killed himself, although one of the soldiers, Sergeant Boston Corbett, claimed to have shot Booth on orders from "the Almighty." The wounded Booth was dragged from the burning barn and died shortly thereafter.

May 1, 1865, executive order issued by President Johnson for trial by military commission of alleged assassins

July 7, 1865, four persons hanged for participation in conspiracy

•They were David E. Herold, Lewis Paine, George A. Atzerodt, and Mrs. Mary Eugenia Jenkins Surratt. Under the guidance of Herold, Paine had carried out the attack on Secretary of State Seward, Apr. 14. Seward, his two sons, Frederick and Augustus, and two other men were wounded. Atzerodt was to have killed Vice President Johnson but lost his nerve and spent the evening roaming the city and drinking. Mrs. Surratt, the keeper of a Washington boarding house, was never conclusively proved to have taken part in the conspiracy, although she undoubtedly knew of its existence.

•Four other men accused in connection with the conspiracy were imprisoned at Fort Jefferson in the Dry Tortugas, Fla. One, Michael O'Laughlin, died in prison of yellow fever, Sept. 23, 1867. The others, Dr. Samuel A. Mudd, Edward Spangler, and Samuel B. Arnold, were pardoned by President Johnson, February, 1869.

DEATH

Date of death: Apr. 15, 1865
•Lincoln was the first of two presidents who died before completing their second terms. The other was McKinley.
•He was the third of eight presidents who died in office.
•He was the first of eight presidents who lay in state in the Capitol Rotunda.
•He was the third of six presidents who lay in state in the White House.
Place of death: Washington, D.C.
•He was the fourth of seven presidents who died in Washington.
Age at death: 56 years, 62 days
Cause of death: Assassination by pistol shot
•He was the first of four presidents who were assassinated.
Place of burial: Springfield, Ill.

•He was the only president buried in Illinois.

THE VICE PRESIDENTS
(15th and 16th)

Note: Lincoln was the fourth of seven presidents who had two vice presidents.

Full name: Hannibal Hamlin (15th)
Date of birth: Aug. 27, 1809
Place of birth: Paris, Me.
•He was the only vice president who was born in Maine.
Religious denomination: Unitarian
•He was the last of three vice presidents who were Unitarians.
Occupation: Lawyer
•He was admitted to the bar, practiced law in Hamden, Me., 1833; member of the Maine state legislature, served three terms as speaker, 1836–1840, 1847; member of the House of Representatives, 1843–1847; member of the Senate, 1848–1857; resigned to become governor of Maine, 1857, but served only a few weeks; returned to the Senate, 1857.
•He was the eighth of 21 vice presidents who served in the House of Representatives before their terms of office.
•He was the seventh of 17 vice presidents who served in the Senate before their terms of office.
•He was the fourth of ten vice presidents who served both in the House of Representatives and the Senate before their terms of office.
•He was the fifth of 12 vice presidents who served both in the House of Representatives and the Senate.
•He was the seventh of 14 vice presidents who served as state governors.
Term of office: Mar. 4, 1861, to Mar. 4, 1865 (4 years)
•He was the seventh of 17 vice presidents who served four-year terms.
•Lincoln and Hamlin were the 17th of 41 president-vice president teams.
Age at inauguration: 51 years, 189 days
State represented: Maine
•He was the only vice president who represented Maine
Political party: Republican
•He was the first of 15 vice presidents who were Republicans
Occupations after term: U.S. senator, diplomat

•He was a member of the Senate, 1869–1881; minister to Spain, appointed by President Garfield, 1881–1882.

•He was the third of six vice presidents who served in the Senate after their terms of office.

•He was the first of four vice presidents who served in the Senate both before and after their terms of office.

Date of death: July 4, 1891

•He was the last of three vice presidents who died on the Fourth of July.

Place of death: Bangor, Me.

•He was the only vice president who died in Maine.

Age at death: 81 years, 311 days

Place of burial: Bangor, Me.

•He was the only vice president who was buried in Maine.

Full name: Andrew Johnson (16th)

• *See* pages 193–203.

•He was the second of three vice presidents named Johnson.

•He was the first vice president who was born in the 19th century.

•He was the second of two vice presidents who were born in North Carolina. The other was King.

•He was the second of two vice presidents who were of no specific religious denomination. The other was Jefferson.

•Lincoln and Johnson was the only president-vice president team of no specific religious denomination.

•Johnson was the ninth of 21 vice presidents who served in the House of Representatives before their terms of office.

•He was the ninth of 17 vice presidents who served in the Senate before their terms of office.

•He was the fifth of ten vice presidents who served in both the House of Representatives and the Senate before their terms of office.

•He was the sixth of 12 vice presidents who served both in the House of Representatives and the Senate.

•He was the fourth of six vice presidents who served in the Senate after their terms of office.

•He was the second of four vice presidents who served in the Senate both before and after their terms of office.

•He was the eighth of 14 vice presidents who served as state governors.

•He was the fifth of 14 vice presidents who served less than one term.

•He was the third of seven vice presidents who served less than one year.

•Lincoln and Johnson were the 18th of 41 president-vice president teams.

•Johnson was the only vice president who represented Tennessee.

•He was the third of 13 vice presidents who represented states that were not their native states.

•He was the seventh of 16 vice presidents who were Democrats. However, he was elected on the National Union-Republican ticket.

•He was the only vice president who died in Tennessee.

•He was the only vice president who was buried in Tennessee.

THE CABINET

State: William Henry Seward of New York, Mar. 6, 1861, to Mar. 4, 1869

Treasury: Salmon Portland Chase of Ohio, Mar. 7, 1861, to June 30, 1864

•William Pitt Fessenden of Maine, July 5, 1864, to Mar. 3, 1865

•Hugh McCulloch of Indiana, Mar. 9, 1865, to Mar. 3, 1869

War: Simon Cameron of Pennsylvania, Mar. 5, 1861, to Jan. 14, 1862

•Edwin McMasters Stanton of Ohio, Jan. 20, 1862, to May 28, 1868

Attorney General: Edward Bates of Missouri, Mar. 5, 1861, to Nov. 24, 1864

•James Speed of Kentucky, Dec. 2, 1864, to July 17, 1866

Navy: Gideon Welles of Connecticut, Mar. 7, 1861, to Mar. 3, 1869

Postmaster General: Montgomery Blair of Maryland, Mar. 5, 1861, to Sept. 23, 1864

•William Dennison of Ohio, Sept. 24, 1864, to July 16, 1866

Interior: Caleb Blood Smith of Indiana, Mar. 5, 1861, to Dec. 31, 1862

•John Palmer Usher of Indiana, Jan. 8, 1863, to May 15, 1865

THE SUPREME COURT

Chief Justice: Salmon Portland Chase of Ohio, appointed, Dec. 6, 1864; confirmed, Dec. 6, 1864

Associate Justices: Noah Haynes Swayne of

Ohio, appointed, Jan. 21, 1862; confirmed, Jan. 24, 1862
•Samuel Freeman Miller of Iowa, appointed, July 16, 1862; confirmed, July 16, 1862

•David Davis of Illinois, appointed, Oct. 17, 1862; confirmed, Dec. 8, 1862
•Stephen Johnson Field of California, appointed, Mar. 6, 1863; confirmed, Mar. 10, 1863

ANDREW JOHNSON

Full name: Andrew Johnson
•He was the first of two presidents named Johnson. He and Lyndon Johnson were not related.
•He was the second of two presidents named Andrew. The other was Jackson.
•He was the second of two presidents who shared the initials of a previous president (Jackson). The other was Monroe.
•He was the 14th of 17 presidents who did not have middle initials or middle names.
Date of birth: Dec. 29, 1808
•He was the second of three presidents who were born in December.
Place of birth: Raleigh, N.C.
•He was the second of two presidents who were born in North Carolina. The other was Polk.
•His birthplace, a small house on the property of Casso's Inn, Fayetteville Street, later was moved to East Cabarrus Street. The house was purchased by the Wake County Committee of the Colonial Dames of America, July 1, 1904, and shortly afterwards was presented to the City of Raleigh and relocated in Pullen Park. It is open to the public daily except Saturdays, Thanksgiving, Christmas Eve and Christmas, 2 to 5 P.M. Admission: adults, 25 cents; children, ten cents.
Family lineage: English-Scottish-Irish
•He was the first of three presidents who were of English-Scottish-Irish ancestry.
Religious denomination: None
•He was the last of three presidents who were of no specific religious denomination.
College: None
•He was the seventh of nine presidents who did not attend college.
•He was the 11th of 15 presidents who were not graduated from college.

PARENTS AND SIBLINGS

Father's name: Jacob Johnson
Date of birth: Apr. 5, 1778
Place of birth: Northumberland County, England
•Johnson's father was the fifth of eight parents of presidents who were born abroad.
•His father was the third of four fathers of presidents who were born abroad.
Occupations: Hostler, janitor, constable
Date of death: Jan. 4, 1812
•Andrew was four years, six days old when

his father died.
Place of death: Raleigh, N.C.
Age at death: 33 years, 274 days

Mother's name: Mary McDonough Johnson
Date of birth: July 17, 1783
Place of birth: *Unknown*
Date of marriage: Sept. 9, 1801
•After the death of his father, Johnson's mother remarried. His stepfather was Turner Daugherty of Raleigh, N.C.
•He was the only president who had a stepfather.
•He was the third of five presidents who had stepparents.
Children: 2 sons
•William was born in 1803 and Andrew in 1808.
•Johnson was the first of three presidents who came from families of two children.
•He was the sixth of ten presidents who were second children.
Date of death: Feb. 13, 1856
Place of death: *Unknown*
Age at death: 72 years, 211 days

MARRIAGE

Date of marriage: May 17, 1827
Place of marriage: Greeneville, Tenn.
•Johnson was the last of three presidents who were married in Tennessee.
Age at marriage: 18 years, 115 days
•He was the president who married at the earliest age.
•He was the only president who was married in his teens.
Years married: 48 years, 75 days

Wife's name: Eliza McCartle Johnson
•She was the 14th of 33 first ladies.
•She was the 18th of 40 wives of presidents.
Date of birth: Oct. 4, 1810
•She was the first of four first ladies who were born in October.
•She was the third of six wives of presidents who were born in October.

Place of birth: Leesburg, Tenn.
•She was the second of two first ladies who were born in Tennessee. The other was Sarah Polk.
•She was the second of two wives of presidents who were born in Tennessee.
Wife's mother: _____ McCartle
Wife's father: _____ McCartle, shoemaker
Age at marriage: 16 years, 213 days
•She was the first lady and wife of a president who was married at the earliest age.
•She was the third of four first ladies who were married in their teens.
•She was the third of five wives of presidents who were married in their teens.
Years younger than husband: 1 year, 279 days
Children: 5; 3 sons, 2 daughters
•Martha was born on Oct. 25, 1828; Charles on Feb. 19, 1830; Mary on May 8, 1832; Robert on Feb. 22, 1834; and Andrew on Aug. 5, 1852.
•Johnson was the second of three presidents who had five children.
•He was the ninth of 19 presidents who had both male and female children.
•He was the 12th of 30 presidents who had children.
Years she survived her husband: 168 days
•She was the ninth of 21 first ladies who survived their husbands.
•She was the tenth of 23 wives of presidents who survived their husbands.
Date of death: Jan. 15, 1876
Place of death: Greene County, Tenn.
•She was the second of two first ladies who died in Tennessee. The other was Sarah Polk.
•She was the last of three wives of presidents who died in Tennessee.
Age at death: 65 years, 103 days
Place of burial: Greene County, Tenn.
•She was the second of two first ladies who were buried in Tennessee. The other was Sarah Polk.
•She was the last of three wives of presidents who were buried in Tennessee.

EARLY YEARS

Jan. 4, 1812, Johnson's father died
1822, apprenticed to tailor, Raleigh, N.C.
•The apprentices were read to as they labored. Johnson was taught the alphabet by

his fellow workers, borrowed books and taught himself to read.
1824, ran away from apprenticeship
•His employer, tailor James J. Selby, offered

a ten dollar reward for his return.

1824, worked as journeyman tailor, Laurens, S.C.

May, 1826, returned to Raleigh

•Although his former employer had closed the tailor shop that he had fled, the possibility of legal action remained. He decided to leave the community.

September, 1826, with mother and stepfather, moved to Greeneville, Tenn.

•Some months later after a series of transient jobs, he learned that the Greeneville tailor had retired. He set up shop there.

May 17, 1827, married Eliza McCartle, Greeneville

Oct. 25, 1828, his first daughter born

•The girl was named Martha Johnson.

1828, elected alderman, Greeneville

•He was reelected in 1829 and in 1830.

Feb. 19, 1830, his first son born

•The boy was named Charles Johnson.

1830, elected mayor, Greeneville

•He held this office for three years

1831, purchased tailor shop, Greeneville

•The shop, a small frame structure, which he moved to its present location, Depot and College Streets, remained in the hands of his heirs until purchased by the State of Tennessee in 1921. It later was enclosed in a brick building. He also bought a small house which still stands across the street from the shop.

•He was the last of nine presidents who owned slaves.

•The Andrew Johnson National Historic Site, consisting of the tailor shop and a museum, the Johnson home on Main Street, and the Andrew Johnson Cemetery on Monument Avenue, is open to the public daily except Christmas, 9 A.M. to 5 P.M. It is administered by the National Park Service. Admission: adults, 50 cents, June 1 through Sept. 15; children under 16, free.

1831, appointed trustee of Rhea Academy by county court

May 8, 1832, his second daughter born

•The girl was named Mary Johnson.

Feb. 22, 1834, his second son born

•The boy was named Robert Johnson.

1835, elected to state legislature

•He nominated himself and was elected to represent adjoining Greene and Washington counties.

1837, defeated for state legislature

•He opposed internal improvements.

1839, reelected to state legislature

1840, made state reputation as orator while campaigning for Van Buren

1841, elected to state senate

•He represented adjoining Greene and Hawkins counties.

NATIONAL PROMINENCE

1843, elected to House of Representatives

•He was the tenth of 17 presidents who were elected to the House.

Dec. 4, 1843, took his seat in House of Representatives

•Johnson was reelected to the House four times, serving in the 28th through the 32nd congresses.

•He was the tenth of 17 presidents who served in the House.

1851, purchased unfinished house on Main Street, Greeneville

•The Johnson home remained in the hands of his heirs until purchased by the federal government in 1941. Restoration was completed in 1958. It is part of the Andrew Johnson National Historic Site.

1851, degree of Master Mason conferred by Greeneville Lodge No. 119, Greeneville

•He was the sixth of 13 presidents who were Masons.

Aug. 5, 1852, his third son born

•The boy was named Andrew Johnson.

1853, elected governor of Tennessee

•He had planned to run for Congress again, but his district was gerrymandered to afford the Whigs an overwhelming majority. He promptly announced his candidacy for the governorship.

•He was the second of two presidents who served as governors of Tennessee. The other was Polk.

•He was the sixth of 13 presidents who were state governors.

1855, reelected governor of Tennessee

1857, elected to Senate

•He was the ninth of 16 presidents who were elected to the Senate.

•He was the seventh of 11 presidents who were elected to both the House and the Senate.

Dec. 7, 1857, took seat in Senate

•He was the ninth of 15 presidents who served in the Senate.

•He was the seventh of ten presidents who served in both the House and the Senate.

May 20, 1858, made celebrated speech in favor of homestead bill

•The bill was passed in 1860, but was vetoed by Buchanan.

1860, supported John C. Breckinridge, southern Democratic candidate for president

Dec. 13, 1860, proposed amendment to Constitution

•He introduced a joint resolution, which proposed to amend the Constitution so as to elect the president and vice president by district votes, to elect senators by direct popular vote, and to limit the terms of federal judges to 20 years. Half of all federal judges were to come from slave states and half from free states.

Dec. 18–19, 1860, denounced secession in celebrated Senate speech on his resolution

•He continued to speak out against secession and for adherence to the Constitution. His most vehement speech, Mar. 2, 1861, referred to secessionists in these terms:

> I would have them arrested and tried for treason, and, if convicted, by the eternal God, they should suffer the penalty of the law at the hands of the executioner.

June 8, 1861, Tennessee seceded from Union

•He had campaigned vigorously to prevent his state from seceding. His life was threatened repeatedly, forcing him to flee across the state line.

•He was the only southerner who remained in the Senate.

Mar. 4, 1862, appointed military governor of Tennessee by Lincoln, commissioned as brigadier general, U. S. Volunteers

•He resigned from the Senate and returned to Nashville, Mar. 12. He organized a provisional government, arranged Union meetings throughout the state, completed the railroad from Nashville to the Tennessee River, and raised 25 regiments for the Union army.

•He was the second of two presidents who were military governors. The other was Jackson.

•He was the sixth of 12 presidents who were generals.

•Johnson was the first of seven presidents who served in the Civil War.

•He was the ninth of 21 presidents who served in the military during wartime.

Mar. 18, 1862, issued proclamation appealing to Tennesseeans to return to their allegiance, to accept "a full and complete amnesty for all past acts and declarations"

Dec. 8, 1862, issued proclamation ordering congressional elections

Dec. 15, 1862, levied assessment upon wealthy Confederate sympathizers

Feb. 20, 1863, issued proclamation that ordered business agents to retain funds of southern firms

June 7, 1864, nominated for vice president, National Union convention, Baltimore, Md.

Nov. 8, 1864, elected vice president

Mar. 3, 1865, resigned commission, U. S. Volunteers

Mar. 4, 1865, took oath as vice president

•He had asked to take the oath in Nashville, but Lincoln requested his return to Washington. Prior to entering the overheated Senate chamber, Johnson drank three brandies. Ill and exhausted by his trip from Tennessee, he showed signs of intoxication during his acceptance speech. Although defended by Lincoln, who sent an investigator to Tennessee to check on his drinking habits, Johnson was labeled a drunk by gossips and political opponents.

THE PRESIDENT (17th)

Term of office: Apr. 15, 1865, to Mar. 4, 1869 (3 years, 323 days)

•Johnson was the sixth of 12 presidents who had served as vice presidents.

•He was the third of eight presidents who, because of the death of their predecessors, did not complete their vice-presidential terms.

•He was the third of four presidents who served only the unexpired terms of their predecessors.

•He was the fifth of nine presidents who served less than one term.

•He was the 11th of 19 presidents who served one term or less than one term.

State represented: Tennessee

•He was the last of three presidents who represented Tennessee.

•He was the sixth of 15 presidents who represented states that were not their native states.

Political party: Democratic

•He was the sixth of 12 presidents who were Democrats, although he was elected on the Republican (National Union) ticket.

Congresses: 39th, 40th

Administration: 20th

Age at taking oath: 56 years, 107 days

•Johnson took the oath of office in his suite in the Kirkwood House, a hotel in Washington, D.C., on Saturday, Apr. 15, 1865. The oath was administered by Chief Justice Salmon P. Chase.

•This was the second of four oath-taking ceremonies at which Chase officiated.

•Johnson was the third of four presidents who did not give inaugural addresses.

THE 20th ADMINISTRATION

1865

Apr. 29, issued executive order discontinuing commercial restrictions on most of South

May 1, issued executive order for trial by military commission of alleged assassins of Lincoln

May 2, issued executive order for arrest of Jefferson Davis

•A reward of $100,000 was offered for the capture of the Confederate president. Davis was apprehended, May 10, near Irwinville, Ga.; he was imprisoned, May 22, Fort Monroe.

May 9, issued executive order that reestablished authority of U.S. in Virginia, recognized Francis Pierpont as governor

May 10, issued proclamation announcing "armed resistance to the authority of the Government in the insurrectionary States may be regarded at an end"

May 15, Secretary of Interior Usher resigned

May 15, appointed his second secretary of interior, James Harlan

May 22, issued executive order that removed commercial restrictions on southern ports.

May 22–23, attended general review of armies of Potomac, Tennessee, and Georgia, Washington, D.C.

May 29, issued first proclamation of amnesty

•Amnesty was granted to all who took an oath of obedience to the Constitution except civil, diplomatic, and military leaders of the Confederacy.

May 29, appointed William Holden as provisional governor of North Carolina

May 30, Associate Justice Catron died

June 13, issued proclamation that removed restrictions on trade east of Mississippi River as of July 1

June 13, appointed William L. Sharkey as provisional governor of Mississippi

June 17, appointed Andrew J. Hamilton and James Johnson as provisional governors of Texas and Georgia

June 21, appointed Lewis E. Parsons as provisional governor of Alabama

June 23, issued proclamation that rescinded blockade as to foreign commerce

June 24, issued proclamation that removed restrictions on trade west of Mississippi River

June 30, appointed Benjamin F. Perry as provisional governor of South Carolina

July 13, appointed William Marvin as provisional governor of Florida

Aug. 29, issued proclamation that lifted all restrictions on southern ports as of Sept. 1

Oct. 12, issued proclamation ending martial law in Kentucky

Dec. 1, issued proclamation that revoked suspension of writ of habeas corpus in northern states

Dec. 4, first session of 39th Congress

•The administration controlled both the Senate and the House of Representatives. The Democrats lost two Senate and 34 House seats. The Senate (52 members) consisted of 42 Unionists and ten Democrats. The House (191 members) consisted of 145 Unionists and 46 Democrats.

Dec. 4, sent his first State of the Union message to Congress

Dec. 18, sent special message on insurgent states, with Grant report, to Congress

Dec. 18, 13th Amendment to Constitution declared ratified

• *See* Constitution, page 643.

Dec. 21, signed special act for relief of Mrs. Abraham Lincoln

•Mrs. Lincoln was granted $25,000.

Dec. 23, relieved Governor Holden of

North Carolina
- He appointed Jonathan Worth as provisional governor.

1866

Feb. 19, vetoed Freedmen's Bureau bill
- This was the first of Johnson's 29 vetoes.
Feb. 22, denounced congressional committee on Reconstruction
- He spoke from the steps of the White House, criticizing the joint committee on Reconstruction, which opposed his moderate policies. The committee of six senators and nine representatives, which he called "an irresponsible central directory" that had assumed "all the powers of Congress," was controlled by the Radicals, who were dominated by Thaddeus Stevens.
Mar. 6, organization of his supporters formed, Washington, D.C.
- The group, which included moderate Republican and Democratic senators, issued a call in June for a National Union convention.
Mar. 27, vetoed civil rights bill
- He held that the bill, which granted citizenship to all persons born in the U.S. except Indians and granted equal civil rights to all citizens, was an unwarranted invasion of states' rights and therefore was unconstitutional.
Apr. 2, issued proclamation that declared insurrection and Civil War at end everywhere but Texas
Apr. 9, civil rights act passed over his veto
- This was the first of his 15 vetoes that were overridden.
Apr. 16, appointed Henry Stanbery as associate justice
- This, Johnson's only appointment to the Supreme Court, was not acted upon by the Senate.
- He was the ninth of 15 presidents who nominated justices not confirmed by the Senate.
- Stanbery was the 14th of 25 men nominated to the Supreme Court who were not confirmed by the Senate.
May 15, vetoed admission of Colorado bill
June 6, issued proclamation warning against participation in Fenian invasion of Canada, ordered strict enforcement of neutrality laws
June 15, vetoed Montana Iron Company

public lands bill
June 16, 14th Amendment to Constitution submitted to states for ratification
June 20, report of joint committee on Reconstruction
- The committee maintained that Congress rather than the chief executive should prevail on questions of Reconstruction and that the southern states were not entitled to representation in Congress.
June 22, sent special message to Congress in which he opposed submission of 14th Amendment to states
July 15, vetoed continuation of Freedmen's Bureau bill
- This act was passed over his veto, July 16.
July 16, Postmaster General Dennison resigned
July 17, Attorney General Speed resigned
July 23, Supreme Court reduced to seven members as vacancies should occur by act of Congress
- This act was designed to prevent Johnson from appointing members of the Court and it nullified his Apr. 16 appointment of Stanbery.
- At the time the Senate refused to confirm Stanbery, the Court consisted of nine members.
July 23, appointed his second attorney general, Henry Stanbery
July 24, Tennessee readmitted
- Congress had made readmission contingent on ratification of the 14th Amendment by Tennessee. The amendment had been ratified by Tennessee, July 19.
July 25, appointed his second postmaster general, Alexander W. Randall
July 27, Secretary of Interior Harlan resigned, effective, Aug. 31
July 27, appointed his third secretary of interior, Orville H. Browning
July 28, vetoed survey of Territory of Montana bill
July 28, first session of 39th Congress adjourned
Aug. 14, received Queen Emma of Sandwich Islands, Hawaii
- He was the first president to receive a queen.
Aug. 14–17, National Union convention, Philadelphia, Pa.
- His supporters adopted by resolution a declaration of principles which vindicated his policies, Aug. 17. However, his attempt to form a moderate party failed.

Aug. 20, issued proclamation that declared insurrection and Civil War at end everywhere in U.S., including Texas

Aug. 28, departed for Chicago, Ill., to take part in ceremony laying cornerstone of monument to Stephen A. Douglas

• Accompanied by members of his cabinet, General Grant, and Admiral Farragut, Johnson made an electioneering tour of the country, visiting and speaking in Philadelphia, New York City, Cleveland, and St. Louis, as well as Chicago.

• This political tour has come to be known as the first "swing around the circle."

Sept. 3, southern and northern Republicans convened, opposed his policies, Philadelphia

Sept. 6, laid cornerstone of Douglas monument, Chicago

Sept. 8, accused "radical Congress" of planning New Orleans race riot

• When the state constitutional convention met in New Orleans, July 30, more than two hundred persons—mostly Negroes—were killed or wounded when fired upon by the police.

Sept. 17, "Soldiers and Sailors" convention, Cleveland, Ohio

• This convention of veterans supported his policies.

Sept. 25–26, Republican veterans convention, Pittsburgh, Pa.

• This convention of veterans opposed his policies.

Nov. 6, election day

• The Republicans won control of both the Senate and the House of Representatives, which gave the Radicals control of Reconstruction legislation.

Dec. 3, second session of 39th Congress

Dec. 3, sent his second State of the Union message to Congress

1867

Jan. 5, vetoed suffrage in District of Columbia bill

Jan. 7, charges of usurpation of power referred to House judiciary committee

• He had been charged with corrupt use of appointment, pardon and veto powers, disposal of public property, and interference in elections by Representative James M. Ashley of Ohio, who had introduced the District of Columbia suffrage bill with Lot

M. Morrill. The charges were referred to the committee on the judiciary by a vote of 108–39.

Jan. 8, suffrage in District of Columbia act passed over his veto

Jan. 21, portion of act of July 17, 1862, repealed

• The pertinent clause authorized the president to proclaim general amnesty.

Jan. 22, next and all succeeding congresses ordered to assemble, Mar. 4, instead of in December

Jan. 29, vetoed bills to admit Colorado and Nebraska as states

Feb. 9, act to admit Nebraska as state passed over his veto

Mar. 1, Nebraska admitted as 37th state

• Nebraska was the only state admitted during his term of office.

• Lincoln, the capital of Nebraska, was the last of four state capitals named for presidents.

Mar. 2, command of army act

• This act provided that the president issue military orders through the general of the army.

Mar. 2, vetoed tenure of office bill

Mar. 2, Tenure of Office Act passed over his veto

• This act prohibited the president from removing civil officers except with the consent of the Senate.

Mar. 2, signed act declaring valid proclamations of president, Mar. 4, 1861 to July 1, 1866, regarding martial law and military trials

Mar. 2, vetoed first Reconstruction bill

Mar. 2, first Reconstruction Act passed over his veto

• This act imposed martial law on the southern states, divided the South into five military districts, and provided that statehood would be restored only after ratification of the 14th Amendment.

Mar. 4, second session of 39th Congress adjourned

Mar. 4, first session of 40th Congress

• The Republicans controlled both the Senate and the House of Representatives. The Democrats gained two Senate and three House seats. The Senate (54 members) consisted of 42 Republicans and 12 Democrats. The House (193 members) consisted of 143 Republicans, 49 Democrats, and one vacancy.

Mar. 23, vetoed second Reconstruction bill

Mar. 23, second Reconstruction Act passed over his veto

Mar. 29, first session of 40th Congress adjourned to July 3

•The first session was continued by repeated adjournments. Congress deemed it advisable "that the President should not be allowed to have control of events for eight months without the supervision of the legislative branch of the government."

Mar. 30, issued proclamation calling special session of Senate, Apr. 1

Mar. 30, Alaska purchase treaty signed

•The treaty, which transferred Alaska to the U.S. on payment of $7,200,000 to Russia, was ratified by the Senate, Apr. 9.

•The transfer of territory occurred, Oct. 18, but Congress refused to appropriate funds until July 27, 1868.

Apr. 1, special session of Senate

•This session adjourned, Apr. 19.

June 20, issued instructions to commanders of southern military districts

July 3, first session of 40th Congress reconvened

July 5, Associate Justice Wayne died

•The death of Wayne reduced the Supreme Court to eight members.

July 19, vetoed third Reconstruction bill and Reconstruction joint resolution

July 19, third Reconstruction Act and Reconstruction joint resolution passed over his vetoes

July 20, first session of 40th Congress adjourned to Nov. 21

Aug. 5, asked for resignation of Secretary of War Stanton

•Stanton refused to resign.

Aug. 12, issued executive order suspending Stanton

Aug. 12, appointed General Ulysses S. Grant as acting secretary of war

Aug. 17, relieved General Philip H. Sheridan as commander of Fifth Military District, Louisiana and Texas

•Johnson appointed Winfield Scott Hancock as commander of the Fifth District.

Aug. 23, refused to accept resignation of Secretary of State Seward

Sept. 7, issued proclamation that granted general amnesty

Nov. 21, first session of 40th Congress reconvened

Nov. 25, judiciary committee report recommended impeachment

•The report of the committee on the judici-

ary on charges brought against the president resolved that he "be impeached for high crimes and misdemeanors."

Dec. 2, first session of 40th Congress adjourned

Dec. 2, second session of 40th Congress

Dec. 3, sent his third State of the Union message to Congress

Dec. 7, resolution to impeach defeated in House

1868

Jan. 13, Senate refused to concur in suspension of Stanton

•This decision was accepted as lawful by Stanton and Acting Secretary Grant, under the Tenure of Office Act.

Feb. 21, removed Stanton, appointed General Lorenzo Thomas as acting secretary

•A Senate resolution declared the removal of Stanton illegal, Feb. 21.

Feb. 21, motion to impeach made in House

•The motion, presented by Representative John Covode of Pennsylvania, was referred to the committee on Reconstruction.

Feb. 22, committee on Reconstruction report recommended resolution for impeachment

Feb. 24, House voted to impeach, 126–47

Feb. 25, impeachment reported at bar of Senate

•Johnson was the only president who was impeached.

Mar. 2, nine articles of impeachment agreed upon in House

Mar. 3, two additional articles of impeachment agreed upon in House

Mar. 5, Senate convened as court of impeachment

•He was summoned to appear and answer charges. The court adjourned to Mar. 13.

Mar. 12, Attorney General Stanbery resigned

•Stanbery resigned to serve as one of the counsel for President Johnson in the impeachment trial.

Mar. 13, court of impeachment formally reopened, adjourned to Mar. 23

•He was given ten days, instead of the 40 he had asked, for preparation of his answer to the charges of violation of the Tenure of Office Act and other irregularities.

Mar. 23, his answer read by counsel

•His answer denied that the removal of

Secretary of War Stanton and his appointment of an acting secretary was illegal. He challenged the constitutionality of the Tenure of Office Act.
• The Tenure of Office Act was declared unconstitutional by the Supreme Court, *Myers v. U.S.*, 1926.
Mar. 25, vetoed amended judiciary bill
Mar. 27, amended judiciary act passed over his veto
Mar. 30, his trial began
May 16, acquitted on 11th article of impeachment
• The Senate voted 35–19 that he was guilty of high misdemeanor as charged. He was acquitted, since a two-thirds vote was necessary to convict. The court adjourned until after the Republican national convention.
May 26, acquitted on second and third articles of impeachment
• The Senate voted 35–19 on both articles, the same result as on May 16, and adjourned *sine die* by a vote of 34–16.
• The decisive vote in all instances was cast by Senator Edmund G. Ross of Kansas. Ross and the other six Republican senators who voted for acquittal paid for their actions with their political careers.
May 28, accepted resignation of Secretary of War Stanton
May 30, appointed his second secretary of war, John M. Schofield
• Schofield took office, June 1.
May 30, reappointed Henry Stanbery as attorney general
• His appointment of Stanbery was rejected by the Senate, June 2.
• Johnson was the third of five presidents whose nominees to the cabinet were rejected by the Senate.
• Stanbery was the sixth of eight nominees to the cabinet who were rejected by the Senate.
June 5, held reception for Chinese embassy, White House
June 20, vetoed admission of Arkansas bill
June 22, admission of Arkansas act passed over his veto
June 25, signed act that provided eight-hour workday for laborers and workmen in government employ
June 25, vetoed southern states admission to Congress bill
June 25, southern states admission to Congress act passed over his veto

• This act admitted North Carolina, South Carolina, Louisiana, Georgia, Alabama, and Florida to representation in Congress.
July 4, issued proclamation of amnesty pardoning all not under presentment or indictment
July 4–9, Democratic national convention, New York City
• *See* Election of 1868, pages 210–211.
• He was the fourth of five presidents who sought but were denied renomination.
July 15, appointed his third attorney general, William M. Evarts
• This was the last of Johnson's six cabinet appointments.
July 20, vetoed exclusion of electoral votes of unreconstructed states bill
July 20, exclusion of electoral votes of unreconstructed states act passed over his veto
July 25, vetoed discontinuance of Freedmen's Bureau bill
July 25, discontinuance of Freedmen's Bureau act passed over his veto
• This act provided for the discontinuance of the bureau as of Jan. 1, 1869.
July 27, second session of 40th Congress adjourned to Sept. 21
• Congress assembled for one day, Sept. 21, adjourned to Oct. 16, reassembled, Oct. 16, and adjourned to Nov. 12.
July 28, 14th Amendment to Constitution declared ratified
• *See* Constitution, pages 643–644.
Nov. 3, election day
• *See* Election of 1868, pages 210–211.
Nov. 12, second session of 40th Congress assembled and adjourned
Dec. 7, third session of 40th Congress
Dec. 9, sent his fourth and last State of the Union message to Congress
Dec. 25, issued proclamation of unconditional pardon and amnesty to all concerned in insurrection
• The treason trial of Jefferson Davis had begun, Dec. 3, in Richmond, Va. After the proclamation of amnesty, the charge was dropped, Feb. 15, 1869.

1869

Feb. 13, vetoed trustees of Negro schools in District of Columbia bill
• This was the last of his 14 vetoes that were not overridden.

Feb. 22, vetoed tariff on copper bill
•This was the last of his 29 vetoes.
Feb. 22, tariff on copper act passed over his veto
•This was the last of his 15 vetoes that were overridden.
•He was the second of two presidents who had a majority of their vetoes negated. The

other was Pierce.
•He was the president who had the most vetoes overridden.
Feb. 26, 15th Amendment to Constitution submitted to states for ratification
Mar. 4, third session of 40th Congress adjourned

THE FORMER PRESIDENT

Mar. 4, 1869, did not attend inauguration of Grant
•Grant had informed the inaugural committee that he would not ride with Johnson or even speak to him.
•Johnson was the third of four presidents who did not attend the inaugurations of their successors.
•His age upon leaving office was 60 years, 65 days.
April, 1869, returned to Greeneville, Tenn.
•During the welcoming ceremonies, he rode in a cavalcade down the main street and under a banner that read: "Welcome Home, Andrew Johnson, Patriot." Eight years earlier, when Tennessee had joined the Confederacy and he had been forced to flee for his life, a banner that read: "Andrew Johnson, Traitor," had flown in the same spot.
1871, unsuccessful candidate for Senate
•He was defeated in the legislature by one vote.
1872, unsuccessful candidate for House of Representatives
January, 1875, elected to Senate
•He was the only former president elected to the Senate.
•He was the second of two former presidents who were elected to Congress. John Quincy Adams was elected to the House in 1830.
Mar. 5, 1875, took seat in Senate
•He was the only former president who served in the Senate.
Mar. 22, 1875, made speech in Senate
•His only speech in the Senate as former president was an attack on Grant's policy toward the readmitted southern states.
Mar. 24, 1875, returned to Greeneville at end of special session
July 5, 1875, joined wife, Carter's Station, Tenn.
•While visiting his daughter, Mary Stover

Brown, whose plantation was in Carter's Station, he suffered a stroke.

DEATH

Date of death: July 31, 1875
Place of death: Carter's Station, Tenn.
•Johnson was the last of three presidents who died in Tennessee.
Age at death: 66 years, 214 days
•He lived six years, 149 days, after the completion of his term.
Cause of death: Stroke
Place of burial: Greeneville, Tenn.
•He was the last of three presidents who were buried in Tennessee.
•The Andrew Johnson Cemetery was donated to the federal government in 1906 by his heirs and was administered by the war department as a national cemetery until 1942. It is now administered by the National Park Service and is part of the Andrew Johnson National Historic Site.

THE VICE PRESIDENT

•Johnson was the third of four presidents who did not have vice presidents.

THE CABINET

State: William Henry Seward of New York, Mar. 6, 1861, to Mar. 4, 1869
Treasury: Hugh McCulloch of Indiana, Mar. 9, 1865, to Mar. 3, 1869
War: Edwin McMasters Stanton of Ohio, Jan. 20, 1862, to May 28, 1868
•John McAllister Schofield of Missouri, June 1, 1868, to Mar. 13, 1869
Attorney General: James Speed of Kentucky, Dec. 2, 1864, to July 17, 1866

•Henry Stanbery of Ohio, July 23, 1866, to Mar. 12, 1868; reappointed, May 30, 1868; rejected by Senate, June 2, 1868
•William Maxwell Evarts of New York, July 15, 1868, to Mar. 3, 1869
Navy: Gideon Welles of Connecticut, Mar. 7, 1861, to Mar. 3, 1869
Postmaster General: William Dennison of Ohio, Sept. 24, 1864, to July 16, 1866
•Alexander Williams Randall of Wisconsin, July 25, 1866, to Mar. 4, 1869
Interior: John Palmer Usher of Indiana, Jan. 8, 1863, to May 15, 1865

•James Harlan of Iowa, May 15, 1865, to Aug. 31, 1866
•Orville Hickman Browning of Illinois, Sept. 1, 1866, to Mar. 3, 1869

THE SUPREME COURT

•Johnson was the last of three presidents who did not name a member of the Court. He appointed Henry Stanbery, Apr. 16, 1866, but the appointment was not acted upon by the Senate.

Eighteenth President

ULYSSES SIMPSON GRANT

Full name: Ulysses Simpson Grant
- His given name was Hiram Ulysses Grant.
- He was the first of four presidents who dropped their first names.
- He was the first of five presidents who changed their names from those they were given at birth.
- He was the fourth of 19 presidents who had middle initials or middle names.

Date of birth: Apr. 27, 1822
- He was the last of four presidents who were born in April.

Place of birth: Point Pleasant, Ohio
- His restored birthplace is in Grant Memorial State Park. A weatherboard cabin, it is a state memorial administered by the Ohio Historical Society. It is open to the public daily, 9:30 A.M. to 12, noon, and 1 to 5 P.M., Apr. 1 to Nov. 1. Admission: adults, 25 cents; children, 15 cents; student and youth groups, and children under 16 accompanied by parents, free.
- He was the first of three consecutive presidents who were born in Ohio.
- He was the first of seven presidents who were born in Ohio.

Family lineage: English-Scottish
- He was the first of two presidents who

were of English-Scottish ancestry. The other was Benjamin Harrison.

Religious denomination: Methodist
- He was the second of four presidents who were Methodists.

College: U.S. Military Academy, West Point, N.Y.
- He was the first of two presidents who went to West Point. The other was Eisenhower.
- He was the 11th of 27 presidents who attended college.

Date of graduation: July 1, 1843
- The academy did not confer degrees at the time.
- He was the seventh of 21 presidents who were graduated from college.

PARENTS AND SIBLINGS

Father's name: Jesse Root Grant
Date of birth: Jan. 23, 1794
Place of birth: near Greensburg, Westmoreland County, Pa.
Occupations: Leather tanner, factory owner
Date of death: June 29, 1873
- Grant was the third of six presidents whose

fathers lived to see their sons' inauguration or oath-taking days. Mr. Grant did not attend the ceremony.

Place of death: Covington, Ky.
Age at death: 79 years, 157 days

Mother's name: Hannah Simpson Grant
Date of birth: Nov. 23, 1798
Place of birth: Montgomery County, Pa.
Date of marriage: June 24, 1821
Children: 6; 3 sons, 3 daughters
• Hiram Ulysses was born in 1822; Samuel Simpson in 1825; Clara in 1828; Virginia Paine in 1832; Orvil Lynch in 1835; and Mary Frances in 1839.
• Grant was the only president who came from a family of six children.
• He was the fourth of eight presidents who were eldest children.
Date of death: May 11, 1883
• He was the fifth of ten presidents whose mothers lived to see their sons' inauguration or oath-taking days. Mrs. Grant did not attend the ceremony.
• He was the first of two presidents whose parents lived to see their son's inauguration days. The other was Kennedy.
Place of death: Jersey City, N.J.
Age at death: 84 years, 169 days

MARRIAGE

Date of marriage: Aug. 22, 1848
Place of marriage: St. Louis, Mo.
• Grant was the first of two presidents who were married in Missouri. The other was Truman.
Age at marriage: 26 years, 117 days
• He was the 13th of 27 presidents who were married in their twenties.
Years married: 36 years, 335 days

Wife's name: Julia Boggs Dent Grant
• She was the 15th of 33 first ladies.
• She was the 19th of 40 wives of presidents.
Date of birth: Jan. 26, 1826
• She was the first of two first ladies who were born in January. The other was Grace Coolidge.
• She was the first of two wives of presidents who were born in January.
Place of birth: St. Louis, Mo.
• She was the first of two first ladies who were born in Missouri. The other was Bess Truman.
• She was the first of two wives of presidents who were born in Missouri.
Wife's mother: Ellen Bray Wrenshall Dent
Wife's father: Frederick Dent, merchant and planter
Age at marriage: 22 years, 209 days
• She was the 12th of 26 first ladies who were married in their twenties.
• She was the 15th of 30 wives of presidents who were married in their twenties.
Years younger than husband: 3 years, 274 days
Children: 4; 3 sons, 1 daughter
• Frederick Dent was born on May 30, 1850; Ulysses Simpson on July 22, 1852; Ellen on July 4, 1855; and Jesse Root on Feb. 6, 1858.
• Grant was the last of four presidents who had four children.
• He was the tenth of 19 presidents who had both male and female children.
• He was the 13th of 30 presidents who had children.
Years she survived her husband: 17 years, 144 days
• She was the tenth of 21 first ladies who survived their husbands.
• She was the 11th of 23 wives of presidents who survived their husbands.
Date of death: Dec. 14, 1902
Place of death: Washington, D.C.
• She was the fifth of nine first ladies who died in Washington.
• She was the fifth of nine wives of presidents who died in Washington.
Age at death: 76 years, 322 days
• She had celebrated her 75th birthday, Jan. 26, 1901.
• She was the seventh of 16 first ladies who lived to be 70.
• She was the seventh of 17 wives of presidents who lived to be 70.
• She was the fifth of 14 first ladies who lived to be 75.
• She was fifth of 15 wives of presidents who lived to be 75.
Place of burial: New York, N.Y.
• She was the only first lady or wife of a president who was buried in New York City.
• She was the second of four first ladies who were buried in New York.
• She was the fourth of seven wives of presidents who were buried in New York.

EARLY YEARS

Fall, 1823, with family, moved to Georgetown, Ohio

1828–1835, attended subscription schools of village, worked on family farm

• Grant was partial to horses. He drove wagons from the age of eight, ploughed and did all the work done with horses at 11.

1836–1837, attended school, Maysville, Ky.

1838–1839, attended school, Ripley, Ohio

Spring, 1839, received appointment to U.S. Military Academy, West Point, N.Y.

• He had no desire to go to West Point; his father had applied for the appointment.

May, 1839, departed for West Point

• He traveled by river steamer, canal packet, and railroad (the first train he had ever seen). In no hurry to reach his destination, he spent five days in Philadelphia and then several more in New York City. "I would have been glad to have had a steamboat or railroad collision, or any other accident happen, by which I might have received a temporary injury sufficient to make me ineligible, for a time, to enter the Academy," he wrote in his *Memoirs.* "Nothing of the kind occurred, and I had to face the music." He arrived at West Point on May 30 or May 31.

June-August, 1841, spent furlough with family, Bethel, Ohio

• His father had sold his business in Georgetown and moved to Bethel, 12 miles to the west. "These ten weeks were shorter than one week at West Point," Grant wrote.

July 1, 1843, graduated from U.S. Military Academy

• Although he was the best horseman of his class and held an equestrian high-jump record that stood for 25 years, his request for assignment to the dragoons—as the cavalry was then called—was denied because of his academic standing. He ranked 21st in the class of 39. He was commissioned as a brevet second lieutenant and was assigned to the Fourth Infantry at Jefferson Barracks, Mo.

• He was the third of four presidents who were professional soldiers.

Sept. 1, 1843, reported to Jefferson Barracks

May, 1844, accompanied regiment to Camp Salubrity, La.

July, 1845, accompanied regiment to New Orleans Barracks

September, 1845, commissioned as second lieutenant

September, 1845, accompanied regiment to Corpus Christi, now in Texas

• His regiment joined the "army of occupation," commanded by General Zachary Taylor.

Mar. 8, 1846, advanced with regiment toward Rio Grande

May 8, 1846, participated in Battle of Palo Alto

May 9, 1846, participated in Battle of Resaca de la Palma

• He was a company commander.

May 13, 1846, war declared

• He was the last of three presidents who served in the Mexican War.

• He was the tenth of 21 presidents who served in the military during wartime.

Sept. 21–25, 1846, participated in capture of Monterey

Mar. 29, 1847, participated in capture of Veracruz

• His regiment had been transferred to the division of General William Worth, under the command of General Winfield Scott.

Apr. 18, 1847, participated in Battle of Cerro Gordo

Aug. 20, 1847, participated in Battle of Churubusco

Sept. 8, 1847, participated in Battle of Molino del Rey

• He was brevetted a first lieutenant for his service in this encounter.

Sept. 13, 1847, participated in Battle of Chapultepec

• He was commended in dispatches of his superior officers and was brevetted captain.

Sept. 14, 1847, entered Mexico City

• He was promoted to the permanent rank of first lieutenant a few days later.

Winter, 1847–1848, served as regimental quartermaster and commissary, Tacubaya

July, 1848, departed for U.S.

• His regiment was sent to Pascagoula, Miss.

Aug. 22, 1848, married Julia Boggs Dent, St. Louis, Mo.

• After his honeymoon he reported to his new post at Sackets Harbor, N.Y. The following April, he was transferred to Detroit, Mich., then back to Sackets Harbor in the spring of 1851.

May 30, 1850, his first son born
•The boy was named Frederick Dent Grant.
July 5, 1852, sailed with regiment for California
•The regiment arrived in Aspinwall, now Colon, Panama, July 12. About one-seventh of the troops died of cholera while crossing the Isthmus of Panama. They arrived in San Francisco in early September; after a few weeks at Benicia Barracks, the regiment was transferred to Fort Vancouver, on the Columbia River, then in Oregon Territory.
July 22, 1852, his second son born
•The boy was named Ulysses Simpson Grant.
Aug 5, 1853, commissioned as captain
•He assumed command of a company stationed at Humboldt Bay, Cal., in September.
1854, resigned from army
•His long separation from his wife and children (he had yet to see his second son), plus the fact that he couldn't afford to bring his family West, led him to excessive drinking, first at Fort Vancouver and then at Humboldt Bay. The situation came to a head when his commanding officer, Colonel Robert C. Buchanan, encountered Grant drunk in public. Buchanan demanded that Grant resign or stand trial; his resignation became effective, July 31.
Aug, 1854, rejoined wife, St. Louis, Mo.
1854–1858, worked farm near St. Louis
•The 60-acre farm, about 12 miles from St. Louis, had been given to Mrs. Grant by her father. Grant cleared the land and built a house there. The farm was never successful.
July 4, 1855, his only daughter born
•The girl was named Ellen Grant.
Nov. 4, 1856, cast first presidential vote
•He voted for Buchanan. "It was evident to my mind that the election of a Republican President in 1856 meant the secession of all the Slave States, and rebellion," he wrote in his *Memoirs*.
Feb. 6, 1858, his third son born
•The boy was named Jesse Root Grant.
Winter, 1858, entered real estate business, St. Louis
•He formed a partnership with his wife's cousin, Harry Boggs. Grant withdrew from the firm early in 1860. While in the real estate business, he sought the post of county engineer, an appointive office. He was not appointed by the county court.
May, 1860, took clerkship in his father's hardware and leather store, Galena, Ill.
•He worked for his younger brother, Simpson. His salary was $800 a year; he drew $1,500 during the 11 months he clerked in the store and later paid back the balance from his army pay.
Apr. 16, 1861, presided at public meeting, Galena
•Lincoln had issued his proclamation that "insurrection" existed and called on the states for seventy-five thousand volunteers, Apr. 15. A company of volunteers was raised; Grant was offered and declined the captaincy. He trained the company and accompanied the unit to Springfield, where they were assigned to a regiment.
May 5, 1861, appointed mustering officer in office of state adjutant general, Springfield
May 24, 1861, requested assignment from U.S. adjutant general
•He received no reply to his request for a regiment.
June 17, 1861, appointed colonel of 21st Illinois Infantry
•The regiment was transferred to Palmyra, Mo., next guarded a section of the Hannibal and St. Joseph Railroad, and later was transferred to Mexico, Mo.
•He was the second of seven presidents who served in the Civil War.
•He was the only president who served in both the Mexican War and the Civil War.
Aug. 7, 1861, appointed brigadier general of volunteers
•His commission was dated May 17.
•He was the seventh of 12 presidents who were generals.
Aug. 26, 1861, assigned command of district of southeastern Missouri, which included southern Illinois
Nov. 7, 1861, attacked Confederate camp, Belmont, Mo.
•He captured the camp, 175 prisoners, and two guns, but fell back when a superior force of Confederates counterattacked. His horse was shot from under him during the engagement. The Union force lost 485 men; the Confederates, 640.
Feb. 6, 1862, captured Fort Henry, Tenn., in cooperation with Commodore Andrew Hull Foote

NATIONAL PROMINENCE

Feb. 16, 1862, captured Fort Donelson, Tenn.
- This was the first Union capture of a prominent strategic point and the beginning of Grant's national reputation. It was here that he answered the request for terms of capitulation with his famed unconditional surrender message. "No terms except unconditional and immediate surrender can be accepted," he replied to Confederate General Simon Bolivar Buckner. "I propose to move immediately upon your works."
- Although he was called "Sam" by his intimates, the coincidence of his initials and the surrender message earned him the nationally hailed nickname, "Unconditional Surrender" Grant. He was promoted to major general. His commission dated from the surrender of Fort Donelson.

Apr. 6–7, 1862, Battle of Shiloh or Pittsburg Landing, Tenn.
- Surprised by a Confederate attack, Union forces retreated nearly to Pittsburg Landing. After a day of bitter fighting, the assault was suspended about 6 P.M., Apr. 6, when the Confederate commander received an inaccurate report that Union reinforcements could not arrive in time to prevent the destruction of Grant's army the following day. The reinforcements did arrive, and Grant counterattacked about 7:30 A.M., Apr. 7. The southerners were forced to withdraw. Both sides claimed victory. The northern claim was valid as the Confederate retreat meant the evacuation of much of Tennessee. Union losses were 1,754 killed and 11,293 wounded or missing. Confederate losses were 1,723 killed and 8,971 wounded or missing.

Oct. 25, 1862, took command of Department of Tennessee
- This command included northern Mississippi, parts of Kentucky and Tennessee.

Nov. 4, 1862, occupied Grand Junction, Tenn.
- This was the first move in the advance on Vicksburg.

Dec. 20, 1862, his advance supply base captured, Holly Springs, Miss.
- About $1,500,000 worth of supplies were destroyed. The Union base commander was dismissed from the service.

Dec. 29, 1862, Union force defeated, Chickasaw Bluffs, Miss.
- He was unable to support the Chickasaw Bluffs operation because of the loss of Holly Springs.

February–April, 1863, unsuccessful preliminary operations, Vicksburg
- An attempt to build a mile-long canal opposite Vicksburg to transport troops around the Confederate batteries for an attack from the south was abandoned in March because of the exceptionally high water. A larger canal project, begun at Duckport and connected by a series of bayous to the Mississippi River 20 miles below Vicksburg was also unsuccessful. Another force attempted to open a route northward through the swamps from Lake Providence, La., to the Mississippi south of Vicksburg; this project also was abandoned in March.
- A complicated waterborne project involved opening the levee at Yazoo Pass, 325 miles north of Vicksburg, so that Union troops could be sent down the Tallahatchie and Yazoo Rivers. Confederate forces stopped this advance by building a fort on the Yazoo, 90 miles north of Vicksburg. The Federal gunboats were halted, Mar. 11, and withdrew six days later. Still another Union force under Admiral William D. Porter attempted a 200-mile trip through Steele's Bayou, but was halted at Rolling Fork.
- Grant had little hope for any of these ventures; they were public relations gestures and a means of maintaining troop morale until the weather improved.

Mar. 29, 1863, began major Vicksburg operation
- His forces crossed to the west side of the Mississippi and began the march south.

Apr. 30, 1863, recrossed Mississippi, 30 miles south of Vicksburg

May 1, 1863, Port Gibson captured

May 3, 1863, occupied Grand Gulf
- The Confederate forces had pulled back to defend Vicksburg. Confederate reinforcements massed at Jackson, 45 miles east of Vicksburg.

May 12, 1863, skirmish at Raymond
- His strategy was to move between the two wings of the enemy, defeating them in turn. This decision was in violation of orders.

May 14, 1863, captured Jackson

May 16, 1863, Battle of Champion's Hill or Baker's Creek

• A Confederate force of about 22,000 men defended Champion's Hill, midway between Jackson and Vicksburg. The hill was captured and lost several times in the most severe fighting of the campaign. Union losses were about 410 killed, with 2,000 wounded and missing; Confederate losses were about 380 killed and 3,400 wounded and missing.

May 17, 1863, Battle of Big Black River

• A Confederate force of four thousand was routed by ten thousand Union troops but managed to destroy the bridges across the river.

May 19, 1863, first assault on Vicksburg

• This attack was repelled.

May 22, 1863, second frontal assault on Vicksburg

• This attack also was repelled. The twenty-two thousand defenders inflicted thirty-two hundred casualties among the thirty-five thousand Union infantry.

May 23–July 4, siege of Vicksburg

• Following the failure of the second assault, he settled down to take the city by siege, his chief weapons being constant bombardment and the defenders' inability to obtain supplies and food.

July 4, 1863, surrender of Vicksburg

• He originally asked for unconditional surrender but paroled the Confederate army of General John C. Pemberton to avoid the delays involved in dealing with twenty thousand prisoners of war, half of whom were unfit because of wounds and sickness. Pemberton believed that he had negotiated better terms by giving Grant the satisfaction of a surrender on the Fourth of July.

• The fall of Vicksburg, which occurred the day after the Union victory at Gettysburg, cut the South in half and opened the Mississippi for resumption of northern trade. It marked the impending death of the Confederacy.

Oct. 16, 1863, appointed commander of new Military Division of Mississippi

• His new command included the departments and armies of the Tennessee, the Cumberland, and Ohio. He received his commission personally from Secretary of War Stanton at Louisville, Ky., Oct. 17 or Oct. 18.

Oct. 23, 1863, assumed new command, Chattanooga, Tenn.

Nov. 23–25, 1863, Battle of Chattanooga

• The Chattanooga campaign culminated in Union victories at Lookout Mountain, Nov. 24, and Missionary Ridge, Nov. 25. As a result, Confederate forces were driven out of Tennessee, and the way was prepared for Sherman's march to the sea.

Mar. 1, 1864, nominated as lieutenant general

• The rank had been revived by an act of Congress, Feb. 29. His nomination was confirmed by the Senate, Mar. 2.

Mar. 9, 1864, received commission as lieutenant general

• The commission was presented personally by President Lincoln at the White House.

Mar. 12, 1864, appointed General in Chief of Armies of U.S.

• He assumed strategic direction of the war.

• He was the first officer in the history of the U.S. Army to attain the rank of full general. The only other president who was a full general was Eisenhower.

Mar. 26, 1864, established headquarters, Culpeper, Va.

May 5–7, 1864, Battle of Wilderness

• This marked the first encounter between troops commanded by Grant and Lee. Although considered a Union victory (albeit a costly one), the battle was far from a defeat for Lee. Union losses were 2,246 killed and 12,073 wounded, while Confederate losses were estimated at 7,750.

May 7–20, 1864, Spotsylvania campaign

• The results of this campaign were also inconclusive. Four Union assaults on well-entrenched Confederate positions between May 9 and May 18 failed. It was in the course of this campaign, May 11, that Grant said: "I propose to fight it out on this line if it takes all summer."

May 23–27, 1864, Battle of North Anna River or Hanover Junction, Va.

• The Confederate position proved too strong; he withdrew to Hanover Town.

May 27–30, 1864, Battle of Totopotomoy Creek, Va.

• Lee again blocked the Union forces.

May 31–June 12, 1864, Battle of Cold Harbor

• This was Lee's last great victory of the war. In the main Union assault, June 3, Grant lost seven thousand men, while the southern losses were no more than fifteen hundred. However, total Confederate losses during the previous month had been about thirty-two thousand, approximately 45 percent of Lee's strength. In the same period, Grant lost about fifty thousand men, roughly 40 percent of his force. Unlike Lee, Grant had no trouble getting replacements.

June 14–16, 1864, moved Army of Potomac to south side of James River

•He had decided to proceed against Richmond from the south via Petersburg, an important Confederate communications center.

June 15–18, 1864, Petersburg campaign

•The four-day assault failed. He gave up trying to take Petersburg by direct assault after losses of about seventeen hundred killed, eighty-five hundred wounded, and twelve hundred missing. The siege that followed lasted until March, 1865.

Mar. 30–Apr. 1, 1865, Battle of Five Forks, Va.

•Union cavalry under General Philip Sheridan won a decisive victory. Lee had concluded that Petersburg and Richmond could not be held and planned to move south to join forces with General Joseph E. Johnston, who was retreating before Sherman in North Carolina. Sheridan's victory at Five Forks, followed by Union victories at Appomattox Station, Apr. 8, and at Appomattox Court House, Apr. 9, denied Lee access to vital rail connections and effectively ended the war.

Apr. 9, 1865, accepted surrender of Lee, Appomattox

•The terms of surrender, drawn up by Grant and accepted by Lee, paroled Confederate officers and men and allowed them to return home with their horses and baggage. Officers were permitted to keep their sidearms. The generous terms of the surrender probably encouraged other Confederate commanders to abandon further hostilities. Johnston surrendered to Sherman, Apr. 26; Richard Taylor surrendered to E. R. S. Canby, Mar 4; and E. Kirby Smith surrendered to Canby, May 26.

•Grant rebuked his men for firing salutes to celebrate the victory. "The war is over," he said, "the rebels are again our countrymen, and the best sign of rejoicing will be to abstain from all demonstrations in the field."

Apr. 10, 1865, reported to Washington, D.C.

June-August, 1865, toured northern U.S., Canada

Aug. 18, 1865, house presented to Grants by citizens of Galena, Ill.

•The Grant Home State Memorial on Bouthillier Street is maintained by the State of Illinois Department of Conservation, Division of Parks and Memorials. It contains many Grant mementos, including White House china. It is open to the public daily except Thanksgiving, Christmas and New Year's Day, 9 A.M. to 5 P.M. There is no admission charge.

December, 1865, made inspection tour of South

•His report was submitted to Congress by President Johnson and became the basis for some Reconstruction laws.

Fall, 1866, refused order to undertake special mission to Mexico

•His refusal of the order by President Johnson was based on his contention that it was a diplomatic mission rather than part of military service, and that he therefore had the right to decline a civil appointment.

Aug. 12, 1867, appointed secretary of war ad interim by Johnson

May 21, 1868, unanimously nominated for president, Republican national convention, Chicago, Ill.

Nov. 3, 1868, election day

• *See* Election of 1868, below.

Dec. 2, 1868, presidential electors cast ballots

•He received 214 of the 294 electoral votes from the 34 states.

• *See* Election of 1868, below.

Feb. 10, 1869, electoral vote tabulated by Congress

•Grant and Colfax were officially declared elected.

ELECTION OF 1868

Republican party, convened, May 20, at Chicago, Ill., nominated Ulysses Simpson Grant of Illinois for president, Schuyler Colfax of Indiana for vice president.

•This was the fourth Republican national convention. It was the second Republican convention in Chicago; it was the third major party convention in Chicago.

Democratic party, convened, July 4, at New York City, nominated Horatio Seymour of Indiana for president, Francis Preston Blair, Jr., of Missouri for vice president.

•This was the tenth Democratic national convention. It was the first Democratic convention in New York City; it was the first of two major party conventions in New York City.

Election day, Tuesday, Nov. 3, 1868
Popular vote: 5,716,082
   Grant, 3,012,833
   Seymour, 2,703,249
Electoral vote: 294, 34 states
   • Grant, 214, 26 states
     (Alabama, 8; Arkansas, 5; California; 5, Connecticut, 6; Florida, 3; Illinois, 16; Indiana, 13; Iowa, 8; Kansas, 3; Maine,

7; Massachusetts, 12; Michigan 8; Minnesota, 4; Missouri, 11; Nebraska, 3; Nevada, 3; New Hampshire, 5; North Carolina, 9; Ohio, 21; Pennsylvania, 26; Rhode Island, 4; South Carolina, 6; Tennessee, 10; Vermont, 5; West Virginia, 5; Wisconsin, 8)
• Seymour, 80, eight states
   (Delaware, 3; Georgia, 9; Kentucky, 11; Louisiana, 7; Maryland, 7; New Jersey, 7; New York, 33; Oregon, 3)
• Votes not cast: 26 three states
   (Mississippi, 10; Texas, 6; Virginia, 10)

THE PRESIDENT (18th)

Term of office: Mar. 4, 1869, to Mar. 4, 1877 (8 years)
•Grant was the seventh of 12 presidents who were elected to second terms.
•He was the seventh of 16 presidents who served more than one term.
•He was the sixth of nine presidents who served two terms.
•He was the fifth of eight presidents who served for eight years.
State represented: Illinois
•He was the second of two presidents who represented Illinois. The other was Lincoln.
•He was the seventh of 15 presidents who represented states that were not their

native states.
Political party: Republican
•He was the second of 14 presidents who were Republicans.
Congresses: 41st, 42nd, 43rd, 44th
Administrations: 21st, 22nd
Age at inauguration: 46 years, 311 days
Inauguration day, Thursday, Mar. 4, 1869
•Grant took the oath of office, administered by Chief Justice Salmon P. Chase, on the east portico of the Capitol.
•This was the second of three inaugurations at which Chase officiated.
•This was the third of four oath-taking ceremonies at which Chase officiated.

THE 21st ADMINISTRATION

1869

Mar. 4, first session of 41st Congress
•The administration controlled both the Senate and the House of Representatives. Senate membership increased by 20 seats; House membership increased by 50 seats. The Republicans gained 19 Senate and 27 House seats; the Democrats lost one Senate seat, gained 14 House seats. The Senate (74 members) consisted of 61 Republicans, 11 Democrats and two vacancies. The House (243 members) consisted of 170 Republicans and 73 Democrats.
•This was the largest Republican majority in the Senate, 50.
Mar. 5, appointed his first secretary of state, Elihu B. Washburne; his first secretary of treasury, Alexander T. Stewart; his first at-

torney general, Ebenezer R. Hoar; his first secretary of navy, Adolph E. Borie; his first postmaster general, John A. J. Creswell; and his first secretary of interior, Jacob D. Cox
•Borie took office, Mar. 9
Mar. 9, Secretary of Treasury Stewart resigned
•Stewart withdrew inasmuch as an act of Sept. 2, 1789, prohibited anyone in the importing business from holding federal office.
Mar. 11, Secretary of State Washburne resigned, effective, Mar. 16
•Unqualified for the cabinet post, Washburne resigned to accept appointment as minister to France.
Mar. 11, appointed his second secretary of state, Hamilton Fish; his second secretary

of treasury, George S. Boutwell; and his first secretary of war, John A. Rawlins

• Boutwell took office, Mar. 12; Rawlins, Mar. 13; and Fish, Mar. 17.

• Rawlins had been Grant's adjutant during the war.

Mar. 18, signed public credit act

• This act provided for the payment of government debts in gold.

Apr. 5, signed amended Tenure of Office Act

• This act was modified but not repealed. The House of Representatives had voted to repeal the act, Jan. 11, in accordance with the known wishes of the president-elect.

Apr. 7, sent special message to Congress concerning claims against Great Britain

• He supported the view that Great Britain should compensate the U.S. for damages inflicted by the Confederate cruisers, *Alabama, Florida,* and *Shenandoah,* which had been built in British shipyards.

Apr. 8, called special session of Senate, Apr. 12

Apr. 10, signed act amending judiciary act

• The act provided that the Supreme Court was to consist of a chief justice and eight associate justices and also authorized the appointment of nine circuit judges.

• This was the last change in the size of the Court.

Apr. 10, first session of 41st Congress adjourned

Apr. 10, vetoed relief of Blanton Duncan bill

• This was the first of his 93 vetoes, the first of his 48 pocket vetoes. More than half of his vetoes (50) were of relief bills.

Apr. 12, special session of Senate

• This session adjourned, Apr. 23.

May 19, issued proclamation on eight-hour workday

• He directed department heads to ascertain that no cuts in wages accompanied the reduction of government workers' hours to eight.

June 22, Secretary of Navy Borie resigned, effective, June 25

June 25, appointed his second secretary of war, George M. Robeson

Aug. 19, recognized Cuban insurgents

• This proclamation was never published. It was pigeonholed by Secretary of State Fish.

Sept. 6, Secretary of War Rawlins died

Sept. 24, Black Friday, gold panic

• An attempt by James Fisk, Daniel Drew, and Jay Gould to corner the gold market

brought ruin to thousands.

Oct. 25, appointed his second secretary of war, William W. Belknap

Dec. 6, second session of 41st Congress

Dec. 6, sent his first State of the Union message to Congress

Dec. 15, Associate Justice Grier resigned, effective, Feb. 1

Dec. 15, appointed Ebenezer R. Hoar as associate justice

• Hoar, the first of Grant's eight appointments to the Supreme Court, was rejected by the Senate, Feb. 3, 1870.

• Grant was the tenth of 15 presidents who nominated justices not confirmed by the Senate.

• Hoar was the 15th of 25 men nominated to the Supreme Court who were not confirmed by the Senate.

Dec. 20, appointed Edwin M. Stanton as associate justice

• Stanton, who was confirmed by the Senate, Dec. 20, was the second of Grant's eight appointments to the Supreme Court.

Dec. 24, Associate Justice Stanton died

• Stanton did not serve on the Supreme Court.

1870

Jan. 24, received Prince Arthur of Great Britain

• Prince Arthur was the third son of Queen Victoria.

Jan 26, signed act readmitting Virginia to representation in Congress

Feb. 7, appointed William Strong and Joseph P. Bradley as associate justices

• Strong, who was confirmed by the Senate, Feb. 18, was the third of Grant's eight appointments to the Supreme Court.

• Bradley, who was confirmed by the Senate, Mar. 21, was the fourth of Grant's eight appointments to the Supreme Court

Feb. 23, signed act readmitting Mississippi to representation in Congress

Mar. 30, 15th Amendment to Constitution ratified

• This was the last amendment ratified in the 19th century.

• *See* Constitution, page 644.

Mar. 30, signed act readmitting Texas to representation in Congress

May 24, issued proclamation that warned against participation in Fenian raids into Canada

May 31, signed first enforcement act
• This was the first Ku Klux Klan act, which provided heavy penalties for infringement upon voting rights under the 14th and 15th amendments.
• Part of this act was declared unconstitutional in 1876.
June 13, sent special message to Congress announcing strict neutrality regarding Cuban revolution
June 15, Attorney General Hoar resigned, effective, July 8
June 22, signed act organizing department of justice
• The department of justice was placed under the direction of the attorney general.
June 23, appointed his second attorney general, Amos T. Akerman
• Akerman took office, July 8.
July 14, signed act providing annual pension of $3,000 for Mrs. Abraham Lincoln
July 14, vetoed southern Union troops bill
July 15, signed act readmitting Georgia to representation in Congress
• This act ended military rule of the South.
July 15, signed act reducing army to peacetime footing
July 15, second session of 41st Congress adjourned
Aug. 22, issued proclamation of neutrality in Franco-Prussian War
Oct. 4, appointed first solicitor general, Benjamin H. Bristow
Oct. 12, issued proclamation forbidding military expeditions against nations at peace with U.S.
Oct. 30, Secretary of Interior Cox resigned, effective, Oct. 31
Nov. 1, appointed his second secretary of interior, Columbus Delano
Dec. 5, third session of 41st Congress
Dec. 5, sent his second State of the Union message to Congress

Note: The official population, according to the ninth census, was 38,558,371.

1871

Feb. 21, signed act providing territorial government for District of Columbia
Feb. 28, signed act providing for federal supervision of elections in cities of more than twenty thousand population
Mar. 3, signed act establishing first Civil Service Commission

• The commission proved ineffective when Congress refused to vote appropriations.
Mar. 3, signed Indian appropriation act
• This act nullified all Indian treaties and made Indians national wards.
Mar. 4, appointed first civil service commissioner, George W. Curtis
• Curtis resigned in 1875 when his recommendations were refused consideration and the commission was discontinued.
Mar. 4, third session of 41st Congress adjourned
Mar. 4, first session of 42nd Congress
• The administration maintained control of the Senate, but lost control of the House of Representatives. The Democrats gained six Senate and 61 House seats. The Senate (74 members) consisted of 57 Republicans and 17 Democrats. The House (243 members) consisted of 134 Democrats, 104 Republicans, and five others.
Mar. 24, issued proclamation against unlawful combinations in South Carolina
• This proclamation was aimed at the Ku Klux Klan.
Apr. 5, sent special message to Congress recommending annexation of Santo Domingo
• The Senate refused to ratify a treaty negotiated by his personal envoy and private secretary, Orville E. Babcock.
Apr. 20, signed second enforcement act
• This was the second Ku Klux Klan act, which authorized the suspension of the writ of habeas corpus when combinations of private persons had successfully defied the 15th Amendment.
• Part of this act was declared unconstitutional, 1883.
Apr. 20, first session of 42nd Congress adjourned
Apr. 20, called special session of Senate, May 10
May 8, Treaty of Washington signed
• The treaty, which consigned the *Alabama* claims to international arbitration, was signed by the U.S. and Great Britain in Washington, D.C. Great Britain was held liable by the tribunal; the U.S. was awarded damages of $15,500,000, 1872.
May 10, special session of Senate
• This session adjourned, May 27.
Oct. 12, issued proclamation ordering Ku Klux Klan in South Carolina to disperse and surrender arms
Oct. 17, issued proclamation suspending writ of habeas corpus in nine South

Carolina counties.

•Federal troops were sent to South Carolina. More than six hundred arrests were made; less than 25 percent of those indicted were convicted.

•This was the first occasion after military rule had ceased on which federal troops were used to maintain order in the South.

Dec. 4, second session of 42nd Congress

Dec. 4, sent his third State of the Union message to Congress

Dec. 13, Attorney General Akerman resigned, effective, Jan. 10, 1872

Dec. 14, appointed his third attorney general, George H. Williams

•Williams took office, Jan. 10, 1872.

1872

Mar. 1, signed act establishing Yellowstone National Park

Mar. 4, received Japanese embassy of 114 persons, White House

Mar. 5, appointed commission to examine plans and proposals for interoceanic canal across Isthmus of Darien, Colombia

May 14, vetoed pension to Mary Ann Montgomery bill

•This was the first of his four vetoes that were overridden.

May 23, nominated for president, Workingmen's national convention, New York City

June 6, renominated for president, Republican national convention, Philadelphia, Pa.

June 8, signed act establishing post office as executive department

June 10, signed act providing for discontinuance of Freedmen's Bureau as of June 30

June 10, second session of 42nd Congress adjourned

June 10, accepted Republican renomination

Sept. 4, Credit Mobilier exposed in New York *Sun*

•Officers of the Credit Mobilier of America, a construction company organized in 1867 to complete the Union Pacific Railroad, had bribed members of Congress by selling them stock at half the market value in return for specific legislation regarding right-of-way and public land grants. Stock was distributed by Representative Oakes Ames of Massachusetts, chief officer of Credit Mobilier, to Speaker of the House Schuyler Colfax (who was serving as vice president

when details of the stock deals became public knowledge), Senator Henry Wilson (who succeeded Colfax as vice president), and Representative James A. Garfield (who later served as president), among others.

Nov. 5, election day

• *See* Election of 1872, below.

Nov. 28, Associate Justice Nelson resigned

Dec. 2, third session of 42nd Congress

Dec. 2, sent his fourth State of the Union message to Congress

•He recommended the appointment of a commission to determine the boundary of Alaska.

Dec. 3, appointed Ward Hunt as associate justice

•Hunt who was confirmed by the Senate, Dec. 11, was the fifth of Grant's eight appointments to the Supreme Court.

Dec. 4, presidential electors cast ballots

•He received 286 of the 352 electoral votes from the 35 states.

• *See* Election of 1872, below.

1873

Jan. 29, vetoed relief of East Tennessee University bill

Jan. 31, signed act abolishing franking privilege

Feb. 12, signed coinage act

•This act made gold the sole monetary standard and omitted all silver currency. Opponents called it "The Crime of '73."

Feb. 12, electoral votes tabulated by Congress

•Grant and Wilson were officially declared elected.

Mar. 3, signed act increasing salaries of president, vice president, members of Congress, cabinet, and Supreme Court, effective Mar. 4.

•This act came to be known as the "Salary Grab Act" and was repealed except for the increases voted the president and members of the Court, 1874.

•Grant was the first recipient of the new salary, $50,000.

Mar. 4, third session of 42nd Congress adjourned

ELECTION OF 1872

Labor Reform party, convened, Feb. 21, at

Columbus, Ohio, nominated David Davis of Illinois for president, Joel Parker of New Jersey for vice president. Davis and Parker declined.
• The Labor Reform party reconvened, Aug. 22, at Philadelphia, Pa., nominated Charles O'Conor of New York for president, Eli Saulsbury of Delaware for vice president. O'Conor and Saulsbury declined.

Prohibition party, convened Feb. 22, at Columbus, Ohio, nominated James Black of Pennsylvania for president, John Russell of Michigan for vice president.
• This was the first Prohibition convention.

Liberal Republican party, convened, May 1, at Cincinnati, Ohio, nominated Horace Greeley of New York for president, Benjamin Gratz Brown of Missouri for vice president.

Workingmen's party, convened, May 23, at New York City, nominated Ulysses Simpson Grant of Illinois for president, Henry Wilson of Massachusetts for vice president.

Republican party, convened, June 5, at Philadelphia, Pa. nominated Ulysses Simpson Grant of Illinois for president, Henry Wilson of Massachusetts for vice president.
• This was the fifth Republican national convention. It was the second Republican convention in Philadelphia; it was the fourth major party convention in Philadelphia.

Revenue Reformers' (liberal Republican) party, convened, June 21, at New York City, nominated William Slocomb Groesbeck of Ohio for president, Frederick Law Olmsted of New York for vice president

Democratic party, convened, July 9, at Baltimore, Md., nominated Horace Greeley of New York for president, Benjamin Gratz Brown of Missouri for vice president.
• This was the 11th Democratic national convention. It was the sixth Democratic convention in Baltimore; it was the 16th major party convention in Baltimore.
• A splinter group, the **Straight-out Democrats**, convened, Sept. 3, at Louisville, Ky., nominated Charles O'Conor of New York for president, John Quincy Adams II of Massachusetts for vice president.

O'Conor and Adams declined; however, the Straight-out Democratic ticket was on the ballots of 23 states.

Election day, Tuesday, Nov. 5, 1872
Popular vote: 6,466,354
  Grant, 3,597,132
  Greeley, 2,834,125
  O'Conor, 29,489
  Black, 5,608
Electoral vote: 352, 35 states
  • Grant, 286, 29 states
    (Alabama, 10; California, 6; Connecticut, 6; Delaware, 3; Florida, 4; Illinois, 21; Indiana, 15; Iowa, 11; Kansas, 5; Maine, 7; Massachusetts, 13; Michigan, 11; Minnesota, 5; Mississippi, 8; Nebraska, 3; Nevada, 3; New Hampshire, 5; New Jersey, 9; New York, 35; North Carolina, 10; Ohio, 22; Oregon, 3; Pennsylvania, 29; Rhode Island, 4; South Carolina, 7; Vermont, 5; Virginia, 11; West Virginia, 5; Wisconsin, 10)
• The 66 votes from six states that would have been cast for Greeley, who died Nov. 29, 1872, were divided:
  • Thomas Andrews Hendricks of Illinois, 42, four states
    (Kentucky, 8 of 12 votes; Maryland, 8; Tennessee, 12; Texas, 8)
• Hendricks also received the votes of six Missouri electors.
  • Benjamin Gratz Brown of Missouri, 18, two states
    (Georgia, 6 of 11 votes; Missouri, 8 of 15 votes)
• Brown also received the votes of four Kentucky electors.
  • Charles Jones Jenkins of Georgia, 2, no states
• Jenkins received the votes of two Georgia electors.
  • David Davis of Illinois, 1, no states
• Davis received the vote of one Missouri elector.

Note: Three of the Georgia electors voted for Greeley, but these votes were not counted.

THE 22nd ADMINSTRATION

1873

Mar. 4, his second inauguration day

• Grant took the oath of office, administered by Chief Justice Salmon P. Chase, on the east portico of the Capitol.

•This was the last of three inaugurations at which Chase officiated.

•This was the last of four oath-taking ceremonies at which Chase officiated.

•Grant's age at his second inauguration was 50 years, 311 days.

•He was the eighth of 21 presidents who were younger than their vice presidents. Grant was ten years, 70 days younger than Wilson.

Mar. 16, Secretary of Treasury Boutwell resigned

Mar. 17, appointed his third secretary of treasury, William A. Richardson

May 7, Chief Justice Salmon P. Chase died

May 22, issued proclamation ordering disorderly bands in Louisiana to disperse

June 29, his father died

July 3, issued proclamation announcing Centennial Exposition of 1876

Aug. 22, with Mrs. Grant, celebrated silver wedding anniversary, White House

•He was the third of five presidents who celebrated their 25th anniversaries while residents of the White House.

Sept. 18, Panic of 1873 began

•The failure of Jay Cooke and Company, a major New York banking firm, set off the panic. The New York Stock Exchange closed, Sept. 20, for ten days. The principal reason was illogical railroad speculation. One of the worst U.S. depressions followed, lasting until 1878.

•This was the fourth of nine U.S. depressions.

Dec. 1, first session of 43rd Congress

•The administration maintained control of the Senate and regained control of the House of Representatives. House membership increased by 57 seats. The Republicans lost three Senate seats, but gained 90 House seats. The Senate (74 members) consisted of 54 Republicans, 19 Democrats, and one other. The House (300 members) consisted of 194 Republicans, 92 Democrats, and 14 others.

Dec. 1, sent his fifth State of the Union message to Congress

Dec. 1, appointed George H. Williams as chief justice

•This, Grant's sixth appointment to the Supreme Court, was withdrawn, Jan. 8, 1874.

•Grant was the second of three presidents who nominated chief justices who were not confirmed by the Senate.

•Williams was the second of four nominees

for chief justice who were not confirmed by the Senate.

•Williams was the 16th of 25 men nominated to the Supreme Court who were not confirmed by the Senate.

1874

Jan. 9, appointed Caleb Cushing as chief justice

•Grant was the last of three presidents who appointed more than one chief justice.

•This, Grant's seventh appointment to the Supreme Court, was withdrawn, Jan. 13.

•He was the only president who nominated two chief justices who were not confirmed by the Senate.

•Cushing was the third of four nominees for chief justice who were not confirmed by the Senate.

•Cushing was the 17th of 25 men nominated to the Supreme Court who were not confirmed by the Senate.

Jan. 19, appointed Morrison R. Waite as chief justice

•Waite, who was confirmed by the Senate, Jan. 21, was the last of Grant's eight appointments to the Supreme Court.

•Only four of his appointees took the oath of office; two were withdrawn, one was rejected, and one died shortly after confirmation.

•He was the fifth of 14 presidents who appointed chief justices.

Jan. 20, appropriation act of 1873 repealed

•The "Salary Grab Act" of Mar. 3, 1873, was repealed, except for the salary increases of the president and justices of the Supreme Court.

Apr. 22, vetoed inflation of currency bill

May 15, issued proclamation ordering disorderly gatherings in Arkansas to disperse

•He recognized Elisha Baxter as governor of Arkansas.

•Election frauds had been charged by proponents of both Baxter, the Republican candidate, and Joseph Brooks, the Liberal Republican candidate.

May 21, attended wedding of his daughter, Nellie, and Algernon Frederick Sartoris, White House

•This was the third of eight White House weddings of daughters of presidents.

•This was the fourth of nine White House weddings of children of presidents.

June 1, Secretary of Treasury Richardson resigned, effective, June 3

June 4, appointed his fourth secretary of treasury, Benjamin H. Bristow

June 20, signed act abolishing territorial government in District of Columbia

• This act provided for a commission of three governing regents.

June 23, first session of 43rd Congress adjourned

June 24, Postmaster General Creswell resigned, effective, July 3

July 3, appointed his second postmaster general, James W. Marshall

Aug. 24, Postmaster General Marshall resigned

Aug. 24, appointed his third postmaster general, Marshall Jewell

Nov. 7, first G.O.P. elephant cartoon published

• The first cartoon to depict the elephant as the symbol of the Republican party was drawn by Thomas Nast and appeared in *Harper's Weekly.* Entitled "Third Term Panic," it showed the elephant, labeled "The Republican Vote," on the verge of plunging into a pit.

• Nast is generally credited with having drawn the first Democratic donkey cartoon, although the donkey had been pictured as the Democratic symbol as early as Jackson's administration. However, Nast's donkey cartoons did much to establish the animal as the party symbol.

Dec. 7, second session of 43rd Congress

Dec. 7, sent his sixth State of the Union message to Congress

Dec. 15, received King Kalakaua of Sandwich Islands, Hawaii

• Grant was the first president to receive a reigning king.

Dec. 21, issued proclamation ordering disorderly gatherings in Mississippi to disperse

• Political strife between state officers and taxpayers led to race riots at a considerable loss of life. About seven hundred Negroes were killed at Vicksburg, Dec. 7.

1875

Jan. 14, signed specie resumption act

• This act provided for the resumption of specie payments by Jan. 1, 1879, and the reduction of greenbacks in circulation to $300,000,000.

Jan. 30, signed reciprocity treaty with Hawaii

• The Senate ratified the treaty, effective, June 3.

Feb. 17, special session of Senate, Mar. 5.

Mar. 1, signed civil rights act guaranteeing Negroes equal rights in public places

• This act also prohibited Negroes from being excluded from jury duty.

Mar. 4, second session of 43rd Congress adjourned

Mar. 5, special session of Senate

• This session adjourned, Mar. 24.

Apr. 22, Attorney General Williams resigned, effective, May 15

May 1, "Whiskey Ring" investigation

• Preferential treatment of certain distillers by internal revenue officials, first exposed by the St. Louis *Democrat*, was uncovered. The investigation by Secretary of Treasury Bristow resulted in more than two hundred indictments; about half pleaded guilty and a dozen fled the country. Only a handful of the others was convicted. Among those acquitted was Orville Babcock.

May 15, appointed his fourth attorney general, Edwards Pierrepont

May 29, "third term" letter published

• He said he had no intention of running for a third term.

July 5, Secretary of Interior Delano resigned

• Grant accepted Delano's resignation, Sept. 22, effective, Nov. 1.

July 31, President Andrew Johnson died

• With the death of Johnson, Grant became the second of four presidents who served for periods when no former president was living.

Sept. 29, voiced opposition to sectarian schools in speech, Des Moines, Iowa

Oct. 19, appointed his third secretary of interior, Zachariah Chandler

Nov. 22, Vice President Wilson died

• Thomas W. Ferry, of Michigan, president pro tempore of the Senate, became acting vice president.

Dec. 6, first session of 44th Congress

• The administration maintained control of the Senate but again lost control of the House of Representatives. The Democrats gained ten Senate and 17 House seats. The Senate (76 members) consisted of 46 Republicans, 29 Democrats, and one other. The House (292 members) consisted of 169

Democrats, 109 Republicans, and 14 others.

Dec. 7, sent his seventh State of the Union message to Congress

• He advocated nonsectarian and compulsory education.

Dec. 9, his private secretary, Orville Babcock, indicted

• Grant's efforts resulted in the acquittal of Babcock, who had been charged with complicity in the "Whiskey Ring" conspiracy.

Dec. 15, anti-third-term resolution passed in House of Representatives by wide margin

1876

Feb. 3, vetoed custody of Indian trust funds bill

Mar. 2, Secretary of War Belknap resigned

• Belknap was impeached by the House on the grounds of gross malfeasance in office, Mar. 2.

• Belknap, whose duties included maintenance of Indian reservations, had awarded his wife an Indian trade post. Mrs. Belknap made an arrangement with a New York contractor, who in turn agreed to allow the incumbent trader to retain the post for $12,000 a year. Mrs. Belknap was to receive half of this amount but died after receiving only $1,500. Her husband continued the arrangement after her death.

• Belknap also contrived similar contracts for several associates, including one who was paid a "salary" of $100,000.

• Belknap was the only member of the cabinet who was impeached.

Mar. 8, appointed his third secretary of war, Alphonso Taft

• Taft was the father of the future president.

Mar. 31, vetoed relief of G. B. Tyler and E. H. Luckett bill

• This was the second of his four vetoes that were overridden.

Apr. 4, Belknap articles of impeachment presented in Senate

Apr. 18, vetoed reduction of presidential salary bill

• The bill was a further repeal of the "Salary Grab Act" of 1873; if signed, it would have reduced the chief executive's salary to $25,000 yearly as of Mar. 4, 1877.

May 4, sent special message to Congress defending his recurrent absence from Washington

• He had been much criticized for spending considerable time at Long Beach, N.J., and justified his absences from the seat of government by citing precedents of previous presidents.

May 7, received Dom Pedro II and Empress Theresa of Brazil, White House

May 10, opened Centennial Exposition, Philadelphia, Pa.

May 22, Attorney General Pierrepont resigned

May 22, appointed his fifth attorney general, Alphonso Taft, and his fourth secretary of war, James D. Cameron

June 20, Secretary of Treasury Bristow resigned

June 26, issued proclamation suggesting public religious services, July 4

July 7, appointed his fifth secretary of treasury, Lot M. Morrill

July 11, Postmaster General Jewell resigned, effective, July 12

July 11, vetoed relief of Nelson Tiffany bill

• This was the third of his four vetoes that were overridden.

July 12, appointed his fourth postmaster general, James N. Tyner

• Tyner was the last of Grant's 25 cabinet appointments.

• He and Franklin D. Roosevelt both appointed 25 men to their cabinets, the largest number of cabinet appointments.

July 20, vetoed post office statutes bill

Aug. 1, Belknap acquitted by Senate

• The vote was 35–25 for conviction, less than the necessary two-thirds. However, 23 of the 25 senators who voted to acquit declared that they had taken such action in the belief that the Senate had no jurisdiction over a cabinet member who had resigned.

• Other members of Grant's cabinet who were involved in scandals included Secretary of Navy Robeson, Attorney General Williams, and Secretary of Treasury Richardson. Robeson accepted kickbacks on naval purchases between 1869 and 1876 of more than $300,000. Williams used government funds for personal expenses during the Panic of 1873. Richardson had appointed an investigator to seek out delinquent taxes who was paid the exorbitant fee of 50 percent of $427,000 collected.

• Robeson remained in the cabinet until the

end of the Grant administration. Williams would have been elevated to the Supreme Court if the Senate had not objected. Richardson, who had resigned in 1874, was appointed to the court of claims.

Aug. 1, Colorado admitted as 38th state
•Colorado was the only state admitted during Grant's term of office.

Aug. 15, first session of 44th Congress adjourned

Aug. 15, vetoed sales of Indian lands bill
•This was the last of his four vetoes that were overridden.

Oct. 17, issued proclamation ordering disorderly gatherings in South Carolina to disperse

Nov. 7, election day
• *See* Election of 1876, page 227.

Dec. 4, second session of 44th Congress

Dec. 5, sent his eighth and last State of the Union message to Congress
•He apologized for his failings while president, ascribing them to inexperience. His

mistakes were "errors of judgment, not of intent," he said.

1877

Jan. 29, signed act establishing electoral commission
•This commission decided the disputed Election of 1876.
• *See* page 227.

Feb. 14, vetoed advertising of executive department bill

Feb. 28, vetoed relief of Edward A. Leland bill
•This was the last of his 45 regular vetoes.

Mar. 3, second session of 44th Congress adjourned

Mar. 3, pocket vetoed five private relief bills, an army commission bill, and a bill to provide a shorthand report for U.S. courts in California
•These were the last of his 48 pocket vetoes.

THE FORMER PRESIDENT

Mar. 5, 1877, attended inauguration of Hayes
•Grant's age upon leaving office was 54 years, 311 days.

May, 1877-September, 1879, made round-the-world trip
•Accompanied by his wife and their youngest son, Jesse, he zigzagged through Europe for 18 months with no planned itinerary, visiting nearly every important city. He was greeted everywhere with ovations, receptions, and special recognition. He was received by Queen Victoria of Great Britain, Leopold II of Belgium, Alfonso XII of Spain, Alexander II of Russia, and Pope Leo XIII.
•He was the fourth of eight former presidents who visited Europe.
•He was the last of three former presidents who met with Popes.
•He decided to extend his journey to Asia and Africa, and visited India, Siam, China, Japan, and Egypt.
•A two-volume account of his travels, *Around the World With General Grant,* by John Russell Young, was published in 1879, and became a bestseller.
•He was the only former president who visited Asia.

•He was the first of two former presidents who visited Africa. The other was Theodore Roosevelt.

Sept. 20, 1879, landed in San Francisco, Cal.
•He made a six-week tour of the West Coast, then journeyed eastward. He arrived in Philadelphia, Nov. 5, two years and six months after he had sailed from that city for Europe.

1880, visited Cuba, West Indies, and Mexico

June 2–8, 1880, unsuccessful candidate for president, Republican national convention, Chicago, Ill.
•He received 304 votes on the first ballot, but anti-third-term forces supported James G. Blaine of Maine, John Sherman of Ohio, and other favorite sons. After 35 ballots, the Blaine and Sherman factions combined to give Garfield the necessary 378 votes.
•Grant was the first president who sought a third term.

1881, moved from Galena to New York City

1881, made second trip to Mexico City

1882, made third trip to Mexico City

May 11, 1883, his mother died

Dec. 24, 1883, injured in fall
•He suffered serious injury when he fell on the ice in front of his residence on East 66th Street, New York City. He was on

crutches for months and walked with a cane for the rest of his life.

May, 1884, firm of Grant and Ward failed

•He was a partner in the brokerage firm, which had been formed by his son, Ulysses, and Ferdinand Ward. Grant invested $100,000, and also reinvested most of his $3,000 monthly income from the firm. When the firm went into bankruptcy, Ward and another officer of the company were indicted and sent to jail. Neither of the Grants were implicated in dishonesty, but both were criticized for negligence.

•Shortly before the scandal broke, Grant had been induced by Ward to raise $150,-000 to save the Marine National Bank. He borrowed the sum from William H. Vanderbilt. He repaid Vanderbilt with his own and his wife's personal property, his war trophies, and gifts received during his world tour.

June, 1884, agreed to write series of articles for *Century* Magazine

•He wrote four articles on the Civil War; the first concerned the Battle of Shiloh. He was to receive $500 an article, but the fees were doubled when the articles added fifty thousand circulation to the issues in which they appeared.

August, 1884, illness diagnosed as cancer at root of tongue

•He had complained of discomfort in his mouth earlier in the summer.

Fall, 1884, began to write memoirs

•He had received several attractive offers from publishers. He accepted a contract offered by Samuel L. Clemens (Mark Twain), part owner of the publishing firm of Charles L. Webster and Company, Feb. 27, 1885. The contract stipulated that Grant was to receive an advance of $25,-000 per volume against a 20 percent royalty.

January, 1885, forced to abandon dictation

•He was in much pain. His weight had dropped from 200 to 145 pounds.

Mar. 3, 1885, nominated as general on retired list with full pay by President Arthur

•Grant's salary was $13,500.

June 26, 1885, moved to Mount McGregor, near Saratoga, N.Y.

•He received thousands of letters and hundreds of visitors.

July 19, 1885, finished his memoirs

•He completed the manuscript four days before his death.

•The two volume *Personal Memoirs of U.S. Grant,* published in 1885–1886, sold more than 300,000 copies. Mrs. Grant received royalties of more than $440,000.

DEATH

Date of death: July 23, 1885

Place of death: Mount McGregor, N.Y.

•Grant was the fourth of eight presidents who died in New York.

Age at death: 63 years, 87 days

•He lived eight years, 141 days, after the completion of his term.

Cause of death: Cancer

Place of burial: New York, N.Y.

•He was the only president who was buried in New York City.

•He was the third of six presidents who were buried in New York.

THE VICE PRESIDENTS
(17th and 18th)

Note: Grant was the fifth of seven presidents who had two vice presidents.

Full name: Schuyler Colfax (17th)

Date of birth: Mar. 23, 1823

Place of birth: New York, N.Y.

•He was the first of two vice presidents who were born in New York City. The other was Theodore Roosevelt.

•He was the fifth of eight vice presidents who were born in New York.

Religious denomination: Dutch Reformed

•He was the second of four vice presidents who were Dutch Reformed.

Occupations: Editor, politician

•He moved to Indiana in his teens, 1836; established a Whig newspaper in South Bend, Ind., in the 1840's; helped form Republican party in the state, 1855; member of the House of Representatives, 1855–1869; speaker of the House, 1863–1869.

•He was the 12th of 21 vice presidents who served in the House of Representatives before their terms of office.

•He was the first of two vice presidents who served as speakers of the House. The other was Garner.

Term of office: Mar. 4, 1869, to Mar. 4, 1873 (4 years)

•He was the eighth of 17 vice presidents

who served four-year terms.
•Grant and Colfax were the 19th of 41 president-vice president teams.
Age at inauguration: 45 years, 346 days
State represented: Indiana
•He was the first of four vice presidents who represented Indiana.
•He was the fourth of 13 vice presidents who represented states that were not their native states.
Political party: Republican
•He was the second of 15 vice presidents who were Republicans.
Occupation after term: Lecturer
Date of death: Jan. 13, 1885
Place of death: Mankato, Minn.
•He was the only vice president who died in Minnesota.
Age at death: 61 years, 296 days
Place of burial: South Bend, Ind.
•He was the first of four vice presidents who were buried in Indiana.

Full name: Henry Wilson (18th)
•His name was Jeremiah Jones Colbath, but he changed it legally to Henry Wilson, 1833.
Date of birth: Feb. 16, 1812
Place of birth: Farmington, N.H.
•He was the only vice president who was born in New Hampshire.
Religious denomination: Congregationalist
•He was the first of four vice presidents who were Congregationalists.
Occupation: Shoe manufacturer
•He was indentured to a farmer as a boy; apprenticed himself to a Natick, Mass., cobbler, 1833; established a shoe factory, 1838; Whig member of Massachusetts house of representatives, most of years between 1841 and 1852; left Whig party and helped form Free-Soil party, 1848; purchased and edited Boston *Republican*, made it a Free-Soil newspaper, 1848–1851; elected to Senate as Know-Nothing (American party), 1854, but withdrew from party, 1855; member of the Senate, 1855–1873; chairman of Senate committee on military affairs during Civil War.
•He was the eighth of 17 vice presidents who served in the Senate before their terms of offices.
Term of office: Mar. 4, 1873, to Nov. 22, 1875 (2 years, 263 days)
•He was the sixth of 14 vice presidents who served less than one term.

•Grant and Wilson were the 20th of 41 president-vice president teams.
Age at inauguration: 61 years, 16 days
State represented: Massachusetts
•He was the third of four vice presidents who represented Massachusetts.
•He was the fifth of 13 vice presidents who represented states that were not their native states.
Political party: Republican
•He was the third of 15 vice presidents who were Republicans.
Date of death: Nov. 22, 1875 (died in office)
•He was the third of six vice presidents who died before completing their first terms.
•He was the fourth of seven vice presidents who died in office.
•He was the only vice president who lay in state in the Capitol Rotunda.
Place of death: Washington, D.C.
•He was the fourth of six vice presidents who died in Washington.
Age at death: 63 years, 279 days
Place of burial: Natick, Mass.
•He was the second of two vice presidents who were buried in Massachusetts. The other was John Adams.

THE CABINET

State: Elihu Benjamin Washburne of Illinois, Mar. 5, 1869, to Mar. 16, 1869
•Hamilton Fish of New York, Mar. 17, 1869, to Mar. 12, 1877
Treasury: Alexander Turney Stewart of New York, Mar. 5, 1869, to Mar. 8, 1869
•George Sewall Boutwell of Massachusetts, Mar. 12, 1869, to Mar. 16, 1873
•William Adams Richardson of Massachusetts, Mar. 17, 1873, to June 3, 1874
•Benjamin Helm Bristow of Kentucky, June 4, 1874, to June 20, 1876
•Lot Myrick Morrill of Maine, July 7, 1876, to Mar. 3, 1877
War: John Aaron Rawlins of Illinois, Mar. 13, 1869, to Sept. 6, 1869
•William Worth Belknap of New York, Oct. 25, 1869, to Mar. 2, 1876
•Alphonso Taft of Ohio, Mar. 8, 1876, to May 22, 1876
•James Donald Cameron of Pennsylvania, May 22, 1876, to Mar. 3, 1877
Attorney General: Ebenezer Rockwood Hoar of Massachusetts, Mar. 5, 1869, to July 8, 1870

•Amos Tappan Akerman of Georgia, July 8, 1870, to Jan. 10, 1872

•George Henry Williams of Oregon, Jan. 10, 1872, to May 15, 1875

•Edwards Pierrepont of New York, May 15, 1875, to May 22, 1876

•Alphonso Taft of Ohio, May 22, 1876, to Mar. 11, 1877

Navy: Adolph Edward Borie of Pennsylvania, Mar. 9, 1869, to June 25, 1869

•George Maxwell Robeson of New Jersey, June 26, 1869, to Mar. 12, 1877

Postmaster General: John Angel James Creswell of Maryland, Mar. 5, 1869, to July 3, 1874

•James William Marshall of Virginia, July 3, 1874, to Aug. 24, 1874

•Marshall Jewell of Connecticut, Aug. 24, 1874, to July 12, 1876

•James Noble Tyner of Indiana, July 12, 1876, to Mar. 12, 1877

Interior: Jacob Dolson Cox of Ohio, Mar. 5, 1869, to Oct. 31, 1870

•Columbus Delano of Ohio, Nov. 1, 1870, to Sept. 30, 1875

•Zachariah Chandler of Michigan, Oct. 19, 1875, to Mar. 11, 1877

THE SUPREME COURT

Chief Justices: George Henry Williams of Oregon, appointed, Dec. 1, 1873; withdrawn, Jan. 8, 1874

•Caleb Cushing of Massachusetts, appointed, Jan. 9, 1874; withdrawn, Jan. 13, 1874

•Morrison Remick Waite of Ohio, appointed, Jan. 19, 1874; confirmed Jan. 21, 1874

Associate Justices: Ebenezer Rockwood Hoar of Massachusetts, appointed, Dec. 15, 1869; rejected by Senate, Feb. 3, 1870

•Edwin McMasters Stanton of Ohio, appointed, Dec. 20, 1869; confirmed, Dec. 20, 1869

•William Strong of Pennsylvania, appointed, Feb. 7, 1870; confirmed, Feb. 18, 1870

•Joseph Paul Bradley of New Jersey, appointed, Feb. 7, 1870; confirmed, Mar. 21, 1870

•Ward Hunt of New York, appointed, Dec. 3, 1872; confirmed, Dec. 11, 1872

Nineteenth President

RUTHERFORD BIRCHARD HAYES

Full name: Rutherford Birchard Hayes
- He was the fifth of 19 presidents who had middle initials or middle names.

Date of birth: Oct. 4, 1822
- He was the second of five presidents who were born in October.

Place of birth: Delaware, Ohio
- He was the second of three consecutive presidents who were born in Ohio.
- He was the second of seven presidents who were born in Ohio.

Family lineage: Scottish
- He was the only president who was of Scottish ancestry.

Religious denomination: attended Methodist Church
- He was the third of four presidents who were Methodists.
- He never formally joined the church.

College: Kenyon College, Gambier, Ohio
- He was the only president who went to Kenyon.
- He was the 12th of 27 presidents who attended college.

Date of graduation: Aug. 3, 1842, Bachelor of Arts
- He was the eighth of 21 presidents who were graduated from college.

Law School: Harvard Law School, Cambridge, Mass.
- He was the first of nine presidents who attended law school.

Date of graduation: Aug. 27, 1845, Bachelor of Laws
- He was the first of three presidents who were graduated from law school.

PARENTS AND SIBLINGS

Father's name: Rutherford Hayes
Date of birth: Jan. 4, 1787
Place of birth: Brattleboro, Vt.
Occupations: Farmer, storekeeper
Date of death: July 20, 1882
- Hayes's father died 77 days before his birth.
- Hayes was the second of two presidents who were born after their fathers' deaths. The other was Jackson.

Place of death: Delaware, Ohio
Age at death: 35 years, 197 days

Mother's name: Sophia Birchard Hayes
Date of birth: Apr. 15, 1792
Place of birth: Wilmington, Vt.

223

Date of marriage: Sept. 13, 1813
Children: 5; 3 sons, 2 daughters
• A son, name unknown, was born in 1814; Lorenzo in 1815; Sarah Sophia in 1817; Fanny Arabella in 1820; and Rutherford Birchard in 1822. The eldest son died in infancy.
• Hayes was the first of four presidents who were fifth children.
• He was the fourth of seven presidents who came from families of five children.
Date of death: Oct. 30, 1866
Place of death: Columbus, Ohio
Age at death: 74 years, 198 days

MARRIAGE

Date of marriage: Dec. 30, 1852
Place of marriage: Cincinnati, Ohio
• Hayes was the first of two presidents who were married in Cincinnati. The other was Taft.
• He was the second of seven presidents who were married in Ohio.
Age at marriage: 30 years, 87 days
• He was the third of six presidents who were married in their thirties.
Years married: 36 years, 177 days

Wife's name: Lucy Ware Webb Hayes
• She was the 16th of 33 first ladies.
• She was the 20th of 40 wives of presidents.
Date of birth: Aug. 28, 1831
• She was the first of three first ladies who were born in August.
• She was the first of four wives of presidents who were born in August.
Place of birth: Chillicothe, Ohio
• She was the first of six first ladies who were born in Ohio.
• She was the first of six wives of presidents

who were born in Ohio.
Wife's mother: Maria Cook Webb
Wife's father: James Webb, physician
Age at marriage: 21 years, 124 days
• She was the 13th of 26 first ladies who were married in their twenties.
• She was the 16th of 30 wives of presidents who were married in their twenties.
Years younger than husband: 8 years, 328 days.
Children: 8; 7 sons, 1 daughter
• Sardis Birchard (later renamed Birchard Austin) was born in 1853; James Webb (later renamed Webb Cook) in 1856; Rutherford Platt in 1858; Joseph Thompson in 1861; George Crook in 1864; Fanny in 1866 or 1867; Scott Russell in 1869 or 1871; and Manning Force in 1873. Three of the children died in infancy: Joseph Thompson in 1863; George Crook in 1866; and Manning Force in 1874.
• Hayes was the only president who had eight children.
• He was the 11th of 19 presidents who had both male and female children.
• He was the 14th of 30 presidents who had children.
Date of death: June 25, 1889
Place of death: Fremont, Ohio
• She was the second of four first ladies who died in Ohio.
• She was the second of four wives of presidents who died in Ohio
Age at death: 57 years, 301 days
Place of burial: Fremont, Ohio
• She was the second of five first ladies who were buried in Ohio.
• She was the second of five wives of presidents who were buried in Ohio.
Years he survived his wife: 3 years, 206 days
• He was the ninth of 14 presidents who survived their wives.

EARLY YEARS

1828–1836, attended schools in Delaware and Norwalk, Ohio
1837, attended Webb Preparatory School, Middletown, Conn.
November, 1838, entered Kenyon College, Gambier, Ohio
Aug. 3, 1842, was graduated from Kenyon College
• Hayes led his class in both his junior and senior years. He received grades of 20 in

four subjects and 19½ in Bible as a senior; 20 was maximum. He was class valedictorian.
1842, began study of law with firm of Sparrow and Matthews, Columbus, Ohio
• He was the 13th of 26 presidents who studied law.
August, 1843, entered Harvard Law School, Cambridge, Mass.
Aug. 27, 1845, was graduated from Har-

vard Law School

1845, received master of arts degree, Kenyon College

1845, admitted to Ohio bar

• He was the 13th of 23 presidents who were lawyers.

April, 1846, began law practice in partnership with Ralph P. Buckland, Lower Sandusky, now Fremont, Ohio

1848–1849, spent winter in Texas for his health

• He suffered a throat ailment. He returned to Ohio when his health was restored.

1850, moved to Cincinnati, Ohio

• He resumed the practice of law.

Dec. 30, 1852, married Lucy Ware Webb, Cincinnati

December, 1853, won new trial for Nancy Farrar

• Nancy Farrar had poisoned ten people and been convicted of murder in 1852. When the case was reviewed by the Ohio supreme court, Hayes's motion for a new trial was granted. He had represented her as insane, unable to determine right from wrong. The second trial was never held; Nancy Farrar was adjudged insane and institutionalized. This was a landmark decision in criminal law.

1856, declined Republican nomination for common pleas judge, Cincinnati

1858, appointed city solicitor by Cincinnati city council

1859, elected city solicitor

April, 1861, defeated for city solicitor

June 27, 1861, commissioned as major in 23rd Ohio Infantry

• He was the third of seven presidents who served in the Civil War.

• He was the 11th of 21 presidents who served in the military during wartime.

July, 1861, his regiment ordered to West Virginia

Sept. 19, 1861, appointed judge advocate of Department of Ohio by General William S. Rosecrans

Oct. 24, 1861, promoted to lieutenant colonel

Sept. 14, 1862, led charge in Battle of South Mountain, Md.

• His regiment lost about half of its men in this phase of the Antietam campaign. He led a charge and held his position, despite a musket ball wound of the left arm.

• He was the third of four presidents who were wounded or injured in action.

Oct. 24, 1862, promoted to colonel

Mar. 17, 1863, assumed command of First Brigade, Third Division, VIII Army Corps

June 28, 1863, assumed command of First Brigade, Scammon's Division

July 18, 1863, attacked Morgan's Raiders, Pomeroy, Ohio

• His troops participated in the attack on the raiding party of General John Hunt Morgan, who was prevented from recrossing the Ohio River at Buffington.

December, 1863, assumed command of First Brigade, Third Division

April, 1864, assumed command of First Brigade, Second Infantry Division

July 23–24, 1864, participated in Battle of Winchester, Va.

August, 1864, nominated for House of Representatives, Republican district convention, Cincinnati

• He rejected the suggestion that he request a furlough to campaign. "An officer fit for duty, who at this crisis would abandon his post to electioneer for a seat in Congress, ought to be scalped," he replied.

Sept. 19, 1864, participated in Battle of Opequon, Va.

NATIONAL PROMINENCE

October, 1864, elected to House of Representatives

• Hayes was the 13th of 17 presidents who were elected to the House.

Oct. 19, 1864, participated in Battle of Cedar Creek, Va.

• After the action, General George Crook congratulated Hayes and said, "Colonel, from this day you will be a brigadier general." He was assigned command of the

division and was promoted to brevet brigadier general a few days later.

• He had received an ankle wound at Cedar Creek, the fourth and last wound of his military service.

• He was the eighth of 12 presidents who were generals.

Mar. 13, 1865, promoted to brevet major general

June 8, 1865, resigned from army

Dec. 4, 1865, took seat in House of Representatives
- He was reelected in 1866, and served in the 39th and 40th congresses.
- He was the 13th of 17 presidents who served in the House.

June, 1867, nominated for governor of Ohio, Republican state convention

October, 1867, elected as governor
- He was inaugurated in January, 1868.
- He was the first of two presidents who served as governors of Ohio. The other was McKinley.
- He was the seventh of 13 presidents who served as state governors.

January, 1872, declined offer of Senate seat
- The Republican majority in the state legislature was controlled by Senator John Sherman. Hayes refused the support of a coalition of anti-Sherman Republicans and Democrats; Sherman was reelected.

July, 1872, nominated for House of Representatives
- Although he wished to retire from public life, he accepted the nomination.

October, 1872, defeated for election to House

1872, declined offer of appointment by Grant as assistant treasurer of U.S.

1873, retired to Fremont

1874, inherited large estate of uncle, Sardis Birchard
- The 25-acre estate, Spiegel Grove, Hayes and Buckland Avenues, Fremont, was given to the State of Ohio by the family in 1909–1910. The Rutherford B. Hayes State Memorial, containing the Hayes home, the Hayes Library and Museum, and the tombs of President and Mrs. Hayes, is administered by the Ohio Historical Society and the Hayes Foundation.
- A National Historic Landmark, the Hayes home is open to the public daily for tours, 9 A.M. to 5 P.M., Wednesdays through Saturdays, and 2 to 5 P.M., Sundays through Tuesdays, except Thanksgiving, Christmas and New Year's Day. Advance reservations required. Admission: adults, $1; children under 16, 50 cents.
- The museum is open to the public daily, 9 A.M. to 5 P.M., and Sundays and holidays, 1:30 to 5 P.M. Admission: adults, 50 cents; children under 16, 15 cents. The library is open for reference and research, 9 A.M. to 5 P.M., Mondays through Fridays, and 9 A.M. to 12, noon, Saturdays. Closed Sun-

days and holidays. Admission: free.
- The iron gates at the six entrances to Spiegel Grove stood at entrances to the White House before and during the Hayes administration.

1875, nominated for governor of Ohio, Republican state convention
- He supported Alphonso Taft but was himself nominated on the first ballot.

October, 1875, elected as governor of Ohio for third time
- His election immediately cast him as a presidential candidate.

Mar. 29, 1876, named "favorite son" candidate for president, Republican state convention

June 16, 1876, nominated for president, Republican national convention, Cincinnati, Ohio

Nov. 7, 1876, election day
- *See* Election of 1876, page 227.

Dec. 6, 1876, presidential electors cast ballots
- Neither candidate received the 185 electoral votes necessary for election; Tilden received 184; Hayes, 165. A total of 20 votes were disputed because of conflicting sets of electoral votes returned by four states, Florida, Louisiana, Oregon, and South Carolina. Charges of fraud were leveled by both parties.
- The constitutional provision that electoral votes be opened by the president of the Senate in the presence of both houses of Congress did not specify by whom the votes should be counted. Since the Republicans had a majority in the Senate and the Democrats in the House of Representatives, further controversy was inevitable. A joint Senate-House committee was formed to devise a plan for some authority whose decision on disputed votes would be final.

Jan. 29, 1877, electoral commission established
- The commission, empowered to make the final decision, was to consist of five members each from the Senate, the House, and the Supreme Court. The Republican-controlled Senate predictably elected three Republicans and two Democrats, while a compensating three Democrats and two Republicans were chosen by the House. The act that established the commission specified four justices of the Supreme Court, two from each party, who were to choose a fifth member, intended to be Jus-

tice David Davis, an independent. Before the commission was formed, Davis was elected to the Senate by the Illinois legislature and resigned from the Court. His place on the commission was filled by Justice Joseph P. Bradley, a Republican. The only two Democrats on the Supreme Court were already members of the commission.

Feb. 1, 1877, electoral commission assembled, Hall of House of Representatives
•Since the states were considered alphabetically, the first dispute to arise was that of Florida. This was settled, Feb. 9, in favor of Hayes by a commission vote of 8–7, along strictly party lines. The disputes regarding the Louisiana, Oregon, and South Carolina votes were settled in identical fashion, Feb. 16, Feb. 23, and Feb. 28.

Mar. 2, 1877, electoral vote tabulated by Congress
•Hayes and Wheeler were officially declared elected.

ELECTION OF 1876

American party, convened, June 9, 1875, at Pittsburgh, Pa., nominated James B. Walker of Illinois for president, Donald Kirkpatrick of New York for vice president.

Prohibition party, convened, May 17, 1876, at Cleveland, Ohio, nominated Green Clay Smith of Kentucky for president, Gideon Tabor Stewart of Ohio for vice president.

Greenback party, convened, May 18, at Indianapolis, Ind., nominated Peter Cooper of New York for president, Newton Booth of Kansas for vice president. Booth declined; Samuel Fenton Cary of Ohio became the party's vice-presidential candidate.
•This was the first Greenback convention.

Republican party, convened, June 14, at Cincinnati, Ohio, nominated Rutherford Birchard Hayes of Ohio for president, William Almon Wheeler of New York for vice president.
•This was the sixth Republican national convention. It was the first Republican convention in Cincinnati; it was the second major party convention in Cincinnati.

Democratic party, convened, June 27, at St. Louis, Mo., nominated Samuel Jones Tilden of New York for president, Thomas Andrews Hendricks of Indiana for vice president.
•This was the 12th Democratic national convention. It was the first Democratic convention in St. Louis; it was the first of five major party conventions in St. Louis.

Election day, Tuesday, Nov. 7, 1876
Popular vote: 8,430,283
   Hayes, 4,036,298
   Tilden, 4,300,590
   Cooper, 81,737
   Smith, 9,522
   Walker, 2,636
•Hayes was the sixth of 15 presidents who were elected without receiving a majority of the popular vote.
•Tilden was the second of three presidential candidates who received a majority of the popular votes, but were defeated in the electoral college.

Electoral vote: 369, 38 states
 • Hayes, 185, 21 states
   (California, 6; Colorado, 3; Florida, 4; Illinois, 21; Iowa, 11; Kansas, 5; Louisiana, 8; Maine, 7; Massachusetts, 13; Michigan, 11; Minnesota, 5; Nebraska, 3; Nevada, 3; New Hampshire, 5; Ohio, 22; Oregon, 3; Pennsylvania, 29; Rhode Island, 4; South Carolina, 7; Vermont, 5; Wisconsin, 10)
 • Tilden, 184, 17 states
   (Alabama, 10; Arkansas, 6; Connecticut, 6; Delaware, 3; Georgia, 11; Indiana, 15; Kentucky, 12; Maryland, 8; Mississippi, 8; Missouri, 15; New Jersey, 9; New York, 35; North Carolina, 10; Tennessee, 12; Texas, 8; Virginia, 11; West Virginia, 5)

THE PRESIDENT (19th)

Term of office: Mar. 4, 1877, to Mar. 4, 1881 (4 years)
•Hayes was the 12th of 19 presidents who served one term or less than one term.
•He was the seventh of ten presidents who served for four years.

State represented: Ohio
•He was the second of six presidents who represented Ohio.

Political party: Republican

•He was the third of 14 presidents who were Republicans
Congresses: 45th, 46th
Administration: 23rd
Age at inauguration: 54 years, 151 days
•He was the ninth of 21 presidents who were younger than their vice presidents. Hayes was three years, 96 days younger than Wheeler.
Inauguration day: Monday, Mar. 5, 1877
•Hayes took the oath of office, administered by Chief Justice Morrison R. Waite, on the steps of the east portico of the Capitol.

•He was the third of five presidents who postponed their oath-taking ceremonies to Monday because Mar. 4 fell on Sunday. However, because the election had been so vigorously disputed, he had taken the oath privately in the White House, Saturday, Mar. 3.
•He was the first president to take the oath in the White House.
•This was the first of three inaugurations at which Waite officiated.
•This was the first of four oath-taking ceremonies at which Waite officiated.

THE 23rd ADMINISTRATION

1877

Mar. 8, appointed his only secretary of state, William M. Evarts; his only secretary of treasury, John Sherman; his first secretary of war, George W. McCrary; his only attorney general, Charles Devens; his first secretary of navy, Richard W. Thompson; his first postmaster general, David M. Key; and his only secretary of interior, Carl Schurz
•Sherman took office, Mar. 10; Evarts, McCrary, Devens, Key, and Schurz, Mar. 12; and Thompson, Mar. 13.
Mar. 29, appointed John M. Harlan as associate justice
•Harlan, who was confirmed by the Senate, Nov. 29, was the first of Hayes's three appointments to the Supreme Court.
Apr. 24, carpetbag rule ended in Louisiana
•Louisiana was the last southern state to regain control of its internal government.
May 5, called special session of Congress, Oct. 15
•The 44th Congress had adjourned without voting army appropriations for the fiscal year ending June 30, 1878.
June 22, issued executive order prohibiting electioneering by government officers
•This order applied to every department of the civil service and prohibited participation in the management of political organizations, caucuses, conventions, and election campaigns. The order also disallowed assessments for political purposes on officers or subordinates.
July 18, issued proclamation against domestic violence in West Virginia
•He issued similar proclamations that con-

cerned Maryland, July 21, and Pennsylvania, July 23. The "domestic violence" was a widespread strike of railroad workers, whose daily wages of $1 to $2.15 for 12 hours had been cut ten to 15 percent.
•He ordered federal troops to these three states, as well as Illinois, to suppress the strikes. The troops occupied major centers of unrest and arrested strike leaders, but not before much violence occurred. During a battle between strikers and state militia in Pittsburgh, July 20–23, many were killed and most of the city was burned to the ground. The militia was forced to fight its way out of the city.
Oct. 15, first session of 45th Congress
•The administration controlled the Senate, but not the House of Representatives. The Republicans lost seven Senate seats, gained 28 House seats. The Senate (76 members) consisted of 39 Republicans, 36 Democrats, and one other. The House (293 members) consisted of 156 Democrats and 137 Republicans.
Nov. 23, Great Britain awarded $5,500,000 for U.S. fishing rights in North Atlantic
•The award was made by the Halifax fisheries commission, which had been created by the Treaty of Washington, 1871.
Dec. 3, first session of 45th Congress adjourned
Dec. 3, second session of 45th Congress
Dec. 3, sent his first State of the Union message to Congress
•He strongly urged the resumption of specie payments.
Dec. 31, with Mrs. Hayes, celebrated silver

wedding anniversary, White House
•Since their anniversary, Dec. 30, fell on a Sunday, the celebration was held the following day. With the entire White House staff in attendance, the wedding ceremony was reenacted by Reverend Lorenzo Dow McCabe, the minister who had married them in 1852. Mrs. Hayes wore her wedding gown.
•He was the fourth of five presidents who celebrated their 25th anniversaries while residents of the White House.

Note: The first telephone was installed in the White House in 1877.

1878

Feb. 28, vetoed Bland-Allison silver bill
•This was the first of his 13 vetoes.
Feb. 28, Bland-Allison silver act passed over his veto
•This act required the treasury department to purchase a minimum of $2,000,000 worth of silver at market price each month.
•This was his only veto that was overridden.
Mar. 6, vetoed special term of courts in Mississippi bill
May 31, signed greenback act
•This act provided that the $346,681,000 outstanding in greenbacks should remain part of the currency.
June 11, signed District of Columbia government act
•This act provided that the district was to be governed by three commissioners appointed by the president—a Republican, a Democrat, and an engineer officer of the army. Residents were to have no elective privileges, local or national.
June 20, second session of 45th Congress adjourned
July 11, suspended Chester A. Arthur as collector of port of New York
Oct. 4, received first resident Chinese embassy, White House
Oct. 7, issued proclamation against domestic violence in New Mexico
•He ordered the military to restore peace and order in the territory, where serious disturbances by outlaw bands had occurred.
Dec. 2, third session of 45th Congress

Dec. 2, sent his second State of the Union message to Congress

1879

Jan. 1, specie payments resumption began
•Specie payments, suspended in 1861, were resumed as authorized by the act of Jan. 14, 1875.
Feb. 15, signed act that allowed women to practice before Supreme Court
•Women who had practiced three years before state supreme courts were eligible for admission to practice before the Supreme Court. The first woman admitted was Belva Ann Bennett Lockwood.
Mar. 1, vetoed Chinese immigration restriction bill
Mar. 3, third session of 45th Congress adjourned
Mar. 3, pocket vetoed relief of certain settlers on public lands bill
•This was his only pocket veto.
Mar. 4, called special session of Congress, Mar. 18
•The 45th Congress had adjourned without voting necessary appropriations for expenses of the government.
Mar. 18, first session of 46th Congress
•The administration lost control of the Senate; the Democrats gained seven seats. The Democrats retained control of the House of Representatives, but lost six seats. The Senate (76 members) consisted of 43 Democrats and 33 Republicans. The House (293 members) consisted of 150 Democrats, 128 Republicans, 14 others, and one vacancy.
•This was the first Congress with Democratic majorities in both chambers since 1857.
Apr. 26, issued proclamation that ordered removal of squatters from Indian Territory
Apr. 29, vetoed army appropriation bill
•He objected to the tacking on of legislative provisions to appropriations bills.
May 12, vetoed military interference at elections bill
May 29, vetoed legislative, executive, and judicial appropriations bill
June 23, signed second army appropriations act
June 23, vetoed payment of marshals bill
•This was the first of four payments of marshals bills he vetoed in 1879 and 1880.

June 30, sent special message to Congress in regard to marshals payments

July 1, first session of 46th Congress adjourned

Dec. 1, second session of 46th Congress

Dec. 1, sent his third State of the Union message to Congress

•He urged suspension of silver coinage, recommended vigorous enforcement of laws against polygamy in Utah Territory, and asked for an appropriation for the civil service commission.

Dec. 10, Secretary of War McCrary resigned

Dec. 10, appointed his second secretary of war, Alexander Ramsey

1880

Feb. 1, sent special message to Congress regarding Ponca Indians

•His Indian policy included preparation for citizenship by industrial and general education, allotment of land in severalty, fair compensation for land not required for allotment, and eventual citizenship.

Feb. 12, issued second proclamation against squatter settlement of Indian Territory

Mar. 8, sent special message to Congress on interoceanic canal

•He stated that the canal must be under U.S. control.

June 2, Postmaster General Key resigned

June 2, appointed his second postmaster general, Horace Maynard

June 5, elected to Phi Beta Kappa, Kenyon College, Gambier, Ohio

•He was the only president who was elected to Phi Beta Kappa while in office.

•He was the third of five presidents who were alumni members of Phi Beta Kappa.

•He was the sixth of 11 presidents who were members of Phi Beta Kappa.

June 15, vetoed payment of marshals bill

•This was the last of four payments of marshals bills he vetoed.

June 16, second session of 46th Congress adjourned

Sept. 8, visited San Francisco, Cal.

•He was the first president to visit the West Coast while in office.

Nov. 4, election day

• *See* Election of 1880, page 237.

Nov. 17, Chinese exclusion treaty signed, Peking

•The treaty authorized the U.S. to "regu-

late, limit or suspend," but not to prohibit, the immigration of Chinese laborers.

Dec. 6, third session of 46th Congress

Dec. 6, sent his fourth and last State of the Union message to Congress

•He reiterated his recommendation of an appropriation for the civil service commission, again urged suspension of silver coinage, and asked for land grants or appropriations to supplement state education funds.

Dec. 14, accepted resignation of Associate Justice Strong

Dec. 15, appointed William B. Woods as associate justice

•Woods, who was confirmed by the Senate, Dec. 21, was the second of Hayes's three appointments to the Supreme Court.

Dec. 20, Secretary of Navy Thompson resigned

Note: The official population, according to the tenth census, was 50,155,783.

1881

Jan. 7, appointed his second secretary of navy, Nathan Goff, Jr.

•Goff was the last of Hayes's ten cabinet appointments.

Jan. 24, accepted resignation of Associate Justice Swayne

Jan. 26, appointed Stanley Matthews as associate justice

•This, the last of Hayes's three appointments to the Supreme Court, was not acted upon by the Senate.

•Hayes was the 11th of 15 presidents who nominated justices not confirmed by the Senate.

•Matthews was the 18th of 25 men nominated to the Supreme Court who were not confirmed by the Senate.

Feb. 22, issued executive order to ban sales of intoxicating liquors at military installations

Mar. 3, vetoed refunding of national debt bill

•This was the last of his 13 vetoes.

Mar. 3, third session of 46th Congress adjourned

Note: He was the last of three presidents who did not seek renomination after their first terms.

THE FORMER PRESIDENT

Mar. 4, 1881, attended inauguration of Garfield
•Hayes's age upon leaving office was 58 years, 151 days.
•After the ceremony he boarded a special train to return to Ohio. The train collided with another near Baltimore, Md. Two passengers were killed and about 20 seriously injured. He was thrown from his Pullman chair but was not hurt. His homeward journey was delayed for a full day by the accident.
March, 1881, retired to Fremont, Ohio
•His principal interests were education, prison reform, and matters pertaining to Civil War veterans. He devoted much time to Negro education in the South and the development of manual training programs in high school systems. He was in great demand as a speaker at Memorial Day services, monument unveilings, and veteran reunions and conventions.
•He owned several farms.
•He was the fifth of six presidents who were farmers, planters, or ranchers after their terms of office.
1889, opposed suggestion former presidents should be appointed to Senate
Apr. 30, 1889, attended celebration of centennial of Washington inauguration, Washington, D.C.
•President Harrison and former President Cleveland also attended.
June 25, 1889, his wife died
Oct. 4, 1892, celebrated his 70th birthday
•He was the 11th of 16 presidents who lived to be 70.
Jan. 14, 1893, suffered heart attack
•He was stricken aboard a train while returning to Fremont from a business trip.

DEATH

Date of death: Jan. 17, 1893
Place of death: Fremont, Ohio
•Hayes was the only president who died in Ohio.
Age at death: 70 years, 105 days
•He lived 11 years, 319 days, after the completion of his term.
Cause of death: Heart attack
Place of burial: Fremont, Ohio
•He was the second of five presidents who were buried in Ohio.

THE VICE PRESIDENT (19th)

Full name: William Almon Wheeler
Date of birth: June 30, 1819
Place of birth: Malone, N.Y.
•Wheeler was the sixth of eight vice presidents who were born in New York.
Religious denomination: Presbyterian
•He was the eighth of 11 vice presidents who were Presbyterians.
College: University of Vermont, Burlington, Vt., 1838–1840
Occupations: Lawyer, banker
•He was admitted to the New York bar, practiced in Malone, 1845; district attorney of Franklin county, 1846–1849; Whig member of state assembly, 1850–1851; Republican member and president pro tempore of state senate, 1858–1859; member of House of Representatives, 1861–1863; presided at New York constitutional convention, 1867–1868; again member of House of Representatives, 1869–1877.
•He was the 13th of 21 vice presidents who served in the House of Representatives before their terms of office.
Term of office: Mar. 4, 1877, to Mar. 4, 1881 (4 years)
•He was the ninth of 17 vice presidents who served four-year terms.
•Hayes and Wheeler were the 21st of 41 president-vice president teams.
Age at inauguration: 57 years, 247 days
State represented: New York
•He was the sixth of ten vice presidents who represented New York.
Political party: Republican
•He was the fourth of 15 vice presidents who were Republicans.
Occupations after term: Lawyer, banker
Date of death: June 4, 1887
Place of death: Malone, N.Y.
•He was the fifth of nine vice presidents who died in New York.
Age at death: 67 years, 339 days
Place of burial: Malone, N.Y.
•He was the fifth of nine vice presidents who were buried in New York.

THE CABINET

State: William Maxwell Evarts of New York, Mar. 12, 1877, to Mar. 7, 1881
Treasury: John Sherman of Ohio, Mar. 10,

1877, to Mar. 3, 1881

War: George Washington McCrary of Iowa, Mar. 12, 1877, to Dec. 10, 1879

•Alexander Ramsey of Minnesota, Dec. 10, 1879, to Mar. 5, 1881

Attorney General: Charles Devens of Massachusetts, Mar. 12, 1877, to Mar. 6, 1881

Navy: Richard Wigginton Thompson of Virginia, Mar. 13, 1877, to Dec. 20, 1880

•Nathan Goff, Jr., of West Virginia, Jan. 7, 1881, to Mar. 6, 1881

Postmaster General: David McKendree Key of Tennessee, Mar. 12, 1877, to June 2, 1880

•Horace Maynard of Tennessee, June 2, 1880, to Mar. 5, 1881

Interior: Carl Schurz of Missouri, Mar. 12, 1877, to Mar. 5, 1881

THE SUPREME COURT

Associate Justices: John Marshall Harlan of Kentucky, appointed, Mar. 29, 1877; confirmed, Nov. 29, 1877

•William Burnham Woods of Georgia, appointed, Dec. 15, 1880; confirmed, Dec. 21, 1880

•Stanley Matthews of Ohio, appointed, Jan. 26, 1881; not acted upon by Senate

JAMES ABRAM GARFIELD

Full name: James Abram Garfield
•He was the last of five presidents named James.
•He was the sixth of 19 presidents who had middle initials or middle names.
Date of birth: Nov. 19, 1831
•He was the fourth of five presidents who were born in November.
Place of birth: Orange, Ohio
•He was the third consecutive president born in Ohio.
•He was the third of seven presidents who were born in Ohio.
•He was the last of seven presidents who were born in log cabins.
•A replica of his log cabin birthplace is on the grounds of Lawnfield, 8095 Mentor Avenue, Mentor, Ohio.
Family lineage: English-French Huguenot
•He was the only president of English-French Huguenot ancestry.
Religious denomination: Disciples of Christ
•He was the first of two presidents who were Disciples of Christ. The other was Lyndon B. Johnson.
College: Williams College, Williamstown, Mass.

•He was the only president who went to Williams.
•He was the 13th of 27 presidents who attended college.
Date of graduation: July 30, 1856, Bachelor of Arts
•He was the ninth of 21 presidents who were graduated from college.

PARENTS AND SIBLINGS

Father's name: Abraham Garfield
•His father was christened Abraham, but called Abram.
Date of birth: Dec. 28, 1799
Place of birth: Worcester, N.Y.
Occupations: Farmer, canal construction supervisor
Date of death: May 8, 1833
•James was one year, 170 days old when his father died.
Place of death: Orange, Ohio
Age at death: 33 years, 131 days

Mother's name: Eliza Ballou Garfield
Date of birth: Sept. 21, 1801

Place of birth: Richmond, N.H.
Date of marriage: Feb. 3, 1820
Children: 5; 3 sons, 2 daughters
• Mehitabel was born in 1821; Thomas in 1822; Mary in 1824; James in 1827; and James Abram in 1831. James died in infancy.
• Garfield was the second of four presidents who were fifth children.
• He was the fifth of seven presidents who came from families of five children.
Date of death: Jan. 21, 1888
• Garfield was the sixth of ten presidents whose mothers lived to see their sons' inauguration or oath-taking days.
• Mrs. Garfield was the first of four mothers of presidents who attended the ceremonies.
• Garfield was the second of three presidents whose mothers survived them.
Place of death: Mentor, Ohio
Age at death: 86 years, 122 days

MARRIAGE

Date of marriage: Nov. 11, 1858
Place of marriage: Hiram, Ohio
• Garfield was the third of seven presidents who were married in Ohio.
Age at marriage: 26 years, 357 days
• He was the 14th of 27 presidents who were married in their twenties.
Years married: 22 years, 312 days

Wife's name: Lucretia Rudolph Garfield
• She was the 17th of 33 first ladies.
• She was the 21st of 40 wives of presidents.
Date of birth: Apr. 19, 1832
• She was the only first lady who was born in April.
• She was the first of two wives of presidents who were born in April. The other was Mary Harrison.
Place of birth: Hiram, Ohio
• She was the second of six first ladies who were born in Ohio.
• She was the second of six wives of presidents who were born in Ohio.
Wife's mother: Arabella Mason Rudolph
Wife's father: Zebulon Rudolph, farmer
Age at marriage: 26 years, 206 days
• She was the 14th of 26 first ladies who were

married in their twenties.
• She was the 17th of 30 wives of presidents who were married in their twenties.
Years younger than husband: 152 days
Children: 7; 5 sons, 2 daughters
• Eliza was born on July 3, 1860; Harry Augustus on Oct. 11, 1863; James Rudolph on Oct. 17, 1865; Mary on Jan. 17, 1867; Irvin McDowell on Aug. 3, 1870; Abram on Nov. 21, 1872; and Edward in 1874. Two of the children died in infancy, Eliza in 1863 and Edward in 1876.
• Garfield was the only president who had seven children.
• He was the 12th of 19 presidents who had both male and female children.
• He was the 15th of 30 presidents who had children.
Years she survived her husband: 36 years, 176 days
• She was the 11th of 21 first ladies who survived their husbands.
• She was the 12th of 23 wives of presidents who survived their husbands.
Date of death: Mar. 14, 1918
Place of death: Pasadena, Cal.
• She was the only first lady or wife of a president who died in California.
Age at death: 85 years, 329 days
• She had celebrated her 85th birthday, Apr. 19, 1917.
• She was the eighth of 16 first ladies who lived to be 70.
• She was the eighth of 17 wives of presidents who lived to be 70.
• She was the sixth of 14 first ladies who lived to be 75.
• She was the sixth of 15 wives of presidents who lived to be 75.
• She was the fourth of nine first ladies who lived to be 80.
• She was the fourth of ten wives of presidents who lived to be 80.
• She was the third of six first ladies who lived to be 85.
• She was the third of seven wives of presidents who lived to be 85.
Place of burial: Cleveland, Ohio
• She was the third of five first ladies who were buried in Ohio.
• She was the third of five wives of presidents who were buried in Ohio.

EARLY YEARS

May 8, 1833, his father died
1841–1847, worked as farm hand
• Garfield attended a district school during
the winter months for several years.
1848, traveled to Cleveland, Ohio
• His favorite reading was adventure stories,
particularly tales of the sea. He went to
Cleveland intent on shipping out as a sailor
on a lake schooner but changed his mind
when he learned what life as a seaman entailed.
1848–1849, worked on Ohio canal boats
Winter, 1849–1850, attended Geauga Seminary, Chester, Ohio
• During vacation he worked as a carpenter.
1850, joined Disciples of Christ church
1851, entered Hiram Eclectic Institute, now
Hiram College, Hiram, Ohio
• He attended the institute for three years,
helping to pay his expenses by teaching in
the English department. He also gave instructions in ancient languages.
• He was the third of seven presidents who
taught school.
September, 1854, entered Williams College,
Williamstown, Mass.
July 30, 1856, was graduated from Williams
College with highest honors in his class
1856–1857, taught Latin and Greek, Hiram
Eclectic Institute
1857–1860, president of Hiram Eclectic Institute
1858, studied law, Hiram
• He was the 14th of 26 presidents who studied law.

Nov. 11, 1858, married Lucretia Rudolph,
Hiram
1859, represented Portage and Summit
Counties, state senate
July 3, 1860, his first daughter born
• The girl was named Eliza Garfield.
1860, admitted to bar, Hiram
• He was the 14th of 23 presidents who were
lawyers.
Aug. 21, 1861, commissioned as lieutenant
colonel, 42nd Regiment, Ohio Volunteers
• Garfield was the fourth of seven presidents
who served in the Civil War.
• He was the 12th of 21 presidents who
served in the military during wartime.
Nov. 27, 1861, promoted to colonel
Dec. 17, 1861, given command of 18th Bri-
gade, Army of Ohio
Jan. 10, 1862, Battle of Middle Creek, Ky.
• His brigade, though outnumbered by more
than two-to-one, routed the Confederate
force commanded by Colonel Humphrey
Marshall.
• Garfield was promoted to brigadier gen-
eral by Lincoln. His commission was dated
Jan. 10.
• He was the ninth of 12 presidents who
were generals.
Apr. 7, 1862, participated in second day's
fighting, Battle of Shiloh, near Pittsburg
Landing, Tenn.
June, 1862, supervised rebuilding of Mem-
phis and Charleston railroad bridges
July 30, 1862, returned to Hiram
• He contracted camp fever and was ill for
two months.

NATIONAL PROMINENCE

September, 1862, elected to House of Rep-
resentatives
• Garfield was the 12th of 17 presidents who
were elected to the House.
Sept. 25, 1862, reported to Washington,
D.C., assigned court-martial duty
• He was assigned the case of General Fitz-
John Porter, Nov. 25.
January, 1863, appointed chief of staff by
General William S. Rosecrans
Sept. 19, 1863, promoted to major general
• He was promoted for gallantry during the
Battle of Chickamauga. He volunteered to
take the news of the defeat on the right

to the commander of the left, General
George H. Thomas. This action was cred-
ited with saving the Army of the Cumber-
land.
Oct. 11, 1863, his first son born
• The boy was named Harry Augustus Gar-
field.
Dec. 5, 1863, resigned his commission
• Although offered the command of a divi-
sion under General Thomas, who had reor-
ganized the Army of the Cumberland,
Garfield resigned to take his seat in the
House of Representatives.
• He was the 12th of 17 presidents who

served in the House of Representatives.

1864, elected to Phi Beta Kappa, Williams College, Williamstown, Mass.

• He was the second of five presidents who were alumni members of Phi Beta Kappa.

• He was the fifth of 11 presidents who were members of Phi Beta Kappa.

Jan. 14, 1864, made his first speech in Congress

• He spoke on a motion to print extra copies of the official report of General Rosecrans. His military reputation had secured him membership on the committee on military affairs.

Nov. 22, 1864, degree of Master Mason conferred, Columbus, Ohio

• The degree was conferred by Columbia Lodge No. 30, at the request of Magnolia Lodge No. 20.

• He was the seventh of 13 presidents who were Masons.

Oct. 17, 1865, his second son born

• The boy was named James Rudolph Garfield.

1865, appointed to ways and means committee

Jan. 17, 1867, his second daughter born

• The girl was named Mary Garfield.

1867, chairman of committee on military affairs

1869, chairman of first committee on banking and currency

Aug. 3, 1870, his third son born

• The boy was named Irvin McDowell Garfield.

1871, chairman of committee on appropriations

Nov. 21, 1872, his fourth son born

• The boy was named Abram Garfield.

1874, his fifth son born

• The boy was named Edward Garfield.

1875, member of ways and means committee

Fall, 1876, purchased farm, Mentor, Ohio

• During the next nine years, the small farmhouse on the property was remodeled and enlarged in three stages. He named the 26-room mansion, Lawnfield.

• Lawnfield, 8095 Mentor Avenue (U.S. 20), was deeded to the Western Reserve Historical Society by his heirs in 1936. The first two floors are furnished with the personal possessions of the Garfield family. A general museum dealing with Lake County history.has been established on the

third floor. A replica of his log cabin birthplace and a small one-story building used in 1880 as the Campaign Office are on the grounds. Operated by the Lake County Historical Society, Lawnfield is open to the public daily except Mondays, May 1 through Oct. 31, 9 A.M. to 5 P.M., and Sundays and holidays, 1 to 5 P.M. Admission: adults, $1; junior and senior high school students, 75 cents; elementary school students, 50 cents.

1876, sent by Grant to witness counting of Louisiana vote

1877, member of electoral commission

• He opposed the formation of the electoral commission, which was created by act of Congress, signed by Grant, Jan. 29.

• However, Garfield was chosen by acclamation as one of the two Republican members of the commission.

Jan. 13, 1880, elected to Senate

• He was elected by the Ohio legislature. His term was to begin, Mar. 4, 1881

• He was the tenth of 16 presidents who were elected to the Senate.

• He was the eighth of 11 presidents who were elected to both the House of Representatives and the Senate.

June 8, 1880, nominated for president, Republican national convention, Chicago, Ill.

• He was nominated on the 36th ballot.

Nov. 2, 1880, election day

• *See* Election of 1880, page 237.

• He was the only president who simultaneously was a member of the House, Senator-elect and President-elect.

Nov. 8, 1880, resigned from House of Representatives

• He had taken his seat in the 38th Congress and had been reelected eight times; he resigned as a member of the 46th Congress.

Dec. 1, 1880, presidential electors cast ballots

• He received 214 of the 369 electoral votes from the 38 states.

• *See* Election of 1880, page 237.

Dec. 23, 1880, declined Senate seat

• He was the only president of the 15 elected to the Senate who did not serve in the upper house.

Feb. 9, 1881, electoral votes tabulated by Congress

• Garfield and Arthur were officially declared elected.

ELECTION OF 1880

Republican party, convened, June 2, at Chicago, Ill., nominated James Abram Garfield of Ohio for president, Chester Alan Arthur of New York for vice president.
• This was the seventh Republican national convention. It was the third Republican convention in Chicago; it was the fourth major party convention in Chicago
Greenback-Labor party, convened, June 9, at Chicago, Ill., nominated James Baird Weaver of Iowa for president, Benjamin Chambers of Texas for vice president.
Prohibition party, convened, June 17, at Cleveland, Ohio, nominated Neal Dow of Maine for president, Henry Adams Thompson of Ohio for vice president.
Democratic party, convened, June 22, at Cincinnati, Ohio, nominated Winfield Scott Hancock of Pennsylvania for president, William Hayden English of Indiana for vice president.
• This was the 13th Democratic national convention. It was the second Democratic convention in Cincinnati; it was the third major party convention in Cincinnati.
American party, nominated John Wolcott Phelps of Vermont for president, Samuel Clarke Pomeroy of Kansas for vice president.

Election day, Tuesday, Nov. 2, 1880
Popular vote: 9,218,958
    Garfield, 4,454,416
    Hancock, 4,444,952
    Weaver, 308,578
    Dow, 10,305
    Phelps, 707
• Garfield was the seventh of 15 presidents who were elected without receiving a majority of the popular vote.
Electoral vote: 369, 38 states
    • Garfield, 214, 19 states
    (Colorado, 3; Connecticut, 6; Illinois, 21; Indiana, 15; Iowa, 11; Kansas, 5; Maine, 7; Massachusetts, 13; Michigan, 11; Minnesota, 5; Nebraska, 3; New Hampshire, 5; New York, 35; Ohio, 22; Oregon, 3; Pennsylvania, 29; Rhode Island, 4; Vermont, 5; Wisconsin, 10)
• He also received the vote of one California elector.
    • Hancock, 155, 19 states
    (Alabama, 10; Arkansas, 6; California, 5 of 6 votes; Delaware, 3; Florida, 4; Georgia, 11; Kentucky, 12; Louisiana, 8; Maryland, 8; Mississippi, 8; Missouri, 15; Nevada, 3; New Jersey, 9; North Carolina, 10; South Carolina, 7; Tennessee, 12; Texas, 8; Virginia, 11; West Virginia, 5)

THE PRESIDENT (20th)

Term of office: Mar. 4, 1881, to Sept. 19, 1881 (199 days)
• Garfield was the president who served the second shortest term.
• He was the sixth of nine presidents who served less than one term.
• He was the 13th of 19 presidents who served one term or less than one term.
State represented: Ohio
• He was the third of six presidents who represented Ohio.
• He was the third of four presidents who succeeded presidents who represented the same state.
Political party: Republican
• He was the fourth of 14 presidents who

were Republicans.
Congress: 47th
Administration: 24th
Age at inauguration: 49 years, 105 days
• He was the tenth of 21 presidents who were younger than their vice presidents. Garfield was one year, 45 days younger than Arthur.
Inauguration day: Friday, Mar. 4, 1881
• Garfield took the oath of office, administered by Chief Justice Morrison R. Waite, on the east portico of the Capitol.
• This was the second of three inaugurations at which Waite officiated.
• This was the second of four oath-taking ceremonies at which Waite officiated.

THE 24th ADMINISTRATION

1881

Mar. 5, appointed his only secretary of state, James G. Blaine; his only secretary of treasury, William Windom; his only secretary of war, Robert T. Lincoln; his only attorney general, Isaac W. MacVeagh; his only secretary of navy, William H. Hunt; his only postmaster general, Thomas L. James; and his only secretary of interior, Samuel J. Kirkwood
• Blaine and Hunt took office, Mar. 7; Windom, Mar. 8.
• Robert Todd Lincoln was the first of two sons of presidents who served in the cabinet. The other was James Rudolph Garfield.
• Garfield was the last of four presidents who made no changes in their cabinets.
Mar. 14, appointed Stanley Matthews as associate justice
• Matthews, who was confirmed by the Senate, May 12, was Garfield's only appointment to the Supreme Court.
Mar. 23, appointed William H. Robertson as collector of port of New York
Mar. 28, received protest of Robertson appointment
• Postmaster General James, representing

Vice President Arthur and Senators Roscoe Conkling and Thomas Platt of New York, presented the formal protest. Robertson was a political opponent of Conkling.
May 2, Robertson appointment tabled
• Republican members of the Senate yielded to Conkling as a matter of senatorial courtesy and agreed to postpone confirmation of Robertson.
May 5, withdrew nominations approved by Conkling
• His countermove was to withdraw those nominations he had made on the advice of Conkling.
May 16, Senators Conkling and Platt resigned
May 18, Collector Robertson confirmed by Senate
May 20, special session of Senate adjourned
July 25, Associate Justice Clifford died

Notes: He was the second of two presidents who did not send State of the Union message to Congress. The other was William Henry Harrison.
• He was the last of seven presidents who did not exercise the veto.

THE ASSASSINATION

July 2, 1881, shot by Charles J. Guiteau in Baltimore and Potomac railroad station, Washington, D.C.
• Scheduled to deliver the commencement address at his alma mater, Williams College, he was passing through the waiting room of the Baltimore and Potomac railroad station at about 9 A.M. when he was shot in the back by Guiteau. A second shot grazed his arm.
• Guiteau is reputed to have shouted, "I am a Stalwart and now Arthur is President!" Stalwarts were members of the conservative wing of the Republican party, led by Roscoe Conkling of New York. The Stalwarts had favored a third term for Grant in 1880.
• The seriously wounded Garfield was taken to the White House, where he remained for two months. Daily bulletins on his progress were published in every city of the

U.S. and in many European capitals. The medical care he received, although the best available at the time, largely was responsible for his death. Repeated probing for the bullet with nonsterile instruments aggravated his condition and eventually led to blood poisoning.
Sept. 6, 1881, removed from White House to Francklyn cottage, Elberon, N.J.
• At his own request, he was moved to Elberon by special train, in the hope that the sea air would aid his recovery. He seemed to rally at first but suffered another setback, Sept. 15.
Sept. 19, 1881, died at 10:35 P.M., Elberon, N.J.
• His last words were, "Oh, Swaim, there is pain here. Oh, oh, Swaim." David G. Swaim was his chief of staff.
Nov. 14, 1881, trial of Guiteau began, Washington, D.C.

•Guiteau had been apprehended at the time of the shooting.
•The murder trial lasted more than ten weeks and was punctuated by frequent outbursts from the defendant.
Jan. 25, 1882, Guiteau found guilty of murder
•Although he pleaded insanity (doubtless correctly), Guiteau was found both sane and guilty by the jury.
Feb. 4, 1882, Guiteau sentenced to be hanged
June 30, 1882, Guiteau hanged, Washington, D.C.

DEATH

Date of death: Sept. 19, 1881
•Garfield was the third of five presidents who died before they completed their first terms.
•He was the fourth of eight presidents who died in office.
Place of death: Elberon, N.J.
•He was the first of two presidents who died in New Jersey. The other was Cleveland.
•He was the second of eight presidents who lay in state in the Capitol Rotunda.
Age at death: 49 years, 105 days
Cause of death: Assassination by pistol shot
•He was the second of four presidents who were assassinated.
Place of burial: Cleveland, Ohio
•He was the third of five presidents who were buried in Ohio.

THE VICE PRESIDENT (20th)

Full name: Chester Alan Arthur
• *See* pages 240–247.
•Arthur was the first of three vice presidents who were born in Vermont.
•He was the third of eight vice presidents who were Episcopalians.

•He was the seventh of 14 vice presidents who served less than one term.
•He was the fourth of seven vice presidents who served less than one year.
•Garfield and Arthur were the 22nd of 41 president-vice president teams.
•Arthur was the seventh of ten vice presidents who represented New York.
•He was the sixth of 13 vice presidents who represented states that were not their native states.
•He was the fifth of 15 vice presidents who were Republicans.
•He was the only vice president who died in New York City.
•He was the sixth of nine vice presidents who died in New York.
•He was the sixth of nine vice presidents who were buried in New York.

THE CABINET

State: James Gillespie Blaine of Maine, Mar. 7, 1881, to Dec. 19, 1881
Treasury: William Windom of Minnesota, Mar. 8, 1881, to Nov. 13, 1881
War: Robert Todd Lincoln of Illinois, Mar. 5, 1881, to Mar. 5, 1885
Attorney General: Isaac Wayne MacVeagh of Pennsylvania, Mar. 5, 1881, to Oct. 24, 1881
Navy: William Henry Hunt of Louisiana, Mar. 7, 1881, to Apr. 16, 1882
Postmaster General: Thomas Lemuel James of New York, Mar. 5, 1881, to Dec. 20, 1881
Interior: Samuel Jordan Kirkwood of Iowa, Mar. 5, 1881, to Apr. 6, 1882

THE SUPREME COURT

Associate Justice: Stanley Matthews of Ohio, appointed, Mar. 14, 1881; confirmed, May 12, 1881

Twenty-first President

CHESTER ALAN ARTHUR

Full name: Chester Alan Arthur
•He was the seventh of 19 presidents who had middle initials or middle names.
Date of birth: Oct. 5, 1830
•He was the third of five presidents who were born in October.
Place of birth: reputedly Fairfield, Vt.
•He was the first of two presidents who were born in Vermont. The other was Coolidge.
•A replica of Arthur's birthplace is on State Route 108, about three and a half miles east of Fairfield Station. Owned by the State of Vermont and operated by the Vermont Board of Historic Sites, it is open to the public daily except Mondays, 10 A.M. to 5 P.M., June 21 to Labor Day, and weekends to Oct. 15. Admission: adults, 50 cents, children under 16, free.

Note: He was probably born in Canada, but since his parents were U.S. citizens, his eligibility for the office of president was not challenged.

Family lineage: English-Scottish-Irish
•He was the second of three presidents who were of English-Scottish-Irish ancestry.

Religious denomination: Episcopalian
•He was the eighth of nine presidents who were Episcopalians.
College: Union College, Schenectady, N.Y.
•He was the only president who went to Union.
•He was the 14th of 27 presidents who attended college.
Date of graduation: July 26, 1848, Bachelor of Arts
•He was the tenth of 21 presidents who were graduated from college.

PARENTS AND SIBLINGS

Father's name: William Arthur
Date of birth: Dec. 5, 1796
Place of birth: near Ballymena, Northern Ireland
•Arthur's father was the sixth of eight parents of presidents who were born abroad.
•Arthur's father was the last of four fathers of presidents who were born abroad.
Occupation: Baptist minister
•Arthur was the first of three presidents whose fathers were clergymen.

240

Date of death: Oct. 27, 1875
Place of death: Newtonville, N.Y.
Age at death: 78 years, 326 days

Mother's name: Malvina Stone Arthur
Date of birth: Apr. 24, 1802
Place of birth: near Berkshire, Vt.
Date of marriage: probably Apr. 12, 1821
Children: 9; 6 daughters, 3 sons
•The exact order of the children's births is unknown. They were: Regina; Jane (born Mar. 14, 1824); Almeda; Ann Eliza; Chester (born Oct. 5, 1830); Malvina; William; George (born May 24, 1836); and Mary.
•Arthur was the third of four presidents who were fifth children.
•He was the fourth of seven presidents who came from families of nine children.
Date of death: Jan. 16, 1869
Place of death: Newtonville, N.Y.
Age at death: 66 years, 262 days

MARRIAGE

Date of marriage: Oct. 25, 1859
Place of marriage: New York, N.Y.
•Arthur was the third of five presidents who were married in New York City.
•He was the fifth of seven presidents who were married in New York.
Age at marriage: 29 years, 20 days
•He was the 15th of 27 presidents who were married in their twenties.
Years married: 20 years, 79 days

Wife's name: Ellen Lewis Herndon Arthur
•She was called Nell.
•She was the 22nd of 40 wives of presidents.
Date of birth: Aug. 30, 1837
•She was the second of four wives of presidents who were born in August.

Place of birth: Fredericksburg, Va.
•She was the fifth of six wives of presidents who were born in Virginia.
Wife's mother: Frances Hansbrough Herndon
Wife's father: Commander William Lewis Herndon, U.S. Navy
Age at marriage: 22 years, 56 days
•She was the 18th of 30 wives of presidents who were married in their twenties.
Years younger than husband: 6 years, 329 days
Children: 3; 2 sons, 1 daughter
•William Lewis Herndon was born on Dec. 10, 1860; Chester Alan on July 25, 1864; and Ellen Herndon on Nov. 21, 1871. William Lewis Herndon died in infancy.
•Arthur was the third of seven presidents who had three children.
•He was the 13th of 19 presidents who had both male and female children.
•He was the 16th of 30 presidents who had children.
Date of death: Jan. 12, 1880
•She was the fourth of five wives of presidents who died before their husbands' terms of office.
•She was the fifth of seven wives of presidents who were not first ladies.
Years he survived his wife: 6 years, 310 days
•Arthur was the tenth of 14 presidents who survived their wives.
Place of death: New York, N.Y.
•She was the first of five wives of presidents who died in New York City.
•She was the third of eight wives of presidents who died in New York.
Age at death: 42 years, 135 days
Place of burial: Albany, N.Y.
•She was the fifth of seven wives of presidents who were buried in New York.

EARLY YEARS

Sept. 5, 1845, entered Union College as sophomore, Schenectady, N.Y.
July 26, 1848, was graduated with Bachelor of Arts degree, Union
•During his sophomore and senior years, Arthur had taught school for a term in Schaghticoke, N.Y.
•He was the fourth of seven presidents who taught school.

•He was elected to Phi Beta Kappa.
•He was the second of three presidents who were members of Phi Beta Kappa elected as undergraduates.
•He was the fourth of 11 presidents who were members of Phi Beta Kappa.
1848, taught school in North Pownal, Vt.
•He also studied law intermittently.

- He was the 15th of 26 presidents who studied law.

1849, appointed principal of North Pownal Academy

1851, awarded master of arts degree, Union College

Nov. 2, 1852, cast first presidential vote

- He voted for Winfield Scott.

Mar. 5, 1853, joined law firm of Culver and Parker as clerk, New York City

May 4, 1854, admitted to bar, New York City

- The firm name became Culver, Parker and Arthur.
- He was the 15th of 23 presidents who were lawyers.

1856, formed law firm with Henry D. Gardiner, New York City

Oct. 25, 1859, married Ellen Lewis Herndon, New York City

Dec. 10, 1860, his first son born

- The boy was named William Lewis Herndon Arthur.

Jan. 1, 1861, appointed state engineer-in-chief

- This position on Governor Edwin D. Morgan's military staff was honorary. Arthur's rank was brigadier general.

Apr. 15, 1861, appointed assistant quartermaster general

Apr. 14, 1862, appointed inspector general

- In May, he inspected the New York troops at Fredericksburg and on the Chickahominy River, Va.
- Arthur was the fifth of seven presidents who served in the Civil War.
- He was the tenth of 12 presidents who were generals.
- He was the 13th of 21 presidents who served in the military during wartime.

June 28, 1862, served as secretary of conference of governors of loyal states, New York City

July 27, 1862, appointed quartermaster general

Dec. 31, 1862, resigned his commission

Jan. 1, 1863, resumed law practice, New York City

July 7, 1863, his first son died

- William Lewis Herndon Arthur lived two years, 209 days.

July 25, 1864, his second son born

- The boy was named Chester Alan Arthur and was called Alan.

1867, appointed member of Republican city executive committee

1868, elected chairman of Republican state executive committee

Jan. 16, 1869, his mother died

1869–1870, appointed counsel to New York City tax commission

NATIONAL PROMINENCE

Nov. 20, 1871, appointed collector of port of New York by Grant

- Arthur was confirmed by the Senate, Dec. 12; he was commissioned for four years, Dec. 16.
- This was his only federal office prior to his election as vice president.
- He was the only president who served as collector of the port of New York.

Nov. 21, 1871, his only daughter born

- The girl was named Ellen Herndon Arthur.

Oct. 27, 1875, his father died

Dec. 17, 1875, reappointed collector of port of New York by Grant

- He was confirmed by the Senate, Dec. 17, and commissioned for four years, Dec. 18.

June 14–16, 1876, attended Republican national convention, Cincinnati, Ohio

- He was a supporter of Roscoe Conkling.

Aug. 23, 1876, chairman of Republican state convention, Saratoga, N.Y.

Sept. 7, 1877, asked to resign as collector of port of New York

- The resignation request was made by Secretary of Treasury Sherman, coupled with the offer of a diplomatic appointment.
- Arthur refused to resign.

Nov. 23, 1877, replied to Jay commission charges

- The Jay commission, appointed, Apr. 14, had made four reports critical of his management of the custom house.

July 11, 1878, suspended as collector of port of New York by Hayes

1878, resumed law practice, New York City

- He was senior member of the firm of Arthur, Phelps, Knevels and Ransom.

Jan. 12, 1880, his wife died

June 2–8, 1880, delegate to Republican national convention, Chicago, Ill.

- As a Conkling Stalwart, he supported

Grant for a third term.
June 8, 1880, nominated as Republican candidate for vice president
•The Garfield forces, in a move to placate Conkling and the Stalwarts, first offered the vice-presidential nomination to Levi P. Morton of New York. Morton wished to confer with Conkling, who was not available. When the Garfield men grew restless and offered the nomination to Arthur, he accepted immediately without waiting for Conkling's endorsement.
July 5, 1880, formally accepted nomination
Nov. 2, 1880, elected vice president
Mar. 4, 1881, took oath as vice president, Senate chamber

THE PRESIDENT (21st)

Term of office: Sept. 20, 1881, to Mar. 4, 1885 (3 years, 166 days)
•Arthur was the seventh of 12 presidents who had served as vice presidents.
•He was the fourth of eight presidents who, because of the death of their predecessors, did not complete their vice-presidential terms.
•He was the last of four presidents who served only the unexpired terms of their predecessors.
•He was the seventh of nine presidents who served less than one term.
•He was the 14th of 19 presidents who served one term or less than one term.
State represented: New York
•He was the third of eight presidents who represented New York.
•He was the eighth of 15 presidents who represented states that were not their native states.
Political party: Republican
•He was the fifth of 14 presidents who were Republicans.
Congresses: 47th, 48th
Administration: 24th
Age at taking oath: 50 years, 350 days
•Arthur took the oath of office at his home, 123 Lexington Avenue, New York City, at 2:05 A.M., Tuesday, Sept. 20, 1881. The oath was administered by Justice John R. Brady of the New York Supreme Court.
•Later that day Arthur wrote a letter, which he addressed to himself at the executive mansion, on the subject of succession. He destroyed the letter once he was in the White House.
•He was the second of two presidents who took the oath of office in New York City. The other was Washington.
•He was the fourth of seven presidents who took the oath of office from an official other than a justice of the Supreme Court.
•On Thursday, Sept. 22, the oath of office was repeated during a private ceremony in the room reserved for the vice president in the Capitol. This oath was administered by Chief Justice Morrison R. Waite. About 40 dignitaries—including former Presidents Hayes and Grant—were present.
•This was the third of four oath-taking ceremonies at which Waite officiated.
•Waite was the first of two officials who administered the oath of office to two presidents in the same year; he had officiated at the inauguration of Garfield, Mar. 4. The other was Chief Justice Stone, who administered the oath to Franklin D. Roosevelt and Truman in 1945.
•Arthur was the last of four presidents who did not give inaugural addresses. His brief speech—only 118 words long—at the private ceremony in the Capitol has been referred to mistakenly as an inaugural address.

THE 24th ADMINISTRATION

1881

Sept. 22, issued proclamation declaring Sept. 26 as day of mourning for President Garfield
Oct. 19, participated in dedication of Revolutionary War monument, Yorktown, Va.
•This was the centennial of the surrender of Cornwallis.
Oct. 24, accepted resignations of Secretary of Treasury Windom and Attorney General MacVeagh
•Windom's resignation became effective, Nov. 13.

Oct. 27, appointed his second secretary of treasury, Charles J. Folger
• Folger took office, Nov. 14.
Dec. 5, first session of 47th Congress
• The administration controlled the House of Representatives, but the tied Senate was organized by the Democrats. The Republicans gained four Senate and 34 House seats. The Senate (76 members) consisted of 37 Republicans, 37 Democrats, and two others. The House (293 members) consisted of 152 Republicans, 130 Democrats, and 11 others.
Dec. 6, sent his first State of the Union message to Congress
Dec. 12, Secretary of State Blaine resigned, effective, Dec. 19
Dec. 12, appointed his second secretary of state, Frederick T. Frelinghuysen
• Frelinghuysen took office, Dec. 19.
Dec. 19, appointed his second attorney general, Benjamin H. Brewster
• Brewster took office, Jan. 2, 1882.
Dec. 19, appointed Horace Gray as associate justice
• Gray, who was confirmed by the Senate, Dec. 20, was the first of Arthur's three appointments to the Supreme Court.
Dec. 20, Postmaster General James resigned
Dec. 20, appointed his second postmaster general, Timothy O. Howe
• Howe took office, Jan. 5, 1882.

1882

Jan. 7, Associate Justice Hunt resigned
• Hunt had been incapacitated for about five years.
Feb. 24, appointed Roscoe Conkling as associate justice
• Conkling, the second of Arthur's three appointments to the Supreme Court, was confirmed by the Senate, Mar. 2, but declined to serve.
• Conkling was the last of seven appointees, confirmed by the Senate, who declined to serve.
• Arthur was the last of four presidents who appointed associate justices who declined to serve
Mar. 13, appointed Samuel Blatchford as associate justice
• Blatchford, who was confirmed by the Senate, Mar. 27, was the last of Arthur's three

appointments to the Supreme Court.
Mar. 22, signed amended antipolygamy act
Mar. 31, signed widows of presidents pension act
• This act, the first of its kind, awarded pensions of $5,000 yearly to the widows of Presidents Polk, Tyler, and Garfield.
Apr. 4, vetoed Chinese immigration bill
• The bill, if enacted, would have prohibited the immigration of Chinese laborers for 20 years—a violation of the treaty of 1880.
• This was the first of his 12 vetoes.
Apr. 6, Secretary of Interior Kirkwood resigned
Apr. 6, appointed his second secretary of interior, Henry M. Teller
Apr. 12, Secretary of Navy Hunt resigned, effective, Apr. 16
Apr. 12, appointed his second secretary of navy, William E. Chandler
• Chandler took office, Apr. 16.
Apr. 17, sent special message to Congress asking for system of supplemental levees on Mississippi River
• Mississippi floods had made eighty-five thousand homeless in March.
Apr. 18, sent special message to Congress concerning proposed Pan-American Peace Congress
• He asked Congress for its opinion of the peace conference, scheduled for Nov. 22; Congress did not reply.
• All North and South American countries had been invited to send representatives to Washington by then Secretary of State Blaine, Nov. 29, 1881.
May 3, issued proclamation against violence of Arizona "cowboys"
May 6, signed Chinese Exclusion Act
• This act, which suspended immigration of Chinese for ten years, was a modified version of the bill he had vetoed, Apr. 4.
May 15, signed tariff commission act
• This act authorized the appointment of a nine-man commission.
May 22, commercial treaty signed with Korea
July 1, vetoed carriage of passengers at sea bill
• He vetoed the bill on the grounds that it was neither correctly nor accurately phrased.
• This was the second of his 12 vetoes.
Aug. 1, vetoed rivers and harbors bill
• He vetoed the bill, authorizing appropriations of $18,743,875, on the grounds that

the amounts were excessive and did not promote commerce among the states but were entirely for the benefit of the localities in which the improvements were proposed.

Aug. 2, rivers and harbors act passed over his veto

• This was his only veto that was overridden.

Aug. 2, signed modified carriage of passengers at sea act

Aug 8, first session of 47th Congress adjourned

Aug. 9, indefinitely postponed proposed Pan-American Peace Congress

• He stated his belief that the convocation should not be held without the express authority of Congress.

Nov. 25, removed postal and government printing officials for involvement in Star Route frauds

• Star Routes were roads over which U.S. mail was carried by wagon or horse. Frauds in the post office department, involving 93 routes, led to more than 25 indictments. No convictions resulted, although the government had been defrauded of about $4,-000,000.

Dec. 4, second session of 47th Congress

Dec. 4, sent his second State of the Union message to Congress

1883

Jan. 16, signed civil service reform act

• This act provided for a bipartisan three-man civil service commission to draw up and administer competitive examinations for federal positions. The first chairman was Dorman B. Eaton, secretary of the Civil Service Reform Association, who had drafted the act for its sponsor, Senator George H. Pendleton of Ohio.

Jan. 20, reciprocal commercial treaty with Mexico signed

• The treaty, signed by General Grant and William H. Trescott for the U.S., was ratified by the Senate, Mar. 11.

Mar. 3, signed repeal of stamp taxes act

• This "Mongrel Tariff" act removed excise taxes from all articles except liquor and tobacco.

Mar. 4, second session of 47th Congress adjourned

Mar. 7, received envoys of Queen of Madagascar

Mar. 25, Postmaster General Howe died

Apr. 3, appointed his third postmaster general, Walter Q. Gresham

May 8, published new civil service regulations

May 24, attended opening of Brooklyn Bridge

June 25, issued executive order that reduced internal revenue districts

• The collection districts were reduced in number from 126 to 83.

Aug. 1, attended opening of Southern Exposition, Louisville, Ky.

Sept. 18, received Korean diplomats, New York City

Sept. 21, sent telegraph message to Emperor of Brazil

• This message opened the telegraphic communication between the U.S. and Brazil.

Sept. 25, attended unveiling of Burnside monument, Bristol, R.I.

• Ambrose E. Burnside, a Union major general during the Civil War, was governor of Rhode Island, 1866–1868, and a member of the Senate, 1875–1881. Burnside died in Bristol, 1881.

• Burnside's whiskers were much copied; originally called "Burnsides" in his honor,. the style came to be known as sideburns.

Nov. 26, attended unveiling of statue of Washington, steps of Sub-Treasury Building, New York City

Dec. 3, first session of 48th Congress

• The administration won control of the Senate but lost control of the House of Representatives. The Republicans gained three Senate seats, lost 33 House seats. Actually, the Republican defeat in the House was much more severe inasmuch as reapportionment had added 33 seats. The Senate (76 members) consisted of 40 Republicans and 36 Democrats. The House (325 members) consisted of 200 Democrats, 119 Republicans, and six others.

Dec. 4, sent his third State of the Union message to Congress

Note: The Panic of 1883, fifth of nine U.S. depressions, was brought on by the decline of agricultural commodities prices.

1884

Jan. 8, sent special message to Congress recommending system for permanent improvement of Mississippi River navigation

Mar. 26, sent special message to Congress in which he asked for appropriations to reconstruct navy, establish army and navy gun factories

Apr. 11, sent special message to Congress recommending annual appropriation of $1,500,000 for armament of fortifications

June 3–6, defeated for renomination, Republican national convention, Chicago, Ill.

• *See* Election of 1884, page 251.

•He was the last of five presidents who sought but were denied renomination.

June 27, signed act that created bureau of labor, department of interior

July 1, issued proclamation that warned squatters against settling on Oklahoma lands

July 2, vetoed relief of Fitz-John Porter bill

•Major General Porter had been court-martialed in 1863 for disobedience of military orders.

July 5, signed act that created bureau of navigation, treasury department

July 7, signed act that created Central and South American commission

July 7, first session of 48th Congress adjourned

July 7, pocket vetoed six private relief and military appointment bills

Aug. 5, attended ceremony when cornerstone laid for pedestal of Statue of Liberty, New York City

Sept. 4, Secretary of Treasury Folger died

Sept. 24, appointed his third secretary of treasury, Walter Q. Gresham

•Gresham, who had been postmaster general, took office, Sept. 25.

Oct. 14, appointed his fourth postmaster general, Frank Hatton

Oct. 28, Secretary of Treasury Gresham resigned, effective, Oct. 30

Oct. 31, appointed his fourth secretary of treasury, Hugh McCulloch

•McCulloch was the first of three secretaries of treasury who served under three presidents.

•He was the second of nine executive officers who served in the cabinets of three presidents; he had served previously under Lincoln and Andrew Johnson.

•McCulloch was the last of Arthur's ten cabinet appointments.

Nov. 4, election day

• *See* Election of 1884, page 251.

Dec. 1, second session of 48th Congress

Dec. 1, sent his fourth and last State of the Union address to Congress

Dec. 16, opened World's Industrial and Cotton Centennial Exposition by telegraph

•The exposition was held in New Orleans, La.

1885

Jan. 31, announced expiration of Treaty of Washington with Great Britain as of July 1

Feb. 3, sent special message to Congress recommending passage of bill creating office of general of army on retired list

•His aim was to appoint former President Grant.

Feb. 25, signed act to prevent and provide penalties for illegal enclosures of public lands

Feb. 26, signed act to prohibit entrance into U.S. of contract laborers

•This act exempted domestics and skilled labor otherwise not obtainable for new industries.

Mar. 3, signed act to appoint one general of army on retired list with rank and full pay

•He appointed Grant, Mar. 3.

Mar. 3, signed amended postal appropriation act

•This act provided $800,000 for contracting with American steamship lines for transportation of foreign mails.

Mar. 3, signed act that appropriated $1,895,000 for four new naval vessels, two cruisers and two gunboats

Mar. 3, second session of 48th Congress adjourned

Mar. 3, pocket vetoed two private bills

•These were the last of his 12 vetoes, eight of which were pocket vetoes.

Note: The first elevator was installed in the White House during the Arthur administration.

THE FORMER PRESIDENT

Mar. 4, 1885, attended inauguration of Cleveland

•Arthur's age upon leaving office was 54 years, 150 days.

Mar. 1885, resumed law practice, New York City

1885, accepted presidency of New York Arcade Railway Company

• The firm was one of several that attempted to construct a subway in New York City. The first American subway was completed in 1897, in Boston, Mass.

February, 1886, advised to retire by physicians

• Examination revealed that he was suffering from Bright's disease. He retired from all business and professional activities. Treatment brought relief, but a heart condition developed.

Nov. 16, 1886, suffered cerebral hemorrhage

DEATH

Date of death: Nov. 18, 1886

Place of death: New York, N.Y.

• Arthur was the second of three presidents who died in New York City.

• He was the fifth of eight presidents who died in New York.

Age at death: 56 years, 44 days

• He lived one year, 259 days after the completion of his term.

Cause of death: Bright's disease, cerebral hemorrhage

Place of burial: Albany, N.Y.

• He was the fourth of six presidents who were buried in New York.

THE VICE PRESIDENT

• Arthur was the last of four presidents who did not have vice presidents.

THE CABINET

State: James Gillespie Blaine of Maine, Mar. 7, 1881, to Dec. 19, 1881

• Frederick Theodore Frelinghuysen of New Jersey, Dec. 19, 1881, to Mar. 6, 1885

Treasury: William Windom of Minnestoa, Mar, 8, 1881, to Nov. 13, 1881

• Charles James Folger of New York, Nov. 14, 1881, to Sept. 4, 1884

• Walter Quintin Gresham of Indiana, Sept. 25, 1884, to Oct. 30, 1884

• Hugh McCulloch of Indiana, Oct. 31, 1884, to Mar. 7, 1885

War: Robert Todd Lincoln of Illinois, Mar. 5, 1881, to Mar. 5, 1885

Attorney General: Isacc Wayne MacVeagh of Pennsylvania, Mar. 5, 1881, to Oct. 24, 1881

• Benjamin Harris Brewster of Pennsylvania, Jan. 2, 1882, to Mar. 5, 1885

Navy: William Henry Hunt of Louisiana, Mar. 7, 1881, to Apr. 16, 1882

• William Eaton Chandler of New Hampshire, Apr. 16, 1882, to Mar. 6, 1885

Postmaster General: Thomas Lemuel James of New York, Mar. 5, 1881, to Dec. 20, 1881

• Timothy Otis Howe of Wisconsin, Jan. 5, 1882, to Mar. 25, 1883

• Walter Quintin Gresham of Indiana, Apr. 3, 1883, to Sept. 24, 1884

• Frank Hatton of Iowa, Oct. 14, 1884, to Mar. 6, 1885

Interior: Samuel Jordan Kirkwood of Iowa, Mar. 5, 1881, to Apr. 6, 1882

• Henry Moore Teller of Colorado, Apr. 6, 1882, to Mar. 3, 1885

THE SUPREME COURT

Associate Justices: Horace Gray of Massachusetts, appointed, Dec. 19, 1881; confirmed, Dec. 20, 1881

• Roscoe Conkling of New York, appointed, Feb. 24, 1882; confirmed, Mar. 2, 1882; declined to serve

• Samuel Blatchford of New York, appointed, Mar. 13, 1882; confirmed, Mar. 27, 1882

Twenty-second President

GROVER CLEVELAND

Full name: Grover Cleveland
•His given name was Stephen Grover Cleveland.
•He was the second of four presidents who dropped their first names.
•He was the second of five presidents who changed their names from those they were given at birth.
•He was the eighth of 19 presidents who had middle initials or middle names.
Date of birth: Mar. 18, 1837
•He was the last of four presidents who were born in March.
Place of birth: Caldwell, N. J.
•He was the only president who was born in New Jersey.
•His birthplace, formerly the manse of the First Presbyterian Church of Caldwell, 207 Bloomfield Avenue, where his father was minister, is administered by the State of New Jersey Department of Conservation and Economic Development. It is open to the public daily except Mondays, 10 A.M. to 12, noon, and 1 to 5 P.M., and Sundays, 2 to 5 P.M. Closed Thanksgiving, Christmas and New Year's Day. Admission: adults, 25 cents; children under 12, free.
Family lineage: English-Irish-French

•He was the only president who was of English-Irish-French ancestry.
Religious denomination: attended Presbyterian Church
•He was the third of six presidents who were Presbyterians.
•He never formally joined the church.
College: None
•He was the eighth of nine presidents who did not attend college.
•He was the 12th of 15 presidents who were not graduated from college.

PARENTS AND SIBLINGS

Father's name: Richard Falley Cleveland
Date of birth: June 19, 1804
Place of birth: Norwich, Conn.
Occupation: Presbyterian minister
•Cleveland was the second of three presidents whose fathers were clergymen. His father's first pastorate was Congregational, but all subsequent were Presbyterian.
Date of death: Oct. 1, 1853
•Grover was 16 years, 197 days old when his father died.
Place of death: Holland Patent, N.Y.

248

Age at death: 49 years, 104 days

Mother's name: Anne Neal Cleveland
Date of birth: Feb. 4, 1806
Place of birth: Baltimore, Md.
Date of marriage: Sept. 10, 1829
Children: 9; 5 daughters, 4 sons
• Anna Neal was born in 1830; William Neal in 1832; Mary Allen in 1833; Richard Cecil in 1835; Stephen Grover in 1837; Margaret Louise Falley in 1838; Lewis Frederick in 1841; Susan Sophia in 1843; and Rose Elizabeth in 1846.
• Cleveland was the last of four presidents who were fifth children.
• He was the fifth of seven presidents who came from families of nine children.
Date of death: July 19, 1882
Place of death: Holland Patent, N.Y.
Age at death: 76 years, 165 days

MARRIAGE

Date of marriage: June 2, 1886
• Cleveland was the only bachelor president who married while in office.
• He was the second of two presidents who were bachelors at inauguration. The other was Buchanan.
• He was the second of three presidents who were married while in office.
Place of marriage: White House, Washington, D.C.
• He was the only president who was married in the White House.
• He was the first of two presidents who were married in Washington. The other was Wilson.
Age at marriage: 49 years, 76 days
• He was the president who married for the first time at the most advanced age.
• He was the second of two presidents who were married in their forties. The other was Madison.
Years married: 22 years, 22 days

Wife's name: Frances Folsom Cleveland
• She was the 18th of 33 first ladies.
• She was the 23rd of 40 wives of presidents.
Date of birth: July 21, 1864
• She was the second of three first ladies who were born in July.
• She was the second of four wives of presidents who were born in July.
Place of birth: Buffalo, N.Y.

• She was the fourth of six first ladies who were born in New York.
• She was the fifth of seven wives of presidents who were born in New York.
Wife's mother: Emma Cornelia Harmon Folsom
Wife's father: Oscar Folsom, attorney
• Folsom was the second of four fathers-in-law of presidents who were attorneys.
Age at marriage: 21 years, 316 days
• She was the youngest first lady.
• She was the 15th of 26 first ladies who were married in their twenties.
• She was the 19th of 30 wives of presidents who were married in their twenties.
Years younger than husband: 27 years, 125 days
Children: 5; 3 daughters, 2 sons
• Ruth was born on Oct. 3, 1891; Esther on Sept. 9, 1893; Marion on July 7, 1895; Richard Folsom on Oct. 28, 1897; and Francis Grover on July 18, 1903.
• Cleveland was the last of three presidents who had five children.
• He was the 14th of 19 presidents who had both male and female children.
• He was the 17th of 30 presidents who had children.

Notes: Mrs. Cleveland married Thomas J. Preston, Jr., a member of the Princeton University faculty, Feb. 10, 1913.
• She was the first of two first ladies who remarried. The other was Jacqueline Kennedy.
• She was the first of two wives of presidents who remarried.

Date of death: Oct. 29, 1947
Place of death: Baltimore, Md.
• She was the only first lady or wife of a president who died in Maryland.
Age at death: 83 years, 100 days
• She had celebrated her 80th birthday, July 21, 1944.
• She was the ninth of 16 first ladies who lived to be 70.
• She was the ninth of 17 wives of presidents who lived to be 70.
• She was the seventh of 14 first ladies who lived to be 75.
• She was the seventh of 15 wives of presidents who lived to be 75.
• She was the fifth of nine first ladies who lived to be 80.
• She was the fifth of ten wives of presidents who lived to be 80.

Years she survived her husband: 39 years, 127 days
• She was the 12th of 21 first ladies who survived their husbands.
• She was the 13th of 23 wives of presidents who survived their husbands.
Place of burial: Princeton, N.J.
• She was the only first lady or wife of a president who was buried in New Jersey.

EARLY YEARS

1841, with family, moved to Fayetteville, N.Y.
1851, with family, moved to Clinton, N.Y.
1853, with family, moved to Holland Patent, N.Y.
Oct. 1, 1853, his father died
1853–1854, worked as clerk and assistant teacher, New York Institute for Blind, New York City
1854, returned to Holland Patent
1855, assisted editor of *American Shorthorn Handbook*
• Cleveland had decided to seek work in Cleveland, Ohio, named for his kinsman, Moses Cleveland, but stopped to visit an uncle, Lewis F. Allen, in Black Rock, now part of Buffalo, N.Y. Allen, founder and editor of the *American Shorthorn Handbook*, hired him as an assistant. He worked on several volumes of the publication—as the preface of the fifth volume, published in 1861, acknowledged.
Aug, 1855, hired as clerk and copyist for law firm, began study of law, Buffalo
• He remained with Rogers, Bowen and Rogers until 1862.
• He was the 16th of 26 presidents who studied law.
1859, admitted to bar, Buffalo
• He was the 16th of 23 presidents who were lawyers.
1859, promoted to managing clerk, Rogers, Bowen and Rogers
Jan. 1, 1863, appointed assistant district attorney, Erie County
• Two of his brothers served in the Union army, but since he was contributing to the support of his mother and sister, he hired a substitute when drafted.
1865, unsuccessful Democratic candidate for district attorney
• He was defeated by the Republican candidate, Lyman K. Bass, an intimate friend and later partner.
1865, formed law firm with Isaac K. Vanderpoel
1869, when Vanderpoel resigned, firm became Lanning, Cleveland and Folsom
1870, elected sheriff of Erie County
Jan. 1, 1871, took office as sheriff
• During his three-year term, he performed all the duties of his office, including the supervision of hangings.
1874, returned to law practice
• One of his partners was Lyman Bass. The firm, Bass, Cleveland and Bissell, prospered. When Bass retired because of ill health, the firm became Cleveland and Bissell
1881, elected mayor of Buffalo
Jan. 1, 1882, took office as mayor
• He was known as the "veto mayor." His use of the veto power nullified nearly $1,000,000 worth of fraudulent sewage and street-cleaning contracts. His attacks on the grafters led the Buffalo *Sunday Times* to endorse him for governor.
July 19, 1882, his mother died

NATIONAL PROMINENCE

Sept. 22, 1882, nominated for governor, Democratic state convention, Syracuse, N.Y.
Nov. 7, 1882, elected as governor of New York
Jan. 1, 1883, took office as governor
• Cleveland was the second of four presidents who served as governors of New York
• He was the eighth of 13 presidents who served as state governors.
July 11, 1884, nominated for president, Democratic national convention, Chicago, Ill.
July 29, 1884, officially notified of nomination
Aug. 18, 1884, formally accepted nomination

• *See* Election of 1884, below.
Dec. 3, 1884, presidential electors cast ballots
• He received 219 of the 401 electoral votes from the 38 states.
• *See* Election of 1884, below.
Jan. 6, 1885, resigned as governor of New York
Feb. 11, 1885, electoral vote tabulated by Congress
• Cleveland and Hendricks were officially declared elected.

ELECTION OF 1884

Anti-Monopoly party, convened, May 14, at Chicago, Ill., nominated Benjamin Franklin Butler of Massachusetts for president. The party's national committee nominated Absolom Madden West of Mississippi for vice president, Aug. 16.
Greenback-Labor party, convened, May 28, at Indianapolis, Ind., nominated Benjamin Franklin Butler of Massachusetts for president, Absolom Madden West of Mississippi for vice president.
Republican party, convened, June 3, at Chicago, Ill., nominated James Gillespie Blaine of Maine for president, John Alexander Logan of Illinois for vice president.
• This was the eighth Republican national convention. It was the fourth Republican convention in Chicago; it was the fifth major party convention in Chicago.
Democratic party, convened, July 8, at Chicago, Ill., nominated Grover Cleveland of New York for president, Thomas Andrews Hendricks of Indiana for vice president
• This was the 14th Democratic national convention. It was the second Democratic convention in Chicago; it was the sixth major party convention in Chicago.
Prohibition party, convened, July 23, at Pittsburgh, Pa., nominated John Pierce St. John of Kansas for president, William Daniel of Maryland for vice president.
National Labor party, convened, July 30, at Chicago, Ill., endorsed the Democratic candidates, Cleveland and Hendricks.
Equal Rights party, convened, Sept. 5, at Des Moines, Iowa, nominated Belva Ann Bennett Lockwood of Washington, D.C. for president.
• Mrs. Lockwood was the first female candidate for the presidency.
Election day, Tuesday, Nov. 4, 1884
Popular vote: 10,095,701
　　Cleveland, 4,914,986
　　Blaine, 4,854,981
　　Butler, 175,365
　　St. John, 150,369
• Cleveland was the eighth of 15 presidents who were elected without receiving a majority of the popular vote.
Electoral vote: 401, 38 states
• Cleveland, 219, 20 states
(Alabama, 10; Arkansas, 7; Connecticut, 6; Delaware, 3; Florida, 4; Georgia, 12; Indiana, 15; Kentucky, 13; Louisiana, 8; Maryland, 8; Mississippi, 9; Missouri, 16; New Jersey, 9; New York, 36; North Carolina, 11; South Carolina, 9; Tennessee, 12; Texas, 13; Virginia, 12; West Virginia, 6)
• Blaine, 182, 18 states
(California, 8; Colorado, 3; Illinois, 22; Iowa, 13; Kansas, 9; Maine, 6; Massachusetts, 14; Michigan, 13; Minnesota, 7; Nebraska, 5; Nevada, 3; New Hampshire, 4; Ohio, 23; Oregon, 3; Pennsylvania, 30; Rhode Island, 4; Vermont, 4; Wisconsin, 11)

THE PRESIDENT (22nd)

Term of office: Mar. 4, 1885, to Mar. 4, 1889 (4 years)
• Cleveland also served as the 24th president. *See* pages 271–278.
State represented: New York
• Cleveland was the last of four presidents who succeeded presidents who represented the same state.
• He was the fourth of eight presidents who represented New York.
• He was the ninth of 15 presidents who represented states that were not their native states.
Political party: Democratic
• He was the first Democrat elected as president since before the Civil War.
• He was the seventh of 12 presidents who were Democrats.
Congresses: 49th, 50th
Administration: 25th

Age at inauguration: 47 years, 351 days
•He was the 11th of 21 presidents who were younger than their vice presidents. Cleveland was 17 years, 192 days younger than Hendricks.
Inauguration day: Wednesday, Mar. 4, 1885
•Cleveland took the oath of office, administered by Chief Justice Morrison R. Waite, on the east portico of the Capitol.
•This was the last of three inaugurations at which Waite officiated.
•This was the last of four oath-taking ceremonies at which Waite officiated.
•Cleveland was the second of two presidents who gave their inaugural addresses as orations without consulting notes or manuscript. The other was Pierce.
•Cleveland also gave his 1893 inaugural address as an oration.

THE 25th ADMINISTRATION

1885

Mar. 5, appointed his only secretary of state, Thomas F. Bayard; his first secretary of treasury, Daniel Manning; his only secretary of war, William C. Endicott; his only attorney general, Augustus H. Garland; his only secretary of navy, William C. Whitney; his first postmaster general, William F. Vilas; and his first secretary of interior, Lucius Q. C. Lamar
•Garland, Vilas, and Lamar took office, Mar. 6; Bayard and Whitney, Mar. 7; Manning, Mar. 8.
Mar. 13, issued proclamation that warned against attempts to settle on Oklahoma lands
Mar. 13, withdrew Nicaragua treaty
•The Zavala-Frelinghuysen draft canal treaty had been signed, Dec. 1, 1884.
Apr. 17, issued proclamation nullifying Arthur executive order
•Arthur, by executive order, had opened reservations on the east bank of the Missouri River in Dakota Territory to settlement.
July 23, issued proclamation ordering cattlemen to vacate Indian lands of Cheyenne and Arapaho reservations
Aug. 7, issued proclamation ordering land office agents to destroy illegal enclosures of public lands
Aug. 8, attended funeral of President Grant, New York City
Nov. 7, issued proclamation ordering all insurgents and unlawful assemblages in Washington Territory to disperse
Nov. 25, Vice President Hendricks died
Dec. 7, first session of 49th Congress
•The administration controlled the House of Representatives. The Democrats lost two Senate and 28 House seats. The Senate (76 members) consisted of 41 Republicans, 34 Democrats, and one vacancy. The House (325 members) consisted of 182 Democrats, 140 Republicans, two others, and one vacancy.
Dec. 8, sent his first State of the Union message to Congress
•Cleveland recommended increased appropriations for the consular and diplomatic service, the suspension of compulsory silver coinage, the extension of civil service reform, improvement of the navy, and urged legislation to determine the order of presidential succession.

1886

Jan. 19, signed act providing order of presidential succession
•This act stated that in case of removal, death, resignation or inability of both the president and the vice president, cabinet officers were to succeed to the presidency in the following order: state, treasury, war, attorney general, postmaster general, and interior. This act remained in effect until 1947.
Mar. 1, sent special message to Senate in which he asserted power of removal of federal officers belonged to president
•He refused to produce documents sought by the Senate on the grounds that the papers were not official but were of a personal and private nature. It was in this message that he used the phrase, "innoculous desuetude," to characterize the Tenure of Office Act: "After an existence of nearly twenty years of almost innocuous desuetude these laws are brought forth."
Mar. 2, sent special message to Congress in which he recommended indemnity for an-

ti-Chinese riots of 1885
• He suggested the indemnity on moral grounds, as he felt that the government was not legally liable for the Rock Springs, Wy., massacre of Sept. 2, 1885. Many of the four hundred Chinese imported to work in the Union Pacific railroad coal mines had been killed during an attack 'by two hundred miners.

Mar. 10, vetoed relief of J. H. McBlair bill
• This was the first of his 414 vetoes during his first term.
• He vetoed more than twice the number of bills vetoed by all of his predecessors. The 13 presidents who had exercised the veto had vetoed a tôtal of 204 bills.
• This was the first of his 61 private relief bill vetoes of his first term.

Apr. 22, sent special message to Congress suggesting commission of labor for settlement of disputes

May 8, vetoed pension of Andrew J. Hill bill
• This was the first of his 282 pension bill vetoes during his first term.

June 2, married Frances Folsom, White House

June 29, signed act legalizing incorporation of national trade unions

July 1, signed act restoring Fitz-John Porter to army
• Porter was recommissioned as a colonel of infantry and retired, Aug. 2.

July 5, vetoed pension to J. Romiser bill

July 7, vetoed right of way to railroads in northern Montana bill

July 9, vetoed public building in Dayton, Ohio, bill

July 14, issued executive order warning officeholders and subordinates against use of official positions to influence political movements

Aug. 3, pension to J. Romiser act passed over his veto
• This was the first of his two vetoes during his first term that were overridden.

Aug. 5, first session of 49th Congress adjourned

Aug. 5, pocket vetoed ten bills
• Seven of the ten vetoes were relief and pension bills. The others were bills to provide for the erection of a public building in Annapolis, Md.; for the distribution of the Official Register; and for payment of the treasury surplus towards the public debt.
• He pocket vetoed 110 bills during his first term.

October, toured West and South
• During the three-week trip, he traveled about five thousand miles. He spoke in Indianapolis, Chicago, Minneapolis, St. Louis, Kansas City, Atlanta, and other cities.

Oct. 28, dedicated Statue of Liberty, New York City

Dec. 6, second session of 49th Congress

Dec. 6, sent his second State of the Union message to Congress
• He urged reduction of the treasury surplus by amendment of the tariff laws, recommended construction of modern navy and coastal defenses, and asked for correction of abuses in the disposition of public lands.

1887

Jan. 29, signed Mexican War pension act

Feb. 3, signed electoral count act
• This act, which was designed to prevent a repetition of the 1876 disputed election, fixed the second Monday in January as the day of meeting of presidential electors at such places as the state legislatures might direct and fixed the second Wednesday in February as the day of counting electoral votes in Congress. Acceptance by Congress of returns certified by executive officers of the states was specified.

Feb. 4, signed Interstate Commerce Commission Act
• The ICC was the first effective regulatory commission.

Feb. 8, signed Indian severalty act
• This act granted Indian families 160 acres apiece, to be held in trust by the government for 25 years as a guarantee against exploitation.

Feb. 11, vetoed dependent pension bill
• The bill would have provided pensions for all honorably discharged veterans who were disabled and dependent upon their own labor. It would have established the precedent of pensions without regard to disability suffered in military service.

Feb. 14, Secretary of Treasury Manning resigned, effective, Mar. 31

Feb. 16, vetoed Texas seed bill
• Several Texas counties had been stricken by drought. In his veto message, he stated that "though the people support the government, the government should not support the people."

Feb. 23, signed act prohibiting importation

of opium from China

Mar. 2, authorized to adopt retaliatory measures in fishery dispute with Canada

Mar. 2, signed Hatch Act

• This act provided subsidies for state agricultural experiment stations. It was written by Norman J. Colman, commissioner of agriculture, and sponsored by Representative William H. Hatch of Missouri.

Mar. 3, public building in Dayton, Ohio, act passed over his veto

• This was the second of his two vetoes during his first term that were overridden.

Mar. 3, Tenure of Office Act repealed

• This act had limited the powers of the president in regard to appointments or removals from office. Passed over the veto of President Andrew Johnson in 1867, it was the basis on which Johnson had been impeached in 1868.

Mar. 3, second session of 49th Congress adjourned

Mar. 3, pocket vetoed 47 bills

• A total of 30 were relief and pension bills. Among the others were bills to provide for public buildings in Monroe, La., and East Saginaw, Mich.; to construct a public road to a national cemetery in Corinth, Miss.; to prevent the employment of convict and alien labor on public works; to authorize the printing of extra copies of the report of the District of Columbia health officer; and to print additional copies of the 1886 edition of the U.S. map.

Mar. 22, appointed first Interstate Commerce Commission

Apr. 1, appointed his second secretary of treasury, Charles S. Fairchild

May 14, Associate Justice Woods died

June 16, revoked war department order to return captured Union and Confederate flags to states

• He had signed the war department order, June 7. Protests from Republican leaders and GAR (Grand Army of the Republic) officials brought about the revocation. The flags were not returned until 1905.

Dec. 5, first session of 50th Congress

• The administration maintained control of the House of Representatives. The Democrats gained three Senate seats but lost 12 House seats. The Senate (76 members) consisted of 39 Republicans and 37 Democrats. The House (325 members) consisted

of 170 Democrats, 151 Republicans, and four others.

Dec. 6, sent his third State of the Union message to Congress

• He devoted his entire message to the tariff and urged its downward revision, emphasizing that protectionist rates had encouraged the establishment of trusts and raised prices.

Dec. 6, appointed Lucius Q. C. Lamar as associate justice

• Lamar, who was confirmed by the Senate, Jan. 16, 1888, was the first of Cleveland's two appointments to the Supreme Court during his first term.

1888

Jan. 7, Secretary of Interior Lamar resigned, effective, Jan. 10

Jan. 16, appointed his second secretary of interior, William F. Vilas

• Vilas had been postmaster general.

Jan. 16, appointed his second postmaster general, Donald M. Dickinson

Mar. 23, Chief Justice Waite died

Apr. 30, appointed Melville W. Fuller as chief justice

• Fuller, who was confirmed by the Senate, July 20, was the second of Cleveland's two appointments to the Supreme Court during his first term.

• He was the sixth of 14 presidents who appointed chief justices of the Supreme Court.

June 1, authorized to appoint general of army

• He appointed Philip H. Sheridan.

June 6, renominated for president by acclamation, Democratic national convention, St. Louis, Mo.

June 13, signed act establishing department of labor

• He was authorized to appoint a commissioner of labor.

July 26, vetoed right-of-way for railroad through Indian lands bill

Aug. 23, sent special message to Congress that outlined plan of retaliation regarding fishery dispute with Canada

Sept. 8, wrote letter of acceptance of Democratic renomination

Sept. 24, vetoed sale of military reservation in Kansas bill

Oct 20, first session of 50th Congress adjourned

Oct. 20, pocket vetoed 22 bills

•Nine were relief and pension bills. Among the others were bills to create the Lincoln district of the Territory of New Mexico; to grant right-of-way to railroads across Indian reservations in Dakota Territory and Indian Territory; and to establish lightships off Sandy Hook, N.J., and Nantucket, Mass.

Nov. 6, election day

• *See* Election of 1888, pages 263–264.

•He was the last of three presidential candidates who received a plurality of the popular vote but were defeated in the electoral college.

Dec. 3, second session of 50th Congress

Dec. 3, sent his fourth State of the Union message to Congress

1889

Jan. 14, presidential electors cast ballots

•Harrison received 233 electoral votes; Cleveland received 168.

• *See* Election of 1888, pages 263–264.

Feb. 9, signed act establishing department of agriculture as executive department

Feb. 12, appointed first secretary of agriculture, Norman J. Colman

•Colman, who had been the sixth and last commissioner of agriculture since Apr. 3, 1885, took office, Feb. 15.

•Colman was the last of Cleveland's 11 cabinet appointments during his first term.

Feb. 13, electoral vote tabulated by Congress

•Harrison and Morton were officially declared elected.

•Cleveland was the fourth of seven presidents who were defeated when they sought reelection.

Mar. 2, vetoed bill to refund direct tax levied by act of Aug. 5, 1861, to states and territories

•This was the last of his 414 vetoes during his first term.

Mar. 3, second session of 50th Congress adjourned

Mar. 3, pocket vetoed 31 bills

•A total of 25 were relief and pension bills. The others were bills to provide for trial by jury in District of Columbia police courts; to create a port of delivery at Port Angeles, Washington Territory; to grant right-of-way to two railway companies through Indian Territory; and to authorize a bridge across the Arkansas River.

•These were the last of his 110 pocket vetoes during his first term.

THE FORMER PRESIDENT

Mar. 4, 1889, attended inauguration of Benjamin Harrison

•Cleveland's age upon leaving office was 51 years, 351 days.

March, 1889, returned to law practice, New York City

Apr. 30, 1889, attended celebration of centennial of Washington inauguration, Washington, D.C.

•President Harrison and former President Hayes also attended.

Feb. 10, 1891, his "silver letter" read at public meeting, New York City

•After leaving the White House, he continued to exert a powerful influence within the Democratic party by public expression of views and private consultation with other party leaders. His most important public act was the "silver letter," in which he opposed a bill pending in Congress for the free and unlimited coinage of silver. He wrote that "the greatest peril would be invited by the adoption of the scheme."

•Most political observers felt at the time that his stand was foolhardy, that his action would defeat the bill but at the cost of cancelling his chances for renomination in 1892. The measure was defeated. However, tariff reform became the principal issue the following year, and his rejuvenation as leader of his party was assured.

Oct. 3, 1891, his first daughter born

•The girl was named Ruth Cleveland.

June 23, 1892, nominated for president, Democratic national convention, Chicago, Ill.

•He was renominated on the first ballot.

Sept. 26, 1892, formally accepted nomination

•"Tariff reform is still our purpose," he said

in his letter of acceptance.

Nov. 8, 1892, election day

• *See* Election of 1892, pages 271–272.

1892, his writings and speeches, edited by George F. Parker, published by Cassell, New York City

Jan. 9, 1893, presidential electors cast ballots

• He received 277 of the 444 electoral votes from the 44 states.

• *See* Election of 1892, pages 271–272.

Feb. 8, 1893, electoral vote tabulated by Congress

• Cleveland and Stevenson were officially declared elected.

THE VICE PRESIDENT (21st)

Full name: Thomas Andrews Hendricks

Date of birth: Sept. 7, 1819

Place of birth: near Zanesville, Ohio

• Hendricks was the first of three vice presidents who were born in Ohio.

Religious denomination: Episcopalian

• He was the fourth of eight vice presidents who were Episcopalians.

College: Hanover College, Hanover, Ind.

Date of graduation: 1841

Occupation: Lawyer

• He was a member of the House of Representatives, 1851–1855; commissioner in general land office, 1855–1859; Senator from Indiana, 1863–1869; governor of Indiana, 1873–1877; Democratic vice presidential candidate, 1876.

• He was the 11th of 21 vice presidents who served in the House of Representatives before their terms of office.

• He was the tenth of 17 vice presidents who served in the Senate before their terms of office.

• He was the sixth of ten vice presidents who served in both the House of Representatives and the Senate before their terms of office.

• He was the eighth of 12 vice presidents who served both in the House of Representatives and the Senate.

• He was the ninth of 14 vice presidents who served as state governors.

Term of office: Mar. 4, 1885, to Nov. 25, 1885 (266 days)

• He was the fifth of seven vice presidents who served less than one year.

• He was the eighth of 14 vice presidents

who served less than one term.

• Cleveland and Hendricks were the 23rd of 41 president-vice president teams.

Age at inauguration: 65 years, 178 days

State represented: Indiana

• He was the second of four vice presidents who represented Indiana.

• He was the seventh of 13 vice presidents who represented states that were not their native states.

Political party: Democratic

• He was the eighth of 16 vice presidents who were Democrats

Date of death: Nov. 25, 1885 (died in office)

• He was the fourth of six vice presidents who died before completing their first terms.

• He was the fifth of seven vice presidents who died in office.

Place of death: Indianapolis, Ind.

• He was the first of two vice presidents who died in Indiana. The other was Fairbanks.

Age at death: 66 years, 79 days

Place of burial: Indianapolis, Ind.

• He was the second of four vice presidents who were buried in Indiana.

THE CABINET

State: Thomas Francis Bayard of Delaware, Mar. 7, 1885, to Mar. 6, 1889

Treasury; Daniel Manning of New York, Mar. 8, 1885, to Mar. 31, 1887

• Charles Stebbins Fairchild of New York, Apr. 1, 1887, to Mar. 6, 1889

War: William Crowninshield Endicott of Massachusetts, Mar. 5, 1885, to Mar. 5, 1889

Attorney General: Augustus Hill Garland of Arkansas, Mar. 6, 1885, to Mar. 5, 1889

Navy: William Collins Whitney of New York, Mar. 7, 1885, to Mar. 5, 1889

Postmaster General: William Freeman Vilas of Wisconsin, Mar. 6, 1885, to Jan. 16, 1888

• Donald McDonald Dickinson of Michigan, Jan. 16, 1888, to Mar. 5, 1889

Interior: Lucius Quintus Cincinnatus Lamar of Mississippi, Mar. 6, 1885, to Jan. 10, 1888

• William Freeman Vilas of Wisconsin, Jan. 16, 1888, to Mar. 5, 1889

Agriculture: Norman Jay Colman of Missouri, Feb. 15, 1889, to Mar. 6, 1889

THE SUPREME COURT

Chief Justice: Melville Weston Fuller of Illinois, appointed, Apr. 30, 1888; confirmed, July 20, 1888

Associate Justice: Lucius Quintus Cincinnatus Lamar of Mississippi, appointed, Dec. 6, 1887; confirmed, Jan. 16, 1888

BENJAMIN HARRISON

Full name: Benjamin Harrison
• He was the second of four presidents who had the same surname as a previous president. He was the grandson of William Henry Harrison.
• He was the only president whose grandfather had been president.
• He was the 15th of 17 presidents who did not have middle initials or middle names.
Date of birth: Aug. 20, 1833
• He was the first of three presidents who were born in August.
Place of birth: North Bend, Ohio
• He was the fourth of seven presidents who were born in Ohio.
• His birthplace was destroyed by fire.
Family lineage: English-Scottish
• He was the second of two presidents who were of English-Scottish ancestry. The other was Grant.
Religious denomination: Presbyterian
• He was the fourth of six presidents who were Presbyterians.
College: Miami University, Oxford, Ohio
• He was the only president who went to Miami.
• He was the 15th of 27 presidents who attended college.

Date of graduation: probably June 24, 1852, Bachelor of Arts
• He was the 11th of 21 presidents who were graduated from college.

PARENTS AND SIBLINGS

Father's name: John Scott Harrison
Date of birth: Oct. 4, 1804
Place of birth: Vincennes, Ind.
Occupation: Farmer
Date of death: May 25, 1878
Place of death: North Bend, Ohio
Age at death: 73 years, 233 days

Father's first wife: Lucretia Knapp Johnson Harrison
Date of birth: Sept. 16, 1804
Place of birth: Boone County, Ky.
Date of marriage: 1824
Children: 3; 2 daughters, 1 son
• Elizabeth was born in 1825, William Henry in 1827, and Sarah Lucretia in 1829. William Henry died in infancy.
• Harrison was the fourth of six presidents who had half brothers or half sisters.
Date of death: Feb. 6, 1830

Place of death: *Unknown*
Age at death: 25 years, 143 days

Mother's name: Elizabeth Ramsey Irwin Harrison
Date of birth: July 18, 1810
Place of birth: Mercersburg, Pa.
Date of marriage: Aug. 12, 1831
• Harrison was the third of five presidents whose mothers were second wives.
Children: 10; 7 sons, 3 daughters
• Archibald Irwin was born in 1832; Benjamin in 1833; Mary Jane in 1835; Anna Symmes in 1837; John Irwin in 1839; Carter Bassett in 1840; Anna Symmes in 1842; John Scott in 1844; James Findlay in 1847; and James Irwin in 1849. Four of the children died in infancy: Anna Symmes in 1838; John Irwin in 1839; James Findlay in 1848; and James Irwin in 1850.
• Benjamin was his mother's second child.
• He was his father's fifth child.
• He was the only president who came from a family of 13 children.
Date of death: Aug. 15, 1850.
• Benjamin was 16 years, 360 days old when his mother died.
Place of death: probably North Bend, Ohio
Age at death: 40 years, 28 days

MARRIAGE

Date of first marriage: Oct. 20, 1853
Place of first marriage: Oxford, Ohio
• Harrison was the fourth of seven presidents who were married in Ohio.
Age at first marriage: 20 years, 61 days
• He was the 16th of 27 presidents who married in their twenties.
Years married: 39 years, 5 days

First wife's name: Caroline Lavinia Scott Harrison
• She was the 19th of 33 first ladies.
• She was the 24th of 40 wives of presidents.
Date of birth: Oct. 1, 1832
• She was the second of four first ladies who were born in October.
• She was the fourth of six wives of presidents who were born in October.
Place of birth: Oxford, Ohio
• She was the third of six first ladies who were born in Ohio.
• She was the third of six wives of presidents who were born in Ohio.

First wife's mother: Mary Potts Neal Scott
First wife's father: John Witherspoon Scott, Presbyterian minister and college professor
• Harrison was the fourth of five presidents who married the daughters of clergymen.
Age at marriage: 21 years, 19 days
• She was the 16th of 26 first ladies who were married in their twenties.
• She was the 20th of 30 wives of presidents who were married in their twenties.
Years older than husband: 323 days
• She was the third of six first ladies who were older than their husbands.
• She was the third of six wives of presidents who were older than their husbands.
Children: 2; 1 son, 1 daughter
• Russell Benjamin was born on Aug. 12, 1854, and Mary Scott on Apr. 3, 1858.
• Harrison was the 15th of 19 presidents who had both male and female children.
• He was the 18th of 30 presidents who had children.
Date of death: Oct. 25, 1892
• She was the second of three first ladies who died while their husbands were in office.
Place of death: White House, Washington, D.C.
• She was the second of three first ladies who died in the White House.
• She was the sixth of nine first ladies who died in Washington.
• She was the sixth of nine wives of presidents who died in Washington.
Age at death: 60 years, 24 days
Place of burial: Indianapolis, Ind.
• She was the only first lady who was buried in Indiana.
• She was the first of two wives of presidents who were buried in Indiana. The other was Mary Harrison.
Years he survived his first wife: 8 years, 139 days
• Harrison was the 11th of 14 presidents who survived their wives.

Date of second marriage: Apr. 6, 1896
• Harrison was the second of two presidents who remarried after the expiration of their terms. The other was Fillmore.
• He was the third of five presidents who remarried.
Place of second marriage: New York, N.Y.
• He was the fourth of five presidents who were married in New York City.
• He was the sixth of seven presidents who

were married in New York.
Age at second marriage: 62 years, 230 days
•He was the only president who was married in his sixties.
•He was the president who married at the most advanced age.
Years married: 4 years, 341 days

Second wife's name: Mary Scott Lord Dimmick Harrison
•Harrison was the fifth of six presidents who married widows. She was the widow of Walter Erskine Dimmick, who had died in 1882.
•She was the second of three widows who became the second wives of presidents.
•She was the sixth of seven wives of presidents who were not first ladies.
•She was the 25th of 40 wives of presidents.
Date of birth: Apr. 30, 1858
•She was the second of two wives of presidents who were born in April. The other was Lucretia Garfield.
Place of birth: Honesdale, Pa.
•She was the only wife of a president who was born in Pennsylvania.
Second wife's mother: Elizabeth Scott Lord
•Harrison's second wife was the niece of his first wife; Caroline Lavinia Scott Harrison and Elizabeth Scott Lord were sisters.
Second wife's father: Farnham Lord, engineer and canal company manager
Age at marriage: 37 years, 341 days
•She was the first of three wives of presidents who married in their thirties.

Years younger than husband: 24 years, 253 days
Children: 1 daughter
•Elizabeth was born on Feb. 21, 1897.
•Harrison was the second of three presidents who had children by both wives.
•He was the fourth of seven presidents who had three children.
Years she survived her husband: 46 years, 298 days
•She was the 14th of 23 wives of presidents who survived their husbands.
Date of death: Jan. 5, 1948
Place of death: New York, N.Y.
•She was the second of five wives of presidents who died in New York City.
•She was the fourth of eight wives of presidents who died in New York.
Age at death: 89 years, 250 days
•She was the wife of a president who lived to the most advanced age.
•She had celebrated her 85th birthday, Apr. 30, 1943.
•She was the tenth of 17 wives of presidents who lived to be 70.
•She was the eighth of 15 wives of presidents who lived to be 75.
•She was the sixth of ten wives of presidents who lived to be 80.
•She was the fourth of seven wives of presidents who lived to be 85.
Place of burial: Indianapolis, Ind.
•She was the second of two wives of presidents who were buried in Indiana. The other was Caroline Harrison.

EARLY YEARS

1836–1847, attended local school, also was tutored at home, North Bend, Ohio
Fall, 1848, entered Farmer's College, near Cincinnati, Ohio
•This preparatory school, originally called Cary's Academy after its founder, later was renamed Belmont College.
Aug. 15, 1850, his mother died
September, 1850, entered Miami University, Oxford, Ohio
•Harrison enrolled in the junior class.
June 24, 1852, was graduated from Miami University
•He ranked fourth in his class. He was an able debater and was president of the Union Literary Society as a senior.
Fall, 1852, began to read law with Bella-

my Storer, senior partner of Storer and Gwynne, Cincinnati
•He was the 17th of 26 presidents who studied law.
Oct. 20, 1853, married Caroline Lavinia Scott, Oxford
1854, admitted to bar, Cincinnati
•He was the 17th of 23 presidents who were lawyers.
April, 1854, his only son born
•The boy was named Russell Benjamin Harrison.
1855, formed law firm with William Wallace, Indianapolis, Ind.
•His partner was the son of David Wallace, who had been governor of Indiana, 1837–1840, and the brother of Lew Wallace, who

later served as a Union major general, governor of New Mexico, and minister to Turkey. Lew Wallace wrote *Ben Hur.*
• The firm was very successful and did considerable divorce work. Indiana, at the time, had a very lenient divorce law. After the state divorce law was amended in 1859, the firm refused marital cases.
1856, joined Republican party
• He campaigned for John Charles Fremont, the first Republican presidential candidate.
May 5, 1857, elected city attorney, Indianapolis
1858, declined to run for state legislature
1858, appointed secretary of Republican state central committee
• He held this post until 1860.
Apr. 3, 1858, his first daughter born
• The girl was named Mary Scott Harrison.
Feb. 5, 1860, nominated for reporter of Indiana supreme court
Oct. 9, 1860, elected as reporter of Indiana supreme court
Jan. 13, 1861, took office as reporter of supreme court
• Elected to a four-year term, he served until he entered military service.
Feb. 11, 1861, member of committee that greeted Lincoln, en route to Washington, Indianapolis
Dec. 11, 1861, formed law firm with William Pinkney Fishback
• His former partner, William Wallace, had been elected county clerk.
July 14, 1862, commissioned as second lieutenant, 70th Indiana Infantry
• Harrison was the sixth of seven presidents who served in the Civil War.
• He was the 14th of 21 presidents who served in the military during wartime.
July 22, 1862, promoted to captain
• He had recruited 85 men.
Aug. 7, 1862, promoted to colonel
• He marched his regiment off to join the Union army at Louisville, Ky., Aug. 13.
Sept. 30, 1862, his regiment's first encounter with enemy, Russellville, Ky.
• The regiment spent the next 15 months in Kentucky and Tennessee.
Jan. 9, 1864, assigned command of First Brigade, First Division, XI Army Corps
Feb. 23, 1864, nominated for reporter of Indiana supreme court
• He did not receive word of his nomination until six weeks later. He accepted by letter, Apr. 27, conditional on his release

from the army.
Feb. 24, 1864, his brigade departed for Georgia from Nashville, Tenn.
• In an army reorganization, he and his Indiana volunteers were transferred to the First Brigade, Third Division, XX Army Corps.
May 14–15, 1864, participated in Battle of Resaca, Ga.
• This was his first time under fire.
May 25–27, 1864, participated in Battle of New Hope Church, Dallas, Ga.
June 16, 1864, participated in action at Golgotha, near Kenesaw Mountain, Ga.
June 29, 1864, assigned command of First Brigade, Third Division, XX Army Corps
• Shortly before this he had been afflicted with a hand infection. He began to wear kid gloves for protection, a habit which cost him votes among the working class in his later life.
July 20, 1864, participated in Battle of Peach Tree Creek, Ga.
• Following this battle he was recommended for promotion to brigadier general by General Joseph Hooker, commanding officer of the XX Corps.
Sept. 1, 1864, fall of Atlanta, Ga.
• The XX Corps entered the evacuated city, Sept. 2. Harrison was ordered to report to Governor Oliver P. Morton of Indiana for special duty.
Sept. 20, 1864, reported to Governor Morton, Indianapolis
• After a brief furlough, he was ordered to devote himself to recruiting. Unofficially, he was encouraged to do some electioneering.
September—October, 1864, made a series of speeches on behalf of state and national Republican candidates, including himself
Oct. 11, 1864, elected reporter of Indiana supreme court
Nov. 9, 1864, departed from Indianapolis to rejoin XX Corps
Dec. 15–16, 1864, participated in Battle of Nashville, Tenn.
Jan. 16, 1865, relieved of duty, given furlough
Jan. 23, 1865, brevetted brigadier general of volunteers
• He was the 11th of 12 presidents who were generals.
Jan. 30, 1865, stricken with scarlet fever, Narrowsburg, N.Y.
• He was bedridden for several weeks.

Feb. 26, 1865, sailed from New York City to rejoin XX Corps

Mar. 2, 1865, arrived at Savannah, Ga.

•He had been ordered to report to General William T. Sherman, but Sherman had long departed for the Carolinas. Harrison was temporarily assigned to command a camp for convalescents and recruits in South Carolina.

Apr. 19, 1865, rejoined XX Corps, Goldsboro, N.C.

•On the day of his arrival, word was received of Lincoln's assassination. Harrison delivered the eulogy at the camp service.

Apr. 26, 1865, witnessed surrender of General Joseph E. Johnston to General Sherman, Durham's Station, N.C.

May 9, 1865, received commission as brigadier general, Richmond, Va.

June 8, 1865, honorably discharged from army

June 16, 1865, returned to Indianapolis

•He resumed his law practice and his duties as reporter of the state supreme court. His law firm was now Porter, Harrison and Fishback. Albert G. Porter later was governor of Indiana.

1870, his partner, William P. Fishback, resigned to assume editorship of Indianapolis *Journal*

•Fishback was succeeded in the firm by Judge Cyrus C. Hines.

May, 1871, served as defense attorney in Milligan case

•Lambdin P. Milligan, a member of the subversive Knights of the Golden Circle (whose password was "Nu-oh-lac," which was Calhoun, backwards), had been tried by a military commission for conspiracy in 1864, and was sentenced to be hanged. The sentence was commuted to life imprisonment. Later, the Supreme Court, in its landmark decision, *Ex parte Milligan*, ruled that the military commission had no jurisdiction, and Milligan was released, Apr. 2, 1866. Milligan brought civil suit against 22 persons involved.

•Harrison was appointed for the defense by President Grant. Since the Supreme Court decision made certain the plaintiff's right of recovery, his task was to mitigate the damages by emphasizing Milligan's treasonable activities. Milligan sued for $100,-000; the jury found in Milligan's favor, May 30, but awarded damages of only $5.

Feb. 22, 1872, defeated for nomination for governor, Republican state convention

•He declined the nomination for Congressman-at-large.

Aug. 4, 1876, nominated for governor by state central committee

•The state convention had nominated Godlove S. Orth, minister to Austria-Hungary, the previous February. Orth withdrew, Aug. 2.

Aug. 7, 1876, accepted nomination for governor

•He knew nothing of the nomination, since he was vacationing in Michigan. He returned, Aug. 5, and was surprised to be greeted by a crowd of five thousand, a brass band, and a cannon.

Oct. 10, 1876, defeated for governor of Indiana by James D. ("Blue Jeans") Williams

•The vote was so close that the outcome was uncertain until three days after the election.

May 25, 1878, his father died

June 28, 1879, appointed to Mississippi River Commission by Hayes

•He declined at first but reconsidered after receiving the official commission and a personal letter from Hayes.

Aug. 4, 1879, met with Hayes, White House

•He formally accepted the commissionership the following day and served to Mar. 3, 1881.

June 2–8, 1880, chairman of Indiana delegation, Republican national convention, Chicago, Ill.

Summer, 1880, campaigned for Garfield and Arthur

•An unreconstructed rebel who was annoyed at Harrison's speech in Bloomington, Ill., pulled a gun, which failed to fire. The dissenter was dragged from the hall.

NATIONAL PROMINENCE

Jan. 18, 1881, elected to Senate

•Harrison was the 11th of 16 presidents who were elected to the Senate.

Mar. 4, 1881, took seat in Senate

•He declined a post in the Garfield cabinet.

•He was the tenth of 15 presidents who served in the Senate.

June 3, 1884, attended Republican national

convention as delegate-at-large, Chicago, Ill.
• He returned to Indianapolis when it became obvious that his name was to be put into nomination. James G. Blaine received the nomination on the fourth ballot.
Feb. 5, 1887, defeated for reelection to Senate
• The Democrats had gained control of the state legislature and had gerrymandered the state. The state senate was deadlocked for 15 ballots and finally elected David Turpie on the 16th.
Feb. 22, 1888, opened campaign for presidency, Detroit, Mich.
• In a speech to the Michigan Club, he said, "I am a dead statesman, but I am a living and rejuvenated Republican." The phrase, "Rejuvenated Republicanism," became the slogan of his backers.
June 25, 1888, nominated for president, Republican national convention, Chicago, Ill.
• He received 83 votes on the first ballot, when John Sherman of Ohio led with 225. Harrison was nominated on the eighth ballot.
Nov. 6, 1888, election day
• *See* Election of 1888, below.
Jan. 14, 1889, presidential electors cast ballots
• He received 233 of the 401 electoral votes from the 38 states.
• *See* Election of 1888, below.
Feb. 13, 1889, electoral vote tabulated by Congress
• Harrison and Morton were officially declared elected.

ELECTION OF 1888

Industrial Reform party, convened, Feb. 22, at Washington, D.C., nominated Albert Redstone of California for president, John Colvin of Kansas for vice president.
Equal Rights party, convened, May 15, at Des Moines, Iowa, nominated Belva Ann Bennett Lockwood of Washington, D.C., for president, Alfred Love of Pennsylvania for vice president. Love declined; Charles Stuart Wells became the party's vice-presidential candidate.
Union Labor party, convened, May 16, at Cincinnati, Ohio, nominated Alson Jenness Streeter of Illinois for president, Charles

Cunningham of Arkansas for vice president.
United Labor party, convened, May 17, at Cincinnati, Ohio, nominated Robert Hall Cowdrey of Illinois for president, William H. T. Wakefield of Kansas for vice president.
Prohibition party, convened, May 31, at Indianapolis, Ind., nominated Clinton Bowen Fisk of New Jersey for president, John Anderson Brooks of Missouri for vice president.
Democratic party, convened, June 5, at St. Louis, Mo., nominated Grover Cleveland of New York for president, Allen Granberry Thurman of Ohio for vice president.
• This was the 15th Democratic national convention. It was the second Democratic convention in St. Louis; it was the second major party convention in St. Louis.
Republican party, convened, June 19, at Chicago, Ill., nominated Benjamin Harrison of Indiana for president, Levi Parsons Morton of New York for vice president.
• This was the ninth Republican national convention. It was the fifth Republican convention in Chicago; it was the seventh major party convention in Chicago.
American party, convened, Aug. 15, at Philadelphia, Pa., nominated James Langdon Curtis of New York for president, Peter Dinwiddie Wigginton of California for vice president.
Election day, Tuesday, Nov. 6, 1888
Popular vote: 11,388,037
　　　Cleveland, 5,540,329
　　　Harrison, 5,439,853
　　　Fisk, 249,506
　　　Streeter, 146,934
　　　Cowdrey, 2,818
　　　Curtis, 1,591
　　　others, 7,006
• Harrison was the ninth of 15 presidents who were elected without receiving a majority of the popular vote.
Electoral vote: 401, 38 states
　• Harrison, 233, 20 states
　　　(California, 8; Colorado, 3; Illinois, 22; Indiana, 15; Iowa, 13; Kansas, 9; Maine, 6; Massachusetts, 14; Michigan, 13; Minnesota, 7; Nebraska, 5; Nevada, 3; New Hampshire, 4; New York, 36; Ohio, 23; Oregon, 3; Pennsylvania, 30; Rhode Island, 4; Vermont, 4; Wisconsin, 11)
　• Cleveland, 168, 18 states

(Alabama, 10; Arkansas, 7; Connecticut, 6; Delaware, 3; Florida, 4; Georgia, 12; Kentucky, 13; Louisiana, 8; Maryland, 8; Mississippi, 9; Missouri, 16;

New Jersey, 9; North Carolina, 11; South Carolina, 9; Tennessee, 12; Texas, 13; Virginia, 12; West Virginia, 6)

THE PRESIDENT (23rd)

Term of office: Mar. 4, 1889, to Mar. 4, 1893 (4 years)
•Harrison was the 15th of 19 presidents who served one term or less than one term.
•He was the eighth of ten presidents who served for four years.
State represented: Indiana
•He was the only president who represented Indiana.
•He was the tenth of 15 presidents who represented states that were not their native states.
Political party: Republican
•He was the sixth of 14 presidents who

were Republicans.
Congresses: 51st, 52nd
Administration: 26th
Age at inauguration: 55 years, 196 days
•He was the 12th of 21 presidents who were younger than their vice presidents. Harrison was nine years, 96 days younger than Morton.
Inauguration day: Monday, Mar. 4, 1889
•Harrison took the oath of office, administered by Chief Justice Melville W. Fuller, on the east portico of the Capitol.
•This was the first of six inaugurations at which Fuller officiated.

THE 26th ADMINISTRATION

1889

Mar. 5, appointed his first secretary of state, James G. Blaine; his first secretary of treasury, William Windom; his first secretary of war, Redfield Proctor; his only attorney general, William H. H. Miller; his only secretary of navy, Benjamin F. Tracy; his only postmaster general, John Wanamaker; his only secretary of interior, John W. Noble; and his only secretary of agriculture, Jeremiah M. Rusk
•Tracy and Rusk took office, Mar. 6; Blaine, Windom, and Noble, Mar. 7.
•Blaine was the only secretary of state who served under three presidents.
•Blaine was the third of nine executive officers who served in the cabinets of three presidents; he served previously under Garfield and Arthur.
•Windom was the second of three secretaries of treasury who served under three presidents.
•Windom was the fourth of nine executive officers who served in the cabinets of three presidents; he served previously under Garfield and Arthur.
Mar. 21, issued proclamation that warned against entering Bering Sea for unlawful hunting of furbearing animals

Mar. 22, Associate Justice Matthews died
Apr. 30, attended celebration of centennial of Washington inauguration, Washington, D.C.
•Former Presidents Hayes and Cleveland also attended.
Nov. 2, North Dakota and South Dakota admitted as 39th and 40th states
•The Dakotas were the first and second of the six states admitted during Harrison's term of office.
Nov. 8, Montana admitted as 41st state
•Montana was the third of six states admitted during his term of office.
Nov. 11, Washington admitted as 42nd state
•Washington was the fourth of six states admitted during his term of office.
Dec. 2, first session of 51st Congress
•The administration controlled both the Senate and the House of Representatives. The Republicans gained eight Senate and 22 House seats. The Senate (84 members) consisted of 47 Republicans and 37 Democrats. The House (330 members) consisted of 173 Republicans, 156 Democrats, and one other.
Dec. 3, sent his first State of the Union message to Congress
Dec. 4, appointed David J. Brewer as associate justice

• Brewer, who was confirmed by the Senate, Dec. 18, was the first of Harrison's four appointments to the Supreme Court.

Note: Electric lighting was installed in the White House in 1889. Irwin Hood ("Ike") Hoover, who installed the system, remained at the White House for 42 years, mostly as chief usher. In his memoirs, "Forty-two Years in the White House," Hoover wrote: "The Harrison family were afraid to turn the lights on and off for fear of getting a shock."

1890

Jan. 7, gave state dinner for vice president and cabinet, White House

Feb. 4, issued proclamation announcing ratification of Samoan treaty

• This treaty, signed June 14, 1889, in Berlin, placed the Samoan islands under joint control of the U.S., Great Britain, and Germany, The agreement provided a fueling station for the expanding American Pacific fleet.

Feb. 10, issued proclamation that opened part of Sioux reservation for settlement

• About eleven million acres of Sioux territory were opened to general settlement; the land had been ceded to the government in 1889.

Feb. 17, issued proclamation against use of Cherokee Strip for grazing under private contracts with Indians

Mar. 12, Senator Ingalls unanimously designated to preside in Senate during future absences of vice president

• This function had never before been exercised by any member of the Senate.

• Senator John J. Ingalls of Kansas had been chosen president pro tem. of the Senate, Feb. 25, 1886, and continued by successive elections until 1890. He resigned, Feb. 19, 1891.

Mar. 15, issued second proclamation against entering Bering Sea for unlawful hunting of furbearing animals

• The president had been authorized by Congress, Mar. 2, 1889, to declare American dominion over the waters of the Bering Sea—a right disputed by Great Britain.

Apr. 26, vetoed increased indebtedness of Ogden, Utah, bill

• This was the first of his 44 vetoes.

May 2, signed act that established Territory of Oklahoma

• The Oklahoma Territory was the last territory established in the continental U.S.

June 27, appointed national commission for World's Columbian Exposition

• Chicago had been chosen as the site of the exposition by the House of Representatives, Feb. 24. The fair, to commemorate the quadricentennial of the discovery of America, was scheduled for 1892.

June 27, signed dependent pension act

• This act granted pensions to Union veterans of 90 days or more service who were disabled and unable to earn a livelihood. Disablement did not have to be traceable to military service. Pensions were also granted to dependent parents, minor children, and widows of veterans.

• During his administration the number of pensioners rose by nearly 300,000 to 970,-000, and the annual appropriation for pensions increased from $81,000,000 to $135,-000,000.

July 2, signed Sherman Anti-Trust Act

• This act, drafted by the Senate judiciary committee, declared:

> . . . every contract, combination in the form of trust or otherwise, or conspiracy, in restraint of trade or commerce among the several states, or with foreign nations, is hereby declared to be illegal.

July 3, Idaho admitted as 43rd state

• Idaho was the fifth of six states admitted during his term of office.

July 10, Wyoming admitted as 44th state

• Wyoming was the last of the six states admitted during his term of office.

• This was the largest number of states admitted during any presidential administration.

July 11, signed act authorizing bridge across Hudson River between New York and New Jersey

July 14, signed Sherman Silver Purchase Act

• This act required the purchase of 4,500,-000 ounces of silver each month by the treasury department, payment to be made in treasury notes redeemable in gold or silver at the option of the department.

July 29, sent special message to Congress in which he recommended legislation to close mails and express lines of U.S. to lottery companies

Aug. 30, signed act authorizing inspection by the department of agriculture of salted pork or bacon for export
•The act also authorized the inspection of imported food, drink, and cattle.
Sept. 19, signed rivers and harbors act
•Appropriations totalled $24,981,295.
Sept. 25, signed act reserving certain California big tree groves as public parks
•This act established the Sequoia and Yosemite national parks.
Oct. 1, signed act establishing weather bureau, department of agriculture
•Weather information previously had been supplied by the army signal corps.
Oct. 1, first session of 51st Congress adjourned
Oct. 1, pocket vetoed 11 bills
•All were relief and pension bills.
•He pocket vetoed 25 bills during his term in office.
Oct. 6, signed McKinley Tariff Act
•This act raised the tariff rates to 49.5 percent, in order to meet the rates of foreign nations.
Oct. 13, Associate Justice Miller died
Dec. 1, second session of 51st Congress
Dec. 1, sent his second State of the Union message to Congress
Dec. 23, appointed Henry B. Brown as associate justice
•Brown, who was confirmed by the Senate, Dec. 29, was the second of Harrison's four appointments to the Supreme Court.
Dec. 24, issued proclamation announcing World's Columbian Exposition, Chicago, Ill.
•The exposition was to open officially May 1, 1893, and close, Oct. 26, 1893.

Note: The official population, according to the 11th census, was 62,947,714.

1891

Jan. 29, Secretary of Treasury Windom died
Feb. 7, signed reapportionment of House of Representatives act
Feb. 25, appointed his second secretary of treasury, Charles Foster
Mar. 3, signed circuit court of appeals act
•This act created nine courts of appeal and provided for nine additional U.S. circuit judges. The nine courts were formally organized, June 16.

Mar. 3, signed international copyright act
•This act gave British, French, Swiss, and Belgian authors protection in the U.S.
Mar. 3, signed forest reserve act
•This act authorized the closing of timber areas to settlers and establishment of national parks.
Mar. 4, second session of 51st Congress adjourned
•The 51st Congress was nicknamed "The Billion Dollar Congress," since it approved appropriations which totalled slightly less than a billion dollars.
Mar. 4, pocket vetoed ten bills
•Four were relief and pension bills.
Apr. 8, opened patent centennial, Washington, D.C.
Apr. 14–Mar 15, toured South and West
May 20, opened to settlement about 1,600,000 acres of Fort Berthold Indian reservation, S.D.
June 15, issued proclamation announcing temporary agreement with Great Britain in Bering Sea dispute
Aug. 13, ordered Cherokee Strip closed
Sept. 10, issued proclamation that set apart forest reserve adjoining Yellowstone National Park, Wy.
Sept. 18, issued proclamation opening 900,000 acres of Indian land in Oklahoma Territory to settlement
Nov. 5, Secretary of War Proctor resigned
Dec. 5, first session of 52nd Congress
•The administration maintained control of the Senate but lost control of the House of Representatives. The Democrats gained two Senate and 75 House seats. The Senate (88 members) consisted of 47 Republicans, 39 Democrats, and two Populists. The House (333 members) consisted of 231 Democrats, 88 Republicans, and 14 others, mostly Populists.
Dec. 9, sent his third State of the Union message to Congress
•He as much as asked for a declaration of war against Chile. Two American sailors had been killed and 17 injured when attacked by a mob in Valparaiso, Oct. 16.
Dec. 17, appointed his second secretary of war, Stephen B. Elkins

1892

Jan. 11, issued proclamation that set apart forest reserve in New Mexico

Jan. 22, Associate Justice Bradley died

Jan. 27, sent special message to Congress regarding Chile

• The Chilean government apologized officially and agreed to pay an indemnity of $75,000 to the heirs of the dead and injured sailors.

Feb. 11, issued proclamation that set apart Pike's Peak forest reserve, Colo.

Feb. 22, Mrs. Harrison presided at first Continental Congress of Daughters of American Revolution, Washington, D.C.

• Harrison's wife was the first president-general of the DAR, which had been organized in Washington, D.C., 1890.

Apr. 11, issued proclamation that opened greater part of Lake Traverse Indian reservation, N.D., to settlement

Apr. 12, issued proclamation opening to settlement Cheyenne and Arapaho Indian lands, Okla.

May 5, signed Chinese Exclusion Act

• This act extended the exclusion laws for an additional ten years and provided for the registration of Chinese laborers.

June 4, Secretary of State Blaine resigned

June 10, renominated for president, Republican national convention, Minneapolis, Minn.

June 20, sent special message to Congress recommending retaliation against Canada for discrimination against U.S. vessels

June 29, appointed his second secretary of state, John W. Foster

• For the first time, the cabinet included two secretaries with the same surname. For close to eight months, Charles Foster and John W. Foster served together in Harrison's cabinet. They were not related.

• John Foster was the last of Harrison's 11 cabinet appointments.

July 13, signed rivers and harbors act

• This act appropriated $21,153,618 and authorized contracts of $31,555,401.

July 14, sent two thousand troops to Idaho

• A lockout involving three thousand striking miners in the Coeur d'Alene mining district had begun, Apr. 1. Several miners were killed, July 11. The troops suppressed the disturbance and withdrew, July 23.

July 19, vetoed circuit courts of appeals bill

July 19, authorized to contract for eight-thousand-ton armed cruiser and nine-thousand-ton coastline battleship

July 19, appointed George Shiras, Jr., as associate justice

• Shiras, who was confirmed by the Senate, July 26, was the third of Harrison's four appointments to the Supreme Court.

July 26, signed act authorizing tolls or prohibition of passage, St. Mary's Falls canal, Mich.

July 27, signed Indian wars pension act

• Veterans of the Black Hawk, Seminole, and Creek wars and the Cherokee disturbance, were granted pensions of $8 a month.

Aug. 3, vetoed bill to provide for bringing suit against U.S. government

Aug. 5, first session of 52nd Congress adjourned

Aug. 5, pocket vetoed bill to lower height of proposed Ohio River bridge between Cincinnati, Ohio, and Covington, Ky.

Aug. 20, issued proclamation that set tolls for St. Mary's Falls canal, Mich.

• He ordered a toll of 20 cents per ton to be collected as of Sept. 1 from foreign vessels bound for any Canadian port, in retaliation for Canadian measures.

Sept. 1, ordered 20-day quarantine of all immigrant vessels from cholera ports

• Cholera was brought to New York City by the Hamburg-American steamship, *Moravia*, Aug. 30. A total of 22 of the 385 steerage passengers had died during the voyage.

Sept. 5, his letter of acceptance of Republican renomination published

Oct. 15, issued proclamation that opened 1,800,000-acre Crow reservation, Mont., to settlement

Oct. 25, Mrs. Harrison died

Nov. 8, election day

• *See* Election of 1892, pages 271–272.

Dec. 4, second session of 52nd Congress

Dec. 6, sent his fourth and last State of the Union message to Congress

Dec. 9, issued proclamation setting apart South Platte forest reserve, Cal.

Dec. 20, issued proclamations setting apart Battlement forest reserve, Colo., and Afognak forest and fish culture reserve, Alaska

1893

Jan. 4, issued proclamation of Mormon amnesty

• The amnesty was extended to those who agreed to future obedience of the anti-polygamy laws.

Jan. 9, presidential electors cast ballots
• Cleveland received 277 electoral votes. Harrison received 145.
• *See* Election of 1892, pages 271–272.
Jan. 23, Associate Justice Lamar died
Feb. 2, appointed Howell E. Jackson as associate justice
• Jackson, who was confirmed by the Senate, Feb. 18, was the last of Harrison's four appointments to the Supreme Court.
Feb. 8, electoral votes tabulated by Congress
• Cleveland and Stevenson were officially declared elected.
• Harrison was the fifth of seven presidents who were defeated when they sought re-election.
Feb. 14, issued proclamation that set apart Sierra forest reserve, Cal.
Feb. 15, submitted Hawaiian treaty of annexation to Senate
Feb. 15, signed national cholera quarantine act
Feb. 20, issued proclamations that set apart Pacific Coast reserve, Wash., and Grand Canyon forest reserve, Ariz.
Feb. 21, suspended part of St. Mary's Falls tolls proclamation of Aug. 20, 1892
Feb. 23, Secretary of State Foster resigned

• Foster resigned to sit on the Bering Sea tribunal, Paris.
Feb. 25, issued proclamation that set apart Trabuco Canon forest reserve, Cal.
Feb. 27, vetoed bill to prescribe number of district attorneys and marshals in judicial district of Alabama
• This was the last of Harrison's 19 regular vetoes.
Mar. 1, signed diplomatic appropriation act
• This act stipulated that American diplomats should hold rank similar to those of ministers from countries to which they were accredited.
Mar. 2, signed interstate railway safety act
Mar. 2, act to prescribe number of district attorneys and marshals in judicial district of Alabama passed over his veto
• This was his only veto that was overridden.
Mar. 4, second session of 52nd Congress adjourned
• This was the first actual billion dollar Congress. Appropriations totalled $1,026,822,-049.72—about $38,000,000 more than appropriated by the 51st Congress, the so-called "Billion Dollar Congress."
Mar. 4, pocket vetoed three bills
• These were the last of Harrison's 25 pocket vetoes.

THE FORMER PRESIDENT

Mar. 4, 1893, attended inauguration of Cleveland
• Harrison's age upon leaving office was 59 years, 196 days.
• He attended a reception in his honor that evening at the home of his former postmaster general, John Wanamaker.
March, 1893, returned to Indianapolis, Ind.
• He resumed the practice of law and soon built one of the best practices in the country. He appeared often before the Supreme Court.
• His home in Indianapolis, 1230 North Delaware Street, a National Historic Landmark, is owned by the Arthur Jordan Foundation and operated by the President Benjamin Harrison Foundation. It is open to the public daily, 10 A.M. to 4 P.M., and Sundays, 12:30 to 4 P.M. Closed from Christmas to New Year's Day. Admission: adults, $1; children, 50 cents.
1893, his public papers and addresses as

president published by Government Printing Office
Spring, 1894, gave series of lectures, Stanford University, Palo Alto, Cal.
• These lectures on constitutional law included "The Development of the National Constitution;" "The Colonial Charters;" "Legal Aspects of the Controversy Between the American Colonies and Great Britain;" "Early Attempts at Union and the Union de Facto;" "The Confederation;" and "The Institution of State Governments."
• He was the first of two former presidents who were law professors. The other was Taft.
Feb. 4, 1896, refused to seek Republican nomination for president
• "There has never been an hour since I left the White House that I have felt a wish to return to it," he wrote John Gowdy of Indianapolis. He would not consent to his

name being presented to the convention.
Apr. 6, 1896, married Mary Scott Lord Dimmick, New York City
• His son and daughter refused to attend his marriage to their first cousin. His second wife was the niece of his first wife and had served as the first lady's secretary in the White House.
Feb. 21, 1897, his second daughter born
• The girl was named Elizabeth Harrison. She was the only child of his second marriage.
• He was the second of three former presidents who became fathers.
1897, his book, *This County of Ours*, published by Scribner, New York City
• Much of the material had appeared as a series of articles in *Ladies Home Journal*, 1896–1897. The book sold about fifteen thousand copies. It was published in England under the title, *The Constitution and Administration of the United States of America*. It also was translated into Spanish.
• He was the eighth of 21 presidents who wrote books that were published during their lifetimes.
1897, appointed chief counsel to represent Venezuela in boundary dispute with Great Britain
• He and his staff prepared for the case for two years.
1898, visited Yellowstone National Park
• The park was still undeveloped.
1899, argued Venezuela case before arbitration tribunal, Paris
• His closing argument lasted 25 hours. Most of the Venezuelan claims, which involved the British Guinea border, were upheld.
November, 1899, returned to U.S.
• Following the trial he and his wife toured France, Belgium, Germany, and England.
• He was the fifth of eight former presidents who visited Europe.
April, 1900, presided at Ecumenical Conference of Foreign Missions, New York City
• He had served as an elder of the Presbyterian Church for 40 years. He served as a lay member of the church's general assembly at times and presided at several important conferences, including this meeting of two thousand delegates.
Nov. 24, 1900, appointed to Permanent Court of Arbitration by McKinley
• The court had been established by the

Hague Conference on Peace, 1899. Harrison was not called upon to act in connection with any case.
1901, his postadministration addresses and writings published by Bobbs-Merrill, Indianapolis
• Compiled by his wife, Mary Lord Harrison, his speeches and articles were published under the title, *Views of An Ex-President.*

DEATH

Date of death: Mar. 13, 1901
Place of death: Indianapolis, Ind.
• Harrison was the only president who died in Indiana.
Age at death: 67 years, 205 days
• He lived eight years and nine days after the completion of his term.
Cause of death: Pneumonia
Place of burial: Indianapolis, Ind.
• He was the only president who was buried in Indiana.

THE VICE PRESIDENT (22nd)

Full name: Levi Parsons Morton
Date of birth: May 16, 1824
Place of birth: Shoreham, Vt.
• Morton was the second of three vice presidents who were born in Vermont.
Religious denomination: Episcopalian
• He was the fifth of eight vice presidents who were Episcopalians.
Occupation: Banker
• His business career began in Hanover, N.Y., about 1845, and Boston, Mass., 1850; dry goods business in New York City, 1854; organized his banking firm, 1863; formed Morton, Bliss and Company, 1869; served as member of House of Representatives, 1879–1881; minister to France, appointed by President Garfield, 1881–1885.
• He was the 15th of 21 vice presidents who served in the House of Representatives before their terms of office.
Term of office: Mar. 4, 1889, to Mar. 4, 1893 (4 years)
• He was the tenth of 17 vice presidents who served four-year terms.
• Harrison and Morton were the 24th of 41 president-vice president teams.
Age at inauguration: 64 years, 292 days

State represented: New York
•He was the eighth of ten vice presidents who represented New York.
•He was the eighth of 13 vice presidents who represented states that were not their native states.
Political party: Republican
•He was the sixth of 15 vice presidents who were Republicans.
Occupations after term: Banker, governor
•He was governor of New York, 1895–1897; organized the Morton Trust Company, 1899.
•He was the tenth of 14 vice presidents who served as state governors.
•He was the only vice president who served as a state governor after his term of office.
Date of death: May 16, 1920
•He was the only vice president who died on his birthday.
Place of death: Rhinebeck, N.Y.
•He was the seventh of nine vice presidents who died in New York.
Age at death: 96 years
Place of burial: Rhinebeck, N.Y.
•He was the seventh of nine vice presidents who were buried in New York.

THE CABINET

State: James Gillespie Blaine of Maine, Mar. 7, 1889, to June 4, 1892
•John Watson Foster of Indiana, June 29, 1892, to Feb. 23, 1893

Treasury: William Windom of Minnesota, Mar. 7, 1889, to Jan. 29, 1891
•Charles Foster of Ohio, Feb. 25, 1891, to Mar. 6, 1893
War: Redfield Proctor of Vermont, Mar. 5, 1889, to Nov. 5, 1891
•Stephen Benton Elkins of West Virginia, Dec. 17, 1891, to Mar. 5, 1893
Attorney General: William Henry Harrison Miller of Indiana, Mar. 5, 1889, to Mar. 6, 1893
Navy: Benjamin Franklin Tracy of New York, Mar. 6, 1889, to Mar. 6, 1893
Postmaster General: John Wanamaker of Pennsylvania, Mar. 5, 1889, to Mar. 6, 1893
Interior: John Willock Noble of Missouri, Mar. 5, 1889, to Mar. 6, 1893
Agriculture: Jeremiah McLain Rusk of Wisconsin, Mar. 6, 1889, to Mar. 6, 1893

THE SUPREME COURT

Associate Justices: David Josiah Brewer of Kansas, appointed, Dec. 4, 1889; confirmed, Dec. 18, 1889
•Henry Billings Brown of Michigan, appointed, Dec. 23, 1890; confirmed, Dec. 29, 1890
•George Shiras, Jr., of Pennsylvania, appointed, July 19, 1892; confirmed, July 26, 1892
•Howell Edmunds Jackson of Tennessee, appointed, Feb. 2, 1893; confirmed, Feb. 18, 1893

GROVER CLEVELAND

Republican party, convened, June 7, at Minneapolis, Minn., nominated Benjamin Harrison of Indiana for president, Whitelaw Reid of New York for vice president.
•This was the tenth Republican national convention. It was the only major convention held in Minneapolis.
Democratic party, convened, June 21, at Chicago, Ill., nominated Grover Cleveland of New York for president, Adlai Ewing Stevenson of Illinois for vice president.
•This was the 16th Democratic national convention. It was the third Democratic convention held in Chicago; it was the eighth major party convention held in Chicago.
Prohibition party, convened, June 29, at Cincinnati, Ohio, nominated John Bidwell of California for president, James Britton Cranfill of Texas for vice president.
People's (Populist) party, convened, July 2, at Omaha, Neb., nominated James Baird Weaver of Iowa for president, James Gaven Field of Virginia for vice president.
•This was the first Populist convention. It

was the only major convention held in Omaha.
Socialist Labor party, convened, Aug. 28, at New York City, nominated Simon Wing of Massachusetts for president, Charles Horatio Matchett of New York for vice president.
Election day, Tuesday, Nov. 8, 1892
Popular vote: 12,074,398
　　Cleveland, 5,556,918
　　Harrison, 5,176,108
　　Weaver, 1,041,028
　　Bidwell, 264,133
　　Wing, 21,164
•Cleveland was the tenth of 15 presidents who were elected without receiving a majority of the popular vote.
•He was the first of two presidents who were elected twice without receiving majorities of the popular vote. The other was Wilson.
•Cleveland was the first of two presidents who received pluralities of the popular vote in three elections. The other was Franklin D. Roosevelt.
Electoral vote: 444, 44 states
　• Cleveland, 277, 23 states

(Alabama, 11; Arkansas, 8; California, 8 of 9 votes; Connecticut, 6; Delaware, 3; Florida, 4; Georgia, 13; Illinois, 24; Indiana, 15; Kentucky, 13; Louisiana, 8; Maryland, 8; Mississippi, 9; Missouri, 17; New Jersey, 10; New York, 36; North Carolina, 11; South Carolina, 9; Tennessee, 12; Texas, 15; Virginia, 12; West Virginia, 6; Wisconsin, 12)
• Cleveland also received the votes of one elector from North Dakota, one from Ohio, and five from Michigan.
  • Harrison, 145, 16 states
    (Iowa, 13; Maine, 6; Massachusetts, 15; Michigan, 9 of 14 votes; Minnesota, 9; Montana, 3; Nebraska, 8; New Hampshire, 4; Ohio, 22 of 23 votes; Oregon,

3 of 4 votes; Pennsylvania, 32; Rhode Island, 4; South Dakota, 4; Vermont, 4; Washington, 4; Wyoming, 3)
• Harrison also received the votes of one elector from North Dakota and one from California.
  • Weaver, 22, four states
    (Colorado, 4; Idaho, 3; Kansas, 10; Nevada, 3)
• Weaver also received the votes of one elector from North Dakota and one from Oregon.

Note: None of the candidates won North Dakota, since the electoral vote in that state was divided evenly between Cleveland, Harrison, and Weaver.

THE PRESIDENT (24th)

Term of office: Mar. 4, 1893, to Mar. 4, 1897 (4 years)
• Cleveland was the eighth of 12 presidents who were elected to second terms.
• Cleveland had served as the 22nd president. *See* pages 248–257.
• He was the eighth of 16 presidents who served more than one term.
• He was the seventh of nine presidents who served two terms.
• He was the only president who served nonconsecutive terms.
• He was the sixth of eight presidents who served for eight years.
Congresses: 53rd, 54th
Administration: 27th

Age at second inauguration: 55 years, 351 days
• He was the 13th of 21 presidents who were younger than their vice presidents. Cleveland was one year, 144 days younger than Stevenson.
• He was the second of two presidents who were younger than both of their vice presidents. The other was Madison.
Second inauguration day: Saturday, Mar. 4, 1893
• Cleveland took the oath of office, administered by Chief Justice Melville W. Fuller, on the east portico of the Capitol.
• This was the second of six inaugurations at which Fuller officiated.

THE 27th ADMINISTRATION

1893

Mar. 5, appointed his first secretary of state, Walter Q. Gresham; his only secretary of treasury, John G. Carlisle; his only secretary of war, David S. Lamont; his first attorney general, Richard Olney; his only secretary of navy, Hilary A. Herbert; his first postmaster general, Wilson S. Bissell; his first secretary of interior, Hoke Smith; and his only secretary of agriculture, Julius S. Morton
• Olney, Bissell, and Smith took office, Mar. 6; Gresham, Carlisle, Herbert, and Morton, Mar. 7.

Mar. 9, withdrew Hawaiian annexation treaty from Senate
Mar. 13, received Prince Kaiulani of Hawaii, White House
Mar. 24, was informed Great Britain and France had elevated representatives in U.S. to rank of ambassador
Mar. 30, appointed Thomas F. Bayard as ambassador to Great Britain
• Bayard, who was confirmed by the Senate, Apr. 3, was the first ambassador of the U.S.
Apr. 27, attended International Columbian naval review, New York City
• Ten nations, including the U.S., were

represented by 36 warships.

May 1, formally opened World's Columbian Exposition, Chicago, Ill.

•This was the official opening of the World's Fair, although it had been open to the general public since Oct. 20, 1892.

June 27, Panic of 1893

•The gold reserve, which had been declining steadily since 1890, had fallen below $90,000,000 in April. Stocks on the New York exchange had dropped sharply, May 5; the market crashed, June 27. The precipitous situation was traceable to the McKinley Tariff Act, which had decreased revenue, and the pension acts, which had depleted the surplus.

•This was the sixth of nine U.S. depressions

June 30, called special session of Congress, Aug. 7

July 1, secretly operated on for cancer

•Most of Cleveland's upper left jaw, part of his palate, and two contiguous teeth were removed during a secret operation aboard the yacht, *Oneida*, owned by Commodore Elias C. Benedict, on Long Island Sound. A second operation to remove additional malignant tissue was performed aboard the yacht, July 17.

•When Cleveland arrived at his summer home in Buzzard's Bay, Mass., it was announced that two ulcerated teeth had been extracted. The details of the cancer operation remained a secret until 1917, when a full account appeared in the *Saturday Evening Post*, written by Dr. William W. Keen of Philadelphia. Keen had assisted Dr. Joseph Bryant of New York City, who had performed the operations.

•An accurate account of the clandestine surgery by E. J. Edwards, who wrote under the pseudonym, *Holland*, was published in the Philadelphia *Press*, Aug. 29. Edwards was denounced as a scandalmongering liar. His source, Dr. Ferdinand Hasbrouck, a young New York City dentist who had administered the new anesthesia, nitrous oxide ("laughing gas"), was discredited by presidential aides. Hasbrouck had bungled a routine extraction, it was said, and had invented the cancer story in revenge for having been discharged.

July 7, Associate Justice Blatchford died

Aug. 7, first session of 53rd Congress

•The administration controlled both the Senate and the House of Representatives. The Democrats gained five Senate seats but lost 11 House seats. The Senate (88 members) consisted of 44 Democrats, 38 Republicans, three others, and three vacancies. The House (357 members) consisted of 220 Democrats, 126 Republicans, and 11 others.

Aug. 8, sent special message to Congress in which he urged repeal of Sherman Silver Purchase Act

Aug. 23, issued proclamation that opened Cherokee Strip, Okla., to settlement, Sept. 16

•This was the largest and best known of the Oklahoma "runs."

•About ninety thousand persons registered as intended settlers on the six million acres and poised on the border, Sept. 16. It is estimated that twenty thousand crossed the border "sooner," as others had done in 1889 and 1891. These land rush violations gave Oklahoma its nickname, the Sooner State.

Sept. 5, addressed Pan-American Medical Congress, Washington, D.C.

•His robust appearance gave credence to the official story that he had a couple of teeth extracted in July, rather than a serious operation. Since the cancer surgery had been performed from inside the mouth, with the aid of a recently developed French cheek retractor, no scar was visible. He also had been fitted with a hard-rubber plug which completely filled the jaw hole.

Sept. 9, his second daughter born

•The girl was named Esther Cleveland.

•Esther was the first of three children born to presidents while in office.

•Esther was the only child of a president who was born in the White House.

Sept. 19, appointed William B. Hornblower as associate justice

•Hornblower, the first of Cleveland's four appointments to the Supreme Court during his second term, was rejected by the Senate, Jan. 15, 1894.

•Cleveland was the 12th of 15 presidents who nominated justices not confirmed by the Senate.

•Hornblower was the 19th of 25 men nominated to the Supreme Court who were not confirmed by the Senate.

Nov. 1, signed act which repealed Sherman Silver Purchase Act

Nov. 3, signed amended Chinese exclusion act

Nov. 3, first session of 53rd Congress adjourned

Dec. 4, second session of 53rd Congress

Dec. 4, sent his first State of the Union message of his second term to Congress

Dec. 18, sent special message to Congress in which he defined his position on Hawaii

• He explained that he would not submit the annexation treaty to the Senate since he considered the provisional government illegal.

1894

Jan. 17, vetoed relief of timber and stone lands purchasers bill

• This was the first of Cleveland's 170 vetoes during his second term.

• This was the first of 44 private relief bills he vetoed during his second term.

• He vetoed 584 bills during his two terms, 105 of which were private relief bills. Only Franklin D. Roosevelt exercised the veto power more often.

Jan. 20, vetoed Hudson River bridge bill

Jan. 22, appointed Wheeler H. Peckham as associate justice

• Peckham, the second of Cleveland's four appointments to the Supreme Court during his second term, was rejected by the Senate, Feb. 16.

• Peckham was the 20th of 25 men nominated to the Supreme Court who were not confirmed by the Senate.

Feb. 19, appointed Edward D. White as associate justice

• White, who was confirmed by the Senate, Feb. 19, was the third of Cleveland's four appointments to the Supreme Court during his second term.

Mar. 29, vetoed coinage of silver bullion bill

Apr. 6, signed act to carry out terms of Bering Sea decision

• The international tribunal had decided, Aug. 15, 1893, that the U.S. had no rights outside the three-mile limit and prohibited sealing within 60 miles of the Pribilof Islands.

June 28, signed Labor Day act

• The first Monday in September was designated a legal holiday.

July 3, ordered U.S. troops to Chicago to enforce federal injunction against Pullman strike

• The Pullman strike, which had begun, May

11, became a general strike and tied up every railroad in the Midwest when the American Railway Union, led by Eugene V. Debs, boycotted the servicing of Pullman cars, June 26. Violence broke out; the railroad association appealed for federal troops to restore order. A federal court issued an injunction which forbade interference with interstate commerce and U.S. mails. Debs was indicted for criminal conspiracy and contempt of court, July 10. The troops were withdrawn, July 20. The union officially ended the walkout, Aug. 3; the strike was broken. Debs was found guilty of contempt and sentenced to six months in prison, Dec. 14.

July 17, signed enabling act to admit Utah as state

July 19, his personal letter to Representative William L. Wilson, in which he condemned the Senate tariff bill, read in House

Aug. 8, recognized new Republic of Hawaii

• The Republic of Hawaii had been proclaimed, July 4.

Aug. 18, signed act that authorized one-million-acre grants to public land states

• The land grants were authorized for irrigation, reclamation, cultivation, and settlement. Funds which accrued to the states as a result of this program were to be used for the reclamation of other lands within the states.

Aug. 27, Tariff Act of 1894 became law without his signature

• The Wilson-Gorman Tariff Act lowered duties to the still highly protective average level of 39.9 percent.

• This act also provided for the first graduated income tax; this section of the act was declared unconstitutional in 1895.

Aug. 28, second session of 53rd Congress adjourned

Aug. 28, pocket vetoed six bills

• Two of the six vetoes were of relief bills. The others were bills to provide for the publishing of District of Columbia railway franchise laws; to amend the District of Columbia revised statutes; to print the agricultural report of 1894; and to authorize a railway through Indian Territory.

• He pocket vetoed 128 bills during his second term. He pocket vetoed 238 bills during his two terms. Only Franklin D. Roosevelt employed the pocket veto power more often.

Sept. 27, issued proclamation that granted amnesty to persons convicted of polygamy under Edmunds act

Sept. 28, issued proclamation that set apart Ashland forest reserve, Ore.

Dec. 3, third session of 53rd Congress

Dec. 3, sent his second State of the Union message of his second term to Congress

Dec. 8, issued proclamation of new Chinese treaty

•The treaty, which regulated immigration, had been ratified by the Senate, Aug. 13.

Dec. 9, issued proclamation of treaty with Japan

Dec. 12, issued executive order that placed internal revenue workers in classified civil service

1895

Feb. 1, vetoed railway right-of-way through San Carlos Indian reservation, Ariz., bill

Feb. 6, decided boundary dispute between Brazil and Argentine Republic

•His decision was in favor of Brazil.

Feb. 7, called J. Pierpont Morgan to White House for gold crisis conference

•The gold reserve had fallen to $41,000,000. Two loans placed with New York bankers had not relieved the situation. A third loan of $62,400,000 was placed with a banking syndicate headed by Morgan and August Belmont.

Feb. 8, sent special message to Congress regarding Morgan-Belmont loan

•He advised Congress that the loan of $62,-400,000 had been made for 30 years at four percent under the act of Jan. 14, 1875.

Feb. 23, vetoed pension to Eunice Putnam bill

•This was the first of 54 pension bills he vetoed during his second term.

•He vetoed 336 pension bills during his two terms.

Mar. 1, accepted resignation of Postmaster General Bissell

Mar. 1, appointed his second postmaster general, William L. Wilson

Mar. 4, third session of 53rd Congress adjourned

Mar. 4, pocket vetoed 57 bills.

•A total of 34 were relief and pension bills. The others included bills to correct military records; to construct a railway bridge across the Sulphur River in Arkansas and

Texas; to authorize two railways through Indian Territory; and to grant the State of Kansas the abandoned Fort Hayes military reservation for the purpose of establishing branches of state colleges.

May 28, Secretary of State Gresham died

June 7, accepted resignation of Attorney General Olney

June 7, appointed his second secretary of state, Richard Olney, and his second attorney general, Judson Harmon

•Harmon took office, June 8; Olney, June 10.

•Olney was the only member of Cleveland's cabinet who headed two executive departments.

June 12, issued proclamation that warned against participation in Cuban filibustering expeditions

•An insurrection against Spanish rule of Cuba had broken out, Feb. 24. Filibustering expeditions organized on American soil were blocked from participation by U.S. naval vessels.

July 7, his third daughter born

•The girl was named Marion Cleveland.

•Marion was the second of three children born to presidents while in office.

Aug. 8, Associate Justice Jackson died

Dec. 2, first session of 54th Congress

•The administration lost control of both the Senate and the House of Representatives. The Democrats lost five Senate and 116 House seats. The Senate (88 members) consisted of 44 Republicans, 39 Democrats, and five others. The House (357 members) consisted of 246 Republicans, 104 Democrats, and seven others.

Dec. 2, sent his third State of the Union message of his second term to Congress

Dec. 3, appointed Rufus W. Peckham as associate justice

•Peckham, who was confirmed by the Senate, Dec., 9, was the last of Cleveland's four appointments to the Supreme Court during his second term.

•Peckham was the last of his six appointments to the Supreme Court during his two terms.

•Peckham was the last of his four appointees who served on the Court.

Dec. 17, laid diplomatic correspondence regarding Venezuelan boundary dispute before Congress

•The dispute between Great Britain and Venezuela concerned the boundary line of British Guiana and dated back to 1814. It would be the duty of the U.S. "to resist by every means in its power" the expropriation of any lands by Great Britain, Cleveland said. He based American interest on the Monroe Doctrine, recommending the appointment of an independent commission to determine the boundary.

1896

Jan. 1, appointed members of Venezuela boundary commission
•The commission, which held its first meeting, Jan. 4, was furnished pertinent information by both Great Britain and Venezuela. A treaty was signed, Feb. 2, 1897, which provided for the submission of the dispute to an arbitration board. The British claims were upheld, and the boundary line was set along the Schomburgk line, Oct. 3, 1899. Venezuela was awarded the mouth of the Orinoco River.
Jan. 4, Utah admitted as 45th state
•Utah was the only state admitted during his term of office.
Feb. 28, Cuban resolution passed in House of Representatives
•The resolution favored the granting of belligerent rights to the Cuban insurrectionists and urged the president to mediate in an attempt to bring peace to Cuba.
Apr. 6, Cuban resolution passed in Senate
•The offer was rejected by Spain, May 22.
June 3, vetoed rivers and harbors bill
June 3, rivers and harbors act passed over his veto
•This was the first of his five vetoes that were overridden during his second term.
June 10, vetoed pension of Francis E. Hoover bill
June 10, pension of Francis E. Hoover act passed over his veto
•This was the second of his five vetoes that were overridden during his second term.
June 11, first session of 54th Congress adjourned
June 11, pocket vetoed 16 bills
•Nine of the 16 vetoes were of relief and pension bills. The others included bills to erect a monument in honor of Samuel Hahnemann in Washington, D.C.; to provide a new division of the eastern judicial district of Texas; to erect a hospital in Biloxi, Miss.; and to extend the time of payments due from settlers and purchasers of

ceded Indian reservations.
July 30, issued second proclamation against Cuban filibusters
Aug. 22, accepted resignation of Secretary of Interior Smith, effective Aug. 31
Aug. 22, appointed his second secretary of interior, David R. Francis
•Francis took office, Sept. 1.
•Francis was the last of Cleveland's 12 cabinet appointments of his second term.
Nov. 3, election day
• See Election of 1896, page 283.
•Cleveland voted for John McCauley Palmer; as a conservative "gold bug" Democrat, he thus avoided voting for William Jennings Bryan.
Dec. 7, second session of 54th Congress
Dec. 7, sent his fourth and last State of the Union message of his second term to Congress

1897

Feb. 6, reduced number of pension agencies
•His executive order reduced the number of agencies by half, which resulted in an operational savings of $160,000.
Feb. 8, vetoed new division of eastern judicial district of Texas bill
Feb. 8, new division of eastern judicial district of Texas act passed over his veto
•This was the third of his five vetoes that were overridden during his second term.
Feb. 22, issued proclamation that set apart forest reserves in six Western states
•The forest reserves, which totalled twenty million acres, were located in California, Wyoming, Montana, Utah, Idaho, and Washington.
Feb. 27, received report of Venezuela boundary commission
Mar. 2, vetoed amended immigration bill
•This amendment provided for a literacy test and prohibited the employment of aliens on U.S. public works projects.
Mar. 3, vetoed pensions to Caroline D. Howatt and Rachel Patton bills
Mar. 3, pensions to Caroline D. Howatt and Rachel Patton acts passed over his veto
•These were the fourth and last of his five vetoes that were overridden during his second term.
Mar. 4, second session of 54th Congress adjourned

Mar. 4, pocket vetoed 49 bills
• A total of 27 were of relief and pension bills. The others included bills to authorize the District of Columbia to accept a be-

quest for use of public white schools, to set aside the Pacific forest reserve as a public park, and to provide delivery of letters in communities without free delivery.

THE FORMER PRESIDENT

Mar. 4, 1897, attended inauguration of McKinley
• Cleveland's age upon leaving office was 59 years, 351 days.
• He was the second of three presidents who participated in four inaugural ceremonies.
Mar. 4, 1897, departed on shooting and fishing trip from Alexandria, Va.
Mar. 18, 1897, joined his wife at new home, Princeton, N.J.
• It was his 60th birthday. He had bought the colonial stone and stucco house shortly before he left the White House. He named the estate, Westland, in honor of his friend, Professor Andrew F. West of Princeton.
Oct. 28, 1897, his first son born
• The boy was named Richard Folsom Cleveland.
• Cleveland was the last of three former presidents who became fathers.
1899, accepted chair of Henry Stafford Little Lectureship in Public Affairs, Princeton University
April, 1900, suffered gastrointestinal attack, Lakehurst, N.J.
May, 1900, his first Saturday Evening Post article published
• He wrote 16 articles for the magazine between 1900 and 1906. His fees ranged up to $2,500.
1901, appointed member of board of trustees, Princeton University
• He was named president of the board in 1904. In this capacity he had frequent conflicts regarding educational philosophy with the president of the university, Woodrow Wilson.
July 18, 1903, his second son born
• The boy was named Francis Grover Cleveland.
1904, his book, Presidential Problems, published by Century Company, New York City
• His book contained a number of his Princeton lectures, including his views on "The Independence of the Executive," "The Government in the Chicago Strike of

1894," and "The Venezuelan Boundary Affair."
• He was the ninth of 21 presidents who wrote books that were published during their lifetimes.
1906, reorganized Equitable Life Assurance Society of U.S., New York City
1906, his book, Fishing and Shooting Sketches, published by Outing Publishing Company, New York City
• A proficient fisherman, he had fished throughout the Northeast and Canada. He was also a collector of guns. While several of the presidents fished, only Hoover pursued the sport with Cleveland's avidity.
Mar. 18, 1907, celebrated his 70th birthday
• He was the 12th of 16 presidents who lived to be 70.
1907, elected president of Association of Presidents of Life Insurance Companies
• His salary was $25,000 yearly.
1907, elected to Phi Beta Kappa
• He was the only former president elected to Phi Beta Kappa.
• He was the last of three presidents who were honorary members of Phi Beta Kappa.
• He was the ninth of 11 presidents who were members of Phi Beta Kappa.
1908, his book, Good Citizenship, published by H. Altemus Company, Philadelphia, Pa.

DEATH

Date of death: June 24, 1908
Place of death: Princeton, N.J.
• Cleveland was the second of two presidents who died in New Jersey. The other was Garfield.
Age at death: 71 years, 98 days
• He lived 19 years, 112 days after the completion of his second term.
Cause of death: Heart attack
Place of burial: Princeton, N.J.
• He was the only president who was buried in New Jersey.

THE VICE PRESIDENT (23rd)

Note: Cleveland was the sixth of seven presidents who had two vice presidents. *See* page 256.

Full name: Adlai Ewing Stevenson
• Stevenson was the grandfather of Adlai E. Stevenson, the Democratic presidential candidate in 1952 and 1956.
Date of birth: Oct. 25, 1835
Place of birth: Christian County, Ky.
• Stevenson was the third of four vice presidents who were born in Kentucky.
Religious denomination: Presbyterian
• He was the ninth of 11 vice presidents who were Presbyterians.
• Cleveland and Stevenson were both Presbyterians. They were the fourth of seven president-vice president teams of the same religious denomination.
Occupation: Lawyer
• He practiced law in Metamora, Ill., 1858, and Bloomington, Ill., after 1868; member of the House of Representatives, 1875–1877 and 1879–1881; first assistant postmaster general, 1885–1889.
• He was the 14th of 21 vice presidents who served in the House of Representatives before their terms of office.
Term of office: Mar. 4, 1893, to Mar. 4, 1897 (4 years)
• He was the 11th of 17 vice presidents who served four-year terms.
• Cleveland and Stevenson were the 25th of 41 president-vice president teams.
Age at inauguration: 57 years, 130 days
State represented: Illinois
• He was the first of two vice presidents who represented Illinois. The other was Dawes.
• He was the ninth of 13 vice presidents who represented states that were not their native states.
Political party: Democratic
• He was the ninth of 16 vice presidents who were Democrats.
Occupation after term: Lawyer
• He was the Democratic vice-presidential candidate, 1900; the gubernatorial candidate, Illinois, 1908.
Date of death: June 14, 1914
Place of death: Chicago, Ill.

• He was the first of two vice presidents who died in Illinois. The other was Dawes.
Age at death: 78 years, 232 days
Place of burial: Bloomington, Ill.
• He was the first of two vice presidents who were buried in Illinois. The other was Dawes.

THE CABINET

State: Walter Quintin Gresham of Indiana, Mar. 7, 1893, to May 28, 1895
• Richard Olney of Massachusetts, June 10, 1895, to Mar. 5, 1897
Treasury: John Griffin Carlisle of Kentucky, Mar. 7, 1893, to Mar. 5, 1897
War: David Scott Lamont of New York, Mar. 5, 1893, to Mar. 5, 1897
Attorney General: Richard Olney of Massachusetts, Mar. 6, 1893, to June 7, 1895
• Judson Harmon of Ohio, June 8, 1895, to Mar. 5, 1897
Navy: Hilary Abner Herbert of Alabama, Mar. 7, 1893 to Mar. 5, 1897
Postmaster General: Wilson Shannon Bissell of New York, Mar. 6, 1893, to Mar. 1, 1895
• William Lyne Wilson of West Virginia, Apr. 4, 1895, to Mar. 5, 1897
Interior: Hoke Smith of Georgia, Mar. 6, 1893 to Aug. 31, 1896
• David Rowland Francis of Missouri, Sept. 1, 1896, to Mar. 5, 1897
Agriculture: Julius Sterling Morton of Nebraska, Mar. 7, 1893, to Mar. 5, 1897

THE SUPREME COURT

Associate Justices: William Butler Hornblower of New York, appointed, Sept. 19, 1893; rejected by Senate, Jan. 15, 1894
• Wheeler Hazard Peckham of New York, appointed, Jan. 22, 1894; rejected by Senate, Feb. 16, 1894
• Edward Douglass White of Louisiana, appointed, Feb. 19, 1894; confirmed, Feb. 19, 1894
• Rufus Wheeler Peckham of New York, appointed, Dec. 3, 1895; confirmed, Dec. 9, 1895

Twenty-fifth President

WILLIAM McKINLEY

Full name: William McKinley
- He was the second of three presidents who were named William.
- He was the sixth of eight presidents who had the same full names as their fathers.
- He was the 16th of 17 presidents who did not have middle initials or middle names.

Date of birth: Jan. 29, 1843
- He was the second of four presidents who were born in January.

Place of birth: Niles, Ohio
- He was the fifth of seven presidents who were born in Ohio.
- His birthplace, now in a marble memorial building, is open to the public daily except Mondays and holidays, 1:30 to 4 P.M., June 1 to Aug. 31, and Saturdays and Sundays only during May, September, and October. Admission: free.

Family lineage: English-Scottish-Irish and English-Scottish-German
- He was the only president who was of English-Scottish-Irish and English-Scottish-German ancestry.

Religious denomination: Methodist
- He was the last of four presidents who were Methodists.

College: Allegheny College, Meadville, Pa.

- He was the only president who went to Allegheny.
- He was the 16th of 27 presidents who attended college.
- He was the fifth of six presidents who attended but were not graduated from college.
- He was the 13th of 15 presidents who were not graduated from college.

Law School: Albany Law School, Albany, N.Y.
- He was the second of nine presidents who attended law school.
- He was the first of six presidents who attended but were not graduated from law school.

PARENTS AND SIBLINGS

Father's name: William McKinley
Date of birth: Nov. 15, 1807
Place of birth: Mercer County, Pa.
Occupations: Manager, founder of blast furnaces
Date of death: Nov. 24, 1892
Place of death: Canton, Ohio
Age at death: 85 years, nine days

279

Mother's name: Nancy Campbell Allison McKinley
Date of birth: Apr. 22, 1809
Place of birth: New Lisbon, now Lisbon, Ohio
Date of marriage: Jan. 6, 1829
Children: 9; 5 daughters, 4 sons
•David Allison was born in 1829; Anna in 1832; James in 18—; Mary in 18—; Helen in 18—; Sarah Elizabeth in 1841; William in 1843; Abbie Celia in 18—; and Abner in 1849. Abbie Celia died in infancy.
•McKinley was the second of two presidents who were seventh children. The other was William Henry Harrison.
•He was the sixth of seven presidents who came from families of nine children.
Date of death: Dec. 12, 1897
•McKinley was the seventh of ten presidents whose mothers lived to see their sons' inauguration or oath-taking days.
•Mrs. McKinley was the second of four mothers of presidents who attended the ceremonies.
Place of death: Canton, Ohio
Age at death: 88 years, 234 days

MARRIAGE

Date of marriage: Jan. 25, 1871
Place of marriage: Canton, Ohio
•McKinley was the fifth of seven presidents who were married in Ohio.
Age at marriage: 27 years, 361 days
•He was the 17th of 27 presidents who were married in their twenties.
Years married: 30 years, 232 days

Wife's name: Ida Saxton McKinley
•She was the 20th of 33 first ladies.
•She was the 26th of 40 wives of presidents.
Date of birth: June 8, 1847
•She was the third of four first ladies who were born in June.
•She was the fourth of five wives of presi-

dents who were born in June.
Place of birth: Canton, Ohio
•She was the fourth of six first ladies who were born in Ohio.
•She was the fourth of six wives of presidents who were born in Ohio.
Wife's mother: Catherine Dewalt Saxton
Wife's father: James Asbury Saxton, banker
Age at marriage: 23 years, 231 days
•She was the 17th of 26 first ladies who were married in their twenties.
•She was the 21st of 30 wives of presidents who were married in their twenties.
Years younger than husband: 4 years, 130 days
Children: 2 daughters
•Katherine was born on Dec. 25, 1871, and Ida on Apr. 1, 1873. Both children died in infancy.
•McKinley was the second of two presidents whose children died before they attained maturity. The other was Pierce.
•He was the first of five presidents who had only female children.
•He was the second of seven presidents who had two children.
•He was the 19th of 30 presidents who had children.
Years she survived her husband: 5 years, 254 days
•She was the 13th of 21 first ladies who survived their husbands.
•She was the 15th of 23 wives of presidents who survived their husbands.
Date of death: May 26, 1907
Place of death: Canton, Ohio
•She was the third of four first ladies who died in Ohio.
•She was the third of four wives of presidents who died in Ohio.
Age at death: 59 years, 352 days
Place of burial: Canton, Ohio
•She was the fourth of five first ladies who were buried in Ohio.
•She was the fourth of five wives of presidents who were buried in Ohio.

EARLY YEARS

1849–1852, attended public schools, Niles, Ohio
1852, with family, moved to Poland, Ohio
1852–1859, attended Union Seminary, Poland

1859–1860, attended Allegheny College, Meadville, Pa.
•McKinley withdrew from college due to illness.
1860, taught school, Poland

- He was the fifth of seven presidents who taught school.
1861, worked as clerk, Poland post office
June 11, 1861, enlisted as private, Company E, 23rd Ohio Infantry
- He was the last of seven presidents who served in the Civil War.
- He was the 15th of 21 presidents who served in the military during wartime.
Sept. 10, 1861, saw first action, Carnifex Ferry, W. Va.
Apr. 15, 1862, promoted to commissary sergeant
Sept. 16, 1862, participated in Battle of Antietam, Md.
Sept. 23, 1862, commissioned as second lieutenant
Feb. 7, 1863, promoted to first lieutenant
July 23–24, 1864, participated in Battle of Winchester, Va.
- During the retreat he and his regiment retrieved a battery of four guns that had been abandoned.
July 25, 1864, promoted to captain
Sept. 19, 1864, participated in Battle of Opequon, Va.
Sept. 22, 1864, participated in Battle of Cedar Creek, Va.
Oct. 19, 1864, participated in Battle of Fishers Hill, Va.
1864–1865, served on staffs of General George Crook and General Winfield S. Hancock
Mar. 14, 1865, promoted to brevet major
May 3, 1865, degree of Master Mason conferred by Hiram Lodge No. 21, Winchester, Va.
- He was the eighth of 13 presidents who were Masons.
July 26, 1865, mustered out of army
1865, studied law with Judge Charles E. Glidden and David M. Wilson, Youngstown, Ohio
- McKinley was the 18th of 26 presidents who studied law.
1866, attended law school, Albany, N.Y.
Mar. 5, 1867, admitted to bar, Warren, Ohio
- He was the 18th of 23 presidents who were lawyers.
1867, began practice of law, Canton, Ohio
1867, made first political speeches
- He advocated Negro suffrage, an unpopular cause in Ohio.
1867, campaigned for Rutherford B. Hayes, who was running for governor
- Hayes, who had been McKinley's commanding officer in the 23rd Ohio Infantry, was elected.
1869, elected prosecuting attorney, Stark County, Ohio
- This was his first public office.
Jan. 25, 1871, married Ida Saxton, Canton, Ohio
1871, defeated when sought reelection as prosecuting attorney
- He lost by 45 votes.
Dec. 25, 1871, his first daughter born
- The girl was named Katherine McKinley.
Apr. 1, 1873, his second daughter born
- The girl was named Ida McKinley.
Aug. 22, 1873, his daughter, Ida, died
1875, again campaigned for Hayes
- Hayes again was elected governor.
June 25, 1876, his daughter, Katherine, died

NATIONAL PROMINENCE

Oct. 5, 1876, elected to House of Representatives
- McKinley was reelected six times and served in the 45th through the 51st congresses.
- He was the 14th of 17 presidents who were elected to the House.
Mar. 4, 1877, took seat in House of Representatives
- He was the 14th of 17 presidents who served in the House.
1880, chairman of Republican state convention
June 2–8, 1880, attended Republican national convention, Chicago, Ill.
- He was appointed to the Republican national committee.
June–November, 1880, campaigned for James A. Garfield
- McKinley spoke in Ohio, New York, Maine, Indiana, and Illinois.
December, 1880, appointed member of House ways and means committee
- He succeeded Garfield.
September, 1881, chairman of committee for Garfield memorial services in House
October, 1882, his election to Congress contested

• He defeated Jonathan Hasson Wallace by eight votes, according to the official count. Wallace contested the election. McKinley took his seat in the 48th Congress and served until May 27, 1884, when the election was reversed and he was succeeded by Wallace.

1884, chairman of Republican state convention

June 3–6, 1884, attended Republican national convention, Chicago, Ill.

• He served as a delegate-at-large.

1884, campaigned for James G. Blaine

• McKinley accompanied Blaine on the candidate's western tour, and also spoke in New York and West Virginia.

October, 1884, elected to House of Representatives

• He defeated David R. Paige by about two thousand votes.

Jan. 19, 1886, delivered memorial address at presentation of Garfield statue to Congress

Apr. 2, 1888, presented minority report of ways and means committee on Mills tariff bill to Congress.

May 18, 1888, delivered tariff speech in Congress

• The speech, in which he held for protection, was reprinted by the Republican national and state committees. Millions of copies were distributed during the 1888 campaign.

June 19–25, 1888, attended Republican national convention, Chicago, Ill.

• He was a delegate-at-large and chairman of the resolutions committee. He endorsed John Sherman.

• When a movement began to place McKinley's name in nomination, he told the convention he was not a candidate. "I do not request, I demand, that no delegate who would not cast reflection upon me shall cast a ballot for me," he said.

December, 1889, defeated for speaker of House

• Thomas Brackett Reed was elected speaker on the third ballot in the Republican caucus.

Dec. 17, 1889, introduced tariff bill

• This was the customs administration act.

1890, chairman of ways and means committee

Apr. 16, 1890, introduced McKinley tariff bill

• Signed by Harrison, Oct. 6, the McKinley

Tariff Act of 1890 raised the tariff rates to 49.5 percent.

Apr. 24, 1890, spoke in Congress in favor of sustaining civil service law

• "The Republican party must take no step backward," he said. "The merit system is here, and it is here to stay."

October, 1890, defeated for reelection to House

• His district had been gerrymandered. He was defeated by John G. Warwick by about three hundred votes.

June, 1891, nominated for governor by acclamation, Republican state convention

• He opened his campaign in Niles and made 135 speeches throughout Ohio prior to election day.

October, 1891, elected governor of Ohio

Jan. 11, 1892, inaugurated as governor

• He was the second of two presidents who served as governors of Ohio. The other was Hayes.

• McKinley was the ninth of 13 presidents who served as state governors.

June 7–10, 1892, permanent chairman of Republican national convention, Chicago, Ill.

• He received 182 votes on the first ballot, on which Harrison had been renominated. McKinley moved to make the nomination of Harrison unanimous, which was done.

June-November, 1892, campaigned for Harrison

October, 1893, reelected governor of Ohio

September-November, 1894, made national speaking tour

• He averaged seven speeches a day during the eight-week tour and addressed about two million people. He traveled more than sixteen thousand miles in special trains.

Jan. 13, 1896, retired as governor

• A movement for his nomination as Republican candidate for president already had begun.

1896, his book, *The Tariff in the Days of Henry Clay and Since,* published by Henry Clay Publishing Company, New York City

• He was the tenth of 21 presidents who wrote books that were published during their lifetimes.

June 17, 1896, nominated for president, Republican national convention, St. Louis, Mo.

Nov. 3, 1896, election day

• *See* Election of 1896, page 283.

Jan. 11, 1897, presidential electors cast ballots
- He received 271 of the 447 electoral votes from the 45 states.
- *See* Election of 1896, below.

Feb. 10, 1897, electoral vote tabulated by Congress
- McKinley and Hobart were officially declared elected.

ELECTION OF 1896

Prohibition party, convened, May 27, at Pittsburgh, Pa., nominated Joshua Levering of Maryland for president, Hale Johnson of Illinois for vice president.

Republican party, convened, June 16, at St. Louis, Mo., nominated William McKinley of Ohio for president, Garret Augustus Hobart of New Jersey for vice president.
- This was the 11th Republican national convention. It was the first Republican convention held in St. Louis; it was the third major party convention held in St. Louis.

Socialist Labor party, convened, July 4, at New York City, nominated Charles Horatio Matchett of New York for president, Matthew Maguire of New Jersey for vice president.

Democratic party, convened, July 7, at Chicago, Ill., nominated William Jennings Bryan of Nebraska for president, Arthur Sewall of Maine for vice president.
- This was the 17th Democratic national convention. It was the fourth Democratic convention held in Chicago; it was the ninth major party convention held in Chicago.

National Silver Republican party, convened, July 22, at St. Louis, Mo., endorsed Democratic candidate Bryan for president, nominated Thomas Edward Watson of Georgia for vice president.

People's (Populist) party, convened, July 25, at St. Louis, Mo., nominated William Jennings Bryan of Nebraska for president, Thomas Edward Watson of Georgia for vice president.

National Democratic (gold Democrats) party, convened, Sept. 2, at Indianapolis, Ind., nominated John McCauley Palmer of Illinois for president, Simon Bolivar Buckner of Kentucky for vice president.

National (free silver) party nominated Charles Eugene Bentley of Nebraska for president, James Haywood Southgate of North Carolina for vice president.

Election day, Tuesday, Nov. 3, 1896

Popular vote: 14,159,540
> McKinley, 7,111,607
> Bryan, 6,731,635 (6,509,052, Democratic; 222,583, People's)
> Palmer, 134,645
> Levering, 131,312
> Matchett, 36,373
> Bentley, 13,968

Electoral vote: 447, 45 states
- McKinley, 271, 23 states
  (California, 8 of 9 votes; Connecticut, 6; Delaware, 3; Illinois, 24; Indiana, 15; Iowa, 13; Kentucky, 12 of 13 votes; Maine, 6; Maryland, 8; Massachusetts, 15; Michigan, 14; Minnesota, 9; New Hampshire, 4; New Jersey, 10; New York, 36; North Dakota, 3; Ohio, 23; Oregon, 4; Pennsylvania, 32; Rhode Island, 4; Vermont, 4; West Virginia, 6; Wisconsin, 12)
- Bryan, 176, 22 states
  (Alabama, 11; Arkansas, 8; Colorado, 4; Florida, 4; Georgia, 13; Idaho, 3; Kansas, 10; Louisiana, 8; Mississippi, 9; Missouri, 17; Montana, 3; Nebraska, 8; Nevada, 3; North Carolina, 11; South Carolina, 9; South Dakota, 4; Tennessee, 12; Texas, 15; Utah, 3; Virginia, 12; Washington, 4; Wyoming, 3)
- Bryan also received the votes of one California and one Kentucky elector.
- The 447 votes for vice-presidential candidates were divided: Hobart, 271; Sewall, 149; Watson, 27.

THE PRESIDENT (25th)

Term of office: Mar. 4, 1897, to Sept. 14, 1901 (4 years, 194 days)
- McKinley was the ninth of 12 presidents who were elected to second terms.
- McKinley was the ninth of 16 presidents who served more than one term.

State represented: Ohio
- He was the fourth of six presidents who represented Ohio.

Political party: Republican

•He was the seventh of 14 presidents who were Republicans.
Congresses: 55th, 56th, 57th
Administrations: 28th, 29th
Age at inauguration: 54 years, 34 days
Inauguration day: Thursday, Mar. 4, 1897

•McKinley took the oath of office, administered by Chief Justice Melville W. Fuller, on the east portico of the Capitol.
•This was the third of six inaugurations at which Fuller officiated.

THE 28th ADMINISTRATION

1897

Mar. 5, appointed his first secretary of state, John Sherman; his only secretary of treasury, Lyman J. Gage; his first secretary of war, Russell A. Alger; his first attorney general, Joseph McKenna; his only secretary of navy, John D. Long; his first postmaster general, James A. Gary; his first secretary of interior, Cornelius N. Bliss; and his only secretary of agriculture, James Wilson
•Sherman, Gage, Long, and Wilson took office, Mar. 6.
Mar. 15, first session of 55th Congress
•The administration controlled both the Senate and the House of Representatives. The Republicans gained two Senate seats but lost 40 House seats. The Senate (90 members) consisted of 46 Republicans, 34 Democrats, and ten others. The House (357 members) consisted of 206 Republicans, 134 Democrats, 16 others, and one vacancy.
Mar. 15, sent special message to Congress in which he urged tariff revision
Apr. 27, spoke at dedication of Grant's Tomb, New York City
May 9, ordered secretary of navy to dispatch cruiser to Honduras to protect American interests
June 4, signed act that created commission to examine all possible canal routes across Nicaragua
June 25, issued proclamation that set apart land reserve, Nogales, Ariz.
July 14, revoked Cleveland's executive order that had reduced number of pension agencies
July 24, authorized to suspend discriminating duties imposed on foreign commerce and vessels
July 24, signed Dingley Tariff Act
•This act imposed the highest tariff up to that time, with average rates at 57 percent. The act replaced the Wilson-Gorman

Tariff Act of 1893, and remained in force until 1909.
July 24, first session of 55th Congress adjourned
Dec. 1, accepted resignation of Associate Justice Field
Dec. 6, second session of 55th Congress
Dec. 6, sent his first State of the Union message to Congress
Dec. 16, appointed Joseph McKenna as associate justice
•McKenna, who was confirmed by the Senate, Jan. 21, 1898, was McKinley's only appointment to the Supreme Court.
Dec. 29, signed act that prohibited killing of seals in Northern Pacific
•This act prohibited seal hunting north of 35 degrees, north latitude, and prohibited importation of sealskins taken elsewhere than the Pribilof Islands.

1898

Jan. 25, accepted resignation of Attorney General McKenna
Jan. 25, appointed his second attorney general, John W. Griggs
Feb. 9, de Lome letter published in New York *Journal*
•Depuy de Lome, Spanish minister to the U.S., resigned when the letter, in which the diplomat described McKinley as "weak and a bidder for the admiration of the crowd," was published. The private letter had been stolen from the mails in Havana by Cuban revolutionists.
Feb. 15, *U.S.S. Maine* destroyed
•The cause of the explosion has never been determined. A total of 260 officers and seamen were killed.
Mar. 2, issued proclamation that set apart Pine Mountain and Zaca Lake forest reserves, Cal.
Mar. 9, signed act that appropriated $50,-000,000 for national defense

Mar. 27, instructed minister to Spain to communicate American desires and intentions

• Minister Stewart L. Woodford notified the Madrid government that the U.S. sought an armistice in Cuba until Oct. 1, and the abolishment of the Spanish concentration camp policy.

Mar. 28, sent special message to Congress with *Maine* report

• The naval court of inquiry reported, Mar. 21, that the battleship had been destroyed by an underwater mine, but that responsibility was impossible to determine.

Apr. 10, notified that Spain had granted armistice in Cuba

• The Spanish government had offered to arbitrate the *Maine* incident and to abolish the concentration camp policy but declined to grant an armistice unless requested by the Cuban insurgents. The armistice was granted, Apr. 9, after much pressure had been exerted by foreign ministers in Madrid.

Apr. 11, sent war message to Congress

• He asked for "forcible intervention" by the U.S. to establish peace in Cuba.

• This was the fifth of seven war messages.

Apr. 18, accepted resignation of Postmaster General Gary, effective, Apr. 21

Apr. 20, signed joint resolution that recognized independence of Cuba

• The resolution demanded Spanish military withdrawal, empowered the employment of U.S. army and navy forces, and disclaimed any territorial ambitions in Cuba.

Apr. 21, Spain broke off diplomatic relations with U.S.

Apr. 21, appointed his second postmaster general, Charles E. Smith

Apr. 22, ordered blockade of Cuban ports

Apr. 23, issued call for 125,000 volunteers

Apr. 24, Spain declared war against U.S.

Apr. 25, U.S. declared war against Spain

• The formal declaration stated that a state of war had existed since Apr. 21.

Apr. 25, Secretary of State Sherman resigned, effective, Apr. 27

• Sherman, an anti-expansionist, resigned in protest against the war declaration.

Apr. 26, appointed his second secretary of state, William R. Day

• Day took office, Apr. 28.

May 1, Battle of Manila Bay

• A Spanish fleet of ten vessels was destroyed or captured. The U.S. Asiatic squadron of four cruisers and two gunboats, under the command of Commodore George Dewey, suffered only eight wounded casualties. The Spanish lost 381 men.

May 10, issued proclamation that set apart Prescott forest reserve, Ariz.

May 11, promoted Dewey to rear admiral

May 16, vetoed relief of administrators of Isaac P. Tice bill

• This was the first of McKinley's 42 vetoes.

• This was the first of 22 private relief bills he vetoed.

May 25, issued call for seventy-five thousand volunteers

May 27, issued proclamation that set apart Pecos River forest reserve, N. Mex.

May 29, Spanish fleet bottled up in harbor of Santiago de Cuba

June 13, signed war revenue act

June 14, expeditionary force sailed for Cuba from Tampa, Fla.

June 20, Guam occupied

• When the *U.S.S. Charleston* fired on the island, June 19, the Spanish commander, who did not know that war had been declared, apologized for not returning the "salute." The Spaniard explained that he had no ammunition.

June 24, Battle of Las Guasimas

• This was the first land battle in Cuba. Marines had engaged in minor skirmishes with the Spaniards after landing at Guantanamo, June 12, 14, and 15.

July 1, signed federal bankruptcy act

July 1, battles of El Caney and San Juan

• The Americans suffered heavy casualties but took the fortified village of El Caney and San Juan Hill, thereby winning command of the heights to the north and east of Santiago. Colonel Theodore Roosevelt commanded the dismounted Rough Riders who took part in the Battle of San Juan Hill.

July 3, Spanish fleet destroyed

• At the cost of one killed and one wounded, the Spanish fleet was demolished when it tried to run the blockade of Santiago harbor. During the four-hour battle along the coast, 474 Spaniards were killed or wounded and 1,750 were taken prisoner.

July 4, Wake Island captured

July 7, signed joint resolution that adopted treaty of annexation of Hawaii

July 8, second session of 55th Congress adjourned

July 8, pocket vetoed bill to provide register for steamer, *Titania*

•This was the first of McKinley's 36 pocket vetoes.

July 9, appointed commission as provided for in Hawaii joint resolution to recommend legislation to Congress

July 17, Santiago surrendered

•The destruction of the Spanish fleet, July 3, and the capture of Santiago and its garrison of twenty-four thousand troops virtually ended the war.

July 21, Nipe occupied

•Four warships bombarded the port. This was the last naval engagement in Cuban waters.

July 25, Puerto Rico occupied

•Ponce, the island's second largest city, fell, July 28.

July 26, Spanish government asked peace terms

•The request for peace was made through French Ambassador Jules Cambon.

July 30, communicated American terms to Spanish government via Cambon

Aug. 9, his terms of peace formally accepted by Spain

Aug. 12, issued proclamation announcing suspension of hostilities

•According to the terms, Spain was to relinquish Cuba and cede Puerto Rico and one of the Ladrone Islands to the U.S. Manila was to be occupied by the U.S., pending the final disposition of the Philippines by treaty.

Aug. 13, surrender of Manila

Aug. 17, issued proclamation that set apart San Francisco Mountains forest reserve, Ariz.

Sept. 8, appointed commission to investigate conduct of war department during hostilities

Sept. 9, appointed peace commission to conclude treaty with Spain

•Secretary of State Day was appointed chairman of the peace commission.

Sept. 16, accepted resignation of Secretary of State Day

Sept. 19, issued proclamation that set apart Black Hills forest reserve, S.D. and Wy.

Sept. 30, appointed his third secretary of state, John M. Hay

Dec. 5, third session of 55th Congress

Dec. 5, sent his second State of the Union message to Congress

Dec. 10, Treaty of Paris signed

•Spain relinquished all claim and title to Cuba, agreed to assume the $400,000,000 Cuban debt, and ceded Puerto Rico, Guam and the Philippines to the U.S. for the payment of $20,000,000.

Dec. 21, accepted resignation of Secretary of Interior Bliss

Dec. 21, appointed his second secretary of interior, Ethan A. Hitchcock

Dec. 21, sent instructions to secretary of war regarding temporary government of Philippines

1899

Jan. 20, appointed first Philippine commission

Feb. 10, issued proclamation that set apart forest reserves in Montana and Utah

Mar. 2, signed act that created naval rank of admiral

•The first admiral of the navy was George Dewey.

Mar. 2, issued proclamation that authorized Mt. Rainier National Park, Wash.

Mar. 2, issued proclamation that set apart forest reserve in New Mexico

Mar. 4, third session of 55th Congress adjourned

Apr. 9, former Associate Justice Field died

May 29, issued executive order that modified civil service rules

July 7, issued call for ten regiments to quell Philippine insurrection

July 19, accepted resignation of Secretary of War Alger, effective, Aug. 1

Aug. 1, appointed his second secretary of war, Elihu Root

Nov. 21, Vice President Hobart died

Dec. 4, first session of 56th Congress

•The administration maintained control of both the Senate and the House of Representatives. The Republicans gained seven Senate seats but lost 21 House seats. The Senate (90 members) consisted of 53 Republicans, 26 Democrats, and 11 others. The House (357 members) consisted of 185 Republicans, 163 Democrats, and nine others.

Dec. 5, sent his third State of the Union message to Congress

1900

Feb. 6, appointed William Howard Taft as chairman of commission to establish civil government in Philippines

Mar. 14, signed gold standard act

Apr. 7, appointed second Philippine commission

• Taft had been named president of the new commission, Mar. 13.

Apr. 10, issued proclamation that opened part of Colville Indian reservation, Wash., to settlers

Apr. 12, signed act that provided for establishment of civil government in Puerto Rico

• This act authorized the president to appoint a governor-general and a council, the upper house of the legislature.

Apr. 30, signed act granting territorial status to Hawaii, effective, June 14

June 7, first session of 56th Congress adjourned

June 7, pocket vetoed two bills

• The bills were to incorporate the National White Cross of America and to amend the revised statutes.

June 20, renominated for president, Republican national convention, Philadelphia, Pa.

Oct. 12, appointed American representatives to Permanent Court of Arbitration, The Hague, Netherlands

Nov. 6, election day

• *See* Election of 1900, below.

Dec. 3, second session of 56th Congress

Dec. 3, sent his fourth and last State of the Union message to Congress

Note: The official population, according to the 12th census, was 75,994,575.

1901

Jan. 14, presidential electors cast ballots

• He received 292 of the 447 electoral votes from the 45 states.

• *See* Election of 1900, below.

Feb. 13, electoral vote tabulated by Congress

• McKinley and Roosevelt were officially declared elected.

Mar. 2, signed amended army appropriation act

• The Spooner amendment authorized the president to establish civil government in the Philippines. Previously he had acted under his war powers.

Mar. 3, signed act that established national

bureau of standards

Mar. 3, second session of 56th Congress adjourned

Mar. 3, pocket vetoed 29 bills

• These were the last of his 36 pocket vetoes. A total of 17 were private relief bills, 11 were correction of military record bills, and one was to grant a power company dam at Knoxville, Tenn.

Note: He was the eighth of 11 presidents who never had a veto overridden.

ELECTION OF 1900

Social Democratic party, convened, Mar. 6, at Indianapolis, Ind., nominated Eugene Victor Debs of Indiana for president, Job Harriman of California for vice president.

People's (Populist, Anti-Fusion) party, convened, May 9, at Cincinnati, Ohio, nominated Wharton Barker of Pennsylvania for president, Ignatius Donnelly of Minnesota for vice president.

Socialist Labor party, convened, June 2, at New York City, nominated Joseph Francis Malloney of Massachusetts for president, Valentine Remmel of Pennsylvania for vice president.

Republican party, convened, June 19, at Philadelphia, Pa., nominated William McKinley of Ohio for president, Theodore Roosevelt of New York for vice president.

• This was the 12th Republican national convention. It was the third Republican convention held in Philadelphia; it was the fifth major party convention held in Philadelphia.

Prohibition party, convened, June 27, at Chicago, Ill., nominated John Granville Woolley of Illinois for president, Henry Brewer Metcalf of Rhode Island for vice president.

Democratic party, convened, July 4, at Kansas City, Mo., nominated William Jennings Bryan of Nebraska for president, Adlai Ewing Stevenson of Illinois for vice president.

• This was the 18th Democratic national convention. It was the only Democratic convention held in Kansas City; it was the first of two major party conventions held in Kansas City.

• Bryan was endorsed by the Fusion Populists.

Union Reform party nominated Seth Hockett Ellis of Ohio for president, Samuel T. Nicholson of Pennsylvania for vice president.

United Christian party nominated Jonah Fitz Randolph Leonard of Iowa for president, David H. Martin of Pennsylvania for vice president.

Election day, Tuesday, Nov. 6, 1900

Popular vote: 13,972,880
  McKinley, 7,219,525
  Bryan, 6,358,737
  Woolley, 209,166
  Debs, 94,864
  Barker, 50,599
  Malloney, 33,332
  Ellis, 5,598
  Leonard, 1,059

Electoral vote: 447, 45 states
  • McKinley, 292, 28 states

(California, 9; Connecticut, 6; Delaware, 3; Illinois, 24; Indiana, 15; Iowa, 13; Kansas, 10; Maine, 6; Maryland, 8; Massachusetts, 15; Michigan, 14; Minnesota, 9; Nebraska, 8; New Hampshire, 4; New Jersey, 10; New York, 36; North Dakota, 3; Ohio, 23; Oregon, 4; Pennsylvania, 32; Rhode Island, 4; South Dakota, 4; Utah, 3; Vermont, 4; Washington, 4; West Virginia, 6; Wisconsin, 12; Wyoming, 3)

• Bryan, 155, 17 states
(Alabama, 11; Arkansas, 8; Colorado, 4; Florida, 4; Georgia, 13; Idaho, 3; Kentucky, 13; Louisiana, 8; Mississippi, 9; Missouri, 17; Montana, 3; Nevada, 3; North Carolina, 11; South Carolina, 9; Tennessee, 12; Texas, 15; Virginia, 12)

THE 29th ADMINISTRATION

1901

Mar. 4, his second inauguration day

• McKinley took the oath of office, administered by Chief Justice Melville W. Fuller, on the east portico of the Capitol.

• This was the fourth of six inaugurations at which Fuller officiated.

Mar. 29, accepted resignation of Attorney General Griggs

Apr. 5, appointed his third attorney general, Philander C. Knox

• Knox was the last of McKinley's 15 cabinet appointments.

Apr. 11, issued proclamation that established San Isabel forest reserve, Colo.

July 4, issued proclamation that set apart Wichita forest reserve, Okla.

July 25, issued proclamation that established free trade between Puerto Rico and U.S.

Aug. 3, issued proclamation that established Payson forest reserve, Utah

Sept. 5, spoke at Pan-American Exposition, Buffalo, N.Y.

THE ASSASSINATION

Sept. 6, 1901, shot by Leon F. Czolgosz in Temple of Music, Pan-American Exposition, Buffalo, N.Y.

• While shaking hands with visitors at a public reception, McKinley was shot twice, in the chest and the stomach. Czolgosz had concealed a .32-caliber revolver under a handkerchief draped around his hand so as to resemble a bandage.

• After emergency surgery at a hospital on the exposition grounds, McKinley was moved to the home of John G. Milburn, his host during his visit to Buffalo. He appeared to make steady improvement until Sept. 12, but then weakened.

Sept. 14, 1901, died at 2:15 A.M., Buffalo, N.Y.

• His last words were: "Good-by, all. Good-by. It is God's way. His will be done."

Sept. 23, 1901, trial of Czolgosz began, Buffalo, N.Y.

• Czolgosz, a 28-year-old anarchist, had been apprehended immediately after the shooting. Indicted for first-degree murder after having been declared sane by a panel of doctors, he made no defense. His lawyers called no witnesses; he refused to testify in his own behalf. The trial lasted only eight hours and 26 minutes, including the impanelling of the jury.

Sept. 24, 1901, Czolgosz convicted of murder

• The jury required only 34 minutes to return the verdict of guilty.

Oct. 29, 1901, Czolgosz electrocuted, Auburn State Prison, Auburn, N.Y.

DEATH

Date of death: Sept. 14, 1901
• McKinley was the second of two presidents who died before they completed their second terms. The other was Lincoln.
• He was the fifth of eight presidents who died in office.
Place of death: Buffalo, N.Y.
• He was the sixth of eight presidents who died in New York.
• He was the third of eight presidents who lay in state in the Capitol Rotunda.
Age at death: 58 years, 228 days
Cause of death: Assassination by revolver shot
• He was the third of four presidents who were assassinated.
Place of burial: Canton, Ohio
• He was the fourth of five presidents who were buried in Ohio.

THE VICE PRESIDENTS
(24th and 25th)

Note: McKinley was the last of seven presidents who had two vice presidents.

Full name: Garret Augustus Hobart (24th)
Date of birth: June 3, 1844
Place of birth: Long Branch, N.J.
• Hobart was the second of two vice presidents who were born in New Jersey. The other was Burr.
Religious denomination: Presbyterian
• He was the tenth of 11 vice presidents who were Presbyterians.
College: Rutgers College, New Brunswick, N.J.
Date of graduation: 1863
Occupation: Lawyer
• He was admitted to the bar, began practice in Paterson, N.J., 1866; served in state assembly, 1872–1874; state senate, 1875–1882; president of state senate, 1881–1882.
Term of office: Mar. 4, 1897, to Nov. 21, 1899 (2 years, 262 days)
• He was the ninth of 14 vice presidents who served less than one term.
• McKinley and Hobart were the 26th of 41 president-vice president teams.
Age at inauguration: 52 years, 274 days
State represented: New Jersey

• He was the only vice president who represented New Jersey.
Political party: Republican
• He was the seventh of 15 vice presidents who were Republicans.
Date of death: Nov. 21, 1899 (died in office)
• He was the fifth of six vice presidents who died before completing their first terms.
• He was the sixth of seven vice presidents who died in office.
Place of death: Paterson, N.J.
• He was the only vice president who died in New Jersey.
Age at death: 55 years, 171 days
Place of burial: Paterson, N.J.
• He was the second of two vice presidents who were buried in New Jersey. The other was Burr.

Full name: Theodore Roosevelt (25th)
• See pages 291–309.
• Roosevelt was the second of two vice presidents who were born in New York City. The other was Colfax.
• He was the seventh of eight vice presidents who were born in New York.
• He was the third of four vice presidents who were Dutch Reformed.
• He was the 11th of 14 vice presidents who served as state governors.
• He was the tenth of 14 vice presidents who served less than one term.
• He was the sixth of seven vice presidents who served less than one year.
• McKinley and Roosevelt were the 27th of 41 president-vice president teams.
• Roosevelt was the ninth of ten vice presidents who represented New York.
• He was the eighth of 15 vice presidents who were Republicans.
• He received the Nobel Peace Prize for 1906.
• He was the first of two vice presidents who received the Nobel Peace Prize. The other was Dawes.
• He was the eighth of nine vice presidents who died in New York.
• He was the eighth of nine vice presidents who were buried in New York.

THE CABINET

State: John Sherman of Ohio, Mar. 6, 1897, to Apr. 27, 1898
• William Rufus Day of Ohio, Apr. 28, 1898, to Sept. 16, 1898

•John Milton Hay of Washington, D.C., Sept. 30, 1898, to July 1, 1905

Treasury: Lyman Judson Gage of Illinois, Mar. 6, 1897, to Jan. 31, 1902

War: Russell Alexander Alger of Michigan, Mar. 5, 1897, to Aug. 1, 1899

•Elihu Root of New York, Aug. 1, 1899, to Jan. 31, 1904

Attorney General: Joseph McKenna of California, Mar. 5, 1897, to Jan. 25, 1898

•John William Griggs of New Jersey, Jan. 25, 1898, to Mar. 29, 1901

•Philander Chase Knox of Pennsylvania, Apr. 5, 1901, to June 30, 1904

Navy: John Davis Long of Massachusetts, Mar. 6, 1897, to Apr. 30, 1902

Postmaster General: James Albert Gary of Maryland, Mar. 5, 1897, to Apr. 21, 1898

•Charles Emory Smith of Pennsylvania, Apr. 21, 1898, to Jan. 9, 1902

Interior: Cornelius Newton Bliss of New York, Mar. 5, 1897, to Dec. 21, 1898

•Ethan Allen Hitchcock of Missouri, Dec. 21, 1898, to Mar. 4, 1907

Agriculture: James Wilson of Iowa, Mar. 6, 1897, to Mar. 5, 1913

THE SUPREME COURT

Associate Justice: Joseph McKenna of California, appointed, Dec. 16, 1897; confirmed, Jan. 21, 1898

Twenty-sixth President

THEODORE ROOSEVELT

Full name: Theodore Roosevelt
- He was the first of two presidents named Roosevelt. He and Franklin D. Roosevelt were fifth cousins.
- He was the seventh of eight presidents who had the same full names as their fathers.
- He was the last of 17 presidents who did not have middle initials or middle names.

Date of birth: Oct. 27, 1858
- He was the fourth of five presidents who were born in October.

Place of birth: New York, N.Y.
- He was the only president who was born in New York City.
- He was the third of four presidents who were born in New York.
- His reconstructed birthplace, a Victorian townhouse at 28 East 20th Street, and the adjacent museum, is administered by the National Park Service in cooperation with the Theodore Roosevelt Association. It is open to the public, 9 A.M. to 4:30 P.M., Mondays through Fridays except Christmas and New Year's Day. Admission: adults, 50 cents; children under 16, free.

Family lineage: Dutch and Scottish-Irish-French Hugenot
- He was the only president who was of Dutch and Scottish-Irish-French Huguenot ancestry.

Religious denomination: Dutch Reformed
- He was the second of two presidents who were Dutch Reformed. The other was Van Buren.

College: Harvard University, Cambridge, Mass.
- He was the third of five presidents who went to Harvard.
- He was the 17th of 27 presidents who attended college.

Date of graduation: June 30, 1880, Bachelor of Arts
- He was the 12th of 21 presidents who were graduated from college.

Law School: Columbia Law School, New York, N.Y.
- He was the first of two presidents who attended Columbia Law School. The other was Franklin D. Roosevelt.
- He was the third of nine presidents who attended law school.
- He was the second of six presidents who attended, but were not graduated from law school.

PARENTS AND SIBLINGS

Father's name: Theodore Roosevelt
Date of birth: Sept. 22, 1831
Place of birth: New York, N.Y.
Occupations: Merchant, glass importer
•Roosevelt's father also was collector of the port of New York.
Date of death: Feb. 9, 1878
•Theodore was 19 years, 105 days old when his father died.
Place of death: New York, N.Y.
Age at death: 46 years, 140 days

Mother's name: Martha Bulloch Roosevelt
Date of birth: July 8, 1834
Place of birth: Hartford, Conn.
Date of marriage: Dec. 22, 1853
Children: 4; 2 sons, 2 daughters
•Anna was born in 1855; Theodore in 1858; Elliott in 1860; and Corinne in 1861.
•Elliott was the father of Anna Eleanor Roosevelt, wife of Franklin D. Roosevelt.
•Roosevelt was the first of two presidents who came from families of four children. The other was Wilson.
•He was the seventh of ten presidents who were second children.
Date of death: Feb. 14, 1884
•Both Roosevelt's mother and his first wife died on this date.
Place of death: New York, N.Y.
Age at death: 49 years, 221 days

MARRIAGE

Date of first marriage: Oct. 27, 1880
•Roosevelt was the second of two presidents who were married on their birthdays. The other was Tyler.
Place of first marriage: Brookline, Mass.
•He was the second of two presidents who were married in Massachusetts. The other was John Adams.
Age at first marriage: 22 years
•He was the 18th of 27 presidents who were married in their twenties.
Years married: 3 years, 110 days
•He was the president who was married for the shortest period of time.

First wife's name: Alice Hathaway Lee Roosevelt
•She was the 27th of 40 wives of presidents.

Date of birth: July 29, 1861
•She was the third of four wives of presidents who were born in July.
Place of birth: Chestnut Hill, Mass.
•She was the second of two wives of presidents who were born in Massachusetts. The other was Abigail Adams.
First wife's mother: Caroline Haskell Lee
First wife's father: George Cabot Lee, banker
Age at marriage: 19 years, 90 days
•She was the fourth of five wives of presidents who were married in their teens.
Years younger than husband: 2 years, 275 days
Children: 1 daughter
•Alice Lee was born on Feb. 12, 1884.
•Roosevelt was the 20th of 30 presidents who had children.
Date of death: Feb. 14, 1884
•She was the last of five wives of presidents who died before their husbands' inaugurations.
•She was the last of seven wives of presidents who were not first ladies.
•Both Roosevelt's first wife and his mother died on this date.
Place of death: New York, N.Y.
•She was the third of five wives of presidents who died in New York City.
•She was the fifth of eight wives of presidents who died in New York.
Age at death: 22 years, 200 days
Place of burial: Cambridge, Mass.
•She was the last of three wives of presidents who were buried in Massachusetts.
Years he survived his first wife: 34 years, 326 days
•Roosevelt was the 12th of 14 presidents who survived their wives.

Date of second marriage: Dec. 2, 1886
•He was the only president who remarried before his term of office.
•He was the fourth of five presidents who remarried.
Place of second marriage: London, England
•He was the second of two presidents who were married abroad. The other was John Quincy Adams.
•He was the second of two presidents who were married in London.
Age at second marriage: 28 years, 36 days
•He was the 19th of 27 presidents who were married in their twenties.

Years married: 32 years, 35 days

Second wife's name: Edith Kermit Carow Roosevelt
•She was the 21st of 33 first ladies.
•She was the 28th of 40 wives of presidents.
Date of birth: Aug. 6, 1861
•She was the second of three first ladies who were born in August.
•She was the third of four wives of presidents who were born in August.
Place of birth: Norwich, Conn.
•She was the only first lady or wife of a president who was born in Connecticut.
Second wife's mother: Gertrude Elizabeth Tyler Carow
Second wife's father: Charles Carow, merchant
Age at marriage: 25 years, 118 days
•She was the 18th of 26 first ladies who were married in their twenties.
•She was the 22nd of 30 wives of presidents who were married in their twenties.
Years younger than husband: 2 years, 283 days
Children: 5; 4 sons, 1 daughter
•Theodore was born on Sept. 13, 1887; Kermit on Oct. 10, 1889; Ethel Carow on Aug. 13, 1891; Archibald Bulloch on Apr. 9, 1894; and Quentin on Nov. 19, 1897.
•Roosevelt was the last of three presidents who had children by both wives.
•He was the third of four presidents who had six children.
•He was the 16th of 19 presidents who had both male and female children.

Years she survived her husband: 29 years, 268 days
•She was the 14th of 21 first ladies who survived their husbands.
•She was the 16th of 23 wives of presidents who survived their husbands.
Date of death: Sept. 30, 1948
Place of death: Oyster Bay, N.Y.
•She was the first of three first ladies who died in New York.
•She was the sixth of eight wives of presidents who died in New York.
Age at death: 87 years, 55 days
•She had celebrated her 85th birthday, Aug. 6, 1946.
•She was the tenth of 16 first ladies who lived to be 70.
•She was the 11th of 17 wives of presidents who lived to be 70.
•She was the eighth of 14 first ladies who lived to be 75.
•She was the ninth of 15 wives of presidents who lived to be 75.
•She was the sixth of nine first ladies who lived to be 80.
•She was the seventh of ten wives of presidents who lived to be 80.
•She was the fourth of six first ladies who lived to be 85.
•She was the fifth of seven wives of presidents who lived to be 85.
Place of burial: Oyster Bay, N.Y.
•She was the third of four first ladies who were buried in New York.
•She was the sixth of seven wives of presidents who were buried in New York.

EARLY YEARS

Spring, 1869-May, 1870, toured Europe with family
•The trip included prolonged visits to England, France, The Netherlands, Switzerland, Austria, and Italy. Roosevelt was a sickly child and suffered from asthma; one purpose of the trip was to improve his health, but no material change occurred. He began a program of body building when he returned to New York City, which he continued for many years with good results.
November, 1872-July, 1873, with family, made second trip abroad
•In addition to visits to several countries

seen on his first European tour, he journeyed to Germany, Egypt, and the Holy Land.
July, 1873, with family, moved into new home, 6 West 57th Street, New York City
•He spent most of the next three years studying with a tutor, Arthur Cutler, in preparation for Harvard.
September, 1876, entered Harvard College, Cambridge, Mass.
Feb. 9, 1878, his father died
June 30, 1880, was graduated from Harvard College
•He ranked 21st in a class of 177, and was a member of Phi Beta Kappa.

•He was the last of three presidents who were members of Phi Beta Kappa elected as undergraduates.

•He was the seventh of 11 presidents who were members of Phi Beta Kappa.

Summer, 1880, went on camping trip to Maine; hunting trip to Illinois, Iowa, and Dakota Territory

Oct. 27, 1880, married Alice Hathaway Lee, Chestnut Hill, Mass.

1880-1882, studied law at Columbia Law School, New York City

•He was the first of three presidents who studied law but did not seek admission to the bar.

•He was the 19th of 26 presidents who studied law.

May-September, 1881, with Mrs. Roosevelt, toured Europe

Nov. 9, 1881, elected to New York state assembly

1882, his first book, *The Naval War of 1812,* published

•He began the book during his senior year at Harvard and completed it following his return from Europe.

•He was the 11th of 21 presidents who wrote books that were published during their lifetimes.

Jan. 2, 1882, took seat in state assembly

•At 23, he was the youngest member of the legislature. He was reelected in 1882 and 1883. He was an unsuccessful candidate for speaker in his third term.

Aug. 1, 1882, commissioned as second lieutenant, New York national guard

Feb. 3, 1883, promoted to captain

•His sporadic attendance during the three years that he was a member of the national guard constituted his total military experience prior to 1898.

Fall, 1883, hunted buffalo in Dakota Territory

•During this trip he bought a share in a cattle ranch for $14,000.

Feb. 12, 1884, his first daughter born

•The girl was named Alice Lee Roosevelt.

Feb. 14, 1884, his mother and his wife died

•The legislature was in session at Albany, Feb. 13, when he received word of the birth of his daughter. He left for home at once and arrived there shortly before midnight to be told by his brother Elliott that both his mother and his wife were dying. His mother died of typhoid fever at 3 A.M.; his wife at 2 P.M. of Bright's disease. A dou-

ble funeral was held, Feb. 16.

Feb. 20, 1884, returned to Albany for remainder of session

June 3-6, 1884, attended Republican national convention, Chicago, Ill.

June 9, 1884, arrived at Medora, Dakota Territory

•He spent nearly two years there, with occasional trips East for business and Christmas visits. He now had two ranches in the territory. His Harvard diction was somewhat incongruous in these surroundings. His exhortation to a cowboy during a roundup, "Hasten forward quickly there," became a local catch phrase, especially popular for encouraging speedy service in saloons.

1884-1885, built Sagamore Hill, Oyster Bay, L.I.

•His 26-room home on Cove Neck Road is administered by the National Park Service in cooperation with the Theodore Roosevelt Association. It is open to the public daily, 9 A.M. to 5 P.M., except Christmas and New Year's Day. Admission: adults, 50 cents; children under 16, free.

1885, his book, *Hunting Trip of a Ranchman,* published by Putnam, New York City

1885, appointed deputy sheriff of Billings County, Dakota Territory

March, 1886, captured three thieves who had stolen his boat

•Since he lacked another boat to pursue the thieves, he and two friends constructed a raft in three days and spent another three days overtaking the thieves.

October, 1886, returned to East

November, 1886, defeated as Republican candidate for mayor, New York City

Dec. 2, 1886, married Edith Kermit Carow, London, England

Mar. 28, 1887, with Mrs. Roosevelt, returned to New York City

1887, his book, *Life of Thomas Hart Benton,* published by Houghton Mifflin, Boston, Mass.

Sept. 13, 1887, his first son born

•The boy was named Theodore Roosevelt.

1888, his book, *Gouverneur Morris,* published by Houghton Mifflin, Boston, Mass.

1888, his book, *Ranch Life and the Hunting Trail,* published by Century, New York City

•This book was illustrated by Frederic Remington.

May 13, 1889, took office as member of U.S. Civil Service Commission

•Appointed by Benjamin Harrison, Roosevelt was reappointed by Cleveland in 1893. He served until May 1, 1895.

1889, first volume of his book, *The Winning of the West, 1769–1807,* published by Putnam, New York City

•The fourth and last volume was published in 1896.

Oct. 10, 1889, his second son born

•The boy was named Kermit Roosevelt.

1891, his book, *New York,* published by Longmans, Green, New York City

Aug. 13, 1891, his second daughter born

•The girl was named Ethel Carow Roosevelt.

Apr. 9, 1894, his third son born

•The boy was named Archibald Bulloch Roosevelt.

1895, *Hero Tales from American History,* published by Century, New York City.

•He wrote this book in collaboration with Henry Cabot Lodge.

May, 1895, appointed to board of police commissioners, New York City

•Shortly afterward he was elected president of the four-man board. Another member was Frederick D. Grant, a son of former President Grant.

Apr. 5, 1897, appointed assistant secretary of navy by McKinley

•Roosevelt was confirmed by the Senate, Apr. 8.

•He was the first of two presidents who served as assistant secretaries of navy. The other was Franklin D. Roosevelt.

Nov. 19, 1897, his fourth son born

•The boy was named Quentin Roosevelt.

Feb. 15, 1898, *U.S.S. Maine* sunk, Havana, Cuba

Feb. 25, 1898, ordered Commodore George Dewey to assemble Asiatic squadron at Hong Kong

•The order included instructions to prevent the departure of the Spanish fleet in the Pacific in the event of war. Roosevelt exceeded his authority in issuing this directive in the absence of his superior, Secretary of Navy Long, a fact that was overlooked after Dewey's victory at Manila Bay, May 1.

Apr. 25, 1898, war declared on Spain

•Offered the colonelcy of the First Volunteer Cavalry Regiment, he declined on the grounds that he lacked military experi-

ence. His suggestion that the post be offered to Captain Leonard Wood was followed. Roosevelt was commissioned as lieutenant colonel of the regiment, which the press nicknamed "The Rough Riders" since its members were recruited largely from among the cowboys of the Southwest.

May 6, 1898, resigned as assistant secretary of navy

May, 1898, trained at army camp near San Antonio, Tex.

•He was the only president who served in the Spanish-American War.

•He was the 16th of 21 presidents who served in the military during wartime.

June 5, 1898, promoted to colonel

June 13, 1898, sailed for Cuba, Tampa, Fla.

June 22, 1898, arrived in Cuba

June 24, 1898, fought first skirmish, Las Guasimas

•There are conflicting reports as to whether his troops were ambushed by retreating Spanish forces. Richard Harding Davis, who called it an ambush at the time in a dispatch to the New York *Herald,* changed his mind by 1910, when he said that "far from anyone running into an ambush, every one of the officers had full knowledge of where he would find the enemy."

July 1, 1898, led charge up one of San Juan hills

•The rise he and his troops charged was called Kettle Hill because sugar kettles abandoned by the Spaniards were found at ·the top. The San Juan blockhouse was on a nearby hill and gave its name to a whole group of hills.

•This was his only major military engagement.

Aug. 1, 1898, signed letter that advocated removal of U.S. troops from Santiago

•The troops, who had occupied Santiago following its surrender, July 17, had been ordered to remain as a matter of military expediency, although they suffered from severe attacks of malaria and yellow fever. The letter was actually a round-robin protest that represented the views of a number of officers, most from the regular army, whose careers would have been prejudiced if they had signed it. The letter was published in the U.S., Aug. 5, and provoked sufficient public outcry to cause withdrawal of the troops.

Aug. 15, 1898, landed at Montauk, L.I.

Sept. 4, 1898, said farewell to troops

NATIONAL PROMINENCE

Nov. 5, 1898, elected governor of New York
• Roosevelt took office in January, 1899.
• He was the third of four presidents who served as governors of New York.
• He was the tenth of 13 presidents who served as state governors
1899, his book, *Rough Riders*, published by Scribner, New York City
June 21, 1900, nominated for vice president, Republican national convention, Philadephia, Pa.
Nov. 6, 1900, elected vice president
• *See* Election of 1900, pages 287–288.
Mar. 4, 1901, took oath of office as vice president

Apr. 24, 1901, degree of Master Mason conferred by Matinecock Lodge No. 806, Oyster Bay, N.Y.
• He was the ninth of 13 presidents who were Masons.
Sept. 6, 1901, McKinley shot
• He was informed of the assassination attempt while attending an outing of the Vermont Fish and Game League and left for Buffalo immediately. By Sept. 10, when McKinley was reported much improved, Roosevelt departed to join his family in the Adirondacks. He was mountain-climbing, Sept. 13, when word arrived that McKinley was dying.

THE PRESIDENT (26th)

Term of office: Sept. 14, 1901, to Mar. 4, 1909 (7 years, 171 days)
• Roosevelt was the eighth of 12 presidents who had served as vice presidents.
• He was the fifth of eight presidents who, because of the death of their predecessors, did not complete their vice-presidential terms.
• He was the first of four presidents who served the unexpired terms of their predecessors and were elected to and served second terms.
• He was the tenth of 16 presidents who served more than one term.
State represented: New York
• He was the fifth of eight presidents who

represented New York.
Political party: Republican
• He was the eight of 14 presidents who were Republicans.
Congresses: 57th, 58th, 59th, 60th
Administrations: 29th, 30th
Age at taking oath: 42 years, 322 days
• Roosevelt took the oath of office at the residence of Ansley Wilcox in Buffalo, N.Y., on Saturday, Sept. 14, 1901. The oath was administered by Judge John R. Hazel of the U.S. District Court.
• He was the fifth of seven presidents who took the oath of office from an official other than a justice of the Supreme Court.
• Roosevelt was the youngest president.

THE 29th ADMINISTRATION

1901

Sept. 14, issued proclamation designating Sept. 19 as day of mourning for President McKinley
Oct. 17, entertained Booker T. Washington, White House
• Roosevelt's reception of the Negro leader caused great indignation throughout the South.
Nov. 19, issued executive order revoking McKinley civil service modification order of May 29, 1899
Nov. 27, authorized application of civil service rules to Indian agencies

Dec. 2, first session of 57th Congress
• The administration controlled both the Senate and the House of Representatives. The Republicans gained three Senate and 13 House seats. The Senate (90 members) consisted of 56 Republicans, 29 Democrats, three others, and two vacancies. The House (357 members) consisted of 198 Republicans, 153 Democrats, five others, and one vacancy.
Dec. 3, sent his first State of the Union message to Congress
• His message of over thirty thousand words called for the regulation of corporations and trusts, an extensive conservation pro-

gram, a more efficient army and an enlarged navy, and the extension of civil service.

Dec. 16, Hay-Pauncefote Treaty ratified
•The treaty with Great Britain, which concerned the Isthmian canal, had been signed, Nov. 18. It provided that the U.S. was to have the sole right of construction, maintenance, and control of the canal and that fortification was permitted. The treaty superceded the Clayton-Bulwer Treaty of 1850.

1902

Jan. 9, accepted resignations of Secretary of Treasury Gage and Postmaster General Smith
•Gage's resignation was effective, Jan. 31.
Jan. 9, appointed his second secretary of treasury, Leslie M. Shaw, and his second postmaster general, Henry C. Payne
•Shaw took office, Feb. 1.
Jan. 20, sent canal commission report to Congress
•The report recommended the purchase of the property and rights to the Panama Canal for $40,000,000.
Mar. 6, signed permanent census bureau act
Mar. 8, signed Philippine tariff act
Mar. 10, accepted resignation of Secretary of Navy Long, effective, Apr. 30
Mar. 10, first antitrust suit, Northern Securities Company
•He had directed Attorney General Knox to bring suit against the railroad holding company, which had been organized by James J. Hill, Nov. 12, 1901.
Mar. 11, vetoed removal of charge of desertion from naval record of John Glass bill
•This was the first of his 82 vetoes.
Mar. 25, issued executive order that provided for evacuation of Cuba
•The formal transfer from American to Cuban control occurred, May. 20.
Apr. 11, issued proclamation that set apart Santa Rita forest reserve, Ariz.
Apr. 16, issued proclamation establishing Niobrara forest reserve, Neb.
Apr. 29, appointed his second secretary of navy, William H. Moody
•Moody took office, May 1.
May 7, issued proclamation that set apart Fort Hall forest reserve, Idaho
May 9, dispatched William Howard Taft to negotiate with Pope Leo XIII for sale of friar lands in Philippines

May 22, issued proclamations that set apart Medicine Bow, Yellowstone, and Teton forest reserves, Wy.
June 7, ordered investigation of coal strike
•Anthracite coal miners, who sought a 20 percent wage increase and an eight-hour day, had gone out on strike, May 12.
July 1, first session of 57th Congress adjourned
July 3, issued proclamation of peace and amnesty in Philippines
July 17, signed conservation act
July 22, issued proclamation that set apart Mount Graham forest reserve, Ariz.
July 26, issued proclamation that set apart Lincoln forest reserve, N. Mex.
July 30, issued proclamation that set apart Chiricahua forest reserve, Ariz.
Aug. 11, appointed Oliver W. Holmes as associate justice
•Holmes, who was confirmed by the Senate, Dec. 4, was the first of Roosevelt's three appointments to the Supreme Court.
Aug. 16, issued proclamation that set apart Little Belt Mountains and Madison forest reserves, Mont.
Aug. 19, began trust policy speaking tour, New England and Middle West
•Enforcement of the antitrust laws was not an attempt to destroy big business, he explained, but corporations must "subserve the public good."
Aug. 20, issued proclamation that set apart Alexander Archipelago forest reserve, Alaska
Sept. 3, suffered minor injuries when his car collided with trolley near Pittsfield, Mass.
Sept. 3, received coal strike report
•The modified demands of the miners, a ten percent wage increase, and an eight to ten-hour day, were refused by the operators.
Sept. 15, Associate Justice Gray died
Oct. 3, invited mine owners and John Mitchell, president of United Mine Workers, to White House
•Roosevelt's request to open the mines pending an examination of the facts by a federal commission was refused by the operators.
Oct. 16, appointed Coal Strike Commission
•The miners agreed to accept the decision of the commission. The strike was declared at an end by Mitchell, Oct. 21.
Dec. 1, second session of 57th Congress

Dec. 2, sent his second State of the Union message to Congress

1903

Jan. 18, sent greetings to King Edward VII of Great Britain
•The message was sent by wireless telegraph from the Marconi station, Wellfleet, Mass.
Feb. 12, signed act increasing Supreme Court salaries
•This act raised the salary of the chief justice to $13,000, and those of associate justices to $12,500.
Feb. 14, signed act establishing department of commerce and labor
Feb. 16, appointed first secretary of commerce and labor, George B. Cortelyou
•Cortelyou took office, Feb. 18.
Feb. 19, accepted resignation of Associate Justice Shiras, effective, Feb. 23
Feb. 19, appointed William R. Day as associate justice
•Day, who was confirmed by the Senate, Feb. 23, was the second of Roosevelt's three appointments to the Supreme Court.
Mar. 3, second session of 57th Congress adjourned
Mar. 3, pocket vetoed six bills
•Four were pension bills, one was a private relief bill, and one concerned alteration of a military record.
•These were the first six of his 40 pocket vetoes.
Mar. 14, was named umpire of claims in case of Great Britain, Germany, and Italy against Venezuela
July 4, sent first message on Pacific cable to Philippines
•He also sent the second message, which went around the world in 12 minutes.
Aug. 12, Hay-Herran Convention rejected by Colombia
•The convention, which had been ratified by the U.S. Senate, would have provided for a six-mile-wide canal zone across the Isthmus of Panama.
Nov. 2, ordered warships to Panama to maintain "free and uninterrupted transit" across Isthmus
Nov. 3, Panama revolution began
Nov. 6, recognized independence of Panama from Colombia
Nov. 9, first session of 58th Congress

•The administration maintained control of both the Senate and the House of Representatives. The Republicans gained two Senate and nine House seats. The Senate (90 members) consisted of 58 Republicans and 32 Democrats. The House (386 members) consisted of 207 Republicans, 178 Democrats, and one vacancy.
Nov. 13, formally received Philippe Bunau-Varilla, minister from Panama
Nov. 18, Hay-Bunau-Varilla treaty signed
•The treaty provided that the Republic of Panama would lease to the U. S. a ten-mile-wide canal zone across the Isthmus in perpetuity for $10,000,000 and an annual fee of $250,000, beginning nine years after the exchange of ratifications. The treaty was ratified by the Senate, Feb. 23, 1904.
Dec. 7, first session of 58th Congress adjourned
Dec. 7, second session of 58th Congress
Dec. 7, sent his third State of the Union message to Congress

1904

Jan. 11, accepted resignation of Secretary of War Root, effective, Jan. 31
Jan. 11, appointed his second secretary of war, William Howard Taft
•Taft took office, Feb. 1.
Feb. 22, sent Admiral George Dewey to investigate conditions in Santo Domingo
•A detachment of U.S. Marines landed on the island, Feb. 26.
Mar. 15, issued executive order establishing Civil War service pension
•All veterans over 62 years of age were to receive a minimum of $6 per month, a maximum of $12 at 70, effective, Apr. 13.
Apr. 27, signed naval construction act
•This act authorized the construction of two first class battleships, two first class cruisers, three scout cruisers, and two colliers.
Apr. 28, signed act creating merchant marine commission
Apr. 28, second session of 58th Congress adjourned
May 13, issued proclamation that opened 382,000 acres of Rosebud reservation, S.D., to settlers, July 1
•This was the last of the large government land grants.
June 21, nominated for president by accla-

mation, Republican national convention, Chicago, Ill.

June 23, had ultimatum, "We want either Perdicaris alive or Raisuli dead," read to Republican delegates

• An elderly American citizen, Ion Perdicaris, had been kidnapped in Tangier by the brigand chieftain, Ahmed ben Mohammed Raisuli, purely as a gesture of defiance of the Sultan of Morocco. Perdicaris was never in danger.

• Roosevelt ordered the message read to the convention, where it received the expected cheers and created the obvious headlines, knowing full well that Perdicaris's release was imminent. The message, dispatched to the U.S. consul general in Tangier, actually had been written by Secretary of State Hay with the aid of a phrase-turning newspaperman, Edward M. Hood.

June 30, accepted resignations of Attorney General Knox, Secretary of Navy Moody, and Secretary of Commerce and Labor Cortelyou

July 1, appointed his second attorney general, William H. Moody; his third secretary of navy, Paul Morton; and his second secretary of commerce and labor, Victor H. Metcalf

Oct. 4, Postmaster General Payne died

Oct. 10, appointed his third postmaster general, Robert J. Wynne

Nov. 8, election day

• *See* Election of 1904, below.

Dec. 5, third session of 58th Congress

Dec. 6, sent his fourth State of the Union message to Congress

• He announced his policy of possible intervention in hemispheric affairs, which has come to be known as the Roosevelt Corollary to the Monroe Doctrine. He said:

> Chronic wrongdoing or an impotence which results in a general loosening of the ties of civilized society, may in America, as elsewhere, ultimately require intervention by some civilized nation, and in the Western Hemisphere the adherence of the United States to the Monroe Doctrine may force the United States, however reluctantly, in flagrant cases of such wrongdoing or impotence, to the exercise of an international police force.

1905

Jan. 9, presidential electors cast ballots

• He received 336 of the 476 electoral votes from the 45 states.

• *See* Election of 1904, below.

Feb. 1, appointed Gifford Pinchot as chief of forest service division, department of agriculture

Feb. 8, electoral vote tabulated by Congress

• Roosevelt and Fairbanks were officially declared elected.

Feb. 26, received report of Panama Canal engineering commission

• The commission recommended the construction of a sea-level canal, which would cost $230,500,000 over a period of 12 years.

Mar. 3, third session of 58th Congress adjourned

Mar. 3, pocket vetoed two bills

• One was an amendment to a District of Columbia smoke prevention bill, and the other was a bill to confirm a lease made by the Seneca Nation Indians of New York.

ELECTION OF 1904

Socialist party, convened, May 1, at Chicago, Ill., nominated Eugene Victor Debs of Indiana for president, Benjamin Hanford of New York for vice president.

Republican party, convened, June 21, at Chicago, Ill., nominated Theodore Roosevelt of New York for president, Charles Warren Fairbanks of Indiana for vice president

• This was the 13th Republican national convention. It was the sixth Republican convention in Chicago; it was the tenth major party convention in Chicago.

Prohibition party, convened, June 29, at Indianapolis, Ind., nominated Silas Comfort Swallow of Pennsylvania for president, George W. Carroll of Texas for vice president.

Socialist Labor party, convened, July 2, at New York City, nominated Charles Hunter Corregan of New York for president, William Wesley Cox of Illinois for vice president.

People's (Populist) party, convened, July 4, at Springfield, Ill., nominated Thomas Edward Watson of Georgia for president,

Thomas Henry Tibbles of Nebraska for vice president.

Democratic party, convened, July 6, at St. Louis, Mo., nominated Alton Brooks Parker of New York for president, Henry Gassaway Davis of West Virginia for vice president.

•This was the 19th Democratic national convention. It was the third Democratic convention held in St. Louis; it was the fourth major party convention held in St. Louis.

Continental party, convened, Aug. 31, at Chicago, Ill., nominated Austin Holcomb of Georgia for president, Albert King of Missouri for vice president.

Election day, Tuesday, Nov. 8, 1904

Popular vote: 13,523,224

    Roosevelt, 7,628,785

    Parker, 5,084,338

    Debs, 402,893

    Swallow, 258,750

    Watson, 114,138

    Corregan, 33,490

    Holcomb, 830

Electoral vote: 476, 45 states

• Roosevelt, 336, 32 states
(California, 10; Colorado, 5; Connecticut, 7; Delaware, 3; Idaho, 3; Illinois, 27; Indiana, 15; Iowa, 13; Kansas, 10; Maine, 6; Massachusetts, 16; Michigan, 14, Minnesota, 11; Missouri, 18; Montana, 3; Nebraska, 8, Nevada, 3; New Hampshire, 4; New Jersey, 12; New York, 39; North Dakota, 4; Ohio, 23; Oregon, 4; Pennsylvania, 34; Rhode Island, 4; South Dakota, 4; Utah, 3; Vermont, 4; Washington, 5; West Virginia, 7; Wisconsin, 13; Wyoming, 13)

•Roosevelt also received the vote of one Maryland elector.

• Parker, 140, 13 states
(Alabama, 11; Arkansas, 9; Florida, 5; Georgia, 13; Kentucky, 13; Louisiana, 9; Maryland, 7 of 8 votes; Mississippi, 10; North Carolina, 12; South Carolina, 9; Tennessee, 12; Texas, 18; Virginia, 12)

•Roosevelt was the second of four presidents who defeated major opponents representing the same state (Parker).

THE 30th ADMINISTRATION

1905

Mar. 4, his inauguration day

•Roosevelt took the oath of office, administered by Chief Justice Melville W. Fuller, on the east portico of the Capitol

•This was the fifth of six inaugurations at which Fuller officiated.

•Roosevelt's age at his second inauguration was 46 years, 128 days.

•He was the 14th of 21 presidents who were younger than their vice presidents. Roosevelt was six years, 169 days younger than Fairbanks.

Mar. 4, special session of Senate

Mar. 6, accepted resignation of Postmaster General Wynne

Mar. 6, appointed his fourth postmaster general, George B. Cortelyou

Mar. 18, special session of Senate adjourned

•The Senate refused to ratify the Santo Domingo protocol, which would have given the U.S. control of custom finances in order to guarantee Santo Domingo's European debts. Roosevelt made a similar ar-

rangement with the bankrupt government, which made Santo Domingo a virtual U.S. protectorate, His action was an example of the Roosevelt Corollary to the Monroe Doctrine.

Mar. 29, accepted resignation of Panama Canal commission

Apr. 1, appointed new Panama Canal commission

May 5, ordered investigation of tobacco trust

May 12, issued proclamation that set apart Chesnimnus forest reserve, Ore.

May 31, accepted resignation of Secretary of Navy Morton, effective, June 30

June 8, sent identical notes urging Russia and Japan to end conflict

•His proposal of a peace conference was accepted. He chose Portsmouth, N.H., as the site of the conference, July 11.

June 20, dismissed minister to Venezuela, Herbert W. Bowen

•Bowen had been recalled, Apr. 29, for having made unfounded charges against his predecessor, F. B. Loomis.

June 23, issued executive order in regard to exemptions from provisions of Chinese exclusion laws
• His order exempted Chinese officials, merchants, students, and travelers.
July 1, Secretary of State Hay died
July 1, appointed his fourth secretary of navy, Charles J. Bonaparte
July 7, appointed his second secretary of state, Elihu Root
• Root took office, July 19.
Aug. 5, met with Russian and Japanese peace commissioners, Oyster Bay, N.Y.
• The peace conference opened at Portsmouth, N.H., Aug. 9.
Aug. 7, ordered federal supervision of yellow fever district, Louisiana
• An epidemic in New Orleans was reported, July 20. The government antimosquito campaign brought the situation under control in October, after about four hundred persons had died.
Aug. 25, submerged in submarine off Oyster Bay, N.Y.
• He was the first of three presidents who submerged in submarines while in office.
Sept. 5, peace treaty signed by representatives of Russia and Japan, Portsmouth, N.H.
• He demurred at supporting Japanese claims for indemnity. However, Japan was given "paramount political, military and economic" interests in Korea, as well as concessions in southern Manchuria.
Nov. 3, received Rear Admiral Prince Louis of Battenburg
• Prince Louis, the commander of a visiting British naval squadron, changed his name during World War I to Mountbatten. He was made Marquess of Milford Haven and married a granddaughter of Queen Victoria. His grandson, made Duke of Edinburgh, married Princess Elizabeth of Great Britain, now Queen Elizabeth II.
Dec. 4, first session of 59th Congress
• The administration controlled both the Senate and the House of Representatives. The Republicans gained 43 House seats. The Senate (90 members) consisted of 58 Republicans and 32 Democrats. The House (386 members) consisted of 250 Republicans and 136 Democrats.
Dec. 5, sent his fifth State of the Union message to Congress

1906

Feb. 17, attended wedding of his daughter, Alice Lee, to Nicholas Longworth, White House
• This was the fourth of eight White House marriages of daughters of presidents.
• This was the fifth of nine White House weddings of children of presidents.
Feb. 19, decided for lock canal for Panama Canal
• Opinion was sharply divided; lock canal proponents were opposed by those who favored a sea-level canal.
Apr. 7, Act of Algeciras
• Convinced that France and Germany had brought Europe close to a general war over the question of Morocco in 1905, Roosevelt intervened at the suggestion of Kaiser Wilhelm II and persuaded both sides to meet in conference, with the U.S. in attendance, at Algeciras, Spain, Jan. 16. He was instrumental in persuading the Germans to agree to allow France to police Morocco in exchange for the assurance of German investment protection. The Act of Algeciras, a major diplomatic victory for France, was ratified by the Senate in 1906 with the proviso that the U.S. was not obligated to enforce its provisions.
Apr. 14, delivered "muckrake" speech
• He first referred to the expose writers of the period as "muckrakers" in his off-the-record speech at the Gridiron Club dinner, Jan. 17. His reference to Bunyan's allegorical figure in *Pilgrim's Progress*, and its application, remained off-the-record for as long as it took the newspapermen and their guests to leave the banquet hall.
• Quick to realize that he had stumbled on yet another catchy figure of speech, he repeated it in his speech at the dedication of the cornerstone of the House of Representatives office building. He declared:

> There is filth on the floor, and it must be scraped up with the muckrake; and there are times and places where this service is the most needed of all the services that can be performed. But the man who never does anything else, who never thinks or speaks or writes, save of his feats with the muckrake, speedily becomes, not a help to society, not an incitement to good,

but one of the most potent forces of evil.

• The attack-word quickly was applied to all of the reform writers, the serious investigators as well as the sensationalists. While many took offense, "muckraker" soon came to be regarded as a term of approval, a categorical badge of honor.

May 28, accepted resignation of Associate Justice Brown

June 4, sent report of president's commission to investigate meat packing industry to Congress

• The report bore out Upton Sinclair's indictment of the meat packers in his novel, *The Jungle.*

June 16, signed enabling act for Oklahoma and Indian Territory to form state

June 23, signed act providing for presidential travel expense account not exceeding $25,000 annually

June 27, issued executive order providing system of consular service examination and promotion

June 29, signed act authorizing lock canal plan

June 29, signed act establishing bureau of immigration and naturalization

June 30, signed Pure Food and Drug Act

June 30, signed Meat Inspection Act

June 30, first session of 59th Congress adjourned

June 30, pocket vetoed nine bills

July 20, appointed pure food commission

Aug. 14, Brownsville, Tex., riot

• During the midnight raid on the town, allegedly by Negro soldiers from nearby Fort Brown, a white bartender was killed and a policeman was wounded. None of the raiders was ever identified.

Aug. 23, tabled Cuban request for U.S. aid

• Tomas Estrada Palma, the first president of Cuba, asked for assistance to put down a revolt that grew out of election disputes. Troops were sent during October and remained for about two weeks before order was restored.

Aug. 27, ordered public printer to use simplified spelling

• When the Spelling Reform Association, headed by his friend, Professor Brander Matthews of Columbia University, proposed three hundred changes in spelling, he ordered the printing office to adopt the new words in official publications. A furor followed. Henry Watterson of the Louis-ville *Courier-Journal* summed up the opposition's arguments in an editorial which stated that the president's name should be spelled "Rucefelt," "the first silabel riming with goose."

Sept. 12, ordered marines to Haiti

Sept. 19, issued proclamation extending eight-hour day to all government workers

Sept. 19, issued proclamation that opened 500,000 acres in Oklahoma Territory to settlers

Nov. 5, punished three companies of Negro troops for Brownsville, Tex., raid of Aug 14

• He ordered more than 160 soldiers discharged without honor and barred from reenlistment after he became convinced that the soldiers had entered into a conspiracy of silence to protect the guilty. Since election day was Nov. 6, his order, which conceivably could have influenced the Negro vote, was withheld for several days.

• Not until Mar. 2, 1909, two days before he left office, did he take further action; he signed a measure appointing a military court to review the individual cases of the discharged soldiers.

Nov. 9, departed for Panama

• He arrived in the Canal Zone, Nov. 15.

• This was the first occasion when a president left the U.S. while in office.

• He was the first of five presidents who visited Panama while in office.

• He was the first of 11 presidents who traveled outside the U.S. while in office.

Nov. 16, inspected Panama Canal

Nov. 21, visited Puerto Rico

• He was the first of seven presidents who visited Puerto Rico while in office.

Nov. 26, returned to Washington, D.C.

Dec. 3, appointed William H. Moody as associate justice

• Moody, who was confirmed by the Senate, Dec. 12, was the last of Roosevelt's three appointments to the Supreme Court.

Dec. 3, second session of 59th Congress

Dec. 3, sent his sixth State of the Union message to Congress

• In his most radical State of the Union message, he said that all big business was engaged in interstate commerce and should eventually be subject to federal controls. He called for government inspection of corporation books.

Dec. 10, officially notified of Nobel Peace Prize

•He was awarded the peace prize for his services in terminating the Russo-Japanese War.

•He was the first American to receive the Nobel Peace Prize.

•He was the first of two presidents who received the Nobel Peace Prize. The other was Wilson.

Dec. 12, accepted resignation of Attorney General Moody, effective, Dec. 17

Dec. 12, accepted resignations of Secretary of Navy Bonaparte and Secretary of Commerce and Labor Metcalf effective, Dec. 16

Dec. 12, appointed his third attorney general, Charles J. Bonaparte; his fifth secretary of navy, Victor H. Metcalf; and his third secretary of commerce and labor, Oscar S. Straus

•Bonaparte, Metcalf, and Straus took office, Dec. 17.

•Straus was the first Jew to serve in the cabinet.

1907

Jan. 14, accepted resignations of Secretary of Treasury Shaw, Postmaster General Cortelyou, and Secretary of Interior Hitchcock

•Shaw's resignation was effective, Mar. 3; Cortelyou's and Hitchcock's resignations were effective, Mar. 4.

Jan. 15, appointed his third secretary of treasury, George B. Cortelyou; his fifth postmaster general, George von L. Meyer, and his second secretary of interior, James R. Garfield

•Cortelyou, Meyer, and Garfield took office, Mar. 4.

•James Rudolph Garfield was the second of two sons of presidents who served in the cabinet. The other was Robert Todd Lincoln.

•George B. Cortelyou was the only member of the cabinet who headed three executive departments. He previously had served as secretary of commerce and labor and postmaster general.

Jan. 26, signed act that prohibited political contributions by corporations

Feb. 20, authorized by immigration act to refuse entry of certain immigrants

•This act authorized refusal of entry to any person carrying a passport of any country

other than the U.S. It was designed to keep out undesirables, the insane and feeble-minded, and others.

Feb. 26, signed act raising salary of vice president from $8,000 to $12,000, effective, Mar. 4, 1909

•Sherman was the first recipient of the new salary.

Mar. 1, signed act amending public printing regulations

•This amendment ended his simplified spelling experiment. "In my own correspondence, I shall continue using the new spelling," he said, and he did.

Mar. 2, endowed Foundation for Promotion of Industrial Peace with Nobel Peace Prize award

Mar. 4, second session of 59th Congress adjourned

Mar. 4, pocket vetoed six bills

Mar. 14, appointed inland waterways commission

•The commission was formed to study forest preservation and commercial waterways.

Mar. 14, issued executive order denying entry to U.S. of Japanese laborers from Hawaii, Mexico, and Canada

Apr. 26, opened Tercentenary Exposition, Jamestown, Va.

Oct. 22, Panic of 1907

•The seventh of nine U.S. depressions was initiated by the failure of the Knickerbocker Trust Company of New York City, which was brought about by reports of an attempt to corner the copper market. The Westinghouse Electric and Manufacturing Company went into receivership the next day, the Pittsburgh Stock Exchange suspended operations, and a number of bank failures followed. J. P. Morgan prevented the closing of the New York Stock Exchange and the failure of the Trust Company of America by means of a personal loan. This and other Morgan loans, which matched the $25,000,000 deposited in New York banks by the treasury department, checked the panic. The crisis passed in December.

Nov. 16, Oklahoma admitted as 46th state

•Oklahoma was the only state admitted during Roosevelt's term of office.

Dec. 1, issued executive order extending merit system to almost one-third of fourth class postmasters

Dec. 2, first session of 60th Congress

•The administration maintained control of both the Senate and the House of Representatives. The Republicans gained three Senate seats but lost 28 House seats. The Senate (92 members) consisted of 61 Republicans, 29 Democrats, and two vacancies. The House (386 members) consisted of 222 Republicans and 164 Democrats.

Dec. 3, sent his seventh State of the Union message to Congress

Dec. 16, dispatched fleet of 16 battleships on world cruise

•His intention was to underline the fact that the U.S. was now second in naval power only to Great Britain.

1908

May 13–15, conference of governors, White House

•He invited the governors and other prominent citizens to discuss the means of conserving natural resources.

May 23, vetoed bill to extend time for construction of dam across Rainy River, Minn.

May 23, act to extend time for construction of dam across Rainy River, Minn., passed over his veto

•This was the only one of his 82 vetoes that was overridden.

May 30, first session of 60th Congress adjourned

June 6, appointed conservation commission

June 19, accepted resignation of Secretary of War Taft, effective, June 30

June 24, President Cleveland died

•With the death of Cleveland, Roosevelt became the third of four presidents who served for periods when no former president was living.

June 29, appointed his third secretary of war, Luke E. Wright

•Wright took office, July 1.

Aug. 10, appointed country life commission

Nov. 3, 1908, election day

• *See* Election of 1908, pages 313–314.

Nov. 30, issued executive order that placed fifteen thousand fourth class postmasters in classified civil service

•This order covered all fourth class postmasters north of the Ohio River and east of the Mississippi River.

Nov. 30, accepted resignation of Secretary of Navy Metcalf

Dec. 1, appointed his sixth secretary of navy, Truman H. Newberry

Dec. 2, second session of 60th Congress

Dec. 8, sent his eighth and last State of the Union message to Congress

Dec. 15, sent special message to Congress in which he asked investigation of New York *World*

•He labeled a series of critical articles that had appeared in the *World* and had been widely reprinted before and after the election "a string of infamous libels." The articles, on the Panama Canal purchase, accused him of lying and charged that insiders, including his brother-in-law, Douglas Robinson, and Charles P. Taft, half brother of President-elect Taft, had siphoned off millions of dollars when the U.S. paid $40,000,000 for the defunct French company. The "real offender," Roosevelt said in his message, was Joseph Pulitzer, publisher of the *World*, and added:

> While the criminal offense of which Mr. Pulitzer has been guilty is in form a libel upon individuals, the great injury done is in blackening the good name of the American people. It should not be left to a private citizen to sue Mr. Pulitzer for libel. He should be prosecuted for libel by the government authorities.

1909

Jan. 27, accepted resignation of Secretary of State Root

Jan. 27, appointed his third secretary of state, Robert Bacon

•Bacon was the last of Roosevelt's 21 cabinet appointments

Feb. 17, federal grand jury indicted Joseph Pulitzer and editors of New York *World*

•A federal indictment was returned in the District of Columbia District Court. Pulitzer was charged on five counts of criminal libel of Roosevelt, Charles P. Taft, Douglas Robinson, J. P. Morgan, Elihu Root, and William N. Cromwell. Cromwell, a New York attorney, had earned a legal fee of $800,000 for his part in the Panama Canal purchase. Totally unjustified, inasmuch as the defendants were summoned to appear for trial in Washington rather than their home districts, the case was dismissed on the ground of jurisdiction, Jan. 25, 1910.

Feb. 21, U.S. fleet returned after world cruise

Feb. 22, reviewed fleet, Hampton Roads, Va.

Mar. 4, signed act increasing salary of president from $50,000 to $75,000

• Taft was the first recipient of the new salary.

Mar. 4, second session of 60th Congress adjourned

Mar. 4, pocket vetoed 17 bills

• These were the last of his 82 vetoes, the last of his 40 pocket vetoes.

THE FORMER PRESIDENT

Mar. 4, 1909, attended inauguration of Taft

• Roosevelt's age upon leaving office was 50 years, 128 days.

• He was the youngest former president.

• He did not ride back to the White House with his successor, as was customary, but instead was escorted to the railroad station by the New York delegation. He and his wife departed for Oyster Bay, L.I.

Mar. 23, 1909, with his son, Kermit, sailed for Africa, Hoboken, N.J.

• They traveled by way of Gibralter and Suez to the east coast of Africa, landing at Mombasa, Kenya. During the next ten months, moving northward, he collected specimens of flora, fauna, and mammals, and hunted big game. This expedition was made under the auspices of the Smithsonian Institution.

• His account of his adventures in Africa appeared as a series of articles in *Scribner's* Magazine. The articles were published by Scribner in 1910 under the title, *African Game Trails.* This book sold more than a million copies.

• He was the second of two former presidents who visited Africa. The other was Grant.

Mar. 14, 1910, arrived at Khartoum, Sudan

• He and his party had traveled more than one thousand miles during the safari.

• He was joined at Khartoum by his wife and their daughter, Ethel.

April–May, 1910, toured Europe

• He and his wife were received by royalty in Italy, The Netherlands, Norway, Sweden, and Germany. In Rome, he caused a stir by refusing an audience with Pope Pius X because of conditions imposed by the papal secretary. At the Sorbonne in Paris, he spoke on the duties of citizenship in a republic. In Christiania (now Oslo), he read a paper before the Nobel Peace Prize committee. In Potsdam, he reviewed the Imperial Guard with Kaiser Wilhelm II and was the first private citizen to review German troops.

• He was the sixth of eight former presidents who visited Europe.

May 20, 1910, served as U.S. representative at funeral of Edward VII, London

June 7, 1910, delivered Romanes lecture, Oxford University

• His lecture was entitled "Biological Analogies in History."

June 18, 1910, returned to U.S.

• He was given a welcoming parade on Fifth Avenue, New York City, that remained unequaled until Charles A. Lindbergh returned from Paris in 1927.

June 30, 1910, met with Taft, Beverly, Mass.

• This was their first meeting since the inauguration of his successor.

Aug. 23, 1910, departed on three-week speaking tour of West

• He toured 16 states in a special railroad train provided by *Outlook* Magazine. Upon his return to the U.S., he had joined Lyman Abbott's magazine as a contributing editor. He had rejected more remunerative offers to accept the $12,000 position.

1910, his book, *The New Nationalism*, published by Outlook Company, New York City

Feb. 24, 1912, announced candidacy for Republican nomination

• "I will accept the nomination for President if it is tendered to me," he wrote in reply to the petition of seven Republican governors, "and I will adhere to this decision until the convention has expressed its preference." Three days earlier upon his arrival in Columbus to address the Ohio constitutional convention, he had told a newspaperman, "My hat is in the ring."

June 22, 1912, defeated for nomination for

president, Republican national convention, Chicago, Ill.

•Taft received 561 votes on the first ballot. Roosevelt received 107 votes, with 60 votes scattered. However, 344 delegates declined to vote.

Aug. 7, 1912, nominated for president, Progressive national convention, Chicago, Ill.

•The Progressive party was popularly known as the Bull Moose party because of his enthusiastic comment that he was "as fit as a bull moose."

•He was the last of three former presidents who were the presidential candidates of minor parties.

Oct. 14, 1912, shot in chest by fanatic, Milwaukee, Wis.

•He was shot by John N. Schrank from six feet away as he entered his car to be driven to a speaking engagement. The bullet pierced Roosevelt's overcoat, passed through a metal spectacles case and his 50-page speech, folded double. It fractured his fourth rib, and lodged just short of his right lung. He insisted upon being driven to the auditorium, where he spoke for almost an hour.

•Schrank later was certified as "suffering from insane delusions grandiose in character," and was committed to a mental institution.

•This was the only assassination attempt on a former president.

Nov. 5, 1912, defeated for presidency by Wilson

• *See* Election of 1912, pages 327–328.

Dec. 27, 1912, delivered address, "History as Literature," annual meeting of American Historical Society, Boston, Mass.

•He was president of the society.

•His address was published by Scribner in 1913, *History as Literature, and Other Essays.*

February, 1913, first installment of his autobiography published, *Outlook* Magazine

• *Theodore Roosevelt, an Autobiography,* was published by Macmillan in the fall of 1913, and was reissued frequently.

May, 1913, sued editor of *Iron Age* Magazine for libel

•During the campaign of 1912, the trade magazine editor had written: "Roosevelt lies and curses in a most disgusting way; he

gets drunk too, and that not infrequently, and all of his intimates know about it." He won the suit easily. Damages were set, at his own request, at six cents.

Oct. 4, 1913, with his son, Kermit, sailed for South America

•He lectured before scientific organizations in Buenos Aires, Argentina; Montevideo, Uruguay; and Rio de Janeiro, Brazil.

•He was the only former president who visited South America.

Oct. 21, 1913, decided to explore unmapped Rio da Duvida (River of Doubt)

•He had agreed to ascend the Paraguay River to collect zoological and botanical specimens for the American Museum of Natural History. Upon his arrival in Rio de Janiero, he heard of the unmapped river that flowed northward toward the Amazon from west central Brazil. He convinced the Brazilian government to sponsor a major expedition.

Feb. 27–Apr. 30, 1914, explored River of Doubt

•He nearly died on this hazardous trip. He suffered intermittent attacks of malaria and dysentary, gashed a leg that became infected, and lost 57 pounds. His temperature rose at times to 105 degrees; "The fever was high and father was out of his mind," Kermit later wrote.

•Other troubles beset the 20-man expedition. Three boats were lost in high water, equipment was lost and discarded, and food ran low. Three men did not complete the journey: one drowned; another went insane and killed a member of the party before disappearing into the jungle. After many hardships the expedition reached Manaus in western Brazil, after having traveled fifteen hundred miles.

•The Brazilian government renamed the River of Doubt in his honor, Teodoro or Rio Roosevelt.

•His account of the expedition, *Through the Brazilian Wilderness,* was published in 1914 by Scribner.

1914, *Life Histories of African Game Animals* published by Scribner, New York City

•He wrote this two-volume work in collaboration with naturalist Edmund Heller.

January, 1915, began series of monthly articles, *Metropolitan* Magazine

1915, his book, *America and the World War,*

published by Scribner, New York City
- These essays originally appeared as a series of nine articles in *The New York Times.*

Apr. 19–May 22, 1915, tried for libel, Syracuse, N.Y.
- He had accused William Barnes, Jr., a New York Republican political leader, of connivance with Tammany Hall bosses. Barnes filed suit for libel, asking $500,000. The first verdict was 11–1 in favor of Roosevelt. The jury then reversed itself and ruled for Barnes and an equal division of costs. When the court ruled this verdict improper, the jury decided for Roosevelt. Roosevelt's defense costs were $52,000.

March, 1916, with Mrs. Roosevelt, vacationed in Trinidad, British West Indies
- From Trinidad, he issued a public statement in which he as much as said that the U.S. would enter the war if he were elected president. He stated that "it would be a mistake to nominate me unless the country has in its mood something of the heroic—unless it feels not only devotion to the ideals but the purpose measurably to realize those ideals in action."

May, 1916, made speaking tour of Midwest
- He made major addresses in Detroit, Mich.; Kansas City, Mo.; and St. Louis, Mo. "It is our purpose this fall to elect an American President and not a viceroy of the German emperor," he declared in St. Louis, a German-American city.

June 8, 1916, unsuccessful nominee for president, Republican national convention, Chicago, Ill.
- Charles Evans Hughes was nominated on the third ballot.

June 10, 1916, declined Progressive nomination for president, Chicago, Ill.
- He had recommended the nomination of Henry Cabot Lodge. Instead, the Bull Moose convention nominated him. He refused on the grounds that his entry into the presidential race would reelect Wilson.

June 28, 1916, his recommendation of Progressive support of Republican candidate Hughes accepted by Progressive national committee
- He campaigned for Hughes.

1916, his book, *Fear God and Take Your Own Part*, published by Doran, New York City

- Much of the contents had appeared in *Metropolitan* Magazine.

Apr. 10, 1917, met with Wilson, requested command of division, White House
- For more than a year, he had been drawing plans for a volunteer division in the event that the U.S. entered the war. Applications for service in the "Roosevelt Division" mounted to 200,000.

May 18, 1917, again requested military command
- He asked Wilson for authority "to raise two divisions for immediate service at the front." His request was refused.

September, 1917, began series of signed editorials in Kansas City *Star*
- He wrote one or two editorials each week of about five hundred words each. He had written more than a hundred for the *Star* prior to his death.

1917, his book, *The Foes of Our Own Household*, published by Doran, New York City

1917, his book, *National Strength and International Duty*, published by Princeton University Press, Princeton, N.J.
- This book consisted of the Henry Stafford Little lectures for 1917.

February, 1918, underwent mastoid operation

July 14, 1918, his son, Quentin, killed in action
- Lieutenant Quentin Roosevelt, a pilot, was shot down while on patrol behind the German lines. Roosevelt's son was buried with military honors by German airmen near the spot where he had crashed in Cambrai, northern France.

Oct. 28, 1918, made last major address
- He spoke in opposition to Wilson's appeal for a Democratic Congress, Carnegie Hall, New York City.

Nov. 11, 1918, admitted to Roosevelt Hospital, New York City
- His illness was diagnosed as inflammatory rheumatism. He returned to Sagamore Hill, Oyster Bay, on Christmas Day.

DEATH

Date of death: Jan. 6, 1919
Place of death: Oyster Bay, N.Y.
- He was the seventh of eight presidents

who died in New York.
Age at death: 60 years, 71 days
• He lived nine years and 309 days after the completion of his term.
Cause of death: Embolism in coronary artery
Place of burial: Oyster Bay, N.Y.
• He was the fifth of six presidents who were buried in New York.

THE VICE PRESIDENT (26th)

Full name: Charles Warren Fairbanks
Date of birth: May 11, 1852
Place of birth: near Unionville Center, Ohio
• Fairbanks was the second of three vice presidents who were born in Ohio.
Religious denomination: Methodist
• He was the first of three vice presidents who were Methodists.
College: Ohio Wesleyan University, Delaware, Ohio
Date of graduation: 1872
Occupation: Lawyer
• He was admitted to the bar in Columbus, Ohio, in 1872; practiced law in Indianapolis, Ind., until 1897; member of Senate, 1897–1905.
• He was the 11th of 17 vice presidents who served in the Senate before their terms of office.
Term of office: Mar. 4, 1905, to Mar. 4, 1909 (4 years)
• He was the 12th of 17 vice presidents who served four-year terms.
• Roosevelt and Fairbanks were the 28th of 41 president-vice president teams.
Age at inauguration: 52 years, 297 days
State represented: Indiana
• He was the third of four vice presidents who represented Indiana.
• He was the tenth of 13 vice presidents who represented states that were not their native states.
Political party: Republican
• He was the ninth of 15 vice presidents who were Republicans.
Occupation after term: Lawyer
• He was the Republican vice-presidential candidate, 1916.
Date of death: June 4, 1918
Place of death: Indianapolis, Ind.
• He was the second of two vice presidents

who died in Indiana. The other was Hendricks.
Age at death: 66 years, 24 days
Place of burial: Indianapolis, Ind.
• He was the third of four vice presidents who were buried in Indiana.

THE CABINET

State: John Milton Hay of Washington, D.C., Sept. 30, 1898, to July 1, 1905
• Elihu Root of New York, July 19, 1905, to Jan. 27, 1909
• Robert Bacon of New York, Jan. 27, 1909, to Mar. 5, 1909
Treasury: Lyman Judson Gage of Illinois, Mar. 6, 1897, to Jan. 31, 1902
• Leslie Mortier Shaw of Iowa, Feb. 1, 1902, to Mar. 3, 1907
• George Bruce Cortelyou of New York, Mar. 4, 1907, to Mar. 7, 1909
War: Elihu Root of New York, Aug. 1, 1899, to Jan. 31, 1904
• William Howard Taft of Ohio, Feb. 1, 1904, to June 30, 1908
• Luke Edward Wright of Tennessee, July 1, 1908, to Mar. 11, 1909
Attorney General: Philander Chase Knox of Pennsylvania, Apr. 5, 1901, to June 30, 1904
• William Henry Moody of Massachusetts, July 1, 1904, to Dec. 17, 1906
• Charles Joseph Bonaparte of Maryland, Dec. 17, 1906, to Mar. 4, 1909
Navy: John Davis Long of Massachusetts, Mar. 6, 1897, to Apr. 30, 1902
• William Henry Moody of Massachusetts, May 1, 1902, to June 30, 1904
• Paul Morton of Illinois, July 1, 1904, to June 30, 1905
• Charles Joseph Bonaparte of Maryland, July 1, 1905, to Dec. 16, 1906
• Victor Howard Metcalf of California, Dec. 17, 1906, to Nov. 30, 1908
• Truman Handy Newberry of Michigan, Dec. 1, 1908, to Mar. 5, 1909
Postmaster General: Charles Emory Smith of Pennsylvania, Apr. 21, 1898, to Jan. 9, 1902
• Henry Clay Payne of Wisconsin, Jan. 9, 1902, to Oct. 4, 1904
• Robert John Wynne of Pennsylvania, Oct. 10, 1904, to Mar. 6, 1905
• George Bruce Cortelyou of New York,

Mar. 6, 1905, to Mar. 4, 1907
•George von Lengerke Meyer of Massachu-
setts, Mar. 4, 1907, to Mar. 5, 1909
Interior: Ethan Allen Hitchcock of Missouri,
Dec. 21, 1898, to Mar. 4, 1907
•James Rudolph Garfield of Ohio, Mar. 4,
1907, to Mar. 5, 1909
Agriculture: James Wilson of Iowa, Mar. 6,
1897, to Mar. 5, 1913
Commerce and Labor: George Bruce Cor-
telyou of New York, Feb. 18, 1903, to June
30, 1904
•Victor Howard Metcalf of California, July
1, 1904, to Dec. 16, 1906

•Oscar Solomon Straus of New York, Dec.
17, 1906, to Mar. 5, 1909

THE SUPREME COURT

Associate Justices: Oliver Wendell Holmes
of Massachusetts, appointed, Aug. 11,
1902; confirmed, Dec. 4, 1902
•William Rufus Day of Ohio, appointed,
Feb. 19, 1903; confirmed, Feb. 23, 1903
•William Henry Moody of Massachusetts,
appointed, Dec. 3, 1906; confirmed, Dec.
12, 1906

WILLIAM HOWARD TAFT

Full name: William Howard Taft
- He was the last of three presidents who were named William.
- He was the ninth of 19 presidents who had middle initials or middle names.

Date of birth: Sept. 15, 1857
- He was the only president who was born in September.

Place of birth: Cincinnati, Ohio
- He was the sixth of seven presidents who were born in Ohio.
- His birthplace, 2038 Auburn Avenue, is not yet open to the public. Under the jurisdiction of the National Park Service, the house has been partially restored. Extensive restoration is planned.

Family lineage: English
- He was the 11th of 12 presidents of English ancestry.

Religious denomination: Unitarian
- He was the last of four presidents who were Unitarians.

College: Yale College, New Haven, Conn.
- He was the only president who went to Yale.
- He was the 18th of 27 presidents who attended college.

Date of graduation: June 27, 1878, Bachelor of Arts

- He was the 13th of 21 presidents who were graduated from college.

Law School: Cincinnati Law School, Cincinnati, Ohio
- He was the fourth of nine presidents who attended law school.

Date of graduation: 1880
- He did not wait for his degree of Bachelor of Laws, which was conferred after he had been admitted to the bar.
- He was the second of three presidents who were graduated from law school.

PARENTS AND SIBLINGS

Father's name: Alphonso Taft
Date of birth: Nov. 5, 1810
Place of birth: near Townshend, Vt.
Occupation: Lawyer
- Taft's father served as judge of the Cincinnati superior court, 1865–1872; was an unsuccessful candidate for the Republican nomination for governor of Ohio, 1875 and 1879; served in Grant's cabinet as secretary of war and attorney general, 1876–1877; was appointed by Arthur as minister to Austria-Hungary, 1882–1884, and minister to Russia, 1884–1885.

•Taft was the only president whose father had served in the cabinet.
•He was the second of three presidents whose fathers had served as ministers plenipotentiary or ambassadors.
Date of death: May 21, 1891
Place of death: San Diego, Cal.
Age at death: 80 years, 197 days

Father's first wife: Fanny Phelps Taft
Date of birth: Mar. 28, 1823
Place of birth: Townshend, Vt.
Date of marriage: Aug. 29, 1841
Children: 5; 4 sons, 1 daughter
•Only two of her children reached maturity; Charles Phelps, who was born in 1843, and Peter Rawson, who was born in 1845.
•Taft was the fifth of six presidents who had half brothers or half sisters.
Date of death: June 2, 1852
Place of death: Cincinnati, Ohio
Age at death: 29 years, 66 days

Mother's name: Louisa Maria Torrey Taft
•Taft's mother was called Louise.
Date of birth: Sept. 11, 1827
Place of birth: Boston, Mass.
Date of marriage: Dec. 26, 1853
•Taft was the fourth of five presidents whose mothers were second wives.
Children: 5; 4 sons, 1 daughter
•Samuel Davenport was born in 1855; William Howard in 1847; Henry Waters in 1859; Horace Dutton in 1861; and Fanny in 1865. Samuel died in infancy.
•William was his mother's second child.
•He was his father's seventh child.
•He was the last of five presidents who came from families of ten children.
Date of death: Dec. 7, 1907
Place of death: Millbury, Mass.
Age at death: 80 years, 87 days

MARRIAGE

Date of marriage: June 19, 1886
Place of marriage: Cincinnati, Ohio
•Taft was the second of two presidents who were married in Cincinnati. The other was Hayes.
•He was the sixth of seven presidents who were married in Ohio.
Age at marriage: 28 years, 277 days
•He was the 20th of 27 presidents who were married in their twenties.
Years married: 43 years, 262 days

Wife's name: Helen Herron Taft
•She was called Nellie.
•She was the 22nd of 33 first ladies.
•She was the 29th of 40 wives of presidents.
Date of birth: June 2, 1861
•She was the last of four first ladies who were born in June.
•She was the last of five wives of presidents who were born in June.
Place of birth: Cincinnati, Ohio
•She was the fifth of six first ladies who were born in Ohio.
•She was the fifth of six wives of presidents who were born in Ohio.
Wife's mother: Harriet Collins Herron
Wife's father: John Williamson Herron, attorney
•Herron was the third of four fathers-in-law of presidents who were attorneys.
Age at marriage: 25 years, 17 days
•She was the 19th of 26 ladies who were married in their twenties.
•She was the 23rd of 30 wives of presidents who were married in their twenties.
Years younger than husband: 3 years, 109 days
Children: 3; 2 sons, 1 daughter
•Robert Alphonso was born on Sept. 8, 1889; Helen Herron on Aug. 1, 1891; and Charles Phelps on Sept. 20, 1897.
•Taft was the fifth of seven presidents who had three children.
•He was the 17th of 19 presidents who had both male and female children.
•He was the 21st of 30 presidents who had children.
Years she survived husband: 13 years, 75 days
•She was the 15th of 21 first ladies who survived their husbands.
•She was the 17th of 23 wives of presidents who survived their husbands.
Date of death: May 22, 1943
Place of death: Washington, D.C.
•She was the seventh of nine first ladies who died in Washington.
•She was the seventh of nine wives of presidents who died in Washington.
Age at death: 81 years, 35 days
•She suffered what in all likelihood was a cerebral hemorrhage on May 17, 1909. She never fully recovered her health.
•She had celebrated her 80th birthday, June 2, 1941.
•She was the 11th of 16 first ladies who lived to be 70.
•She was the 12th of 17 wives of presidents

who lived to be 70.
•She was the ninth of 14 first ladies who lived to be 75.
•She was the tenth of 15 wives of presidents who lived to be 75.
•She was the seventh of nine first ladies who lived to be 80.
•She was the eighth of ten wives of presidents who lived to be 80.

Place of burial: Arlington National Cemetery, Arlington, Va.
•She was the only first lady or wife of a president who was buried in Arlington.
•She was the last of six first ladies who were buried in Virginia.
•She was the last of seven wives of presidents who were buried in Virginia.

EARLY YEARS

June 5, 1874, was graduated from Woodward High School, Cincinnati, Ohio
•Taft ranked second in his class.
June 27, 1878, was graduated from Yale College, New Haven, Conn.
•He ranked second in his class of 132 members. His salutatory address was entitled "The Professional and Political Prospects of the College Graduate."
1878, entered Cincinnati Law School, Cincinnati
•He attended law school until 1880.
•He was the 20th of 26 presidents who studied law.
1879-1880, covered courts as reporter for Cincinnati *Commercial*
•He was the first of three presidents who worked as newspapermen as young men.
May 5, 1880, admitted to bar, Columbus, Ohio
•He was the 19th of 23 presidents who were lawyers.
Jan. 3, 1881, appointed assistant prosecutor, Hamilton County, Ohio
March, 1882, appointed collector of internal revenue by Arthur
•Taft served until January, 1883.
•He was the only president who served as a collector of internal revenue. He served in the first district of Ohio.
1883-1884, practiced law in partnership with Harlan Page Lloyd, Cincinnati
•Lloyd was a former partner of Taft's father.

Jan. 1, 1885, appointed assistant county solicitor, Hamilton County
June 19, 1886, married Helen Herron, Cincinnati
March, 1887, appointed judge, Cincinnati superior court
April, 1888, elected to full judicial term, Cincinnati superior court
•This was his only elective office prior to the presidency.
Sept. 8, 1889, his first son born
•The boy was named Robert Alphonso Taft.
Feb. 14, 1890, appointed U.S. solicitor general by Harrison
Aug. 1, 1891, his only daughter born
•The girl was named Helen Herron Taft.
Mar. 21, 1892, appointed U.S. circuit judge by Harrison
•He was appointed for the sixth judicial circuit—the federal districts of Ohio, Michigan, Kentucky, and Tennessee. He also became an ex officio member of the circuit court of appeals.
March, 1893, succeeded to senior U.S. circuit judge of sixth circuit
1896, served as professor of law of real property and dean of Cincinnati Law School
•He was a member of the law school faculty until 1900.
•He was the only president who taught law before his term of office.
Sept. 20, 1897, his second son born
•The boy was named Charles Phelps Taft.

NATIONAL PROMINENCE

Feb. 6, 1900, appointed chairman of commission to establish civil government in Philippines by McKinley
Mar. 13, 1900, appointed president of second Philippine commission by McKinley
June 4, 1900, arrived in Manila, Philippines

July 4, 1901, appointed governor-general of Philippines by McKinley
•He was the only president who served as governor-general of the Philippines.
January, 1902, returned to Washington, D.C.

June 5, 1902, received by Pope Leo XIII, Rome, Italy
• This was the first of his many assignments as Roosevelt's representative. The American offer to purchase friar lands in the Philippines was rejected; the matter was not successfully terminated until November, 1903.
Aug. 22, 1902, returned to Manila
Oct. 27, 1902, declined appointment to Supreme Court
Jan. 7, 1903, again declined appointment to Supreme Court
Dec. 23, 1903, departed from Manila
• He had been summoned by Roosevelt to succeed Elihu Root as secretary of war.
Jan. 6, 1904, received by Emperor of Japan, Tokyo
Feb. 1, 1904, took office as secretary of war, Washington, D.C.
• He was the second of two presidents who served as secretary of war. The other was Monroe.
• Taft was the seventh of eight presidents who served in the cabinet.
November-December, 1904, made troubleshooting trip to Panama
July-September, 1905, escorted congressional delegation to Philippines
July 27–29, 1905, conferred with prime minister of Japan, Count Taro Katsura, Tokyo
• The secret Taft-Katsura agreement stipulated that the U.S. would not contest Japanese aims in Korea in return for Japan's pledge to stay out of the Philippines. The agreement was approved by Roosevelt, July 31, but the arrangement was not publicized.
1905, served as acting secretary of state during illness of John Hay
Dec. 1, 1905, began diet
• He lost 70 pounds during the next 19 months. His weight was 320 pounds when he began his supervised diet. He weighed 250 in July, 1906.
• The heaviest of all presidents, he weighed 300 to 332 pounds while in office.
• Six feet tall, he was the tenth of 14 presidents who were that height or taller.
January, 1906, again declined appointment to Supreme Court
• He was quite anxious to join the Court, but declined for the third time because he felt his work in the war department and his involvement in the Panama Canal and Phil-

ippine situations were unfinished. Also, Mrs. Taft opposed his accepting the appointment as associate justice; she fervently desired him to run for president in 1908.
Sept. 29-Oct. 13, 1906, served as provisional governor of Cuba
• He was the only president who served as provisional governor of Cuba.
1906, his first book, *Four Aspects of Civic Duty*, published by Scribner, New York City
• This book was a collection of his Yale lectures on the responsibilities of citizenship.
• He was the 12th of 21 presidents who wrote books that were published during their lifetimes.
September-December, 1907, made round-the-world trip
• He visited the Philippines, Japan, Russia, and Germany, before returning to the U.S.
April-May, 1908, made troubleshooting trip to Panama
June 18, 1908, nominated for president, Republican national convention, Chicago, Ill.
• He was nominated on the first ballot.
June 30, 1908, resigned as secretary of war
Nov. 3, 1908, election day
• *See* Election of 1908, below.
Jan. 11, 1909, presidential electors cast ballots
• He received 321 of the 483 electoral votes from the 46 states.
• *See* Election of 1908, below.
Jan. 29-Feb. 7, 1909, visited Panama
Feb. 10, 1909, electoral vote tabulated by Congress
• Taft and Sherman were officially declared elected.
Feb. 18, 1909, made Mason "at sight" by Grand Lodge of Ohio
• He was the tenth of 13 presidents who were Masons.

ELECTION OF 1908

People's (Populist) party, convened, Apr. 2, at St. Louis, Mo., nominated Thomas Edward Watson of Georgia for president, Samuel W. Williams of Indiana for vice president.
United Christian party, convened, May 1, at Rock Island, Ill., nominated Daniel Braxton Turney of Illinois for president,

Lorenzo S. Coffin of Iowa for vice president.

Socialist party, convened, May 10, at Chicago, Ill., nominated Eugene Victor Debs of Indiana for president, Benjamin Hanford of New York for vice president.

Republican party, convened, June 16, at Chicago, Ill., nominated William Howard Taft of Ohio for president, James Schoolcraft Sherman of New York for vice president.

• This was the 14th Republican national convention. It was the seventh Republican convention held in Chicago; it was the 11th major party convention held in Chicago.

Democratic party, convened, July 7, at Denver, Colo., nominated William Jennings Bryan of Nebraska for president, John Worth Kern of Indiana for vice president.

• This was the 20th Democratic national convention. It was the only major party convention held in Denver.

Prohibition party, convened, July 15, at Columbus, Ohio, nominated Eugene Wilder Chafin of Illinois for president, Aaron Sherman Watkins of Ohio for vice president.

Socialist Labor party, convened, July 24, at New York City, nominated August Gillhaus of New York for president, Donald L. Monro of Virginia for vice president.

Independence Party, convened, July 27, at Chicago, Ill., nominated Thomas Louis Hisgen of Massachusetts for president, John Temple Graves of Georgia for vice president.

Election day Tuesday, Nov. 3, 1908
Popular vote: 14,891,788
    Taft, 7,679,114
    Bryan, 6,410,665
    Debs, 420,890
    Chafin, 253,840
    Hisgen, 83,651
    Watson, 29,146
    Gillhaus, 14,021
    Turney, 461
Electoral vote 483, 46 states
• Taft, 321, 29 states
    (California, 10; Connecticut, 7; Delaware, 3; Idaho, 3; Illinois, 27; Indiana, 15; Iowa, 13; Kansas, 10; Maine, 6; Massachusetts, 16; Michigan, 14; Minnesota, 11; Missouri, 18; Montana, 3; New Hampshire, 4; New Jersey, 12; New York, 39; North Dakota, 4; Ohio, 23; Oregon, 4; Pennsylvania, 34; Rhode Island, 4; South Dakota, 4; Utah, 3; Vermont, 4; Washington, 5; West Virginia, 7; Wisconsin, 13; Wyoming, 3)
• Taft also received the votes of two Maryland electors.
• Bryan, 162, 17 states
    (Alabama, 11; Arkansas, 9; Colorado, 5; Florida, 5; Georgia, 13; Kentucky, 13; Louisiana, 9; Maryland, 6 of 8 votes; Mississippi, 10; Nebraska, 8; Nevada, 3; North Carolina, 12; Oklahoma, 7; South Carolina, 9; Tennessee, 12; Texas, 18; Virginia, 12)
• Bryan was the only major party presidential candidate who was defeated three times.

THE PRESIDENT (27th)

Term of office: Mar. 4, 1909, to Mar. 4, 1913 (4 years)
• Taft was the 16th of 19 presidents who served one term or less than one term.
• He was the ninth of ten presidents who served for four years.
State represented: Ohio
• He was the fifth of six presidents who represented Ohio.
Political party: Republican
• He was the ninth of 14 presidents who were Republicans.
Congresses: 61st, 62nd
Administration: 31st
Age at inauguration: 51 years, 170 days

• He was the 15th of 21 presidents who were younger than their vice presidents. Taft was one year, 326 days younger than Sherman.
Inauguration day: Thursday, Mar. 4, 1909
• Taft took the oath of office, administered by Chief Justice Melville W. Fuller, in the Senate chamber of the Capitol. The ceremony was to have been held on the east portico of the Capitol, but a blizzard brought about a change in plans. "I always said it would be a cold day when I became President," he quipped.
• This was the last of six inaugurations at which Fuller officiated.

•Taft was the last of three presidents who took the oath of office in the Senate chamber.

•This was the last of five inaugural ceremonies in the Senate chamber.

•The inaugural address was 5,428 words long, the second longest ever made. The lengthiest inaugural address was delivered by William Henry Harrison.

•A precedent was set when Mrs. Taft rode back from the inaugural ceremony to the White House with her husband:

THE 31st ADMINISTRATION

1909

Mar. 5, appointed his only secretary of state, Philander C. Knox; his only secretary of treasury, Franklin MacVeagh; his first secretary of war, Jacob M. Dickinson; his only attorney general, George W. Wickersham; his only secretary of navy, George von L. Meyer; his only postmaster general, Frank H. Hitchcock; his first secretary of interior, Richard A. Ballinger; his only secretary of agriculture, James Wilson; and his only secretary of commerce and labor, Charles Nagel

•Knox, Wilson, and Nagel took office, Mar. 6; MacVeagh, Mar. 8; and Dickinson, Mar. 12.

•Knox was the fifth of nine executive officers who served in the cabinets of three presidents; Knox had served as attorney general under McKinley and Theodore Roosevelt.

•Wilson was the only secretary of agriculture who served under three presidents.

•Wilson was the sixth of nine executive officers who served in the cabinets of three presidents; Wilson had served as secretary of agriculture under McKinley and Theodore Roosevelt.

Mar. 15, first session of 61st Congress

•The administration controlled both the Senate and the House of Representatives. The Democrats gained three Senate and eight House seats. The Senate (92 members), consisted of 59 Republicans, 32 Democrats, and one vacancy. The House (391 members) consisted of 219 Republicans and 172 Democrats.

Mar. 16, sent special message to Congress in which he urged "prompt revision" of tariff

•The Payne tariff bill was introduced in the House on the following day.

Mar. 26, issued executive order restoring Marine Corps to Navy under same conditions as prevailed prior to Roosevelt order

Mar. 27, appointed budget committee of cabinet members to supervise all estimates for federal expenses

May 13, issued executive order establishing central committee to purchase all government supplies.

May 22, issued executive orders opening 700,000 acres of government land to settlement in Idaho, Montana, and Washington

May 25, abolished Council of Fine Arts created by Roosevelt

June 1, opened Alaska-Yukon-Pacific Exposition in Seattle, Wash., by pressing gold telegraph key, White House

June 10, presented gold medals given by Aero Club of America to Orville and Wilbur Wright

•A Wright aircraft, the first plane purchased by the government, was accepted by the U.S. Army, Aug. 2.

June 16, sent special message to Congress in which he recommended two percent tax on net incomes of corporations

•Taft called for the submission to the states of an amendment to the Constitution to permit a federal income tax.

July 12, 16th Amendment to Constitution submitted to states for ratification

July 16, informed delegation of congressmen of his attitude in favor of downward revision of tariff

Aug. 5, signed Payne-Aldrich Tariff Act

•This act, which lowered 650 and raised 220 tariff schedules, and left 1,150 unchanged, was the first revision in tariff laws since the Dingley Act of 1897.

Aug. 5, first session of 61st Congress adjourned

Aug. 7, began summer vacation, Beverly, Mass.

Aug. 19, dismissed seven West Point cadets for hazing

Aug. 21, issued executive order reducing army by ten percent

•The force was to be maintained at eighty thousand men.

Sept. 11, appointed first tariff commission

Sept. 14, advocated establishment of central bank in speech to Boston Chamber of Commerce, Boston, Mass.

Sept. 15, upheld Secretary of Interior Ballinger in public lands controversy; ordered dismissal of land office agent, Louis R. Glavis

• Glavis had accused Ballinger of impropriety.

Sept. 15, began thirteen-thousand-mile trip around country

Sept. 16, advocated appointment of commission to investigate and remedy court delays, Chicago, Ill.

Sept. 17, referred to Payne-Aldrich Tariff Act as "best bill the Republican party ever passed," Winona, Minn.

• This was the most self-damaging phrase he uttered as president. It was to come back to haunt him time after time, especially during the campaigns of 1910 and 1912.

Sept. 20, recommended changes in interstate commerce and antitrust laws

Sept. 21, defended corporations tax, Denver, Colo.

Sept. 23, opened Gunnison irrigation tunnel in Colorado

• When he pressed a golden bell on a silver plate in Montrose, Cal., which opened the floodgates of the Gunnison tunnel, he set in motion the greatest irrigation project yet undertaken by the government. The six-mile tunnel, which measured 11 by 13 feet through solid rock, cost $3,000,000 and took ten years to complete.

Sept. 26, preached before large audience in Morman Tabernacle, Salt Lake City, Utah

Sept. 27, descended twelve hundred feet in copper mine, Butte, Mont.

• A Philadelphia newspaperman wrote that he had set the "presidential underground record."

Oct. 16, exchanged friendly meetings with President Porfirio Diaz of Mexico, El Paso, Tex., and Ciudad Juarez, Mexico

• Taft was the first of seven presidents who visited Mexico while in office.

• He was the second of 11 presidents who traveled outside the U.S. while in office.

Oct. 24, Associate Justice Peckham died

Oct. 25–30, journeyed down Mississippi River, St. Louis, Mo., to New Orleans, La.

Nov. 10, returned to Washington, D.C.

• During his 13,000-mile swing around the country, he made more than 250 speeches and was much encouraged by his recep-

tion. "The one note that I could hear everywhere," he wrote his wife, Oct. 24, "was that of contentment and satisfaction with conditions, and such a note is inconsistent with the defeat of the party in power."

Nov. 26, approved regulations for collection of corporations tax

Dec. 6, second session of 61st Congress

Dec. 7, sent his first State of the Union message to Congress

Dec. 13, appointed Horace H. Lurton as associate justice

• Lurton, who was confirmed by the Senate, Dec. 20, was the first of Taft's six appointments to the Supreme Court.

Notes: Taft was the first president to receive an annual salary of $75,000. The salary increase had been authorized by an act of Mar. 4, 1909.

• The first White House automotive fleet was purchased in 1909. It consisted of a 1908 White Steamer limousine, two 1908 Pierce-Arrow Vandelettes, and a 1908 Baker electric.

1910

Jan. 1, 5,575 guests attended New Year's Day reception, White House

Jan. 7, ordered removal of Gifford Pinchot, chief of forest service

• Taft appointed H. S. Graves of the Yale Forestry School as chief of the forest service, Jan. 12.

Jan. 28, announced his decision not to drop antitrust suit against Union Pacific and Southern Pacific railroads

Feb. 24, announced five measures he considered "must" legislation to redeem party pledges

• The measures involved postal savings banks, conservation, anti-injunction, interstate commerce law amendments, and the Arizona and New Mexico statehood bills.

Mar. 17, gave six speeches, including talk to Republican editors, Chicago, Ill.

• A poll taken in February by the Chicago *Tribune* of Republican editors west of the Alleghenies had revealed that 2,886 disapproved and only 812 approved of the Payne-Aldrich Tariff Act.

Mar. 20, conferred with W. S. Fielding, Canadian finance minister, regarding tariff relations, Albany, N.Y.

Mar. 26, tariff dispute with Canada settled during conference with Minister Fielding, White House

Mar. 28, vetoed bill to amend military record of Aaron Cornish

•This was the first of his 30 regular vetoes.

Mar. 28, Associate Justice Brewer died

Mar. 31, issued proclamations extending minimum rates of tariff to all nations

Apr. 1, issued executive order that placed assistant postmasters of first and second class post offices in classified service list

Apr. 9, spoke on party solidarity to League of Republican Clubs, Washington, D.C.

•"No man has the right to read another out of the party," he said, an obvious reference to the Insurgent Republicans. He added: "He reads himself out if he is disloyal and if he can not by his own works show his colors."

Apr. 13, was hissed during address to convention of National American Woman Suffrage Association, Washington, D.C.

•He was the first president to address the suffragists.

•The hissing incident occurred when he said that he was not altogether in sympathy with the suffragist movement, that he thought one of the dangers was that women as a whole were not interested in the vote and that the power of the ballot would be controlled by the "less desirable class" of women.

Apr. 14, tossed out first ball of Washington Nationals-Philadelphia Athletics baseball game

•He was the first of 11 presidents who officially opened baseball seasons.

Apr. 25, appointed Charles Evans Hughes as associate justice

•Hughes, who was confirmed by the Senate, May 2, was the second of Taft's six appointments to the Supreme Court.

May 10, appointed Theodore Roosevelt as special ambassador to represent U.S. at funeral of King Edward VII of Great Britain, London

May 31, ordered Attorney General Wickersham to file petition alleging conspiracy in restraint of trade against railroads of Western Traffic Association

•The railway association had announced a general increase in freight rates, effective, June 1.

June 4, declared socialism to be future

American problem, Jackson, Mich.

•Jackson was the birthplace of the Republican party.

June 6, conferred with western railroad officials who agreed to suspend projected rate increases until railroad act went into effect

June 7, met with eastern railroad representatives who also agreed to suspend increases until railroad act became effective

June 20, signed railroad act

June 21, signed Arizona and New Mexico statehood act

June 25, signed postal savings system act

June 25, signed rivers and harbors act

June 25, second session of 61st Congress adjourned

June 25, pocket vetoed three bills

•These were the first of his nine pocket vetoes.

June 28, departed Washington for summer home, Beverly, Mass.

June 30, met with Theodore Roosevelt, Beverly

•This was their first meeting since Taft's inauguration.

July 3, ordered withdrawn from public settlement 8,495,731 acres of water power sites, oil, coal, and phosphate lands in Alaska

July 4, Chief Justice Fuller died

Sept. 21, ordered withdrawn from public settlement 69,055 acres of coal lands in Colorado, 1,327 acres of power sites in California

Oct. 9, received Home Rule Irish members of British Parliament, White House

Nov. 8, election day

•The Republicans lost control of the House of Representatives for the first time in 16 years. The Democrats gained ten seats in the Senate, giving them actual control with help from the Insurgent Republicans.

Nov. 20, accepted resignation of Associate Justice Moody

Nov. 10–11, made inspection tour of Panama Canal

•He was the second of five presidents who visited Panama while in office.

•This was the first of his two trips to Panama while in office.

Nov. 25, ordered tax returns of corporations made public

•The net income of 262,490 corporations subject to the tax was $3,125,480,000 for the fiscal year that had ended June 30. The tax yielded $26,872,270.

Dec. 5, third session of 61st Congress
Dec. 6, sent his second State of the Union message to Congress
Dec. 12, appointed Edward D. White as chief justice, Willis Van Devanter and Joseph R. Lamar as associate justices
•White, who was confirmed by the Senate, Dec. 12, was the third of Taft's six appointments to the Supreme Court
•Van Devanter and Lamar, who were confirmed by the Senate, Dec. 15, were the fourth and fifth of his six appointments to the Supreme Court.
•Taft was the first president since Washington to promote an associate justice to the chief justiceship.
•White, who had been appointed by Cleveland in 1894, was the first of three associate justices who were appointed and confirmed as chief justices.
•Taft was the seventh of 14 presidents who appointed chief justices.

Note: The official population according to the 13th census, was 91,972,266.

1911

Jan. 12, sent special message to Congress in which he asked appropriation of $5,000,000 to begin fortification of Panama Canal
Mar. 4, third session of 61st Congress adjourned
Mar. 4, pocket vetoed two bills
•These were the fourth and fifth of his nine pocket vetoes.
Mar. 7, accepted resignation of Secretary of Interior Ballinger
Mar. 7, appointed his second secretary of interior, Walter L. Fisher
Apr. 4, first session of 62nd Congress
•The administration ostensibly controlled the Senate—although control actually was in the hands of a Democratic-Insurgent Republican coalition—but lost control of the House. The Democrats gained ten Senate and 56 House seats. The Senate (92 members) consisted of 49 Republicans, 42 Democrats, and one vacancy. The House (391 members) consisted of 228 Democrats, 162 Republicans, and one Socialist.
•The Socialist representative, Victor L. Berger of Milwaukee, Wis., was the first member of his party elected to Congress.
May 16, accepted resignation of Secretary

of War Dickinson
May 16, appointed his second secretary of war, Henry L. Stimson
•Stimson was the last of Taft's 11 cabinet appointments.
•Seven of the nine original members of his cabinet remained in office for four years.
June 19, with Mrs. Taft, celebrated silver wedding anniversary, White House
•He and his wife received thousands of guests during the night garden party.
•He was the last of five presidents who celebrated their 25th anniversaries while residents of the White House.
July 26, signed Canadian reciprocity act
•This reciprocal agreement, which provided for free trade on some American and Canadian products and reduced duties on others, was defeated when a newly-elected Canadian Parliament rejected it, Sept. 21.
Aug. 15, vetoed resolution admitting Arizona and New Mexico as states
•He objected to certain provisions of their constitutions.
Aug. 17, vetoed wool bill
•This revision of schedule K of the Payne-Aldrich Tariff Act had been passed by the Democratic and Insurgent Republican coalition.
Aug. 21, signed joint resolution for admission of Arizona and New Mexico
Aug. 22, vetoed cotton bill
Aug. 22, first session of 62nd Congress adjourned
Sept. 15–Nov. 12, made cross-country speaking tour
Oct. 14, Associate Justice Harlan died
Nov. 9, spoke at dedication of Lincoln Memorial, Frankfort, Ky.
Dec. 4, second session of 62nd Congress
Dec. 7, sent his third State of the Union message to Congress

1912

Jan. 6, signed proclamation of admission of New Mexico as 47th state
•New Mexico was the first of two states admitted during his term of office.
Jan. 16, warned Cuban government U.S. would intervene if military continued to interfere in political affairs
Jan. 18, pardoned Charles W. Morse
•Morse, who had been convicted of misappropriating funds of the Bank of North

America, had been sentenced in 1908 to 15 years in federal prison.

• Taft had believed the army surgeons who reported that Morse could not live "as long as six months" but later admitted he had been deceived. Morse lived for many years.

Feb. 2, sent special message to Congress in which he recommended appointment of international commission to study world prices

Feb. 5, ordered four battalions of troops to Mexican border

Feb. 14, signed proclamation of admission of Arizona as 48th state

• Arizona was the second of two states admitted during his term of office.

• Taft was the first president of the 48 states, which comprised the U.S. until 1959.

Feb. 19, appointed Mahlon Pitney as associate justice

• Pitney, who was confirmed by the Senate, Mar. 13, was the last of Taft's six appointments to the Supreme Court.

• Only Washington and Franklin D. Roosevelt appointed more members of the Supreme Court. Taft and Jackson appointed the same number of members of the Court, six.

Mar. 2, issued proclamation warning Americans to observe neutrality laws, abstain from participation in Mexican disturbances

Mar. 14, issued executive order prohibiting exportation of war materials to Mexico

Mar. 27, Mrs. Taft and Viscountess Chinda, wife of Japanese ambassador, planted first two cherry trees on west side of Tidal Basin, Potomac Park, Washington, D.C.

• The cherry trees, three thousand in 12 varieties, were given to the City of Washington by the City of Tokyo.

Apr. 17, appointed Julia C. Lathrop as director of new federal Children's Bureau

• This was the first appointment of a woman to a major federal post.

May 13, 17th Amendment to Constitution submitted to states for ratification

June 22, renominated for president, Republican national convention, Chicago, Ill.

• Taft was nominated on the first ballot. He received 561 votes; Roosevelt, 107; La Follette, 41; Cummins, 17; and Hughes, two. However, 344 delegates declined to vote.

Aug. 1, accepted Republican nomination

Aug. 9, vetoed compromise wool tariff schedule bill

• This bill was passed over his veto by the House of Representatives, Aug. 13, but no action was taken by the Senate.

Aug. 14, vetoed steel and iron schedule bill

Aug. 15, vetoed legislative, executive and judicial appropriation bill

• He objected to a provision to abolish the Court of Commerce.

Aug. 24, signed Panama Canal act which exempted American coastal vessels from canal tolls

Aug. 26, second session of 62nd Congress adjourned

Aug. 26, pocket vetoed two bills

• These were the sixth and seventh of his nine pocket vetoes.

Sept. 2, created National Oil Reserve No. 1, which contained 38,969 acres, Elks Hill, Cal.

Oct. 14, reviewed fleet of 123 warships, Hudson River, New York City

Oct. 30, Vice President Sherman died, Utica, N.Y.

Nov. 1, granted exclusive interview to Louis Seibold of New York *World*

• This interview was not published because Taft withheld permission. A stenographic transcript of the interview was found years later among the Taft Papers, Library of Congress, by biographer Henry F. Pringle.

Nov. 5, election day

• *See* Election of 1912, pages 327–328.

Nov. 13, signed proclamation fixing Panama Canal toll rates

Dec. 2, third session of 62nd Congress

Dec. 3, sent his fourth and last State of the Union message to Congress

Dec. 5, issued executive order declaring land and waters within Panama Canal Zone as military reservation

Dec. 19, departed from Washington on short trip to Canal Zone

• This was the second of his two visits to Panama.

1913

Jan. 13, presidential electors cast ballots

• Wilson received 435 electoral votes; Roosevelt, 88, and Taft, eight.

• *See* Election of 1912, pages 327–328.

Feb. 1, proposed amendment to Constitution to limit tenure of offices of president and vice president to one term of six years passed by Senate, 47–23

Feb. 11, action on proposed constitutional amendment postponed indefinitely by House of Representatives

Feb. 12, electoral votes tabulated by Congress

• Wilson and Marshall were officially declared elected.

• Taft was the sixth of seven presidents who were defeated when they sought reelection.

Feb. 14, vetoed immigration bill containing literacy test for immigrants

• This bill was passed over his veto by the Senate, 72–18, Feb. 18, but the veto was sustained in the House of Representatives, 213–114, Feb. 19.

Feb. 23, gave farewell dinner for Washington news correspondents, White House

• Attended by 40 guests, this affair was the first of its kind in the executive mansion.

Feb. 25, 16th Amendment to Constitution ratified

• *See* Constitution, page 644.

Feb. 28, vetoed Webb-Kenyon bill

• He considered the bill, which prohibited interstate shipment of liquor into dry states, unconstitutional.

Mar. 1, Webb-Kenyon Act passed over his veto

• This was the only one of his 39 votes that was overridden.

Mar. 1, attended farewell function, National Press Club, Washington, D.C.

Mar. 3, met for final time with White House correspondents, discussed successes and failures of his administration

• He told the reporters that he was proudest of the fact that he had named six of the nine members of the Supreme Court. "And I have said to them, damn you, if any of you die, I'll disown you," he added.

Mar. 3, with Mrs. Taft, exchanged courtesy calls with President-elect and Mrs. Wilson

Mar. 4, signed act establishing department of labor

• The department of commerce and labor was to be continued as the department of commerce.

Mar. 4, third session of 62nd Congress adjourned

Mar. 4, pocket vetoed two bills

• These were the last of his 39 vetoes, the eighth and last of his nine pocket vetoes.

THE FORMER PRESIDENT

Mar. 4, 1913, attended inauguration of Wilson

• Taft's age upon leaving office was 55 years, 170 days.

• "I wish you a successful administration and the carrying out of all your aims," he said to Wilson after the inaugural address. "We will all be behind you."

Mar. 4, 1913, with Mrs. Taft, departed from Washington aboard 3:10 P.M. train for Augusta, Ga.

• During his stay in Augusta, he played golf almost daily.

• He was the first president who played golf.

Apr. 1, 1913, arrived in New Haven, Conn., to take up duties as Kent professor of law, Yale University

• He was the second of two former presidents who were law professors. The other was Benjamin Harrison.

Sept. 4, 1913, elected president of American Bar Association

May–November, 1914, Mrs. Taft's memoirs serialized in *Delineator* Magazine

• Her book, *Recollections of Full Years*, was published by Dodd-Mead in 1914.

• Mrs. Taft was the first of four first ladies who wrote their memoirs for publication. The others were Edith Wilson, Eleanor Roosevelt, and Lady Bird Johnson.

Apr. 13, 1915, served with Roosevelt as pallbearer at services for Professor Thomas A. Lounsbury of Yale, New Haven, Conn.

• It was the first meeting of the two former presidents since 1911. While the amenities were observed, the meeting was far from a reconciliation.

1916, his lectures on presidency published

• *The Presidency: Its Duties, Its Powers, Its Opportunities and Its Limitations*, a collection of three lectures delivered at the University of Virginia in January, 1915, was published by Scribner.

• *Our Chief Magistrate and His Powers*, a collection of substantially the same lectures, slightly expanded, delivered at Columbia University, New York City, was published by Columbia University Press, also in 1916.

Apr. 8, 1918, appointed as joint chairman, with Frank P. Walsh, of National War Labor Board by Wilson

May 5, 1918, reconciled with Roosevelt

• They met by chance in the dining room of the Blackstone Hotel in Chicago, Ill. As the onlookers cheered, they shook hands. "I've seen old Taft," said Roosevelt afterwards, "and we're in perfect harmony on everything."

Jan. 8, 1919, attended Roosevelt funeral

June 30, 1921, appointed and confirmed as chief justice of Supreme Court

• Appointed by Harding, Taft was the only president who accepted an appointment to the Supreme Court. In 1811, John Quincy Adams was appointed as an associate justice by Jefferson but declined to serve.

Oct. 3, 1921, administered oath as chief justice by Associate Justice McKenna

• Taft was the only president who served as chief justice of the U.S.

Dec. 27, 1922, presided at first annual Conference of Senior Circuit Court Judges

Mar. 4, 1925, administered oath of office to Coolidge

• Taft was the only former president who administered the presidential oath of office. He administered the oath to Coolidge and Hoover.

Oct. 25, 1926, delivered majority opinion, *Myers v. United States*

• By a vote of six to three, the Supreme Court upheld the removal by President Wilson in 1920 of Frank S. Myers, postmaster at Portland, Ore. This was the first Court decision upon presidential removal powers and it declared an act of Congress passed in 1876, which provided that postmasters "shall be appointed and may be removed by the President with the advice and consent of the Senate," was an unconstitutional invasion of the executive authority.

• This decision also pronounced unconstitutional the Tenure of Office Act of 1867, which had been the basis for the impeachment of President Andrew Johnson.

Sept. 15, 1927, celebrated his 70th birthday

• He was the 13th of 16 presidents who lived to be 70.

Mar. 4, 1929, administered oath of office to Hoover

• This was the second inauguration at which Taft officiated.

• He was the second of three presidents who participated in four inaugural ceremonies.

Feb. 3, 1930, resigned from Supreme Court due to illness

DEATH

Date of death: Mar. 8, 1930

Place of death: Washington, D.C.

• He was the sixth of seven presidents who died in Washington.

• He was the fifth of eight presidents who lay in state in the Capitol Rotunda.

Age at death: 72 years, 174 days

• Taft lived 17 years and four days after the completion of his term.

Cause of death: Debility

Place of burial: Arlington National Cemetery, Arlington, Va.

• He was the first of two presidents who were buried in Arlington. The other was Kennedy.

• He was the sixth of seven presidents who were buried in Virginia.

THE VICE PRESIDENT (27th)

Full name: James Schoolcraft Sherman

Date of birth: Oct. 24, 1855

Place of birth: Utica, N.Y.

• Sherman was the last of eight vice presidents who were born in New York.

Religious denomination: Dutch Reformed

• He was the last of four vice presidents who were Dutch Reformed.

College: Hamilton College, Clinton, N.Y.

Date of graduation: 1878

Occupation: Lawyer

• He was mayor of Utica, 1884–1885; member of the House of Representatives, 1887–1891 and 1893–1909; chairman of the House committee on Indian affairs for 14 years.

• He was the 16th of 21 vice presidents who served in the House of Representatives before their terms of office.

Term of office: Mar. 4, 1909, to Oct. 30, 1912 (3 years, 240 days)

• He was the 11th of 14 vice presidents who served less than one term.

• Taft and Sherman were the 29th of 41 president-vice president teams.

Age at inauguration: 53 years, 131 days

State represented: New York

• He was the last of ten vice presidents who

represented New York.
Political party: Republican
•He was the tenth of 15 vice presidents who were Republicans.
Date of death: Oct. 30, 1912 (died in office)
•He was the only vice president nominated for a second term who died prior to election day. Nicholas Murray Butler, nominated by the Republican national committee, received the electoral votes that would have been cast for Sherman had he lived.
•He was the last of six vice presidents who died during their first terms.
•He was the last of seven vice presidents who died in office.
Place of death: Utica, N.Y.
•He was the last of nine vice presidents who died in New York.
Age at death: 57 years, 6 days
Place of burial: Utica, N.Y.
•He was the last of nine vice presidents who were buried in New York.

THE CABINET

State: Philander Chase Knox of Pennsylvania, Mar. 6, 1909, to Mar. 5, 1913
Treasury: Franklin MacVeagh of Illinois, Mar. 8, 1909, to Mar. 5, 1913
War: Jacob McGavock Dickinson of Tennessee, Mar. 12, 1909, to May 21, 1911
•Henry Lewis Stimson of New York, May 22, 1911, to Mar. 4, 1913
Attorney General: George Woodward Wick-

ersham of New York, Mar. 6, 1909, to Mar. 5, 1913
Navy: George von Lengerke Meyer of Massachusetts, Mar. 6, 1909, to Mar. 4, 1913
Postmaster General: Frank Harris Hitchcock of Massachusetts, Mar. 5, 1909, to Mar. 4, 1913
Interior: Richard Achilles Ballinger of Washington, Mar. 5, 1909, to Mar. 13, 1911
•Walter Lowrie Fisher of Illinois, Mar. 13, 1911, to Mar. 4, 1913
Agriculture: James Wilson of Iowa, Mar. 6, 1897, to Mar. 5, 1913
Commerce and Labor: Charles Nagel of Missouri, Mar. 6, 1909, to Mar. 4, 1913

THE SUPREME COURT

Chief Justice: Edward Douglass White of Louisiana, appointed, Dec. 12, 1910; confirmed, Dec. 12, 1910
Associate Justices: Horace Harmon Lurton of Tennessee, appointed, Dec. 13, 1909; confirmed, Dec. 20, 1909
•Charles Evans Hughes of Massachusetts, appointed, Apr. 25, 1910; confirmed, May 2, 1910
•Willis Van Devanter of Wyoming, appointed, Dec. 12, 1910; confirmed, Dec. 15, 1910
•Joseph Rucker Lamar of Georgia, appointed, Dec. 12, 1910; confirmed, Dec. 15, 1910
•Mahlon Pitney of New Jersey, appointed, Feb. 19, 1912; confirmed, Mar. 13, 1912

Twenty-eighth President

WOODROW WILSON

Full name: Woodrow Wilson
- His given name was Thomas Woodrow Wilson.
- He was the second of two presidents who were named Thomas. The other was Jefferson.
- He was the third of four presidents who dropped their first names.
- He was the third of five presidents who changed their names from those they were given at birth.
- He was the tenth of 19 presidents who had middle initials or middle names.

Date of birth: Dec. 28, 1856
- He was the last of three presidents who were born in December.

Place of birth: Staunton, Va.
- He was the last of eight presidents who were born in Virginia.
- His birthplace, the former Presbyterian manse at 24 North Coalter Street, is owned and maintained by the Woodrow Wilson Birthplace Foundation, Inc. It is open to the public daily except Thanksgiving, Christmas and New Year's Day, 9 A.M. to 5 P.M. It is closed on Sundays during December, January, and February. Admission: adults, $1; children, ten to 16 years of age,

50 cents. Groups of ten or more: adults, 80 cents; children, 35 cents.

Family lineage: Scottish-Irish
- He was the last of four presidents who were of Scottish-Irish ancestry.

Religious denomination: Presbyterian
- He was the fifth of six presidents who were Presbyterians.

College: College of New Jersey, now Princeton University, Princeton, N.J.
- He was the second of three presidents who went to Princeton.
- He was the 19th of 27 presidents who attended college.

Date of graduation: June 18, 1879, Bachelor of Arts
- He was the second of two presidents who were graduated from Princeton. The other was Madison.
- He was the 14th of 21 presidents who were graduated from college.

Law school: University of Virginia, Charlottesville, Va.
- He was the fifth of nine presidents who attended law school.
- He was the third of six presidents who attended, but were not graduated from law school.

PARENTS AND SIBLINGS

Father's name: Joseph Ruggles Wilson
Date of birth: Feb. 28, 1822
Place of birth: Steubenville, Ohio
Occupation: Presbyterian minister
• Wilson was ths last of three presidents whose fathers were clergymen.
Date of death: Jan. 21, 1903
Place of death: Princeton, N.J.
Age at death: 80 years, 327 days

Mother's name: Janet Woodrow Wilson
Date of birth: Dec. 20, 1826
Place of birth: Carlisle, England
• Wilson's mother was the seventh of eight parents of presidents who were born abroad.
• His mother was the third of four mothers of presidents who were born abroad.
Date of marriage: June 7, 1849
Children: 4; 2 sons, 2 daughters
• Marion Williamson was born on Oct. 20, 1851; Annie Josephson on Sept. 8, 1853; Thomas Woodrow on Dec. 28, 1856; and Joseph Ruggles on July 20, 1867.
• Wilson was the second of two presidents who came from families of four children. The other was Theodore Roosevelt.
• He was the fourth of five presidents who were third children.
Date of death: Apr. 15, 1888
Place of death: Clarksville, Tenn.
Age at death: 61 years, 117 days

MARRIAGE

Date of first marriage: June 24, 1885
Place of first marriage: Savannah, Ga.
• He was the only president who was married in Georgia.
Age at first marriage: 28 years, 178 days
• He was the 21st of 27 presidents who were married in their twenties.
Years married: 29 years, 43 days

First wife's name: Ellen Louise Axson Wilson
• She was the 23rd of 33 first ladies.
• She was the 30th of 40 wives of presidents.
Datre of birth: May 15, 1860
• She was the last of three first ladies who were born in May.
• She was the last of three wives of presidents who were born in May.

Place of birth: Savannah, Ga.
• She was the only first lady or wife of a president who was born in Georgia.
First wife's mother: Margaret Hoyt Axson
First wife's father: Samuel Axson, Presbyterian minister
• Wilson was the last of five presidents who married the daughters of clergymen.
Age at marriage: 25 years, 40 days
• She was the 20th of 26 first ladies who were married in their twenties.
• She was the 24th of 30 wives of presidents who were married in their twenties.
Years younger than husband: 3 years, 139 days
Children: 3 daughters
• Margaret Woodrow was born on Apr. 16, 1886; Jessie Woodrow on Aug. 28, 1887; and Eleanor Randolph on Oct. 5, 1889.
• Wilson was the second of five presidents who had only female children.
• He was the sixth of seven presidents who had three children.
• He was the 22nd of 30 presidents who had children.
Date of death: Aug. 6, 1914
Place of death: White House, Washington, D.C.
• She was the last of three first ladies who died in the White House.
• She was the last of three first ladies who died while their husbands were in office.
• She was the eighth of nine first ladies who died in Washington.
• She was the eighth of nine wives of presidents who died in Washington.
Age at death: 54 years, 83 days
Place of burial: Rome, Ga.
• She was the only first lady or wife of a president who was buried in Georgia.
Years he survived his first wife: 9 years, 181 days
• Wilson was the 13th of 14 presidents who survived their wives.

Date of second marriage: Dec. 18, 1915
• He was the last of three presidents who married while in office.
• He was the last of five presidents who remarried.
Place of second marriage: Washington, D.C.
• He was the second of two presidents who were married in Washington. The other was Cleveland.
Age at second marriage: 58 years, 355 days
• He was the last of three presidents who

were married in their fifties.
Years married: 8 years, 47 days

Second wife's name: Edith Bolling Galt Wilson
- Wilson was the last of six presidents who married widows. She was the widow of Norman Galt of Washington, D. C., who had died in 1908.
- She was the last of three widows who became the second wives of presidents.
- She was the 24th of 33 first ladies.
- She was the 31st of 40 wives of presidents.

Date of birth: ·Oct. 15, 1872
- She was the third of four first ladies who were born in October.
- She was the fifth of six wives of presidents who were born in October.

Place of birth: Wytheville, Va.
- She was the last of three first ladies who were born in Virginia.
- She was the last of six wives of presidents who were born in Virginia.

Second wife's mother: Sallie White Bolling
Second wife's father: William Holcombe Bolling, attorney and judge
- Bolling was the second of two fathers-in-law of presidents who were judges. The other was the father of Anna Harrison.
- Bolling was the last of four fathers-in-law of presidents who were attorneys.

Age at marriage: 43 years, 64 days
- She was the only first lady who married in her forties.
- She was the second of two wives of presidents who married in their forties. The other was Caroline Fillmore.

Years younger than husband: 15 years, 291 days

Children: None
- Wilson was the second of two presidents

who had children by their first wives only. The other was Fillmore.

Years she survived her husband: 37 years, 328 days
- She was the 16th of 21 first ladies who survived their husbands.
- She was the 18th of 23 wives of presidents who survived their husbands.

Date of death: Dec. 28, 1961
- She was the only first lady or wife of a president who died on her husband's birthday.

Place of death: Washington, D.C.
- She was the last of nine first ladies who died in Washington.
- She was the last of nine wives of presidents who died in Washington.
- Wilson was the only president whose two wives died in the same community.

Age at death: 89 years, 74 days
- She had celebrated her 85th birthday, Oct. 15, 1957.
- She was the 12th of 16 first ladies who lived to be 70.
- She was the 13th of 17 wives of presidents who lived to be 70.
- She was the tenth of 14 first ladies who lived to be 75.
- She was the 11th of 15 wives of presidents who lived to be 75.
- She was the eighth of nine first ladies who lived to be 80.
- She was the ninth of ten wives of presidents who lived to be 80.
- She was the fifth of six first ladies who lived to be 85.
- She was the sixth of seven wives of presidents who lived to be 85.

Place of burial: Washington, D.C.
- She was the only first lady or wife of a president who was buried in Washington.

EARLY YEARS

November, 1857, with family, moved to Augusta, Ga.
1870, with family, moved to Columbia, S.C.
1873, entered Davidson College, Davidson, N.C.
- Wilson left college after a few months because of ill health.
June, 1874, returned to Columbia, S.C.
October, 1874, with family, moved to Wilmington, N.C.
September, 1875, entered College of New

Jersey, now Princeton University, Princeton, N.J.
November, 1877, his first article published in college publication, *Nassau Literary* Magazine
- His subject was Bismarck.
October, 1878, his prize essay published, *Nassau Literary* Magazine
- His subject was William Pitt, the first Earl of Chatham.
June 18, 1879, was graduated from College

of New Jersey.

August, 1879, his first national magazine article published, *International Review*

• The article, "Cabinet Government in the United States," recommended seats in Congress for cabinet members, with or without vote, to offset the imbalance of committee control of the Senate and House of Representatives.

September, 1879, entered law school, University of Virginia, Charlottesville, Va.

• He left law school in 1880 because of ill health.

• He was the 21st of 26 presidents who studied law.

1880, returned to Wilmington, N.C.

June, 1882, moved to Atlanta, Ga.

October, 1882, admitted to bar, Atlanta

• He formed a partnership with Edward Ireland Renick, with whom he had attended law school.

• He was the 20th of 23 presidents who were lawyers.

1883, abandoned practice of law

September, 1883, enrolled as graduate student, Johns Hopkins University, Baltimore, Md.

January, 1885, his first book, *Congressional Government; A Study in American Politics*, published by Houghton Mifflin, Boston, Mass.

• He was the 13th of 21 presidents who wrote books published during their lifetimes.

June 24, 1885, married Ellen Louise Axson, Savannah, Ga.

September, 1885, accepted position as associate professor of history, Bryn Mawr College, Bryn Mawr, Pa.

• Bryn Mawr, chartered in 1880, opened in 1885 with a group curriculum plan modeled on Johns Hopkins.

Apr. 16, 1886, his first daughter born

• The girl was named Margaret Woodrow Wilson.

June, 1886, received degree of doctor of philosophy in political science, Johns Hopkins

• His book, *Congressional Government,* served as his Ph.D. thesis.

• He was the only president who earned a doctoral degree.

1887, began series of lectures, Johns Hopkins

• He journeyed from Bryn Mawr to Baltimore each week and gave 25 lectures during the series.

Aug. 28, 1887, his second daughter born

• The girl was named Jessie Woodrow Wilson.

1887, unsuccessful applicant for post of first assistant secretary of state

Apr. 15, 1888, his mother died

1888, accepted position as professor of history, Wesleyan University, Middletown, Conn.

1889, his book, *The State; Elements of Historical and Practical Politics,* published by Heath, Boston, Mass.

1889, elected to Phi Beta Kappa, Wesleyan

• He was the second of three presidents who were honorary members of Phi Beta Kappa.

• He was the eighth of 11 presidents who were members of Phi Beta Kappa.

Oct. 5, 1889, his third daughter born

• The girl was named Eleanor Randolph Wilson.

1890, accepted position as professor of jurisprudence and political economy, College of New Jersey, now Princeton

1893, his biography, *George Washington,* published by Harper, New York City

1893, his book of essays, *An Old Master, and Other Political Essays,* published by Scribner, New York City

1896, name of College of New Jersey changed to Princeton University

1896, his book of essays, *More Literature, and Other Essays,* published by Houghton Mifflin, Boston, Mass.

1898, revised edition of his book, *The State,* published by Heath, Boston, Mass.

1901, his article, "When a Man Comes to Himself," published as book by Harper, New York City

• The 37-page book originally appeared as an article in *Century* Magazine. He wrote 35 magazine articles, in addition to his books, while at Princeton.

1902, his five-volume *A History of the American People* published by Harper, New York City

June 9, 1902, unanimously elected president of Princeton by trustees

• He was the first layman to hold the post since the institution was founded in 1746.

Oct. 25, 1902, took office as president of Princeton

• He was the first of two presidents who were presidents of major colleges or universities. The other was Eisenhower.

Jan. 21, 1903, his father died

Feb. 3, 1906, first mentioned as presidential possibility

•He was suggested as a potential candidate by George Harvey, president of the publishing firm, Harper & Bros., and editor of *Harper's Weekly*, in a speech at the Lotus Club, New York City.

1907, withdrew as candidate for Senate

•He had indicated interest in the seat but withdrew from the New Jersey race when it became apparent that he would be opposed by the progressive wing of the Democratic party.

Oct. 17, 1907, trustees of Princeton requested withdrawal of his "quad" plan

•In June, the trustees had approved his plan to substitute a number of quadrangles—dormitories where students of all classes were to live, study, and eat together—for the exclusive eating clubs reserved for senior and junior class students. The alumni objected; his plan was dropped in 1908.

NATIONAL PROMINENCE

Jan. 18, 1908, endorsed for president in New York *World* editorial

•The editorial was written by George Harvey.

October, 1909, elected president of Short Ballot Association

•This national group subscribed to the theory that reduction of the number of elected city officials would lead to more efficient municipal government.

July 15, 1910, agreed to run for governor of New Jersey

•Wilson published a statement that he would accept the nomination if supported by "a decided majority of the thoughtful Democrats" of the state.

Sept. 15, 1910, nominated for governor, Democratic state convention, Trenton, N.J.

Oct. 20, 1910, resigned as president of Princeton

Nov. 8, 1910, elected governor

Nov. 26, 1910, first "Wilson for President" club organized, Staunton and Norfolk, Va.

Jan. 17, 1911, inaugurated as governor

•He was the only president who served as governor of New Jersey.

•He was the 11th of 13 presidents who served as state governors.

July 2, 1912, nominated for president, Democratic national convention, Baltimore, Md.

•He was nominated on the 46th ballot.

Nov. 5, 1912, election day

• *See* Election of 1912, below.

Jan. 13, 1913, presidential electors cast ballots

•He received 435 of the 531 electoral votes from the 48 states.

• *See* Election of 1912, below.

Feb. 12, 1913, electoral vote tabulated by Congress

•Wilson and Marshall were officially declared elected.

ELECTION OF 1912

Socialist Labor party, convened, Apr. 7, at New York City, nominated Arthur Edward Reimer of Massachusetts for president, August Gillhaus of New York for vice president.

Socialist party, convened, May 12, at Indianapolis, Ind., nominated Eugene Victor Debs of Indiana for president, Emil Seidel of Wisconsin for vice president.

Republican party, convened, June 18, at Chicago, Ill., nominated William Howard Taft of Ohio for president, James Schoolcraft Sherman of New York for vice president.

•This was the 15th Republican national convention. It was the eighth Republican convention held in Chicago; it was the 12th major party convention held in Chicago.

Democratic party, convened, June 25, at Baltimore, Md., nominated Woodrow Wilson of New Jersey for president, Thomas Riley Marshall of Indiana for vice president.

•This was the 21st Democratic national convention. It was the ninth Democratic convention held in Baltimore; it was the 17th major party convention held in Baltimore.

Prohibition party, convened, July 10, at Atlantic City, N.J., nominated Eugene Wilder Chafin of Illinois for president, Aaron Sherman Watkins of Ohio for vice president.

Progressive ("Bull Moose") party, convened, Aug. 5, at Chicago, Ill., nominated Theodore Roosevelt of New York for president, Hiram Warren Johnson of California for vice president.
•This was the 13th major party convention held in Chicago.
Election day, Tuesday, Nov. 5, 1912
Popular vote: 15,087,242
    Wilson, 6,283,019
    Roosevelt, 4,119,507
    Taft, 3,484,956
    Debs, 962,573
    Chafin, 207,928
    Reimer, 29,259
•Wilson was the 11th of 15 presidents who were elected without receiving a majority of the popular vote.
Electoral vote: 531, 48 states
    • Wilson, 435, 40 states
    (Alabama, 12; Arizona, 3; Arkansas, 9; Colorado, 6; Connecticut, 7; Delaware, 3; Florida, 6; Georgia, 14; Idaho, 4; Illinois, 29; Indiana, 15; Iowa, 13; Kansas,

10; Kentucky, 13; Louisiana, 10; Maine, 6; Maryland, 8; Massachusetts, 18; Mississippi, 10; Missouri, 18; Montana, 4; Nebraska, 8; Nevada, 3; New Hampshire, 4; New Jersey, 14; New Mexico, 3; New York, 45; North Carolina, 12; North Dakota, 5; Ohio, 24; Oklahoma, 10; Oregon, 5; Rhode Island, 5; South Carolina, 9; Tennessee, 12; Texas, 20; Virginia, 12; West Virginia, 8; Wisconsin, 13; Wyoming, 3)
•Wilson also received the votes of two California electors.
    • Roosevelt, 88, six states
    (California, 11 of 13 votes; Michigan, 15; Minnesota, 12; Pennsylvania, 38; South Dakota, 5; Washington, 7)
    • Taft, 8, two states
    (Utah, 4; Vermont, 4)
•The eight votes for the Republican vice-presidential candidate, Sherman, who had died, Oct. 30, were transferred to Nicholas Murray Butler.

THE PRESIDENT (28th)

Term of office: Mar. 4, 1913, to Mar. 4, 1921 (8 years)
•He was the tenth of 12 presidents who were elected to second terms.
•He was the 11th of 16 presidents who served more than one term.
•He was the eighth of nine presidents who served two terms.
•Wilson was the sixth of eight presidents who served for eight years.
State represented: New Jersey
•He was the only president who represented New Jersey.
•He was the 11th of 15 presidents who represented states that were not their native states.

Political party: Democratic
•He was the eighth of 12 presidents who were Democrats.
Congresses: 63rd, 64th, 65th, 66th
Administrations: 32nd, 33rd
Age at inauguration: 56 years, 66 days
•He was the 16th of 21 presidents who were younger than their vice presidents. Wilson was two years, 289 days younger than Marshall.
Inauguration day, Tuesday, Mar. 4, 1913
•Wilson took the oath of office, administered by Chief Justice Edward Douglass White, on the east portico of the Capitol.
•This was the first of three inaugurations at which White officiated.

THE 32nd ADMINISTRATION

1913

Mar. 5, appointed his first secretary of state, William Jennings Bryan; his first secretary of treasury, William G. McAdoo; his first secretary of war, Lindley M. Garrison; his first attorney general, James C. McReynolds; his only secretary of navy, Josephus

Daniels; his only postmaster general, Albert S. Burleson; his first secretary of interior, Franklin K. Lane; his first secretary of agriculture, David F. Houston; his first secretary of commerce, William C. Redfield; and his only secretary of labor, William B. Wilson
•Redfield was the first secretary of com-

merce; William B. Wilson was the first secretary of labor.

• Wilson was the first of two presidents who appointed namesakes to his cabinet. The other was Kennedy.

• The president and William B. Wilson were not related.

• McAdoo, Houston, and William B. Wilson took office, Mar. 6.

Mar. 11, announced U.S. would no longer lend support to special interests

• His statement amounted to a refusal of recognition of the Huerta government of Mexico.

Mar. 15, held first press conference, White House

• This was the first regular press conference, open to all accredited correspondents. He agreed to meet with the press twice a week.

Mar. 18, announced withdrawal of American participation in proposed six-power loan to China for construction of Hukuang railway

Apr. 7, first session of 63rd Congress

• The administration controlled both the Senate and the House of Representatives. The Democrats gained nine Senate and 62 House seats. The Senate (96 members) consisted of 51 Democrats, 44 Republicans, and one vacancy. The House (435 members) consisted of 290 Democrats, 127 Republicans, and 18 others.

Apr. 8, appeared in person before joint session of Congress to deliver special tariff message

• This was the first time that a president had made a personal appearance before Congress since 1800. Jefferson had set the precedent of sending presidential messages—which were read by clerks—in 1801.

Apr. 22, protested against California legislation excluding aliens from land ownership

• The state assembly had passed an alien land bill, directed against the Japanese, Apr. 16. The state senate substituted a stronger bill, which specifically prohibited land ownership by Japanese, Apr. 21. Despite Wilson's appeal for a veto, the senate bill was signed by Governor Hiram Johnson, May 19.

May 2, formally recognized Republic of China

May 26, issued public statement denouncing "industrious and insidious" lobby

• After the House of Representatives passed the Underwood tariff bill, May 8, a highly organized campaign to defeat the bill in the Senate was begun by lobbyists representing the wool, sugar, cotton, and other interests. Wilson said:

It is of serious interest to the country that the people at large should have no lobby and be voiceless in these matters, while great bodies of astute men seek to create an artificial opinion and to overcome the interests of the public for their private profit.

May 31, issued proclamation of adoption of 17th Amendment

• This amendment provided for the direct elections of members of the Senate by popular vote.

• *See* Constitution, page 644.

June 23, sent special message to Congress asking legislation to decentralize banking system

• The control of the system of banking, he said:

. . . must be public, not private, must be vested in the Government itself, so that the banks may be the instruments, not the masters, of business and of individual enterprise and initiative.

July 14, conferred with railroad management and labor representatives

• Agreements were reached that averted a strike of conductors and trainmen.

July 15, signed Newlands Act

• The Newlands Arbitration Act, which replaced the Erdman Act of 1898, provided for a four-man board of mediation and conciliation to be appointed by the president, which was to act at the request of either management or labor in railroad labor disputes.

July 23, acknowledged segregation policy

• Postmaster General Burleson had suggested segregation of all Negroes in federal service at a cabinet meeting, Apr. 11. Shortly thereafter the post office and treasury departments began to segregate, demote, and discharge Negro workers.

• In a letter to Oswald Garrison Villard, publisher of the New York *Evening Post* and the *Nation*, as well as a founder of the National Association for the Advancement of Colored People, Wilson insisted that the segregation policy was "as much in the interest of the negroes as for any other reason," and added:

My own feeling is, by putting certain bureaus and sections in the charge of negroes we are rendering them more safe in their possession of office and less likely to be discriminated against.

• Not until Villard and other progressive editors, clergymen, and civic leaders mounted publicity campaigns against segregation in the federal government was the policy reversed.

• This was the first instance of officially sanctioned discrimination against Negroes in the federal service since the Civil War period. As the first southern-born president since Andrew Johnson, whose cabinet included four southern-born members, Wilson was severely criticized for his complacency in this matter. Even his strongest editorial supporter, Frank Cobb of the New York *World*, wrote later:

Mr. Wilson ought to have set his heel upon this presumptuous Jim-Crow government the moment it was established. He ought to set his heel upon it now. It is a reproach to his Administration and to the great political principles which he represents.

Aug. 4, appointed special envoy to Mexico, John Lind

• Convinced that Ambassador Henry Lane Wilson had aided the Huerta *coup d'etat*, he had sent William Bayard Hale to Mexico City as his personal representative in May. In July, he called Ambassador Wilson home and dismissed him.

Aug. 8, addressed circular note to governments with representatives in Mexico

• Wilson urged the foreign powers to convince Victoriano Huerta of the necessity of accepting U.S. mediation. He had instructed Lind to press for an immediate armistice and free election, that Huerta should not be a candidate for the presidency, and that all factions should abide by the results of the election.

Aug. 27, addressed joint session of Congress, outlined his Mexican policy

• He announced that Huerta had rejected his proposals, Aug. 16, and declared the U.S. now would institute a policy of "watchful waiting."

• Wilson was informed by Lind that evening

that Huerta had conceded that, under the Mexican constitution, he could not be a candidate to succeed himself.

Oct. 3, signed Underwood Tariff Act

• This act reversed tariff policy that had prevailed since Civil War days, reduced rates by roughly ten percent to 24 to 26 percent, and placed iron, steel, wool, and subsequently sugar on the free list.

• The act also instituted the first income tax under the 16th Amendment, the third income tax law. It sanctioned a maximum income tax of seven percent on net incomes over $500,000 and a one percent tax on corporate net incomes.

Oct. 27, defined his Latin American policy, Mobile, Ala.

• Huerta had arrested 110 members of the Mexican chamber of deputies, Oct. 10, and set up a military dictatorship. Huerta was "elected" president of Mexico, Oct. 26; meanwhile, in the northern provinces, Venustiano Carranza had established a provisional government at Hermosillo, Sonora.

• Great Britain, which had recently converted its navy from coal to oil and depended upon Mexico for its oil supply, recognized the Huerta government. So did 16 other foreign governments.

• Wilson emphasized his opposition to the Huerta regime in his Mobile speech and foresaw the day when Latin America (meaning Mexico) would be free from the control of foreign concessionaires (meaning Great Britain). His intention, he added, was the development of constitutional government in Mexico, and he emphasized that the U.S. "would never again seek one additional foot of territory by conquest."

Nov. 7, addressed supplemental circular note to governments with representatives in Mexico

• He stated that his immediate duty was "to require Huerta's retirement," and that the U.S. would "now proceed to employ such means as may be necessary to secure this result."

Nov. 25, attended wedding of his daughter, Jessie Woodrow, to Francis Bowes Sayre, White House

• This was the fifth of eight White House weddings of daughters of presidents.

• This was the sixth of nine White House weddings of children of presidents.

Dec. 1, vetoed private bill to reinstate dis-

missed West Point cadet
•This was the first of his 44 vetoes.
Dec. 1, first session of 63rd Congress adjourned
Dec. 1, second session of 63rd Congress
•There was no recess.
Dec. 2, delivered his first State of the Union address to Congress
•He was the first president to deliver his State of the Union message in person since John Adams.
Dec. 23, signed Owen-Glass Federal Reserve Act
•This act, which established the federal reserve system, represented the first comprehensive reorganization of the national banking system since 1863. The Owen-Glass act established 12 regional banks coordinated by a seven-member federal reserve board. All national and certain state banks were to be members of the system.

1914

Jan. 20, delivered special message to Congress recommending legislation to strengthen Sherman Anti-Trust Act
Jan. 27, issued executive order establishing permanent civil government for Panama Canal Zone, effective, Apr. 1
Feb. 3, issued proclamation lifting embargo on exportation of arms to Mexico
•This committed the U.S. to support of the Carranza faction.
Mar. 5, delivered special message to Congress in which he recommended repeal of tolls-exemption clause of Panama Canal act of 1912
•This was a reversal of his campaign position regarding the act of Aug. 24, 1912, which exempted U.S. coastal shipping from paying canal tolls. The British had protested the clause as a contravention of the Hay-Pauncefote treaty.
Mar. 12, signed act authorizing the construction, maintenance and operation of one thousand miles of railways in Alaska
Mar. 28, signed amended copyright act
Apr. 9, Tampico incident
•An unarmed party from the U.S.S. Dolphin, which had served as the presidential yacht during Cleveland's two terms, was arrested in a restricted zone. The Americans were released promptly, and apolo-

gies were made. On the basis that two of the party had been taken at gunpoint from an American vessel—a whaleboat—Admiral Henry T. Mayo demanded, over and above a formal apology, that an American flag be hoisted ashore and saluted with 21 guns. Huerta refused to salute the American flag. Informed of the incident, Wilson supported Admiral Mayo.
Apr. 20, delivered special message to Congress on Mexican situation
•He asked for permission to use armed force if necessary and received a standing ovation. The House of Representatives passed a resolution that day approving the use of force; similar action was taken by the Senate, Apr. 22.
Apr. 21, ordered seizure of custom house, Veracruz, Mexico
•This action was ordered upon receipt of information that a German ship with munitions for Huerta was due to land in Veracruz within hours. The city was shelled and occupied. Mexican casualties were about 200 killed and 300 wounded; American losses were 19 killed and 47 wounded.
Apr. 22, Mexico severed diplomatic relations with U.S.
Apr. 25, received arbitration offer from ABC powers (Argentina, Brazil, and Chile)
May 7, attended wedding of his daughter, Eleanor Randolph, to Secretary of Treasury McAdoo, White House
•He was the only president who had two daughters who were married in the White House.
•He was the only president whose daughter married a member of the cabinet.
•This was the sixth of eight White House weddings of daughters of presidents.
•This was the seventh of nine White House weddings of children of presidents.
May 20, ABC conference began, Niagara Falls, Ontario, Canada
•Representatives of the U.S. and the Huerta government met with mediators from the ABC powers.
June 15, appointed federal reserve board
June 15, signed amended Panama Canal act
•This act repealed the tolls-exemption clause of the 1912 act.
June 24, ABC mediation plan accepted by U.S.
•The plan, which called for the retirement of Huerta, the establishment of a Mexican provisional government, and no indemnity

to the U.S. for Veracruz occupational costs, was rejected by the Mexicans. Huerta was forced to resign, July 15.

July 12, Associate Justice Lurton died

July 28–Aug. 6, World War I began

Aug. 4, issued proclamations of neutrality in wars between Austria-Hungary and Serbia, Germany and Russia, Germany and France
• He issued similar proclamations regarding Great Britain and Germany, Aug. 5, and Austria-Hungary and Russia, Aug. 7.

Aug. 4, offered mediation by U.S. as signatory of Hague convention to warring nations

Aug. 6, Mrs. Wilson died

Aug. 15, Panama Canal opened to traffic
• The canal was opened officially by presidential proclamation, July 12, 1915.
• The total cost of the canal, which took seven years to construct, was $336,650,-000.

Aug. 18, signed ship registry act
• This act repealed the requirement that foreign-built ships be less than five years old when admitted to U.S. registry.

Aug. 18, issued proclamation of neutrality in war between Germany and Belgium
• He issued similar proclamations regarding Japan and Germany, Aug. 24, and Japan and Austria-Hungary, Aug. 27.

Aug. 18, made public appeal to U.S. citizens to be "impartial in thought as well as in action"

Aug. 19, appointed James C. McReynolds as associate justice
• McReynolds, who was confirmed by the Senate, Aug. 29, was the first of Wilson's three appointments to the Supreme Court.

Aug. 29, accepted resignation of Attorney General McReynolds

Aug. 29, appointed his second attorney general, Thomas W. Gregory

Sept. 4, addressed joint session of Congress, requested legislation to assure additional revenue of $100,000,000
• The administration tax bill relied exclusively on new excise taxes, but the southern congressional bloc revised the measure drastically. Wilson signed the revised bill, Oct. 22.

Sept. 5, issued executive order providing for government operation of all wireless stations

Sept. 5, submitted plan for settlement of Colorado strike to operators and miners
• The plan was accepted by the miners,

Sept. 15; it was rejected by the operators, Sept. 23.

Sept. 26, signed Federal Trade Commission Act
• This act, designed to prevent monopolies and discourage unfair competition in interstate commerce, established a five-man bipartisan board that replaced the board of corporations.

Oct. 15, signed Clayton Anti-Trust Act
• This act, designed to supplement the Sherman Anti-Trust Act, was hailed by labor as its "Magna Carta." Supreme Court decisions later weakened the labor provisions of the measure.

Oct. 22, signed war revenue act

Oct. 24, second session of 63rd Congress adjourned

Nov. 3, election day
• The Republicans gained 59 seats in the House of Representatives; the Democrats gained five Senate seats.

Nov. 13, issued proclamation of neutrality of Panama Canal Zone

Nov. 16, 12-bank federal reserve system began operations

Nov. 29, appointed Colorado mine strike commission
• The United Mine Workers ended the strike, Dec. 8.

Dec. 7, third session of 63rd Congress

Dec. 8, delivered his second State of the Union message to Congress

1915

Jan. 17, his grandson, Francis B. Sayre, Jr., born in White House

Jan. 26, signed act establishing Rocky Mountain National Park, Colo.

Jan. 28, vetoed immigration bill
• This bill included a mandatory literacy test and restrictions that would have denied entry to political refugees.

Jan. 28, signed act establishing U.S. Coast Guard
• The Coast Guard replaced the revenue cutter service, which had been established in 1790, and the life saving service, which had been established in 1871.

Jan. 30, dispatched his representative, Colonel Edward M. House, to confer with Allied and Central Power officials regarding American mediation
• Colonel House remained abroad until June

5, but accomplished little.

Feb. 10, sent "strict accountability" note to Germans

• He revised and approved the note, signed by Secretary of State Bryan. The U.S. note protested the German proclamation of Feb. 4, which declared the waters around the British Isles a war zone and announced that after Feb. 18, "neutral vessels cannot always be prevented from suffering from the attacks intended for enemy ships."

Feb. 22, appointed members of Federal Trade Commission

Mar. 3, signed. amended federal reserve bank act

Mar. 4, third session of 63rd Congress adjourned

Apr. 30, signed act creating naval oil reserve No. 3, near Casper, Wy.

• The 9,481-acre reserve was popularly known as Teapot Dome.

May 5, U.S. Marines landed in Santo Domingo

• This was the first step toward military occupation of Santo Domingo. Occupation was completed, Nov. 29; it continued until 1924.

May 7, *Lusitania* sunk by submarine

• The British transatlantic steamer was sunk about 15 miles off the southwestern Irish coast by the German submarine, U-20.

• A total of 1,198 of the 1,959 passengers and crew died, including 124 Americans.

May 8, issued first public statement regarding *Lusitania*

• The message, released by his secretary, Joseph P. Tumulty, read:

Of course the President feels the distress and the gravity of the situation to the utmost, and is considering very earnestly, but very calmly, the right course of action to pursue. He knows that the people of the country wish and expect him to act with deliberation as well as with firmness.

May 10, delivered "too proud to fight" speech, Philadelphia, Pa.

• Addressing four thousand recently naturalized citizens in Convention Hall, he said:

The example of America must be the example not merely of peace because it will not fight, but of peace because peace is the healing and elevating influence of the world and strife is not. There is

such a thing as a man being too proud to fight. There is such a thing as a nation being so right that it does not have to convince others by force that it is right.

May 13, sent first *Lusitania* note to Germans

• His note of protest, signed by Bryan, condemned the German submarine campaign, upheld the right of American citizens to travel on the high seas, and reiterated the "strict accountability" position. The German reply, dated May 28, maintained that the *Lusitania* was armed and carried Canadian troops. The steamer was not armed, carried no troops; however, the cargo included 4,200 cases of cartridges and 1,250 cases of empty steel shrapnel shells.

May 17, reviewed Atlantic fleet of U.S. Navy, New York City harbor

June 2, issued warning to Mexican factions to halt civil war or face American intervention

• After Huerta had been deposed, Carranza expressed his willingness to step down as leader of the Constitutionalists and aid in the establishment of a civil government representing all factions. Pancho Villa, who declared war against Carranza in September, 1914, gained American support. Carranza's forces defeated the Villista army decisively in April, 1915, and forced Villa to retreat to the northern provinces.

June 8, accepted resignation of Secretary of State Bryan, effective, June 9

• Wilson and Bryan disagreed about what should be the contents of the second *Lusitania* note.

June 9, sent second *Lusitania* note to Germans

• He said the Imperial German Government was "misinformed" about the steamer being armed and carrying troops and reiterated the American demands of May 13. The note was signed by Acting Secretary of State Robert Lansing.

June 24, appointed his second secretary of state, Robert Lansing

July 1, signed act reorganizing department of agriculture

July 12, received text of German reply to second *Lusitania* note

• The German position had not changed.

July 21, sent third *Lusitania* note to Germans

• Over Lansing's signature, Wilson termed the German reply to the second note "very unsatisfactory." He added that repetition of acts in contravention of U.S. neutral rights would be regarded as "deliberately unfriendly."

• Although this had the sound of being virtually an ultimatum, his position on submarine warfare had changed from condemnatory to acceptance according to the rules of cruiser warfare. Berlin was informed through diplomatic channels that no reply to the third note was expected.

July 28, ordered military occupation of revolution-torn Haiti

• U.S. Marines landed July 28; order was restored by Aug. 1. A puppet government was formed, and a ten-year treaty that made Haiti a semiprotectorate was signed, Sept. 16.

Sept. 1, *Arabic* pledge made by German ambassador

• Ambassador Johann von Bernstorff, in response to protests made after two Americans were killed when the British steamer, *Arabic*, was sunk, Aug. 19, pledged on his own authority:

> Liners will not be sunk by our submarines without warning . . . provided that the liners do not try to escape or offer resistance.

Oct. 6, his engagement to Mrs. Galt announced

• He and Mrs. Edith Bolling Galt had met at the White House the previous March. They had been introduced by his cousin, Helen Woodrow Bones.

Oct. 9, attended World Series, Philadelphia, Pa.

• He, Mrs. Galt, and her mother, Mrs. William H. Bolling, attended the second game of the Philadelphia Phillies-Boston Red Sox series.

• He was the first of four presidents who attended the World Series while in office.

• He was the first of two presidents who attended World Series games outside Washington, D.C., while in office. The other was Hoover.

Oct. 19, recognized Carranza government of Mexico

• He reluctantly recognized the Constitutionalist government after Villa's armies were decisively defeated in northern Mexico.

Oct. 20, approved embargo on arms to Mexico, except to districts controlled by Carranza

Nov. 4, spoke on preparedness program, Manhattan Club, New York City

• He stressed the defensive nature of his program. This speech set off a wave of opposition, particularly from Progressives.

Dec. 6, first session of 64th Congress

• The administration retained control of both the Senate and the House of Representatives. The Democrats gained five seats in the Senate but lost 59 House seats. The Senate (96 members) consisted of 56 Democrats, 39 Republicans, and one other. The House (435 members) consisted of 231 Democrats, 193 Republicans, eight others, and three vacancies.

Dec. 7, delivered his third State of the Union message to Congress

• He outlined a comprehensive national defense program.

Dec. 17, signed extension of 1914 emergency war tax act

Dec. 18, married Mrs. Edith Bolling Galt, Washington, D.C.

Dec. 28, his representative, Colonel House, sailed for Europe

1916

Jan. 2, Associate Justice Lamar died

Jan. 3, returned to Washington after honeymoon

Jan. 27, opened preparedness campaign, New York City

• He outlined his program in speeches before the Railway Business Association, the New York Federation of Churches, and the Motion Picture Board of Trade.

Jan. 28, appointed Louis D. Brandeis as associate justice

• Brandeis, who was confirmed by the Senate, June 1, was the second of Wilson's three appointments to the Supreme Court.

• Brandeis was the first Jew named to the Court. Anti-Semitism played a part but was not the principal element in the four-month furor that occurred before his confirmation, the longest and one of the dirtiest political battles ever fought over a presidential appointment. A leading advocate of public regulation of private enterprise, Brandeis had helped frame such regulatory measures as the antitrust and federal trade commission acts and had believed in and fought for collective bargaining, minimum wage and maximum hour legislation. Brandeis was a dangerous radical in the eyes of the proponents of the laissez-faire system of economics and political life, and they fought his confirmation with every weapon they could muster.

Jan. 29-Feb. 4, toured Middle West
- Wilson delivered major addresses in Pittsburgh, Cleveland, Milwaukee, Des Moines, Topeka, Kansas City, and St. Louis. Great crowds greeted him enthusiastically, everywhere except in Topeka. He said that he was not committed to any specific program; he declared that the country must prepare not for aggressive war, but for defense of the U.S. and the rest of the western hemisphere. In his climactic speech in St. Louis, he called for "incomparably the greatest navy in the world."

Feb. 10, accepted resignation of Secretary of War Garrison, effective, Mar. 5
- Wilson refused to endorse Garrison's plan for compulsory enlistment and federal control of the national guard.

Feb. 29, demanded defeat of McLemore and Gore resolutions
- The McLemore resolution, introduced by Representative Jeff McLemore of Texas, Feb. 17, requested the president to warn Americans not to travel on armed vessels. The Gore resolution, introduced by Senator Thomas P. Gore of Oklahoma, Feb. 25, asked the denial of passports to Americans who sought passage on armed vessels and demanded protection of American trade in noncontraband.
- The Gore resolution was tabled, Mar. 3; the McLemore resolution was tabled, Mar. 7.

Mar. 6, appointed his second secretary of war, Newton D. Baker
- Baker took office, Mar. 9.

Mar. 9, notified of Villa raid on Columbus, N. Mex.
- Shortly after dawn that morning, Villa led more than one thousand of his guerillas across the border. At least 17 Americans were killed in the raid on the border town. A troop of American cavalry drove the Villistas off, pursued them about 15 miles into Mexico, and killed and wounded about 70.

Mar. 10, ordered expedition against Villa
- "An adequate force will be sent at once in pursuit of Villa with the single object of capturing him and putting a stop to his forces," he announced. "This can and will

be done in entirely friendly aid of the constituted authorities in Mexico and with scrupulous respect for the sovereignty of that republic."
- Under the command of Brigadier General John J. Pershing, four thousand troops entered Mexico, Mar. 15.

Apr. 18, sent ultimatum to Germans after *Sussex* crisis
- The *Sussex*, an unarmed French channel vessel, was torpedoed in the English Channel, Mar. 24. Four of the injured passengers were Americans. Regarding the incident as a violation of the *Arabic* pledge, Wilson dispatched this ultimatum:

  Unless the Imperial Government should now immediately declare its purpose to abandon its present methods of submarine warfare against passenger and freight-carrying vessels, the Government of the United States can have no choice but to sever diplomatic relations with the German Empire.

Apr. 19, delivered address explaining ultimatum to joint session of Congress

May 9, mobilized national guards of Texas, Arizona, and New Mexico for border duty
- A band of two hundred of Villa's men had raided Glen Springs and Boquillas, Tex., May 5–6; three American soldiers and a nine-year-old boy were killed.
- On May 5, Wilson had approved, but did not release, a statement that the Pershing expedition was gradually to be withdrawn inasmuch as there was no large body of Villistas within four hundred miles of the border.

May 9, received German apology for sinking of *Sussex*
- The note of regret regarding the "deplorable incident" followed a note of May 4 that had announced that naval authorities had been instructed to conduct submarine operations everywhere according to the general rules of international law concerning visit and search. The German apology ended the crisis.

May 29, signed executive order adopting official presidential flag
- The flag contained the presidential seal in bronze upon a blue background and a large white star in each of the four corners.

June 3, signed army reorganization act
- The regular army was increased to 206,000 men, with provisions for additional expan-

sion by presidential order to 254,000 men, as well as expansion of the now-federalized national guard to 425,000 men. The act also provided authority to draft men during wartime to bring the regular army to legal strength.

June 10, accepted resignation of Associate Justices Hughes
• Hughes had been nominated for president by the Republican national convention, Chicago, Ill., June 7.

June 15, renominated for president, Democratic national convention, St. Louis, Mo.

June 21, learned of Carrizal incident
• Two troops of U.S. cavalry, under orders from General Pershing not to enter any place garrisoned by Mexican government troops, attempted to pass through Carrizal, a village in Chihauhua, where between 120 and 200 Mexican soldiers were stationed. Although warned by the local commander, General Felix Gomez, that orders were to fire on Americans moving in any direction but north, the American commander, Captain Charles T. Boyd, rashly ordered his troops forward. At least 14 Americans—including Boyd—were killed, and 25 others were captured. About 30 Mexicans were killed, while more than 40 were wounded.
• Wilson first learned of the Carrizal clash when he heard newsboys shouting "Extra!" outside the White House, and sent an aide for a newspaper.

June 25, demanded release of Carrizal prisoners, asked assurances U.S. troops would not face future attacks by Mexican troops
• The Mexicans ordered the release of the American prisoners, June 28.

June 30, spoke on Mexican situation, New York Press Club, New York City
• He said he was the spokesman, at least for the time being, of those people who did not want war with Mexico and that he was not the servant of those with Mexican investments. He summed up his position with two rhetorical questions:

> Do you think the glory of America would be enhanced by a war of conquest in Mexico?
> Do you think that any act of violence by a powerful nation like this against a weak and distracted neighbor would reflect distinction upon the annals of the United States?

July 11, signed good roads act
• This act established the bureau of roads in the department of agriculture and authorized assistance to state highway programs that met federal standards.

July 14, appointed John H. Clarke as associate justice
• Clarke, who was confirmed by the Senate, July 24, was the last of Wilson's three appointments to the Supreme Court.

July 17, signed federal farm loan act
• This act provided long-term credit for farmers, much as the federal reserve act had provided relief to industry and commerce. Twelve farm loan banks were established, capitalized at $750,000 each, from which members of cooperative farm loan associations could secure loans at low rates of interest.

July 27, appointed federal farm loan board

Aug. 8, sent treaty for purchase of Danish West Indies to Senate
• The treaty, which transferred the Virgin Islands to the U.S. for $25,000,000, was ratified by the Senate, Sept. 7. Ratifications were exchanged, Jan. 17, 1917, and the transfer of the islands was accepted, Mar. 31, 1917.

Aug. 18, vetoed army appropriations bill
• He objected to a provision in the revised articles of war that exempted retired officers from court-martial. The bill was rewritten to his specifications, and he signed the act, Aug. 29.

Aug. 29, recommended legislation to avert railroad strike to joint session of Congress
• The railroads and the four brotherhoods had been deadlocked since June on the eight-hour workday issue. He met with both sides, Aug. 14, without success; a nationwide strike was called for Sept. 4. The legislation he recommended included the eight-hour day, approval of increased freight rates if warranted by increased operating costs, and the immediate enlargement of the Interstate Commerce Commission. He also asked for the power to take control of the railroads and draft into military service such crews and management officials necessary for efficient operation.

Aug. 29, signed naval appropriations act

Aug. 29, signed Philippine Islands organic act
• The act conferred Filipino citizenship upon those who had been Spanish subjects

as of Apr. 11, 1899, established a legislature, a bill of rights, and male suffrage. Executive power was vested in the governor-general, who was to be appointed by the president.

Sept. 1, signed child labor act
• This act, forbidding interstate shipments of products of child labor, was declared unconstitutional by the Supreme Court, June 3, 1918.

Sept. 2, officially notified of nomination as Democratic candidate for president, Long Branch, N.J.

Sept. 3, signed Adamson Eight-Hour Act
• This act specified eight hours as a day's labor on railroads operating in interstate commerce.

Sept. 4, accepted Lincoln birthplace memorial, Hodgenville, Ky.

Sept. 7, signed shipping act
• This act, which marked the rejuvenation of the American merchant marine, authorized the U.S. Shipping Board, which was empowered to construct, purchase, lease or requisition vessels through the Emergency Fleet Corporation, capitalized at $50,000,000.

Sept. 8, signed revenue act
• This act increased the maximum tax on incomes to 14 percent, increased the maximum tax on estates to ten percent, and lowered income tax exemptions. The act also increased the tax on munitions manufacturers to a maximum of 12½ percent.

Sept. 8, first session of 64th Congress adjourned

Sept. 8, pocket vetoed appropriation for arming and equipping militia of Georgia bill
• This was the first of his 11 pocket vetoes.

Sept. 8, addressed National American Woman Suffrage Association, Atlantic City, N.J.
• He stated that woman suffrage was inevitable and that he would fight for the cause.

Sept. 23, delivered first of series of "front porch" campaign speeches, Long Branch, N.J.

Sept. 29, sent O'Leary telegram
• One of the highlights of the campaign was the reaction to a telegram Wilson sent to Jeremiah A. O'Leary, president of an anti-British, pro-German group called the American Truth Society:

I would feel deeply mortified to have you or anybody like you vote

for me. Since you have access to many disloyal Americans and I have not, I will ask you to convey this message to them.

Nov. 4, delivered final campaign speech, Long Branch, N.J.

Nov. 5, wrote confidential letter regarding possibility of resigning
• He outlined the course he intended to follow in the event that he was defeated in a letter to Secretary of State Lansing:

I would ask your permission to invite Mr. Hughes to become Secretary of State and would then join the Vice President in resigning, and thus open to Mr. Hughes the immediate succession to the presidency.

Nov. 7, election day
• *See* Election of 1916, pages 338–339.

Dec. 4, second session of 64th Congress

Dec. 5, delivered his fourth State of the Union message to Congress

Dec. 18, sent peace note to all belligerents
• He requested both Allied and Central Powers to state their war aims. The Germans made no reply, and the response of the Allies was patently unrealistic.

1917

Jan. 8, presidential electors cast ballots
• He received 277 of the 531 electoral votes from the 48 states.
• *See* Election of 1916, pages 338–339.

Jan. 22, delivered "peace without victory" speech to Senate
• He said:

Victory would mean peace forced upon the loser, a victor's terms imposed upon the vanquished. It would be accepted in humiliation, under duress, at an intolerable sacrifice, and would leave a sting, a resentment, a bitter memory upon which terms of peace would rest, not permanently, but only as upon quicksand. Only a peace between equals can last, only a peace the very principle of which is equality and a common participation in a common benefit.

• He proposed a league of nations, "a concert of power":

I am proposing, as it were, that the nations should with one accord adopt the doctrine of President Monroe as the doctrine of the world.

Jan. 28, ordered General Pershing to withdraw his command from Mexico
• This order was transmitted officially by Secretary of War Baker.

Jan. 29, vetoed immigration bill that included literacy test

Jan. 31, informed of German submarine decree
• Ambassador von Bernstorff informed Secretary of State Lansing that, effective, Feb. 1, German submarines would sink all ships in a broad war zone without warning. Only neutral ships already at sea would be safe during a short period of grace. One U.S. passenger ship would be allowed to sail weekly between New York City and Falmouth, England, provided the vessels were properly marked and carried no contraband. This latter edict was modified, Feb. 2.

Feb. 3, severed diplomatic relations with Germany
• Wilson stated:

We do not desire any hostile conflict with the Imperial German Government. . . . We shall not believe that they are hostile to us unless and until we are obliged to believe it; and we propose nothing more than the reasonable defense of the undoubted rights of our people.

Feb. 5, immigration act passed over his veto
• This was the first of his six vetoes that were overridden.

Feb. 14, electoral vote tabulated by Congress
• Wilson and Marshall were officially declared elected.

Feb. 23, signed vocational education act

Feb. 25, received text of Zimmerman telegram

Feb. 26, asked joint session of Congress for emergency powers
• He requested legislation authorizing the arming of American merchant vessels.

Feb. 27, called sinking of *Laconia* "overt act"
• The British liner, *Laconia*, was torpedoed without warning off the Irish coast, Feb. 25. Two Americans died.

Feb. 28, decided to authorize publication of Zimmerman telegram
• A cipher telegram from Foreign Secretary Alfred Zimmerman to the German minister to Mexico, Heinrich von Eckhardt, Jan. 16, stated that if war broke out between the U.S. and Germany an alliance with Mexico would be proposed upon the following terms:

Joint conduct of the war. Joint conclusion of peace. Ample financial support and an agreement on our part that Mexico shall gain back by conquest the territory lost to her at a prior period in Texas, New Mexico, and Arizona.

• The telegram also suggested that President Venustiano Carranza of Mexico be requested to prevail upon Japan to desert the Allies and switch to the German side.
• British Intelligence had intercepted the message. A copy had been given to U.S. Ambassador Walter Hines Page in London, Feb. 24, who forwarded it to the state department. A paraphrased version of the telegram was given to the Associated Press state department correspondent, Edward M. Hood. The story was published, Mar. 1, and created the desired sensation.

Mar. 1, sent report to Senate that declared Zimmerman telegram authentic
• German-American spokesmen immediately had labeled the telegram a forgery. Zimmerman admitted its authenticity, Mar. 3.

Mar. 2, signed organic act for Puerto Rico
• This act established Puerto Rico as a U.S. territory and conferred citizenship on its inhabitants.

Mar. 4, second session of 64th Congress adjourned
• The armed ship bill, which had passed in the House of Representatives, 403–13, Mar. 1, did not come to a vote in the Senate. Senator Robert M. La Follette of Wisconsin led the filibuster which lasted from Feb. 28 to adjournment.

ELECTION OF 1916

Socialist Labor party, convened, Apr. 23, at New York City, nominated Arthur Edward Reimer of Massachusetts for president, Caleb Harrison of Illinois for vice president.

Republican party, convened, June 7, at Chicago, Ill., nominated Charles Evans Hughes of New York for president, Charles Warren Fairbanks of Indiana for vice president.
• This was the 16th Republican national convention. It was the ninth Republican convention held in Chicago; it was the 14th major party convention held in Chicago.
Progressive ("Bull Moose") party, convened, June 7, at Chicago, Ill., nominated Theodore Roosevelt of New York for president, John Milliken Parker of Louisiana for vice president.
• Roosevelt declined the nomination and instead supported Hughes.
Democratic party, convened, June 14, at St. Louis, Mo., nominated Woodrow Wilson of New Jersey for president, Thomas Riley Marshall of Indiana for vice president.
• This was the 22nd Democratic national convention. It was the fourth Democratic convention held in St. Louis; it was the fifth major party convention held in St. Louis.
Prohibition party, convened, July 19, at St. Paul, Minn., nominated James Franklin Hanly of Indiana for president, Ira David Landrith of Tennessee for vice president.
Socialist party did not hold a national convention but rather nominated candidates by mail referendum: Allen Louis Benson of New York for president, George Ross Kirkpatrick of New Jersey for vice president.
Election day, Tuesday, Nov. 7, 1916
Popular vote: 18,480,949
    Wilson, 9,129,606

Hughes, 8,532,221
Benson, 585,113
Hanly, 220,606
Reimer, 13,403
• Wilson was the 12th of 15 presidents who were elected without receiving a majority of the popular vote.
• He was the second of two presidents who were elected twice without receiving majorities of the popular vote. The other was Cleveland.
Electoral vote: 531, 48 states
  • Wilson, 277, 30 states
    (Alabama, 12; Arizona, 3; Arkansas, 9; California, 13; Colorado, 6; Florida, 6; Georgia, 14; Idaho, 4; Kansas, 10; Kentucky, 13; Louisiana, 10; Maryland, 8; Mississippi, 10; Missouri, 18; Montana, 4; Nebraska, 8; Nevada, 3; New Hampshire, 4; New Mexico, 3; North Carolina, 12; North Dakota, 5; Ohio, 24; Oklahoma, 10; South Carolina, 9; Tennessee, 12; Texas, 20; Utah, 4; Virginia, 12; Washington, 7; Wyoming, 3)
• Wilson also received the vote of one West Virginia elector.
  • Hughes, 254, 18 states
    (Connecticut, 7; Delaware, 3; Illinois, 29; Indiana, 15; Iowa, 13; Maine, 6; Massachusetts, 18; Michigan, 15; Minnesota, 12; New Jersey, 14; New York, 45; Oregon, 5; Pennsylvania, 38; Rhode Island, 5; South Dakota, 4; Vermont, 4; West Virginia, 7 of 8 votes; Wisconsin, 13)

THE 33rd ADMINISTRATION

1917

Mar. 5, his second inauguration day
• Wilson took the oath of office, administered by Chief Justice Edward Douglass White, on a platform on the east portico of the Capitol.
• He was the fourth of five presidents who postponed their oath-taking ceremonies until Monday because Mar. 4 fell on Sunday. However, he had taken the oath in a private ceremony in the President's Room of the Capitol, Mar. 4. This oath had been administered by White.
• This was the second of three inaugurations at which White officiated.

Mar. 6, advised by Secretary of State Lansing that he could arm merchant vessels without congressional approval
• He announced his decision to arm the vessels, Mar. 9.
Mar. 21, called special session of Congress, Apr. 2
Mar. 24, issued proclamation suspending eight-hour day for government workers, provided for overtime pay
Mar. 25, issued executive order calling up national guard of eastern states
Mar. 31, issued executive order establishing general munitions board
Apr. 2, first session of 65th Congress
• The administration retained control of the

Senate but organized the House of Representatives only with the help of other parties. The Democrats lost three Senate and 21 House seats. The Senate (96 members) consisted of 53 Democrats, 42 Republicans, and one other. The House (435 members) consisted of 216 Republicans, 210

Democrats, and nine others.

Apr. 2, delivered war message to Congress
• He asked for a declaration of war, vilified the German submarine campaign as "warfare against mankind," and declared, "The world must be made safe for democracy."
• This was the sixth of seven war messages.

WORLD WAR I

1917

Apr. 6, signed joint declaration of war resolution
• The resolution was passed in the Senate, 82–6, Apr. 4, and in the House, 373–50, Apr. 6.

Apr. 6, issued proclamation announcing state of war

Apr. 14, issued executive order establishing committee on public information
• He appointed George Creel as chairman of the committee, which consisted of the secretaries of state, war, and navy.

Apr. 24, signed Liberty Loan Act
• This act authorized an issue of bonds to be sold by public subscription. Secretary of Treasury McAdoo issued $2,000,000,000 worth of 3½ percent convertible gold bonds in June.

May 10, appointed General Pershing as commanding general of American Expeditionary Force, effective, May 26

May 14, authorized army strengthened to 223,000 men

May 16, issued executive order establishing air production board

May 18, signed Selective Service Act
• This act authorized the registration and classification of all men between the ages of 21 and 30.

May 18, issued executive order dispatching one division to France
• The first American troops landed in Saint-Nazaire, France, June 26.

May 19, appointed Herbert Hoover as food controller

May 23, issued proclamation of neutrality of Panama Canal

June 5, first draft registration enrolled more than 9,500,000 men

June 15, signed Espionage Act
• This act provided imprisonment of up to 20 years and fines up to $10,000 for aiding the enemy, obstructing recruitment, or

refusal of military service. The act also empowered the postmaster general to refuse mailing privileges to newspapers and other publications considered seditious.

July 3, issued executive order calling all national guard for military service

July 9, issued proclamation placing export of foods and other products under government control

July 13, issued executive order drafting 678,000 men into military service
• The drawing for the first draft was made, July 20.

July 18, issued executive order imposing censorship on transatlantic cables

July 28, war industries board established by council of national defense
• The war industries board succeeded the general munitions board.

Aug. 10, signed food and fuel control act
• This act empowered the president to fix the prices of wheat, coal, coke, and other products and to license producers and distributors. The act prohibited the use of foodstuffs in the manfacture of distilled liquors and prohibited the importation of liquors.

Aug. 10, appointed Herbert Hoover as food administrator

Aug. 21, fixed price of bituminous coal

Aug. 23, appointed Harry A. Garfield as fuel administrator

Aug. 23, fixed price of anthracite coal

Sept. 7, issued proclamation prohibiting export of currency or bullion

Sept. 19, issued executive order establishing labor mediation commission

Sept. 19, fixed price of copper

Sept. 24, fixed prices of iron, iron ore, steel

Oct. 1, second Liberty bond issue
• Secretary of Treasury McAdoo issued $3,-800,000,000 of four percent convertible gold bonds in November.

Oct. 3, signed new war revenue act
• This act authorized a graduated income

tax on personal incomes of $1,000, beginning at four percent, increased the corporation tax to six percent, and instituted a graduated excess profits tax of 20 to 60 percent for individuals and corporations. The act also provided for increased excise taxes and increased postal rates.

Oct. 6, signed trading with enemy act

•This act empowered the president to impose an embargo on imports and to control exports. The act also created the office of alien property custodian.

Oct. 6, first session of 65th Congress adjourned

Oct. 12, appointed first alien property custodian, A. Mitchell Palmer

Nov. 7, issued proclamation licensing production of bakery items

Nov. 16, issued proclamation requiring registration of enemy aliens

•Aliens were denied admission to the District of Columbia, the Panama Canal Zone, and all waterfront zones.

Nov. 27, issued executive order conveying price-fixing powers to food administration

Dec. 4, second session of 65th Congress

Dec. 4, delivered his fifth State of the Union message to Congress

Dec. 11, issued proclamation announcing state of war with Austria-Hungary

•Congress had passed a joint resolution that declared war on Austria-Hungary, Dec. 7.

Dec. 18, signed joint resolution submitting 18th Amendment to Constitution to states

Dec. 26, issued proclamation placing railroads under government control

•Secretary of Treasury McAdoo was appointed director general of the railroad administration.

1918

Jan. 8, listed his "14 Points" for peace in address to Congress

•The 14 Points, which he considered "the only possible program" for peace when the war ended, were:

1. open convenants openly arrived at
2. freedom of the seas
3. removal of trade barriers
4. armament reduction
5. impartial adjustment of colonial claims
6. evacuation of Russia and independent determination of Russian national policy

7. evacuation and restoration of Belgium
8. evacuation and restoration of France, including Alsace-Lorraine
9. readjustment of Italian borders
10. opportunity of autonomous development for the people of Austria-Hungary
11. readjustment of borders of Rumania, Serbia, and Montenegro
12. self-determination for peoples under Turkish rule and freedom of the Dardenelles
13. establishment of a free Poland, with access to the sea
14. establishment of "a general association of nations"

Jan. 26, issued proclamation establishing one "meatless," two "wheatless," and two "porkless" days per week

Feb. 2, issued executive order providing for control of enemy property

Feb. 14, ordered investigation of irregularities in shipbuilding

Mar. 4, appointed Bernard M. Baruch as chairman of reorganized war industries board

Mar. 7, authorized distinguished service medal for U.S. Army

Mar. 19, signed act establishing daylight saving time throughout U.S.

Mar. 20, issued proclamation confiscating 40 Dutch vessels

•The vessels, which were berthed in U.S. ports, were placed in government service at full, but delayed, compensation.

Mar. 21, signed railroad control act

•This act provided for compensation to be paid to the railroads during the period of government management. The period was to end no later than 21 months after ratification of a peace treaty.

Mar. 25, third Liberty bond issue

•Secretary of Treasury McAdoo issued $4,-200,000,000 of four and one-half percent convertible gold bonds in May.

Mar. 29, approved selection of General Ferdinand Foch of France as supreme commander of Western Front

•Foch was formally appointed, Apr. 14.

Mar. 29, appealed to governor of California for clemency for Tom Mooney

•Labor leader Mooney had been sentenced to death for the bombing during the 1916 Preparedness Day parade in San Francisco. Mooney's sentence was commuted to life imprisonment; he was pardoned unconditionally in 1938.

Apr. 4, issued proclamation establishing war finance corporation

Apr. 8, issued proclamation establishing national war labor board

•He appointed Frank P. Walsh and former President Taft as joint chairmen.

Apr. 10, signed export trade associations act

Apr. 11, issued proclamation assuming control of four principal Atlantic coastline steamship companies

May 16, signed Sedition Act

•This amendment to the Espionage Act of 1917 provided heavy penalties for making or conveying false statements that interfered with the prosecution of the war and for "disloyal" language about the American government, the Constitution, and the flag. The act, which was aimed principally at Socialists and pacifists, resulted in the trial and imprisonment of Eugene V. Debs and others.

May 20, issued executive order reorganizing signal corps

May 20, signed act authorizing reorganization of executive department

June 1, issued executive order concerning conscientious objectors

•Conscientious objectors were exempted from military service and assigned agricultural work or positions with the American Friends Service Committee (Quakers).

June 8, issued executive order establishing war labor policies board

•He appointed Felix Frankfurter as chairman.

June 25, Battle of Belleau Wood ended

•More than twenty-seven thousand American troops participated in this first major U.S. action. The Fourth U.S. Marine Brigade played a large part in recapturing Belleau Wood.

July 4, reiterated war aims, Mount Vernon, Va.

July 18–Aug. 6, second Battle of Marne

•About eighty-five thousand U.S. troops participated in blunting the German offensive. This was the turning point of the war.

July 18, signed act authorizing government control of American shipping for duration of war

July 22, issued proclamation placing telephone and telegraph systems under government control

Aug. 2, was notified state of war existed between Russia and U.S.

•American affairs in Russia were put in the hands of the Swedish consul general, Aug. 5.

Sept. 12–Sept. 16, Battle of St. Mihiel

•This was the first distinctly American offensive. About 550,000 American troops, with French and British aid, cut off the St. Mihiel salient, which removed a German threat. U.S. casualties were about 7,000.

Sept. 16, rejected Austro-Hungarian note on peace terms

Sept. 26–Nov. 11, Meuse-Argonne offensive

•More than 1,200,000 American troops were employed in the general offensive. The objective, the cutting of the Sedan-Mezieres railroad—the main supply route for the German armies—was achieved at a cost of 120,000 U.S. casualties.

Sept. 27, set forth "five particulars," including League of Nations, in New York City address

Sept. 30, endorsed woman suffrage amendment to Constitution in address to Senate

Oct. 5, armistice requested by Prince Max of Baden, Imperial Chancellor of Germany

•A similar request, asking for an armistice prior to a peace conference based on the 14 Points, was made by Austria-Hungary, Oct. 7.

Oct. 18, proposed recognition of independence of Czechs and Yugoslavs in note to Austria-Hungary

Oct. 23, agreed to submit German proposals to Allies

Oct. 25, his open letter to American people asked for election of Democratic Congress

Oct. 26, accused by Republicans of using war as "party asset"

•A joint appeal for the election of a Republican Congress was made by former Presidents Roosevelt and Taft, Oct. 31.

Nov. 5, election day

•The Republicans won control of both the Senate and the House of Representatives.

Nov. 5, Allies agreed to accept 14 Points as basis for armistice

•Wilson threatened separate action by the U.S. if the British and the French continued to vacillate. The Allies insisted, however, in reserving the right to discuss freedom of the seas at the peace conference and demanded German reparation for war damages in addition to the restoration of invaded territory.

Nov. 9, appointed Herbert Hoover to represent U.S. in organization of food relief in Europe

Nov. 9, Kaiser Wilhelm II of Germany abdicated

Nov. 11, armistice signed

• World War I had ended.

1918

Nov. 18, announced he would attend Paris peace conference

Nov. 21, second session of 65th Congress adjourned

Nov. 21, accepted resignation of Secretary of Treasury McAdoo, effective, Dec. 15

Dec. 2, third session of 65th Congress

Dec. 2, delivered his sixth State of the Union message to Congress

Dec. 4, sailed from Hoboken, N.J. for peace conference

Dec. 13, arrived at Brest, France

• He was the first of four presidents who visited France while in office.

• He was the first of seven presidents who visited Europe while in office.

• He was the third of 11 presidents who traveled outside the U.S. while in office.

• This was the first of his four visits to France while in office.

Dec. 16, accepted honorary citizenship of Paris

Dec. 16, appointed his second secretary of treasury, Carter Glass

Dec. 26–Dec. 31, visited England

• He was the first of five presidents who visited England while in office.

1919

Jan. 2–Jan. 6, visited Italy

• He conferred with King Victor Emmanuel II in Rome and met with Pope Benedict XV in the Vatican.

• He was the first of six presidents who visited Italy while in office.

• He was the first of five presidents who met with Popes while in office.

Jan. 7, returned to Paris

• This was the second of his four visits to France while in office.

Jan. 18, addressed opening session of Paris Peace Conference

Jan. 25, League of Nations included in peace settlement

• He led the fight for the League and convinced the other members of the "Big Four" (Georges Clemenceau of France, David Lloyd George of Great Britain, and Vittorio Orlando of Italy) that the international organization was central to the issues—but only after yielding major concessions.

Jan. 29, 18th Amendment ratified, effective Jan. 16, 1920

• *See* Constitution, page 644.

Feb. 14, submitted draft covenant of League of Nations to plenary session

• He presided at meetings of the commission that drew up the covenant, Feb. 3–14. The principal writers of the covenant were David Hunter Miller, legal adviser to Colonel House, and Lord Robert Cecil of Great Britain.

Feb. 15, sailed for U.S.

Feb. 24, arrived at Boston, Mass.

Feb. 26, met with members of Senate and House foreign relations committees

• A statement of opposition, which rejected the League, was signed by 37 Republican senators, as well as two senators-elect, Mar. 2. The statement, called the Senatorial Round-Robin, was read in the Senate, Mar. 4.

Mar. 4, third session of 65th Congress adjourned

Mar. 4, defended League in New York City address

• He insisted that it would be an impossibility to "dissect the covenant from the treaty without destroying the whole vital structure."

Mar. 4, accepted resignation of Attorney General Gregory

Mar. 5, appointed his third attorney general, A. Mitchell Palmer

Mar. 5, sailed for France

Mar. 14, arrived in Paris

• On his arrival he was presented with French demands, which included severe reparations for war damage to French property and either the Allied occupation of the Rhineland or the creation of a buffer state in the region.

• This was the third of his four visits to France while in office.

Apr. 3, became ill

May 19, first session of 66th Congress

• The administration lost control of both the Senate and the House of Representatives. The Democrats lost six Senate and 19

House seats. The Senate (96 members) consisted of 48 Republicans, 47 Democrats, and one other. The House (435 members) consisted of 237 Republicans, 191 Democrats, and seven others.

June 4, 19th Amendment to Constitution submitted to states for ratification

June 18–19, visited Belgium

•He was the first of three presidents who visited Belgium while in office.

June 20, returned to Paris

•This was the last of his four visits to France while in office.

June 28, Treaty of Versailles signed

June 29, sailed for U.S.

July 8, arrived in New York City

July 10, submitted covenant of League of Nations with Treaty of Versailles to Senate for ratification

July 12, issued proclamation prohibiting exportation of arms to Mexico

July 12, vetoed agricultural appropriations bill, which included repeal of daylight saving time clause

July 25, issued proclamation placing embargo on arms and ammunition to Mexico

Aug. 15, vetoed repeal of daylight saving time bill

Aug. 20, daylight saving time repeal act passed over his veto

•This was the second of his six vetoes that were overridden.

Aug. 25, suggested four-cents-per-hour increase for railroad shopmen

•This offer was accepted, Sept. 21, which averted a railroad strike.

Sept. 4, began speaking tour in defense of League of Nations

•He delivered more than 35 speeches in 29 cities during his 9,500-mile tour of the West.

Sept. 22, steel strike began

•The most serious of the labor crises that followed the discontinuation of federal labor agencies (more than 4,000,000 wage earners went out on strike in 1919, compared with slightly more than 1,200,000 in 1918), the steel strike was called by the American Federation of Labor when U.S. Steel refused to confer with union leaders. The strike was a failure and was abandoned, Jan. 9, 1920.

Sept. 26, became seriously ill

•He suffered a nervous breakdown in Pueblo, Colo., and was forced to cancel the remainder of his speaking tour.

Oct. 2, suffered stroke, Washington, D.C.

Oct. 6, national industrial conference convened, Washington, D.C.

•The conference, which he had called, ended without result, Oct. 23, in disagreement regarding collective bargaining.

Oct. 27, vetoed Volstead prohibition enforcement bill

Oct. 28, Volstead Act passed over his veto

•This was the third of his six vetoes that were overridden.

Oct. 30, issued executive order restoring coal price and distribution powers to fuel administration

Oct. 31, Secretary of Commerce Redfield resigned

Nov. 19, first session of 66th Congress adjourned

Nov. 21, issued proclamation reestablishing functions of food administration under attorney general

Dec. 1, second session of 66th Congress

Dec. 5, delivered his seventh State of the Union message to Congress

Dec. 16, appointed his second secretary of commerce, Joshua W. Alexander

Dec. 24, issued proclamation returning railroads and express companies to private operation, effective, Mar. 1, 1920

1920

Jan. 12, announced recall of American troops from Russia

Jan. 21, appointed American members of Permanent Court of International Arbitration, The Hague, Netherlands

Feb. 1, Secretary of Treasury Glass resigned

Feb. 2, accepted resignation of Secretary of Agriculture Houston

Feb. 2, appointed his second secretary of agriculture, Edwin T. Meredith

Feb. 2, appointed his third secretary of treasury, David F. Houston

Feb. 13, accepted resignation of Secretary of State Lansing

Feb. 13, issued executive order returning commercial radio to private ownership

Feb. 29, Secretary of Interior Lane resigned

Mar. 15, appointed his second secretary of interior, John B. Payne

Mar. 22, appointed his third secretary of state, Bainbridge Colby

•Colby, who took office, Mar. 23, was the

last of Wilson's 20 cabinet appointments.

Mar. 23, issued executive order abolishing price-fixing of coal, effective, Apr. 1

May 27, vetoed joint resolution declaring war with Germany at end

June 4, vetoed budget bill on constitutional grounds

• He objected to a clause providing for the removal of the comptroller general—a presidential appointee—by Congress.

June 5, second session of 66th Congress adjourned

June, depression began

• A drastic drop in export trade led to heavy inventories, wage cuts, and business failures. Unemployment rose steadily during the next 18 months, topping 4,500,000. The effects were felt longer in agriculture.

• This was the eighth of nine U.S. depressions.

Aug. 26, issued proclamation announcing ratification of 19th Amendment

• *See* Constitution, page 644.

Oct. 3, asked voters for endorsement of League of Nations in November election

Nov. 2, election day

• *See* Election of 1920, pages 351–352.

Dec. 6, third session of 66th Congress

Dec. 7, sent his eighth and last State of the Union message to Congress

Dec. 10, awarded Nobel Peace Prize

• His award was accepted by U.S. Minister Albert Schmedeman in Christiania, now Oslo, Norway.

• Wilson was the second of two presidents who were awarded the Nobel Peace Prize. The other was Theodore Roosevelt.

Dec. 14, presented deed to new house to Mrs. Wilson

• Built in 1915, the red brick Georgian house at 2340 S Street, N.W., Washington; D.C., was designed by Waddy B. Wood. An elevator and a billiard room were installed, a brick garage with a large porch above it was constructed, and iron gates were placed at the drive entrance. Some partitions were changed and stacks built for his

library of eight thousand volumes. The Woodrow Wilson House is a property of the National Trust for Historic Preservation. It is open to the public daily except Christmas, 10 A.M. to 5 P.M. Admission: adults, 50 cents; students and military, 25 cents.

Note: The official population, according to the 14th census, was 105,710,620.

1921

Jan. 3, vetoed joint resolution to reinstitute War Finance Corporation

Jan. 4, War Finance Corporation joint resolution passed over his veto

• This was the fourth of his six vetoes that were overridden.

Jan. 31, refused to commute sentence of Eugene V. Debs

• The commutation was recommended by Attorney General Palmer.

Feb. 5, vetoed army enlistment bill

Feb. 7, army enlistment act passed over his veto

• This act directed the secretary of war to cease enlisting men in the regular army except for those who had served two or more enlistments.

• This was the fifth of his six vetoes that were overridden.

Feb. 24, vetoed amendment to 1914 act to provide drainage of Indian allotments of Five Civilized Tribes

Mar. 2, Indian act amendment passed over this veto

• This was the last of his six vetoes that were overridden.

Mar. 4, third session of 66th Congress adjourned

Mar. 4, pocket vetoed immigration and army appropriations bills

• These were the last of Wilson's 44 vetoes and his 11 pocket vetoes.

THE FORMER PRESIDENT

Mar. 4, 1921, rode to Capitol with President-elect Harding

• Wilson's age at leaving office was 64 years, 66 days.

• He and Mrs. Wilson did not stay for his

successor's inauguration or inaugural address but quietly left the Capitol by a side door. They drove to their new home, 2340 S Street, N.W.

• He was the last of four presidents who did

not attend the inaugurations of their successors.

June, 1921, admitted to bar, Washington, D.C. and New York City

•He had formed a law partnership with his last secretary of state, Bainbridge Colby. He refused most of the business offers made to the law firm. He used the only fee that he accepted to buy an electric automobile for Mrs. Wilson.

Apr. 12, 1922, broke with Tumulty

•His former secretary had read a "message" to a Democratic dinner in New York City, Aug. 8, that was interpreted as his endorsement of James M. Cox as the party's presidential candidate in 1924. He repudiated the message in a letter to *The New York Times*, published, Apr. 14. "I did not send any message whatever to that dinner nor authorize anyone to convey a message," he wrote. He never saw Tumulty again.

1922, accepted Order of White Eagle from Polish government

•This was the only foreign decoration that he accepted.

Aug. 5, 1923, attended funeral of President Harding

Nov. 10, 1923, made only radio address

Nov. 11, 1923, made last public speech

•He told a large Armistice Day crowd in front of his home:

> I have seen fools resist Providence before and I have seen their destruction, and it will come upon these again, utter destruction and contempt; that we shall prevail is as sure as that God reigns.

Fall, 1923, *President Wilson's Case for the League of Nations* published by Princeton University Press, Princeton, N.J.

•Compiled with his approval by Hamilton Foley, the book consisted of Wilson's official explanation of the League covenant and the Treaty of Versailles to the Senate foreign affairs committee and his speeches of 1919.

Dec. 28, 1923, his 67th birthday

•He received a custom-built Rolls Royce and a purse to cover improvements on his home from friends. The specially built automobile had an unusually high top and wide doors. It featured orange trim on black, the Princeton colors.

January, 1924, developed digestive disturbance

DEATH

Date of death: Feb. 3, 1924

Place of death: Washington, D.C.

•Wilson was the sixth of seven presidents who died in Washington.

Age at death: 67 years, 37 days

•He lived two years and 336 days after the completion of his term.

Cause of death: Apoplexy

Place of burial: Washington, D.C.

•He was the only president who was buried in Washington.

THE VICE PRESIDENT (28th)

Full name: Thomas Riley Marshall

Date of birth: Mar. 14, 1854

Place of birth: North Manchester, Ind.

•Marshall was the only vice president who was born in Indiana.

Religious denomination: Presbyterian

•He was the last of 11 vice presidents who were Presbyterians.

•Wilson and Marshall were both Presbyterians. They were the fifth of seven president-vice president teams of the same religious denomination.

College: Wabash College, Crawfordsville, Ind.

Date of graduation: 1873

Occupation: Lawyer

•He was admitted to the bar, 1875; practiced in Columbia City, Ind.; prominent member of Democratic party in state for many years; governor of Indiana, 1909–1913.

•He was the 12th of 14 vice presidents who served as state governors.

Term of office: Mar. 4, 1913, to Mar. 4, 1921 (8 years)

•Marshall was the fifth of seven vice presidents who were elected to two terms.

•He was the third of five vice presidents who served two terms.

•He was the second of three vice presidents who served eight years.

•Wilson and Marshall were the 30th of 41 president-vice president teams.

•They were the third of five president-vice president teams that were reelected.

•They were the first of two Democratic president-vice president teams that were reelected. The other was Roosevelt and Garner.

Age at inauguration: 58 years, 355 days
State represented: Indiana
• He was the last of four vice presidents who represented Indiana.
Political party: Democratic
• He was the tenth of 16 vice presidents who were Democrats.
Occupation after term: Lawyer
Date of death: June 1, 1925
Place of death: Washington, D.C.
• He was the fifth of six vice presidents who died in Washington.
Age at death: 71 years, 79 days
Place of burial: Indianapolis, Ind.
• He was the last of four vice presidents who were buried in Indiana.

THE CABINET

State: William Jennings Bryan of Nebraska, Mar. 5, 1913, to June 9, 1915
• Robert Lansing of New York, June 24, 1915, to Feb. 13, 1920
• Bainbridge Colby of New York, Mar. 23, 1920, to Mar. 4, 1921
Treasury: William Gibbs McAdoo of New York, Mar. 6, 1913, to Dec. 15, 1918
• Carter Glass of Virginia, Dec. 16, 1918, to Feb. 1, 1920
• David Franklin Houston of Missouri, Feb. 2, 1920, to Mar. 3, 1921
War: Lindley Miller Garrison of New Jersey, Mar. 5, 1913, to Mar. 5, 1916
• Newton Diehl Baker of Ohio, Mar. 9, 1916, to Mar. 4, 1921
Attorney General: James Clark McReynolds

of Tennessee, Mar. 5, 1913, to Aug. 29, 1914
• Thomas Watt Gregory of Texas, Aug. 29, 1914, to Mar. 4, 1919
• Alexander Mitchell Palmer of Pennsylvania, Mar. 5, 1919, to Mar. 5, 1921
Navy: Josephus Daniels of North Carolina, Mar. 5, 1913, to Mar. 5, 1921
Postmaster General: Albert Sidney Burleson of Texas, Mar. 5, 1913, to Mar. 5, 1921
Interior: Franklin Knight Lane of California, Mar. 5, 1913, to Feb. 29, 1920
• John Barton Payne of Illinois, Mar. 15, 1920, to Mar. 4, 1921
Agriculture: David Franklin Houston of Missouri, Mar. 6, 1913, to Feb. 2, 1920
• Edwin Thomas Meredith of Iowa, Feb. 2, 1920, to Mar. 4, 1921
Commerce: William Cox Redfield of New York, Mar. 5, 1913, to Oct. 31, 1919
• Joshua Willis Alexander of Missouri, Dec. 16, 1919, to Mar. 4, 1921
Labor: William Bauchop Wilson of Pennsylvania, Mar. 6, 1913, to Mar. 5, 1921

THE SUPREME COURT

Associate Justices: James Clark McReynolds of Tennessee, appointed, Aug. 19, 1914; confirmed, Aug. 29, 1914
• Louis Dembitz Brandeis of Massachusetts, appointed, Jan. 28, 1916; confirmed, June 1, 1916
• John Hessin Clarke of Ohio, appointed, July 14, 1916; confirmed, July 24, 1916

Twenty-ninth President

WARREN GAMALIEL HARDING

Full name: Warren Gamaliel Harding
• He was the 11th of 19 presidents who had middle initials or middle names.
Date of birth: Nov. 2, 1865
• He was the last of five presidents who were born in November.
• He and Polk were the only presidents who were born on the same day of the year.
Place of birth: Corsica, now Blooming Grove, Ohio
• He was the last of seven presidents who were born in Ohio.
Family lineage: Scottish-Irish and English-Dutch
• He was the only president who was of Scottish-Irish and English-Dutch ancestry.
Religious denomination: Baptist
• He was the first of two presidents who were Baptists. The other was Truman.
College: Ohio Central College, Iberia, Ohio
• He was the only president who went to Ohio Central, which no longer exists.
• He was the 20th of 27 presidents who attended college.
• He was the last of six presidents who attended, but were not graduated from college.

• He was the 14th of 15 presidents who were not graduated from college.

PARENTS AND SIBLINGS

Father's name: George Tryon Harding
Date of birth: June 12, 1843
Place of birth: Corsica, Ohio
Occupation: Physician
• Harding was the only president whose father was a doctor.
Date of death: Nov. 19, 1928
• He was the first of two presidents whose fathers survived them. The other was Kennedy.
• Harding was the fourth of six presidents whose fathers lived to see their sons' inauguration or oath-taking days. Dr. Harding did not attend the ceremony.
Place of death: Santa Ana, Cal.
Age at death: 84 years, 160 days

Mother's name: Phoebe Elizabeth Dickerson Harding
Date of birth: Dec. 21, 1843
Place of birth: near Corsica, Ohio

348

Date of marriage: May 7, 1864
Children: 8; 5 daughters, 3 sons
• Warren Gamaliel was born in 1865; Charity Malvina in 1867; Mary Clarissa in 1868; Eleanor Priscilla in 1872; Charles Alexander in 1874; Abigail Victoria in 1876; George Tryon in 1878; and Phoebe Caroline in 1879.
• Harding was the second of two presidents who came from families of eight children. The other was Tyler.
• He was the fifth of eight presidents who were eldest children.
Date of death: May 20, 1910
Place of death: *Unknown*
Age at death: 66 years, 150 days

Father's second wife: Eudora Kelley Luvisi Harding
• Harding was the third of four presidents who had stepmothers.
• He was the fourth of five presidents who had stepparents.
Date of birth: Sept. 25, 1868
Place of birth: near Bartonia, Ind.
Date of marriage: Nov. 23, 1911
Place of marriage: Anderson, Ind.
Date of divorce: Oct. 5, 1916
Date of death: July 24, 1955
Place of death: Union City, Ind.
Age at death: 86 years, 302 days

Father's third wife: Mary Alice Severns Harding
• Harding was the only president whose father married three times.
Date of birth: Nov. 13, 1869
Place of birth: Marion, Ohio
Date of marriage: Aug. 11, 1921
• Harding was the only president whose father remarried during his term in office.
Place of marriage: Monroe, Mich.
Date of death: Nov. 27, 1964
Place of death: Marion, Ohio
Age at death: 95 years, 14 days

MARRIAGE

Date of marriage: July 8, 1891
Place of marriage: Marion, Ohio
• Harding was the last of seven presidents who were married in Ohio.
Age at marriage: 25 years, 248 days
• He was the 22nd of 27 presidents who

were married in their twenties.
Years married: 32 years, 25 days

Wife's name: Florence Kling De Wolfe Harding
• She had married Henry De Wolfe in 1880; they were divorced in 1885.
• Harding was the second of two presidents who married divorcees. The other was Jackson.
• She was the 25th of 33 first ladies.
• She was the 32nd of 40 wives of presidents.
Date of birth: Aug. 15, 1860
• She was the last of three first ladies who were born in August.
• She was the last of four wives of presidents who were born in August.
Place of birth: Marion, Ohio
• She was the last of six first ladies who were born in Ohio.
• She was the last of six wives of presidents who were born in Ohio.
Wife's mother: Louisa Bouton Kling
Wife's father: Amos Kling, banker and merchant
Age at marriage: 30 years, 327 days
• She was the first of two first ladies who were married in their thirties. The other was Bess Truman.
• She was the second of three wives of presidents who were married in their thirties.
Years older than husband: 5 years, 79 days
• She was her husband's senior by more years than any other first lady or wife of a president.
• She was the fourth of six first ladies who were older than their husbands.
• She was the fourth of six wives of presidents who were older than their husbands.
Children: None
• Harding was the last of six presidents who were childless.
• *See* page 351, Oct. 22, 1919.
• Mrs. Harding had one son by her previous marriage, Marshall Eugene De Wolfe.
• Harding was the last of three presidents who had stepchildren.
Years she survived her husband: 1 year, 111 days
• She was the 17th of 21 first ladies who survived their husbands.
• She was the 19th of 23 wives of presidents who survived their husbands.
Date of death: Nov. 21, 1924
Place of death: Marion, Ohio

• She was the last of four first ladies who died in Ohio.

• She was the last of four wives of presidents who died in Ohio.

Age at death: 64 years, 98 days

Place of burial: Marion, Ohio

• She was the last of five first ladies who were buried in Ohio.

• She was the last of five wives of presidents who were buried in Ohio.

EARLY YEARS

1871, with family, moved to Caledonia, Ohio

• Harding attended the local school, worked at odd jobs, and learned the printer's trade in the shop of the Caledonia *Argus*. His father had an interest in the weekly.

1879–1882, attended Ohio Central College, Iberia, Ohio

• He played the alto horn in the school band, was a member of the debating team, and edited the yearbook.

1882, taught school

• He taught for one term in a country school, which was two miles from Marion, Ohio. His salary was $30 a month.

• He was the sixth of seven presidents who taught school.

1882, joined family in Marion

• His family had moved to Marion while he was teaching. He read law for a few weeks and then sold insurance for a short time.

1883, worked for Marion *Mirror*

• He set type, wrote minor news stories and sold advertisements. His salary was $7 a week.

• He was the second of three presidents who were newspapermen.

1884, with two partners, purchased Marion *Star*

• He, John Warwick, and John Seickle bought the failing daily newspaper for $300 and assumed its mortgage. The first edition under this new management was published, Nov. 26. A front-page box announced: "We have purchased the 'Star' and we will stay." The announcement was signed "Star Publishing Co."

• He was the only president who was a newspaper publisher.

1886, assumed full control of *Star*

• Seickle had given up his partnership in the newspaper earlier. When Warwick objected to Harding's plan to install a telephone, Harding bought out Warwick and ordered the phone.

• The struggling paper survived, partially because of political advertising. Originally independent, the *Star* became a Republican journal and won its share of official state notices.

Nov. 2, 1886, appointed member of Republican county committee

July 8, 1891, married Florence Kling De Wolfe, Marion

• Shortly after their marriage, he became ill. His wife ran the *Star* while he stayed at home. "I went down there intending to help out for a few days," she later told an interviewer, "and remained fourteen years." She organized a force of delivery boys and also managed the advertising department. One of her newsboys later wrote:

> Mrs. Harding in those days ran the show. . . . It was her energy and business sense which made the *Star* . . . . Her husband was the front. He was . . . very affable; very much of a joiner and personally popular . . . . (but) it was she who was the real driving force in the success that the Marion *Star* was unquestionably making in its community.

• The ex-newsboy was Norman Thomas, who was to be the Socialist candidate for the presidency six times, 1928–1948.

• The Harding home and museum, 380 Mount Vernon Avenue, is open to the public daily, 10 A.M. to 5 P.M., and Sundays, 1 to 6 P.M., June 1 through Sept. 30, and daily except Mondays, Thanksgiving, Christmas, and New Year's Day, 1 to 5 P.M., Oct. 1 through May 31. Privately owned, the home and museum is maintained by the Harding Memorial Association. Admission: adults, 75 cents; children under 16, 35 cents.

1892, defeated for county auditor

1899, elected to state senate

1901, reelected to state senate

• He served as floor leader during his second term.

1903, elected lieutenant governor of Ohio
1905, declined renomination for lieutenant
governor
May 20, 1910, his mother died
Nov. 8, 1910, defeated as Republican candi-

date for governor
June 21, 1912, nominated William Howard
Taft for reelection, Republican national
convention, Chicago, Ill.

NATIONAL PROMINENCE

Nov. 3, 1914, elected to Senate
•Harding was the 12th of 16 presidents who
were elected to the Senate.
Dec. 6, 1915, took seat in Senate
•He was the 11th of 15 presidents who
served in the Senate.
June 7–10, 1916, served as temporary chair-
man, Republican national convention,
Chicago, Ill.
•He delivered the keynote speech.
February, 1919, first "Harding for Presi-
dent" club organized, Toledo, Ohio
•The response was meager.
Oct. 6, 1919, expressed preference for Sen-
ate
•In a private letter, he wrote that he would
prefer to remain in the Senate, "a position
far more to my liking than the Presidency
possibly could be."
Oct. 22, 1919, his illegitimate child born,
Asbury Park, N.J.
•His mistress, Nan Britton, originally from
Marion, named the child Elizabeth Ann
Christian.
Nov. 1, 1919, informed Republican state advisory committee he was candidate for reelection to Senate
Dec. 15, 1919, announced his candidacy for
president in letter to Republican county
committee
•He had been prevailed upon to change his
mind by Mrs. Harding and Harry M.
Daugherty, Ohio member of Republican
national committee.
Feb. 21, 1920, his nomination predicted by
Daugherty
•Harding had entered three primaries,
where he made poor showings. In Ohio, he
won by less than fifteen thousand votes
over Leonard Wood. While he would receive the support of 39 of Ohio's 48 delegates to the convention, a split delegation
from his home state was hardly considered
an auspicious beginning. In Indiana, he did
not win a single delegate. And in Montana,
he received only a handful of votes, 723 of

more than 40,000.
•Despite these disappointments, Daugh-
erty, his campaign manager, told *The New
York Times*:
> I don't expect Senator Harding to
> be nominated on the first, second,
> or third ballots, but I think we can
> afford to take chances that, about
> eleven minutes after two, Friday
> morning of the convention, when
> ten or twenty weary men are sit-
> ting around a table, someone will
> say, 'Who will we nominate?' At
> that decisive time the friends of
> Harding will suggest him and can
> well afford to abide by the result.

June 12, 1920, nominated for president,
Republican national convention, Chicago,
Ill.
•When a deadlock developed between
Leonard Wood and Frank O. Lowden, 15
party leaders gathered and agreed upon
him as the nominee, as Daugherty had pre-
dicted.
Aug. 27, 1920, degree of Master Mason con-
ferred by Marion Lodge No. 70, Marion
•He was the 11th of 13 presidents who were
Masons.
Nov. 2, 1920, election day
• *See* Election of 1920, below.
Jan. 10, 1921, presidential electors cast bal-
lots
•He received 404 of the 531 electoral votes
from the 48 states.
• *See* Election of 1920, below.
Feb. 9, 1921, electoral votes tabulated by
Congress
•Harding and Coolidge were officially de-
clared elected.

ELECTION OF 1920

Socialist Labor party, convened, May 5, at
New York City, nominated William Wesley
Cox of Missouri for president, August Gill-

haus of New York for vice president.

Socialist party, convened, May 8, at New York City, nominated Eugene Victor Debs of Indiana for president, Seymour Stedman of Illinois for vice president.

•Debs was in federal prison when nominated, serving a ten-year sentence for violation of the espionage and sedition acts of 1917 and 1918.

Republican party, convened, June 8, at Chicago, Ill., nominated Warren Gamaliel Harding of Ohio for president, Calvin Coolidge of Massachusetts for vice president.

•This was the 17th Republican national convention. It was the tenth Republican convention held in Chicago; it was the 15th major party convention held in Chicago.

Democratic party, convened, June 28, at San Francisco, Cal., nominated James Middleton Cox of Ohio for president, Franklin Delano Roosevelt of New York for vice president.

•This was the 23rd Democratic national convention. It was the first of two Democratic conventions held in San Francisco; it was the first of three major party conventions held in San Francisco.

Farmer Labor party, convened, July 11, at Chicago, Ill., nominated Parley Parker Christensen of Utah for president, Maximilian Sebastian Hayes of Ohio for vice president.

Single Tax party, convened, July 12, at Chicago, Ill., nominated Robert Charles Macauley of Pennsylvania for president, Richard George Barnum of Ohio for vice president.

Prohibition party, convened, July 21, at Lincoln, Neb., nominated Aaron Sherman Watkins of Ohio for president, David Leigh Colvin of New York for vice president.

Election day, Tuesday, Nov. 2, 1920
Popular vote: 27,141,304
    Harding, 16,153,115
    Cox (D), 9,133,092
    Debs, 915,490
    Christensen, 265,229
    Watkins, 189,339
    Cox (SL), 30,594
    others, 54,445
Electoral vote: 531, 48 states
  • Harding, 404, 37 states
    (Arizona, 3; California, 13; Colorado, 6; Connecticut, 7; Delaware, 3; Idaho, 4; Illinois, 29; Indiana, 15; Iowa, 13; Kansas, 10; Maine, 6; Maryland, 8; Massachusetts, 18; Michigan, 15; Minnesota, 12; Missouri, 18; Montana, 4; Nebraska, 8; Nevada, 3; New Hampshire, 4; New Jersey, 14; New Mexico, 3; New York, 45; North Dakota, 5; Ohio, 24; Oklahoma, 10; Oregon, 5; Pennsylvania, 38; Rhode Island, 5; South Dakota, 5; Tennessee, 12; Utah, 4; Vermont, 4; Washington, 7; West Virginia, 8; Wisconsin, 13; Wyoming, 3)
  • Cox, 127, 11 states
    (Alabama, 12; Arkansas, 9; Florida, 6; Georgia, 14; Kentucky, 13; Louisiana, 10; Mississippi, 10; North Carolina, 12; South Carolina, 9; Texas, 20; Virginia, 12)
•Harding was the third of four presidents who defeated major opponents representing the same state (Cox).

THE PRESIDENT (29th)

Term of office: Mar. 4, 1921, to Aug. 2, 1923 (2 years, 151 days)
•Harding was the eighth of nine presidents who served less than one term.
•He was the 17th of 19 presidents who served one term or less than one term.
State represented: Ohio
•He was the last of six presidents who represented Ohio.
Political party: Republican
•He was the tenth of 14 presidents who were Republicans.
Congress: 67th
Administration: 34th

Age at inauguration: 55 years, 122 days
Inauguration day: Friday, Mar. 4, 1921
•Harding took the oath of office, administered by Chief Justice Edward Douglass White, on the east portico of the Capitol.
•This was the last of three inaugurations at which White officiated.
•He was the first president to ride to his inauguration in an automobile.
•His inauguration was the first at which a public address system was used. It was also the first inauguration that was described over the radio.

THE 34th ADMINISTRATION

1921

Mar. 4, appointed his only secretary of state, Charles Evans Hughes; his only secretary of treasury, Andrew W. Mellon; his only secretary of war, John W. Weeks; his only attorney general, Harry M. Daugherty; his only secretary of navy, Edwin Denby; his first postmaster general, William H. Hays; his first secretary of interior, Albert B. Fall; his only secretary of agriculture, Henry C. Wallace; his only secretary of commerce, Herbert C. Hoover; and his only secretary of labor, James J. Davis

• Hughes, Weeks, Daugherty, Hays, Fall, Wallace, Hoover, and Davis took office, Mar. 5; Denby, Mar. 6.

Mar. 22, held first press conference

• He revived the biweekly press conference that had been instituted but abandoned by Wilson. Sessions were held on Tuesdays at 1 P.M. and Fridays at 4 P.M., to give morning and afternoon papers equal opportunity.

• He was the first president to make his press conference permanent as well as regular.

Mar. 23, appointed commission to investigate conditions in Philippines

Apr. 2, Order of the Elephant dinner, White House

• His guests were the newspaper correspondents who had covered his front porch campaign in Marion. Toward the end of the campaign, he had been their guest at a dinner at which the newsmen had concocted the Order of the Elephant, Local 1, Marion, Ohio.

Apr. 11, first session of 67th Congress

• The administration controlled both the Senate and the House of Representatives. The Republicans gained 11 Senate and 63 House seats. The Senate (96 members) consisted of 59 Republicans and 37 Democrats. The House (435 members) consisted of 300 Republicans, 132 Democrats, one other, and two vacancies.

• This was the Congress in which the Republican party held its largest majority in the House (168).

Apr. 11, opened telephone line between U.S. and Cuba

May 10, issued executive order transferring management of naval oil reserves from navy to interior departments

• The oil reserves involved were Elk Hills and Buena Vista Hills, Cal., and Teapot Dome, Wy.

May 19, Chief Justice White died

May 19, signed first immigration quota act

• This act initiated the quota system, stipulating that not more than three percent of any nationality, as recorded in the 1910 census, were to be admitted during any given year. Total annual immigration was set at 357,000.

May 20, received Madame Marie Sklodowska Curie, co-discoverer of radium, White House

• He presented Madame Curie with a capsule of radium valued at $100,000, a gift from the women of the U.S.

May 23, attended brief services for six thousand war dead, whose bodies had been returned from France, army pier, Hoboken, N.J.

May 27, signed emergency tariff act

• This act raised rates on the majority of agricultural products.

June 10, signed budget and accounting act

• This act created a budget bureau in the treasury department. The president was directed to submit a budget estimate at each regular session of Congress, present a statement of the financial condition of the government, and when advisable to recommend tax, loan, and other financial legislation. The act also created a general accounting office, to be headed by the comptroller general.

June 10, appointed national prohibition commissioner, Roy A. Haynes of Ohio

June 21, appointed first director of budget bureau, Charles G. Dawes

June 30, appointed William Howard Taft as chief justice

• Taft, who was confirmed by the Senate, June 30, was the first of Harding's four appointments to the Supreme Court.

• Harding was the only president who appointed a former president to the Supreme Court.

• He was the eighth of 14 presidents who appointed chief justices.

July 1, appointed General John J. Pershing as chief of staff

Aug. 9, U.S. veterans bureau established

• This independent unit, which assumed the

administration of all veterans' relief, was directly responsible to the president.
•He appointed Charles R. Forbes as director.

Aug. 11, his father remarried
•Dr. George T. Harding married Alice Severns in Monroe, Mich. After escorting his bride to her home, his father ordered his chauffeur to drive him to his residence, saying, "Well, Alice, I'll see you later, I guess." Dr. Harding was 78; his wife was 52. The White House announced that the wedding had come as a complete surprise to the president. This was his father's third marriage.

Aug. 11, formally invited Great Britain, France, Italy, and Japan to discuss limitation and reduction of armaments at Washington conference
•China also was invited to discuss Pacific and Far Eastern problems.

Aug. 15, signed packers and stockyards act
Aug. 24, signed grain futures trading act
Aug. 24, peace treaty with Austria signed, Vienna
•This and subsequent peace treaties declared that World War I had ended, July 2.

Aug. 25, peace treaty with Germany signed, Berlin
Aug. 29, peace treaty with Hungary signed, Budapest
Aug. 30, issued proclamation ordering marching miners of West Virginia to return home
•Federal troops were sent into the state, ending the miners' strike, Sept. 2.

Nov. 5, issued proclamation establishing Armistice Day, Nov. 11, as legal holiday
Nov. 11, attended burial ceremony at Tomb of Unknown Soldier, Arlington National Cemetery, Arlington, Va.
Nov. 12, welcomed delegates to Conference for Limitation of Armaments
Nov. 14, issued proclamation of termination of war with Germany as of July 2
Nov. 23, first session of 67th Congress adjourned
Nov. 30, established question box for press conference
•This decision, which modified the free exchange theory, was the result (it was explained by George Christian, his press secretary) of conflicting interpretations of his refusal to reply to certain questions in the past, as well as the presence of an increased number of correspondents who

were drawn to Washington by the armaments conference.
•Under the new rule, reporters submitted questions in writing prior to conferences, which the president would or would not answer, as he saw fit. Oral questions pursuing subjects raised by previous replies to written questions were permitted.

Dec. 5, second session of 67th Congress
Dec. 6, delivered his first State of the Union message to Congress
Dec. 13, Four-Power Pacific Treaty signed, Washington, D.C.
•The U.S., Great Britain, France, and Japan agreed to respect the rights of the others regarding specific Pacific island possessions. When ratified by the Senate, by only four votes, it was stipulated that "there is no commitment to armed forces, no alliance, no obligation to join in any defense."

Dec. 20, erred regarding Four-Power Treaty
•In answer to a written question at his 1 P.M. press conference as to whether the treaty provisions applied to the main islands of Japan, he replied that they did not. This view was diametrically opposed to that held by Secretary of State Hughes. The *faux pas* caused a worldwide flurry. At 7:15 P.M., a formal statement of correction was issued.

Dec. 23, pardoned Eugene V. Debs and others
•Debs and 23 others convicted of violation of the espionage and other wartime laws were pardoned as of Christmas Day. Debs had served two years and eight months of his ten-year sentence.

1922

Feb. 6, Five-Power Treaty signed, Washington, D.C.
•The U.S., Great Britain, France, Italy, and Japan agreed upon a ten-year naval armament program, during which no new capital ships were to be constructed, and established a ratio of capital ships. On a ratio of five, the U.S. and Great Britain were ranked at five, Japan, three, and France and Italy, 1.7.

Feb. 6, Nine-Power Treaty signed, Washington, D.C.
•All of the nations represented at the conference guaranteed the independence and

territorial integrity of China and reiterated the "open door" principle.

Feb. 18, signed cooperative marketing act
•This act exempted cooperatives and agricultural producers from antitrust laws.

Feb. 21, appointed foreign debt funding commission
•He appointed Secretaries Hughes, Mellon, and Hoover, and Representative Harold Burton.

Mar. 4, Postmaster General Hays resigned

Mar. 4, appointed his second postmaster general, Hubert Work

Mar. 4, issued proclamation prohibiting export of arms or munitions to China

Mar. 20, issued executive order withdrawing all American troops from Germany by July 1

Mar. 31, issued executive order reorganizing bureau of engraving and printing
•He dismissed the director, James L. Wilmeth, and 25 others "for the good of the service."

Apr. 7, naval reserve No. 3, Teapot Dome, secretly leased to Harry F. Sinclair
•Secretary of Interior Fall leased the reserve, without competitive bid, to Sinclair, who reassigned it to the Mammoth Oil Company for $160,000,000 in stock.
•The Supreme Court declared the Teapot Dome lease invalid, Oct. 10, 1927.

Apr. 11, appointed World War foreign debt commission
•He appointed Secretary of Treasury Mellon as chairman.

Apr. 25, Elk Hills naval reserve secretly leased to Edward L. Doheny
•The Supreme Court declared the Elk Hills lease invalid, Feb. 28, 1927.

May 26, signed act establishing federal narcotics control board

June 14, dedicated Francis Scott Key memorial, Baltimore, Md.
•The dedication ceremony was broadcast by radio.
•He was the first president to speak on radio while in office.

June 17, received Filipino delegation led by Manuel Quezon
•He rejected the appeal for full independence, June 22.

July 1, issued executive order concerning German dye and drug patents
•He ordered the alien property custodian to secure the patents from the Chemical Foundation of New York City on the grounds that the price paid had been insufficient to protect the interests of the former German owners. The foundation refused to comply; the case dragged on in the federal courts for years.

July 10, proposed settlement in coal strike
•The strike of anthracite and bituminous coal miners had begun, Apr. 1, when the operators proposed a wage cut. The wage scale agreement of 1920 had expired, Mar. 31. The bituminous miners returned to work, Aug. 30; the anthracite miners, Sept. 2. Little was accomplished by the strike.

July 31, proposed settlement of railroad shopmen strike
•His proposal to refer the matter to the railroad labor board was rejected by the operators, who refused to allow the workers to return with their seniority rights unimpaired.

Aug. 7, made second railroad shopmen strike settlement proposal
•His proposal to refer the seniority question to the railroad labor board was accepted by the operators but rejected by the shopmen.
•The railroad strike ended, Sept. 11, after the railroad labor board decision to restore seniority rights was accepted by both sides. The strike cost the railroads about 20 percent of their 1923 income, while costing the government about $2,000,000 for deputies employed to preserve order.

Sept. 4, Associate Justice Clarke resigned

Sept. 5, appointed George Sutherland as associate justice
•Sutherland, who was confirmed by the Senate, Sept. 5, was the second of Harding's four appointments to the Supreme Court.

Sept. 19, vetoed soldiers' bonus bill
•This was the only bill that Congress attempted to pass over his veto. The House of Representatives voted to override the veto, 258–54, Sept. 20. The Senate voted to override the veto, 44–28, Sept. 20, which was four votes less than the necessary two-thirds.
•This was the fourth of his six vetoes.
•His previous vetoes concerned consolidation of lands within the Clearwater, St. Joe, and Selway national forests; an amendment to an act to incorporate a Masonic relief association in the District of Columbia; and an amendment to a judiciary act.

Sept. 21, signed Fordney-McCumber Tariff Act
- This act returned the tariff to levels in excess of the rates of 1909 on manufactured goods. High duties were placed on farm products.

Sept. 22, second session of 67th Congress adjourned

Sept. 22, vetoed amendment to department of agriculture appropriations act
- This was the fifth of his six vetoes, his only pocket veto.

Oct. 10, appointed coal commission
- He appointed John Hays Hammond as chairman.

Oct. 26, issued executive order directing prohibition agents not to act outside three-mile limit

Oct. 27, first Navy Day
- His proclamation established Navy Day as an annual holiday.

Nov. 13, Associate Justice Day resigned

Nov. 20, met with governor of Louisiana regarding Ku Klux Klan activities in that state

Nov. 20, third session of 67th Congress

Nov. 21, appealed for financial assistance for merchant marine

Nov. 23, appointed Pierce Butler as associate justice
- Pierce, who was confirmed by the Senate, Dec. 21, was the third of Harding's four appointments to the Supreme Court.

Dec. 4, third session of 67th Congress adjourned

Dec. 4, fourth session of 67th Congress

Dec. 7, received Georges Clemenceau, war premier of France, White House

Dec. 8, delivered his second State of the Union message to Congress

Dec. 11, Elk Hills naval reserve secretly leased to Edward L. Doheny by second agreement with Secretary of Interior Fall

Dec. 31, Associate Justice Pitney resigned

1923

Jan. 3, vetoed pension bill
- This bill concerned pension increases for veterans of the Civil War, the Mexican War, and the War of 1812, and also for veterans' widows.
- This was the last of Harding's six vetoes.
- He was the ninth of 11 presidents who never had a veto overridden.

Jan. 10, issued executive order ending American army occupation of Rhine

Jan. 24, appointed Edward T. Sanford as associate justice
- Sanford, who was confirmed by the Senate, Jan. 29, was the last of Harding's four appointments to the Supreme Court.

Jan. 29, Charles R. Forbes, director of veterans bureau, resigned under charges of mismanagement
- Forbes, who was indicted for fraud, conspiracy, and bribery, was sentenced to two years in federal prison and fined $10,000, Feb. 4, 1925.

Feb. 15, ordered troops to Mexican border

Feb. 24, sent special message to Congress urging consent to U.S. membership in World Court
- On the advice of the secretary of state, Harding asked for the consent of the Senate to join the court, with the understanding that such action would not involve any legal relation to the League of Nations.

Feb. 27, Postmaster General Work resigned

Feb. 27, appointed his third postmaster general, Harry S. New

Feb. 27, issued executive order setting apart thirty-five thousand square miles in Alaska as naval oil reserve

Mar. 4, Secretary of Interior Fall resigned

Mar. 4, fourth session of 67th Congress adjourned

Mar. 5, appointed his second secretary of interior, Hubert Work
- Work was the last of Harding's 13 cabinet appointments.

Mar. 27, issued executive order instructing tariff commission to investigate high price of sugar
- The commission report, Apr. 19, stated that the high price of sugar was not due to the tariff.

June 20, began transcontinental speaking tour
- He made the first of a series of speeches in St. Louis, Mo., July 21. He also spoke in Hutchinson, Kan.; Denver, Colo.; Cheyenne, Wy.; Salt Lake City, Utah; Pocatello, Ida.; Yellowstone Park, Wy.; Portland, Ore.; and Spokane and Tacoma, Wash.

July 5, sailed for Alaska aboard navy transport, *U.S.S. Henderson*, Tacoma

July 8, arrived in Alaska
- His first stop was the Indian village of Metlakatla on the Island of Annette, where he

was greeted by Governor Scott Bone. The same day, the ship proceeded to Ketchikan, where the Hardings celebrated their 32nd wedding anniversary.

•Harding and his party visited Wrangell, July 9; Juneau, July 10; Skagway, June 11; and Seward, July 13. From Seward, the group traveled north by train to Anchorage, July 14, and Fairbanks, the northernmost stop, July 16. They returned to Seward, July 17.

•After two days of rest aboard the *Henderson,* they sailed to Valdez, July 19; Cordova, July 20; made a side trip by train to Childs Glacier, July 21; and visited Sitka, their last stop in Alaska, July 22.

•He was the first of five presidents who visited Alaska while in office.

July 22, sailed from Sitka for Vancouver, British Columbia, Canada

July 26, spoke at banquet, Vancouver

•He was the first of seven presidents who visited Canada while in office.

•He was the fourth of 11 presidents who traveled outside the U.S. while in office.

July 26, sailed from Vancouver for Seattle

•During the night, in a thick fog, the *Henderson* rammed one of the escorting destroyers. No serious damage or injuries resulted.

July 27, arrived in Seattle, Wash.

•He made a speech at a Seattle stadium during the day and later addressed a delayed Press Club luncheon. En route to California that night by train he suffered an attack of ptomaine poisoning. Consequently, he made no personal appearances in Oregon; plans for a side trip to Yosemite Park were cancelled.

July 29, arrived in San Francisco, Cal.

•His illness caused the cancellation of his California speaking program.

DEATH

Date of death: Aug. 2, 1923

•He was the fourth of five presidents who died before they completed their first terms.

•He was the sixth of eight presidents who died in office.

Place of death: San Francisco, Cal.

•He was the only president who died in California.

•He was the fourth of six presidents who lay in state in the White House.

•He was the fourth of eight presidents who lay in state in the Capitol Rotunda.

Age at death: 57 years, 273 days

Cause of death: Apoplexy

•He was the third of four presidents who died of natural causes while in office.

Place of burial: Marion, Ohio

•He was the last of five presidents who were buried in Ohio.

THE VICE PRESIDENT (29th)

Full name: Calvin Coolidge

• *See* pages 359–371.

•Coolidge was the last of three vice presidents who were born in Vermont.

•He was the second of four vice presidents who were Congregationalists.

•He was the 13th of 14 vice presidents who served as state governors.

•He was the 12th of 14 vice presidents who served less than one term.

•Harding and Coolidge were the 31st of 41 president-vice president teams.

•Coolidge was the last of four vice presidents who represented Massachusetts.

•He was the 11th of 13 vice presidents who represented states that were not their native states.

•He was the 11th of 15 vice presidents who were Republicans.

•He was the second of two vice presidents who died in Massachusetts. The other was John Adams.

•He was the only vice president who was buried in Vermont.

THE CABINET

State: Charles Evans Hughes of New York, Mar. 5, 1921, to Mar. 4, 1925

Treasury: Andrew William Mellon of Pennsylvania, Mar. 4, 1921, to Feb. 12, 1932

War: John Wingate Weeks of Massachusetts, Mar. 5, 1921, to Oct. 13, 1925

Attorney General: Harry Micajah Daugherty of Ohio, Mar. 5, 1921, to Mar. 28, 1924

Navy: Edwin Denby of Michigan, Mar. 6, 1921, to Mar. 10, 1924

Postmaster General: William Harrison Hays of Indiana, Mar. 5, 1921, to Mar. 4, 1922

•Hubert Work of Colorado, Mar. 4, 1922, to

Feb. 27, 1923
•Harry Stewart New of Indiana, Feb. 27, 1923, to Mar. 5, 1929

Interior: Albert Bacon Fall of New Mexico, Mar 5, 1921, to Mar. 4, 1923
•Hubert Work of Colorado, Mar. 5, 1923, to July 24, 1928

Agriculture: Henry Cantwell Wallace of Iowa, Mar. 5, 1921, to Oct. 25, 1924

Commerce: Herbert Clark Hoover of California, Mar. 5, 1921, to Aug. 21, 1928

Labor: James John Davis of Pennsylvania, Mar. 5, 1921, to Nov. 30, 1930

THE SUPREME COURT

Chief Justice: William Howard Taft of Ohio, appointed, June 30, 1921; confirmed, June 30, 1921

Associate Justices: George Sutherland of Utah, appointed, Sept. 5, 1922; confirmed, Sept. 5, 1922
•Pierce Butler of Minnesota, appointed, Nov. 23, 1922; confirmed, Dec. 21, 1922
•Edward Terry Sanford of Tennessee, appointed, Jan. 24, 1923; confirmed, Jan. 29, 1923

Thirtieth President

CALVIN COOLIDGE

Full name: Calvin Coolidge
- His given name was John Calvin Coolidge.
- He was the last of four presidents who dropped their first names.
- He was the fourth of five presidents who changed their names from those they were given at birth.
- He was the fourth of five presidents named John.
- He was the last of eight presidents who had the same full names as their fathers.
- He was the 12th of 19 presidents who had middle initials or middle names.

Date of birth: July 4, 1872
- He was the only president who was born on the Fourth of July.
- He was the second of two presidents who were born in July. The other was John Quincy Adams.

Place of birth: Plymouth, Vt.
- He was the second of two presidents who were born in Vermont. The other was Arthur.
- His birthplace and the Coolidge Homestead, across the street from his birthplace, are on state route 100-A. Owned by the State of Vermont, both are under the jurisdiction of the Division of Historic Sites.

Both are open to the public daily, 9 A.M. to 6 P.M., May 29 to Oct. 24. Admission: adults, 50 cents.

Family lineage: English
- He was the last of 12 presidents who were of English ancestry.

Religious denomination: Congregationalist
- He was the only president who was a Congregationalist.

College: Amherst College, Amherst, Mass.
- He was the only president who went to Amherst.
- He was the 21st of 27 presidents who attended college.

Date of graduation: June 26, 1895, Bachelor of Arts
- He was the 15th of 21 presidents who were graduated from college.

PARENTS AND SIBLINGS

Father's name: John Calvin Coolidge
Date of birth: Mar. 31, 1845
Place of birth: Plymouth, Vt.
Occupations: Farmer, storekeeper, justice of the peace
Date of death: Mar. 18, 1926

•Coolidge was the fifth of six presidents whose fathers lived to see their sons' inauguration or oath-taking days.

•John Coolidge was the first of two fathers of presidents who attended the ceremonies. The other was Joseph Kennedy.

•Mr. Coolidge, a justice of the peace and notary public, administered the oath of office.

Place of death: Plymouth, Vt.

Age at death: 80 years, 352 days

Mother's name: Victoria Josephine Moor Coolidge

Date of birth: Mar. 14, 1846

Place of birth: Pinney Hollow, Vt.

Date of marriage: May 6, 1868

Children: 2; 1 son, 1 daughter

•John Calvin was born in 1872, and Abigail Gratia in 1875.

•Coolidge was the second of three presidents who came from families of two children.

•He was the sixth of eight presidents who were eldest children.

Date of death: Mar. 14, 1885

•Mrs. Coolidge died on her birthday.

•Calvin was 12 years, 253 days old, when his mother died.

Place of death: Plymouth, Vt.

Age at death: 39 years

Father's second wife: Caroline Brown Coolidge

Date of birth: Jan. 22, 1857

Place of birth: probably Plymouth, Vt.

Date of marriage: Sept. 9, 1891

•Calvin was 19 years, 67 days old, when his father remarried.

•He was the second of two presidents who had stepmothers before they reached maturity. The other was Lincoln.

•He was the last of four presidents who had stepmothers.

•He was the last of five presidents who had stepparents.

Children: None

Date of death: May 19, 1920

Place of death: Plymouth, Vt.

Age at death: 63 years, 117 days

MARRIAGE

Date of marriage: Oct. 4, 1905

Place of marriage: Burlington, Vt.

•Coolidge was the only president who was married in Vermont.

Age at marriage: 33 years, 92 days

•He was the fourth of six presidents who were married in their thirties.

Years married: 27 years, 93 days

Wife's name: Grace Anna Goodhue Coolidge

•She was the 26th of 33 first ladies.

•She was the 33rd of 40 wives of presidents.

Date of birth: Jan. 3, 1879

•She was the second of two first ladies who were born in January. The other was Julia Grant.

•She was the second of two wives of presidents who were born in January.

Place of birth: Burlington, Vt.

•She was the only first lady or wife of a president who was born in Vermont.

Wife's mother: Elmira Barnett Goodhue

Wife's father: Andrew Goodhue, steamboat inspector

Age at marriage: 26 years, 274 days

•She was the 21st of 26 first ladies who were married in their twenties.

•She was the 25th of 30 wives of presidents who were married in their twenties.

Years younger than husband: 6 years, 183 days

Children: 2 sons

•John was born on Sept. 7, 1906, and Calvin was born on Apr. 13, 1908.

•Coolidge was the fourth of six presidents who had only male children.

•He was the third of seven presidents who had two children.

•He was the 23rd of 30 presidents who had children.

Years she survived her husband: 24 years, 184 days

•She was the 18th of 21 first ladies who survived their husbands.

•She was the 20th of 23 wives of presidents who survived their husbands.

Date of death: July 8, 1957

Place of death: Northampton, Mass.

•She was the last of three first ladies who died in Massachusetts.

•She was the last of three wives of presidents who died in Massachusetts.

Age at death: 78 years, 186 days

•She had celebrated her 75th birthday, Jan. 3, 1954.

•She was the 13th of 16 first ladies who lived to be 70.

•She was the 14th of 17 wives of presidents who lived to be 70.
•She was the 11th of 14 first ladies who lived to be 75.
•She was the 12th of 15 wives of presidents who lived to be 75.

Place of burial: Plymouth, Vt.
•She was the only first lady or wife of a president who was buried in Vermont.

EARLY YEARS

Mar. 14, 1885, his mother died
1890, his sister died
June, 1890, was graduated from Black River Academy, Ludlow, Vt.
•Coolidge planned to enter Amherst College in the fall but failed the entrance examination, due to illness. He enrolled in St. Johnsbury Academy, Vt., for a brush-up course.
Sept. 9, 1891, his father remarried
1891, entered Amherst College, Amherst, Mass.
June 26, 1895, graduated from Amherst
September, 1895, began study of law in office of Hammond and Field, Northampton, Mass.
•He was the 22nd of 26 presidents who studied law.
1896, won $150 gold medal in Sons of American Revolution essay contest
•His essay was on the principles of the American Revolution.
1897, admitted to bar, Northampton, Mass.
•He was the 21st of 23 presidents who were lawyers.
1898, elected to common council, Northampton
•He served two terms on the council.
1898, elected vice president of Northampton savings bank

1899–1902, city solicitor, Northampton
1904, appointed chairman of Republican county committee, Hampshire County
Oct. 4, 1905, married Grace Goodhue, Burlington, Vt.
1905, defeated as candidate for Northampton board of education
•This was his only defeat at the polls.
Sept. 7, 1906, his first son born
•The boy was named John Coolidge.
1906, elected to Massachusetts house of representatives
•When he took his seat in January, 1907, he presented a note to the speaker from Richard Irwin, a former state senator from Northampton: "Like a singed cat he is better than he looks."
•He served two terms in the house, 1907–1908.
Apr. 13, 1908, his second son born
•The boy was named Calvin Coolidge.
1909, resumed law practice, Northampton
1910–1911, mayor of Northampton
•He served two terms as mayor.
1911, elected to Massachusetts senate
•He served four terms in the state senate, 1912–1915. He served as president of the senate, 1914–1915.
1915, elected lieutenant governor of Massachusetts

NATIONAL PROMINENCE

November, 1918, elected governor of Massachusetts
Jan. 1, 1919, took office as governor
•Coolidge was the only president who served as governor of Massachusetts.
•He was the 12th of 13 presidents who served as state governors.
Feb. 24, 1919, welcomed President Wilson, Boston, Mass.
•Wilson and his official party landed in Boston on the first return trip from the Paris Peace Conference.
Sept. 8, 1919, refused to intervene in Boston

police crisis
•The members of the Boston police department had voted, 1,134–2, to strike, earlier in the day. He refused to sponsor a compromise plan, as suggested by Mayor Andrew J. Peters and others; Coolidge also balked at calling out the state guard. That evening he encountered Peters at the Commonwealth Armory; angry words were exchanged, and then the mayor of Boston hit the governor of Massachusetts in the left eye.
Sept. 9, 1919, Boston police strike began

• Two nights of rioting followed. Mayor Peters, who had learned that he had the authority to call out those state guard units within city limits, did so, and also issued a call for citizen volunteers. Guardsmen opened fire on rioters in Scollay Square, killing three, Sept. 10. At least three others were killed before the mobs dispersed.

Sept. 11, 1919, called out state guard

• He issued executive orders that called out the militia and placed the Boston police department under his control.

Sept. 12, 1919, replied to Samuel Gompers of AFL

• When the president of the American Federation of Labor requested the reinstatement of the policemen-strikers, Coolidge made his celebrated reply: "There is no right to strike against the public safety by anybody, anywhere, any time." The statement earned him a national reputation.

November, 1919, reelected governor of Massachusetts

• He was elected by a plurality of about 125,000, in contrast to his plurality of 16,773 the previous year.

1919, received honorary degree of Doctor of Laws, Amherst College, Amherst, Mass.

June 11, 1920, received 35 votes for president on first ballot, Republican national convention, Chicago, Ill.

• His votes had dwindled to five on the tenth and last ballot.

June 12, 1920, nominated for vice president

Nov. 2, 1920, elected as vice president

Mar. 4, 1921, inaugurated as vice president

1921, elected to Phi Beta Kappa, Amherst College, Amherst, Mass.

• He was the fourth of five presidents who were alumni members of Phi Beta Kappa.

• He was the tenth of 11 presidents who were members of Phi Beta Kappa.

THE PRESIDENT (30th)

Term of office: Aug. 3, 1923, to Mar. 4, 1929 (5 years, 213 days)

• Coolidge was the ninth of 12 presidents who had served as vice presidents.

• He was the sixth of eight presidents who, because of the death of their predecessors, did not complete their vice-presidential terms.

• He was the second of four presidents who served the unexpired terms of their predecessors and were elected to and served second terms.

• He was the 12th of 16 presidents who served more than one term.

State represented: Massachusetts

• He was the third of four presidents who represented Massachusetts.

• He was the 12th of 15 presidents who represented states that were not their native states.

Political party: Republican

• He was the 11th of 14 presidents who were Republicans.

Congresses: 68th, 69th, 70th

Administrations: 34th, 35th

Age at taking oath: 51 years, 30 days

• Coolidge took the oath of office in the sitting room of the Coolidge home in Plymouth Notch, Vt., on Friday, Aug. 3, 1923. The oath was administered by his father, John C. Coolidge, a justice of the peace.

• He was the only president who took the oath of office from his father.

• He was the sixth of seven presidents who took the oath of office from an official other than a justice of the Supreme Court.

• He took the oath of office for a second time in his suite of the Willard Hotel, Washington, D.C., Aug. 21. The oath was administered by Justice Adolph August Hoehling of the District of Columbia Supreme Court.

THE 34th ADMINISTRATION

1923

Aug. 24, appointed commission to investigate imminent coal strike

• Negotiations between the anthracite oper-

ators and miners had broken down.

Aug. 31, recognized Obregon government of Mexico

• Diplomatic relations with Mexico were resumed, Sept. 3.

Sept. 1, anthracite coal strike began in Pennsylvania
• The strike ended, Sept. 8, when the operators and miners accepted the terms recommended by the federal commission, headed by Governor Gifford Pinchot. A ten percent wage increase was accepted, but the operators balked at accepting the closed shop rule. The miners returned to work, Sept. 18.
Nov. 5, received David Lloyd George, war prime minister of England, White House
Dec. 3, first session of 68th Congress
• The administration maintained control of both the Senate and the House of Representatives. The Democrats gained six Senate and 75 House seats. The Senate (96 members) consisted of 51 Republicans, 43 Democrats, and two others. The House (435 members) consisted of 225 Republicans, 207 Democrats, and three others.
Dec. 6, delivered his first State of the Union message to Congress
• Coolidge supported U.S. adherence to the World Court, Mellon's tax reduction program, and the enforcement of prohibition. He advocated cuts in government spending and a hands-off policy toward business. He opposed the cancellation of war debts and the veterans' bonus.
• This State of the Union message was broadcast by radio.
• He was the first president to appear on radio in his official capacity.
Dec. 11, accepted invitation of U.S. participation in reparations conference
Dec. 15, appointed experts to investigate financial condition of Germany
• He appointed Charles G. Dawes, H. M. Robinson, and Owen D. Young.

1924

Jan. 7, issued proclamation prohibiting sale of munitions to Mexican rebels.
Jan. 17, said "After all, the chief business of America is business," Washington, D.C.
• While this single sentence has been cited innumerable times as the sum of his philosophy, he also said in the same speech to the American Society of Newspaper Editors:
   It is only those who do not understand our people who believe that our national life is entirely ab-

sorbed by material motives. We make no concealment of the fact that we want wealth, but there are many other things that we want very much more. We want peace and honor, and that charity which is so strong an element of all civilization. The chief ideal of the American people is idealism. I cannot repeat too often that America is a nation of idealists.
Jan. 27, denied charge that corrupt officials were being protected
• The chairman of the Democratic national committee had stated, Jan. 26, that Republicans in office involved in the Teapot Dome and other scandals were being shielded from prosecution.
Feb. 8, signed joint resolution charging former Secretary of Interior Fall and Secretary of Navy Denby with fraud and corruption in execution of 1922 oil leases
• The resolution instructed the president to institute court action to cancel the Sinclair and Doheny leases in Wyoming and California.
Feb. 18, accepted resignation of Secretary of Navy Denby, effective, Mar. 10
Feb. 21, refused to remove Governor-General Leonard Wood of Philippines
• His letter to Manuel Roxas, chairman of the Philippine independence commission, who had demanded Wood's removal, was published, Mar. 5. He added that the Philippines were not ready for independence.
Feb. 24, sent special message to Congress urging adherence to Permanent Court of International Justice
Mar. 7, issued proclamation raising tariff rates on wheat and wheat products
Mar. 14, appointed Secretary of Commerce Hoover as chairman of St. Lawrence-Great Lakes waterways commission
Mar. 19, appointed his second secretary of navy, Curtis D. Wilbur
Mar. 28, asked for and received resignation of Attorney General Daugherty
Apr. 7, appointed his second attorney general, Harlan F. Stone
May 2, issued proclamation prohibiting export of arms and munitions to Cuban rebels.
May 3, vetoed pension increase for Civil War and Spanish-American War veterans bill

•This was the first of Coolidge's 50 vetoes.

May 9, accepted resignation of William J. Burns, head of Secret Service

•Burns had been charged with spying on members of Congress.

May 15, vetoed soldiers' bonus bill

May 19, soldiers' bonus act passed over his veto

•This was the first of his four vetoes that were overridden.

June 2, signed act authorizing secretary of interior to issue certificates of citizenship to Indians

June 2, signed act reducing income taxes by 25 percent

•This act also increased estate taxes to the highest level yet imposed.

June 7, issued executive order providing regulations for reformed foreign service

•This order set up the foreign service personnel board and an executive committee, a board of examiners, and a foreign service school and school board.

June 7, vetoed postal salaries bill

•This bill called for salary increases that would have cost $68,000,000 annually.

June 7, first session of 68th Congress adjourned

June 12, nominated for president, Republican national convention, Cleveland, Ohio

July 7, his son, Calvin, died, Washington, D.C.

•Calvin Coolidge was the fourth of five children of presidents who died during their fathers' terms of office.

Aug. 11, posed for newsreels

•He was the first president to pose for campaign newsreel films. The pictures, taken on the White House grounds, were shown in theaters across the country, along with films taken of Democratic candidate Davis and Progressive candidate La Follette.

Oct. 25, Secretary of Agriculture Wallace died

Nov. 4, election day

• See Election of 1924, page 365.

Nov. 7, appointed commission to investigate agricultural conditions

Nov. 22, appointed his second secretary of agriculture, Howard M. Gore

Dec. 1, second session of 68th Congress

Dec. 3, delivered his second State of the Union message to Congress

Dec. 19, appointed federal oil conservation board

•The board consisted of Secretary of War Weeks, Secretary of Navy Wilbur, Secretary of Interior Work, and Secretary of Commerce Hoover.

1925

Jan. 5, accepted resignation of Attorney General Stone, effective, Mar. 1

Jan. 5, Associate Justice McKenna resigned

Jan. 5, appointed Harlan F. Stone as associate justice

•Stone, who was confirmed by the Senate, Feb. 5, was Coolidge's only appointment to the Supreme Court.

Jan. 10, accepted resignation of Secretary of State Hughes, effective, Mar. 4

Jan. 10, appointed Charles B. Warren as attorney general

Jan. 12, presidential electors cast ballots

•He received 382 of the 531 electoral votes from the 48 states.

• See Election of 1924, page 365.

Jan. 19, exchanged greetings with King Alfonso XIII on new cable between U.S. and Spain

Feb. 2, signed air mail act

Feb. 11, electoral vote tabulated by Congress

•Coolidge and Dawes were officially declared elected.

Feb. 16, appointed his second secretary of state, Frank B. Kellogg

•Kellogg took office, Mar. 5.

Feb. 18, accepted resignation of Secretary of Agriculture Gore, effective, Mar. 4

•Gore had been elected governor of West Virginia.

Feb. 18, appointed his third secretary of agriculture, William M. Jardine

•Jardine took office, Mar. 5.

Feb. 25, signed postal pay and rate increase act

•This act raised rates for second class matter —which increased revenue by $60,000,-000—and increased postal department salaries by $68,000,000.

Mar. 2, Supreme Court decision in Grossman case held president had power of pardon regarding persons who had been found guilty of contempt of court

Mar. 4, signed executive and legislative salaries act

•This act raised the salaries of the vice president, members of the cabinet, and the speaker of the House from $12,000 to $15,000, and the salaries of members of Congress from $7,500 to $10,000.

Mar. 4, second session of 68th Congress adjourned

Mar. 4, pocket vetoed four bills

• Three of these measures would have authorized certain Indian tribes to submit treaty claims to the Court of Claims, and the other was a private relief bill.

• A total of 30 of his 50 vetoes were pocket vetoes.

ELECTION OF 1924

Commonwealth Land (Single Tax) party, convened, Feb. 8, at Chicago, Ill., nominated William James Wallace of New Jersey for president, John Cromwell Lincoln of Ohio for vice president.

Socialist Labor party, convened, May 11, at New York City, nominated Frank Thomas Johns of Oregon for president, Verne L. Reynolds of Maryland for vice president.

American party, convened, June 3, at Columbus, Ohio, nominated Gilbert O. Nations of Washington, D.C., for president, Charles H. Randall of California for vice president.

Prohibition party, convened, June 5, at Columbus, Ohio, nominated Herman P. Faris of Missouri for president, Marie C. Brehm of California for vice president.

Republican party, convened, June 10, at Cleveland, Ohio, nominated Calvin Coolidge of Massachusetts for president, Charles Gates Dawes of Illinois for vice president.

• This was the 18th Republican national convention. It was the first of two Republican conventions held in Cleveland; it was the first of two major party conventions held in Cleveland.

Democratic party, convened, June 24, at New York City, nominated John William Davis of West Virginia for president, Charles Wayland Bryan of Nebraska for vice president.

• This was the 24th Democratic national convention. It was the second of two Democratic conventions held in New York City; it was the second of two major party conventions held in New York City.

Progressive (farmer-labor-liberal coalition) party, convened, July 4, at Cleveland, Ohio, nominated Robert Marion La Follette of Wisconsin for president, Burton Kendall Wheeler of Montana for vice president.

• La Follette and Wheeler were endorsed by the Socialist party, a faction of the Farmer-Labor party, and the American Federation of Labor.

Workers' (Communist) party, convened, July 11, at New York City, nominated William Zebulon Foster of Illinois for president, Benjamin Gitlow of New York for vice president.

• A Farmer-Labor group had nominated Duncan MacDonald of Illinois for president, William Bouck of Washington for vice president, June 19. MacDonald and Bouck withdrew, July 10; Foster and Gitlow became the nominees.

Election day, Tuesday, Nov. 4, 1924

Popular vote: 29,116,161
 Coolidge, 15,725,016
 Davis, 8,386,704
 La Follette, 4,832,532
 Faris, 57,551
 Johns, 38,958
 Foster, 33,360
 Nations, 24,340
 Wallace, 2,778
 others, 4,922

Electoral vote: 531, 48 states
• Coolidge, 382, 35 states
 (Arizona, 3; California, 13; Colorado, 6; Connecticut, 7; Delaware, 3; Idaho, 4; Illinois, 29; Indiana, 15; Iowa, 13; Kansas, 10; Kentucky, 13; Maine, 6; Maryland, 8; Massachusetts, 18; Michigan, 15; Minnesota, 12; Missouri, 18; Montana, 4; Nebraska, 8; Nevada, 3; New Hampshire, 4; New Jersey, 14; New Mexico, 3; New York, 45; North Dakota, 5; Ohio, 24; Oregon, 5; Pennsylvania, 38; Rhode Island, 5; South Dakota, 5; Utah, 4; Vermont, 4; Washington, 7; West Virginia, 8; Wyoming, 3)
• Davis, 136, 12 states
 (Alabama, 12; Arkansas, 9; Florida, 6; Georgia, 14; Louisiana, 10; Mississippi, 10; North Carolina, 12; Oklahoma, 10; South Carolina, 9; Tennessee, 12; Texas, 20; Virginia, 12)
• La Follette, 13, one state
 (Wisconsin, 13)

THE 35th ADMINISTRATION

1925

Mar. 4, his inauguration day
• Coolidge took the oath of office, administered by Chief Justice William Howard Taft, on the east portico of the Capitol.
• This was the first of two inaugurations at which the oath of office was administered by a former president.
• This was the first of two inaugurations at which Taft officiated.
• This was the first inauguration broadcast on radio.
• Coolidge's age at his inauguration was 53 years, 244 days. He was the 17th of 21 presidents who were younger than their vice presidents. Coolidge was six years, 311 days younger than Dawes.
Mar. 4, special session of Senate
Mar. 10, Senate rejected Charles B. Warren as attorney general
• Warren, who was considered by some as a representative of the sugar trust, was rejected by the Senate, 41–39.
• This was the first time in 57 years that the Senate had refused to concur with the wishes of a president regarding membership in the cabinet.
• Coolidge was the fourth of five presidents whose nominees to the cabinet were rejected by the Senate.
• Warren was the seventh of eight nominees to the cabinet who were rejected by the Senate.
Mar. 12, reappointed Charles B. Warren as attorney general
Mar. 16, Senate again rejected Warren
• The vote was 46–39.
Mar. 17, appointed his third attorney general, John G. Sargent
• Sargent took office, Mar. 18.
Mar. 18, special session of Senate adjourned
Mar. 19, issued executive order transferring patent office from department of interior to department of commerce
Mar. 26, appointed commission to investigate possible use of facilities at Muscle Shoals, Ala.
June 4, issued executive order transferring bureau of mines from department of interior to department of commerce
July 16, issued executive order remitting last of Boxer indemnity to China
• This sum, more than $6,100,000, was set apart as a fund for the education of Chinese students in U.S. colleges and universities.
Sept. 12, appointed national air board
• The board was assigned the task of investigating the proper role of the government in aeronautics.
Oct. 13, accepted resignation of Secretary of War Weeks, effective, Oct. 14
Oct. 14, appointed his second secretary of war, Dwight F. Davis
Dec. 2, received national air board report
• The board recommended the appointment of assistant secretaries of war, navy, and commerce for aviation affairs, and also expressed disapproval of a unified air service.
Dec. 7, first session of 69th Congress
• The administration maintained control of both the Senate and the House of Representatives. The Republicans gained three Senate and 22 House seats. The Senate (96 members) consisted of 54 Republicans, 40 Democrats, one other, and one vacancy. The House (435 members) consisted of 247 Republicans, 183 Democrats, and five others.
Dec. 7, delivered his third State of the Union message to Congress
Dec. 21, sent special message to Congress recommending adherence to World Court

1926

Feb. 26, signed revenue act
• This act reduced personal income and inheritance taxes and repealed the publicity clause that related to income tax returns.
Apr. 2, appointed commission to investigate economic and political conditions in Philippines
• He appointed Carmi A. Thompson as chairman.
May 8, issued executive order authorizing employment of state and local officers as prohibition agents
May 20, signed air commerce act
• This act placed civil aviation under the control of the department of commerce.
May 25, signed public buildings act
• This act authorized the expenditure of $165,000,000 over a period of five years for the construction of federal buildings, in-

cluding $50,000,000 for buildings in the District of Columbia.

June 14, appointed board of mediation

July 2, signed act creating army air corps

July 3, signed pension act

•This act provided an additional $65 a month for Mexican and Civil War veterans who were receiving less than $72, an additional $90 for total disability, and $50 for widows.

July 3, first session of 69th Congress adjourned

July 3, pocket vetoed five bills

Sept. 15, issued proclamation prohibiting illegal shipment of arms and ammunition to Nicaragua

Nov. 11, said question of adherence of U.S. to World Court was "closed incident," Kansas City, Mo.

•The Senate had approved adherence but attached five reservations, Jan. 27. One reservation, which related to advisory opinions, was not acceptable to members of the court. Consequently, the U.S. did not join the World Court.

Dec. 4, received report of Philippine commission

•The Thompson report recommended that the independence of the Philippines be postponed.

Dec. 6, second session of 69th Congress

Dec. 7, delivered his fourth State of the Union message to Congress

Dec. 10, Vice President Dawes awarded Nobel Peace Prize

1927

Jan. 10, sent special message to Congress in which he defended intervention in Nicaragua

•He declared that Mexico was attempting to establish a regime hostile to the U.S. in Nicaragua.

Feb. 3, appointed first minister to Canada, William Phillips

•He received Charles V. Massey, the first Canadian minister to the U.S., Feb. 18.

Feb. 10, invited Great Britain, France, Italy, and Japan to naval conference in Geneva, Switzerland

•Great Britain and Japan accepted; France and Italy declined.

Feb. 23, signed radio control act

•This act created the federal radio commis-

sion, which was empowered to set regulations and to issue and revoke station licenses.

Feb. 25, signed national bank consolidation act

•This act provided for the indefinite extension of charters of federal reserve banks and authorized national banks to establish branches.

Feb. 25, vetoed McNary-Haugen farm relief bill

•This bill had been defeated in the House of Representatives, 1924, and in the House and Senate, 1926. Coolidge accompanied his veto message—in which he condemned the measure as "a tax for the special benefit of particular groups"—with a statement from Attorney General Sargent that the bill was unconstitutional.

Feb. 25, signed act granting U.S. citizenship to certain inhabitants of Virgin Islands

Mar. 2, signed naval appropriation act

•This act provided for the construction of three cruisers that had been authorized in 1924, and fixed the personnel of the navy at 83,200 men.

Mar. 2, moved from White House

•During extensive and necessary renovation of the White House, he and Mrs. Coolidge lived in the residence of Mrs. Eleanor Patterson, Dupont Circle, Washington, D.C., and then vacationed in the Black Hills. They moved into the enlarged White House upon their return from South Dakota, Sept. 11.

Mar. 4, signed amended organic act of Puerto Rico

Mar. 4, second session of 69th Congress adjourned

Mar. 4, pocket vetoed two bills

Apr. 2, issued executive order returning naval oil reserves to navy department

•This order revoked the Harding order of May 10, 1921, which had transferred the Elk Hills and Buena Vista Hills, Cal., and Teapot Dome, Wy., reserves from the navy department to the interior department.

Apr. 6, vetoed act of legislature of Philippines

•This act, which authorized a plebiscite on independence for the islands, had been passed by the legislature over the veto of Governor-General Wood.

Apr. 7, appointed Henry L. Stimson as his personal representative to negotiate for end of hostilities in Nicaragua

Apr. 22, appointed committee to cooperate with Red Cross in relief of Mississippi Valley flood district
•The committee consisted of five cabinet members, headed by Secretary of Commerce Hoover. More than 600,000 persons in six states needed assistance. This was the worst flood to date in the area and it inundated more than 4,400,000 acres. Several hundred inhabitants drowned.
June 11, presented distinguished flying cross to Charles A. Lindbergh, White House
•Lindbergh had made the first solo nonstop flight from New York City to Paris, May 20–21.
June 20-Aug. 4, Geneva naval conference
•The conference of representatives of the U.S., Great Britain, and Japan ended in a stalemate. The American proposal that the 5–5–3 ratio of the Washington Conference of 1921 be extended to cruisers, destroyers, and submarines was not accepted.
July 2, appointed General F. R. McCoy to supervise Nicaraguan election, as arranged by Stimson
Aug. 2, withdrew as candidate for reelection
•His succinct statement, "I do not choose to run for President in nineteen twenty-eight," was released to the press at Rapid City, S.D. He and his wife were vacationing at State Lodge in the Black Hills at the time.
•He made his startling announcement on what he considered the fourth anniversary of his succession to the presidency. His predecessor had died about 7:30 P.M., Aug. 2, 1923; he had taken the oath of office a few minutes before 3 A.M., Aug. 3, 1923.
Dec. 5, first session of 70th Congress
•The administration maintained control of both the Senate and the House of Representatives. The Republicans lost six Senate and ten House seats. The Senate (96 members) consisted of 48 Republicans, 47 Democrats, and one other. The House (435 members) consisted of 237 Republicans, 195 Democrats, and three others.
Dec. 5, delivered his fifth State of the Union message to Congress
Dec. 12, removed W. S. Hill, member of shipping board
•Hill had accepted a sizeable loan from a West Coast shipping company.

1928

Jan. 16, delivered opening address at Pan-American Conference, Havana, Cuba
•He was the first of two presidents who visited Cuba while in office. The other was Truman.
•He was the fifth of 11 presidents who traveled outside the U.S. while in office.
•This was his only visit to a foreign country while in office.
Feb. 4, dedicated National Press Club building, Washington, D.C.
Mar. 9, signed amended antitrust act
•This amendment permitted limited interlocking of bank directorates.
Mar. 10, signed settlement of war claims act
•This act provided for the eventual return of property of German, Austrian, and Hungarian citizens seized during the war, held by the alien property custodian, and stipulated payment of claims.
Apr. 28, appointed first emergency board to investigate railroad dispute
May 15, vetoed revised McNary-Haugen farm relief bill
May 15, signed flood control act
•This act appropriated $325,000,000 for a ten-year flood control program in the Mississippi Valley.
May 22, signed merchant marine act
•This act doubled the ship construction loan fund to $250,000,000 to encourage private shipping and authorized the sale of certain government vessels.
May 24, three acts passed over his vetoes
•These measures provided retirement benefits for certain army officers, amended a post office compensation act, and granted rent, fuel, and equipment allowances for fourth class postmasters.
•These were the second, third, and last of his four vetoes that were overridden.
May 29, signed revenue act reducing income tax
•This act, which cut the personal income tax to a maximum of 12 percent, also reduced or repealed a variety of taxes on automobiles, wine, theater tickets, and club dues. The act reduced governmental revenue by an estimated $222,500,000.
May 29, first session of 70th Congress adjourned
May 29, pocket vetoed three bills
July 20, accepted resignation of Secretary of Interior Work, effective, July 24

July 20, appointed his second secretary of interior, Roy O. West
• West took office, July 25.
Aug. 21, accepted resignation of Secretary of Commerce Hoover
Aug. 21, appointed his second secretary of commerce, William F. Whiting
• Whiting took office, Aug. 22.
• Whiting was the last of Coolidge's ten cabinet appointments.
Sept. 29, appointed emergency board to investigate western railroad dispute
• The board recommended a six percent wage increase for the conductors and trainmen of 47 western railroads, which was accepted by the railway workers.
Nov. 6, election day
• See Election of 1928, pages 375–376.
Nov. 24, announced U.S. would renew negotiations for membership in World Court
Dec. 3, second session of 70th Congress
Dec. 4, sent his sixth and last State of the Union message to Congress
Dec. 21, signed Boulder Dam act
• This act appropriated $165,000,000 for the construction of a 726-foot dam at Boulder Canyon on the Colorado River at the Nevada-Arizona border. The highest dam in the U.S., it was called Hoover Dam in 1932–1933 and was officially so renamed in 1947.

1929

Jan. 7, entertained James Lucey, White House
• The invitation to Lucey, an old friend who was known as the "Philosopher Cobbler" of Northampton, Mass., had been extended in 1923.
Feb. 13, signed naval appropriation act
• This act appropriated $274,000,000 for 15 10,000-ton cruisers and an aircraft carrier.
Feb. 22, made final public address, George Washington University, Washington, D.C.
• Speaking at commencement exercises, he characterized Washington as the best businessman of his day. Coolidge emphasized that it had been Jefferson, not Washington, who warned against "entangling alliances"; he urged national "detachment" to assure world peace.
Mar. 2, signed amended prohibition enforcement act
• This act increased the penalties for violators (including first offenders) of the prohibition laws.
Mar. 4, second session of 70th Congress adjourned
Mar. 4, pocket vetoed 16 bills
• These were the last of his 50 vetoes, his 30 pocket vetoes.

THE FORMER PRESIDENT

Mar. 4, 1929, attended inauguration of Hoover
• Coolidge's age upon leaving office was 56 years, 243 days.
• Following the ceremony he and Mrs. Coolidge departed for their home at 21 Massasoit Street, Northampton, Mass. It was half of a double house that they had first rented when they were married in 1905. Over the years the rent had increased from $25 to $36 a month.
• Shortly after their return to Northampton, he bought The Beeches, a 12-room house with nine acres of lawn and woods, on the outskirts of town.
April, 1929, first installment of his autobiography published, Cosmopolitan Magazine
• Written before he left the White House, The Autobiography of Calvin Coolidge was published by Cosmopolitan Book Cor-

poration, New York City, after it had appeared as a three-part magazine series. He was paid $75,000 for his life story.
• He was the 14th of 21 presidents who wrote books that were published during their lifetimes.
July 24, 1929, attended White House ceremony when Kellogg-Briand peace pact proclaimed in effect by Hoover
• This was the only occasion when he visited the White House after his term of office.
June 30, 1930, his first column published, New York Herald Tribune and other newspapers
• The column, "Thinking Things Over with Calvin Coolidge," appeared daily in the Herald Tribune and nearly two hundred other papers. He quickly grew tired of writing the feature and refused to even consider renewing his one-year contract

with the McClure Newspaper Syndicate. He was paid $203,045 for the series of two-hundred-word articles.
• He was the only president who was a syndicated newspaper columnist, although several others wrote articles for the press.
Oct. 6, 1931, delivered radio address on insurance
• After he left the White House, he was elected to the board of directors of the New York Life Insurance Company. In his radio talk, which had been prepared by a New York Life public relations man, he warned listeners against the type of insurance man who constantly suggested alterations in their policies. The address was printed and distributed in pamphlet form by New York Life.
Feb. 8, 1932, sued by St. Louis, Mo., insurance man
• Lewis B. Tebbetts filed suit against him and New York Life for $100,000 each, alleged that his reputation as an "honest insurance agent" had been damaged by the former president's remarks on the radio as reprinted in the insurance company pamphlet. The suit was settled for $2,500.
Nov. 7, 1932, spoke at Republican rally, Madison Square Garden, New York City
• He also made a 15-minute speech for Hoover on the radio that evening.

DEATH

Date of death: Jan. 5, 1933
Place of death: Northampton, Mass.
• Coolidge was the second of two presidents who died in Massachusetts. The other was John Adams.
Age at death: 60 years, 185 days
• He lived three years, 307 days, after the completion of his term.
Cause of death: Coronary thrombosis
Place of burial: Plymouth, Vt.
• He was the only president who was buried in Vermont.

THE VICE PRESIDENT (30th)

Full name: Charles Gates Dawes
Date of birth: Aug. 27, 1865
Place of birth: Marietta, Ohio
• Dawes was the last of three vice presidents who were born in Ohio.

Religious denomination: Congregationalist
• He was the third of four vice presidents who were Congregationalists.
• Coolidge and Dawes were both Congregationalists. They were the sixth of seven president-vice president teams of the same religious denomination.
College: Marietta College, Marietta, Ohio
Date of graduation: 1884
• He graduated from Cincinnati Law School, Cincinnati, Ohio, 1886.
Occupations: Lawyer, banker
• He was admitted to the bar, 1886, and practiced law in Lincoln, Neb, until 1894; member of Republican national executive committee, 1896; comptroller of currency, treasury department, 1897–1901; organized Central Trust Company of Illinois, 1902; served in army, member of General John Pershing's staff, 1917–1919; first director of bureau of the budget, 1921; chairman of reparations committee to investigate German budget, 1923–1924; the Dawes plan, which reduced reparations payments and stabilized German finances, was adopted, Aug. 20, 1924.
• He was awarded the Nobel Peace Prize for 1925, Dec. 10, 1926.
• He was the second of two vice presidents who were awarded the Nobel Peace Prize. The other was Theodore Roosevelt.
Term of office: Mar. 4, 1925, to Mar. 4, 1929 (4 years)
• He was the 13th of 17 vice presidents who served four-year terms.
• Coolidge and Dawes were the 32nd of 41 president-vice president teams.
Age at inauguration: 59 years, 189 days
State represented: Illinois
• He was the second of two vice presidents who represented Illinois. The other was Stevenson.
• He was the 12th of 13 vice presidents who represented states that were not their native states.
Political party: Republican
• He was the 12th of 15 vice presidents who were Republicans.
Occupations after term: Banker, diplomat
• He was ambassador to Great Britain, appointed by Hoover, 1929–1932; president of the Reconstruction Finance Corporation, 1932–1933.
Date of death: Apr. 23, 1951
Place of death: Evanston, Ill.
• He was the second of two vice presidents

who died in Illinois. The other was Stevenson.

Age at death: 85 years, 239 days
Place of burial: Chicago, Ill.
•He was the second of two vice presidents who were buried in Illinois. The other was Stevenson.

THE CABINET

State: Charles Evans Hughes of New York, Mar. 5, 1921, to Mar. 4, 1925
•Frank Billings Kellogg of Minnesota, Mar. 5, 1925, to Mar. 28, 1929
Treasury: Andrew William Mellon of Pennsylvania, Mar. 4, 1921, to Feb. 12, 1932
War: John Wingate Weeks of Massachusetts, Mar. 5, 1921, to Oct. 13, 1925
•Dwight Filley Davis of Missouri, Oct. 14, 1925, to Mar. 5, 1929
Attorney General: Harry Micajah Daugherty of Ohio, Mar. 5, 1921, to Mar. 28, 1924
•Harlan Fiske Stone of New York, Apr. 7, 1924, to Mar. 1, 1925
•Charles B. Warren of Michigan, appointed, Jan. 10, 1925; rejected by Senate, Mar. 10, 1925; appointed, Mar. 12, 1925; rejected by Senate, Mar. 16, 1925
•John Garibaldi Sargent of Vermont, Mar.

18, 1925, to Mar. 5, 1929
Navy: Edwin Denby of Michigan, Mar. 6, 1921, to Mar. 10, 1924
•Curtis Dwight Wilbur of California, Mar. 19, 1924, to Mar. 4, 1929
Postmaster General: Harry Stewart New of Indiana, Feb. 27, 1923, to Mar. 5, 1929
Interior: Hubert Work of Colorado, Mar. 5, 1923, to July 24, 1928
•Roy Owen West of Illinois, July 25, 1928, to Mar. 4, 1929
Agriculture: Henry Cantwell Wallace of Iowa, Mar. 5, 1921, to Oct. 25, 1924
•Howard Mason Gore of West Virginia, Nov. 22, 1924, to Mar. 4, 1925
•William Marion Jardine of Kansas, Mar. 5, 1925, to Mar. 4, 1929
Commerce: Herbert Clark Hoover of California, Mar. 5, 1921, to Aug 21, 1928
•William Fairfield Whiting of Massachusetts, Aug. 22, 1928, to Mar. 4, 1929
Labor: James John Davis of Pennsylvania, Mar. 5, 1921, to Nov. 30, 1930

THE SUPREME COURT

Associate Justice: Harlan Fiske Stone of New York, appointed, Jan. 5, 1925; confirmed, Feb. 5, 1925

HERBERT CLARK HOOVER

Full name: Herbert Clark Hoover
•He was the 13th of 19 presidents who had middle initials or middle names.
Date of birth: Aug. 10, 1874
•He was the second of three presidents who were born in August.
Place of birth: West Branch, Iowa
•He was the first president born west of the Mississippi River.
•He was the only president who was born in Iowa.
•His birthplace on Downey Street is two blocks north from the West Branch exit of Interstate 80.
•His father sold the birthplace cottage in 1879. His sons acquired it in 1935 and it was restored to its 1874 appearance in 1939. Designated a National Historic Site, Aug. 12, 1965, it is administered by the National Park Service. It is open daily except Thanksgiving, Christmas, and New Year's Day, 9 A.M. to 5 P.M., and Sundays, 10 A.M. to 5 P.M. (Sept. 16 to May 15, 2 to 5 P.M.) Admission: free.
Family lineage: Swiss-German
•He was the first of two presidents who were of Swiss-German ancestry. The other was Eisenhower.
Religious denomination: Society of Friends

•He was the first of two presidents who were Quakers. The other was Nixon.
College: Stanford University, Stanford, Cal.
•He was the only president who went to Stanford.
•He was the 22nd of 27 presidents who attended college.
Date of graduation: May 29, 1895, Bachelor of Arts
•He was the 16th of 21 presidents who were graduated from college.

PARENTS AND SIBLINGS

Father's name: Jesse Clark Hoover
Date of birth: Sept. 2, 1846
Place of birth: West Milton, Ohio
Occupations: Blacksmith, farm equipment salesman
Date of death: Dec. 10, 1880
•Herbert was six years, 122 days old, when his father died.
Place of death: West Branch, Iowa
Age at death: 34 years, 99 days

Mother's name: Huldah Randall Minthorn Hoover
Date of birth: May 4, 1848

Place of birth: Burgersville, Ontario, Canada
•His mother was the last of four mothers of presidents who were born abroad.
•She was the last of eight parents of presidents who were born abroad.
Date of marriage: Mar. 12, 1870
Children: 3; 2 sons, 1 daughter
•Theodore Jesse was born in 1871, Herbert Clark in 1874, and May in 1876.
•Hoover was the fourth of five presidents who came from families of three children.
•He was the eighth of ten presidents who were second children.
Date of death: Feb. 24, 1883
•Herbert was eight years, 198 days old, when his mother died.
•He was the second of two presidents who were orphans. The other was Jackson.
Place of death: West Branch, Iowa
Age at death: 34 years, 296 days

MARRIAGE

Date of marriage: Feb. 10, 1899
Place of marriage: Monterey, Cal.
•Hoover was the first of two presidents who were married in California. The other was Nixon.
Age at marriage: 24 years, 184 days
•He was the 23rd of 27 presidents who were married in their twenties.
Years married: 44 years, 331 days

Wife's name: Lou Henry Hoover
•She was the 27th of 33 first ladies.
•She was the 34th of 40 wives of presidents.
Date of birth: Mar. 29, 1874
•She was the third of four first ladies who were born in March.
•She was the fourth of five wives of presidents who were born in March.
Place of birth: Waterloo, Iowa
•She was the first of two first ladies who were born in Iowa. The other was Mamie Eisenhower.
•She was the first of two wives of presidents who were born in Iowa.

Wife's mother: Florence Weed Henry
Wife's father: Charles Henry, banker
Age at marriage: 24 years, 318 days
•She was the 22nd of 26 first ladies who were married in their twenties.
•She was the 26th of 30 wives of parents who were married in their twenties.
Years older than husband: 134 days
•She was the fifth of six first ladies who were older than their husbands.
•She was the fifth of six wives of presidents who were older than their husbands.
Children: 2 sons
•Herbert Clark was born on Aug. 4, 1903, and Allan Henry on July 17, 1907. Both sons were born in London, England.
•Hoover was the second of three presidents who had children who were born abroad.
•He was the fifth of six presidents who had only male children.
•He was the fourth of seven presidents who had two children.
•He was the 24th of 30 presidents who had children.
Date of death: Jan. 7, 1944
Place of death: New York, N.Y.
•She was the first of two first ladies who died in New York City. The other was Eleanor Roosevelt.
•She was the second of three first ladies who died in New York.
•She was the fourth of five wives of presidents who died in New York City.
•She was the seventh of eight wives of presidents who died in New York.
Age at death: 68 years, 284 days
Place of burial: Palo Alto, Cal.
•She was the only first lady or wife of a president who was buried in California.
•A few days after her husband's burial in 1964, the body of Mrs. Hoover was reinterred at West Branch, Iowa.
•She was the only first lady or wife of a president who was buried in Iowa.
Years he survived his wife: 20 years, 287 days
•Hoover was the last of 14 presidents who survived their wives.

EARLY YEARS

Dec. 10, 1880, his father died
Feb. 24, 1883, his mother died
•Following the death of his mother, Hoover lived for a time with his uncle, Allan

Hoover, on a farm near West Branch, Iowa.
1884, moved to Newberg, Ore.
•He lived with his mother's brother, Dr.

Henry John Minthorn.

1885, with Minthorns, moved to Salem, Ore.

• He worked as an office boy while attending high school.

May 29, 1895, was graduated from Stanford University, Palo Alto, Cal.

• He was a member of the first class to be graduated from Stanford.

1895–1896, worked as mine laborer, California

• His first mining job, he later wrote, was "pushing a car in the lower levels of the Reward mine for $5.00 a day, on a ten-hour night shift and a seven-day week."

1897–1901, worked as mining engineer, western Australia and China

Feb. 10, 1899, married Lou Henry, Monterey, Cal.

1900, directed food relief for victims of Boxer Rebellion

• He was then employed as chief engineer at the imperial mines of China.

1901–1914, employed as mining engineer

• His engineering assignments took him all over the world: Australia, China, France, India, England, Hawaii, New Zealand, South Africa, Canada, Germany, Malay States, Russia, and the U.S.

Aug. 4, 1903, his first son born

• The boy was named Herbert Clark Hoover, Jr.

July 17, 1907, his second son born

• The boy was named Allan Henry Hoover.

1908, formed consulting engineering firm, offices in New York City and principal foreign cities

1909, his first book, *Principles of Mining*, published by Hill, New York City

• The text was based on two series of lectures he had delivered at Columbia University, New York City, and Stanford University.

• He was the 15th of 21 presidents who wrote books that were published during their lifetimes.

1912, elected trustee, Stanford University

• He was the first alumnus to be elected a trustee. He served until 1961, when he became trustee emeritus.

1912, translation of *De Re Metallica* published in London, England

• Written by Georg Agricola, *De Re Metallica* was published in Latin in 1556. The work traced the development of mining methods, geology, mineralogy, and mining law from the earliest times to the 16th century.

• The 640-page English translation was a joint venture; he edited the book from his wife's translation.

1914, organized American Relief Committee, London, England

• As chairman, he expedited the return of 120,000 U.S. citizens who were stranded in Europe at the outbreak of World War I. "I did not realize it at the moment, but on Monday, August 3rd, my engineering career was over forever," he wrote in his memoirs. "I was on the slippery road of public life."

October, 1914, formed Committee for Relief of Belgium and Northern France

• He directed the relief of ten million persons in the area, victims of the German occupation and the Allied blockade. He obtained agreements for the protection of the food, clothing, and medical supplies from all belligerents. He probably was the only American allowed to move freely between London, Paris, Brussels, and Berlin.

NATIONAL PROMINENCE

May 19, 1917, appointed U.S. food administrator by Wilson

• The U.S. Grain Corporation, the sugar equalization board, and the food purchase board pioneered methods of mobilizing food resources in wartime.

Nov. 9, 1918, appointed director-general of Relief and Reconstruction of Europe by Wilson

• All of Europe faced famine and pestilence. Hoover's organization of four thousand American workers and many thousands of local assistants worked in 30 countries, supervising the distribution of forty-six million tons of food during 1918–1920. More than nineteen million tons of food were supplied by the U.S. Total cost of the relief and reconstruction program was $3,287,-000,000.

1919, served as member and alternate chairman of Supreme Economic Council, member of committee of economic advisors to American delegation to Paris Peace Conference

1919, founded Hoover Institution on War, Revolution and Peace, Stanford University

• The institution's initial aim was to preserve "an historical collection on the Great War." From 1919 to 1922, aided by his contribution of $150,000, institution workers searched Europe for significant records of World War I and peace negotiations. The collection grew so large that the Hoover War Library was established on the Stanford campus, 1922.

Mar. 5, 1921, appointed secretary of commerce by Harding

• Hoover was the only president who served as secretary of commerce.

• He was the only president who served in the cabinet in a position other than secretary of state or secretary of war.

• He was the last of eight presidents who served in the cabinet.

1922, his book, *American Individualism*, published by Doubleday, Page, New York City

Aug. 3, 1923, retained as secretary of commerce by Coolidge

June 14, 1928, nominated for president, Republican national convention, Kansas City, Mo.

• He was nominated on the first ballot.

Oct. 22, 1928, made "rugged individualism" speech, New York City

• He condemned the Democratic platform as state socialism and endorsed free competition and private initiative.

Nov. 6, 1928, election day

• *See* Election of 1928, below.

November—December, 1928, made goodwill tour of Central and South America

• As president-elect, he visited Honduras, Costa Rica, Nicaragua, El Salvador, Ecuador, Peru, Chile, Argentina, Uruguay, and Brazil.

Dec. 23, 1928, returned to U.S.

Jan. 14, 1929, presidential electors cast ballots

• He received 444 of the 531 electoral votes from the 48 states.

• *See* Election of 1928, below.

Feb. 13, 1929, electoral votes tabulated by Congress

• Hoover and Curtis were officially declared elected.

ELECTION OF 1928

Socialist party, convened, Apr. 13, at New York City, nominated Norman Thomas of New York for president, James Hudson Maurer of Pennsylvania for vice president.

Workers' (Communist) party, convened, May 27, at New York City, nominated William Zebulon Foster of Illinois for president, Benjamin Gitlow of New York for vice president.

Republican party, convened, June 12, at Kansas City, Mo., nominated Herbert Clark Hoover of California for president, Charles Curtis of Kansas for vice president.

• This was the 19th Republican national convention. It was the only Republican convention held in Kansas City; it was the second of two major party conventions held in Kansas City.

Democratic party, convened, June 26, at Houston, Tex., nominated Alfred Emanuel Smith of New York for president, Joseph Taylor Robinson of Arkansas for vice president.

• This was the 25th Democratic national convention. It was the only major party convention held in Houston.

Farmer Labor party, convened, July 11, at Chicago, Ill., nominated George William Norris of Nebraska for president, Will Vereen of Georgia for vice president. Norris declined the nomination. Frank Elbridge Webb of California later became the party's nominee.

Prohibition party, convened, July 12, at Chicago, Ill., nominated William Frederick Varney of New York for president, James Arthur Edgerton of Virginia for vice president.

Socialist Labor party nominated Verne L. Reynolds of New York for president, Jeremiah D. Crowley of New York for vice president.

Election day, Tuesday, Nov. 6, 1928

Popular vote: 36,805,951
    Hoover, 21,437,277
    Smith, 15,007,698
    Thomas, 265,583
    Foster, 46,896
    Reynolds, 21,586
    Varney, 20,101
    Webb, 6,810

Electoral vote: 531, 48 states
  • Hoover, 444, 40 states
    (Arizona, 3; California, 13; Colorado, 6; Connecticut, 7; Delaware, 3; Florida, 6; Idaho, 4; Illinois, 20; Indiana, 15; Iowa, 13; Kansas, 10; Kentucky, 13; Maine, 6; Maryland, 8; Michigan, 15; Minnesota,

12; Missouri, 18; Montana, 4; Nebraska, 8; Nevada, 3; New Hampshire, 4; New Jersey, 14; New Mexico, 3; New York, 45; North Carolina, 12; North Dakota, 5; Ohio, 24; Oklahoma, 10; Oregon, 5; Pennsylvania, 38; South Dakota, 5; Tennessee, 12; Texas, 20; Utah, 4; Vermont, 4; Virginia, 12; Washington, 7; West Virginia, 8; Wisconsin, 13; Wyoming, 3)
• Smith, 87, eight states
(Alabama, 12; Arkansas, 9; Georgia, 14; Louisiana, 10; Massachusetts, 18; Mississippi, 10; Rhode Island, 5; South Carolina, 9)

THE PRESIDENT (31st)

Term of office: Mar. 4, 1929, to Mar. 4, 1933 (4 years)
• Hoover was the 18th of 19 presidents who served one term or less than one term.
• He was the last of ten presidents who served for four years.
• He was the last president whose term ended on Mar. 4.
State represented: California
• He was the only president who represented California.
• He was the 13th of 15 presidents who represented states that were not their native states.
Political party: Republican
• He was the 12th of 14 presidents who were Republicans.

Congresses: 71st, 72nd
Administration: 36th
Age at inauguration: 54 years, 206 days
• He was the 18th of 21 presidents who were younger than their vice presidents. Hoover was 14 years, 197 days younger than Curtis.
Inauguration day: Monday, Mar. 4, 1929
• Hoover took the oath of office, administered by Chief Justice William Howard Taft, on the east portico of the Capitol.
• This was the second of two inaugurations at which the oath of office was administered by a former president.
• This was the second of two inaugurations at which Taft officiated.

THE 36th ADMINISTRATION

1929

Mar. 5, appointed his only secretary of state, Henry L. Stimson; his first secretary of war, James W. Good; his only attorney general, William D. Mitchell; his only secretary of navy, Charles F. Adams; his only postmaster general, Walter F. Brown; his only secretary of interior, Ray L. Wilbur; his only secretary of agriculture, Arthur M. Hyde; and his first secretary of commerce, Robert P. Lamont
• Hoover did not submit the names of Secretary of Treasury Mellon and Secretary of Labor Davis, who had served under Coolidge. The Senate, after confirming the others, adopted a resolution directing the judiciary committee to investigate whether a secretary of treasury could legally hold over from the previous administration; the body then adjourned. The committee reported that Mellon had the legal right to retain the cabinet post.

• Good and Hyde took office, Mar. 6; Stimson, Mar. 29.
• Mellon was the last of three secretaries of treasury who served under three presidents. He was the seventh of nine executive officers who served in the cabinets of three presidents. He had served previously under Harding and Coolidge.
• Davis was the only secretary of labor who served under three presidents. He was the eighth of nine executive officers who served in the cabinets of three presidents. He had served previously under Harding and Coolidge.
Mar. 14, issued executive order regarding income tax refunds
• He ordered that all decisions of internal revenue tax refunds over $20,000 were to be open for public inspection.
Mar. 25, announced White House horses turned over to army
• In an economy move, he ordered the seven horses quartered in the White House

stables transferred to Fort Myers, Va. A black charger, the personal property of Coolidge, was shipped to Northampton, Mass.

Mar. 25, announced presidential yacht, *Mayflower*, decommissioned

• A fisherman, but no yachtsman, he ordered the vessel sent to the Philadelphia navy yard. He made his first fishing trip to Madison, Va., Apr. 6.

Mar. 28, Secretary of Treasury Mellon took oath of office

Apr. 15, first session of 71st Congress

• The administration controlled both the Senate and the House of Representatives. The Republicans gained eight Senate and 30 House seats. The Senate (96 members) consisted of 56 Republicans, 39 Democrats, and one other. The House (435 members) consisted of 267 Republicans, 163 Democrats, one other, and four vacancies.

Apr. 16, sent special message to Congress on farm relief and tariff revision

• He recommended legislation to establish a federal farm board with funds to assist cooperative associations, tariff readjustment, and asked the repeal of the national origins provision of an immigration law which was to go into operation, July 1.

Apr. 16, Senate confirmed former Vice President Dawes as ambassador to Great Britain

Apr. 21, informed chairman of Senate agriculture committee that export debenture plan for farm relief was unworkable

• The export debenture plan, backed by the farm bloc, would have provided that the difference between domestic and world prices be met by use of customs receipts.

Apr. 22, decried rising crime rate, New York City

• In an address to the Associated Press, he stated that life and property in the U.S. were endangered relatively more than in any other civilized country, adding that violations of the prohibition laws accounted for only eight percent of crime.

May 20, appointed commission to investigate law enforcement

• The first meeting of the commission was held at the White House, May 28.

May 27, pocket veto upheld by Supreme Court

• The Supreme Court unanimously affirmed the decision of the U.S. Court of Claims in which the right of the president to prevent enactment of legislation by pocket veto was upheld.

May 30, warned against international arms race

• In a Memorial Day address at Arlington National Cemetery, he stated that every major country had strengthened its navy since the Kellogg-Briand pact was signed in 1927. "We are still borne on the tide of competitive building." he said.

June 11, accused Senate of delaying farm relief

June 15, signed agricultural marketing act

• Administration farm measures without the debenture plan passed in the House of Representatives three times between Apr. 25 and June 13, but were blocked in the Senate. When he made it explicit that he would veto any bill that contained the plan, senatorial opposition ended.

• This act established the federal farm board, a revolving fund of $500,000,000 for low-interest loans, and also provided for price support.

June 18, signed census and reapportionment act

• This act authorized the president to declare a reapportionment of Congress after each census if the legislature had failed to act. Congress had not taken such action since 1911.

June 25, issued proclamation announcing agreement among six states regarding Boulder Canyon project

July 15, addressed first meeting of farm board, stressed necessity of establishment of farm cooperatives

July 24, issued proclamation declaring Kellogg-Briand pact in effect

• The White House ceremony was attended by former President Coolidge, former Secretary of State Kellogg, and representatives of 45 nations. A total of 62 nations had or shortly thereafter pledged themselves to renounce war as a national policy.

July 24, announced U.S. would not lay keels of three cruisers as planned

• His decision followed the British announcement of suspension of major naval construction.

Aug. 17, began vacation at fishing camp, near Madison, Va.

• When greeted by a crowd on his arrival at Madison, he good-naturedly asked for privacy while on vacation:

It is generally realized and accepted that prayer is the most personal of all human relationship[s]. On such occasions as that, men and women are entitled to be alone and undisturbed. Next to prayer, fishing is the most personal relationship of man, and, of more importance than the fact itself, everybody concedes that the fish will not bite in the presence of the public and the press.

- Rapidan Camp, now known as Camp Hoover, is located within the boundary of Shenandoah National Park, at the confluence of two streams, Mill Prong and Laurel Prong, which join to form the Rapidan River. The Rapidan tract was purchased and the camp structures were built by the President with his own funds. A detachment of U.S. Marines was stationed nearby for security.
- After he left the White House, he offered Rapidan Camp to succeeding presidents but the location did not prove popular with President Franklin D. Roosevelt. The camp was deeded to the federal government as a portion of Shenandoah National Park, which was established in 1935. Only three of the original structures, including the President's Cabin, remain. The camp can be hiked to from the Big Meadows area of the Skyline Drive. On the eastern park boundary, route 649 from Criglersville, Va., leads to the camp. This road is chained off at the park line but the public can walk into the camp area. The buildings are not open to the public.

Aug. 29, greeted commander of Graf Zeppelin, Dr. Hugo Eckener
- The German Zeppelin had just completed a 21-day round-the-world trip.

Sept. 6, stated he would tolerate no interference in naval reduction program from those with financial interests in shipbuilding
- He endorsed the investigation of lobbyists for American shipbuilders, who were accused of exerting undue influence during the unsuccessful 1927 Geneva naval disarmament conference.

Oct. 7, gave state dinner for British prime minister, J. Ramsay MacDonald, White House
- He and MacDonald had conferred at his Virginia fishing camp, Oct. 5–6. Mac-

Donald addressed a joint session of Congress, Oct. 7, after invitations to a five-power naval conference were issued by the British government. The U.S., France, Italy, and Japan were invited to the proposed January, 1930, London meeting.

Oct. 9, released joint statement with Prime Minister MacDonald after five days of private meetings
- They expressed complete accord regarding the Kellogg-Briand pact and agreed to begin conversations to solve "old historical problems" inasmuch as war between the U.S. and Great Britain was "unthinkable."

Oct. 11, received Polish delegation on 150th anniversary of death of Revolutionary hero, General Casimir Pulaski

Oct. 12, attended World Series game, Philadelphia, Pa.
- He attended the final game of the five-game series, which was won by the Philadelphia Athletics over the Chicago Cubs.
- He was the second of four presidents who attended the World Series while in office.
- He was the second of two presidents who attended World Series games outside Washington, D.C., while in office. The other was Wilson.

Oct. 21, attended Edison golden jubilee, Dearborn, Mich.
- Thomas A. Edison reenacted the discovery of the electric light in the same laboratory in which he had worked in Menlo Park, N.J., 50 years before. The laboratory had been moved to Greenfield Village in Dearborn, Henry Ford's reproduction of an early American community. Greenfield Village was not completed until 1933.

Oct. 22–23, traveled down Ohio River on stern-wheel steamboat
- He traveled from Cincinnati, Ohio, to Louisville, Ky., during the Ohio Waterway celebration of the completion of the one-thousand-mile, nine-feet-deep canalized waterway from Pittsburgh, Pa., to the Mississippi River.

Oct. 23, announced five-year inland waterways program, Louisville, Ky.
- During an address at the Louisville Memorial to the War Dead, he stated that the millions saved by naval reduction would be used to improve navigation of the Mississippi and its tributaries. He also declared in favor of the St. Lawrence deepwater route to the Atlantic.

Oct. 24, stock market broke

•About thirteen million shares changed hands, climaxing a downward trend which had prevailed for weeks. The following day, Hoover said:

The fundamental business of the country, that is the production and distribution of commodities, is on a sound and prosperous basis.

Oct. 29, stock market crashed

•More than sixteen million shares were sold during Wall Street's blackest day. By mid-November, $30,000,000,000 in paper value of listed stocks had been wiped out. During the next three years, losses increased to about $75,000,000,000.

•This was the worst and last of nine U.S. depressions.

Oct. 30, presented Madame Marie Sklodow-ska Curie with $50,000 draft, White House

•The money was a gift from Madame Curie's American friends for the purchase of a gram of radium.

Nov. 18, Secretary of War Good died

Nov. 19, pledged aid by heads of 12 major railroads

•The railway leaders pledged to maintain full employment and maximum programs of new construction and improvement.

Nov. 22, first session of 71st Congress adjourned

Nov. 23, telegraphed appeal to 48 governors to help offset possible unemployment.

Dec. 2, second session of 71st Congress

Dec. 2, sent his first State of the Union message to Congress

•In his twelve-thousand-word message, he declared that business was sound, pledged an income tax reduction, and requested tariff legislation and a stronger prohibition law.

Dec. 4, sent budget message to Congress

•He submitted a budget of $3,830,445,000, and recommended an income tax cut of $160,000,000.

Dec. 6, appointed his second secretary of war, Patrick J. Hurley

•Hurley took office, Dec. 9.

Dec. 16, signed joint resolution reducing income tax revenue

•The $160,000,000 reduction applied only to 1929 incomes, payable in 1930.

Dec. 24, fire at White House

•The interior and contents of the executive offices were destroyed, but the official papers were saved. During the reconstruction, he occupied the office of General John Pershing in the War, State, and Navy Building next door. He returned to the White House, Apr. 15, 1930.

1930

Jan. 2, with Mrs. Hoover, shook hands with more than sixty-three hundred New Year's Day callers

Jan. 7, held breakfast conference with delegates to London Naval Limitation Conference, White House

•The delegates sailed, Jan. 9.

Jan. 13, sent special message to Congress outlining six specific recommendations for immediate legislation to strengthen prohibition enforcement

Jan. 15, hosted White House dinner for former premier of South Africa, Jan Smuts

Jan. 24, issued executive order banning importation of parrots

•Psittacosis, an acute infectious virus disease which affects parrots, can be transmitted to humans.

Feb. 3, Chief Justice Taft resigned

Feb. 3, appointed Charles Evans Hughes as chief justice

•Hughes, who was confirmed by the Senate, Feb. 13, was the first of Hoover's four appointments to the Supreme Court.

•Hughes, who had been appointed by Taft in 1910 and who had resigned in 1916, was the second of three chief justices who had served as associate justices.

•Hoover was the ninth of 14 presidents who appointed chief justices.

Feb. 9, fished at Long Key, Fla.

Feb. 22, attended Washington's Birthday ceremonies, Alexandria and Mount Vernon, Va.

Mar. 8, Associate Justice Sanford died

Mar. 22, appointed John J. Parker as associate justice

•Parker, the second of Hoover's four appointments to the Supreme Court, was rejected by the Senate, 41–39, May 7.

•Hoover was the 13th of 15 presidents who nominated justices not confirmed by the Senate.

•Parker was the 21st of 25 men nominated to the Supreme Court not confirmed by the Senate.

Apr. 22, vetoed bill to authorize coinage of silver 50-cent pieces in commemoration of 75th anniversary of Gadsden Purchase

•This was the first of his 21 regular vetoes.
Apr. 30, received London Naval Treaty of 1930 from Secretary of State Stimson
•The treaty had been signed by the U.S., Great Britain, France, Italy, and Japan, Apr. 22.
May 1, sent naval treaty to Senate for ratification
May 9, appointed Owen J. Roberts as associate justice
•Roberts, who was confirmed by the Senate, May 20, was the third of Hoover's four appointments to the Supreme Court.
May 20, reviewed U.S. Navy off Virginia shore
May 28, vetoed soldiers, sailors, and nurses pension bill
May 30, delivered Memorial Day address, Gettysburg, Pa.
June 2, soldiers, sailors, and nurses pension act passed over his veto
•This act provided pensions for veterans of the Spanish-American War, the Philippine Insurrection, and the Boxer Rebellion.
•This was the first of his three vetoes that were overridden.
June 6, directed Secretary of State Stimson to refuse to turn over correspondence on London naval treaty to Senate foreign relations committee
June 12, received Dr. Julio Prestes, president-elect of Brazil, White House
June 26, vetoed World War I veterans' pension bill
•This bill, an amendment to the veterans act of 1924, would have provided $102,000,000 in pensions.
July 3, second session of 71st Congress adjourned
July 3, pocket vetoed three bills
July 4, signed $145,000,000 rivers and harbors act
July 7, special session of Senate to consider London naval treaty
July 11, again directed Secretary of State Stimson to refuse to turn over naval treaty correspondence to Senate
July 21, Senate ratified naval treaty
July 21, special session of Senate adjourned
July 22, signed naval treaty
Aug. 27, pushed button lighting Lindbergh beacon, Chicago, Ill., from White House
•The beacon was said to be the brightest light in the world.
Sept. 17, recognized new governments of Argentina, Boliva, and Peru

•The U.S. now had established diplomatic relations with all Latin American republics.
Oct. 1, attended World Series game, Philadelphia, Pa.
•He attended the opening game between the Philadelphia Athletics and the St. Louis Cardinals. The Athletics won the six-game series.
Oct. 6, addressed American Legion national convention, Boston, Mass.
Oct. 6, addressed American Federation of Labor national convention, Boston
Oct. 7, addressed 50,000 people at 150th anniversary of Battle of King's Mountain, S.C.
Oct. 17, appointed cabinet committee to investigate unemployment
Oct. 22, issued executive order prohibiting shipping of arms and ammunition to Brazilian revolutionaries
Nov. 9, accepted Democratic offer of nonpartisan cooperation to combat economic crisis
Nov. 28, accepted resignation of Secretary of Labor Davis, effective, Nov. 30
Nov. 28, appointed his second secretary of labor, William N. Doak
•Doak took office, Dec. 9.
Dec. 1, third session of 71st Congress
Dec. 2, sent his second State of the Union message to Congress
•He requested legislation to accelerate "the greatest program of waterway, harbor, flood control, public building, highway and airway improvement in all our history," estimated to cost between $100,000,000 and $150,000,000.
Dec. 10, sent World Court protocols to Senate, urged ratification
Dec. 20, signed $116,000,000 emergency construction to aid unemployed act
Dec. 20, signed $45,000,000 drought relief act
Dec. 22, signed $150,000,000 farm board appropriation act
Dec. 31, announced ratification of London naval treaty by Senate

Note: The official population, according to the 15th census, was 122,775,046.

1931

Jan. 1, with Mrs. Hoover, shook hands with

6,429 visitors at New Year's Day reception, White House

Jan. 9, refused Senate request to return confirmations of three new members of federal power commission

Jan. 20, sent special message to Congress voicing his opposition to repeal of 18th Amendment

Feb. 12, broadcast Lincoln's Birthday address

Feb. 22, worshipped in George Washington's pew, Old Christ Episcopal Church, Alexandria, Va.

Feb. 26, vetoed veterans' bonus bill

Feb. 27, veterans' bonus act passed over his veto

• This act authorized loans of 50 percent on the adjusted compensation certificates provided for by the act of 1924.

• This was the second of his three vetoes that were overridden.

Mar. 3, vetoed Muscle Shoals joint resolution

• This resolution would have created a corporation to operate government properties at Muscle Shoals, Ala.

Mar. 4, third session of 71st Congress adjourned

Mar. 23, visited Puerto Rico

• He was the second of seven presidents who visited Puerto Rico while in office.

Mar. 25, visited Virgin Islands

• He was the first of four presidents who visited the Virgin Islands while in office.

• He did not travel outside the continental U.S. while president except for this trip to Puerto Rico and the Virgin Islands.

• He was the only president since McKinley who did not visit a foreign country during his term of office.

Apr. 11, attended funeral of Speaker of House Nicholas Longworth, Cincinnati, Ohio

Apr. 29, entertained king and queen of Siam, White House

May 30, delivered Memorial Day address, Gettysburg, Pa.

June 16, spoke at dedication of Harding tomb, Marion, Ohio

• He said:

Warren Harding had a dim realization that he had been betrayed by a few men whom he trusted, by men whom he had believed were his devoted friends. It was later proved to the courts of the land that these men had betrayed not only the friendship and trust of their staunch and loyal friend, but they had betrayed their country. That was the tragedy of the life of Warren Harding.

June 17, rededicated reconstructed Lincoln Tomb, Springfield, Ill.

June 20, proposed moratorium of war reparations and war debts

• The stock market rallied momentarily.

Sept. 21, spoke against veterans' bonus, American Legion national convention, Detroit, Mich.

Oct. 19, spoke at ceremony commemorating 150th anniversary of Cornwallis's surrender, Yorktown, Va.

Nov. 11, dedicated Memorial to War Dead, Washington, D.C.

Dec. 7, first session of 72nd Congress

• The administration lost control of the House of Representatives. The Democrats gained eight Senate and 57 House seats. The Senate (96 members) consisted of 48 Republicans, 47 Democrats, and one Independent. The House (435 members) consisted of 220 Democrats, 214 Republicans, and one other.

Dec. 8, sent his third State of the Union message to Congress

• He proposed the establishment of a lending agency to provide emergency financing to banks and railroads.

Dec. 23, signed moratorium of war reparations and war debts

1932

Jan. 4, urged Congress to speed up legislation to stimulate national credit

Jan. 5, received representatives of unemployed "army," White House

• About eighteen thousand unemployed, led by a Catholic priest, Reverend James R. Cox of Pittsburgh, Pa., gathered in Washington.

Jan. 12, Associate Justice Holmes resigned

Jan. 14, Postmaster General Brown announced President Hoover would seek reelection, after White House conference

Jan. 22, signed Reconstruction Finance Corporation act

• This act authorized the RFC, which was capitalized at $500,000,000 and authorized to issue up to $2,000,000,000 worth of tax-exempt bonds for the purpose of extending emergency financing to banks, insurance companies, railroads, and farm mortgage associations. The RFC was established, Feb. 2, with Charles G. Dawes as president.

Jan. 23, signed land banks expansion act
•This act authorized the expansion of land banks capital by $125,000,000.

Feb. 3, appealed for halt to hoarding
•He estimated that about $1,300,000,000 in U.S. currency was being hoarded.

Feb. 3, accepted resignation of Secretary of Treasury Mellon, effective, Feb. 12

Feb. 8, appointed his second secretary of treasury, Ogden L. Mills
•Mills took office, Feb. 13.

Feb. 15, appointed Benjamin N. Cardozo as associate justice
•Cardozo, who was confirmed by the Senate, Feb. 24, was the last of Hoover's four appointments to the Supreme Court.

Feb. 22, addressed joint session of Congress on bicentennial of Washington's birthday

Feb. 27, signed credit expansion act
•The Glass-Steagall act made about $750,-000,000 of the gold supply available for purposes other than currency support and broadened the acceptability of commercial paper for rediscount by the Federal Reserve System.

Mar. 3, 20th Amendment submitted to states

Mar. 23, signed anti-injunction act
•The Norris-La Guardia Act forbade federal injunctions against strikers without evidence of danger or injury to interests against which strikes were called and also provided for trial by jury for persons cited for violations of injunctions.

Apr. 4, sent special message to Congress in which he proposed joint executive department-congressional commission to study governmental economics and recommend legislation

Apr. 25, addressed governors' conference, Richmond, Va.
•He emphasized that state governments shared responsibility for the economy.

Apr. 27, vetoed omnibus pension bill
•This bill was a composite of 367 individual bills, 186 of which originated in the House of Representatives and 181 in the Senate.

May 5, sent special message to Congress regarding delay in balancing budget
•In response to favorable public sentiment,

he issued a supplementary statement condemning legislative delay and lobby interference, May 6:
> It is an issue of the people against delays and destructive legislation which impair the credit of the United States. It is also an issue between the people and the locust swarm of lobbyists who haunt the halls of Congress, seeking special privilege for special groups.

May 11, vetoed amendment to Tariff Act of 1930 bill

May 13, asked federal law enforcement agencies to make Lindbergh kidnapping "never-to-be-forgotten case" until justice done
•The body of 20-month-old Charles A. Lindbergh, Jr., kidnapped from Hopewell, N.J., Mar. 1, had been found, May 12.

May 31, Supreme Court decided president could sign bills after final adjournment of Congress

June 6, signed $1,118,500,000 tax act

June 10, refused request of business leader group to revive council of national defense

June 16, renominated for president, Republican national convention, Chicago, Ill.

July 11, vetoed unemployment relief bill

July 15, cut his own salary by 20 percent
•The vice president and the cabinet announced that 15 percent of their salaries would be returned to the government.
•Hoover donated his presidential salary to charity.
•He was the first of two presidents who did so. The other was Kennedy.

July 16, first session of 72nd Congress adjourned

July 21, signed relief and construction act
•This act authorized the RFC to raise its debt ceiling to $3,000,000,000. The RFC was given power to lend $1,500,000,000 to states and local communities for the construction of self-liquidating public works. An additional $300,000,000 was provided for temporary loans to states unable to finance relief programs.

July 21, signed amended veterans administration act
•This act provided that 215,000 World War I veterans could borrow half the value of their bonus certificates, effective, July 25.

July 22, signed Federal Home Loan Bank Act
•He had recommended this measure in his

third State of the Union message.
July 28, called out army against bonus army
•The first contingent of the "Bonus Expeditionary Force"—veterans seeking immediate and full payment of their adjusted compensation certificates—arrived in Washington, May 29. The bonus army grew to about seventeen thousand. After the Senate defeated the bonus bill, June 17, the government provided funds to return the veterans to their homes. About two thousand refused to leave and clashed with the Washington police sent to evict them. Two veterans and two policemen were killed; many were injured. The federal troops used infantry, cavalry, and tanks to remove the veterans.
Aug. 7, Secretary of Commerce Lamont resigned
Aug. 8, appointed his second secretary of commerce, Roy D. Chapin
•Chapin was the last of Hoover's 14 cabinet appointments.
Aug. 11, formally accepted Republican nomination for president
•He announced that he favored changes in the 18th Amendment, principally that the states should determine the provisions of liquor sale laws.
Sept. 3, directed Postmaster General Brown to reinstate Gary, Ind. postal employee who had been discharged after introducing bonus payment resolution at American Legion convention
Sept. 11, released bonus army report
•The department of justice report concerned the veterans who had applied for loans to return to their homes. The report alleged that 1,069 of the 4,723 who applied for travel funds had police records.
Sept. 26, laid cornerstone of new post office department building, Washington, D.C.
•He used the trowel Washington had used to lay the cornerstone of the Capitol in 1793.
Oct. 4, offered comprehensive agricultural rehabilitation program during campaign speech, Des Moines, Iowa
Oct. 7, appealed for female vote in radio speech, White House
Oct. 13, laid cornerstone of new Supreme Court building, Washington, D.C.
Nov. 7, made final radio appeal of campaign, Elko, Nev.

Nov. 8, election day
•*See* Election of 1932, page 392.
Nov. 12, invited President-elect Roosevelt to White House to confer on European nations' request to further defer war debt payments
•The conference was held, Nov. 22. Hoover notified Great Britain, France, Belgium, Poland, and Czechoslovakia that the war debt deferments question would have to be answered by Congress.
Dec. 5, second session of 72nd Congress
Dec. 6, sent his fourth and last State of the Union message to Congress
•He urged balancing the budget by reorganization of the government and recommended a 25 percent manufacturers' sales tax.

1933

Jan. 5, former President Coolidge died
•With the death of Coolidge, Hoover became the last of four presidents who served for periods when no former president was living.
Jan. 7, attended Coolidge funeral, Northampton, Mass.
Jan. 9, presidential electors cast ballots
•Roosevelt received 472 electoral votes. Hoover received 59.
•*See* Election of 1932, page 392.
Jan. 13, vetoed Philippine independence bill
Jan. 13, Philippine independence act passed over his veto
•This act enabled the people of the Philippines to adopt a constitution and form a government to provide for their independence.
•This was the last of his three vetoes that were overridden.
Jan. 24, vetoed deficiency bill
Feb. 6, 20th Amendment declared ratified
•*See* Constitution, page 644.
Feb. 8, electoral votes tabulated by Congress
•Roosevelt and Garner were officially declared elected.
•Hoover was the last of seven presidents who were defeated when they sought reelection.
Feb. 20, 21st Amendment sent to states for ratification
•This amendment called for the repeal of

the 18th Amendment.

Feb. 25, signed amended banking act
•This act assigned the protection of national bank deposits to the comptroller of the currency.

Mar. 4, second session of 72nd Congress adjourned

Mar. 4, pocket vetoed seven bills
•These were the last of his 37 vetoes, the last of his 16 pocket vetoes.

THE FORMER PRESIDENT

Mar. 4, 1933, attended inauguration of Franklin D. Roosevelt
•Hoover's age upon leaving office was 58 years, 206 days.
•He was the only living former president from Mar. 4, 1933, to Mar. 4, 1953.

March, 1933, retired to his home, Palo Alto, Cal.

1934, *The State Papers and Other Public Writings of Herbert Hoover*, edited by William Starr Myers, published in two volumes by Doubleday, Doran, New York City

1936, appointed chairman of Boys Club of America

1938, made extended trip to Europe
•He was the guest of the governments of Austria, Belgium, Czechoslovakia, Estonia, Finland, France, Latvia, and Poland. He also visited Germany.
•He was the seventh of eight former presidents who visited Europe.

1938, his book, *Addresses Upon the American Road, 1933–1938*, published by Scribner, New York City

1939, appointed chairman of Commission for Polish Relief

1939, appointed chairman of Finnish Relief Fund

1940, his book, *Further Addresses Upon the American Road, 1938–1940*, published by Scribner, New York City

1940, appointed chairman of Committee on Food for Small Democracies

1942, *The Problems of Lasting Peace* published by Doubleday, Doran, New York City
•He wrote this book in collaboration with Hugh Gibson.

1942, appointed chairman of Belgian Relief Fund

1943, his book, *America's First Crusade*, published by Scribner, New York City

Jan. 7, 1944, his wife died

Aug. 10, 1944, celebrated his 70th birthday
•He was the 14th of 16 presidents who lived to be 70.

May 28, 1945, visited White House at invitation of Truman
•This was his first visit to the White House since Mar. 4, 1933.

1946, appointed coordinator of Food Supply for World Famine by Truman

1946, his book, *Addresses Upon the American Road; World War II, 1941–1945*, published by Van Nostrand, New York City

Jan. 21, 1947, accepted Truman invitation to conduct study of food and economic conditions in Germany and central Europe

Feb. 27, 1947, submitted report on food conditions in Europe to Truman
•He recommended that the U.S. allot $475,-000,000 to supply food, seed, and other products to German civilians for the period up to July 1, 1948.

1947, Boulder Dam officially renamed Hoover Dam

July 7, 1947, first Hoover Commission established
•The Commission on Organization of the Executive Branch of the Government was established by an act of Congress.

Apr. 1, 1949, final report of Hoover Commission submitted
•The comprehensive recommendations of the commission led to the Reorganization Act of 1949.

June 5, 1949, rebuked Republican national committee for misuse of his Hoover Commission speeches
•He charged that his "objective and nonpartisan" talks on reorganization had been rebroadcast with unauthorized additions by Republican congressmen.

1949, declined appointment to Senate
•Governor Thomas E. Dewey of New York had offered to appoint Hoover to the Senate to complete the term of Senator Robert F. Wagner, who had resigned, June 28.

Aug. 10, 1949, warned against excessive taxation, Palo Alto, Cal.
•On his 75th birthday, in a speech before an audience of ten thousand at Stanford Uni-

versity, he cautioned against excessive taxation, which he blamed on "the multitude of pressure groups among our own citizens," and state and municipal governments that demanded federal funds.

•He was the eighth of ten presidents who lived to be 75.

1949, his book, *Addresses Upon the American Road, 1945–1948*, published by Van Nostrand, New York City

Apr. 28, 1950, called for expulsion of U.S.S.R. and Soviet bloc from United Nations in speech to American Newspaper Publishers Association, New York City

Dec. 20, 1950, advocated American defenses be limited to western hemisphere, plus England in Europe, and Japan, Formosa, and Philippines in Pacific

1951, his book, *Addresses Upon the American Road, 1948–1950*, published by Stanford University Press

1951–1952, his memoirs published by Macmillan, New York City

•His autobiographical observations were published in three volumes: *Years of Adventure, 1874–1920; The Cabinet and the Presidency, 1920–1933;* and *The Great Depression, 1929–1941.*

July 7, 1952, addressed Republican national convention, Chicago, Ill.

•This was the last of his many convention speeches. He had spoken to all of the Republican conventions since he had left the White House.

July 24, 1953, appointed to 12-member Commission on Government Operations by Eisenhower

•He agreed to serve as chairman, Aug. 10. This second Hoover Commission functioned until June 30, 1955.

Aug. 10, 1954, celebrated his 80th birthday

•He was the fifth of six presidents who lived to be 80.

Dec. 11, 1955, urged Congress to establish office of administrative vice president

•He suggested that the post be filled by presidential appointment.

1955, his book, *Addresses Upon the American Road, 1950–1955*, published by Stanford University Press

1958, his book, *The Ordeal of Woodrow Wilson*, published by McGraw-Hill, New York City

Aug. 10, 1959, celebrated his 85th birthday

•He was the third of four presidents who lived to be 85.

1959–1961, his three-volume *An American Epic* published by H. Regnery, Chicago, Ill.

•This work concerned his relief activities during and after World War I.

1961, his book, *Addresses Upon the American Road, 1955–1960*, published by Caxton, Caldwell, Ida.

Aug. 10, 1962, Herbert Hoover Presidential Library and Museum dedicated, West Branch, Iowa

•The presidential library and museum was built by the Herbert Hoover Birthplace Foundation, with help from related institutions. The grounds and the buildings were deeded to the federal government in 1964. The library and the museum are administered by the National Archives and Records Service, General Services Administration. It is open daily except Thanksgiving, Christmas and New Year's Day, 9 A.M. to 5 P.M., and Sundays, 10 A.M. to 5 P.M. (Sept. 16 to May 15, 2 to 5 P.M.) Admission: adults, 50 cents; children under 15, free.

Aug. 10, 1964, celebrated his 90th birthday

•He was the second of two presidents who lived to be 90. The other was John Adams, who outlived him by 136 days.

DEATH

Date of death: Oct. 20, 1964

Place of death: New York, N.Y.

•Hoover was the last of three presidents who died in New York City.

•He was the last of eight presidents who died in New York.

•He was the sixth of eight presidents who lay in state in the Capitol Rotunda.

Age at death: 90 years, 71 days

•He lived 31 years, 230 days, after the completion of his term.

•He was the president who lived longest after the completion of his term.

Cause of death: Internal hemorrhage

Place of burial: West Branch, Iowa

•He was the only president who was buried in Iowa.

THE VICE PRESIDENT (31st)

Full name: Charles Curtis

•Curtis was the only vice president who shared the initials of a previous vice presi-

dent (Coolidge).
Date of birth: Jan. 25, 1860
Place of birth: on Indian ground, now North Topeka, Kan.
•He was the only vice president who was born in Kansas.
Religious denomination: Episcopalian
•He was the sixth of eight vice presidents who were Episcopalians.
Occupation: Lawyer
•He was admitted to the Kansas bar, 1881, practiced in Topeka; county attorney for Shawnee County, 1884–1888; member of House of Representatives, 1893–1907; member of Senate, 1907–1913 and 1915–1929.
•He was the 17th of 21 vice presidents who served in the House of Representatives before their terms of office.
•He was the 12th of 17 vice presidents who served in the Senate before their term of office.
•He was the seventh of ten vice presidents who served in both the House of Representatives and the Senate before their terms of office.
•He was the ninth of 12 vice presidents who served in both the House of Representatives and the Senate.
Term of office: Mar. 4, 1929, to Mar. 4, 1933 (4 years)
•Curtis was the 14th of 17 vice presidents who served four-year terms.
•He was the last vice president whose term of office ended on Mar. 4.
•Hoover and Curtis were the 33rd of 41 president-vice president teams.
•They were the second of two president-vice president teams that were defeated when they sought reelection. The other team was Van Buren and Johnson.
Age at inauguration: 69 years, 38 days
State represented: Kansas
•He was the only vice president who represented Kansas.
Political party: Republican
•He was the 13th of 15 vice presidents who were Republicans.
Occupation after term: Lawyer
Date of death: Feb. 8, 1936
Place of death: Washington, D.C.
•He was the last of six vice presidents who died in Washington.

Age at death: 76 years, 14 days
Place of burial: Topeka, Kan.
•He was the only vice president who was buried in Kansas.

THE CABINET

State: Henry Lewis Stimson of New York, Mar. 29, 1929, to Mar. 4, 1933
Treasury: Andrew William Mellon of Pennsylvania, Mar. 4, 1921, to Feb. 12, 1932
•Ogden Livingston Mills of New York, Feb. 13, 1932, to Mar. 4, 1933
War: James William Good of Illinois, Mar. 6, 1929, to Nov. 18, 1929
•Patrick Jay Hurley of Oklahoma, Dec. 9, 1929, to Mar. 3, 1933
Attorney General: William DeWitt Mitchell of Minnesota, Mar. 5, 1929, to Mar. 4, 1933
Navy: Charles Francis Adams of Massachusetts, Mar. 5, 1929, to Mar. 4, 1933
Postmaster General: Walter Folger Brown of Ohio, Mar. 5, 1929, to Mar. 4, 1933
Interior: Ray Lyman Wilbur of California, Mar. 5, 1929, to Mar. 4, 1933
Agriculture: Arthur Mastick Hyde of Missouri, Mar. 6, 1929, to Mar. 4, 1933
Commerce: Robert Patterson Lamont of Illinois, Mar. 5, 1929, to Aug. 7, 1932
•Roy Dikeman Chapin of Michigan, Aug. 8, 1932, to Mar. 4, 1933.
Labor: James John Davis of Pennsylvania, Mar. 5, 1921, to Nov. 30, 1930
•William Nuckles Doak of Virginia, Dec. 9, 1930, to Mar. 4, 1933.

THE SUPREME COURT

Chief Justice: Charles Evans Hughes of New York, appointed, Feb. 3, 1930; confirmed, Feb. 13, 1930
Associate Justices: John Johnston Parker of North Carolina, appointed, Mar. 22, 1930; rejected by Senate, May 7, 1930
•Owen Josephus Roberts of Pennsylvania, appointed, May 9, 1930; confirmed, May 20, 1930.
•Benjamin Nathan Cardozo of New York, appointed, Feb. 15, 1932; confirmed, Feb. 24, 1932.

Thirty-second President

FRANKLIN DELANO ROOSEVELT

Full name: Franklin Delano Roosevelt
•He was the second of two presidents named Franklin. The other was Pierce.
•He was the third of four presidents who had the same surname as a previous president. He and Theodore Roosevelt were fifth cousins.
•He was the 14th of 19 presidents who had middle initials or middle names.
Date of birth: Jan. 30, 1882
•He was the third of four presidents who were born in January.
Place of birth: Hyde Park, N.Y.
•He was the last of four presidents who were born in New York.
•His birthplace is on the New York-Albany Post Road (U.S. 9), two miles south of Hyde Park and four miles north of Poughkeepsie. It was designated a National Historic Site, Jan. 15, 1944. A gift from President Roosevelt, the site then consisted of 33 acres containing the home and outbuildings. Title to the area was accepted by the secretary of the interior, Nov. 21, 1945, when Mrs. Roosevelt and her children waived their life interests in the house and grounds. The site was formally dedicated, Apr. 12, 1946, the first anniversary of

President Roosevelt's death. Now containing 187 acres, it is administered by the National Park Service. It is open to the public daily, except Mondays and Tuesdays during the months of December through March. Admission: adults, 50 cents; children under 16, free.
•The Franklin D. Roosevelt Library and Museum, adjacent to the Roosevelt home, is administered by the National Archives and Records Service, General Services Administration. It contains, in addition to documents and manuscripts pertaining to the Roosevelt years, his ship models and marine print collections. It is open to the public daily except Christmas, 9 A.M. to 5 P.M. Admission: adults, 50 cents; children under 16, free.
Family lineage: Dutch and French-Dutch
•He was the only president who was of Dutch and French-Dutch ancestry.
Religious denomination: Episcopalian
•He was the last of nine presidents who were Episcopalians.
College: Harvard University, Cambridge, Mass.
•He was the fourth of five presidents who attended Harvard.

•He was the 23rd of 27 presidents who attended college.

Date of graduation: June 24, 1903, Bachelor of Arts

•He was the fourth of five presidents who were graduated from Harvard.

•He was the 17th of 21 presidents who were graduated from college.

Law School: Columbia Law School, New York, N.Y.

•He was the second of two presidents who went to Columbia Law. The other was Theodore Roosevelt.

•He was the sixth of nine presidents who attended law school.

•He was the fourth of six presidents who attended but were not graduated from law school.

PARENTS AND SIBLINGS

Father's name: James Roosevelt
Date of birth: July 16, 1828
Place of birth: Hyde Park, N.Y.
Occupations: Lawyer, financier
Date of death: Dec. 8, 1900
•Franklin was 18 years, 312 days old, when his father died
Place of death: New York, N.Y.
Age at death: 72 years, 145 days

Father's first wife: Rebecca Brien Howland Roosevelt
Date of birth: Jan. 15, 1831
Place of birth: *Unknown*
Date of marriage: 1853
Place of marriage: *Unknown*
Children: 1 son
•James Roosevelt was born in 1854.
•Roosevelt was the last of six presidents who had half brothers or half sisters.
Date of death: Aug. 21, 1876
Place of death: *Unknown*
Age at death: 45 years, 219 days

Mother's name: Sara Delano Roosevelt
Date of birth: Sept. 21, 1854
Place of birth: near Newburgh, N.Y.
Date of marriage: Oct. 7, 1880
•Roosevelt was the last of five presidents whose mothers were second wives.
Place of marriage: Algonac, family home near Newburgh, N.Y.
Children: 1 son
•Franklin Delano was born in 1882.

•He was his mother's only child.
•He was his father's second child.
•Roosevelt was the last of three presidents who came from families of two children.
•He was the third of five presidents who had male siblings only.
Date of death: Sept. 7, 1941
•Roosevelt was the eighth of ten presidents whose mothers lived to see their sons' inauguration or oath-taking days.
•Mrs. Roosevelt was the third of four mothers of presidents who attended the ceremonies.
Place of death: Hyde Park, N.Y.
Age at death: 86 years, 351 days

MARRIAGE

Date of marriage: Mar. 17, 1905
Place of marriage: New York, N.Y.
•Roosevelt was the last of five presidents who were married in New York City.
•He was the last of seven presidents who were married in New York.
Age at marriage: 23 years, 46 days
•He was the 24th of 27 presidents who were married in their twenties.
Years married: 40 years, 26 days

Wife's name: Anna Eleanor Roosevelt Roosevelt
•She was his fifth cousin once removed.
•She was the 28th of 33 first ladies.
•She was the 35th of 40 wives of presidents.
Date of birth: Oct. 11, 1884
•She was the last of four first ladies who were born in October.
•She was the last of six wives of presidents who were born in October.
Place of birth: New York, N.Y.
•She was the second of two first ladies who were born in New York City. The other was Elizabeth Monroe.
•She was the second of two wives of presidents who were born in New York City.
•She was the fifth of six first ladies who were born in New York.
•She was the sixth of seven wives of presidents who were born in New York.
Wife's mother: Anna Eleanor Hall Roosevelt
Wife's father: Elliott Roosevelt, sportsman
Age at marriage: 20 years, 157 days
•She was the 23rd of 26 first ladies who were married in their twenties.
•She was the 27th of 30 wives of presidents

who were married in their twenties.
Years younger than husband: 2 years, 254 days.
Children: 6; 5 sons, 1 daughter
•Anna Eleanor was born on May 3, 1906; James on Dec. 23, 1907; Franklin Delano on Mar. 18, 1909; Elliott on Sept. 23, 1910;/ Franklin Delano on Aug. 17, 1914; and John Aspinwell on Mar. 13, 1916. Her third child, Franklin Delano, died in infancy, Nov. 8, 1909.
•Roosevelt was the last of three presidents who had children who were born abroad. His fifth child, Franklin Delano, was born in Campobello, New Brunswick, Canada.
•He was the last of four presidents who had six children.
•He was the 18th of 19 presidents who had both male and female children.
•He was the 25th of 30 presidents who had children.
Years she survived her husband: 17 years, 209 days
•She was the 19th of 21 first ladies who survived their husbands.
•She was the 21st of 23 wives of presidents who survived their husbands.

Date of death: Nov. 7, 1962
Place of death: New York, N.Y.
•She was the second of two first ladies who died in New York City. The other was Lou Hoover.
•She was the last of five wives of presidents who died in New York City.
•She was the last of three first ladies who died in New York.
•She was the last of eight wives of presidents who died in New York.
Age at death: 78 years, 27 days
•She had celebrated her 75th birthday, Oct. 11, 1959.
•She was the 14th of 16 first ladies who lived to be 70.
•She was the 15th of 17 wives of presidents who lived to be 70.
•She was the 12th of 14 first ladies who lived to be 75.
•She was the 13th of 15 wives of presidents who lived to be 75.
Place of burial: Hyde Park, N.Y.
•She was the last of four first ladies who were buried in New York.
•She was the last of seven wives of presidents who were buried in New York.

EARLY YEARS

Winter, 1887, met President Cleveland, White House
•Roosevelt and his parents had spent most of the winter in Washington. Cleveland had offered his father a diplomatic post, which was declined. Just before the family returned to Hyde Park, his father took him to the White House. According to family legend, Cleveland patted him on the head and said, "My little man, I am making a strange wish for you. It is that you may never be President of the United States."
1891, attended school for brief time, Bad Nauheim, Germany
•His early education, both at his Hyde Park home and on trips abroad with his parents, was supervised by tutors and governesses. His family made frequent trips to England, France, and Germany.
September, 1896, entered Groton School, Groton, Mass.
•He was graduated from Groton in June, 1899.
September, 1900, entered Harvard University, Cambridge, Mass.

Dec. 8, 1900, his father died
June 24, 1903, was graduated from Harvard University
•A member of the class of 1904, he completed the requirements for a bachelor's degree in three years. He remained at Harvard for an extra year in order to serve as editor-in-chief of the Harvard *Crimson* and studied history and economics in the graduate school.
September, 1904, entered Columbia Law School, New York City
•He attended Columbia Law School until June, 1907.
•He was the 23rd of 26 presidents who studied law.
Mar. 17, 1905, married Anna Eleanor Roosevelt, New York City
•The bride was given away by her uncle, President Theodore Roosevelt. The date of the wedding had been determined by the fact that "Uncle Ted" planned to be in New York City that day to review the St. Patrick's Day parade.
June, 1905, with wife, toured Europe

•At the end of his first year in law school, he and his wife departed on a honeymoon trip and visited England, France, Italy, Switzerland, and Germany. In the course of the trip, he received word that he had failed two courses at Columbia, which he made up by reexamination in the fall.

May 3, 1906, his first daughter born
•The girl was named Anna Eleanor Roosevelt.

Spring, 1907, admitted to bar, New York City
•Having passed the bar examination, he decided against completing his studies at Columbia Law School.
•He was the 22nd of 23 presidents who were lawyers.

1907, engaged as junior clerk by law firm of Carter, Ledyard and Milburn, New York City

Dec. 23, 1907, his first son born
•The boy was named James Roosevelt.

Fall, 1908, moved into house at 49 East 65th Street, New York City
•His mother had built two adjoining houses at Nos. 47 and 49. She occupied No. 47 and presented No. 49 to her son and his wife.

Mar. 18, 1909, his second son born
•The boy, who was named Franklin Delano, died, Nov, 8.

Sept. 23, 1910, his third son born
•The boy was named Elliott Roosevelt.

Nov. 8, 1910, elected to New York state senate
•He took his seat in January, 1911. During his first term as state senator, he met Louis McHenry Howe, Albany correspondent for the New York *Herald*, who became his political adviser and confidant.

Nov. 28, 1911, degree of Master Mason conferred by Holland Lodge No. 8, New York City
•He was the 12th of 13 presidents who were Masons.

Nov. 5, 1912, reelected as state senator

NATIONAL PROMINENCE

April, 1913, appointed assistant secretary of navy by Wilson
•Roosevelt served under Secretary Daniels until 1920.
•He was the second of two presidents who served as assistant secretaries of navy. The other was Theodore Roosevelt.

Aug. 17, 1914, his fourth son born
•The boy was named Franklin Delano Roosevelt.

September, 1914, defeated in Democratic primary for Senate by Ambassador James W. Gerard
•Gerard, ambassador to Germany, won the primary by better than two-to-one.

Mar. 13, 1916, his fifth son born
•The boy was named John Aspinwall Roosevelt.

1917, attempted to enlist in navy
•His request for active service was denied by Wilson, who told Daniels, "Neither you nor I nor Franklin Roosevelt has the right to select the place of service to which our country has assigned us."

1918, declined to run for governor of New York

July 9, 1918, departed for tour of European naval bases
•He returned in September, having inspected naval bases in England, France, and Italy. He contracted double pneumonia and was carried ashore in New York City on a stretcher.

October, 1918, again requested active service
•Wilson again refused and informed him of the German armistice offer by Prince Max of Baden.

Jan. 5, 1919, departed for Europe
•His second trip to Europe as assistant secretary was to oversee the dismantling of the naval establishment.
•He and Mrs. Roosevelt learned of the death of Theodore Roosevelt while at sea.

Feb. 15, 1919, sailed for U.S. aboard *George Washington* with Wilson
•They arrived in Boston, Feb. 24.

July 6, 1920, nominated for vice president, Democratic national convention, San Francisco, Cal.

Aug. 6, 1920, resigned as assistant secretary of navy

Nov. 2, 1920, election day
• *See* Election of 1920, pages 351–352.

1920, returned to law practice
•He became a partner in the firm of Emmet, Marvin and Roosevelt, New York City. He also took a position as vice presi-

dent in charge of the New York office of the Fidelity and Deposit Company of Maryland, a surety bond firm.

Aug. 10–11, 1921, stricken by anterior poliomyelitis, Campobello, New Brunswick, Canada

• While cruising with his family, Aug. 10, he noticed a fire on a small island. He and his children beat out the flames. Afterwards, he went for a swim in the ice-cold waters of the bay. When he returned to his summer home, he found that the mail had arrived; in his wet swimsuit, he sat and read the letters and newspapers. Though he felt a chill, he was so tired that he decided not to dress and went directly to bed. The next morning his left leg would not operate correctly. When he could feel no reaction in either leg, doctors were summoned.

Aug. 12, 1921, examined by Dr. William W. Keen

• Dr. Keen, who was vacationing in the area, was summoned to diagnose and he concluded that a blood clot from a sudden congestion had settled in the lower spinal cord. He prescribed massage, stating that recovery would probably occur within a matter of months. Several days later, Keen altered his diagnosis from a blood clot to a lesion in the spinal cord. He submitted a bill for $600. The disease was not determined as poliomyelitis until after examination by other doctors.

• In 1893, Dr. Keen had assisted in the secret operation for cancer of President Cleveland.

June 26, 1924, made nominating speech for Alfred E. Smith, Democratic national convention, New York City

• This was the first "Happy Warrior" speech.

October, 1924, made first visit to Warm Springs, Ga.

• On the recommendation of George Foster Peabody, the banker and philanthropist, Roosevelt decided to try the benefits of treatment in the warm waters of the springs. He had found that swimming was the best exercise inasmuch as water relieved the weight from his legs. "Water got me into this fix," he is reported to have said, "water will get me out again!"

1924, formed new law partnership with D. Basil O'Connor, New York City

1926, declined to run for Senate

1928, his book, *The Happy Warrior, Alfred E. Smith*, published, Houghton Mifflin, Boston, Mass.

• This was the only campaign biography written by a president.

• He was the 16th of 21 presidents who wrote books that were published during their lifetimes.

June 28, 1928, nominated Alfred E. Smith, Democratic national convention, Houston, Tex.

• This was the second "Happy Warrior" speech.

Sept. 25, 1928, nominated for governor, Democratic state convention, Rochester, N.Y.

• Convinced that Smith would lose to Hoover and that running for governor was political suicide, Roosevelt had gone to Warm Springs to emphasize his intention to concentrate on the recovery of the use of his legs. Smith prevailed upon him to run with the argument that no other Democrat could hold the state.

Nov. 6, 1928, elected governor of New York

• He won by about 25,000 votes, while Smith was losing the state by 100,000.

Jan. 1, 1929, took office as governor

• He was the last of four presidents who served as governors of New York.

• He was the last of 13 presidents who served as state governors.

1929, elected to Phi Beta Kappa, Harvard University, Cambridge, Mass.

• He was the last of five presidents who were alumni members of Phi Beta Kappa.

• He was the last of 11 presidents who were members of Phi Beta Kappa.

Nov. 4, 1930, reelected governor

• He won reelection by what was then the largest majority in the history of the state, 725,000.

July 1, 1932, nominated for president, Democratic national convention, Chicago, Ill.

• He was nominated on the fourth ballot.

July 2, 1932, flew to Chicago to accept nomination

• He set a precedent by appearing at the convention to accept the nomination rather than waiting several weeks for the formal ceremony. A ten-passenger three-engine plane flew him from Albany to Chicago, with stops for fuel in Buffalo and Cleveland. In his acceptance speech, he said his decision to come to the convention might have been "unprecedented and unusual, but these are unprecedented and unusual times." In summing up his program, he declared, "I pledge you, I pledge myself, to a new deal for the American people."

Nov. 8, 1932, election day
• *See* Election of 1932, below.

Jan. 9, 1933, presidential electors cast ballots
• He received 472 of the 531 electoral votes from the 48 states.
• *See* Election of 1932, below.

Feb. 8, 1933, electoral vote tabulated by Congress
• Roosevelt and Garner were officially declared elected.

Feb. 15, 1933, his assassination attempted by Giuseppe Zangara, Miami, Fla.
• Zangara, an unemployed bricklayer, fired six shots from about 12 yards away. Roosevelt, who had just finished speaking to a crowd in Bay Front Park, was sitting in the back seat of his open touring car. He was uninjured, but five others were wounded, including Mayor Anton Cermak of Chicago. Cermak died, Mar. 6. Zangara was captured at the scene of the assassination attempt, was tried, and found guilty of the murder of Cermak. Zangara was electrocuted at Raiford, Fla., Mar. 20.
• This was the only assassination attempt on a president-elect.

ELECTION OF 1932

Socialist Labor party, convened, Apr. 30, at New York City, nominated Verne L. Reynolds of New York for president, John W. Aiken of Massachusetts for vice president.

Socialist party, convened, May 21, at Milwaukee, Wis., nominated Norman Thomas of New York for president, James Hudson Maurer of Pennsylvania for vice president.

Communist party, convened, May 28, at Chicago, Ill., nominated William Zebulon Foster of New York for president, James William Ford of Alabama for vice president.

Republican party, convened, June 14, at Chicago, Ill., nominated Herbert Clark Hoover of California for president, Charles Curtis of Kansas for vice president.
• This was the 20th Republican national convention. It was the 11th Republican convention held in Chicago; it was the 16th

major convention held in Chicago.

Democratic party, convened, June 27, at Chicago, Ill., nominated Franklin Delano Roosevelt of New York for president, John Nance Garner of Texas for vice president.
• This was the 26th Democratic national convention. It was the fifth Democratic convention held in Chicago; it was the 17th major convention held in Chicago.

Prohibition party, convened, July 5, at Indianapolis, Ind., nominated William David Upshaw of Georgia for president, Frank Stewart Regan of Illinois for vice president.

Farmer Labor party, convened, July 9, at Omaha, Neb., nominated Jacob Sechler Coxey of Ohio for president, Julius J. Reiter of Minnesota for vice president.

Liberty party, convened, Aug. 17, at St. Louis, Mo., nominated William Hope Harvey of Arkansas for president, Frank B. Hemenway of Washington for vice president.

Election day, Tuesday, Nov. 8, 1932
Popular vote: 39,754,675
    Roosevelt, 22,829,501
    Hoover, 15,760,684
    Thomas, 884,649
    Foster, 103,253
    Upshaw, 81,872
    Harvey, 53,247
    Reynolds, 34,038
    Coxey, 7,431
Electoral vote: 531, 48 states
• Roosevelt, 472, 42 states
  (Alabama, 11; Arizona, 3; Arkansas, 9; California, 22; Colorado, 6; Florida, 7; Georgia, 12; Idaho, 4; Illinois, 29; Indiana, 14; Iowa, 11; Kansas, 9; Kentucky, 11; Louisiana, 10; Maryland, 8; Massachusetts, 17; Michigan, 19; Minnesota, 11; Mississippi, 9; Missouri, 15; Montana, 4; Nebraska, 7; Nevada, 3; New Jersey, 16; New Mexico, 3; New York, 47; North Carolina, 13; North Dakota, 4; Ohio, 26; Oklahoma, 11; Oregon, 5; Rhode Island, 4; South Carolina, 8; South Dakota, 4; Tennessee, 11; Texas, 23; Utah, 4; Virginia, 11; Washington, 8; West Virginia, 8; Wisconsin, 12; Wyoming, 3)
• Hoover, 59, six states
  (Connecticut, 8; Delaware, 3; Maine, 5; New Hampshire, 4; Pennsylvania, 36; Vermont, 3)

THE PRESIDENT (32nd)

Term of office: Mar. 4, 1933, to Apr. 12, 1945 (12 years, 39 days)
• Roosevelt was the 11th of 12 presidents who were elected to second terms.
• He was the 13th of 16 presidents who served more than one term.
• He was the only president who was elected to and served three terms.
• He was the only president who served more than two terms.
• He was the only president who was elected to a fourth term.
State represented: New York
• He was the sixth of eight presidents who represented New York.
Political party: Democratic
• He was the ninth of 12 presidents who were Democrats.

Congresses: 73rd, 74th, 75th, 76th, 77th, 78th, 79th
• He was the only president who served with more than four congresses.
Administrations: 37th, 38th, 39th, 40th
• He was the only president who had more than two administrations.
Age at inauguration: 51 years, 33 days
• He was the 19th of 21 presidents who were younger than their vice presidents. Roosevelt was 13 years, 69 days younger than Garner.
Inauguration day: Saturday, Mar. 4, 1933
• Roosevelt took the oath of office, administered by Chief Justice Charles Evans Hughes, on the east portico of the Capitol.
• This was the first of three inaugurations at which Hughes officiated.

THE 37th ADMINISTRATION

1933

"The Hundred Days"

Mar. 4, appointed his first secretary of state, Cordell Hull; his first secretary of treasury, William H. Woodin; his first secretary of war, George H. Dern; his first attorney general, Homer S. Cummings; his first secretary of navy, Claude A. Swanson; his first postmaster general, James A. Farley; his only secretary of interior, Harold L. Ickes, his first secretary of agriculture, Henry A. Wallace; his first secretary of commerce, Daniel C. Roper; and his only secretary of labor, Frances Perkins
• Woodin took office, Mar. 5.
• Miss Perkins was the first of two female members of the cabinet. The other was Oveta Culp Hobby.
Mar. 6–9, bank holiday
• He issued a proclamation, Mar. 5, which declared a four-day bank holiday. All transactions by banks, trust companies, credit unions, and building and loan associations were suspended. An embargo was placed on the export of gold, silver, and currency.
Mar. 8, held first press conference
• He agreed to meet with the press twice weekly. The written question rule, instituted in 1921, was abolished. Direct quotation was still not permitted—except in

rare instances—but paraphrasing was allowed.
• This was the first of his 998 press conferences. During his first term, he held 337 such conferences.
Mar. 9, first session of 73rd Congress
• The administration controlled both the Senate and the House of Representatives. The Democrats gained 12 Senate and 97 House seats. The Senate (96 members) consisted of 59 Democrats, 36 Republicans, and one Farmer Laborite. The House (435) consisted of 313 Democrats, 117 Republicans, and five Farmer Laborites.
Mar. 9, signed Emergency Banking Relief Act
• This act, which gave him broad discretionary powers over banking and currency, was introduced, passed, and signed in less than eight hours. The secretary of the treasury was authorized to call in all gold and gold certificates; hoarding and exporting gold were prohibited.
Mar. 12, broadcast his first "fireside chat"
• This was the first of his eight radio reports to the nation during his first term. The phrase, "fireside chat," has been attributed to radio commentator Robert Trout and Harry C. Butcher, then the Washington manager of the Columbia Broadcasting System and later naval aide to General Dwight D. Eisenhower. In this first radio

report, Roosevelt explained, in the simplest terms, what was being done to end the financial emergency.
- "Everybody understood him," quipped Will Rogers, "even the bankers."

Mar. 20, signed economy act
- This act cut veterans' pensions, reduced federal salaries by 15 percent, and reorganized several government agencies. Opposed by a large bloc of Democrats in the House of Representatives, the bill passed with the aid of 69 Republican votes, 266–138, Mar. 11. It passed in the Senate, 62–13, Mar. 15.
- He believed this act would save $500,000,000; the actual saving was about $240,000,000.

Mar. 22, signed beer-wine revenue act
- This act amended the Volstead Act of 1919, and legalized the sale of wine and beer that contained no more than 3.2 percent of alcohol. The act went into effect, Apr. 7.

Mar. 27, issued executive order abolishing federal farm board
- All federal agricultural agencies were consolidated in the Farm Credit Administration.

Mar. 31, signed Civilian Conservation Corps Reconstruction Relief Act
- This act created 250,000 road construction, soil erosion, flood control, national park, and reforestation jobs for young men between the ages of 18 and 25. Those employed received $30 weekly—$25 of which was sent to their families. The CCC employed more than 2,000,000 by the end of 1941.

Apr. 5, extended deadline for turning in gold coins and certificates to May 1
- Anyone who had coins or certificates valued at $100 or more was required to exchange them for other money. As of Apr. 5, about $630,000,000 in gold or certificates had been turned in. However, $600,000,000 in certificates plus $400,000,000 in bullion and coins still were hoarded. On May 1, the hoarded total was still about $700,000,000.

Apr. 12, his nominee as minister to Denmark, Ruth Bryan Owen, confirmed by Senate
- Mrs. Owen, the daughter of William Jennings Bryan, was the first female American diplomatic officer.

Apr. 19, gold standard abandoned

- This brought about a decline in the dollar value abroad, but commodity, stock, and silver prices increased on American exchanges.

Apr. 21, conferred with Prime Minister J. Ramsay MacDonald of Great Britain, White House
- This was the first of a series of conversations on world economic conditions with MacDonald, Premier Edouard Herriot of France, and representatives of Canada, Argentina, Italy, and numerous other countries. The talks extended over a period of months.

May 7, promised "partnership" of government and industry
- In a fireside chat, he said the government would use the inflation legislation only to permit debtors to repay "in the same kind of dollar which they borrowed."

May 12, signed Federal Emergency Relief Act
- This act created a national relief system, administrated by Harry L. Hopkins. Half of the $500,000,000 appropriation was allotted to the states; half was distributed on the basis of $1 federal aid for every $3 of state or local funds spent on relief or unemployed.

May 13, signed Agricultural Adjustment Act
- This act was designed to raise farm prices by cash subsidies or rental payments in exchange for curtailment of production and by establishing parity prices for certain basic commodities. Funds came from taxes levied on farm product processors; this feature of the AAA was declared unconstitutional by the Supreme Court, 1936.

May 16, proposed international disarmament agreement, treaty of nonaggression, to 54 nations
- He also sent an explanatory special message to Congress.

May 18, signed Tennessee Valley Authority Act
- This act authorized the TVA to construct dam and power plants and to produce and sell electric power and nitrogen fertilizers in a seven-state region. This ended the controversy that had extended over 13 years about the disposition of the $165,000,000 wartime power and munitions plant at Muscle Shoals.

May 27, signed Federal Securities Act
- This act required most new securities is-

sued to be registered with the Federal Trade Commission.

May 27, authorized postal savings system to purchase $100,000,000 worth of government bonds

June 5, abandonment of gold standard completed
- He signed the gold repeal joint resolution —which cancelled the gold clause in all federal and private obligations—making all debts and contractual agreements payable in legal tender.

June 13, signed Home Owners Refinancing Act
- This act authorized the Home Owners Loan Corporation (HOLC) to refinance nonfarm mortgage debts. HOLC made loans on about one million mortgages by June, 1936.

June 16, signed National Industrial Recovery Act
- This act created the National Recovery Administration (NRA) and established regulatory codes for control of numerous industries. Employers were exempted from antitrust action; employees were guaranteed collective bargaining and minimum wages and hours. The second section of the act established the Public Works Administration (PWA), which provided employment by public works construction.
- NRA affected five hundred industrial fields and twenty-two million employees; PWA spent more than $4,000,000,000 on thirty-four thousand public works. Hugh S. Johnson was appointed administrator of NRA; Secretary of Interior Ickes was appointed administrator of PWA.
- In 1935, the NIRA was declared unconstitutional by the Supreme Court.

June 16, signed banking act of 1933
- The Glass-Steagall Act created the Federal Bank Deposit Insurance Corporation, which guaranteed bank deposits under $5,000, separated investment from commercial banking to halt speculation with deposits, and widened the powers of the Federal Reserve Board.

June 16, signed Farm Credit Act
- This act reorganized agricultural credit activities to conform with his executive order of Mar. 27, and consolidated the Farm Credit Administration, the federal farm board, and the federal farm loan board into a single agency.

June 16, signed emergency railroad transportation act
- This act created the office of federal coordinator of transportation, repealed the "recapture" clause of the transportation act of 1920, and gave the Interstate Commerce Commission supervision of railroad holding companies.

June 16, allocated $238,000,000 to navy department for construction of 32 new vessels

June 16, first session of 73rd Congress adjourned

June 16, pocket vetoed amendment to federal farm loan act
- This was the first of his 635 vetoes, the first of his 263 pocket vetoes.
- Roosevelt exercised the veto power more often than any other president. However, Cleveland vetoed 583 bills during his eight years in office.

June 16, departed on first vacation
- He took a train to Boston, Mass., where he boarded the *Amberjack II* and set sail for Campobello, New Brunswick, Canada.

- "The Hundred Days" had ended.

June 29, arrived at Campobello
- He was the second of seven presidents who visited Canada while in office.
- He was the sixth of 11 presidents who traveled outside the U.S. while in office.
- This was the first of his seven visits to Canada while in office.

July 3, refused to commit U.S. to gold standard
- In a message to the World Monetary and Economic Conference, London, he said the U.S. would not support a currency-stabilizing program proposed by the gold-bloc nations, France, Belgium, The Netherlands, Italy, Poland, and Switzerland. He added that the proposal was "a purely artificial and temporary experiment, affecting the monetary exchange of a few nations only," and suggested that the conference turn its attention to "more real and permanent financial stability."

July 9, signed cotton textile code
- This code abolished child labor, established the 40-hour week as of July 17, and fixed the minimum weekly wage at $12 in the South and $13 in the North.

July 11, appointed council to coordinate rehabilitation programs
- The council consisted of the cabinet and

the heads of the special federal agencies established by Congress. The nation was divided into ten regional zones.

July 12, ordered Postmaster General Farley to place all postmasters under civil service rules

July 14, issued executive order imposing processing tax of 4.2 cents per pound on cotton, effective, Aug. 1

July 16, issued executive orders applying cotton textile code to manufacture of rayon, cotton thread, and silk

July 19, ended vacation at Campobello

• He boarded a U.S. destroyer at Campobello and transferred in American waters to the new cruiser, *U.S.S. Indianapolis*, so as to observe the vessel's speed test run down the Atlantic coast.

July 24, made NRA appeal in fireside chat

• He asked the people to sign up individually under the emergency industrial codes. Blanks were mailed to five million employers.

Aug. 1, NRA blue eagle made official appearance

• The emblem was a sign of acceptance by employers of the NRA codes on work hours and wages.

Aug. 3, approved contracts for naval construction program

• The navy department awarded contracts to private shipyards for 21 ships. An additional 16 ships were to be built in federal navy yards. The contracts totalled $130,-000,000.

Aug. 5, appointed National Labor Board

• He appointed Senator Robert F. Wagner of New York as chairman of the board, which was empowered to decide collective bargaining disagreements.

Aug. 10, issued executive order to federal contractees to conform to NRA codes or face cancellation

Aug. 19, signed NRA codes for steel, oil, and lumber industries

Aug. 27, signed code for automobile industry

Aug. 29, issued executive order modifying embargo on newly-mined gold to permit restricted sale and export at world price

Sept. 10, sent warships to Cuba

• Cuba, beset by economic chaos due to the collapse of sugar prices, had been the scene of unrest for years. Dictator Gerardo Machado was forced out of office, Aug. 12, and a second army coup turned out his

successor, Carlos Manuel de Cespedes, Sept. 5. The U.S. refused to recognize the government of Ramon Grau San Martin, who became president, Sept. 10. Eight destroyers and 15 other U.S. naval vessels were in Cuban waters, Sept. 15.

Sept. 18, signed code for bituminous coal industry

Sept. 21, issued executive order authorizing AAA to buy $75,000,000 worth of surplus clothing materials and food for distribution among unemployed

Oct. 2, visited Century of Progress Exposition, Chicago, Ill.

• While in Chicago to attend the World's Fair, he also addressed the American Legion national convention.

Oct. 3, signed codes for banking, shoe, retail motor vehicle, and retail lumber industries

Oct. 7, removed Republican member of Federal Trade Commission, William E. Humphrey

• In July he had requested the resignation of Humphrey, who refused. Humphrey had been appointed to a seven-year term in 1931 by Hoover.

Oct. 9, conferred with President Harmodio Arias of Panama, White House

• He and Arias announced in a joint statement, Oct. 17, the termination of U.S. government practices that had interfered with native business in Panama.

Oct. 18, issued executive order organizing Commodity Credit Corporation

• The agency, organized under the AAA, was authorized to use $3,000,000 of RFC funds for loans to farmers on crops, principally cotton.

Oct. 20, released correspondence with Mikhail Kalinin, president of the Central Executive Committee of the U.S.S.R.

• He had called Kalinin, Oct. 10, and had invited a Russian representative to discuss ending "the present abnormal relations" between the two countries. Kalinin accepted the invitation, Oct. 17.

Oct. 22, announced new gold policy

• In a fireside chat, he announced that he had authorized the Reconstruction Finance Corporation to establish a government market for U.S. newly-mined gold and to buy or sell gold on the world market. The new gold policy went into effect, Oct. 25. The price set by the government was $31.36 per ounce. The gold value of the dollar was marked at about 66 cents.

Oct. 23, issued executive order revising retail code
•Local retail stores and local service industries that employed fewer than five persons in communities of twenty-five hundred population or less were exempted from the retail code and reemployment agreement.
Nov. 7, received Maxim M. Litvinov, Soviet commissar of foreign affairs, White House
Nov. 8, appointed Harry L. Hopkins as head of Civil Works Administration
•The CWA, an emergency unemployment relief program, was established to place 4,-000,000 unemployed persons on federal, state, and local work projects. The agency spent $933,000,000 on 180,000 projects and was terminated in March, 1934.
Nov. 15, granted leave of absence to Secretary of Treasury Woodin
•Woodin was in ill health.
•Roosevelt appointed Henry Morgenthau, Jr., governor of the Farm Credit Administration, as acting secretary; Undersecretary Dean Acheson resigned.
Nov. 15, signed code for air transport industry
Nov. 16, recognized U.S.S.R.
•The establishment of diplomatic relations was effected by an exchange of letters with Litvinov.
Nov. 17, signed codes for newsprint, paper and pulp, hotel, food, and grocery industries
Nov. 27, signed code for motion picture industry, Warm Springs, Ga.
Nov. 27, signed temporary code for liquor industry
•This code, which was to be administered by the AAA, placed the liquor industry under virtual government control.
Dec. 5, 21st Amendment declared ratified
•This repealed the 18th Amendment, the liquor prohibition amendment.
•See Constitution, pages 644–645.
Dec. 20, accepted resignation of Secretary of Treasury Woodin, effective, Dec. 31
Dec. 20, appointed his second secretary of treasury, Henry Morgenthau, Jr.
•Morgenthau took office, Jan. 1, 1934.
Dec. 21, issued executive order providing for purchase of newly-mined U.S. silver
•Half of the silver was to be coined, the other half deposited in the treasury.
Dec. 24, restored civil rights to fifteen hundred persons who had served prison terms

for violations of Selective Service Act during World War I
Dec. 30, issued proclamation relinquishing federal control of state banks not members of federal reserve system
•The government continued control of transactions in foreign exchange and gold payments.

1934

Jan. 3, second session of 73rd Congress
Jan. 3, delivered his first State of the Union message to Congress
Jan. 4, sent budget message to Congress
•He estimated that total expenditures for the fiscal year ending June 30 would be $10,569,000,000, with receipts of about $3,260,000,000. He forecast that the 1935 deficit would drop to about $2,000,000,-000.
Jan. 8, received credentials of first U.S.S.R. ambassador, Alexander Troyanovsky
Jan. 11, signed liquor tax act
Jan. 15, sent special message to Congress requesting additional gold legislation
•He asked for authority to impound all gold in the treasury and to devalue the dollar to a maximum of 60 cents and a minimum of 50 cents.
Jan. 30, first Birthday Balls held
•Funds raised at the balls were donated to the Georgia Warm Springs Foundation. He accepted a check for $1,000,000 on behalf of the infantile paralysis foundation, May 9.
Jan. 30, signed gold reserve act
Jan. 31, issued proclamation setting price of gold and value of dollar
•Gold was priced at $35 per fine troy ounce, less one-fourth of one percent mint charge; the value of the dollar was fixed at 59.06 cents.
•The government took title to all gold held by federal reserve banks, in return for which new gold certificates were given the banks. The dollar profit on this gold, estimated at about $2,793,000,000, was credited to the treasury. A fund of $2,000,000,-000 of this profit was set up to stabilize the dollar on the international exchange and to support the government bond market.
Jan. 31, signed Farm Mortgage Refinancing Act
•This act established the Federal Farm Mortgage Corporation, which was author-

ized to issue $2,000,000,000 in bonds to further the refinancing of farm debts.

Feb. 2, issued executive order establishing export-import bank for trade with U.S.S.R.

Feb. 9, ordered cancellation of all airmail contracts as of Feb. 19, assigned army to carry mails until new contracts drawn

Feb. 15, signed civil works emergency relief act

• This act authorized $950,000,000 for a civil works and direct relief program under the Federal Emergency Relief Administration (FERA) until the end of the fiscal year of 1935. About 2,500,000 unemployed were assisted before direct relief was returned to state and local agencies in January, 1935.

Feb. 17, signed code for daily newspapers

Feb. 23, signed crop loan act

• This act authorized the Farm Credit Administration to extend crop production and harvesting loans during 1934. About $37,900,000 was loaned to agricultural producers.

Feb. 27, issued executive order establishing NRA board of review

• He appointed Clarence Darrow as board chairman.

Mar. 1, vetoed relief bill

• This was the first of his 342 vetoes of private relief bills.

Mar. 5, outlined program to create one million new jobs

• He told a Washington audience of business and industrial leaders that the new jobs could be created if a general ten percent increase in wages was coupled with a ten percent decrease in hours.

Mar. 9, issued executive order establishing export-import bank for trade with Cuba

Mar. 15, issued executive order excluding from future government contracts all companies and individuals that did not certify compliance with NRA codes

Mar. 20, signed code for grain exchanges

Mar. 27, signed naval parity act

• This act authorized the construction of one hundred naval vessels and one thousand aircraft over a five-year period. Congress did not appropriate sufficient funds.

Mar. 27, vetoed independent executive offices bill

Mar. 28, independent executive offices act passed over his veto

• This act granted $228,000,000 in additional allowances to World War I veterans and $125,000,000 in salary increases to government employees.

• This was the first of his nine vetoes that were overridden.

Mar. 31, signed Philippine Independence Act

• This act provided for independence of the islands in 1944, after formation of a transitional government with a Filipino chief executive. Acceptance was voted by the Filipino legislature, Apr. 30.

Apr. 1, conducted Easter services aboard Astor yacht, off Great Abaco Island, Bahamas

• He was a guest aboard the yacht, *Nourmahal*, owned by Vincent Astor. The religious services were attended by the officers and men of the destroyer, *U.S.S. Ellis*, as well as by Astor's guests and crew.

• Roosevelt did not go ashore at Nassau, when the yacht visited the port, Mar. 30.

Apr. 7, signed Jones-Connally Act, at sea

• This act added to the list of agricultural commodities subject to the AAA act, including cattle, grain sorghums, barley, peanuts, and flax.

Apr. 13, returned to Washington, D.C.

• He was met at the railroad station by two hundred members of the House of Representatives and 30 senators, while a brass band played "Happy Days Are Here Again." The representatives had marched to the station from the Capitol, but the senators, who refused to march, arrived individually.

Apr. 13, signed debt default act

• This act prohibited loans to foreign governments that defaulted on war debts.

Apr. 14, issued executive order providing for approval of all budgets and assessments of code authorities by Hugh S. Johnson

Apr. 17, conferred with President Stenjo Vincent of Haiti about ending U.S. financial control of country

• The Haitian financial situation was stabilized with U.S. aid. American troops were withdrawn, Aug. 6.

Apr. 21, signed cotton control act

• This act authorized the fixing of a limitation on the cotton crop and provided for state and county quotas. A departure from the voluntary principle of the AAA, the act authorized a tax of not less than five cents a pound and as much as 50 percent of the value of excess cotton prior to being sent to market.

Apr. 28, signed home owners loan act

•This act guaranteed the principal and interest of the $2,000,000,000 in Home Loan Bank Corporation bonds authorized for refinancing of home mortgages.

May 9, signed Jones-Costigan Act

•This act added sugar cane and sugar beets to the list of agricultural commodities subject to the AAA act and provided for a processing tax on sugar, effective, June 8. A limitation on these sugar crops was authorized, and the secretary of agriculture was empowered to impose quotas on sugar imports.

•The tax features of this act were invalidated by the Supreme Court, 1936.

May 18, signed crime control acts

•Six new crime laws resulted, which for the first time empowered the government to punish persons who assaulted federal agents on duty, who crossed state lines to evade prosecution or to avoid giving testimony, who incited or participated in federal penal institution riots, who robbed member banks of the federal reserve system, or who sent extortion or kidnap notes across state lines. The death penalty was authorized for convicted kidnappers who had failed to return their victims unharmed, and the passage of seven days became presumptive evidence that a kidnapping victim had been transported across a state line.

May 24, signed Municipal Bankruptcy Act

May 28, issued proclamation prohibiting sale of arms or munitions to Bolivia or Paraguay, engaged in Chaco War

May 30, gave Memorial Day address, Gettysburg, Pa.

May 31, reviewed fleet off entrance to New York harbor

•Aboard the *U.S.S. Indianapolis*, he reviewed the fleet of 81 warships south of Ambrose Channel, which is 25 miles from New York City. The naval line stretched for 12 miles and took 90 minutes to pass. After the review, the *Indianapolis* led the fleet into the Hudson River.

June 6, signed Federal Securities Exchange Act

•This act established the Securities and Exchange Commission (SEC), and authorized the licensing of stock exchanges. The SEC was empowered to regulate trading in securities. The Federal Reserve Board was empowered to set margin requirements.

June 7, signed corporate bankruptcy act

June 12, signed airmail act

June 12, signed reciprocal tariff act

June 12, signed farm mortgage foreclosure act

June 13, announced only partial payments were contemplated in suggestion to Great Britain for settling war debt with goods in kind

•Great Britain announced the suspension of war debt installment payments to U.S., June 4. The British said they could not accept the goods in kind suggestion, June 27. Only Finland paid her war debt, $166,538, which was the total received by the U.S. of about $175,000,000 owed in new obligations and $300,000,000 in accrued unpaid accounts, June 15.

June 14, directed issuance of silver certificates

•The silver certificates were to be issued against the accumulated stocks of that metal. The value of silver was placed at $1.29 an ounce.

June 15, signed national guard act

•This act established the national guard as part of the army in wartime or in a national emergency declared by Congress.

June 18, signed free zone act

•This act established free zones in New York City and other ports.

June 18, second session of 73rd Congress adjourned

June 19, signed Communications Act of 1934

•This act established the Federal Communications Commission (FCC), which replaced the Federal Radio Commission. The act transferred control of communications from the ICC to the FCC, which was authorized to regulate interstate and foreign telegraph, cable, and radio.

June 19, signed silver purchase act

•This act authorized the purchase of that amount of silver that would equal one-third of the value of the treasury's gold holdings.

June 19, signed labor disputes joint resolution

•This resolution established the Labor Relations Board, which superseded the NLB.

June 20, received honorary degree of doctor of laws, Yale University, New Haven, Conn.

June 26, White House statement on pocket vetoes

•He desired to take a more affirmative position than just withholding his signature from bills passed in the final ten days of a session. Therefore, he wrote "Disapproved and signature withheld" on each bill and appended brief statements giving reasons for disapproval.

June 27, signed Railroad Retirement Act of 1934
• This act was invalidated by the Supreme Court, 1935.

June 27, signed Railway Labor Act
• This act established a national railroad adjustment board and upheld the rights of workers to organize and bargain collectively.

June 28, signed tobacco control act

June 28, signed Federal Farm Bankruptcy Act
• This act was invalidated by the Supreme Court, 1935.

June 28, signed national housing act
• This act established the Federal Housing Administration (FHA), which insured loans for new construction, repairs, and improvements of farm properties and small business plants. The act increased HOLC borrowing power by $3,000,000,000.

June 29, issued executive order prohibiting shipment of arms or military equipment to Cuba except under state department license

June 30, issued executive order abolishing NRA board of review

June 30, appointed members of Labor Relations Board, Securities and Exchange Commission, Federal Communications Commission

July 1, began cruise to Hawaii
• He boarded the new cruiser, *U.S.S. Houston*, off Annapolis, Md., accompanied by two of his sons, Franklin, Jr., and John.

July 5, landed at Cap Haitien, Haiti
• He was the only president who visited Haiti while in office.

July 6, landed at Mayaguez, Puerto Rico; motored to San Juan
• He was the third of seven presidents who visited Puerto Rico while in office.

July 7, landed at St. Thomas, Virgin Islands
• He was the second of four presidents who visited the Virgin Islands while in office.

July 10, landed at Cartagena, Colombia
• He was the first of two presidents who visited Colombia while in office. The other was Kennedy.
• He was the first of five presidents who

visited South America while in office.

July 11, traveled through Panama Canal
• He was the only president who traveled through the canal while in office
• He was the third of four presidents who visited Panama while in office.
• This was the first of his four visits to Panama while in office.

July 13, fished at Cocos Island, off Costa Rica

July 17, asked to intervene in general strike, San Francisco, Cal.
• The nation's first general strike grew out of a longshoremen's strike that had begun, May 9, and ended, July 29.

July 21, issued executive order authorizing $75,000,000 reforestation program for drought area, from Canadian border to Texas

July 24–25, fished at Kailua and Hilo, Hawaii

July 26, reviewed army and naval forces, Honolulu
• He was the first of five presidents who visited Hawaii while in office.
• This was the first of his two visits to Hawaii while in office.

July 28, departed from Hawaii

Aug. 1, occupation of Haiti ended officially
• The occupation had lasted 19 years. The last contingent of U.S. Marines departed, Aug. 15.

Aug. 2, anchored off Astoria, Ore.

Aug. 3, landed at Portland, Ore.
• He inspected the site of the proposed power and navigation dam at Bonneville on the Columbia River, 40 miles above Portland. The dam was completed in 1937.

Aug. 3–8, toured drought states

Aug. 9, issued executive order recalling all silver to mints within 90 days
• His order applied to all stocks of silver except coins and fabricated silver held under license or owned by foreign governments or central banks.

Aug. 10, returned to Washington, D.C.

Aug. 10, issued proclamation authorizing waiving of import duties on hay and other forage, effective, Aug. 20

Aug. 22, issued executive order reducing hours of 200,000 cotton garment industry workers by ten percent, increased wages by ten percent

Aug. 24, issued proclamation announcing reciprocal tariff treaty with Cuba
• The treaty reduced import and export duties for both nations on sugar, rum, to-

bacco, and other commodities.

Aug. 26, departed for month's vacation, Hyde Park, N.Y.

Sept. 5, appointed special board of inquiry to investigate textile strike

•The strike had begun, Sept. 1. About 400,-000 of the industry's 735,000 employees were on strike by Sept. 15. He appealed to them, Sept. 22, to return to work pending adjustments suggested by the board of inquiry. The United Textile Workers voted to end the strike immediately, Sept. 22; his proposal for a six-month truce was formally accepted, Oct. 3.

Sept. 24, accepted resignation of NRA Administrator Hugh S. Johnson

•He appointed a five-man National Industrial Recovery Board to replace Johnson. He named W. Averell Harriman as NRA administrative officer and Donald M. Nelson as code administration director.

Sept. 30, called for armistice between management and labor in fireside chat

Oct. 12, reissued executive order reducing hours, increasing wages of cotton garment industry workers

•The cotton garment industry had refused to abide by his order of Aug. 22, but finally agreed to reduce hours from 40 to 36 weekly if current wages were maintained.

Oct. 31, consolidated Executive Council and National Emergency Council

•He appointed Donald Richberg as chairman of the 33-member council.

Nov. 6, election day

•The Democrats made gains in both the Senate and the House of Representatives.

Nov. 14, linked all fiscal agencies by establishing loan committee under Secretary of Treasury Morgenthau

Nov. 16, dedicated monument to pioneers, Harrodsburg, Ky.

Nov. 16, inspected TVA project, Norris, Tenn.

Nov. 16, departed for Warm Springs, Ga.

Dec. 11, attended Gridiron Club dinner, Washington, D.C.

•The Gridiron Club is composed of leading members of the Washington press corps. The principal speakers at their off-the-record affairs usually are a prominent member of the opposition party and the president.

•In a departure from custom, the opposition speech was given by H.L. Mencken of the Baltimore *Sun*. In reply, the president engaged in what seemed to be a diatribe against the American press, which he said was shot through with "stupidity, cowardice and philistinism," and staffed by men "who could not pass the entrance examination for Harvard and Tuskegee, or even Yale." It was several minutes before the audience came to realize that he was quoting from Mencken's essay, "Journalism in America."

1935

Jan. 3, first session of 74th Congress

•The administration maintained control of both the Senate and the House of Representatives. The Democrats gained ten Senate and nine House seats. The Senate (96 members) consisted of 69 Democrats, 25 Republicans, one Farmer Laborite, and one Progressive. The House (435 members) consisted of 322 Democrats, 102 Republicans, seven Progressives, three Farmer Laborites, and one vacancy.

•This was the first Congress to convene under the provisions of the 20th Amendment.

• *See* Constitution, page 644.

Jan. 4, delivered his second State of the Union message to Congress

•He outlined an extensive program that included national public works projects to provide 3,500,000 jobs ("The Federal Government must and shall quit this business of relief."), unemployment and old-age insurance, slum clearance and housing, and a more realistic use of natural resources.

Jan. 16, sent special message to Congress asking U.S. adherence to World Court

•The Senate voted for participation in the court, 52–36, Jan. 29. This vote fell seven short of the two-thirds necessary for ratification.

Jan. 31, signed act extending RFC for two years

Feb. 4, signed act authorizing issuance of "baby bonds"

Feb. 8, issued executive order withdrawing all remaining public lands from use

•This order affected about 1,200,000 acres, which completed withdrawal from settlement, location, sale, or entry of the entire 165,695,000 acres of public domain.

Mar. 24, signed Philippine Independence Act

• The Tydings-McDuffie Act duplicated much of the content of the Hawes-Cutting Act of Jan. 13, 1933, but provided for the removal of U.S. military bases and left the status of naval bases to future negotiation. After the act was accepted unanimously by the Filipino legislature, May 1, a constitutional convention was scheduled for July 30 in Manila.

Apr. 8, signed emergency relief appropriation act

• This $4,880,000,000 program established the Works Progress Administration (WPA), renamed in 1939 the Works Projects Administration. Direct relief ended with the WPA, which provided for a gigantic national works program for jobless "employables." Harry L. Hopkins was appointed administrator, May. 6.

• During its eight-year existence, WPA employed more than 8,500,000 individuals on 1,400,000 projects, at a cost of about $11,-000,000,000. Much waste and inefficiency resulted, but the tangible results of the WPA included more than 650,000 miles of highways, 125,000 public buildings, 8,000 parks, 850 airports, as well as the construction or repair of 124,000 bridges.

Apr. 27, signed soil conservation act

• This act established the soil conservation service of the department of agriculture.

May 1, issued executive order establishing Resettlement Administration

• The RA was authorized to grant loans for the purchase of farm lands by sharecroppers and tenants, and lend assistance in soil erosion, flood control, and reforestation. RA established a series of "Greenbelt towns," including Greenbelt, Md.; Greenhills, Ohio, and Greendale, Wis. Undersecretary Rexford G. Tugwell was appointed administrator.

May 6, Supreme Court declared Railroad Retirement Act of 1934 unconstitutional

May 10, received Admiral Richard E. Byrd, White House

• Admiral Byrd had just returned from his second expedition to the Antarctic.

May 11, issued executive order establishing Rural Electrification Administration

• The REA was authorized to finance electricity production and the building of light and power lines in rural areas not served by private utility companies.

May 22, vetoed soldiers' bonus bill

• The bill provided for immediate payment of the $2,200,000,000 of the adjusted service certificates held by World War I veterans. Under the adjusted compensation act of 1924, they were not due to mature until 1945.

• He established a precedent by delivering his veto message in person before a joint session of Congress. The House of Representatives voted to override the veto, 322–98, May 22, but it was sustained by the Senate, 54–40, May 23.

May 27, Supreme Court declared National Industrial Recovery Act of 1933 unconstitutional

May 31, retorted to Supreme Court NIRA decision

• He examined the decision for an hour and 25 minutes during a press conference. It was "more important than any decision probably since the Dred Scott case," he said, adding that it had turned back the Constitution to "the horse and buggy days."

June 1, ordered all 411 pending NRA cases in court dropped on advice of Attorney General Cummings

June 7, issued executive order establishing National Resources Committee

June 19, sent special tax message to Congress

• He requested legislation to provide higher taxes on very large incomes (both individual and corporate), an inheritance tax, and higher estate and gift taxes.

June 26, issued executive order establishing National Youth Administration

• Part of the WPA, the NYA provided a work-relief and employment program for those between the ages of 16 and 25, as well as part-time jobs for needy school, college, and graduate students.

July 5, signed labor relations act

• The Wagner-Connery Act established a new National Labor Relations Board, which was empowered to supervise elections at the request of the employees, certify trade unions, and issue cease and desist orders to employers adjudged unfair. The act upheld the right of workers to join labor organizations and bargain collectively.

July 26, commuted sentences of 151 alien convicts

• This was the first of a series of mass commutation orders issued for reasons of economy and congestion of federal penal institutions. The 151 aliens, including one woman, were deported.

Aug. 9, signed motor carrier act

• This act placed buses and trucks engaged in interstate commerce under the authority of the ICC, except carriers of livestock, farm products, fish, and newspapers.

Aug. 13, signed war pension act

• This act restored five thousand persons to the pension rolls—veterans and widows of veterans of the Spanish-American War, the Boxer Rebellion and the Philippine Insurrection—at a cost of $45,580,000.

Aug. 14, signed Social Security Act

• This act established a federal-state cooperative system of unemployment compensation. A federal payroll tax was levied on all employers of eight persons or more; each state administered its own program. An old-age pension plan for those 65 years or older was instituted on the national level. The act also authorized grants to help the states meet the cost of state old-age pension programs and grants to assist state relief programs for the destitute blind, the crippled, and dependent and delinquent children.

Aug. 23, signed banking act of 1935

Aug. 26, first session of 74th Congress adjourned

Aug. 27, signed act banning suits against government for alleged losses due to dollar devaluation, effective, Jan. 1, 1936

Aug. 28, signed public utility holding company act

Aug. 29, signed Railroad Retirement Act of 1935

• This act replaced the 1934 act invalidated by the Supreme Court, May 6.

Aug. 29, signed limited three-year farm mortgage moratorium act

• This act replaced the Federal Farm Bankruptcy Act of 1934, invalidated by the Supreme Court, 1935.

Aug. 30, signed Bituminous Coal Conservation Act

• This act fixed the price of soft coal and authorized a 15 percent tax on the selling price at mine sites. Operators who complied with the soft coal code were granted 90 percent refunds.

• This act was invalidated by the Supreme Court, 1936.

Aug. 30, signed Revenue Act of 1935

• This act included the wealth tax recommendations he had made in his special tax revision message of June 19; a surtax on

incomes over $50,000 and estates over $40,000, as well as an increase in gift tax rates. Taxes on incomes in excess of $1,-000,000 graduated sharply, to 75 percent of incomes of $5,000,000 or more. Higher corporation taxes for all firms except the smallest were established. An inheritance tax feature that he had requested was eliminated from the bill prior to passage.

Aug. 31, signed joint resolution for mandatory ban on arms shipments to belligerents

• U.S. citizens were warned that travel on belligerent vessels was undertaken at their own risk.

Aug. 31, signed amended TVA act

Sept. 6, stated experimental phase of New Deal nearing end

• Roy W. Howard, chairman of the board of Scripps-Howard newspapers had requested a word of reassurance to quiet the fears of the business community. In response, Roosevelt said that the "substantial completion" of the experimental stage of his administration would lead to a "breathing spell."

Sept. 17, congratulated first president of Philippine Commonwealth, Manuel Quezon

Sept. 25, issued proclamation listing implements of war affected under neutrality resolution of Aug. 31

• All manufacturers, exporters, and importers were ordered to register with the state department before Nov. 29.

Sept. 26, departed for West Coast

• He spoke in several cities along the way, including Fremont, Neb.; Boulder Dam; and Los Angeles, Cal.

Oct. 2, witnessed tactical maneuvers of U.S. Navy, off San Diego, Cal.

• From the bridge of the *U.S.S. Houston*, he reviewed the largest tactical maneuvers in U.S. naval history to date, in which 50,000 men, 129 warships, and 449 planes were involved. A sham attack on a flotilla of four ships, led by the *Houston*, was staged.

Oct. 5, issued proclamation, through state department, imposing embargo on arms and ammunition to Italy or Ethiopia

• Italy had invaded Ethiopia, Oct. 3.

Oct. 6, issued proclamation warning Americans travel on Italian or Ethiopian ships was undertaken at own risk

Oct. 11, fished at Cocos Island, off Costa Rica

Oct. 16, landed at Balboa, Panama Canal Zone

•He inspected Madden Dam.

•This was the second of Roosevelt's four visits to Panama while in office.

•Vice President Garner sailed for the Philippines, Oct. 16, from Seattle, Wash. This was the first time that the president and the vice president were out of the country simultaneously.

Oct. 22, landed at Charleston, S.C.

Oct. 24, returned to Washington, D.C.

Oct. 30, urged end of Ethiopian war, suggested cessation of all trade with Italy

Nov. 14, signed proclamation certifying independence of Philippines and election of officers

•Vice President Garner attended the inauguration of President Quezon.

Nov. 17, rejected Knights of Columbus demand

•The American Catholic society for men had insisted that the administration halt the "persecution of religion by the Mexican government."

Nov. 29, federal dole ended

•The government had doled out $3,694,-000,000 since May, 1933.

1936

Jan. 3, second session of 74th Congress

Jan. 3, delivered his third State of the Union message to Congress

•He challenged the critics of the New Deal to repeal his administration's measures if they could.

Jan. 6, Supreme Court invalidated AAA as invasion of states' rights

•The Court ruled that the processing tax was a means of regulating crop production. The Court ordered $200,000,000 of impounded processing taxes returned to suing processors, Jan. 13.

Jan. 24, vetoed adjusted compensation bill

Jan. 27, Adjusted Compensation Act passed over his veto

•This act authorized nine-year interest-bearing bonds, which were convertible into cash at any time. More than $1,500,-000,000 in soldiers' bonus bonds were distributed to three million World War I veterans, June 15.

•This was the second of his nine vetoes that were overridden.

Feb. 15, White House announced he had proposed conference to "determine how

the maintenance of peace among the American republics may be safeguarded"

•The Inter-American Conference for the Maintenance of Peace was scheduled for Dec. 1, Buenos Aires, Argentina.

Feb. 21, issued executive order placing Kure Island under control of navy department

•Kure had been under Hawaiian control.

Feb. 29, signed amended neutrality resolution

•This amendment prohibited loans or credits to belligerents, but a "Monroe Doctrine" clause exempted American nations engaged in war with nations outside the western hemisphere.

Feb. 29, signed soil conservation and domestic allotment act

•This act, which replaced the AAA, substituted benefit payments to farmers who practiced soil conservation for the contracts for crop production control, which had been invalidated by the Supreme Court. Farmers leased lands withdrawn from use to the government through their county associations and were compensated for checking erosion.

Mar. 4, pushed button putting Norris Dam, Norris, Tenn., in service

•Norris Dam was named for Senator George W. Norris of Nebraska, sponsor of bills that created the Tennessee Valley Authority.

•Norris also wrote the 20th Amendment to the Constitution.

• See Constitution, page 644.

Apr. 6, Supreme Court ruled against SEC in test case but did not decide constitutionality

Apr. 13, granted interview to major general relieved of command for criticizing WPA

•Major General Johnson Hagood was restored to active duty and reassigned. Hagood served one full day at his new post, May 4. He then requested and was granted retirement.

May 18, Supreme Court invalidated Bituminous Coal Conservation Act of 1935

May 25, Supreme Court invalidated Municipal Bankruptcy Act of 1934

June 10, spoke at Arkansas centennial ceremonies, Little Rock, Ark.

June 11–12, spoke at Texas centennial ceremonies, Houston, San Antonio, Austin, and Dallas, Tex.

June 14, attended memorial to George R. Clark, Revolutionary hero, Vincennes, Ind.

June 14, visited Lincoln birthplace, Hodgenville, Ky.

June 20, signed Federal Anti-Price-Discrimination Act

•This act, which affected chain stores engaged in interstate commerce, prohibited low prices that tended to reduce competition and promote monopoly.

June 20, second session of 74th Congress adjourned

June 22, signed Revenue Act of 1936

•This act added a surtax of from seven to 27 percent on undistributed corporation profits.

June 26, signed Merchant Marine Act

•This act created the Maritime Commission, which superseded the shipping board; it also provided outright subsidies in place of ocean mail contracts and set labor standards for seamen.

June 26, renominated by acclamation, Democratic national convention, Philadelphia, Pa.

June 27, made acceptance speech before crowd of 105,000, Franklin Field, Philadelphia, Pa.

•It was in this speech that he employed the phrases, "economic royalists" and "rendezvous with destiny."

•Speaking of the Old Guard Republicans, he said:

These economic royalists complain that we seek to overthrow the institutions of America. What they really complain about is that we seek to take away their power.

•In the same address he said:

Governments can err, Presidents do make mistakes, but the immortal Dante tells us that divine justice weighs the sins of the cold-blooded and the sins of the warm-hearted in different scales.

Better the occasional faults of a Government that lives in a spirit of charity than the constant omissions of a Government frozen in the ice of its own indifference.

There is a mysterious cycle in human events. To some generations much is given. Of other generations much is expected. This generation of Americans has a rendezvous with destiny.

June 27, pushed button opening Great Lakes Exposition, Cleveland, Ohio

June 30, signed government contracts act

•This act provided that employees of firms with government contracts should be paid prevailing wages, to be determined by the labor department. Convict and child labor were prohibited from working on government contracts.

July 8, received report from AFL alleging Supreme Court NRA decision cost almost 840,000 jobs

July 11, spoke at dedication of $60,300,000 Triborough Bridge, New York City

July 20, issued executive order placing all first, second, and third class postmasters under civil service

July 31, conferred with Canadian leaders, Quebec, Canada

•After a stay at Campobello, he met with the governor general, Lord Tweedsmuir, and Prime Minister Mackenzie King. A "good neighbor" policy was formulated.

•This was the second of Roosevelt's seven visits to Canada while in office.

Aug. 14, set forth foreign policy of neutrality, Chautauqua, N.Y.

Aug. 27, Secretary of War Dern died

Aug. 30, instructed state department to protest attempted bombing of *U.S.S. Kane*

•An unidentified plane dropped a bomb near the destroyer off the Spanish coast. Representations were made to the Spanish government and the rebel leaders. General Francisco Franco later apologized for the incident.

Sept. 16, formally accepted invitation to be presidential candidate of American Labor party

Sept. 25, appointed his second secretary of war, Harry H. Woodring

Sept. 29, made opening address of campaign, state Democratic convention, Syracuse, N.Y.

•He said:

The true conservative seeks to protect the system of private property and free enterprise by correcting such injustices and inequalities as arise from it.

Oct. 1, defended deficit as investment in human welfare, Pittsburgh, Pa.

Oct. 9, defended his reciprocal trade treaties as aid to agriculture and world peace, St. Paul, Minn.

Oct. 14, told business leaders he had saved

them, not harmed them, "believe it or not," Chicago, Ill.

Oct. 16, charged Wall Street with using stockholders' money to finance campaign against his reelection, Cleveland, Ohio

Oct. 26, dedicated new $625,000 chemistry building, Howard University, Washington, D.C.

• He pledged his administration to the guarantee that "among American citizens there should be no forgotten men and no forgotten races."

Oct. 28, spoke at Statue of Liberty, New York City

• This was the 50th anniversary of the dedication of the Statue of Liberty.

Nov. 3, election day

• *See* Election of 1936, page 407.

Nov. 10, issued executive order regarding exportation of military aircraft

• He directed that the state department should be governed by the war department policy, which did not permit the exporting of planes of types contracted for by the army until such contracts had been substantially filled.

Nov. 12, pushed button that opened $77,-000,000 San Francisco-Oakland bridge, Cal.

Nov. 18, embarked for South America aboard *U.S.S. Indianapolis*, Charleston, S.C.

Nov. 27, arrived at Rio de Janeiro, Brazil

• He was the first of three presidents who visited Brazil while in office.

• This was the first of his three visits to Brazil while in office.

Nov. 30, arrived at Buenos Aires, Argentina

• He was the first of two presidents who visited Argentina while in office. The other was Eisenhower.

Dec. 1, addressed opening session of Inter-American Conference for Maintenance of Peace, Buenos Aires

• He called for a union of American nations so constituted that in case of aggression from Europe it could stand "shoulder to shoulder," prepared to consult together for mutual safety.

Dec. 2, sailed for U.S.

Dec. 3, visited Montevideo, Uruguay

• He was the first of three presidents who visited Uruguay while in office.

Dec. 14, presidential electors cast ballots

• He received 523 of the 531 electoral votes from the 48 states.

• See Election of 1936, page 407.

Dec. 15, landed at Charleston, S.C.

• He returned to Washington by train the same day.

1937

Jan. 5, first session of 75th Congress

• The administration maintained control of both the Senate and the House of Representatives. The Democrats gained six Senate and 11 House seats. The Senate (96 members) consisted of 75 Democrats, 17 Republicans, two Farmer Laborites, one Progressive, and one Independent. The House (435 members) consisted of 333 Democrats, 89 Republicans, seven Progressives, five Farmer Laborites, and one vacancy.

• This was the Congress in which the Democrats held the largest Senate majority—58. This surpassed the previous record majority of 50 in 1869.

• This was the Congress in which the Democrats held the largest House majority—244. This surpassed the previous record majority of 220 in 1935.

Jan. 6, electoral votes tabulated by Congress

• Roosevelt and Garner were officially declared elected.

Jan. 6, delivered his fourth State of the Union message to Congress

• He maintained that no Constitutional amendment was necessary to attain the objectives of a better social order. "The judicial branch is asked by the people to do its part in making democracy successful," he said.

Jan. 8, signed joint resolution placing embargo on shipment of arms and munitions to Spain

• The Spanish Civil War had commenced in Spanish Morocco, July 18, 1936.

• The embargo worked to the advantage of the rebels who were receiving military supplies from Italy and Germany.

Jan. 12, sent special message to Congress asking for legislation to reorganize executive branch

• He asked for the establishment of two new cabinet-level departments—social welfare and public works. He suggested redesignation of the department of interior as the department of conservation and the abolition of the office of comptroller general.

He also requested authorization to appoint six administrative assistants.

ELECTION OF 1936

Socialist Labor party, convened, Apr. 26, at New York City, nominated John W. Aiken of Massachusetts for president, Emil F. Teichert of New York for vice president.

Prohibition party, convened, May 5, at Niagara Falls, N.Y., nominated David Leigh Colvin of New York for president, Claude A. Watson of California for vice president.

Socialist party, convened, May 23, at Cleveland, Ohio, nominated Norman Thomas of New York for president, George Nelson of Wisconsin for vice president.

Republican party, convened, June 9, at Cleveland, Ohio, nominated Alfred Mossman Landon of Kansas for president, Frank Knox of Illinois for vice president.

• This was the 21st Republican national convention. It was the second of two Republican conventions held in Cleveland; it was the second of two major conventions held in Cleveland.

Democratic party, convened, June 23, at Philadelphia, Pa., nominated Franklin Delano Roosevelt of New York for president, John Nance Garner of Texas for vice president.

• This was the 27th Democratic national convention. It was the first Democratic convention held in Philadelphia; it was the sixth major convention held in Philadelphia.

Communist party, convened, June 24, at New York City, nominated Earl Russell Browder of Kansas for president, James

William Ford of New York for vice president.

Note: William Lemke of North Dakota announced, June 19, that he was the **Union** party candidate for president and that his running mate was Thomas Charles O'-Brien of Massachusetts. Lemke was endorsed by the first convention of the National Union for Social Justice, which convened, Aug. 14, at Cleveland, Ohio.

Election day, Tuesday, Nov. 3, 1936
Popular vote: 45,652,300
    Roosevelt, 27,757,333
    Landon, 16,684,231
    Lemke, 892,267
    Thomas, 187,833
    Browder, 80,171
    Colvin, 37,677
    Aiken, 12,788
Electoral vote: 531, 48 states
• Roosevelt, 523, 46 states
    (Alabama, 11; Arizona, 3; Arkansas, 9; California, 22; Colorado, 6; Connecticut, 8; Delaware, 3; Florida, 7; Georgia, 12; Idaho, 4; Illinois, 29; Indiana, 14; Iowa, 11; Kansas, 9; Kentucky, 11; Louisiana, 10; Maryland, 8; Massachusetts, 17; Michigan, 19; Minnesota, 11; Mississippi, 9; Missouri, 15; Montana, 4; Nebraska, 7; Nevada, 3; New Hampshire, 4; New Jersey, 16; New Mexico, 3; New York, 47; North Carolina, 13; North Dakota, 4; Ohio, 26; Oklahoma, 11; Oregon, 5; Pennsylvania, 36; Rhode Island, 4; South Carolina, 8; South Dakota, 4; Tennessee, 11; Texas, 23; Utah, 4; Virginia, 11; Washington, 8; West Virginia, 8; Wisconsin, 12; Wyoming, 3)
• Landon, 8, two states
    (Maine, 5; Vermont, 3)

THE 38th ADMINISTRATION

1937

Jan. 20, his second inauguration day
• Roosevelt took the oath of office, administered by Chief Justice Charles Evans Hughes, on the east portico of the Capitol.
• This was the first inauguration to take place on January 20, under the provisions of the 20th Amendment.
• *See* Constitution, page 644.

• This was the second of three inaugurations at which Chief Justice Hughes officiated.
Feb. 5, sent special message to Congress recommending judiciary reorganization
• Roosevelt submitted legislation drawn in the department of justice that proposed the increase of membership of the Supreme Court from nine to as many as 15, if justices declined to retire at the age of 70. Also recommended was the addition of

as many as 50 federal judges of all classes, the submission of appeals of lower court decisions regarding constitutionality directly to the Supreme Court, and the assignment of district judges wherever necessary to speed up court proceedings.

Mar. 1, signed Reciprocal Trade Agreements Act

• This act extended the period during which he could negotiate agreements under the Trade Agreement Act of 1934 to June, 1940.

Mar. 1, signed Supreme Court Retirement Act

• This act permitted the retirement of justices at 70 years of age or over, with full pay for life. Retired justices could later be called for special service in lower courts by the chief justice.

Mar. 9, explained Court reorganization plan during fireside chat

• The reorganization bill was designed to restore the balance of power among the three branches of government, he said, and added that the courts had "cast doubts on the ability of the elected Congress to protect us against catastrophe by meeting squarely our modern social and economic conditions." Opponents had charged that the bill was an attempt to "pack" the Supreme Court.

Apr. 2, announced government would curtail purchases in durable goods

• He said the prices of steel, copper, and other basic products had risen faster than wages.

Apr. 20, sent budget message to Congress asking $1,500,000,000 for relief in fiscal year beginning July 1

Apr. 26, signed Guffey-Vinson Coal Act

• This act replaced the Guffey-Snyder Bituminous Coal Conservation Act of 1935, which had been invalidated in 1936. It put bituminous coal production under federal control, provided for a revenue tax of one percent per ton, and imposed a penalty tax of 19.5 percent of the sales price on noncode members.

Apr. 28, departed Washington for Gulf of Mexico fishing trip

• He boarded the *Potomac* at New Orleans, La., Apr. 29. The cruise ended at Galveston, Tex., May 11. He returned to Washington, May 14.

May 1, signed Neutrality Act of 1937

• This act authorized the president to list products over and beyond munitions to be paid for on delivery. It also defined travel on vessels of belligerents as unlawful.

May 18, accepted resignation of Associate Justice Van Devanter, effective, June 2

June 1, sent special message to Congress asking for termination of oil-depletion clause of income tax law

June 1, vetoed bill to extend government insurance for World War I veterans

June 1, act to extend government insurance for veterans passed over his veto

• This act extended the privilege of renewing the expiring five-year policies for another five-year period.

• This was the third of his nine vetoes that were overridden.

June 24, signed railway pension act

June 30, attended wedding of son, Franklin, to Ethel du Pont, near Wilmington, Del.

July 9, stated government employees had no right to strike

July 13, vetoed bill to extend for one year interest rate of three and one-half percent on certain federal land-bank loans

July 22, his judiciary reorganization bill returned to Senate judiciary committee

• This marked defeat of the measure. However, the resignation of Associate Justice Van Devanter—a member of the conservative anti-New Deal Court bloc—and the most recent Court decisions amounted to a form of victory. New Deal legislation had been upheld, including the Frazier-Lemke Farm Mortgage Moratorium Act, the Social Security Act, and the Wagner Labor Relations Act.

July 22, act to extend interest rate on certain farm land-bank loans passed over his veto

• This was the fourth of his nine vetoes that were overridden.

Aug. 12, appointed Hugo L. Black as associate justice

• Black, who was confirmed by the Senate, Aug. 17, was the first of Roosevelt's nine appointments to the Supreme Court.

Aug. 18, signed Miller-Tydings enabling act

• This act, which amended the antitrust laws to legalize fair trade laws enacted in various states, was a "rider" to a District of Columbia appropriations measure. He expressed his disapproval of the act but reluctantly signed it.

Aug. 21, first session of 75th Congress adjourned

Aug. 26, signed judicial procedure reform act
• This act provided for lower court procedure reform but did not allow for the appointment of new judges, as he had recommended.
Aug. 26, signed Revenue Act of 1937
Sept. 1, signed act that extended modified Jones-Costigan Act of 1934 to 1940
Sept. 1, signed National Housing Act
• The Wagner-Steagall Act established the U.S. Housing Authority under the department of interior to make low-interest 60-year loans to local agencies that contributed ten percent of slum clearance and housing projects.
Sept. 14, issued executive order prohibiting transport of war materials to China and Japan in government-owned merchant ships
• Private owners were notified that they entered the Asian war zone at their own risk. This order benefited Japan inasmuch as she had a large merchant fleet.
Sept. 22, began western tour
Sept. 25, visited Yellowstone National Park
Sept. 30, visited Victoria, British Columbia, Canada
• This was the third of his seven visits to Canada while in office.
Oct. 5, delivered "quarantine" speech, Chicago, Ill.
• He pledged his administration to a "concerted effort" with other nations to "quarantine" the aggressors. He warned that the U.S. was menaced by a "reign of terror and international lawlessness" that had "reached a stage where the very foundations of civilization are threatened."
Oct. 11, received Vittorio Mussolini, son of Italian dictator, White House
Oct. 12, issued proclamation calling Congress into extra session, Nov. 15
Nov. 15, second session of 75th Congress
Nov. 15, sent special message to Congress in which he recommended legislation for governmental reorganization; wages and hours regulation; tax relief for small business; agricultural aid and conservation; and development of natural resources programs
Nov. 18, had abscessed tooth extracted
Nov. 25, observed Thanksgiving Day, White House
• He had postponed his Thanksgiving trip to Warm Springs, Ga., due to discomfort

from tooth pain.
Nov. 28, departed for fishing trip in Florida waters
• He returned to the White House, Dec. 6.
Dec. 21, second session of 75th Congress adjourned
• None of his recommendations had been acted upon during the short session. A coalition of southern Democratic conservatives and Republicans blocked the administration programs.
Dec. 21, accused majority of press and minority of business leaders of repetitious obstructionism
• He said that the opposition had much to do with the prevailing economic conditions.
Dec. 31, issued proclamation that reduced price of newly-minted domestic silver from 77.57 to 64.64 cents per ounce

1938

Jan. 3, third session of 75th Congress
Jan. 3, delivered his fifth State of the Union message to Congress
• He called for cooperation between government and business to raise the national income.
Jan. 3, sent budget message to Congress
• He estimated expenditures for the fiscal year ending June 30, 1939, at $7,070,558,-000; receipts at $6,120,952,000; and a deficit of $949,606,000.
Jan. 5, accepted resignation of Associate Justice Sutherland, effective, Jan. 17
Jan. 6, opposed Ludlow resolution, which called for national referendum as prerequisite to war declaration
• The resolution, sponsored by Representative Louis Ludlow of Indiana, was returned to committee, Jan. 10.
Jan. 8, reiterated readiness to battle industrial autocrats
• In his Jackson Day address, he stated he was still ready to combat the "mere handful" of businessmen, industrialists and bankers who were contending "to the last ditch to retain such autocratic control of the industry and finances of the country as they now possess."
Jan. 9, German customs banned volumes of his recent speeches, Swiss border
Jan. 15, appointed Stanley F. Reed as associate justice
• Reed, who was confirmed by the Senate,

Jan. 25, was the second of Roosevelt's nine appointments to the Supreme Court.

Jan. 28, sent special defense armaments message to Congress

•He stated national defense was "inadequate," and requested funds for two new battleships and two new cruisers, as well as a variety of smaller vessels. He also asked for appropriations to purchase army ammunition and antiaircraft materials.

Feb. 4, signed amended federal housing act

Feb. 16, signed Agricultural Adjustment Act of 1938

•This measure was a modified form of the Agricultural Adjustment Act of 1933, but without the processing tax system declared unconstitutional in 1936. The act established the "ever-normal granary" plan of Secretary of Agriculture Wallace. It also established the Federal Crop Insurance Corporation (FCIC), capitalized at $100,-000,000, to insure wheat crops.

Mar. 7, directed U.S. flags raised on Canton and Enderbury Islands

•Two of the Phoenix Islands, Canton and Enderbury, assumed importance with the establishment of trans-Pacific air routes, being situated on a direct line between Hawaii and New Caledonia. The U.S. claim was disputed by Great Britain but was settled amicably in 1939, when the islands were placed under joint control for 50 years.

Mar. 22, dismissed Arthur E. Morgan, chairman of TVA

•Morgan had refused to submit to the president details of charges made by other TVA officials against the administration, maintaining the investigation should be conducted by Congress rather than by the executive department.

Apr. 8, held special press conference for business trade-paper editors

•"As far as powers go, I figured out the other day that there is not a single power I have that Hoover and Coolidge did not have," he told the business editors.

Apr. 14, sent special message to Congress outlining series of recommendations to combat recession

•In what amounted to a reversal of his deflationary policies, he asked for a $3,000,-000,000 spending program, including $1,-250,000,000 to double the WPA rolls to 3,000,000; $175,000,000 for the Farm Security Administration; $75,000,000 for

the National Youth Administration; and $50,000,000 for the Civilian Conservation Corps.

•That evening, during a fireside chat, he said the recession, which had set in early the previous summer, had been caused by overproduction and price rises, despite government warnings.

Apr. 18, pardoned Dr. Francis E. Townsend

•The originator of the Townsend Plan, who had been found guilty of contempt of Congress, had come to Washington to pay the $100 fine and to serve the 30-day federal prison sentence. He had walked out on the House of Representatives committee that was investigating his old-age pension plan, May 21, 1936.

•The Townsend Plan proposed a $200 monthly pension in scrip, to be spent during the month, to retired persons over 60 years old. The funds were to be raised by a sales tax.

Apr. 21, addressed Daughters of American Revolution, Washington, D.C.

•He shocked the members of the society—reactionary by nature—by underlining the fact that "all of us, and you and I especially, are descended from immigrants and revolutionists."

•He did not, as legend has it, begin his speech with the salutation: "Fellow Immigrants!"

Apr. 25, sent special message on federal and state tax exemptions to Congress

•He recommended termination of the reciprocal tax exemptions for federal and state employees and owners of government and state bonds.

Apr. 29, sent special message to Congress in which he recommended "thorough study" of concentration of economic power in U.S. industry and effect of concentration upon decline of competition

May 12, asserted federal courts had modified their views to fit times, in letter to director of American Law Institute

May 17, signed Naval Expansion Act of 1938

•This act authorized a ten-year, $1,090,-656,000 naval construction program.

May 27, Revenue Act of 1938 became law without his signature

•He sharply criticized those provisions of the act concerning undistributed profits and capital gains. The undistributed profits tax of 1936 was repealed and was replaced by a 19 percent corporation tax that could be further reduced by payment of dividends out of taxable income.

• This was the first time he withheld his signature without exercising the veto power.

June 2, addressed graduation class, U.S. Naval Academy, Annapolis, Md.

June 15, vetoed extension of interest rates on farm loans bill

June 16, extension of farm loans interest rate act passed over his veto

• This was the fifth of his nine vetoes that were overridden.

June 16, third session of 75th Congress adjourned

June 18, attended wedding of Anne Lindsay Clark and his son, John, Nahant, Mass.

June 21, signed emergency relief appropriation act

June 23, signed Civil Aeronautics Act

• This act established the Civil Aeronautics Authority (CAA) to supervise all but military air transportation.

June 24, signed Food, Drug, and Cosmetic Act

• This act imposed stringent labeling and advertising regulations on food, drugs, and cosmetics and superseded the Pure Food Act of 1906.

June 24, announced plans for active participation in Democratic primary campaign

• In a fireside chat, he made clear his plans to support liberal Democrats, to purge party of "yes but fellows." In his role as party leader, he said:

   . . . charged with the responsibility of the definitely liberal declaration of principles set forth in the 1936 Democratic platform, I feel that I have every right to speak in those few instances where there may be a clear issue between candidates for a Democratic nomination involving these principles, or involving a clear misuse of my name.

• He asked for the defeat of such conservative incumbents as Senators Walter F. George of Georgia, "Cotton Ed" Smith of South Carolina, and Millard F. Tydings of Maryland, and Representative John J. O'-Connor of New York. All but O'Connor were reelected.

June 25, signed Fair Labor Standards Act

• This wage-and-hours act raised the minimum wage of workers in interstate commerce from 25 to 40 cents an hour and limited hours to 44 per week plus time and

a half for overtime. The act also prohibited labor by children under 16 years of age and hazardous jobs to youths under 18.

June 30, laid cornerstone of federal building, New York World's Fair, New York City

July 3, dedicated memorial shaft to "peace eternal in a nation united," joint reunion of Blue and Gray, Gettysburg, Pa.

• More than 1,800 GAR and Confederate veterans, as well as 150,000 spectators, attended the ceremonies on the 75th anniversary of the last day of the Battle of Gettysburg.

July 3, sent message to Conference on Economic Conditions in South, Washington, D.C.

• "It is my conviction that the South presents right now the nation's No. 1 economic problem," he said.

July 7, began campaign tour

July 8, spoke at 150th anniversary ceremonies of opening of Northwest Territory, Marietta, Ohio

July 9, Associate Justice Cardozo died

July 14, reviewed U.S. fleet of 63 warships, San Francisco, Cal.

July 16, finished campaign tour, Los Angeles and San Diego, Cal.

• Leaving San Diego, he boarded the *U.S.S. Houston* and began a 19-day Pacific fishing trip.

Aug. 4–5, visited Panama and Panama Canal Zone

• He inspected the canal zone defenses and part of the Pan-American highway system.

• This was the third of his four visits to Panama while in office.

Aug. 9, arrived at Pensacola, Fla.

• He returned to Washington, Aug. 12.

Aug. 18, with Prime Minister Mackenzie King, dedicated Thousand Islands Bridge connecting Canada and U.S. at Clayton, N.Y.

Aug. 18, visited Canada

• He received an honorary degree of doctor of civil laws at Queens University, Kingston, Ontario. "We in the Americas are no longer a faraway continent, to which the eddies of controversies beyond the seas could bring no interest or no harm," he said.

• This was the fourth of his seven visits to Canada while in office.

Aug. 31, received Douglas "Wrong-Way" Corrigan, White House

• Refused permission to fly the Atlantic in his

nine-year-old plane, Corrigan flew from Brooklyn to Dublin, Ireland, July 17–18, claiming he had started for Los Angeles.

Sept. 26, appealed to European leaders to continue negotiations regarding Czechoslovakian crisis

• His pleas to Chancellor Adolf Hitler of Germany, President Eduard Benes of Czechoslovakia, Prime Minister Neville Chamberlain of Great Britain, and Premier Edouard Daladier of France were to no avail.

Sept. 27, again appealed to Hitler for peaceful solution of crisis

• He also appealed to Premier Benito Mussolini of Italy to intervene with Hitler. The German chancellor was adamant in his demand that Czechoslovakia yield the Sudetenland. The Czech area and all important Czech fortresses were ceded to Germany as a result of the Munich Agreement, Sept. 30.

Nov. 4, dedicated Will Rogers Memorial, Claremore, Okla.

• He spoke by radio from Hyde Park, N. Y.

Nov. 8, election day

• He suffered a major defeat that saw the liberal Democratic-Independent faction in Congress reduced by half. The Republicans made their first congressional gains since 1928.

Nov. 14, ordered Ambassador Hugh Wilson home from Berlin for "consultation"

• In retaliation, the German ambassador to the U.S., Hans H. Dieckhoff, was recalled, Nov. 18.

Nov. 18, announced German refugees in U.S. on visitors' permits should not be forced to return

• He said that he would request revision of the immigration quotas to permit more refugees to enter the country. At the time, between twelve thousand and fifteen thousand refugees were in the U.S. on visitors' permits.

Dec. 10, announced plans for Franklin D. Roosevelt Library, Hyde Park

Dec. 15, spoke at groundbreaking ceremonies, Thomas Jefferson Memorial, Washington, D.C.

Dec. 23, Secretary of Commerce Roper resigned

Dec. 24, lit community Christmas tree, Lafayette Park

Dec. 24, appointed his second secretary of commerce, Harry L. Hopkins

1939

Jan. 2, Attorney General Cummings resigned

Jan. 2, appointed his second attorney general, Frank Murphy

Jan. 3, first session of 76th Congress

• The administration maintained control of both the Senate and the House of Representatives. The Republicans gained six Senate and 81 House seats. The Senate (96 members) consisted of 69 Democrats, 23 Republicans, two Farmer Laborites, one Progressive, and one Independent. The House (435 members) consisted of 262 Democrats, 170 Republicans, two Progressives, and one Farmer Laborite.

Jan. 4, delivered his sixth State of the Union message to Congress

• He defended the New Deal, saying that the nation had "passed through the period of internal conflict in the launching of our program of social reform." He reiterated his request for reorganization legislation, which had been defeated in the 75th Congress. He denounced the European dictatorships and called for support of his national defense program.

Jan. 5, sent annual budget message to Congress

• He estimated expenditures for the fiscal year ending June 30, 1940, at $8,995,663,-200; receipts at $5,669,320,000; and a deficit of $3,326,343,200. He requested $1,-319,558,000 for national defense.

Jan. 5, appointed Felix Frankfurter as associate justice

• Frankfurter, who was confirmed by the Senate, Jan. 17, was the third of Roosevelt's nine appointments to the Supreme Court.

Jan. 7, urged "real Democrats" to stick together, Jackson Day dinner, Washington, D.C.

• In an appeal to Democrats to remain the liberal party, he charged:

> Republican impotence has caused powerful interests, opposed to genuine democracy, to push their way into the Democratic party, hoping to paralyze it by dividing its councils.

• He said Republican gains in Congress had spiked the previously advanced arguments for the lack of a Republican program, but maintained the GOP would remain conservative.

Jan. 31, conferred secretly with Senate military affairs committee on foreign policy

•He had approved English and French purchase of munitions in 1938, but ordered the details suppressed. These facts became public after a French official was killed in the crash of a new model American bomber in California. Following the secret talk with the senators, a report circulated that he had designated the American eastern frontier as "the Rhine."

Feb. 3, denounced "Rhine" report as "deliberate lie"

•"The American foreign policy has not changed and it is not going to change," he told his press conference. He proceeded to outline U.S. policy:

    Number 1: We are against any entangling alliances, obviously

    Number 2: We are in favor of the maintenance of world trade for everybody—all nations—including ourselves.

    Number 3: We are in complete sympathy with any and every effort made to reduce or limit armaments.

    Number 4: As a nation—as American people—we are sympathetic with the peaceful maintenance of political, economic and social independence of all nations in the world.

Feb. 7, signed deficiency relief act

•He had requested $875,000,000 for WPA. This act provided an appropriation of $725,000,000; he immediately issued a message in which he asked for an additional $150,000,000.

Feb. 13, accepted resignation of Associate Justice Brandeis

Feb. 16, sent special message to Congress urging federal aid to combat water pollution.

•He said the time for the federal government to exert vigorous leadership in this area was long overdue.

Feb. 18, opened Golden Gate Exposition, San Francisco, Cal.

•He participated in the opening ceremonies by radio from Key West, Fla.

Feb. 19, boarded *U.S.S. Houston* to join fleet maneuvers, Key West, Fla.

Mar. 3, disembarked at Charleston, S.C.

•Upon his return he expressed satisfaction with the naval maneuvers in the Caribbean.

Mar. 4, asked again for additional $150,000,000 for WPA

•Congress voted an appropriation of $100,000,000. He signed the act, Apr. 13.

Mar. 17, edited and approved official condemnation of invasion of Czechoslovakia

•Germany had invaded Czechoslovakia, Mar. 14.

Mar. 20, appointed William O. Douglas as associate justice

•Douglas, who was confirmed by the Senate, Apr. 4, was the fourth of Roosevelt's nine appointments to the Supreme Court.

Apr. 1, issued proclamation ending embargo on sales of arms and ammunition to Spain

•The U.S. recognized the Franco regime. The Spanish Civil War had ended when the Loyalists surrendered, Mar. 29.

Apr. 3, signed Administrative Reorganization Act of 1939

•This act regrouped some of the many federal agencies, boards, commissions, and other units that had been formed over the years; others were eliminated.

Apr. 9, "I'll be back in the fall if we don't have a war," he said upon leaving Warm Springs, Ga., for Washington, D.C.

Apr. 14, asked Hitler and Mussolini for pledge not to attack or invade nations of Europe and Middle East

•Roosevelt suggested a 25-year pact and promised a world disarmament conference and international trade agreements. Hitler rejected the appeal, Apr. 28.

Apr. 25, sent special message to Congress submitting Plan I for regrouping government units under Reorganization Act.

Apr. 26, signed $549,000,000 war department appropriation act

•He issued an executive order for the purchase of 571 military aircraft at an estimated cost of $50,000,000.

Apr. 26, sent special message to Congress in which he asked immediate construction of additional naval bases in Pacific, Alaska, Puerto Rico, and continental U.S.

Apr. 27, sent special message to Congress asking for $1,477,000,000 for WPA and $123,000,000 for Farm Security Administration, for fiscal year ending June 30, 1940

Apr. 30, opened New York World's Fair, New York City

May 5, received President Anastasio Somoza of Nicaragua, White House

May 6, urged coal wage dispute settlement

• He met with representatives of the bituminous coal industry and the United Mine Workers, May 9. An agreement was signed, May 10, which provided that the UMW was the exclusive bargaining agency for employees.

May 9, sent special message to Congress submitting Plan II under Reorganization Act

May 10, participated by radio in dedication of Museum of Modern Art, New York City

June 8, welcomed King George VI and Queen Elizabeth of Great Britain, White House

• This was the first U.S. visit by British sovereigns.

June 11, served hot dogs and beer during picnic for British royal couple, Hyde Park, N.Y.

June 12, addressed graduating class, U.S. Military Academy, West Point, N.Y.

• "We seek peace by honorable and pacific conduct," he said, but this course "must never be mistaken for weakness on the part of the United States."

June 30, signed Emergency Relief Appropriation Act of 1939

• He signed this act reluctantly and cited several objectionable features, including the abolishment of the federal theater project, the reduction of security wages in the North and West in favor of the South, the limitation of administrative expenses to 3.4 percent, and the requirement that project workers other than veterans should be laid off for 30 days after 18-month WPA employment.

• This act changed the name of the Works Progress Administration to the Works Projects Administration.

June 30, signed agricultural appropriation act

July 1, issued executive order declaring Plans I and II of Reorganization Act in effect

• These plans consolidated 24 former units and established the Federal Security Agency, the Federal Works Agency, and the Federal Loan Agency.

July 6, signed monetary act fixing legal price of newly-mined silver at 71.11 cents an ounce

• This act continued his authority to reduce the gold content of the dollar and con-

tinued his power to control exchange rates by use of the $2,000,000,000 stabilization fund.

July 7, Secretary of Navy Swanson died

July 14, sent special message to Congress asking revision of neutrality laws

July 14, condemned WPA strikes

• In protest of provisions of the Emergency Relief Appropriation Act of 1939, seventy-five thousand skilled WPA construction workers had struck for shorter hours, July 6–12. Several thousand of the strikers were dismissed when they failed to return to work.

July 18, released public statement on necessity of revision of neutrality laws

• After Roosevelt had been informed by Senate leaders that no action could be expected during the current session, the White House announced that the president and the secretary of state took the position that failure by the Senate to take action

> . . . would weaken the leadership of the United States in exercising its potent influence in the cause of preserving the peace among the nations in the event of a new crisis in Europe between now and next January.

Aug. 2, signed Hatch Act

• This act prohibited federal officeholders from active participation in political campaigns, which he said was "at least a step in the right direction."

Aug. 5, first session of 76th Congress adjourned

Aug. 11, signed act for construction of additional Panama Canal facilities

Aug. 24, appealed to Hitler and President Ignaz Moszicki of Poland for settlement of differences by arbitration or conciliation

• Hitler had long demanded Danzig and the Polish Corridor.

• Roosevelt cut short a fishing trip in Canadian waters aboard the *U.S.S. Tuscaloosa* upon receiving word of the signing of the German-Russian nonaggression pact, Aug. 23.

Sept. 1, asked belligerents to ban bombing of civilian populations and undefended cities

• Germany invaded Poland, Sept. 1; Great Britain and France declared war on Germany, Sept. 3.

Sept 3, broadcast to nation on European war

• "As long as it remains within my power to prevent, there will be no blackout of peace in the United States," he said in his fireside chat. He added: "This nation will remain a neutral nation, but I cannot ask that every American remain neutral in thought as well." The latter statement was an obvious reference to Wilson's 1914 appeal to U.S. citizens to be "impartial in thought as well as in action."

Sept. 5, issued proclamation of neutrality

Sept. 5, issued proclamation prohibiting exportation of arms and ammunition to belligerents

Sept. 8, issued proclamation of limited national emergency

Sept. 8, issued executive order of reorganization of executive office of president

• The realignment included such principal divisions as the White House office, the national resources planning board, the liaison office for personnel management, the office of government reports, and the bureau of the budget. The order also provided for the appointment of six administrative assistants.

Sept. 13, issued proclamation calling special session of Congress, Sept. 21

Sept. 17, informed of invasion of Poland by U.S.S.R.

Sept. 21, second session of 76th Congress

Sept. 21, urged repeal of embargo provisions of neutrality act during address to Congress

Sept. 30, appealed for labor accord in letter to William Green, president of AFL

• He made a similar appeal to John L. Lewis of the CIO, Oct. 6.

Oct. 11, received report on possibility of atomic bomb from Alexander Sachs

• He had received a letter from Albert Einstein two months earlier about the possibility of developing a nuclear fission bomb. Sachs, an economist and student of science, brought him up to date on recent developments in the field, both in the U.S. and Germany.

• The first step undertaken was Roosevelt's appointment of an advisory committee on uranium.

Oct. 18, issued proclamation restricting use of U.S. territorial waters by foreign submarines

• All belligerents were ordered to stay out of U.S. waters and ports except the Panama Canal Zone.

Oct. 26, defined political philosophies during radio address to New York *Herald Tribune* Forum, New York City

• He said:

There are, therefore, two distinct dangers to democracy. There is the peril from those who seek the fulfillment of fine ideals at a pace that is too fast for the machinery of the modern body politic to function—people who by insistence on too great speed foster an oligarchic form of government such as Communism, or Naziism or Fascism. The other group which represents an equal danger is composed of that small minority which complains that the democratic processes are inefficient as well as being too slow, people who would have the whole of government put into the hands of a little group of those who have proved their efficiency in lines of specialized science or specialized private business, but who do not see the picture as a whole. They equally, and in most cases unconsciously too, are in effect advocating the oligarchic form of government—Communism, or Naziism or Fascism.

Extreme Rightists and extreme Leftists ought not to be taken out by us and shot against the wall, for they sharpen the argument, and make us realize the value of the democratic middle course—especially if that middle course, in order to keep up with the times is, and I quote what I have said before, "just a little bit left of center."

I am reminded of four definitions:

A Radical man is a man with both feet firmly planted—in the air.

A Conservative is a man with two perfectly good legs who, however, has never learned to walk forward.

A Reactionary is a somnambulist walking backwards.

A Liberal is a man who uses his legs and his hands at the behest— at the command—of his head.

Oct. 31, issued proclamation establishing Thanksgiving Day as Thursday, Nov. 23 —one week ahead of customary date

•His Thanksgiving Day proclamation created a furor among traditionalists. His purpose had been to lengthen the shopping period between Thanksgiving and Christmas.

Nov. 3, second session of 76th Congress adjourned

Nov. 4, signed Neutrality Act of 1939

•This act repealed the arms embargo and authorized the exporting of arms and ammunition to belligerents on a "cash and carry" basis.

Nov. 4, issued proclamation of neutrality under new act

Nov. 15, laid cornerstone of Jefferson Memorial, Washington, D.C.

Nov. 16, Associate Justice Butler died

Nov. 19, laid cornerstone of Franklin D. Roosevelt Library, Hyde Park, N.Y.

Nov. 23, Thanksgiving Day

•A total of 25 states observed the holiday on the date he had proclaimed as Thanksgiving Day. The other 23 observed the following Thursday, Nov. 30.

Dec. 1, condemned Russian invasion of Finland

•Finland had been invaded by the U.S.S.R., Nov. 30.

Dec. 10, issued executive order extending $10,000,000 credit to Finland to purchase supplies in U.S.

Dec. 23, appointed Myron C. Taylor as his personal representative to Vatican

1940

Jan. 2, appointed his second secretary of navy, Charles Edison

Jan. 3, third session of 76th Congress

Jan. 3, delivered his seventh State of the Union message to Congress

•"The first President of the United States warned us against entangling foreign alliances," he said. "The present President of the United States subscribes to and follows that precept."

•It had been Jefferson, not Washington, who expressed apprehension of "entangling alliances"; Washington had warned against "permanent alliances."

Jan. 3, sent budget message to Congress

•He estimated expenditures for the fiscal year ending June 30, 1941, at $8,424,000,-000; receipts at $5,548,000,000; and a deficit of $2,176,000,000, after recovery of

$700,000,000 excess capital funds from government corporations.

Jan. 4, accepted resignation of Attorney General Murphy, effective, Jan. 18

Jan. 4, appointed his third attorney general, Robert H. Jackson

•Jackson took office, Jan. 18.

Jan. 4, appointed Frank Murphy as associate justice

•Murphy, who was confirmed by the Senate, Jan. 16, was the fifth of Roosevelt's nine appointments to the Supreme Court.

Jan. 8, warned Democrats that 1940 elections would be lost if party failed to hold independent voters, Jackson Day dinner, Washington, D.C.

Jan. 30, sent special message to Congress recommending construction by FWA of 50 small hospitals in needy areas

•He asked for $7,500,000 to $10,000,000 for the Public Health Service to build the 100-bed hospitals.

Feb. 9, announced Sumner Welles, undersecretary of state, would confer with leaders of Great Britain and France, Germany, and Italy

Feb. 13, sent special message to Congress urging immediate appropriation of $15,-000,000 for strategic war materials

Feb. 27, inspected Panama Canal

•He visited the Canal Zone during a two-week vacation cruise aboard the *U.S.S. Tuscaloosa.* Upon his return he asked Congress for funds for additional antiaircraft installations and defense planes for the vulnerable canal, but these requests were not acted upon.

•This was the last of his four visits to Panama while in office.

Mar. 14, explained mission of Myron C. Taylor as his personal representative to Pope Pius XII

•The appointment had created concern in Protestant circles. In a letter to Reverend George A. Buttrick, president of the Federal Council of the Churches of Christ in America, Roosevelt denied that the appointment constituted inauguration of formal diplomatic relations with the Vatican.

Mar. 15–Apr. 1, confined to White House with intestional influenza

Apr. 2, sent special message to Congress proposing Plan III to carry out provisions of Reorganization Act

Apr. 6, vetoed bill requiring deportation of alien drug addicts

• In his veto message, he said addiction must be regarded as "a lamentable disease, rather than a crime."

Apr. 10, issued executive order prohibiting transactions in $267,000,000 worth of Norwegian and Danish credits and assets in U.S.

• Germany had invaded Norway and Denmark, Apr. 9.

Apr. 11, sent special message to Congress proposing Plan IV to carry out provisions of Reorganization Act

• The House of Representatives rejected the fourth government reorganization order, which proposed the transfer of the CAA to the commerce department and the abolishment of the air safety board, May 8.

Apr. 12, signed act continuing reciprocal trade agreements program

Apr. 13, condemned invasion of Norway and Denmark

Apr. 18, sent special message to House in which he requested authority to use relief appropriations of $975,000,000 in eight-month period, rather than 12-month period, beginning July 1, due to business decline

Apr. 25, vetoed Philippine travel pay bill

May 2, Philippine travel pay act passed over his veto

• This was the sixth of his nine vetoes that were overridden.

May 11, issued proclamation of neutrality in war between Germany and The Netherlands, Belgium, and Luxembourg

• Germany had invaded the Low Countries, May 10.

May 11, issued executive order prohibiting transactions in $1,619,000,000 worth of Dutch credits and assets in U.S.

• This order also placed similar controls on the $760,000,000 in Belgian assets and the $48,000,000 in Luxembourg assets.

May 16, asked Congress for $1,182,000,000 in additional appropriations for national defense

• "We stand ready not only to spend millions for defense," he said in his address to the joint session, "but to give our service and even our lives for the maintenance of our American liberties."

May 22, sent special message to Congress proposing Plan V to carry out provisions of Reorganization Act

May 26, emphasized need for national defense program during fireside chat

May 31, sent special message to Congress in which he asked additional $1,277,741,170 for national defense, authority to call up national guard and reserves

June 3, received appeal for military supplies from Prime Minister Churchill

• Winston Churchill had succeeded Neville Chamberlain as prime minister of Great Britain, May 11. Roosevelt responded to the British appeal by releasing surplus stocks of arms and ammunition, as well as aircraft. About $43,000,000 worth of military supplies were shipped to Great Britain during June.

June 10, issued proclamation of neutrality in war between Italy and France and Great Britain

• Germany had invaded France in force, June 5. Italy declared war on France and Great Britain and invaded southern France, June 10.

June 10, condemned Italy for invasion of France

• "On this tenth day of June, 1940, the hand that held the dagger has stuck it into the back of its neighbor," he said at the University of Virginia, Charlottesville, Va. He also outlined American policy:

In our American unity, we will pursue two obvious and simultaneous causes: we will extend to the opponents of force the material resources of this nation, and at the same time we will harness and speed up the use of those resources in order that we ourselves in the Americas may have equipment and training equal to the task of any emergency and every defense.

June 11, sent special message to Congress asking additional $50,000,000 for relief of refugees

• Refugee relief was included in the Emergency Relief Appropriation Act of 1940, which he signed, June 26.

June 11, signed navy department appropriation act

• This act provided appropriations totaling $334,216,560, as well as $137,937,362 for contract authorizations.

June 13, signed war department appropriation act

• This act provided appropriations totaling $611,770,364, as well as $252,229,636 for contract authorizations.

June 20, accepted resignation of Secretary

of War Woodring

June 20, accepted resignation of Secretary of Navy Edison, effective, June 24

June 20, appointed his third secretary of war, Henry L. Stimson, and his third secretary of navy, Frank Knox

• Both Stimson and Knox were prominent Republicans. Stimson had served as secretary of war under Taft and secretary of state under Hoover. Knox, the publisher of the Chicago *Daily News*, had been the Republican vice-presidential candidate in 1936.

• Stimson took office, July 10; Knox, July 11.

• Stimson was the last of nine executive officers who served in the cabinets of three presidents.

June 21, act to provide for alterations of certain bridges passed over his veto

• This was the seventh of his nine vetoes that were overridden.

June 25, signed Revenue Act of 1940

• This act provided for tax measures drawn to yield $994,300,000 yearly.

June 26, signed Emergency Relief Appropriation Act of 1940

June 29, signed Alien Registration Act

• The Smith Act required all aliens to submit to registration and fingerprinting. Registration began Aug. 27; about five million persons were registered by Dec. 26. The act was designed to combat subversive activities and made unlawful the advocacy of violent overthrow of the government and membership in groups dedicated to such aims.

• This was the first peacetime legislation that contained antisedition provisions since the Alien and Sedition Acts of 1798.

July 1, sent special message to Congress recommending enactment of steeply-graduated excess profits tax

July 2, issued proclamation prohibiting exportation of war materials and strategic raw products except by state department license

July 4, turned over his repository of personal and official papers to government archives, Hyde Park, N.Y.

July 5, outlined Four Freedoms during press conference

July 10, sent special message to Congress asking additional $4,848,171,957 for national defense

July 18, renominated for president, Democratic national convention, Chicago, Ill.

• He made his acceptance speech to the convention by radio from the White House, 12:25 A.M., July 19.

• He was the only president nominated for a third term.

July 20, signed $4,000,000,000 two-ocean navy appropriations act

July 22, sent special message to Congress asking additional $500,000,000 for Export-Import Bank for loans to Latin American nations

July 29, inspected Norfolk Navy Yard, Norfolk, Va.

• This was the first of a series of inspection tours of military installations and defense plants within 12-hours travel-time from the White House.

July 29, sent special message to Congress in which he again asked national guard ordered into active service

Aug. 8, accepted resignation of Postmaster General Farley, effective, Aug. 31

Aug. 8, appointed his second postmaster general, Frank C. Walker

• Walker took office, Sept. 10.

Aug. 17, accepted resignation of Secretary of Agriculture Wallace, effective, Sept. 4

• Wallace had been nominated as the Democratic vice-presidential candidate, July 18.

Aug. 19, appointed his second secretary of agriculture, Claude R. Wickard

• Wickard took office, Sept. 5.

Aug. 20, named Roy W. Howard as individual who refused call for government service

• There had been much speculation as to the identity of the man alluded to in his acceptance speech of July 19. Talking about the beginnings of the defense program, he had said:

> Regardless of party, regardless of personal convenience, they came —they answered the call. Every single one of them, with one exception has come to the nation's Capital to serve the nation.

• He identified Howard, publisher of the Scripps-Howard newspapers and board chairman of United Press, in answer to a question during his press conference.

Aug. 23, signed Investment Company Act of 1940

Aug. 25, accepted resignation of Secretary of Commerce Hopkins, effective, Sept. 18

Aug. 25, appointed his third secretary of commerce, Jesse H. Jones

•Jones took office, Sept. 19.

Aug. 26, issued executive order coordinating facilities of Grand Coulee and Bonneville dam projects

Aug. 27, signed act authorizing induction of national guard into federal service

•This act limited the use of the national guard to the western hemisphere, territories and possessions of the U.S., and the Philippines.

Sept.2, dedicated $36,000,000 Chickamauga Dam and artificial lakes of TVA, near Chattanooga, Tenn.

•He also dedicated 200,000 acres of timberland in Great Smoky National Park.

Sept. 3, sent special message informing Congress of acquisition of naval and air bases from Great Britain in exchange for 50 overage destroyers

•The bases in Newfoundland and Bermuda were outright gifts to the U.S., while those in the Bahamas, Jamaica, St. Lucia, Trinidad, Antigua, and British Guiana were acquired on 99-year leases.

•He cited the Louisiana Purchase as precedent for the defense agreement. Not a treaty, it did not require ratification by the Senate.

Sept. 16, signed Selective Training and Service Act

•The Burke-Wadsworth Act authorized the first peacetime selective service program. All men between the ages of 21 and 36 were required to register, Oct. 16.

Sept. 17, signed act authorizing RFC to make $10,000,000 loans to finance development of manganese and other strategic and critical minerals

Sept. 19, signed act combining all interstate commerce regulations, except air traffic, within ICC

Sept. 26, issued proclamation banning exportation of scrap iron and steel to any nation outside western hemisphere except Great Britain, effective, Oct. 16

•This order was aimed directly at Japan, who protested the ban as an "unfriendly act," Oct. 8.

Sept. 28, dedicated new National Airport, Washington, D.C.

Oct. 8, signed excess profits tax-amortization act

Oct. 10, signed ratification of Act of Havana

•The Act of Havana, unanimously approved by delegates of the 21 republics of the Pan-American Union, July 30, stipulated that the American republics, individually or collectively, could take possession of European colonies in the western hemisphere endangered by aggression. The act was designed to prevent German encroachment and made the Monroe Doctrine multipartite.

Oct. 17, sent special message to Congress recommending earliest possible development of International Rapids section of St. Lawrence River

Oct. 18, announced series of five campaign speeches

•Since his renomination he had insisted that his presidential duties during such critical times precluded active participation in the political campaign. The mounting strength of Wendell L. Willkie, his Republican opponent, brought about this change of mind. Roosevelt announced that he would speak out against the "misrepresentations" of "Republican orators."

•He delivered major addresses in Philadelphia, Oct. 23; New York City, Oct. 28; Boston, Oct. 30; Brooklyn, Nov. 1; and Cleveland, Nov. 2.

Oct. 29, witnessed selection of first draft numbers, Washington, D.C.

•More than 16,000,000 men between 21 and 36 had registered, Oct. 16. The draft called for the training of 1,200,000 troops over a one-year period.

Oct. 31, dedicated National Institute of Health, Bethesda, Md.

Nov. 5, election day

• See Election of 1940, page 420.

Nov. 11, laid cornerstone of Naval Medical Center, Bethesda, Md.

Nov. 15, issued proclamation of neutrality in war between Italy and Greece

•Italy had invaded Greece, Oct. 28.

Nov. 19, appealed to William Green of AFL for labor peace

•John L. Lewis, founder and president of the CIO, had resigned, Nov. 18. The new president of the CIO, Philip Murray, warned the administration not "to force shotgun agreements between the CIO and the AFL," Nov. 22.

Nov. 26, signed Ramspeck Act

•This act empowered the president to place more than 200,000 employees of "temporary" government agencies under the merit system after noncompetitive examinations.

Dec. 2, signed act that amended Sedition

Act of 1918 to make sabotage federal offense in peacetime as well as wartime

Dec. 5, again urged development of Great Lakes-St. Lawrence Seaway project

Dec. 13, conferred with Duke of Windsor, Governor General of Bahamas, aboard *U.S.S. Tuscaloosa* off Bahamas during vacation cruise

Dec. 16, presidential electors cast ballots

• He received 449 of the 531 electoral votes from the 48 states.

• *See* Election of 1940, below.

Dec. 18, vetoed Logan-Walter bill

• This bill would have subjected rulings and regulations of administrative agencies to court review.

Dec. 20, established Office of Production Management

• He appointed William S. Knudsen as director of the OPM, which had been organized to coordinate defense production and to expedite material aid to the anti-Axis nations "short of war."

Dec. 29, delivered fireside chat on national security

• "There can be no appeasement with ruthlessness," he said and added that the U.S. "must be the great arsenal of democracy."

Note: The official population, according to the 16th census, was 131,669,275.

1941

Jan. 3, third session of 76th Congress adjourned

Jan. 3, first session of 77th Congress

• The administration maintained control of both the Senate and the House of Representatives. The Republicans gained five Senate seats, while the Democrats gained four House seats. The Senate (96 members) consisted of 66 Democrats, 28 Republicans, one Progressive, and one Independent. The House (435 members) consisted of 266 Democrats, 161 Republicans, three Progressives, one Farmer Laborite, one American Laborite, and three vacancies.

Jan. 6, electoral votes tabulated by Congress

• Roosevelt and Wallace were officially declared elected.

Jan. 6, delivered his eighth State of the Union message to Congress

• He outlined and recommended the lend-lease program of aid to the Allies. He also

defined the Four Freedoms: freedom of speech and expression; freedom of worship; freedom from want; and freedom from fear.

Jan. 14, pocket vetoed bill for relief of Mr. and Mrs. Max von der Porten

• This was his only veto that was not accompanied by a message or statement of reason for rejection.

• This bill was passed during the third session of the 76th Congress.

ELECTION OF 1940

Socialist party, convened, Apr. 7, at Washington, D.C., nominated Norman Thomas of New York for president, Maynard C. Krueger of Illinois for vice president.

Socialist Labor party, convened, Apr. 28, at New York City, nominated John W. Aiken of Massachusetts for president, Aaron M. Orange of New York for vice president.

Prohibition party, convened, May 10, at Chicago, Ill., nominated Roger Ward Babson of Massachusetts for president, Edgar V. Moorman of Illinois for vice president.

Communist party, convened, June 2, at New York City, nominated Earl Russell Browder of Kansas for president, James William Ford of New York for vice president.

Republican party, convened, June 24, at Philadelphia, Pa., nominated Wendell Lewis Willkie of Indiana for president, Charles Linza McNary of Oregon for vice president.

• This was the 22nd Republican national convention. It was the fourth Republican convention held in Philadelphia; it was the seventh major convention held in Philadelphia.

Democratic party, convened, July 15, at Chicago, Ill., nominated Franklin Delano Roosevelt of New York for president, Henry Agard Wallace of Iowa for vice president.

• This was the 28th Democratic national convention. It was the sixth Democratic convention held in Chicago; it was the 18th major convention held in Chicago.

Election day, Thursday, Nov. 5, 1940

Popular vote: 49,897,781

    Roosevelt, 27,313,041

    Willkie, 22,348,480

    Thomas, 116,410

    Babson, 58,708

Browder, 46,259
Aiken, 14,883
Electoral vote: 531, 48 states
• Roosevelt, 449, 38 states
(Alabama, 11; Arizona, 3; Arkansas, 9; California, 22; Connecticut, 8; Delaware, 3; Florida, 7; Georgia, 12; Idaho, 4; Illinois, 29; Kentucky, 11; Louisiana, 10; Maryland, 8; Massachusetts, 17; Minnesota, 11; Mississippi, 9; Missouri, 15; Montana, 4; Nevada, 3; New Hampshire, 4; New Jersey, 16; New Mexico,

3; New York 47; North Carolina, 13; Ohio, 26; Oklahoma, 11; Oregon, 5; Pennsylvania, 36; Rhode Island, 4; South Carolina, 8; Tennessee, 11; Texas, 23; Utah, 4; Virginia, 11; Washington, 8; West Virginia, 8; Wisconsin, 12; Wyoming, 3)
• Willkie, 82, ten states
(Colorado, 6; Indiana, 14; Iowa, 11; Kansas, 9; Maine, 5; Michigan, 19; Nebraska, 7; North Dakota, 4; South Dakota, 4; Vermont, 3)

THE 39th ADMINISTRATION

1941

Jan. 20, his third inauguration day
• Roosevelt took the oath of office, administered by Chief Justice Charles Evans Hughes, on the east portico of the Capitol.
• This was the last of three inaugurations at which Chief Justice Hughes officiated.
• He was the last of 21 presidents who were younger than their vice presidents. Roosevelt was six years, 251 days younger than Wallace.
Jan. 31, Associate Justice McReynolds retired
Feb. 12, sent special message to Congress requesting additional $10,000,000 for TVA
Feb. 24, sent special message to Congress requesting $150,000,000 for housing facilities in defense centers
Mar. 11, signed Lend-Lease Act
Mar. 12, sent special message to Congress requesting $7,000,000,000 to finance lend-lease program
Mar. 17, dedicated National Gallery of Art, Washington, D.C.
• The gallery, the largest marble building in the world, was built with funds provided by Andrew W. Mellon, who also contributed his collection of paintings.
Mar. 19, issued executive order establishing National Defense Mediation Board
• The board was established within the OEM to settle labor disputes that interfered with the defense program.
Mar. 27, signed defense aid supplemental appropriation act
• This act authorized an initial appropriation of $7,000,000,000 in arms and other equipment for nations whose defense was con-

sidered vital to the U.S. Total aid granted under this lend-lease appropriation act prior to and during World War II was more than $50,000,000,000.
Apr. 5, signed independent offices appropriation act
• This act provided the additional $10,000,-000 for TVA and other funds.
Apr. 7, issued executive order forming USO
• The United Service Organizations for National Defense included the Salvation Army, YMCA, YWCA, Catholic Community Service, Jewish Welfare Board, and Travelers Aid Society.
Apr. 10, announced agreement with Denmark providing for U.S. military bases in Greenland
Apr. 11, informed Prime Minister Churchill that "sea frontier of the U.S." would be extended to cover North Atlantic west of West Longitude 26°
Apr. 11, issued executive order establishing Office of Price Administration and Civilian Supply within OEM
Apr. 21, urged resumption of bituminous coal mining
• About 85 percent of the coal production had been curtailed by a UMW strike of 400,000 miners, Apr. 2. The strike ended, Apr. 30, although negotiations continued. A new contract beneficial to labor was signed, July 6, the terms of which were retroactive to Apr. 1.
Apr. 23, issued executive order extending civil service classification to additional 100,000 federal workers.
Apr. 30, made radio speech regarding defense savings bonds and stamps
• Series E, F, and G bonds were placed on sale, May 1.

May 1, recommended legislation to provide $3,500,000,000 in additional taxes

May 4, dedicated birthplace of Woodrow Wilson as national shrine, Staunton, Va.

May 5, issued executive order for increased production of heavy bomber aircraft

• Production of five hundred bombers a month in June, 1943, was his goal, which was accomplished three months ahead of schedule. Production during June, 1941, was nine bombers.

May 14, sent special message to Congress requesting additional $22,500,000 to train defense workers

May 15, declared Vichy collaboration with Germany menace to western hemisphere

• France had signed an armistice with Germany, June 22, 1940.

• The Vichy government of Marshal Henri Philippe Petain had been established, July 2, 1940.

May 20, issued executive order establishing Office of Civilian Defense within OEM

May 20, announced discontinuation of Thanksgiving policy

• He admitted the trial of observing Thanksgiving on the next-to-last Thursday in November had failed to benefit retail sales. Thanksgiving was returned to the last Thursday in November.

May 20, sent special message to Congress in which he requested legislation to build pipeline from Texas to Middle Atlantic refineries

• The proposed pipeline would eliminate the danger of submarine attack on coastal vessels and would release the tankers for overseas duty.

May 26, signed crop loan act

• This act provided that the government would lend growers of wheat, corn, rice, cotton, and tobacco up to 85 percent of parity.

May 27, issued proclamation of unlimited national emergency

• Widespread German military success in Europe, the Balkans, and Africa necessitated the placing of U.S. military and civilian defenses in readiness to repel any acts or threats of aggression toward the western hemisphere, he explained during a radio broadcast.

June 2, accepted resignation of Chief Justice Charles Evans Hughes, effective, July 1

June 2, sent special message to Congress again urging speedy authorization of St.

Lawrence Seaway project

June 6, signed act permitting requisition of idle foreign vessels in American waters

June 9, issued executive order of seizure by army of North American Aviation Company plant, Inglewood, Cal.

• The order was brought on by a wildcat strike. It was rescinded after the company and the United Automobile Workers agreed to accept recommendations of the National Defense Mediation Board, July 1.

• This was the first of three defense plants that he ordered seized by the army or the navy prior to Pearl Harbor.

June 12, accepted resignation of Attorney General Jackson, effective, July 10

June 12, appointed Harlan F. Stone as chief justice

• Stone, who was confirmed by the Senate, June 27, was the sixth of Roosevelt's nine appointments to the Supreme Court.

• Stone, who had been appointed by Coolidge in 1925, was the last of three chief justices who had served as associate justices.

• Roosevelt was the tenth of 14 presidents who appointed chief justices.

June 12, appointed James F. Byrnes and Robert H. Jackson as associate justices

• Byrnes, who was confirmed by the Senate, June 12, was the seventh of Roosevelt's nine appointments to the Supreme Court.

• Jackson, who was confirmed by the Senate, July 7, was the eighth of his nine appointments to the Supreme Court.

June 12, issued executive order to OPM to take steps to bar discrimination in defense work

June 14, issued executive order prohibiting transactions in U.S. credits and assets by Germany, Italy, and 14 other European countries

June 16, issued executive order to state department to close German and Italian consulates in U.S. by July 10

• U.S. consulates in European countries controlled by the Axis were ordered closed in retaliation.

June 20, sent special message to Congress in which he announced sinking of *Robin Moor* in South Atlantic

• The *Robin Moor*, victim of a German submarine, was the first American merchant ship sunk by the Nazis. "It is a warning that the United States may use the high seas of the world only with Nazi consent," he said, and added, "We are not yielding and we do not propose to yield."

June 21, sent special message to Congress asking for legislation that would authorize requisitioning of inventories of vital materials for national defense

June 24, promised U.S. aid to U.S.S.R.

•Germany had invaded the Soviet Union, June 22.

June 26, sent special message to Congress in which he requested $300,000,000 for 75,000-unit defense housing program

June 28, signed act that authorized $150,-000,000 for housing and community facilities in defense centers

•This act was later amended to provide a total of $530,000,000 for defense center housing and community facilities.

June 28, issued executive order establishing Office of Scientific Research and Development

June 30, dedicated Franklin D. Roosevelt Library, Hyde Park, N.Y.

July 7, informed Congress of landing of U.S. troops in Iceland, Trinidad, and British Guiana

July 11, his appointment of William J. Donovan as coordinator of information announced

July 13, sent his personal representative, Harry L. Hopkins, to confer with Prime Minister Churchill in London

•The Atlantic Conference was agreed upon during the Churchill-Hopkins meetings.

July 17, issued proclamation of blacklisting of eighteen hundred Latin American firms and persons for aiding Germany and Italy

•This blacklist grew to more than 15,400 firms and persons by 1944.

July 21, sent special message to Congress in which he urged extension of one-year military training by selectees

July 25, approved mission to Moscow by Harry L. Hopkins

•Hopkins arrived in Moscow, July 30, for the three-day series of conferences with Premier Joseph V. Stalin and other Soviet officials.

July 26, issued executive order nationalizing Philippine armed forces for duration of emergency

•The Filipino troops were placed under the command of General Douglas A. MacArthur, who was appointed commander-in-chief of U.S. forces in the Far East.

July 26, issued executive order prohibiting transactions in U.S. credits and assets by Japan and China

•This order halted the shipment of U.S. scrap iron and gasoline to Japan. Great Britain took similar action. Japan retaliated with similar decrees.

July 30, sent special message to Congress in which he requested price control legislation to avert inflation

July 30, signed act authorizing construction of oil pipelines

•The shortage of steel delayed this project. The "Big Inch" (24-inch) pipeline extended 1,254 miles between Longview, Tex., and Phoenixville, Pa., and was completed in the summer of 1943. The "Little Inch" (20-inch) pipeline extended 1,475 miles between Beaumont, Tex., and Linden, N.J., and was completed in December, 1943.

July 30, issued executive order establishing Economic Defense Board

July 30, issued executive order establishing Office of Coordinator of Inter-American Affairs

•The first coordinator was Nelson A. Rockefeller.

Aug. 9–12, met with Prime Minister Churchill aboard U.S.S. Augusta and H.M.S. Prince of Wales at sea, near Argentia, Newfoundland, Canada

Aug. 14, announced Atlantic Charter

•The charter, an eight-point joint declaration of the aims of the English-speaking democracies drafted at the secret meetings at sea, emphasized that postwar order should be based on the principles of freedom, justice, security, and access to raw materials and natural resources.

•Not a treaty or pact, the charter contained neither formal seals nor signatures.

Aug. 15, joint Roosevelt-Churchill message to Stalin delivered by American and British ambassadors, Moscow

•They asked for a conference in Moscow to enable Allied powers to apportion their joint resources in order to mobilize the greatest striking power against Nazism.

Aug. 18, signed service extension act

•This act authorized the extension of training and active military service to 18 months. This legislation passed in the House of Representatives by a single vote, 203–202, after passing in the Senate, 45–30.

Aug. 21, reported to Congress on Atlantic Conference

Sept. 1, gave radio address on foreign policy

•He said:

> I know that I speak the conscience and determination of the American people when I say that we shall do everything in our power to crush Hitler and his Nazi forces.

Sept. 3, issued executive order establishing Office of Defense Health and Welfare Services

Sept. 5, appointed his fourth attorney general, Francis Biddle

Sept. 7, his mother died

Sept. 11, announced "shoot-on-sight" policy after torpedo attack on *U.S.S. Greer* by German submarine

•The destroyer, which was not damaged, was carrying mail to Iceland when attacked.

•In a fireside chat, Roosevelt said:

> We have sought no shooting war with Hitler. We do not seek it now. But neither do we want peace so much that we are willing to pay for it by permitting him to attack our naval and merchandise ships while they are on legitimate business.

•He announced that German and Italian ships that entered American defensive waters would do so at their own peril and he warned that "when you see a rattlesnake poised to strike, you do not wait until he has struck before you crush him."

Sept. 20, signed tax act designed to raise $3,553,400,000 in revenue

•This was the largest tax increase in U.S. history. The act provided for new and higher levies in all categories, including $1,382,100,000 in corporate and excess profits taxes and $1,144,000,000 in individual income taxes.

Sept. 26, spoke during Liberty Fleet Day ceremonies

•During the day, 14 Liberty ships were launched from shipyards on the Atlantic, Pacific, and Gulf coasts.

Oct. 9, received report of British scientists from Dr. Vannevar Bush that atomic bomb could be constructed from U-235

Oct. 9, sent special message to Congress requesting authorization to arm merchant ships, revision of Neutrality Act of 1939

Oct. 11, proposed Anglo-American pooling of research facilities to develop atomic bomb

•Details of this agreement were withheld from the public.

Oct. 14, signed Lanham Act

•This act authorized $150,000,000 for defense housing—half of the amount he had requested, June 26.

Oct. 16, signed act authorizing requisitioning of inventories of vital materials for national defense.

Oct. 24, issued executive order establishing Office of Facts and Figures

Oct. 26, asked John L. Lewis of United Mine Workers to avert strike in captive coal mines

•The strike began Oct. 27, the issue being the union shop in captive coal mines—those owned by and producing only for steel companies. The fifty-three thousand miners returned to work, Nov. 3; the dispute was referred to the National Defense Mediation Board.

Oct. 28, issued executive order establishing Lend-Lease Administration

Nov. 7, declared U.S.S.R. defense vital to U.S.

•A lend-lease credit of $1,000,000 was granted the Soviet Union, Nov. 6.

Nov. 13, sent special message to Congress again requesting revision of Neutrality Act of 1939

Nov. 18, suggested two alternatives to steel companies and striking coal miners

•When the National Defense Mediation Board voted, Nov. 10, against the union shop in captive coal mines, 9–2, the two dissenting members, representatives of the CIO, resigned. The miners struck again, Nov. 17. The strike spread to many commercial mines in Pennsylvania, West Virginia, and Kentucky. Roosevelt offered two alternatives—the suspension of the union shop issue during the period of national emergency or binding arbitration.

Nov. 22, appointed three-man board of arbitration in coal strike

•He appointed John R. Steelman, who represented the public; Benjamin F. Fairless, who represented management; and John L. Lewis of the UMW. The board decided in favor of the union shop system for captive mines, 2–1, Dec. 7.

Nov. 24, announced U.S. troops sent to Dutch Guiana to protect bauxite mines

•Nearly two-thirds of the bauxite used by

the U.S. aluminum industry in the manufacture of aircraft parts was mined in Dutch Guiana.

Nov. 29, spoke at Warm Springs Foundation dinner, Warm Springs, Ga.

• It was his custom to spend Thanksgiving in Georgia. His annual trip to Warm Springs was postponed for nearly a week by the press of official business. He had spent Thanksgiving, Nov. 27, in Washington.

Dec. 3, announced defense of Turkey vital to U.S., directed lend-lease aid be furnished

Dec. 6, sent personal appeal to Emperor Hirohito of Japan for peace in Pacific

Dec. 7, Pearl Harbor attacked by Japanese

• The sneak attack on the Hawaiian naval base by Japanese air and naval forces began at 7:55 A.M., and continued for nearly two hours. Among the 19 U.S. warships sunk or severely damaged were five of the eight battleships at anchor. About 150 U.S. aircraft were destroyed. More than 2,400 were killed—including 68 civilians—and about 1,200 were wounded. The Japanese lost 28 planes and three midget submarines.

• The Japanese also attacked the Philippines, Guam, and Midway Island, as well as Hong Kong and the Malay Peninsula, Dec. 7. Guam fell, Dec. 11; Hong Kong, Dec. 25. Midway withstood the assault.

Dec. 8, addressed joint session of Congress, asked for declaration of war against Japan

• His address began:

> Yesterday, December 7, 1941—a date which will live in infamy—the United States of America was suddenly and deliberately attacked by naval and air forces of the Empire of Japan.

• A state of war was declared in 33 minutes. There was one dissenting vote, that of Representative Jeanette Rankin of Montana. Mrs. Rankin also had voted against the war resolution of 1917.

• This was the last of the seven war messages.

WORLD WAR II

1941

Dec. 9, made fireside chat from White House

• He said during this worldwide broadcast:

> We are now in the midst of a war, not for conquest, not for vengeance, but for a world in which this nation, and all that this nation represents, will be safe for our children. We propose to eliminate the danger from Japan, but it would serve us ill if we accomplished that and found that the rest of the world was dominated by Hitler and Mussolini. So, we are going to win the war and we are going to win the peace that follows.

Dec. 11, sent special message to Congress asking that state of war be recognized between Germany and Italy and U.S.

• Germany and Italy had declared war on the U.S., Dec. 11.

• Congress unanimously passed joint resolutions; Mrs. Rankin voted "present" in both instances.

Dec. 18, issued executive order appointing commission to investigate attack on Pearl Harbor

• He appointed Associate Justice Roberts as chairman. The Roberts Commission submitted its report, Jan. 23, 1942.

Dec. 18, issued executive order establishing Office of Defense Transportation

Dec. 19, issued executive order establishing Office of Censorship

• He appointed Byron Price, executive news editor of the Associated Press, as director.

Dec. 22, signed amended Selective Service Act

• Military conscription was extended to include all men from 20 to 44, and the act also provided for the registration of all between 18 and 64.

Dec. 22, White House announced arrival of Prime Minister Churchill and staff

Dec. 23, held joint press conference with Churchill

• Asked how long he estimated the war would last, the prime minister replied, "If we manage it well, it will only take half as long as if we manage it badly."

Dec. 24, signed $512,000,000 appropriation act to provide housing, sanitary systems, and schools for war workers and families in expanding industrial areas

Dec. 27, White House statement summarized conferences with Churchill

• The Arcadia Conference—as the series of Anglo-American meetings was designated —reaffirmed that Germany was the primary target.

Dec. 28, issued proclamation pledging resources of U.S. to support of Philippines

• "I give to the people of the Philippines my solemn pledge that their freedom will be redeemed and their independence established and protected," he said.

• The Japanese had invaded the Philippines, Dec. 10; Manila fell, Jan. 2, 1942.

1942

Jan. 1, signed joint declaration of United Nations pledging cooperation for victory, White House

• This declaration, a product of the Arcadia Conference, was signed by 26 allied nations. He made the last change in the document, substituting "United Nations" for "Associated Powers."

Jan. 2, first session of 77th Congress adjourned

Jan. 2, informed of fall of Manila

Jan. 5, second session of 77th Congress

Jan. 5, submitted budget message to Congress

• He estimated expenditures for the fiscal year ending June 30, 1943, at $58,927,902,-000, including war expenditures of $52,-786,186,000. He estimated receipts at $17,852,090,000.

Jan. 6, delivered his ninth State of the Union message to Congress

• "The militarists of Berlin and Tokyo started this war," he said. "But the massed, angered forces of common humanity will finish it."

Jan. 12, issued executive order establishing National War Labor Board

• This was the wartime successor to the National Defense Mediation Board. The new board had the power to adjust labor disputes, including the authority to impose mediation. The NDMB had been empowered only to recommend mediation.

Jan. 14, sent special message to Congress recommending legislation to handle private claims against federal government

• He recommended that executive departments and independent agencies be authorized to adjust tort claims up to $1,000, and that U.S. district courts be authorized to handle claims up to $7,500.

Jan. 16, issued executive order establishing War Production Board

• The WPB superseded the Supply Priorities and Allocations Board. He ordered the functions formerly exercised by the Office of Production Management transferred to the WPB, Jan. 24.

Jan. 16, supported continuation of wartime professional baseball

Jan. 24, Roberts Commission attributed Pearl Harbor defeat to failures of military commanders, Rear Admiral Husband Kimmel and Lieutenant General Walter Short

Jan. 24–17, Battle of Macassar Strait

• This was the first major sea battle of World War II. A sizeable Japanese invasion convoy was severely damaged by Allied sea and air forces in the strait between Borneo and Celebes, Indonesia.

Jan. 30, signed Emergency Price Control Act of 1942

Feb. 2, Supreme Court ruled presidential foreign policy cannot be disregarded by courts or upset by states

Feb. 7, approved $500,000,000 lend-lease aid to China

Feb. 7, issued executive order establishing War Shipping Administration

Feb. 9, vetoed bill to provide for registration of certain foreign propaganda agencies

• The bill, a proposed amendment to the Alien Registration Act of 1940, would have restricted representatives of friendly nations in U.S.

Feb. 15, informed of fall of Singapore

Feb. 23, made fireside chat on war progress

• This was one of his most effective radio addresses. He spoke candidly of U.S. losses in the Pacific and reverses to be expected in the future, but he assured the people of ultimate victory.

• During this fireside chat, a Japanese submarine surfaced off Golata, Cal., and shelled an oil refinery. Slight damage was reported, but no casualties.

Feb. 24, issued executive order establishing National Housing Agency

Feb. 27–28, battles of Java Sea and Sunda Strait

• Four Allied cruisers, including the *U.S.S. Houston*, and four destroyers were sunk by the Japanese at the cost of one badly damaged destroyer and four transports.

Feb. 28, issued executive order reorganizing war department
•This order established three major commands under the secretary of war and the general staff: the army ground forces; the army air forces; and the services of supply, later renamed the army service forces.

Mar. 11, issued executive order establishing Office of Alien Property Custodian

Mar. 11, sent report on first year of lend-lease to Congress

Mar. 12, issued executive order reorganizing navy department

Mar. 14, appealed to state governors to conserve rubber by lowering speed limits

Mar. 17, White House announced departure from Philippines of General Douglas A. MacArthur
•Roosevelt had ordered MacArthur to Australia when it became obvious that Bataan could not hold out against the Japanese. MacArthur, his family, and about 15 members of his staff slipped out of Luzon by PT boat, boarded two flying fortresses on the north coast of Mindanao and were flown to Australia.

Mar. 18, issued executive order establishing War Relocation Authority
•His executive order of Feb. 19 had authorized the establishment of military areas from which "any or all persons" could be removed. A military zone that included about half of California, two-thirds of Washington and Oregon, and less than half of Arizona was established, Mar. 3. All persons of Japanese descent were required to evacuate this area. About 110,000 Japanese and Japanese-Americans were housed in ten detention centers outside the military zone.

Mar. 20, approved suspension of some antitrust proceedings for duration of war

Mar. 25, awarded Congressional Medal of Honor to General MacArthur

Apr. 10, received message of surrender of Bataan
•Bataan fell, Apr. 9. Several thousand troops under General Jonathan M. Wainwright withdrew to Corregidor Island in Manila Bay.
•The "death march" of American and Filipino prisoners began, Apr. 10. Forced to march about 85 miles in six days, thousands died or were killed during the or-

deal. At least fifty-two hundred Americans and a larger number of Filipinos died.

Apr. 18, Tokyo bombed by American B-25's
•The raid by 16 carrier-based bombers was not officially confirmed until May 19, when he decorated General James H. Doolittle at the White House. Only minor damage was inflicted on the Japanese capital and other cities that were bombed, but the raid bolstered American morale.

Apr. 18, issued executive order establishing War Manpower Commission

Apr. 21, told press conference Doolittle planes had been based in "Shangri-La"
•The White House refused to confirm Japanese reports of the Tokyo raid. For military reasons, the role of the *U.S.S. Hornet*, the aircraft carrier from which the B-25's had been launched, was suppressed.
•Toward the end of the war, a new carrier was christened the *U.S.S. Shangri-La*. Shangri-La was the Tibetan locale in James Hilton's popular novel, *Lost Horizon*.

Apr. 21, presented Congressional Medal of Honor to Lieutenant Edward H. O'Hara, U.S.N., White House
•This was the first time that he personally presented the highest award for extraordinary valor in combat.

Apr. 27, sent special message to Congress in which he outlined seven-point economic stabilization program
•He recommended an extensive taxation program, ceilings on prices and rents, curtailment of installment buying, rationing, and limitation of personal incomes to $25,-000 annually.

Apr. 27, registered in fourth draft
•He was among thirteen million men between the ages of 45 and 64 who registered.

Apr. 28, announced during fireside chat several hundred thousand U.S. soldiers and sailors had been dispatched "thousands of miles from home" to "bases and battlefields"

May 6, surrender of Corregidor

May 7–8, Battle of Coral Sea
•This American victory halted the Japanese advance. This was the first naval battle in history in which all fighting was done by carrier-based planes without engagement by surface ships.

May 12, received President Manuel Quezon of Philippines, White House

May 14, signed act establishing Women's

Army Auxiliary Corps
• This was the first time that women were enlisted for noncombat military service. More than sixty-five thousand officers and enlisted women joined the WAAC in little more than a year. The status of the corps was changed from auxiliary to regular component of the army, July 1, 1943, and its name changed to Women's Army Corps (WAC).

May 16, commuted prison sentence of Earl Browder
• The Communist party presidential candidate in 1936 and 1940 had served 14 months of a four-year sentence for passport fraud.

May 27, sent special message to Congress in which he requested additional $600,000,-000 for war housing

May 28, sent greetings to *Yank* on publication of first issue
• *Yank* was an army weekly magazine. The editorial staff consisted entirely of enlisted men.

May 29-June 1, conferred with Soviet Foreign Minister Vyacheslav M. Molotov, White House
• The White House announced, June 11, that "full understanding was reached with regard to the urgent tasks of creating a second front in Europe in 1942." Molotov had insisted on the phrase, "in 1942," although it was unlikely.

June 3–6, Battle of Midway
• This was the first major defeat of the Japanese navy, which lost four carriers, 12 or more other vessels, 275 planes, and more than 4,500 men. The Americans lost a carrier and a destroyer, 150 planes, and about 300 men.

June 5, signed joint resolution of state of war between U.S. and Hungary, Rumania, and Bulgaria

June 5, warned Japanese of retaliation in kind in event of use of poison gas
• The Japanese were reported to have used gas in various localities in China.

June 10, received King George of Greece, White House

June 12, made radio appeal for scrap rubber campaign
• More than 300,000 tons of scrap rubber were collected, June 15–30.

June 13, issued executive order establishing Office of War Information
• This order consolidated the Office of Facts

and Figures, the Office of Government Reports, and the Coordinator of Information within the OEM.

June 13, issued military order establishing Office of Strategic Services

June 20–25, conferred with Prime Minister Churchill, Hyde Park, N.Y., and White House
• They discussed the advisability of a North African landing rather than a cross-Channel operation.

June 24, received King Peter II of Yugoslavia, White House

July 2, issued military order establishing military commission to try eight captured German saboteurs
• The eight had landed from German submarines—four in Amagansett, L.I., June 13, and four in Ponte Vedra Beach, Fla., June 17. They were captured by the FBI in New York City and Chicago, Ill., June 20–27. All were found guilty, Aug. 3. Six were electrocuted, Aug. 8, in the District of Columbia jail. Roosevelt commuted the sentences of the other two to life imprisonment and 30 years.

July 28, told press conference U.S. armed forces had grown to four million men

July 29, attended wedding of Mrs. Louise Gill Macy and Harry L. Hopkins, Oval Study, White House

July 30, signed act establishing Women Appointed for Voluntary Emergency Service (WAVES), women's branch of navy

July 30, warned neutral nations against providing asylum to war criminals
• He cautioned the neutrals against giving asylum to Hitler, Mussolini, and Tojo and their "gangs" when the enemy leaders attempted to "escape their just deserts."

Aug. 8–9, Battle of Savo Island
• Three U.S. heavy cruisers and an Australian heavy cruiser were lost in this battle, a defeat that severely endangered the U.S. Marine force that had landed on Guadalcanal, Aug. 7. The Guadalcanal campaign continued for the next six months.

Aug. 21, announced appointment of Wendell L. Willkie as special emissary to Near East and Russia

Aug. 31, dedicated Naval Medical Center, Bethesda, Md.
• He had helped draft the plans for the center.

Sept. 3, spoke to International Student Assembly from White House

• "The Nazis, the Fascists, and the militarists of Japan have nothing to offer to youth—except death," he said during the 31-language radio broadcast.

Sept. 7, sent special message to Congress in which he reiterated his seven-point anti-inflation program

Sept. 7, explained his anti-inflation program during fireside chat

• He threatened to use his executive power if Congress did not act, explaining that "if the vicious spiral of inflation ever gets under way, the whole economic system will stagger."

Sept. 17, issued executive order providing for coordination of rubber program

• A complete synthetic rubber industry was developed during the next 18 months.

Sept. 17, began 12-state inspection tour of war plants, army, navy, and air force training camps

Sept. 23, his personal representative, Wendell L. Willkie, met with Stalin, Moscow

• Willkie called for a second front "at the earliest possible moment," Sept. 26.

Oct. 1, returned to Washington, D.C.

• Roosevelt's 8,754-mile inspection tour had taken him to the West Coast and back.

Oct. 2, signed Stabilization Act of 1942

• This act established the Office of Economic Stabilization and imposed civilian purchasing power controls by fixing farm prices, urban and rural rents, wages, and salaries. A limit of $25,000 was placed on annual salaries.

Oct. 3, accepted resignation of Associate Justice Byrnes

Oct. 3, issued executive order appointing first director of economic stabilization, James F. Byrnes

Oct. 7, announced plan to try war criminals after war

• He emphasized that no mass reprisals were contemplated. He said that punishment would be meted out to "ringleaders responsible for the organized murder of thousands of innocent persons and the commission of atrocities."

Oct. 9, sent special message to Congress in which he asked for establishment of Veterans' Rehabilitation Service

Oct. 10, signed act that repealed clause of Neutrality Act of 1939, which required U.S. citizens living abroad to return every two years to retain citizenship

Oct. 11–12, Battle of Cape Esperance

• The Japanese lost a carrier and four destroyers in this engagement in the Solomon Islands.

Oct. 12, gave fireside chat on homefront

• During an extensive report on his recent inspection tour, he said that the minimum age for selective service would be lowered from 20 to 18.

Oct. 14, received report from Wendell L. Willkie on 31,000-mile trip to Near East, Russia, and China

Oct. 21, signed act designed to yield $7,000,000,000 in increased income tax revenue

Oct. 23, Mrs. Roosevelt arrived in England

• The first lady returned from her trip to the British Isles, Nov. 18.

Nov. 2, sent special message to Congress in which he urged integration of war production with Canada

Nov. 7, broadcast to French people regarding invasion of North Africa

• U.S. and British forces landed, Nov. 8, at Casablanca, Oran, and Algiers, French North Africa. These major ports and airfields were secured within 48 hours.

Nov. 12–15, naval battle of Guadalcanal

• The Japanese lost two battleships, a cruiser, two destroyers, and ten transports; the U.S. lost two cruisers and seven destroyers. This victory insured the success of American ground forces on Guadalcanal. The Japanese abandoned the island in early February, 1943.

Nov. 13, signed act lowering draft age to 18

• When he signed this act, he announced that he would appoint a committee to study postwar educational opportunities for servicemen.

Nov. 23, signed act establishing *Semper Paratus* ("Always Ready") Service (SPARS), women's branch of coast guard

Nov. 30, approved order of OES Director Byrnes to remove ceiling on farm wages

• The purpose of this order was to expedite the retention and recruitment of needed agricultural workers.

Nov. 30, opened first war loan drive

• The first drive resulted in sales of $12,947,000,000, Nov. 30–Dec. 23.

Dec. 2, issued executive order establishing Petroleum Administration for War

Dec. 4, declared WPA had earned "honorable discharge," announced discontinuation of WPA projects

Dec. 5, issued executive order centralizing war food policies under department of agriculture

Dec. 16, second session of 77th Congress adjourned

•The 77th Congress had been in session since Jan. 3, 1941, except for two days in January, 1942. The Congress had voted appropriations of about $215,000,000,000—all but $15,000,000,000 for defense and war purposes. "My truly sincere thanks for all that you have accomplished during these difficult two years," he said.

Dec. 24, signed joint resolution increasing pay of about 1,277,000 government workers

•This resolution provided for the adoption of the 48-hour week. Time and a half was to be paid for over 40 hours or a flat ten percent increase for those government workers whose duties could not be fitted to an overtime schedule.

1943

Jan. 6, first session of 78th Congress

•The administration maintained control of both the Senate and the House of Representatives. The Republicans gained nine Senate and 46 House seats. The Senate (96 members) consisted of 58 Democrats, 37 Republicans, and one Progressive. The House (435 members) consisted of 220 Democrats, 207 Republicans, two Progressives, one Farmer Laborite, one American Laborite, and four vacancies.

Jan. 6, submitted annual budget message to Congress

•He estimated expenditures for the fiscal yearing ending June 30, 1944, at $104,-124,000,000, including $100,000,000,000 for war expenditures; receipts at $51,000,-000,000; and the deficit at about $53,000,-000,000. He was deliberately vague so as not to reveal actual expenditures to the enemy.

Jan. 7, delivered his tenth State of the Union message to Congress

•He informed Congress of military and naval production progress:

The state of this Nation is good—
the heart of this Nation is sound—
the spirit of this Nation is strong—
the faith of this Nation is eternal.

Jan. 9, secretly left Washington

Jan. 11, appointed Wiley B. Rutledge as associate justice

•Rutledge, who was confirmed by the Senate, Feb. 8, was the last of Roosevelt's nine appointments to the Supreme Court.

•He had appointed all members of the current Supreme Court except Associate Justice Roberts, a 1930 Hoover appointee.

•Roosevelt and Washington appointed an equal number of associate justices who served on the Court—eight. Only Washington appointed more associate justices—nine.

•Only Washington appointed more justices—13. Only Washington appointed more justices who served on the Court—11.

Jan. 11, flew from Miami, Fla., to Trinidad, British West Indies

•He was the first president to travel outside the U.S. during wartime.

•He was the first of two presidents who visited Trinidad while in office. The other was Truman.

•This was the first of his two visits to Trinidad while in office.

Jan. 12, flew from Trinidad to Belem, Brazil

•This was the second of his three visits to Brazil while in office.

Jan. 13, flew from Brazil to Bathurst, Gambia

•Gambia was then a British crown colony and protectorate.

•He was the only president to visit Gambia while in office.

•This was the first of his two visits to Gambia while in office.

•He was the first of two presidents to visit Africa while in office. The other was Eisenhower.

Jan. 14, flew from Gambia to Casablanca, French Morocco

•He was the third of five presidents who visited war zones while in office.

•He was the first president to visit a war zone since Lincoln.

•He was the first of two presidents to visit Morocco while in office. The other was Eisenhower.

Jan. 14–21, conferred with Prime Minister Churchill, Casablanca

•He and Churchill reached agreement on the invasion of Sicily and Italy, and decided to launch around-the-clock air assaults against the Germans. General Eisenhower was appointed supreme commander of Al-

lied operations in North Africa.
- Both Stalin and Chiang Kai-shek had been invited to the conference but did not attend.

Jan. 21, motored northeast to review American troops in Rabat and Port Lyautey, Morocco
- He lunched in the open with twenty thousand soldiers of the Fifth Army.

Jan. 24, held joint press conference with Churchill, Casablanca
- They announced that the war would be fought until the "unconditional surrender" of Germany, Italy, and Japan.

Jan. 24, with Churchill, motored to Marrakesh, Morocco

Jan. 25, flew from Marrakesh to Bathurst, Gambia
- This was the second of his two visits to Gambia while in office.

Jan. 26, spent most of day aboard *U.S.S. Memphis,* also made trip up Gambia River aboard British lend-lease tug, *H.M.S. Aimwell*

Jan. 27, visited Liberia
- He flew from Bathurst to Roberts Field, then motored the 50 miles to the capital, Monrovia, where he lunched with President Edwin Barclay. He inspected American Negro troops in Liberia and also visited some of the sixty-nine thousand acres of Firestone rubber plantations, before turning to Bathurst.
- Monrovia was founded in 1822 by the American Colonization Society and was named for President Monroe.
- Roosevelt was the only president who visited Liberia while in office.

Jan. 27, flew from Gambia to Natal, Brazil

Jan. 28–29, conferred with President Getulio Vargas of Brazil, Natal
- He and Vargas conferred aboard a U.S. destroyer in Potengi River Harbor; he also inspected military installations.
- This was the last of his three visits to Brazil while in office.

Jan. 29, flew from Brazil to Trinidad
- This was the second of his two visits to Trinidad while in office.

Jan. 30, flew from Trinidad to Miami, Fla.

Jan. 31, trained to Washington, D.C.
- He had traveled 16,965 miles during his 23-day trip.

Feb. 1, sent treaty for relinquishment of extraterritorial rights in China to Congress
- The Chinese treaty was unanimously

ratified by the Senate, Feb. 11.

Feb. 4, congratulated Stalin on Russian victory at Stalingrad
- The Germans had surrendered Stalingrad, Feb. 2.

Feb. 5, issued executive order establishing interdepartmental committee within department of justice to consider cases of subversive activities by federal employees
- This committee considered 671 cases by Sept. 30, 1945. Only 24 discharges resulted; 143 cases were suspended because of resignations or other reasons; 104 cases received the attention of other agencies; disciplinary action was taken in three cases.

Feb. 6, urged Congress not to repeal $25,-000 net salary limitation

Feb. 9, issued executive order establishing 48-hour minimum work week in war plants

Feb. 12, paraphrased Lincoln's "we cannot escape history" speech in address to White House Correspondents Association.
- He said:

    Again—we cannot escape history. We have supreme confidence that, with the help of God, honor will prevail. We have faith that future generations will know that here, in the middle of the twentieth century, there came a time when men of good will found a way to unite, and produce, and fight to destroy the forces of ignorance, and intolerance, and slavery, and war.

Feb. 15, reiterated his support for $25,000 net salary limitation

Feb. 19, held joint press conference with Madame Chiang Kai-shek, White House

Feb. 20, opposed plan to require Senate confirmation of federal employees whose annual salaries exceeded $4,500
- This proposal was an attempt by Senator Kenneth D. McKellar of Tennessee to gain patronage control of TVA personnel. The McKellar maneuver was unsuccessful.

Feb. 22, sent message of admiration to Marshal Stalin on 25th anniversary of Red Army

Mar. 2–3, battle of Bismarck Sea
- A Japanese fleet of ten warships and 12 transports was destroyed, as well as more than 60 Japanese planes.

Mar. 9, sent special message to Congress in which he recommended amendment to organic act for Puerto Rico

•The proposed amendment would have authorized Puerto Ricans to elect their own governor.

Mar. 9, issued executive order defining foreign information functions of OWI

•Squabbling between officials of the OWI and the OSS led to this modification of the OSS executive order of June 13, 1942. Closer cooperation resulted.

Apr. 2, vetoed Bankhead farm bill

•This bill would have excluded government benefit payments from the calculation of parity prices for ceiling purposes. Farmers would have been given "an unwarranted bonus at the expense of the consumers," he said in his veto message, which would have caused "an inflationary tornado."

•Although the bill had been passed by huge majorities in the Senate, 78–2, and the House of Representatives, 149–40, his veto was not overridden.

Apr. 7, opened second war loan drive

•The second drive resulted in sales of $18,555,000,000, Apr. 12–May 1.

Apr. 7, issued executive order establishing committee for congested production areas

•War-worker congestion had led to many problems in production centers. The committee designated 18 areas where it concentrated its efforts, obtaining necessary priorities to solve housing, food, health, fuel, and transportation problems.

Apr. 8, issued executive order to "hold the line" on prices and wages

•This order halted price increases in agricultural commodities, as well as wage and salary increases. The OPA succeeded in rolling back the prices of 39 commodities within two months.

Apr. 11, criticized rider method of legislation

•He refused to sign the Public Debt Act of 1943, because of a rider terminating his authority to limit net yearly salaries to $25,000. Rather than veto the bill and nullify the basic content—which raised the public debt limit from $125,000,000,000 to $210,000,000,000—he allowed it to become law without his signature.

Apr. 13, spoke at dedication of Thomas Jefferson Memorial, Washington, D.C.

Apr. 13, departed on inspection tour of training camps

•He visited the Marine Corps training station at Parris Island, S.C., Apr. 14; Maxwell Field, Ala., and Fort Benning, Ga., Apr. 15.

Apr. 15–16, visited Warm Springs, Ga.

•This was his first visit to Warm Springs since Nov. 30, 1941.

Apr. 17, visited WAAC training center, Fort Oglethorpe, Ga.; and Camp Forrest, Tenn.

Apr. 18, visited Camp Joseph T. Robinson, Ark., and Camp Gruber, Okla.

Apr. 19, issued executive order establishing Solid Fuels Administration for War

•This order centralized authority concerning solid fuels, which included anthracite, bituminous, subbituminous, and lignitic coals.

Apr. 19, visited Douglas Aircraft assembly plant, Tulsa, Okla.

Apr. 20, visited Mexico

•He conferred with President Manuel Avila Camacho in Monterrey.

•He was the second of seven presidents who visited Mexico while in office.

Apr. 21, accompanied by President Avila, visited Naval Training Center, Corpus Christi, Tex.

Apr. 21, instructed department of state to make public formal protest to Japanese of execution of Tokyo raiders

•A total of 80 airmen had participated in the 16-plane Tokyo raid, Apr. 18, 1942. One was killed, two were reported missing, five were interned in Russia, and 64 returned through China. Two of the B-25's were forced down in Japan; eight airmen were captured. Three were executed, Oct. 15, 1942. The other five were imprisoned; one died of malnutrition and dysentery, Dec. 1, 1942; and four were liberated after VJ-Day.

Apr. 22–28, continued inspection tour of training camps

•He visited installations in Texas, Colorado, Kansas, Nebraska, Missouri, Indiana, and Kentucky.

Apr. 29, returned to Washington, D.C.

•He had traveled 7,652 miles during his 17-day trip.

May 1, issued executive order to secretary of interior to seize coal mines

•A general strike of 450,000 bituminous coal miners and 80,000 anthracite miners began, May 1.

May 2, gave fireside chat on mine seizure

•On his way to the Oval Room, he was informed that John L. Lewis of the United Mine Workers and Secretary of Interior Ickes had reached agreement for the miners to return to work, May 4, for a 15-day truce period. Roosevelt delivered the speech anyway. "There can be no one among us—no one faction—powerful enough to interrupt the forward march of our people to victory," he said.

May 12–25, conferred with Prime Minister Churchill, White House
•This two-week conference was officially designated Trident. The target date for the invasion of France was set at May 1, 1944. Much of the discussion was given to coordinating the air offensive against Germany. General Eisenhower was ordered to push the campaign in the Mediterranean area until Italy was forced to withdraw from the war.
•Plans also were drawn for the war in the Pacific. It was decided to build up Chinese materiel by flying "over the hump" from India to China; intensified campaigns against the Marshall Islands, some of the Carolines, the rest of the Solomons, and New Guinea were also blueprinted.

May 13, sent special message to Congress in which he asked additional appropriation for war housing

May 25, held joint press conference with Prime Minister Churchill, White House

May 26, telegraphed union leaders to end rubber strike in Akron, Ohio
•He threatened seizure if the strike didn't end by noon, May 27. The workers returned to their jobs.

May 27, issued executive order establishing new committee on fair employment practice as independent unit within OEM

May 27, issued executive order establishing Office of War Mobilization
•He appointed James F. Byrnes as director.

June 7, spoke to delegates to United Nations Conference on Food and Agriculture, White House
•"Freedom from want and freedom from fear go hand in hand," he said.

June 8, again warned enemy against use of poison gas
•He promised "full and swift retaliation in kind" if poison gas was used.

June 9, signed pay-as-you-go income tax act
•A 20 percent withholding of taxable income became effective, July 1, for all wage and salary earners. This act also provided for the cancellation of 75 percent of individuals' 1942 or 1943 tax, whichever was lowest.

June 11, appealed by radio to citizens of Italy to oust Mussolini, quit Axis

June 11, held special press conference for business paper editors

June 21, issued proclamation directing dispersal of Detroit rioters
•A total of 34—including 25 Negroes—were killed, and more than seven hundred were injured during the race riots. About thirteen hundred were arrested—85 percent of whom were young Negroes.

June 23, called action of UMW leaders "intolerable"
•The third interruption of coal production by the UMW had ended, June 22. "The action of the leaders of the United Mine Workers coal miners has been intolerable," he said, and added that he intended to ask Congress to raise the draft limit to 65 in order to induct those who interrupted work in plants, mines, and other establishments owned or operated by the government.

June 25, vetoed war labor disputes bill

June 25, War Labor Disputes Act passed over his veto
•The Smith-Connally Anti-Strike Act made illegal strikes in plants seized by the government and provided criminal penalties for those who instigated, directed or aided such strikes. It also made unions liable for failure to give 30-day notice of intention to strike.
•This was the eighth of his nine vetoes that were overridden.

June 30, issued executive order transferring WPA functions to Federal Works Agency
•This order officially terminated the WPA and ordered its $130,000,000 of remaining funds turned back to the treasury department.
•During its eight years of existence, the WPA had employed more than 8,500,000 individuals on more than 1,400,000 projects at a total cost of about $11,000,000,-000.

July 2, vetoed bill that would have imposed restrictions on Commodity Credit Corporation

July 7, signed final amendment to Lanham Act
•The Lanham Act of 1941 had provided for the original $150,000,000 war housing appropriation. Additional appropriations added up to $1,200,000,000 for defense and wartime housing of workers in essential industries. Roosevelt's May 13 request

for another $400,000,000 had been reduced by one-fourth.

July 9, announced invasion of Sicily during state dinner for General Henri Giraud

• The invasion of Sicily began, July 10, and ended successfully, Aug. 17, at a cost of seventy-four hundred U.S. casualties.

• Giraud and Charles de Gaulle were co-presidents of the French Committee of National Liberation.

July 10, assured Pope Pius XII neutral status of Vatican City and papal domains throughout Italy would be respected

July 15, issued executive order establishing Office of Economic Warfare

• This order abolished the Board of Economic Warfare and transferred various subsidiary corporations of the Reconstruction Finance Corporation to the OEW.

• His action brought to an end the public controversy over responsibility for an alleged lag in war production that had raged for months between Vice President Wallace (who had been chairman of the Board of Economic Warfare) and Secretary of Commerce Jones (who headed the RFC).

July 25, informed of resignation of Mussolini

• King Victor Emmanuel III of Italy announced the resignation of Mussolini and his cabinet and the appointment of Marshal Pietro Badoglio as head of government.

July 27, issued summation of 1944 budget

• He estimated expenditures at $106,000,-000,000; receipts at $38,000,000,000; and the deficit at $68,000,000,000.

July 28, gave fireside chat on war progress, plans for peace

• "The first crack in the Axis has come," he said.

Aug. 9, White House announced his return from Canadian fishing trip

• During his one-week stay in Canada, he lived in a special Canadian Pacific Railway train on a siding at the water's edge of the northern shore of Lake Huron.

• This was the fifth of his seven visits to Canada while in office.

Aug. 12, pledged independence of Philippines as soon as Japanese power destroyed

Aug. 13–15, held preliminary conversations with Prime Minister Churchill prior to Quebec conference, Hyde Park, N.Y.

Aug. 17–24, conferred with Prime Minister Churchill, Quebec, Canada

• The first Quebec conference, which was designated as Quadrant, resulted in the decision to supplement the Normandy invasion of 1944 by a diversionary operation in southern France. The Southeast Asia Command was established. The chiefs of the naval staffs reported that the Battle of the Atlantic had turned to the Allies' favor.

• This was the sixth of Roosevelt's seven visits to Canada while in office.

Aug. 25, addressed Canadian Parliament, Ottawa

Aug. 31, promoted General Eisenhower to permanent rank of major general

Sept. 3, informed of successful invasion of Italy by Allies

• The British Eighth Army crossed the Strait of Messina between Sicily and Italy.

Sept. 8, informed of unconditional surrender of Italy

• The U.S. Fifth Army made amphibious landings, Sept. 9, from seven hundred Allied ships at Salerno.

Sept. 8, gave fireside chat on third war loan drive

• The third drive resulted in sales of $18,-944,000,000, Sept. 9–Oct. 2.

Sept. 17, sent special message to Congress on war progress

Sept. 25, issued executive order establishing Foreign Economic Administration

Sept. 28, sent special message to Congress in which he recommended self-government for Puerto Rico

Oct. 4, received Ambassador Andrei Gromyko of U.S.S.R.

Oct. 6, sent special message to Congress in which he requested authority to proclaim free Philippines

Oct. 11, sent special message to Congress urging repeal of Chinese exclusion laws

Oct. 13, issued joint statement with Churchill and Stalin acknowledging Italian government pledge to submit to will of Italian people after Germans driven from country

• King Victor Emmanuel III, through Marshal Badoglio, had declared war against Germany, Oct. 13.

Oct. 14, gave dinner for President Elie Lescot of Haiti, White House

Oct. 27, sent special message to Congress in which he urged legislation for education of war veterans

Nov. 1, again ordered Secretary of Interior Ickes to seize coal mines

• The mines had been returned to the operators by Oct. 12. The fourth wartime strike of coal miners brought on the new seizure order.

•Ickes negotiated a 37½-cent hourly wage increase, Nov. 3, which was approved by the National War Labor Board and the UMW, Nov. 5.

Nov. 1, sent special message to Congress on food program

•This message elaborated on the fundamental principles and details of his stabilization program. He explained that subsidies would cost $800,000,000 during 1943, but that billions had been saved by the government and consumers. Prices had increased 13 percent, but food prices, except for fresh vegetables and fruits, had advanced only four percent. Fresh vegetables and fruits had increased 58 percent between September, 1942, and May, 1943.

Nov. 9, spoke at ceremony of signing by 44 nations of agreement creating United Nations Relief and Rehabilitation Administration (UNRRA), White House

Nov. 11, sent special message to Congress on reverse lend-lease

•He said that Great Britain had agreed to stop collecting dollars for raw materials and foodstuffs supplied to the U.S. Instead, the commodities would be counted as reverse lend-lease, offsetting U.S. aid.

Nov. 13, signed act extending terms of President Manuel Quezon and Vice President Sergio Osmena of Philippines until Japanese expulsion

Nov. 13, departed aboard U.S.S. Iowa for North Africa, Hampton Roads, Va.

Nov. 20, arrived in Oran, Algeria

•He was the only president who visited Algeria while in office.

•This was the first of his two visits to Algeria while in office.

•This was the second of his three visits to Africa while in office.

Nov. 21, flew to Tunis

•He and General Eisenhower toured the battlefields.

•Roosevelt was the first of two presidents who visited Tunis while in office. The other was Eisenhower.

•This was the first of his two visits to Tunis while in office.

Nov. 22–26, conferred with Prime Minister Churchill and Generalissimo Chiang Kai-shek, Cairo, Egypt

•The first Cairo conference concerned the war against Japan. The three leaders agreed that Japan was to be stripped of all Pacific islands acquired since 1914, as well as Manchuria, Formosa, Korea, and the Pescadores.

•He was the only president who visited Egypt while in office.

•This was the first of his three visits to Egypt while in office.

Nov. 27, flew from Egypt to Teheran, Iran

Nov. 28–Dec. 1, conferred with Prime Minister Churchill and Marshal Stalin, Teheran, Iran

•The Teheran conference primarily concerned the planned invasion of France and Soviet support of the assault by offensive action on the eastern front. Stalin agreed to enter the war against Japan, but no specific date was agreed upon.

•Roosevelt was the first of two presidents who visited Iran while in office. The other was Eisenhower.

•He was the first of four presidents who visited Asia while in office.

Dec. 1, vetoed bill that would have designated December 7 as Armed Services Honor Day

Dec. 1–2, visited Camp Amirabad, Iran

•He reviewed American troops of the Persian Gulf Command.

Dec. 2, flew from Iran to Cairo, Egypt

•This was the second of his three visits to Egypt while in office.

Dec. 4–6, conferred with Prime Minister Churchill and President Ismet Inonu of Turkey, Cairo, Egypt

•The second Cairo conference reaffirmed the "traditional relations of friendship" between Turkey and the U.S., Great Britain and the U.S.S.R. It was a failure in the sense that Turkey did not agree to enter the war against Germany. Inonu maintained his position of neutrality until January, 1945.

Dec. 7, flew from Egypt to Tunis

•In Tunis, he announced the appointment of General Eisenhower as supreme commander of the planned invasion of western Europe.

•This was the second of Roosevelt's two visits to Tunis while in office.

Dec. 8, with Eisenhower, flew from Tunis to Malta

•He paid tribute to the heroism of the Maltese. Malta became the most bombed spot in the world during World War II, undergoing twelve hundred air raids.

• He was the only president who visited Malta while in office.

• This was the first of his two visits to Malta while in office.

• He was the second of seven presidents who visited Europe while in office.

• He was the first of three presidents who visited four foreign continents while in office.

Dec. 9, with Eisenhower, flew from Malta to Sicily

• He landed in Castelvetrano, reviewed American troops, and decorated General Mark Clark and five other officers of the Fifth Army.

• He was the only president who visited Sicily while in office.

• He was the second of six presidents who visited Italy while in office.

Dec. 10, boarded *U.S.S. Iowa* for return cruise to U.S.

• He arrived in Washington, Dec. 17.

Dec. 10, announced he had signed amendment to draft law placing fathers at bottom of eligible lists

Dec. 17, signed act that repealed Chinese exclusion laws

• This act repealed the laws passed between 1882 and 1913 barring Chinese immigration to the U.S. It made the Chinese subject to regular quotas established by the immigration act of 1924 and made Chinese residents eligible for naturalization as American citizens.

Dec. 18, called operators and union officials to White House conference, Dec. 19, in attempt to avert railroad strike

Dec. 19, met with 15 management representatives and five union officials for three hours, White House

• Two of the five brotherhoods—representing the engineers and the trainmen— agreed to accept his offer to arbitrate, Dec. 24.

Dec. 21, first session of 78th Congress adjourned

Dec. 24, made fireside chat on Teheran and Cairo conferences

Dec. 27, issued executive order to U.S. Army to seize railroads

• Three of the five brotherhoods had refused his offer to arbitrate; these unions came to terms, Jan. 14, 1944. The government relinquished control of the railroads, Jan. 18, 1944.

1944

Jan. 10, second session of 78th Congress

Jan. 10, submitted annual budget message to Congress

• He estimated expenditures for the fiscal year ending June 30, 1945, at $11,115,000,-000 including $90,000,000,000 for war purposes; receipts at $40,769,000,000; and the deficit at $59,346,000,000.

Jan. 11, sent his 11th State of the Union message to Congress

• He set forth his "Economic Bill of Rights," which included recommendations for tax legislation to reduce exorbitant war profits, a cost-of-food law with a floor and a ceiling on farm product prices, and reenactment of the stabilization statute. He also asked for a national service law.

• This was his only State of the Union message that he did not deliver in person. Suffering from influenza, he was confined to the White House by his physician. He broadcast his message to the nation that evening.

Jan. 11, major Allied air offensive against Europe began

• The British and American air strikes built steadily. More than two thousand tons of bombs were dropped on Berlin by eight hundred B-17's, Mar. 6.

Jan. 18, announced settlement of railroad strike

• The government relinquished control of the railroads at midnight, after a settlement involving a wage increase of nine to 11 cents an hour had been agreed upon. The railroads' annual wage cost increased by about ten percent to $3,500,000,000.

Jan. 18, opened fourth war loan drive

• The fourth drive resulted in sales of $16,-730,000,000, Jan. 18–Feb. 15.

Jan. 22, issued executive order establishing war refugee board

Jan. 22, Allied campaign in central Italy began

• The campaign began with costly amphibious landings at Anzio. Severe fighting continued for almost four months before Cassino, a key position in the German Gustav Line, was taken and the road to Rome opened, May 18.

Jan. 25, sent special message to Congress in which he recommended legislation to provide for absentee balloting by members of armed forces

Jan. 31, U.S. forces invaded Marshall Islands
•Roi and Namur were secured, Feb. 3; Kwajalein, Feb. 6; and Eniwetok, Feb. 22.
Feb. 5, held special press conference for Negro Newspaper Publishers Association
Feb. 18, vetoed cost-of-living bill
•In his veto message, he said the bill to extend the Commodity Credit Corporation to June 30, 1945, was inflationary and would raise the cost-of-living substantially. While he favored the continuation of the corporation, he felt the bill as drawn would, in effect, repeal the Stabilization Act of 1942.
Feb. 19, issued executive order establishing Surplus War Property Administration
Feb. 22, vetoed revenue bill
•In his veto message, he said that the $2,-315,200,000 tax bill was "wholly ineffective," and would actually raise slightly less than $1,000,000,000. "The bill is replete with provisions that not only afford indefensible special privileges to favored groups, but sets dangerous precedents," he said. He characterized the legislation as "a tax relief bill providing relief not for the needy but for the greedy." Majority Leader Alben W Barkley, who called the veto message an insult to Congress and an attack on his integrity, resigned.
Feb. 23, sent "Dear Alben" letter to Barkley
•He asked the Kentucky senator to reconsider resigning and expressed the hope that if the majority leader resigned that the Democratic members of the Senate "will immediately and unanimously re-elect you." Barkley was reelected, unanimously.
Feb. 24, issued executive order establishing Retraining and Reemployment Administration in OWM
Feb. 25, Revenue Act of 1944 passed over his veto
•This was the last of his nine vetoes that were overridden.
Feb. 28, signed act extending Commodity Credit Corporation to July 1, 1945
Feb. 29, U.S. forces invaded Admiralty Islands
•Los Negros was seized, Feb. 29; Lorengau fell, Mar. 18.
Mar. 14, condemned Nazi use of Rome as military center
Mar. 15, asked governors to supply necessary information on pending soldier vote bill

•The bill provided that members of the armed forces must make their own applications for state absentee ballots, that the federal form was available for those who applied for but did not get state ballots in time and whose governors had certified that the federal form was legal under state laws. Within a week, 47 of the 48 governors replied, some inconclusively. About three-fourths of the governors said that the federal form was not authorized by existing laws of their states.
Mar. 24, asked frontiers opened "to all victims of oppression"
•He again said that war criminals would be tried and punished.
Mar. 31, sent special message to Congress on soldier vote bill
•He said that the bill was wholly inadequate, but that he would allow the act to become law without his signature.
Apr. 8, departed for vacation at Hobcaw Barony, near Georgetown, S.C.
•Hobcaw Barony was a plantation owned by Bernard M. Baruch. He was still feeling the effects of the flu he had contracted after his return from Teheran. During February and March, his physician had put him on a diet and he had lost 15 pounds. His normal weight was between 185 and 190 pounds.
•His absence from Washington led to many rumors about his health, most of which were malicious.
Apr. 25, issued executive order to Secretary of Commerce Jones to seize Montgomery Ward plants and facilities
•Between 1942 and 1944, Montgomery Ward officials repeatedly rejected directive orders of the NWLB. When the company's president, Sewell Avery, defied the executive order for six hours, he was carried bodily out of his Chicago, Ill., office and deposited on the sidewalk. The plants were returned to management, May 9—the same day that employees voted recognition of the CIO union.
Apr. 28, Secretary of Navy Knox died
May 7, returned to White House after month vacation at Hobcaw Barony
May 17, addressed Conference of International Labor Organization, White House
•He had taken part in the first ILO conference in Washington, 1919. The ILO was the only organization connected with the League of Nations to survive the period

between World War I and World War II.
• He had signed the joint resolution that authorized U.S. membership in the ILO, June 19, 1934.

May 17, signed lend-lease extension act

May 19, his fourth secretary of navy, James V. Forrestal, took office
• Forrestal was the last secretary of navy who was a member of the cabinet.

May 20, announced Vice President Wallace had departed on special mission to China

May 21, issued executive order to war department to seize Montgomery Ward subsidiary
• The Hummer Manufacturing Company, a war plant subsidiary of Montgomery Ward in Springfield, Ill., was seized for failure of the parent company to comply with an NWLB directive of Apr. 14.

May 29, signed simplified tax act
• This act extended the application of the withholding tax to provide for the collection at source from those with salaries or wages under $5,000.

June 5, gave fireside chat on fall of Rome
• Rome had been occupied by the U.S. Fifth Army and the British Eighth Army, June 4.

June 6, D-Day
• The invasion of France, Operation Overlord, was the largest amphibious military operation of all time. About 175,000 men were involved in the spearhead assault along the 60-mile line in Normandy from the Orne River to the Cotentin Peninsula. Between 4,500 and 5,000 ships, including more than 1,500 landing craft, were used, supported by about 9,000 aircraft.
• Allied casualties on D-Day were more than 10,000, including about 6,600 Americans, between 2,500 and 3,000 British, and about 1,000 Canadians. German casualties were estimated at between 4,000 and 9,000.
• About 1,000,000 men, more than 560,000 tons of supplies and about 170,000 vehicles had landed in Normandy by July 1.

June 9, held special press conference for business paper editors

June 10, signed act raising national debt limit to $260,000,000,000

June 12, sent special message to Congress regarding refugee policy
• He informed Congress that one thousand refugees who had fled their homelands in southern Italy would be brought to the U.S. Most were women and children; they were housed in an emergency camp, Fort Oswego, N.Y.

June 12, gave fireside chat to open fifth war loan drive
• The fifth drive resulted in sales of $20,639,000,000, June 12–July 8.

June 15, U.S. forces landed in Mariana Islands
• The Japanese air and naval base of Saipan was attacked, June 15, and was captured after severe fighting, July 9. Guam was attacked, July 20, and taken, Aug. 10. Tinian was attacked, July 23, and taken, Aug. 1. The Marianas campaign was completed, Aug. 10.

June 16, air offensive began against Japanese home islands
• The first raid by B-29's was made against Kyushu, southernmost of the four main islands of Japan.

June 19–20, Battle of Philippine Sea
• In the battle—fought exclusively by carrier-based planes—the Japanese lost three carriers and about two hundred planes. Several Japanese battleships and cruisers were severely damaged.

June 22, signed Servicemen's Readjustment Act
• The GI Bill of Rights provided that veterans with 90 days of active service between Sept. 15, 1940, and July 25, 1947, could qualify for education or training for one year plus time served, with a maximum of four years allowed. The act also provided for loans at interest of not more than four percent for up to 50 percent backing of purchases of businesses, business and farming equipment. Veterans were guaranteed unemployment insurance for a full year, with a maximum of $20 per week allowed (the "52–20 Club").

June 29, signed two Philippine joint resolutions
• One established the Philippine Rehabilitation Commission. The other set policy for the granting of independence to the Philippines, permitting U.S. acquisition of air and army bases.

June 30, signed Stabilization Extension Act

July 1, signed Public Health Service Act of 1944

July 11, announced he would accept nomination for fourth term
• "If the convention should ... nominate me for the Presidency, I shall accept," he wrote Robert E. Hannegan, chairman of

the Democratic national committee. "If the people elect me, I will serve."

July 14, stated position on renomination of Vice President Wallace

• "I personally would vote for his renomination if I were a delegate to the convention," he wrote Senator Samuel D. Jackson of Indiana, who was to be permanent chairman of the convention. "At the same time, I do not wish to appear in any way as dictating to the convention." Hannegan, who wanted Senator Harry S. Truman of Missouri as the vice-presidential nominee, leaked the letter to the press, July 17. This maneuver made it plain that the president was not demanding Wallace's renomination.

July 18, U.S. forces captured St. Lo

• The breakthrough from St. Lo—the road center connecting Normandy and Brittany —led to the overrunning of Brittany, Aug. 10.

July 19, endorsed Truman and Douglas as acceptable vice-presidential nominees

• In a letter to Hannegan, dated July 19 but written before he left Washington, Roosevelt said that he would "be very glad to run" with either Associate Justice William O. Douglas or Senator Truman. Hannegan conferred with the president aboard his special train during his Chicago stopover, July 15. When Hannegan came out of the private car, he informed Grace Tully, the president's private secretary, that "the President wants you to retype this letter and switch these names so it will read 'Harry Truman or Bill Douglas.'"

July 19, arrived in San Diego, Cal.

• He had left Washington, July 13, spent the following day at Hyde Park, N.Y., and then boarded his private train for the trip to the West Coast.

July 20, renominated for president, Democratic national convention, Chicago, Ill.

• He made his acceptance speech by radio, speaking to the convention from his train, San Diego.

• He was the only president nominated for a fourth term.

July 21, boarded cruiser, *U.S.S. Baltimore*, at San Diego for voyage to Pearl Harbor

July 26, arrived at Pearl Harbor, Oahu, Hawaii

• He conferred for three days with General Douglas A. MacArthur, Southwest Pacific Allied commander, and Admiral Chester W. Nimitz, commander of the Pacific fleet.

• While in Hawaii, he reviewed Seventh Division veterans of Attu and Kwajalien, visited wounded who had just arrived from Saipan, and inspected a dozen naval and military establishments.

• His visit to Schofield Barracks, July 27, occurred on the tenth anniversary of his first visit to Hawaii while in office.

• This was the second of his two visits to Hawaii while in office.

July 29, held press conference, Honolulu, Hawaii

Aug. 3, arrived in Alaska

• After a four-day cruise from Hawaii, he arrived at Adak, the naval air base in the Aleutian Islands. Fog and rain prevented the *Baltimore* from putting in at Dutch Harbor, but he did inspect the naval air and submarine base at Kodiak Island. He "played hookey," as he put it, when he fished for three hours off Juneau, and caught one halibut and one flounder.

• He was the second of five presidents who visited Alaska while in office.

Aug. 12, arrived at Bremerton, Wash.

• He reviewed his Pacific inspection trip in a radio address from the Puget Sound Navy Yard. He spoke from the slanted forecastle deck of a destroyer, in the face of a stiff wind. He was uncomfortable standing in his braces, which he had not worn in more than a year, and spoke poorly. The bad reaction to the broadcast led to a revival of the rumors concerning his health.

Aug. 15, U.S. forces invaded southern France

• The Seventh Army landed between the mouth of the Rhone River and Cannes and drove up the Rhone Valley.

Aug. 18, lunched with Senator Truman, White House

• This was his first meeting with his running mate.

Aug. 23, received delegates to Dumbarton Oaks conference

• Representatives of the U.S., Great Britain, U.S.S.R., and China had met at Dumbarton Oaks, an estate in Georgetown, Washington, D.C., Aug. 21. The framework for what ultimately was to become the United Nations Organization was devised at the conference, which concluded, Oct. 7.

Aug. 25, hailed liberation of Paris

Aug. 29, again urged legislation for self-government of Puerto Rico

Sept. 11–16, conferred with Prime Minister Churchill, Quebec, Canada
• The second Quebec conference set the zones of occupation and postwar treatment of Germany. The Morgenthau Plan, which would have reduced Germany to the status of an agricultural nation, was tentatively approved.
• This was the last of his seven visits to Canada while in office.
Sept. 12, U.S. forces entered Germany
• The Americans crossed into Germany near Eupen and Trier.
Sept. 14, U.S. forces invaded Palau Islands
• Peleliu and Augaur were taken during the campaign, which ended, Oct. 13. Babelthuap, occupied by thirty thousand Japanese troops, was bypassed.
Sept. 16, held joint press conference with Prime Ministers Churchill and King, Quebec
Sept. 18, requested study of war agency liquidation, administrative reorganization for peace
Sept. 21, sent special message to Congress in which he recommended Missouri River development plan
Sept. 22, signed department of agriculture organic act of 1944
• This act substantially strengthened the Rural Electrification Administration.
Sept. 23, requested study of methods to aid veterans who wished to engage in farming
• More than one million members of the armed forces had indicated their intent to reestablish themselves as farmers and ranchers.
Sept. 23, made "Fala speech," Teamsters Union, Washington, D.C.
• Although he had told the press that the speech to the Teamsters "won't be very political," this was the highlight of the 1944 campaign. Aware that Thomas E. Dewey had made inroads while he remained aloof and also aware that the question of his health had become of paramount importance, Roosevelt began:
> Well, here we are again—after four years—and what years they have been! I am actually four years older —which seems to annoy some people. In fact, millions of us are more than eleven years older than when we started in to clear up the mess that was dumped in our laps in 1933.

• The most memorable portion of the speech, however, concerned his dog:
> These Republican leaders have not been content with attacks on me, or my wife, or on my sons. No, not content with that, they now include my little dog, Fala. Well, of course, I don't resent attacks, and my family doesn't resent attacks, but Fala *does* resent them. You know, Fala is Scotch, and being a Scottie, as soon as he learned that the Republican fiction writers in Congress and out had concocted a story that I had left him behind on the Aleutian Islands and had sent a destroyer back to find him—at a cost to the taxpayers of two or three, or eight or twenty million dollars—his Scotch soul was furious. He has not been the same dog since. I am accustomed to hearing malicious falsehoods about myself —such as that old, worm-eaten chestnut that I have represented myself as indispensable. But I think I have the right to resent, to object to libelous statements about my dog.

Oct. 3, signed Surplus Property Act of 1944
• This act established the Surplus Property Board to dispose of the estimated $100,-000,000,000 in surplus property. He signed it reluctantly and called the legislation poorly drawn.
Oct. 3, issued executive order expanding Office of War Mobilization to Office of War Mobilization and Reconversion
Oct. 4, announced 2,300,000 long tons of food and other civilian supplies shipped to Italy since invasion of Sicily
Oct. 5, called for end of poll taxes
• "The right to vote must be open to our citizens irrespective of race, color or creed —without tax or artificial restriction of any kind," he said in a radio address from the White House.
Oct. 9, congratulated Dumbarton Oaks conferees
• "The task of planning the great design of security and peace has been well begun," he said of the conference that had ended, Oct. 7.
Oct. 20, U.S. forces invaded Philippine Islands
• The drive to retake the islands began when

forces under General Douglas A. MacArthur invaded Leyte.

Oct. 21, Aachen captured
•Aachen was the first sizable German city taken by the Allies.

Oct. 23–26, Battle of Leyte Gulf
•This second battle of the Philippine Sea resulted in the decisive defeat of the Japanese. There were three engagements; the Japanese lost two battleships, four carriers, nine cruisers, and nine destroyers. When the remainder of the Japanese fleet withdrew, the U.S. controlled the Philippine Sea.

Oct. 27, made major campaign speech, Shibe Park, Philadelphia, Pa.
•He spoke also in Wilmington, Del., and Camden, N.J.

Oct. 28, made major campaign speech, Soldier Field, Chicago, Ill.
•He spoke also in Fort Wayne, Ind.

Oct. 29, made campaign speech by radio, White House

Nov. 4, made major campaign speech, Fenway Park, Boston, Mass.
•He spoke also in Bridgeport and Hartford, Conn., and Springfield, Mass.

Nov. 6, made election eve radio address, Hyde Park, N.Y.

Nov. 7, election day
•"I am glad to be here on this election day again—I might say again and again and again!" he told neighbors who gathered at his Hyde Park home to congratulate him on his reelection.
•This was the first wartime election since 1864.
• *See* Election of 1944, page 442.

Nov. 19, opened sixth war loan drive
•The sixth drive resulted in sales of $21,-621,000,000, Nov. 20–Dec. 16.

Nov. 21, accepted resignation of Secretary of State Hull, effective, Nov. 30

Nov. 21, appointed his second secretary of state, Edward R. Stettinius, Jr.
•Stettinius took office, Dec. 1.

Dec. 1, ordered heads of executive departments and independent agencies to refrain from public statements indicating early end of war

Dec. 16–26, Battle of Bulge
•A last-ditch German counteroffensive advanced about 50 miles in the Ardennes before being checked. The surprise attack cost more than seventy thousand American casualties, including at least eight thousand killed. The Allied line was not restored until Jan. 21, 1945.

Dec. 18, presidential electors cast ballots
•He received 432 of the 531 electoral votes from the 48 states.
• *See* Election of 1944, page 442.

Dec. 19, second session of 78th Congress adjourned

Dec. 19, said "I am going down the whole line a little left of center," in reply to press conference question as to whether he was going right or left politically

Dec. 21, convention with Canada for avoidance of double taxation and prevention of estate-taxes evasion ratified

Dec. 22, characterized newspaper columnists as "unnecessary excrescence on our civilization"
•The reporters at his press conference roared with laughter when correspondent May Craig interposed, "But you have one in the family!"
•Mrs. Roosevelt's column, "My Day," appeared in more than 150 newspapers.

Dec. 27, issued executive order to seize Montgomery Ward and Company properties
•This second seizure of the company followed a strike against one of Montgomery Ward's retail stores in Detroit, Mich., Dec. 9, when the firm refused to comply with the NWLB order to raise wages considered substandard.
•The Circuit Court of Appeals upheld the constitutional power of the president to seize the plants, June 8, 1945. The properties were returned to the company by a Truman executive order, Aug. 25, 1945.

Dec. 29, pocket vetoed bill to abolish Jackson Hole national monument
•He had established Jackson Hole as a national monument by executive order, Mar. 15, 1943. More than 173,000 acres, Jackson Hole is located in west Wyoming at the south end of Grand Teton National Park.
•This was the last of his 263 pocket vetoes.
•He employed the pocket veto power more often than any other president.

1945

Jan. 3, first session of 79th Congress
•The administration maintained control of both the Senate and the House of Representatives. The Republicans gained one Senate seat; the Democrats gained 23 House seats. The Senate (96 members) con-

sisted of 57 Democrats, 38 Republicans, and one Progressive. The House (435 members) consisted of 243 Democrats, 190 Republicans, one Progressive, and one American Laborite.

Jan. 3, submitted annual budget message to Congress

• He "tentatively" estimated expenditures for the fiscal year ending June 30, 1946, at $83,000,000,000, including $70,000,000,-000 for war purposes; receipts at $41,300,-000,000; and the deficit at $41,700,000,-000.

• He estimated that the national debt would be $252,000,000,000 by June 30, 1945; $292,000,000,000 by June 30, 1946.

• He listed war expenditures as $6,700,000,-000 in 1941; $28,300,000,000 in 1942; $75,-100,000,000 in 1943; $89,700,000,000 in 1944; and $89,000,000,000 in 1945.

Jan. 5, electoral vote tabulated by Congress

• Roosevelt and Truman were officially declared elected.

Jan. 6, delivered his 12th and last State of the Union message to Congress

• "International cooperation on which enduring peace must be based is not a one-way street," he said. He broadcast excerpts from the speech that evening.

ELECTION OF 1944

Prohibition party, convened, Nov. 12, 1943, at Indianapolis, Ind., nominated Claude A. Watson of California for president, Andrew Johnson of Kentucky for vice president.

Socialist Labor party, convened, Apr. 29, 1944, at Detroit, Mich., nominated Edward A. Teichert of Pennsylvania for president, Arla A. Albaugh of Ohio for vice president.

Communist party, convened, May 19, at New York City, nominated no candidates.

Socialist party, convened, June 2, at Reading, Pa., nominated Norman Thomas of New York for president, Darlington Hoopes of Pennsylvania for vice president.

Republican party, convened, June 26, at Chicago, Ill., nominated Thomas Edmund Dewey of New York for president, John William Bricker of Ohio for vice president.

• This was the 23rd Republican national convention. It was the 12th Republican convention held in Chicago; it was the 19th major party convention held in Chicago

Democratic party, convened, July 19, at Chicago, Ill., nominated Franklin Delano Roosevelt of New York for president, Harry S. Truman of Missouri for vice president.

• This was the 29th Democratic national convention. It was the seventh Democratic convention held in Chicago; it was the 20th major party convention held in Chicago.

Election day: Tuesday, Nov. 7, 1944

Popular vote: 47,969,016
    Roosevelt, 25,612,610
    Dewey, 22,017,617
    Thomas, 79,003
    Watson, 74,779
    Teichert, 45,336
    others, 139,671

Electoral vote: 531, 48 states
• Roosevelt, 432, 36 states
    (Alabama, 11; Arizona, 4; Arkansas, 9; California, 25; Connecticut, 8; Delaware, 3; Florida, 8; Georgia, 12; Idaho 4; Illinois, 28; Kentucky, 11; Louisiana, 10; Maryland, 8; Massachusetts, 16; Michigan, 19; Minnesota, 11; Mississippi, 9; Missouri, 15; Montana, 4; Nevada, 3; New Hampshire, 4; New Jersey, 16; New Mexico, 4; New York, 47; North Carolina, 14; Oklahoma, 10; Oregon, 6; Pennsylvania, 35; Rhode Island, 4; South Carolina, 8; Tennessee, 12; Texas, 23; Utah, 4; Virginia, 11; Washington, 8; West Virginia, 8)
• Dewey, 99, 12 states
    (Colorado, 6; Indiana, 13; Iowa, 10; Kansas, 8; Maine, 5; Nebraska, 6; North Dakota, 4; Ohio, 25; South Dakota, 4; Vermont, 3; Wisconsin, 12; Wyoming, 3)

• Roosevelt was the last of four presidents who defeated major opponents representing the same state (Dewey).

THE 40th ADMINISTRATION

1945

Jan. 20, his fourth inauguration day

• Roosevelt took the oath of office, administered by Chief Justice Harlan F. Stone, on the south portico of the White House.

•This was the only inauguration at which Stone officiated.

•This was the first of two oath-taking ceremonies at which Stone officiated. The chief justice administered the oath to Truman less than three months later.

•This was the only time that an inauguration was held at the White House.

•Roosevelt was the last of three presidents who participated in four inaugural ceremonies.

•His fourth inaugural address lasted slightly more than five minutes and contained only 559 words. He said:

> We have learned to be citizens of the world, members of the human community. We have learned the simple truth, as Emerson said, that "The only way to have a friend is to be one."

•This was the second shortest inaugural address. Washington had delivered the shortest inaugural address (135 words), Mar. 4, 1793.

Jan. 22, departed from Washington for Yalta conference

Feb. 2, arrived at Valletta, Malta

•He made the ten-day voyage aboard the cruiser, *U.S.S. Quincy*.

•This was the second of his two visits to Malta while in office.

Feb. 3, flew from Malta to Yalta, Crimea, U.S.S.R.

•He was accompanied on the fourteen-hundred-mile plane trip by Prime Minister Churchill, who had met him at Malta.

•Roosevelt was the only president who visited Russia while in office.

Feb. 3–11, conferred with Prime Minister Churchill and Premier Stalin, Yalta

•The Crimean conference reaffirmed the "unconditional surrender" policy, and agreement was reached on a Declaration of Liberated Europe, which pledged the three powers to support postwar governments formed by free elections. In exchange for entering the war against Japan "in two or three months after Germany has surrendered," the Soviet Union was awarded the Kurile Islands, half of Sakhalin Island, and an occupation zone in Korea, as well as rights in Manchuria, Dairen, and Port Arthur. The U.S. and Great Britain agreed to recognize the autonomy of Outer Mongolia. Eastern Poland was awarded to the Soviet Union, the eastern border being fixed on the Curzon Line; Poland was to be given additional German territory to the north and west.

•It was agreed that a conference to draft the charter of the United Nations Organization would convene in San Francisco, Cal., Apr. 25. The U.S. and Great Britain supported the Russian request for three votes in the UN; the U.S.S.R. agreed to support a U.S. request for three votes if asked for in the future. The Russian position was that the Ukraine and Byelorussia, while constituent parts of the Soviet Union, should be accorded full membership in the UN as though they were independent nations. This arrangement remained secret until late March; no logical reason for withholding details of the agreement has ever been advanced.

Feb. 12, flew from Yalta to Egypt

•During the next three days, he conferred aboard the *U.S.S. Quincy* in Great Bitter Lake with King Farouk I of Egypt, King Ibn Saud of Saudi Arabia, and Emperor Haile Selassie of Ethiopia.

•This was the last of Roosevelt's three visits to Egypt while in office.

•This was the last of his three visits to Africa while in office.

Feb. 14, traveled through Suez Canal to Alexandria, Egypt

•Prime Minister Churchill came aboard the *Quincy* at Alexandria. This was their last meeting.

Feb. 17, traveled from Alexandria to Algiers, Algeria

•This was the second of his two visits to Algeria while in office.

Feb. 28, arrived in Washington, D.C.

•His trip to Yalta was the last of his 24 trips outside the United States while in office.

•He was the president who traveled most often outside the U.S. while in office. He visited 19 countries while in office. Only Eisenhower visited more countries while in office, 28.

Feb. 28, appointed delegates to UN conference in San Francisco

•He appointed Secretary of State Stettinius, Cordell Hull, Senator Tom Connally, Senator Arthur H. Vandenberg, Representative Sol Bloom, Representative Charles A. Eaton, Harold Stassen, and Dean Virginia Gildersleeve of Barnard College.

Mar. 1, addressed Congress on Yalta conference

Mar. 1, accepted resignation of Secretary of Commerce Jones

Mar. 2, appointed his fourth secretary of commerce, Henry A. Wallace
• Wallace was the last of Roosevelt's 25 cabinet appointments.
• Roosevelt and Grant both appointed 25 men to their cabinets, the largest number of cabinet appointments.
Mar. 10, signed act granting insurance companies moratorium under antitrust acts
Mar. 26, sent special message to Congress in which he urged strengthening of trade agreements act
Mar. 29, vetoed relief of Charles R. Hooper bill
• This was the last of his 635 vetoes. More than half of his vetoes—342—concerned private relief bills.
Apr. 5, held final press conference, Little White House, Warm Springs, Ga.
• This was the last of his 998 press conferences.
• This was the largest number of press conferences held by a president.

DEATH

Date of death: Apr. 12, 1945
• Roosevelt was the only president who died during his fourth term.
• He was the seventh of eight presidents who died in office.
Place of death: Warm Springs, Ga.
• He was the only president who died in Georgia.
• He died in the Little White House in Warm Springs, which has been preserved as he left it. Officially entitled Franklin D. Roosevelt's Little White House and Museum, it is owned by the State of Georgia and administered by the Franklin D. Roosevelt Warm Springs Memorial Commission. It is open to the public daily, 9 A.M. to 5 P.M., and weekends during June, July and August, 9 A.M. to 6 P.M. Admission: adults, $1.25; children under 13, active military and dependents, and groups of 15 or more, 75 cents. Children under six, free.
• He was the fifth of six presidents who lay in state in the White House.
Age at death: 63 years, 72 days
Cause of death: Cerebral hemorrhage
• He was the last of four presidents who died of natural causes while in office.
Place of burial: Hyde Park, N.Y.
• He was the last of six presidents who were buried in New York.

THE VICE PRESIDENTS
(32nd, 33rd and 34th)

Note: Roosevelt was the only president who had three vice presidents.

Full name: John Nance Garner (32nd)
Date of birth: Nov. 22, 1868
Place of birth: near Detroit, Tex.
• Garner was the first of two vice presidents who were born in Texas. The other was Lyndon Johnson.
Religious denomination: Methodist
• He was the second of three vice presidents who were Methodists.
Occupation: Lawyer
• He was admitted to the Texas bar, 1890; member of the Texas legislature, 1898–1902; member of House of Representatives, 1903–1933; speaker of the House, 1931–1933.
• He was the 18th of 21 vice presidents who served in the House of Representatives before their terms of office.
• He was the second of two vice presidents who served as speaker of the House. The other was Schuyler Colfax.
Term of office: Mar. 4, 1933, to Jan. 20, 1941 (7 years, 322 days)
• Garner was the sixth of seven vice presidents who were elected to second terms.
• He was the fourth of five vice presidents who served two terms.
• He was the last of four vice presidents who served more than seven years.
• Roosevelt and Garner were the 34th of 41 president-vice president teams.
• They were the fourth of five president-vice president teams that were reelected.
• They were the second of two Democratic president-vice president teams that were reelected. The other team was Wilson and Marshall.
• Garner was the first vice president whose term ended on January 20.
Age at inauguration: 64 years, 102 days
State represented: Texas
• He was the first of two vice presidents who represented Texas. The other was Lyndon Johnson.
Political party: Democratic
• He was the 11th of 16 vice presidents who were Democrats.
Occupation after term: Retired
Date of death: Nov. 7, 1967
Place of death: Uvalde, Tex.

• He was the only vice president who died in Texas.

Age at death: 98 years, 350 days

• He was the vice president who lived to the most advanced age.

Place of burial: Uvalde, Tex.

• He was the only vice president who was buried in Texas.

Full name: Henry Agard Wallace (33rd)
Date of birth: Oct. 7, 1888
Place of birth: Adair County, Iowa

• Wallace was the only vice president who was born in Iowa.

Religious denomination: Episcopalian

• He was the seventh of eight vice presidents who were Episcopalians.

• Roosevelt and Wallace were both Episcopalians. They were the last of seven president-vice president teams of the same religious denomination.

College: Iowa State College, Ames, Iowa
Date of graduation: 1910
Occupations: Editor, author, geneticist

• He was associate editor of *Wallace's Farmer*, the farm journal established by his grandfather, Henry Wallace, 1910–1924; wrote several books, including *Agricultural Prices*, 1920, and *Corn and Corn Growing*, with E. N. Bressman, 1923; editor of *Wallace's Farmer*, succeeding his father, Henry Cantwell Wallace (who had been secretary of agriculture under Presidents Harding and Coolidge), 1924–1933; developed and marketed hybrid seed corn; secretary of agriculture, appointed by President Roosevelt, 1933–1941.

• He was the last of four vice presidents who served in the cabinet.

Term of office: Jan. 20, 1941, to Jan. 20, 1945 (4 years)

• He was the 15th of 17 vice presidents who served four-year terms.

• Roosevelt and Wallace were the 35th of 41 president-vice president teams.

Age at inauguration: 52 years, 105 days
State represented: Iowa

• He was the only vice president who represented Iowa.

Political party: Democratic

• He was the 12th of 16 vice presidents who were Democrats.

Occupations after term: Editor, author, geneticist, politician

• He was secretary of commerce, appointed by Roosevelt, 1945–1946; editor of *New Republic*, the liberal weekly, 1946–1948;

presidential candidate of leftist Progressive party, polled 1,157,172 votes, 1948; resigned from Progressive party, 1950. He wrote more than a dozen books, including *The Century of the Common Man* (1943), and *Toward World Peace* (1948). As a geneticist, he worked extensively on hens' eggs, strawberries, and gladioli.

• He was the second of two vice presidents who served in the cabinet both before and after their terms of office. The other was John C. Calhoun.

Date of death: Nov. 18, 1965
Place of death: Danbury, Conn.

• He was the only vice president who died in Connecticut.

Age at death: 77 years, 42 days
Place of burial: Des Moines, Iowa

• He was the only vice president who was buried in Iowa.

Full name: Harry S. Truman (34th)
• *See* pages 447–486.

• Truman was the only vice president who was born in Missouri.

• He was the second of two vice presidents who were Baptists. The other was Richard Mentor Johnson.

• He was the 14th of 17 vice presidents who served in the Senate before their terms of office.

• He was the 13th of 14 vice presidents who served less than one term.

• He was the last of seven vice presidents who served less than one year.

• Roosevelt and Truman were the 36th of 41 president-vice president teams.

• Truman was the only vice president who represented Missouri.

• He was the 13th of 16 vice presidents who were Democrats.

THE CABINET

State: Cordell Hull of Tennessee, Mar. 4, 1933, to Nov. 30, 1944
• Edward Reilly Stettinius, Jr., of Virginia, Dec. 1, 1944, to June 27, 1945
Treasury: William Hartman Woodin of New York, Mar. 5, 1933, to Dec. 31, 1933
• Henry Morgenthau, Jr., of New York, Jan. 1, 1934, to July 22, 1945
War: George Henry Dern of Utah, Mar. 4, 1933, to Aug. 27, 1936
• Harry Hines Woodring of Kansas, Sept. 25, 1936, to June 20, 1940

•Henry Lewis Stimson of New York, July 10, 1940, to Sept. 21, 1945

Attorney General: Homer Stille Cummings of Connecticut, Mar. 4, 1933, to Jan. 2, 1939

•Frank Murphy of Michigan, Jan. 2, 1939, to Jan. 18, 1940

•Robert Houghwout Jackson of New York, Jan. 18, 1940, to July 10, 1941

•Francis Biddle of Pennsylvania, Sept. 5, 1941, to June 30, 1945

Navy: Claude Augustus Swanson of Virginia, Mar. 4, 1933, to July 7, 1939

•Charles Edison of New Jersey, Jan. 2, 1940, to June 24, 1940

•Frank Knox of Illinois, July 11, 1940, to Apr. 28, 1944

•James Vincent Forrestal of New York, May 19, 1944, to Sept. 17, 1947

Postmaster General: James Aloysius Farley of New York, Mar. 4, 1933, to Aug. 31, 1940

•Frank Comerford Walker of Pennsylvania, Sept. 10, 1940, to May 8, 1945

Interior: Harold LeClaire Ickes of Illinois, Mar. 4, 1933, to Feb. 15, 1946

Agriculture: Henry Agard Wallace of Iowa, Mar. 4, 1933, to Sept. 4, 1940

•Claude Raymond Wickard of Indiana, Sept. 5, 1940, to June 29, 1945

Commerce: Daniel Calhoun Roper of South Carolina, Mar. 4, 1933, to Dec. 23, 1938

•Henry Lloyd Hopkins of New York, Dec. 24, 1938, to Sept. 18, 1940

•Jesse Holman Jones of Texas, Sept. 19, 1940, to Mar. 1, 1945

•Henry Agard Wallace of Iowa, Mar. 2, 1945 to Sept. 20, 1946

Labor: Frances Perkins (Wilson) of New York, Mar. 4, 1933, to June 30, 1945

THE SUPREME COURT

Chief Justice: Harlan Fiske Stone of New York, appointed, June 12, 1941; confirmed, June 27, 1941

Associate Justices: Hugo Lafayette Black of Alabama, appointed, Aug. 12, 1837; confirmed Aug. 17, 1937

•Stanley Forman Reed of Kentucky, appointed, Jan. 15, 1938; confirmed, Jan. 25, 1938

•Felix Frankfurter of Massachusetts, appointed, Jan. 5, 1939; confirmed, Jan. 17, 1939

•William Orville Douglas of Connecticut, appointed, Mar. 20, 1939; confirmed, Apr. 4, 1939

•Frank Murphy of Michigan, appointed, Jan. 4, 1940; confirmed, Jan. 16, 1940

•James Francis Byrnes of South Carolina, appointed, June 12, 1941; confirmed, June 12, 1941

•Robert Houghwout Jackson of New York, appointed, June 12, 1941; confirmed, July 7, 1941

•Wiley Blount Rutledge of Iowa, appointed, Jan. 11, 1943; confirmed, Feb. 8, 1943

Thirty-third President

HARRY S. TRUMAN

Full name: Harry S. Truman
- He was the only president whose middle initial did not represent a middle name.
- He was the 15th of 19 presidents who had middle initials or middle names.

Date of birth: May 8, 1884
- He was the first of two presidents who were born in May. The other was Kennedy.

Place of birth: Lamar, Mo.
- He was the only president who was born in Missouri.
- The Harry S. Truman Birthplace, 1009 Truman Street (U.S. 71), was purchased in 1957 by the United Automobile Workers and given to the State of Missouri. A State Historic Site, it is administered by the Missouri State Park Board. It is open to the public daily except Mondays, 10 A.M. to 4 P.M., and Sundays, 12, noon, to 6 P.M. Admission: free.

Family lineage: English-Scottish-Irish
- He was the last of three presidents who were of English-Scottish-Irish ancestry.

Religious denomination: Baptist
- He was the second of two presidents who were Baptists. The other was Harding.

College: None
- He was the only president of the 20th century who did not attend college.
- He was the last of nine presidents who did not attend college.
- He was the last of 15 presidents who were not graduated from college.

Law School: Kansas City School of Law, Kansas City, Mo., now School of Law, University of Missouri at Kansas City
- He was the seventh of nine presidents who attended law school.
- He was the fifth of six presidents who attended, but were not graduated from law school.

PARENTS AND SIBLINGS

Father's name: John Anderson Truman
Date of birth: Dec. 5, 1851
Place of birth: Jackson County, Mo.
Occupations: Farmer, livestock salesman-trader
Date of death: Nov. 3, 1914
Place of death: Kansas City, Mo.
Age at death: 62 years, 333 days

Mother's name: Martha Ellen Young Truman
Date of birth: Nov. 25, 1852
Place of birth: Jackson County, Mo.
•The farm on which Truman's mother was born was located in what is now Kansas City.
Date of marriage: Dec. 28, 1881
Place of marriage: Jackson County, Mo.
Children: 3; 2 sons, 1 daughter
•Harry S. was born in 1884, John Vivian in 1886, and Mary Jane in 1889.
•Truman was the last of five presidents who came from families of three children.
•He was the seventh of eight presidents who were eldest children.
Date of death: July 26, 1947
•Truman was the ninth of ten presidents whose mothers lived to see their sons' inauguration or oath-taking days. Mrs. Truman did not attend the ceremony.
Place of death: Grandview, Mo.
Age at death: 94 years, 243 days

MARRIAGE

Date of marriage: June 28, 1919
Place of marriage: Independence, Mo.
•Truman was the second of two presidents who were married in Missouri. The other was Grant.
Age at marriage: 35 years, 51 days
•He was the fifth of six presidents who married in their thirties.

Wife's name: Elizabeth Virginia Wallace Truman
•She was called Bess.

•Her maiden name was the same as that of her husband's predecessor as vice president. She and Henry A. Wallace were not related.
•She was the 29th of 33 first ladies.
•She was the 36th of 40 wives of presidents.
Date of birth: Feb. 13, 1885
•She was the second of two first ladies who were born in February. The other was Louisa Adams.
•She was the second of two wives of presidents who were born in February.
Place of birth: Independence, Mo.
•She was the second of two first ladies who were born in Missouri. The other was Julia Grant.
•She was the second of two wives of presidents who were born in Missouri.
Wife's mother: Madge Gates Wallace
Wife's father: David Willock Wallace, farmer
Age at marriage: 34 years, 135 days
•She was the first lady and wife of a president who married for the first time at the most advanced age.
•She was the second of two first ladies who married in their thirties. The other was Florence Harding.
•She was the last of three wives of presidents who married in their thirties.
Years younger than husband: 281 days
Children: 1 daughter
•Mary Margaret was born Feb. 17, 1924
•Truman was the only president who had an only child.
•He was the third of five presidents who had only female children.
•He was the 26th of 30 presidents who had children.

EARLY YEARS

1885, with family, moved to farm near Harrisonville, Mo.
1887, with family, moved to farm near what is now Grandview, Mo.
December, 1890, with family, moved to Independence, Mo.
1892, began schooling, Independence
•Although he had been able to read the large-print family Bible since the age of five, Truman could not read the fine-print school books until he was fitted with thick-lensed glasses.
January, 1894, contracted diphtheria

•The illness resulted in a temporary paralysis of his arms and legs. His mother pushed him in a baby carriage for several months before he recovered.
July 4–6, 1900, served as page, Democratic national convention, Kansas City Mo.
1901, was graduated from Independence high school
•Family financial reverses prevented his attending college.
•He studied briefly for admission to West Point until he learned that his eyesight would prevent his passing the U.S. Military

Academy physical examination.

1901, worked as timekeeper for railroad construction contractor

• His salary was $35 a month. The job ended in June, 1902.

1902, worked in Kansas City *Star* mailroom

• His salary was $7 a week.

1902, with family, moved to Kansas City, Mo.

1903, worked as clerk for National Bank of Commerce, Kansas City

• His salary was $35 a month.

1904, worked as bookkeeper, Union National Bank, Kansas City

• When his parents moved to a farm near Clinton, Mo., later that year, he lived for a time with his father's sister, Emma Colgan, and then moved to a boarding house where another of the boarders was Arthur Eisenhower, a bank clerk and brother of Dwight David Eisenhower. Truman supplemented his $60 a month salary by working Saturday afternoons as an usher at the Grand Theater, Kansas City.

June 14, 1905, became charter member of Battery B, Missouri National Guard

• He served in the unit for six years.

1906, left Kansas City to manage family farm near Grandview

• His parents had moved to this farm, which was owned by his grandmother, after the corn crop of the Clinton farm was washed out by flood. He managed the farm for more than ten years.

1906, served as election clerk, Grandview

• His father was election judge for the precinct.

• This was Truman's first contact with the Pendergast machine, which controlled Democratic politics in Kansas City and Jackson County.

Mar. 18, 1909, degree of Master Mason conferred by Belton Lodge No. 450, Grandview

• He was the last of 13 presidents who were Masons.

Nov. 3, 1914, his father died

• Truman succeeded to his father's political post as road overseer of eastern Jackson County, but later lost the job over a procedural matter.

1915, appointed postmaster, Grandview

• He gave his monthly salary of $50 to his assistant, Ella Hall.

• He was the second of two presidents who were postmasters. The other was Lincoln.

1915, invested and lost $2,000 in lead and zinc mine, Commerce, Okla.

1916, invested $5,000 in Kansas oil venture

• He borrowed the money on five ten-month notes cosigned by his mother. After a series of dry wells, the company began drilling in 1917 on a 320-acre plot leased near Eureka, Kan. Shortly before the U.S. entered World War I, the company sold this lease to the Empire Company, who continued drilling an abandoned well and struck oil. The Empire Company later became the Cities Service Oil Company. "There was never a dry hole found on that three hundred and twenty acres," he said years later. "It was the famous Teeter Pool."

May 22, 1917, rejoined national guard

• He joined the newly formed 2nd Missouri Field Artillery. He was elected first lieutenant of Battery F.

Aug. 5, 1917, sworn into federal military service

• His national guard unit became the 129th Field Artillery of the 35th Division.

• He was the second of two presidents who served in the military during World War I. The other was Eisenhower.

• He was the 17th of 21 presidents who served in the military during wartime.

Sept. 26, 1917, assigned to Camp Doniphan, Fort Sill, Okla.

• He served as regimental canteen officer.

Mar. 30, 1918, sailed for France aboard *George Washington*

• His regiment landed at Brest, Apr. 13.

May, 1918, read of his promotion to captain in *The New York Times*

• He did not receive official notice of his promotion until October. He requested retroactive pay, but was refused on the grounds that he had not "accepted" the commission earlier.

July, 1918, assumed command of Battery D, 129th Field Artillery

Sept. 6, 1918, first combat experience in Vosges Mountains, Alsace, now France

• He also participated in the battle of St. Mihiel, the first major U.S. offensive, Sept. 12–16, and the Meuse-Argonne offensive, which began, Sept. 26.

Nov. 11, 1918, fired last round, 10:45 a.m., northeast of Verdun

Apr. 9, 1919, sailed from Brest aboard German liner, *Zeppelin*

•He arrived in New York City, Apr. 20.

May 6, 1919, discharged with rank of major, Camp Funston, Kan.

June 28, 1919, married Elizabeth Virginia Wallace, Independence

•After a short honeymoon in Chicago and Port Huron, Mich., they moved into a house in Independence, which they shared with her mother and grandmother.

Nov. 29, 1919, opened men's haberdashery, Independence

•His partner was Edward Jacobson, who had been his assistant at Camp Doniphan. The firm of Truman and Jacobson began with $35,000 worth of merchandise. Sales during the first year were more than $70,000, but business deteriorated during the 1921 business slump. The store closed in 1922. The partners, to avoid bankruptcy, made agreements with their creditors to pay off indebtedness as soon as possible. They continued to diminish their obligations over a period of years.

Nov. 7, 1922, elected county judge of eastern district, Jackson County

•This position was administrative rather than judicial.

•Each county was administered by two judges representing districts and a presiding judge elected by the county as a whole. He took office in January, 1923.

1923–1925, during academic years, attended Kansas City School of Law

•He was the 24th of 26 presidents who studied law.

•He was the second of three presidents who studied law, but did not seek admission to the bar.

Feb. 17, 1924, his only daughter born

•The girl was named Mary Margaret Truman.

Nov. 4, 1924, defeated when ran for reelection as county judge

•This was the only election that he lost.

1925, took job as membership salesman, Kansas City Automobile Club

•He sold about one thousand memberships in one year, clearing about $5,000 after expenses.

Nov. 2, 1926, elected presiding judge, Jackson County

•This position entailed supervision of a multimillion dollar budget and the appointment of nine hundred county employees.

1929, became Democratic leader of eastern Jackson County

•His predecessor, Michael Pendergast, had died. Pendergast was the brother of the political boss, Thomas J. ("Big Tom") Pendergast.

Nov. 4, 1930, reelected presiding judge, Jackson County

October, 1933, appointed dollar-a-year Reemployment Director of Missouri by Harry L. Hopkins

Aug. 7, 1934, won Democratic primary for Senate

NATIONAL PROMINENCE

Nov. 6, 1934, elected to Senate

•Truman defeated the Republican incumbent, Roscoe Conkling Patterson, by 262,-000 votes.

•He was the 13th of 16 presidents who were elected to the Senate.

Jan. 3, 1935, took office in Senate

•He was appointed to the appropriations and interstate commerce committees.

•He was the 12th of 15 presidents who served in the Senate.

1937, appointed vice chairman of Senate subcommittee investigating railroad financing

•When the hearings finally ended in January, 1939, he and committee counsel Max Lowenthal drafted legislation to regulate the finances of railroads. This became law

as the Transportation Act of 1940.

1940, declined appointment to Interstate Commerce Commission

•This appointment was intended to clear the way for Governor Lloyd Stark of Missouri to run for his Senate seat. Stark was supported by President Roosevelt.

Aug. 6, 1940, won Democratic primary for Senate

•He defeated Stark by 7,967 votes.

Nov. 5, 1940, reelected to Senate

•He defeated the Republican candidate, Manvel Davis, by about forty-four thousand votes.

January, 1941, completed thirty-thousand-mile defense construction projects investigation trip

•The original impetus for the tour was a

complaint about the construction of Fort Leonard Wood, Rolla, Mo. Conditions there prompted him to continue his investigation.

Feb. 10, 1941, denounced defense construction program in Senate speech

• His resolution for the appointment of an investigating committee was approved, Mar. 1. He was appointed chairman, but his request for a $25,000 budget was voted down. The Truman Committee began with a $15,000 budget.

August, 1941, Truman Committee report revealed waste of more than $100,000,000 in billion-dollar military camp construction program

December, 1941, his request for military duty denied

January, 1942, Truman Committee voted appropriation of $100,000 for second-year budget

Nov. 26, 1943, made national radio broadcast on results of Truman Committee investigations

• While active, the committee produced 32 reports at a cost of $400,000, which purportedly saved the federal government about $15,000,000,000.

1943, refused chairmanship of Democratic National Committee

1944, named in poll of Washington newspaper correspondents as second only to President Roosevelt in contribution to U.S. war effort

July 14, 1944, agreed to nominate James F. Byrnes as vice-presidential candidate

July 21, 1944, nominated for vice president, Democratic national convention, Chicago, Ill.

Nov. 7, 1944, elected vice president

Jan. 20, 1945, took oath as vice president, White House

• The oath was administered by Truman's predecessor, Henry A. Wallace.

THE PRESIDENT (33rd)

Term of office: Apr. 12, 1945, to Jan. 20, 1953 (7 years, 283 days)

• Truman was the tenth of 12 presidents who had served as vice presidents.

• He was the seventh of eight presidents who, because of the deaths of their predecessors, did not complete their vice-presidential terms.

• He was the third of four presidents who served the unexpired terms of their predecessors and were elected to and served second terms.

• He was the 14th of 16 presidents who served more than one term.

State represented: Missouri

• He was the only president who represented Missouri.

Political party: Democratic

• He was the tenth of 12 presidents who were Democrats.

Congresses: 79th, 80th, 81st, 82nd

Administrations: 40th, 41st

Age at taking oath: 60 years, 339 days

• Truman took the oath of office in the Cabinet Room of the White House on Thursday, Apr. 12, 1945. The oath was administered by Chief Justice Harlan F. Stone.

• This was the second of two oath-taking ceremonies at which Stone officiated.

• Stone was the second of two officials who administered the oath of office to two presidents in the same year; he had officiated at the fourth inauguration of Franklin D. Roosevelt, Jan. 20. The other was Chief Justice Waite, who administered the oath to Garfield and Arthur in 1881.

• Truman was the oldest vice president who succeeded to the presidency.

THE 40th ADMINISTRATION

1945

Apr. 14, moved into Blair House

• Truman and his family resided in the governmental guest residence until May 7.

Apr. 15, attended Roosevelt burial, Hyde Park, N.Y.

Apr. 16, addressed joint session of Congress

• He pledged to continue the policies of his predecessor.

Apr. 17, held first press conference

• He was applauded at the end of the news conference by the 348 reporters who had gathered in his office.

Apr. 19, vetoed private relief bill
•This was the first of his 250 vetoes.
Apr. 23, conferred with Molotov and Gromyko, White House
•He bluntly told Foreign Minister Vyacheslav M. Molotov and Ambassador Andrei A. Gromyko that the U.S.S.R. had not lived up to agreements made at Yalta and that the U.S. would not approve admission of the Polish government, as then constituted, to the UN. When Molotov said, "I have never been talked to like this," Truman quickly replied, "Carry out your agreements and you won't get talked to like this."
Apr. 25, briefed on atomic bomb project by Secretary of War Stimson
•He had not known of the existence of the project until after he had taken the oath as president.
Apr. 28, by telephone, addressed opening session of United Nations
•He appealed to the delegates from 46 nations, who met in San Francisco, to "rise above personal interests" and establish an international organization that would "redeem the terrible sacrifices of the last six years."
May 8, accepted resignation of Postmaster General Walker
May 8, V-E Day
•He announced the end of hostilities in Europe in a special radio broadcast. In a separate statement, he called upon Japan to surrender unconditionally.
June 1, sent special message to Congress in which he outlined plans for campaign against Japan
June 2, signed act authorizing war department to resume acceptance of enlistments in regular army
June 18, greeted General Eisenhower on return from Europe, Washington, D.C.
June 26, witnessed signing of charter of United Nations, San Francisco, Cal.
June 27, accepted resignation of Secretary of State Stettinius
June 29, accepted resignation of Secretary of Agriculture Wickard
June 29, appointed his second secretary of state, James F. Byrnes
•Byrnes took office, July 3.
June 30, accepted resignations of Attorney General Biddle, Secretary of Labor Perkins
June 30, appointed his second secretary of agriculture, Clinton P. Anderson

July 1, appointed his second attorney general, Thomas C. Clark; his second postmaster general, Robert E. Hannegan; and his second secretary of labor, Lewis B. Schwellenbach
July 5, accepted resignation of Associate Justice Roberts, effective, July 31
July 7, sailed for Potsdam conference aboard *U.S.S. Augusta*, Newport News, Va.
July 15, arrived at Antwerp, Belgium
•He was met at Antwerp by General Eisenhower, driven to Brussels, and then flown to Berlin.
•He was the second of three presidents who visited Belgium while in office.
•He was the first of five presidents who visited Germany while in office.
•He was the third of seven presidents who visited Europe while in office.
•He was the seventh of 11 presidents who traveled outside the U.S. while in office.
July 16, informed of successful atomic bomb explosion at Alamogordo, New Mex.
July 16, informally received Premier Joseph V. Stalin, Potsdam, Germany
July 17–Aug. 2, presided at Tri-partite Conference, near Potsdam
•He, Prime Minister Churchill, and Stalin met until July 25.
•The new British prime minister, Clement R. Atlee, took the place of Churchill, July 28.
July 17, briefed on successful atomic bomb test
•Secretary of State Stimson flew from Washington to Berlin to inform him of the details of the test in New Mexico.
July 19, played piano at state dinner for Churchill and Stalin
•He played Beethoven's Minuet in G.
July 20, witnessed raising of flag over headquarters of U.S. Group Control Council, Berlin
•The flag had flown over the Capitol, Dec. 7, 1941.
July 22, accepted resignation of Secretary of Treasury Morgenthau
July 23, appointed his second secretary of treasury, Frederick M. Vinson
July 26, issued joint proclamation with Churchill that again called for unconditional surrender of Japan
•The proclamation obliquely warned Japan that she faced "prompt and utter destruction," that the Allied forces were "poised to strike the final blows."

Aug. 2, with Atlee and Stalin, issued communique outlining peace terms for Germany

Aug. 2, flew to Plymouth, England; sailed for U.S. aboard *U.S.S. Augusta*

• He and King George VI exchanged visits aboard *H.M.S. Renown* and the *Augusta*, Plymouth Roads.

• Truman was the second of five presidents who visited England while in office.

Aug. 3, announced "no secret agreements of any kind" made at Potsdam

• He made this statement aboard the *Augusta*.

Aug. 4, White House announced he had signed Bretton Woods act

• The act authorized the U.S. to participate in the Food and Agricultural Organization of the UN and increased Export-Import Bank lending authority from $700,000,000 to $3,500,000,000.

Aug. 5, first atomic bomb dropped on Hiroshima, Japan

• "We have spent $2,000,000,000 on the greatest scientific gamble in history—and won," he announced 16 hours later. About eighty thousand persons were killed, and 60 percent of the city was obliterated.

Aug. 7, arrived at Newport News, Va., traveled by special train to Washington, D.C.

Aug. 8, signed United Nations charter

Aug. 9, second atomic bomb dropped on Nagasaki, Japan

Aug. 9, received Japanese offer of surrender

• The Japanese interpreted the Potsdam surrender ultimatum to mean that the Japanese emperor could remain on the throne.

Aug. 10, replied to Japanese offer of surrender

• On behalf of the Allies, he said Hirohito would be permitted to retain the throne for the time being, but that ultimately the emperor's future must be determined by popular election.

Aug. 14, Japan surrendered unconditionally

Aug. 18, issued executive order easing wage controls

• He urged employers and unions to continue to accept War Labor Board decisions.

Aug. 21, issued executive order terminating lend-lease

• The U.S. supplied total aid of $41,208,000,-000 to foreign nations in four years and five months, through May 31. Reverse lend-lease returned $5,500,000,000.

Aug. 22, received provisional president of

France, General Charles de Gaulle, White House

Aug. 23, criticized Generalissimo Francisco Franco of Spain

Aug. 23, issued executive order of seizure of Illinois Central Railroad to avert strike

Aug. 27, proposed draft extension for two years

• In a special message to Congress, he asked for the continuation of the draft in regard to men between 18 and 25.

Aug. 29, released findings of army and navy inquiry boards that had investigated attack on Pearl Harbor

Aug. 30, sent special message to Congress in which he recommended writing off lend-lease debts

Aug. 31, issued executive order abolishing Office of War Information

• The order transferred the OWI's foreign information division to the state department as of Sept. 15.

Sept. 1, Japan formally surrendered to Allies

• The ceremony took place aboard the *U.S.S. Missouri* in Tokyo Bay.

• World War II had ended.

1945

Sept. 2, V-J Day

• He issued a proclamation, Sept. 1, in which he urged the observation of V-J Day as a symbol of "victory of liberty over tyranny." He also asked the nation to remember "our departed gallant leader, Franklin D. Roosevelt, defender of democracy, architect of world peace and cooperation."

Sept. 6, submitted extensive legislative program to Congress

Sept. 10, awarded Medal of Honor to General Jonathan Wainwright, White House

Sept. 18, appointed Harold H. Burton as associate justice

• Burton, who was confirmed by the Senate, Sept. 19, was the first of Truman's four appointments to the Supreme Court.

Sept. 21, accepted resignation of Secretary of War Stimson

• Truman announced that he had approved the recommendation of Stimson that the war be officially designated as World War II.

Sept. 25, sent special message to Congress in which he asked reduction of army budget by $28,692,772,000

Sept. 27, appointed his second secretary of war, Robert P. Patterson

Oct. 1, issued executive order reorganizing navy department

Oct. 3, sent special message to Congress in which he urged prompt organization of Atomic Energy Commission

Oct. 4, issued executive order to navy for seizure of 26 oil companies

• Strikes had curtailed one-third of the U.S. refinery production.

Oct. 4, issued executive order abolishing War Production Board as of Nov. 3

Oct. 8, stated U.S. would not give away engineering abilities that produced atomic bomb, Union City, Tenn.

Oct. 23, sent special message to Congress in which he urged legislation to provide military training of one year for all males between 17 and 20

Oct. 25, signed executive order changing design of presidential flag

• The design was altered so that the American eagle was looking toward the olive branch of peace and circled by stars representing the 48 states.

Oct. 27, reviewed 47 warships in Hudson River, New York City

• The U.S. must hold the atomic bomb as "a sacred trust," he said in his Navy Day speech to a Central Park crowd estimated at one million persons. He urged cooperation between nations to avoid atomic destruction.

Nov. 10, conferred with Prime Minister Atlee of Great Britain and Prime Minister King of Canada on atomic bomb, Washington, D.C.

• They announced the future sharing of information on the practical applications of atomic energy with other members of the United Nations, on a reciprocal basis, "just as soon as effective enforceable safeguards against its use for destructive purposes can be devised."

Nov. 20, appointed General Eisenhower as chief of staff of army, Fleet Admiral Chester W. Nimitz as chief of naval operations

Nov. 28, received progress report on Allied policy for Germany

• His special representative, Bryon Price, reported that the policy formulated at Potsdam was meeting opposition, particularly from France. The French were seeking economic dismemberment of Germany.

Nov. 29, stated Big Three meetings no longer necessary

• He told a press conference that the United Nations could supervise matters previously debated and decided at tri-partite conferences.

Dec. 3, sent special message to Congress asking for legislation to avert strikes during reconversion

• He urged legislation similar to the Railway Labor Act and the authorization of federal fact-finding boards to investigate industrial disputes. According to his plan, strikes would be unlawful while investigations were being conducted.

• Philip Murray, CIO president, attacked Truman's plan as "the first step of ever more savage legislative repression" which could eventually "destroy labor union organizations."

Dec. 6, issued joint statement with Prime Minister Atlee announcing writing off of $25,000,000,000 in lend-lease aid to Great Britain and granting of $3,750,000,000 U.S. loan, subject to ratification by Congress and Parliament

Dec. 12, announced appointment of three-man fact-finding board to investigate General Motors strike

Dec. 12, announced comprehensive program to provide housing for veterans and displaced war workers

Dec. 15, called for truce in Chinese civil war

• He sent General Marshall as temporary ambassador to act as mediator between the Chinese Nationalists and Communists.

Dec. 18, signed act authorizing appropriation of $1,350,000,000 for United Nations Relief and Rehabilitation Administration during 1946

Dec. 19, sent special message to Congress outlining unification of army, navy, and air force departments into departments of national defense

Dec. 19, appointed four delegates to first General Assembly of United Nations

Dec. 21, first session of 79th Congress adjourned

Dec. 22, pocket vetoed bill that would have rescinded $51,000,000,000 in war appropriations

• This bill contained a rider that provided for the return of the U.S. Employment Service to the states within one hundred days.

• This was the first of his 70 pocket vetoes.

Dec. 31, signed act authorizing appropriation of $160,000,000 for emergency housing for veterans, servicemen, and families

Dec. 31, issued executive order terminating War Labor Board

• This order established the National Wage Stabilization Board in place of the NWLB.

1946

Jan. 3, criticized "handful" of congressional leaders for "distressingly slow" progress on reconversion program

Jan. 10, asked United Automobile Workers and General Motors to accept compromise wage increase

• His fact-finding board recommended a 19½-cents-an-hour wage increase. General Motors rejected the proposal, Jan. 11, and offered a 15-cent increase. The union accepted the board report, Jan. 13.

Jan. 12, asked United Steelworkers for one-week postponement of strike scheduled for midnight, Jan. 13

• U.S. Steel and the union agreed to resume bargaining at the White House, Jan. 16.

Jan. 14, second session of 79th Congress

Jan. 14, sent special message to Congress asking for cancellation of $6,000,000,000 in war contracts

Jan. 15, announced U.S. would demand full trusteeship of captured Japanese islands considered vital to American security

Jan. 17, proposed 18½-cents-an-hour wage increase to avert steel strike

• The union accepted the proposal, but U.S. Steel rejected the suggested compromise, Jan. 18. Only one steel producer, Henry J. Kaiser—who employed less than four thousand men—contracted with the union to pay the 18½-cent increase, Jan. 19.

Jan. 20, steel strike began

• About 750,000 steel workers went on strike, closing mills in 29 states. This was the largest strike to date under the jurisdiction of a single union.

• An additional 900,000 workers in major industries were off their jobs when the steel strike began—including more than 260,000 meat industry, 200,000 automotive, 200,000 electrical, and 50,000 transportation employees.

Jan. 21, sent his first State of the Union message to Congress

• His message was the first of its kind, a joint State of the Union and budget message.

• His 25,000-word message called for the renewal of price and rent control since inflation was "our chief worry"; suggested "substantial" wage increases in most industries; argued against tax reduction; and recommended the extension of social security and the continuation of farm subsidies. He submitted a budget of $35,800,000,000.

Jan. 23, awarded Medal of Honor to Commander Joseph T. O'Callaghan, White House

• Reverend O'Callaghan was the first chaplain to receive the medal.

Jan. 24, rejected proposal to call conference of industrial leaders to formulate national wage policy

• The suggestion had come from Benjamin F. Fairless, president of the U.S. Steel Corporation, in a radio address, Jan. 23. Truman criticized management and labor alike and again recommended acceptance of the 18½-cents-an-hour increase.

Jan. 24, issued executive order of seizure and operation of 134 meat-packing plants

Jan. 30, sent special message to Congress recommending approval of $4,400,000,000 loan to Great Britain

Jan. 31, informed Congress total lend-lease aid to allies since 1941 inception was $46,040,000,000

Jan. 31, stated atomic energy control would be placed in civilian hands as soon as possible

Feb. 5, issued executive order of seizure of Port of New York tugboat system

• The strike of tugboat workers in New York, Feb. 4, continued until Feb. 13. A state of emergency existed; schools and nonessential businesses closed, priorities on fuel and food were established, and a "brownout" was ordered.

Feb. 6, issued executive order prohibiting use of wheat for beer and alcohol as part of program to supply food for distressed districts of Europe

Feb. 10, received former Prime Minister Churchill of Great Britain, White House

Feb. 13, accepted resignation of Secretary of Interior Ickes, effective, Feb. 15

• Ickes was the last member of Franklin D. Roosevelt's original cabinet to resign.

Feb. 14, announced new national wage-price policy

• He appointed Chester Bowles, head of the

OPA, as director of the Office of Economic Stabilization, Feb. 21.

Feb. 15, steel strike ended

• The 26-day strike ended when U.S. Steel accepted the 18½-cents-an-hour wage increase he had recommended, Jan. 17.

• A price rise of $5 a ton resulted.

Feb. 20, signed modified full-employment act

Feb. 26, appointed his second secretary of interior, Julius A. Krug

• Krug took office, Mar. 18.

Mar. 1, endorsed policy statement limiting foreign loans to $3,250,000,000 until June 30, 1947

• The policy statement of the National Advisory Council on International Monetary and Financial Problems did not effect the pending credit of $3,750,000,000 to Great Britain.

Mar. 4, with Winston Churchill, departed for Fulton, Mo.

• Churchill advocated an Anglo-American association to deter Russian ambitions in a speech at Westminster College, Fulton, Mar. 5. This was the "iron curtain" speech. "From Stettin in the Baltic to Trieste in the Adriatic, an iron curtain has descended across the continent," said Churchill.

Mar. 7, issued executive order reopening all public lands in U.S. and Alaska to settlement, except those which contained "substantial" deposits of fissionable materials

Mar. 8, appointed emergency board to investigate railroad dispute

Mar. 25, welcomed delegates to first meeting of UN Security Council in interim headquarters, Hunter College, New York City

Mar. 28, appointed military "brain trust" to help formulate national defense program

Apr. 1, soft coal strike began

Apr. 6, urged unification of armed forces, universal military training, and extension of draft for one year

• In an Army Day speech in Chicago, Ill., he warned of a possible Middle East conflict between Great Britain and Russia and pledged U.S. military support of UN.

Apr. 12, attended dedication of birthplace of Franklin D. Roosevelt as national shrine, Hyde Park, N.Y.

Apr. 18, his fact-finding board recommended 16-cents-an-hour increase for railroad engineers and trainmen

Apr. 19, warned "millions will surely die un-less we eat less," appealing to Americans to tighten belts

Apr. 20, conferred with John L. Lewis of United Mine Workers regarding soft coal strike

Apr. 22, Chief Justice Stone died

Apr. 22–23, witnessed naval maneuvers one hundred miles off Virginia capes from aboard aircraft carrier, *U.S.S. Franklin D. Roosevelt*

Apr. 29, issued executive order returning seized meat-packing plants and facilities to owners

May 3, signed veterans priority act

• This act provided that honorably discharged veterans had first call—after the government—on surplus property.

May 4, received report that soft coal strike had developed into "national disaster"

• The Office of War Mobilization and Reconversion report added that the effects of the strike would "spread rapidly through the economy" and would seriously damage the reconversion progress.

May 6, sent special message to Congress on hemispheric defense

• He proposed that the U.S. organize, equip, and train armed forces of other American republics.

May 6, sent war department budget to Congress

• The budget of $7,246,000,000 included $200,000,000 allocated for "atomic service."

May 9, stated soft coal strike was nearing status of strike against government

• Dimouts in 22 eastern states were requested by federal authorities to conserve soft coal supplies.

May 9, electrical workers' strike ended

• The 115-day strike, the longest major postwar work stoppage, ended when the Westinghouse Electric Corporation agreed to an 18-cents-an-hour wage increase.

May 11, received honorary degree of Doctor of Laws, Fordham University, New York City

May 14, signed act to continue selective service to July 1

May 14, called representatives of railroads and trainmen unions to White House conference in effort to avert strike scheduled for May 18

May 16, submitted comprehensive reorganization plan for Federal Security Agency to Congress

May 16, signed return of war dead act
•The program to return the war dead to the U.S., which was to commence in late 1946, would cost about $200,000,000.

May 17, issued executive order of seizure of nation's railroads
•He directed the Office of Defense Transportation to operate the railroads and appealed to the workers to stay on duty.

May 18, announced five-day truce in imminent railroad strike

May 21, issued executive order of seizure of soft coal mines

May 23, railroad strike began
•When the 250,000 members of the two railroad brotherhoods walked off their jobs, the national total of strikers rose to about 960,000.

May 24, threatened to call out troops "and use every means within my power" if railroad workers remained off jobs
•"The fact is that the action of this small group of men has resulted in millions of other workers losing their wages," he said in a national radio broadcast. The strike, he added, "touches not only the welfare of a class but virtually concerns the well-being and the very life of all our people."

May 25, railroad strike ended
•The strike ended on terms that he suggested, an 18½-cents-an-hour wage increase. Union officials condemned governmental interference and called his radio address of the previous night "very unfair."
•Later in the day, he appeared before a joint session of Congress, where he requested temporary emergency powers to break strikes against the government in any industry. He specifically asked for authority to draft strikers into the armed services. The House of Representatives immediately passed the legislation he sought. The Senate, however, rejected the bill for emergency authority, May 29.

May 29, soft coal strike ended
•The union won most of its demands, including a welfare and retirement fund financed by the operators. The 45-day strike cost an estimated $2,000,000,000. Lost production was estimated at ninety million tons of coal and eighteen million tons of steel.

May 31, stated military services and War Shipping Administration would be used to operate ships if maritime strike called

June 1, received honorary degree of Doctor of Laws, Washington College, Chestertown, Md.

June 3, received new Russian ambassador, Nikolai V. Novikov

June 6, accepted resignation of Secretary of Treasury Vinson, effective, June 23

June 6, appointed Frederick M. Vinson as chief justice
•Vinson, who was confirmed by the Senate, June 20, was the second of Truman's four appointments to the Supreme Court.
•Truman was the 11th of 14 presidents who appointed chief justices.

June 6, appointed his third secretary of treasury, John W. Snyder
•Snyder took office, June 25.

June 7, hard coal strike ended
•The nine-day strike of anthracite miners ended with the union winning an 18½-cents-an-hour wage increase, as well as a health and welfare fund.

June 11, vetoed labor dispute bill
•The House of Representatives attempted to override the veto but fell five votes short of the necessary two-thirds, 255–135, June 11.

June 11, appointed special cabinet committee to study Palestine question

June 14, informed Congress total lend-lease aid to all nations from Mar. 31, 1941, to Dec. 31, 1945, was $49,096,000,000

June 15, submitted to Congress 12-point program for merger of army and navy into single department of defense
•He said that the plan to place the army, navy, and air force under a single chief of staff had been discarded; instead he proposed retention of the three chiefs of staff.

June 20, said he favored Baruch plan for international control of atomic energy
•The plan of Bernard M. Baruch did not include the right of veto by the Big Five powers, as did the Russian proposal.

June 27, reported U.S. had shipped 5,500,-000 tons of grain to famine areas during first six months of 1946

June 29, vetoed amended OPA extension bill

June 29, signed amended Selective Service Act
•This act extended the draft until Mar. 31, 1947, but exempted 18-year-olds and fathers.

July 1, attended joint session of Congress

called to pay tribute to memory of Franklin D. Roosevelt

July 2, conferred with four American members of Jewish Agency

• He said that he hoped the transfer of 100,-000 homeless European Jews to Palestine would proceed "with all dispatch."

July 3, appointed fact-finding board to investigate first national commercial airlines strike, called by mechanics

July 4, issued proclamation of recognition of Republic of Philippines

July 15, signed joint resolution ratifying $3,-750,000,000 British loan agreement

July 24, signed $2,000,000,000 navigation, electric-power, irrigation, and flood control act

July 25, sent special message to Congress announcing he had signed OPA revival act

• This act renewed the Office of Price Administration until June 30, 1947. He said that he had signed it "reluctantly," although he felt it was better than the bill he had vetoed, June 29. He added that he would be forced to call a special session of Congress if the law did not check inflation. Price controls were gradually eliminated by the act.

July 31, signed act raising price of silver from 71.11 to 90.5 cents an ounce

Aug. 1, vetoed tidelands oil bill

• This bill would have transferred title to the states of those lands under navigable waters that extended three miles from coastlines.

Aug. 1, signed act that established five-man civilian board for atomic energy control and development

Aug. 2, second session of 79th Congress adjourned

Aug. 3, directed department heads to cut expenditures by $2,200,000,000

• His revised budget for the year ending June 30, 1947, was $41,500,000,000, as compared with his January estimate of $35,800,000,000.

Aug. 8, signed act increasing pensions of 2,-000,000 veterans of World War I and II, as well as 400,000 dependents, by 20 percent

Aug. 9, signed terminal leave pay act

• This act provided $2,700,000,000 for payment of terminal leave to fifteen million discharged members of armed forces.

Aug. 12, signed act that established New York City aquarium as national shrine

• The act authorized the department of the interior to accept the 135-year-old aquarium.

Aug. 13, signed act raising salaries of ambassadors and ministers

• The salaries of high-ranking ambassadors were raised to $25,000 annually, while the minimum salaries for ministers were raised to $15,000.

Aug. 16, departed on vacation cruise in New England waters aboard presidential yacht, *Williamsburg*

• After two days of being stormbound at Quonset Point, R.I., he decided against the contemplated cruise to Maine and ordered his captain to sail for Bermuda.

Aug. 22, arrived in Bermuda

• He was the first of four presidents who visited Bermuda while in office.

Sept. 2, returned to Washington D.C.

• The 18-day cruise was the first actual vacation of his 16 months in office.

Sept. 20, asked for resignation of Secretary of Commerce Wallace

• He had been embarrassed by a speech made by Wallace in New York City, Sept. 12, which had advocated a foreign policy diametrically opposed to his own. Worse, Truman had lied during the controversy which followed. At a press conference, Sept. 12, when asked by reporters who had seen advance copies of the Wallace speech if he had approved it, he answered affirmatively. Two days later he issued a statement that was immediately recognized as the transparent fabrication it was. He said:

> It was my intention to express the
> thought that I approved the right
> of the Secretary of Commerce to
> deliver the speech. I did not intend
> to indicate that I approved the
> speech as indicating a statement of
> the foreign policy of this country.

When Secretary of State Byrnes, who was attending the Paris Peace Conference, threatened to resign, Truman fired Wallace.

Sept. 22, appointed his second secretary of commerce, W. Averell Harriman

• Harriman took office, Oct. 7.

Sept. 25, reported 71 percent of supplies distributed by United Nations Relief and Rehabilitation Administration had been provided by U.S.

Sept. 26, refused to request decontrol of meat prices to halt meat shortage

• He said that the shortage had been caused by the sale of livestock during the suspension of OPA in July and August and by the failure of Congress to enact proper legislation.

Sept. 28, visited U.S. Military Academy, West Point, N.Y.

• He told the cadet corps that he was certain "we are going to have a permanent peace."

Oct. 8, sent message to AFL national convention in Chicago, Ill., in which he urged labor to cooperate with industry and government to meet most compelling national need, "full, sustained production"

Oct. 14, announced lifting of all price controls on livestock and meat products to relieve meat shortage

• In a national broadcast from the White House, he charged that the meat crisis had been caused by

> . . . a few men in Congress who, in the service of selfish interests, have been determined for some time to wreck controls, no matter what the cost might be to our people.

Oct. 23, opened meeting of United Nations General Assembly, Flushing Meadows Park, New York City

• After just peace settlements had been made, the United Nations "can and will prevent war between nations and remove the fear of war," he said, and pointed out that the UN should guard against being splintered because of differences in political philosophies and economic and social systems. He was congratulated by Foreign Minister Molotov of the U.S.S.R. on having made "a great speech."

Oct. 24, announced federal spending for public works projects would exceed previous estimate of $900,000,000 by $165,000,-000

Oct. 25, issued proclamation lifting tariff on foreign lumber and lumber products to speed up federal housing program

Oct. 28, appointed five-man civilian Atomic Energy Commission, with David E. Lilienthal as chairman

Nov. 5, election day

• The Democrats suffered major losses in the Senate and the House of Representatives and in gubernatorial elections.

Nov. 6, declined to comment on Democratic defeats at polls

Nov. 7, declined to comment on Fulbright suggestion that he resign

• Senator J. William Fulbright, a first-term Democrat from Arkansas, proposed that he "should appoint a Republican Secretary of State and resign from office." While he made no public comment, Truman privately referred to the Arkansan as "Senator Halfbright."

Nov. 9, issued executive order terminating all price controls except ceilings on rent, sugar, and rice

Nov. 11, pledged full cooperation to incoming Republican Congress

• In his first postelection statement, he said:

> As President of the United States, I am guided by a simple formula: to do in all cases, from day to day, without regard to narrow political considerations, what seems to me to be best for the welfare of all our people. Our search for that welfare must always be based upon a progressive concept of government.

Nov. 17, decided to fight John L. Lewis and UMW "on all fronts"

• Lewis had called a strike of the 400,000 soft coal miners against the government-operated mines for Nov. 20.

Nov. 20, directed department of justice to proceed against Lewis for contempt of court when union leader defied court order to avert walkout

Nov. 21, made dive in submarine, off Key West, Fla.

• He made a short voyage aboard the captured German submarine, *U-2513*, during naval exercises, while vacationing at Key West.

• He was the first of two presidents who traveled by submarine while in office. The other was Eisenhower.

• He was the second of three presidents who submerged in submarines while in office.

Nov. 24, flew to Grandview, Mo., for surprise visit with his mother on eve of her 94th birthday

Nov. 26, hosted diplomatic dinner, White House

• This dinner marked the opening of the first full social season at the White House since 1939. There had been a seven-year suspension of state dinners and a five-year suspension of state receptions because of the war.

Nov. 30, attended Army-Navy football game, Philadelphia, Pa.

Dec. 7, soft coal strike ended

• John L. Lewis and the UMW had been found guilty of civil as well as criminal contempt of court, Dec. 3. The strike had caused massive layoffs in major industries, including seventy thousand steel, fifty thousand railroad, and forty thousand automotive workers. A dimout ordered by the government had darkened 21 states. In a surprise move, Lewis called off the strike.

Dec. 12, issued executive order merging remaining wartime economic agencies into Office of Temporary Controls

Dec. 18, announced U.S. policy regarding China unchanged

•The U.S. would continue efforts to bring about peace between Chiang Kai-shek's Nationalists and the Chinese Communists, he said.

Dec. 25, spent Christmas with family, Independence, Mo.

Dec. 31, issued proclamation officially ending hostilities of World War II

•He explained that the proclamation did not end the state of war, or the states of emergency declared by President Franklin D. Roosevelt, Sept. 8, 1939, and May 27, 1941.

1947

Jan. 3, first session of 80th Congress

•The administration lost control of both the Senate and the House of Representatives. The Republicans gained 13 Senate and 56 House seats. The Senate (96 members) consisted of 51 Republicans and 45 Democrats. The House (435 members) consisted of 246 Republicans, 188 Democrats, and one American Laborite.

•This was the first time in 18 years that the Republicans controlled Congress.

Jan. 6, delivered his second State of the Union message to Congress

•He outlined his labor program and requested legislation for the unification of the military services, universal military training, and health insurance. He recommended the establishment of a department of welfare. He asked for continuance of excise taxes to permit balancing of the budget.

Jan. 7, accepted resignation of Secretary of State Byrnes, effective, Jan. 21

Jan. 7 appointed his third secretary of state, George C. Marshall

•Marshall took office, Jan. 21.

Jan. 8, submitted economic report to Congress

•He recommended the extension of rent control; higher social security benefits; a broader application of minimum wage regulations; and the maintenance of taxes at 1946 levels.

Jan. 10, submitted budget message to Congress

•The proposed budget was $37,730,000,-000, which included $11,256,000,000 for military appropriations.

Jan. 15, called for legislation to implement Bill of Rights in speech to Committee on Civil Rights

Jan. 16, reported agreement of army and navy to his unification plan under secretary of defense

Jan. 17, sent special message to Congress calling for repeal of $564,000,000 in appropriations for several departments

Jan. 23, his invitation to head mission to study food and economic situations in Germany and central Europe accepted by former President Hoover

Feb. 3, sent special message to Congress asking extension of some of his wartime controls for additional year

•The controls concerned food, freight car allocation, and certain imports and exports.

Feb. 5, submitted report to Congress on first year of UN

•He called for "genuinely national, bipartisan" support of the United Nations.

Feb. 5, again asked for legislation to change line of presidential succession

•He favored the succession of an elective officer, the speaker of the House, rather than an appointive officer, the secretary of state.

Feb. 14, flew to Grandview, Mo.

•His 94-year-old mother had fractured her hip in a fall at home.

Feb. 17, diverted seven thousand tons of food to Rumania

•The food, intended for U.S. occupation forces in Europe, was sent to Moldavia province, where 500,000 people faced starvation.

Feb. 19, sent special message to Congress requesting repeal of certain wartime emergency laws

•He asked for the repeal of 24 laws, as well as the temporary extension of ten laws, to accelerate the termination of emergencies proclaimed in 1939 and 1941.

Feb. 21, urged appropriation of $350,000,000 for food and other supplies for people of liberated countries, recommended distribution by U.S. rather than international agency

Feb. 24, sent special message to Congress urging legislation to authorize U.S. participation in International Refugee Organization

Feb. 25, ordered revision of reciprocal trade program to meet Republican objections

Feb. 26, sent draft of bill to Congress for merger of army, navy, and air force under secretary of defense

Mar. 2, departed for Mexico

• He was welcomed by President Miguel Aleman in Mexico City, Mar. 3.

• He was the third of seven presidents who visited Mexico while in office.

Mar. 3, sent special message to Congress recommending Selective Service Act be allowed to lapse, Mar. 31

• He also recommended that all members of the armed forces except volunteers be discharged by June 30.

Mar. 4, placed wreath at monument of young heroes of Battle of Chapultepec

• About one hundred boy cadets had defended the Mexican Military College on the fortified hill of Chapultepec, Sept. 13, 1847, shortly before the fall of Mexico City to U.S. troops under Scott.

Mar. 6, returned to U.S. from Mexico, received honorary degree from Baylor University, Waco, Tex.

Mar. 7, conferred with cabinet regarding crisis in Greece

• The Greek government had appealed to the U.S. for financial assistance, arms, and technical experts to avert economic and political collapse, Mar. 4.

Mar. 12, addressed joint session of Congress, outlined "Truman Doctrine"

• He asked for an appropriation of $400,000,000 to extend economic and political aid to the governments of Greece and Turkey. He said:

> I believe that it must be the policy of the United States to support free peoples who are resisting attempted subjugation by armed minorities or by outside pressures.

Mar. 12–18, vacationed in Key West, Fla.

Mar. 18, sent special message to Congress in which he proposed extension of export controls to June 30, 1948

Mar. 22, issued executive order directing department heads and FBI to thoroughly investigate loyalty of federal employees and applicants for government jobs

Mar. 24, 22nd Amendment to Constitution submitted to states for ratification

Mar. 26, recommended price cuts to industry, warned of potential inflation

Mar. 31, signed act that extended sugar rationing and price controls for seven months

Apr. 1, sent special message to Congress requesting rent control be extended to June 30, 1948

Apr. 5, declared his faith in United Nations, but asserted "Truman Doctrine" necessary

• In a Jefferson Day address in Washington, D.C., he maintained that the activities of the UN necessarily had to be supplemented by such programs as his proposed aid to Greece and Turkey to avert war.

Apr. 15, sent special message to Congress recommending revision of Neutrality Act of 1939 to bar sales of arms and implements of war to aggressor nations

Apr. 15, conferred Medal of Merit on former Secretary of State Hull

• During the ceremony at the naval hospital in Bethesda, Md., he referred to Hull as the "father of the United Nations."

Apr. 19, opposed tax reduction in immediate future, cited possibility of inflation

Apr. 21, reiterated his stand on necessity of price reduction to avoid inflation in speech to Associated Press, New York City

Apr. 26, issued executive order transferring unspecified number of U.S. naval vessels to Chinese government

Apr. 27, received report of Secretary of State Marshall on Moscow peace conference

• Marshall reported that the U.S. must insure the survival of Germany and Austria as independent nations or face the probability of a Communist-dominated Europe

Apr. 29, greeted President Aleman of Mexico, Washington, D.C.

Apr. 30, signed act changing name of Boulder Dam to Hoover Dam

May 9, sent special message to Congress in which he recommended appropriation of $24,900,000 to finance investigation into loyalty of federal employees

May 11, spent Mother's Day with bedridden mother, Grandview, Mo.

May 14, signed act outlawing portal-to-portal back-pay lawsuits of labor unions

May 17, flew to Grandview, Mo.

• His mother had suffered a relapse.

May 19, sent special message to Congress in which he urged legislation for comprehensive public health program

May 22, signed $400,000,000 Greek-Turkish aid act, Kansas City, Mo.

• He said:

> In extending the aid requested by two members of the United Nations, the United States is helping to further aims and purposes identical with those of the United Nations. Our aim in this instance is evidence not only that we pledge our support to the UN, but that we act to support it.

May 23, sent special message to Congress in which he requested extension of certain wartime powers

• He asked for a continuation of controls on production and export of tin and tin products, quinine and quinidine, manila and agave fibers, antimony, and cinchona bark to June 30, 1948.

May 27, sent special message to Congress in which he requested legislation to streamline housing and home financing programs

May 29, returned to Washington, D.C.

May 31, signed act providing $350,000,000 for reconstruction and feeding of liberated nations

June 1, received report of advisory commission on universal training

• The report called U.S. military forces a "hollow shell," recommended compulsory training of all youths at age of 18 or when high school was completed.

June 3, announced U.S. ready to negotiate hemispheric mutual assistance pact since differences with Argentina regarding Nazi influence had been settled

June 5, sent special message to Congress asking legislation for compulsory military training

June 5, denounced Communist coup ousting moderate government of Hungary

June 7, attended reunion of 35th Division, Kansas City, Mo.

• He castigated the House of Representatives for slashing expenditures for the interior and agriculture departments in a speech to his World War I comrades.

June 10–12, visited Canada

• He was the third of seven presidents who visited Canada while in office.

June 11, addressed joint session of Canadian Parliament, Ottawa

June 14, formally signed peace treaties with Italy, Hungary, Rumania, and Bulgaria

• He criticized Hungary, Rumania, and Bulgaria for having failed to establish governments that were "truly representative of the people," as stipulated in the Yalta agreement.

June 16, vetoed income tax reduction bill

• He called the proposed $4,000,000,000 tax cut ill-timed, beneficial only to those with large incomes.

• The House of Representatives came within two votes of overriding his veto, 268–137, June 17.

June 17, called for standardization of driving-license laws

• He told the Highway Conference in Washington, D.C., that the lack of standardization was "a travesty on public safety," that the high accident toll was "a national disaster."

June 20, vetoed labor-management relations bill

• The House of Representatives passed the measure over his veto, without debate, 331–83.

• In a radio address, he called the bill a "shocking piece of legislation," which was "bad for labor, bad for management and bad for the country."

June 21, Democratic filibuster to delay Senate vote to override veto of labor-management relations bill failed

June 22, appointed nonpartisan committee under Secretary of Commerce Harriman to determine resources available to implement Marshall Plan

• Secretary of State Marshall, in a June 5 speech at Harvard University, had outlined the European Recovery Program, which came to be known as the Marshall Plan. Marshall stipulated that the nations of Europe would be expected to increase their industrial production and give other evidence of self-aid rather than place their reliance only on U.S. assistance. "Our policy is not directed against any country or doctrine, but against hunger, poverty, desperation and chaos," said the secretary of state, and added:

> The role of this country should consist of friendly aid in the drafting of

a European program and of later support of such a program so far as it may be practical for us to do so. The program should be a joint one, agreed to by a number, if not all, European nations.

June 23, labor-management relations act passed over his veto
• The Senate voted to override his veto, 68–25.
• This was the Taft-Hartley Act, which banned the closed shop and the secondary boycott, stipulated that employers could sue unions for breached contracts and strike damages, and ended the check-off system of union-dues collection. The act also required a 60-day "cooling off" period before strikes, required unions to file public financial statements, and required union leaders to sign oaths stating that they were not Communists.
• This was the first of his 12 vetoes that were overridden.

June 24, appealed to members of National Labor Relations Board for fair administration of Taft-Hartley law
• The immediate response to the new labor law was a series of wildcat strikes by soft coal miners in ten states. About 185,000 walked out, thereby cutting coal production 40 percent.

June 26, pledged himself to "faithfully" administer Taft-Hartley law, appealed to labor and management to comply with provisions

June 26, vetoed wool support bill
• This bill would have increased the tariff on wool by means of import fees.

June 30, signed act extending federal rent control to Mar. 1, 1948
• Since rent control was scheduled to expire at midnight, he approved what he termed "a most unsatisfactory law." The act provided for up to 15 percent increases if owners and tenants signed 18-month leases.

July 1, criticized, but signed treasury-post office departmental appropriations act

July 4, criticized Russian obstructionism in Independence Day speech, Monticello, Va.
• The Paris Three-Power Conference on the Marshall Plan had ended in discord, July 2, which split Europe into Western and Soviet blocs.

July 5, announced U.S. had shipped more than 18,430,000 long tons of grains and other foods during fiscal year that ended June 30
• This was the largest volume of food shipped abroad by any one country in 12 months.

July 7, sent special message to Congress asking admission of "substantial number" of nearly one million survivors of Nazi terror in central Europe

July 16, sent special message to Congress requesting appropriation of $250,000,000 as first step of ten-year, $4,000,000,000, Mississippi Valley flood control program

July 18, again vetoed income tax reduction bill
• The House of Representatives voted to override the veto, 299–108, July 18, but the Senate vote was five short of the necessary two-thirds, 57–36, July 18.

July 18, signed presidential succession act
• This act provided that the speaker of the House and the president pro tempore of the Senate succeeded to the presidency prior to members of the cabinet.

July 18, accepted resignation of Secretary of War Patterson

July 18, appointed his third secretary of war, Kenneth C. Royall
• Royall took office, July 19.

July 19, signed act accepting trusteeship of Pacific Islands formerly mandated to Japan

July 21, sent midyear economic report to Congress
• He said that predictions of a depression and a recession had proven false—civilian production had risen to $225,000,000,000 and employment had passed sixty million —but, he added, the threat of inflation remained.

July 25, signed act terminating 175 war statutes, placed time limit on benefits for World War II veterans

July 26, signed armed services unification act

July 26, appointed first secretary of defense, James V. Forrestal
• Forrestal took office, Sept. 17.

July 26, his mother died

July 27, first session of 80th Congress adjourned

July 28, attended funeral of mother, Kansas City, Mo.

July 30–Aug. 8, pocket vetoed 19 bills

Aug. 4, signed act granting Puerto Rico right to elect governor by popular vote

Aug. 7, signed act putting armed services

promotions on merit basis

Aug. 20, forecast record surplus of $4,700,-000,000 at end of fiscal year, June 30, 1948

Aug. 28, exchanged letters of cooperation with Pope Pius XII

•He and the Pope pledged to work together for world peace to combat "collectivism."

Aug. 31, departed for Rio de Janeiro, Brazil

•He made one stop en route, Trinidad, British West Indies

•He was the second of two presidents who visited Trinidad while in office. The other was Franklin D. Roosevelt.

Sept. 1, arrived in Rio de Janeiro

•He was the second of three presidents who visited Brazil while in office.

•He was the second of five presidents who visited South America while in office.

Sept. 2, addressed final session of Inter-American Conference for the Maintenance of Continental Peace and Security, Petropolis, Brazil

•He stated that while he was confident that the international "difficulties" would not lead to war, "our military strength will be retained as evidence of the seriousness with which we view our obligations."

•The Treaty of Rio de Janeiro, a mutual defense pact, was signed by 19 American nations in the Brazilian capital, following the closing session of the conference.

Sept. 3, announced lifting of export ban on radioactive isotopes

•He announced the decision, which would enable foreign scientists to conduct medical and biological experiments, in a message to the International Cancer Research Congress, St. Louis, Mo.

Sept. 5, addressed Brazilian Congress, Rio de Janeiro

Sept. 6, narrowly escaped injury when his car skidded on wet road, high on Tijuca Peak, Rio de Janeiro

Sept. 7, departed from Rio de Janeiro for U.S., aboard *U.S.S. Missouri*

Sept. 17, directed first secretary of defense, James V. Forrestal, to take oath of office

•Truman radioed the order for Forrestal to take the oath of office five days ahead of schedule from the *Missouri*. The White House announced that the change of plans was due to "the whole general international situation."

Sept. 19, arrived at Norfolk, Va.

Sept. 20, returned to Washington, D.C.,

from Norfolk, aboard presidential yacht, *Williamsburg*

Sept. 29, informed Congressional leaders at White House conference that $580,000,-000 was needed in emergency aid if France and Italy were to survive coming winter "as free and independent nations"

Oct. 1, announced U.S. consumption of bread and meat must be reduced to meet minimum needs of distressed countries

•A saving of 100,000,000 bushels of grain would be necessary during the next nine months, he said at the first meeting of the Citizens Food Committee.

Oct. 5, asked nation to observe meatless Tuesdays, use no eggs or poultry on Thursdays, and eat one slice of bread less per day

•He and his family observed the first peacetime meatless day, Oct. 7.

Oct. 15, ordered cancellation of all state dinners during winter season to aid food conservation program

Oct. 23, called special session of Congress, Nov. 17

•He called the special session to provide legislation to combat rising prices and to provide emergency aid for Europe until the Marshall Plan was put into effect. He explained his reasons in a radio address, Oct. 24.

Oct. 25, declared state of Maine disaster area

•Forest fires had caused damage estimated at $30,000,000.

Nov. 14, announced all but extreme federal employee disloyalty cases would be heard by newly formed Loyalty Review Board, promised no "witch hunts"

Nov. 17, second session of 80th Congress

•In an address to a joint session of Congress, he proposed a ten-point anti-inflation program and asked for $597,000,000 in emergency aid for France, Italy, and Austria. His anti-inflation program included limited price and wage controls, stronger rent control legislation, and consumer rationing of scarce commodities.

Nov. 25, accepted resignation of Postmaster General Hannegan

Nov. 26, commuted prison sentence of Mayor James M. Curley of Boston, Mass.

•Curley had served five months of a six-to-18-month term for mail fraud in the federal correctional institution, Danbury, Conn.

Dec. 13, vowed appropriate action would be

taken if Italy's independence threatened "directly or indirectly"

•U.S. occupation troops withdrew from Italy, Dec. 14.

Dec. 16, appointed his third postmaster general, Jesse M. Donaldson

Dec. 19, sent special message to Congress in which he urged authorization of $17,000,000,000 to finance Marshall Plan for four-year period

Dec. 19, second session of 80th Congress adjourned

Dec. 23, signed act providing $540,000,000 in stopgap aid for France, Italy, Austria, and China

Dec. 23, granted full pardons to 1,523 men convicted of Selective Service Act violations during World War II

1948

Jan. 6, third session of 80th Congress

Jan. 7, delivered his third State of the Union message to Congress

•His message urged passage of the Marshall Plan legislation, asked statehood for Hawaii and Alaska, and proposed a $40 cost-of-living credit for each taxpayer and dependent to be financed by increased corporations profit taxes. He also asked for a minimum pay increase from 40 to 75 cents an hour.

Jan. 12, sent budget message to Congress

•He submitted a budget of $39,669,000,000 to meet the "unprecedented challenge of totalitarianism abroad" and domestic realities.

Jan. 26, urged approval of St. Lawrence Seaway project

Jan. 29, sent special message to Congress in which he demanded $6,800,000,000 for Marshall Plan or rejection of European recovery program

Feb. 1, submitted ten-point civil rights program to Congress

Feb. 5, warned of possible economic chaos, urged passage of his ten-point anti-inflation program of Nov. 17, 1947

Feb. 7, attended ceremonies marking retirement of General Eisenhower and induction of General Omar N. Bradley as general of army

Feb. 9, sent special message to Congress proposing extension of federal aid to state highway construction program

•He asked $1,000,000,000 to extend the highway program two years beyond the expiration date, June 30, 1949.

Feb. 16, sent special message to Congress stating additional funds for military aid to Greece and Turkey would be needed

Feb. 19, warned international conditions were too serious "to put an isolationist in the White House"

•He spoke at two Jefferson-Jackson dinners in Washington, D.C., attracting record crowds of Democrats despite boycotts by southern members of the party who opposed his civil rights program.

Feb. 20, flew to Key West, Fla., first stop on vacation and Caribbean inspection tour

•He visited Puerto Rico, the Virgin Islands, and the U.S. naval base at Guantanamo, Cuba, Feb. 21–25.

•He was the fourth of seven presidents who visited Puerto Rico while in office.

•He was the third of four presidents who visited the Virgin Islands while in office.

•He was the second of two presidents who visited Cuba while in office. The other was Coolidge.

Feb. 23, sent special message to Congress in which he asked extension of rent control until Apr. 30, 1949

Feb. 24, issued executive order to investigate steel industry price rises

Mar. 5, recommended dismantling of War Assets Administration, transfer of its duties to Federal Works Agency

Mar. 8, authorized announcement of his candidacy for presidency "if nominated"

Mar. 15, issued executive order to all federal departments and agencies to ignore congressional subpoenas or court orders for confidential data

•This order grew out of the investigation into the loyalty of Dr. Edward U. Condon, director of the Bureau of Standards.

•No files were to be turned over to congressional investigators until he had authorized their release.

Mar. 16, appointed fact-finding board to investigate strike of 100,000 packinghouse workers

•The strike had cut meat production by 50 percent.

Mar. 16, issued executive order transferring 29 merchant ships to Italy

•The vessels—14 of which were Italian ships seized during the war—were given to Italy as a token of renewed friendship.

Mar. 17, urged swift enactment of European Recovery Program, universal military training, and temporary restoration of draft in speech to joint session of Congress

• Russia had "destroyed the independence and democratic character of a whole series of nations in Eastern and Central Europe" and intended to dominate Western Europe if not combatted, he said.

Mar. 23, appointed fact-finding board to investigate soft coal strike

• Coal production fell 90 percent when 360,-000 members of the UMW walked off their jobs in support of John L. Lewis's demand for a $100-a-month pension to be paid by the operators.

Mar. 25, told press he intended to campaign for reelection despite revolt of southern Democrats, growing labor opposition, and Henry Wallace's third-party movement

Mar. 30, signed act extending rent control in modified form for additional year

Apr. 2, vetoed $4,800,000,000 tax reduction bill

Apr. 2, tax reduction act passed over his veto

• This was the second of his 12 vetoes that were overridden.

Apr. 3, signed $6,098,000,000 foreign aid act

• This act established the Economic Cooperation Administration, and provided $5,300,000,000 for the first year of the Marshall Plan, which he declared was "America's answer to the challenge facing the free world today."

Apr. 5, vetoed bill to exclude vendors of newspapers and magazines from social security benefits

• His veto message declared the measure a threat to the entire social security system.

Apr. 6, appointed Paul G. Hoffman as first economic cooperation administrator

Apr. 8, sent special message to Congress requesting export-import lending power be increased by $500,000,000 to finance Latin American industrialization program

Apr. 17, again urged passage of his ten-point anti-inflation program in speech to American Society of Newspaper Editors

Apr. 20, exclusion of newspaper and magazine vendors from social security benefits act passed over his veto

• This was the third of his 12 vetoes that were overridden.

Apr. 22, accepted resignation of Secretary of Commerce Harriman

• Truman appointed Harriman as chief representative of ECA in Europe, with rank of ambassador-at-large.

Apr. 22, appointed his third secretary of commerce, Charles Sawyer

• Sawyer took office, May 6.

May 1, called for compulsory health insurance legislation in address to National Health Assembly, Washington, D.C.

May 10, issued executive order of seizure of nation's railroads

• The railroad workers remained on their jobs.

May 10, accepted resignation of Secretary of Agriculture Anderson

May 12, White House called "fire trap"

• The fire-fighting facilities of the executive mansion were termed inadequate, according to a report of a special committee of the National Fire Protection Association.

May 13, sent special message to Congress asking for an additional appropriation of $2,434,441,000 to strengthen armed services

May 14, recognized provisional Jewish government as "de facto authority of the new State of Israel"

May 15, vetoed bill to amend Atomic Energy Act of 1946

• The bill provided that future members or general managers of the Atomic Energy Commission must first by investigated with respect to character, associations, and loyalty by the FBI. His veto message called the bill an "unwarranted encroachment" on his executive powers.

May 21, signed military aircraft act

• This act provided an appropriation of $3,-198,100,000 for procurement of a 70-group air force.

May 24, sent special message to Congress urging expansion of social security system to include twenty million workers not previously covered

May 25, received Chaim Weizmann, president of Israel

• This was the first official call of Weizmann as president.

June 2, urged to withdraw from presidential race

• In reply to a letter from a resident of his own state, he wrote that he "was not brought up to run from a fight."

June 2, appointed his third secretary of agriculture, Charles F. Brannan

June 3, began "non-political" transcontinental speaking tour

June 4, called for broad social security program, criticized amended bill for admission of displaced persons pending in Congress, Chicago, Ill.

June 5, criticized congressmen who favored farm program while campaigning, opposed same legislation in House of Representatives and Senate, Omaha, Neb.

June 7, warned against private power interests and congressional allies, Pocatello, Idaho

June 8, criticized Congress for cutting back farm and housing programs, Butte, Mont.

June 9, assailed 80th Congress as "the worst we've ever had since the first one met," Spokane, Wash.

June 10, Secretary of Labor Schwellenbach died

June 12, vetoed bill to exempt railroad rate agreements approved by ICC from antitrust laws

June 12, warned U.S.S.R. that entire free world, not just U.S., opposed policies, Berkeley, Cal.

• He said the U.S. refused to "gamble" with peace by making bilateral agreements with the U.S.S.R. and would act only through the United Nations, in an address at the University of California.

June 14, vetoed social security joint resolution

• His veto message stated that 750,000 persons would be deprived of old-age and unemployment benefits.

June 14, social security joint resolution passed over his veto

• This was the fourth of his 12 vetoes that were overridden.

June 14, vetoed $1,000,000,000 supplemental appropriations for Federal Security Agency bill

• His veto message objected to a rider that would have transferred the U.S. Employment Service to the Federal Security Agency.

June 14, demanded Congress remain in session until price control and other major legislation passed, Los Angeles, Cal.

June 16, supplemental appropriations for Federal Security Agency act passed over his veto

• This act provided funds for the Social Security Administration, some sections of the Public Health Service, and the U.S. Employment Service.

• This was the fifth of his 12 vetoes that were overridden.

June 17, act to exempt railroad rate agreements from antitrust laws, if approved by ICC, passed over his veto

• This was the sixth of his 12 vetoes that were overridden.

June 18, returned to Washington, D.C.

• Throughout his "non-political" speaking tour, he had sharply criticized the Republican majority of the 80th Congress for having devoted its energies to the "special interests."

June 20, second session of 80th Congress adjourned

June 24, made decision to resist blockade of Berlin

• In retaliation to his June 18 order of currency reform in the American zone of Germany, the Soviets sealed off Berlin to all land traffic.

June 24, signed peacetime draft act

• The act required men between the ages of 19 and 25 to serve 21 months. Eighteen-year-olds who enlisted for one year were exempted from further service.

June 25, reluctantly signed act admitting 205,000 displaced persons and refugees to U.S. over two-year period

• He condemned the act as "flagrantly discriminatory."

June 25, signed act raising salary of vice president from $15,000 to $20,000

• This act also increased the presidential travel expense account from $25,000 to $40,000, annually.

June 26, ordered Berlin airlift

• He ordered all planes in the European command into service to supply food and other necessities for the citizens of Berlin. The airlift was maintained for 320 days, until the Russians admitted defeat and terminated the blockade, May 12, 1949.

June 28, signed foreign aid act

• This act, which he called highly satisfactory, provided $6,030,710,228 for the European recovery program and other foreign aid.

June 30, criticized Congress for failure to provide funds for TVA steam-generating plant

July 1, received President Romulo Gallegos of Venezuela, White House

July 1, reluctantly signed housing act

• He condemned the Republican measure for having "failed miserably to meet the urgent need of the people."

July 1, reiterated his intention to run for reelection, despite southern opposition and Wallace third-party movement

July 2, largest federal surplus for any fiscal year announced

•Secretary of Treasury Snyder announced a surplus of $8,419,469,843 for fiscal year 1948, the largest in U.S. history.

July 3, announced two principal aims of U.S., peace with justice and viable United Nations

•He spoke at the ceremony which marked the 100th anniversary of the laying of the cornerstone of the Washington Monument, July 4, 1848.

July 3, reluctantly signed federal employee salary increase act

•He said the increases were inadequate and unfair and blamed Congress for failure to pass his program to decrease the cost of living.

July 3, reluctantly signed agricultural act

•He said Congress had failed to cope with the farm problems.

July 15, nominated for president, Democratic national convention, Philadelphia, Pa.

•In his acceptance speech, he announced a special session of Congress, July 26.

July 19, conferred with diplomatic and military leaders about Berlin crisis

July 20, issued proclamation ordering 9,-500,000 men between ages of 18 and 25 to register for military service

July 26, third session of 80th Congress

July 26, issued two executive orders in which he directed end of discrimination in armed forces and civil government "as rapidly as possible"

July 27, outlined ten administration proposals, including eight-point anti-inflation program, in address to special session of Congress

•He proposed civil rights, housing, federal aid to education, and increased old age insurance legislation; as well as a rise in the minimum hourly wage from 40 to 75 cents; a broader federal employee wage increase; admission of additional displaced persons; approval of the international wheat agreement; and approval of a $65,000,000 loan for the United Nations headquarters.

July 31, dedicated Idlewild International Airport, New York City

•Idlewild, the world's largest air terminal,

was renamed John F. Kennedy International Airport, 1963.

Aug. 3, sent special message to Congress in which he proposed $4,300,000,000 excess-profits tax

Aug. 5, denounced Congressional investigation of subversives as "red herring" to divert attention from Republican campaign to defeat his anti-inflation program

Aug. 7, third session of 80th Congress adjourned

•During the 11-day session, a limited housing bill was passed, as were two of his eight anti-inflation proposals. A $65,000,000 loan for UN headquarters also was approved.

Aug. 10, signed housing act

Aug. 11, appointed his third secretary of labor, Maurice J. Tobin

•Tobin took office, Aug. 13.

Aug. 11, signed United Nations $65,000,000 loan act

Aug. 12, characterized special session as "do-nothing session" during news conference

Aug. 15, forecast $1,545,000,000 deficit for fiscal 1949 during midyear budget review

Aug. 16, reluctantly signed act tightening controls on consumer and bank credits

•He called the measure a "feeble response" to the need for anti-inflationary legislation.

Aug. 21–29, took precampaign vacation cruise in Florida waters

Sept. 1, denounced Taft-Hartley Act

•He called for the repeal of the act, said it "unfairly restricts labor unions and their members."

Sept 6, formally opened campaign, Detroit, Mich.

•He set the tone for his campaign by assailing the "do-nothing" 80th Congress and warned of a depression if the Republicans were victorious.

Sept. 13, expressed apprehension over reluctance of scientists to enter governmental service

•The possibility of "smears" was the reason, he told the centennial meeting of the American Association for the Advancement of Science.

Oct. 21, promised to work for repeal of Taft-Hartley Act, increase of minimum hourly wage from 40 to 75 cents, during major radio campaign address

Oct. 28, issued executive order releasing $154,817,000 of air force funds for purchase of 125 bombers and other aircraft

Oct. 30, ended campaign, St. Louis, Mo.

Nov. 1, broadcast from his home, Independence, Mo.

• He said the outcome of the election would affect the U.S. for years to come and characterized the Democratic party as "the party of the people" and the Republican party as "the party of privilege."

Nov. 2, election day

• See Election of 1948, below.

Nov. 3, pledged himself to "continue to serve the American people to the best of my ability," Independence, Mo.

Nov. 5, returned to White House

Nov. 7–21, vacationed in Key West, Fla.

• During his visit the main throughfare of Key West was renamed Truman Avenue.

Nov. 16, outlined his domestic program for second administration, Key West, Fla.

• The repeal of the Taft-Hartley Act and the passage of the civil rights program were his principal objectives, he said. He added that he would work for those measures—still not acted upon—that he had outlined in his 21-point continuation of the New Deal program, Sept. 6, 1945.

Dec. 1, received Madame Chiang Kai-shek, White House

Dec. 8, greeted President Carlos Prio Socrarras of Cuba, Washington Airport

Dec. 9, reiterated his charge that House Un-American Activities Committee investigation of alleged Communist activities was "red herring"

Dec. 13, presidential electors cast ballots

• Truman received 303 of the 531 electoral votes from the 48 states.

• See Election of 1948, below.

Dec. 31, fourth session of 80th Congress met and adjourned

1949

Jan. 1, recognized Republic of Korea

Jan. 3, first session of 81st Congress

• The administration regained control of both the Senate and the House of Representatives. The Democrats gained nine Senate and 75 House seats. The Senate (96 members) consisted of 54 Democrats and 42 Republicans. The House (435 members) consisted of 263 Democrats, 171 Republicans, and one American Laborite.

Jan. 5, delivered his fourth State of the Union message to Congress

• He outlined an eight-point anti-inflation program; a seven-year plan for one million low-rent housing units; additional social security and universal military training legislation; and again asked repeal of the Taft-Hartley Act and an increased minimum hourly wage of 75 cents.

Jan. 6, electoral votes tabulated by Congress

• Truman and Barkley were officially declared elected.

Jan. 7, accepted resignation of Secretary of State Marshall, effective, Jan. 20

Jan. 7, appointed his fourth secretary of State, Dean G. Acheson

• Acheson took office, Jan. 21.

Jan. 10, submitted $41,858,000,000 budget to Congress

• He estimated a deficit of $873,000,000 for fiscal 1950. He asked for $6,000,000,000 in additional taxes.

Jan. 17, sent special message to Congress asking additional powers to reorganize executive department agencies

Jan. 19, announced opposition to changes in electoral college system

Jan. 19, signed act raising salaries of president and vice president, effective, Jan. 20

• The salary of the president was increased from $75,000 to $100,000 annually, and a $50,000 expense account, tax free, was granted. The salary of the vice president was increased from $20,000 to $30,000 annually.

• Truman and Barkley were the first recipients of the new salaries.

ELECTION OF 1948

Prohibition party, convened, June 26, 1947, at Winona Lake, Ind., nominated Claude A. Watson of California for president, Dale H. Learn of Pennsylvania for vice president.

Socialist Labor party, convened, May 2, 1948 at New York City, nominated Edward A. Teichert of Pennsylvania for president, Stephen Emery of New York for vice president.

Socialist party, convened, May 7, at Reading, Pa., nominated Norman Thomas of New York for president, Tucker Powell Smith of Michigan for vice president.

Republican party, convened, June 21, at Philadelphia, Pa., nominated Thomas Edmund Dewey of New York for president,

Earl Warren of California for vice president.
- This was the 24th Republican national con-vention. It was the fifth Republican convention held in Philadelphia; it was the eighth major party convention held in Philadelphia.

Socialist Workers party, convened, July 2, at New York City, nominated Farrell Dobbs of New York for president, Grace Carlson of Minnesota for vice president.

Democratic party, convened, July 12, at Philadelphia, Pa., nominated Harry S. Truman of Missouri for president, Alben William Barkley of Kentucky for vice president.
- This was the 30th Democratic national convention. It was the second Democratic convention held in Philadelphia; it was the ninth major party convention held in Philadelphia.

States' Rights Democratic (Dixiecrat) party, convened, July 17, at Birmingham, Ala., nominated James Strom Thurmond of South Carolina for president, Fielding Lewis Wright of Mississippi for vice president.

Progressive party, convened, July 23, at Philadelphia, Pa., nominated Henry Agard Wallace of Iowa for president, Glen Hearst Taylor of Idaho for vice president.

Communist party, convened, Aug. 2, at New York City, endorsed the Progressive party ticket of Wallace and Taylor.

Election day, Tuesday, Nov. 2, 1948
Popular vote: 48,790,445

Truman, 24,179,345
Dewey, 21,991,291
Thurmond, 1,176,125
Wallace, 1,157,326
Thomas, 139,572
Watson, 103,900
Teichert, 29,272
Dobbs, 13,614
- Truman was the 13th of 15 presidents who were elected without receiving a majority of the popular vote.

Electoral vote: 531, 48 states
- Truman, 303, 28 states
  (Arizona, 4; Arkansas, 9; California, 25; Colorado, 6; Florida, 8; Georgia, 12; Idaho, 4; Illinois, 28; Iowa, 10; Kentucky, 11; Massachusetts, 16; Minnesota, 11; Missouri, 15; Montana, 4; Nevada, 3; New Mexico, 4; North Carolina, 14; Ohio, 25; Oklahoma, 10; Rhode Island, 4; Tennessee, 11 of 12 votes; Texas, 23; Utah, 4; Virginia, 11; Washington, 8; West Virginia, 8; Wisconsin, 12; Wyoming, 3)
- Dewey, 189, 16 states
  (Connecticut, 8; Delaware, 3; Indiana, 13; Kansas, 8; Maine, 5; Maryland, 8; Michigan, 19; Nebraska, 6; New Hampshire, 4; New Jersey, 16; New York, 47; North Dakota, 4; Oregon, 6; Pennsylvania, 35; South Dakota, 4; Vermont, 3)
- Thurmond, 39, four states
  (Alabama, 11; Louisiana, 10; Mississippi, 9; South Carolina, 8)
- Thurmond also received the vote of one Tennessee elector.

THE 41st ADMINISTRATION

1949

Jan. 20, his inauguration day
- Truman took the oath of office, administered by Chief Justice Frederick Moore Vinson, on the east portico of the Capitol.
- This was the first of two inaugurations at which Chief Justice Vinson officiated.
- Truman's age at his inauguration was 64 years, 257 days.
- He was the 20th of 21 presidents who were younger than their vice presidents. Truman was six years, 175 days younger than Barkley.

Feb. 1, differentiated between "controlled economy" and "planned economy" in ad-

dress before National Planning Commission
- He urged support of his and the Hoover Commission's proposals to realign the federal government structure, rejected "controlled economy" as totalitarian.

Feb. 3, stated Premier Stalin welcome at White House, but reiterated his position against negotiations with Soviets outside UN
- Stalin had declared, Jan. 30, that he had "no objections" to meeting with Truman "at a mutually acceptable place" to discuss world affairs.

Feb. 11, appointed General Eisenhower as head of Joint Chiefs of Staff and special consultant to Secretary of Defense Forrestal

Feb. 15, sent special message to Congress in which he proposed eight-point anti-inflation program
•He urged wage, price, and production controls and a tax increase of $4,000,000,000.
Feb. 17, sent special message to Congress asking $5,400,000 for reconstruction of White House
Feb. 24, stated he would making national speaking tour if necessary to fight "special interests" combatting his legislative program
Feb. 28, Republicans supported, southern Democrats opposed his plan to strengthen antifilibuster rules
•Southern Democratic senators filibustered against the proposed amendment, which was withdrawn by administration leaders, Mar. 14.
Mar. 3, accepted resignation of Secretary of Defense Forrestal, effective, Mar. 27
Mar. 3, appointed his second secretary of defense, Louis A. Johnson
•Johnson took office, Mar. 28.
Mar. 14, photographs taken from blimp at Key West, Fla., ordered confiscated by his press secretary, Charles G. Ross
•Ross maintained the pictures of the president and Chief Justice Vinson violated presidential security and privacy. After editing, some of the pictures were released, Mar. 17.
Mar. 21, stigmatized real estate lobby as "real enemy of the American home" in address to U.S. Conference of Mayors
Mar. 22, Senate confirmed his appointment of James Boyd as director of bureau of mines
•John L. Lewis of the United Mine Workers had called a two-week strike in protest of the appointment.
Mar. 23, welcomed Winston Churchill, Washington, D.C.
Mar. 28, awarded Distinguished Service Medal to former Secretary of Defense Forrestal
Mar. 30, signed extension of federal rent control act
•He called the act, which extended rent control for 15 months, "a crushing defeat for the real estate lobby."
Mar. 31, criticized Senator Walter F. George (D., Ga.) for opposition to proposed tax increase

•He maintained that a budget deficit was more dangerous than higher taxes. George had warned that a "sizable depression" would follow if the $4,000,000,000 tax increase was passed, Mar. 29.
Mar. 31, opposed proposed $1,600,000,000 increase in $15,000,000,000 defense budget
•The appropriation increase was recommended by the chairman of the House of Representatives services committee, Carl Vinson.
Apr. 4, attended signing of North Atlantic Treaty by 12 nations, Washington, D.C.
•He said:
> We are like a group of householders, living in the same locality, who decide to express their community of interests by entering into a formal association for their mutual self-protection.
•The 12 nations were Belgium, Canada, Denmark, France, Great Britain, Iceland, Italy, Luxembourg, The Netherlands, Norway, Portugal, and the U.S.
Apr. 6, declared he would order use of atomic bomb again if necessary to protect U.S. and democracies
Apr. 12, sent special message to Senate in which he asked ratification of North Atlantic Treaty
Apr. 12, received report from Secretary of State Acheson explaining only Congress could declare war; U.S. was not "automatically" at war if North Atlantic signatory was attacked
Apr. 13, sent special message to Congress asking establishment of Columbia Valley Administration
Apr. 19, signed $5,430,000,000 European recovery act
•The appropriation for the 15 months ending June 30, 1950, was $150,000,000 less than requested.
Apr. 22, submitted national compulsory health insurance program to Congress
Apr. 26, proposed $157,800,000 cut in European recovery program because of price reductions
Apr. 27, his compulsory health insurance program shelved
Apr. 28, sent special message to Congress in which he recommended U.S. join International Trade Organization
May 5, cited defeat of Wood labor bill as administration victory

•The bill, submitted as a substitute for the Taft-Hartley Act, was sponsored by Representative John S. Wood of Georgia.

May 9, sent special message to Congress asking legislation to reorganize executive department as recommended by Hoover Commission

May 12, submitted report on U.S. 1948 participation in UN to Congress

•He and Secretary of State Acheson expressed faith in the international organization while admitting disappointments during 1948, which they implied were attributable to excessive Soviet vetoes.

May 18, welcomed President Eurico Gaspar Dutra of Brazil, Washington, D.C.

May 22, expressed shock at suicide of former Secretary of Defense Forrestal

•Forrestal, who had suffered a mental and physical breakdown attributed to overwork, "was as truly a casualty of war as if he had died on the firing line," Truman said.

June 16, declared anyone in executive department who contributed to wave of hysteria brought about by spy and loyalty investigations would be fired

June 17, again denounced "real estate lobby" for opposition to low-rent housing and slum clearance program

•He had estimated the program would cost $10,000,000, and called the $20,000,000,-000 estimate by real estate spokesmen a "distortion" and "misrepresentation."

June 20, signed reorganization act

•This act authorized him to reorganize the executive department as recommended by the Hoover Commission. He submitted seven proposals to Congress, including a bill to convert the Federal Security Agency into a new department of welfare under a secretary of cabinet rank.

June 24, sent special message to Congress in which he requested $45,000,000 to provide technical aid to underdeveloped areas under Point IV program

June 30, declared he would continue to fight for repeal of Taft-Hartley Act

•A modified version of the labor law had been passed by Congress over administration opposition.

July 1, received budget report from Secretary of Treasury Snyder revealing deficit of $1,811,000,000

•The deficit for the fiscal year that ended June 30 was a peacetime record and exceeded his forecast by $1,211,000,000.

July 11, submitted midyear economic report to Congress, admitted decline in economy

•He reversed his stand on deficit spending and dropped demands for $4,000,000,000 in additional taxes and wage and price controls. He said there could be "no greater folly" than seeking to balance the budget during the current "moderate downward trend."

July 13, admitted nation had serious unemployment problem, denied existence of depression

•He had recommended deficit spending, he said in a national radio address, to maintain essential programs.

July 19, Associate Justice Murphy died

July 25, signed North Atlantic Treaty

•The NATO treaty had been ratified by the Senate, July 21.

July 25, sent special message to Congress in which he asked $1,450,000,000 for military aid to NATO signatories, the Philippines, Korea, and Iran

•"So long as the danger of aggression exists, it is necessary to think in terms of the forces required to prevent it," he said.

July 28, appointed Thomas C. Clark as associate justice

•Clark, who was confirmed by the Senate, Aug. 18, was the third of Truman's four appointments to the Supreme Court.

Aug. 8, welcomed President Elpidio Quirino of the Philippines, Washington, D.C.

Aug. 16, his proposal for department of welfare defeated in Senate by coalition of Republicans and southern Democrats

Aug. 24, accepted resignation of Attorney General Clark

Aug. 24, appointed his third attorney general, J. Howard McGrath

Aug. 24, issued proclamation that declared North Atlantic pact in effect

Aug. 25, indicated he would not run for reelection in 1952, but said it was too early to make decision

Sept. 1, stated he would retain Major General Harry Vaughan as military aide

•Vaughan had been accused of using undue influence on behalf of personal and business associates.

Sept. 10, Associate Justice Rutledge died

Sept. 15, private relief act passed over his veto

•This was the seventh of his 12 vetoes that

were overridden.

Sept. 15, appointed Sherman Minton as associate justice

• Minton, who was confirmed by the Senate, Oct. 4, was the last of Truman's four appointments to the Supreme Court.

Sept. 23, announced Soviet possession of atomic bomb

Sept. 26, signed extension of Reciprocal Trade Agreements Act

Oct. 11, welcomed Prime Minister Jawaharlal Nehru of India, Washington, D.C.

Oct. 16, vetoed bill that would have provided ten-year rehabilitation program for Navajo and Hopi Indians

• His objection was based on that portion of the bill that transferred the Indian reservations from federal to state jurisdiction.

Oct. 18, issued executive order authorizing Atomic Energy Commission to withdraw $30,000,000 from reserve fund for new construction at Oak Ridge, Tenn., and Hanford, Wash., atomic plants

Oct. 19, first session of 81st Congress adjourned

Oct. 24, attended laying of cornerstone of United Nations headquarters, New York City

• The U.S. had supported international control of atomic energy since the first nuclear explosion, he said, that would
  . . . assure effective prohibition of atomic weapons, and at the same time would promote the peaceful use of atomic energy by all nations.

Nov. 1, forecast deficit of $5,500,000,000 for fiscal year ending June 30, 1950

Nov. 3, attended centennial of Minnesota territory, St. Paul, Minn.

Nov. 10, accepted resignation of Secretary of Interior Krug, effective, Dec. 1

Nov. 10, appointed his third secretary of interior, Oscar L. Chapman

• Chapman took office, Dec. 1.

Nov. 16, issued executive order authorizing Federal Housing Administration loans of $20,375,000 for low-rent housing in 27 states, District of Columbia and Puerto Rico

Nov. 16, welcomed Shah Mohammed Reza Pahlevi of Iran, Washington, D.C.

Nov. 23, accepted resignation of AEC chairman, David E. Lilienthal

• He had strongly supported Lilienthal, the first chairman of the Atomic Energy Commission, who had been under almost con-

tinuous attack since his appointment in 1946.

Dec. 2, issued executive order to FHA to deny financial assistance to new housing projects with racial, religious, or color restrictions

Dec. 19, issued executive order prohibiting low-altitude flying over Superior National Forest, Minn.

• Hunters had been stalking wild game in the national forest by airplane.

Dec. 21, dedicated carillon given by American Veterans of World War II, Arlington National Cemetery

Dec. 25, celebrated Christmas with family, Independence, Mo.

Dec. 27, recognized United States of Indonesia

1950

Jan. 3, second session of 81st Congress

Jan. 4, delivered his fifth State of the Union message to Congress

• He reiterated his request for enactment of such Fair Deal legislation as compulsory health insurance and repeal of the Taft-Hartley Act. He stated that he would seek tax revision to aid business and industrial investment.

Jan. 5, announced U.S. would not grant military aid to Chinese Nationalists to defend Formosa, but economic aid would continue

Jan. 9, submitted $42,439,000,000 budget message to Congress

• He estimated the deficit for fiscal 1951 at $5,133,000,000.

Jan. 14, approved recall of U.S. consular officials from Red China

Jan. 21, refused to comment on Hiss trial decision

• Alger Hiss was found guilty of perjury, New York City.

Jan. 23, sent special tax message to Congress

• He asked for legislation to reduce excise taxes, and raise gift, estate, and corporation taxes.

Jan. 31, announced he had ordered Atomic Energy Commission to "continue its work on all forms of atomic weapons," including H-bomb

Feb. 2, rejected theory that U.S. should seek agreement with Russia on international control of nuclear weapons

•He told the press that failures to reach agreement with the U.S.S.R. in the past ruled out the possibility of the U.S. initiating negotiations.

Feb. 5, sent special message to Congress in which he urged legislation to cancel charters of dubious GI schools

•A Veterans Administration report had revealed that many of the fifty-six hundred schools that had benefited from GI enrollment since 1944 lacked competent teaching staffs and training facilities.

Feb. 14, stated U.S.S.R. was untrustworthy, had broken 39 of 40 agreements made with U.S. since 1945

Feb. 15, pledged full-scale campaign against underworld, following meeting of federal, state, and local law-enforcement officers

Feb. 16, chided Republicans for "motheaten" political tactics, Jefferson-Jackson dinner, Washington, D.C.

•He said that the GOP had opposed progress since 1933, and that the opposition party tactic of dragging out the "same moth-eaten scarecrow of 'socialism'" was "an insult to the intelligence of the American people."

Mar. 2, lunched with Li Tsung-jen, deposed Chinese Nationalist president

•Li had assumed the presidency when Chiang Kai-shek retired, Jan. 21, 1949. Chiang resumed the presidency, Mar. 1; Li denounced Chiang as a "dictator."

Mar. 6, issued proclamation postponing Panama Canal toll increase until Apr. 1, 1951

•This act, which increased tolls from 90 cents to $1 a ton, had been approved in 1948. This was the fourth time the increase had been postponed.

Mar. 12, sailed for Key West, Fla., aboard *Williamsburg*

•He arrived in Key West, Mar. 16, after a stormy voyage aboard the presidential yacht.

Mar. 16, signed act repealing all federal taxes on oleomargarine

Mar. 18, issued proclamation regarding national census

•He pledged that data gathered by census-takers would not be employed as the basis for tax increase legislation. He also stated that no one's privacy would be invaded.

Apr. 3, sent special message to Congress on farm price-support program

•He urged a complete review of the program rather than "patching it up with makeshift legislation."

Apr. 6, sent special message to Congress in which he asked unemployment insurance coverage for six million additional persons

•He also requested that unemployment benefits be raised by 20 percent.

Apr. 12, greeted President Gabriel Gonzalez Videla of Chile, Washington, D.C.

Apr. 14, granted full pardon to former Mayor James M. Curley of Boston, Mass.

•Truman had commuted Curley's six-to-18-month sentence for mail fraud after the former mayor had served five months in federal prison, 1947.

Apr. 15, vetoed bill to amend National Gas Act of 1938

•This bill would have exempted sales of natural gas by independent producers from the rate-fixing authority of the Federal Power Commission.

•In his veto message, he said that "unlike purchasers of coal and oil, purchasers of natural gas cannot easily move from one producer to another in search of lower prices."

Apr. 18, announced he and Secretary of State Acheson would solicit foreign policy views of Republican members of Congress

•The bipartisan foreign policy theory had been bolstered by the appointment of Republican statesman, John Foster Dulles, as a consultant to Acheson, Apr. 6.

Apr. 19, signed act authorizing $88,570,000, ten-year rehabilitation program for Navajo and Hopi Indians

•He pointed out that he had vetoed a similar measure in 1949 because the bill would have placed the two tribes under state court jurisdiction.

May 2, urged Senate to approve U.S.-Canadian treaty for joint development of Niagara and St. Lawrence power

May 2, called "worst president, but one of the cleverest politicians ever to occupy the White House" by Harold B. Stassen, president of University of Pennsylvania and contender for Republican presidential nomination

•Asked for comment, he laughed and said he would let history decide.

May 4, forecast Cold War would not develop into shooting war

•At a press conference, he promised to reduce the 1951 defense budget

May 10, signed act creating National

Science Foundation "to promote the development of new scientific knowledge
and new scientific talent"

May 15, challenged Republicans "to come
out with something and be a real opposition"

•His entire cabinet joined him at the closing
rally of the three-day National Democratic
Conference and Jefferson Jubilee, Chicago,
Ill.

May 17, spoke at Library of Congress ceremonies on occasion of publication of first
of 52 volumes of papers of Thomas Jefferson

May 19, again urged extension of Selective
Service Act

•He said that if Congress had passed his universal military training program in 1945,
there would have been no Cold War.

May 20, reviewed first Armed Forces Day
parade, Washington, D.C.

May 22, signed $1,800,000,000 rivers and
harbors act

May 25, announced agreement with Great
Britain and France to regulate arms sales
in Middle East

May 29, conferred with UN Secretary General Trygve Lie, White House

•Lie had just returned from Moscow, where
he had conferred with Stalin on the ways
and means of ending the Cold War.

June 1, sent special message to Congress in
which he asked $1,222,500,000 in military
aid for Europe and Asia

June 5, signed Foreign Economic Aid act

•This act, which authorized $3,200,000,000
for five foreign aid programs, was "a major
contribution to peace and freedom in the
world," he said.

June 6, denounced "creeping socialism"
propaganda campaign of administration
opponents

•He said:
  Nothing could be farther from the
  truth. The record shows that government action in recent years has
  been the salvation of private enterprise.

June 10, attended reunion of his World War
I unit, St. Louis, Mo.

•In his address to the 35th Division veterans, he predicted that the Cold War would
last "for many years."

June 16, signed amendment to displaced
persons act of 1948

•The number of European refugees eligible

to enter the U.S. was raised from 205,000
to 415,000.

June 17, signed executive order releasing
federal income tax files to special Senate
committee investigating interstate crime

June 24, informed of invasion of South
Korea by North Korea

June 26, announced U.S. would support UN
against North Korean "act of aggression"

June 27, announced he had ordered U.S. air
and sea forces "to give the Korean government troops cover and support"

June 30, signed act extending selective service until July 9, 1951

June 30, vetoed bill to amend Hatch Act

•The bill proposed modifications of penalties and restrictions of the Hatch Act,
which prohibited federal office holders
from political campaign participation.

July 7, sent special message to Congress in
which he asked $260,000,000 to accelerate
H-bomb production

July 12, signed act providing free postage
for combat-area servicemen

July 18, issued executive order establishing
credit controls on public housing

July 21, issued executive order to 14 federal
departments and agencies to reduce
spending

July 25, sent special message to Congress
asking tax increase of $5,000,000,000

•He asked legislation to provide a $3,000,-
000,000 increase in personal income taxes,
$1,500,000,000 in corporate taxes, and
$500,000,000 from revised tax statutes.

July 26, submitted midyear economic report to Congress

•He indicated that he would request further tax increases and price controls in the
future and urged moderation on the part
of business, labor, and consumers.

July 27, announced previously requested
reduction of excise taxes would be postponed due to Korean War

Aug. 1, signed act granting U.S. citizenship
and limited self-government to Guam

•Guam had been ceded to the U.S. by Spain,
1898.

Aug. 3, signed act raising armed forces to
any necessary level during national emergency

Aug. 8, signed act authorizing $350,000,000
naval modernization program

•The program included construction of a
nuclear submarine.

Aug. 18, appointed Lieutenant General

Walter Bedell Smith as director of CIA
• The CIA had been severely criticized for failure to anticipate the invasion of South Korea.
Aug. 25, issued executive order to seize railroads to avert strike of trainmen and yardmen
Aug. 28, signed new Social Security Act
• He also sent a special message to Congress in which he asked $134,000,000 to finance provisions of the act. An additional ten million workers were covered by the new measure.
Aug. 30, his condemnatory letter about U.S. Marines inserted in *Congressional Record*
• When a Republican congressman from California demanded that he add a marine to the Joint Chiefs of Staff, he wrote in reply:
> The Marine Corps is the Navy's police force, and as long as I am President that is what it will remain. They have a propaganda machine that is almost equal to Stalin's.
• Indignant protests were heard from all parts of the country, which led him to write letters of apology to the Marine Corps commandant, General Clifton B. Gates, and the Commander of the Marine Corps League, Clay Nixon.
Sept. 1, outlined Asian policy in TV-radio address
• "We do not want Formosa or any part of Asia for ourselves," he said. General Douglas A. MacArthur had declared Formosa should be part of American defenses in a letter released Aug. 28.
• "We do not believe in aggressive or preventive war," Truman added. Secretary of Navy Francis P. Matthews had advocated preventive war, Aug. 25.
Sept. 7, addressed Marine Corps national convention, Washington, D.C.
• He was greeted warmly by the veterans despite his recent remarks about the Marine Corps.
Sept. 8, signed Defense Production Act
• This act authorized him to establish priorities, allocate materials, stabilize prices and wages, and regulate consumer credit and construction, until June 30, 1951.
Sept. 9, signed act authorizing drafting of doctors and dentists under age of 51
Sept. 9, explained Defense Production Act during national radio address
Sept. 12, accepted resignation of Secretary

of Defense Johnson, effective, Sept. 19
Sept. 12, appointed his third secretary of defense, George C. Marshall
• Marshall took office, Sept. 21.
Sept. 14, vetoed bill to grant outpatient treatment by VA to veterans of Spanish-American War, Boxer Rebellion and Philippine insurrection
Sept. 14, proposed initial discussions regarding Japanese peace treaty
Sept. 18, submitted report on defenses against nuclear, biological, and chemical warfare to Congress
• The report had been prepared by the National Securities Resources Board.
Sept. 19, act to grant outpatient treatment to veterans of Spanish-American War, Boxer Rebellion and Philippine insurrection passed over his veto
• This was the eighth of his 12 vetoes that were overridden.
Sept. 22, vetoed Internal Security bill
Sept. 23, Internal Security Act of 1950 passed over his veto
• The McCarran Act provided for the registration of Communist party members and Communist front organization officers with the department of justice and also denied Communists the right to work for the federal government or in defense work. The Supreme Court ruled that individuals may refuse to register as members of the Communist party, Nov. 15, 1965.
• This was the ninth of his 12 vetoes that were overridden.
Oct. 9, issued executive order to ECA to set up long-range rehabilitation projects for Korean public utilities, mines, and harbors
Oct. 13, visited Hawaii, inspected Pearl Harbor
• He was the second of five presidents who visited Hawaii.
Oct. 15, conferred with General Douglas A. MacArthur, Wake Island
• He was the first of two presidents who visited Wake Island. The other was Eisenhower.
Oct. 24, spoke at fifth anniversary ceremonies, United Nations, Flushing Meadows, N.Y.
Nov. 1, his assassination attempted, Washington, D.C.
• Two members of the Puerto Rican nationalist movement tried to shoot their way into Blair House, his temporary residence,

with the intention of killing him. One of the attackers, Griselio Torresola of New York City, was shot to death; the other, Oscar Collazo of New York City, was wounded and captured. During the gun battle in front of Blair House, a White House guard, Private Leslie Coffelt of Arlington, Va., was mortally wounded, and two other guards, Private Joseph Downs and Private Donald T. Birdzell, were seriously wounded. Private Coffelt died in the hospital.

• This was the second unsuccessful attempt on the life of a president. The first occurred in 1835, when Richard Lawrence attempted to kill Jackson.

Nov. 4, attended funeral of Private Coffelt, Fort Meyer, Va.

Nov. 14, requested corporation excess profits tax

• In letters to the chairmen of the Senate and House of Representatives finance committees, he urged immediate legislation to raise an additional $4,000,000,000 by means of an excess profits tax on corporations engaged in defense work.

Nov. 16, assured Chinese Communists that U.S. would abide by UN policy not to cross Korean border into China

• Despite the fact that UN forces were being attacked "from a privileged sanctuary," he stated that "we have never at any time entertained any intention to carry hostilities into China."

Nov. 18, issued executive order to Export-Import Bank and ECA to allocate $33,600,-000 worth of food supplies as emergency aid to Yugoslavia.

Nov. 30, acknowledged seriousness of entry of Chinese Communist troops in Korea, asserted UN troops would not withdraw

• UN forces suffered major losses and were driven into general retreat, Nov. 26, when 200,000 Chinese troops crossed the Manchurian border.

Dec. 8, conferred with Prime Minister Atlee, Washington, D.

• Their joint statement declared "there can be no thought of appeasement or of rewarding aggression, whether in the Far East or elsewhere."

Dec. 15, declared U.S.S.R. willing to bring world to "brink of a general war"

• He said that the Korean War and the entry of the Chinese into the conflict was evidence of Russian intentions.

Dec. 16, issued proclamation of national emergency

Note: The official population, according to the 19th census, was 150,697,361.

1951

Jan. 2, second session of 81st Congress adjourned

Jan. 3, first session of 82nd Congress

• The administration maintained control of both the Senate and the House of Representatives. The Democrats lost six Senate and 35 House seats. The Senate (96 members) consisted of 48 Democrats, 46 Republicans, one Democratic-Liberal, and one vacancy. The House (435 members) consisted of 228 Democrats, 205 Republicans, one Democratic-Liberal, and one Independent.

Jan. 8, delivered his sixth State of the Union message to Congress

• He denounced the new imperialism of Russia, asked for legislation to expand military and economic aid, and urged the production of fifty thousand modern military aircraft and thirty-five thousand tanks annually.

Jan. 15, issued executive order permitting men between 18 and 26 years of age to volunteer for 21-month service prior to draft call

Jan. 23, appointed internal security commission

• He denied that the Commission on Internal Security and Individual Rights, which was to study "the operation of the government employee and security programs," had been formed to bypass the congressional investigations he had opposed.

Jan. 30, conferred with Premier Rene Pleven of France, Washington, D.C.

• Continued support of UN action in Korea, and U.S. aid to French forces and nationalist armies of Vietnam, Cambodia, and Laos were announced after the conference.

Feb. 26, 22nd Amendment to Constitution ratified

• This amendment limited future presidents to two terms.

• *See* Constitution, page 645.

Mar. 21, received manpower report from Secretary of Defense Marshall

• Marshall reported that the armed forces

had doubled to 2,900,000 men since South Korea had been attacked nine months earlier.

Mar. 26, opened fourth meeting of foreign ministers of 21 American republics, Washington, D.C.

Mar. 31, issued executive order amending selective service regulations to exempt high-grade college students

Apr. 17, issued executive order reconstituting Wage Stabilization Board under Defense Production Act

Apr. 17, issued executive order empowering Secretary of State Acheson to supervise allocation of foreign aid funds

Apr. 25, signed armed services free insurance act

• This act provided $10,000 life insurance policies to all members of the armed forces, retroactively to June 27, 1950.

• Families of men killed in Korea would receive $92.90 monthly for ten years.

Apr. 28, issued executive order authorizing discharge of federal employees if "reasonable doubt" of loyalty uncovered

May 21, sent special message to Congress in which he requested supplemental appropriations of $1,090,000,000

• About 80 percent was appropriated for stockpiling strategic materials.

May 31, signed supplemental appropriation act providing $6,442,668,000 for defense

• This appropriation brought the total of military appropriations for the fiscal year to more than $42,200,000,000.

June 2, signed supplemental appropriation act providing $365,000,000 for federal agencies

June 15, signed act providing $190,000,000 for India to buy U.S. grain

June 16, signed two-year extension of Reciprocal Trade Agreements Act

June 19, signed act extending selective service to July 1, 1955, laid groundwork for universal military training program

• He appointed a five-man National Security Training Commission to draw up the UMT program.

June 30, signed act extending price, wage, and rent controls for one month

July 2, received budget surplus report for fiscal 1951 from Secretary of Treasury Snyder

• The surplus of $3,510,000,000 for the fiscal year that had ended June 30 was the second highest on record to date.

July 9, sent special message to Congress in which he called for official termination of state of war between U.S. and Germany

July 12, signed act authorizing government to hire Mexican farm workers to fill U.S. jobs vacated by workers who had entered military service or defense industries

July 18, signed federal flood aid act

• He had proclaimed Kansas, Missouri, and Oklahoma as disaster areas after severe floods hit the Missouri Valley area, July 11. The appropriation was $25,000,000.

July 23, sent midyear economic report to Congress, urged stronger price, wage, and rent controls

• He asked for a $10,000,000,000 tax increase, citing the Council of Economic Advisers report that placed defense expenditures at $35,000,000,000 annually, which would rise to more than $50,000,000,000 by Jan. 1, 1952.

July 31, signed amended Defense Production Act

• He criticized the measure, which he said would bring about higher prices.

Aug. 1, issued proclamation suspending tariff reductions for U.S.S.R., Communist China, and their satellites

Aug. 6, vetoed bill to establish pension rates for veterans

Aug. 7, sent special message to Congress in which he urged continuation of financial support of UN, Pan-American Union, other international organizations

• He said reductions in the $30,000,000 budget item would harm U.S. leadership in world affairs.

Aug. 14, during radio broadcast, attacked unnamed "scandalmongers and character assassins" in Congress who charged government infested by Communists

• Senator Joseph McCarthy (R., Wis.), the obvious target, demanded and received free time to reply from the three major radio networks.

Aug. 16, signed joint resolution appropriating $950,000 to department of labor to transport Mexican farm workers to U.S.

Aug. 17, issued executive order releasing twenty-five thousand tons of stockpiled copper to alleviate defense production shortage

Aug. 29, issued executive order establishing Defense Materials Procurement Agency

Sept. 12, accepted resignation of Secretary of Defense Marshall

Sept. 17, appointed his fourth secretary of defense, Robert A. Lovett

Sept. 18, act to establish pension rate for veterans passed over his veto

•This was the tenth of his 12 vetoes that were overridden.

Sept. 25, issued executive order strengthening security regulations for all federal departments and agencies

•This order was challenged by the American Society of Newspaper Editors and other groups as being suppressive.

Sept. 28, conferred with Prime Minister Louis St. Laurent of Canada on proposed St. Lawrence Seaway

•While he favored joint participation, Truman inferred that he would support Canadian construction of the project if Congress did not act.

Oct. 10, signed Mutual Security Act, which authorized $7,483,400,000 for foreign aid

Oct. 18, denied assertion by General MacArthur "secret plan" had existed to swap Formosa and UN seat for Chinese Communists for peace in Korea

Oct. 18, vetoed bill to provide automobiles for disabled veterans

Oct. 20, act to provide automobiles for disabled veterans passed over his veto

•This was the 11th of 12 vetoes that were overridden.

Oct. 20, first session of 82nd Congress adjourned

Oct. 24, issued proclamation formally declaring state of war between U.S. and Germany had terminated, Oct. 19, 1951

Oct. 31, welcomed Princess Elizabeth and Prince Philip of Great Britain, White House

Nov. 5, conferred with General Eisenhower on NATO and SHAPE

•SHAPE was Supreme Headquarters, Allied Powers in Europe.

Nov. 7, urged U.S.S.R. to endorse disarmament program submitted to UN by Great Britain, France, and U.S.

Nov. 13, announced Near East aid program

•Iran, Iraq, Jordan, Egypt, Syria, Israel, Lebanon, and Saudi Arabia were the beneficiaries of $160,000,000 in economic and technical aid to raise living standards in the Near East.

Nov. 23, issued executive order cancelling all tariff concessions to U.S.S.R. and Poland as of Jan. 5, 1952

Dec. 29, issued executive order authorizing

15-man commission to study and recommend legislation on health needs

1952

Jan. 2, issued executive order authorizing reorganization of internal revenue bureau

•Widespread corruption had been uncovered in the bureau.

Jan. 3, issued executive order creating 11-man commission to study Missouri River land and water conservation

Jan. 7–8, conferred with Prime Minister Churchill of Great Britain, White House

•Churchill addressed a joint session of Congress, Jan. 17, saying he had come to the U.S. "not for gold, but for steel." It was announced, Jan. 18, that the U.S. would sell Great Britain 1,000,000 tons of steel in 1952 for $125,000,000, while Great Britain would sell 55,100,000 pounds of aluminum and 20,000 tons of tin to the U.S. for $61,-864,000.

Jan. 8, second session of 82nd Congress

Jan. 9, delivered his seventh State of the Union message to Congress

•He asked for enactment of his Fair Deal measures, emphasizing the civil rights program. He urged a new farm price-support program, federal aid to education by means of grants to the states, and statehood for Alaska and Hawaii.

Jan. 16, submitted annual economic report to Congress

•He forecast a deficit of between $12,000,-000,000 and $14,000,000,000 if taxes were not increased for the fiscal year ending June 30, 1953.

Jan. 21, submitted budget message to Congress

•He called for expenditures of $85,400,-000,000, and repeated his forecast of a huge deficit, which he pinpointed at $14,450,-000,000. His budget included $52,400,-000,000 for military expenditures and $10,500,000,000 for foreign aid. He again asked for tax revisions to reduce the projected deficit.

Jan. 30, refused to release state department papers to Senate internal security subcommittee

Feb. 1, appointed Newbold Morris to investigate government corruption

•Morris announced that his first investigation would concern the justice department, which was protested by Attorney General McGrath. Morris was discharged by McGrath, Apr. 3; a few hours later, McGrath submitted his resignation, upon request.

Feb. 5, authorized $478,160,000 economic aid to Great Britain from Mutual Security program fund

Feb. 11, sent special message to Congress in which he urged extension of defense production act to June, 1954

Feb. 19, issued executive order outlining rules for conscientious objectors

Mar. 4, dedicated first sea-going Voice of America transmitting vessel

Mar. 6, sent special message to Congress in which he asked $7,900,000,000 for arms and military supplies for free nations

Mar. 7, submitted annual report on Mutual Security program, again urged adoption of arms and supplies legislation

Mar. 17, *Mr. President*, book based on his personal papers by William Hillman, published, Farrar, Straus and Young, New York City

Mar. 23, issued executive order authorizing $4,300,000 of Mutual Security funds to aid refugees from Iron Curtain nations who enlisted in NATO forces

Mar. 24, sent special message to Congress asking admission of 300,000 European refugees to U.S. during next three years

Mar. 27, with family, moved back into White House

•The Trumans had resided in Blair House since November, 1948, when extensive renovation of the White House had begun.

Mar. 29, announced he would not seek re-election

•He announced at the Jefferson-Jackson dinner in Washington:

I shall not be a candidate for reelection. I have served my country long and I think efficiently and honestly. I shall not accept a renomination. I do not feel that it is my duty to spend another four years in the White House.

Apr. 2, welcomed Queen Juliana and Prince Bernard of The Netherlands, Washington, D.C.

Apr. 3, accepted resignation of Attorney General McGrath, effective, Apr. 7

Apr. 3, stated he would not run for Senate or House of Representatives after term

•He said that he planned to write and lecture.

Apr. 8, issued executive order to Secretary of Commerce Sawyer to seize and operate steel mills to avert national strike

Apr. 11, approved request of General Eisenhower to be relieved as Supreme Commander of NATO, June 1

Apr. 15, signed peace treaty with Japan

•Ratified by the Senate, Mar. 20, the treaty went into effect, Apr. 28.

Apr. 17, held his 300th press conference

•He told members of the American Society of Newspaper Editors that the presidency was a continuing office and that he would not run for reelection since he did not believe that any man was indispensable in any position.

Apr. 22, public tours of White House resumed

Apr. 24, signed $25,000,000 flood relief act

•More serious than the floods of 1951, the Missouri River overflow and subsequent overflows from the Mississippi and Red rivers extended from Montana and South Dakota to Kansas and Missouri. Damage was estimated at $300,000,000.

May 5, sent special message to Congress outlining $1,500,000,000 flood damage insurance plan

May 15, appointed his fourth attorney general, James P. McGranery

•McGranery took office, May 27

•McGranery was the last of Truman's 24 cabinet appointments.

May 19, criticized American Medical Association for "socialized medicine" campaign against social security legislation

•The administration bill, which would have increased benefits by $5 a month, was rejected by the House of Representatives.

May 20, announced development of atomic artillery piece at convocation that concluded 150th anniversary celebration of U.S. Military Academy, West Point, N.Y.

May 23, issued executive order returning 195 railroads to private owners

•The railroads had been operated by the army since Aug. 27, 1950. The railroads and three unions signed 16-month contracts recommended by his special assistant, John R. Steelman.

May 26, criticized utilities for propagandizing against public power

•He did not oppose private ownership, he said, but denounced the public relations tactics, which were charged off as operational expenditures.

May 29, vetoed tidelands oil bill
• This bill would have returned submerged oil lands of the continental shelf to the states, which he called "a free gift of immensely valuable resources."

June 14, dedicated keel of first atomic submarine, *Nautilus*, Groton, Conn.

June 18, criticized Senate for returning St. Lawrence Seaway bill to committee

June 20, signed compromise arms and military supplies for free nations act
• He had requested $7,900,000,000; Congress voted $6,448,000,000.

June 25, vetoed bill to revise laws relating to immigration, naturalization, and nationality

June 27, act to revise laws relating to immigration, naturalization, and nationality passed over his veto
• This was the last of his 12 vetoes that were overridden. Only Andrew Johnson had more vetoes overridden.

July 2, dedicated Bull Shoals Dam, Ozark Mountains

July 3, signed Puerto Rico constitution act
• Puerto Rico became the first overseas U.S. commonwealth, July 25.

July 7, second session of 82nd Congress adjourned

July 15, signed supplemental appropriations act
• This omnibus measure for $11,793,776,000 was 20 percent less than he had requested. For political reasons, he said, Congress had created the illusion of economy.

July 16, signed new GI Bill of Rights

July 19, submitted his midyear economic report to Congress
• He forecast a budget deficit of $10,000,000,000 for fiscal 1953. The deficit for 1952, announced July 1, had been $4,016,640,000.

July 24, commuted death sentence of Oscar Collazo to life imprisonment
• Collazo, along with another Puerto Rican nationalist, had attempted to assassinate him at Blair House, Nov. 1, 1950. Collazo was convicted for the murder of Private Leslie Coffelt, a White House guard.

July 25, flew to Democratic national convention after Adlai E. Stevenson nominated, Chicago, Ill.
• Truman received the votes of six delegates on the first and second ballots, although he

was not a candidate. Stevenson was nominated on the third ballot.

Aug. 8, issued executive order directing Civil Service Commission to merge all governmental loyalty programs

Aug. 28, received report that NATO goals for 1952 could not be met, dollar deficit endangered Western European stability
• Substantial U.S. investment plus increased U.S. imports from Europe would be necessary, reported Ambassador William H. Draper, Jr., special U.S. representative in Europe.

Sept. 4, issued executive order establishing commission to study immigration policies

Sept. 27, issued executive order to Federal Trade Commission to prepare study of how consumer dollar spent

Sept. 29, opened whistle-stop campaign for Stevenson, North Dakota
• The White House had announced that he would tour 20 states, and would speak in 75 to 100 communities during his 8,500-mile political tour.

Nov. 4, election day
• *See* Election of 1952, page 491.

Nov. 18, conferred with President-elect Eisenhower, White House
• They discussed in general terms the transfer of government affairs to the incoming administration.

Dec. 18, received report of Commission on Health Needs
• Among the many recommendations of the commission was the establishment of a cabinet-level post of health and security.

Dec. 26, reviewed his years in office during press conference
• He stated that his most important decision had been U.S. intervention in Korea.

1953

Jan. 3, first session of 83rd Congress
• The Republicans controlled both the Senate and the House of Representatives. The Republicans gained one Senate and 16 House seats. The Senate (96 members) consisted of 47 Republicans, 46 Democrats, one Democratic-Liberal, one Independent, and one vacancy. The House (435 members) consisted of 221 Republicans, 212 Democrats, one Independent, and one vacancy.

Jan. 7, sent his eighth and last State of the

Union message to Congress
Jan. 8, welcomed Prime Minister Churchill, White House
Jan. 9, submitted his budget message to Congress
• He forecast a deficit of $9,900,000,000 for the fiscal year beginning, July 1. He opposed tax cuts in 1953.

Jan. 9, issued executive order authorizing a loyalty system to investigate U.S. citizens in UN positions
Jan. 14, submitted his annual economic report to Congress
Jan. 15, expressed optimism regarding world peace in farewell address

THE FORMER PRESIDENT

Jan. 20, 1953, attended inauguration of Eisenhower
• Truman's age upon leaving office was 68 years, 257 days.
• Following the ceremony, he and his wife had luncheon with Dean Acheson and later boarded a train for Independence, Mo. When a reporter asked him what he had done on his first day at home, he replied, "I took the suitcases up to the attic."
Nov. 16, 1953, defended his appointment of late Harry Dexter White as board member of International Monetary Fund, during radio broadcast
• He had been accused by Attorney General Brownell of appointing White despite knowledge of an FBI report that White was a spy for the U.S.S.R., Nov. 6. Representative Harold H. Velde, chairman of the House committee on un-American activities, ordered a subpoena issued to Truman. Truman refused to appear before the committee, cited precedents, and said he was willing to answer questions about his acts as an individual, but not as president.
• During the broadcast, he said:
  I have been accused, in effect, of knowingly betraying the security of the United States. The charge is, of course, a falsehood.
• Brownell later said that when he had charged laxity in the White appointment there had been "no intention of impugning the loyalty of any high official of the prior administration."
May 8, 1954, celebrated his 70th birthday
• He was the 15th of 16 presidents who lived to be 70.
June 20, 1954, underwent emergency surgery for removal of appendix and gall bladder, Kansas City, Mo.
• His condition became serious from an infection not related to the operation, June 27, but his rapid recovery permitted his

return to his home in Independence, July 9.
Feb. 13, 1955, Mrs. Truman's 70 birthday
• She was the 15th of 16 first ladies who lived to be 70.
• She was the 16th of 17 wives of presidents who lived to be 70.
Apr. 18, 1955, appeared before Senate foreign relations committee
• The hearings concerned possible revision of the UN charter. Truman strongly supported the UN, saying that unlimited war would have resulted without the international organization. He opposed both U.S. withdrawal and U.S.S.R. expulsion from the UN.
May 8, 1955, broke ground for Harry S. Truman Library, Independence, Mo.
• The ceremony was held on his 71st birthday.
June 20, 1955, attended tenth anniversary meeting of UN, War Memorial Opera House, San Francisco, Cal.
1955, his book, *Year of Decisions*, published, Doubleday, New York City
• This was the first volume of his memoirs. A second volume, *Years of Trial and Hope*, was published in 1956.
• He was the 17th of 21 presidents who wrote books that were published during their lifetimes.
Apr. 21, 1956, attended wedding of his daughter, Margaret, to Elbert Clifton Daniel, Independence, Mo.
• Mr. Daniel was assistant to the foreign news editor of *The New York Times*. Mr. Daniel is now associate editor of *The Times*.
May 11, 1956, with Mrs. Truman, sailed for Europe
• The Trumans visited France, Italy, Austria, Belgium, The Netherlands, and England.
• He was the last of eight former presidents who visited Europe.
June 20, 1956, awarded honorary degree of

Doctor of Civil Law, Oxford University, Oxford, England

•The Latin citation addressed him as "Harricum Truman," referred to him as the "truest of allies." Student cheers of "Give 'em hell, Harricum" followed the ceremony.

July 6, 1957, attended dedication of Harry S. Truman Library, Independence, Mo.

•The Harry S. Truman Library is administered by the National Archives and Records Service, General Services Administration. It includes a museum and a reproduction of his White House office. The museum is open to the public daily except Thanksgiving, Christmas, and New Year's Day, 9 A.M. to 5 P.M., and Sundays, 10 A.M. to 5 P.M. (2 to 5 P.M., Sept. 16 to May 15). Offices, research areas, and Mr. Truman's suite are not open to the public. Admission: adults, 50 cents; children under 16 and school groups for which application is made in advance, free.

•The library was given to the federal government by the city of Independence and friends.

Mar. 14, 1958, defended decision to drop atomic bombs on Hiroshima and Nagasaki

•In reply to criticism from the City Council of Hiroshima, he said his decision had prevented the loss of 250,000 American and 250,000 Japanese lives—the estimated casualties if an Allied invasion of Japan had been necessary, adding:

> The need for such a fateful decision, of course, never would have arisen had we not been shot in the back by Japan at Pearl Harbor.

May 26, 1958, with Mrs. Truman, sailed for Europe

•They visited Spain, France, and Italy.

1959, his birthplace in Lamar, Mo., restored and presented to State of Missouri by United Auto Workers

May 8, 1959, celebrated his 75th birthday

•He was the ninth of ten presidents who lived to be 75.

Feb. 13, 1960, Mrs. Truman's 75th birthday

•She was the 13th of 14 first ladies who lived to be 75.

•She was the 14th of 15 wives of presidents who lived to be 75.

Oct. 10, 1960, quoted by Associated Press as saying anyone who voted for Nixon and Lodge "ought to go to hell" and Nixon "never told the truth in his life"

•He allegedly made the remarks during a campaign speech in San Antonio, Tex. He later denied having made the first statement, but added "they can't challenge" the second.

Nov. 10, 1961, met with former President Eisenhower, Truman Library

•This was their first significant conversation since Nov. 18, 1952, when he had briefed his successor at the White House. They had met briefly and exchanged handshakes at the funeral of General George C. Marshall in 1959.

Nov. 18, 1961, attended funeral of Representative Sam Rayburn, Bonham, Tex.

•Rayburn had served in the House of Representatives for nearly 49 years, longer than any other member. He held the post of speaker for 17 years, more than twice the tenure of the previous record holder, Henry Clay.

•The Rayburn funeral was attended by four consecutive presidents: former Presidents Truman and Eisenhower, President Kennedy, and then-Vice President Johnson.

Nov. 25, 1963, attended funeral of President Kennedy, Washington, D.C.

Mar. 12, 1964, with Mrs. Lyndon B. Johnson, represented United States at funeral of King Paul I of Greece, Athens

May 8, 1964, celebrated his 80th birthday

•He was the last of six presidents who lived to be 80

Feb. 13, 1965, Mrs. Truman's 80th birthday

•She was the last of nine first ladies who lived to be 80.

•She was the last of ten wives of presidents who lived to be 80.

July 30, 1965, witnessed signing of Medicare Act by President Johnson, Independence, Mo.

•The ceremony was held in Independence to honor the fact that he had been the first president to send a legislative message to Congress on the nation's health needs, Nov. 19, 1945.

Jan. 20, 1966, attended ceremony at Truman Library dedicating Harry S. Truman Center for Advancement of Peace at Hebrew University, Jerusalem

•On this occasion, President Johnson presented the first two Medicare cards to Mr. and Mrs. Truman.

July 30, 1966, hospitalized for stomach ailment, later announced as colitis

May 8, 1967, celebrated his 83rd birthday quietly at home
• For the first time since he left the White House, he did not attend the annual birthday luncheon given by friends in Kansas City, Mo.
Nov. 25, 1967, made rare public appearance at Shrine parade, Independence
• He reviewed the parade from an armchair on his front porch.
Mar. 16, 1968, arrived for two-week visit at Key West, Fla.
• This was his 12th visit to the Florida resort since 1946.
Apr. 18, 1968, portrait of Mrs. Truman added to White House Gallery of First Ladies
• The Trumans did not attend the ceremony. They were represented by their daughter and son-in-law, Mr. and Mrs. Clifton Daniel, and their four grandsons.
Feb. 20, 1969, hospitalized with intestinal flu, Kansas City, Mo.
• He spent five days in Research Hospital.
Mar. 21, 1969, visited by President Nixon, Independence
• At the Truman Library, he accepted the Steinway piano on which he had frequently played in the White House.
Mar. 22, 1969, with Mrs. Truman, arrived in Key West, Fla., for two-week vacation
May 8, 1969, celebrated his 85th birthday
• He was the last of four presidents who lived to be 85.
June 28, 1969, with Mrs. Truman, celebrated their 50th wedding anniversary
• He was the last of four presidents who celebrated their golden wedding anniversaries.
Feb. 13, 1970, Mrs. Truman's 85th birthday
• She was the last of six first ladies who lived to be 85.
• She was the last of seven wives of presidents who lived to be 85.
Mar. 11, 1970, nine-week exhibition of photographs, films and memorabilia of his White House years opened, Hallmark Gallery, New York City
Apr. 9, 1970, his portrait presented to National Portrait Gallery, Washington, D.C.
• The portrait by Greta Kempton was commissioned by former Secretary of Treasury John W. Snyder and a group of 15 Truman cabinet members, appointees and friends. Other Truman portraits by Miss Kempton

(Mrs. A. M. McNamara) hang in the White House, the state capitol at Jefferson, Mo., and the Masonic Consistory in St. Louis, Mo.
Apr. 13, 1970, observed 25th anniversary of his elevation to presidency, Independence
• Seven of his cabinet and White House advisers visited him to pay their respects, Apr. 11.
Jan. 21, 1971, hospitalized for stomach ailment, later announced as colitis, Kansas City, Mo.
• This was the sixth time he was hospitalized since he left the White House.
May 6, 1971, refused to accept Congressional Medal of Honor
• "I do not consider that I have done anything which should be the reason for any award, congressional or otherwise," he said in a letter to his congressman. Congress had planned to present the medal on May 8, his 87th birthday.

THE VICE PRESIDENT (35th)

Full name: Alben William Barkley
Date of birth: Nov. 24, 1877
• Barkley was the last vice president who was born in the 19th century.
Place of birth: near Lowes, Ky.
• He was the last of four vice presidents who were born in Kentucky.
Religious denomination: Methodist
• He was the last of three vice presidents who were Methodists.
College: Marvin College, Clinton, Ky.
Date of graduation: 1897
• He graduated from the University of Virginia Law School, Charlottesville, Va., 1903.
Occupation: Lawyer
• He was admitted to the Kentucky bar, 1903; prosecuting attorney of McCracken Co., Ky., 1905–1909; county judge, 1909–1913; House of Representatives, 1913–1927; Senate, 1927–1949; had been majority leader of Senate, 1937–1946.
• He was the 19th of 21 vice presidents who served in the House of Representatives before their term of office.
• He was the 13th of 17 vice presidents who served in the Senate before their terms of office.
• He was the eighth of ten vice presidents

who served in both the House of Representatives and the Senate before their terms of office.
• He was the tenth of 12 vice presidents who served both in the House of Representatives and the Senate.
Term of office: Jan. 20, 1949, to Jan. 20, 1953 (4 years)
• He was the 16th of 17 vice presidents who served four-year terms.
• Truman and Barkley were the 37th of 41 president-vice president teams.
Age at inauguration: 71 years, 57 days
• He was the oldest vice president at inauguration.
State represented: Kentucky.
• He was the last of three vice presidents who represented Kentucky.
Political party: Democratic
• He was the 14th of 16 vice presidents who were Democrats.
Occupation after term: U.S. Senator
• He was reelected to the Senate, 1954.
• He was the fifth of six vice presidents who served in the Senate after their terms in office.
• He was the third of four vice presidents who served in the Senate both before and after their terms in office.
Date of death: Apr. 30, 1956
Place of death: Lexington, Va.
• He was the last of three vice presidents who died in Virginia.
Age at death: 78 years, 157 days
Place of burial: Paducah, Ky.
• He was the last of three vice presidents who were buried in Kentucky.

THE CABINET

State: Edward Reilly Stettinius, Jr., of Virginia, Dec. 1, 1944, to June 27, 1945
• James Francis Byrnes of South Carolina, July 3, 1945, to Jan. 21, 1947
• George Catlett Marshall of Pennsylvania, Jan. 21, 1947, to Jan. 20, 1949
• Dean Gooderham Acheson of Connecticut, Jan. 21, 1949, to Jan. 20, 1953
Treasury: Henry Morgenthau, Jr., of New York, Jan. 1, 1934, to July 22, 1945
• Frederick Moore Vinson of Kentucky, July 23, 1945, to June 23, 1946
• John Wesley Snyder of Missouri, June 25, 1946, to Jan. 20, 1953

War: Henry Lewis Stimson of New York, July 10, 1940, to Sept. 21, 1945
• Robert Porter Patterson of New York, Sept. 27, 1947, to July 18, 1947
• Kenneth Claiborne Royall of North Carolina, July 19, 1947, to Sept. 17, 1947
Defense: James Vincent Forrestal of New York, Sept. 17, 1947, to Mar. 27, 1949
• Louis Arthur Johnson of West Virginia, Mar. 28, 1949, to Sept. 19, 1950
• George Catlett Marshall of Pennsylvania, Sept. 21, 1950, to Sept. 12, 1951
• Robert Abercrombie Lovett of New York, Sept. 17, 1951, to Jan. 20, 1953
Attorney General: Francis Biddle of Pennsylvania, Sept. 5, 1941, to June 30, 1945
• Thomas Campbell Clark of Texas, July 1, 1945, to Aug. 24, 1949
• James Howard McGrath of Rhode Island, Aug. 24, 1949, to Apr. 7, 1952
• James Patrick McGranery of Pennsylvania, May 27, 1952, to Jan. 20, 1953
Navy: James Vincent Forrestal of New York, May 19, 1944, to Sept. 17, 1947
Postmaster General: Frank Comerford Walker of Pennsylvania, Sept. 10, 1940, to May 8, 1945
• Robert Emmet Hannegan of Missouri, July 1, 1945, to Nov. 25, 1947
• Jesse Monroe Donaldson of Missouri, Dec. 16, 1947, to Jan. 20, 1953
Interior: Harold LeClaire Ickes of Illinois, Mar. 4, 1933, to Feb. 15, 1946
• Julius Albert Krug of Wisconsin, Mar. 18, 1946, to Dec. 1, 1949
• Oscar Littleton Chapman of Colorado, Dec. 1, 1949, to Jan. 20, 1953
Agriculture: Claude Raymond Wickard of Indiana, Sept. 5, 1940, to June 29, 1945
• Clinton Presba Anderson of New Mexico, June 30, 1945, to May 10, 1948
• Charles Franklin Brannan of Colorado, June 2, 1948, to Jan. 20, 1953
Commerce: Henry Agard Wallace of Iowa, Mar. 2, 1945, to Sept. 20, 1946
• William Averell Harriman of New York, Oct. 7, 1946, to Apr. 22, 1948
• Charles Sawyer of Ohio, May 6, 1948, to Jan. 20, 1953
Labor: Frances Perkins (Wilson) of New York, Mar. 4, 1933, to June 30, 1945
• Lewis Baxter Schwellenbach of Washington, July 1, 1945, to June 10, 1948
• Maurice Joseph Tobin of Massachusetts, Aug. 13, 1948, to Jan. 20, 1953

THE SUPREME COURT

Chief Justice: Frederick Moore Vinson of Kentucky, appointed, June 6, 1946; confirmed, June 20, 1946

Associate Justices: Harold Hitz Burton of Ohio, appointed, Sept. 18, 1945; confirmed, Sept. 19, 1945

- Thomas Campbell Clark of Texas, appointed, July 28, 1949; confirmed, Aug. 18, 1949.
- Sherman Minton of Indiana, appointed, Sept. 15, 1949; confirmed, Oct. 4, 1949

Thirty-fourth President

DWIGHT DAVID EISENHOWER

Full name: Dwight David Eisenhower
- His given name was David Dwight Eisenhower.
- He was the only president who transposed his first and middle names.
- He was the last of five presidents who changed their names from those they were given at birth.
- He was the 16th of 19 presidents who had middle initials or middle names.

Date of birth: Oct. 14, 1890
- He was the last of five presidents who were born in October.
- He was the last president who was born in the 19th century.

Place of birth: Denison, Tex.
- He was the first of two presidents who were born in Texas. The other was Lyndon Johnson.
- His birthplace, the Eisenhower Birthplace State Park, Lamar Avenue and Day Street, is under the supervision of the Texas Parks and Wildlife Department. It is open to the public daily except Christmas, June 1 through Aug. 31, 8 A.M. to 6 P.M., and Sept. 1 through May 31, 10 A.M. to 12, noon, and 1 to 5 P.M. Admission: adults, 25 cents; children under 12, ten cents; children under six, free.

Family lineage: Swiss-German
- He was the second of two presidents who were of Swiss-German ancestry. The other was Hoover.

Religious denomination: Presbyterian
- He was the last of six presidents who were Presbyterians.

College: U.S. Military Academy, West Point, N.Y.
- He was the second of two presidents who went to West Point. The other was Grant.
- He was the 24th of 27 presidents who attended college.

Date of graduation: June 12, 1915, Bachelor of Science
- An act of Congress, signed May 25, 1933, and amended, July 8, 1937, conferred the degree of Bachelor of Science retroactively by certificate upon all qualified living graduates of the U.S. Military Academy.
- He was the second of two presidents who were graduated from the academy. The other was Grant.
- He was the 18th of 21 presidents who were graduated from college.

487

PARENTS AND SIBLINGS

Father's name: David Jacob Eisenhower
Date of birth: Sept. 23, 1863
Place of birth: Elizabethville, Pa.
Occupations: Mechanic, gas company manager
Date of death: Mar. 10, 1942
Place of death: Abilene, Kan.
Age at death: 78 years, 168 days

Mother's name: Ida Elizabeth Stover Eisenhower
Date of birth: May 1, 1862
Place of birth: Mount Sidney, Va.
Date of marriage: Sept. 23, 1885
Place of marriage: Lecompton, Kan.
Children: 7 sons
• Arthur was born on Nov. 11, 1886; Edgar on Jan. 19, 1889; David Dwight on Oct. 14, 1890; Roy on Aug. 9, 1892; Paul on May 12, 1894; Earl on Feb. 1, 1898; and Milton on Sept. 15, 1899. Paul died in infancy, Mar. 16, 1895.
• Eisenhower was the second of two presidents who came from families of seven children. The other was William Henry Harrison.
• He was the last of five presidents who were third children.
• He was the fourth of five presidents who had male siblings only.
Date of death: Sept. 11, 1946
Place of death: Abilene, Kan.
Age at death: 84 years, 133 days

MARRIAGE

Date of marriage: July 1, 1916
Place of marriage: Denver, Colo.
• Eisenhower was the only president who was married in Colorado.
Age at marriage: 25 years, 261 days
• He was the 25th of 27 presidents who were married in their twenties.
Years married: 52 years, 270 days

Wife's name: Marie Geneva Doud Eisenhower
• She was called Mamie.
• She was the 30th of 33 first ladies.
• She was the 37th of 40 wives of presidents.
Date of birth: Nov. 14, 1896
• She was the last of three first ladies who were born in November.
• She was the last of three wives of presidents who were born in November.
Place of birth: Boone, Iowa
• She was the second of two first ladies who were born in Iowa. The other was Lou Hoover.
• She was the second of two wives of presidents who were born in Iowa.
Wife's mother: Elvira Mathilda Carlson Doud
Wife's father: John Sheldon Doud, meat packer
Age at marriage: 19 years, 230 days
• She was the last of four first ladies who were married in their teens.
• She was the last of five wives of presidents who were married in their teens.
Years younger than husband: 6 years, 31 days
Children: 2 sons
• Doud Dwight was born on Sept. 24, 1917, and John Sheldon Doud on Aug. 3, 1922. Doud Dwight died in infancy, Jan. 2, 1921.
• Eisenhower was the last of six presidents who had only male children.
• He was the fifth of seven presidents who had two children.
• He was the 27th of 30 presidents who had children.

Notes: She was the 20th of 21 first ladies who survived their husbands.
• She was the 22nd of 23 wives of presidents who survived their husbands.
• She was the last of 14 first ladies who lived to be 75.
• She was the last of 15 wives of presidents who lived to be 75.

EARLY YEARS

1891, with family, moved to Abilene, Kan.
1905, suffered from blood poisoning
• An infection set in after he had severely skinned a knee. The attending doctor recommended amputation of the leg but

Eisenhower refused to allow it.
1910, was graduated from Abilene High School, Abilene, Kan.
June 12, 1915, was graduated from U.S. Military Academy, West Point, N.Y.

•He ranked 65th in studies and 95th in deportment in the class of 164 members.
•He was the last of four presidents who were professional soldiers.
Sept. 5, 1915, assigned to 19th Infantry, Fort Sam Houston, San Antonio, Tex.
July 1, 1916, married Marie Geneva Doud, Denver Colo.
July 1, 1916, promoted to first lieutenant
Apr. 6, 1917, war declared
•He was the first of two presidents who served in the military during World War I. The other was Truman.
•He was the 18th of 21 presidents who served in the military during wartime.
Sept. 24, 1917, his first son born
•The boy was named Doud Dwight Eisenhower.
Jan. 2, 1921, his first son died
Aug. 3, 1922, his second son born
•The boy was named John Sheldon Doud Eisenhower.
1922–1924, stationed in Panama Canal Zone
1925–1926, attended Command and General Staff School, Fort Leavenworth, Kan.
•He was graduated first in the class of 275 members.
1928, attended Army War College, Washington, D.C.
1929-1932, served on staff of assistant secretary of war, Washington, D.C.

1932-1934, served on staff of General Douglas A. MacArthur, army chief of staff, Washington, D.C.
1935-1939, served on staff of General MacArthur, Philippine Islands
Nov. 30, 1939, received pilot's license
•He was the only president licensed to fly an airplane.
Jan. 5, 1940, assumed duties as regimental executive officer, 15th Infantry Regiment, Third Infantry Division, Fort Lewis, Wash.
November, 1940, appointed chief of staff, Third Infantry Division, Fort Lewis
March, 1941, appointed chief of staff, IX Army Corps, Fort Lewis
June, 1941, assumed duties as chief of staff, III Army Corps, Fort Sam Houston, San Antonio, Tex.
September, 1941, promoted to temporary rank of brigadier general
•He was the last of 12 presidents who were generals.
Dec. 7, 1941, Japanese attacked Pearl Harbor
•He was the first of four presidents who served in the military during World War II.
•He was the only president who served in both World War I and World War II.
Feb. 16, 1942, appointed assistant chief of staff, War Plans Division, War Department General Staff

NATIONAL PROMINENCE

Mar. 27, 1942, promoted to temporary rank of major general
•This promotion accompanied his assignment as the first chief of Operations Division, War Department General Staff.
June 11, 1942, appointed commanding officer of European Theater of Operations
•Eisenhower assumed command of the ETO, June 24, London, England.
July 7, 1942, promoted to temporary rank of lieutenant general
Nov. 7, 1942, Allied commander-in-chief, invasion of North Africa
Feb. 11, 1943, promoted to temporary rank of general
•He was the 12th officer in the history of the U.S. Army to attain the rank of full general. The first was Grant.
Dec. 24, 1943, designated as Supreme Commander, Allied Expeditionary Forces
•His appointment was announced by Presi-

dent Franklin D. Roosevelt during a radio broadcast.
•His orders from the combined chiefs of staff, Washington, D. C., were:
  You will enter the continent of Europe and, in conjunction with the other United Nations, undertake operations aimed at the heart of Germany and the destruction of her armed forces . . .
May 17, 1944, decided Operation Overlord, Allied invasion of Europe, would begin June 5, June 6, or June 7
June 4, 1944, postponed D-Day, scheduled for June 5, 24 hours because of unfavorable weather conditions
•Earlier that day he had written a communique for release in case the invasion failed. It read:
  Our landings in the Cherbourg-Havre area have failed to gain a

satisfactory foothold and I have withdrawn the troops. My decision to attack at this time and place was based on the best information available. The troops, the air and Navy did all that bravery and devotion to duty could do. If there is any blame or fault attached to the attempt, it is mine alone.

June 6, 1944, D-Day
• As supreme commander, Eisenhower commanded nearly 3,000,000 Allied troops, including 1,700,000 Americans. No American had ever commanded so many men from so many countries.
• *See* page 438.

May 7, 1945, accepted surrender of German army, Rheims, France

1945-1948, served as army chief of staff

Apr. 20, 1946, visited his birthplace, Denison, Tex.
• This was his first visit to his birthplace. He had no recollection of the house at Lamar Avenue and Day Street, as his parents had moved from it when he was a baby. When he enrolled at the U.S. Military Academy, he gave Tyler, Tex., as his birthplace. It was not until 1946 that he learned that he had been born in Denison. The Denison *Herald* was chiefly responsible for establishing the facts.

June 22, 1947, his boyhood home dedicated as national shrine, Abilene, Kan.

June 24, 1947, accepted appointment as president of Columbia University, New York City
• He announced his intention of assuming the university post upon release from active duty.

Feb. 7, 1948, retired from U.S. Army

July 5, 1948, declared he "could not accept nomination for any public office or participate in a partisan political contest"
• An Eisenhower-for-president campaign was gaining strength throughout the country. Anti-Truman Democratic leaders in several states—notably Georgia, Virginia, and New Jersey—had called for Eisenhower's nomination.

Oct. 12, 1948, installed as president, Columbia University
• He was the second of two presidents who were presidents of major colleges or universities. The other was Wilson.

Nov. 18, 1948, his book, *Crusade in Europe,* published, Doubleday, New York City

• He was the 18th of 21 presidents who wrote books that were published during their lifetimes.

Feb. 11, 1949, appointed head of joint chiefs of staff and principal consultant to Secretary of Defense Forrestal by President Truman
• He took a leave of absence from Columbia.

December, 1950, bought Gettysburg, Pa., farm
• A national historic site, the 230-acre farm was deeded to the U. S. in Eisenhower's will, with the proviso that Mrs. Eisenhower had the right to occupy the residence as long as she desired.
• The Eisenhower farm is not open to the public.

Dec. 19, 1950, appointed Supreme Commander of European Defense by foreign ministers of NATO nations, Brussels, Belgium

Apr. 2, 1951, assumed duties of Supreme Commander, NATO

Nov. 3-6, 1951, conferred with President Truman, Washington, D.C.

Jan. 7, 1952, announced he would accept Republican nomination for president if drafted
• This was the first time he publicly identified himself as a Republican.

Apr. 2, 1952, requested to be relieved as NATO commander by June

May 30, 1952, relinquished NATO command to General Matthew B. Ridgway

June 4, 1952, made first major political speech, Abilene, Kan.

July 11, 1952, nominated for president, Republican national convention, Chicago, Ill.
• He was nominated on the first ballot.

July 13, 1952, submitted resignation as officer of U.S. Army
• His resignation was accepted, July 18.

Aug. 5, 1952, outlined ten-point program for domestic prosperity without war, annual meeting of Veterans of Foreign Wars, Los Angeles, Cal.

Aug. 25, 1952, addressed American Legion national convention, New York City

Sept. 17, 1952, addressed American Federation of Labor convention, New York City
• The delegates to the AFL convention endorsed his Democratic opponent, Adlai E. Stevenson, Sept. 23. This was the first time the union convention endorsed a presidential candidate.

Oct. 14, 1952, disclosed income of $888,303 since 1942

• The major portion, $635,000, was royalties for his book, *Crusade in Europe*. He paid 25 percent capital gains taxes on his literary earnings.

Oct. 24, 1952, pledged he would go to Korea if elected to seek "early and honorable" end to war, Detroit, Mich.

Nov. 4, 1952, election day

• *See* Election of 1952, below.

Nov. 17, 1952, submitted resignation as president and trustee of Columbia University, effective, Jan. 19, 1953

Nov. 18, 1952, conferred with President Truman, White House

• They discussed the transfer of government business to the new administration.

Nov. 29, 1952, departed for Korea

• He made a three-day tour of inspection, Dec. 2–4. Details of the trip were kept secret until Dec. 5, when he was on his way back to the U.S.

Dec. 15, 1952, presidential electors cast ballots

• He received 442 of the 531 electoral votes from the 48 states.

• *See* Election of 1952, below.

Jan. 6, 1953, electoral votes tabulated by Congress

• Eisenhower and Nixon were officially declared elected.

ELECTION OF 1952

Prohibition party, convened, Nov. 13, 1951, at Indianapolis, Ind., nominated Stuart Hamblen · of Oklahoma for president, Enoch Arden Holtwick of Illinois for vice president.

Socialist Labor party, convened, May 4, 1952, at New York City, nominated Eric Hass of New York for president, Stephen Emery of New York for vice president.

Socialist party, convened, May 30, at Cleveland, Ohio, nominated Darlington Hoopes of Pennsylvania for president, Samuel Herman Friedman of New York for vice president.

Progressive party, convened, July 4, at Chicago, Ill., nominated Vincent William Hallinan of California for president, Charlotta A. Bass of New York for vice president.

Republican party, convened, July 7, at Chicago, Ill., nominated Dwight David Eisenhower of New York for president, Richard Milhous Nixon of California for vice president.

• This was the 25th Republican national convention. It was the 13th Republican convention held in Chicago; it was the 21st major party convention held in Chicago.

Socialist Workers party, convened, July 20, at New York City, nominated Farrell Dobbs of New York for president, Myra Tanner Weiss of New York for vice president.

Democratic party, convened, July 21, at Chicago, Ill., nominated Adlai Ewing Stevenson of Illinois for president, John Jackson Sparkman of Alabama for vice president.

• This was the 31st Democratic national convention. It was the eighth Democratic convention held in Chicago; it was the 22nd major party convention held in Chicago.

Election day, Tuesday, Nov. 4, 1952

Popular vote: 61,714,924
  Eisenhower, 33,936,234
  Stevenson, 27,314,992
  Hallinan, 140,023
  Hamblen, 72,969
  Hass, 30,376
  Hoopes, 20,203
  Dobbs, 10,306
  others, 189,821

Electoral vote: 531, 48 states

• Eisenhower, 442, 39 states
  (Arizona, 4; California, 32; Colorado, 6; Connecticut, 8; Delaware, 3; Florida, 10; Idaho, 4; Illinois, 27; Indiana, 13; Iowa, 10; Kansas, 8; Maine, 5; Maryland, 9; Massachusetts, 16; Michigan, 20; Minnesota, 11; Missouri, 13; Montana, 4; Nebraska, 6; Nevada, 3; New Hampshire, 4; New Jersey, 16; New Mexico, 4; New York, 45; North Dakota, 4; Ohio, 25; Oklahoma, 8; Oregon, 6; Pennsylvania, 32; Rhode Island, 4; South Dakota, 4; Tennessee, 11; Texas, 24; Utah, 4; Vermont, 3; Virginia, 12; Washington, 9; Wisconsin, 12; Wyoming, 3)

• Stevenson, 89, nine states
  (Alabama, 11; Arkansas, 8; Georgia, 12; Kentucky, 10; Louisiana, 10; Mississippi, 8; North Carolina, 14; South Carolina, 8; West Virginia, 8)

THE PRESIDENT (34th)

Term of office: Jan. 20, 1953, to Jan. 20, 1961 (8 years)
• Eisenhower was the last of 12 presidents who were elected to second terms.
• He was the last of nine presidents who served two terms.
• He was the 15th of 16 presidents who served more than one term.
• He was the last of eight presidents who served for eight years.
• He was the first president whose term of office was limited to eight years by the provisions of the 22nd Amendment.
State represented: New York
• He was the seventh of eight presidents who represented New York.
• He was the 14th of 15 presidents who represented states that were not their native states.
Political party: Republican
• He was the only Republican president of the 20th century who won two successive elections.
• He was the 13th of 14 presidents who were Republicans.
Congresses: 83rd, 84th, 85th, 86th
Administrations: 42nd, 43rd
Age at inauguration: 62 years, 98 days
Inauguration day: Tuesday, Jan. 20, 1953
• Eisenhower took the oath of office, administered by Chief Justice Frederick M. Vinson, on the east portico of the Capitol.
• This was the second of two inaugurations at which Vinson officiated.

THE 42nd ADMINISTRATION

1953

Jan. 21, appointed his first secretary of state, John Foster Dulles; his first secretary of treasury, George M. Humphrey; his first secretary of defense, Charles E. Wilson; his first attorney general, Herbert Brownell; his only postmaster general, Arthur E. Summerfield; his first secretary of interior, Douglas McKay; his only secretary of agriculture, Ezra T. Benson; his first secretary of commerce, Sinclair Weeks; and his first secretary of labor, Martin P. Durkin.
• Wilson refused to divest himself of his General Motors stock, valued at $2,500,000. After Wilson changed his mind and agreed to sell his stock, he was confirmed by the Senate, Jan. 26, and took office, Jan. 28.
Jan. 26, issued executive order establishing nine-member International Information Activities Board
Feb. 2, delivered his first State of the Union message to Congress
• Eisenhower announced that he had ended U.S. Navy patrolling of the Formosa Straits and requested the extension of rent control, passage of the Hawaii statehood bill and amendments to the Taft-Hartley Act.
Feb. 6, issued executive order suspending all wage controls and most consumer goods price controls
Feb. 7, signed act creating post of undersecretary of state for administration
• This was the first act he signed.
Feb. 17, placed budget reduction ahead of tax relief during first news conference
Feb. 19, favored establishment of Air Force Academy, similar to West Point and Annapolis
Mar. 23, with Congressional leaders, decided to allow RFC to expire, June 30
Mar. 26, met with Premier Rene Mayer of France, Washington, D.C.
• Additional U.S. aid to finance the French war in Indochina was agreed upon in principal, since Eisenhower considered the conflict a part of the struggle against Communism rather than a colonial war.
Apr. 1, issued executive order withdrawing civil service protection from 134,000 federal jobs.
Apr. 1, signed act creating department of health, education and welfare
• This was the first executive department established in 40 years. The department of labor had been created, Mar. 4, 1913.
Apr. 2, declared he would determine U.S. combat strength, not Secretary of Defense Wilson
Apr. 7, welcomed Chancellor Konrad Adenauer, White House
Apr. 11, appointed first secretary of health, education and welfare, Oveta Culp Hobby
• Mrs. Hobby was the second of two female members of the cabinet. The other was Frances Perkins.

Apr. 12, reported appointment of his brother, Milton S. Eisenhower, as his personal representative to make fact-finding tour of Latin America

Apr. 16, made his first major foreign policy address, Washington, D.C.

•He proposed the international limitation of military forces, international control to promote the peaceful use of atomic power, and the banning or limiting of other weapons in a speech to the American Society of Newspaper Editors.

Apr. 18, decided to put up presidential yacht, *Williamsburg*

•After service for American Red Cross entertaining of wounded servicemen, which ended July 30, the yacht was put into the "mothball fleet."

Apr. 27, issued executive order establishing new federal employee security program

Apr. 30, proposed $8,500,000,000 cut in Truman defense and foreign aid programs

Apr. 30, issued military reorganization plan giving additional control to civilian officials of defense department

May 4, greeted 44 state and five territorial governors who met at his request, Washington, D.C.

May 7, submitted defense budget to Congress

•He proposed a military budget of $43,200,-000,000, which was $2,300,000,000 less than proposed by Truman.

May 19, sent special message in which he recommended tax revisions to Congress

•He asked extension of the excess profits tax beyond June 30; repeal of the five percent cut in corporation taxes scheduled for Apr. 1, 1954; continuation of the 11 percent increase on personal income taxes; postponement of the old-age security tax increase; and extension of excise tax rates scheduled for reduction, Apr. 1, 1954.

May 22, signed offshore lands act

•This act conferred title to submerged coastal lands to the states. This ended the tidelands oil deposits controversy that began when President Franklin D. Roosevelt claimed the lands for the federal government in 1937.

June 2, issued executive order that established International Organizations Employees Loyalty Board

•This order extended the provisions of the new loyalty check system to cover U.S. citizens employed by the UN and other international organizations.

June 14, dedicated home of President Theodore Roosevelt, Sagamore Hill, as national shrine, Oyster Bay, N.Y.

June 14, denounced "book burning" at commencement exercises, Dartmouth College, Hanover, N.H.

•However, he expressed his belief that books that advocated the overthrow of the government should be removed from state department libraries overseas, June 17.

June 15, vetoed two private relief bills

•These were the first and second of his 181 vetoes.

June 17, expressed opposition to Tennessee Valley Authority

•He said he favored the elimination of the dominant federal role in TVA, which he cited as a prime example of "creeping socialism."

June 19, denied final clemency plea for Julius and Ethel Rosenberg

•Mr. and Mrs. Rosenberg "may have condemned to death tens of millions of innocent people," he said. Convicted of conspiracy to commit espionage and supplying atomic data to the U.S.S.R. in 1951, the Rosenbergs were executed at Sing Sing Prison, Ossining, N.Y., that evening.

June 25, signed act granting one million bushels of wheat to Pakistan to avert starvation

June 30, sent special message to Congress in which he asked authority to use surplus food supplies for emergency relief to friendly nations

July 24, appointed President Hoover to 12-member commission on government operations

•The committee was formed to study federal functions and determine which should be taken over by state and local governments. Hoover accepted the chairmanship, Aug. 10.

July 27, Korean War ended

•An armistice was signed at Panmunjom by representatives of the commands of the United Nations and the North Koreans and Chinese Communists.

•In a radio report to the nation, he said:

We must not now relax our guard nor cease our quest. Throughout the coming months, during the period of prisoner screening and exchange, and during the possibly longer period of the political conference which looks toward the unification of Korea, we and our United Nations allies must be vigilant against the possibility of untoward developments.

July 29, received report of Milton S. Eisenhower on fact-finding trip to South America

July 30, sent special message to Congress in which he asked Congress to raise national debt statutory ceiling by $15,000,000,000

•His request was tabled by the Senate finance committee, Aug. 1.

Aug. 4, first session of 83rd Congress adjourned

Aug. 6, cited accomplishments of his administration during first six months

•In a radio report to the nation, he noted the termination of "futile" economic controls; the Korea rebuilding program; the reorganization of the defense department; the emergency drought aid program; the program to admit additional refugees; the wheat gift to Pakistan; simplification of custom regulations; the arming of allies program; and the extension of "onerous" but necessary taxes.

Aug. 6, pocket vetoed bill to repeal federal tax on motion picture admissions

•This was the first of his 108 pocket vetoes.

Aug. 12, issued executive order calling for across-the-board expenditure reduction in all departments and agencies

Sept. 5, announced $45,000,000 grant to Iran

•A coup had restored Shah Mohammed Reza Pahlevi to power and ousted dictatorial Premier Mohammed Mossadegh, Aug. 19.

Sept. 8, Chief Justice Vinson died

Sept. 10, accepted resignation of Secretary of Labor Durkin

Sept. 30, appointed Earl Warren as chief justice

•Warren, who was confirmed by the Senate, Mar. 1, 1954, was the first of Eisenhower's five appointments to the Supreme Court.

•Eisenhower was the 12th of 14 presidents who appointed chief justices.

Oct. 7, decided all future statements regarding nuclear bombs must conform with decisions of National Security Council or be submitted for White House clearance

•Conflicting statements about the Russian hydrogen bomb from administration officials led to this ruling.

Oct. 8, appointed his second secretary of labor, James P. Mitchell

•Mitchell took office, Oct. 9.

Oct. 14, issued executive order making refusal of government employees to testify before congressional committees on ground of possible self-incrimination basis for dismissal

Oct. 14, announced emergency aid of $9,-000,000 had been allotted to Bolivia

Oct. 15, promised comprehensive farm program by early 1954 in speech to Future Farmers of America, Kansas City, Mo.

Oct. 19, dedicated Falcon Dam, Mexico

•He was the fourth of seven presidents who visited Mexico while in office.

•He was the eighth of 11 presidents who traveled outside the U.S. while in office.

•This was the first of his three visits to Mexico while in office.

Nov. 5, empowered New York State Power Authority to develop St. Lawrence River hydroelectric project with Canada

Nov. 12, announced formation of U.S.-Canadian committee on trade and economic affairs

Nov. 13–14, visited Canada

•He conferred with Canadian officials and addressed the Canadian Parliament, Ottawa, Nov. 14. He stressed the mutual responsibility for defense of the North American continent and expressed the hope that the Senate would authorize participation in the St. Lawrence Seaway project.

•He was the fourth of seven presidents who visited Canada while in office.

•This was the first of his three visits to Canada while in office.

Nov. 15, returned to Washington, D.C.

Dec. 2, stated U.S. always would have "differences of opinions" with allies and nations it aided, but must not "grow weary of the processes of negotiation and adjustment"

Dec. 4–8, met with Prime Minister Churchill of Great Britain, Premier Joseph Laniel of France, Bermuda

•The European Defense Community was endorsed, exchange of atomic energy information was discussed, and continued aid to the French in Indochina was pledged.

•Eisenhower was the second of four presidents who visited Bermuda while in office.

•This was the first of his two visits to Bermuda while in office.

Dec. 8, addressed General Assembly of United Nations, New York City
• He proposed an international pool of atomic stockpiles to counter the "fearful trend to atomic military buildup." The U.S.S.R. entered preliminary discussions, Jan. 11, 1954, but the talks broke down in May when the Soviets declared participation must follow the prohibition of atomic weapons.

Dec. 16, held first presidential news conference that was broadcast in full

Dec. 19, endorsed long-range plan of defense department to emphasize air power and continental defense
• Army strength was to be reduced by one-third and the navy and marines were to be reduced by 15 percent.

Dec. 22, ordered withdrawal of security clearance for Dr. J. Robert Oppenheimer
• Oppenheimer, who had directed the development of the atomic bomb, chose to face charges of Communist affiliations and opposition to the development of the hydrogen bomb when he was suspended by the Atomic Energy Commission. A report that the AEC had voted, 4–1, against reinstating Oppenheimer was released, June 29, 1954.

1954

Jan. 4, declared U.S. "must not and need not tolerate a boom-and-bust" economy
• In reply to Democratic charges that the country was already in a recession, he pledged during a TV and radio report that the administration would use "every legitimate means" to sustain prosperity.

Jan. 6, second session of 83rd Congress

Jan. 7, delivered his second State of the Union message to Congress
• He reiterated his determined stand to meet renewed aggression in Korea; requested authority to share certain nuclear knowledge with allies; urged a constitutional amendment to permit 18-year-olds to vote; and maintained that federal spending would be reduced by $5,000,000,000 during the next fiscal year.

Jan. 11, sent special farm program message to Congress
• Designed to offset "unbalanced farm production," the program would provide for the allotment of federally-stored farm products to school lunch programs and national emergency, foreign aid, and disaster relief stockpiles, he said.

Jan. 11, sent special message to Congress outlining 15 recommended revisions of Taft-Hartley Act

Jan. 14, sent special message to Congress proposing increased social security benefits
• He also asked legislation to provide coverage for an additional ten million workers, including self-employed professionals and farmers and those state and local government employees who wished to participate.

Jan. 18, sent special message to Congress in which he proposed $25,000,000 limited federal reinsurance service to encourage health insurance organizations to offer broader protection
• This plan was rejected in the House of Representatives, July 13.

Jan. 21, sent budget message to Congress
• He proposed a budget of $62,642,000,000, which would result in a deficit of $2,928,-000,000.

Jan. 25, sent special low-cost housing message to Congress
• He proposed the erection of thirty-five thousand additional units yearly.

Jan. 26, stated libel and slander laws protected individuals accused of being "communistic"

Jan. 27, welcomed President Celal Bayar of Turkey, White House
• Bayar was the first president of Turkey to visit the U.S.

Jan. 28, sent annual economic report to Congress
• He said that a serious recession was not in the offing, and that the current business decline and employment fall-off would soon abate. A department of commerce estimate of 1,850,000 unemployed, Jan. 5, had been contradicted by a census bureau estimate for January of 3,087,000.

Feb. 24, sent special message to Congress proposing nine-point, $350,000,000 federal employee pay rise, voluntary insurance, and pension plan program

Feb. 25, reported acceptance of arms aid by Pakistan, rejection of similar aid by India

Feb. 25, Bricker amendment to Constitution defeated in Senate
• He opposed the proposed amendment, which would have limited the treaty-mak-

ing powers of the president.

Mar. 8, submitted report to Congress on shipments of arms and military equipment to allies

• The U.S., by means of the Mutual Security Act, had shipped arms and equipment valued at $3,800,000,000 in 1953, which was about half of the total involved since October, 1949.

Mar. 10, stated that U.S. would not become involved in Indochina war unless Congress declared war

Mar. 15, opposed Democratic proposals to increase individual income tax exemptions

Mar. 24, declared FBI files would not be released to congressional committees "while he was President"

• Senator Joseph R. McCarthy, chairman of the Senate permanent investigations subcommittee, had stated that this policy hindered his campaign against Communists in government.

Mar. 29, Secretary of State Dulles stated Communist aggression in Southeast Asia must be met with united action, regardless of risks involved

• He had approved the Dulles speech, which was delivered to the Overseas Press Club, New York City.

Mar. 30, sent special message to Congress in which he requested decreased tariff rates on many goods, modifications of "Buy American" act, extension of Reciprocal Trade Agreements Act

Apr. 1, signed Air Force Academy Act

Apr. 5, warned nation against "hysterical thinking" during TV-radio address

• He criticized the excessive use of investigatory powers by congressional committees, but added that public opinion, "the most powerful of all forces," would end any threats to the democratic system.

Apr. 22, McCarthy hearings began

• The army department filed 29 charges of misconduct against Senator McCarthy, who retaliated with 46 countercharges. The 36-day hearings were carried on national television.

May 3, submitted lend-lease report to Congress

• The U.S. collected $48,374,745 on outstanding debts during 1953.

May 13, signed St. Lawrence Seaway Act

May 17, racial segregation in public schools declared unconstitutional by Supreme Court

May 21, his proposal to lower voting age to 18 defeated in Senate

May 25, received Emperor Haile Selassie of Ethiopia, White House

May 31, criticized "demagogues thirsty for personal power" during speech at bicentennial of Columbia University, New York City

June 17, McCarthy hearings ended

• Senator McCarthy was condemned but not censured by the Senate, Dec. 2.

June 22, emphasized importance of Japan in speech to National Editorial Association, Washington, D.C.

• He said that the fall of Japan to Communism would be disastrous inasmuch as that country was the key to the defense of the western Pacific.

June 25–29, conferred with Prime Minister Churchill, White House.

July 1, opposed admission of Communist China to United Nations

• He said he would do his utmost to prevent the admission of Red China to the UN.

July 21, voiced disapproval of armistice agreement signed by French and Communist Vietminh in Geneva

• He said that the U.S. accepted the truce, which ended the war in Vietnam and Laos after seven and a half years of fighting, and would not employ force to alter the terms.

Aug. 10, opposed return of $500,000,000 in German assets seized during World War II

Aug. 12, stated "recent decline in economic activity had come to a halt" in midyear survey of business conditions

Aug. 17, stated U.S. Seventh Fleet would defend Formosa from attack by Communist China

Aug. 20, second session of 83rd Congress adjourned

Aug. 24, signed Communist control act, outlawing Communist party

• He also signed seven other anti-Communist acts.

Sept. 6, disclosed U.S. had joined five nations to form international agency to investigate peacetime uses of atomic energy

• He announced the agreement with Great Britain, Canada, France, Australia, and South Africa during ceremonies in Denver, Colo., when he employed radioactive and electronic devices to break ground for the first commercial atomic energy plant at Shippingport, Pa.

Sept. 8, Southeast Asia defense treaty

signed, Manila, the Philippines

Oct. 9, Associate Justice Jackson died

Oct. 25, cabinet meeting seen and heard on television and radio for first time

Oct. 28, conferred with Chancellor Konrad Adenauer, White House

• He and Adenauer endorsed reunification of Germany "only by peaceful means."

Oct. 30, announced U.S. would send $8,-585,000 worth of food and grain to West and East Germany, Czechoslovakia, Hungary, and Yugoslavia

• Summer floods had caused hazardous conditions.

Nov. 2, election day

• The Democrats won control of the Senate and the House of Representatives in the off-year elections.

Nov. 4–6, Queen Mother Elizabeth of Great Britain visited White House

Nov. 10, appointed John M. Harlan as associate justice

• Harlan, who was confirmed by the Senate, Mar. 16, 1955, was the second of Eisenhower's five appointments to the Supreme Court.

Nov. 11, dedicated Eisenhower Memorial Museum, Abilene, Kan.

Dec. 4, his program for peaceful use of atomic energy unanimously adopted by UN General Assembly

Dec. 17, appointed Joseph M. Dodge as chairman of council of foreign economic policies

1955

Jan. 5, first session of 84th Congress

• The administration lost control of both the Senate and the House of Representatives. The Democrats gained two Senate and 18 House seats. The Senate (96 members) consisted of 49 Democrats and 47 Republicans. The House (435 members) consisted of 230 Democrats, 203 Republicans, and two vacancies.

Jan. 6, delivered his third State of the Union message to Congress

• He urged the creation of a reserve training program, a federal aid program to add public school classrooms, and an increase in the minimum hourly wage from 75 to 90 cents. He also reiterated a number of legislative requests made in his 1954 State of the Union message.

Jan. 10, sent special message to Congress in which he asked three-year extension of Reciprocal Trade Agreements Act provision to reduce tariffs in return for trade concessions by foreign countries

Jan. 12, "massive retaliation" policy outlined by Secretary of State Dulles

• Dulles said that the president and the National Security Council had decided "to depend primarily upon a great capacity to retaliate instantly by means and at places of our choosing."

Jan. 13, sent special message to Congress requesting continuation of current Selective Service System for four years

Jan. 17, sent budget message to Congress

• He proposed a budget of $62,410,000,000, which would result in a deficit of $2,410,-000,000.

Jan. 20, opposed tax reduction in 1955 in annual economic report to Congress

Jan. 24, sent special message to Congress in which he asked emergency powers to defend Formosa and Pescadores

• The powers were granted by joint resolution, Jan. 28.

• The Seventh Fleet assisted the evacuation of twenty-five thousand Chinese Nationalist troops and seventeen thousand civilians from Tachens, Feb. 6–11.

Feb. 2, stated his proposed 140,000 reduction of army ground forces correct on long-range basis

• His plan had been severely criticized by General Matthew B. Ridgway, army chief of staff, Jan. 31.

Feb. 8, sent special message to Congress proposing three-year, $7,000,000,000, federal-state-local school construction program

Mar. 2, signed act raising salaries of vice president, congressmen, and judiciary

• The salary of the vice president was raised from $30,000 to $35,000. Congressmen's salaries were raised from $15,000 to $22,-500 annually, as of Mar. 1, the first increase since 1946. The chief justice's salary was raised from $25,500 to $35,000, those of associate justices from $25,000 to $35,000.

Mar. 5, issued executive order instituting seven changes in federal employee security program

• The principal change gave accused employees statements of charges and the right to face and question their accusers.

Mar. 10, stated U.S. would maintain troops

in Europe if West Germany's sovereignty and right to rearm was ratified

Mar. 15, Secretary of State Dulles modified "massive retaliation" policy

•Dulles said small nuclear weapons, rather than hydrogen bombs, would be employed in event of war.

Mar. 31, signed armed forces pay increase act

•An appropriation of $745,000,000 provided for pay raises for 1,700,000 members of the armed forces.

Apr. 13, signed agreement to share atomic weapon information with NATO nations

Apr. 25, proposed plan to construct atomic-powered merchant ship

•His proposal was rejected by the joint congressional atomic energy committee, June 13.

Apr. 27, announced he and Georgi K. Zhukov, Soviet defense minister, had been corresponding for three weeks

•He expressed the hope that the exchange of views might lead to "some betterment of the world situation."

May 20, vetoed post office wage increase bill

•The bill provided for an 8.8 percent increase; he again recommended a 7.6 percent rise.

June 10, signed revised post office wage increase act

•The act provided for an eight percent increase.

June 13, conferred with Chancellor Adenauer of West Germany, White House

June 20, attended tenth anniversary of United Nations, San Francisco, Cal.

•The UN charter had been signed in San Francisco, June 24, 1945.

June 24, issued executive order to Atomic Energy Commission to distribute 440 pounds of enriched uranium to 22 nations

July 11, issued executive order of cancellation of AEC contract with Dixon-Yates utilities group to build private power plant, West Memphis, Ark.

•This order ended the public *vs.* private power controversy that followed his executive order directing that the contract be negotiated, June 17, 1954.

July 13, accepted resignation of Secretary of Health, Education and Welfare Hobby, effective, July 31

July 18–23, attended Geneva Conference, Geneva, Switzerland

•The summit conference was held at the Palace of Nations. He conferred with Prime Minister Anthony Eden of Great Britain, Premier Edgar Faure of France, and Premier Nikolai A. Bulganin of the U.S.S.R.

•Eisenhower was the only president who visited Switzerland while in office.

•He was the fourth of seven presidents who visited Europe while in office.

Aug. 1, appointed his second secretary of health, education and welfare, Marion B. Folsom

Aug. 2, first session of 84th Congress adjourned

Sept. 24, suffered heart attack, Denver, Colo.

•The attack was described as "moderate" by Dr. Paul Dudley White. The stock market plummeted, Sept. 26, when stock values dropped by more than $12,000,000,000, the largest loss since 1929. Both Republican and Democratic leaders were convinced that his illness would remove him as a candidate for reelection in 1956.

Oct. 11, conferred with Secretaty of State Dulles on foreign policy matters, Denver

•Eisenhower also wrote Premier Nikolai A. Bulganin regarding inspection for control of armaments in both the U.S. and the U.S.S.R. Bulganin accepted the preliminary plan, Oct. 23.

Oct. 29, endorsed farm program of Secretary Benson

•He stated that he would not endorse a return to high fixed price supports.

Nov. 11, returned to Washington, D.C.

•He said:

I am happy that the doctors have given me a parole, if not a pardon, and I expect to be back at my accustomed duties, although they say I must ease and not bulldoze my way into them.

Nov. 14, departed for Gettysburg, Pa.

•He spent the next five weeks recuperating at his Gettysburg home. Aides Sherman Adams and James C. Hagerty accompanied him.

Nov. 18, received report on unsuccessful Geneva conference from Secretary of State Dulles

•Dulles read a speech prepared for the president on TV-radio that evening.

Nov. 28, addressed White House Conference on Education

•His speech was filmed at Gettysburg.

While education must not be centrally controlled, he said, federal leadership, credit, and funds were necessary.

Dec. 20, returned to Washington, D.C.

Dec. 28, flew to Key West, Fla., for two-week vacation

1956

Jan. 3, second session of 84th Congress

Jan. 5, sent his fourth State of the Union message to Congress

•He stated that government spending had been reduced by $10,000,000,000, that taxes had been reduced by $7,500,000,000, and that a balanced budget was in the offing.

Jan. 8, returned to Washington, D.C.

Jan. 12, sent special message to Congress outlining aid-to-education program

•He requested federal grants of $250,000,-000 annually for five years, to be matched by state funds; loans of $250,000,000 annually for five years for federal purchase of school construction bonds.

Jan. 16, sent budget message to Congress

•He proposed a budget of $66,300,000,000, which would result in a surplus of $400,-000,000.

Jan. 28, rejected Soviet offer of treaty of friendship and cooperation

•The treaty was proposed by Premier Bulganin in a personal letter, Jan. 25. Eisenhower's reply stated that the terms offered were covered by the UN charter.

Jan. 30–Feb. 1, conferred with Prime Minister Sir Anthony Eden, White House

•He and Eden issued a joint statement that warned Asian and African nations against acceptance of Soviet political or economic aid.

Feb. 8, sent special message to Congress asking revision of immigration laws

•He requested a quota rise of about sixty-five thousand entries, of which five thousand would be available without regard to nationality.

Feb. 14, his doctors reported he had made "good recovery" from coronary thrombosis

•Dr. White and a board of five doctors reported he could "carry on an active life satisfactorily for another five or ten years."

Feb. 16, issued executive order exempting fathers and men 26 or older from draft

Feb. 17, vetoed bill to amend natural gas act

•The bill would have cancelled federal regulation of natural gas production. He subscribed to the basic objectives of the bill but instead suggested passage of a bill that included "specific language protecting consumers in their right to fair prices."

Feb. 22, issued executive order authorizing sale or lease of $1,000,000,000 worth of U-235

Feb. 28, conferred with President Giovanni Gronchi of Italy, White House

•Gronchi was the first Italian chief of state to visit the U.S.

Feb. 29, announced during news conference he would run for second term

•In a TV-radio address that evening he explained:

> The work that I set out four years ago to do has not yet reached the stage of development and fruition that I then hoped could be accomplished within the period of a single term in this office.

•He discussed his heart attack, his curtailed work schedule, emphasizing that

> . . . there is not the slightest doubt that I can now perform as well as I ever have all of the important duties of the Presidency.

Mar. 6, released letter to Premier Bulganin in which he proposed agreement to halt production of fissionable material for war

Mar. 19, sent special message on foreign aid to Congress

•He requested $4,800,000,000, emphasized need for long-range commitments.

Mar. 26–28, chaired informal "good neighbor" conference with Prime Minister Louis St. Laurent of Canada and President Adolfo Ruiz Cortines of Mexico, White Sulphur Springs, W. Va.

Mar. 29, accepted resignation of Secretary of Interior McKay, effective, Apr. 15

Apr. 9, sent personal messages and copies of U.S. pledge to oppose aggression in Middle East to Israeli and Egyptian governments

Apr. 21, suggested U.S.S.R. could right Stalin's wrongdoings by dismantling puppet rule in satellite nations

•His speech to the American Society of Newspaper Editors contained his first comment on the downgrading of Stalin, which had commenced at the 20th Congress of the Soviet Communist Party in Moscow, Feb. 14–25.

May 11–12, pronounced fit after extensive physical examination at Walter Reed Army Hospital, Washington, D.C.

May 16, received President Sukarno of Indonesia, White House

May 28, appointed his second secretary of interior, Frederick A. Seaton

•Seaton took office, June 5.

June 8, suffered ileitis attack

•He underwent an operation at Walter Reed Hospital, June 9, which was termed successful. Ileitis is an inflammation of the ileum, the lower section of the small intestine.

June 14, visited by Chancellor Adenauer, Walter Reed hospital

June 30, left hospital for Gettysburg farm

July 1, with Mrs. Eisenhower, celebrated 40th wedding anniversary, Gettysburg

July 15, received delegation of Republican congressional leaders, authorized them to announce he was still running for reelection

July 15, returned to White House

July 19, White House announced balanced budget

•A surplus of $1,754,000,000 for fiscal 1956 was announced.

July 21–23, visited Panama

•He and the presidents of 18 American republics conferred in Panama City, where they signed the Panama Declaration, calling for "inter-American cooperative efforts to seek the solution of economic problems and to raise the living standards of the continent."

•He was the last of four presidents who visited Panama while in office.

July 27, second session of 84th Congress adjourned

Aug. 1, held first news conference in two months

•He said, when questioned about his health, that he had "no doubts" about his ability to serve a second term.

Aug. 7, released his letter of reply to Premier Bulganin

•Bulganin had called upon U. S. and European allies to reduce armed forces in Germany, June 6.

•He said troop reduction could not be dealt with "as an isolated matter." He added that he was perplexed by Soviet diplomacy. Referring to the Geneva agreement on German reunification by free elections, he said:

I am perplexed as to how we can work together constructively if agreements which are negotiated at the highest level after the most thorough exploration do not seem dependable.

Aug. 22, renominated for presidency, Republican national convention, San Francisco, Cal.

Sept. 3, released labor department report stating "level of the economy has never been higher in peace or war."

Sept. 7, Associate Justice Minton retired

Sept. 12, officially opened campaign with picnic supper for five hundred Republican leaders, Gettysburg

Sept. 29, appointed William J. Brennan, Jr., as associate justice

•Brennan, who was confirmed by the Senate, Mar. 19, 1957, was the third of Eisenhower's five appointments to the Supreme Court.

Oct. 15, issued executive order authorizing continuation of U.S. economic aid to Yugoslavia

Oct. 28, warned Israel against taking "forceful initiative" in Middle East

Oct. 28, pronounced in "excellent health" after thorough examination at Walter Reed medical center, Washington, D.C.

Oct. 30, asked Prime Minister Eden and Premier Guy Mollet to halt Anglo-French intervention in Egypt

•Egypt had seized the Suez Canal, July 27. Three months of futile negotiations followed. Israel attacked Egypt, Oct. 29, and penetrated to the bank of the canal in three days. Great Britain and France sent a joint demand to Egypt and Israel to cease fighting and withdraw ten miles from the canal, Oct. 30. Israel complied, but Egypt rejected the ultimatum.

Oct. 30, deplored military intervention in Egypt by Great Britain, France, and Israel

•He called the British and French bombing of Egyptian airfields an "error," adding "there will be no United States involvement in the present hostilities," in a nationwide TV-radio report. He expressed the hope that the UN could end the crisis.

•After five days of bombings, British and French troops invaded Egypt, Nov. 5. Port Said and Port Faud were quickly captured. The fighting ended, Nov. 7, with the acceptance of a UN cease-fire appeal.

Nov. 6, election day

• *See* Election of 1956, below.

Nov. 8, offered asylum to five thousand Hungarian refugees.

• The Hungarian revolution had begun, Oct. 23, and was crushed by Soviet troops and tanks, Nov. 4.

Nov. 13, stated U.S., through UN, would oppose any Soviet military intervention in Middle East

Nov. 17, announced AEC would sell nuclear materials to cooperating nations at prices charged domestic users.

Nov. 17, issued statement of denial that Suez crisis had split NATO

Dec. 1, announced 21,500 Hungarian refugees would be given asylum

Dec. 16, received Prime Minister Jawaharlal Nehru of India, White House

• Eisenhower and Nehru conferred for four days in Washington and Gettysburg.

Dec. 17, presidential electors cast ballots

• He received 457 of the 531 electoral votes from the 48 states.

• *See* Election of 1956, below.

1957

Jan. 1, announced quota of Hungarian refugees had been raised to unspecified number

Jan, 2, rejected Soviet proposal for five-nation summit conference, stated he preferred to work through UN

Jan. 3, first session of 85th Congress

• The administration controlled neither the Senate nor the House of Representatives. The Democrats gained four House seats. The Senate (96 members) consisted of 49 Democrats and 47 Republicans. The House (435 members) consisted of 234 Democrats, 200 Republicans, and one vacancy.

Jan. 7, electoral votes tabulated by Congress

• Eisenhower and Nixon were officially declared elected.

Jan. 10, sent his fifth State of the Union message to Congress

Jan. 13–15, made 4,600-mile air tour of Midwest and Southwest drought area

ELECTION OF 1956

Prohibition party, convened, Sept. 4, 1955, at Milford, Ind., nominated Enoch Arden Holtwick of Illinois for president, Edward M. Cooper of California for vice president.

Socialist Labor party, convened, May 5, 1956, at New York City, nominated Eric Hass of New York for president, Georgia Cozzini of Wisconsin for vice president.

Socialist party, convened, June 8, at Chicago, Ill., nominated Darlington Hoopes of Pennsylvania for president, Samuel Herman Friedman of New York for vice president.

Democratic party, convened, Aug. 13, at Chicago, Ill., nominated Adlai Ewing Stevenson of Illinois for president, Estes Kefauver of Tennessee for vice president.

• This was the 32nd Democratic national convention. It was the ninth Democratic convention held in Chicago; it was the 23rd major party convention held in Chicago.

Socialist Workers party, convened Aug. 19, at New York City, nominated Farrell Dobbs of New York for president, Myra Tanner Weiss of New York for vice president.

Republican party, convened, Aug. 20, at San Francisco, Cal., nominated Dwight David Eisenhower of New York for president, Richard Milhous Nixon of California for vice president.

• This was the 26th Republican national convention. It was the first Republican convention held in San Francisco; it was the second major party convention held in San Francisco.

States' Rights party, convened, Oct. 15, at Richmond, Va., nominated Thomas Coleman Andrews of Virginia for president, Thomas Harold Werdel of California for vice president.

States' Rights party of Kentucky nominated Harry Flood Byrd of Virginia for president, William Ezra Jenner of Indiana for vice president.

Texas Constitution party nominated William Ezra Jenner of Indiana for president, Joseph Bracken Lee of Utah for vice president.

Election day, Tuesday Nov. 6, 1956

Popular vote: 62,065,469
     Eisenhower, 35,590,472
     Stevenson, 26,031,322
     Andrews, 167,826
     Byrd, 134,128
     Hass, 44,450
     Holtwick, 41,937
     Jenner, 30,999

Dobbs, 5,707
Hoopes, 1,763
others, 16,865
Electoral vote: 531, 48 states
• Eisenhower, 457, 41 states
(Arizona, 4; California, 32; Colorado,
6; Connecticut, 6; Delaware, 3; Flori-
da, 10; Idaho, 4; Illinois, 27; Indiana,
13; Iowa, 10; Kansas, 8; Kentucky, 10;
Louisiana, 10; Maine, 5; Maryland, 9;
Massachusetts, 16; Michigan, 20; Min-
nesota, 11; Montana, 4; Nebraska, 6;
Nevada, 3; New Hampshire, 4; New
Jersey, 16; New Mexico, 4; New York,

45; North Dakota, 4; Ohio, 25; Okla-
homa, 8; Oregon, 6; Pennsylvania, 32;
Rhode Island, 4; South Dakota, 4;
Tennessee, 11; Texas, 24; Utah, 4; Ver-
mont, 3; Virginia, 12; Washington, 9;
West Virginia, 8; Wisconsin, 12; Wyo-
ming, 3)
• Stevenson, 73, seven states
(Alabama, 10 of 11 votes; Arkansas, 8;
Georgia, 12; Mississippi, 8; Missouri, 13;
North Carolina, 14; South Carolina, 8)
• Walter Burgwyn Jones, 1, no states
•Jones received the vote of one Alabama
elector.

THE 43rd ADMINISTRATION

1957

Jan. 20, took oath of office privately, White
House
Jan. 21, his second inauguration day
•Eisenhower took the oath of office pub-
licly, administered by Chief Justice Earl
Warren, on the east plaza of the Capitol.
•This was the first of four inaugurations at
which Chief Justice Warren officiated.
•Eisenhower was the last of five presidents
who postponed their oath-taking ceremonies to Monday because inauguration day
fell on Sunday.
Jan. 23, sent annual economic report to
Congress
•Price increases accounted for $21,500,-
000,000, half of the gains in the 1956 production of goods and services, he said.
Jan. 28, sent special message to Congress in
which he proposed emergency school program
•He asked $325,000,000 for each of the next
four years in federal grants for school construction and authorization for federal purchase of $750,000,000 of local school
bonds.
Jan. 30, stated he would not seek third term
•He would not run for reelection even if the
constitutional amendment barring more
than two presidential terms was repealed,
he said during a news conference.
Jan. 31, accepted resignation of Associate
Justice Reed, effective, Feb. 25
Jan. 31, sent special message to Congress in
which he urged revision of McCarran-Wal-
ter Act of 1952 to permit doubling of immigration quotas
Feb. 9, U.S.-Saudi Arabia pact announced

•In a joint statement, he and Ibn Saud announced renewal for five years of the U.S.
lease of Dhahran air field in exchange for
military aid.
Feb. 25–27, met with Premier Guy Mollet of
France, White House
•He and Mollet reaffirmed U.S. and French
adherence to the principles endorsed by
the UN Security Council regarding the operation of the Suez Canal.
Mar. 2, appointed Charles E. Whittaker as
associate justice
•Whittaker, who was confirmed by the Senate, Mar. 19, was the fourth of Eisenhower's five appointments to the Supreme
Court.
Mar. 9, signed Middle East doctrine joint
resolution
•This resolution authorized the president to
institute military assistance programs to
those Middle Eastern nations that requested help. The use of $200,000,000 of
Mutual Security funds was authorized
prior to June 30, 1958.
Mar. 21–24, conferred with Prime Minister
Harold Macmillan of Great Britain, Bermuda
•He and Macmillan announced the reaffirmation of U.S.-British "responsibility to
seek to coordinate their foreign policies."
The alliance had been under stress as a
result of differences over Middle Eastern
policy since the Suez crisis.
•This was the second of his two visits to Bermuda while in office.
Mar. 25, appointed Mrs. Katherine Brownell Oettinger as director of Children's
Bureau
•Prior to the appointment of Mrs. Oet-

tinger, who was the mother of two sons, the 45-year-old bureau always had been headed by spinsters.

Mar. 27, maintained reductions of his $71,-800,000,000 budget would jeopardize U.S. security

Mar. 29, proposed presidential disability amendment

•The suggested amendment provided that presidential powers could be delegated to the vice president by written declaration of inability to serve. Approval of a majority of the cabinet would be necessary before the vice president became acting president. Written declaration of ability to resume office by the president would cancel the arrangement.

Apr. 3, appointed Mrs. Anne W. Wheaton as associate press secretary

•Mrs. Wheaton was the first woman to hold the post.

Apr. 16, his brother, Edgar, criticized size of budget

•When asked for comment on his older brother's disapproval of his fiscal policies, he laughed and replied, "Edgar has been criticizing me since I was five years old."

May 8, greeted President Ngo Dinh Diem of South Vietnam, White House

May 9, received report of his special ambassador to Middle East, James P. Richards

•Richards had visited 15 nations, allocating $120,000,000 in military aid.

May 12, visited Gettysburg battlefield with Field Marshal Viscount Montgomery

•Emotional protests were heard from the South when it became known that he and Montgomery had agreed that the Union and Confederate commanders at Gettysburg, General George G. Meade and General Robert E. Lee, should have been "sacked." On May 15, he said in reply:

I consider in my book are [sic] about four top Americans of the past. They are Franklin, Washington, Lincoln and Lee, and anybody whoever tries to put me in any other relationship with respect to General Lee is mistaken.

May 14, appealed for support of his budget in TV-radio speech

•He said:

No great reductions in it are possible unless Congress eliminates or curtails existing federal programs, or all of us demand less service from the government, or unless we

are willing to gamble with the safety of our country.

May 14, military aid to Yugoslavia resumed

•He approved the state department order for $100,000,000 in military assistance, including two hundred jet planes, and stated that Yugoslavia "is and firmly intends to remain independent." U.S. aid had been halted in 1956, when Yugoslavia and the U.S.S.R. reconciled.

May 21, again appealed for support of his budget on TV-radio

•He said:

To cripple our programs for mutual security in the false name of "economy" can mean nothing less than a weakening of our nation.

May 26–28, conferred with Chancellor Adenauer of West Germany, Washington, D.C. and Gettysburg

May 29, accepted resignation of Secretary of Treasury Humphrey, effective, July 29

May 29, appointed his second secretary of treasury, Robert B. Anderson

•Anderson took office, July 29.

June 6, witnessed conclusion of carrier-to-carrier, ocean-to-ocean flight.

•Four Navy jets flew from the carrier, *U.S.S. Bon Homme Richard*, off San Diego, Cal., to the carrier, *U.S.S. Saratoga*, off the Florida coast. He was aboard the *Saratoga*.

June 9, his "mild stomach upset" caused stock market drop, June 10.

•He returned to work, June 11; the market returned to normal.

June 13, issued executive order freeing young men in ready reserve programs from draft liability

June 19, conferred with Prime Minister Nobusuke Kishi of Japan, White House

•A joint statement that U.S. military forces in Japan would be substantially reduced was released, June 21.

June 24, received report that H-bomb radioactive fallout had been reduced by 95 percent

June 24, proposed federal-state commission to examine interdependent functions and revenues of state and federal governments in address to annual Governors Conference, Williamsburg, Va.

July 3, warned against efforts to oversimplify Algerian situation, declared role of U.S. was to strive "behind the scenes" for settlement of such problems

•Senator John F. Kennedy had stated that the administration should support Algeria and end its tacit support of French repression of the Algerian rebellion, July 2.

July 3, announced release of 131,560 pounds of U-235 as fuel for nuclear plants in U.S. and abroad

July 10, conferred with Prime Minister Hussein Shaheed Suhrawardy of Pakistan, Washington, D.C.

July 12, flew by helicopter from White House lawn to secret relocation center during national civil defense test

• He was the first president to fly in a helicopter while in office

July 16, with his approval, Secretary of Defense Wilson ordered armed forces reduced by 100,000 by Jan. 1, 1958

July 29, signed ratification papers that formalized U.S. membership in International Atomic Energy Agency

Aug. 7, accepted resignation of Secretary of Defense Wilson

• Wilson's resignation became effective, Oct. 8.

Aug. 7, appointed his second secretary of defense, Neil H. McElroy

• McElroy took office, Oct. 9.

Aug. 21, announced U.S. had agreed to two-year suspension of nuclear tests

• This was a concession to the U.S.S.R. Earlier, the U.S. had suggested a ten-month suspension.

Aug. 24, piloted his two-engine airplane for short while en route from Washington to Gettysburg

• He was the only president to fly an airplane while in office.

Aug. 30, first session of 85th Congress adjourned

Sept. 3, minimized importance of Russian ICBM

• "The big thing to remember," he said "is that a mere tested vehicle is a long ways from actual production." The U.S.S.R. had announced the successful test, Aug. 26.

Sept. 19, with his approval, Secretary of Defense Wilson ordered armed forces reduced by additional 100,000 during 1958

Sept. 26, made dive in atomic submarine, *Seawolf*, off Newport, R.I.

• The dive was made to a depth of 60 feet.

• He was the second of two presidents who traveled by submarine while in office. The other was Truman.

• He was the last of three presidents who submerged in submarines while in office.

Oct. 10, breakfasted with Komla Agbeli Gbedemah, finance minister of Ghana, White House

• Gbedemah had been ordered out of a restaurant in Dover, Del., and was told "colored people are not allowed to eat in here," Oct. 7.

Oct. 17, greeted Queen Elizabeth II and Prince Philip, Duke of Edinburgh, National Airport, Washington, D.C.

• His gift to the British royal couple was a portrait he had painted of their son, Prince Charles. A second gift from the Eisenhowers was a porcelain of Prince Philip playing polo. The gifts for the Eisenhowers were a table with an inlaid copy of the D-Day battle plan and a pair of porcelain warblers.

Oct. 23–25, conferred with Prime Minister Macmillan, White House

Oct. 24, accepted resignation of Attorney General Brownell, effective, Nov. 8

Oct. 24, appointed his second attorney general, William P. Rogers

• Rogers took office, Nov. 8.

Nov. 10–11, underwent annual physical checkup, Walter Reed Army Hospital, Washington, D.C.

• His doctors reported that his general condition was excellent.

Nov. 25, suffered stroke

• He suffered a blood vessel blockage in his brain, which was described as a mild stroke. The stock market dropped by $4,-470,000,000 in about 20 minutes, Nov. 26, but fully recovered the following day.

• He made a quick recovery and returned to work, Dec. 9.

Dec. 10, received letter from Premier Bulganin proposing East-West conference

• Bulganin stated that the U.S.S.R. was willing to end nuclear testing as of Jan. 1, 1958.

Dec. 15, rejected appeal by Prime Minister Nehru of India to U.S. and U.S.S.R. to end nuclear testing as evidence of intention to disarm

Dec. 16–19, attended heads of government NATO meeting, Paris, France

• All 15 of the NATO nations, except Portugal, were represented by the heads of their governments. He told the meeting:

I assure you in the most solemn terms that the United States would come, at once and with all appropriate force, to the assistance of any NATO nation subject to armed attack.

• He was the second of four presidents who visited France while in office.
• This was the first of his four visits to France while in office.

1958

Jan. 7, second session of 85th Congress
Jan. 9, delivered his sixth State of the Union message to Congress
Jan. 12, replied to Bulganin's call for East-West conference
• He said the summit conference should follow meetings on lower levels "so that it could be ascertained that such a top-level meeting would, in fact, hold good hope of advancing the cause of peace and justice in the world."
Jan. 13, sent budget message to Congress
• He estimated expenditures for the fiscal year ending June 30, 1959, at $73,900,000, and receipts at $74,400,000,000, which would result in a surplus of $500,000,000.
Jan. 20, sent economic report to Congress
• Price increases accounted for a "considerable part" of the five percent gains in the 1957 production of goods and services and personal incomes, he said.
Feb. 11, issued executive order to Postmaster General Summerfield to seek $2,000,-000,000 appropriation for building and equipment modernization program
Feb. 12, stated U.S. economy was not facing "prolonged downswing"
Feb. 17, chided Bulganin for instituting "repetitive public debate"
• In a letter to the Soviet premier, Eisenhower said he doubted the value of "continuing to write speeches to each other." He reiterated his position in favor of lower level meetings to lay the groundwork for a summit conference.
Feb. 25, spoke at bipartisan foreign aid rally, Washington, D.C.
• Others who participated, appealing for the support of foreign-aid programs, included former President Truman, Vice President Nixon, and Adlai E. Stevenson.
Feb. 26, stated he and Vice President Nixon had "clear understanding" in event of his disability·
• Details of the agreement were released by the White House, Mar. 3. The inability to serve would be determined by the president "if possible." Otherwise, the vice

president would make the decision "after such consultation as seems to him appropriate." The president alone would decide when the inability had ended. In such instances, the vice president would assume the title of acting president.
Mar. 5, suggested business slump would end when general public resumed purchases
• He told a news conference:
   In other words, the private economy has a way of steering its own course, and the federal government and the state governments are not themselves the most important factor in those dips and upturns of the economy.
Apr. 2, sent special message to Congress in which he proposed National Aeronautics and Space Agency
Apr. 3, sent special message to Congress in which he proposed major reorganization of defense department
• His plan strengthened the role of the secretary of defense, detached the joint chiefs of staff from their individual services and assigned them to assist the secretary "in his exercise of direction over unified commands."
Apr. 4, received note from Premier Nikita Sergeyevich Khrushchev urging suspension of U.S. nuclear testing
• Khrushchev had succeeded Bulganin as Soviet premier, Mar. 27.
Apr. 8, rejected Khrushchev proposal, suggested U.S.-U.S.S.R. study of technical aspects of nuclear disarmament
Apr. 8, stated unemployment "leveling off"
• The rise in unemployment during March had been the smallest of the past five months. "These statistics indicate a slowing up of the downturn," he said.
• The recession had begun in August, 1957. The Federal Reserve Board reported, Apr. 14, that the industrial production index had dropped during March to the lowest level since the 1953–1954 recession.
Apr. 17, appealed for support of defense department modernization plan
• He maintained that the plan would establish "clear-cut civilian responsibility, unified strategic planning and direction and completely unified combat commands." His address to a joint meeting of the American Society of Newspaper Editors and the International Press Institute in Washington was televised.

Apr. 28, urged Khrushchev to support U.S. plan for international Arctic inspection zone
- The U.S. resolution was approved by ten of the 11 members of the UN Security Council but was vetoed by the U.S.S.R.

May 3, released note to 11 nations asking treaty to preserve Antarctica for scientific research

May 15, greeted Vice President Nixon, National Airport, Washington, D.C.
- The vice president's 18-day goodwill tour of eight South American nations had been disrupted repeatedly by mob violence.

May 31, U.S.S.R. agreed to his proposal of technical talks on nuclear disarmament

June 3, received note requesting expansion of U.S.-U.S.S.R. trade from Premier Khrushchev

June 4, received President Theodor Heuss of West Germany, White House
- Heuss was the first German head of state to visit the U.S.

June 7, received Prime Minister Macmillan of Great Britain, White House

June 18, lauded Sherman Adams, told news conference "I need him"
- Assistant to the President Adams, who was under attack for alleged preferential treatment of Bernard Goldfine, a Boston industrialist, admitted he had been imprudent, June 17.

July 2, received Khrushchev suggestion of technical talks
- The proposal closely paralleled U.S. proposals made earlier in the year. The Soviet premier also suggested an aerial inspection plan previously rejected by the U.S. as inadequate.

July 7, signed Alaska statehood act

July 8–11, visited Canada
- He conferred with Prime Minister John Diefenbaker, and addressed the Canadian Parliament in Ottawa.
- This was the second of his three visits to Canada while in office.

July 15, sent special message to Congress in which he announced he had ordered U.S. Marines to Lebanon
- The pro-West monarchy of Iraq had been overthrown, July 14. In the belief that the U.S.S.R. and the United Arab Republic planned a similar coup in Lebanon, he had sent troops at the request of President Camille Chamoun of Lebanon. The marines

landed unopposed, July 15–16. The American force of marine and army units in Lebanon numbered more than fourteen thousand, Aug. 5. The last American troops left Lebanon, Oct. 25.

July 31, Secretary of Health, Education and Welfare Folsom retired

Aug. 1, appointed his third secretary of health, education and welfare, Arthur S. Flemming

Aug. 8, awarded presidential citation to officers and crew of *Nautilus*, nuclear submarine that made first undersea crossing of North Pole, Aug. 3
- This was the first presidential citation awarded in peacetime.

Aug. 13, addressed UN General Assembly, New York City
- He presented his "framework of a plan for peace" in the Middle East.

Aug. 22, stated U.S. would suspend nuclear testing for one year if U.S.S.R. would halt future testing and negotiate for nuclear control system
- He said American representatives could meet with spokesmen for other nuclear powers by the end of October. He added that U.S. testing would be suspended at the opening of negotiations. Khrushchev accepted the proposal to start talks in Geneva, Oct. 31.

Aug. 24, second session of 85th Congress adjourned

Aug. 25, signed act authorizing pension for former presidents
- This act provided former presidents with pensions of $25,000 yearly, suitable office accommodations and necessary staff.
- A limit of $50,000 was set on the accumulative salaries of each staff.

Aug. 27, told news conference offshore islands more important to defense of Formosa than three years earlier
- The islands had been subjected to intensive shelling by Chinese Communist shore batteries, beginning Aug. 23.

Sept. 8, warned Communist China not to use "armed force to achieve territorial ambitions"
- U.S. warships had begun to escort Chinese Nationalist supply convoys to Quemoy, Sept. 7. Khrushchev had said that an attack on Communist China would be considered an attack on the U.S.S.R.

Sept. 11, warned against appeasement of

Chinese Communists in TV-radio address
- The U.S. would not "retreat in the face of armed aggression, which is part and parcel of a continuing program of using armed force to conquer new regions," he said.
- American and Chinese Communist representatives conferred in Warsaw, Poland, Sept. 15. The talks became deadlocked; the U.S. demanded a cease-fire while the Chinese Communists contended that the Formosan matter was an "internal affair."

Sept. 22, accepted resignation of Sherman Adams
- Eisenhower said that Adams still had his "complete trust, confidence and respect."

Oct. 7, accepted resignation of Associate Justice Burton, effective, Oct. 13

Oct. 7, appointed Potter Stewart as associate justice
- Stewart, who was confirmed by the Senate, May 5, 1959, was the last of Eisenhower's five appointments to the Supreme Court.

Oct. 24, accepted resignation of Secretary of Commerce Weeks, effective, Nov. 10

Oct. 24, appointed his second secretary of commerce, Lewis L. Strauss
- Strauss took office, Nov. 13.

Nov. 7, announced U.S. would continue suspension of nuclear testing
- The U.S.S.R. had tested nuclear weapons on Nov. 1 and Nov. 3. "If there is not shortly a corresponding renunciation by the Soviet Union, the United States will be obligated to reconsider its position," he added.

Nov. 10, announced U.S. would continue $900,000,000 yearly aid to Southeast Asia
- He presented a program of trade expansion, technical aid, and loans to the needy countries of the area in an address to the Colombo Plan Consultative Committee, Seattle, Wash.

Dec. 3, issued executive order transferring Jet Propulsion Laboratory, Pasadena, Cal., from defense department to NASA
- The National Aeronautics and Space Administration had also sought control of the Ballistic Missile Agency, Huntsville, Ala. His order continued army operation of the missile agency but permitted NASA use of the Alabama facility on a cooperative plan.

Dec. 9, received letter from Khrushchev asserting U.S.S.R. had ICBM with 8,500-mile range and compact hydrogen bomb
- The letter was delivered by Senator Hu-

bert H. Humphrey, who had met with the Soviet premier for eight hours in the Kremlin, Dec. 1.

Dec. 16, recorded Christmas message for broadcast from satellite
- The tape recording was placed aboard an Atlas missile that went into orbit from Cape Canaveral, Fla., Dec. 18.
- This message was the first broadcast from space to earth of a human voice.

1959

Jan. 3, issued proclamation of admission of Alaska as 49th state
- Alaska was the first of two states admitted during his term of office.

Jan. 3, issued executive order adding 49th state to flag, effective, July 4
- The new flag had seven staggered rows of seven stars each.

Jan. 3, signed executive order adding 49th star to presidential flag

Jan. 7, first session of 86th Congress
- The administration controlled neither the Senate nor the House of Representatives. The Democrats gained 15 Senate and 50 House seats. The Senate (98 members) consisted of 64 Democrats and 34 Republicans. The House (436 members) consisted of 283 Democrats and 153 Republicans.
- These were the largest majorities since the 75th Congress, 1937–1938.

Jan. 9, delivered his seventh State of the Union message to Congress

Jan. 19, submitted balanced budget message to Congress
- He estimated expenditures for the fiscal year ending June 30, 1960, at $77,030,000,-000, and receipts at $77,100,000,000, which would result in a surplus of $70,-000,000. The deficit for the previous year was $12,891,000,000, he said.

Jan. 20, urged cooperation of labor in fight against inflation
- In his annual economic report to Congress, he asked the cooperation of labor, management, and consumers, but stressed the "particularly critical role" of labor leaders.

Jan. 21, greeted President Arturo Frondizi of Argentina, White House

Jan. 28, sent special labor message to Congress
- He asked legislation to

. . . safeguard workers' funds in union treasuries against misuse; to protect the rights and freedoms of individual union members, including the basic right to free and secret election of officers; to advance true and responsible collective bargaining; to protect the public and innocent third parties from unfair and coercive practices such as boycotting and blackmail picketing.

Jan. 29, sent special farm message to Congress

• He asked legislation to end high price supports and suggested supports between 75 and 90 pecent of the average market prices during the past three years.

Feb. 4, scoffed at Soviet ICBM accuracy claim as propaganda

• The Soviet intercontinental missiles "cannot be stopped by any anti-aircraft weapons" and can carry nuclear warheads "precisely to any point on the globe," announced Marshal Rodion L. Malinovsky, Soviet minister of defense, Feb. 3.

Feb. 6, rejected Khrushchev invitation to visit Russia

• A White House statement discounted the sincerity of the invitation, which had been included in a hostile speech in Moscow, Feb. 5.

Feb. 6, asked Shah of Iran to reject new Soviet nonaggression treaty, sign economic and defense agreement with U.S.

• The Shah announced that Iran would sign the U.S. agreement, Feb. 21. Iran renounced the 1921 treaty with the U.S.S.R. that permitted the movement of Russian troops into Iran in the event of invasion by a third nation, Mar. 2.

Feb. 7, received Mayor Willy Brandt of West Berlin, White House

Feb. 8, White House announced his approval of $10,000,000 military aid to Indonesia

Feb. 12, sent special message to Congress in which he asked rise in U.S. contributions to World Bank and International Monetary Fund

• He urged legislation to increase the U.S. subscription to the World Bank by $3,175,-000,000, and the monetary fund by $1,-375,000,000.

Feb. 19–20, visited Mexico

• He flew to Acapulco for conferences with President Adolfo Lopez Mateos. They jointly announced an agreement to build the Diablo Dam on the Rio Grande, 150 miles west of San Antonio, Tex.

• This was the second of his three visits to Mexico while in office.

Feb. 25, said West would not "give an inch" in Berlin

• Khrushchev had rejected the proposal of a Big Four foreign ministers conference on Germany in a Kremlin speech, Feb. 24. Eisenhower said the Western allies would not

. . . give one single inch in the preservation of our rights and of discharging our responsibilities in this particular region, especially Berlin.

• Several proposals were made and rejected by both sides during the next month. The U.S.S.R. agreed, Mar. 30, to a Big Four foreign ministers conference in Geneva, to which advisers from East and West Germany were to be invited, May 11.

Mar. 10, issued executive order imposing mandatory controls on imports of crude or unfinished petroleum products except under department of interior license

Mar. 11, received President Jose Maria Lemus of El Salvador, White House

Mar. 16, expressed willingness to meet with Soviet leaders if foreign ministers conference proved successful

• In a TV-radio report to the nation, he said:
We shall continue to exercise our right of peaceful passage to and from West Berlin. We will not be the first to breach the peace; it is the Soviets who threaten the use of force to interfere with such free passage.

Mar. 18, signed Hawaii Statehood Act

Mar. 20–22, conferred on German situation with Prime Minister Macmillan, White House and Camp David, near Thurmont, Md.

Mar. 23, received King Hussein of Jordan, White House

Apr. 4, addressed North Atlantic Council, Washington, D.C.

• The council—the foreign ministers of the 15 NATO nations—ended its three-day meeting on the tenth anniversary of the signing of the North Atlantic Treaty. "Since NATO was formed, there has been no further Communist advance in Europe, either by political or military means," he said.

Apr. 14, dedicated Robert A. Taft Memorial Bell Tower, Capitol grounds, Washington, D.C.

Apr. 15, accepted resignation of Secretary of States Dulles, effective, Apr. 22

Apr. 18, appointed his second secretary of state, Christian A. Herter

• Herter took office, Apr. 22.

Apr. 23, appointed Dulles as special consultant to president

• He presented the commission to Dulles in Walter Reed Hospital, where the former secretary of state was under treatment for cancer. Dulles died at the hospital, May 24.

May 4, welcomed Sir Winston Churchill, White House

May 11, received King Baudouin of Belgium, White House

May 28, conferred with Big Four foreign ministers, White House

• The foreign ministers conference had opened in Geneva, May 11, and then recessed for the funeral of former Secretary of State Dulles, May 27. Eisenhower met with Foreign Ministers Selwyn Lloyd of Great Britain, Maurice Couve de Murville of France, and Andrei A. Gromyko of the Soviet Union, and Secretary of State Herter. Eisenhower urged continued efforts to break the impasse. The conference reopened in Geneva, remained deadlocked, and recessed indefinitely, Aug. 5.

June 8, addressed dinner for Republican members of Congress, Washington, D.C.

June 19, Senate rejected Lewis L. Strauss as secretary of commerce

• This was the first time in 34 years that the Senate had refused to concur with a president's wishes regarding membership in the cabinet. The Senate had rejected the appointment of Charles B. Warren as attorney general by President Coolidge, Mar. 10, 1925.

• Eisenhower was the last of five presidents whose nominees to the cabinet were rejected by the Senate.

• Strauss was the last of eight nominees to the cabinet who were rejected by the Senate. The vote was 49–46.

June 26, with Queen Elizabeth II, dedicated St. Lawrence Seaway, St. Lambert, Quebec, Canada

• This was the last of his three visits to Canada while in office.

June 29, visited Soviet Exhibition of Science, Technology and Culture, the Coli-

seum, New York City

• He was greeted by Frol R. Koslov, Soviet first deputy premier. The exhibition was formally opened later in the day by Koslov and Vice President Nixon.

June 30, conferred with Koslov, White House

June 30, Secretary of Commerce Strauss resigned

• Although unconfirmed, Strauss had served as secretary for seven months.

July 4, 49-star flag officially raised for first time, Independence Hall, Philadelphia, Pa.

• He had sent the flag, which was the original made by the quartermaster's department. The flag was later taken to Alaska, the 49th state, in an oak box made from the wood of an Independence Square tree.

July 8, called racial segregation "morally wrong"

• His press conference comment came after the Reverend Dr. Martin Luther King, Jr., had said that "the President should state not only that integration is the law of the land but that segregation is morally wrong."

July 21, *N.S. Savannah*, first atomic merchant ship, christened by Mrs. Eisenhower, Camden, N.J.

• The nuclear ship was named for the first steam vessel to cross the Atlantic, May-June, 1819.

Aug. 3, announced he would meet with Khrushchev in both Moscow and Washington in fall

Aug. 10, appointed his third secretary of commerce, Frederick H. Mueller

Aug. 21, issued proclamation of statehood of Hawaii

• He also exhibited for the first time the 50-star flag that would become official, July 4, 1960. The stars were arranged in nine staggered rows—five rows of six stars each and four of five stars each.

• Hawaii was the second of two states that were admitted during his term office.

Aug. 21, signed executive order adding 50th star to presidential flag

Aug. 26–27, visited West Germany, conferred with Chancellor Adenauer

• He was the second of five presidents who visited Germany while in office.

Aug. 27-Sept. 2, visited England, Scotland

• He conferred with Prime Minister Macmillan in London and at Chequers, the official country home of the British prime minister. He and Macmillan flew to Scotland, Aug. 28, for an overnight visit with Queen Elizabeth II at Balmoral Castle. He also gave a dinner in London for his wartime associates, including Sir Winston Churchill.

• He was the third of five presidents who visited England while in office.

• He was the only president who visited Scotland while in office.

• This was the first of his two visits to Scotland while in office.

Sept. 2–4, visited France, conferred with President de Gaulle

• He also conferred with Premier Antonio Segni of Italy in Paris.

• This was the second of his four visits to France while in office.

Sept. 4–7, visited Scotland

• He spend the weekend at Culzean Castle on the Firth of Clyde. His nine-room apartment in the castle was a gift given him by the Scottish people after World War II.

• This was the second of his two visits to Scotland while in office.

Sept. 7, returned to U.S.

• He said at the National Airport, Washington, that "every troublesome little problem" had been discussed during his trip. "I am quite certain that for the moment at least everything is going splendidly," he added.

Sept. 8, received report of Federal Commission on Civil Rights

• The commission recommended legislation to appoint temporary federal vote registrars where local officials failed to register Negro voters.

Sept. 9, vetoed civil functions appropriations bill

Sept. 10, civil functions appropriations act passed over his veto

• This was the first of his two vetoes that were overridden.

Sept. 14, hosted luncheon for Princess Beatrix of The Netherlands, White House

Sept. 15, received Premier Khrushchev, White House

• This was the first visit to the U.S. of a Russian head of state.

Sept. 15, first session of 86th Congress adjourned

Sept. 17, praised de Gaulle's Algerian proposal

• De Gaulle had offered the people of Al-

geria three choices—secession, autonomy, or integration—within four years of the restoration of peace. The French president favored integration, "out-and-out identification with France, such as is implied in the equality of rights."

Sept. 19, decribed congressional session as "disappointing"

• He criticized the Democratic majority for failure to increase interest ceilings on long-term government bonds; rejection of the administration farm program; Mutual Security Program cutbacks; and the passage of "extravagant" public works programs.

Sept. 22, issued executive order to treasury department to increase interest rates to four and one-half percent on Series E and Series H savings bonds

Sept. 25–27, conferred with Khrushchev, Camp David

• They agreed to reopen negotiations on Berlin and announced that "all outstanding international questions should be settled not by the application of force but by peaceful means through negotiations."

Sept. 28, told press conference Khrushchev had removed many of his objections to summit meeting

Sept. 30, received Premier Antonio Segni and Foreign Minister Giuseppe Pella of Italy, White House

Oct. 6, issued executive order that invoked Taft-Hartley Act in dock strike

• The seventy thousand members of the International Longshoremen's Association had gone on strike, Oct. 1, closing Atlantic and Gulf of Mexico ports.

Oct. 9, issued executive order that invoked Taft-Hartley Act in steel strike

• The United Steelworkers of America went out on strike against 12 companies, producers of 85 percent of U.S. steel, July 15. The steel strike, the sixth since World War II, lasted until Nov. 7, when the Supreme Court upheld the 80-day Taft-Hartley injunction. The 116-day stoppage was the longest nationwide steel strike.

Oct. 9, received President Adolfo Lopez Mateos of Mexico, White House

Oct. 21, announced transfer of Army Ballistics Missile Agency to NASA

Oct. 28, announced tentative agreement reached with Macmillan, Adenauer and de Gaulle regarding Western summit meeting in December

Oct. 29, approved New York City as site of 1964 World's Fair

Dec. 1, Secretary of Defense McElroy resigned

Dec. 2, appointed his third secretary of defense, Thomas S. Gates
- Gates was the last of Eisenhower's 21 cabinet members.

Dec. 3, departed on 19-day "peace and goodwill" tour of 11 countries on three continents

Dec. 4–5, visited Italy
- He conferred with President Giovanni Gronchi and Premier Segni in Rome and with Pope John XXIII at the Vatican.
- He was the third of six presidents who visited Italy while in office.
- He was the second of five presidents who met with Popes while in office.

Dec. 6–7, visited Turkey
- He conferred with President Celal Bayer and Premier Adnan Menderes in Ankara.
- He was the only president who visited Turkey while in office.
- He was the second of four presidents who visited Asia while in office.

Dec. 8, visited Pakistan
- He conferred with President Mohammed Ayub Khan in Karachi.
- He was the first of three presidents who visited Pakistan while in office.

Dec. 9, visited Afghanistan
- He conferred with King Mohammed Zahir in Kabul.
- He was the only president who visited Afghanistan while in office.

Dec. 9–14, visited India
- He conferred with President Rajendra Prasad and Prime Minister Nehru in New Delhi and also addressed the Indian Parliament.
- He was the first of two presidents who visited India while in office. The other was Nixon.

Dec. 14, visited Iran
- He conferred with Shah Mohammed Reza Pahlevi and addressed the Iranian Parliament in Teheran.
- He was the second of two presidents who visited Iran while in office. The other was Franklin D. Roosevelt.

Dec. 14–15, visited Greece
- He conferred with King Paul and Premier Constantine Karamanlis and addressed the Chamber of Deputies in Athens.
- Eisenhower was the only president who visited Greece while in office.

Dec. 17, visited Tunisia
- En route from Athens to Toulon aboard the cruiser, U.S.S. Des Moines, he flew by helicopter to Tunis for a breakfast meeting with President Habib Bourguiba.
- He was the only president who visited the Republic of Tunisia while in office.
- He was the second of two presidents who visited Tunis while in office. The other was Franklin D. Roosevelt, who met with General Eisenhower in the city when Tunisia was a French protectorate.
- He was the second of two presidents who visited Africa while in office. The other was Franklin D. Roosevelt.

Dec. 18–21, visited France, attended Western summit meeting
- He disembarked from the Des Moines at Toulon, where he trained to Paris. During the conferences with Macmillan, de Gaulle, and Adenauer, it was decided to invite Khrushchev to an East-West summit conference.
- This was the third of Eisenhower's four visits to France while in office.

Dec. 22, visited Spain
- He flew to Torrejon Air Base, near Madrid. He conferred with Generalissimo Francisco Franco in Madrid.
- He was the first of two presidents who visited Spain while in office. The other was Nixon.

Dec. 22, visited Morocco
- He conferred with King Mohammed V in Casablanca. It was announced that U.S. military forces would be withdrawn from Morocco by Jan. 1, 1964.
- He was the second of two presidents who visited Morocco while in office. The other was Franklin D. Roosevelt.

Dec. 22, returned to U.S.

Dec. 23, during Christmas message, explained purpose of his trip had been "to improve the climate in which diplomacy might work more successfully"

Dec. 29, announced U.S. would end voluntary ban on nuclear testing, Dec. 31
- The failure of East-West talks in Geneva led to the decision. He said:
  Although we consider ourselves free to resume nuclear weapon testing, we shall not resume nuclear weapons tests without announcing our intention in advance of any resumption.

1960

Jan. 6, second session of 86th Congress

Jan. 7, delivered his eighth State of the Union message to Congress

Jan. 18, submitted budget message to Congress

• He estimated expenditures for the fiscal year ending June 30, 1961, at $79,800,000,-000, and receipts at $84,000,000,000, which would result in a surplus of $4,200,-000,000. To achieve the surplus, he proposed legislation to raise the postal rate by one cent and the gasoline tax by a half-cent.

Jan. 19, attended signing of U.S.-Japanese security treaty, White House

• This treaty superseded the U.S.-Japanese treaty of Sept. 8, 1951.

Jan. 20, submitted economic report to Congress

• He asked repeal of the four and one-half percent interest rate ceiling on government bonds.

Jan. 26, reiterated U.S. Cuban policy

• Premier Fidel Castro had delivered a lengthy TV-radio harangue, Jan. 19–20, in which he accused the U.S. of hostility toward Cuba. He expressed regret at Castro's "unwarranted attacks" during a press conference but underlined U.S. policy against retaliation or intervention.

Feb. 3, stated U.S. should share nuclear weapons with allies

Feb. 9, sent special farm message to Congress

• He asked for reexamination of the price support programs. "I will approve any constructive solution that the Congress wishes to develop," he said.

Feb. 16, sent special foreign aid message to Congress

• He asked for $2,175,000,000 in economic assistance and $2,000,000,000 in military aid.

Feb. 17, described U.S. defenses as "awesome"

• Democratic leaders had long accused the administration of misleading statements about the strength of national defenses. During a press conference, he said, "Our defense is not only strong, it is awesome, and it is respected elsewhere."

Feb. 18, issued executive order to attorney general to seize ships and aircraft carrying arms and munitions to Cuba and other Latin American nations

Feb. 21, again denied existence of "missile gap"

• He said:
> We have forged a trustworthy shield of peace—an indestructible force of incalculable power, ample for today and constantly developing to meet the needs of tomorrow.

Feb. 22, departed on goodwill tour of Latin America

Feb. 22–23, visited Puerto Rico

• He was the first of three presidents who visited the Commonwealth of Puerto Rico while in office.

• He was the fifth of seven presidents who visited Puerto Rico while in office.

• This was the first of this two trips to Puerto Rico while in office.

Feb. 23–25, visited Brazil

• He flew to Brasilia, where he was greeted by President Juscelino Kubitschek. He and Kubitschek signed the Declaration of Brasilia and proclaimed a "hemispheric crusade for economic development." He addressed a joint session of the Brazilian senate and chamber of deputies in Rio de Janeiro, Feb. 24. He visited Sao Paulo, Feb. 25.

• He was the last of three presidents who visited Brazil while in office.

• He was the third of five presidents who visited South America while in office.

• He was the second of three presidents who visited four foreign continents while in office.

Feb. 26–28, visited Argentina

• He conferred with President Arturo Frondizi and addressed the Argentine congress in Buenos Aires. He and Frondizi issued the Declaration of San Carlos de Bariloche in that resort city on Lake Nahuel Huapi, Feb. 28.

• He was the second of two presidents who visited Argentina while in office. The other was Franklin D. Roosevelt.

Feb. 29-Mar. 1, visited Chile

• He conferred with President Jorge Alessandri and addressed the Chilean congress in Santiago.

• He was the only president who visited Chile while in office.

Mar. 2–3, visited Uruguay

• He conferred with President Benito Nardone and addressed the Uruguayan congress in Montevideo.

• He was the second of three presidents who visited Uruguay while in office.

Mar. 3–7, visited Puerto Rico

• This was the second of his two visits to Puerto Rico while in office.

Mar. 7, returned to Washington, D.C.

Mar. 10, conferred with Premier David Ben-Gurion of Israel, White House

Mar. 15, conferred with Chancellor Adenauer of West Germany, White House

• He and Adenauer issued a joint statement of reaffirmation of their "determination to continue their efforts to achieve the reunification of Germany in peace and freedom."

Mar. 16, endorsed candidacy for president of Vice President Nixon

Mar. 16, proposed biracial conferences throughout South to ease tensions caused by Negro sit-in campaigns

• Organized sit-ins to protest segregation had begun, Feb. 1, in Greensboro, N.C., lunchcounters and quickly spread throughout the South. He said:

> I am deeply sympathetic with the efforts of any group to enjoy the rights . . . of equality that they are guaranteed by the Constitution.

Apr. 5, received President Alberto Lleras Camargo of Colombia, White House

Apr. 16, released economic growth report on 1960's

• The report of the Cabinet Committee on Price Stability for Economic Growth predicted "great expansion" during the next ten years. He called the report "encouraging," but warned against complacency.

Apr. 19, issued executive order granting ten percent wage increases to skilled and semiskilled Panamanian workers in Canal Zone

Apr 22–24, conferred with President de Gaulle, Washington and Camp David

Apr. 27, rejected Khrushchev theory on Berlin

• The Soviet premier had contended that Western rights in Berlin could be invalidated if the U.S.S.R. signed a separate peace treaty with East Germany. Eisenhower countered with a statement that the U.S. would not give up its "juridicial position" in Berlin.

May 4, signed agreement to sell seventeen million tons of grain to India

May 5, informed of Khrushchev announce-

ment of downing of U-2 plane over Russia

• The U-2 reconnaissance flights had begun in 1956. Eisenhower had been informed that one of the planes was overdue and presumed lost, May 1, but his advisers were certain that the Soviets would never admit their inability over a period of four years to halt the "spy plane" flights.

• Khrushchev announced to the Supreme Soviet, the two-chamber legislature, that the American plane had been shot down, May 1. Confident that self-destroying mechanisms in the U-2 had obliterated any evidence of espionage—including its pilot —NASA announced that a weather plane was missing in Turkey, and the state department added that "no deliberate attempt to violate Soviet air space" had ever been made.

May 6, signed Civil Rights Act of 1960

May 7, informed of Khrushchev announcement of capture of U-2 pilot

• Khrushchev told the Soviet legislature that the U-2 had been shot down by rocket at an altitude of sixty-five thousand feet near Sverdlovsk and that the captured pilot, Francis Gary Powers, had confessed to espionage. The fact that the "uninjured pilot of our reconnaissance plane, along with much of his equipment intact, was in Soviet hands," Eisenhower later wrote, was "unbelievable."

• The state department released a statement that

> . . . in endeavoring to obtain information now concealed behind the Iron Curtain, a flight over Soviet territory was probably undertaken by an unarmed civilian U-2 plane.

May 7, announced plans to resume underground nuclear tests

May 9, Secretary of State Herter announced U-2 program had been ordered by President Eisenhower

• Khruschev warned of rocket retaliation against those countries that served as bases for U-2 planes. The U.S. would defend its allies, said a state department spokesman, May 10.

May 11, defended U-2 flights as "distasteful but vital"

• He said:

> No one wants another Pearl Harbor. This means that we must have knowledge of military forces and preparations around the world.

Secrecy in the Soviet Union makes this essential.

•However, he ordered future U-2 flights cancelled.

May 14, signed Mutual Security Authorization Act

•This act provided appropriations totalling $1,366,200,000, which was $88,700,000 less than requested.

May 14, departed for Paris summit conference

May 15, met with President de Gaulle and Prime Minister Macmillan, Elysee Palace, Paris

•He was informed that Khrushchev would not attend the summit conference until he apologized for the U-2 flights, ended the flights, and punished those responsible. He told de Gaulle and Macmillan that the flights had been halted, but refused to meet the other conditions.

May 16, met with Khrushchev, de Gaulle, and Macmillan, Elysee Palace

•Khrushchev refused to acknowledge this meeting as the opening session of the summit conference. He maintained that it was a preliminary meeting to determine whether the summit conference would be held. The Soviet leader repeated his three demands and added that the invitation to President Eisenhower to visit the U.S.S.R., June 10–19, had been withdrawn.

•In reply, Eisenhower restated the reasons for the overflights and informed Khrushchev that the flights would not be resumed. He said:

I have come to Paris to seek agreements with the Soviet Union which would eliminate the necessity for all forms of espionage, including overflights. I see no reason to use this incident to disrupt the conference.

•He added that he planned to submit to the UN a proposal for a UN aerial surveillance system in all nations prepared to accept such inspection.

•This was the last of his four visits to France while in office.

May 17, met with de Gaulle and Macmillan, Elysee Palace

•Khrushchev refused to attend.

May 19–20, visited Portugal

•He conferred with President Americo Tomas and Premier Antonio de Oliveira Salazar in Lisbon.

•He was the first of three presidents who visited Portugal while in office.

May 20, returned to U.S.

May 25, reported to nation on U-2 incident and abortive summit conference

•He again called the overflights necessary and blamed Khrushchev for wrecking the Paris Conference. During his TV-radio talk he said:

We must continue businesslike dealings with the Soviet leaders on outstanding issues and improve the contacts between our own and the Soviet peoples, making clear that the path of reason is still open if the Soviets will but use it.

June 3, conferred with Prime Minister Diefenbaker of Canada, White House

June 8, signed military construction authorization act

•This act provided appropriations totalling $1,185,320,000 for military construction within and outside the U.S.

June 12, departed on Asian tour

June 12–13, visited Alaska

•He flew to Anchorage.

•He was the first of three presidents who visited the 49th state while in office.

•He was the third of five presidents who visited Alaska while in office.

June 13, made refueling stop, Wake Island

•He was the second of two presidents who visited Wake Island while in office. The other was Truman.

•This was the first of his two visits to Wake Island while in office.

June 14–16, visited Philippines

•He was greeted by President Carlos Garcia and addressed a joint session of the Philippine congress in Manila.

•While in Manila, anti-American riots occurred in Tokyo. He was informed, June 16, that the Japanese government had "postponed" its invitation for his visit.

•He was the first of three presidents who visited the Philippines while in office.

June 16, 23rd Amendment submitted to states

•This amendment proposed presidential voting rights for residents of the District of Columbia.

• See Constitution, page 645.

June 16, sailed from Manila for Taiwan aboard *U.S.S. St. Paul*

June 18–19, visited Formosa

•He conferred with Generalissimo Chiang

Kai-shek in Taipei, Taiwan. The Chinese Communists subjected the offshore islands of Matsu and Quemoy to heavy bombardment prior to his arrival and at his departure "to show the great Chinese people's contempt and scorn for Eisenhower."
•He was the only president who visited Formosa while in office.

June 19, flew to Okinawa
•He conferred with Lieutenant General Donald P. Booth, the American high commissioner, and Seisaku Ota, chief representative of the Ryukyuan people, in Naha.
•He was the only president who visited Okinawa while in office.

June 19–20, visited Korea
•He conferred with Prime Minister Huh Chung and addressed the Korean general assembly in Seoul.
•He was the first of two presidents who visited Korea while in office. The other was Johnson.

June 20, made refueling stop, Wake Island
•This was the second of his two visits to Wake Island while in office.

June 20–25, visited Hawaii
•He was the first of three presidents who visited the 50th state while in office.
•He was the third of five presidents who visited Hawaii while in office.

June 26, returned to Washington, D.C.

June 30, vetoed seven and one-half percent federal employees pay increase bill

July 1, federal employees pay increase act passed over his veto
•This was the second of his two vetoes that were overridden.

July 6, issued proclamation cancelling 95 percent of Cuban sugar exports to U.S. during remainder of 1960
•The quota slash, which involved 856,000 tons of sugar, was in answer to the Castro government's "deliberate policy of hostility toward the United States," he said.

July 9, warned U.S.S.R. "establishment of a regime dominated by international communism in the Western Hemisphere" would never be permitted
•Khrushchev had threatened to retaliate with rockets if the U.S. intervened militarily in Cuba.

July 14, approved state department announcement that Monroe Doctrine was as valid as when declared in 1823.
•Khrushchev had said that the Monroe Doctrine was dead, July 12.

July 20, announced budget surplus of $1,068,000,000 for fiscal year that ended June 30

July 21, announced he had instructed Ambassador Henry Cabot Lodge to request early meeting of UN Disarmament Commission
•The U.S. proposed to shut down its uranium and plutonium production plants and to transfer 33 tons of U-235 to an international stockpile if the U.S.S.R. would do likewise, Aug. 16. The Soviets rejected both propositions.

July 26, addressed Republican national convention, Chicago, Ill.

Aug. 1, met with Republican presidential and vice-presidential candidates, Richard M. Nixon and Henry Cabot Lodge, Summer White House, Newport, R.I.

Aug 12, his prerecorded message bounced off *Echo I* satellite
•The message was sent by radio from Goldstone, Cal., and received in Holmdel, N.J.
•*Echo I* was the first communications satellite to orbit the earth.

Aug. 19, U-2 pilot, Francis Gary Powers, convicted of espionage, sentenced to ten years' "deprivation of freedom," Moscow
•Eisenhower expressed regret at the "severity" of Powers' sentence.

Sept. 1, second session of 86th Congress adjourned

Sept. 2, signed Mutual Security Appropriation Act
•This act provided $3,722,350,000 for the fiscal year ending June 30, 1962.

Sept. 17, issued executive order to fly Panamanian flag and U.S. flag in Canal Zone plaza

Sept. 22, addressed UN General Assembly, New York City

Sept. 29, addressed Republican rally, Chicago, Ill.
•The campaign speech was seen and heard by thirty-eight thousand Republicans at dinners in 36 cities by closed-circuit television.

Oct. 2, rejected appeal by neutralist leaders to meet with Khrushchev
•In reply to a UN resolution by Prime Minister Nehru of India, President Sukarno of Indonesia, President Nasser of the United Arab Republic, President Tito of Yugoslavia, and President Kwame Nkrumah of Ghana, he wrote:

If the Soviet Union seriously desires a reduction in tensions it can readily pave the way for useful negotiations by actions in the United Nations and elsewhere.

•Khrushchev said he would meet with Eisenhower if the U.S. apologized for "unprecedented treacherous acts," Oct. 4.

•Nehru withdrew the neutralist resolution, Oct. 6.

Oct. 14, celebrated his 70th birthday

•He was the last of 16 presidents who lived to be 70.

Oct. 19, approved ten-year U.S.-Canadian Columbia River water power and storage agreement

Oct. 24, with President Adolfo Lopez Mateos of Mexico, announced imminent construction of Amistad Dam on Rio Grande, Ciudad Acuna, Mexico

•This was the last of his three visits to Mexico while in office.

•This was the last of his 16 trips outside the U.S. while in office. Only Franklin D. Roosevelt made more trips outside the U.S. while in office, 24.

•Eisenhower was the president who visited the most foreign countries while in office, 28.

Oct. 28, addressed Republican rally, Philadelphia, Pa.

•In the closing days of the campaign, he added several cities to his speaking schedule. He spoke in Cleveland and Pittsburgh, Nov. 1, and joined the Republican candidates for a series of appearances in New York City, Nov. 2.

Nov. 1, stated U.S. would take necessary steps to defend naval base at Guantanamo, Cuba

Nov. 8, election day

• *See* Election of 1960, pages 523–524.

Nov. 16, issued executive order to all federal agencies to minimize foreign spending

•This order was brought on by the drastic outflow of gold. Since 1957, the U.S. had spent $10,000,000,000 abroad in excess of funds derived from foreign sources.

Nov. 16, ordered naval air and surface units to patrol Central American waters off Guatemala and Nicaragua

•Guatemala and Nicaragua had requested U.S. assistance after uprisings in both countries, allegedly led by Castro sympathizers.

Dec. 2, issued executive order providing $1,000,000 of Mutual Security funds for Cuban refugee relief and resettlement in Florida

Note: The official population, according to the 18th census, was 179,323,175.

1961

Jan. 3, announced U.S. had severed diplomatic relations with Cuba

•He said that the Castro government had demanded the reduction of state department personnel in Cuba to 11 persons, adding:

> This calculated action on the part of the Castro Government is only the latest of a long series of harassments, baseless accusations and vilification. There is a limit to what the United States in self-respect can endure. That limit has now been reached.

Jan. 3, first session of 87th Congress

•The Democrats controlled both the Senate and the House of Representatives. The Republicans gained two Senate and 23 House seats. The Senate (100 members) consisted of 64 Democrats and 36 Republicans. The House (437 members) consisted of 261 Democrats and 176 Republicans.

Jan. 16, sent his ninth and last State of the Union message to Congress

•In his final State of the Union message, he reviewed his eight years in office.

Jan. 16, submitted his final budget message to Congress

•He estimated expenditures for the fiscal year ending June 30, 1962, at $80,900,000,-000 and receipts at $82,300,000,000, which would result in a surplus of $1,400,-000,000.

Jan. 17, gave farewell address on TV-radio, White House

•He warned:

> In the councils of government, we must guard against the acquisition of unwarranted influence, whether sought or unsought, by the military-industrial complex.

Jan. 18, recommended earlier inauguration at final press conference

•The requirement that an outgoing president submit State of the Union and budget messages that do not necessarily agree with the views of the incoming chief executive is "a little bit silly," he said, adding:

> I think that we ought to get a Constitutional amendment to change the time of the inauguration and to give dates for election and assumption of office in such a fashion that a new President ought to have at least 80 days or something of that kind before he meets his first Congress.

THE FORMER PRESIDENT

Jan. 20, 1961, attended inauguration of Kennedy, retired to Gettysburg, Pa.
- Eisenhower's age upon leaving office was 70 years, 98 days.
- He was the oldest man to serve as president.

Mar. 22, 1961, act signed by President Kennedy restored his rank of general of army

Oct. 3, 1961, warned against overemphasis on race with U.S.S.R. to moon
- In a secret speech to the Naval War College, he said he believed "to make the so-called race to the moon a major element in our struggle to show that we are superior to the Russians is getting our eyes off the right target." He added that "some day humans are going to circle the moon, take some pictures of it, and maybe even get to a planet and back if there is time."

Nov. 10, 1961, met with former President Truman, Harry S. Truman Library, Independence, Mo.
- This was their first significant conversation since Nov. 18, 1952, when, as president-elect, he had been briefed by Truman at the White House. They had met briefly at the funeral of General George C. Marshall in 1959.

Nov. 18, 1961, attended funeral of Representative Sam Rayburn, Bonham, Tex.

May 1, 1962, dedicated Dwight D. Eisenhower Library, Abilene, Kan.
- The library, on Southeast Fourth Street, two miles south of the Abilene exit from Interstate 70, was erected with private funds and given to the federal government. It is administered by the National Archives and Records Service, General Services Administration. It is open to the public daily except Thanksgiving, Christmas and New Year's Day, 9 A.M. to 5 P.M. The library is across the street from the Eisenhower Museum and his boyhood home, where he lived from 1891 to 1910.

The museum and the home, including their contents, were given to the federal government by the Eisenhower Foundation in 1966. Admission to the exhibit areas of the library and the museum is by joint ticket: adults, 50 cents; children under 16, free. There is no admission charge to enter the Eisenhower home.

Nov. 19, 1963, rededicated national cemetery, Gettysburg, Pa.
- This was the 100th anniversary of the dedication by Lincoln.

Oct. 14, 1965, celebrated his 75th birthday
- He was the last of ten presidents who lived to be 75.

Oct. 14, 1965, first volume of his presidential memoirs, *Mandate for Change*, published by Doubleday, New York City
- It sold more than 300,000 copies.

Nov. 9, 1965, suffered second heart attack, Augusta, Ga.
- At nearby Fort Gordon Army Hospital, doctors described the mild attack as a coronary insufficiency.

Nov. 10, 1965, suffered third heart attack, Fort Gordon Army Hospital
- This was a more severe attack than that of the previous day—a myocardial infarction. He had recovered sufficiently to be transferred to Walter Reed Army Medical Center, Washington, Nov. 23, where he completed his recuperation.

Apr. 20, 1966, his book, *Waging Peace*, published by Doubleday, New York City
- This second volume of his presidential memoirs sold more than eighty thousand copies.

July 1, 1966, with Mrs. Eisenhower, celebrated 50th wedding anniversary.
- He was the third of four presidents who celebrated their golden wedding anniversaries.

Nov. 14, 1966, Mrs. Eisenhower's 70th birthday
- She was the last of 16 first ladies who lived to be 70.

• She was the last of 17 wives of presidents who lived to be 70.

June 16, 1967, his book, *At Ease: Stories I Tell to Friends*, published by Doubleday, New York City

• This anecdotal account of his early years and rise to national prominence, prior to his nomination in 1952, sold more than 2,335,000 copies.

Feb. 6, 1968, scored hole-in-one, Palm Springs, Cal.

• An avid golfer before, during and after his term of office, he usually scored in the nineties, but frequently dipped into the eighties in 1963–1965. This was his only hole-in-one.

Apr. 29, 1968, suffered fourth heart attack, Palm Desert, Cal.

• He was treated at March Air Force Base Hospital until May 14, when he was transferred to Walter Reed Army Medical Center, Washington.

• He suffered his fifth heart attack in the hospital, June 15; his sixth, Aug. 6, and his seventh, Aug. 16. His condition was described as "extremely critical," but he made slow but steady improvement.

Feb. 22, 1969, acute intestinal obstruction developed

• Surgery to relieve the obstruction was performed, Feb. 23. His doctors said that the obstruction was caused by scar tissue that had built up either from his 1923 appendectomy or his 1966 gall bladder operation.

Feb. 28, 1969, contracted pneumonia

Mar. 15, 1969, suffered congestive heart failure

DEATH

Date of death: Mar. 28, 1969

Place of death: Washington D.C.

• Eisenhower was the last of seven presidents who died in Washington.

• He was the last of eight presidents who lay in state in the Capitol Rotunda.

Age at death: 78 years, 165 days

• He lived eight years, 67 days, after the completion of his term.

Cause of death: Heart disease

Place of burial: Abilene, Kan.

• He was the only president who was buried in Kansas.

THE VICE PRESIDENT (36th)

Full name: Richard Milhous Nixon

• *See* pages 581–634.

• Nixon was the only vice president who was born in California.

• He was the first vice president who was born in the 20th century.

• He was the second youngest vice president. The youngest was Breckinridge.

• He was the only vice president who was a Quaker.

• He was the last of 21 vice presidents who served in the House of Representatives before their terms of office.

• He was the 16th of 17 vice presidents who served in the Senate before their terms of office.

• He was the last of ten vice presidents who served in both the House of Representatives and the Senate before their terms of office.

• He was the last of 12 vice presidents who served in both the House of Representatives and the Senate.

• He was the last of seven vice presidents who were elected to second terms.

• He was the last of five vice presidents who served two terms.

• He was the last of three vice presidents who served eight years:

• Eisenhower and Nixon were the 38th of 41 president-vice president teams.

• They were the last of five president-vice president teams that were reelected.

• They were the only Republican president-vice president team that was reelected.

• Nixon was the only vice president who represented California.

• He was the 14th of 15 vice presidents who were Republican.

THE CABINET

State: John Foster Dulles of New York, Jan. 21, 1953, to Apr. 22, 1959

• Christian Archibald Herter of Massachusetts, Apr. 22, 1959, to Jan. 20, 1961

Treasury: George Magoffin Humphrey of Ohio, Jan. 21, 1953, to July 29, 1957

• Robert Bernard Anderson of Connecticut, July 29, 1957, to Jan. 20, 1961

Defense: Charles Erwin Wilson of Michigan, Jan. 28, 1953, to Oct. 8, 1957

•Neil Hesler McElroy of Ohio, Oct. 9, 1957,
to Dec. 1, 1959
•Thomas Sovereign Gates, Jr., of Pennsyl-
vania, Dec. 2, 1959, to Jan. 20, 1961
Attorney General: Herbert Brownell, Jr., of
New York, Jan. 21, 1953, to Nov. 8, 1957
•William Pierce Rogers of Maryland, Nov.
8, 1957, to Jan. 1961
Postmaster General: Arthur Ellsworth Sum-
merfield of Michigan, Jan. 21, 1953, to Jan.
20, 1961
Interior: Douglas McKay of Oregon, Jan. 21,
1953, to Apr. 15, 1956
•Frederick Andrew Seaton of Nebraska,
June 5, 1956, to Jan. 20, 1961
Agriculture: Ezra Taft Benson of Utah, Jan.
21, 1953, to Jan. 20, 1961
Commerce: Sinclair Weeks of Massachu-
setts, Jan. 20, 1953, to Nov. 10, 1958
•Lewis Lichtenstein Strauss of New York,
Nov. 13, 1958, to June 30, 1959; rejected
by Senate, June 19, 1959
•Frederick Henry Mueller of Michigan,
Aug. 10, 1959, to Jan. 20, 1961
Labor: Martin Patrick Durkin of Illinois, Jan.
21, 1953, to Sept. 10, 1953
•James Paul Mitchell of New Jersey, Oct. 9,

1953, to Jan. 20, 1961
Health, Education and Welfare: Oveta Culp
Hobby of Texas, Apr. 11, 1953, to July 31,
1955
•Marion Bayard Folsom of New York, Aug.
1, 1955, to July 31, 1958
•Arthur Sherwood Flemming of Ohio, Aug.
1, 1958, to Jan. 20, 1961

THE SUPREME COURT

Chief Justice: Earl Warren of California, appointed, Sept. 30, 1853; confirmed, Mar. 1,
1954
Associate Justices: John Marshall Harlan of
New York, appointed, Nov. 10, 1954; confirmed Mar. 16, 1955
•William Joseph Brennan of New Jersey, appointed, Sept. 29, 1956; confirmed, Mar.
19, 1957
•Charles Evans Whittaker of Missouri, appointed, Mar. 2, 1957; confirmed, Mar. 19,
1957
•Potter Stewart of Ohio, appointed, Oct. 7,
1958; confirmed, May 5, 1959

Thirty-fifth President

JOHN FITZGERALD KENNEDY

Full name: John Fitzgerald Kennedy
•He was the last of five presidents named John.
•He was the 17th of 19 presidents who had middle initials or middle names.
Date of birth: May 29, 1917
•He was the second of two presidents who were born in May. The other was Truman.
•He was the first president who was born in the 20th century.
Place of birth: Brookline, Mass.
•He was the last of three presidents who were born in Massachusetts.
•His birthplace, 83 Beals Street, is privately owned. It is not open to the public.
Family lineage: Irish
•He was the only president who was of Irish ancestry.
Religious denomination: Roman Catholic
•He was the only president who was a Catholic.
Colleges: Princeton University, Princeton, N.J., and Harvard University, Cambridge, Mass.
•He was the last of three presidents who went to Princeton.
•He was the last of five presidents who went to Harvard.

•He was the 25th of 27 presidents who attended college.
Date of graduation: June 20, 1940, Bachelor of Science cum laude
•He was the 19th of 21 presidents who were graduated from college.
•He was the last of five presidents who were graduated from Harvard.

PARENTS AND SIBLINGS

Father's name: Joseph Patrick Kennedy
Date of birth: Sept. 6, 1888
Place of birth: Boston, Mass.
Occupations: Real estate owner, financier, banker, diplomat
•Kennedy's father was ambassador to the Court of St. James's, 1937–1941.
•Kennedy was the last of three presidents whose fathers had been ministers plenipotentiary or ambassadors.
Date of death: Nov. 18, 1969
•Kennedy was the last of six presidents whose fathers lived to see their sons' inauguration or oath-taking days.
•Joseph Kennedy was the second of two fathers of presidents who attended the cere-

monies. The other was John Coolidge.
- Kennedy was the second of two presidents whose fathers survived them. The other was Harding.

Place of death: Hyannis Port, Mass.
Age at death: 81 years, 73 days

Mother's name: Rose Fitzgerald Kennedy
Date of birth: July 22, 1890
Place of birth: Boston, Mass.
Date of marriage: Oct. 7, 1914
Place of marriage: Boston, Mass.
Children: 9; 5 daughters, 4 sons
- Joseph was born in 1915; John Fitzgerald in 1917; Rosemary in 1919; Kathleen in 1920; Eunice in 1921; Patricia in 1924; Robert Francis in 1925; Jean in 1928; and Edward Moore in 1932.
- Kennedy was the last of seven presidents who came from families of nine children.
- He was the ninth of ten presidents who were second children.

Notes: He was the last of ten presidents whose mothers lived to see their sons' inauguration or oath-taking days.
- Mrs. Kennedy was the last of four mothers of presidents who attended the ceremonies.
- Kennedy was the last of three presidents whose mothers survived them.

MARRIAGE

Date of marriage: Sept. 12, 1953
Place of marriage: Newport, R.I.
- Kennedy was the only president who was married in Rhode Island.

Age at marriage: 36 years, 106 days
- He was the last of six presidents who were married in their thirties.

Years married: 10 years, 71 days

Wife's name: Jacqueline Lee Bouvier Kennedy
- She was called Jackie.

- She was the 31st of 33 first ladies.
- She was the 38th of 40 wives of presidents.

Date of birth: July 28, 1929
- She was the last of three first ladies who were born in July.
- She was the last of four wives of presidents who were born in July.

Place of birth: Southampton, N.Y.
- She was the last of six first ladies who were born in New York.
- She was the last of seven wives of presidents who were born in New York.

Wife's mother: Janet Lee Bouvier
Wife's father: John Vernon Bouvier, stockbroker

Age at marriage: 24 years, 46 days
- She was the 24th of 26 first ladies who were married in their twenties.
- She was the 28th of 30 wives of presidents who were married in their twenties.

Years younger than husband: 12 years, 60 days

Children: 3; 2 sons, 1 daughter
- Caroline Bouvier was born on Nov. 27, 1957; John Fitzgerald on Nov. 25, 1960; and Patrick Bouvier on Aug. 7, 1963. Patrick Bouvier died in infancy, Aug. 9, 1963.
- Kennedy was the last of seven presidents who had three children.
- He was the last of 19 presidents who had both male and female children.
- He was the 28th of 30 presidents who had children.

Notes: She was the last of 21 first ladies who survived their husbands.
- She was the last of 23 wives of presidents who survived their husbands.
- Mrs. Kennedy married Aristotle Socrates Onassis, a Greek shipping executive, considered one of the wealthiest men in the world, Oct. 20, 1968.
- She was the second of two first ladies who remarried. The other was Frances Cleveland.
- She was the second of two wives of presidents who remarried.

EARLY YEARS

1922–1931, attended private schools in Brookline, Mass.; Riverdale, Bronx, N.Y.; and New Milford, Mass.
1931–1935, attended Choate School, Wallingford, Conn.

- Kennedy ranked 64th in his graduating class of 112 members.

Summer, 1935, attended London School of Economics, London, England
- While in London, he contracted jaundice.

Sept. 23, 1935, entered Princeton University, Princeton, N.J.
- His illness delayed his entrance, and a recurrence of the ailment caused him to drop out of college, Dec. 12.

Sept. 5, 1936, entered Harvard University, Cambridge, Mass.

May 29, 1938, received $1,000,000 trust fund from father on 21st birthday

1939, toured Europe
- He did not attend Harvard during the second semester of his junior year. He served as secretary to his father, who was U.S. ambassador to the Court of St. James's, and traveled throughout Europe, from France to Russia. He was in London when Germany invaded Poland, Sept. 1.

June 20, 1940, was graduated from Harvard University

Fall, 1940, studied briefly at Stanford University Graduate School of Business Administration, Palo Alto, Cal.

1940, his first book, *Why England Slept*, published by Funk, New York City
- This book was an expansion of his senior thesis at Harvard, an analysis of England's lack of preparation for World War II.
- He was the 19th of 21 presidents who wrote books that were published during their lifetimes.

Oct. 5, 1941, commissioned as ensign, U.S. Navy
- He was not called for duty until 1942, and attended PT boat training school.
- He was the first of three presidents who served in the U.S. Navy.
- He was the second of four presidents who served in World War II.
- He was the 19th of 21 presidents who served in the military during wartime.

March, 1943, sailed for South Pacific
- He assumed command of the PT-109 in April in the Solomon Islands. His rank was lieutenant (j.g.).

Aug. 2, 1943, PT-109 rammed and sunk by Japanese destroyer, *Amagiri*, Solomon Islands
- Two of the 13 crew members went down with the stern section of the PT boat. He

was thrown backward against the wall of the cockpit by the impact. He succeeded in marshalling the survivors, only one of whom was seriously injured. When the floating forward section seemed about to sink, they swam to the nearest islet. He towed the injured man by a life preserver strap during the four-hour swim.
- When he and the crew swam to a larger island across a two-mile inlet, Aug. 4, he again towed the injured crew member. The following day he and another of the men swam to a nearby island, where they found a case of hard candy on a wrecked Japanese vessel. When they returned they were met by a group of natives. He scratched a message on the shell of a cocoanut, which the natives carried to Allied agents in the area.
- He and his crew were rescued, Aug. 8.
- He received the Purple Heart, the Navy Medal, and the Marine Medal for this action.
- He was the last of four presidents who were wounded or injured in action.

December, 1943, returned to U.S.
- He was hospitalized for malaria and a back ailment. The injuries he suffered in the ramming of the PT-109 aggravated a back ailment sustained during a school football game.

1944, underwent disc operation, Chelsea Naval Hospital, near Boston, Mass.

April, 1945, discharged from U.S. Navy

1945, worked as reporter, International News Service
- Among his assignments was the first United Nations meeting in San Francisco, Cal., Apr. 24.
- He was the last of three presidents who were newspapermen.

1945, edited limited edition of *As We Remember Joe*, privately printed tribute to his brother, Joseph P. Kennedy, Jr.
- His older brother, a Navy pilot, was killed in action over England, Aug. 12, 1944. The edition of 150 copies was distributed to relatives and friends.

NATIONAL PROMINENCE

Nov. 5, 1946, elected to House of Representatives
- Kennedy was the 16th of 17 presidents

who were elected to the House.

Jan. 3, 1947, took seat in House of Representatives

•Twice reelected, he served in the 80th, 81st, and 82nd congresses.

•He was the 16th of 17 presidents who served in the House.

Nov. 4, 1952, elected to Senate

•He defeated Senator Henry Cabot Lodge by seventy thousand votes.

•He was the 15th of 16 presidents who were elected to the Senate.

•He was the tenth of 11 presidents who were elected both to the House of Representatives and the Senate.

Jan. 3, 1953, took seat in Senate

•He was the 14th of 15 presidents who served in the Senate.

•He was the ninth of ten presidents who served in both the House and the Senate.

Sept. 12, 1953, married Jacqueline Lee Bouvier, Newport, R.I.

October, 1954, underwent operation for spinal fusion, Hospital for Special Surgery, New York City

•The condition of his back had deteriorated to the point that he had to use crutches. The operation was only partially successful; a second operation was necessary in February, 1955.

Jan. 1, 1956, his second book, *Profiles in Courage*, published by Harper, New York City

•He had researched and written the book during his long convalescence from the spinal operations. A bestseller, the book was awarded the Pulitzer Prize for Biography, 1957.

•He was the only president who won a Pulitzer Prize.

Aug. 17, 1956, unsuccessful candidate for nomination as vice president, Democratic national convention, Chicago, Ill.

•He showed surprising strength but lost to Senator Estes Kefauver of Tennessee when votes were switched after the second ballot.

Nov. 27, 1957, his only daughter born

•The girl was named Caroline Bouvier Kennedy.

Nov. 4, 1958, reelected to Senate

July 14, 1960, nominated for president, Democratic national convention, Los Angeles, Cal.

•He was nominated on the first ballot.

Nov. 8, 1960, election day

• *See* Election of 1960, below.

Nov. 25, 1960, his first son born

•The boy was named John Fitzgerald Kennedy, Jr.

Dec. 19, 1960, presidential electors cast ballots

•He received 303 of the 537 electoral votes from the 50 states.

• *See* Election of 1960, below.

Jan. 6, 1961, electoral vote tabulated by Congress

•Kennedy and Johnson were officially declared elected.

ELECTION OF 1960

Prohibition party, convened, Sept. 1, 1959, at Winona Lake, Ind., nominated Rutherford Losey Decker of Missouri for president, Earle Harold Munn of Michigan for vice president.

National States' Rights party, convened, Mar. 19, 1960, at Dayton, Ohio, nominated Orval Eugene Faubus of Arkansas for president, John Geraerdt Crommelin of Alabama for vice president.

Socialist Labor party, convened, May 7, at New York City, nominated Eric Hass of New York for president, Georgia Cozzini of Wisconsin for vice president.

Democratic party, convened, July 11, at Los Angeles, Cal., nominated John Fitgerald Kennedy of Massachusetts for president, Lyndon Baines Johnson of Texas for vice president.

•This was the 33rd Democratic national convention. It was the only Democratic convention held in Los Angeles; it was the only major party convention held in Los Angeles.

Republican party, convened, July 25, at Chicago, Ill., nominated Richard Milhous Nixon of California for president, Henry Cabot Lodge of Massachusetts for vice president.

•This was the 27th Republican national convention. It was the 14th Republican convention held in Chicago; it was the 24th major party convention held in Chicago.

Socialist Workers party nominated Farrell Dobbs of New York for president, Myra Tanner Weiss of New York for vice president.

Election day, Tuesday, Nov. 8, 1960

Popular vote: 68,837,285

    Kennedy, 34,227,096

    Nixon, 34,108,546

Faubus, 214,195
Hass, 46,478
Decker, 45,919
Dobbs, 39,541
Byrd, 116,248 (unpledged Democrats, Mississippi)
others, 39,262
•Kennedy was the 14th of 15 presidents who were elected without receiving a majority of the popular vote.
Electoral vote: 537, 50 states
  • Kennedy, 303, 22 states
    (Arkansas, 8; Connecticut, 8; Delaware, 3; Georgia, 12; Hawaii, 3; Illinois, 27; Louisiana, 10; Maryland, 9; Massachusetts, 16; Michigan, 20; Minnesota, 11; Missouri, 13; Nevada, 3; New Jersey, 16; New Mexico, 4; New York, 45; North Carolina, 14; Pennsylvania, 32; Rhode Island, 4; South Carolina, 8; Texas, 24; West Virginia, 8)
•Kennedy also received the votes of five Alabama electors.

• Nixon, 219, 26 states
  (Alaska, 3; Arizona, 4; California, 32; Colorado, 6; Florida, 10; Idaho, 4; Indiana, 13; Iowa, 10; Kansas, 8; Kentucky, 10; Maine, 5; Montana, 4; Nebraska, 6; New Hampshire, 4; North Dakota, 4; Ohio, 25; Oklahoma, 7 or 8 votes; Oregon, 6; South Dakota, 4; Tennessee, 11; Utah, 4; Vermont, 3; Virginia, 12; Washington, 9; Wisconsin, 12; Wyoming, 3)
• Byrd, 15, two states
  (Alabama, 6 of 11 votes; Mississippi, 8)
•Byrd also received the vote of one Oklahoma elector.

Note: Senator Harry F. Byrd of Virginia received the unpledged votes of Democratic electors in Mississippi and Alabama, as well as the vote of one Oklahoma Republican elector who defected although pledged to Nixon.

THE PRESIDENT (35th)

Term of office: Jan. 20, 1961, to Nov. 22, 1963 (2 years, 306 days)
•Kennedy was the last of nine presidents who served less than one term.
•He was the last of 19 presidents who served one term or less than one term.
State represented: Massachusetts
•He was the last of four presidents who represented Massachusetts.
Political party: Democratic
•He was the 11th of 12 presidents who were Democrats.
Congresses: 87th, 88th
Administration: 44th
Age at inauguration: 43 years, 236 days
•He was the youngest man elected to the presidency.
•He was 43 years, 163 days old, when elected.

•He was the second youngest to take the oath of office; the youngest was Theodore Roosevelt.
•He was the last of 21 presidents who were younger than their vice presidents. Kennedy was eight years, 275 days younger than Johnson.
Inauguration day: Friday, Jan. 20, 1961
•Kennedy took the oath of office, administered by Chief Justice Earl Warren, on a platform on the renovated east front of the Capitol.
•This was the second of four inaugurations at which Warren officiated.

Note: Kennedy was the second of two presidents who donated their salaries to charity. The other was Hoover.

THE 44th ADMINISTRATION

1961

Jan. 21, appointed his only secretary of state, Dean Rusk; his only secretary of treasury, Douglas Dillon; his only secretary of defense, Robert S. McNamara; his only at-

torney general, Robert F. Kennedy; his first postmaster general, J. Edward Day; his only secretary of interior, Stewart L. Udall; his only secretary of agriculture, Orville L. Freeman; his only secretary of commerce, Luther H. Hodges; his first secretary of labor, Arthur J. Goldberg; and his first secretary of health, education and welfare, Abraham A. Ribicoff

•Kennedy was the only president who appointed a brother to the cabinet.

•He was the second of two presidents who appointed namesakes to the cabinet. The other was Wilson.

Jan. 25, announced release of RB-47 fliers by Russians at first press conference

•The two airmen, Captain Freeman Olmstead and Captain John McKone, were the surviving crewmen of a jet reconnaissance plane shot down by the Russians over the Bering Sea, July 1, 1960.

•This was the first presidential press conference seen and heard on live television. The audience was estimated at sixty million persons.

Jan. 30, delivered his first State of the Union message to Congress

Feb. 2, sent special message to Congress on economy

•He asked for an increase in minimum social security benefits from $33 to $43, temporary extension of unemployment insurance for long-term unemployed, and an increase in the minimum wage to $1.15 an hour.

Feb. 3, issued executive order providing $4,000,000 federal assistance program for Cuban refugees

•About sixty-five thousand Cuban refugees were involved, about half of whom were in the Miami area of Florida.

Feb. 6, sent special message to Congress urging establishment of program to encourage foreign travel in U.S. and the reduction of duty-free allowances for American tourists from $500 to $100

Feb. 9, sent special message to Congress in which he proposed federal health insurance program for aged

•He also suggested federal scholarships for medical and dental students and federal grants for medical, dental, and nursing school construction and improvement.

Feb. 15, pledged support of NATO

Feb. 15, received cable on disarmament from Premier Khrushchev

•The Russian leader said agreement between the U.S. and the U.S.S.R. on disarmament "would be a great joy for all people on earth, and a great boon for the whole of mankind."

Feb. 20, sent special message to Congress in

which he proposed $5,625,000,000 federal aid-to-education program

Mar. 1, issued executive order creating Peace Corps pilot program; sent special message to Congress in which he proposed permanent Peace Corps

•He appointed Sargent Shriver as director of the Peace Corps, Mar. 4. Shriver was his brother-in-law.

Mar. 6, issued executive order on equal opportunity in government employment and government contracting

Mar. 8, sent special message to Congress in which he asked separate bill for private school loans

•In an effort to protect his school-aid program, which was under attack in Catholic circles since it barred aid to sectarian schools at the elementary and secondary levels, he proposed separate legislation.

Mar. 13, offered ten-year plan to raise living standards in Latin America

•This was the Alliance for Progress program.

•He asked Congress for the $500,000,000 authorized in 1960 for the Inter-American Fund for Social Progress, Mar. 14.

Mar. 22, sent special message to Congress in which he urged formation of single foreign aid agency

Mar. 23, stated U.S. position on Laos during televised news conference

•He said:

We are faced with a clear and one-sided threat of a change in the internationally agreed position of Laos. This threat runs counter to the will of the Laotian people, who wish only to be independent and neutral. It is posed rather by the military operation of internal dissident elements directed from outside the country. This is what must end, if peace is to be achieved in Southeast Asia.

Mar. 24 and Mar. 28, sent special budget revision messages to Congress

•He estimated expenditures of $80,693,000,000, with a deficit of $2,169,000,000 for fiscal 1961, and $81,433,000,000, with a deficit of $2,826,000,000 for fiscal 1962. He said the Eisenhower estimates of $79,000,000 and $1,468,000,000 surpluses were mistaken.

•He asked nearly $2,000,000,000 more than

requested by his predecessor for defense appropriations; proposed increased Polaris submarine and Minuteman ICBM programs; a reduction of the B-70 supersonic bomber program; cancellation of the nuclear plane program; and abandonment of 73 military bases.

Mar. 26, met with Prime Minister Macmillan of Great Britain, Key West, Fla.

• They issued a joint appeal to the U.S.S.R. for a "constructive reply" to Western proposals regarding Laos.

• He discussed the Laotian situation with Foreign Minister Gromyko at the White House, Mar. 27.

Mar. 30, appointed Vice President Johnson as chairman of National Advisory Council for Peace Corps

Apr. 3, 23rd Amendment to Constitution ratified

• *See* Constitution, page 645.

Apr. 4–8, conferred with Prime Minister Macmillan, issued joint statement of "high level of agreement," White House

Apr. 11–12, conferred with Chancellor Adenauer of West Germany, White House

Apr. 12, congratulated U.S.S.R. on first manned flight in extraterrestrial space

• Major Yuri Gagarin was the pilot of *Vostok I*, the first manned spacecraft to go into orbit around the earth.

Apr. 17–20, Bay of Pigs fiasco

• About fourteen hundred anti-Castro Cuban exiles, who were trained and equipped by the CIA, landed on the beaches of western central Cuba, at Bahia de Cochinos (Bay of Pigs) in Las Villas province. The invasion was a spectacular failure; more than twelve hundred were captured.

• He assumed full responsibility. "There's an old saying," he said during his Apr. 21 press conference, "that victory has a hundred fathers and defeat is an orphan," and added, "I am the responsible officer of the government."

Note: While Kennedy referred to the phrase, "victory has a hundred fathers and defeat is an orphan," as an old saying, it is likely that he remembered it from the motion picture, "The Desert Fox." In the film, the phrase is voiced by Leo Carroll, who portrayed Field Marshal Gerd von Rundstedt, the World War II German commanding officer. "The Desert Fox" was the story of Field Marshal Irwin Rommel. The

screenplay was written by Nunnally Johnson.

• On Apr. 25, the White House issued this statement:

> President Kennedy has stated from the beginning that as President he bears sole responsibility. . . . He has stated it on all occasions and he restates it now. . . . The President is strongly opposed to anyone within or without the administration attempting to shift the responsibility.

• This was the worst defeat of his administration. His prestige suffered immeasurably. Privately, according to his special counsel, Theodore C. Sorenson, he said:

> How could I have been so far off base? All my life I've known better than to depend on the experts. How could I have been so stupid, to let them go ahead?

Apr. 20–28, discussed Cuban situation with Republican leaders

• He conferred with former Vice President Nixon, White House; with Senator Barry Goldwater at Camp David, Md., Apr. 21; former President Eisenhower, Apr. 22; Governor Nelson Rockefeller, Apr. 25; and former President Hoover in New York City, Apr. 28.

Apr. 20, declared U.S. would not "abandon" Cuba to Communists

• "But let the record show that our patience is not inexhaustible," he told the American Society of Newspaper Editors, adding:

> Should it ever appear that the inter-American doctrine of non-interference merely conceals or excuses a course of non-action; if the nations of this hemisphere should fail to meet their commitments against outside Communist penetration, then I want it clearly understood that this government will not hesitate in meeting its primary obligations, which are the security of our nation.

Apr. 21, announced first project of Peace Corps, road building in Tanganyika

Apr. 22, appointed Maxwell D. Taylor to investigate CIA role in Cuban invasion

May 3, conferred with President Habib Bourguiba of Tunisia, White House

May 5, reactivated President's Board of

Consultants on Foreign Intelligence

May 5, watched first launching of manned American spacecraft, White House
- He telephoned his congratulations to Commander Alan B. Shepard, Jr., who was aboard the *U.S.S. Lake Champlain* after the suborbital flight.

May 8, presented Distinguished Service Medal of NASA to Commander Shepard, White House

May 16–17, made state visit to Canada; addressed Canadian Parliament, Ottawa
- He was the fifth of seven presidents who visited Canada while in office.
- He was the ninth of 11 presidents who traveled outside the U.S. while in office.

May 20, ordered Attorney General Robert Kennedy "to take all necessary steps" after Freedom Riders attacked and beaten in Montgomery, Ala.
- Attorney General Kennedy ordered four hundred U.S. marshals to the Alabama state capital and an additional two hundred marshals, May 22.
- Among the 20 or more injured in Montgomery was President Kennedy's personal representative, John Siegenthaler.

May 25, delivered special message to Congress in which he asked legislation for moon project, expanded military strength, increased foreign aid
- In what he called his second State of the Union message, he said:
  I believe that this nation should commit itself to achieving the goal, before this decade is out, of landing a man on the moon and returning him safely to the earth. No single space project in this period will be more impressive to mankind or more important for the long-range exploration of space.

May 26, vetoed relief bill for William Joseph Vincent
- This was the first of his 21 vetoes.

May 30, conferred with Prime Minister David Ben-Gurion of Israel, New York City

May 31, arrived in Paris, en route to Vienna meeting with Premier Khrushchev
- He met with President Charles de Gaulle on six occasions during his three-day visit to Paris.
- He was the third of four presidents who visited France while in office.
- He was the fifth of seven presidents who visited Europe while in office.

June 3–4, met with Premier Khrushchev, Vienna, Austria
- He was the only president who visited Austria while in office.

June 4–5, visited England
- He met with Prime Minister Macmillan and dined with Queen Elizabeth II.
- He was the fourth of five presidents who visited England while in office.
- This was the first of his two visits to England while in office.

June 6, made television and radio report on Khrushchev conference, White House
- He said there had been
  . . . no discourtesy, no loss of tempers, no threats or ultimatums by either side; no advantage or concession was either gained or given; no major decision was either planned or taken; no spectacular progress was either achieved or pretended.
- He added that, while views contrasted sharply, "at least the channels of communication were opened more fully."

June 9, began using crutches
- It was announced that he had strained his back during a tree-planting ceremony in Ottawa in May. He discarded the crutches, June 23.

June 12–13, conferred with Premier Amintore Fanfani of Italy, White House

June 20–22, conferred with Premier Hayato Ikeda of Japan, White House
- He and Ikeda issued a joint announcement of the establishment of the U.S.-Japan Committee on Trade and Economic Affairs, to be composed of cabinet members of both nations.

June 23, heard report of Ambassador Adlai E. Stevenson on economic and political conditions in South America
- Stevenson, who had visited ten countries, said conditions had worsened, that while the Alliance for Progress program "attracted universal enthusiasm," U.S. popularity had suffered because of the Cuban invasion.

June 26, appointed General Maxwell D. Taylor as his military representative
- Taylor, a former chief of staff, was recalled to active duty.

June 26, appointed fact-finding board to investigate maritime strike
- A quarter of the merchant fleet had been idle since June 15.

June 28, replied to Khrushchev threat to sign separate peace treaty with East Germany
• He said:
> The Soviets would make a grave mistake if they suppose that Allied unity and determination could be determined by threat or fresh aggressive acts.

July 11–13, conferred with President Mohammed Ayub Khan of Pakistan, White House
• A state dinner in honor of President Ayub Khan was held under a canopied pavilion at Mount Vernon, July 11.

July 20, issued executive order transferring responsibility for civilian defense from Office of Civil and Defense Mobilization to defense department
• A national fallout shelter program was visualized.

July 25, announced large-scale military buildup because of Berlin crisis
• "We cannot and will not permit the Communists to drive us out of Berlin—either gradually or by force," he said in a national TV-radio address. He said he was asking Congress for an additional $3,247,000,000 for the armed forces, was ordering draft calls doubled, and was seeking congressional authorization to recall certain reserve units.

Aug. 1–2, conferred with Premier Chen Cheng of Nationalist China, White House
• He reaffirmed U.S. support for UN membership for Nationalist China and opposition to admission of Red China, Aug. 2.

Aug. 10, revealed pre-inaugural agreement with Vice President Johnson regarding any period of inability to perform duties of his office
• According to the agreement, which was similar to the Eisenhower-Nixon understanding, the vice president would serve as acting president during the period of inability.

Aug. 17, Alliance for Progress accord signed, Inter-American Economic and Social Conference, Punta del Este, Uruguay
• The alliance, which he had proposed, Mar. 13, was signed by the U.S. and 19 Latin American nations.

Aug. 18, announced he had ordered fifteen-hundred-man battle group to reinforce five-thousand-man U.S. garrison, West Berlin
• The East German government had closed off all crossing points to West Berlin beginning, Aug. 13, and had erected a wall of concrete blocks along most of the 25-mile border.

Aug. 21, heard report of Vice President Johnson on West Berlin trip
• Johnson had flown to Germany as his representative, Aug. 18, to reassure the citizens of West Berlin that the U.S. would honor its obligations.

Aug. 30, sent General Lucius D. Clay to West Berlin as his personal representative, with rank of ambassador

Sept. 1, White House replied to U.S.S.R. announcement of resumption of nuclear weapons testing
• The statement declared that the Russian announcement of Aug. 31 was "a form of atomic blackmail." It added that he was confident the size of the U.S. nuclear weapons stockpile and delivery systems were wholly adequate for defense needs.

Sept. 3, issued joint statement with Prime Minister Macmillan to Premier Khrushchev
• The U.S. and Great Britain, they said, agreed "not to conduct nuclear tests which take place in the atmosphere and produce radioactive fallout."

Sept. 5, ordered resumption of U.S. nuclear tests without fallout in laboratories and underground
• Khruschev rejected the U.S.-Great Britain proposal to end all tests, Sept. 9.

Sept. 6, warned steel industry of possible grave consequences of price rise

Sept. 13, received delegation from Belgrade conference, informed neutralist leaders talks with Khrushchev would begin when "they could serve a useful purpose"
• Representatives of 25 nonaligned nations met in Belgrade, Yugoslavia, Sept. 1–5, and appealed to the U.S. and the U.S.S.R. to begin negotiations "to establish a safe peace."

Sept. 22, signed Peace Corps Act
• This act established the corps on a permanent basis and authorized $40,000,000 for fiscal 1962 operations.

Sept. 25, addressed United Nations General Assembly, New York City
• He said the West would stand firm on Berlin and invited the Soviets to enter "a peace race." He stressed the need for disarmament negotiations, adding that the "logical place to begin is a treaty assuring the end of nuclear tests of all kinds."

Sept. 26, first session of 87th Congress adjourned

Oct. 3, signed extension of National Defense Education Act

•He signed this compromise school-aid act "with extreme reluctance," criticized the lack of teacher-training provisions, and cited as undesirable the continuation of aid to impacted areas, "which gives more money to more schools for more years than either logic or economy can justify."

•Impacted areas were school districts in which parents worked or lived on federal property or had increased school enrollments because of federal activity.

Oct. 3, pocket vetoed bill to increase within-grade longevity pay for postal workers

•This was the first of his nine pocket vetoes.

Oct. 6, conferred with Foreign Minister Gromyko, White House

•Nothing constructive came from the two-hour conference.

Oct. 11, announced he was dispatching General Maxwell D. Taylor to South Vietnam

•Taylor, his special military adviser, conferred with President Ngo Dinh Diem and South Vietnamese and U.S. military officers, Oct. 18–25. After hearing Taylor's secret report, Kennedy assured Ngo of continued U.S. assistance, Oct. 26.

Nov. 2, announced U.S. would prepare to resume atmospheric nuclear testing

•The largest nuclear explosion to date—the force of which was in excess of 50 megatons—had been set off by the U.S.S.R. in the Soviet Arctic, Oct. 30.

Nov. 6–9, conferred with Prime Minister Jawaharlal Nehru of India, Newport, R.I. and Washington, D.C.

•He and Nehru issued a joint statement of agreement "on the urgent need for a treaty banning nuclear tests with necessary provision for inspection and control."

Nov. 14, conferred with General Chung Hee Park, commander of South Korean military government

•He pledged continued economic aid to South Korea, as well as armed assistance in the event of another Communist attack.

Nov. 18, attended funeral of Sam Rayburn, speaker of House, Bonham, Tex.

•Rayburn, who had died Nov. 16, had served for nearly 49 years, longer than any other member of the House of Representatives.

•Rayburn held the post of speaker for 17 years, which was another record perfor-

mance. As speaker, Rayburn served more than twice as long as Henry Clay.

Nov. 25, interviewed by Izvestia editor, Aleksei I. Adzhubei, Hyannis Port, Mass.

•This unique interview was published in the Moscow edition of Izvestia, Nov. 28. During the two-hour interview, he gave the U.S. position on Berlin, disarmament, and nuclear testing, and assigned responsibility for the major tensions of the day to the U.S.S.R. The interviewer, Adzhubei, was the son-in-law of Premier Khrushchev.

Nov. 28, issued executive order to treasury department to halt sale of silver

Dec. 5, urged physical fitness program for young, New York City

Dec. 6, asked support of his program to liberalize foreign trade policies, New York City

•He asked for replacement of the Reciprocal Trade Agreements Act in a speech before the National Association of Manufacturers.

Dec. 15, visisted Puerto Rico

•He was the second of three presidents who visited the Commonwealth of Puerto Rico while in office.

•He was the sixth of seven presidents who visited Puerto Rico while in office.

Dec. 16, visited Caracas, Venezuela

•He and President Romulo Betancourt signed a communique of U.S.-Venezuelan cooperation within the terms of the Alliance for Progress and witnessed the signing of a $10,000,000 loan to the Venezuelan Workers Bank for Housing by the U.S. Development Loan Fund.

•He was the only president who visited Venezuela while in office.

•He was the fourth of five presidents who visited South America while in office.

Dec. 17, visited Bogota, Colombia

•He and President Alberto Lleras Camargo dedicated a housing development, an Alliance for Progress project.

•He was the second of two presidents who visited Colombia while in office. The other was Franklin D. Roosevelt.

Dec. 21–22, conferred with Prime Minister Macmillan, Bermuda

•He and Macmillan agreed that preparations for resumption of atmospheric nuclear testing should be made.

•He was the third of four presidents who visited Bermuda while in office.

Dec. 25, pledged firm U.S. stand on Berlin

•"The bonds which tie us have been tested

before: we are at your side now—as before," he told the people of West Berlin in a taped TV message broadcast in that city. "We shall stay."

1962

Jan. 3, announced increase of army from 14 to 16 divisions

Jan. 10, second session of 87th Congress

Jan. 11, delivered his second State of the Union message to Congress

•He requested a new trade expansion act that would permit tariff cuts to meet the challenge of the Common Market; the creation of a new department of urban affairs and housing; and enactment of school-aid legislation that had been rejected during the first session. He also asked for standby authority to reduce income tax rates; extension of corporation and excise tax rates; and the withholding of taxes on dividend and interest income. A health insurance program for the aged; increased postal rates; and federal assistance for public fallout shelters were among his other requests.

Jan. 18, submitted balanced budget to Congress

•The proposed budget, $92,537,000,000, included increases for national security and space activities. He estimated a surplus of $463,000,000, during fiscal 1963, after receipts of $93,000,000,000.

Jan. 22, submitted economic report to Congress, maintained economy "had regained its momentum"

Jan. 22, announced $25,000,000 credit granted Dominican Republic

•President Joaquin Balaguer of the Dominican Republic resigned, Jan. 16, and was replaced by a military junta that did not win U.S. support. A second coup led by air force officers installed Rafael Bonnelly as president. Bonnelly, who had served as vice president of the Dominican council of state and had been scheduled to succeed Balaguer, was acceptable to the U.S.

Jan. 25, submitted draft of trade expansion bill to Congress

Jan. 31, sent special message to Congress proposing agricultural program "to replace the present patchwork of short-run emergency measures"

•He proposed controls on acreage and sales of major surplus crops, wheat and feed grains; controls on milk marketing; an expanded rural renewal and education program; and conversion of fifty million acres of crop lands into forest and recreation areas.

Feb. 1, proposed welfare reforms program to Congress

•The $193,000,000 program would place "more stress on services," he said, "instead of relief."

Feb. 6, sent special message to Congress again proposing school-aid legislation

•The five-year, $5,700,000,000 program, similar to his 1961 program, was designed to aid public elementary and secondary schools. Private and parochial schools were excluded.

Feb. 7, repeated his belief federal aid to parochial schools would be unconstitutional

Feb. 7, condemned John Birch Society as "totally alien" to both major political parties

Feb. 7, sent special message to Congress proposing legislation to establish $1,000,-000,000 global communications satellite system operated by privately-owned corporation

Feb. 14, stated U.S. training missions in South Vietnam instructed to protect themselves if necessary, but were "not combat troops in the generally understood sense of the word"

•The U.S. Military Assistance Command had been announced, Feb. 8, which the defense department said demonstrated American determination to prevent a Communist takeover of South Vietnam.

Feb. 20, congratulated Lieutenant Colonel John H. Glenn, Jr., first American in orbit

•He telephoned Glenn, who was aboard the U.S.S. Noa, after the three-orbit trip in space. The Glenn flight embarked the U.S. on "the new ocean," Kennedy said in a White House statement, and added, "I believe the United States must sail on it and be in a position second to none."

Mar. 2, announced U.S. atmospheric nuclear testing would resume in late April if U.S.S.R. did not agree to treaty

•Khrushchev declined. The U.S. test series began, Apr. 25, near Christmas Island, largest atoll in the Pacific.

Mar. 7, proposed U.S.-U.S.S.R. cooperative program of space exploration in letter to Khrushchev

• Khrushchev instructed Soviet delegates to the UN Committee on Peaceful Uses of Outer Space to meet with American members, Mar. 20.

Mar. 13, sent special message to Congress in which he requested $4,878,000,000 for economic and military foreign aid

Mar. 29, accepted resignation of Associate Justice Whittaker

Mar. 30, appointed Byron R. White as associate justice

• White, who was confirmed by the Senate, Apr. 11, was the first of Kennedy's two appointments to the Supreme Court.

Apr. 5, sent special message to Congress proposing, three-year, $500,000,000, urban transportation program and a cutback in intercity transportation federal aid

Apr. 11, denounced steel price rise

• A $6-a-ton price increase was announced, Apr. 10, by U.S. Steel, and seven other steel companies immediately followed suit. During his press conference, he attacked the increases as "wholly unjustifiable," and added:

> Some time ago I asked every American to consider what he would do for his country and I asked the steel companies. In the last 24 hours, we had their answer.

• Attorney General Kennedy ordered an investigation, Apr. 12; the Federal Trade Commission began a separate inquiry. Administration officials prevailed upon other major steel companies to hold the line. Secretary of Defense McNamara shifted procurement of steel for defense production to firms that had not raised prices. The eight steel companies, including U.S. Steel, capitulated, Apr. 13, and cancelled the price rise.

Apr. 21, opened Century 21 Exposition, Seattle, Wash.

• He opened the exposition by pressing a golden telegraph key in Palm Beach, Fla. This was the first World's Fair to be held in the U.S. in 22 years.

Apr. 28–29, conferred with Prime Minister Macmillan, White House

May 12, ordered task force of Seventh Fleet toward Indochinese peninsula

• Northern Laos had fallen to Communist rebels, May 3–12.

May 15, ordered four thousand U.S. troops to Thailand

• He said he acted at the invitation of the Thai government.

May 20, during televised speech, denounced American Medical Association for opposition to his program of medical care for aged under social security, New York City

May 22–24, conferred with President Felix Houphouet-Boigny of Ivory Coast, White House

• He announced a $5,000,000 loan to the Ivory Coast for the establishment of a development bank, which amount was to be matched by the West African government.

May 28, stock market broke

• In the worst one-day drop since 1929, prices on the New York Stock Exchange fell $20,800,000. Prices rebounded the next day, restoring about 65 percent of the losses. The remainder of the losses were restored by June 1.

June 5, welcomed Archbishop Makarios, President of Cyprus, White House

June 7, announced he would ask "across-the-board" personal and income tax cut, effective, Jan. 1, 1963

June 11, attacked "myths" during speech at Yale University commencement exercises, New Haven, Conn.

• He said:

> . . . the greatest enemy of truth is very often not the lie—deliberate, contrived and dishonest—but the myth, persistent, persuasive and unrealistic.

• Among the myths he discredited were those that insisted the federal bureaucracy had grown more rapidly than the economy as a whole, that federal deficits create inflation and budget surpluses prevent inflation, and that the federal debt was growing at a dangerous rate.

June 14, expressed hope Laotian settlement would lead to more amicable relations between U.S. and U.S.S.R.

• A coalition government representing pro-Western, neutralist, and pro-Communist factions had been announced, June 11, in Khang Khay, Laos. He and Khrushchev had agreed a year earlier at Vienna to support a neutral and independent Laos.

June 27, requested support of Supreme Court decision outlawing recitation of official prayer in New York public schools

June 27, maintained U.S. position unchanged regarding defense of Formosa and Pescadores
• The Chinese Communists had massed large military forces opposite the offshore islands of Matsu and Quemoy, which were held by Nationalist China.
June 29–July 1, visited Mexico
• He and President Adolfo Lopez Mateos announced they had reached agreement that the U.S. would make a $20,000,000 agricultural loan to Mexico.
• He was the fifth of seven presidents who visited Mexico while in office.
July 23–24, conferred with President Carlos Julio Arosemena Monroy of Ecuador, White House
July 25, endorsed Puerto Rican plebescite proposal
• In a letter to Governor Luis Munoz Marin, he approved the governor's proposal for a plebescite in which Puerto Ricans could vote for independence, statehood, or a revised commonwealth status with the U.S.
Aug. 13, announced his decision against immediate tax cut
• In a TV-radio talk from the White House, he renewed his pledge for an "across-the-board" tax cut at "the right time," and said he would introduce tax reduction legislation in the next congressional session. Several of his economic advisers had joined the clamor for an immediate tax cut.
Aug. 27, 24th Amendment to Constitution submitted to states for ratification
Aug. 29, accepted resignation of Associate Justice Frankfurter
Aug. 29, accepted resignation of Secretary of Labor Goldberg, effective, Sept. 20
Aug. 29, appointed Arthur J. Goldberg as associate justice
• Goldberg, who was confirmed by the Senate, Sept. 25, was the second of Kennedy's two appointments to the Supreme Court.
Aug. 30, appointed his second secretary of labor, W. Willard Wirtz
• Wirtz took office, Sept. 25.
Aug. 30, signed compromise Filipino war damage act
Sept. 4, announced Cuban military arsenal had been bolstered by large-scale deliveries of Soviet equipment
• He said the U.S. would use "whatever means may be necessary" to prevent Castro "from taking action against any part of the western hemisphere."

Sept. 11–12, made inspection tour of space installations
• Accompanied by U.S. and British space officials, he visited Huntsville, Ala.; Cape Canaveral, Fla.; Houston, Tex.; and St. Louis, Mo. He outlined his space program in an address at Rice University, Houston.
Sept. 13, denounced church burnings in Georgia and Mississippi shooting as "cowardly" and "outrageous"
• The incidents were attempts to discourage Negro vote registration. "I don't know any more outrageous action which I've seen occur in this country for a good many months or years," he said. He guaranteed protection to registrars, adding, "if it requires extra legislation, and extra force, we shall do that."
Sept. 13, stated no further licenses for exporting U-2 planes had been or would be issued
• A National Chinese U-2, purchased directly from the American manufacturer in 1960, had been shot down over Communist China, Sept. 9.
Sept. 30, asked compliance with federal law of University of Mississippi students and citizens of state
• His telecast plea did not halt the rioting, which had begun after James H. Meredith had taken up residence at the all-white university. The riot raged for 15 hours, during which two persons were killed and 375 injured, including 165 U.S. marshals. Order was restored with the help of 3,000 federal troops. The Negro youth registered and began classes.
Oct. 2, urged campaign to prevent spread of Castroism in Latin America during address to foreign ministers of Organization of American States, White House
Oct. 13, second session of 87th Congress adjourned
Oct. 16, informed of Cuban missile build-up
• Conclusive proof that the Soviet Union was preparing offensive missile bases in Cuba had been obtained by U-2 overflight of the island.
Oct. 18, conferred with Foreign Minister Gromyko, White House
• The Russian foreign minister, after a lengthy discussion of Berlin, turned the subject to Cuba and said that Soviet assistance was "contributing to the defense capabilities of Cuba" and "training by

Soviet specialists of Cuban nationals in handling defensive armaments was by no means offensive."

• Kennedy responded to this flat lie by sending for and reading aloud his Sept. 13 news conference warning against offensive missiles in Cuba:

If at any time the Communist build-up in Cuba were to endanger or interfere with our security in any way . . . or if Cuba should ever . . . become an offensive military base of significant capacity for the Soviet Union, then this country would do whatever must be done to protect its own security and that of its allies.

Oct. 20, cancelled campaign tour because of "cold," Chicago, Ill.

Oct. 22, announced naval and air quarantine of Cuba, White House

• Close surveillance of Soviet activity in Cuba had revealed, he said in an 18-minute nationally-telecast speech, that "a series of offensive missile sites is now in preparation on that imprisoned island." With the object of preventing the use of these missiles against the U.S. "or any other country," he outlined the steps he had taken or ordered—quarantine, continuous surveillance, and action if needed. "We will not prematurely or unnecessarily risk the costs of world-wide nuclear war in which even the fruits of victory would be ashes in our mouth, but neither will we shrink from that risk at any time it must be faced," he said. The quarantine would be continued, he added, until the missiles had been dismantled and removed from Cuba under UN supervision.

Oct. 23, pocket vetoed relief bills for Richard C. Collins and Mrs. Helenita K. Stevenson

• These were the eighth and last of his nine pocket vetoes.

Oct. 24, ordered quarantine put into effect

• A special naval force was formed to control the sea lanes to Cuba, which included the destroyer, *U.S.S. Joseph P. Kennedy, Jr.*, named for his late brother. Patrol planes reported 18 Russian merchant ships en route to Cuba. One tanker was stopped, Oct. 25, but permitted to proceed inasmuch as it carried only oil; the navy also stopped and cleared a Russian-chartered freighter, Oct. 26.

Oct. 25–26, was informed Russian ships had reversed course

• U.S. planes followed the vessels all the way to Soviet ports.

Oct. 28, reached agreement with Khrushchev ending Cuban crisis

• In return for the halt of construction of the missile bases and the removal of the Soviet weapons, he pledged that the U.S. would not invade Cuba.

Nov. 2, announced Soviet missile bases being dismantled and "progress is now being made toward restoration of peace in the Caribbean" in television and radio report to nation, White House

Nov. 7, U.S. and U.S.S.R. agreed missiles would be counted at sea

• Premier Castro had rejected international inspection of missile sites, Nov. 1.

Nov. 8, was informed all known missiles had been dismantled

Nov. 13, welcomed Chancellor Konrad Adenauer of West Germany, White House

Nov. 20, ordered naval quarantine ended

• He announced that Premier Khrushchev had agreed to withdraw all Soviet jet bombers from Cuba within 30 days.

Dec. 18–21, conferred with Prime Minister Macmillan, Nassau, Bahamas

• He was the first of two presidents who visited the Bahamas while in office. The other was Nixon.

1963

Jan. 9, first session of 88th Congress

• The administration maintained control of both the Senate and the House of Representatives. The Democrats gained three Senate seats and lost three House seats. The Senate (100 members) consisted of 67 Democrats and 33 Republicans. The House (435 members consisted of 257 Democrats, 177 Republicans, and one vacancy.

Jan. 14, delivered his third and last State of the Union message to Congress

• He proposed a permanent tax cut; a three-year tax reform program; a domestic Peace Corps; extension of social security to include health programs for retired workers; and civil rights legislation to insure voting rights and the right to counsel in federal courts.

Jan. 17, sent budget message to Congress

• He proposed a budget of $98,800,000,000, which would result in a deficit of $11,900,-000,000.

Jan. 19, appointed three-man mediation board to attempt to settle East and Gulf coasts longshoremen's strike

• The board recommended a 39-cent-per-hour package, which was accepted by both sides. The 34-day strike ended, Jan. 26, and cost an estimated $800,000,000.

Jan. 20, ordered nuclear testing halt since private talks with U.S.S.R. being held

• The talks between the U.S., Great Britain, and the U.S.S.R. broke off, Jan. 31.

Jan. 24, submitted his economic report to Congress

• He forecast continued moderate expansion.

Jan. 24, sent special tax reduction message to Congress

• His program was designed to provide a $11,040,000,000 reduction for individuals and a $3,400,000,000 reduction for corporations.

Jan. 29, sent special education message to Congress

• He asked for $1,215,000,000 for the proposed education legislation.

Jan. 31, sent special farm message to Congress

• He asked for $1,900,000,000 for the proposed farm aid.

Feb. 5, sent special message on mental health aid to Congress

Feb. 6, issued executive order prohibiting ships carrying federally-financed cargoes to trade with Cuba

Feb. 14, sent special message in which he proposed youth conservation corps to Congress

Feb. 19, received President Romulo Betancourt of Venezuela, White House

Feb. 21, sent special message on medical care for aged to Congress

Mar. 11, sent special manpower message to Congress

• He said full employment was the nation's "most pressing internal challenge" and urged a tax cut to combat unemployment.

Mar. 18–20, conferred with six Central American presidents, San Jose, Costa Rica

• In a speech at the opening of the conference with the presidents of Costa Rica, El Salvador, Guatemala, Honduras, Panama, and Nicaragua, Kennedy said:

We will build a wall around Cuba—not a wall of mortar or brick or barbed wire, but a wall of dedicated men determined to protect their own freedom and sovereignty.

• He was the first of two presidents who visited Costa Rica while in office. The other was Lyndon B. Johnson.

Apr. 2, sent special message on foreign aid to Congress

• He requested $4,525,000,000 for foreign aid, which was $420,000,000 less than he had asked for foreign aid in his Jan. 17 budget message.

Apr. 9, proclaimed Sir Winston Churchill honorary citizen of U.S., White House

Apr. 11, declared his opposition to announced steel price rises but indicated he would not oppose selected steel product increases.

• The steel companies "acted with some restraint," he said, Apr. 19.

May 9–10, conferred with Prime Minister Lester B. Pearson of Canada, Hyannis Port, Mass.

• Pearson announced that Canada would accept U.S. nuclear warheads for missiles installed in Canada and for Canadian NATO forces, May 11.

May 18, participated in 30th anniversary of TVA, Muscle Shoals, Ala.

May 23, issued executive order that gave power to secretary of agriculture to restrict export and import of wheat

• His wheat control program had been defeated by referendum, May 21.

June 4, addressed delegates from more than one hundred nations to World Food Congress, Washington, D.C.

• He said:

We have the ability, we have the means, we have the capacity to eliminate hunger from the face of the earth. We need only the will.

June 5, endorsed supersonic transport plane program in commencement address, U.S. Air Force Academy, Colorado Springs, Colo.

June 10, proposed "strategy of peace," American University, Washington, D.C.

• He announced that the U.S., Great Britain, and the U.S.S.R. had agreed to confer in Moscow on the nuclear test-ban treaty and that the U.S. would not conduct atmospheric tests "so long as other states do not do so."

June 11, signed executive order federalizing Alabama National Guard

• Governor George C. Wallace had defied a federal court order and a presidential appeal by blocking the door of the University of Alabama and preventing the enrollment of two Negro students. Wallace also refused to stand aside when ordered by Deputy Attorney General Nicholas deB. Katzenbach. The governor complied when the order was repeated by the commander of the National Guard.

June 19, sent special message to Congress in which he proposed civil rights legislation

• His omnibus bill provided for equal access to restaurants, hotels and retail establishments in interstate commerce and authorized the attorney general to institute school integration suits when requested by those unable to sue.

June 23–26, visited West Germany

• He conferred with Chancellor Adenauer, emphasized the U.S. commitment to Europe in an address in Frankfurt, and was greeted by a crowd of one million people when he visited West Berlin. At the city hall, after having been made an honorary citizen of the city, he made his celebrated *"Ich bin ein Berliner"* speech.

• He was the third of five presidents who visited Germany while in office.

June 26–29, visited Ireland

• He made a sentimental journey to his family's ancestral home, County Wexford. He also addressed a joint session of the Irish Parliament, Dublin.

• He was the first of two presidents who visited Ireland while in office. The other was Nixon.

June 29–30, visited England

• He met with Prime Minister Macmillan at Birch Grove, Sussex.

• He also visited the Edensor grave of his sister, Kathleen, who had been killed in a 1948 plane crash.

• This was the second of his two visits to England while in office.

July 1–2, visited Italy

• He conferred with President Antonio Segni and Pope Paul VI in Rome.

• He was the fourth of six presidents who visited Italy while in office.

• He was the third of five presidents who met with Popes while in office.

July 3, returned to Washington, D.C.

July 10, succeeded in postponing railroad strike

• He won the delay with a last-minute appeal to give him time to submit legislation to Congress. On July 22, he asked Congress to authorize the ICC to decide what changes in work rules were necessary.

July 18, sent special message to Congress proposing legislation to tax American investments abroad

• This legislation was designed to slow the gold outflow and to improve the U.S. balance-of-payments position.

July 26, made TV address to nation on test-ban treaty

• After nearly five years of negotiations, an agreement to halt nuclear tests, in the atmosphere, outer space, and under water, had been initialed, July 25, in Moscow by representatives of the U.S., Great Britain, and the U.S.S.R.

• The treaty was signed at the Kremlin, Aug. 5; it was ratified by the Senate, Sept. 24.

Aug. 7, his second son born

• The boy was named Patrick Bouvier Kennedy.

• He was the second of two presidents who became fathers while in office. The other was Cleveland.

• Patrick was the last of three children born to presidents while in office.

Aug. 9, his son, Patrick, died

• The boy, who had been born more than five weeks prematurely, succumbed to a respiratory ailment.

• Patrick Bouvier Kennedy was the last of five children of presidents who died during their fathers' terms of office.

Aug. 28, signed joint resolution averting railroad strike

• A nationwide railroad strike had been scheduled for midnight.

• The resolution, which provided for an arbitration board to decide the size of train crews and the legitimacy of diesel locomotive firemen in freight and yard service, was passed and signed in a matter of hours.

• This was the first time that compulsory arbitration was imposed in a peacetime labor dispute.

Aug. 28, met with Negro leaders while 200,000 marched in support of effective civil rights laws, White House

• The highlight of the peaceful demonstration was an address by Reverend Dr. Martin Luther King, Jr., at the Lincoln Memorial ("I have a dream . . .").

Aug. 30, "hot line" installed

• This was the direct link between Washington and Moscow that made possible an exchange of messages between the heads of state in a matter of minutes.

Sept. 2, criticized South Vietnamese repression of Buddhists as "very unwise"

• During a televised interview, he said that U.S. military assistance would continue but added "changes in policy and perhaps in personnel" of the government of President Ngo Dinh Diem were necessary if popular support by the South Vietnamese people was to be regained.

Sept. 10, signed executive order terminating drafting of married men

Sept. 10, accepted resignation of Postmaster General Day

Sept. 10, appointed his second postmaster general, John A. Gronouski

• Gronouski took office, Sept. 30.

• Gronouski was the last of Kennedy's 13 cabinet appointments.

Sept. 10, again federalized Alabama National Guard

• Governor Wallace had used state troopers to block public school integration below the college level, Sept. 2–9. When all five U.S. district judges in Alabama signed an order that prohibited Wallace and the state troops from barring Negro students, the governor replaced the troopers with national guardsmen. The delaying tactics ended with the federalization of the guard.

Sept. 12, applauded school desegregation in 157 southern cities during previous two weeks

Sept. 12, with Mrs. Kennedy, celebrated tenth wedding anniversary, Newport, R.I.

Sept. 19, sent Kenneth C. Royall, former secretary of army, and Earl H. Blaik, former West Point football coach, to Birmingham, Ala., as his personal representatives to help mediate racial dispute

• Racial rioting had followed the bombing of a Negro church in Birmingham, Sept. 15. Four Negro girls were killed and 20 other Negroes were injured in the bombing which occurred during Sunday services. "It is regrettable that public disparagement of law and order has encouraged violence which has fallen on the innocent," he said in an obvious reference to Governor Wallace, Sept. 16. Kennedy's actions were praised by Dr. Martin Luther King, Jr., and six other Negro leaders after a White House conference.

Sept. 20, saluted "pause in the cold war"

during speech to General Assembly of UN, New York City.

• He spoke of the "special responsibility to the world" that required the U.S. and the U.S.S.R. "to concentrate less on our differences and more on the means of resolving them peacefully." He proposed cooperation in space, including a joint expedition to the moon.

• Foreign Minister Gromyko had made a conciliatory address, Sept. 19, in which he suggested an 18-nation summit conference in Moscow during 1964 to negotiate a "general and complete disarmament" treaty.

Sept. 24–29, made "non-political" tour of 11 western states

• He attacked the conservative position of such critics as Senator Barry Goldwater in an address at the Mormon Tabernacle, Salt Lake City, Utah, saying:

> If we were to resign from the United Nations, break off with all countries of whom we disapprove, end foreign aid, call for the resumption of atmospheric nuclear testing and turn our back on the rest of mankind, we would not only be abandoning American influence in the world—we would be inviting a Communist expansion which every Communist power would welcome. Our policy would not have much deterrent effect in a world where nations determined to defend their own independence could no longer count on America.

Oct. 9, announced his approval of sale of $250,000,000 worth of U.S. wheat to U.S.S.R.

Oct. 10, issued proclamation declaring nuclear test ban treaty in effect

Nov. 1–2, military coup overthrew South Vietnamese government of President Ngo Dinh Diem

• Diem and his brother, secret police chief Ngo Dinh Nhu, were killed, Nov. 2. The U.S. recognized the new government, headed by former Vice President Nguyen Ngoc Tho as premier, Nov. 7.

Nov. 15, called unemployment "most important domestic issue" in speech to AFL-CIO convention, New York City

Nov. 18, denied administration "anti-business," sought support for tax cut legislation in speech to Florida Chamber of Commerce, Tampa, Fla.

Nov. 19, vetoed relief bill for Dr. James T. Mattux
- This was the last of his 21 vetoes.
- He was the tenth of 11 presidents who

never had a veto overriden.

Nov. 21, departed for three-day trip to Texas

Nov. 22, addressed Fort Worth Chamber of Commerce, flew to Dallas

THE ASSASSINATION

Nov. 22, 1963, shot from ambush while riding in motorcade, Dallas, Tex.
- On the second day of a political fence-mending tour of Texas, Kennedy was riding in a motorcade from Love Field, Dallas, to the downtown Merchandise Mart where he was to address a luncheon group, when he was shot in the head. Mortally wounded, he was rushed to Parkland Hospital, about five minutes away, but emergency treatment by a team of physicians proved unsuccessful. The time of his death officially was fixed at 1 P.M. (CST).
- Governor John B. Connally of Texas, riding in the same car, also was seriously wounded. Connally recovered.
- Efforts to locate the source of the shots were inconclusive, although they were believed by many to have come from a six-story building, the Texas School Book Depository. A search of the building revealed an Italian-made carbine.
- At about 1:15 P.M., a Dallas policeman, J. D. Tippit, was found shot to death beside his patrol car about three miles from where the president was shot. Acting on a tip from a suspicious cashier, police surrounded a nearby movie theater and there arrested Lee Harvey Oswald. Oswald earlier had been questioned at the book depository and released when he was identified as an employee. He was charged with the murder of the policeman and, after long hours of interrogation, also charged with the murder of the president.

Nov. 24, 1963, Oswald shot in Municipal Building, Dallas, Tex.
- The accused assassin was being moved from the city jail to the county jail, before the eyes of millions watching on television, when he was shot and killed by Jack Rubenstein, also known as Jack Ruby, a Dallas nightclub owner.

Nov. 29, 1963, special commission to investigate assassination appointed by President Johnson
- The commission, headed by Chief Justice Earl Warren, included Senator Richard B. Russell (D., Ga); Senator John Sherman Cooper (R., Ky.); Representative Hale Boggs (D., La.); Representative Gerald R. Ford (R., Mich.); Allen W. Dulles, former director of the CIA; and John J. McCloy, former adviser to President Kennedy. The Warren Commission met for the first time, Dec. 5.

Feb. 17, 1964, trial of Ruby began, Dallas, Tex.
- Ruby was found guilty of the murder of Oswald, Mar. 14. He was sentenced to death.

Sept. 27, 1964, Warren Commission report released
- The most significant conclusion contained in the 888-page report was that the assassination was not the result of a conspiracy, that Lee Harvey Oswald was the sole assassin.
- The commission concluded that President Kennedy had been shot by Oswald from the sixth floor of the Texas School Book Depository with the Italian carbine found there. The gun had been identified as the property of Oswald, purchased from a Chicago mail-order house.
- Although the purpose of the appointment of the Warren Commission had been to quiet controversy about the assassination of President Kennedy, its lengthy report probably generated more controversy than it quieted.

Oct. 5, 1966, murder conviction of Ruby reversed
- The Texas Court of Criminal Appeals reversed the 1964 decision and ordered a new trial outside Dallas County. The three appeals judges wrote separate opinions and held that inadmissable evidence had been allowed.

Jan. 3, 1967, Ruby died, Dallas, Tex.
- Ruby, who died in Parkland Hospital, had cancer, but his death was attributed to a blood clot in the lungs.

DEATH

Date of death: Nov. 22, 1963
• Kennedy was the last of five presidents who died before they completed their first terms.
• He was the last of eight presidents who died in office.
• He was the seventh of eight presidents who lay in state in the Capitol Rotunda.
• He was the last of six presidents who lay in state in the White House.
Place of death: Dallas, Tex.
• He was the only president who died in Texas.
Age at death: 46 years, 177 days
• He was the president who died at the youngest age.
Cause of death: Assassination by rifle shot
• He was the last of four presidents who were assassinated.
Place of burial: Arlington National Cemetery, Arlington, Va.
• He was the second of two presidents who were buried in Arlington. The other was Taft.
• He was the last of seven presidents who were buried in Virginia.

THE VICE PRESIDENT (37th)

Full name: Lyndon Baines Johnson
• *See* pages 539–580.
• Johnson was the second of two vice presidents who were born in Texas. The other was Garner.
• He was the last of three vice presidents named Johnson.
• He was the only vice president who was a Disciple of Christ.
• He was the 20th of 21 vice presidents who served in the House of Representatives before their terms of office.
• He was the 15th of 17 vice presidents who served in the Senate before their terms of office.
• He was the ninth of ten vice presidents who served in both the House of Representatives and the Senate before their terms of office.
• He was the 11th of 12 vice presidents who served in both the House of Representa-
tives and the Senate.
• He was the last of 14 vice presidents who served less than one term.
• Kennedy and Johnson were the 39th of 41 president-vice president teams.
• Johnson was the second of two vice presidents who represented Texas. The other was Garner.
• He was the 15th of 16 vice presidents who were Democrats.

THE CABINET

State: David Dean Rusk of New York, Jan. 21, 1961, to Jan. 20, 1969
Treasury: Clarence Douglas Dillon of New Jersey, Jan. 21, 1961, to Apr. 1, 1965
Defense: Robert Strange McNamara of Michigan, Jan. 21, 1961, to Feb. 29, 1968
Attorney General: Robert Francis Kennedy of Massachusetts, Jan. 21, 1961, to Sept. 3, 1964
Postmaster General: James Edward Day of California, Jan. 21, 1961, to Sept, 10, 1963
• John Austin Gronouski of Wisconsin, Sept. 30, 1963, to Aug. 30, 1965
Interior: Stewart Lee Udall of Arizona, Jan. 21, 1961, to Jan. 20, 1969
Agriculture: Orville Lothrop Freeman of Minnesota, Jan. 21, 1961, to Jan. 20, 1969
Commerce: Luther Hartwell Hodges of North Carolina, Jan. 21, 1961, to Jan. 15, 1965
Labor: Arthur Joseph Goldberg of Washington, D.C., Jan. 21, 1961, to Sept. 20, 1962
• William Willard Wirtz of Illinois, Sept. 25, 1962, to Jan. 20, 1969
Health, Education and Welfare: Abraham Alexander Ribicoff of Connecticut, Jan. 21, 1961, to July 13, 1962
• Anthony Joseph Celebrezze of Ohio, July 31, 1962 to July 27, 1965

THE SUPREME COURT

Associate Justices: Byron Raymond White of Colorado, appointed, Mar. 30, 1962; confirmed, Apr. 11, 1962
• Arthur Joseph Goldberg of Illinois, appointed, Aug. 29, 1962; confirmed, Sept. 25, 1962

Thirty-sixth President

LYNDON BAINES JOHNSON

Full name: Lyndon Baines Johnson
• He was the only president with the same surname as a previous president who was not related to that predecessor.
• He was the last of four presidents who had the same surname as a previous president.
• He was the 18th of 19 presidents with middle initials or middle names.
Date of birth: Aug. 27, 1908
• He was the last of three presidents who were born in August.
Place of birth: near Stonewall, Tex.
• He was the second of two presidents who were born in Texas. The other was Eisenhower.
Family lineage: English-*unknown*
• The origin of the Johnson line is unknown. The line has been traced only to his great-great-grandfather, John Johnson, who was born in 1764, place unknown. John Johnson died in Oglethorpe County, Ga., 1828.
Religious denomination: Disciples of Christ
• He was the second of two presidents who were Disciples of Christ. The other was Garfield.
College: Southwest Texas State Teachers College, now Southwest Texas State College, San Marcos, Tex.

• He was the only president who went to Southwest Texas State.
• He was the 26th of 27 presidents who attended college.
Date of graduation: Aug. 18, 1930. Bachelor of Science
• He was the 20th of 21 presidents who were graduated from college.
Law School: Georgetown Law School, Washington, D.C.
• He was the eighth of nine presidents who attended law school.
• He was the last of six presidents who attended, but were not graduated from law school.

PARENTS AND SIBLINGS

Father's name: Sam Ealy Johnson
Date of birth: Oct. 11, 1877
Place of birth: Buda, Hays County, Tex.
Occupations: Farmer, trader
• Johnson's father was also a member of the Texas state legislature and an inspector for the Texas railroad commission.
Date of death: Oct. 23, 1937
Place of death: Austin, Tex.

Age at death: 60 years, 12 days

Mother's name: Rebekah Baines Johnson
Date of birth: June 26, 1881
Place of birth: McKinney, Tex.
Date of marriage: Aug. 20, 1907
Place of marriage: Fredericksburg, Tex.
Children: 5; 3 daughters, 2 sons
• Lyndon Baines was born in 1908; Rebekah
  Luruth in 1910; Josefa Hermine in 1912;
  Sam Houston in 1914; and Lucia Huffman
  in 1916.
• Johnson was the sixth of seven presidents
  who came from families of five children.
• He was the last of eight presidents who
  were eldest children.
Date of death: Sept. 12, 1958
Place of death: Austin, Tex.
Age at death: 77 years, 78 days

MARRIAGE

Date of marriage: Nov. 17, 1934
Place of marriage: San Antonio, Tex.
• Johnson was the only president who was
  married in Texas.
Age at marriage: 26 years, 82 days
• He was the 26th of 27 presidents who were
  married in their twenties.

Wife's name: Claudia Alta Taylor Johnson
• She was called Lady Bird.

• She was the 33rd first lady.
• She was the 40th wife of a president.
Date of birth: Dec. 22, 1912
• She was the second of two first ladies who
  were born in December. The other was
  Mary Lincoln.
• She was the second of two wives of presi-
  dents who were born in December.
Place of birth: Karnack, Tex.
• She was the only first lady or wife of a presi-
  dent who was born in Texas.
Wife's mother: Minnie Pattillo Taylor
Wife's father: Thomas Jefferson Taylor,
  storekeeper and rancher
Age at marriage: 21 years, 330 days
• She was the 25th of 26 first ladies who were
  married in their twenties.
• She was the 29th of 30 wives of presidents
  who were married in their twenties.
Years younger than husband: 4 years, 117
  days
Children: 2 daughters
• Lynda Bird was born on Mar. 19, 1944, and
  Lucy Baines on July 2, 1947. Lucy changed
  the spelling of her name to Luci when she
  was a child.
• Johnson was the fourth of five presidents
  who had only female children.
• He was the sixth of seven presidents who
  had two children.
• He was the 29th of 30 presidents who had
  children.

EARLY YEARS

1913, entered public school, Johnson City,
  Tex.
1924, was graduated from Johnson City
  High School, Johnson City, Tex.
• After graduation, Johnson went to California with a group of friends who eventually separated to find jobs when their
  money ran out. After holding a variety of
  odd jobs, he hitchhiked back to Johnson
  City, where he worked for a time on a road
  gang.
1927, entered Southwest Texas State Teachers College, San Marcos, Tex.
• He worked as a janitor and part-time secretary to the college president to help pay his
  expenses.
Aug. 18, 1930, was graduated from Southwest Texas State Teachers College, now
  Southwest Texas State College

• Although he had three months of pre-col-
  lege studies to make up when he entered,
  he finished in three and one-half years, including a year out of college when he
  taught grade school in Cotulla, Tex.
• He was the last of seven presidents who
  taught school.
1930–1931, taught public speaking and debate, Sam Houston High School, Houston,
  Tex.
Nov. 24, 1931, appointed secretary to Representative Richard M. Kleberg
• Kleberg, a member of the family who owns
  the vast King Ranch, had been elected to
  represent the 14th Congressional District
  of Texas in a special election.
1933, elected speaker of "Little Congress,"
  organization of congressional secretaries
Sept. 19, 1934, entered Georgetown Uni-

versity Law School, Washington, D.C.
•He was the 25th of 26 presidents who studied law.
Nov. 17, 1934, married Claudia Alta Taylor, San Antonio, Tex.
July 25, 1935, appointed state director of National Youth Administration by President Roosevelt
•Johnson resigned as secretary to Representative Kleberg and discontinued his law

studies. He served as Texas director of the NYA until 1937.
•He was the last of three presidents who studied law but did not seek admission to the bar.
Mar. 1, 1937, announced his candidacy for House of Representatives
•A special election was scheduled after the death of Representative James P. Buchanan.

NATIONAL PROMINENCE

Apr. 10, 1937, elected to House of Representatives
•Johnson represented the Tenth Congressional District of Texas.
•He was the 15th of 17 presidents who were elected to the House.
Apr. 11, 1937, met President Roosevelt, accompanied presidential party across Texas
May 14, 1937, took seat in House of Representatives
•He first served in the 75th Congress. He was appointed to the naval affairs committee.
•He was the 15th of 17 presidents who served in the House.
Oct. 23, 1937, his father died
Nov. 8, 1938, reelected to House
•He was reelected five times, serving in the 76th, 77th, 78th, 79th, and 80th congresses.
Nov. 4, 1941, defeated in special election for Senate
•A special election was scheduled after the death of Senator Morris Sheppard. Johnson was defeated by Governor W. Lee ("Pappy") O'Daniel by 1,311 votes.
Dec. 9, 1941, commissioned as lieutenant commander, U.S. Navy
•He was the first member of Congress to enter the armed forces after Pearl Harbor.
•He was the second of three presidents who served in the U.S. Navy.
•He was the third of four presidents who served in World War II.
•He was the 20th of 21 presidents who served in the military during wartime.
June 9, 1942, received Silver Star for gallantry in action, New Guinea
•He was decorated personally by General Douglas A. MacArthur.
1942, ordered back to Washington, D.C.
•President Roosevelt ordered all members

of Congress in the armed forces to return to their offices.
Mar. 19, 1944, his first daughter born
•The girl was named Lynda Bird Johnson.
July 2, 1947, his second daughter born
•The girl was named Lucy Baines Johnson.
Nov. 2, 1948, elected to Senate
•He had defeated former Governor Coke Stevenson in the Democratic primary by 87 votes.
•He was the 14th of 16 presidents who were elected to the Senate.
•He was the ninth of 11 presidents who were elected both to the House of Representatives and the Senate.
Jan. 3, 1949, took seat in Senate
•He was the 13th of 15 presidents who served in the Senate.
•He was the eighth of ten presidents who served both in the House of Representatives and the Senate.
Jan. 2, 1951, elected majority whip of Senate
1951, began buying LBJ Ranch
•He purchased the first 231 acres from an aunt, Mrs. Clarence Martin.
Jan. 3, 1953, elected minority leader of Senate
•"If you're in an airplane flying somewhere, you don't run up to the cockpit and attack the pilot," he said. "Mr. Eisenhower is the only President we've got."
Nov. 2, 1954, reelected to Senate
Jan. 5, 1955, elected majority leader of Senate
July 2, 1955, suffered serious heart attack while en route to Middleburg, Va.
•He did not return to the Senate until December.
Aug. 16, 1956, nominated for president as favorite-son candidate, Democratic national convention, Chicago, Ill.

• Adlai E. Stevenson was nominated on the first ballot.

1958, presented U.S. resolution calling for peaceful exploration of outer space to UN at request of President Eisenhower

Sept. 12, 1958, his mother died

July 13, 1960, defeated for presidential nomination, Democratic national convention, Los Angeles, Cal.

• He received 409 votes. Kennedy, with 806 votes, was nominated on the first ballot.

July 14, 1960, nominated for vice president by acclamation

Nov. 6, 1960, elected vice president

• He also was elected to the Senate for a third term.

Jan. 3, 1961, took oath of office as member of Senate, immediately resigned

Jan. 20, 1961, took oath of office as vice president

Apr. 3, 1961, attended independence ceremonies, Dakar, Republic of Senegal

May, 1961, visited Far East and Southeast Asia

• He conferred with President Ngo Dinh Diem of South Vietnam; President Carlos P. Garcia of the Philippines; President Chiang Kai-shek of the Republic of China; Mohammed Ayub Khan of Pakistan; and Prime Minister Jawaharlal Nehru of India.

September, 1961, conferred with Chancellor Konrad Adenauer and Mayor Willy Brandt, West Berlin, Germany

July, 1962, attended tenth anniversary of Commonwealth of Puerto Rico ceremonies, San Juan

August–September, 1962, visited Middle East

• He conferred with Shah Mohammed Reza Pahlevi of Iran; President Cemal Gursel of Turkey; King Paul I of Greece; and the president of Cyprus, Archbishop Makarios.

February, 1963, attended inauguration of President Juan Bosch of Dominican Republic, Santo Domingo

June, 1963, represented President Kennedy at funeral of Pope John XXIII, Rome, Italy

• Johnson had paid a courtesy call on Pope John in September, 1962.

Nov. 21, 1963, accompanied President Kennedy to Texas

THE PRESIDENT (36th)

Term of office: Nov. 22, 1963, to Jan. 20, 1969 (5 years, 59 days)

• Johnson was the 11th of 12 presidents who had served as vice presidents.

• He was the last of eight presidents who, because of the deaths of their predecessors, did not complete their vice-presidential terms.

• He was the last of four presidents who served the unexpired terms of their predecessors and also were elected to and served second terms.

• He was the last of 16 presidents who served more than one term.

State represented: Texas

• He was the only president who represented Texas.

Political party: Democratic

• He was the last of 12 presidents who were Democrats.

Congresses: 88th, 89th, 90th, 91st

Administrations: 44th, 45th

Age at taking oath: 55 years, 87 days

• Johnson took the oath of office aboard the presidential jet, Air Force One, at Love Field, Dallas, Tex., on Friday, Nov. 22, 1963. The oath of office was administered by Sarah T. Hughes, U.S. District Judge for the northern district of Texas.

• Johnson was the last of seven presidents who took the oath of office from an official other than a justice of the Supreme Court.

• He was the only president who took the oath of office from a female official.

• This was the only oath-taking ceremony that was held in an airplane.

THE 44th ADMINISTRATION

1963

Nov. 23, issued proclamation designating Nov. 25 as a day of mourning for President Kennedy

Nov. 25, marched in Kennedy funeral procession from White House to St. Matthew's Cathedral

Nov. 27, addressed joint session of Congress

• "All I have I would have given gladly not

to be standing here today," Johnson began, and added:

> An assassin's bullet has thrust upon me the awesome burden of the Presidency. I am here today to say I need your help. I cannot bear this burden alone. I need the help of all Americans in all America.

Nov. 29, issued executive order appointing special commission to investigate Kennedy assassination
• He appointed Chief Justice Earl Warren as chairman.

Dec. 4, met with labor and business leaders, urged cooperation and support of economic, civil rights, and medicare programs

Dec. 5, announced presidential succession agreement with Speaker John W. McCormack in event of disability
• Representative McCormack would serve as acting president in the event of Johnson's disability, according to the agreement, which was similar to the Eisenhower-Nixon and Kennedy-Johnson agreements.

Dec. 11, ordered budget reductions in all executive departments
• He emphasized in an address to defense department officials that their department was responsible for about half of the national budget and that it was their responsibility to "achieve the biggest savings."

Dec. 17, made his first address to United Nations
• Referring to President Kennedy, he said:
> My nation has lost a great leader, this organization has lost a great friend, world peace has lost a great champion. . . . I have come here today to make it unmistakably clear that the assassin's bullet which took his life did not alter his nation's purpose. We are more than ever opposed to the doctrine of hate and violence in our own land and around the world.

Dec. 20, first session of 88th Congress adjourned

Dec. 22, spoke briefly at Lincoln Memorial services officially ending month-long period of national mourning for President Kennedy

Dec. 27–28, conferred with Chancellor Ludwig Erhard of West Germany, Johnson City, Tex.

Dec. 31, pocket vetoed bill to amend Tariff Act of 1930 to require certain packages of imported articles to be marked to indicate country of origin
• This was the first of his 14 pocket vetoes, the first of his 30 vetoes.

1964

Jan. 7, second session of 88th Congress

Jan. 8, delivered his first State of the Union message to Congress
• He announced a $500,000,000 government spending reduction would be included in the next budget and said nuclear weapon production would be reduced by 25 percent. He also announced an extensive antipoverty program.

Jan. 9, conferred by telephone with President Robert Chiari of Panama
• Violence in the Panama Canal Zone led to the death of 21 Panamanians and four American soldiers, Jan. 9–10. Panama severed diplomatic relations with the U.S.; Chiari insisted upon "complete revision" of canal treaties.

Jan. 14, gave his first state dinner in honor of President Antonio Segni of Italy, White House

Jan. 16, dispatched Attorney General Kennedy to investigate means of halting undeclared war between Indonesia and Malaysia
• A cease-fire agreement was negotiated by Attorney General Kennedy.

Jan. 18, replied to Khrushchev proposal to end territorial and frontier disputes
• The U.S. would be interested in specific disarmament programs, Johnson said, rather than "vague declarations of principle that oppose some wars but not all." The Khrushchev plan of Jan. 2 would have outlawed the presence of U.S. military forces in South Korea, South Vietnam, and elsewhere, while permitting Communist conduct of "just" anticolonial actions.

Jan. 20, submitted economic report to Congress
• He warned against inflationary results of price or wage increases and urged an $11,000,000,000 tax cut.

Jan. 21, submitted budget message to Congress
• Defense spending was to be decreased by $1,100,000,000 and agricultural costs were to be reduced by $1,300,000,000 in the $97,900,000,000 budget.

Jan. 21–22, conferred with Prime Minister

Lester B. Pearson of Canada, White House
•Agreement on a power and flood-control program for the Columbia River Basin was announced, as well as the establishment of an international park on Campobello Island, the New Brunswick summer home of President Franklin D. Roosevelt.
Jan. 23, signed act that renamed National Cultural Center as John F. Kennedy Center for the Performing Arts
Feb. 1, voiced disagreement with de Gaulle proposal to neutralize former French possessions—Cambodia, Laos, North and South Vietnam
•He said the U.S. would continue its present policy in Southeast Asia.
Feb. 4, 24th Amendment to Constitution ratified
• *See* Constitution, page 645.
Feb. 5, sent special message on truth-in-lending and truth-in-packaging legislation to Congress
Feb. 7, issued executive order to defense department to discharge those among 2,500 Cuban civilians employed at Guantanamo who refused to live or spend earned dollars at naval base
Feb. 10, sent special message on medical care for aged to Congress
Feb. 12–13, conferred with Prime Minister Sir Alec Douglas-Home of Great Britain, Washington
Feb. 21–22, conferred with President Adolfo Lopez Mateos of Mexico, Palm Springs, Cal.
•Johnson and Mateos agreed to seek a mutually satisfactory solution to the Colorado River salinity problem.
Feb. 26, signed long-range tax reduction act
•Individual tax rates were reduced from a range of 20 to 91 percent to a range of 16 to 77 percent. Corporation taxes were reduced from 52 to 50 percent in 1964, and to 48 percent in 1965. Reductions over the two-year period totalled $11,545,000,000.
Feb. 29, announced development of 2,000-mile-per-hour jet plane
Mar. 9, sent special message on manpower problems to Congress
•He requested the formation of a special commission on automation.
Mar. 11, signed Coast Guard construction program act
•The appropriation of $93,299,000 was for 27 new ships, 17 helicopters, and shore installations.

Mar. 16, stated Panama dispute still unsolved
•Although the U.S. and Panama had agreed to accept settlement of their differences by an OAS five-nation committee, Mar. 12, Johnson and President Chiari disagreed about ground rules. "As of this moment, I do not believe that there has been a genuine meeting of minds between the two presidents of the two countries," Johnson said.
Mar. 16, sent special message to Congress in which he outlined his "war on poverty" program
•He suggested legislation to provide training for 380,000 youths at a cost of $962,500,000 for the first year. The program would be conducted by the planned Office of Economic Opportunity, and would be directed by Sargent Shriver of the Peace Corps.
Mar. 19, sent special message to Congress on foreign aid
•He proposed the smallest foreign aid appropriation since the Marshall Plan had been instituted—$2,400,000,000 for economic aid and $1,000,000,000 for military aid.
Mar. 23, vetoed bill to confer jurisdiction on court of claims to hear claim of R. Gordon Finney, Jr.
•This was the first of his 16 regular vetoes.
Mar. 23, stated wage and price restraint was responsibility of both labor and management, United Auto Workers national convention, Atlantic City, N.J.
Mar. 25, disagreed with Fulbright foreign policy proposals
•Senator J. William Fulbright, chairman of the Senate foreign relations committee, had suggested U.S. positions on Cuba and Panama were too rigid. "We are clinging to old myths in the face of new realities," Fulbright said.
Mar. 26, U.S. policy of continued support of South Vietnam reiterated by Secretary of Defense McNamara
•He had approved the McNamara speech, in which the defense secretary rejected the possibilities of "withdrawal" or "neutralization."
Mar. 28, declared Alaska disaster area
•A severe earthquake had caused $750,000,000 worth of damage in Alaska, Mar. 27. The toll of 117 dead and missing was considered low by experts, who declared

the quake the most powerful in North American history, worse than the 1906 San Francisco earthquake.

Apr. 4, refused to discuss U.S.-Panama dispute at press conference
• The U.S. and Panama had agreed to resume diplomatic relations, Apr. 3, in order to seek "prompt elimination" of causes of conflict. He demurred at discussing the differences prior to formal conferences.

Apr. 8, met funeral train of General Douglas MacArthur, Washington
• Johnson laid a wreath at the coffin in the Capitol Rotunda.

Apr. 14–15, conferred with King Hussein of Jordan, White House

Apr. 16, urged legislation to investigate construction of sea-level canal between Atlantic and Pacific oceans
• While several alternate routes were to be studied, he said the first study would be made in cooperation with the government of Colombia.

Apr. 20, announced reduction of nuclear materials production
• He and Khrushchev simultaneously announced cutbacks in the production of plutonium and enriched uranium for military use.

Apr. 22, dedicated Federal Pavilion, New York World's Fair

Apr. 24, made flying tour of Appalachia
• He suggested a $228,000,000 program to relieve poverty in the 360 counties of the ten-state Appalachian region.

May 7–8, revisited Appalachia
• "We will not win our war against poverty until the conscience of the entire nation is aroused," he said. He spoke in Maryland, Ohio, West Virginia, Tennessee, North Carolina, and Georgia.

May 11, signed $40,000,000 loan to Alliance for Progress
• He announced that assistance to Latin American nations since December, 1963, totalled more than $430,000,000.

May 14, received plan for additional military and economic aid to South Vietnam from Secretary of Defense McNamara and General Maxwell D. Taylor, chairman of joint chiefs of staff
• McNamara and Taylor had just returned from Saigon.

June 1–2, conferred with Premier Levi Eshkol of Israel, Washington
• Eshkol was the first Israeli premier to

make an official visit to the U.S.

June 3, stated U.S. stronger than "combined might of all the nations in the history of the world"
• In an address to the 78th commencement of the U.S. Coast Guard Academy, New London, Conn., he said American military strength had been built "not to destroy but to save, not to put an end to civilization but rather to try to put an end to conflict."

June 4, warned Turkey not to invade Cyprus
• Turkey announced postponement of its plans to land troops on Cyprus, June 5.

June 12, conferred with Chancellor Ludwig Erhard of West Germany, White House

June 22–23, conferred with Premier Ismet Inonu of Turkey, Washington

June 24–25, met with Premier George Papandreou of Greece, Washington
• Johnson's attempts to mediate the Turkish-Greek dispute over Cyprus were unsuccessful.

July 2, signed Civil Rights Act of 1964
• This act included among its many provisions the controversial public accommodations and equal employment opportunity clauses. During the 83 days of debate in the Senate, cloture was invoked for the first time on a civil rights measure.

July 6, signed mass transit act
• This act provided $375,000,000 over three years for urban area construction aid for subway, bus, and rail systems.

July 11, signed space administration appropriations act
• This act provided $5,227,500,000 for NASA during fiscal 1965. This included $2,600,000,000 for the *Apollo* project.

July 22, conferred with Prince Abdul Rahman, prime minister of Malaysia, White House
• U.S. support of Malaysia was announced a few days later.

July 24, conferred with Senator Barry Goldwater, Republican presidential nominee, on campaign tactics
• After the meeting, which had been requested by Goldwater, a joint statement was released:

> The President met with Senator Goldwater and reviewed the steps he had taken to avoid the incitement of racial tensions. Senator Goldwater expressed his position, which was that racial tensions

should be avoided. Both agreed upon this position.

July 24, again refused to consider de Gaulle proposal to neutralize Cambodia, Laos, North and South Vietnam
- The French president had suggested an international conference to investigate the means whereby the U.S., the U.S.S.R., and Communist China could pull out of the Southeast Asia peninsula. "We do not believe in a conference called to ratify terror," he said.

July 30, eliminated cabinet members and high officials who consulted with cabinet from consideration as Democratic vice-presidential candidates
- This political move ruled out the possibility

that Attorney General Kennedy would become Johnson's running mate.

Aug. 1, signed military construction act
- This act provided construction appropriations of $1,535,000,000.

Aug. 4, announced U.S. air attacks on North Vietnamese oil depot and PT boat bases
- He claimed in a televised announcement that the bombing raid was a retaliatory action for attacks by North Vietnamese PT boats on U.S. destroyers in the Gulf of Tonkin, in international waters, Aug. 2 and Aug. 4. He said that the *U.S.S. Maddox* was attacked, Aug. 2, and the *Maddox* and the *U.S.S. Turner Joy* were attacked, Aug. 4.
- The North Vietnamese denied that the Aug. 4 incident had occurred.

THE VIETNAM WAR

1964

Aug. 6, conferred with Secretary General U Thant of UN, White House
- Without making direct reference to the attack on North Vietnam, Johnson told Thant, "This nation has acted and this nation will always act when necessary in self-defense."

Aug. 7, signed joint resolution that authorized him to repel any armed attack against U.S. military forces by all necessary means
- The resolution, which authorized military assistance to any of the SEATO signatories, was approved in the House of Representatives, 416–0, and in the Senate, 88–2. This later came to be known as the Gulf of Tonkin Resolution.

Aug. 12, condemned racial violence in speech before 87th annual meeting of American Bar Association, New York City
- He said:

  We will not permit any part of America to become a jungle, where the weak are the prey of the strong and the many. Such acts must be stopped—whether they occur in Mississippi or in the State of New York.

- Racial violence had erupted in Harlem, July 18, during which one Negro was killed, five others wounded, and 81 civilians and 35 policemen were injured. The bodies of three civil rights workers, one of whom was Negro, had been found near

Philadelphia, Miss., Aug. 4. The trio, who had disappeared, June 22, had been shot to death.

Aug. 12, signed military pay increase act
- This act provided for pay raises of 2.5 percent for all military personnel with more than two years of service. The act affected both enlisted and commissioned personnel on active duty and in the reserve. The annual cost would be about $207,000,000.

Aug. 13, signed highway aid act

Aug. 14, signed federal employees salary reform act
- The salary of the vice president was raised from $35,000 to $43,000. Justices of the Supreme Court received $4,500 increases: the chief justice's salary was raised to $40,-000, associate justices to $39,500. Members of Congress were increased by $7,500 to $30,000. Executive department positions were regulated at five levels, from $26,000 to $35,000. The raises for classified employees averaged 4.3 percent. All increases were retroactive to July 1, except those of members of Congress, whose raises were effective Jan. 1, 1965.

Aug. 19, his net worth listed at $3,484,098 as of July 31, 1964
- At his direction, a New York accounting firm released the financial statement listing the net worth of the Johnson family in terms of original purchase value. The principal asset was the Texas Broadcasting Corporation, operator of Austin radio and television stations.

Aug. 26, renominated by acclamation, Democratic national convention, Atlantic City, N.J.

• He flew to Atlantic City, where, in an unprecedented act, he appeared before the delegates and stated that he had decided Senator Hubert H. Humphrey was "the best equipped man in this nation to be President if something happened to the President." He had announced his choice of Humphrey as the Democratic vice-presidential nominee prior to his departure from Washington.

Aug. 30, signed Economic Opportunity Act of 1964

• This act established the Office of Economic Opportunity (OEO), authorized $947,500,-000 for fiscal 1965. With state and local community cooperation, job corps training centers and conservation camps were to be provided for male and female youths between the ages of 16 and 21.

Sept. 2, signed housing act

• This act authorized $1,100,500,000 for four housing programs.

Sept. 3, signed wilderness act

• This act set apart 9,200,000 acres of forest lands as a federal wilderness system.

Sept. 7, opened campaign with Labor Day speech, Detroit, Mich.

Sept. 16, met with Prime Minister Lester B. Pearson of Canada, Vancouver, British Columbia

• Johnson attended ceremonies related to the Columbia River treaty.

• He was the sixth of seven presidents who visited Canada while in office.

• He was the tenth of 11 presidents who traveled outside the U.S. while in office.

• This was the first of his three visits to Canada while in office.

Sept. 17, announced U.S. had developed and installed two new weapon systems and over-horizon radar

• The two antisatellite systems were the Nike-Zeus and Thor rockets.

Sept. 26, received racial disorder report from FBI

• The FBI reported that there had been "no systematic planning or organization" of any of the riots in New York City and eight other northern cities.

Oct. 3, second session of 88th Congress adjourned

Oct. 13, signed act expanding ROTC program to include twelve hundred schools

Oct. 16, signed omnibus education act

• This act extended the National Defense Education Act for three years to July 30, 1968.

Oct. 18, praised deposed Khrushchev

• While Johnson was careful in his praise of the former Soviet premier, who had been deposed, Oct. 14, he made mention of Khrushchev's participation in the nuclear test-ban treaty, the establishment of the Washington-Moscow hot line, and the agreement to ban nuclear weapons from space. "In these actions, he demonstrated good sense and sober judgment," he said.

Oct. 20, issued proclamation of 30-day mourning period for former President Hoover

• Hoover had died in New York City earlier in the day.

Oct. 31, promised "Great Society" as he ended campaign, New York City

• In a speech given at Madison Square Garden, he said:

> This nation, this people, this generation, has man's first opportunity to create the Great Society. It can be a society of success without squalor—beauty without barrenness—works of genius without the wretchedness of poverty. We can open the doors of learning, of fruitful labor and rewarding leisure—not just to the privileged few, but to everyone.

Nov. 3, election day

• *See* Election of 1964, pages 548–549.

Dec. 2, opposed interest rise

• He urged the banks to maintain present lending rates in a speech to the Business Council, Washington.

Dec. 7–8, conferred with Prime Minister Harold Wilson of Great Britain, White House

Dec. 16, announced 162 antipoverty projects in all 50 states

• This was the second allotment of poverty funds, totalling $82,600,000. The first allotment—$35,000,000 for 120 projects—had been announced in late November.

Dec. 17, presidential electors cast ballots

• Johnson received 486 of the 538 electoral votes from the 50 states.

• *See* Election of 1964, pages 548–549.

Dec. 18, announced new sea-level canal in Central America or Colombia would be constructed

•He also stated the U.S. had proposed a new treaty with Panama to replace the 1903 canal zone treaty. The site of the present canal was one of four possible routes for the new canal, he said.

Dec. 30, urged disarmament agreement in New Year's greetings message to Soviet leaders

1965

Jan. 4, first session of 89th Congress
•The administration maintained control of both the Senate and the House of Representatives. The Democrats gained one Senate and 38 House seats. The Senate (100 members) consisted of 68 Democrats and 32 Republicans. The House (435 members) consisted of 295 Democrats and 140 Republicans.

Jan. 4, delivered his second State of the Union message to Congress
•He outlined his comprehensive Great Society program.
•Delivered at 9 P.M., this was the first State of the Union message telecast during "prime time."

Jan. 6, electoral votes tabulated by Congress
•Johnson and Humphrey were officially declared elected.

Jan. 7, sent special health plan message to Congress
•He urged legislation to provide medicare for the aged, more efficient programs for the young and the mentally retarded, and proposed 32 regional medical centers to coordinate research and treatment of cancer, heart disease, and strokes.

Jan. 12, sent special education message to Congress
•He urged legislation to provide $1,515,-000,000 for educational purposes during the fiscal year beginning July 1. About two-thirds of the funds were asked as grants for public schools serving underprivileged children.

Jan. 12–13, conferred with Premier Eisaku Sato of Japan, White House

Jan. 13, sent special immigration message to Congress
•He proposed to abolish immigration quotas based on national origin.

Jan. 14, submitted $3,380,000,000 foreign aid program to Congress

Jan. 15, accepted resignation of Secretary of

Commerce Hodges

Jan. 15, appointed his second secretary of commerce, John T. Connor
•Connor took office, Jan. 18.

Jan. 17, announced third antipoverty allotment, $101,960,000 for 88 projects

Jan. 18, announced plan to replace Polaris missile program
•He asked for $2,000,000,000 to develop the Poseidon missile system.

ELECTION OF 1964

Socialist Workers party, convened, Dec. 28, 1963, at New York City, nominated Clifton DeBerry of New York for president, Edward Shaw of New York for vice president.

National States' Rights party, convened, Mar. 2, 1964, at Louisville, Ky., nominated John Kasper of Tennessee for president, J. B. Stoner of Georgia for vice president.

Socialist Labor party, convened May 2, at New York City, nominated Eric Hass of New York for president, Henning A. Blomen of Massachusetts for vice president.

Republican party, convened, July 13, at San Francisco, Cal., nominated Barry Morris Goldwater of Arizona for president, William Edward Miller of New York for vice president.
•This was the 28th Republican national convention. It was the second Republican convention held in San Francisco; it was the third major party convention held in San Francisco.

Democratic party, convened, Aug. 24, at Atlantic City, N.J., nominated Lyndon Baines Johnson of Texas for president, Hubert Horatio Humphrey of Minnesota for vice president.
•This was the 34th Democratic national convention. It was the only Democratic convention held in Atlantic City; it was the only major party convention held in Atlantic City.

Prohibition party, convened, Aug. 26, at Chicago, Ill., nominated Earle Harold Munn of Michigan for president, Mark Shaw of Massachusetts for vice president.

Election day, Tuesday, Nov. 3, 1964

Popular vote: 70,440,367
    Johnson, 43,167,895
    Goldwater, 27,146,969
    Hass, 42,642
    Munn, 23,267

DeBerry, 22,249
Kasper, 6,957
others, 30,388
Electoral vote: 538, 50 states and District of Columbia
• Johnson, 486, 44 states and District of Columbia
(Alaska, 3; Arkansas, 6; California, 40; Colorado, 6; Connecticut, 8; Delaware, 3; District of Columbia, 3; Florida, 14; Hawaii, 4; Idaho, 4; Illinois, 26; Indiana, 13; Iowa, 9; Kansas, 7; Kentucky, 9; Maine, 4; Maryland, 10; Massachusetts, 14; Michigan, 21; Minnesota, 10; Mis-souri, 12; Montana, 4; Nebraska, 5; Nevada, 3; New Hampshire, 4; New Jersey, 14; New Mexico, 4; New York, 43; North Carolina, 13; North Dakota, 4; Ohio, 26; Oklahoma, 8; Oregon, 6; Pennsylvania, 29; Rhode Island, 4; South Dakota, 4; Tennessee, 11; Texas, 25; Utah, 4; Vermont, 3; Virginia, 12; Washington, 9; West Virginia, 7; Wisconsin, 12; Wyoming, 3)
• Goldwater, 52, six states
(Alabama, 10; Arizona, 5; Georgia, 12; Louisiana, 10; Mississippi, 7; South Carolina, 8)

THE 45th ADMINISTRATION

1965

Jan. 20, inauguration day
• Johnson took the oath of office, administered by Chief Justice Earl Warren, on the east portico of the Capitol.
• This was the third of four inaugurations at which Chief Justice Warren officiated.
Jan. 25, sent budget message to Congress
• He estimated expenditures for the fiscal year ending June 30, 1966, at $99,700,000,-000; receipts at $94,400,000,000; and a deficit of $5,300,000,000.
Jan. 28, proposed constitutional amendments on presidential disability, electoral college reforms
Feb. 4, sent special farm message to Congress
• His program called for the continuation of federal farm price supports with some modifications.
Feb. 4, opposed de Gaulle call for UN charter revision
• He declared that the troubles within the UN were "traceable not to the United Nations Charter, but to those countries which have violated either the spirit or the letter of the Charter."
Feb. 7, ordered air strikes against North Vietnam
• The air attacks were in retaliation for Vietcong guerrilla attacks on American installations.
Feb. 8, sent special message on natural beauty to Congress
• He said:
We must rescue our cities and countryside . . . with the same pur-pose and vigor with which, in other areas, we moved to save the forests and the soil.
Feb. 9, conferred with Reverend Dr. Martin Luther King, Jr., pledged swift action on voting rights legislation
Feb. 10, asked reduction of duty-free exemption on purchases abroad by Americans
Feb. 17, defended Vietnam policy in speech to National Industrial Conference Board, Washington
• He said the U.S. sought "no wider war."
Mar. 2, sent special housing and urban development message to Congress
• He proposed the creation of a cabinet department of housing and urban development and urged direct rent subsidies for middle-income families to encourage construction of 500,000 new dwellings during the next four years.
Mar. 4, called unemployment "intolerably high" in annual manpower report to Congress
• He called for support of his education and antipoverty programs to help lower the five percent unemployment level.
Mar. 4, asked legislation for high-speed railroad system between Boston, New York City, and Washington, D.C.
Mar. 8–9, first U.S. combat troops landed in South Vietnam
• Two battalions of marines, more than 3,-500 men, were dispatched to defend the Danang air base. U.S. technical advisers in Vietnam numbered 23,500.
Mar. 9, deplored brutality toward Selma-Montgomery marchers

•He criticized the harassment of Negro marchers in Alabama "when they sought to dramatize their deep and sincere interest in attaining the precious right to vote."

Mar. 13, conferred with Governor George C. Wallace of Alabama, White House

•After the right of Negro demonstrators to hold a mass march to Montgomery was upheld in federal court, Governor Wallace announced that Alabama was "financially unable" to mobilize the National Guard to protect the marchers, Mar. 19.

Mar. 15, addressed joint session of Congress, urged voting rights legislation

•In his address to the unusual night session of Congress, which was televised, he said:
    What happened in Selma is part of a far larger movement which reaches into every section and state of America. It is the effort of American Negroes to secure for themselves the full blessings of American life. Their cause must be our cause, too. Because it's not just Negroes, but really it's all of us, who must overcome the crippling legacy of bigotry and injustice.

•He closed with the rallying slogan of the civil rights movement: "And we shall overcome."

Mar. 17, submitted his voting rights legislation to Congress

•The proposed bill was drafted with the assistance of Democratic and Republican leaders.

Mar. 20, federalized Alabama National Guard

•The thirty-two hundred marchers, including many white supporters from throughout the country, began the 54-mile march from Selma to Montgomery, Mar. 21. The participants had grown to twenty-five thousand when the march ended in the state capital. After twice refusing to receive a delegation of the marchers, Governor Wallace finally saw the group, Mar. 30. Wallace refused to call a biracial conference on civil rights.

Mar. 26, called for full investigation of Ku Klux Klan

•He announced the arrest of four Klansmen for the murder of Mrs. Viola Gregg Liuzzo of Detroit, Mich., a white civil rights worker who had been shot to death near Selma, Mar. 25. In a televised report to the nation, Johnson stigmatized the KKK as "a hooded society of bigots" and warned members "to get out of the Ku Klux Klan and return to a decent society before it is too late."

Apr. 2, increased U.S. military and economic aid to South Vietnam

Apr. 5, sent proposed revisions of farm program to Congress

•The suggested legislation was designed to reduce federal costs by $200,000,000 and add $100,000,000 to farm income by raising consumer costs by $300,000,000.

Apr. 7, stated U.S. was prepared to participate in "unconditional discussions" to end Vietnam War, Johns Hopkins University, Baltimore Md.

Apr. 15, conferred with Prime Minister Harold Macmillan of Great Britain, White House

Apr. 19, conferred with Premier Aldo Moro and Foreign Minister Amintore Fanfani of Italy, White House

Apr. 28, sent four hundred marines to Dominican Republic

•A military coup overthrew the U.S.-supported government, Apr. 24–25. In a televised speech, May 2, Johnson charged that Communist leaders, some trained in Cuba, had taken over the revolt. Additional U.S. military units were sent until more than nineteen thousand troops were on duty there.

May 7, spoke on television by satellite to European audiences commemorating 20th anniversary of VE-Day

•VE-Day was May 8.

May 17, asked $4,000,000,000 reduction in excise taxes

May 18, sent special labor message to Congress

•He asked repeal of "right to work" section of Taft-Hartley Act, broadening of $1.25 minimum wage coverage, and extension of unemployment benefit time.

June 1, asked Congress for $89,000,000 foreign aid for Southeast Asia

June 1, explained Dominican Republic action

•During a press conference, he said the U.S. had intervened to protect American lives. He announced the withdrawal of two thousand marines.

June 3, asked Congress to eliminate silver in dimes and quarters, lower silver from 90 to 40 percent in half dollars

•He explained that U.S. silver reserves

would be depleted in three years if regular coinage was continued.

June 4, described eventual role of Negro in America, Howard University, Washington, D.C.

•He said:

> We seek not just freedom but opportunity—not just legal equity but human ability—not just equality as a right and a theory, but equality as a fact and a result.

June 8, his authorization to commit U.S. ground troops to combat in South Vietnam reported by state department

•An additional twenty-one thousand U.S. troops were being sent to Vietnam, Defense Secretary McNamara said, June 16.

June 25, appealed to UN to aid Vietnam negotiations, San Francisco, Cal.

•During ceremonies marking the 20th anniversary of the signing of the UN Charter, he also urged creation of an international peace force, and called for war on international poverty.

•The charter had been signed in San Francisco, June 26, 1945.

July 2, proposed National Teachers Corps for urban slum and rural poverty areas in address to National Educational Association, New York City

July 6, 25th Amendment to Constitution submitted to states for ratification

July 11, issued first-year report on Civil Rights Act of 1964

•He said 60 percent of the southern and border-state school districts had complied with the provisions of the act, which had been signed, July 2, 1964.

July 12, informed by U.S.S.R. of desire to resume Disarmament Committee meetings in Geneva, Switzerland

•The conference, which had recessed in September, 1964, met, July 27.

July 20, accepted resignation of Associate Justice Goldberg, effective, July 25

•Johnson appointed Goldberg as ambassador to the UN, July 20, to succeed Adlai E. Stevenson, who had died in London, England, July 14.

July 20, called for "continuing flow of ideas from universities and private groups," Second White House Conference on Education

July 27, accepted resignation of Secretary of Health, Education and Welfare Celebrezze

July 27, appointed his second secretary of health, education and welfare, John W. Gardner

•Gardner took office, Aug. 18.

July 28, announced troop buildup in Vietnam, doubling of draft

•An additional 50,000 men were sent to South Vietnam, which brought the U.S. commitment to 125,000 troops. The monthly draft was increased from 17,000 to 35,000.

•Johnson said at a press conference:

> We do not want an expanding struggle with consequences that no one can foresee, nor will we bluster or bully or flaunt our power. But we will not surrender and we will not retreat.

July 28, appointed Abe Fortas as associate justice

•Fortas, who was confirmed by the Senate, Aug. 11, was the first of Johnson's four appointments to the Supreme Court.

Aug. 4, sent special message to Congress in which he asked $1,700,000,000 in additional defense appropriations for Vietnam War

Aug. 9–11, briefed members of Congress on Vietnam War

•He stated his belief that there was "no substantial division" in Congress or throughout the country on his Vietnam policy, Aug. 9.

Aug. 20, declared no justification existed for Watts riots

•More than 35 were killed and several hundred injured during the six-day riots in the 140-block Watts section of Los Angeles, Cal., Aug. 11–16. Negro mobs raged through the area, looting and burning entire blocks. "Neither old wrongs nor new fears can ever justify arson or murder," he said.

Aug. 29, announced settlement of 75-day shipping strike

•His proposal for settlement was accepted, including a 3.2 percent wage and benefits increase for members of the three unions involved.

Aug. 30, accepted resignation of Postmaster General Gronouski

Aug. 30, appointed his second postmaster general, Lawrence F. O'Brien

•O'Brien took office, Nov. 3.

Sept. 3, announced settlement of steel dispute

•A three-year agreement, which included a 48-cents-an-hour wage and benefits increase, was signed by union and industry leaders, Sept. 6. Johnson had called the labor and management representatives to Washington, Aug. 30, from Pittsburgh, Pa., where they had been deadlocked since May 1. His suggestions hastened the final decisions.

Sept. 4, recognized provisional government of Dominican Republic

•He approved $20,000,000 in economic aid to the new government headed by Hector Garcia-Godoy.

Sept. 9, signed act that established department of housing and urban development

•This act created the first new cabinet post in 12 years; the department of health, education and welfare had been formed in 1953.

•The 11th cabinet-level department came into being 60 days later, Nov. 9.

Sept. 24, announced new treaty being drawn to supersede 1903 canal agreement with Panama

Oct. 4, met with Pope Paul VI, New York City

•Pope Paul, the first head of the Roman Catholic Church to visit the U.S., addressed the UN, celebrated mass in Yankee Stadium, and visited the Vatican Pavilion at the New York World's Fair.

•Johnson was the only president who met with a Pope in the U.S.

•He was the fourth of five presidents who met with Popes while in office.

•This was the first of his two meetings with Pope Paul while in office.

Oct. 8, underwent gall bladder operation, Bethesda Naval Hospital, Md.

•He had his gall bladder removed, as well as a kidney stone from the right ureter, during the two hour, 15 minute, operation.

Oct. 21, returned to White House from hospital

Oct. 22, signed Highway Beautification Act

•This $320,000,000 measure was popularly called the "Lady Bird Act." Mrs. Johnson suggested the bill to her husband, traveled throughout the country to speak on the subject, and asked for the votes of innumerable legislators. Under the act, 20 percent of federal highway grants would be denied those states that did not agree to control billboards and junkyards along interstate and primary highways by Jan. 1, 1968.

Oct. 22, first session of 89th Congress adjourned

Oct. 23, flew to Texas ranch to continue recuperation

Oct. 28, signed $4,200,000,000 Public Works Appropriation Act

Oct. 29, signed federal employees salary increase act

•The 1,700,000 federal workers were given a 3.6 percent pay raise at a yearly cost of $641,500,000.

Nov. 3, attended oath-taking ceremony of Postmaster General O'Brien, Hye, Tex.

•Johnson had mailed his first letter in the Hye general store (which doubles as the post office) in 1912, when he was four years old.

•O'Brien was the first cabinet officer who took the oath of office outside the capital.

Nov. 8, signed Higher Education Act of 1965, San Marcos, Tex.

•He signed the measure in the gymnasium of his alma mater, Southwest Texas State College. This act provided $160,000,000 for the first year of the federal program of direct scholarships to needy college students.

Nov. 10, won "aluminum war"

•Announced price rises by Alcoa and three smaller aluminum producers were rescinded after the government retaliated with threats to sell stockpiled aluminum.

Nov. 11, held first major foreign affairs review since operation, LBJ Ranch

•He met with Secretary of State Rusk, Defense Secretary McNamara, Undersecretary of State George W. Ball, and Special Assistant McGeorge Bundy.

Nov. 14, returned to White House after 22-day convalescence at ranch

Nov. 16, issued executive order to federal agencies to halt "inequities" in pay scales of blue-collar government employees

•He ordered adjustment of pay rates for about 617,000 workers, about 80 percent of whom were employed by the defense department.

Nov. 17, with his wife, gave dinner dance for Princess Margaret and Earl of Snowden of Great Britain, White House

•It was also the Johnsons' 31st wedding anniversary. He gave Lord Snowden "a little senior advice" during his after-dinner remarks. "I have learned that only two things are necessary to keep one's wife happy," he said. "First, let her think she's having her way. And second, let her have it."

Dec. 10, his approval of construction of 210 new jet bombers announced by Secretary of Defense McNamara

•The FB-111, a strategical and tactical bomber, would replace the B-52 and B-58 wings of the Strategic Air Command.

Dec. 14–15, conferred with President Mohammed Ayub Khan of Pakistan, White House

Dec. 15, congratulated *Gemini 6* and *Gemini 7* astronauts and other NASA personnel involved in first manned rendezvous in space

Dec. 20, conferred with Chancellor Ludwig Erhard of West Germany, White House

Dec. 29, sent emissaries to Ottawa, London, Paris, Rome, Warsaw, Belgrade, and Moscow in major peace drive

•His press secretary announced that the U.S. desired to settle the Vietnam War at the conference table.

1966

Jan. 10, second session of 89th Congress

Jan. 12, delivered his third State of the Union message to Congress

•He declared that the U.S. would stay in Vietnam "until aggression has stopped" and called for the continuation of the Great Society domestic program. He proposed legislation to accelerate corporation and individual income tax collections and to prohibit racial discrimination in housing sales or rentals. He suggested a constitutional amendment to increase the term of office of members of the House of Representatives to four years and asked for the creation of a cabinet-level department of transportation.

Jan. 13, appointed first secretary of housing and urban development, Robert C. Weaver

•Weaver, who took office, Jan. 18, was the first Negro member of the cabinet.

Jan. 24, sent budget message to Congress

•He estimated expenditures for the fiscal year ending June 30, 1967, at $112,847,000,000; receipts at $111,000,000,000; and a deficit of $1,847,000,000.

Jan. 27, sent annual economic report to Congress

•He forecast continued economic growth, reduced unemployment.

Jan. 31, announced U.S. resumption of bombing raids on North Vietnam

•In a TV-radio address, he said the bombings had been resumed after a 37-day pause because the U.S. peace drive had been rejected by North Vietnam and Red China.

Feb. 1, submitted $3,380,000,000 foreign aid program to Congress

Feb. 2, sent special international education and health message to Congress

•He requested $524,000,000 to expand the nutrition program in underdeveloped nations, to conduct an antimalaria program, and to supply birth control and family planning aid where requested.

Feb. 6–8, conferred with Premier Nguyen Cao Ky of South Vietnam, Honolulu, Hawaii

•He and Ky issued the Honolulu Declaration, which pledged the U.S. and South Vietnam to fight aggression and continue the "unending quest for peace."

•This was Johnson's first overseas trip while in office.

•He was the second of three presidents who visited the state of Hawaii while in office.

•He was the fourth of five presidents who visited Hawaii while in office.

•This was the first of his six visits to Hawaii while in office.

Feb. 10, sent special message on Food for Freedom program to Congress

•He recommended a yearly appropriation of $3,300,000,000 for the five-year antifamine program. He also asked for the establishment of national food and fiber reserves for emergency use.

Feb. 23, sent special message on conservation to Congress

•He requested $50,000,000 for the first year of his clean river program, emphasizing that unchecked pollution would result in a "barren America."

Feb. 26, appointed Andrew F. Brimmer to Federal Reserve Board

•Brimmer, who had been assistant secretary of commerce for economic affairs, was the first Negro to serve on the FRB.

Mar. 1, sent special health and education message to Congress

•He asked $41,000,000 for the first year of the health projects, which included grants to train additional specialists for understaffed health services. He also recommended the expansion of education projects under the Higher Education Facilities Act and the Elementary and Secondary Education Act.

Mar. 1, asked Communists for peaceful end to Southeast Asia conflict, pledged substantial aid to both North and South Vietnam

• U.S. forces committed to Vietnam numbered 235,000, the defense department announced, Mar. 2.

Mar. 2, sent special message to Congress in which he proposed cabinet-level department of transportation

• He suggested the coordination of ten agencies concerned with the control of highways, waterways and airlanes. He also asked for $200,000,000 to develop a 2,000-mile-per-hour aircraft.

Mar. 2, decorated cryptologist Frank Byron Rowlett

• Rowlett, who had broken the Japanese code in 1941, was awarded the National Security Medal.

Mar. 7, recommended 3.2 percent pay raise for 1,800,000 federal employees

• The cost of the recommended pay increase was $485,000,000, effective, Jan. 1, 1967.

Mar. 12, met with 38 state governors and governors of Puerto Rico, Guam, and Virgin Islands, White House

• He thanked the governors for their unanimous resolution of support of the administration's policy in Vietnam.

Mar. 21, recommended truth-in-packaging, truth-in-lending and child-safety legislation to Congress

• The three proposals concerned consumer protection. The packaging bill called for explicit labeling of the contents of retail products; the lending bill called for exact information regarding rate of interest charges; and the safety bill called for more stringent regulations regarding children's clothing and medicines.

Mar. 28–29, conferred with Mrs. Indira Gandhi, prime minister of India, White House

• Mrs. Gandhi, the daughter of Jawaharlal Nehru, was the widow of Feroze Gandhi. Her husband was not related to Mohandas K. Gandhi.

Apr. 4, appealed to eight thousand members of firemen and engineers union to return to work

• The walkout which had begun, Mar. 31, affected rail service in 38 states. The brotherhood returned to work after his appeal.

Apr. 14–15, visited Mexico

• He dedicated a statue of Lincoln, a gift of the U.S., in Mexico City, and reaffirmed

this country's commitment to the Alliance for Progress.

• He was the sixth of seven presidents who visited Mexico while in office.

• This was the first of his three visits to Mexico while in office.

Apr. 28, sent 1966 civil rights bill to Congress

• He proposed legislation that would ban discrimination in the sale and renting of housing. This was his first civil rights proposal that concerned a national problem, rather than merely inequities limited to southern states.

• He also asked for legislation to end discrimination in the selection of federal and state juries and to empower the attorney general to initiate suits to force desegregation of public facilities.

May 4, asked anti-inflation suggestions of President's Advisory Committee on Labor-Management

• He acknowledged that "disquieting signs are beginning to appear" in the economy.

May 5, announced 15 percent increase in 1967 wheat acreage

• The addition of 7,700,000 acres to the national wheat acreage allotment under the price support program was the first increase since 1961. The 1967 acreage allotment was set at 59,300,000 acres. The increase was necessary because of reserve depletions by famine aid to India and other nations and by increased commercial exports.

May 7, called for UN space treaty

• He announced that the U.S. would seek a treaty through the UN to prevent any nation from claiming sovereignty to the moon and other celestial bodies. The treaty, he added, also should outlaw nuclear weapons in space.

May 11, called for support of his policies in Vietnam by intellectuals, Princeton, N.J.

• During dedication ceremonies for the Woodrow Wilson School of Public and International Affairs at Princeton University, Johnson replied to the May 5 charges by Senator J. William Fulbright that the U.S. was "succumbing to the arrogance of power" by confusing "its power with virtue and its major responsibilities with a universal mission."

• In his reply, Johnson said:

The exercise of power in this century has meant for all of us in the

United States not arrogance but agony. We have used our power not willingly and recklessly ever, but always reluctantly and with restraint.... The responsible intellectual ... knows above all that his task is, in the language of the current generation, "to cool it," to bring what my generation called "not heat but light" to public affairs.

May 12, visited Vietnam wounded, decorated two officers and two enlisted men, Walter Reed Army Hospital

• He presented Purple Hearts to the four soldiers during his visit to two wards. While at the hospital, he also visited former President Eisenhower, who was being treated for arthritis, and Senator Everett Dirksen, who was recovering from a broken hip.

May 13, signed $2,788,000,000 supplemental appropriation act

• This act provided $1,168,000,000 for military and civilian federal employee pay increases; funds for federal contributions to public assistance programs; veterans' compensations and pensions; elementary and secondary education activities and the Teacher Corps; health insurance for the aged; the rent supplement program; and post office operations.

May 15, White House picketed by more than ten thousand antiwar demonstrators

May 17, formally accepted Hirshhorn art collection, White House

• He asked Congress to authorize the construction of a museum near the National Gallery of Art to house the four thousand paintings and sixteen hundred pieces of sculpture donated to the government by Joseph Herman Hirshhorn. The collection was valued at between $25,000,000 and $50,000,000.

May 17, attacked critics of his Vietnam policy as "Nervous Nellies," Chicago, Ill.

• He told a Democratic party fund-raising dinner:

There will be some Nervous Nellies and some who will become frustrated and bothered and break rank under the strain. And some will turn on their leaders and on their country and on our own fighting men.

• He later denied that he meant to indicate that some citizens were less patriotic than others, May 21. He said that he wanted to emphasize the fact that "because we have dissent does not mean that we have dissected, and because we do have differences does not mean that we are torn to pieces."

May 26, sent special message to Congress on need for new controls on campaign donations

• He proposed disclosure of campaign fund sources in primary and general elections for federal office, as well as a limitation of $5,000 from any one contributor. He asked that members of Congress be required to disclose all gifts and income for personal service. He also suggested that individual contributors should be allowed to deduct the first $100 from taxable income.

May 26, denounced white supremacy policies of Rhodesia, South Africa, and Portuguese territories in Africa

June 2, praised *Surveyor I* operational team

• *Surveyor I* made the first U.S. lunar landing and sent back more than eleven thousand television pictures of the moon surface. Launched, May 30, *Surveyor* landed on the moon, June 2, and operated until July 14, when its batteries went dead. The Soviet *Luna 9* had made the first lunar landing in February but sent back only ten photographs before becoming inoperative.

June 18, appointed Dr. Samuel M. Nabrit as member of Atomic Energy Commission

• Dr. Nabrit, president of Texas Southern University, was the first Negro member of the AEC.

June 21, received King Faisal of Saudi Arabia, White House

June 27, ordered medical review

• After meeting with 23 officials in government medicine, he expressed concern that too much research was being carried on "for the sake of research alone," rather than resulting in tangible benefits.

June 30, announced escalation of Vietnam War would continue, Omaha, Neb.

• He said that U.S. air strikes on military targets in North Vietnam "will continue to impose a growing burden and a high price on those who wage war against the freedom of their neighbors." The first U.S. bombing raids on Hanoi, capital of North Vietnam, and the principal port of Haiphong had been carried out, June 29.

June 30, renewed his call for peace conference, Des Moines, Iowa

•He said that if the leaders of North Vietnam

>... will only let me know when and where they would like to ask us directly what can be done to bring peace to South Vietnam, I will have my closest and most trusted associates there in a matter of hours.

June 30, expressed confidence in success of Medicare program

•Medicare, the program to pay part of the hospital bills of citizens over 65 through Social Security, as well as part of the doctors' bills of those who joined the voluntary program, went into effect July 1.

July 2, appointed commission to study Selective Service System

•He appointed a 20-man National Advisory Commission on Selective Service to study the draft system and make recommendations for reform. Critics of the draft system had called it inequitable.

July 4, signed act that widened public's right to examine governmental records

•He said:

>I have always believed that freedom of information is so vital that only the national security, not the desire of public officials or private citizens, should determine when it must be restricted.

July 4, signed act that created American Revolution Bicentennial Commission

•The commission was established to plan the official celebration of the 200th anniversary of American independence in 1976.

July 13, replica of his birthplace opened to public, near Stonewall, Tex.

•The house in which he was born had deteriorated; the site and several acres of surrounding land had been acquired in 1963, and construction of the replica by the Johnson City Foundation had begun in 1964. The restored stone and wood frame farmhouse of five rooms and two stone fireplaces is on the edge of the LBJ Ranch, near the Pedernales River.

July 19, cautioned congressional leaders against "add-on" appropriations

•He summoned the Democratic chairmen and ranking Republican members of the Senate and House of Representatives appropriations committees to the White House, where he warned against additional "add-on" legislation. Congressional

appropriations beyond administration requests totalled nearly $1,000,000,000, he said.

July 23, warned Negroes that riots impede reforms, Indianapolis, Ind.

•Racial tensions had caused riots in Omaha, Neb., July 3–5; Chicago, Ill., July 12–15; Brooklyn, N.Y., July 15–22; Jacksonville, Fla., July 18; and Cleveland, Ohio, July 18–23.

•In a speech at the Indianapolis Athletic Club, he said:

>Riots in the streets do not bring about lasting reforms. They tear at the very fabric of the community. They set neighbor against neighbor and create walls of distrust and fear between them. They make reform more difficult by turning away the very people who can and must support reform. They start a chain reaction the consequences of which always fall most heavily on those who begin them.

July 26, endorsed recommendation- that more Negroes be promoted to officer ranks in armed forces

•The recommendation had been made by Whitney M. Young, Jr., executive director of the National Urban League, who had recently returned from an inspection trip to South Vietnam to investigate the status of Negro servicemen.

July 29, received Prime Minister Harold Wilson of Great Britain, White House

July 29, announced settlement of 22-day airline strike

•Five major airlines had been shut down by a strike of more than thirty-five thousand mechanics and ground workers, July 7. The settlement was rejected by the rank and file of the union, July 31, and the strike continued.

Aug. 2, urged prompt enactment of gun-control legislation

•His call for enactment of gun-control legislation, which had been under consideration for months, came the day after a University of Texas student, Charles J. Whitman, killed 14 persons and wounded 30 others during 90 minutes of sniping from the top of the university's 27-story tower. Whitman was shot to death by police officers.

Aug. 2, received President Zalman Shazar of Israel, White House

Aug. 3, attended Washington Redskins-Baltimore Colts football game, Washington, D.C.

•He was the first president to attend a professional football game while in office. This was a pre-season game.

Aug. 5, signed $5,000,000,000 space authorization act

Aug. 5, warned that government might have to slash spending "in those areas where prices are rising in an inflationary way"

•The steel industry had announced a 2.1 percent price rise, Aug. 2. Administration spokesmen denounced the increase as "irresponsible" and "inflationary," but no governmental action to roll back the price hike was taken, as had been done in 1965.

Aug. 6, attended wedding of his daughter, Luci Baines Johnson, to Patrick John Nugent, Shrine of the Immaculate Conception, Washington, D.C.

•Miss Johnson was the first daughter of a president in 52 years who was married while her father was in office; Eleanor Wilson had married William McAdoo, May 7, 1914.

Aug. 9, stated steel price rise would net steel firms $50,000,000 after taxes

Aug. 11, issued executive order that widened role of department of housing and urban development

•This order authorized Secretary Weaver to take certain actions to coordinate federal urban programs for which there had been no statutory authority in the past.

Aug. 17, called for economic integration of 19 Latin American nations

•"Effective unity—and not separation—is vital to the needs of expanding populations," he said on the fifth anniversary of the Alliance for Progress. He promised U.S. assistance to the proposed common market for Latin America.

Aug. 21–22, conferred with Prime Minister Lester B. Pearson of Canada, Campobello Island, New Brunswick

•Johnson cruised aboard the *U.S.S. Northampton* from Portland, Me., to Campobello Island. Between conferences, he and Pearson laid the cornerstone of a visitors' center at the summer home of President Franklin D. Roosevelt.

•This was the second of his three visits to Canada while in office.

Aug. 24, signed act that prohibited use of stolen pets in medical research

Sept. 8, sent special message to Congress in which he asked 16-month suspension of seven percent business tax credit and accelerated depreciation allowance on commercial construction

Sept. 8, rejected de Gaulle call for withdrawal of U.S. military forces from South Vietnam

•"We are willing to do anything we can to achieve peace, but it is not a one-way street," Johnson said.

Sept. 21, announced he had accepted resignation of Attorney General Katzenbach, effective, Oct. 2

•Johnson appointed Katzenbach as undersecretary of state, Sept. 21.

Sept. 21, signed act that set maximum interest rates on savings and loan deposits and differential interest rates on various types of bank savings

Sept. 22, offered to stop bombing of North Vietnam if Hanoi would pledge to match de-escalation

•The U.S. proposal was presented to the UN General Assembly by Ambassador Arthur Goldberg.

Sept. 23, signed act that raised minimum wage to $1.40 per hour, effective, Feb. 1, 1967, and to $1.60 per hour, effective, Feb. 1, 1968

•This act provided the 1967 increase for 3,800,000 workers and the 1968 increase for an additional 2,100,000 workers.

Sept. 26, conferred with Chancellor Ludwig Erhard of West Germany, White House

Sept. 27, appealed to Soviet people for new era of friendship between U.S. and U.S.S.R.

•His call for understanding was made in the tenth anniversary issue of the magazine, *Amerika*. The issue of sixty thousand copies was distributed to Russian newsstands under the terms of the Soviet-American cultural exchange agreement.

Sept. 28, received President Leopold S. Senghor of Senegal, White House

Oct. 7, suggested reduction of Soviet and U.S. military forces in Germany, New York City

•After his speech to the National Conference of Editorial Writers, Johnson conferred with Secretary General U Thant at the UN on Vietnam and other issues.

Oct. 13, rejected Thant suggestion that U.S. suspend bombing of North Vietnam as first step toward negotiated settlement

Oct. 15, signed seven conservation acts
- These acts established Guadalupe National Park in Texas, the Big Horn Canyon national recreation area in Montana, and the Pictured Rocks National Lakeshore in Michigan; increased the acreage of Point Reyes National Seashore in California; permitted the government to accept the donation of Wolf Trap Farm in Virginia; set up a program for the preservation of additional historic properties; and authorized a fund of $15,000,000 to provide for the protection of fish and wildlife threatened with extinction.

Oct. 16, signed act that created department of transportation
- This department was the 12th cabinet unit.

Oct. 17, flew to Hawaii, en route to Asia
- This was the second of his six visits to Hawaii while in office.

Oct. 17, signed act that extended U.S. exclusive fishing zone from three to 12 miles off coast
- This act was designed to prevent encroachment by Russian and Japanese fishing fleets, but did not extend the sovereignty of the U.S. beyond the traditional three-mile limit.

Oct. 18, flew to Pago Pago from Hawaii
- He was the only president who visited American Samoa while in office.
- This was the first of his two visits to American Samoa while in office.

Oct. 19, flew to Ohakea Airbase, New Zealand
- From Ohakea, the nearest airfield to Wellington capable of handling large jet aircraft, he was driven the one hundred miles to the capital. While in New Zealand, Johnson conferred with Prime Minister Keith J. Holyoake and the Governor-General, Sir Bernard Fergusson.
- He was the only president who visited New Zealand while in office.

Oct. 21, flew to Canberra, Australia
- During his three-day visit to Australia, he visited Canberra, Melbourne, Sydney, and Brisbane.
- He was the only president who visited Australia while in office.
- This was the first of his two visits to Australia while in office.

Oct. 22, second session of 89th Congress adjourned

Oct. 23, flew to Manila, Philippines

- He attended the seven-nation Manila Conference. Called at the invitation of President Ferdinand E. Marcos of the Philippines, the conference was attended by President Johnson, Prime Minister Harold E. Holt of Australia, Prime Minister Keith J. Holyoake of New Zealand, President Chung Hee Park of Korea, Prime Minister Thanom Kittikachorn of Thailand, and Premier Nguyen Cao Ky of South Vietnam. A statement signed by the seven nations at the end of the conference, Oct. 25, pledged their intention to "continue our military and all other efforts" in South Vietnam "as long as may be necessary, in close consultation among ourselves, until aggression is ended."
- Johnson was the second of three presidents who visited the Philippines while in office.
- He was the third of four presidents who visited Asia while in office.

Oct. 26, made surprise trip from Manila to South Vietnam
- "I came here today for one good reason," he told troops at Camranh Bay, "simply because I could not come to this part of the world and not come to see you." He spent two hours and 24 minutes at the base before flying back to Manila.
- He was the first of two presidents who visited South Vietnam while in office. The other was Nixon.
- He was the fourth of five presidents who visited war zones while in office.
- He was the second of three presidents to travel outside the U.S. during wartime.

Oct. 27, flew to Utapao Air Base, Thailand, from Manila
- After spending the night at the beach house of Prime Minister Thanom Kittikachorn at Bang Saen, Johnson was welcomed in Bangkok by King Phumiphol Aduldej. While in Thailand, he pledged to increase American aid from $40,000,000 to $60,000,000 for the fiscal year ending June 30, 1968.
- He was the only president who visited Thailand while in office.

Oct. 30, flew to Kuala Lumpur, Malaysia, from Thailand
- He conferred with Prime Minister Abdul Rahman. In a speech delivered in Kuala Lumpur, Johnson warned Communist China that any atomic military power that nation developed "can—and will—be deterred." China had announced a successful

test of a nuclear warhead missile, Oct. 28.
• He was the only president who visited Malaysia while in office.
Oct. 31, flew to Seoul, South Korea, from Malaysia
• He conferred with President Chung Hee Park at Blue House, the blue-roofed Korean counterpart of the White House.
• He was the second of two presidents who visited Korea while in office. The other was Eisenhower.
Nov. 1, flew to Anchorage, Alaska, from Korea
• He was the fourth of five presidents who visited Alaska while in office.
• He was the second of three presidents who visited the state of Alaska.
Nov. 2, returned to Washington, D.C.
• During his 17-day trip to Asia, he had visited seven countries.
Nov. 3, signed eight major domestic acts
• These measures authorized almost $15,-000,000 in federal aid for urban renewal, education, health care, antipollution, and consumer protection. He also signed 121 minor acts that had accumulated during his Asian tour.
Nov. 4, flew to LBJ Ranch to begin "reduced schedule of activity"
• On Nov. 3, it had been announced that he would soon undergo throat and abdomen surgery.
Nov. 13, reluctantly signed foreign investors tax act
• While he approved of the measure's main provision to induce more foreign investments in U.S. stocks and bonds by means of more favorable tax treatment, he criticized a variety of amendments that favored special interest groups. This act also provided that taxpayers could choose to have $1 of their income tax allocated to presidential campaigns.
Nov. 16, underwent double operation, Bethesda Naval Hospital, Bethesda, Md.
• A benign polyp was removed from his throat, and a small ventral hernia was repaired. The hernia was a defect in abdomenal scar tissue, a result of his gall bladder operation of 1965. The double operation took only 53 minutes, without complications.
Nov. 19, left hospital, departed for LBJ Ranch
Nov. 25, allocated $1,053,410,000 to states for school aid program in low-income areas

Nov. 29, announced cancellation or delay of $5,300,000,000 in federal programs
• This announcement was made during his first official visit to his ten-room office in the Federal Office Building, Austin, Tex.
Dec. 3, conferred with President Gustavo Diaz Ordaz of Mexico, Ciudad Acuna, Mexico
• Johnson and Diaz Ordaz inspected the $78,000,000 Amistad Dam on the Rio Grande, which was still under construction.
• This was the second of his three visits to Mexico while in office.
Dec. 14, White House announced resignation of Press Secretary Bill D. Moyers
• Moyers, the last of his original group of presidential assistants, resigned to become publisher of the Long Island newspaper, *Newsday*. Moyers's resignation became effective, Jan. 31, 1967.

1967

Jan. 5, issued executive order that banned most trade between U.S. and Rhodesia
Jan. 5, his rejection of officially commissioned portrait revealed
• The portrait by Peter Hurd, commissioned by the White House Historical Association, had been rejected more than one year earlier, reported the Washington *Post*. He was quoted as describing the painting as "the ugliest thing I ever saw."
Jan. 10, first session of 90th Congress
• The administration maintained control of both the Senate and the House of Representatives. The Republicans gained four Senate and 47 House seats. The Senate (100 members) consisted of 64 Democrats and 36 Republicans. The House (435 members) consisted of 248 Democrats and 187 Republicans.
Jan. 10, appointed first secretary of transportation, Alan S. Boyd
• Boyd took office, Jan. 16.
Jan. 10, delivered his fourth State of the Union message to Congress
• He recommended legislation to provide a six percent surcharge on personal and corporate income taxes to finance the Vietnam War and continue the Great Society domestic programs.
• This was the first State of the Union message broadcast on four national television

networks, the three established chains of NBC, CBS and ABC, and a special group of 70 National Educational Television stations.

Jan. 12, accepted resignation of Secretary of Commerce Connor, effective, Jan. 31

Jan. 17, announced defense budget of about $73,000,000,000 for fiscal year ending June 30, 1968

• He also said he would request a supplemental appropriation of $9,000,000,000 for additional military expenditures prior to June 30, 1967.

Jan. 20, sent special message to Congress in which he asked two-year extension of Appalachia region development program

Jan. 23, sent special message on "older Americans" to Congress

• He asked for legislation to raise social security payments, extension of Medicare, and revision of the tax structure to halt "discrimination against older Americans who are willing and able to work."

Jan. 24, sent budget message to Congress

• He estimated expenditures for the fiscal year ending June 30, 1968, at $169,200,-000,000; receipts at $167,100,000,000; and a deficit of $2,100,000,000. The direct cost of the Vietnam War was listed at $21,900,-000,000.

Jan. 26, sent annual economic report to Congress

• The 3.2 percent guidepost for wage increases was abandoned.

• He called on business and labor to exercise "utmost restraint and responsibility" in wage and price decisions.

Jan. 27, participated in signing of space treaty with Great Britain and U.S.S.R.

• The treaty limited the use of outer space for military purposes and outlawed claims of national sovereignty.

Jan. 30, sent special message on air pollution to Congress

• He urged passage of the proposed air quality bill, which would establish pollution control standards and emission limits on industry.

Jan. 31, sent special message on veterans' benefits to Congress

• He asked for legislation to expand benefits for veterans, including veterans of the Vietnam War, by $250,000,000 yearly.

Feb. 6, sent special message on crime to Congress

• He asked for passage of the proposed safe streets and crime control bill, which would provide $50,000,000 in federal grants to the states in 1968 for crime control. He also asked the banning of all wiretapping except in instances involving national security.

Feb. 8, sent special message on needy children to Congress

• He asked for expansion of the preschool Head Start program to include children in the first, second, and third grades.

Feb. 8–9, conferred with Foreign Minister Willy Brandt of West Germany, White House

Feb. 9, sent special message on foreign aid to Congress

• He proposed foreign aid appropriations of $3,100,000,000 for each of the next two fiscal years.

Feb. 10, 25th Amendment to Constitution ratified

• *See* Constitution, page 645.

Feb. 13, received Emperor Haile Selassie of Ethiopia, White House

Feb. 15, appointed panel to investigate CIA participation in financing foreign activities of nongovernmental organizations

• More than 30 American organizations secretly had received CIA funds for overseas operations from 1952 to 1966. The preliminary report of the panel found that the CIA activities had been directed by the National Security Council, Feb. 23.

Feb. 15, sent special message on civil rights to Congress

• He again packaged all of his proposals for civil rights legislation in one bill, including the housing provision that had been defeated by filibuster in the Senate in 1966.

Feb. 16, sent special message on aid to consumers to Congress

• He proposed a program to protect shoppers, investors, and medical patients, including a modified version of the truth-in-lending legislation. He also asked for legislation to require independent annual audits of private welfare and pension funds.

Feb. 21, sent special message on patent reform to Congress

• He recommended that the life of a patent be extended from 17 to 20 years from issuance.

Feb. 28, appointed his third attorney general, Ramsey Clark

• To avoid any possible conflict of interest,

Associate Justice Tom C. Clark, father of the nominee, announced that he would resign from the Supreme Court during or at the end of the current session.

•Clark took office, Mar. 10. His father resigned from the Court, June 12.

•The Clarks were the first father and son who served as attorneys general. Tom C. Clark had been appointed by Truman.

•Ramsey Clark was the only son of a Supreme Court justice who was appointed and served as attorney general.

Feb. 28, sent special message on education and health to Congress

•He asked for $9,000,000 to create a Corporation for Public Television, free of government control. He also requested major expansion of the Teacher Corps.

Mar. 9, refused to disclose his political plans

•During a press conference, he said:

I'm not ready to make a decision about my future after January, 1969, at this time. I think that, down the road several months from now, there will be an appropriate time for an announcement.

•This was the first presidential press conference to be televised live in color from the White House.

Mar. 13, sent special message to Congress in which he urged a 30 percent annual increase in aid to Latin America

•He asked for an additional $300,000,000 annually for five years, over and above the $1,000,000,000 invested each year since the Alliance for Progress began in 1961.

Mar. 14, conferred with Premier Chung Il Kwon of South Korea, White House

•He pledged to modernize the military equipment of Korean forces, both in Korea and South Vietnam.

Mar. 15, addressed joint session of Tennessee legislature, Nashville, Tenn.

•He also visited the homes of Presidents Jackson and Polk.

Mar. 17, issued executive order that released $791,000,000 of federal funds for highway construction, flood control, and other projects

Mar. 17, deferred plans to merge labor and commerce departments

•In a special message to Congress, he announced that he had referred the matter to the President's Advisory Committee on Labor-Management Policy. His efforts to combine the departments had met strong

opposition from labor and small business groups.

•The commerce and labor department had been reorganized and two cabinet-level departments created in 1913.

Mar. 20–21, conferred with Premier Nguyen Cao Ky and Nguyen Van Thieu, chief of state of South Vietnam, Agana, Guam.

•Johnson was the first of two presidents who visited Guam while in office. The other was Nixon.

Mar. 21, visited Hawaii, en route from Guam to Washington, D.C.

•This was the third of his six visits to Hawaii while in office.

Mar. 29, directed CIA to halt covert financial assistance to all private organizations

Mar. 31, signed consular convention with U.S.S.R.

•The Senate had ratified the treaty, which permitted negotiations for the reestablishment of consulates outside the capitals of the two countries, Mar. 16.

•This was the first bilateral treaty between the U.S. and the U.S.S.R. since the Russian Revolution of 1917.

Apr. 3, received President Cevdet Sunay of Turkey, White House

Apr. 4, signed $12,200,000,000 supplemental appropriation act for military operations in Southeast Asia

Apr. 5, sent special message to Congress recommending federal pay increase of four and one-half percent, higher postal rates

Apr. 8, attended opening game of baseball season, Washington, D.C.

•He threw out the first ball of the Washington Senators-New York Yankees game.

Apr. 11, arrived in Montevideo, Uruguay

•He was the last of three presidents who visited Uruguay while in office.

•He was the last of five presidents who visited South America while in office.

Apr. 12–14, attended conference of western hemisphere leaders, Punta del Este, Uruguay

•The formation of a Latin American common market was called for in the Declaration of the Presidents of the Americas, Apr. 14. The declaration was signed by all of the presidents and foreign ministers of the 19 countries represented except Otto Arosemena Gomez, interim president of Ecuador.

Apr. 14, visited Surinam, en route from Uruguay to San Antonio, Tex.
•He spent only slightly more than an hour in Surinam.
•He was the only president who visited Surinam while in office.
Apr. 23–26, visited West Germany
•He attended the funeral of Konrad Adenauer, first chancellor of West Germany, in Cologne, Apr. 25. While in Bonn, Johnson conferred with President Heinrich Luebke and Chancellor Kurt Georg Kiesinger.
•Johnson was the fourth of five presidents who visited Germany while in office.
•He was the sixth of seven presidents who visited Europe while in office.
•He was the last of three presidents who visited four continents while in office.
Apr. 29, authorized Secretary of Transportation Boyd to sign contracts for prototypes of commercial supersonic transport
•Two models of the jet airliner—capable of carrying 300 passengers at 1,750 miles per hour—were authorized. This involved a government investment of $1,144,000,000 over a four-year period.
May 2, sent special message to Congress requesting $75,000,000 for antipoverty summer programs
May 15, conferred with six New England governors on regional problems, Windsor Locks, Conn.
May 23, appointed his third secretary of commerce, Alexander Trowbridge
•Trowbridge took office, June 14.
May 25, sent special message to Congress in which he proposed most of presidential campaign costs be absorbed by federal treasury
May 25, visited Expo 67, Montreal, Canada
•He participated in United States Day ceremonies at Expo 67, and later conferred with Prime Minister Lester B. Pearson at Harrington Lake and Ottawa.
•This was the last of Johnson's three visits to Canada while in office.
June 2, conferred with Prime Minister Harold Wilson of Great Britain on Middle East crisis, White House
•President Gamal Abdel Nasser of the United Arab Republic had forced the withdrawal of a UN emergency force from the Sinai Peninsula, May 19, and proclaimed a blockade of Israeli ships and cargoes bound for Israel through the Gulf of Aqaba, May 22.

•Israel attacked Syria, Jordan, and the United Arab Republic, June 5. In six days, Israel had routed her enemies, occupied territory four times the size of the Jewish state, killed 35,000 Arabs and captured additional thousands, and destroyed the 450-plane Arab air force and about 650 Soviet-built tanks.
June 9, formed cabinet-level committee to study problems of needy Mexican-Americans
June 13, appointed Thurgood Marshall as associate justice
•Marshall, who was confirmed by the Senate, Aug. 30, was the second of Johnson's four appointments to the Supreme Court.
•Marshall was the first Negro member of the Supreme Court.
June 19, proposed five-point plan for Middle East
•He called on the Israelis and the Arabs to recognize each other's rights on land and sea, the restoration or resettlement of refugees, and the designation of borders that would insure mutual safety.
June 23, conferred with Premier Aleksei N. Kosygin of U.S.S.R., Glassboro, N.J.
•Johnson and Kosygin talked at the residence of Dr. Thomas E. Robinson, president of Glassboro State College, for five and a half hours.
•This was his first meeting with the Soviet chief of state.
June 25, again conferred with Kosygin, Glassboro
•This session lasted four and a half hours. Although Johnson described the two conferences as "useful," little of substance came out of the meetings.
June 26, signed act that extended and expanded federal mental health program
June 26, signed saline water conversion program act
June 27, received King Phumiphol Aduldej of Thailand, White House
June 28, conferred with King Hussein of Jordan, White House
June 29, signed act that extended National Teacher Corps
June 30, signed Military Selective Service Act of 1967
•This act extended the draft for four years.
June 30, issued executive order that authorized secretary of defense to draft 19-year-olds first
June 30, signed act that set the permanent

national debt limitation at $358,000,000,-000, effective, July 1
•This act provided for a temporary increase in the debt limit of $7,000,000,000 for the fiscal year ending June 30, 1968.
July 13, announced slight increase of U.S. troops in Vietnam planned
•The authorized number of troops in Vietnam was 480,000.
July 18, signed act ending railroad strike
•Six shopcraft unions had walked out, July 16. The wage dispute affected 95 percent of the nation's trackage and was the first national railroad strike since 1946.
•The act provided for the appointment of a presidential mediation board that would recommend a settlement within 60 days. This settlement would go into effect 30 days later if negotiations were fruitless.
•The board recommended a five and one-half percent annual wage increase in September that was accepted by the unions and, reluctantly, by the operators. The settlement went into effect, Oct. 15.
July 24, issued executive order that sent forty-seven hundred federal paratroopers to quell Detroit riot
•The bloodiest racial disorder of the summer occurred in Detroit, Mich., July 23–30. More than 40 persons were killed and about two thousand injured. When the ghetto riot ended, the homes of about five thousand had been destroyed.
July 27, appointed special advisory commission on civil disorders "to investigate the origin of the recent disorders in our cities"
•In a nationwide television address, he proclaimed July 30 as a national day of prayer for reconciliation.
Aug. 3, sent special budget message to Congress in which he asked for ten percent surcharge on personal and corporate income taxes
•He said the tax surcharge would raise $7,-400,000,000 prior to June 30, 1968, and would reduce the deficit to "manageable proportions." He estimated that the deficit, "without a tax increase and tight expenditure control," could exceed $28,000,-000,000.
•He also announced that 45,000 additional troops would be sent to Vietnam, which would raise the total commitment to 525,-000 men.
Aug. 12, vetoed bill to raise life insurance coverage for federal employees

•He had recommended an insurance bill that would have cost $13,000,000 a year. This bill, which would have increased the government contribution for each employee from 33⅓ to 40 percent, would have cost $61,000,000 the first year and more in future years.
Aug. 15–16, conferred with Chancellor Kurt Georg Kiesinger of West Germany, White House
•Agreement was reached that neither the U.S. nor West Germany would reduce or shift troops in Europe prior to consultation with each other and NATO.
Aug. 16, asked Congress to restore $425,-000,000 cut from his model cities program budget
Aug. 18, challenged Congress to void controversial Gulf of Tonkin Resolution of 1964
•Johnson had been challenged by Senator J. William Fulbright and other critics of his Vietnam policy that he had exceeded his executive authority. Johnson told his press conference audience that "the machinery is there any time the Congress desires to withdraw its view of the matter" and "we're well within the rights of what Congress said in its resolution and the remedy is there if we have acted unwisely or improperly."
•However, he emphasized that withdrawal of the Gulf of Tonkin Resolution would not change his Vietnam policy. "We stated then, and we repeat now," he said, "we did not think the resolution was necessary to do what we did and what we're doing."
Aug. 22, received Shah Mohammed Reza Pahlevi of Iran, White House
Aug. 28, issued executive order that reduced interest-equalization tax on foreign stock and bond purchases
Aug. 31, signed veterans' benefits act
•This new veterans' act extended increased educational, job training, and other benefits to about five million former servicemen, including veterans of the Vietnam War. The measure was expected to cost $285,600,000 during the first year.
•This act also established Aug. 5, 1964 as the formal beginning of the Vietnam War.
Sept. 7, issued executive order that established New England River Basins Commission
Sept. 11, received King Constantine II of Greece, White House

Sept. 14, asked for support of his anticrime and gun-control programs, Kansas City, Mo.

• During a speech to the International Association of Chiefs of Police, he denounced urban rioters and advocates of violence, saying, "much can explain but nothing can justify the riots of 1967."

Sept. 18, received President Giuseppe Saragat of Italy, White House

Sept. 20, asked transportation department to devise long-range air traffic control system

Sept. 27, signed food stamp act

Sept. 29, offered to halt bombing of North Vietnam if peace talks followed, San Antonio, Tex.

• His offer was rejected by North Vietnam.

Oct. 2, attended oath-taking ceremony of Associate Justice Marshall

Oct. 3, signed Vocational Rehabilitation Act of 1967

Oct. 4, signed act that created commission to recommend means of control of pornography

Oct. 10, invited U.S.S.R. to end "competitive spacemanship" by cooperative space exploration

• He spoke at a White House ceremony at which 13 nations, including Great Britain and the U.S.S.R., deposited notices of ratification of the outer-space treaty. The treaty had been signed, Jan. 27, and the Senate had consented to ratification, Apr. 25.

Oct. 11, signed act that authorized $170,-000,000 for Appalachia aid program

Oct. 13, issued executive order strengthening procedures designed to end discrimination against female federal employees

Oct. 26, received President Gustavo Diaz Ordaz of Mexico, White House

Oct. 28, attended transfer of El Chamizal from U.S. to Mexico, Ciudad Juarez

• Johnson and President Gustavo Diaz Ordaz attended the formal exchange of the 437-acre tract of land, as provided for in the Chamizal treaties of 1963 and 1967.

• The land dispute had begun shortly after an 1848 treaty fixed the Rio Grande as the boundary between the two countries.

• When the river changed course, about six hundred acres of Mexican territory were added to El Paso, Tex. A three-man commission—representatives of the U.S., Mexico and Canada—ruled in 1911 that the land belonged to Mexico, but the U.S.

refused to abide by the decision. President Adolfo Lopez Mateos raised the issue when President Kennedy visited Mexico in 1962, with the result that the 437-acre compromise was reached in 1963.

• This was the last of Johnson's three visits to Mexico while in office.

Nov. 3, signed $10,000,000,000 appropriation act for HUD and independent agencies

• He criticized Republican members of the House of Representatives for cuts in the rent supplements and model cities programs. The act provided less than half of the $662,000,000 requested for the model cities program and only $10,000,000 of the $40,000,000 requested for the rent supplements program.

Nov. 7, signed act that created Corporation for Public Broadcasting

• This act created the nonprofit, public corporation to improve the quality of noncommercial television.

Nov. 8, signed act providing for equal military promotion opportunities for women

• This act assured eventual promotion of female members of the armed forces to the ranks of general and admiral.

Nov. 8, received King Hussein of Jordan, White House

Nov. 10–11, made five-thousand-mile tour of eight military installations

• He visited bases in Virginia, California, and Kansas. During a speech to the officers and men of the aircraft carrier, *U.S.S. Enterprise*, off San Diego, Cal., he invited the leaders of North Vietnam to meet with him on a "neutral ship on a neutral sea."

Nov. 15, signed Foreign Assistance Act of 1967 authorizing $2,674,614,000 in foreign aid

Nov. 18, pledged not to devalue dollar

• Great Britain had devalued the pound from $2.80 to $2.40, which he called "a healthy and constructive development in international financial markets."

Nov. 20, signed act that created National Commission on Product Safety

Nov. 20, took part in ceremonies marking U.S. population at 200,000,000

• The population had reached 100,000,000 in 1915 and 150,000,000 in 1950. The U.S. was the fourth nation to pass the 200,000,-000 mark. China is estimated to have a population of about 800,000,000; India has more than 500,000,000; and the U.S.S.R.

has about 250,000,000.

Nov. 21, signed air quality act

•This act authorized a three-year, $428,-000,000 program to combat air pollution.

•He said:

Either we stop poisoning our air, or we become a nation in gas masks, groping our way through dying cities and a wilderness of ghost towns.

Nov. 27, ordered across-the-board reductions in spending by most government agencies

•An expenditure reduction of about $4,-000,000,000 was sought, the amount promised by administration officials in return for congressional consideration of his proposed ten percent tax increase.

Dec. 2, offered to widen international inspection of all civilian and government nuclear plants except defense facilities

Dec. 6, appealed to industry to hold line on price increases

•He blamed both business and labor for the wage-price spiral in a speech to the Business Council in Washington:

Yet business says it is labor's responsibility to break the spiral, and labor says it is yours. I say it is everyone's responsibility. It is the responsibility of government, of labor and of business.

Dec. 8, vetoed bill to grant masters of certain U.S. vessels liens on vessels for wages and other disbursements

•This was the last of his 16 regular vetoes.

Dec. 9, attended wedding of his daughter, Lynda Bird, to Charles Spittall Robb, White House

•This was the seventh of eight White House weddings of daughters of presidents.

•This was the eighth of nine White House weddings of children of presidents.

Dec. 12, appealed to labor to help stop wage-price spiral

•He credited the labor leadership with salvaging some legislation and accused House Republicans of blocking many key bills in a speech to the national convention of the AFL-CIO, Bal Harbour, Fla.

Dec. 15, signed act that extended Civil Rights Commission for five years

•This was the only civil rights legislation passed during 1967.

Dec. 15, signed wholesome meat act

•This act provided for federal inspection of meat plants engaged in intrastate com-

merce after two months and applied the federal system after two years in those states that had not developed programs at least equal to the federal system.

•Among those present at the signing ceremony was Upton Sinclair, whose novel, *The Jungle*, had led to the first meat inspection act in 1906.

Dec. 15, first session of 90th Congress adjourned

Dec. 16, issued proclamation that put first-year Kennedy Round tariff reductions into effect, Jan. 1, 1968

•The tariff reductions applied to almost six thousand items and ranged up to 50 percent over a five-year period. The reciprocal reductions averaged 35 percent.

•The tariff conferences were called Kennedy Round since the Trade Expansion Act, which authorized U.S. participation, was passed during the Kennedy administration.

Dec. 16, signed act that increased pay of postal workers by six percent, military personnel by 5.6 percent, and federal civilian employees by 4.5 percent

•He also signed a new postal rate schedule that raised first class mail from five to six cents, postcards from four to five cents, and domestic air mail from eight to ten cents, effective, Jan. 7, 1968.

Dec. 19, asserted that peace initiatives were province of Saigon government

•He encouraged South Vietnamese leaders to proceed with informal peace talks with the National Liberation Front, the political arm of the Vietcong. He added that he was not "so soft-headed and pudding-headed" as to halt "our half of the war" without reciprocity by Hanoi.

Dec. 19, departed for Australia

•On this trip, which was his second to Asia, Johnson retraced the route he had followed in October, 1966, making stops in Honolulu, Hawaii, and Pago Pago, American Samoa.

•This was the fourth of his six visits to Hawaii while in office.

•This was the second of his two visits to American Samoa while in office.

Dec. 21, arrived in Canberra, Australia

•He conferred with President Nguyen Van Thieu of South Vietnam in Canberra.

•This was the second of Johnson's two visits to Australia while in office.

Dec. 22, attended memorial service for Aus-

tralian Prime Minister Harold Holt, Melbourne, Australia
• Holt had vanished while swimming in the surf of Portsea, near Melbourne, Dec. 17.
• While in Australia, Johnson conferred with representatives of nations that had sent troops to Vietnam.
Dec. 23, visited Korat, Thailand
• He spoke to U.S. airmen at the Royal Thai Air Force base at dawn.
• This was the second of his two visits to Thailand while in office.
Dec. 23, visited U.S. military base, Camranh Bay, South Vietnam
• This was the second of his two visits to South Vietnam while in office.
Dec. 23, visited Karachi, Pakistan
• He conferred with President Mohammed Ayub Khan.
• Johnson was the second of three presidents who visited Pakistan while in office.
Dec. 23, visited Italy
• He conferred with President Giuseppe Saragat at Castel Porziano, 20 miles south of Rome, and with Pope Paul VI in the Vatican Palace.
• Johnson was the first of two presidents who conferred with a Pope on two occasions while in office. The other was Nixon.
• This was the second of his two meetings with Pope Paul while in office.
• He was the fifth of six presidents who visited Italy while in office.
Dec. 24, visited Azores
• He was the first of two presidents who visited the Azores while in office. The other was Nixon.
• He was the second of three presidents who visited Portugal while in office.
Dec. 24, returned to Washington, D.C.
• He had traveled about twenty-seven thousand miles during his around-the-world trip in 112 hours.
Dec. 25, celebrated Christmas, White House
• This was the first Christmas that the Johnson family spent in the White House.
Dec. 27, departed for LBJ Ranch

1968

Jan. 1, imposed mandatory restrictions on dollar investments abroad, Johnson City, Tex.
• He reported at a news conference that the

balance of payments had declined to a net deficit of more than $3,500,000,000 in 1967. He requested citizens to defer "nonessential" travel outside the western hemisphere for the next two years.
• This was the first time that mandatory controls were established on U.S. private investment in foreign countries.
Jan. 2, signed foreign aid appropriation act, San Antonio, Tex.
• This act appropriated $2,290,000,000 for foreign aid for the fiscal year ending June 30.
Jan. 2, signed act providing $9,300,000,000 in continued aid to elementary and secondary schools, San Antonio, Tex.
• This act provided funds for a two-year period ending June 30, 1970.
Jan. 2, signed omnibus social security act, San Antonio, Tex.
• This act raised the pensions of twenty-four million persons by at least 13 percent and gradually raised the social security taxes of seventy-eight million persons.
Jan. 7–8, conferred with Premier Levi Eshkol of Israel, LBJ Ranch
Jan. 14, returned to Washington, D.C.
Jan. 15, conferred with former Prime Minister Harold Macmillan of Great Britain, White House
Jan. 15, second session of 90th Congress
Jan. 17, delivered his fifth State of the Union message
• In his televised 9 P.M. address, he declared that U.S. bombing of North Vietnam "would stop immediately if talks would take place promptly and with reasonable hopes they would be productive." He demanded reciprocity, saying, "the other side must not take advantage of our restraint as they have in the past."
• He also proposed a budget of $186,000,000,000 for the fiscal year ending June 30, 1969, and projected deficits of $20,000,000,000 in fiscal 1968 and $8,000,000,000 in fiscal 1969.
Jan. 19, announced his appointment of Clark M. Clifford as secretary of defense, effective, Mar. 1
Jan. 23, sent special message to Congress in which he asked $2,090,000,000 for manpower programs in the year beginning July 1
Jan. 24, sent special message to Congress urging passage of civil rights legislation
Jan. 25, accepted resignation of Secretary of

Health, Education and Welfare Gardner, effective, Mar. 1

Jan. 25, ordered 14,787 Air Force and Navy reservists to active duty

• This order was prompted by the seizure of the *U.S.S. Pueblo*, a virtually unarmed, 179-foot intelligence ship, and its crew of 83 officers and men. It had been captured by four North Korean patrol boats and escorted into the port of Wonsan, Jan. 23.

Jan. 26, called *Pueblo* seizure "wanton and aggressive act" during brief television report to nation

Jan. 27, made surprise visit to National Press Club

• The occasion was the inauguration of the NPC president, Allan Cromley of the Oklahoma City *Daily Oklahoman*. During his remarks, Johnson quoted Thomas Jefferson:

    . . . were it left to me to decide whether we should have a government without newspapers or newspapers without a government, I should not hesitate a moment to prefer the latter.

• However, Johnson reminded the correspondents, "Jefferson said this before he became President."

Jan. 29, sent budget message to Congress

Jan. 30, sent special message to Congress proposing increased benefits for veterans, including special pay for training veterans as school teachers

Feb. 1, sent annual economic report to Congress

• He again urged a ten percent surcharge on income taxes and said that failure to raise taxes would result in a "feverish boom that could generate an unacceptable acceleration of price increases, a possible financial crisis, and perhaps ultimately a recession period."

Feb. 1, signed executive order permitting election of chief executive of Ryukyu Islands by popular vote

• The Ryukyus, including Okinawa, had been seized by the U.S. from Japan at the end of World War II.

Feb. 4, sent special message on education to Congress

• He proposed expansion of federal aid to elementary, secondary, and higher education so that every qualified young person could have "all the education he wants and

can absorb." He asked for $3,500,000,000 for the program.

Feb. 6, sent special message on consumer protection to Congress

• He urged legislation to protect the "poor, elderly, ignorant" against fraudulent home improvement contracts and other "sales rackets."

Feb. 7, sent special message on crime control to Congress

• His 22-point anticrime program included proposed legislation to deal with inciters of riots, manufacturers and possessors of illegal LSD, and interstate gamblers.

Feb. 8, conferred with Prime Minister Harold Wilson of Great Britain, White House

Feb. 8, sent special message on foreign aid to Congress

• He requested appropriations of $2,500,000 for economic aid and $540,000,000 for military aid during the fiscal year beginning July 1. He also urged a $100,000,000 appropriation for immediate emergency military assistance to South Korea.

Feb. 12, reiterated his San Antonio offer for peace talks with North Vietnam

• He held a question-and-answer session with 11 college students in the White House.

Feb. 12, placed wreath at Lincoln Memorial, Washington, D.C.

• He compared his ordeals with those of the Civil War leader. "Sad but steady—always convinced of his cause—he stuck it out," Johnson said of President Lincoln. "Sad but steady, so will we."

Feb. 16, told press conference he did not believe North Vietnam had ever wanted to negotiate for peace

• He reasserted his confidence in General William C. Westmoreland, American commander in Vietnam. He denied that the use of nuclear weapons in Vietnam was under consideration.

Feb. 16, accepted resignation of Secretary of Commerce Trowbridge, effective, Mar. 1

Feb. 16, appointed his fourth secretary of commerce, C. R. Smith

• Smith took office, Mar. 6.

Feb. 17–18, toured military installations

• He made surprise visits to Fort Bragg, N.C., and El Toro Marine Corps Naval Air Station, Cal., to bid farewell to members of the 82nd Airborne Infantry Division and the Fifth Marine Division. These two divisions supplied 10,500 men requested by General Westmoreland.

•Johnson spent the night aboard the *U.S.S. Constellation*, off San Diego, Cal.

Feb. 18, conferred with former President Eisenhower, Palm Desert, Cal.

•"I really honestly believe he has been as helpful to me as any one person since I have been President," he said of General Eisenhower.

Feb. 19, returned to Washington, D.C.

Feb. 19, conferred with Manlio Brosio, Secretary-General of NATO, White House

Feb. 21, conferred with Secretary General U Thant of United Nations, White House

Feb. 22, sent special message on urban problems to Congress

•He submitted an extensive public-private plan for rebuilding the residential centers of cities during the next ten years. He proposed housing and urban development legislation with a goal of twenty-six million housing units, including housing built by private industry. This program would eventually cost $10,000,000,000.

Feb. 23, proposed waiving of visas for tourists and businessmen from certain—principally western European—nations

•This proposal was aimed at reducing the balance of payments deficit.

Feb. 26, sent urban mass transit reorganization plan to Congress

•This plan would transfer most of the $190,-000,000 program from the department of housing and urban development to the department of transportation.

Feb. 27, sent special farm message to Congress

•This program, designed to give additional federal protection to farmers, included the permanent extension of the Food and Agriculture Act of 1965. He asked for an appropriation of about $7,300,000,000 during fiscal 1969.

Feb. 27, addressed convention of National Rural Electric Cooperative Association, Dallas, Tex.

•This was his first visit to Dallas since the assassination of President Kennedy.

Feb. 29, addressed National Governors Conference, White House

•He asked the governors to help "forge the strongest and most effective federal-state campaign for public order."

Feb. 29, made impromptu appearance at "Discover America" fashion show, State

Dining Room, White House

•The 43 wives of the governors attending the National Governors Conference and a group of fashion designers were the guests of Mrs. Johnson.

•This was the first fashion show held in the White House.

Mar. 1, signed Fire Research and Safety Act

•This act launched new studies into the causes of fires and expanded fire prevention and control programs, including public education.

Mar. 1, visited Manned Spacecraft Center installations, Houston, Tex.

Mar. 2, spoke at roll-out ceremonies of C5A Galaxy, Marietta, Ga.

•The C5A, a four-engine, 246-foot transport jet, is the world's largest aircraft, capable of carrying seven hundred fully-equipped infantrymen.

Mar. 2, flew to Raney Air Force Base, Puerto Rico

•This was his first vacation trip while in office.

•He was the last of three presidents who visited the Commonwealth of Puerto Rico while in office.

•He was the last of seven presidents who visited Puerto Rico while in office.

Mar. 4, returned to Washington, D.C.

Mar. 4, sent special health message to Congress

•He proposed a $15,600,000,000 "Health in America" program. He asked price limits on drugs used in Medicare, Medicaid, and maternal care programs.

Mar. 4, met with copper management and labor representatives, White House

•The copper strike had begun, July 15, and involved sixty thousand workers in 26 unions against the four major copper producers—Kennecott, Anaconda, Phelps-Dodge, and the American Smelting and Refining Company.

Mar. 5, White House aides announced his decision not to enter any presidential primaries

•He had decided not to enter any of the 15 primaries except those three where state laws would make his candidacy automatic.

•In Wisconsin, Nebraska, and Oregon, the name of every person prominently mentioned for the presidency is listed unless he signs an affidavit that he is not a candidate.

Mar. 6, sent special message regarding American Indians to Congress

•He urged legislation to provide $500,000,-000 to raise the standard of living of 600,-000 Indians, and promised a federal policy of "partnership—not paternalism."

Mar. 8, sent special conservation message to Congress

•He requested legislation to provide $1,-200,000,000 to assure pure water, clear air, and oil-free shores. He asked for stiff sanctions to prevent oil spillages from polluting beaches and waterways and urged federal legislation to reclaim land scarred by strip mining.

•He also proposed outright federal purchase of 67,000 acres along the 390-mile shoreline of the Potomac River. The cost of the Potomac project was estimated at $65,-500,000—the most expensive land preservation program in U.S. history.

Mar. 18, addressed National Farmers' Union convention, Minneapolis, Minn.

•He called for a program "of national austerity to insure that our economy will prosper and our fiscal position will be sound."

Mar. 18, signed act removing gold cover from paper currency

•This act freed $10,700,000,000, the gold equivalent to 25 percent of the value of outstanding federal reserve notes.

Mar. 20, again asked Congress for prompt passage of ten percent income tax surcharge

Mar. 22, appointed his third secretary of health, education and welfare, Wilbur J. Cohen

•Cohen took office, May 16.

Mar. 22, appointed General William C. Westmoreland as army chief of staff

•He said General Westmoreland would be replaced as commander of American forces in Vietnam before July 2.

Mar. 26, said solutions to racial problems should begin in South, White House

•He told a delegation of southern Baptist leaders that there is no southern problem and no northern problem, but only an American problem. "But because much of that American problem began in the region which you and I call home, I would like to see the solutions begin there, too," he said.

Mar. 29, asked Congress to set aside nearly one million acres in 24 new wilderness areas to preserve "solitude and splendor of the land"

•He said the new wilderness areas would be

extracted from national forests, national wildlife refuges, and the national parks and monuments systems, in 13 states.

Mar. 31, approved plan to reduce government overseas personnel by initial 12 percent to ease balance of payments deficit

•He estimated the savings at between $12,-000,000 to $15,000,000 during fiscal 1969, and between $20,000,000 to $22,000,000 in future years.

Mar. 31, announced he would not seek nomination for second term

•"I shall not seek, and I will not accept, the nomination of my party for another term as your President," he said during a nationally televised speech about the Vietnam War. Prior to his surprise announcement, he had stated that he had ordered a halt in the air and naval bombardment of almost 90 percent of North Vietnam and invited the Hanoi government to join him in a "series of mutual moves toward peace."

•It was later learned that he had been planning his political announcement for some time and had considered including the withdrawal statement in his State of the Union message.

Apr. 1, addressed annual convention of National Association of Broadcasters, Chicago, Ill.

Apr. 2, sent second annual report of Appalachian Regional Commission to Congress

•He said that "a strong beginning" had been made to improve the economy of Appalachia.

Apr. 2, conferred with Vice President Humphrey and Democratic congressional leaders, White House

Apr. 3, conferred individually with Vice President Humphrey and Senator Robert F. Kennedy, White House

•Johnson promised to provide all presidential candidates with full intelligence briefings on international developments, his press secretary said.

Apr. 3, announced North Vietnam and U.S. had agreed to establish contact between their representatives

Apr. 4, informed of assassination of Reverend Dr. Martin Luther King, Jr.

•He deplored the "brutal slaying" in a brief television statement and asked every citizen to "reject the blind violence that has struck Dr. King, who lived by nonviolence." He proclaimed Sunday, Apr. 7, as a national day of mourning for the Nobel

Prize winner and civil rights leader.
- Dr. King was killed by a sniper's bullet in Memphis, Tenn. His killer, James Earl Ray, was arrested at an airport in London, England, June 8. Ray pleaded guilty to the murder in Memphis, Mar. 10, 1969, and was sentenced to 99 years in prison.

Apr. 5, attended memorial service for Dr. King, Washington Cathedral

Apr. 5, ordered four thousand army and National Guard troops into Washington, D.C.
- A wave of Negro rioting and looting had followed the assassination of Dr. King. At least six persons were killed and 350 injured in Washington during two days of disorder.
- Racial violence flared in 125 cities, principally Washington, Baltimore, Chicago, and Kansas City, Mo. Between 45 and 50 persons were killed, more than 2,600 were injured, and more than 21,000 were arrested. Property damage exceeded $65,-000,000.

Apr. 5, attended investiture of Most Reverend Terence J. Cooke as seventh Roman Catholic archbishop of New York, St. Patrick's Cathedral, New York City

Apr. 5, conferred with UN Secretary General U Thant, New York City

Apr. 6–7, conferred with General William C. Westmoreland, White House
- Upon leaving the White House, Westmoreland said that "militarily, we have never been in a better relative position in South Vietnam."

Apr. 8, received formal message stating willingness of North Vietnam to establish contact with U.S.

Apr. 9, reviewed Vietnam situation with Secretary of State Rusk, Secretary of Defense Clifford, and Ellsworth Bunker, U.S. ambassador to South Vietnam, Camp David, Md.

Apr. 10, appointed General Creighton W. Abrams as successor to General Westmoreland, commander of American forces in Vietnam

Apr. 10, accepted resignation of Postmaster General O'Brien

Apr. 10, appointed his third postmaster general, W. Marvin Watson
- Watson took office, Apr. 26.

Apr. 11, ordered 24,500 military reservists to active duty
- The call-up was announced by Secretary of Defense Clifford, who said 10,000 of the

reservists would be sent to Vietnam as entire units. Clifford also announced a ceiling of 549,500 for U.S. strength in Vietnam.

Apr. 11, signed Civil Rights Act of 1968
- This act was designed to end racial discrimination in the sale and rental of 80 percent of U.S. homes and apartments. It also gave federal protection to civil rights workers.

Apr. 12, flew to LBJ Ranch
- En route, he signed an act to provide an emergency appropriation of $28,000,000 to continue unemployment compensation for returning Vietnam veterans and former federal employees.

Apr. 15, flew to Honolulu, Hawaii
- He was briefed by the military commanders of the Pacific, Apr. 16.
- This was the fifth of his six visits to Hawaii while in office.

Apr. 17, conferred with President Chung Hee Park of South Korea, Honolulu

Apr. 18, briefed former President Eisenhower on Hawaii conferences, March Air Force Base, near Riverside, Cal.

Apr. 18, flew to LBJ Ranch

Apr. 19, declared Trust Territories of Pacific major disaster area
- He ordered the allocation of $2,500,000 in federal aid to help repair typhoon damage on Saipan and other islands.

Apr. 22, returned to Washington, D.C.

Apr. 22, signed act providing for elected school board for District of Columbia
- The school board members previously were elected by the judges of the Federal District Court.

Apr. 23, proposed preparation of five-year plan to speed up development of transport, power, and communications networks of Latin America, White House
- He spoke at the signing ceremony of the amended treaty of the Organization of American States, which had been given unanimous assent by the Senate, Apr. 10.

Apr. 24, pleaded for national unity, Chicago, Ill.
- He told a Democratic fund-raising dinner audience:

    However strong, however prosperous, however just its purposes or noble its cause, no nation can long endure when citizen is turned against citizen, cause against cause, section against section, generation against generation by the mean

and selfish spirit of partisanship.
. . . Let us look to the victories that
have been won for the people. Let
us look to the advances we have
made together in unity and understanding and let us, too, take courage—to renew and sustain that
"battle which their fathers began."

•The quotation was from Lincoln's comment about the authors of the Declaration
of Independence.

Apr. 25, received King Olav V of Norway,
White House

Apr. 27, dedicated Fishtrap Dam, near Pike-
ville, Ky.

•The dam, designed as a flood control and
recreation project at a cost of $55,700,000,
is a part of the Big Sandy River Basin development program. The 195-foot-high
rock dam stretches 1,100 feet across Levisa
Fork Valley.

May 2, designated tornado-devastated counties of Ohio and Kentucky as major disaster areas

•He ordered the allocation of $270,000 in
federal aid to Ohio and $375,000 to Ken-
tucky.

May 3, announced U.S. and North Vietnam
had agreed to meet in Paris for preliminary talks on ending Vietnam War, May 10

May 3, urged Congress to "bite the bullet,"
pass tax increase for good of country

May 3, briefed former President Truman on
proposed peace talks and developments in
Korea, Europe, and NATO, Independence, Mo.

•Johnson explained that he would not be
able to visit Mr. Truman on May 8, the
former president's 84th birthday.

May 3, opened National Collection of Fine
Arts, Washington, D.C.

•The Old Patent Office Building, which had
been restored at a cost of $6,000,000 was
renamed the Fine Arts and Portrait Galler-
ies Building. The collection is a branch of
the Smithsonian Institution.

May 5, agreed to accept $4,000,000,000 re-
duction in budget to expedite approval of
tax increase

•In his strongest attack on Congress, May 3,
he had accused some members of "blackmail" in stalling his tax increase proposal
and had said the appropriation cuts demanded as the price for the ten percent
income tax surcharge ($6,000,000,000)
would "bring chaos to the government."

May 5, announced he would appoint commission of past and present cabinet members and White House Fellows to study
office of Presidency

May 8–9, conferred with Prime Minister
Thanom Kittikachorn of Thailand, White
House

May 14, dedicated Hall of Heroes, Pentagon, Washington, D.C.

•The hall contains more than thirty-two
hundred nameplates honoring Medal of
Honor winners.

May 16, conferred with President Habib
Bourguiba of Tunisia, White House

May 21, sent special message to Congress
requesting additional $3,900,000,000 for
increased costs of Vietnam War and military and civilian pay increases

May 22, signed joint resolution for comprehensive study and investigation of automobile insurance system

•The measure authorized an appropriation
of up to $2,000,000.

May 23, declared U.S. would not be defeated on battlefield while peace talks
went on in Paris

•He said:

  We shall not permit the enemy's
  mortars and rockets to go unan-
  swered and to permit him to
  achieve a victory that would make
  a mockery of the negotiations.

May 27, sent special message to Congress
asking extension of his tariff-cutting authority

•"A nation restricts imports only at the risk
of its own exports," he said. "Restriction
begets restriction."

May 29, signed "truth-in-lending" act

May 29, advocated vote for 18-year-olds
during commencement address, Texas
Christian University, Fort Worth, Tex.

•He received an honorary degree of Doctor
of Laws, his 35th honorary degree.

May 30, reluctantly offered to accept $6,-
000,000,000 reduction of expenditures to
get tax increase

•Without a tax increase, he said, "The gates
of economic chaos, I think, could open,"
and added, "I deeply regret that we are
faced with such a choice."

May 31, announced immediate raise of U.S.
Savings Bonds interest rate

•The rate of interest was increased from
4.15 to 4.25 percent.

June 4, addressed commencement exercises, Glassboro State College, Glassboro, N.J.

•He declared that "some progress" had been made since his 1967 conferences with Premier Kosygin of the U.S.S.R. at Glassboro. He called for cooperation between the U.S. and the Soviet Union to help solve the conflicts in Vietnam and the Middle East and to reach new disarmament agreements.

June 4, conferred with President Jose Joaquin Trejos Fernandez of Costa Rica, White House

June 4, signed authorization of U.S. support for $1,000,000,000 increase in capital funds for Inter-American Development Bank

June 5, notified of shooting of Senator Robert F. Kennedy

•Senator Kennedy, brother of assassinated President John F. Kennedy, was shot in the Hotel Ambassador, Los Angeles, Cal., shortly after midnight by Sirhan Beshara Sirhan, a 24-year-old Jordanian Arab. Kennedy died, June 6.

•Sirhan, who had been seized immediately after he shot the Democratic presidential candidate, was found guilty of first-degree murder, Apr. 17, 1969, and was sentenced to death in the gas chamber. He was transferred to San Quentin Prison's death row, May 23, 1969.

June 5, ordered Secret Service to protect all presidential candidates and their families

•"There are no words equal to the horror of this tragedy," Johnson said about the shooting of Senator Kennedy. He appointed a commission to investigate the circumstances and causes of violence in the U.S.

June 6, proclaimed Sunday, June 9, as day of mourning for Senator Kennedy

June 6, appealed to Congress for more stringent gun-control legislation

June 8, attended funeral service for Senator Kennedy, St. Patrick's Cathedral, New York City

•He flew back to Washington after the church service, where he met the funeral train at the end of its nine-hour journey from New York. He also attended the Kennedy burial ceremony at Arlington National Cemetery.

June 11, visited former President Eisenhower, Walter Reed Army Hospital, Washington, D.C.

June 11, signed executive orders raising pay

of 5,500,000 federal classified employees and military personnel, effective, July 1

•The pay raises ranged from 3 to 8.8 percent.

June 11–12, conferred with Shah of Iran, White House

June 12, addressed UN General Assembly, New York City

•He hailed approval of the Nuclear Non-Proliferation Treaty as probably "the most important step toward peace" in United Nations history. He spoke shortly after the General Assembly voted in support of the treaty, 95–4, with 21 abstentions.

June 13, proclaimed formal ratification of U.S.-U.S.S.R. agreement permitting mutual establishment of consulates

June 15, announced reorganization of Public Health Service

•He signed an executive order, effective, July 1, creating the consumer protection and environmental service in the department of health, education and welfare to coordinate the $15,600,000,000 federal health programs. This order consolidated 15 separate agencies.

June 19, reluctantly signed Omnibus Safety Crime Control Act of 1968

•This act authorized federal grants to improve local law enforcement and methods. It provided controls on the sale of handguns—"a halfway measure," he said, since it omitted rifles and shotguns.

June 20, signed act designating Federal City College as land grant institution

•Federal City College, in Washington, D.C., was the 69th land grant institution. In lieu of an actual grant of land, the college was to receive special federal money grants annually.

June 21, attended oath-taking ceremony of Frederick Delli Quadri, director of Children's Bureau of HEW, White House

•Delli Quadri was the first man to head the Children's Bureau.

June 21, approved CAB order awarding Moscow-to-New York route for Soviet airline, Aeroflot

June 24, sent special message to Congress asking legislation for registering and licensing every gun in U.S.

•The proposed legislation called for licensing by the states but provided for federal licensing in states that did not meet minimal standards within two years.

June 26, announced resignation of Chief

Justice Warren, effective as of confirmation of successor

June 26, appointed Associate Justice Abe Fortas as chief justice

•Johnson was the 13th of 14 presidents who appointed chief justices.

•This, the third of Johnson's four appointments to the Supreme Court, was withdrawn, Oct. 2.

•Johnson was the last of three presidents who appointed chief justices who were not confirmed by the Senate.

•He was the 14th of 15 presidents who appointed justices who were not confirmed by the Senate.

•Fortas was the last of four nominees for chief justice who were not confirmed by the Senate.

•Fortas was the 22nd of 25 men nominated to the Supreme Court who were not confirmed by the Senate.

June 26, appointed William Homer Thornberry as associate justice

•This, the last of Johnson's four appointments to the Supreme Court, was withdrawn, Oct. 2.

•Thornberry was the 23rd of 25 men nominated to the Supreme Court who were not confirmed by the Senate.

June 26, sent proposed 26th Amendment to Congress

•The amendment would extend the right to vote to 18-year-olds.

June 26, sent special message to Congress requesting $98,600,000 to carry out provisions of Crime Control Act

June 28, signed act providing for ten percent surcharge on individual and corporate income taxes

June 28, signed act changing dates of observance of Washington's Birthday, Memorial Day, and Veterans Day and making Columbus Day legal holiday

•Although this act officially applied only to federal and District of Columbia employees, most states observe the federal legal holidays.

•Effective Jan. 1, 1971, Washington's Birthday was to be celebrated on the third Monday in February, Memorial Day on the last Monday in May, Columbus Day on the second Monday in October, and Veterans Day on the fourth Monday in October. With Labor Day being the first Monday in September, there were now five three-day holiday weekends.

July 1, signed Nuclear Non-Proliferation Treaty, White House

•He announced that the U.S. and the U.S.S.R. had agreed to confer in the "nearest future" regarding the limitation and reduction of both offensive and defensive antimissile systems. A total of 57 nations signed the treaty in Moscow, London, and Washington, D.C.

July 3, attended oath-taking ceremony of General William C. Westmoreland, 25th chief of staff of army

•General Westmoreland had been succeeded as commander of U.S. forces in Vietnam by General Creighton W. Abrams, June 10.

July 4, attended Fourth of July celebration, Hemisfair, San Antonio, Tex.

July 6, visited El Salvador

•He was greeted in San Salvador by President Fidel Sanchez Hernandez of El Salvador, President Julio Cesar Mendez Montenegro of Guatemala, President Oswaldo Lopez Arellano of Honduras, President Anastasio Somoza Debayle of Nicaragua, and President Jose Joaquin Trejos Fernandez of Costa Rica.

•Johnson announced a $30,000,000 loan to the Central American development bank and loans totalling $35,000,000 to the individual Central American nations.

•He was the only president who visited El Salvador while in office.

July 8, visited Nicaragua, Costa Rica, Honduras, and Guatemala

•At the conclusion of his two-day meeting with the five Central American presidents, he flew them to their individual capitals in Air Force One.

•He was the only president who visited Nicaragua while in office.

•He was the second of two presidents who visited Costa Rica while in office. The other was Kennedy.

•He was the only president who visited Honduras while in office.

•He was the only president who visited Guatemala while in office.

July 8, flew to LBJ Ranch

July 15, signed land and water conservation fund act, White House

•This act doubled federal funds for new parks and recreation areas to $200,000,000 annually for five years.

July 18–20, visited Hawaii

•He conferred with President Nguyen Van

Thieu of South Vietnam in Honolulu, July 19–20. At the end of the conference, Johnson said:

> The United States will not support the imposition of a "coalition government," or any other form of government, on the people of South Vietnam. The people of South Vietnam—and only the people of South Vietnam—have the right to choose the form of their government.

• This was the last of his six visits to Hawaii while in office.

July 20, returned to LBJ Ranch

July 23, addressed Governors Conference, Cincinnati, Ohio

July 26, signed act appropriating $1,400,-000,000 to interior department conservation programs

• He said that he had signed 278 "significant" conservation and beautification measures—50 of which were "major"—since he took office.

July 27, signed three acts improving benefits for veterans

July 29, signed act extending Food for Peace Program for two years

• This act provided $6,200,000,000 in food aid and placed new emphasis on aid to nations adopting birth-control programs.

July 31, assailed "unjustified" five percent across-the-board price increase by Bethlehem Steel Corporation

• After four other firms joined Bethlehem, he ordered first the Pentagon and then all federal agencies to buy only from companies that held the price line. Bethlehem and the other steel companies cut the increase in half, Aug. 7.

Aug. 1, signed omnibus housing act

• This act authorized a $5,300,000,000 program for the construction or rehabilitation of more than 1,700,000 housing units during the next three years.

Aug. 2, visited former President Eisenhower, Walter Reed Army Hospital, Washington, D.C.

Aug. 9, signed act continuing through 1974 program of federal grants to help finance collection and publication of American historical documents

Aug. 13, signed Natural Gas Pipeline Safety Act

Aug. 13, signed act providing mandatory standards for construction and alteration of buildings financed with federal funds

• This act ensured that physically handicapped persons would have ready access to and use of the buildings.

Aug. 14, signed act providing for three-year study of metric system

Aug. 14, termed nation "healthy" in address before annual convention of National Medical Association, Houston, Tex.

• He said:

> There are some who say that we Americans are on our deathbed and that we haven't done anything to cure ourselves. Others say we are in bad health because we have prescribed too much medicine—or the wrong kind. I disagree. America, I believe, is essentially healthy. Because we have shown that our remedies are taking hold, we must work harder than ever toward our goals.

Aug. 21, denounced Soviet occupation of Czechoslovakia

• More than 200,000 Soviet troops invaded Czechoslovakia, Aug. 20–21. Seven nations, including the U.S., demanded condemnation of the invasion by the United Nations Security Council. Only Hungary voted with the U.S.S.R., but the 10–2 vote was nullified by the Soviet Union's 105th veto.

Aug. 23, signed act providing for local election of governor of Virgin Islands beginning in 1970

• Previously the governor was appointed by the president.

Aug. 29, called for Democratic party unity behind Vice President Humphrey as "especially well-qualified" presidential candidate

• Humphrey had been nominated by the Democratic national convention shortly before the announcement.

• Johnson did not attend the convention in Chicago. He was the first president in 24 years who failed to attend his party's national convention.

Sept. 9, dedicated new department of housing and urban development building, Washington, D.C.

Sept. 11, greeted Prime Minister Errol Barrow of Barbados, White House

Sept. 11, invited three major presidential candidates to send representatives to

White House to "promote the orderly transfer of the executive power"

Sept. 17, declared his unqualified support of Vice President Humphrey

• The endorsement, designed to put to rest rumors that he was less than enthusiastic about the Democratic nominee, was made in a telegram to the Texas Democratic Party convention in Austin.

Sept. 22, signed act authorizing $900,000,-000 contribution to Inter-American Development Bank during next three years

Sept. 23, signed act authorizing hostile-fire pay to 81 military crew members of *U.S.S. Pueblo*

• Two of the 83 men aboard the *Pueblo* were civilian oceanographers.

Sept. 27, signed act appropriating $1,750,-000,000 for military construction programs

Sept. 30, signed act authorizing $1,300,000,-000 in water development of Colorado River Basin

Oct. 1, signed act creating Flaming Gorge National Recreation Area

• Flaming Gorge is a 201,250-acre lake and scenic area straddling the Utah-Wyoming border.

Oct. 2, signed acts establishing Redwood National Park, Cal., and National Cascades National Park, Wash.

• The 58,000-acre Redwood and 1,200,000-acre National Cascades were the 34th and 35th national parks.

Oct. 2, signed act establishing national system of urban and rural trails

• The first two trails designated were the Appalachian, extending from Mount Katahdin, Me., to Mount Oglethorpe, Ga., and the Pacific Crest, stretching from the Mexican to the Canadian borders.

Oct. 2, signed act establishing national wild and scenic rivers system

• This act preserved sections of eight rivers and provided for studies of 27 others.

Oct. 2, withdrew appointment of Associate Justice Fortas as chief justice

• Johnson acted after receiving a request for withdrawal from Justice Fortas. He called the Senate action in blocking the nomination "historically and constitutionally tragic."

Oct. 4, visited former President Eisenhower, Walter Reed Army Hospital, Washington, D.C.

Oct. 9–10, conferred with Prime Minister

Keith J. Holyoake of New Zealand, White House

Oct. 10, made first political speech of campaign

• During his endorsement of the Humphrey-Muskie ticket on NBC-radio, Johnson said the Republicans threatened the domestic programs of his and earlier Democratic administrations.

Oct. 11, visited former President Truman, Independence, Mo.

Oct. 14, second session of 90th Congress adjourned

Oct. 16, signed acts authorizing $7,300,000,-000 for higher education during next three years and $3,200,000,000 for vocational education during next four years

Oct. 16, shared dais with Democratic and Republican presidential nominees, Hubert H. Humphrey and Richard M. Nixon, Alfred E. Smith Memorial Foundation dinner, New York City

Oct. 17, signed act authorizing $71,900,-000,000 for defense during fiscal year which began July 1

• This was the largest single spending measure ever voted by Congress.

Oct. 17, signed act authorizing $1,750,000,-000 for foreign aid

• This act appropriated $1,400,000,000 for economic aid and $375,000,000 for military assistance. This was the lowest amount approved for foreign aid.

Oct. 21, signed $493,000,000 supplemental appropriation act

• This act authorized a $5,000,000 grant for construction of Eisenhower College, Seneca Falls, N.Y.

Oct. 23, signed act banning mail-order sale of rifles, shotguns, and all ammunition, effective, Dec. 16

• He protested that the act "still fell short" of the restrictions needed.

Oct. 23, signed act broadening educational benefits for veterans

• This act extended educational benefits to widows of veterans for the first time.

Oct. 25, signed act prohibiting manufacture, sale, or distribution of LSD or similar drugs

Oct. 30, pocket vetoed bill to amend Merchant Marine Act of 1936 to create an independent Federal Maritime Administration

• This was the last of his 14 pocket vetoes, the last of his 30 vetoes.

• He was the last of 11 presidents who never had a veto overridden.

Oct. 31, ordered halt of air, naval and artillery bombardment of North Vietnam, Nov. 1

Nov. 5, election day

• He voted in Johnson City, Tex.

• For the first time in 30 years, his name was not on the ballot.

• *See* Election of 1968, pages 588–589.

Nov. 8, accepted resignation of Secretary of Treasury Fowler, effective, Dec. 20

Nov. 11, conferred with President-elect Nixon, White House

Nov. 20, conferred with Vice President-elect Agnew, White House

Nov. 22, welcomed 54 new U.S. citizens, White House

• This was the first naturalization ceremony at the White House.

Nov. 26, flew to LBJ Ranch

Dec. 8, gave dinner for 23 *Apollo* astronauts and James E. Webb, former administrator of NASA, White House

Dec. 11, gave last state dinner of his administration in honor of Sheik Sabah al-Salim al Sabah, Emir of Kuwait, White House

Dec. 12, again conferred with President-elect Nixon, White House

Dec. 13, with President Gustavo Diaz Ordaz of Mexico, officiated at border-changing ceremony, El Paso, Tex.

• They met in the middle of a bridge between El Paso and Ciudad Juarez, Mexico. The ceremony marked the return of the disputed Chamizal area to Mexico, which was accomplished by diverting the Rio Grande.

Dec. 16, lit national Christmas tree, on Ellipse behind White House

Dec. 17, presented with album of U.S. stamps issued since he entered government service

• The album, containing more than six hundred stamps, was a personal gift from Postmaster General Watson.

Dec. 18, entered Bethesda Naval Hospital, Bethesda, Md., for treatment of flu-like ailment

• He returned to the White House, Dec. 22.

Dec. 19, authorized expansion of airline service across Pacific

• Five American airlines were awarded the international routes.

Dec. 22, crew of *U.S.S. Pueblo* released

• Commander Lloyd M. Bucher and 81 surviving members of his crew were released at Panmunjom. One crew member, Seaman Duane D. Hodges, had been killed when the ship was seized.

Dec. 27, flew to LBJ Ranch

1969

Jan. 1, accepted resignation of Secretary of Housing and Urban Development Weaver

Jan. 2, appointed his second secretary of housing and urban development, Robert C. Wood

• Wood took office, Jan. 7.

• Wood was the last of Johnson's 14 cabinet appointments.

Jan. 3, returned to Washington, D.C.

Jan. 3, first session of 91st Congress

• The Democrats maintained control of both the Senate and the House of Representatives. The Republicans gained seven Senate and four House seats. The Senate (100 members) consisted of 57 Democrats and 43 Republicans. The House (435 members) consisted of 244 Democrats and 191 Republicans.

Jan. 6, electoral votes tabulated by Congress

• Nixon and Agnew were officially declared elected.

• Vice President Humphrey was the last of three presidential candidates who officially announced the elections of their opponents.

Jan. 9, awarded NASA Distinguished Service Medal to *Apollo 8* astronauts

• Astronauts Frank Borman, James A. Lovell, Jr., and William A. Anders were the first men to orbit the moon, Dec. 24, during the six-day mission, Dec. 21–27.

Jan. 14, delivered his sixth and last State of the Union message

• The Vietnam and Middle East conflicts, as well as the difficulties of dealing with the Communist powers, he declared, were parts of the griefs of office. "Several Presidents have already sought to deal with them," he said during the televised evening joint session. "One or more Presidents will try to resolve or contain them in years to come."

• This was the first time an outgoing president had personally delivered his State of the Union message since John Adams had in 1801.

Jan. 15, sent his sixth and last budget to Congress
- He estimated expenditures for the fiscal year ending June 30, 1970, at $195,272,-000,000; receipts at $198,686,000,000; and a surplus of $3,414,000,000.

Jan. 16, presented Medal of Honor to four members of armed forces, White House
- These were the last of the 38 Medals of Honor he presented during his term of office.

Jan. 17, held last press conference, National Press Club
- In bantering tone, he bade farewell to the newspapermen:
   I will tell you what I am going to do. I am going down to the ranch Monday afternoon and I am going to sit on that front porch in a rocking chair for about ten minutes. Then I am going to read a little and write a little. Then I am going to put on my hat and go out and find Walter Lippmann.

Jan. 17, sent special message to Congress regarding federal pay scales
- He recommended raises of $19,500 annually for the vice president and speaker of the House, $20,000 for the Democratic and Republican leaders of the House of Representatives and Senate and the president pro tempore of the Senate, and $12,-500 for members of Congress.
- In his budget message, he had requested these salary increases, as well as raises of $25,000 for cabinet members, $22,500 for the Chief Justice of the U.S., and $20,500 for associate justices of the Supreme Court.

Jan. 17, signed act increasing salary of president from $100,000 to $200,000 annually, effective, Jan. 20

Jan. 18, sent third annual report of Appalachian Regional Commission to Congress
- He said the six-year program, although only half completed, had proved successful.

Jan. 20, signed executive order creating Marble Canyon National Park in Arizona and Colorado

Jan. 20, awarded Medal of Freedom to 20 Americans
- Among the recipients of the highest civilian award were W. Averell Harriman, chief negotiator at the Paris peace talks, and Harriman's deputy, Cyrus R. Vance.

THE FORMER PRESIDENT

Jan. 20, 1969, attended inauguration of Nixon
- Johnson's age upon leaving office was 60 years, 146 days.
- He was the first president who left office under the provisions of the Presidential Transition Act of 1963. He was allowed $375,000 for expenses during the first six months of his post-presidency.
- Under the Former Presidents Act of 1958, as amended, he receives a lifetime pension of $60,000 annually and a maximum of $65,000 for office expenditures.

Jan. 20, 1969, retired to LBJ ranch
- He attended a farewell luncheon at the Bethesda, Md., home of former Secretary of Defense Clifford before flying from Andrews Air Force Base, Md., to Texas in Air Force One.
- He was the last of six presidents who were farmers, planters, or ranchers after their terms of office.

Jan. 27, 1969 publication plans regarding his memoirs announced
- The first volume of his memoirs, originally scheduled for publication in 1970, was postponed until 1971. The proceeds of this and ensuing volumes, to be published by Holt, Rinehart and Winston, will benefit the Lyndon B. Johnson Public Affairs Foundation at the University of Texas.

February, 1969, his first magazine article since he became president published, *Reader's Digest*
- This and a second article, published in the March issue of *Reader's Digest*, were condensed from a thirty-thousand-word commentary on his White House years that appeared in the Encylopaedia Brittanica's *Book of the Year 1969*, published, Mar. 1.

Mar. 1, 1969, attended funeral of former President Eisenhower, Washington, D.C.

July 16, 1969, appeared on CBS-TV with Walter Cronkite, prior to *Apollo 11* launching
- This was his first public appearance since leaving office.

Dec. 11, 1969, visited President Nixon, White House

•This was his first visit to the White House since leaving office.

Dec. 27, 1969, appeared on first of three hour-long CBS-TV interviews

•He said he had no doubt that he would have been reelected if he had sought the presidency in 1968.

•This series of telecasts was culled from about 20 hours of taped interviews by Walter Cronkite during October.

Feb. 6, 1970, appeared on second of three CBS-TV interviews

•He said Secretary of State Rusk proposed the unconditional halt in the bombing of North Vietnam, Mar. 31, 1968.

Mar. 2, 1970, entered Brooke General Army Hospital, San Antonio, Tex.

•He had suffered chest pains since Feb. 20, brought on by hardening of the coronary arteries. He returned to the LBJ Ranch, Mar. 13.

Apr. 4, 1970, with Mrs. Johnson, attended wedding of Victoria White and Blaine Perkins Kerr, Jr., Washington, D.C.

•The bride was the daughter of columnist William S. White, Johnson's longtime confidant and biographer. White's book, *The Professional: Lyndon B. Johnson*, had been published in 1964.

Apr. 5, 1970, attended religious services, White House

Apr. 6, 1970, visited President Nixon, White House

Apr. 8, 1970, visited House of Representatives

May 1, 1970, made first public address, Democratic fund-raising dinner, Chicago, Ill.

May 2, 1970, appeared on last of three CBS-TV interviews

•He asserted that some of the Kennedy holdovers in 1963 had "undermined the Administration and bored from within to create problems for us."

June 13, 1970, attended dedication of his birthplace and boyhood home as national historical sites

Aug. 29, 1970, attended dedication of LBJ State Park, across Pedernales River from LBJ Ranch

Sept. 3, 1970, attended state dinner for President Gustavo Diaz Ordaz of Mexico, Coronado, Cal.

Oct. 28, 1970, Mrs. Johnson's book, *A White*

House Diary, published by Holt, Rinehart and Winston, New York

•She was the last of four first ladies who published their memoirs.

Jan. 24–Feb. 7, 1971, with Mrs. Johnson, visited Acapulco, Mexico

•They were the guests of former President Miguel Aleman of Mexico.

Oct. 14, 1971, with Mrs. Johnson, attended rededication ceremonies of Eisenhower Museum, Abilene, Kan.

•The Eisenhower Museum had doubled in size during the previous 18 months.

Oct. 14, 1971, with Mrs. Johnson, visited former President and Mrs. Truman, Independence, Mo.

Nov. 1, 1971, his book, *The Vantage Point: Perspectives of the Presidency, 1963–1969*, published, Holt, Rinehart and Winston, New York City

•He was the 20th of 21 presidents who wrote books that were published during their lifetimes.

Nov. 13–15, 1971, with Mrs. Johnson, stayed at Blair House, Washington, D.C.

•This was the first time that the Johnsons accepted the hospitality of President Nixon and stayed at Blair House, the executive guest mansion, during a visit to Washington.

Nov. 14, 1971, with Mrs. Johnson, attended worship services, White House

Nov. 15, 1971, gave his first post-presidential on-the-record newspaper interview, Blair House, Washington, D.C.

•He said that his silence on major issues did not necessarily indicate endorsement of Nixon administration policy. He added that he would support the 1972 Democratic nominee. The interview with Marianne Means of King Features Syndicate appeared in newspapers, Dec. 1–2.

Nov. 15, 1971, delivered address, "America Tomorrow: Will We Hang Together or Hang Separately?," New York University Graduate School of Business, New York City

•He warned of the dangers of isolationism in his speech to about four hundred Wall Street executives. Graduate school students heard and saw the address on closed-circuit television in their classrooms.

•His fee of $25,000 was donated to his alma mater, Southwest Texas State University, and the Lyndon B. Johnson Library.

Dec. 20, 1971, announced his papers on

education would be opened for review, Jan. 26, 1972
• The 250,000 papers concerning his education programs would be the first documents to be opened for public and scholarly review at the Lyndon B. Johnson Presidential Library, he said. A second set of documents, his civil rights papers, are to be opened later in 1972.

THE VICE PRESIDENT (38th)

Full name: Hubert Horatio Humphrey
Date of birth: May 27, 1911
Place of birth: Wallace, S.D.
• Humphrey was the only vice president born in South Dakota.
Religious denomination: Congregationalist
• He was the last of four vice presidents who were Congregationalists.
College: University of Minnesota, Minneapolis, Minn.
Date of graduation: June 17, 1939, Bachelor of Arts
• He had received a degree from the Denver College of Pharmacy, Denver, Colo., 1933.
• He received his Masters of Art degree from Louisiana State University, Baton Rouge, 1940.
Occupation: Politician
• He was elected mayor of Minneapolis in 1945 and 1947; was elected to the Senate in 1948, 1954, and 1960. He was selected as assistant majority leader by the Democratic members of the Senate, 1961.
• He was the 16th of 17 vice presidents who served in the Senate before their terms of office.
Term of office: Jan. 20, 1965, to Jan. 20, 1969 (4 years)
• He was the last of 17 vice presidents who served four-year terms.
• Johnson and Humphrey were the 40th of 41 president-vice president teams.
Age at inauguration: 53 years, 238 days
State represented: Minnesota
• He was the only vice president who represented Minnesota.
• He was the last of 13 vice presidents who represented states that were not their native states.
Political party: Democratic
• He was the last of 16 vice presidents who were Democrats.

Occupations after term: College professor, U.S. Senator
• He taught at the University of Minnesota, Minneapolis, and Macalester College, St. Paul, Minn., 1969–1970; was reelected to the Senate, 1970.
• He was the last of six vice presidents who served in the Senate after their terms of office.
• He was the last of four vice presidents who served in the Senate both before and after their terms of office.

THE CABINET

State: David Dean Rusk of New York, Jan. 21, 1961, to Jan. 20, 1969
Treasury: Clarence Douglas Dillon of New Jersey, Jan. 21, 1961 to Apr. 1, 1965
• Henry Hamill Fowler of Virginia, Apr. 1, 1965, to Dec. 20, 1968
• Joseph William Barr of Indiana, Dec. 21, 1968, to Jan. 20, 1969
Defense: Robert Strange McNamara of Michigan, Jan. 21, 1961, to Feb. 29, 1968
• Clark McAdams Clifford of Maryland, Mar. 1, 1968, to Jan. 20, 1969
Attorney General: Robert Francis Kennedy of Massachusetts, Jan. 21, 1961, to Sept. 3, 1964
• Nicholas deBelleville Katzenbach of Illinois, Feb. 13, 1965, to Oct. 3, 1966
• William Ramsey Clark of Texas, Mar. 10, 1967, to Jan. 20, 1969
Postmaster General: John Austin Gronouski of Wisconsin, Sept. 30, 1963, to Aug. 30, 1965
• Lawrence Francis O'Brien of Massachusetts, Nov. 3, 1965, to Apr. 10, 1968
• William Marvin Watson of Texas, Apr. 26, 1968, to Jan. 20, 1969
Interior: Stewart Lee Udall of Arizona, Jan. 21, 1961, to Jan. 20, 1969
Agriculture: Orville Lothrop Freeman of Minnesota, Jan. 21, 1961, to Jan. 20, 1969
Commerce: Luther Hartwell Hodges of North Carolina, Jan. 21, 1961, to Jan. 15, 1965
• John Thomas Connor of New Jersey, Jan. 18, 1965, to Jan. 31, 1967
• Alexander Buel Trowbridge of New York, June 14, 1967, to Mar. 1, 1968
• Cyrus Rowlett Smith of New York, Mar. 6, 1968, to Jan. 20, 1969
Labor: William Willard Wirtz of Illinois,

Sept. 25, 1962, to Jan. 20, 1969

Health, Education and Welfare: Anthony Joseph Celebrezze of Ohio, July 31, 1962, to July 27, 1965
•John William Gardner of New York, Aug. 18, 1965, to Mar. 1, 1968
•Wilbur Joseph Cohen of Maryland, May 16, 1968, to Jan. 20, 1969

Housing and Urban Development: Robert Clifton Weaver of New York, Jan. 18, 1966, to Jan. 1, 1969
•Robert Colwell Wood of Massachusetts, Jan. 7, 1969, to Jan. 21, 1969

Transportation: Alan Stevenson Boyd of Florida, Jan. 16, 1967, to Jan. 20, 1969

THE SUPREME COURT

Chief Justice: Abe Fortas of Tennessee, appointed, June 26, 1968; withdrawn, Oct. 2, 1968

Associate Justices: Abe Fortas of Tennessee, appointed, July 28, 1965; confirmed, Aug. 11, 1965
•Thurgood Marshall of New York, appointed, June 13, 1967; confirmed, Aug. 30, 1967
•William Homer Thornberry of Texas, appointed, June 26, 1968; withdrawn, Oct. 2, 1968

Thirty-seventh President

RICHARD MILHOUS NIXON

Full name: Richard Milhous Nixon
•He was the last of 19 presidents who had middle initials or middle names.
Date of birth: Jan. 9, 1913
•He was the last of four presidents who were born in January.
Place of birth: Yorba Linda, Cal.
•He was the only president who was born in California.
Family Lineage: English-Scottish-Irish and English-Scottish-Irish-Welsh
•He was the only president who was of English-Scottish-Irish and English-Scottish-Irish-Welsh ancestry.
Religious denomination: Society of Friends
•He was the second of two presidents who were Quakers. The other was Hoover.
College: Whittier College, Whittier, Cal.
•He was the last of 27 presidents who attended college.
Date of graduation: June 9, 1934, Bachelor of Arts
•He was the last of 21 presidents who were graduated from college.
•He was the only president who was graduated from Whittier.
Law School: Duke University Law School, Durham, N.C.

•He was the last of nine presidents who attended law school.
Date of graduation: June 7, 1937, Bachelor of Laws
•He was the last of three presidents who were graduated from law school.

Father's name: Francis Anthony Nixon
Date of birth: Dec. 3, 1878
Place of birth: Elk Township, Vinton County, Ohio
Occupations: Grocer, gas station operator
Date of death: Sept. 4, 1956
Place of death: La Habra, Cal.
Age at death: 77 years, 276 days

Mother's name: Hannah Milhous Nixon
Date of birth: Mar. 7, 1885
Place of birth: near Butlerville, Jennings County, Ind.
Date of marriage: June 25, 1908
Children: 5 sons
•Harold Samuel was born on June 1, 1909; Richard Milhous on Jan. 9, 1913; Francis Donald on Nov. 23, 1914; Arthur Burdg on

581

May 26, 1918; and Edward Calvert on May 3, 1930. Harold Samuel died Mar. 7, 1933, and Arthur Burdg died Aug. 10, 1925.
•Nixon was the last of seven presidents who came from families of five children.
•He was the last of ten presidents who were second children.
•He was the last of five presidents who had male siblings only.
Date of death: Sept. 30, 1967
Place of death: Whittier, Cal.
Age at death: 82 years, 207 days

MARRIAGE

Date of marriage: June 21, 1940
Place of marriage: Riverside, Cal.
•Nixon was the second of two presidents who were married in California. The other was Hoover.
Age at marriage: 27 years, 164 days
•He was the last of 27 presidents who were married in their twenties.

Wife's name: Thelma Catherine Ryan Nixon
•She was called Pat.
•She was the last of 33 first ladies.
•She was the last of 40 wives of presidents.
Date of birth: Mar. 16, 1912
•Her nickname, Pat, came about because she was born on the eve of St. Patrick's Day. Her father arrived home from work after midnight and, learning of his daugh-

ter's birth, called her "St. Patrick's Babe in the Morn."
•Mrs. Nixon always celebrated her birthday on St. Patrick's Day.
•She was the last of four first ladies who were born in March.
•She was the last of five wives of presidents who were born in March.
Place of birth: Ely, Nev.
•She was the only first lady or wife of a president who was born in Nevada.
Wife's mother: Kate Halbertstadt Bender Ryan
Wife's father: William Ryan, miner and truck farmer
Age at marriage: 28 years, 97 days
•She was the last of 26 first ladies who were married in their twenties.
•She was the last of 30 wives of presidents who were married in their twenties.
Years older than husband: 299 days
•She was the last of six first ladies who were older than their husbands.
•She was the last of six wives of presidents who were older than their husbands.
Children: 2 daughters
•Patricia was born on Feb. 21, 1946, and Julie was born on July 5, 1948.
•Nixon was the last of five presidents who had only female children.
•He was the last of seven presidents who had two children.
•He was the last of 30 presidents who had children.

EARLY YEARS

1917, nearly killed in fall from buggy
•Nixon suffered a severe skull gash from above his forehead to the back of his neck when he was struck by a wheel of the buggy. The nearest hospital was 25 miles away; only a dash in the only automobile in Yorba Linda saved his life. He has always parted his hair on the right to hide the scar.
1917, nearly died of pneumonia
1919–1922, attended elementary school, Yorba Linda
1922, with family, moved to Whittier, Cal.
•His father's lemon grove in Yorba Linda had failed.
•Whittier was named for John Greenleaf Whittier, the Quaker poet.
1922–1930, attended elementary and secondary school, Whittier

•After school and during the summers, he worked at odd jobs, pumped gas, and helped out in his father's grocery-gasoline station.
•While in high school, he worked for three weeks each of two summers as a barker for a wheel-of-chance game at the "Slippery Gulch Rodeo" in Prescott, Ariz. He was a shill for a concession that was a legal front for a backroom poker and dice gambling room. He was paid one dollar an hour.
Aug. 10, 1925, his seven-year-old brother, Arthur Burdg, died of tubercular meningitis
Winter, 1929–1930, suffered severe attack of undulant fever
•He was absent much of his senior year in high school but maintained his grades.

June 5, 1930, was graduated from Whittier High School

•He was graduated with honors and was awarded the Harvard Club of California Prize as the outstanding all-around student of his class. The prize was a book, a biography of Dean Le Baron Russell Briggs of Harvard.

Sept. 17, 1930, entered Whittier College

Mar. 7, 1933, his older brother, Harold Samuel, died of tuberculosis

June 9, 1934, was graduated from Whittier College

•He was president of his freshman class and, as a senior, president of the student body. He was a member of the debating team, the glee club, and the drama club, and played on the second-string football team.

•He was graduated second in the class of 109 members.

Sept. 18, 1934, entered Duke University Law School, Durham, N.C.

•He received a full-tuition scholarship and a National Youth Administration job, which paid 35 cents an hour. He maintained his scholarship status for the three-year course of study.

•He was the last of 26 presidents who studied law.

December, 1936, applied for jobs with Wall Street law firms, New York City

•During the Christmas holidays, he and two other Duke seniors, Harlan Leathers and William Perdue, applied for positions with a number of the more prominent New York City law firms.

May, 1937, applied for position as special agent of Federal Bureau of Investigation

June 7, 1937, was graduated from Duke University Law School

•He was elected to membership in the Order of Coif, the national scholastic fraternity for honor law students, and was graduated third in the class of 26 members.

June, 1937, applied for position with law firm of Wingert and Bewley, Whittier

•In a letter to the author, Thomas W. Bewley wrote:

> At our first interview he expressed a keen desire to get in the actual practice of law and have some experience in politics. . . . He immediately identified himself with the Republican causes in the community.

Nov. 9, 1937, admitted to California bar, San Francisco, Cal.

•He was the last of 23 presidents who were lawyers.

•He was taken into the firm of Wingert and Bewley. His beginning salary was about $250 a month. His superior, Thomas Bewley, city attorney of Whittier, also appointed him to the post of assistant city attorney.

Jan. 1, 1939, became partner in law firm

•The reorganized firm was named Bewley, Knoop and Nixon. Nixon opened a branch office in La Habra, Cal., and was appointed town attorney of La Habra. His combined salaries rose to about $6,000 annually.

1940, elected president of Citra-Frost Company, Whittier

•He and a group of Whittier businessmen, who invested $10,000, formed the company to market frozen whole orange juice. The firm failed about 18 months later.

June 21, 1940, married Thelma Catherine Ryan, Riverside, Cal.

Jan. 9, 1942, applied for job with Office of Price Administration, Washington, D.C.

•He was hired to write and coordinate regulations for tire rationing in the Office for Emergency Management. His beginning salary was $61 a week.

June 15, 1942, commissioned as lieutenant, junior grade, U. S. Navy

•His appointment in the Naval Reserve dated from May 22. He received aviation indoctrination training at the Naval Air Station, Quonset Point, R. I.

•He was the last of three presidents who served in the U.S. Navy.

•He was the last of four presidents who served in World War II.

•He was the last of 21 presidents who served in the military during wartime.

Oct. 27, 1942, reported for duty at Naval Reserve Aviation Base, Ottumwa, Iowa

•He was detached from this command, May 7, 1943.

June 30, 1943, reported for duty, Fleet Air Command, Noumea, New Caledonia

•He was assigned to Headquarters Squadron, MAG 25, and reported for duty, July 1. He served as officer in charge of the South Pacific Combat Air Transport Command on Bougainville and Green islands until July 2, 1944.

Oct. 1, 1943, promoted to lieutenant, senior grade

Aug. 9, 1944, returned to U.S.
•He reported for duty at Fleet Air Wing 8, Alameda, Cal.
Dec. 30, 1944, reported for duty, Bureau of Aeronautics, Navy Department, Washington, D.C.
•He was assigned to renegotiating contracts with aircraft firms in Baltimore, Md.
Oct. 3, 1945, promoted to lieutenant commander
Dec. 4, 1945, accepted endorsement of Committee of One Hundred
•The committee had been formed to decide upon a candidate to run against Representative H. Jerry Voorhis, who had represented the Twelfth District for ten years. Nixon had returned to California from Baltimore to be interviewed by 77 members of the committee.
Feb. 21, 1946, his first daughter born
•The girl was named Patricia Nixon.
Mar. 10, 1946, discharged from active duty, U.S. Naval Reserve
•He was mustered out as a lieutenant commander.
Mar. 19, 1946, filed in Republican and Democratic primaries as candidate for House of Representatives
•Cross-filing was permitted in California.
•Voorhis won the Democratic nomination and received a substantial vote in the Republican primary. In the overall count, Voorhis received about seven thousand votes more than Nixon.

NATIONAL PROMINENCE

Nov. 5, 1946, elected to House of Representatives
•Nixon was the last of 17 presidents who were elected to the House.
Jan. 3, 1947, took seat in House of Representatives
•He served in the 80th and 81st congresses.
•He was the last of 17 presidents who served in the House.
July 5, 1948, his second daughter born
•The girl was named Julie Nixon.
Aug. 5, 1948, appointed chairman of subcommittee of House committee on un-American activities
•The subcommittee was appointed to investigate charges made by Whittaker Chambers, a senior editor of *Time* Magazine and a former Communist. Chambers had named several former government officials, including Alger Hiss, as members of an underground Communist group, Aug. 3. Hiss, a former state department official, denied the allegations, Aug. 5.
Aug. 17, 1948, Whittaker Chambers and Alger Hiss testified during executive session of subcommittee, New York City
•Hiss, who had previously claimed he did not know Chambers, identified his accuser as "George Crosley," a free-lance writer he had known in the late 1930's.
Aug. 25, 1948, Chambers and Hiss testified during public session of House committee on un-American activities, Washington, D.C.
Aug. 27, 1948, Chambers repeated charge Hiss was Communist on radio program, "Meet the Press"
•Hiss filed a $50,000 slander suit against Chambers, Sept. 27, based on statements made on "Meet the Press," but the suit was never brought to trial. Chambers's testimony before the House of Representatives committee had been privileged.
Nov. 2, 1948, reelected to House
Dec. 15, 1948, Hiss indicted on two counts of perjury by federal grand jury, New York City
•Hiss was indicted for denying that he had ever given government documents to Chambers.
May 31–July 8, 1949, first Hiss trial
•The jury failed to agree. The jury stood 8–4 for conviction but the minority held for acquittal.
Nov. 17, 1949–Jan. 21, 1950, second Hiss trial
•Hiss was found guilty on both counts of perjury and was sentenced to five years in prison. He served three years, eight months in federal prison, Lewisburg, Pa., and was released in November, 1954.
Nov. 7, 1950, elected to Senate
•Nixon was the last of 16 presidents who were elected to the Senate.
•He was the last of 11 presidents who were elected both to the House of Representatives and the Senate.
Dec. 4, 1950, took oath as member of Senate
•Senator Sheridan Downey had resigned.
Jan. 3, 1951, took seat in Senate

- He was the last of 15 presidents who served in the Senate.
- He was the last of ten presidents who served both in the House of Representatives and the Senate.

July 11, 1952, nominated by acclamation for vice president, Republican national convention, Chicago, Ill.

Sept. 18, 1952, confirmed reports he had accepted $18,235 during past two years from political supporters

Sept. 23, 1952, defended expense fund and gave details of his financial status during national TV-radio speech
- Under pressure to resign as the vice-presidential nominee, he chose instead to explain and defend the fund on national television:

> Not one cent of the $18,000 or any other money of that type ever went to my personal use. Every penny of it was used to pay for political expenses that I did not think should be charged to the taxpayers of the United States.

- The response was overwhelmingly favorable to Nixon's position, and the Republican national committee voted to retain him.
- This came to be known as the "Checkers speech." At one point, he said:

> We did get something, a gift, after the nomination. . . . It was a little cocker spaniel dog . . . black and white, spotted, and our little girl Tricia, the six-year-old, named it Checkers. And you know, the kids, like all kids, loved the dog, and I just want to say this, right now, that regardless of what they say about it, we are going to keep it.

Nov. 4, 1952, election day
- *See* Election of 1952, page 491.

Nov. 11, 1952, resigned from Senate, effective, Jan. 1, 1953

Jan. 20, 1953, took oath as vice president

June 1, 1953, promoted to commander, U.S. Naval Reserve

Dec. 23, 1953, reported on ten-week, 45,000-mile Asian tour
- Nixon reported that President Eisenhower's foreign policy program had put the Communists "for the first time . . . on the defensive all over the world."

Feb. 6–Mar. 5, 1955, made goodwill tour of Caribbean nations

Sept. 30, 1955, presided at cabinet meeting
- President Eisenhower had suffered a heart attack, Sept. 24.
- Nixon called the cabinet meeting to expedite routine business.

Feb. 13, 1956, called Supreme Court decision on school desegregation accomplishment of Eisenhower administration
- He made this claim because the decision had been delivered by "a great Republican Chief Justice, Earl Warren."
- Nixon was criticized by Democratic leaders for placing the Supreme Court in the political arena during the election campaign.

Apr. 26, 1956, announced he would seek renomination for vice-presidency

Aug. 22, 1956, renominated for vice-presidency, Republican national convention, San Francisco, Cal.

Sept. 4, 1956, his father died

Nov. 6, 1956, election day
- *See* Election of 1956, pages 501–502.

Jan. 20, 1957, took vice-presidential oath of office privately, East Room, White House

Jan. 21, 1957, took oath of office, east plaza, Capitol
- The inaugural ceremony had been postponed because Jan. 20 fell on Sunday.

Feb. 26, 1958, presidential disability agreement announced by President Eisenhower
- Details of the agreement were released by the White House, Mar. 3. The inability to serve would be determined by the president "if possible." Otherwise, the vice president would make the decision "after such consultation as seems to him appropriate." The president alone would decide when the inability had ended. In such instances the vice president would assume the title of acting president.

Apr. 27–May 15, 1958, toured eight South American nations
- Nixon visited Argentina, Uruguay, Paraguay, Bolivia, Peru, Ecuador, Colombia, and Venezuela. Mob violence erupted at several stops along the route, including Lima, Peru, and Caracas, Venezuela.
- On May 8, in Lima, he and his interpreter, Colonel Vernon Walters, and a Secret Service agent, John Sherwood, were stoned by a crowd near the entrance to the University of San Marcos, and Nixon and his party were spat upon as they returned to their hotel.
- On May 13, outside Caracas, they were

again spat upon at the airport, and were harassed continuously en route from the airport to the city. The cars in which he and Mrs. Nixon were riding were stoned and clubbed. When the motorcade was forced to stop, a mob of two hundred closed in and attempted to overturn the limousines. Foreign Minister Oscar Garcia Velutini of Venezuela, who was sitting on Nixon's left, and Colonel Walters and Agent Sherwood, who occupied the jump-seats, were struck by flying glass. Once able to proceed, the motorcade abandoned the planned route and they took refuge in the American embassy.

• On May 14, Nixon and his party flew to San Juan, Puerto Rico, and on May 15, returned to Washington, D.C. He was greeted at National Airport by President Eisenhower and the cabinet.

June 27, 1959, with Queen Elizabeth II of Great Britain, dedicated $650,000,000 St. Lawrence hydroelectric project, Massena, N.Y.

June 29, 1959, with First Deputy Premier Frol R. Koslov of U.S.S.R., formally opened Soviet Exhibition of Science, Technology and Culture, New York City

July 23–Aug. 2, 1959, visited U.S.S.R.

• His purpose in visiting Moscow was to formally open the American National Exhibition. He met with Premier Khrushchev in the Kremlin, July 24, and then escorted the Soviet premier on a preview tour of the exhibition.

• He and Khrushchev carried on a running debate on the relative merits of the capitalistic and communistic systems over a period of two hours while inspecting the displays at the exhibition. The exchanges verged on the insulting, but neither took offense. The highlight of the verbal battle took place in a model American home and has come to be known as the "kitchen conference."

• Nixon and Khrushchev engaged in a second marathon debate at the premier's dacha, about 20 miles outside Moscow, July 26. They talked for six hours.

• While in the Soviet Union, Nixon and his party visited Leningrad and the industrial centers of Novosibirsk in West Siberia and Sverdlovsk in the Ural Mountains.

• Back in Moscow, he made an unprecedented, 30-minute television and radio address to the Russian people, Aug. 1. He called for "a just peace based on mutual respect rather than the peace of surrender or dictation by either side."

Aug. 3–5, 1959, visited Poland

Jan. 9, 1960, agreed to have his name entered in Republican presidential primaries

Mar. 16, 1960, endorsed for president by President Eisenhower

July 27, 1960, nominated for president, Republican national convention, Chicago, Ill.

• He was nominated on the first ballot.

Aug. 2, 1960, opened campaign in home-town, Whittier

Sept. 26, 1960, first Nixon-Kennedy television debate, Chicago, Ill.

• Devoted exclusively to domestic policy, the first debate was watched by nearly 70,000,000 people. The consensus of opinion was that Kennedy "won" the debate, not because of content but because of style and personal appearance.

• This was the first televised debate of presidential candidates.

Oct. 7, 1960, second debate, Washington, D.C.

• This debate was watched by about 51,000,000 people.

Oct. 13, 1960, third debate

• Nixon spoke from a studio in Los Angeles and Kennedy from New York City.

• This debate was watched by about 48,000,000 people.

Oct. 21, 1960, fourth and final debate, New York City

• This debate, which was devoted exclusively to foreign policy, was watched by about 48,000,000 people—almost 22,000,000 less than had watched the first debate.

• The consensus of opinion was that Nixon "won" the second, third, and fourth debates. However, in his book, Six Crises, Nixon wrote: "Looking back on all four of them, there can be no question but that Kennedy had gained more from the debates than I."

• He was referring to the fact that, prior to the debates, Kennedy was thought of as politically immature by many of the electorate because of his youth and lack of executive department experience.

Nov. 8, 1960, election day

• See Election of 1960, pages 523–524.

Jan. 6, 1961, electoral votes tabulated by Congress

•As vice president, he officially declared Kennedy and Johnson elected.

•He was the second of three presidential candidates who officially announced the elections of their opponents.

Feb. 28, 1961, returned to California

Mar. 10, 1961, stated he would not run for governorship of California in 1962

Mar. 13, 1961, joined law firm of Adams, Duque and Hazeltine as counsel, Los Angeles

Apr. 20, 1961, conferred with President Kennedy regarding Cuban situation, White House

•This conference followed the Bay of Pigs fiasco. Asked by Kennedy for his advice, Nixon replied: "I would find a proper legal cover and I would go in."

May 1, 1961, contracted with Los Angeles *Times-Mirror* Syndicate for series of newspaper articles

•The contract stipulated that he was to receive $40,000 for ten articles. The series (11 articles in all; he wrote an extra one of his own volition) appeared in newspapers throughout the country, June 20 to Apr. 6, 1962.

May 1–11, 1961, made Midwest speaking tour

•He spoke in Chicago, Detroit, Des Moines, Columbus, and Oklahoma City. He called for a Kennedy-Khrushchev summit meeting and criticized the Democratic farm programs.

June 15, 1961, moved his family to Beverly Hills, Cal.

Sept. 27, 1961, announced his candidacy for governorship of California, Los Angeles

Mar. 29, 1962, his book, *Six Crises*, published by Doubleday, New York City

•He was the last of 21 presidents who wrote books that were published during their lifetimes.

June 5, 1962, nominated for governor in Republican primary

•He defeated Joseph Shell, Republican leader of the state assembly and leading member of the John Birch Society, by two-to-one.

Nov. 5, 1962, defeated in gubernatorial election by incumbent, Governor Edmund G. ("Pat") Brown

Nov. 6, 1962, bitterly denounced press during "last" press conference, Los Angeles

•As his press secretary, Herbert Klein, was conceding the election in the ballroom of the Beverly Hilton Hotel, Nixon walked in at about 10:20 A.M. and moved up to the microphone. "Good morning, gentlemen," he said. "Now that Mr. Klein has made his statement, and now that all the members of the press are so delighted that I have lost, I'd like to make a statement of my own."

•What followed was an emotional, bitter, 15-minute harangue. He accused Governor Brown of having slandered him and attacked the press for the treatment he had received during the campaign:

> One last thing. At the outset I said a couple of things with regard to the press that I noticed some of you looked a little irritated about. . . . Never in my sixteen years of campaigning have I complained to a publisher, to an editor, about the coverage of a reporter. I believe a reporter has got a right to write it as he feels it. . . . I will say to a reporter sometimes that I think, well, look, I wish you would give my opponent the same going over that you give me. . . .
> I think that it's time that our great newspapers have at least the same objectivity, the same fullness of coverage, that television has. And I can only thank God for television and radio for keeping the newspapers a little more honest. . . .
> But as I leave you, I want you to know—just think how much you're going to be missing. You won't have Nixon to kick around any more, because, gentlemen, this is my last press conference. . . .

Mar. 14, 1963, resumed law practice, Los Angeles

May 2, 1963, announced he would move to New York City

•He said he would join the law firm of Mudge, Stern, Baldwin, and Todd as general counsel, June 1, and would become a general partner of the firm after he had completed the six-month residence requirement for admission to the New York bar.

June 12–Aug. 1, 1963, with family, toured Europe

Nov. 21–22, 1963, visited Dallas, Tex.

•By coincidence, he was in Dallas on business on the day that President Kennedy was killed. Nixon departed by air before the shooting occurred and did not learn of the assassination until he arrived in New York City early in the afternoon.

Dec. 5, 1963, admitted to New York bar, Albany

Dec. 15, 1963, became general partner of law firm

• The name of the firm was changed to Nixon, Mudge, Rose, Guthrie and Alexander, Jan. 1, 1964.

Mar. 22–Apr. 15, 1964, made round-the-world business trip

July 15, 1964, introduced Republican presidential candidate, Barry Goldwater, Republican national convention, San Francisco, Cal.

Sept. 4, 1964, registered as voter, New York City

September–November, 1964, campaigned for Goldwater

• He campaigned in 36 states, traveled more than 50,000 miles.

Apr. 10, 1965, visited Moscow

Aug. 25–Sept. 12, 1965, toured Asia

Apr. 27, 1966, argued first case before Supreme Court

• His clients, the James Hill family of Philadelphia, had sued Time, Inc., for invasion of privacy following the publication of a picture story in the Feb. 28, 1955, issue of *Life* Magazine. The Hills were awarded $30,000 in compensatory damages by the New York Court of Appeals. When Time, Inc., appealed, the Supreme Court agreed to hear the case.

• Nixon made a second oral presentation before the Supreme Court in October.

• The Supreme Court decided, 5–4, against his clients, but also concluded that the jury had been improperly instructed. Nixon announced that the case would be retried, but an out-of-court settlement was reached in 1967.

July–August, 1966, with family, made round-the-world trip

September–November, 1966, campaigned in 35 states for 86 Republican congressional candidates

Jan. 1, 1967, name of law firm changed to Nixon, Mudge, Rose, Guthrie, Alexander and Mitchell

• His new partner was John Mitchell, whom he later appointed as his first attorney general.

Mar. 6–25, 1967, toured Europe

Apr. 3–24, 1967, toured Asia

May 5–16, 1967, toured South America

June 5–24, 1967, toured Middle East

Sept. 30, 1967, his mother died

Aug. 8, 1968, nominated for president, Republican national convention, Miami Beach, Fla.

Nov. 5, 1968, election day

• *See* Election of 1968, below.

Dec. 16, 1968, presidential electors cast ballots

• He received 301 of the 538 electoral votes from the 50 states.

• *See* Election of 1968, below.

Dec. 22, 1968, with Mrs. Nixon, attended wedding of their daughter, Julie, to David Eisenhower, Marble Collegiate Church, New York City

• His son-in-law was the grandson of President Eisenhower.

Jan. 1, 1969, name of law firm changed to Mudge, Rose, Guthrie and Alexander

Jan. 6, 1969, electoral votes tabulated by Congress

• Nixon and Agnew were officially declared elected.

• Humphrey was the last of three presidential candidates who officially announced the elections of their opponents.

ELECTION OF 1968

Republican party, convened, Aug. 5, at Miami Beach, Fla., nominated Richard Milhous Nixon of New York for president, Spiro Theodore Agnew of Maryland for vice president.

• This was the 29th Republican national convention. It was the only Republican convention held in Miami Beach; it was the only major party convention held in Miami Beach.

Democratic party, convened, Aug. 26, at Chicago, Ill., nominated Hubert Horatio Humphrey of Minnesota for president, Edmund Sixtus Muskie of Maine for vice president.

• This was the 35th Democratic national convention. It was the tenth Democratic convention held in Chicago; it was the 25th major party convention held in Chicago.

• George Corley Wallace of Alabama announced his candidacy, Feb. 8, 1968. On May 7, a slate of Wallace Alabama elector candidates was elected, making him the Democratic candidate from that state. On Oct. 3, Wallace named Curtis Emerson LeMay of California as his vice-presidential running mate. The Wallace third party was named the **American Independent** party.

Election day, Tuesday, Nov. 5, 1968

Popular vote: 73,211,562

    Nixon, 31,785,480

    Humphrey, 31,275,165

    Wallace, 9,906,473

    others, 244,444

•Nixon was the last of 15 presidents who were elected without receiving a majority of the popular vote.

Electoral vote: 538, 50 states and District of Columbia

  • Nixon, 301, 32 states

    (Alaska, 3; Arizona, 5; California, 40; Colorado, 6; Delaware, 3; Florida, 14; Idaho, 4; Illinois, 26; Indiana, 13; Iowa, 9; Kansas, 7; Kentucky, 9; Missouri, 12; Montana, 4; Nebraska, 5; Nevada, 3; New Hampshire, 4; New Jersey, 17; New Mexico, 4; North Carolina, 12 of 13 votes; North Dakota, 4; Ohio, 26; Oklahoma, 8; Oregon, 6; South Carolina, 8; South Dakota, 4; Tennessee, 11; Utah, 4; Vermont, 3; Virginia, 12; Wisconsin, 12; Wyoming, 3)

• Humphrey, 191, 13 states and District of Columbia

    (Connecticut, 8; District of Columbia, 3; Hawaii, 4; Maine, 4; Maryland, 10; Massachusetts, 14; Michigan, 21; Minnesota, 10; New York, 43; Pennsylvania, 29; Rhode Island, 4; Texas, 25; Washington, 9; West Virginia, 7)

• Wallace, 46, five states

    (Alabama, 10; Arkansas, 6; Georgia, 12; Louisiana, 10; Mississippi, 7)

•Wallace also received the vote of one North Carolina elector.

THE PRESIDENT (37th)

Term of office: Jan. 20, 1969—

•Nixon was the last of 12 presidents who had served as vice presidents.

•He was the second of two presidents who had previously served as vice president for two terms. The other was John Adams.

•He was the last of four presidents who served after the completion of their vice-presidential terms.

•He was the only president who served after but not immediately upon the completion of his vice-presidential term.

•He was the only president who, having served as vice president, did not succeed to the presidency upon the death of his predecessor or the completion of his vice-presidential term.

State represented: New York

•He was the last of eight presidents who represented New York.

•He was the last of 15 presidents who represented states that were not their native states.

Political party: Republican

•He was the last of 14 presidents who were Republicans.

Congresses: 91st, 92nd

Administration: 46th

Age at inauguration: 56 years, 11 days

Inauguration day: Monday, Jan. 20, 1969

•Nixon took the oath of office, administered by Chief Justice Earl Warren, on the east plaza of the Capitol.

•This was the last of four inaugurations at which Warren officiated.

THE 46th ADMINISTRATION

1969

Jan. 20, appointed his first secretary of state, William P. Rogers; his first secretary of treasury, David M. Kennedy; his first secretary of defense, Melvin R. Laird; his first attorney general, John N. Mitchell; his first postmaster general, Winton M. Blount; his first secretary of interior, Walter J. Hickel; his first secretary of agriculture, Clifford M. Hardin; his first secretary of commerce, Maurice H. Stans; his first secretary of labor, George P. Schultz; his first secretary of health, education and welfare, Robert H. Finch; his first secretary of housing and urban development, George W. Romney;

and his first secretary of transportation, John A. Volpe

• All but Hickel took office, Jan. 22. The confirmation of Hickel was delayed on grounds of doubt about his position on the conservation issue and about his reportedly close ties with the oil industry. Hickel was confirmed, Jan. 23, and took office, Jan. 24.

Jan. 21, discussed Latin American problems with Galo Plaza, Secretary-General of Organization of American States

• This was Nixon's first meeting with a foreign official while in office.

Jan. 23, issued executive order that created Urban Affairs Council

• The council consisted of seven cabinet officers and the vice president.

Jan. 23, appointed Arthur F. Burns to newly-created post of counselor to president, with cabinet rank

• Burns had served as chairman of the council of economic advisors during the Eisenhower administration.

Jan. 24, rescinded President Johnson's executive order awarding trans-Pacific airline routes

• Nixon asked the Civil Aeronautics Board to resubmit the recommendations it had made to President Johnson. Johnson's rejection of some recommendations of the CAB Examiner and substitution of other airlines, with whose executives he had been on friendly terms, had given rise to charges of "cronyism."

Jan. 26, attended interdenominational religious service conducted by Reverend Billy Graham, East Room, White House

Jan. 27, held first news conference, White House

Jan. 30, sent his first special message to Congress, requesting extension of authority to reorganize executive branch of government

Jan. 31, issued statement endorsing congressional representation for District of Columbia

• In the same statement, he also endorsed the proposal for preventive detention of "hard core" criminal suspects.

Feb. 2, visited former President Eisenhower, Walter Reed Hospital

Feb. 5, sent special message to Senate, urging prompt ratification of Nuclear Non-Proliferation Treaty

• He had opposed ratification in 1968, in the

wake of the Soviet invasion of Czechoslovakia.

Feb. 7, flew to Key Biscayne, Fla.

• This was the first of his many visits to Key Biscayne while in office.

Feb. 10, returned to Washington, D.C.

Feb. 11, received American tennis team, winners of Davis Cup, White House

Feb. 14, salaries of cabinet officers and members of Congress increased

• The salaries of cabinet officers were increased from $35,000 to $60,000 yearly, and those of members of Congress from $30,000 to $42,500. The increases had become effective 30 days after the recommendation of President Johnson.

Feb. 15, renamed two presidential yachts, *Patricia* and *Julie*, in honor of his daughters

Feb. 15–17, with family, spent weekend at Camp David, Md.

• This was his first visit to the presidential retreat.

Feb. 17, conferred with Ambassador Anatoly F. Dobrynin of U.S.S.R., White House

Feb. 19, sent special message to Congress requesting extension of Economic Opportunity Act

• Contrary to his campaign statements promising sweeping changes, he retained President Johnson's budget request of $2,000,000,000 for programs of the OEO, including the Job Corps and Head Start.

Feb. 20, appointed John S.D. Eisenhower as ambassador to Belgium

• The new ambassador was the son of the former president.

Feb. 20, sent special message to Congress urging constitutional amendment to reform electoral system

• While the message did not call for abolition of the electoral college, it did recommend abolition of individual electors, allocation of electoral votes within each state on a basis proportional to the popular vote, and the reduction from 50 percent to 40 percent of the electoral vote plurality required to choose a president. In the event no candidate received the required 40 percent, a runoff election between the two leading candidates was to decide on the basis of total popular vote, rather than the currently-specified choice by the House of Representatives.

Feb. 23, departed on eight-day tour of five European capitals

•He was the last of 11 presidents who traveled outside the U.S. while in office.

Feb. 23–24, visited Belgium

•He conferred with King Baudouin I and Premier Gaston Eyskens in Brussels.

•Nixon was the last of three presidents who visited Belgium while in office.

•He was the last of seven presidents who visited Europe while in office.

Feb. 24–26, visited England

•He conferred with Prime Minister Harold Wilson both at Chequers and at No. 10 Downing Street, the official residences of the prime minister. Together, they were luncheon guests of Queen Elizabeth II. Nixon also visited the House of Commons.

•He was the only president who visited the British Parliament while in office.

•He was the last of five presidents who visited England while in office.

•This was the first of his three visits to England while in office.

Feb. 26, visited West Germany

•He conferred with President Heinrich Luebke and Chancellor Kurt Georg Kiesinger in Bonn.

•Nixon was the last of five presidents who visited Germany while in office.

Feb. 27, visited West Berlin

Feb. 27–28, visited Italy

•He conferred with President Giuseppe Saragat in Rome.

•Nixon was the last of six presidents who visited Italy while in office.

•This was the first of his four visits to Italy while in office.

Feb. 28–Mar. 2, visited France

•He conferred with President Charles de Gaulle in Paris. He also met with Henry Cabot Lodge, U.S. chief negotiator at the Vietnam peace talks, and South Vietnamese leaders, including Vice President Nguyen Cao Ky.

•Nixon was the last of four presidents who visited France while in office.

•This was the first of his two visits to France while in office.

Mar. 2, returned to Italy for meeting with Pope Paul VI, Vatican City

•Nixon was the last of five presidents who met with Popes while in office.

•This was the first of his two meetings with Pope Paul while in office.

•This was the second of his four visits to Italy while in office.

Mar. 2, returned to Washington, D.C.

Mar. 4, held 55-minute TV-radio news conference regarding his European trip

Mar. 5, met with President Emile-Derlin Zinsou of Dahomey, White House

Mar. 7, presented Medal of Honor to three Army enlisted men wounded in Vietnam, White House

Mar. 13, wired congratulations to *Apollo 9* astronauts on splashdown

•The ten-day mission of astronauts James A. McDivitt, Russell L. Schweickart and David R. Scott successfully tested the docking capabilities of the lunar module. *Apollo 9* made 151 revolutions of the earth over a period of 241 hours, one minute. Nixon praised the mission as "ten days that thrilled the world."

Mar. 14, announced support of modified Sentinel antiballistic missile program

•The new program, which he described as a "safeguard system," was designed to protect U.S. missile sites rather than major population centers, as had been the goal of the original Sentinel system recommended by President Johnson.

Mar. 17, received credentials of new British ambassador, John Freeman, White House

•As editor of the *New Statesman*, Freeman had once written that Mr. Nixon was "a man of no principle whatsoever."

Mar. 19, visited former President Eisenhower, Walter Reed Army Hospital

Mar. 19, hosted 20th anniversary dinner of Chowder and Marching Club, White House

•The club, founded in 1949 by 15 freshmen Republican members of the 88th Congress, is composed of 40 members who either are or were members of the House of Representatives. He was a charter member.

Mar. 21, with Mrs. Nixon, visited former President and Mrs. Truman, Independence, Mo.

•At the Truman Library, he presented the former president with the Steinway piano on which Truman had frequently played "The Missouri Waltz" while in the White House. He played a few bars of the song for the Trumans and others. As he sat down at the piano, he explained: "I play everything in the key of G by ear."

Mar. 21, flew to California

•He and Mrs. Nixon had the use of a private estate, loaned for the weekend, in San Clemente, where they were known to be seeking a place to use as a vacation White House. While in California, he made a helicopter tour of the Santa Barbara beach damaged by leakage from an offshore oil well and visited the mission of San Juan Capistrano.

Mar. 23, returned to Washington, D.C.

Mar. 24, conferred with Prime Minister Pierre Elliott Trudeau of Canada, White House

•This was the first official visit of Nixon's administration.

•An official visit is a full-scale visit by a foreign head of government at the official invitation of the president.

Mar. 26, sent special message to Congress requesting one-year extension of ten percent income tax surcharge

Mar. 27, signed reorganization act

•He dropped the practice of using a number of pens to sign official papers, explaining that to do so made his signature "so scrambled" as to be unrecognizable. He continued the custom of giving souvenir pens to guests at signing ceremonies.

Mar. 28, former President Eisenhower died

•In a special message to Congress, Nixon officially announced the death of General Eisenhower. He proclaimed Mar. 31 as a national day of mourning. In a statement issued by the White House, he described the former president as a man "who spoke with a moral authority seldom equaled in American public life." After cancelling all appointments for the next five days, he drove to Walter Reed Army Hospital, where he joined members of the Eisenhower family. Later, he went by helicopter to Camp David, Md.

Mar. 30, delivered eulogy for former President Eisenhower, Capitol Rotunda

•Nixon had been selected to deliver the eulogy by General Eisenhower.

•He was the only president who delivered the eulogy for another president.

Mar. 31, conferred with President Charles de Gaulle of France and King Baudouin I of Belgium, White House

Mar. 31, attended funeral services for former President Eisenhower, Washington Cathedral Church of St. Peter and St. Paul

Mar. 31, gave reception for foreign dignitaries who attended Eisenhower funeral

Apr. 1, met individually with 12 foreign leaders

•In the order of appearance, they were

Premier Mariano Rumor of Italy; Foreign Minister Joseph Luns of The Netherlands; Prime Minister John G. Gorton of Australia; Chancellor Kurt Georg Kiesinger of West Germany; Premier Chung Il Kwon of South Korea; Premier Marcello Caetano of Portugal; Vice President Nguyen Cao Ky of South Vietnam; Shah Mohammed Reza Pahlevi of Iran; President Habib Bourguiba of Tunisia; President Ferdinand E. Marcos of the Philippines; Premier Suleyman Demirel of Turkey; and former Premier Nobusuke Kishi of Japan.

Apr. 2, attended Eisenhower burial services, Abilene, Kan.

Apr. 2, flew to Key Biscayne, Fla.

•He and his family spent the Easter weekend in Key Biscayne.

Apr. 4, commerce department announced appointment of his brother, Edward C. Nixon, as chairman of federal field committee for development planning in Alaska

•His brother declined the post "for personal reasons," Apr. 8.

Apr. 5, appointed five-man advisory council on government reorganization

Apr. 6, returned to Washington, D.C.

Apr. 7, attended opening game of baseball season, Washington, D.C.

•He threw out the first ball of the Washington Senators-New York Yankees game.

•He was the last of 11 presidents who officially opened baseball seasons.

Apr. 8, conferred with King Hussein of Jordan, White House

Apr. 10, addressed NATO Council, Washington, D.C.

•The meeting of foreign and defense ministers of NATO nations commemorated the 20th anniversary of the signing of the North Atlantic Treaty, Apr. 4, 1949.

Apr. 11, announced revised award of transPacific airline routes

Apr. 14, sent special message outlining domestic plans to Congress

•The message outlined a ten-point legislative program that included an increase in social security benefits; reorganization of the post office department; tax reform; anticrime measures; and home rule for the District of Columbia.

•He had decided against delivering a State of the Union message and informed Congress in general terms of his domestic goals.

Apr. 14, addressed Organization of American States, Washington, D.C.

• In his first major speech on Latin American affairs, he said the Alliance for Progress, founded in 1961 by President Kennedy, was a "great concept," but that it had failed to stimulate sufficient economic growth. Its accomplishments, he added, were "disconcerting."

Apr. 15, sent special budget message to Congress

• He proposed a budget of $192,900,000,-000, which would result in a surplus of $5,-800,000,000, provided the ten percent income tax surcharge was extended.

Apr. 17, predicted election of woman president within "next 50 years" during East Room reception for League of Women Voters, White House

Apr. 18, announced continuation of reconnaissance flights off North Korea

• A Navy EC121 electronic intelligence plane with 31 men aboard was shot down by North Korean jets, Apr. 15. U.S. radar indicated that the plane was 90 miles off North Korea at the time.

Apr. 21, sent special message on tax reform to Congress

• He proposed that the ten percent income tax surcharge be reduced to five percent, Jan. 1, 1970, provided substitute revenue could be generated through repeal of the seven percent investment tax credit to business.

Apr. 23, sent special message on organized crime to Congress

• He asked for $61,000,000 and legislation making it a federal crime to engage in major illicit gambling operations.

Apr. 24, sent special message requesting postal rate increase to Congress

• He suggested an increase from six to seven cents for first class mail and from five to six cents for first class postcards, as well as increases in second and third class rates.

Apr. 26, crowned daughter, Tricia, queen of Azalea Festival, Norfolk, Va.

Apr. 29, presented Presidential Medal of Freedom to Edward Kennedy ("Duke") Ellington, White House dinner

• The musician-composer was honored on his 70th birthday. Ellington's father had once been a part-time butler at the White House.

• This was the first Freedom Medal, the highest civilian medal, presented by President Nixon.

May 3, attended Kentucky Derby, Louisville, Ky.

• He was the only president who attended the Kentucky Derby. He also attended a Derby as vice president.

May 6, conferred with Prime Minister John G. Gorton of Australia, White House

May 6, sent special message proposing $1,-000,000,000 increase in federal food aid programs to Congress

May 12, conferred with General Creighton W. Abrams, U.S. commander in Vietnam, White House

May 12, his personal financial statement released by White House

• His net worth was listed at $596,900. His total assets, chiefly real estate, were listed at $980,400; his liabilities, $383,500, primarily notes, loans and mortgages.

• The statement indicated that he had agreed to sell his New York City apartment for $326,000, and to purchase residential property in San Clemente, Cal., for $340,-000. The purchase price of two houses in Key Biscayne, Fla., was given as $252,800.

May 13, sent special message to Congress urging adoption of lottery system for draft

• The proposed system would limit liability to the draft to a one-year period following a young man's 19th birthday or the end of a college deferment. Draft priority would be established by a lottery drawing based on dates of birth.

May 14, made nationally-televised report on Vietnam War

• He proposed a gradual and mutual withdrawal from South Vietnam of all foreign troops, including those of the U.S. and North Vietnam.

May 15, accepted resignation of Associate Justice Fortas

• Fortas had been under increasing pressure to resign because of his association with the Wolfson Foundation, involving his agreement to accept a fee of $20,000 yearly for life. Fortas received one payment of $20,-000 in January, 1966, and returned it in December, 1966, after Louis Wolfson was twice indicted for stock fraud.

• Fortas was the only justice of the Supreme Court to resign under pressure.

May 17, observed Armed Forces Day naval exercises from aboard *U.S.S. Saratoga*, off Norfolk, Va.

May 18, watched launch of *Apollo 10* on

television, Camp David, Md.

May 20, received King Baudouin I and Queen Fabiola of Belgium, White House

May 21, appointed Warren E. Burger as chief justice

• Burger, who was confirmed by the Senate, June 9, was the first of Nixon's six appointments to the Supreme Court.

• He was the last of 14 presidents who appointed chief justices.

May 25, attended ecumenical religious service conducted by Terence Cardinal Cooke, White House

May 26, telephoned congratulations to *Apollo 10* astronauts aboard *U.S.S. Princeton*, in Pacific

• *Apollo 10*, manned by Colonel Thomas Stafford of the Air Force, Commander Eugene Cernan and Commander John Young of the Navy, was launched, May 18. Stafford and Cernan, in the lunar module, made two orbits of the moon, and approached within fifty thousand feet of its surface, in this successful dress rehearsal for a moon landing.

May 27, sent special message to Congress requesting conversion of post office department from cabinet agency to self-sustaining government-owned corporation

May 27, conferred with Premier Petrus de Jong and Foreign Minister Joseph Luns of Netherlands, White House

May 28, sent special message on foreign aid to Congress

• He requested appropriations of $2,200,-000,000 for economic assistance and $375,-000,000 for military grants. He said he would ask in separate legislation for $275,-000,000 to finance credit sales of military weapons and equipment.

May 28, addressed graduating class of FBI National Academy, White House

• This was the only time the FBI commencement exercises were held at the White House. FBI Director J. Edgar Hoover presented him with a mounted agent's badge; Nixon recalled that he had submitted an FBI application in 1937 but "never heard anything about it."

May 29, signed executive order establishing Council on Environmental Quality

• He said the cabinet-level council would "provide the focal point for this administration's efforts to protect all of our natural resources."

June 2, articles of incorporation of Richard M. Nixon Foundation filed, Sacramento, Cal.

• One purpose of the nonprofit corporation was to be the construction of a presidential library and museum.

June 3, asked Congress to extend antipoverty program for two years

June 3, spoke at dedication of Karl E. Mundt Library, General Beadle State College, Madison, S.D.

• Student revolutionaries, he said, propelled by a "self-righteous moral arrogance" and aided by "permissive" faculties, threatened to undermine the American education system.

• This was his first speech on a college campus while in office.

• Senator Mundt (R., S. D.), a leading conservative, had given his papers to the college library.

• General Beadle State College became Dakota State College, July 1.

June 4, spoke at commencement exercises, U.S. Air Force Academy, Colorado Springs, Colo.

• In this speech, he attacked the "new isolationists," as he labeled critics of his military and foreign policy.

June 4, flew to San Clemente, Cal.

• This was his first visit to his new summer home. The Nixons had purchased a seaside Spanish-style mansion and five acres of land for $340,000, the previous month.

June 7, flew to Honolulu, Hawaii

• He was the last of three presidents who visited the state of Hawaii while in office.

• He was the last of five presidents who visited Hawaii while in office.

• This was the first of his two visits to Hawaii while in office.

June 8, conferred with President Nguyen Van Thieu of South Vietnam, Midway Island

• Nixon announced that 25,000 of the 540,000-man American military force in Vietnam would be withdrawn before the end of August.

• He was the only president who visited Midway while in office.

June 10, returned to Washington, D.C.

June 12, received President Carlos Lleras Restrepo of Colombia, White House

June 16, sent special message to Congress requesting increased user taxes to finance $5,000,000,000 airways and airport improvement program

June 17, White House announced he had ordered comprehensive review of U.S. chemical and biological warfare policies

June 19, during televised news conference, expressed hope all U.S. ground combat troops could be withdrawn from Vietnam by end of 1970

June 23, spoke at oath-taking ceremony of Chief Justice Burger

• In his remarks, Nixon praised the Supreme Court and retiring Chief Justice Earl Warren.

• He was the only president to address the Supreme Court while in office. However, he began his speech by saying, "I am honored to appear today, not as President of the United States but as a member of the Bar admitted to practice before this Court."

• A precedent was set when Chief Justice Warren administered the oath to his successor, Chief Justice Burger.

June 27, visited Canada

• He joined Prime Minister Trudeau at ceremonies marking the tenth anniversary of the opening of the St. Lawrence Seaway, Massena, N.Y., and Montreal.

• Nixon was the last of seven presidents who visited Canada while in office.

June 28, returned to Washington, D.C.

June 29, attended religious services conducted by Rabbi Louis Finkelstein, White House

• This was the first time the White House services were conducted by a rabbi.

June 30, hosted dinner for *Apollo 10* astronauts, White House

July 4, visited Bahamas

• He made an overnight visit to Grand Cay after serving as grand marshal of a Fourth of July parade in Key Biscayne, Fla.

• He was the second of two presidents who visited the Bahamas while in office. The other was Kennedy.

July 7, cancelled plans for July 15 dinner with *Apollo 11* astronauts

• Dr. Charles Berry, the astronauts' chief physician, had advised against the event, scheduled for the night before the launch, on grounds of possible germ contamination.

July 8–9, conferred with Emperor Haile Selassie of Ethiopia, White House

• Haile Selassie was the only state visitor to be received at the White House by four presidents. They were Presidents Eisenhower, Kennedy, Johnson, and Nixon.

July 8, sent special message to Congress asking for broader coverage and improved benefits under unemployment compensation system

July 9, ordered ten percent reduction in U.S. military and civilian personnel abroad

• The reduction, to be put into effect during the next year, did not apply to military forces serving with NATO or in Berlin, South Korea, or Southeast Asia. A total of 14,900 military and 5,100 civilians were involved.

July 11, administration bill for preventive detention sent to Congress

• The measure called for up to 60 days imprisonment without bail of defendants in federal criminal actions if their release was adjudged dangerous to the community. The bill would apply particularly to the District of Columbia, where all criminal cases come under federal jurisdiction.

July 14, sent special message on narcotics to Congress

• This message recommended stiffer penalties for violations of narcotics laws. Justice department officials said he would ask adoption of a "no-knock" clause permitting federal agents, armed with search warrants, to enter suspected premises without knocking or identifying themselves.

July 18, sent special message on world population problems to Congress

• In the first presidential message on this subject, he recommended a program to control U.S. population growth by making birth control information available to all American women of child-bearing age.

July 20, lunar module *Eagle* landed first men on moon, 4:17:40 P.M. (EDT)

• He spoke by radio-telephone to Neil A. Armstrong—the first man to walk on the moon's surface—and Edwin E. Aldrin, Jr., as they stood beside their landing craft in the Sea of Tranquility. The third astronaut, Michael Collins, remained aloft guiding *Apollo 11* in orbit.

July 22, flew to San Francisco, Cal.

July 23, flew to Johnston Island, American atoll in Pacific

• Johnston Island is about seven hundred miles southwest of Hawaii. He spent the night aboard the *U.S.S. Arlington*, a communications ship.

• He was the only president who visited Johnston Island while in office.

July 24, witnessed splashdown of *Apollo 11* from flag bridge of carrier, *U.S.S. Hornet*
- After greeting the astronauts through a window of their isolation trailer, he flew back to Johnston Island by helicopter, then on to Guam aboard Air Force One.
- He was the second of two presidents who visited Guam while in office. The other was Lyndon B. Johnson.

July 26–27, visited Philippines
- He conferred with President Ferdinand E. Marcos in Manila.
- Nixon was the last of three presidents who visited the Philippines while in office.

July 27–28, visited Indonesia
- He conferred with President Suharto in Jakarta.
- Nixon was the only president who visited Indonesia while in office.

July 28–30, visited Thailand
- He was greeted by King Phumiphol Aduldej and Queen Sirikit in Bangkok. During his visit, Nixon conferred with Prime Minister Thanom Kittikachorn, SEATO Secretary General Jesus Vargas, and a group of U.S. ambassadors to Southeast Asia nations.
- He was the second of two presidents who visited Thailand while in office. The other was Lyndon B. Johnson.
- This was the first of Nixon's two visits to Thailand while in office.

July 30, visited South Vietnam
- He conferred with President Nguyen Van Thieu in Saigon and visited American troops in Di An. Nixon spent five and a half hours in South Vietnam.
- He was the only president who visited Saigon while in office.
- He was the second of two presidents who visited South Vietnam while in office. The other was Lyndon B. Johnson.
- He was the last of five presidents who visited war zones while in office.
- He was the last of three presidents to travel outside the U.S. during wartime.

July 30, returned to Thailand
- This was the second of his two visits to Thailand while in office.

July 31–Aug. 1, visited India
- He conferred with Prime Minister Indira Gandhi in New Delhi.
- Nixon was the second of two presidents who visited India while in office. The other was Eisenhower.

Aug. 1–2, visited Pakistan
- He conferred with President Agha Mo-

hammad Yahya Khan in Lahore.
- Nixon was the last of three presidents who visited Pakistan while in office.

Aug. 2–3, visited Rumania
- He received a most enthusiastic welcome from a crowd estimated at 100,000 people, who lined the 12-mile route from the airport to Bucharest. He conferred with President Nicolae Ceausescu.
- Nixon was the only president who visited Rumania while in office.
- This was the first visit by a president to a Communist country since Franklin D. Roosevelt visited Russia in 1945.

Aug. 3, visited England
- He conferred with Prime Minister Harold Wilson at Mildenhall Air Force Base during a two-hour refueling stop.
- This was the second of his three visits to England while in office.

Aug. 3, returned to Washington, D.C.

Aug. 7, sent special message on mass transportation to Congress
- He asked for the expenditure of $10,000,-000,000 over a 12-year period.

Aug. 7–8, conferred with Chancellor Kurt Georg Kiesinger of West Germany, White House

Aug. 8, proposed minimum federal standards for welfare assistance and federal-state revenue-sharing program, during TV-radio speech

Aug. 9, flew to San Clemente, Cal.

Aug. 11, sent special message to Congress urging prompt adoption of welfare reform proposals outlined in his Aug. 8 speech

Aug. 13, sent special message to Congress on revenue-sharing with states
- His plan called for the distribution of $5,-000,000,000 by 1976, and more in future years. Tax funds would be distributed to state and local governments without restrictions on use, he said.

Aug. 13, hosted state dinner for *Apollo 11* astronauts, Los Angeles, Cal.
- The largest state dinner in history, the affair was attended by 1,440 guests, including the Supreme Court, the cabinet (with the exception of Attorney General Mitchell), 44 governors, 50 astronauts, and diplomats from more than 80 nations.

Aug. 18, appointed Clement F. Haynsworth, Jr., as associate justice
- Haynsworth, the second of Nixon's six appointments to the Supreme Court, was rejected by the Senate, 55–45, Nov. 21.

•Nixon was the last of 15 presidents who nominated justices not confirmed by the Senate.

•Haynsworth was the 24th of 25 men nominated to the Supreme Court not confirmed by the Senate.

Aug. 21–22, conferred with President Chung Hee Park of South Korea, San Francisco, Cal.

Aug. 27, dedicated Lady Bird Johnson Grove, Redwood National Park, near Orick, Cal.

•Following a luncheon in honor of former President Johnson's 61st birthday at San Clemente, President and Mrs. Nixon and former President and Mrs. Johnson boarded Air Force One for the eight-hundred-mile trip to northern California. The three-hundred-acre grove lies near the Pacific Coast in the western sector of the national park.

Sept. 1, addressed national governors conference, Colorado Springs, Colo.

Sept. 5, Mrs. Nixon dedicated Pat Nixon Park on site of her childhood home, Cerritos, Cal.

•The eight-room frame house, which was to be refurnished as a children's library and museum, and the surrounding four and a half acres of land, had been purchased from her brother, Tom Ryan, for $140,000, which was raised by a local bond issue.

Sept. 8, visited Mexico

•He and President Gustavo Diaz Ordaz of Mexico dedicated the Amistad Dam on the Rio Grande, between Del Rio, Tex. and Ciudad Acuna, Mexico.

•Nixon was the last of seven presidents who visited Mexico while in office.

•This was the first of his two visits to Mexico while in office.

Sept. 8, returned to Washington, D.C.

•He had spent most of his 31-day working vacation at the Western White House, San Clemente, Cal.

Sept. 9, delivered eulogy at memorial service for Senator Everett McKinley Dirksen, Capitol Rotunda

•Senator Dirksen of Illinois, the minority leader, had died, Sept. 7.

Sept. 12, White House announced resumption of B-52 bombing raids in South Vietnam

•The 36-hour suspension, said Press Secretary Ronald L. Ziegler, was to test whether the temporary truce called by North Viet-

nam after the death of President Ho Chi Minh had any "political significance." Ziegler added that enemy action was back to pre-truce levels.

•Ho Chi Minh had died in Hanoi, Sept. 3.

Sept. 16, announced plans to withdraw additional thirty-five thousand U.S. troops from South Vietnam by Dec. 15

•The first withdrawal of twenty-five thousand men, announced June 8, had been completed in August.

Sept. 15, signed act raising salaries of vice president, speaker of House, president pro tempore of Senate, and majority and minority leaders

•This act increased the salaries of the vice president and the speaker from $43,000 to $62,500 per year, while the salaries of the leaders and the president pro tempore were raised from $42,500 to $49,500.

Sept. 16, conferred with Prime Minister Keith J. Holyoake of New Zealand, White House

Sept. 18, addressed General Assembly of United Nations, New York City

•He said "the time had come for the other side to respond" and called upon delegates "to persuade Hanoi to move seriously into the negotiations which could end this war."

Sept. 19, announced cancellation of draft calls for fifty thousand men in November and December

•He also said that he would institute a random selection system by executive order if Congress did not act on his lottery-system proposal.

Sept. 22, issued executive order establishing collective bargaining commission for construction industry

Sept. 23, announced his decision to proceed with development of supersonic transport plane

Sept. 25, sent special message on social security program to Congress

•He recommended a ten percent increase in benefits, effective, Mar. 1, 1970, and automatic increases based on the cost of living.

Sept. 25–26, conferred with Premier Golda Meir of Israel, White House

Sept. 30, signed act appropriating $8,700,-000,000 for treasury and post office departments, and executive office

Sept. 30, endorsed proposed constitutional

amendment providing for direct election of presidents
- This was a reversal of his previous position on the proposed amendment. He urged the Senate to adopt the amendment, which had been passed by the House of Representatives, 339–70, Sept. 18.
- He had expressed his original position in a special message to Congress, Feb. 20.

Oct. 3, invoked provisions of Railway Labor Act to prevent national rail strike

Oct. 7, conferred with Premier Souvanna Phouma of Laos, White House

Oct. 10, relieved Lieutenant General Lewis B. Hershey as director of Selective Service System, effective, Feb. 16, 1970
- Hershey, who had directed the draft system since 1941, had become a highly controversial figure because of his policy of urging local draft boards to hasten the induction of antiwar protesters. Hershey was promoted to the rank of four-star general and appointed presidential adviser on manpower mobilization, Feb. 16, 1970.

Oct. 11, sent special message to Congress appealing for cooperation between administration and Democratic-controlled Congress for prompt enactment of his domestic program
- In his conciliatory appeal, he admitted that he might have been at fault for delay in submitting his legislative program. However, he added, neither side is "without fault for the delay of vital legislation."

Oct. 13, reiterated his refusal to be influenced by public demonstrations against war in Vietnam
- "If a President—any President—allowed his course to be set by those who demonstrate, he would betray the trust of all the rest," he said. The statement came two days before a nationwide antiwar protest.
- During his Sept. 26 news conference, he had said of criticism from the campuses that "under no circumstances, will I be affected whatever by it."

Oct. 21, received Shah of Iran, White House

Oct. 23, sent special message to Congress proposing ten-year program to rebuild U.S. merchant marine

Oct. 28–29, campaigned in support of Republican gubernatorial candidates, Virginia and New Jersey
- He spoke in behalf of Linwood Holton in Salem, Va., and in support of William T. Cahill in Morristown and Hackensack, N.J.

Both were elected.

Oct. 30, pledged to support and enforce Supreme Court decision on desegregation
- The Court had ruled unanimously that school districts must end segregation "at once" and operate integrated systems "now and hereafter," Oct. 29. The Court thereby rejected the argument of the justice department that delays were permissible in requiring integration in some districts and that providing a continuing education should take precedence over the enforcement of social justice.
- This decision replaced the 1956 decision that school desegregation should proceed with "all deliberate speed."

Nov. 3, spoke on Vietnam
- During his TV-radio address, he asked for the support of the "great silent majority" of Americans as he pursued a secret plan for withdrawal of all U.S. ground combat troops. He blamed the North Vietnamese for lack of progress in the Paris peace talks.

Nov. 4, hosted state dinner for Prince Philip of Great Britain, White House

Nov. 13, made separate visits to House of Representatives and Senate
- He conveyed his appreciation to supporters of his Vietnam policies and asked for understanding and "constructive criticism" from opponents. His visits to the Capitol occurred on the first of three days of antiwar demonstrations in Washington by the New Mobilization Committee to End the War in Vietnam and other groups.
- He was the only president who made separate speeches to the House and the Senate on the same day.

Nov. 14, attended launching of *Apollo 12*, Cape Kennedy, Fla.
- He was the only president who was present for a spacecraft launching while in office.

Nov. 19–21, conferred with Premier Eisaku Sato of Japan, White House
- The U.S. agreed to return Okinawa to Japan in 1972.

Nov. 24, signed Nonproliferation of Nuclear Weapons Treaty, White House
- The treaty was ratified simultaneously by President Nikolai V. Podgorny of the U.S.S.R. in Moscow.

Nov. 25, renounced U.S. use of bacteriological weapons, ordered destruction of existing stockpiles
- He also renounced U.S. use of chemical

weapons except for defense and asked the Senate to ratify the 1925 Geneva Protocol banning chemical warfare.

Nov. 25, signed act extending aid-to-Appalachia program for two years
• The act provided $268,500,000 in grants and loans for health, conservation, education, housing and mining projects in the 13-state area.

Nov. 26, signed draft lottery act
• The act was a single sentence that removed the ban on a lottery inserted by Congress in 1968.
• The lottery, the first since 1942, was held, Dec. 1.

Nov. 28, signed appropriation acts totalling $24,600,000,000
• The acts provided funds for 17 departments, administrations, and agencies.

Dec. 2, signed act establishing Cincinnati, Ohio, home of President Taft as national historical site

Dec. 2, signed act establishing Johnson City, Tex., birthplace and childhood home of President Lyndon B. Johnson as national historical sites

Dec. 2, signed act providing funds to preserve and develop Gettysburg, Pa. farm of President Eisenhower
• The Eisenhower farm had previously been designated a historical site.

Dec. 4, threatened to call Congress into special session after Christmas if major appropriation bills not passed

Dec. 6, attended Texas-Arkansas football game, Fayetteville, Ark.
• Texas won, 15–14. He presented the winners with a plaque naming them the No. 1 team in the nation during the 100th year of college football.

Dec. 8, signed joint resolution providing continuing appropriations until adjournment of 91st Congress or until enactment of pertinent bills

Dec. 9, was awarded 13th Gold Medal Award of National Football Foundation and Hall of Fame, New York City
• He was the fourth president to receive the sports award. The others were Eisenhower, Hoover, and Kennedy.

Dec. 11, conferred with former President Johnson, White House

Dec. 15, announced further reduction of troop strength in Vietnam
• In a national TV-radio address, he said 50,-000 troops would be withdrawn by Apr.

15, 1970, which would bring the troop level below 434,000—a reduction of about 110,000 since he took office.

Dec. 22, allocated $1,000,000 in federal aid to three states for flood and storm damage
• Pennsylvania received $850,000; Colorado, $100,000, and South Dakota, $50,000.

Dec. 23, first session of 91st Congress adjourned

Dec. 24, reluctantly signed act authorizing anti-inflation credit controls
• He said that such controls, if invoked, could "take the nation a long step toward a directly controlled economy."

Dec. 29, signed appropriations acts for state, commerce, justice, and transportation departments, supplemental appropriations acts for treasury and HEW departments

Dec. 30, signed Tax Reform Act of 1969
• Calling the act "unbalanced," he said: "The tax reforms, on the whole, are good; the effect on the budget and on the cost of living is bad."

Dec. 30, signed Federal Coal Mine Health and Safety Act of 1969

Dec. 30, signed $69,200,000,000 appropriations act for defense department

Dec. 30, departed for San Clemente, Cal.

Dec. 31, signed act extending Economic Opportunity Act for two years

Dec. 31, signed act extending Export Control Act for two years

Dec. 31, signed act authorizing $1,972,000,-000 for foreign aid
• "I submitted the lowest aid request in history and regret that this act reduced that request substantially," he said, and added, "Further large cuts in the appropriations bill would have serious consequences for United States foreign policy."

1970

Jan. 1, signed act creating Council on Environmental Quality

Jan. 3, flew by helicopter from San Clemente to North Hollywood for golf game with actors Bob Hope, James Stewart, and Fred MacMurray

Jan. 8, registered as voter, Santa Ana, Cal.

Jan. 8, returned to Washington, D.C.

Jan. 19, second session of 91st Congress

Jan. 19, appointed G. Harrold Carswell as associate justice
• Carswell, the third of Nixon's six appoint-

ments to the Supreme Court, was rejected by the Senate, 51–45, Apr. 8.

• Carswell was the last of 25 men nominated to the Supreme Court who were not confirmed by the Senate.

Jan. 22, delivered his first State of the Union message to Congress

• He placed "first priority" on world peace and a "just" settlement of the Vietnam War, but stressed the necessity of preserving the environment against pollution of all varieties.

Jan. 24, presented Medal of Freedom to Eugene Ormandy, conductor of Philadelphia Orchestra, Philadelphia, Pa.

• Nixon attended the gala anniversary concert celebrating the 113th anniversary of the Philadelphia Academy of Music, the 70th anniversary of the Philadelphia Orchestra, and the ceremonial celebration of Ormandy's 70th birthday. Mr. Ormandy was born Nov. 18, 1899.

Jan. 26, vetoed $19,700,000,000 HEW-Labor appropriation bill

• He signed the veto message on television, condemning the money bill that appropriated $1,100,000,000 more than he had requested as inflationary, untimely, and misdirected.

• His veto was sustained by the House of Representatives, 226–191, 52 votes short of the required two-thirds needed to override the veto, Jan. 28. He promptly invited the 191 House members who voted to sustain his veto to a private reception at the White House that evening.

Jan. 27–28, conferred with Prime Minister Harold Wilson of Great Britain, White House

Jan. 30, sent first economic report to Congress

• He asked the support of Congress in setting a "prudent" fiscal policy and opposed "overly long and overly severe restraint" in the Federal Reserve Board's monetary policy.

Jan. 30, attended induction of his son-in-law, David Eisenhower, into Naval Reserve, White House

Feb. 2, sent budget message to Congress

• He estimated expenditures for the fiscal year ending June 30, 1971, at $200,800,-000,000; receipts as $202,100,000,000; and a surplus of $1,300,000,000.

Feb. 4, signed executive order requiring all federal agencies to conform to federal standards for air and water quality by end of 1972

Feb. 5, accompanied by five of eight cabinet members who made up Urban Affairs Council and other administration officials, met with mayors of ten middle-size cities, Indianapolis, Ind.

• A ten-point policy to deal with the problems of the cities was outlined by Daniel Patrick Moynihan, counselor to the president.

• This was the first time a president had held such a meeting outside Washington, D.C.

Feb. 6, met with governors of Illinois, Indiana, Michigan, and Wisconsin and three nominees to Council on Environmental Quality, Chicago, Ill.

Feb. 10, sent special message on environment to Congress

• He called for "expanded government action" in water pollution control, air pollution control, solid waste disposal, and an increase of park lands and open space. He said:

> Like those in the last century who tilled a plot of land to exhaustion and then moved on to another, we in this century have too casually and too long abused our natural environment.

Feb. 10, signed act providing $2,500,000,-000 for foreign aid and Peace Corps

• The appropriation of $1,800,000,000 for foreign aid was only a slight increase ($50,-000,000) over the amount appropriated in the previous fiscal year—which had been the lowest appropriation for the program since its inception.

Feb. 11, announced third nuclear-powered aircraft carrier would be named for President Eisenhower

Feb. 14, banned production or use of toxins for germ warfare purposes

• This decision closed a loophole, found by defense department officials, in his Nov. 25 ban of bacteriological weapons.

Feb. 18, sent special message on foreign policy to Congress

• Referred to as the first annual report on the state of the world, the 119-page, 40,000-word report was entitled, "A New Strategy for Peace." He disavowed isolationism, but stressed that "a more balanced and realistic American role in the world is essential if American commitments are to be sustained over the long pull."

Feb. 19, honored artist Andrew Wyeth, White House dinner

• An exhibit of Wyeth paintings was held in the East Room, Feb. 20.

• This was the first one-man show in the White House.

Feb. 22, attended full-length performance of *1776*, White House

• *1776* was the Broadway musical about the drafting of the Declaration of Independence.

Feb. 24, welcomed President Georges Pompidou of France, White House

Feb. 26, sent special message to Congress on outmoded and nonessential federal programs

• He proposed the elimination or fundamental change of 57 programs. He had the authority to eliminate 43 of the programs, costing $1,400,000,000, but congressional action was required for the other 14 programs, costing $1,100,000,000.

• Among the programs marked for elimination was the 73-year-old Board of Tea Experts. It was time, he said, to "upset the teacart." However, the board of tea tasters was reappointed, May 12.

Feb. 27, sent special message asking major changes in labor laws to Congress

• He asked for legislation to provide wider presidential powers in preventing transportation strikes, which would require major changes in the Railway Labor Act of 1926 and Taft-Hartley Act of 1947.

Mar. 2, attended dinner for President Pompidou of France, New York City

• He publicly apologized to the French leader for the behavior of pro-Israel demonstrators in Chicago, Ill., Feb. 28.

Mar. 3, sent special message to Congress asking emergency legislation to avert rail strike, scheduled for Mar. 5

Mar. 4, signed act providing 37-day moratorium on strikes and lockouts in rail dispute

Mar. 5, signed proclamation formally placing Nonproliferation of Nuclear Weapons Treaty into effect

• Similar ceremonies were held simultaneously in London and Moscow.

Mar. 6, signed act appropriating $19,400,-000,000 for departments of labor and health, education and welfare

• Although this act appropriated only $300,-

000,000 less than the measure he had vetoed, Jan. 26, a Senate provision empowered him to further reduce the funds by $347,000,000.

Mar. 6, confirmed reports of U.S. air action over Laos

• He said he had authorized air combat operations to counter a Communist offensive, but added that there were "no plans for introducing ground combat forces into Laos." He disclosed that he had requested the assistance of the U.S.S.R. and Great Britain in restoring the neutrality of Laos, as provided for in the 1962 Geneva accord.

Mar. 11, addressed about two thousand Republicans at $1,000-a-plate fund-raising dinner, Washington, D.C.

Mar. 11, announced $12,400,000 program for fiscal 1971 warning nation's youth about dangers of drugs

Mar. 12, appointed Curtis W. Tarr as director of Selective Service System

• Tarr, an assistant secretary of the Air Force, succeeded General Lewis B. Hershey.

Mar. 12, sent special message to Congress proposing two new executive branch agencies

• The program, which would become effective, Aug. 9, would establish the office of management and budget, replacing the bureau of the budget, and the domestic council, superseding the urban affairs council, the rural affairs council, and the cabinet committee on the environment, advisory groups established in 1969.

Mar. 17, announced release of $1,500,000,-000 in construction funds, frozen since Sept. 4, 1970

• This constituted a shift in fiscal policy. He cited progress in the fight against inflation as reason for the change in policy.

Mar. 18, donated oval table for Cabinet Room, White House

• The mahogany and cowhide table, 22 feet long and seven feet wide, cost $4,500. Matching chairs were paid for from federal funds.

Mar. 19, signed act renaming White House police as Executive Protection Service

• The service, enlarged from 250 to 850 members, was placed under the director of the Secret Service, and given the added duties of protecting foreign diplomatic missions.

Mar. 23, declared state of national emergency in postal strike, ordered regular army and reserves to deliver mail, if necessary

• The strike of nearly 200,000 postal employees began in New York City, Mar. 18, and, despite a federal injunction, quickly spread throughout the nation, except the South. The strikers returned to their jobs, Mar. 24–25.

• This was the largest strike against the federal government.

Apr. 1, signed act prohibiting cigarette advertising on television and radio, effective, Jan. 2, 1971

Apr. 3, sent special message to Congress requesting increase in first class postage rate from six to ten cents

• The increase was necessary, he said, to pay a six percent salary increase for federal employees.

Apr. 6, attended opening game of baseball season, Washington, D.C.

• The press of official duties prevented his arrival until the fifth inning. The ceremonial first ball was thrown out by his son-in-law, David Eisenhower.

Apr. 7, presented Medal of Honor to families of 21 servicemen killed in Vietnam

Apr. 9, stated his next appointee to Supreme Court would be "from outside the South"

• The Senate had rejected his nomination of G. Harrold Carswell, 51–45, Apr. 8. Nixon accused the Senate of "regional discrimination" in the rejections of Haynsworth and Carswell.

Apr. 10–11, conferred with Chancellor Willy Brandt of West Germany, White House

Apr. 11, watched telecast of *Apollo 13* launching aboard presidential yacht, *Sequoia*

Apr. 14, appointed Harry A. Blackmun as associate justice

• Blackmun, who was confirmed by the Senate, May 12, was the fourth of Nixon's six appointments to the Supreme Court.

Apr. 14, briefed on problems of *Apollo 13* mission, Goddard Space Flight Center, Greenbelt, Md.

• The most perilous conditions in U.S. space flight history had developed following an explosion aboard the spacecraft, at a distance of some 205,000 miles from earth, Apr. 13. The rupture of oxygen tanks in the command and service module had caused failure of the main fuel cells and forced the

three astronauts—Capt. James A. Lovell, Jr., Fred W. Haise, Jr., and John L. Swigert, Jr.—to take refuge in the lunar module. They stayed in the lunar module for most of the remainder of their journey around the moon and back to earth and ultimately maneuvered their crippled spacecraft to a successful splashdown in the South Pacific, Apr. 17.

Apr. 15, signed act giving six percent salary increase to civilian employees of federal government, retroactive to Dec. 27, 1969

• The estimated cost of the increase was $2,-600,000,000.

Apr. 16, sent special message to Congress on postal reform, asking for increase in first class postal rate from six to eight cents

• This message nullified his Apr. 3 request for an increase to ten cents.

Apr. 18, flew to Honolulu, Hawaii, to present Medal of Freedom to *Apollo 13* astronauts

• En route to Hawaii, he visited NASA headquarters in Houston, Tex., where he presented the medal, the highest civilian award, to the ground operations crew for the mission.

• This was the second of his two visits to Hawaii while in office.

Apr. 19, flew to San Clemente, Cal.

Apr. 20, made national telecast on Vietnam, San Clemente

• He announced plans for further U.S. troop reductions of 150,000 within the next year, which would reduce the troops in Vietnam to 284,000.

Apr. 22, presented Medal of Freedom to seven journalists, White House

• The journalists were Earl C. Behrens, political editor of the San Francisco *Chronicle;* Edward T. Folliard, retired White House correspondent of the Washington *Post;* Arthur Krock, retired Washington correspondent of *The New York Times;* David Lawrence, syndicated columnist and editor of *U.S. News and World Report;* George Gould Lincoln, columnist of the Washington *Evening Star;* Raymond Moley, syndicated columnist and former editor of *Newsweek* Magazine; and Adela Rogers St. Johns, retired reporter for the Hearst newspapers.

• Nixon also presented a posthumous Medal of Freedom to Bill Henry, columnist of the Los Angeles *Times*, who had died Apr. 13.

Apr. 23, signed executive order abolishing

future draft deferments based on father-
hood or occupation
• In a special message to Congress, he asked
for authority to end undergraduate student deferments. He also pledged to move
away from conscription and toward a
volunteer army.
Apr. 30, announced he was sending U.S.
combat troops into Cambodia
• On national television, he described the
action as a necessary extension of the Vietnam War designed to eliminate a major
Communist staging and communications
area. He estimated that the operation
would be completed in six to eight weeks.
May 4, deplored death of four students at
Kent State University, Kent, Ohio
• The four students, two young men and two
young women, were shot to death by National Guardsmen during an antiwar
demonstration. Eight other students were
wounded.
May 5, met with members of Senate and
House of Representatives armed services
committees, and Senate foreign relations
and House foreign affairs committees,
White House
• He pledged that he would not order
American troops to advance deeper than
21 miles into Cambodian territory without
first seeking congressional approval. He
said the troops would be withdrawn in
three to seven weeks.
May 6, met with six Kent State University
students, White House
May 6, received letter from Secretary of Interior Hickel complaining administration
was failing young people of nation
May 7, discussed problems of student unrest
with presidents of eight universities, White
House
May 8, defended U.S. action in Cambodia
during nationally-televised news conference
May 9, paid impromptu dawn visit to group
of protesting students on steps of Lincoln
Memorial
• He spoke to a group of eight students on a
variety of subjects, principally the war and
racial problems. His presence attracted
others and the group grew to about 50 during the hour he spent at the Lincoln
Memorial. Later in the day, more than seventy-five thousand antiwar demonstrators,
mostly students from the more than two
hundred colleges and universities on strike

since the Kent State killings, massed on the
Ellipse, south of the White House.
May 12, signed amendment to Historic
Preservation Act of 1966 authorizing $32,-
000,000 for preservation of historic areas
during next three years
May 15, appointed first two women gener-
als in U.S. Army
• Colonel Anna Mae Hays, chief of the Army
Nurse Corps, and Colonel Elizabeth P.
Hoisington, director of the Women's Army
Corps, were promoted to the temporary
rank of brigadier general.
May 16, expressed regret at deaths of two
Negro youths killed in confrontation with
police on campus of Jackson State College,
Jackson, Miss., May 14
May 20, issued revised budget statement
• He projected a deficit of $1,300,000,000
for the fiscal year ending June 30, 1971. He
had estimated a surplus of $1,300,000,000
in his budget message, Feb. 2.
May 20, met with 15 presidents of predomi-
nantly Negro colleges, White House
May 21, expressed confidence in economy
during meeting with Bernard Lasker,
chairman of New York Stock Exchange
• Stock prices had fallen to the lowest level
since Jan. 2, 1963.
May 26, met with President Suharto of Indonesia, White House
May 26, attended reception for retiring
Speaker John W. McCormack
• McCormack served longer continuously as
speaker than any of his predecessors. He
served for eight and a half years, second
only to Sam Rayburn in total service. Rayburn had served as speaker for 17 years,
but not continuously.
May 27, signed act renaming Kaysinger
Bluff Dam and Reservoir, Mo., after former
President Truman
May 27, gave dinner for business and financial leaders, White House
• The stock market had reached its lowest
level since Nov. 19, 1962, May 26, but rallied strongly for its largest one-day advance to date, 32.04 points.
May 28, addressed overflow crowd of
eighty-eight thousand at Billy Graham
rally, University of Tennessee stadium,
Knoxville, Tenn.
June 3, made televised address on Cambodia
• He called the move into Cambodia "the
most successful operation of this long and

difficult war" and reiterated his promises that action in Cambodia by U.S. troops would be completed by the end of June.

June 5, named Henry Cabot Lodge as his personal envoy to Vatican

• Mr. Lodge was the second U.S. representative to maintain regular contact with the Vatican. President Franklin D. Roosevelt had sent Myron Taylor to the Vatican as his personal envoy in 1939.

June 6, accepted resignation of Secretary of Health, Education and Welfare Finch

• Finch was appointed to the White House staff with the title of counselor to the president.

June 6, appointed his second secretary of health, education and welfare, Elliot L. Richardson

• Richardson took office, June 24.

June 10, accepted resignation of Secretary of Labor Shultz

• Shultz was appointed to the new office of management and budget as director, effective, July 1.

June 10, appointed his second secretary of labor, James D. Hodgson

• Hodgson took office, July 2.

June 13, appointed nine-member commission to inquire into causes and consequences of campus unrest

• He appointed William W. Scranton as chairman.

June 17, made televised address on economy

• While rejecting wage-price controls, he asked the support of business and labor in moderating demands.

June 21, with Mrs. Nixon, celebrated 30th wedding anniversary, Camp David, Md.

June 22, signed act lowering voting age from 21 to 18, but called for Supreme Court test of its constitutionality

• The measure was a rider on a bill extending for five years the protection of the Voting Rights Act of 1965 against racial discrimination.

• *See* Constitution, 26th Amendment, page 645.

June 22, vetoed medical facilities construction and modernization bill

June 24, Senate repealed Gulf of Tonkin Resolution, 81–10

June 25, addressed 50th anniversary convention of United States Jaycees, St. Louis, Mo.

June 26, held briefing for 38 newspaper and broadcasting executives, San Clemente, Cal.

June 30, issued statement announcing successful completion of U.S. ground action in Cambodia

June 30, medical facilities construction and modernization act passed over his veto

• The three-year extension of the Hill-Burton Act authorized $2,790,000,000 for hospital construction and modernization of medical facilities.

• This was the first of his vetoes that were overridden.

• This was the first time since July 1, 1960, that Congress had overridden a presidential veto.

July 1, signed act raising national debt ceiling by $18,000,000,000 to $395,000,000,-000

July 1, signed executive order implementing major reorganization of White House staff

July 1, interviewed by three television commentators on foreign policy, Hollywood, Cal.

• During the televised "conversation," he announced the appointment of David K. E. Bruce as chief U.S. negotiator at the Paris peace talks.

• He was interviewed by John Chancellor of NBC, Eric Sevareid of CBS, and Howard K. Smith of ABC.

July 2, attended oath-taking ceremony of Secretary of Labor Hodgson, San Clemente, Cal.

• Hodgson was the second cabinet officer who took the oath of office outside Washington, D.C. The first was Postmaster General O'Brien, who took the oath of office in Hye, Tex., Nov. 3, 1965.

July 6, returned to Washington, D.C.

July 9, sent special messages to Congress transmitting reorganization plans to establish two agencies

• The plans proposed the establishment of the Environmental Protection Agency (EPA) as a new, independent agency within the executive branch, and the National Oceanic and Atmospheric Administration (NOAA) in the department of commerce.

July 10, Senate again repealed Gulf of Tonkin Resolution, 57–5

• This measure, unlike the June 24 measure, was cast as a concurrent resolution—like the Gulf of Tonkin Resolution itself—requiring no presidential action.

July 10, conferred with Secretary General U Thant of United Nations, White House

• A White House dinner marked the 25th anniversary of the United Nations. The UN charter had been signed, June 26, 1945.

July 13, signed 17 acts to permit disposal of excess stocks of strategic materials

July 13, entertained 34 members of his graduating class from Whittier College, White House

July 14, met with governors of 13 states of Appalachian region, Louisville, Ky.

July 14, attended All-Star baseball game, Cincinnati, Ohio

July 16, welcomed Prince Charles and Princess Anne of Great Britain, White House

• Prince Charles was the third Prince of Wales to visit the White House.

July 18, issued statement admonishing Congress about overspending, asked firm ceiling on total expenditures

July 23, welcomed President Urho Kekkonen of Finland, White House

July 23, attended luncheon with editorial board of Washington *Evening Star*

July 24, signed Emergency Home Financing Act

• This act authorized a $250,000,000 subsidy for the federal home loan banks.

July 24, met with governors of five Plains states, Fargo, N.D.

• Five cabinet officers joined the discussion of rural area problems with the governors of Iowa, Nebraska, North Dakota, Minnesota, and South Dakota.

July 24, conferred with members of hierarchy of Mormon Church, Salt Lake City, Utah

July 29, signed District of Columbia crime control act, San Clemente, Cal.

July 30, held televised news conference, Los Angeles, Cal.

• This was the first presidential news conference televised from outside Washington, D.C., during prime time.

Aug. 3, described Charles Manson as "guilty, directly or indirectly, of eight murders, without reason," Denver, Colo.

• Manson and three female codefendents were then on trial in Los Angeles, Cal., for the Sharon Tate "cult murders" of Aug. 9, 1969. They were convicted of first degree murder, Jan. 25, 1971, and condemned to death in the gas chamber, Mar. 29, 1971.

Aug. 4, greeted President Joseph Desire Mobutu of Congo, White House

Aug. 6, presented Medal of Honor posthumously to families of nine members of armed forces, White House

Aug. 6, received first-day album of six-cent Eisenhower stamps, White House

• Postmaster General Blount also presented an album containing the first sheet of the new stamps to Mrs. Dwight D. Eisenhower.

Aug. 10, signed act extending unemployment insurance coverage to 4,800,000 additional workers

• This act brought the total of U.S. workers covered by unemployment insurance to 63,500,000.

Aug. 11, vetoed independent offices appropriations bill

• This bill would have provided $18,100,-000,000 for the department of housing and urban development, NASA, and several other agencies, exceeding his budget request by $541,000,000.

Aug. 11, vetoed $4,400,000,000 Office of Education appropriations bill

• This bill exceeded his budget request by $453,000,000.

• In identical veto messages, he condemned the independent offices and education appropriations bill as inflationary and added, "I have drawn the line against increased spending."

Aug. 12, signed Postal Reorganization Act

• This act provided the means to replace the post office department with an independent government agency.

• He signed the act in the presence of six former postmasters general—James A. Farley, Arthur E. Summerfield, J. Edward Day, John A. Gronouski, Lawrence F. O'-Brien, and W. Marvin Watson.

Aug. 12, signed act increasing veterans' disability benefits by about 11 percent

• This act exceeded his budget request of $3,000,000,000 by about $218,000,000. He ordered reductions equaling $218,000,000 in other programs, including Medicaid, the Atomic Energy Commission, the General Services Administration, and federal land acquisition.

Aug. 14, met with leaders of seven state advisory committees on public education, New Orleans, La.

Aug. 17, signed act extending Defense Production Act to June 30, 1972

• He reluctantly signed the act, expressing

disapproval of that portion of the bill that authorized him to establish controls on prices, rents, wages, and salaries. "I have previously indicated that I did not intend to exercise such authority if it were given to me," he added.

Aug. 18, $4,400,000,000 Office of Education appropriations act passed over his veto

• This was the second of his vetoes that were overridden.

Aug. 18, briefed editors of New York *Daily News* on foreign and domestic issues, New York City

Aug. 19, sent special message to Senate transmitting Geneva Protocol of 1925 for ratification

• The protocol prohibits nations that have ratified it from being the first to use chemical or biological weapons in war. Originally submitted to the Senate in 1926, it was returned to President Truman in 1947. The United States is the only major military power which is not a party to the protocol.

Aug. 20–21, visited Mexico

• He conferred with President Gustavo Diaz Ordaz at Puerto Vallarta. They announced that they had agreed to a resolution of all current border disputes.

• This was the second of Nixon's two visits to Mexico while in office.

Aug. 21, flew to San Clemente, Cal.

Aug. 22, new flag policy at White House announced

• The flag would be flown over the White House day and night instead of from sunrise to sunset. It is legal to fly the flag at night if it is illuminated.

Aug. 24, briefed western states editors and publishers on foreign policy, San Clemente

Aug. 31, Senator J. William Fulbright and Senator George S. McGovern appeared on NBC television program, "Reply to the President"

• The program was the first broadcast by a major network in compliance with a ruling by the FCC, Aug. 14, that ordered equal time for rebuttal of the president's Indochina policy. Senator Fulbright said the Paris peace talks were deadlocked because the administration was unwilling to make the "key concessions" necessary to break the stalemate.

Sept. 2, hailed relatively smooth desegregation of hundreds of southern school districts, San Clemente

Sept. 3, hosted state dinner in honor of President Gustavo Diaz Ordaz of Mexico, Coronado, Cal.

Sept. 4, issued proclamation regarding display of flag at White House during day and night, except in inclement weather, San Clemente

Sept. 6, returned to Washington, D.C.

Sept. 7, gave Labor Day dinner for 75 labor leaders and wives, White House

Sept. 8, signed act providing additional $75,000 for Franklin Delano Roosevelt Memorial Commission

Sept. 11, announced plan for corps of specially trained guards to police domestic and overseas flights of U.S.-flag airlines to deal with "menace of air piracy"

Sept. 11, sent special message on his legislative program to Congress

• He complained that fewer than a dozen of the 59 measures he recommended had received full approval. "The record of this moment is that Congress has not responded," he said.

Sept. 14, appointed seven members of board of trustees of John F. Kennedy Center for Performing Arts

• One of the new members was his daughter, Patricia, who was appointed for a ten-year, unpaid term.

Sept. 14, sent special message to Congress requesting $28,000,000 for recruiting and training twenty-five hundred security guards for commercial planes

Sept. 15, declined to avert General Motors strike

• The strike by the United Automobile Workers affected 321,510 workers in the U.S. and 22,100 in Canada.

Sept. 15, sent special message to Congress proposing reform of foreign assistance program

Sept. 16, urged end to violence and intolerance in nationally-televised speech, Manhattan, Kan.

• He delivered the first annual Alfred M. Landon Lecture on Public Issues at Kansas State University.

• Mr. Landon, the Republican candidate for president in 1936, was present.

Sept. 16–17, met with newspaper and television officials, Chicago, Ill.

• He met with midwestern regional news media representatives, Sept. 16, and with the editorial boards of the Chicago *Sun-Times, Daily News, Tribune*, and *Chicago Today*, and the editors of three Polish language newspapers, Sept. 17.

Sept. 17, spoke to 140 persons prior to their naturalization, Chicago

Sept. 18, met with Prime Minister Golda Meir of Israel, White House

Sept. 18, signed executive order blocking threatened nationwide railway strike for 60 days

Sept. 22, signed act giving District of Columbia elected nonvoting delegate to House of Representatives

•Washington, D.C. was without representation in Congress except for four years, 1871–1875, when the city was given the same right to a nonvoting House delegate as that of all pre-statehood American territories.

•This act provided for an election within seven months.

Sept. 23, sent special message to Senate asking ratification of convention terminating Bryan-Chamorro Treaty of 1914

•The treaty concerned an interoceanic canal route through Nicaragua. The U.S. did not exercise its rights under the agreement.

Sept. 26, signed executive order amending selective service regulations

•This order forbade the induction of men who had reached their 26th birthdays unless they had already been issued induction orders.

Sept. 27–28, visited Italy

•He conferred with President Giuseppe Saragat in Rome, Sept. 27 and Sept. 28, and met with Pope Paul VI in the Vatican, Sept. 28.

•While in Rome, Nixon greeted 31 American hostages who had been released by Arab guerrillas in Jordan. The Americans had been among the two hundred passengers aboard three jetliners hijacked over Europe and flown to the Jordanian desert near Amman, Sept. 6.

•This was the third of Nixon's four visits to Italy while in office.

•This was the second of his two meetings with Pope Paul while in office.

•Nixon was the second of two presidents who conferred with a Pope on two occasions while in office. The other was Lyndon B. Johnson.

Sept. 28, flew by helicopter to aircraft carrier, *U.S.S. Saratoga*, in Mediterranean

•Once aboard the *Saratoga*, he was informed of the death of President Gamal

Abdel Nasser of Egypt. Nixon cancelled the Sixth Fleet firepower demonstration scheduled for Sept. 29.

Sept. 29, flew by helicopter to cruiser, *U.S.S. Springfield*

•He conferred with commanders of Sixth Fleet units aboard the flagship.

Sept. 29–30, visited Italy

•He spent the night at President Saragat's residence in Naples, the Villa Roseberry. He conferred with officers of the NATO Southern Command and 13 U.S. ambassadors to Mideast countries in Naples.

•This was the last of his four visits to Italy while in office.

Sept. 30–Oct. 2, visited Yugoslavia

•He conferred with President Josip Broz Tito in Belgrade. Together, they visited Zagreb, capital of Croatia, and the tiny village of Kumravec, Tito's birthplace, Oct. 1.

•Nixon was the only president who visited Yugoslavia while in office.

Oct. 2–3, visited Spain

•He conferred with General Francisco Franco in Madrid.

•Nixon was the second of two presidents who visited Spain while in office. The other was Eisenhower.

Oct. 3, visited England

•He conferred with Prime Minister Edward Heath and Queen Elizabeth at Chequers, the country home of the prime minister.

•This was the last of Nixon's three visits to England while in office.

Oct. 3–5, visited Ireland

•He conferred with his chief negotiators at the Paris peace talks, Ambassadors David K. E. Bruce and Philip C. Habib, in Knocklong, Oct. 4. He met with President Eamon de Valera and Prime Minister John Lynch in Dublin, Oct. 5.

•En route to Dublin, Nixon had visited Timahoe, County Kildare, where his maternal sixth great-grandfather supposedly is buried. He dedicated a slanting stone slab on small pillars to the memory of the Quaker community.

•Mrs. Nixon had visited with "more cousins than I knew about" in Ballinrobe, County Mayo, the previous day.

•Nixon was the second of two presidents who visited Ireland while in office. The other was Kennedy.

Oct. 5, returned to Washington, D.C.

Oct. 6, announced Emergency Community

Facilities Act would become law without his signature

•He criticized Congress for "lavish spending" and "fiscal recklessness" for authorizing $1,000,000,000 in federal sewer and water construction grants. He had requested $150,000,000 for the program in his budget.

Oct. 7, signed $19,900,000,000 defense weapons authorization act

•This act also empowered him to sell an unlimited amount of arms to Israel—to balance Soviet arms shipments to Arab states.

Oct. 7, asked Hanoi and Vietcong to join in standstill ceasefire throughout Indochina during nationwide television address

•He also called for an Indochina peace conference to negotiate an end to the fighting in Laos and Cambodia as well as South Vietnam.

Oct. 8, dedicated Oceanographic Science Center of Atlantic Commission, Skidaway Island, near Savannah, Ga.

Oct. 12, began campaign for Republican congressional and gubernatorial candidates, Hartford, Conn.

•The White House announced that he would stump in about 17 states prior to the Nov. 3 elections, Oct. 14.

Oct. 12, met with news executives from northeastern states attending administration briefing on foreign policy, Hartford

•He announced that forty thousand U.S. troops would be withdrawn from Vietnam before Christmas.

Oct. 12, vetoed bill limiting political spending on radio and television advertising

Oct. 15, signed Organized Crime Control Act

•This act established federal control over interstate shipment of explosives, authorized the FBI to enter bombing investigations, and permitted the death penalty in cases of bombings resulting in fatalities.

Oct. 15, signed Urban Mass Transportation Assistance Act

•This act authorized a gradual commitment of $10,000,000,000 over 12 years for new and improved bus and subway systems in urban areas.

Oct. 15, signed joint resolution extending spending authority for departments and agencies whose fiscal 1971 budgets had not been acted upon by Congress

•When Congress recessed until after the elections, Oct. 14, only half of the 14 regular appropriations bills had been acted upon.

Oct. 16, met with Bishop James E. Walsh, White House

•Bishop Walsh had recently been released after 12 years' imprisonment in Red China.

Oct. 17, campaigned in Vermont, New Jersey, Pennsylvania, and Wisconsin

Oct. 19, campaigned in Ohio, North Dakota, and Missouri

Oct. 20, campaigned in Tennessee, North Carolina, and Indiana

Oct. 21, signed Merchant Marine Act of 1970

•This act authorized the construction of three hundred U.S. merchant ships in the 1970's and extended operating subsidies to most ship operators.

Oct. 21, met with Prime Minister of Laos, Prince Souvanna Phouma, White House

Oct. 22, met with Foreign Minister Andrei Gromyko of U.S.S.R., White House

Oct. 23, addressed 25th anniversary session of United Nations General Assembly, New York City

•He appealed to the leaders of the U.S.S.R. to join with the U.S. in keeping the competition between the two countries peaceful despite "very profound and fundamental differences."

Oct. 24, campaigned in Maryland

Oct. 24, rejected recommendations of commission on obscenity and pornography as "morally bankrupt"

•The commission's report, submitted on Sept. 30, called for the elimination of all legal restraints on the purchase by consenting adults of sexually explicit books, pictures, or films.

Oct. 24, met with Prime Minister Eisaku Sato of Japan, White House

Oct. 24, hosted dinner commemorating 25th anniversary of United Nations, White House

•Among the 99 guests representing 31 countries were 28 heads of state and heads of government.

Oct. 25, met with six foreign leaders, White House

•He conferred, in separate meetings, with Archbishop Makarios III, president of Cyprus; Agha Mohammad Yahya Khan, president of Pakistan; Demetrio B. Lakas, president of Panama; Emperor Haile Selassie I of Ethiopia; C.K. Yen, vice president and premier of the Republic of China; and

Cheng Heng, chief of state of Cambodia.

Oct. 26, met with President Nicolae Ceausescu of Rumania, White House

Oct. 26, ordered federal vehicles must be operated on low-lead or unleaded gasoline whenever practical

• He also asked the 50 governors to use the same restriction with state-owned cars.

• The federal government buys more than 900,000,000 gallons of gasoline yearly— one-half of one percent of all gasoline purchased in the U.S.

Oct. 26, signed Resource Recovery Act of 1970

• This act authorized $462,750,000 over three years to help states and cities plan and construct systems for solid waste disposal and recovery.

Oct. 26, signed Legislative Reorganization Act of 1970

• This act provided that committee hearings, with the exception of the appropriations committee, would be open unless national security was involved or the character of witnesses or others could be affected adversely. The act also provided that a record vote could be demanded on any issue by as few as 20 members of the House of Representatives.

Oct. 27, signed Comprehensive Drug Abuse Prevention and Control Act of 1970

• This act stiffened penalties for professional drug traffickers and extended federal controls over previously unregulated drugs.

Oct. 27–28, campaigned in Florida

Oct. 28, campaigned in Texas

Oct. 29, campaigned in Illinois, Minnesota, Nebraska, and California

• His motorcade was stoned in San Jose, Cal., an incident he mentioned with regularity during his subsequent campaign speeches. In most instances, he referred to the rock-throwers as "the violent few," but in Salt Lake City, Oct. 31, he said:
  . . . there were 3,000 people inside the hall listening to the President of the United States . . . and 1,000 ugly demonstrators outside shouting their four-letter obscenities at those who went in, terrorizing the people who were going in, throwing bricks, rocks, and chains at the cars that went by.

Oct. 30, campaigned in California

Oct. 31, campaigned in Arizona, New Mexico, Nevada, and Utah

• His last campaign appearance was at the Mormon Tabernacle, Salt Lake City. He had made campaign speeches in 23 states, beginning in Savannah, Ga., Oct. 8—the most extensive midterm electioneering engaged in by any president.

• Throughout his campaign touring, he emphasized the law-and-order theme and his urgent need for support in the House of Representatives and Senate to carry out his programs.

Nov. 1, his election appeal broadcast at half-time of regionally-televised professional football games

• "It is time for the great silent majority to stand up and be counted," he concluded.

Nov. 2, signed act extending authorizations for four federal health programs

Nov. 3, election day

• He voted in San Clemente, Cal.

Nov. 4, claimed "victory" in midterm election

• He said that the Republican gain of two or three in the Senate (the Indiana election was still undecided) and the Democratic gain of nine seats in the House of Representatives added up to a victory for the administration. He quoted columnist Walter Lippmann as saying that "when the party in power loses little or anything in an off-year election, it has to be called a victory."

• Nixon also said:
  I believe that our hand has been strengthened . . . I believe the chances to win a full generation of peace have been increased as a result of the fact that the President can now speak with a stronger voice because he will have stronger backing in the United States Senate than previously was the case.

Nov. 5, met with Prime Minister Lee Kuan Yew of Singapore, White House

Nov. 5, held background briefing of nine newspaper columnists, White House

Nov. 6, gave reception for descendents of Presidents John Adams and John Quincy Adams, White House

Nov. 8, met with leaders of New York Conservative party, Grand Cay, Bahamas

Nov. 12, attended memorial services for General Charles de Gaulle, Notre Dame Cathedral, Paris

• Nixon met with President Georges Pompidou of France at the Elysee Palace and with President Nikolai V. Podgorny of the U.S.S.R. at a reception given by the French government for heads of state who had attended the memorial services.

•This was the second of Nixon's two visits to France while in office.

Nov. 12, returned to Washington, D.C.

Nov. 13, met with President-elect Luis Echeverria Alvarez of Mexico, White House

Nov. 16, met with eight newly-elected senators, White House

•During the day, he met with Republican Senators-elect J. Glenn Beall, Jr., of Maryland; William E. Brock 3rd of Tennessee; William V. Roth, Jr., of Delaware; Robert Taft, Jr., of Ohio; and Lowell P. Weicker, Jr., of Connecticut; Democratic Senators-elect Lloyd Bentsen of Texas and Hubert H. Humphrey of Minnesota; and Conservative-Republican Senator-elect James Buckley of New York.

Nov. 17, met with Mayor Klaus Schuetz of West Berlin, White House

Nov. 17, attended gala preview of "To Save A Heritage" exhibition, Pennsylvania Academy of Fine Arts, Philadelphia, Pa.

Nov. 18, sent special message to Congress requesting $1,005,000,000 in supplemental foreign assistance programs

•He asked for $500,000,000 in military and economic aid for Israel; $155,000,000 for Cambodia; $150,000,000 for South Korea; $100,000,000 for Turkey, Greece and Taiwan; $65,000,000 for Vietnam; $13,000,-000 for Indonesia; and $5,000,000 for Lebanon. He also asked for $17,000,000 to offset shortages in anticipated recoveries of funds from past years' programs.

Nov. 25, new external lighting system at White House put in operation

•This was the first change in the external lighting of the White House since 1902.

Nov. 25, dismissed Secretary of Interior Hickel, effective immediately

•Ronald L. Ziegler, the presidential press secretary, stated that:

> The President feels that the required elements for a good and continued relationship which must exist between the President and his Cabinet members simply did not exist in this case.

•Ziegler added that Secretary Hickel was not dismissed because of any "specific instance" of mismanagement at the interior

department but because the relationship between the president and the secretary lacked "essential elements of mutual confidence."

•This was the first overt dismissal of a cabinet member since the Truman administration. Truman asked for and received the resignations of Secretary of Commerce Henry A. Wallace in 1946 and Attorney General James H. McGrath in 1952. Other cabinet members undoubtedly were asked to submit their resignations since 1952 but the details of such instances were not publicly acknowledged.

Nov. 25, announced he would appoint Rogers C.B. Morton as his second secretary of interior

•Morton took office, Jan. 29, 1971.

Nov. 26, hosted Thanksgiving Day luncheon for more than one hundred servicemen and women from military hospitals, White House

Nov. 30, signed Agricultural Act of 1970

•This act established for the first time a ceiling on subsidy payments. The ceiling of $55,000 a year on each of three basic crops —cotton, wheat, and feed grains—affected only about eleven hundred of the nation's nearly three million farms. Most of those affected were cotton growers.

Nov. 30, ordered investigation of Coast Guard refusal to grant asylum to Lithuanian sailor who leaped from Soviet fishing boat

•The sailor had jumped from the Soviet craft directly onto the Coast Guard cutter, *Vigilant,* off Martha's Vineyard, Mass., Nov. 23. After several hours of consultation, Soviet crewmen were permitted to board the cutter and seize the defector.

Dec. 3, presented four Young American Medals, White House

•He presented the medals to three youths and the parents of a young boy who lost his life saving a friend. As he gave the award to Debra Jean Sweet of Madison, Wis., the nineteen-year-old girl said, "Mr. President, I find it hard to believe in your sincerity in giving the awards until you get us out of Vietnam." Nixon replied, "We're doing the best we can."

Dec. 3, pledged U.S. would not reduce its forces in Europe "unless there is reciprocal action from our adversaries"

•Nixon's message was read by Secretary of State Rogers at the opening session of the

North Atlantic Council (NATO foreign ministers), Brussels, Belgium.

Dec. 4, announced measures designed to reduce oil prices and halt rising costs in construction industry, New York City

• In an address to the National Association of Manufacturers, he said that he had ordered the interior department to assume responsibilities for the production of oil and gas on federal offshore lands, responsibilities previously controlled by the states. He also said he had ordered an increase in imports of Canadian oil, previously restricted by bilateral agreement.

• Regarding the construction industry, he said that legislation might be required to change the pattern of collective bargaining in the industry and he raised the possibility of federal intervention in wage negotiations on federally-sponsored construction projects.

Dec. 5, urged reversal of Senate's disapproval of SST

• The Senate had refused to provide $290,-000,000 to continue work on two prototypes of the 1,800-mile-per-hour jetliner, Dec. 3. He said that this "devastating mistake" would waste the $700,000,000 previously spent on the supersonic transport project, deal a "mortal blow" to the aerospace industry, and would relegate the U.S. to second place in aviation. He added that it would cost $278,000,000 in contract terminations to close down the project—only slightly less than the amount sought.

Dec. 8, met with King Hussein of Jordan, White House

Dec. 10, declared bombing of North Vietnam military targets would be resumed if level of fighting in South Vietnam was increased by foe while American troops were being withdrawn

• During a nationally-televised news conference, he also said he would order the bombing of missile and military complexes in North Vietnam if U.S. reconnaissance planes were fired upon.

Dec. 10, defended his position on campus unrest

• In a letter to William W. Scranton, chairman of the Commission on Campus Unrest, Nixon took issue with the commission's contention that "only the President can offer the compassionate, reconciling moral leadership that can bring the country together again." In his long-awaited re-

sponse to the Sept. 26 report of the commission, Nixon said that he had come to know "the immense moral authority of the Presidency," and said that he had "tried to exercise that authority to bring an end to violence and bitterness." However, he added:

> Moral authority in a great and diverse nation such as ours does not reside in the Presidency alone. There are thousands upon thousands of individuals—clergy, teachers, public officials, scholars, writers —to whom segments of the nation look for moral, intellectual and political leadership.

Dec. 11, met with Defense Minister Moshe Dayan of Israel, White House

Dec. 12, signed $2,037,814,000 military construction appropriations act

Dec. 13, urged passage of his Family Assistance Plan, opening session of White House Conference on Children

• The program would provide a minimum income of $1,600 yearly plus $800 in food stamps for a family of four. He said:

> In terms of its consequences for children, I think it can be fairly said to be the most important piece of social legislation in the history of this nation.

Dec. 14, announced Secretary of Treasury Kennedy would resign, Feb. 1, 1971, to assume duties in state department as ambassador-at-large

Dec. 14, appointed his second secretary of treasury, John B. Connally

• Connally took office, Feb. 11, 1971.

Dec. 15, signed act restoring use of forty-eight thousand acres of Carson National Forest, N. Mex., to Taos Pueblo Indians

• The tract includes Blue Lake, sacred to the Taos Pueblos, which has been used by the tribe for religious and tribal purposes since the 14th century. The land was appropriated by the government in 1906.

Dec. 15, attended ceremony marking attainment of trillion-dollar ($1,000,000,-000,000) gross national product, department of commerce auditorium

Dec. 16, vetoed employment and manpower bill

• He said the $9,500,000,000 bill would have provided "dead-end jobs in the public sector," and added that "W.P.A.-type jobs" were an "inappropriate and ineffective response to the problems of the seventies."

Dec. 17, signed $17,700,000,000 appropriations act for independent agencies and department of housing and urban development

• This was a compromise measure that appropriated $400,000,000 less than the bill he vetoed, Aug. 11.

Dec. 17–18, met with Prime Minister Edward Heath of Great Britain, White House and Camp David, Md.

Dec. 22, directed cabinet to intensify efforts to provide housing, education, and jobs for minority groups

Dec. 22, signed Agriculture and Related Agencies Appropriation Act of 1971

Dec. 23, issued executive order providing for establishment of federal permit program to regulate discharge of waste into waterways

• The permits, issued by the Army Corps of Engineers, could not be obtained unless the industries received certification from state and interstate agencies that the discharges met existing water quality standards.

• His action was based on a reevaluation of the Refuse Act of 1899. This act originally was intended to keep the waterways clear of obstructions that would impede navigation.

Dec. 24, pocket vetoed bill for relief of Miloye M. Sokitch

Dec. 24, pocket vetoed bill to promote training in family medicine

• This bill would have authorized $233,000,-000 in special grants to hospitals and medical schools over three years for the establishment of new departments to teach "family practice medicine." He withheld his signature, claiming the federal government already had at least four programs that could be used to train general practitioners and that the bill represented "the wrong approach to the solution of the nation's health programs."

Dec. 26, signed Family Planning Services and Population Research Act

• This act authorized a three-year program for funding public and private nonprofit organizations in advising people on birth control and the use of contraceptives.

Dec. 29, signed Occupational Safety and Health Act

• This act authorized the secretary of labor to set safety standards for factories, construction sites, farms, and other places of business.

Dec. 29, announced appointment of Edmund G. ("Pat") Brown as member of Franklin Delano Roosevelt Memorial Commission

• Brown had defeated Nixon for the governorship of California in 1962.

Dec. 30, signed Securities Investor Protection Act

• This act established the Securities Investment Protection Corporation to insure securities and cash deposited with brokerage firms against loss from financial failure or difficulties of such firms. Protection was limited to $50,000 an account, with a limit of cash coverage of $20,000.

Dec. 30, his pocket veto of bill to promote training in family medicine challenged by group of Democratic senators and members of House of Representatives

• The six legislators contended that he had acted illegally in pocket vetoing the bill, Dec. 24, during the short Christmas recess. Congress had recessed, Dec. 22; the Senate returned from recess, Dec. 28, and the House, Dec. 29.

• This was an attempt to force a Supreme Court test of the president's power to use the pocket veto during brief recesses within a session of Congress. This procedure had been used sporadically by previous presidents, but had never been tested in court. In 1938, however, the Supreme Court had ruled that a brief House recess did not prevent the president from returning a formal veto message to Congress.

Dec. 31, signed International Financial Institutions Act

Dec. 31, signed Clean Air Act of 1970

• This act set a six-year deadline for the automotive industry to develop an engine that is nearly free of pollution.

Dec. 31, approved mergers of airlines

• The mergers, which had already been approved by the Civil Aeronautics Board (CAB), combined American Airlines with Trans Caribbean Airways and Northwest Airlines with Northeast Airlines. American and Northwest are the surviving corporations.

Note: The official population according to the 19th census, was 204,765,770.

1971

Jan. 1, vetoed federal "blue collar" employees pay bill
• This bill would have given blue collar workers a four percent pay raise, and would have added $130,000,000 to the combined paychecks of about 800,000 government employees who do janitorial, mechanical, and other labor, mainly in defense installations.
Jan. 2, signed Omnibus Crime Control Act of 1970
Jan. 2, second session of 91st Congress adjourned
Jan. 4, pocket vetoed bill to provide special retirement benefits for federal firefighters
• This bill would have enabled federal firefighters to retire earlier than most other government employees on the grounds that their duties are especially hazardous. "I do not believe that this preferential legislation is wise or justifiable," he said.
Jan. 4, interviewed by four television network commentators, White House
• In the one-hour television interview, he said that his plan for sharing federal revenue with state and local governments would make up "the major thrust" of his State of the Union message, and he predicted significant improvements in the economy during 1971 and a "very good year" in 1972.
• He was interviewed by Eric Sevareid of CBS, Howard K. Smith of ABC, John Chancellor of NBC, and Nancy Dickerson of Public Broadcasting System.
Jan. 5, characterized 91st Congress as one that would be remembered "not for what it did, but for what it failed to do"
• Congress, he said, had failed to act on welfare reform, federal revenue-sharing, and a host of other "excellent proposals" before adjournment. He was especially critical of the Senate, which he said had presented the American people with "the spectacle of a legislative body that had seemingly lost the capacity to decide and the will to act."
Jan. 5, flew to West Coast White House, San Clemente, Cal.
Jan. 6, signed act authorizing $550,000,000 in military and economic aid to six Asian and Middle East nations

• About half of the funds, $255,000,000, was allocated for Cambodia. Korea was to receive $150,000,000; South Vietnam, $65,000,000; and the rest was divided among Indonesia, Jordan, and Lebanon.
Jan. 8, signed act establishing Voyageurs National Park, Minn.
Jan. 8, signed act creating Chesapeake and Ohio Canal National Historic Park along Potomac River
• The act authorized an eventual expenditure of $37,000,000 for land acquisition, restoration, and development. The 20,000-acre park will stretch 184 miles from Washington, D.C., to Cumberland, Md.
Jan. 8, signed federal pay reform act
• This act transferred the authority to set government classified pay from Congress to the president.
Jan. 8, signed two executive orders granting $2,200,000,000 in pay increases to 4,000,000 military personnel and federal "white collar" workers
• One order increased the base pay of 2,700,000 military personnel by 7.9 percent, retroactive to Jan. 1. The second order provided for average pay increases of 5.96 percent for 1,300,000 federal civilian employees.
Jan. 8, signed act raising pensions for former presidents and widows of presidents
• The presidential pension was raised from $25,000 to $60,000 annually. The pension of widows of presidents was increased from $10,000 to $20,000 annually.
Jan. 11, signed act easing cost of food stamps to poor, restricted program to families whose able-bodied adults were willing to accept work
• The new program, which will run until July, 1973, will provide low-cost food for 8,800,000 people. The work provision requires able-bodied adults under 65, except mothers and students, to register for and accept work at wages of at least $1.30 an hour.
Jan. 12, signed act authorizing $200,000,000 in easy credit sales of U.S. arms to foreign allies
• This act also included repeal of the Gulf of Tonkin Resolution of 1964.
Jan. 12, condemned decision of Bethlehem Steel Corporation to raise prices on some products, indicated government might permit increases in steel imports to dis-

suade other steel producers from following suit
- Bethlehem Steel, the nation's second largest producer, had announced plans for increases of 11 to 13 percent by Mar. 1 on items accounting for one-sixth of the steel industry's total production.
- The United States Steel Corporation, the largest producer, announced price increases of 6.8 percent on major construction projects, Jan. 16. The other producers increased their prices by a like amount.

Jan. 14, proposed agency to enlist service of youth, University of Nebraska, Lincoln, Neb.
- He called upon the young and the old alike to "forge an alliance of the generations" in an address on the role of youth in American society to nine thousand students and faculty members. He also said he would ask Congress for authority to combine the Peace Corps, Volunteers in Service to America (VISTA), and other federal agencies into a new volunteer service corps "that will give young Americans an expanded opportunity" to serve the poor in this country and abroad.

Jan. 15, spoke at dedication of Dwight D. Eisenhower National Republican Center, Washington, D.C.
- He said:
  By itself, neither political party in this country can win an election. . . . I would like the Republican party to be the party of the open door, a party with its doors open to all people of all races and of all parties, those who share our great ideals about the future of America and the future of the world.

Jan. 16, directed Attorney General Mitchell to prepare comprehensive reform of federal criminal laws for submission to Congress

Jan. 19, ordered halt to further construction of Cross Florida Barge Canal "to prevent potentially serious environmental damages"
- About $50,000,000 in federal funds had been spent to build nearly one-third of the proposed 107-mile canal.

Jan. 21, first session of 92nd Congress
- The administration controlled neither the Senate nor the House of Representatives. The Republicans gained two Senate seats, but lost 12 House seats. The Senate (100

members) consisted of 54 Democrats, 44 Republicans, one Independent-Democrat and one Conservative-Republican. The House (435 members) consisted of 255 Democrats, 179 Republicans, and one vacancy.

Jan. 22, delivered his second State of the Union message to Congress
- In his nationally-televised message, he presented "six great goals" to "change the framework of government itself—to reform the entire structure of American government." He called for a "peaceful revolution" to turn power back to the people and make government at all levels more responsive to the "new needs of a new era."
- The more revolutionary of his proposals were an annual $16,000,000,000 revenue-sharing plan to rescue state and local governments "from the brink of financial crisis," and a "sweeping reorganization" of the executive branch, which would retain the departments of state, treasury, defense, and justice, and consolidate the others into four new departments—human resources, community development, natural resources, and economic development.
- He also called for welfare reform, new programs to clean the air and water, improved health care including a cancer cure program, and an expansionary, "full employment" budget. He limited his message to "the domestic side of the nation's agenda."

Jan. 22, confirmed report he "never" watched himself on television
- Mrs. Nixon had said, three days earlier, that he did not watch his speeches and statements on television because he believed it would make him too self-conscious about his appearance. He explained that he did not watch himself for fear that he might become more concerned about "how I look" than what he had to say. He added that he also did not watch the television news programs, but preferred to read summaries prepared by his staff.

Jan. 23, paid his respects at bier of Senator Richard B. Russell, capitol rotunda, Atlanta, Ga.
- Senator Russell, the dean of the Senate, died in Washington, D.C., Jan. 21. He had served in the Senate for 38 years.

Jan. 26, welcomed Prince Juan Carlos and Princess Sophia of Spain, White House
- Juan Carlos, pretender to the Spanish

throne, had been named by Generalissimo Franco as his successor.

Jan. 26, presented with copy of first national atlas, White House

• Produced by the U.S. Geological Survey with the cooperation of more than 80 federal agencies, the first official national atlas weighed 14 pounds, contained 765 maps. The 431-page atlas cost $100 a copy.

Jan. 26, sent special message to Congress resubmitting 40 legislative proposals previously submitted to 91st Congress

Jan. 27, appointed George Malcolm White as architect of Capitol

• White was the first architect of the Capitol who was a registered architect.

Jan. 28, sent special message to Congress on draft reform

• He asked for $1,500,000,000 in military pay increases, mainly in the lower grades, to assist in attracting more volunteers. He also asked for a two-year extension of the draft to July 1, 1973. "We shall make every endeavor to reduce draft calls to zero by that time," he said.

Jan. 29, sent second budget message to Congress

• He estimated expenditures for the fiscal year ending June 30, 1971, at $229,200,-000,000; receipts at $217,600,000; and a deficit of $11,600,000,000.

• For the first time, the budget was based on the "full employment" principle, a new economic idea that suggested that the federal government should expend what it would collect if business were normal and unemployment low rather than expend the amount of revenue actually expected during the fiscal year. Nixon said:

> The full employment budget idea is in the nature of a self-fulfilling prophecy: By operating as if we were at full employment, we will help to bring about that full employment.

His budget message also estimated the deficit for fiscal 1971 at $18,600,000,000. In his first budget message of Feb. 2, 1970, he had forecast a small surplus for fiscal 1971.

Jan. 29, flew to Caneel Bay, St. John, Virgin Islands

• He was the last of four presidents who visited the Virgin Islands while in office.

Feb. 1, sent his annual economic report to Congress, called for "orderly expansion"

• He said:

> I do not intend to impose wage and price controls which would substitute new, growing and more vexatious problems for the problems of inflation. Neither do I intend to rely upon an elaborate facade that seems to be wage and price control but is not.

• The accompanying report of his Council of Economic Advisers predicted decreases in unemployment from 6 to 4.5 percent and in the rate of inflation from 5.5 to 3 percent by mid-1972.

Feb. 1, returned from four-day visit to Virgin Islands

Feb. 2, sent special message to Congress proposing establishment of federal executive service

• The plan would revise practices of appointing and removing federal employees in the three highest grades of the civil service, GS-16 to GS-18.

Feb. 3, sent special message to Congress requesting legislation to prevent strikes in transportation industry

• A similar request made a year earlier had been ignored by Congress.

Feb. 3, entertained Jacqueline Kennedy Onassis and her children at family dinner, White House

• This was Mrs. Onassis's first visit to the White House since shortly after the assassination of President Kennedy. She viewed the official portraits of her first husband and herself, which had recently been added to the White House collection.

Feb. 4, sent special message to Congress proposing $5,000,000,000 for general revenue-sharing with state and local governments

Feb. 8, sent special message to Congress outlining his environmental protection program for 1971

Feb. 9, declared California disaster area

• A major earthquake had occurred in the Los Angeles area earlier in the day.

Feb. 9, telephoned congratulations to *Apollo 14* astronauts

• The astronauts, Captain Alan B. Shepard, Jr., and Commander Edgar D. Mitchell of the Navy, and Major Stuart A. Roosa of the Air Force, were aboard the *U.S.S. New Orleans* in the South Pacific after their successful nine-day mission to the moon.

Feb. 11, signed executive order establishing new federal holiday schedule

•The new holiday schedule is:
  Washington's Birthday, the third Monday in February
  Memorial Day, the last Monday in May
  Columbus Day, the second Monday in October
  Veterans Day, the fourth Monday in October

Feb. 11, flew to Key Biscayne, Fla.

•He returned to Washington, Feb. 15.

Feb. 17, held unscheduled news conference, White House

•He spoke of the "present success" of the South Vietnamese action in Laos, supported by U.S. air power, and declared that he would place no limitation on the use of air power except to bar nuclear weapons.

Feb. 18, sent special message to Congress proposing comprehensive national health policy

•The plan would require employers to provide minimum health care insurance at an estimated annual cost of $2,500,000,000, emphasizing private rather than public financing of the program.

Feb. 18, spoke at dedication of Woodrow Wilson International Center for Scholars, Smithsonian Institution Building, Washington, D.C.

Feb. 18, conferred with Prime Minister Emilio Colombo of Italy, White House

Feb. 22, sent special message on higher education to Congress

•He asked that funds available for guaranteed loans to college students be increased from $970,000,000 to $1,500,000,000, beginning July 1. He proposed that a larger portion of the low-interest bank loans go to students from families earning less than $10,000 a year.

•Commenting on the failure of Congress to act on his proposals of the previous year, he said, "I repeat the commitment which I made in my message of last year: that no qualified student who wants to go to college should be barred by lack of money."

Feb. 23, suspended provisions of Davis-Bacon Act of 1931 requiring contractors on federal construction projects to pay prevailing wage rates

Feb. 24, sent special message to Congress proposing legislative program for consumer protection

Feb. 25, sent his second annual report on state of world to Congress

•The 180-page, 65,000-word report was entitled, "Building for Peace." In it, Nixon said:

  Our experience of the Nineteen-Sixties has underlined the fact that we should not do more abroad than domestic opinion can sustain. But we cannot let the pendulum swing in the other direction, sweeping us toward an isolationism which could be disastrous as excessive zeal.

•It was in this report that he referred to the People's Republic of China, using the official name of the mainland China nation, for the first time. No previous president had ever employed the official name, but had referred to "Communist China" or "Peking" when discussing mainland China.

Feb. 26, attended swearing-in ceremony of George Bush as U.S. ambassador to United Nations

Feb. 26, accepted portraits of John Quincy Adams and Mrs. Adams for White House collection

•The portraits by Gilbert Stuart were the gift of John Quincy Adams of Dover, Mass., the great-great-grandson of President Adams.

Mar. 1, addressed joint session of Iowa state legislature, Des Moines, Iowa

•He also met with the governors of Iowa, Illinois, Missouri, and Wisconsin in Des Moines.

Mar. 1, denounced bombing of Capitol as "shocking act of violence"

•The explosion on the ground floor of the Capitol at 1:32 A.M. was preceded by a telephoned warning that the bombing was in protest against U.S. involvement in Laos. Damage originally was estimated at $200,-000, but the actual cost of repairing the damage was about half that amount.

Mar. 2, sent special message to Congress asking for $500,000,000 in special revenue-sharing for law enforcement assistance

Mar. 4, sent special message to Congress asking for $2,000,000,000 in special revenue-sharing for manpower

•In a shift of administration policy, the message included a proposal to permit the use of federal funds to ease unemployment by creation of temporary public service jobs. He had vetoed a bill with much the same goal, Dec. 16, 1970.

Mar. 4, defended U.S. involvement in Laos

during televised news conference, White House

•He said:

The purpose of the Laos campaign . . . like the purpose of Cambodia, is to reduce American forces, to reduce our casualties. And I should point out that that's exactly what this administration has done. We've kept every promise that we've made. We've reduced our forces. We have reduced our casualties. We're going to continue to reduce our forces, and we are getting out of Vietnam in a way that Vietnam will be able to defend itself.

Mar. 5, sent special message to Congress asking for $2,000,000,000 in special revenue-sharing for urban community development

Mar. 9, exclusive interview by C. L. Sulzberger of *The New York Times* published

•In this unusual, on-the-record interview, he said: "This war is ending. I seriously doubt if we will ever have another war. This is probably the very last one."

Mar. 10, sent special message to Congress asking for $1,100,000,000 in special revenue-sharing for rural development

•This plan received a major setback when the Senate voted to extend the Appalachian Regional Development Commission for four years, Mar. 11. In his special message, he had proposed that the commission be abolished and its programs be merged into a new revenue-sharing plan.

Mar. 11, addressed National Conference on Judiciary, Williamsburg, Va.

•He called for "genuine reform" of the court system to bring about faster, more efficient administration of justice.

Mar. 12, presented commissions to graduating class, Naval Officer Candidate School, Newport, R.I.

•His son-in-law, David Eisenhower, was a member of the class.

Mar. 16, announced engagement of his daughter, Tricia, to Edward Ridley Finch Cox

•The engagement was announced at an "Irish Evening at the White House" celebrating the visit of Prime Minister John M. Lynch of Ireland and the 59th birthday of Mrs. Nixon.

Mar. 17, signed act increasing social security

benefits by ten percent, retroactive to Jan. 1

•This act also increased the ceiling on the national debt from $395,000,000,000 to $430,000,000,000.

Mar. 18, sent special message to Congress asking for $2,566,000,000 in special revenue-sharing for transportation

Mar. 19, attended funeral services for Thomas E. Dewey, New York City

•Dewey, the unsuccessful Republican candidate for president in 1944 and 1948, died in Miami, Fla., Mar. 16.

Mar. 22, discussed "last war" statement during live television interview by Howard K. Smith of ABC

•During the one-hour interview in the White House Library, he said:

When I made the statement with regard to this possibly being the last war, I also, as you will note in my interview with Mr. Sulzberger, very strongly indicated the necessity for the United States to play its destined role because of our power, economically and otherwise, as the peace-keeping nation, the major peace-keeping nation in the free world.

Now, if the United States doesn't play that role, there will be another war. I mean by that, for example, for one thing, that how we end the war in Vietnam will have a great effect on whether there will be another war like that.

If the war in Vietnam is ended in a way that it's considered to be an American defeat or a reward for those who engage in aggression, or an encouragement to the hard-liners in the Communist world, then they will do it again.

And, if they hit somebody that's an ally of the United States, like the Philippines or Thailand, we'll be drawn in.

•This was the first live television presidential interview by a single reporter on one network in prime time.

Mar. 23, 26th Amendment to Constitution submitted to states for ratification

Mar. 24, called Senate vote to end further funding of supersonic transport aircraft "severe blow" to aerospace industry

•The Senate had voted, 51–46, to reject an

amendment to provide $134,000,000 to continue federal funding for the SST.

Mar. 24, sent special message to Congress transmitting reorganization plan for merging Peace Corps, VISTA, and seven other voluntary service programs

Mar. 25, sent special message proposing comprehensive reorganization of executive branch

• The present departments of labor, interior, agriculture, commerce, transportation, housing and urban development, and health, education and welfare would be replaced by four new departments—natural resources, community development, human resources, and economic affairs. The proposal would not effect the departments of state, treasury, defense, and justice, or the post office department. The post office department was to be restructured as an independent corporation, July 1.

Mar. 25, met with members of Black Caucus, White House

• The group, consisting of 12 Negro members of the House of Representatives and the non-voting representative of the District of Columbia, had sought the meeting for more than a year, and had boycotted the State of the Union message to publicize its position. A list of more than 60 recommendations for the betterment of blacks and other minorities was presented.

Mar. 26, flew to San Clemente, Cal.

Mar. 29, signed executive order imposing system of "constraints" to prevent inflationary increases in construction costs

• This order was designed to keep negotiated wage increases in the construction industry to an annual level of about six percent. In 1970, wage increases in the industry had averaged between 15 and 18 percent.

• The order also reinstated provisions of the Davis-Bacon Act, which requires contractors in federally-funded projects to pay union scale wages. He had suspended these provisions, Feb. 23.

Mar. 31, reversed administration policy on bills to limit campaign spending

• Testifying before the Senate communications subcommittee, Deputy Attorney General Richard G. Kleindienst supported most provisions of pending legislation to impose ceilings on campaign expenditures for all communications media. Nixon had vetoed a bill limiting campaign spending

on radio and television, Oct. 12, 1970.

Apr. 1, ordered First Lieutenant William L. Calley, Jr., released from stockade and returned to quarters at Fort Benning, Ga.

• Calley had been convicted on charges of murdering South Vietnamese civilians at Mylai, Mar. 29, and sentenced to life imprisonment, Mar. 31, thus ending the longest court-martial in U.S. history. On Apr. 3, the White House announced the president's decision that before any final sentence was carried out in the Calley case the president would personally review and decide the case.

Apr. 3, directed policy on abortions at military hospitals correspond with laws of states where located

Apr. 5, represented at opening of baseball season by former prisoner of war

• Master Sergeant Daniel L. Pitzer of Fairview, W. Va., who had been a prisoner of the Viet Cong for four years, threw out the first ball of the opening game between the Washington Senators and the Oakland Athletics.

Apr. 5, returned to Washington, D.C.

Apr. 6, sent special message to Congress asking for $3,000,000,000 in special revenue-sharing for education

• This was the sixth and last of his special revenue-sharing messages.

Apr. 7, promised withdrawal of additional 100,000 troops from Vietnam by Dec. 1, during national TV-radio address

• Between May 1 and Dec. 1, 100,000 American troops would be withdrawn from Vietnam, he said, reducing the total number of troops there from 540,000, when he took office, to 184,000.

• He refused to fix a deadline for total U.S. withdrawal, explaining:

> If the United States should announce that we will quit regardless of what the enemy does, we would have thrown away our principal bargaining counter to win the release of American prisoners of war, we would remove the enemy's strongest incentive to end the war sooner by negotiation, and we will have given enemy commanders the exact information they need to marshal their attacks against our remaining forces at their most vulnerable time.

Apr. 13, appointed John A. Scali as special consultant to president on communications policy relating to foreign affairs

•Scali, chief diplomatic correspondent for ABC News, had served as unofficial go-between in talks with Soviet diplomats during the 1962 Cuban missile crisis, acting at the direction of President Kennedy and Secretary of State Rusk.

Apr. 14, announced relaxation of U.S. trade embargo with People's Republic of China

•In addition to providing for export of specific nonstrategic goods to Communist China, the program would also ease restrictions on currency exchange and expedite visas for Chinese visitors to the U.S.

Apr. 15, conferred with Prime Minister Ahmed Laraki of Morocco, White House

Apr. 16, interviewed by panel of newsmen, American Society of Newspaper Editors national convention, Washington, D.C.

•He reiterated his reasons for refusing to fix a deadline for total U.S. withdrawal from Vietnam. He also characterized recent criticism of Director J. Edgar Hoover of the FBI as "unfair and malicious."

Apr. 19, addressed Republican Governors' Conference, Williamsburg, Va.

Apr. 19, addressed 80th Continental Congress of Daughters of American Revolution, Constitution Hall, Washington, D.C.

•He was the first president in 17 years to address the DAR annual meeting. President Eisenhower had done so in 1954. "I felt it was high time another President did so," Nixon said.

Apr. 21, sent special message to Congress requesting $3,300,000,000 in foreign aid for fiscal year commencing July 1

Apr. 21, accepted honorary membership in U.S. Table Tennis Association

•The highly-publicized visit to mainland China by the U.S. table tennis team had been privately criticized by Vice President Agnew. The White House had officially denied a rift between the president and the vice president on the subject, Apr. 20.

Apr. 22, presented Medal of Honor posthumously to members of families of three servicemen, White House

Apr. 26, addressed annual meeting of U.S. Chamber of Commerce, Washington, D.C.

•He said that "the worst of inflation is behind us," and predicted that the country was on its way "to a period of solid, substantial expansion."

Apr. 28, transmitted to Congress 14 proposals for additions to Wilderness System

•The proposed additions would expand the wilderness system by 1,800,000 acres in nine states.

Apr. 29, held news conference, White House

•During the televised news conference, he reiterated his refusal to set a date for total withdrawal of U.S. troops from Vietnam, and said that a "residual force" would be maintained for as long as North Vietnam held American prisoners of war.

Apr. 30, met with former Prime Minister Harold Wilson of Great Britain, White House

Apr. 30, spoke at ceremonies welcoming fifteen hundred officers and men of First Marine Division back from Vietnam, Camp Pendleton, Cal.

May 1, held news conference, San Clemente, Cal.

•He said he would seek a tax cut if necessary to keep the economy on an upward curve.

•This news conference was limited to questions on domestic policy.

May 2, made national radio broadcast on agriculture

•This 14-minute speech was recorded at Palm Springs, Cal.

May 3, 6,892 antiwar protesters and others arrested in Washington, D.C.

•Between twelve thousand and fifteen thousand demonstrators attempted to disrupt the operations of the government. They were turned back by more than ten thousand federal troops, National Guardsmen, and Washington, Capitol and park police. A majority of the mass arrests were dragnet maneuvers by metropolitan police and those arrested were persons who had not been actively involved in the demonstrations.

May 4, 2,680 antiwar demonstrators arrested in Washington, D.C.

May 5, more than one thousand antiwar demonstrators arrested in Washington, D.C.

•More than 10,500 persons were arrested during the three-day turmoil.

May 5, sent special message to Congress urging creation of independent legal service corporation

May 6, "disappointed" by United States Steel Corporation's announcement of 6.25 percent price rise on one-third of all

American steel shipments

• White House Press Secretary Ziegler, who reported his reaction, added that "no action is contemplated" by the administration.

May 7, addressed farm leaders at day-long "Salute to Agriculture," White House

May 10, made helicopter tour of proposed Gateway National Recreation Area in New York Harbor

• He was accompanied by Secretary of Interior Morton, the governors of New York and New Jersey, and the mayors of New York City and Newark, N.J.

May 11, pledged his direct leadership of a national campaign to conquer cancer

May 11, received report from Secretary of State Rogers on Middle East

• The Rogers report was described by White House aides as "cautiously optimistic" about the prospects of agreement between Israel and Egypt regarding the reopening of the Suez Canal, closed since 1967.

May 14, planted California sequoia tree on south grounds, White House

May 14, signed act increasing appropriation for Commission on Marijuana and Drug Abuse from $1,000,000 to $4,000,000

May 14, signed act to authorize United States Postal Service to receive fees for execution of applications for passports

May 15, stated unilateral withdrawal of U.S. troops from Europe would be "error of historic dimensions"

• Senator Mike Mansfield of Montana, the Senate majority leader, had proposed that the 310,000-man American NATO force be reduced by 50 percent by Dec. 31.

• The White House released a bipartisan list of 24 former top officials who supported the president's position. Former President Lyndon Johnson opposed any reduction of NATO forces, May 15, as did former President Truman, May 16.

May 17, sent special message to Congress asking for emergency legislation to halt nationwide railway strike

• The Brotherhood of Railroad Signalmen had gone on strike that morning and other rail unions respected the picket lines, shutting down virtually all of the nation's railroads.

May 18, signed joint resolution ordering striking railroad workers to return to work immediately

• The joint resolution established a mora-

torium on signalmen strikes or lockouts extending to Oct. 1. It also provided for an interim wage increase of 13.5 percent.

May 18, issued response to 60 demands of Black Caucus

• "In many cases, we have found a basic accord between your recommendations and our policies," he wrote to Representative Charles C. Diggs, Jr., of Michigan, chairman of the caucus. Representative Diggs called the response "deeply disappointing," May 23.

May 19, ordered federal loan and feed assistance to drought-stricken areas in Southwest

May 20, announced U.S.-U.S.S.R. accord on scope of strategic arms limitation talks

• The official statement, issued simultaneously in Washington and Moscow, said that the two governments had agreed to "concentrate this year" on reaching agreement "for the limitation of the deployment of antiballistic missile systems (ABMs)" and "certain measures with respect to the limitation of offensive strategic weapons."

• "This agreement is a major step in breaking the stalemate on nuclear arms talks," said Nixon. His remarks were broadcast on radio and television. Soviet Premier Alexei Kosygin avoided any personal association with the announcement. In Moscow, an announcer read the statement as part of a regular newscast.

May 22, spoke at dedication ceremonies of Lyndon Baines Johnson Library and School of Public Affairs, Austin, Tex.

May 25, dedicated Tennessee-Tombigbee Waterway, Mobile, Ala.

• The project, connecting the Tennessee and Tombigbee rivers, provided a shorter waterway link between the eastern Gulf Coast and the Tennessee, Ohio and upper Mississippi river valleys. The Tennessee-Tombigbee Waterway Authority was authorized in 1946, but funds to begin construction were not appropriated until 1970. The federal cost was about $346,-000,000.

May 25, spoke to editors and publishers from 12 southern states, Birmingham, Ala.

• During the first of four regional briefings on domestic policy, he said:

> I have nothing but utter contempt
> for the double hypocritical stand-
> ard of Northerners who look at the
> South and point the finger and say,

"Why don't those Southerners do something about their race problem?"

May 25, signed Second Supplemental Appropriations Act of 1971

•This act included an appropriation of $100,000,000 to launch an intensive campaign to find a cure for cancer.

May 27, welcomed King Faisal of Saudi Arabia, White House

May 29, addressed corps of cadets, U.S. Military Academy, West Point, N.Y.

June 1, pledged "highest priority attention" to drug problem, reiterated his support of Washington police suppression of May demonstrators, during TV-radio news conference, White House

•Drug addiction, he said, was "not simply a problem of Vietnam veterans; it's a national problem." He again voiced his opposition to legalizing marijuana, which would "encourage more and more of our young people to start down that long, dismal road that leads to hard drugs and eventually self-destruction." Addicted veterans had been estimated at about 35,000.

•He characterized those arrested during the May 3–5 demonstrations as "vandals and hoodlums and lawbreakers" and said it was "an exaggeration" to suggest that constitutional rights had been suspended. Charges against about 3,000 of the more than 10,500 arrested had been dropped or dismissed by the courts: charges against almost all of the others were later dropped or dismissed.

•In response to a political question, he announced that he had decided "as a matter of policy" that the presidential press conference "is not a proper forum to comment on any partisan political matters or political questions."

June 2, met with President Anastasio Somoza of Nicaragua, White House

June 3, with Attorney General Mitchell and FBI Director Hoover, met with representatives of International Association of Chiefs of Police and National Sheriffs' Association to discuss problem of police slayings

•A total of 51 policemen had been killed in the line of duty during the first five months of 1971.

June 4, sent special message on energy resources to Congress

•He asked for the acceleration of oil and gas lease sales on the Outer Continental Shelf, an additional $15,000,000 for sulfur oxide control demonstration projects, and an additional $27,000,000 for the AEC liquid metal fast breeder reactor program during fiscal 1972.

June 5, dedicated McClellan-Kerr Arkansas River Navigation System, Catoosa, Okla.

•The $1,200,000,000 inland waterway, which opened the Arkansas and Verdigris rivers to shipping from the Mississippi, was named for Senator John L. McClellan of Arkansas and Senator Robert S. Kerr of Oklahoma.

June 10, ended embargo on trade with Communist China

•The export of 47 categories of nonstrategic items was authorized and all controls on imports from China were terminated.

June 11, issued policy statement on equal housing

•The government would continue to enforce prohibitions against racial discrimination in housing, but would not attempt to change local zoning or "to impose federally assisted housing upon any community," he said.

June 12, attended wedding of his daughter, Patricia, to Edward Finch Cox, White House Rose Garden

•This was the only White House wedding held on the grounds. The previous eight weddings there had been held indoors.

•This was the last of eight White House weddings of daughters of presidents.

•This was the last of nine White House weddings of children of presidents.

June 14, White House refused comment on "Pentagon Papers"

•A series of articles on a secret study, made in the Pentagon, of American participation in the Vietnam War, began in *The New York Times*, June 13. Attorney General Mitchell asked *The Times* to refrain from further publication of the documents, June 14; *The Times* refused to halt publication voluntarily. U.S. District Judge Murray I. Gurfein ordered a halt to the publication of the papers, June 15.

•This was the first attempt by the U.S. Government to enjoin publication on the grounds of "national security."

June 15, conferred with Chancellor Willy Brandt of Germany, White House

June 15, presented Medal of Honor to seven members of armed forces, White House

June 17, his statement read by Secretary of State Rogers at signing ceremony of treaty returning Okinawa to Japan

,•Okinawa and the other Ryukyu Islands were to be returned to Japan on an unspecified date in 1972 if the treaty was ratified by the Japanese Diet and the Senate.

June 17, signed executive order establishing special action office for drug abuse prevention within executive department

June 17, sent special message to Congress asking additional $155,000,000 for drug abuse prevention and control

June 18, met with President Leopold Sedar Senghor of Senegal, White House

June 18, spoke to editors and publishers from 12 eastern states and District of Columbia, Rochester, N.Y.

•This was the second of four regional briefings on domestic policy.

June 21, met with executive board of International Brotherhood of Teamsters, Miami Beach, Fla.

•He met with newly-installed President Frank E. Fitzsimmons and 40 teamsters officials. James R. Hoffa, serving a prison term in Lewisburg, Pa., for jury tampering, had resigned, June 20.

•This was the first time since 1944 that a president had addressed the teamsters union or its leaders.

June 22, addressed 120th annual convention of American Medical Association, Atlantic City, N.J.

•He attacked a bipartisan liberal proposal for national health insurance.

•He was the last of four presidents who addressed the AMA. The others, all Republicans, were McKinley in 1897, Coolidge in 1927, and Eisenhower in 1959.

June 22, had ordered review of all procedures for classifying documents, Press Secretary Ziegler announced

•Ziegler said such presidential directives to the National Security Council ordinarily are not made public, but interest in the Pentagon Papers had caused disclosure of the Jan. 15 order.

June 23, announced 47-volume Pentagon study of U.S. involvement in Vietnam would be made available to Congress

•The top secret classification of the Pentagon Papers was not changed. "Since the documents relate primarily to the Johnson and Kennedy periods," said Press Secre-

tary Ziegler, "President Nixon pointed out that he is not in a position to vouch for their accuracy or completeness."

June 23, announced establishment of special committee to develop proposals for comprehensive policy regarding cable television

June 24, dedicated plaque to memory of his mother, Jennings County Courthouse, Vernon, Ind.

•The house in which his mother was born had burned in 1968. It had been located about four and one-half miles southeast of Vernon.

June 25, called for reform of regulations regarding nursing homes in address to combined conventions of National Retired Teachers Association and American Association of Retired Persons, Chicago, Ill.

•Too many nursing homes, he said, are "little more than warehouses for the unwanted" and "dumping grounds for the dying."

June 29, designated Secretary of Treasury Connally as his "chief economic spokesman"

•Secretary Connally told a White House press conference that the president had come to "certain basic conclusions" regarding the economy and that the president felt it "very important to clear up whatever confusion, whatever misunderstanding there might be in the minds of the people."

•Connally added:

He has come to the conclusion that, number one, he's not going to institute a wage-price review board; number two, he's not going to impose mandatory wage and price controls; number three, he's not going to ask the Congress for any tax relief; and number four, that he's not going to increase fiscal spending.

June 29, vetoed $5,600,000,000 public works bill

•He said the bill, which would have provided $2,000,000,000 for an accelerated public works program, was a "costly and time-consuming method of putting unemployed persons to work." He urged that Congress salvage other provisions of the bill, including a $2,700,000,000 authorization for the Appalachian development program and a $550,000,000 authorization for the Economic Development Administration.

June 30, Supreme Court upheld *The New York Times* and Washington *Post* regarding Pentagon Papers

• By a vote of 6–3, the Supreme Court held that any attempt by the government to block news articles prior to publication bears "a heavy burden of presumption against its constitutionality" and that "the government has not met that burden."

June 30, signed executive order establishing volunteer agency, Action

• The Peace Corps, the National Voluntary Action program, and five smaller agencies were merged into Action.

June 30, announced Turkey had agreed to eliminate cultivation of opium poppies by June, 1972.

• Prime Minister Nihat Erim announced the decision in Ankara. Drug experts estimated 60 percent or more of the heroin illegally imported into the U.S. in recent years had been processed from opium poppies grown in Turkey.

June 30, congratulated young citizens on ratification of 26th Amendment

• The amendment guaranteed the right of 18-year-olds to vote in state and local as well as federal elections. It applied to about 11,000,000 young men and women between 18 and 21. The ratification had been accomplished in record time, 99 days. Congress had sent the proposed amendment to the states, Mar. 23.

• *See* Constitution, page 645.

June 30, draft act expired

• It was the first lapse in the draft since 1948.

July 1, post office department became U.S. Postal Service

• No longer a member of the cabinet, Postmaster General Blount retained the title as head of the new interdependent government agency. In the future, the postmaster general will serve at the discretion of a presidentially-appointed and congressionally-approved board of directors.

July 1, signed Micronesian Claims Act of 1971

July 3, spoke at ceremonies designating next five years as Bicentennial Era, Exhibition Hall, National Archives

July 5, presided at certification ceremonies marking formal adoption of 26th Amendment, White House

• He and three 18-year-old members of a singing group, Young Americans in Concert, officially witnessed the certification by General Services Administrator Robert Kunzig.

July 6, spoke to editors and publishers from 11 Midwest states, Kansas City, Mo.

• This was the third of four regional briefings on domestic policy.

July 6, flew to San Clemente, Cal.

July 8, signed proclamation ordering 50 American flags around Washington Monument flown day and night except in inclement weather

• The Washington Monument thus joined a small group of locations, including the White House and the Capitol, where the flag is displayed around the clock.

July 8, budget projection of $11,600,000,-000 deficit for fiscal 1972 raised by at least $7,000,000,000

• The new projection was disclosed by Paul W. McCracken, chairman of the President's Council of Economic Advisers.

July 9, cancelled budget request for $235,-000,000 in SST funds in fiscal 1972

• He also asked Congress for an appropriation of $58,500,000 to repay airlines for contributions made to the supersonic transport project.

July 11, signed Office of Education and Related Agencies Appropriation Act

• This act provided $5,100,000,000 for fiscal 1972, the largest appropriation in the history of the Office of Education.

July 12, signed Emergency Employment Act of 1971

• This public works act authorized the expenditure of $2,250,000,000 over two years to provide city and state jobs for 150,-000 unemployed. He immediately requested the appropriation of $1,000,000,-000, the amount authorized for fiscal 1972.

• Nixon said the act "met the objections to the bill that I vetoed last year," referring to an employment and manpower bill he had vetoed, Dec. 16, 1970, on the grounds that it would have provided "dead-end jobs in the public sector." The Emergency Employment Act of 1971, he added, would provide "transitional" jobs and the "employment will be real and steadying; it will not be a dead-end entrapment in permanent public subsidy."

• This was the first general public employment act since the Works Progress Administration of 1935 (renamed Works Projects Administration, 1939).

July 15, announced his intention to visit People's Republic of China at invitation of Premier Chou En-lai

• He made the announcement in a surprise TV-radio appearance from Los Angeles. Arrangements for the trip had been made by Henry A. Kissinger, his assistant for national security affairs, during a secret visit to Peking, July 9–11.

• In an obvious reference to Nationalist China, Nixon said:

> Our action in seeking a new relationship with the People's Republic of China will not be at the expense of our old friends. It is not directed against any other nation. We seek friendly relations with all nations. Any nation can be our friend without being any other nation's enemy. I have taken this action because of my profound conviction that all nations will gain from a reduction of tensions and a better relationship between the United States and the People's Republic of China.

July 17, met with his special consultant for narcotics and dangerous drugs, Dr. Jerome H. Jaffe, San Clemente

• Afterwards, Dr. Jaffe told the press that tests of servicemen leaving Vietnam indicated 4.5 percent are heroin users, rather than the ten to 20 percent estimated earlier by some observers.

July 18, returned to Washington, D.C.

July 19, proposed new independent agency, Consumer Safety Administration, to replace Food and Drug Administration

July 21, accepted resignation of Dr. Glenn T. Seaborg, chairman of AEC

• Dr. Seaborg, who had shared the 1951 Nobel Prize for chemistry, had been chairman of the Atomic Energy Commission since March, 1961.

• Nixon nominated James R. Schlesinger as chairman of the AEC. Schlesinger was confirmed, Aug. 6.

July 22, sent Seabed Arms Control Treaty to Senate for ratification

• The treaty prohibits the emplacement of nuclear weapons and other weapons of mass destruction on the seabed beyond the 12-mile coastal zone. Secretary of State Rogers had signed the agreement, Feb. 11. Great Britain, the U.S.S.R., and 66 other

nations also signed the treaty.

July 22, asked Congress for $12,100,000 to improve conditions on Snake and Columbia rivers in Washington

July 27, presented first Eisenhower silver dollar to Mrs. Dwight D. Eisenhower, White House

• It was the first silver dollar minted in the U.S. in 36 years.

July 28, accepted resignation of David K. E. Bruce as head of U.S. delegation to Paris peace talks, effective, July 31

• He announced his intention of nominating William J. Porter, ambassador to Korea, to replace Bruce.

July 28, budget deficit of $23,200,000,000 for fiscal 1971 announced

• It was the second highest deficit since World War II, exceeded only by the $25,200,000,000 deficit for fiscal 1968.

July 30, redesignated Air Force One, his official plane, as *Spirit of '76*, in honor of national bicentennial celebration of U.S. independence, Andrews Air Force Base

July 30, addressed annual banquet of Professional Football Hall of Fame, Canton, Ohio

July 31, spoke at dedication ceremonies of Rathbun Dam, near Centerville, Iowa

Aug. 2, Secretary of State Rogers announced U.S. support for seating of People's Republic of China in UN

• This ended 20 years of U.S. resistance to the admission of Red China to the United Nations. The U.S. "will oppose any action to expel the Republic of China or otherwise deprive it of representation in the United Nations," Rogers added.

Aug. 2, White House spokesman criticized steel price rise

• The United States Steel Corporation and other major steel producers announced an eight percent price rise on most products, Aug. 2. The previous day, the industry reached a labor agreement calling for wage increases of about 31 percent over a three-year period.

Aug. 3, asked Congress for $636,000 during fiscal 1972 to declassify World War II documents

• The General Services Administration estimated the project would require five years and $6,000,000 to screen the 160,000,000 pages of secret documents.

Aug. 3, issued statement disavowing HEW plan for busing children to achieve racial

balance in school system of Austin, Tex.
- He instructed Secretary of Health, Education and Welfare Richardson to draft an amendment to the proposed emergency school assistance bill that would "expressly prohibit the expenditure of any of those funds for busing."
- He also stated:

    I am against busing as that term is commonly used in school desegregation cases. I have consistently opposed the busing of our nation's schoolchildren to achieve a racial balance, and I am opposed to the busing of children simply for the sake of busing. Further, while the executive branch will continue to enforce the orders of the court, including court-ordered busing, I have instructed the Attorney General and the Secretary of Health, Education, and Welfare that they are to work with individual school districts to hold busing to the minimum required by law.

Aug. 5, signed executive order establishing National Business Council for Consumer Affairs

Aug. 5, signed act extending Public Works and Economic Development Act of 1965 and Appalachian Regional Development Act of 1965
- The act authorized $3,900,000,000 for development programs in Appalachia and five other regions. The Appalachian program received $1,500,000,000.
- Other regions aided were the Upper Great Lakes, Atlantic Coastal Plains, Ozark Mountains, New England, and the Four Corners of New Mexico, Arizona, Colorado and Utah.

Aug. 5, met with editors and publishers of farm publications, White House

Aug. 6, departed for weekend visit to New Hampshire and Maine
- He spoke in Manchester and Nashua, N.H.; visited the Greenbriar Nursing Home in Nashua, where he outlined administration plans for upgrading nursing homes and extended care facilities; spoke in Bangor, Me.; and journeyed to Minot Island in Penobscot Bay. He was accompanied by Mrs. Nixon and their daughter and son-in-law, Ensign and Mrs. David Eisenhower.

Aug. 7, telephoned congratulations to *Apollo 15* astronauts

- Colonel David R. Scott, Lieutenant Colonel James B. Irwin, and Major Alfred M. Worden, all of the Air Force, were aboard the *U.S.S. Okinawa*, a helicopter carrier, following their 12-day moon exploration mission. They had splashed down in the Pacific, about 330 miles north of Hawaii.

Aug. 8, returned to Washington, D.C.

Aug. 9, signed joint resolution authorizing $1,000,000,000 appropriation for Emergency Employment Act of 1971

Aug. 9, signed Emergency Loan Guarantee Act
- This act guaranteed $250,000,000 of private loans to the Lockheed Aircraft Corporation.

Aug. 10, signed $20,900,000,000 appropriation act for department of labor, department of health, education and welfare, and ten independent and related agencies

Aug. 10, signed $18,300,000,000 appropriation act for department of housing and urban development, NASA, and ten smaller agencies
- He also signed appropriation acts for the departments of state, justice, commerce, interior, transportation, and related agencies, totalling $23,100,000,000.

Aug. 11, signed $2,300,000,000 appropriation act for Atomic Energy Commission

Aug. 11, signed 24 acts authorizing disposal of various metallic elements, fibers, rare-earth materials, tools, and other supplies from national stockpile

Aug. 15, outlined new economic policy during TV-radio address to nation
- "The time has come for a new economic policy for the United States," he said. "It's targets are unemployment, inflation, and international speculation."
- He ordered a 90-day freeze on wages and prices, established a Cost of Living Council to administer the program and recommend measures to stabilize the economy when the freeze ended, and called on corporations to extend the freeze to all dividends.
- He said the U.S. would no longer convert foreign-held dollars into gold, thereby changing the 25-year-old international monetary system.
- He asked Congress to repeal the seven percent automobile excise tax, to put into effect the $50 personal tax exemption increase on Jan. 1, 1972, and to establish an investment tax credit of ten percent for

one year to be followed by a permanent five percent credit on investments made in new American machinery and equipment.

•He announced a ten percent surcharge on all imports, except those that are not subject to duty and those not limited by quota.

•He said he would reduce federal spending in the current fiscal year by $4,700,000,000 by a five percent cut in federal employment, a six-month freeze on federal pay rise schedules, and a ten percent reduction in foreign aid.

•He also said he would ask Congress to postpone the implementation of his revenue-sharing and welfare reform proposals for three months and one year, respectively.

•He made an oblique reference to Franklin D. Roosevelt's economic policies of "The Hundred Days" in 1933 when he said:

> The range of actions I have taken and proposed tonight—on the job front, on the inflation front, on the monetary front—is the most comprehensive new economic policy to be undertaken in this nation in four decades.

Aug. 15, signed executive order stabilizing prices, rents, wages and salaries for 90 days

Aug. 15, issued proclamation declaring national emergency

Aug. 16, stock market soared

•In reaction to the announced new economic program, the New York Stock Exchange rose 32.93 points, the largest one-day gain in history. The previous one-day record, 32.04 points, had been set May 27, 1970.

Aug. 16, accepted resignation of John S. D. Eisenhower as ambassador to Belgium

Aug. 17, met with bipartisan group of congressional leaders seeking support of his economic policies

Aug. 17, pledged his support of efforts to help parochial schools in address to annual meeting of Knights of Columbus, New York City

•At a time when private and parochial schools are closing "at the rate of one a day," he said, "we must resolve to stop that trend and turn it around."

•He was the first president to address the Knights of Columbus, the largest American Roman Catholic fraternal and charitable order.

Aug. 17, vetoed bill to provide retirement benefits to totally disabled District of Co-

lumbia policemen and firemen

•Similar bills had been vetoed by President Eisenhower in 1959 and by President Kennedy in 1961.

Aug. 18, signed act establishing Lincoln home as national historical site, Springfield, Ill.

•Nixon signed the act in the Old Capitol Building, a restoration of the chamber where Lincoln had served as a member of the Illinois legislature.

Aug. 19, addressed national convention of Veterans of Foreign Wars, Dallas, Tex.

Aug. 19, arrived at San Clemente, Cal.

•During his cross-country trip from New York City, he had spoken in Springfield, Ill.; Idaho Falls, Ida.; Grand Teton National Park, Wy.; and Dallas, Tex.

Aug. 20, directed health, education and welfare department to develop work-welfare program in three states

•He ordered demonstration projects in California, Illinois, and New York that would require employable welfare recipients to participate in community work programs when jobs in the private sector were not available.

Aug. 24, conferred with William J. Porter, new chief negotiator at Paris peace talks, San Clemente

Aug. 27, conferred with Kenneth Rush, ambassador to Germany, San Clemente

•Afterwards, the White House announced the president had approved a draft of the four-power agreement on access to Berlin.

Aug. 31, invoked executive privilege in refusing to disclose long-range plans for foreign military aid to Senate foreign relations committee

•The committee had voted to suspend all aid unless the plans were made available or disclosure was specifically forbidden by the president.

•This was only the second time he had invoked the power of executive privilege. He had refused access to certain FBI files, requested by a House of Representatives government operations subcommittee, in June, 1970.

Aug. 31, conferred with HEW Secretary Richardson regarding school busing policies

•It was their first meeting since Nixon's disavowal of HEW plans for extensive busing in Austin, Tex., Aug. 3. Afterwards, Richardson said that administration policies on busing had always been "perfectly clear" to him.

Aug. 31, sent special message to Congress asking six-month delay of pay increases for federal civilian and military employees

• He requested the postponement of the pay raises for 1,300,000 white-collar employees and 2,900,000 military employees, he said, "to continue to set an example for the American people in our striving to achieve prosperity in peacetime." The increases had been scheduled for Jan. 1, 1972.

Sept. 1, extended six-month delay of pay increases to include 600,000 federal blue-collar employees

• The estimated saving in federal spending from the six-month pay freeze, affecting 4,800,000 employees, was about $1,300,000,000.

Sept. 3, spoke at dedication ceremonies for Air Force Museum, Wright-Patterson Air Force Base, Dayton, Ohio

• Later in the evening, he addressed 40,000 members of the Associated Milk Producers in McCormick Place, Chicago, Ill.

Sept. 3, returned to Washington, D.C.

Sept. 6, called upon all citizens to dedicate themselves to "a new prosperity without war and without inflation," during Labor Day speech, Camp David, Md.

Sept. 9, announced 90-day wage-price freeze would not be extended beyond scheduled expiration date, Nov. 13

• In an address to a joint session of Congress, he said the freeze would be replaced by a stabilization program that would be developed in cooperation with representatives of Congress, business, labor, and agriculture. "Let us bear in mind that prosperity is a job for everyone—and that fighting inflation is everybody's business," he added.

• The address, his third to a joint session of Congress, was broadcast live on television and radio.

Sept. 9, attended opening performance at Concert Hall of John F. Kennedy Center for Performing Arts, Washington, D.C.

• He had not attended the gala premiere of the Center's Opera House, the previous evening. Instead, he had relinquished the president's box to members of the Kennedy family.

Sept. 10, met with labor leaders, White House

• After the two-hour meeting, the first with labor leaders since the announcement of the wage-price freeze, it was announced that labor would support the creation of a board representing labor, management, and the public to control wages and prices without government interference after the expiration of the freeze.

Sept. 10, met with Minister for Foreign Affairs Takeo Fukuda of Japan, White House

Sept. 13, met with business leaders to discuss new economic policy, White House

Sept. 14, met with Prince Hitachi and Princess Hanako of Japan, White House

Sept. 14, met with agricultural leaders to discuss new economic policy, White House

Sept. 16, said Phase Two of his economic policy would "have teeth in it," but declined to give details, during impromptu news conference, White House

Sept. 17, accepted resignation of Associate Justice Black

• Black served on the Supreme Court for 34 years, longer than all other justices except Chief Justice John Marshall and Associate Justice Stephen J. Field.

Sept. 21, sent special message to Senate asking ratification of agreement to return Okinawa to Japan

Sept. 21, met with King Olav V of Norway, White House

Sept. 21, appointed Robert M. Duncan as associate judge of U.S. Court of Military Appeals

• Duncan, who was appointed for a term of 15 years, was the first Negro appointed to the Court of Military Appeals, the final appellate tribunal in court-martial conventions.

Sept. 23, accepted resignation of Associate Justice Harlan

Sept. 24, announced approval of agreements with U.S.S.R. to guard against accidental or unauthorized use of nuclear weapons and to modernize Washington-Moscow "hot line" by shifting from teleprinter cable to satellite communication

• Both agreements were signed by Secretary of State Rogers and Foreign Minister Gromyko in Washington, Sept. 30.

Sept. 25, signed act repealing Emergency Detention Act of 1950

• This act had provided for the establishment of detention camps for those thought likely to engage in espionage or sabotage in times of national emergency. Six such camps had been established, but none had been put into operation.

Sept. 25, departed for Pacific Northwest and Alaska

Sept. 25, met with chief negotiators in West Coast dock strike, Portland, Ore.

• He asked for a speedy solution to the walkout that had idled ports since July 1.

Sept. 26, met with Emperor Hirohito of Japan, Elmendorf Air Force Base, Anchorage, Alaska

• It was the first meeting between an American president and a Japanese emperor. The brief meeting was largely ceremonial. Hirohito was the first reigning monarch in Japan's 2,600-year history to travel outside of his native land.

• Nixon was the last of five presidents who visited Alaska while in office.

• Nixon was the last of three presidents who visited the state of Alaska while in office.

Sept. 28, signed act authorizing extension of draft and military pay raise

• The pay increase, scheduled for Oct. 1, was declared subject to the 90-day wage-price freeze.

Sept. 28, attended funeral services for former Justice Black, Washington, D.C.

• Justice Black had died, Sept. 25, eight days after his retirement from the Supreme Court.

Sept. 29, met with Foreign Minister Gromyko of U.S.S.R., White House

Sept. 30, met with Prince Souvanna Phouma, prime minister of Laos, White House

Sept. 30, conferred with leaders of nine education organizations, White House

• The educators recommended that the federal share of public education costs be increased from $3,500,000,000 to $17,500,-000,000.

Sept. 30, gave farewell reception for Douglas B. Cornell of Associated Press, White House

• Cornell retired as White House correspondent after covering seven presidents over a period of 44 years.

• As the reception was ending, Mrs. Nixon made the surprise announcement that Cornell and Helen Thomas, White House correspondent for United Press International, would marry, Oct. 16.

Oct. 1, sent special message to Congress requesting total appropriation of $250,-000,000 for relief and rehabilitation of East Pakistan refugees in India and for

humanitarian aid in East Pakistan

Oct. 4, signed executive order invoking Taft-Hartley Act in dock strike

• Virtually all seaports were shut down when East Coast and Gulf port longshoremen struck, Oct. 1, joining members of the West Coast union, on strike since July 1.

• This was the first time he had invoked the Taft-Hartley Act.

Oct. 5, met with Prime Minister Tun Abdul Razak of Malaysia, White House

Oct. 5, signed act extending loan authority of Farmers Home Administration

• This act increased the appropriation for farm loans by $82,000,000 to $350,-000,000, increased the appropriation for water supply and waste disposal systems by about $45,000,000 to $300,000,000, and made possible the doubling of loans to Indian tribes.

Oct. 6, ordered attorney general to seek injunctions for 80-day cooling-off period in West Coast and port of Chicago dock strikes

• The injunctions were granted by federal judges that evening.

Oct. 7, made TV-radio address on Phase Two of his economic program

• He announced that the 90-day wage-price freeze of Aug. 15 would be followed by an indefinite period of government supervision to limit prices, wages and rents, without direct control of profits. He added that he would appoint a Price Commission and a Pay Board to seek voluntary compliance, and a Cost of Living Council to impose government sanctions "where necessary."

Oct. 8, spoke at Mountain States Forest Festival, Davis-Elkins College, Elkins, W. Va.

• West Virginia was the 50th state he had visited while in office.

• He was the only president who visited all 50 states while in office.

• He was the second of two presidents who visited all of the states of the Union while in office. The other was Franklin D. Roosevelt, who visited the then 48 states.

Oct. 11, met with Foreign Minister Aldo Moro of Italy, White House

Oct. 12, announced he would meet with Soviet leaders in Moscow during latter part of May, 1972, White House

Oct. 12, issued statement on death of former Secretary of State Acheson

• He referred to Acheson, who had served under President Truman, as "one of the towering figures of his time" and a man "of rare intellect, of rigorous conscience, and of profound devotion to his country."

•During the 1954 congressional campaign, Nixon had charged that Truman and Acheson were "traitors to the high principles in which many of the nation's Democrats believed" and that "real Democrats are outraged by the Truman-Acheson-Stevenson gang's defense of Communism in high places."

Oct. 12, signed executive order authorizing Senate committee on commerce to inspect 1939–1972 tax returns to aid in investigation of organized crime

Oct. 13, sent special message to Congress urging expansion of minority business enterprise program

•He requested more than $106,000,000 during the next 18 months for the program that provides loans to minority businesses.

Oct. 15, spoke at Billy Graham Day ceremonies, Charlotte Coliseum, Charlotte, N.C.

Oct. 18, spoke at dedication ceremonies, Center for Cancer Research, Fort Detrick, Md.

•The Fort Detrick laboratories previously had been used for research in biological warfare weapons.

Oct. 18, attended opening of Eisenhower Theater, John F. Kennedy Center for Performing Arts, Washington, D.C.

•The eleven-hundred-seat Eisenhower Theater was the third and last of the major halls of the Kennedy Center for Performing Arts to open.

Oct. 19, met with Prime Minister (Mrs.) Sirimavo Bandaranaike of Ceylon, White House

Oct. 20, stock market, in prolonged slump, retreated to pre-Nixon rally level

•The Dow-Jones industrial average closed off 12.78 points, at 855.65, the lowest level since Aug. 16.

Oct. 21, appointed Lewis F. Powell, Jr., and William H. Rehnquist as associate justices

•He announced the appointments on television and radio from the White House. The nominations were officially submitted to the Senate, Oct. 22.

•Neither of the nominees had been included in the list of six sent to the American Bar Association's federal judiciary committee, Oct. 13. Leakage of that list to the press led Nixon to discontinue the

practice of asking the ABA, through the attorney general, for advance opinions on nominees.

•Powell, who was confirmed by the Senate, Dec. 6, was the fifth of Nixon's six appointments to the Supreme Court.

•Rehnquist, who was confirmed by the Senate, Dec. 10, was the last of Nixon's six appointments to the Supreme Court.

Oct. 22, announced appointment of 15-man Pay Board and seven-man Price Commission

•He appointed George H. Boldt as chairman of the Pay Board and C. Jackson Grayson, Jr., as chairman of the Price Commission.

Oct. 24, requested national commitment to veterans of Vietnam War during Veterans Day radio address, Camp David, Md.

Oct. 26, Secretary of State Rogers issued statement welcoming admission of People's Republic of China to United Nations

•The General Assembly of the UN had voted overwhelmingly to admit Communist China and expel the Republic of China, Oct. 25, a major diplomatic defeat for the U.S. The vote had been 76–35, with 17 abstentions.

•Rogers's statement, which had been approved by Nixon, expressed regret at the expulsion of Nationalist China:

> We think that this precedent, which has the effect of expelling 14 million people on Taiwan from representation in the United Nations, is a most unfortunate one, which will have many adverse effects in the future.

Oct. 27, authorized AEC to proceed with planned underground test of five-megaton nuclear warhead on Amchitka Island, Aleutians

•Congress had barred the controversial test before mid-1972 unless it was authorized by the president.

Oct. 28 and Oct. 30, met with President Tito of Yugoslavia, White House

Oct. 29, informed by Postmaster General Blount of his intention to submit his resignation to board of governors of U.S. Postal Service

•The postmaster general had ceased to be a member of the cabinet, June 30.

Oct. 30, criticized Senate rejection of foreign aid bill

•The Senate had rejected the $3,300,000,-

000 foreign aid authorization bill, 41–27, Oct. 29.

• He said the vote was "a highly irresponsible action which undoes 25 years of constructive bipartisan foreign policy and produces unacceptable risks to the national security."

Nov. 2, designated Mrs. Nixon as his special representative at inauguration of President William R. Tolbert of Liberia, Jan. 3, 1972

Nov. 2, met with Prime Minister William McMahon of Australia, White House

Nov. 4, met with Dr. Kofi A. Busia, prime minister of Ghana, White House

Nov. 4–5, met with Prime Minister Indira Gandhi of India, White House

Nov. 5, White House announced two U.S. grain companies would sell $136,000,000 worth of corn and other livestock feed grains to Soviet Union

• No American grain had been sold to Russia since 1964.

Nov. 5, announced reorganization of U.S. intelligence community

• CIA Director Richard Helms was assigned additional authority in planning, coordinating, and evaluating all intelligence programs.

Nov. 6, informed of successful underground nuclear test on Amchitka Island, Aleutians

Nov. 8, Pay Board voted, 10–5, to set 5.5 percent standard for wage increases during Phase Two

• The five labor members voted against the 5.5 standard.

Nov. 9, redecorated Red Room of White House opened to public

• The Red Room had been closed for seven weeks during the refurbishing, which cost more than $100,000. The room got its name during the Polk administration, when the upholstery was done over in red.

Nov. 9, signed executive order authorizing House of Representatives committee on public works to inspect 1960–1972 tax returns

Nov. 9, addressed 20 Republican fund-raising dinners

• He spoke at dinners in New York City and Chicago, and his remarks were broadcast on closed-circuit television to similar dinners in other cities.

Nov. 11, placed wreath on Tomb of Unknowns, Arlington National Cemetery

• This was the 50th anniversary of the burial of the first Unknown Soldier, a World War I casualty. In 1958, Unknowns from World War II and Korea were buried in Arlington Cemetery.

Nov. 11, accepted resignation of Secretary of Agriculture Hardin

Nov. 11, appointed his second secretary of agriculture, Earl L. Butz

• Nixon said the plan to abolish the department of agriculture had been altered. Peripheral activities of the department would be transferred to new departments, he said, but a streamlined department of agriculture would be retained.

• Butz took office, Dec. 2.

Nov. 11, stock market fell to lowest point of year

• The Dow-Jones industrial average closed off 11.24 points, at 814.91. This was the lowest level since Dec. 3, 1970, when it closed at 808.53.

Nov. 12, announced forty-five thousand additional U.S. troops would be withdrawn from South Vietnam prior to Feb. 1, 1972

• The U.S. combat role, "as far as an offensive situation is concerned, is already concluded," he said, during an unscheduled press conference. "American troops are now in a defensive position."

• This withdrawal would reduce American troop strength in South Vietnam to 139,000.

Nov. 15, U.S. recorded largest balance of payments deficit in history in third quarter

• A commerce department spokesman said the deficit doubled from the second to the third quarter, and reached $12,100,000,000 after seasonal adjustment. The January through September payments deficit, $23,400,000,000, far surpassed any yearly deficit in U.S. history.

Nov. 17, signed Military Procurement Authorization Act of 1971

• This act authorized an appropriation of $21,300,000,000. Nixon emphasized the fact that Section 601 of the act, the so-called "Mansfield Amendment," did not represent his policies, and said that he would ignore it. The amendment called upon the president to end U.S. involvement in Vietnam "at a date certain," subject only to the release of American prisoners of war.

Nov. 18, signed Comprehensive Health Manpower Training Act of 1971

• This act authorized the expenditure of

$750,000,000 for the construction of medical education and research facilities over a period of three years. It also authorized $763,000,000 over three years for grants to medical and health professions schools.

Nov. 18, signed Nurse Training Act of 1971

• This act authorized the expenditure of $120,000,000 over three years for the construction and expansion of nurse training facilities. It also authorized $248,000,000 over three years for grants to nursing schools.

Nov. 19, addressed AFL-CIO convention, Bal Harbour, Fla.

• Discarding his prepared text, he appealed to organized labor for its cooperation with his Phase Two economic controls. He added:

> I want a program that is fair to all elements of this society, fair to organized labor, particularly. . . . But as President of all the American people, it is my duty to do what I think is best for all the American people. And . . . whatever some of you may think, a great majority of the American people, and a majority of union members, want to stop the rise in the cost of living— and that is what we are going to do. In order to stop the rise in the cost of living, we want the participation of business, we want the participation of labor, we want the participation of consumers, and all the other areas of the society. We hope we get it. But whether we get that participation or not, it is my obligation as President of the United States to make this program of stopping the rise in the cost of living succeed, and to the extent that my powers allow it, I shall do exactly that.

Nov. 23, announced he would propose legislation to acquire 547,000 acres of Big Cypress Swamp, Fla., as national reserve

Nov. 24, flew to San Clemente, Cal.

Nov. 25, directed attorney general to seek injunctions for 80-day cooling-off period in Atlantic and Gulf Coast dock strikes

• The injunctions were granted by federal judges, Oct. 26.

Nov. 27, spoke at dedication ceremonies, Eisenhower Memorial Hospital, Palm Desert, Cal.

Nov. 27, White House announced he would meet with Prime Minister Eisaku Sato of Japan in San Clemente, Jan. 6–7, 1972

Nov. 28, returned to Washington, D.C.

Nov. 30, White House announced he and Mrs. Nixon would visit Peking, Hangchow, and Shanghai during their seven-day visit to China, Feb. 21–28, 1972

Nov. 30, authorized Export-Import Bank to finance sales of U.S. goods to Rumania

• This ended a three-year ban on government-backed credits to Communist-bloc nations.

Dec. 1, spoke at 50th National 4-H Congress, Chicago, Ill.

• He told the assembly of youth, many of whom would vote for the first time in 1972:

> The young in America are no longer going to be treated as a mass or a bloc in this country—neither as a generation apart nor as a generation idolized. You deserve better than that. And you will have better, for America is rapidly moving to take you, the young, into full partnership as individuals in our society.

Dec. 2, spoke at final session of second White House Conference on Aging, Washington, D.C.

• He said:

> The entire nation has a high stake in a better life for its older citizens simply because we need you. We need the resources which you alone can offer. We are speaking, after all, of a proven generation, one that has brought this country through the most turbulent period in human history. Your skills, your wisdom, your values and your faith —these are among the most valuable resources this nation possesses.

Dec. 2, met with Prime Minister Golda Meir of Israel, White House

Dec. 2, spoke at oath-taking ceremony for Secretary of Agriculture Butz, White House

Dec. 3, White House announced he would submit budget based on "full employment" concept for fiscal 1973, Key Biscayne, Fla.

Dec. 6, met with Prime Minister Pierre Elliott Trudeau of Canada, White House

• This was the first of a series of consultations with allied leaders prior to his trips to

China and the Soviet Union in 1972.

Dec. 7, met with President Emilio Garrastazu Medici of Brazil, White House

Dec. 8, sent special message to Congress outlining pension reform program

Dec. 9, vetoed child-care bill

• This bill proposed extension of the Economic Opportunity Act of 1964, creation of a National Legal Services Corporation, and establishment of a comprehensive child development program. The "laudable" purpose of the child-care amendment, he said in his veto message, "is overshadowed by the fiscal irresponsibility, administrative unworkability, and family-weakening implications of the system it envisions."

Dec. 10, signed Revenue Act of 1971

• This act increased the personal income tax exemption for individuals from $650 to $675 for 1971 income and $750 for 1972 income, repealed the seven percent excise tax on automobiles, and increased the standard deduction for those taxpayers who do not itemize deductions from 13 percent with a $1,500 ceiling to 15 percent with a $2,000 ceiling.

• Nixon reiterated his opposition "on principle" to a provision of the act for a $1 tax checkoff plan for financing presidential campaigns, applicable to the 1976 campaign. "I am confident that, with the time now allowed for reconsideration, this provision . . . will not become operative," he said.

Dec. 12, flew to Azores

• He met with Prime Minister Marcello Caetano of Portugal in the residence of the U.S. military commander of Lajes Field, Terceira Island.

• He was the second of two presidents who visited the Azores while in office. The other was Lyndon B. Johnson.

• He was the last of three presidents who visited Portugal while in office.

Dec. 13–14, met with President Georges Pompidou of France, Angra do Heroismo, Terceira Island, Azores

Dec. 14, returned to Washington, D.C.

Dec. 15, signed act providing equality of treatment for married women federal employees

Dec. 15, signed Navajo Community College Act

Dec. 15, signed Supplemental Appropriations Act of 1972

Dec. 15, signed act to protect wild horses and burros on public land

• Only about ninety-five hundred unbranded and unclaimed horses and about eleven thousand free-roaming burros remain on public lands.

Dec. 15, signed Veterans Disability and Death Pension Act of 1971

• Pensions for about 2,200,000 veterans and survivors were raised by an average of 6.5 percent.

Dec. 15, signed Veterans Dependency and Indemnity Compensation Act of 1971

• This act provided for increased monthly compensation benefits for about 290,500 widows, children, and dependent parents of veterans. The increases ranged from five to ten percent.

Dec. 17, first session of 92nd Congress adjourned

Dec. 18, announced international agreement to devalue dollar by 7.89 percent, raise values of other major currencies

• His announcement came at the end of the two-day meeting of the Group of Ten, the finance ministers and central bankers of the ten leading industrial nations, at the Smithsonian Institution, Washington, D.C.

• He said the Group of Ten had reached "the most significant monetary agreement in the history of the world."

• The last significant agreement of this kind, he added, was the Bretton Woods Conference of 1944.

Dec. 18, met with Deputy Prime Minister Zulfikar Ali Bhutto of Pakistan, White House

Dec. 18, signed Alaska Native Claims Settlement Act

Dec. 18, signed act establishing Capital Reef National Park, Utah

Dec. 20, met with Prime Minister Edward Heath of Great Britain, Hamilton, Bermuda

• He was the last of four presidents who visited Bermuda while in office.

Dec. 20, signed proclamation removing ten percent surcharge on imports

• He announced that he had signed the proclamation following his meeting with Prime Minister Heath. Actually, he had signed the document en route to Bermuda.

Dec. 21, again met with Prime Minister Heath, Hamilton

Dec. 21, returned to Washington, D.C.

Dec. 22, signed Economic Stabilization Act Amendments of 1971

• This act extended his authority to control wages and prices through Apr. 30, 1973.

• He said:

> I hope and expect, however, that before that date we will see the end of the inflationary psychology that developed in the 1960's, achieve lasting price stability, end controls, and return to reliance on free market forces.

Dec. 22, signed executive orders raising pay of federal civilian employees and military personnel

• The orders provided for a 5.5 percent pay rise for more than one million federal white-collar civilian employees and about three million military personnel, effective Jan. 1, 1972.

Dec. 23, signed National Cancer Act of 1971

• This act authorized the expenditure of $1,-600,000,000 over three years for cancer research and related activities.

Dec. 23, commuted sentence of James R. Hoffa

• The former president of the International Brotherhood of Teamsters, who was serving an eight-year term for jury tampering and a five-year term for pension fund fraud in the federal penitentiary at Lewisburg, Pa., had served four years, 291 days.

• Hoffa was released under a conditional commutation of sentence that specified that he could not "engage in the direct or indirect management of any labor organization" until Mar. 6, 1980, when his full term would have ended.

Dec. 27–28, White House Christmas tree and decorations viewed by 23,975 evening visitors

• This was the second year that candlelight holiday tours were conducted. Tourists were admitted between 6:30 and 10 P.M. The previous year, the holiday tours attracted 17,789 visitors.

Dec. 28, signed act requiring able-bodied welfare workers to register for jobs or job training

Dec. 28–29, met with Chancellor Willy Brandt of West Germany, Key Biscayne, Fla.

Dec. 29, reluctantly signed act providing $454,000,000 in extra benefits for 732,000 unemployed

THE VICE PRESIDENT (39th)

Full name: Spiro Theodore Agnew

Date of birth: Nov. 9, 1918

Place of birth: Baltimore, Md.

• He was the only vice president who was born in Maryland.

Religious denomination: Episcopalian

• He was the last of eight vice presidents who were Episcopalians.

College: Johns Hopkins University, Baltimore, Md.

• He attended Johns Hopkins from February, 1937, to February, 1939. He also attended McCoy College, the night school of Johns Hopkins, for three years, 1952–1955.

Law school: University of Baltimore Law School, Baltimore, Md.

• He attended the evening course of the Baltimore Law School for two years, 1939–1941, and left to enter military service. In 1945, he again enrolled at the law school. He received his Bachelor of Laws degree, June 12, 1947.

Date of graduation: 1947

Occupations: Lawyer, teacher, politician

• He practiced law; taught night courses at the University of Baltimore Law School for seven years, 1959–1966; was elected county executive of Baltimore County in 1962 and served for four years, 1963–1967; was elected governor of Maryland in 1966 and served for two years, 1967–1969.

• He was the last of 14 vice presidents who served as state governors.

Term of office: Jan. 20, 1969—

• Nixon and Agnew were the last of 41 president-vice president teams.

Age at inauguration: 50 years, 72 days

State represented: Maryland

• He was the only vice president who represented Maryland.

Political party: Republican

• He was the last of 15 vice presidents who were Republicans.

THE CABINET

State: William Pierce Rogers of Maryland, Jan. 22, 1969

Treasury: David Matthew Kennedy of Illinois, Jan. 22, 1969, to Feb. 1, 1971

• John Bowden Connally of Texas, Feb. 11, 1971

Defense: Melvin Robert Laird of Wisconsin, Jan. 22, 1969

Attorney General: John Newton Mitchell of New York, Jan. 22, 1969

Postmaster General: Winton Malcolm Blount of Alabama, Jan. 22, 1969, to June 30, 1971

Interior: Walter Joseph Hickel of Alaska, Jan. 24, 1969, to Nov. 25, 1970

• Rogers Clark Ballard Morton of Maryland, Jan. 29, 1971

Agriculture: Clifford Morris Hardin of Nebraska, Jan. 22, 1969, to Nov. 11, 1971

• Earl Lauer Butz of Indiana, Dec. 2, 1971

Commerce: Maurice Hubert Stans of New York, Jan. 22, 1969

Labor: George Pratt Schultz of Illinois, Jan. 22, 1969, to July 1, 1970

• James Day Hodgson of California, July 2, 1970

Health, Education and Welfare: Robert Hutchinson Finch of California, Jan. 22, 1969, to June 6, 1970

• Elliot Lee Richardson of Massachusetts, June 24, 1970

Housing and Urban Development: George Wilcken Romney of Michigan, Jan. 22, 1969

Transportation: John Anthony Volpe of Massachusetts, Jan. 22, 1969

THE SUPREME COURT

Chief Justice: Warren Earl Burger of Virginia, appointed, May 21, 1969; confirmed, June 9, 1969

Associate Justices: Clement Furman Haynsworth, Jr., of South Carolina, appointed, Aug. 18, 1969; rejected by Senate, Nov. 21, 1969

• George Harrold Carswell of Florida, appointed, Jan. 19, 1970; rejected by Senate, Apr. 8, 1970

• Harry Andrew Blackmun of Minnesota, appointed, Apr. 14, 1970; confirmed, May 12, 1970

• Lewis Franklin Powell, Jr., of Virginia, appointed, Oct. 22, 1971; confirmed, Dec. 6, 1971

• William Hubbs Rehnquist of Arizona, appointed, Oct. 22, 1971; confirmed, Dec. 10, 1971

APPENDIXES

THE CONSTITUTION

We, the People of the United States, in order to form a more perfect union, establish justice, insure domestic tranquility, provide for the common defence, promote the general welfare, and secure the blessing of liberty to ourselves and our posterity, do ordain and establish this Constitution for the United States of America.

ARTICLE I.

Section 1. All legislative powers herein granted shall be vested in a Congress of the United States, which shall consist of a Senate and House of Representatives.

Section 2. The House of Representatives shall be composed of members chosen every second year by the people of the several states, and the electors in each state shall have the qualifications requisite for electors of the most numerous branch of the state legislature.

No person shall be a representative who shall not have attained to the age of twenty-five years, and been seven years a citizen of the United States, and who shall not, when elected, be an inhabitant of that state in which he shall be chosen.

Representatives and direct taxes shall be apportioned among the several states which may be included within this Union, according to their respective numbers, [which shall be determined by adding to the whole number of free persons, including those bound to service for a term of years, and excluding Indians not taxed, three-fifths of all other persons.][1] The actual enumeration shall be made within three years after the first meeting of the Congress of the United States, and within every subsequent term of ten years, in such manner as they shall by law direct. The number of representatives shall not exceed one for every thirty thousand, but each state shall have at least one representative; and until such enumeration shall be made, the state of New Hampshire shall be entitled to chuse three, Massachusetts eight,

Rhode-Island and Providence Plantations one, Connecticut five, New-York six, New-Jersey four, Pennsylvania eight, Delaware one, Maryland six, Virginia ten, North-Carolina five, South-Carolina five, and Georgia three.

When vacancies happen in the representation from any state, the Executive authority thereof shall issue writs of election to fill such vacancies.

The House of Representatives shall chuse their Speaker and other officers; and shall have the sole power of impeachment.

Section 3. The Senate of the United States shall be composed of two senators from each state, [chosen by the legislature thereof,][2] for six years; and each senator shall have one vote.

Immediately after they shall be assembled in consequence of the first election, they shall be divided as equally as may be into three classes. The seats of the senators of the first class shall be vacated at the expiration of the second year, of the second class at the expiration of the fourth year, and of the third class at the expiration of the sixth year, so that one-third may be chosen every second year; [and if vacancies happen by resignation, or otherwise, during the recess of the Legislature of any state, the Executive thereof may make temporary appointments until the next meeting of the Legislature, which shall then fill such vacancies.][3]

No person shall be a senator who shall not have attained to the age of thirty years, and been nine years a citizen of the United States, and who shall not, when elected, be an inhabitant of that state for which he shall be chosen.

The Vice-President of the United States shall be President of the Senate, but shall have no vote, unless they be equally divided.

The Senate shall chuse their other officers, and also a President pro tempore, in the absence of the Vice-President, or when he shall exercise the office of President of the United States.

[1]Superseded by Section 2 of the 14th Amendment.
[2]Superseded by Clause 1 of the 17th Amendment.
[3]Modified by Clause 2 of the 17th Amendment.

The Senate shall have the sole power to try all impeachments. When sitting for that purpose, they shall be on oath or affirmation. When the President of the United States is tried, the Chief Justice shall preside: And no person shall be convicted without the concurrence of two-thirds of the members present.

Judgment in cases of impeachment shall not extend further than to removal from office and disqualification to hold and enjoy any office of honor, trust or profit under the United States; but the party convicted shall nevertheless be liable and subject to indictment, trial, judgment and punishment, according to law.

Section 4. The times, places and manner of holding elections for senators and representatives, shall be prescribed in each state by the legislature thereof; but the Congress may at any time by law make or alter such regulations, except as to the places of chusing Senators.

The Congress shall assemble at least once in every year, and such meeting shall [be on the first Monday in December,][4] unless they shall by law appoint a different day.

Section 5. Each house shall be the judge of the elections, returns and qualifications of its own members, and a majority of each shall constitute a quorum to do business; but a smaller number may adjourn from day to day, and may be authorized to compel the attendance of absent members, in such manner, and under such penalties as each house may provide.

Each house may determine the rules of its proceedings, punish its members for disorderly behaviour, and, with the concurrence of two-thirds, expel a member.

Each house shall keep a journal of its proceedings, and from time to time publish the same, excepting such parts as may in their judgment require secrecy; and the yeas and nays of the members of either house on any question shall, at the desire of one-fifth of those present, be entered on the journal.

Neither house, during the session of Congress shall, without the consent of the other, adjourn for more than three days, nor to any other place than that in which the two houses shall be sitting.

Section 6. The senators and representatives shall receive a compensation for their services, to be ascertained by law, and paid out of the treasury of the United States. They shall in all cases, except treason, felony and breach of the peace, be privileged from arrest during their attendance at the session of their respective houses, and in going to and returning from the same; and for any speech or debate in either house, they shall not be questioned in any other place.

No senator or representative shall, during the time for which he was elected, be appointed to any civil office under the authority of the United States, which shall have been created, or the emoluments whereof shall have been encreased during such time; and no person holding any office under the United States, shall be a member of either house during his continuance in office.

Section 7. All bills for raising revenue shall originate in the house of representatives; but the senate may propose or concur with amendments as on other bills.

Every bill which shall have passed the house of representatives and the senate, shall, before it become a law, be presented to the president of the United States; if he approve he shall sign it, but if not he shall return it, with his objections to that house in which it shall have originated, who shall enter the objections at large on their journal, and proceed to reconsider it. If after such reconsideration two-thirds of that house shall agree to pass the bill, it shall be sent, together with the objections, to the other house, by which it shall likewise be reconsidered, and if approved by two-thirds of that house, it shall become a law. But in all such cases the votes of both houses shall be determined by yeas and nays, and the names of the persons voting for and against the bill shall be entered on the journal of each house respectively. If any bill shall not be returned by the President within ten days (Sundays excepted) after it shall have been presented to him, the same shall be a law, in like manner as if he had signed it, unless the Congress by their adjournment prevent its return, in which case it shall not be a law.

Every order, resolution, or vote to which the concurrence of the Senate and House of Representatives may be necessary (except on a question of adjournment) shall be presented to the President of the United States; and before the same shall take effect, shall be approved by him, or, being disapproved by him, shall be repassed by two-thirds of the Senate and House of Representatives, according to the rules and limitations prescribed in the case of a bill.

Section 8. The Congress shall have power

To lay and collect taxes, duties, imposts and excises, to pay the debts and provide for the common defence and general welfare of the United States; but all duties, imposts and excises shall be uniform throughout the United States;

To borrow money on the credit of the United States;

To regulate commerce with foreign nations, and among the several states, and with the Indian tribes;

To establish an uniform rule of naturalization, and uniform laws on the subject of bankruptcies throughout the United States;

To coin money, regulate the value thereof, and of foreign coin, and fix the standard of weights and measures;

[4]Superseded by Section 2 of the 20th Amendment.

To provide for the punishment of counterfeiting the securities and current coin of the United States;

To establish post offices and post roads;

To promote the progress of science and useful arts, by securing for limited times to authors and inventors the exclusive right to their respective writings and discoveries;

To constitute tribunals inferior to the supreme court;

To define and punish piracies and felonies committed on the high seas, and offences against the law of nations;

To declare war, grant letters of marque and reprisal, and make rules concerning captures on land and water;

To raise and support armies, but no appropriation of money to that use shall be for a longer term than two years;

To provide and maintain a navy;

To make rules for the government and regulation of the land and naval forces;

To provide for calling forth the militia to execute the laws of the union, suppress insurrections and repel invasions;

To provide for organizing, arming, and disciplining, the militia, and for governing such part of them as may be employed in the service of the United States, reserving to the States respectively, the appointment of the officers, and the authority of training the militia according to the discipline prescribed by Congress;

To exercise exclusive legislation in all cases whatsoever, over such district (not exceeding ten miles square) as may, by cession of particular States, and the acceptance of Congress, become the seat of the government of the United States, and to exercise like authority over all places purchased by the consent of the legislature of the states in which the same shall be, for the erection of forts, magazines, arsenals, dock-yards, and other needful buildings;—And

To make all laws which shall be necessary and proper for carrying into execution the foregoing powers, and all other powers vested by this constitution in the government of the United States, or in any department or officer thereof.

Section 9. The migration or importation of such persons as any of the states now existing shall think proper to admit, shall not be prohibited by the Congress prior to the year one thousand eight hundred and eight, but a tax or duty may be imposed on such importation, not exceeding ten dollars for each person.

The privilege of the writ of habeas corpus shall not be suspended, unless when in cases of rebellion or invasion the public safety may require it.

No bill of attainder or ex post facto law shall be passed.

No capitation, or other direct, tax shall be laid, unless in proportion to the census or enumeration herein before directed to be taken.[5]

No tax or duty shall be laid on articles exported from any state. No preference shall be given by any regulation of commerce or revenue to the ports of one state over those of another: nor shall vessels bound to, or from, one state, be obliged to enter, clear, or pay duties in another.

No money shall be drawn from the treasury, but in consequence of appropriations made by law; and a regular statement and account of the receipts and expenditures of all public money shall be published from time to time.

No title of nobility shall be granted by the United States:—And no person holding any office of profit or trust under them, shall, without the consent of the Congress, accept of any present, emolument, office, or title, of any kind whatever, from any king, prince, or foreign state.

Section 10. No state shall enter into any treaty, alliance, or confederation; grant letters of marque and reprisal; coin money; emit bills of credit; make any thing but gold and silver coin a tender in payment of debts; pass any bill of attainder, ex post facto law, or law impairing the obligation of contracts, or grant any title of nobility.

No state shall, without the consent of the Congress, lay any imposts or duties on imports or exports, except what may be absolutely necessary for executing its inspection laws; and the net produce of all duties and imposts, laid by any state on imports or exports, shall be for the use of the Treasury of the United States; and all such laws shall be subject to the revision and control of the Congress. No state shall, without the consent of Congress, lay any duty of tonnage, keep troops, or ships of war in time of peace, enter into any agreement or compact with another state, or with a foreign power, or engage in war, unless actually invaded, or in such imminent danger as will not admit of delay.

II.

Section 1. The executive power shall be vested in a president of the United States of America. [He shall hold his office during the term of four years,][6] and, together with the vice-president, chosen for the same term, be elected as follows.

Each state shall appoint, in such manner as the legislature thereof may direct, a number of electors, equal to the whole number of senators and representatives to which the state may be entitled in the Congress: but no senator or representative, or person holding an office of trust or profit under the United States, shall be appointed an elector.

[The electors shall meet in their respective states, and vote by ballot for two persons, of

---

[5]Modified by the 16th Amendment.

[6]Modified by the 22nd Amendment.

whom one at least shall not be an inhabitant of the same state with themselves. And they shall make a list of all the persons voted for, and of the number of votes for each; which list they shall sign and certify, and transmit sealed to the seat of the government of the United States, directed to the president of the senate. The president of the senate shall, in the presence of the senate and house of representatives, open all the certificates, and the votes shall then be counted. The person having the greatest number of votes shall be the president, if such number be a majority of the whole number of electors appointed; and if there be more than one who have such majority, and have an equal number of votes, then the house of representatives shall immediately chuse by ballot one of them for president; and if no person have a majority, then from the five highest on the list the said house shall in like manner chuse the president. But in chusing the president, the votes shall be taken by states, the representation from each state having one vote; a quorum for this purpose shall consist of a member or members from two-thirds of the states, and a majority of all the states shall be necessary to a choice. In every case, after the choice of the president, the person having the greatest number of votes of the electors shall be the vice-president. But if there should remain two or more who have equal votes, the senate shall chuse from them by ballot the vice-president.][7]

The Congress may determine the time of chusing the electors, and the day on which they shall give their votes; which day shall be the same throughout the United States.

No person except a natural born citizen, or a citizen of the United States, at the time of the adoption of this constitution, shall be eligible to the office of president; neither shall any person be eligible to that office who shall not have attained to the age of thirty-five years, and been fourteen years a resident within the United States.

[In case of the removal of the president from office, or of his death, resignation, or inability to discharge the powers and duties of the said office, the same shall devolve on the vice-president, and the Congress may by law provide for the case of removal, death, resignation or inability, both of the president and vice-president, declaring what officer shall then act as president, and such officer shall act accordingly, until the disability be removed, or a president be elected.][8]

The president shall, at stated times, receive for his services, a compensation, which shall neither be encreased nor diminished during the period for which he shall have been elected, and he shall not receive within that period any other emolument from the United States, or any of them.

Before he enter on the execution of his office,

he shall take the following oath or affirmation:

"I do solemnly swear (or affirm) that I will faithfully execute the office of president of t ie United States, and will to the best of my ability, preserve, protect and defend the constitution of t ie United States."

Section 2. The president shall be commander in chief of the army and navy of the United States, and of the militia of the several States, when called into the actual service of the United States; he may require the opinion, in writing, of the principal officer in each of the executive departments, upon any subject relating to the duties of their respective offices, and he shall have power to grant reprieves and pardons for offences against the United States, except in cases of impeachment.

He shall have power, by and with the advice and consent of the senate, to make treaties, provided two-thirds of the senators present concur; and he shall nominate, and by and with the advice and consent of the senate, shall appoint ambassadors, other public ministers and consuls, judges of the supreme court, and all other officers of the United States, whose appointments are not herein otherwise provided for, and which shall be established by law. But the Congress may by law vest the appointment of such inferior offices, as they think proper, in the president alone, in the courts of law, or in the heads of departments.

The president shall have power to fill up all vacancies that may happen during the recess of the senate, by granting commissions which shall expire at the end of their session.

Section 3. He shall from time to time give to the Congress information of the state of the union, and recommend to their consideration such measures as he shall judge necessary and expedient; he may, on extraordinary occasions, convene both houses, or either of them, and in case of disagreement between them, with respect to the time of adjournment, he may adjourn them to such time as he shall think proper; he shall receive ambassadors and other public ministers; he shall take care that the laws be faithfully executed, and shall commission all the officers of the United States.

Section 4. The president, vice-president and all civil officers of the United States, shall be removed from office on impeachment for, and conviction of, treason, bribery, or other high crimes and misdemeanors.

III.

Section 1. The judicial power of the United States, shall be vested in one supreme court, and in such inferior courts as the Congress may from time to time ordain and establish. The judges, both of the supreme and inferior courts, shall hold

[7]Superseded by the 12th Amendment.

[8]Modified by the 25th Amendment.

their offices during good behaviour, and shall, at stated times, receive for their services, a compensation, which shall not be diminished during their continuance in office.

Section 2. The judicial power shall extend to all cases, in law and equity, arising under this constitution, the laws of the United States, and treaties made, or which shall be made, under their authority; to all cases affecting ambassadors, other public ministers and consuls;—to all cases of admiralty and maritime jurisdiction; to controversies to which the United States shall be a party; to controversies between two or more States;—[between a state and citizens of another state;][9]— between citizens of different States,—between citizens of the same state claiming lands under grants of different States, [and between a state, or the citizens thereof, and foreign States, citizens or subjects.][10]

In all cases affecting ambassadors, other public ministers and consuls, and those in which a state shall be party, the supreme court shall have original jurisdiction. In all the other cases before mentioned, the supreme court shall have appellate jurisdiction, both as to law and fact, with such exceptions, and under such regulations as the Congress shall make.

The trial of all crimes, except in cases of impeachment, shall be by jury; and such trial shall be held in the state where the said crimes shall have been committed; but when not committed within any state, the trial shall be at such place or places as the Congress may by law have directed.

Section 3. Treason against the United States, shall consist only in levying war against them, or in adhering to their enemies, giving them aid and comfort. No person shall be convicted of treason unless on the testimony of two witnesses to the same overt act, or on confession in open court.

The Congress shall have power to declare the punishment of treason, but no attainder of treason shall work corruption of blood, or forfeiture except during the life of the person attainted.

IV.

Section 1. Full faith and credit shall be given in each state to the public acts, records, and judicial proceedings of every other state. And the Congress may by general laws prescribe the manner in which such acts, records and proceedings shall be proved, and the effect thereof.

Section 2. The citizens of each state shall be entitled to all privileges and immunities of citizens in the several states.

A person charged in any state with treason, felony, or other crime, who shall flee from justice,

and be found in another state, shall, on demand of the executive authority of the state from which he fled, be delivered up, to be removed to the state having jurisdiction of the crime.

[No person held to service or labour in one state, under the laws thereof, escaping into another, shall, in consequence of any law or regulation therein, be discharged from such service or labour, but shall be delivered up on claim of the party to whom such service or labour may be due.][11]

Section 3. New states may be admitted by the Congress into this union; but no new state shall be formed or erected within the jurisdiction of any other state; nor any state be formed by the junction of two or more states, or parts of states, without the consent of the legislatures of the states concerned as well as of the Congress.

The Congress shall have power to dispose of and make all needful rules and regulations respecting the territory or other property belonging to the United States; and nothing in this Constitution shall be so construed as to prejudice any claims of the United States, or of any particular state.

Section 4. The United States shall guarantee to every state in this union a Republican form of government, and shall protect each of them against invasion; and on application of the legislature, or of the executive (when the legislature cannot be convened) against domestic violence.

V.

The Congress, whenever two-thirds of both houses shall deem it necessary, shall propose amendments to this constitution, or, on the application of the legislatures of two-thirds of the several states, shall call a convention for proposing amendments, which, in either case, shall be valid to all intents and purposes, as part of this constitution, when ratified by the legislatures of three-fourths of the several states, or by conventions in three-fourths thereof, as the one or the other mode of ratification may be proposed by Congress; Provided, that no amendment which may be made prior to the year one thousand eight hundred and eight shall in any manner affect the first and fourth clauses in the ninth section of the first article; and that no state, without its consent, shall be deprived of its equal suffrage in the senate.

VI.

All debts contracted and engagements entered into, before the adoption of this Constitution, shall be as valid against the United States under this Constitution, as under the confederation.

This constitution, and the laws of the United States which shall be made in pursuance thereof;

[9]Modified by the 11th Amendment.
[10]Modified by the 11th Amendment.

[11]Superseded by the 13th Amendment.

and all treaties made, or which shall be made, under the authority of the United States, shall be the supreme law of the land; and the judges in every state shall be bound thereby, any thing in the constitution or laws of any state to the contrary notwithstanding.

The senators and representatives beforementioned, and the members of the several state legislatures, and all executive and judicial officers, both of the United States and of the several States, shall be bound by oath or affirmation, to support this constitution; but no religious test shall ever be required as a qualification to any office or public trust under the United States.

VII.

The ratification of the conventions of nine States, shall be sufficient for the establishment of this constitution between the States so ratifying the same.

[*Done in Convention by the unanimous consent of the States present the seventeenth day of September in the year of our Lord one thousand seven hundred and eighty-seven and of the Independence of the United States of America the twelfth. In witness whereof we have hereunto subscribed our Names.*]

(signatures omitted)

THE AMENDMENTS

Amendments of the Constitution of the United States of America, proposed by Congress, and ratified by the legislatures of the several states, pursuant to the fifth Article of the Constitution:

1st AMENDMENT

Congress shall make no law respecting an establishment of religion, or prohibiting the free exercise thereof; or abridging the freedom of speech, or of the press; or the right of the people peaceably to assemble, and to petition the Government for a redress of grievances.

2nd AMENDMENT

A well regulated Militia, being necessary to the security of a free State, the right of the people to keep and bear Arms, shall not be infringed.

3rd AMENDMENT

No Soldier shall, in time of peace be quartered in any house, without the consent of the Owner, nor in time of war, but in a manner to be prescribed by law.

4th AMENDMENT

The right of the people to be secure in their persons, houses, papers, and effects, against unreasonable searches and seizures, shall not be violated, and no Warrants shall issue, but upon probable cause, supported by Oath or affirmation, and particularly describing the place to be searched, and the persons or things to be seized.

5th AMENDMENT

No person shall be held to answer for a capital, or otherwise infamous crime, unless on a presentment or indictment of a Grand Jury, except in cases arising in the land or naval forces, or in the Milita, when in actual service in time of War or public danger; nor shall any person be subject for the same offence to be twice put in jeopardy of life or limb; nor shall be compelled in any criminal case to be a witness against himself, nor be deprived of life, liberty, or property, without due process of law; nor shall private property be taken for public use, without just compensation.

6th AMENDMENT

In all criminal prosecutions, the accused shall enjoy the right to a speedy and public trial, by an impartial jury of the State and district wherein the crime shall have been committed, which district shall have been previously ascertained by law, and to be informed of the nature and cause of the accusation; to be confronted with the witnesses against him; to have compulsory process for obtaining witnesses in his favor, and to have the Assistance of Counsel for his defence.

7th AMENDMENT

In Suits at common law, where the value in controversy shall exceed twenty dollars, the right of trial by jury shall be preserved, and no fact tried by a jury, shall be otherwise re-examined in any Court of the United States, than according to the rules of the common law.

8th AMENDMENT

Excessive bail shall not be required, nor excessive fines imposed, nor cruel and unusual punishments inflicted.

9th AMENDMENT

The enumeration in the Constitution, of certain rights, shall not be construed to deny or disparage others retained by the people.

10th AMENDMENT

The powers not delegated to the United States by the Constitution, nor prohibited by it to the States, are reserved to the States respectively, or to the people.

11th AMENDMENT

The Judicial power of the United States shall not be construed to extend to any suit in law or equity, commenced or prosecuted against one of the United States by Citizens of another State, or by Citizens or Subjects of any Foreign State.

12th AMENDMENT

The Electors shall meet in their respective states, and vote by ballot for President and Vice-President, one of whom, at least, shall not be an inhabitant of the same state with themselves; they shall name in their ballots the person voted for as President, and in distinct ballots the person voted for as Vice-President, and they shall make distinct lists of all persons voted for as President, and of all persons voted for as Vice-President, and of the number of votes for each, which lists they shall sign and certify, and transmit sealed to the seat of the government of the United States, directed to the President of the Senate;—The President of the Senate shall, in the presence of the Senate and House of Representatives, open all the certificates and the votes shall then be counted;— The person having the greatest number of votes for President, shall be the President, if such number be a majority of the whole number of Electors appointed; and if no person have such majority, then from the persons having the highest numbers not exceeding three on the list of those voted for as President, the House of Representatives shall choose immediately, by ballot, the President. But in choosing the President, the votes shall be taken by states, the representation from each state having one vote; a quorum for this purpose shall consist of a member or members from two-thirds of the states, and a majority of all the states shall be necessary to a choice. [And if the House of Representatives shall not choose a President whenever the right of choice shall devolve upon them, before the fourth day of March next following, then the Vice-President shall act as President, as in the case of the death or other constitutional disability of the President.][12]—The person having the greatest number of votes as Vice-President, shall be the Vice-President, if such number be a majority of the whole number of Electors appointed, and if no person have a majority, then from the two highest numbers on the list, the Senate shall choose the Vice-President; a quorum for the purpose shall consist of two-thirds of the whole number of Senators, and a majority of the whole number shall be necessary to a choice. But no person constitutionally ineligible to the office of President shall be eligible to that of Vice-President of the United States.

13th AMENDMENT

Section 1. Neither slavery nor involuntary servitude, except as a punishment for crime whereof

[12]Superseded by Section 3 of the 20th Amendment.

the party shall have been duly convicted, shall exist within the United States, or any place subject to their jurisdiction.

Section 2. Congress shall have power to enforce this article by appropriate legislation.

14th AMENDMENT

Section 1. All persons born or naturalized in the United States, and subject to the jurisdiction thereof, are citizens of the United States and of the State wherein they reside. No State shall make or enforce any law which shall abridge the privileges or immunities of citizens of the United States; nor shall any State deprive any person of life, liberty, or property, without due process of law; nor deny to any person within its jurisdiction the equal protection of the laws.

Section 2. Representatives shall be apportioned among the several States according to their respective numbers, counting the whole number of persons in each State, excluding Indians not taxed. But when the right to vote at any election for the choice of electors for President and Vice President of the United States, Representatives in Congress, the Executive and Judicial officers of a State, or the members of the Legislature thereof, is denied to any of the male inhabitants of such State, [being twenty-one years of age,][13] and citizens of the United States, or in any way abridged, except for participation in rebellion, or other crime, the basis of representation therein shall be reduced in the proportion which the number of such male citizens shall bear to the whole number of [male citizens twenty-one years of age][14] in such State.

Section 3. No person shall be a Senator or Representative in Congress, or elector of President and Vice President, or hold any office, civil or military, under the United States, or under any State, who, having previously taken an oath, as a member of Congress, or as an officer of the United States, or as a member of any State legislature, or as an executive or judicial officer of any State, to support the Constitution of the United States, shall have engaged in insurrection or rebellion against the same, or given aid or comfort to the enemies thereof. But Congress may by a vote of two-thirds of each House, remove such disability.

Section 4. The validity of the public debt of the United States, authorized by law, including debts incurred for payment of pensions and bounties for services in suppressing insurrection or rebellion, shall not be questioned. But neither the

[13]Superseded by Section 1 of the 26th Amendment.
[14]Superseded by Section 1 of the 19th Amendment and Section 1 of the 26th Amendment.

United States nor any State shall assume or pay any debt or obligation incurred in aid of insurrection or rebellion against the United States, or any claim for the loss or emancipation of any slave; but all such debts, obligations and claims shall be held illegal and void.

Section 5. The Congress shall have power to enforce, by appropriate legislation, the provisions of this article.

15th AMENDMENT

Section 1. The right of citizens of the United States to vote shall not be denied or abridged by the United States or by any State on account of race, color, or previous condition of servitude.

Section 2. The Congress shall have power to enforce this article by appropriate legislation.

16th AMENDMENT

The Congress shall have power to lay and collect taxes on incomes, from whatever source derived, without apportionment among the several States, and without regard to any census or enumeration.

17th AMENDMENT

The Senate of the United States shall be composed of two Senators from each State, elected by the people thereof, for six years; and each Senator shall have one vote. The electors in each State shall have the qualifications requisite for electors of the most numerous branch of the State legislatures.

When vacancies happen in the representation of any State in the Senate, the executive authority of such State shall issue writs of election to fill such vacancies: *Provided,* That the legislature of any State may empower the executive thereof to make temporary appointments until the people fill the vacancies by election as the legislature may direct.

This amendment shall not be so construed as to affect the election or term of any Senator chosen before it becomes valid as part of the Constitution.

18th AMENDMENT[15]

Section 1. After one year from the ratification of this article the manufacture, sale, or transportation of intoxicating liquors within, the importation thereof into, or the exportation thereof from the United States and all territory subject to the jurisdiction thereof for beverage purposes is hereby prohibited.

Section 2. The Congress and the several States shall have concurrent power to enforce this article by appropiate legislation.

Section 3. This article shall be inoperative unless it shall have been ratified as an amendment

[15]Repealed by the 21st Amendment.

to the Constitution by the legislatures of the several States, as provided in the Constitution, within seven years from the date of the submission hereof to the States by the Congress.

19th AMENDMENT

The right of citizens of the United States to vote shall not be denied or abridged by the United States or by any State on account of sex.

Congress shall have power to enforce this article by appropriate legislation.

20th AMENDMENT

Section 1. The terms of the President and Vice President shall end at noon on the 20th day of January, and the terms of Senators and Representatives at noon on the 3d day of January, of the years in which such terms would have ended if this article had not been ratified; and the terms of their successors shall then begin.

Section 2. The Congress shall assemble at least once in every year, and such meeting shall begin at noon on the 3d day of January, unless they shall by law appoint a different day.

Section 3. If, at the time fixed for the beginning of the term of the President, the President elect shall have died, the Vice President elect shall become President. If a President shall not have been chosen before the time fixed for the beginning of his term, or if the President elect shall have failed to qualify, then the Vice President elect shall act as President until a President shall have qualified; and the Congress may by law provide for the case wherein neither a President elect nor a Vice President elect shall have qualified, declaring who shall then act as President, or the manner in which one who is to act shall be selected, and such person shall act accordingly until a President or Vice President shall have qualified.

Section 4. The Congress may by law provide for the case of the death of any of the persons from whom the House of Representatives may choose a President whenever the right of choice shall have devolved upon them, and for the case of the death of any of the persons, from whom the Senate may choose a Vice President whenever the right of choice shall have devolved upon them.

Section 5. Sections 1 and 2 shall take effect on the 15th day of October following the ratification of this article.

Section 6. This article shall be inoperative unless it shall have been ratified as an amendment to the Constitution by the legislatures of three-fourths of the several States within seven years from the date of its submission.

21st AMENDMENT

Section 1. The eighteenth article of amendment to the Constitution of the United States is hereby repealed.

Section 2. The transportation or importation into any State, Territory, or possession of the

United States for delivery or use therein of intoxicating liquors, in violation of the laws thereof, is hereby prohibited.

Section 3. This article shall be inoperative unless it shall have been ratified as an amendment to the Constitution by conventions in the several States, as provided in the Constitution, within seven years from the date of the submission hereof to the States by the Congress.

22nd AMENDMENT

Section 1. No person shall be elected to the office of the President more than twice, and no person who has held the office of President, or acted as President, for more than two years of a term to which some other person was elected President shall be elected to the office of the President more than once. But this Article shall not apply to any person holding the office of President when this Article was proposed by the Congress, and shall not prevent any person who may be holding the office of President, or acting as President, during the term within which this Article becomes operative from holding the office of President or acting as President during the remainder of such term.

Section 2. This article shall be inoperative unless it shall have been ratified as an amendment to the Constitution by the legislatures of three-fourths of the several States within seven years from the date of its submission to the States by the Congress.

23rd AMENDMENT

Section 1. The District constituting the seat of Government of the United States shall appoint in such manner as the Congress may direct:

A number of electors of President and Vice President equal to the whole number of Senators and Representatives in Congress to which the District would be entitled if it were a State, but in no event more than the least populous State; they shall be in addition to those appointed by the States, but they shall be considered, for the purposes of the election of President and Vice President, to be electors appointed by a State; and they shall meet in the District and perform such duties as provided by the twelfth article of amendment.

Section 2. The Congress shall have power to enforce this article by appropriate legislation.

24th AMENDMENT

Section 1. The right of citizens of the United States to vote in any primary or other election for President or Vice President, for electors for President or Vice President, or for Senator or Representative in Congress, shall not be denied or abridged by the United States or any State by reason of failure to pay any poll tax or other tax.

Section 2. The Congress shall have power to enforce this article by appropriate legislation.

25th AMENDMENT

Section 1. In case of removal of the President from office or of his death or resignation, the Vice President shall become President.

Section 2. Whenever there is a vacancy in the office of the Vice President, the President shall nominate a Vice President who shall take office upon confirmation by a majority vote of both Houses of Congress.

Section 3. Whenever the President transmits to the President pro tempore of the Senate and the Speaker of the House of Representatives his written declaration that he is unable to discharge the powers and duties of his office, and until he transmits to them a written declaration to the contrary, such powers and duties shall be discharged by the Vice President as Acting President.

Section 4. Whenever the Vice President and a majority of either the principal officers of the executive departments or of such other body as Congress may by law provide, transmit to the President pro tempore of the Senate and the Speaker of the House of Representatives their written declaration that the President is unable to discharge the powers and duties of his office, the Vice President shall immediately assume powers and duties of the office as Acting President.

Thereafter, when the President transmits to the President pro tempore of the Senate and the Speaker of the House of Representatives his written declaration that no inability exists, he shall resume the powers and duties of his office unless the Vice President and a majority of either the principal officers of the executive department or of such other body as Congress may by law provide, transmit within four days to the President pro tempore of the Senate and the Speaker of the House of Representatives their written declaration that the President is unable to discharge the powers and duties of his office. Thereupon Congress shall decide the issue, assembling within forty-eight hours for that purpose if not in session. If the Congress, within twenty-one days after receipt of the latter written declaration, or, if Congress is not in session, within twenty-one days after Congress is required to assemble, determines by two-thirds vote of both Houses that the President is unable to discharge the powers and duties of his office, the Vice President shall continue to discharge the same as Acting President; otherwise, the President shall resume the powers and duties of his office.

26th AMENDMENT

Section 1. The right of citizens of the United States, who are eighteen years of age or older, to vote shall not be denied or abridged by the United States or by any State on account of age.

Section 2. The Congress shall have power to enforce this article by appropriate legislation.

CHRONOLOGICAL KEY

TO

CONSTITUTIONAL AMENDMENTS

ADMINISTRATIONS

	Page
1st (1789–1793), Washington	15–19
2nd (1793–1797), Washington	19–24
3rd (1797–1801), J. Adams	32–36
4th (1801–1805), Jefferson	45–47
5th (1805–1809), Jefferson	48–49
6th (1809–1813), Madison	58–60
7th (1813–1817), Madison	61–63
8th (1817–1821), Monroe	71–73
9th (1821–1825), Monroe	74–75
10th (1825–1829), J. Q. Adams	83–85
11th (1829–1833), Jackson	96–99
12th (1833–1837), Jackson	100–103
13th (1837–1841), Van Buren	108–110
14th (1841–1845), W. H. Harrison/Tyler	119/125–128
15th (1845–1849), Polk	135–138

AMENDMENTS

	Page
1st–10th,	18
11th,	21
12th,	47

CONGRESSES

	Page
1st (1789–1791),	14–17
2nd (1791–1793),	18–19
3rd (1793–1795),	20–22
4th (1795–1797),	22–24
5th (1797–1799),	32–34
6th (1799–1801),	34–36
7th (1801–1803),	46–47
8th (1803–1805),	47–48
9th (1805–1807),	48–49
10th (1807–1809),	49
11th (1809–1811),	58–59
12th (1811–1813),	59–60
13th (1813–1815),	61–62
14th (1815–1817),	62–63
15th (1817–1819),	71–72
16th (1819–1821),	72–73
17th (1821–1823),	74
18th (1823–1825),	74–75
19th (1825–1827),	84
20th (1827–1829),	84–85
21st (1829–1831),	96–97
22nd (1831–1833),	98–99
23rd (1833–1835),	100–101
24th (1835–1837),	101–102
25th (1837–1839),	109
26th (1839–1841),	110
27th (1841–1843),	125–126
28th (1843–1845),	127–128
29th (1845–1847),	135–137
30th (1847–1849),	137–138

ADMINISTRATIONS		AMENDMENTS		CONGRESSES	
Page		Page		Page	
38th (1937–1941), 407–420 F. D. Roosevelt				75th (1937–1939), 406–411 76th (1939–1941), 412–420	
39th (1941–1945), 421–442 F. D. Roosevelt				77th (1941–1943), 420–430 78th (1943–1945), 430–441	
40th (1945–1949), 442–444/451–469 F. D. Roosevelt/Truman				79th (1945–1947), 441–458 80th (1947–1949), 460–469	
41st (1949–1953), 470–482 Truman		22nd,	477	81st (1949–1951), 469–477 82nd (1951–1953), 477–481	
42nd (1953–1957), 492–501 Eisenhower				83rd (1953–1955), 481–496 84th (1955–1957), 497–500	
43rd (1957–1961), 502–517 Eisenhower				85th (1957–1959), 501–506 86th (1959–1961), 507–515	
44th (1961–1965), 524–537/542–548 Kennedy/L. B. Johnson		23rd, 24th,	526 544	87th (1961–1963), 516–532 88th (1963–1965), 533–537, 542–547	
45th (1965–1969), 549–577 L. B. Johnson		25th,	560	89th (1965–1967), 548–558 90th (1967–1969), 559–575	
46th (1969–1973), 589–633				91st (1969–1971), 576–577, 589–613	
Nixon		26th,	623	92nd (1971–1973), 614–	

MAJOR ACTS AND TREATIES

NOTE: act (with small a)—common or subject title
Act (with capital A)—formal title
treaty (with small t)—common or subject title
Treaty (with capital T)—formal title

PRE-PRESIDENTIAL

GEORGE WASHINGTON

JOHN ADAMS

THOMAS JEFFERSON

JAMES MADISON

JAMES MONROE

JOHN QUINCY ADAMS

ANDREW JACKSON

MARTIN VAN BUREN

HARRY S. TRUMAN

DWIGHT DAVID EISENHOWER

JOHN FITZGERALD KENNEDY

LYNDON BAINES JOHNSON

RICHARD MILHOUS NIXON

STATISTICAL SUMMARY

ADMINISTRATIONS

CABINETS:

Made most appointments [2]: Grant and F. D. Roosevelt (25)

Had appointments rejected by Senate [5] (8): Jackson (Taney); Tyler (Caleb Cushing, Henshaw, Porter, Green); A. Johnson (Stanbery); Coolidge (Warren); Eisenhower (Strauss)

Made no changes during administration [4]: W. H. Harrison; Taylor, Pierce, Garfield

Retained cabinet full term (4 years): Pierce

Members of cabinets:

First female: Secretary of Labor Frances Perkins (F. D. Roosevelt)

First Jew: Secretary of Commerce and Labor Oscar S. Straus (T. Roosevelt)

First Negro: Secretary of Housing and Urban Development Robert C. Weaver (L. B. Johnson)

Relatives of presidents (3) [3]:
    Brother: Attorney General Robert F. Kennedy (Kennedy)
    Sons (2): Secretary of War Robert T. Lincoln (Garfield); Secretary of Interior James R. Garfield (T. Roosevelt)

Same surname: Secretary of State John Watson Foster and Secretary of Treasury Charles Foster (B. Harrison)

Served in three cabinets (9): Crittenden (Attorney General: W. H. Harrison, Tyler, Fillmore); McCulloch (Secretary of Treasury: Lincoln, A. Johnson, Arthur); Blaine (Secretary of State: Garfield, Arthur, B. Harrison); Windom (Secretary of Treasury: Garfield, Arthur, B. Harrison); Knox (Secretary of State: Taft; Attorney General: McKinley, T. Roosevelt); James Wilson (Secretary of Agriculture: McKinley, T. Roosevelt, Taft); Mellon (Secretary of Treasury: Harding, Coolidge, Hoover); Davis (Secretary of Labor: Harding, Coolidge, Hoover); Stimson (Secretary of State: Hoover; Secretary of War: Taft, F. D. Roosevelt)

Served in three executive departments: Cortelyou (Secretary of Treasury, Postmaster General, Secretary of Commerce and Labor: T. Roosevelt)

Presidents who served in cabinets [8]: Jefferson, Madison, Monroe, J. Q. Adams, Van Buren, Buchanan, Taft, Hoover

President who served in two cabinets: Hoover (Secretary of Commerce: Harding, Coolidge)

President who served in two cabinet positions: Monroe (Secretary of State and Secretary of War: Madison)

Cabinet positions held by presidents:
    Secretary of State [6]: Jefferson (Washington); Madison (Jefferson); Monroe (Madison); J. Q. Adams (Monroe); Van Buren (Jackson); Buchanan (Polk)

Secretary of War [2]: Monroe (Madison); Taft (T. Roosevelt)
Secretary of Commerce: Hoover (Harding, Coolidge)
Presidents who were members of sub-cabinets [2]: T. Roosevelt (Assistant Secretary of Navy: McKinley); F. D. Roosevelt (Assistant Secretary of Navy: Wilson)

COMPOSITION OF CONGRESS:

When president took office:

Did not have majority in Senate [3]: Taylor, Cleveland (first term), Nixon
Did not have majority in House of Representatives [3]: Taylor, Hayes, Nixon
Did not have majority in Senate and House [2]: Taylor, Nixon

At start of second term:

Did not have majority in Senate and House: Eisenhower

SUPREME COURT

Did not appoint members of Court [3]: W. H. Harrison, Taylor, A. Johnson

Chief justices:

Appointed chief justices [14]: Washington, J. Adams, Jackson, Lincoln, Grant, Cleveland (first term), Taft, Harding, Hoover, F. D. Roosevelt, Truman, Eisenhower, L. B. Johnson, Nixon
Appointed more than one chief justice [3]: Washington, J. Adams, Grant
Appointed more than one who served: Washington
Made most appointments: Washington (4)
Appointed chief justices who were confirmed by Senate but declined to serve [2] (2): Washington (William Cushing); J. Adams (Jay)
Made appointments not confirmed by Senate [3] (4): Washington (Rutledge); Grant (Williams, Caleb Cushing); L. B. Johnson (Fortas)
  Appointed two chief justices not confirmed by Senate: Grant
Appointed chief justices who had served as associate justices [3] (4): Washington (Rutledge, William Cushing); Taft (White); F. D. Roosevelt (Stone)
Appointed former president as chief justice: Harding (Taft)
President who served as chief justice: Taft

Associate justices:

Made most appointments: Washington (9)
Appointed most who served [2]: Washington and F. D. Roosevelt (8)
Appointed associate justices who were confirmed by Senate but declined to serve [4] (5): Washington (Harrison); Madison (Lincoln, J. Q. Adams); Jackson (Smith); Arthur (Conkling)
  Appointed more than one who declined to serve: Madison
Made appointments not confirmed by Senate [14] (21): Madison (Wolcott); J. Q. Adams (Crittenden); Jackson (Taney); Tyler (Spencer, Walworth, King, Read); Polk (Woodward); Fillmore (Bradford, Badger, Micou); Buchanan (Black); A. Johnson (Stanbery); Grant (Hoar); Hayes (Matthews); Cleveland (second term) (Hornblower, Peckham); Hoover (Parker); L. B. Johnson (Thornberry); Nixon (Haynsworth, Carswell)
  Appointed most not confirmed by Senate: Tyler (4)

POLITICAL PARTY AFFILIATION:

Presidents:

Democratic [12]: Jackson, Van Buren, Polk, Pierce, Buchanan, A. Johnson, Cleveland, Wilson, F. D. Roosevelt, Truman, Kennedy, L. B. Johnson
  First Democrat elected following Civil War: Cleveland
Democratic-Republican [4]: Jefferson, Madison, Monroe, J. Q. Adams
Federalist [2]: Washington, J. Adams
Republican [14]: Lincoln, Grant, Hayes, Garfield, Arthur, B. Harrison, McKinley, T. Roosevelt, Taft, Harding, Coolidge, Hoover, Eisenhower, Nixon
  First Republican reelected in 20th century: Eisenhower
Whig [4]: W. H. Harrison, Tyler, Taylor, Fillmore

Vice presidents:

Democratic (16) [12]: Calhoun (Jackson); Van Buren (Jackson); R. M. Johnson (Van Buren); Dallas (Polk); King (Pierce); Breckinridge (Buchanan); A. Johnson (Lincoln); Hendricks (Cleveland); Stevenson (Cleveland); Marshall (Wilson); Garner (F. D. Roosevelt); Wallace (F. D. Roosevelt); Truman (F. D. Roosevelt); Barkley (Truman); L. B. Johnson (Kennedy); Humphrey (L. B. Johnson)
Democratic-Republican (6) [5]: Jefferson (J. Adams); Burr (Jefferson); Clinton (Jefferson); Gerry (Madison); Tompkins (Monroe); Calhoun (J. Q. Adams)
Democratic-Republican and Democratic: Calhoun (J. Q. Adams, Jackson)
Federalist: J. Adams (Washington)
Republican (15) [13]: Hamlin (Lincoln); Colfax (Grant); H. Wilson (Grant); Wheeler (Hayes); Arthur (Garfield); Morton (B. Harrison); Hobart (McKinley); T. Roosevelt (McKinley); Fairbanks (T. Roosevelt); Sherman (Taft); Coolidge (Harding); Dawes (Coolidge); Curtis (Hoover); Nixon (Eisenhower); Agnew (Nixon)
Whig (2) [2]: Tyler (W. H. Harrison); Fillmore (Taylor)

PRESIDENT-VICE PRESIDENT TEAMS (41):

Democratic (15): Jackson-Calhoun, Jackson-Van Buren, Van Buren-R. M. Johnson, Polk-Dallas, Pierce-King, Buchanan-Breckinridge, Cleveland-Hendricks, Cleveland-Stevenson, Wilson-Marshall, F. D. Roosevelt-Garner, F. D. Roosevelt-Wallace, F. D. Roosevelt-Truman, Truman-Barkley, Kennedy-L. B. Johnson, L. B. Johnson-Humphrey
Democratic-Republican (6): Jefferson-Burr, Jefferson-Clinton, Madison-Clinton, Madison-Gerry, Monroe-Tompkins, J. Q. Adams-Calhoun
Federalist: Washington-J. Adams
Federalist and Democratic-Republican: J. Adams-Jefferson
Republican (16): Lincoln-Hamlin, Lincoln-A. Johnson, Grant-Colfax, Grant-H. Wilson, Hayes-Wheeler, Garfield-Arthur, B. Harrison-Morton, McKinley-Hobart, McKinley-T. Roosevelt, T. Roosevelt-Fairbanks, Taft-Sherman, Harding-Coolidge, Coolidge-Dawes, Hoover-Curtis, Eisenhower-Nixon, Nixon-Agnew
Whig (2): W. H. Harrison-Tyler, Taylor-Fillmore
Teams reelected (5):
  Democratic (2): Wilson-Marshall, F. D. Roosevelt-Garner
  Democratic-Republican: Monroe-Tompkins
  Federalist: Washington-J. Adams
  Republican: Eisenhower-Nixon
Teams defeated when ran for reelection (2): Van Buren-R. M. Johnson, Hoover-Curtis
President who had different party affiliation than vice president: J. Adams
President who had three vice presidents: F. D. Roosevelt (Garner, Wallace, Truman)
Presidents who had two vice presidents [7]: Jefferson (Burr, Clinton); Madison (Clinton, Gerry); Jackson (Calhoun, Van Buren); Lincoln (Hamlin, A. Johnson); Grant (Colfax, H. Wilson); Cleveland (Hendricks, Stevenson); McKinley (Hobart, T. Roosevelt)
Presidents who did not have vice presidents [4]: Tyler, Fillmore, A. Johnson, Arthur
President whose two vice presidents died in office: Madison (Clinton, Gerry)
Vice president chosen by Senate: R. M. Johnson (Van Buren)
Vice president who resigned: Calhoun (Jackson)

ASSASSINATIONS

Presidents assassinated [4]: Lincoln, Garfield, McKinley, Kennedy
Attempted assassinations:
  Of presidents [2]: Jackson, Truman
  Of president-elect: F. D. Roosevelt
  Of former president: T. Roosevelt

AUTHORS

Wrote books [21]: Washington, J. Adams, Jefferson, Madison, Monroe, J. Q. Adams, Buchanan, B. Harrison, Cleveland, McKinley, T. Roosevelt; Taft, Wilson, Coolidge, Hoover, F. D. Roosevelt, Truman, Eisenhower, Kennedy, L. B. Johnson, Nixon
Poet: J. Q. Adams

BIRTH DATES

See VITAL STATISTICS; FIRST LADIES; WIVES OF PRESIDENTS

BIRTH PLACES

See VITAL STATISTICS; FIRST LADIES; WIVES OF PRESIDENTS

BURIAL SITES

See VITAL STATISTICS; FIRST LADIES; WIVES OF PRESIDENTS

CABINETS

See ADMINISTRATIONS

CAPITAL CITIES NAMED FOR PRESIDENTS

State capitals (4): Jackson, Miss.; Jefferson City, Mo.; Madison, Wis.; Lincoln, Neb.
Foreign capital: Monrovia, Liberia

CHILDREN

See FAMILY RELATIONSHIPS

COMMANDER-IN-CHIEF OF ARMY

See MILITARY SERVICE; FORMER PRESIDENTS

CONFEDERACY

President who served in Provisional Congress of Confederation: Tyler
President who was elected to Congress of Confederation: Tyler
Vice president who served as secretary of war: John Cabell Breckinridge
Associate justice of Supreme Court who served as assistant secretary of war: John Archibald Campbell
Cabinet member who served as general: Secretary of War John Buchanan Floyd

Son of president who served as general: Richard Taylor

CONGRESS

See ADMINISTRATIONS, COMPOSITION OF CONGRESS; POLITICAL EXPERIENCE PRIOR TO OFFICE; FORMER PRESIDENTS; FORMER VICE PRESIDENTS

CONSTITUTION

Signers [2]: Washington, Madison

CONTINENTAL CONGRESS

Members [5]: Washington, J. Adams, Jefferson, Madison, Monroe

CONVENTIONS

First political convention: Anti-Masonic (Baltimore, 1831)

Political parties that held conventions:

Anti-Masonic (2): Baltimore (1831); Harrisburg (1835)
Constitutional Union: Baltimore (1860)
Democratic (35): Baltimore (1832, 1836, 1840, 1844, 1848, 1852); Cincinnati (1856); Baltimore (1860); Chicago (1864); New York City (1868); Baltimore (1872); St. Louis (1876); Cincinnati (1880); Chicago (1884); St. Louis (1888); Chicago (1892, 1896); Kansas City (1900); St. Louis (1904); Denver (1908); Baltimore (1912); St. Louis (1916); San Francisco (1920); New York City (1924); Houston (1928); Chicago (1932); Philadelphia (1936); Chicago (1940, 1944); Philadelphia (1948); Chicago (1952, 1956); Los Angeles (1960); Atlantic City (1964); Chicago (1968)
Free-Soil: Buffalo (1848)
Greenback: Indianapolis (1876)
Liberty: Buffalo (1843)
National Republican: Baltimore (1831)
National Union: *See* Republican (1864)
Peoples (Populist): Omaha (1892)
Progressive: Philadelphia (1948)

Progressive (Bull Moose): Chicago (1912)
Prohibition: Columbus (1872)
Republican (29): Philadelphia (1856); Chicago (1860); Baltimore (1864); Chicago (1868); Philadelphia (1872); Cincinnati (1876); Chicago (1880, 1884, 1888); Minneapolis (1892); St. Louis (1896); Philadelphia (1900); Chicago (1904, 1908, 1912, 1916, 1920); Cleveland (1924); Kansas City (1928); Chicago (1932); Cleveland (1936); Philadelphia (1940); Chicago (1944); Philadelphia (1948); Chicago (1952); San Francisco (1956); Chicago (1960); San Francisco (1964); Miami Beach (1968)
Whig (5): Harrisburg (1839); Baltimore (1844); Philadelphia (1848); Baltimore (1852, 1856)

Convention sites:

Atlantic City: Democratic, 1964
Baltimore (17):
   Anti-Masonic: 1831
   Democratic (9): 1832, 1836, 1840, 1844, 1848, 1852, 1860, 1872, 1912
   Democratic (Southern): 1860
   Constitutional Union: 1860
   National Republican: 1831
   Republican (National Union): 1864
   Whig (3): 1844, 1852, 1856
Buffalo (2):
   Liberty: 1843
   Free-Soil: 1848
Charleston, S. Carolina: Democratic, 1860 (adjourned without agreement)
Chicago (25):
   Democratic (10): 1864, 1884, 1892, 1896, 1932, 1940, 1944, 1952, 1956, 1968
   Progressive (Bull Moose): 1912
   Republican (14): 1860, 1868, 1880, 1884, 1888, 1904, 1908, 1912, 1916, 1920, 1932, 1944, 1952, 1960
Cincinnati (3):
   Democratic (2): 1856, 1880
   Republican: 1876
Cleveland (2): Republican, 1924, 1936
Denver: Democratic, 1908
Harrisburg, Pa. (2):
   Anti-Masonic: 1835
   Whig: 1839
Houston: Democratic, 1928
Kansas City, Mo. (2):
   Democratic: 1900
   Republican: 1928

Los Angeles: Democratic, 1960
Miami Beach: Republican, 1968
Minneapolis: Republican, 1892
New York City (2): Democratic, 1868, 1924
Omaha: Peoples (Populist), 1892
Philadelphia (10):
   American (Know Nothing): 1856
   Democratic (2): 1936, 1948
   Progressive: 1948
   Republican (5): 1856, 1872, 1900, 1940, 1948
   Whig: 1848
St. Louis, Mo. (5):
   Democratic (4): 1876, 1888, 1904, 1916
   Republican: 1896
San Francisco (3):
   Democratic: 1920
   Republican (2): 1956, 1964

DEATH

See **ASSASSINATIONS; FIRST LADIES; VITAL STATISTICS; WIVES OF PRESIDENTS**

DECLARATION OF INDEPENDENCE

Signers [2]: J. Adams, Jefferson

DEPRESSIONS (9)

Dates and presidents in office: 1819 (Monroe); 1837 (Van Buren); 1857 (Buchanan); 1873 (Grant); 1883 (Arthur); 1893 (Cleveland); 1907 (T. Roosevelt); 1920 (Wilson); 1929 (Hoover)

EDUCATION

PRESIDENTS:

College:

Attended college [27]: J. Adams, Jefferson, Madison, Monroe, J. Q. Adams, W. H. Harrison, Tyler, Polk, Pierce, Buchanan, Grant, Hayes, Garfield, Arthur, B. Harrison, McKinley, T. Roosevelt, Taft, Wilson, Harding, Coolidge, Hoover, F. D. Roosevelt, Eisenhower, Kennedy, L. B. Johnson, Nixon

Graduated [21]: J. Adams, Madison, J. Q. Adams, Polk, Pierce, Buchanan, Grant, Hayes, Garfield, Arthur, B. Harrison, T. Roosevelt, Taft, Wilson, Coolidge, Hoover, F. D. Roosevelt, Eisenhower, Kennedy, L. B. Johnson, Nixon

Attended but were not graduated [6]: Jefferson, Monroe, W. H. Harrison, Tyler, McKinley, Harding

Did not attend college [9]: Washington, Jackson, Van Buren, Taylor, Fillmore, Lincoln, A. Johnson, Cleveland, Truman

> *Only president in 20th century who did not attend:* Truman

Colleges attended:
> *Allegheny:* McKinley
> *Amherst:* Coolidge
> *Bowdoin:* Pierce
> *Dickinson:* Buchanan
> *Hampden-Sydney:* W. H. Harrison
> *Harvard* [5]: J. Adams, J. Q. Adams, T. Roosevelt, F. D. Roosevelt, Kennedy
> *Johns Hopkins:* Wilson
> *Kenyon:* Hayes
> *Miami (Ohio):* B. Harrison
> *New Jersey: See* Princeton
> *North Carolina:* Polk
> *Ohio Central:* Harding
> *Princeton* [3]: Madison, Wilson, Kennedy
> *Southwest Texas State Teachers:* L. B. Johnson
> *Stanford:* Hoover
> *Union:* Arthur
> *U. S. Military Academy (West Point)* [2]: Grant, Eisenhower
> *Whittier:* Nixon
> *William and Mary* [3]: Jefferson, Monroe, Tyler
> *Williams:* Garfield
> *Yale:* Taft

Graduate Studies:

Attended law school [9]: Hayes, McKinley, T. Roosevelt, Taft, Wilson, F. D. Roosevelt, Truman, L. B. Johnson, Nixon

Graduated from law school [3]: Hayes, Taft, Nixon

Attended but were not graduated [6]: McKinley, T. Roosevelt, Wilson, F. D. Roosevelt, Truman, L. B. Johnson

Law schools attended:
> *Albany:* McKinley
> *Cincinnati:* Taft

> *Columbia* [2]: T. Roosevelt, F. D. Roosevelt
> *Duke:* Nixon
> *Georgetown:* L. B. Johnson
> *Harvard:* Hayes
> *Kansas City:* Truman
> *Virginia:* Wilson

Received Ph.D: Wilson

Studied law [26]: J. Adams, Jefferson, Monroe, J. Q. Adams, Jackson, Van Buren, Tyler, Polk, Fillmore, Pierce, Buchanan, Lincoln, Hayes, Garfield, Arthur, Cleveland, B. Harrison, McKinley, T. Roosevelt, Taft, Wilson, Coolidge, F. D. Roosevelt, Truman, L. B. Johnson, Nixon

Studied medicine: W. H. Harrison

Phi Beta Kappa:

Elected to Phi Beta Kappa [11]: J. Q. Adams, Pierce, Van Buren, Arthur, Garfield, Hayes, T. Roosevelt, Wilson, Cleveland, Coolidge, F. D. Roosevelt

Elected as undergraduates [3]: J. Q. Adams, Arthur, T. Roosevelt

Alumni members [5]: Pierce, Garfield, Hayes, Coolidge, F. D. Roosevelt

Honorary members [3]: Van Buren, Wilson, Cleveland

Elected while in office: Hayes

VICE PRESIDENTS:

See **VICE PRESIDENTS**

ELECTIONS

Elected unanimously: Washington

Received electoral votes of all states [2]: Washington, Monroe

Received majority of popular vote in three elections: F. D. Roosevelt

Received majority of popular vote in four elections: F. D. Roosevelt

Elected without receiving majority of popular vote [15]: J. Q. Adams, Polk, Taylor, Buchanan, Lincoln, Hayes, Garfield, Cleveland, B. Harrison, Cleveland, Wilson (two terms), Truman, Kennedy, Nixon

Elected twice without receiving majority of popular vote [2]: Cleveland, Wilson

Received plurality of popular vote in three elections [2]: Cleveland, F. D. Roosevelt

Defeated in electoral college while receiving plurality of popular vote [3]: Jackson, Tilden, Cleveland

Elections decided by House of Representatives [2]: Jefferson, J. Q. Adams

Election decided by Electoral Commission: Hayes

Reelected unanimously: Washington

Defeated when sought reelection [7]: J. Adams, J. Q. Adams, Van Buren, Cleveland, B. Harrison, Taft, Hoover

Sought but were denied renomination [5]: Tyler, Fillmore, Pierce, A. Johnson, Arthur

First president to announce his own election: Adams

First tabulation of popular vote: 1824 (J. Q. Adams-Jackson)

First election held on same day in all states: 1848 (Taylor)

First time electoral votes cast under provisions of 12th Amendment: 1804 (Jefferson)

FAMILY RELATIONSHIPS

FAMILY POSITION:

Eldest child [8]: J. Adams, Madison, Polk, Grant, Harding, Coolidge, Truman, L. B. Johnson

Second child [10]: Monroe, J. Q. Adams, Fillmore, Buchanan, Lincoln, A. Johnson, T. Roosevelt, Hoover, Kennedy, Nixon

Third Child [5]: Jefferson, Jackson, Taylor, Wilson, Eisenhower

Fifth child [4]: Hayes, Garfield, Arthur, Cleveland

Sixth child: Tyler

Seventh child [2]: W. H. Harrison, McKinley

Father's second child: F. D. Roosevelt

Father's third child: Van Buren

Father's fifth child [2]: Washington, B. Harrison

Father's seventh child [2]: Pierce, Taft

Mother's only child: F. D. Roosevelt

Mother's eldest child: Washington

Mother's second child [2]: B. Harrison, Taft

Mother's sixth child [2]: Van Buren, Pierce

Member of family of two children [3]: A. Johnson, Coolidge, F. D. Roosevelt

Member of family of three children [5]: J. Adams, Jackson, Lincoln, Hoover, Truman

Member of family of four children [2]: T. Roosevelt, Wilson

Member of family of five children [7]: Monroe, J. Q. Adams, Van Buren, Hayes, Garfield, L. B. Johnson, Nixon

Member of family of six children: Grant

Member of family of seven children [2]: W. H. Harrison, Eisenhower

Member of family of eight children [2]: Tyler, Harding

Member of family of nine children [7]: Taylor, Fillmore, Pierce, Arthur, Cleveland, McKinley, Kennedy

Member of family of ten children [5]: Washington, Jefferson, Madison, Polk, Taft

Member of family of 11 children: Buchanan

Member of family of 13 children: B. Harrison

Orphans [2]: Jackson, Hoover

LINEAGE:

Dutch: Van Buren

Dutch, French-Dutch: F. D. Roosevelt

Dutch, Scottish-Irish and French Huguenot: T. Roosevelt

English [12]: Washington, J. Adams, Madison, J. Q. Adams, W. H. Harrison, Tyler, Taylor, Fillmore, Pierce, Lincoln, Taft, Coolidge

English-French Huguenot: Garfield

English-Irish-French: Cleveland

English-Scottish [2]: Grant, B. Harrison

English-Scottish-Irish [3]: A. Johnson, Arthur, Truman

English-Scottish-Irish, English-Scottish-German: McKinley

English-Scottish-Irish, English-Scottish-Irish-Welsh: Nixon

English-unknown: L. B. Johnson

Irish: Kennedy

Scottish: Hayes

Scottish-Irish [4]: Jackson, Polk, Buchanan, Wilson

Scottish-Irish, English-Dutch: Harding

Scottish-Welsh: Monroe

Swiss-German [2]: Hoover, Eisenhower

Welsh-Scottish-Irish: Jefferson

PARENTS OF PRESIDENTS:

Born abroad (8) [7]:
   Mothers (4): Jefferson, Jackson, Wilson, Hoover
   Fathers (4): Jackson, Buchanan, A. Johnson, Arthur

Presidents who had stepparents [5]: Fillmore, Lincoln, A. Johnson, Harding, Coolidge
> Stepmothers [4]: Fillmore, Lincoln, Harding, Coolidge
> Stepfather: A. Johnson

President who had stepbrother and stepsisters: Lincoln

Mothers of presidents:

Were second wives (5): Washington, Pierce, B. Harrison, Taft, F. D. Roosevelt
Lived to inauguration or oath-taking day (10): Washington, J. Adams, Madison, Polk, Grant, Garfield, McKinley, F. D. Roosevelt, Truman, Kennedy
Attended inauguration (4): Garfield, McKinley, F. D. Roosevelt, Kennedy
Survived sons (3): Polk, Garfield, Kennedy
Died same day as son's wife: T. Roosevelt
Died on her birthday: Coolidge

Fathers of presidents:

Born on Feb. 29: Jefferson
Lived to inauguration or oath-taking day (6): J. Q. Adams, Fillmore, Grant, Harding, Coolidge, Kennedy
Attended inauguration: Kennedy
Administered oath of office to son: Coolidge
Married three times: Harding
Remarried during son's term of office: Harding
Signed Declaration of Independence (2): J. Q. Adams, W. H. Harrison
Positions or occupations:
> Cabinet member: Taft
> Clergymen (3): Arthur, Cleveland, Wilson
> Collector of Port of New York: T. Roosevelt
> Doctor: Harding
> Governors (3): W. H. Harrison, Tyler, Pierce
> Ministers plenipotentiary or ambassadors (3): J. Q. Adams, Taft, Kennedy
Survived sons (2): Harding, Kennedy

SIBLINGS:

Had twin siblings: Jefferson
Had male siblings only [5]: J. Adams, Jackson, F. D. Roosevelt, Eisenhower, Nixon

Had half brothers and half sisters [6]: Washington, Van Buren, Pierce, B. Harrison, Taft, F. D. Roosevelt

RELATIONSHIPS TO OTHER PRESIDENTS:

Father was president: J. Q. Adams
Grandfather was president: B. Harrison
Son was president: J. Adams
Grandson was president: W. H. Harrison
Second cousins: Madison, Taylor
Fifth cousins: T. Roosevelt, F. D. Roosevelt

MARRIAGE:

Bachelor: Buchanan
Bachelor at inauguration [2]: Buchanan, Cleveland

Age of presidents at marriage:

Youngest: A. Johnson
Teens: A. Johnson
Twenties [27]: Washington, J. Adams, Jefferson, Monroe, Jackson, Van Buren, W. H. Harrison, Tyler, Polk, Taylor, Fillmore, Pierce, Grant, Garfield, Arthur, B. Harrison, McKinley, T. Roosevelt, T. Roosevelt (second marriage), Taft, Wilson, Harding, Hoover, F. D. Roosevelt, Eisenhower, L. B. Johnson, Nixon
Thirties [6]: J. Q. Adams, Lincoln, Hayes, Coolidge, Truman, Kennedy
Forties [2]: Madison, Cleveland
Fifties [3]: Tyler (second marriage), Fillmore (second marriage), Wilson (second marriage)
Sixties: B. Harrison (second marriage)
Oldest: B. Harrison
Oldest at first marriage: Cleveland

Marital data:

Shortest marriage: T. Roosevelt
Longest marriage: J. Adams
Celebrated 25th anniversary (in office) [5]: Polk, Fillmore, Grant, Hayes, Taft
Celebrated 50th anniversary [4]: J. Adams, J. Q. Adams, Eisenhower, Truman
Married in office [3]: Tyler (second marriage), Cleveland, Wilson (second marriage)
Married on birthday [2]: Tyler, T. Roosevelt
Married on New Year's Day [2]: Jefferson, Polk

Married fifth cousin once removed: F. D. Roosevelt

Married widows [6]: Washington, Jefferson, Madison, Fillmore (second marriage), B. Harrison (second marriage), Wilson (second marriage)

Married divorcees [2]: Jackson, Harding

Married daughters of clergymen [5]: J. Adams, Fillmore, Pierce, B. Harrison, Wilson

Married daughters of judges [2]: W. H. Harrison, Wilson

Married daughters of attorneys [4]: Jefferson, Cleveland, Taft, Wilson

Married daughter of U.S. Senator: Tyler

Married daughter of diplomat: J. Q. Adams

Remarried [5]: Tyler, Fillmore, B. Harrison, T. Roosevelt, Wilson

  Before term: T. Roosevelt
  During term [2]: Tyler, Wilson
  After term [2]: Fillmore, B. Harrison

Place of marriage:

Abroad (London, England) [2]: J. Q. Adams, T. Roosevelt (second marriage)

California [2]: Hoover, Nixon

Colorado: Eisenhower

Georgia: Wilson

Illinois: Lincoln

Kentucky: Taylor

Massachusetts [2]: J. Adams, T. Roosevelt

Mississippi: Jackson (first ceremony)

Missouri [2]: Grant, Truman

New Hampshire: Pierce

New York [7]: Monroe, Van Buren, Tyler, Fillmore (twice), Arthur, B. Harrison, F. D. Roosevelt

  New York City [5]: Monroe, Tyler (second marriage), Arthur, B. Harrison (second marriage), F. D. Roosevelt

Ohio [7]: W. H. Harrison, Hayes, Garfield, B. Harrison, McKinley, Taft, Harding

  Cincinnati [2]: Hayes, Taft

Rhode Island: Kennedy

Tennessee [3]: Jackson (second ceremony), Polk, A. Johnson

Texas: L. B. Johnson

Vermont: Coolidge

Virginia [4]: Washington, Jefferson, Madison, Tyler

Washington, D. C. [2]: Cleveland, Wilson (second marriage)

  White House: Cleveland

CHILDREN:

Had children [30]: J. Adams, Jefferson, Monroe, J. Q. Adams, Van Buren, W. H. Harrison, Tyler, Taylor, Fillmore, Pierce, Lincoln, A. Johnson, Grant, Hayes, Garfield, Arthur, Cleveland, B. Harrison, McKinley, T. Roosevelt, Taft, Wilson, Coolidge, Hoover, F. D. Roosevelt, Truman, Eisenhower, Kennedy, L. B. Johnson, Nixon

Had male and female children [19]: J. Adams, Jefferson, Monroe, J. Q. Adams, W. H. Harrison, Tyler, Taylor, Fillmore, A. Johnson, Grant, Hayes, Garfield, Arthur, Cleveland, B. Harrison, T. Roosevelt, Taft, F. D. Roosevelt, Kennedy

Had male children only [6]: Van Buren, Pierce, Lincoln, Coolidge, Hoover, Eisenhower

Had female children only [5]: McKinley, Wilson, Truman, L. B. Johnson, Nixon

Had one child: Truman

Had two children [7]: Fillmore, McKinley, Coolidge, Hoover, Eisenhower, L. B. Johnson, Nixon

Had three children [7]: Monroe, Pierce, Arthur, B. Harrison, Taft, Wilson, Kennedy

Had four children [4]: J. Q. Adams, Van Buren, Lincoln, Grant

Had five children [3]: J. Adams, A. Johnson, Cleveland

Had six children [4]: Jefferson, Taylor, T. Roosevelt, F. D. Roosevelt

Had seven children: Garfield

Had eight children: Hayes

Had ten children: W. H. Harrison

Had 15 children: Tyler

Had most children before inauguration: W. H. Harrison (10)

Children born abroad [3]: J. Q. Adams, Hoover, F. D. Roosevelt

Child born on July 4: J. Q. Adams

Children born while father in office [2] (3): Cleveland (2), Kennedy

Child born while father president-elect: Kennedy

Child born in White House: Cleveland

Children by two wives [3]: Tyler, B. Harrison, T. Roosevelt

Had illegitimate child: Harding

Had stepchildren [3]: Washington, Madison, Harding

Adopted child: Jackson

Named children for previous presidents: J. Q. Adams

Children who married in White House [8] (9):

    Daughters [7] (8): Monroe, Tyler, Grant, T. Roosevelt, Wilson (2), L. B. Johnson, Nixon

    Son: J. Q. Adams

Daughter married cabinet member: Wilson

Childless [6]: Washington, Madison, Jackson, Pierce, Buchanan (bachelor), Harding (no legitimate child)

Children died before maturity [2]: Pierce, McKinley

Children died during father's terms [5]: J. Adams, Jefferson, Lincoln, Coolidge, Kennedy

Child died in White House: Lincoln

NAMES OF PRESIDENTS

Changed [5]: Grant, Cleveland, Wilson, Coolidge, Eisenhower

Dropped first name [4]: Grant, Cleveland, Wilson, Coolidge

Transposed first and middle names: Eisenhower

Had same first names:

    Andrew [2]: Jackson, Johnson

    Franklin [2]: Pierce, Roosevelt

    James [5]: Madison, Monroe, Polk, Buchanan, Garfield

    John [5]: J. Adams, J. Q. Adams, Tyler, Coolidge, Kennedy

    Thomas [2]: Jefferson, Wilson

    William [3]: Harrison, McKinley, Taft

Had middle names [18]: J. Q. Adams, W. H. Harrison, Polk, Grant, Hayes, Garfield, Arthur, Cleveland, Taft, Wilson, Harding, Coolidge, Hoover, F. D. Roosevelt, Eisenhower, Kennedy, L. B. Johnson, Nixon

Did not have middle names [17]: Washington, J. Adams, Jefferson, Madison, Monroe, Jackson, Van Buren, Tyler, Taylor, Fillmore, Pierce, Buchanan, Lincoln, A. Johnson, B. Harrison, McKinley, T. Roosevelt

Had middle initial only: Truman

Had same name as father [8]: J. Adams, Madison, Jackson, Tyler, Buchanan, McKinley, T. Roosevelt, Coolidge

Had same surname as previous president [4]: J. Q. Adams, B. Harrison, F. D. Roosevelt, L. B. Johnson

Had same surname as previous president, not related: L. B. Johnson

Had same initials as previous president [2]: Madison (Monroe), A. Johnson (Jackson)

RELIGION:

Baptist [2]: Harding, Truman

Congregationalist: Coolidge

Disciples of Christ [2]: Garfield, L. B. Johnson

Dutch Reformed [2]: Van Buren, T. Roosevelt

Episcopalian [9]: Washington, Madison, Monroe, W. H. Harrison, Tyler, Taylor, Pierce, Arthur, F. D. Roosevelt

Methodist [4]: Polk, Grant, Hayes, McKinley

Presbyterian [6]: Jackson, Buchanan, Cleveland, B. Harrison, Wilson, Eisenhower

Roman Catholic: Kennedy

Society of Friends (Quakers) [2]: Hoover, Nixon

Unitarian [4]: Adams, J. Q. Adams, Fillmore, Taft

No specific denomination [3]: Jefferson, Lincoln, A. Johnson

FIRST LADIES

Related to presidents: Anna Eleanor Roosevelt (niece of T. Roosevelt, fifth cousin of F. D. Roosevelt)

MARITAL DATA:

Age at marriage:

    Youngest: Eliza Johnson

    Teens (4): Abigail Adams, Elizabeth Monroe, Eliza Johnson, Marie (Mamie) Eisenhower

    Twenties (26): Martha Washington, Dorothea (Dolley) Madison, Louisa Adams, Anna Harrison, Letitia Tyler, Julia Tyler, Sarah Polk, Margaret Taylor, Abigail Fillmore, Jane Pierce, Mary Lincoln, Julia Grant, Lucy Hayes, Lucretia Garfield, Frances Cleveland, Caroline Harrison, Ida McKinley, Edith Roosevelt, Helen Taft, Ellen Wilson, Grace Coolidge, Lou Hoover, Anna Eleanor Roosevelt, Jacqueline Kennedy, Claudia (Lady Bird) Johnson, Thelma (Pat) Nixon

    Thirties (2): Florence Harding, Elizabeth (Bess) Truman

Forties: Edith Wilson
Older than husband (6): Martha Washington, Abigail Fillmore, Caroline Harrison, Florence Harding, Lou Hoover, Thelma (Pat) Nixon
Most senior to husband: Florence Harding
Oldest at marriage (first or only wife): Elizabeth (Bess) Truman
Age at husband's inauguration:
 Youngest: Frances Cleveland
 Oldest: Anna Harrison
Widows at marriage to presidents (3): Martha Washington, Dorothea (Dolley) Madison, Edith Wilson
Survived by husbands (9): Abigail Adams, Elizabeth Monroe, Letitia Tyler, Abigail Fillmore, Sarah Polk, Lucy Hayes, Caroline Harrison, Ellen Wilson, Lou Hoover
Survived husbands (21): Martha Washington, Dorothea (Dolley) Madison, Louisa Adams, Anna Harrison, Julia Tyler, Sarah Polk, Margaret Taylor, Mary Lincoln, Eliza Johnson, Julia Grant, Lucretia Garfield, Frances Cleveland, Ida McKinley, Edith Roosevelt, Helen Taft, Edith Wilson, Florence Harding, Grace Coolidge, Anna Eleanor Roosevelt, Marie (Mamie) Eisenhower, Jacqueline Kennedy
Remarried after death of president (2): Frances Cleveland, Jacqueline Kennedy

VITAL STATISTICS:

Age:

Lived longest: Anna Harrison
Reached age of 70 (16): Martha Washington, Abigail Adams, Dorothea (Dolley) Madison, Louisa Adams, Anna Harrison, Sarah Polk, Julia Grant, Lucretia Garfield, Frances Cleveland, Edith Roosevelt, Helen Taft, Edith Wilson, Grace Coolidge, Anna Eleanor Roosevelt, Elizabeth (Bess) Truman, Marie (Mamie) Eisenhower
Reached age of 75 (14): Dorothea (Dolley) Madison, Louisa Adams, Anna Harrison, Sarah Polk, Julia Grant, Lucretia Garfield, Frances Cleveland, Edith Roosevelt, Helen Taft, Edith Wilson, Grace Coolidge, Anna Eleanor Roosevelt, Elizabeth (Bess) Truman, Marie (Mamie) Eisenhower
Reached age of 80 (9)): Dorothea (Dolley) Madison, Anna Harrison, Sarah Polk, Lucretia Garfield, Frances Cleveland, Edith

Roosevelt, Helen Taft, Edith Wilson, Elizabeth (Bess) Truman
Reached age of 85 (6): Anna Harrison, Sarah Polk, Lucretia Garfield, Edith Roosevelt, Edith Wilson, Elizabeth (Bess) Truman

Dates of birth:

January (2): Julia Grant, Grace Coolidge
February (2): Louisa Adams, Elizabeth (Bess) Truman
March (4): Abigail Fillmore, Jane Pierce, Lou Hoover, Thelma (Pat) Nixon
April: Lucretia Garfield
May (3): Dorothea (Dolley) Madison, Julia Tyler, Ellen Wilson
June (4): Martha Washington, Elizabeth Monroe, Ida McKinley, Helen Taft
July (3): Anna Harrison, Frances Cleveland, Jacqueline Kennedy
August (3): Lucy Hayes, Edith Roosevelt, Florence Harding
September (2): Sarah Polk, Margaret Taylor
October (4): Eliza Johnson, Caroline Harrison, Edith Wilson, Anna Eleanor Roosevelt
November (3): Abigail Adams, Letitia Tyler, Marie (Mamie) Eisenhower
December (2): Mary Lincoln, Claudia (Lady Bird) Johnson

Places of birth:

Abroad (London, England): Louisa Adams
Connecticut: Edith Roosevelt
Georgia: Ellen Wilson
Iowa (2): Lou Hoover, Marie (Mamie) Eisenhower
Kentucky: Mary Lincoln
Maryland: Margaret Taylor
Massachusetts: Abigail Adams
Missouri (2): Julia Grant, Elizabeth (Bess) Truman
Nevada: Thelma (Pat) Nixon
New Hampshire: Jane Pierce
New Jersey: Anna Harrison
New York (6): Elizabeth Monroe, Letitia Tyler, Abigail Fillmore, Frances Cleveland, Anna Eleanor Roosevelt, Jacqueline Kennedy
 New York City (2): Elizabeth Monroe, Eleanor Roosevelt
North Carolina: Dorothea (Dolley) Madison
Ohio (6): Lucy Hayes, Lucretia Garfield, Caroline Harrison, Ida McKinley, Helen Taft, Florence Harding

Tennessee (2): Sarah Polk, Eliza Johnson
Texas: Claudia (Lady Bird) Johnson
Vermont: Grace Coolidge
Virginia (3): Martha Washington, Letitia Tyler, Edith Wilson

Dates of death:

On husband's birthday: Ellen Wilson
During husband's terms of office (3): Letitia Tyler, Caroline Harrison, Ellen Wilson

Places of death:

California: Lucretia Garfield
Illinois: Mary Lincoln
Maryland: Frances Cleveland
Massachusetts (3): Abigail Adams, Jane Pierce, Grace Coolidge
Mississippi: Margaret Taylor
New York (3): Edith Roosevelt, Lou Hoover, Anna Eleanor Roosevelt
    New York City (2): Lou Hoover, Anna Eleanor Roosevelt
Ohio (4): Anna Harrison, Lucy Hayes, Ida McKinley, Florence Harding
Tennessee (2): Sarah Polk, Eliza Johnson
Virginia (3): Martha Washington, Elizabeth Monroe, Julia Tyler
Washington, D. C. (9): Dorothea (Dolley) Madison, Louisa Adams, Letitia Tyler, Abigail Fillmore, Julia Grant, Caroline Harrison, Helen Taft, Ellen Wilson, Edith Wilson
    White House (3): Letitia Tyler, Caroline Harrison, Ellen Wilson

Places of burial:

California: Lou Hoover
Georgia: Ellen Wilson
Illinois: Mary Lincoln
Indiana: Caroline Harrison
Iowa: Lou Hoover (reinterred, 1964)
Kentucky: Margaret Taylor
Massachusetts (2): Abigail Adams, Louisa Adams
New Hampshire: Jane Pierce
New Jersey: Frances Cleveland
New York (4): Abigail Fillmore, Julia Grant, Edith Roosevelt, Anna Eleanor Roosevelt
    New York City: Julia Grant
Ohio (5): Anna Harrison, Lucy Hayes, Lucretia Garfield, Ida McKinley, Florence Harding

Tennessee (2): Sarah Polk, Eliza Johnson
Vermont: Grace Coolidge
Virginia (6): Martha Washington, Dorothea (Dolley) Madison, Elizabeth Monroe, Letitia Tyler, Julia Tyler, Helen Taft
    Arlington National Cemetery: Helen Taft
Washington, D. C.: Edith Wilson

See also WIVES OF PRESIDENTS

FORMER PRESIDENTS

Lived shortest period after term: Polk
Lived longest period after term: Hoover
Did not attend inaugurations of successors (4): J. Adams, J. Q. Adams, A. Johnson, Wilson

Occupations:

Newspaper columnist: Coolidge
Farmers, planters or ranchers (6): Washington, Jefferson, Madison, Jackson, Hayes, L. B. Johnson
Law professors (2): B. Harrison, Taft

Political activities and offices:

Presidential candidates of minor parties (3): Van Buren, Fillmore, T. Roosevelt
Elected to and served in Congress (2): J. Q. Adams (House of Representatives); A. Johnson (Senate)
Defeated as candidate for House: A. Johnson
Defeated as candidate for Senate (2): J. Q. Adams, A. Johnson
Held office in Confederacy: Tyler

Supreme Court:

Served as Chief Justice: Taft

Military service:

Generals (3): Washington, Grant, Eisenhower
Commander-in-chief of army: Washington

Travel:

Africa (2): Grant, T. Roosevelt
Asia: Grant

Europe (8): Van Buren, Fillmore, Pierce, Grant, B. Harrison, T. Roosevelt, Hoover, Truman

South America: T. Roosevelt

FORMER VICE PRESIDENTS

Served in cabinets (2): Calhoun (State); Wallace (Commerce)

ServedinSenate (6): Calhoun, Breckinridge, Hamlin, A. Johnson, Barkley, Humphrey

Served as governor: Morton

Served as state legislator: R. M. Johnson

Served in Confederate cabinet: Breckinridge (War)

FRATERNAL ORGANIZATIONS

Members of Masons [13]: Washington, Monroe, Jackson, Polk, Buchanan, A. Johnson, Garfield, McKinley, T. Roosevelt, Taft, Harding, F. D. Roosevelt, Truman

GENERALS

See MILITARY SERVICE; FORMER PRESIDENTS

GOVERNORS

See POLITICAL EXPERIENCE PRIOR TO OFFICE; FORMER VICE PRESIDENTS

HOUSE OF REPRESENTATIVES

See ADMINISTRATIONS; POLITICAL EXPERIENCE PRIOR TO OFFICE; FORMER PRESIDENTS

IMPEACHMENT

President who was impeached and acquitted: A. Johnson

Member of Supreme Court who was impeached and acquitted: Associate Justice Samuel Chase

Member of cabinet who was impeached and acquitted: Secretary of War Belknap

INAUGURATIONS

Inaugural addresses:

Did not deliver [4]: Tyler, Fillmore, A. Johnson, Arthur

Gave as oration [2]: Pierce, Cleveland

Longest: W. H. Harrison

Second longest: Taft

Shortest: Washington (1793)

Second shortest: F. D. Roosevelt (1945)

Dates of Inaugurations:

Only ceremony on Apr. 30: Washington (1789)

First ceremony on Mar. 4: Washington (1793)

First ceremony on Jan. 20: F. D. Roosevelt (1937)

Inauguration day postponed from Sunday to Monday [5]: Monroe, Taylor, Hayes, Wilson, Eisenhower

>First ceremony on Mar. 5: Monroe (1821)
>First ceremony on Jan. 21: Eisenhower (1957)

Inaugural statistics:

Automobile first used: Harding

Public address system first used: Harding

Broadcasts:
>First description on radio: Harding
>First direct radio broadcast: Coolidge
>First television broadcast: Truman

Oath of office administered in airplane: L. B. Johnson

First oath taken privately: Hayes

Oldest president to take oath: W. H. Harrison

Youngest president to take oath: T. Roosevelt

Presidents who participated in four inaugural ceremonies [3]: Cleveland, Taft, F. D. Roosevelt

Inaugural and oath-taking sites:

Inaugurated in two cities: Washington

Oath taken outside national capital [4]: Arthur (New York City); T. Roosevelt (Buffalo, N. Y.); Coolidge (Plymouth, Vt.); L. B. Johnson (Dallas, Tex.)

Capital cities where oath taken:
  New York City [2]: Washington, Arthur
  Philadelphia [2]: Washington, J. Adams
  First in Washington, D. C.: Jefferson
Locales where oath taken:
  First in Capitol: Jefferson
  First on east portico of Capitol: Monroe
  In House chamber [5] (6): J. Adams,
  Madison (twice), Monroe, J. Q. Adams,
  Jackson
  In Senate chamber [3] (5): Washington
  (twice), Jefferson (twice), Taft
  In White House: [2] F. D. Roosevelt
  (1945), Truman (1945)

Oath of office:

Administered by Chief Justices:
  Oliver Ellsworth: J. Adams
  John Marshall [5] (9): Jefferson (twice);
  Madison (twice); Monroe (twice); J. Q.
  Adams; Jackson (twice)
  Roger B. Taney [7]: Van Buren, W. H.
  Harrison, Polk, Taylor, Pierce, Bu-
  chanan, Lincoln
  Salmon P. Chase [3] (4): Lincoln; A.
  Johnson; Grant (twice)
  Morrison R. Waite [4]: Hayes; Garfield;
  Arthur (second ceremony); Cleveland
  Melville W. Fuller [5] (6): B. Harrison;
  Cleveland; McKinley (twice); T. Roose-
  velt (1905); Taft
  Edward D. White [2] (3): Wilson (twice);
  Harding
  William H. Taft [2]: Coolidge (1925);
  Hoover
  Charles Evans Hughes (3): F. D. Roose-
  velt
  Harlan Stone [2]: F. D. Roosevelt, Tru-
  man
  Frederick M. Vinson [2]: Truman, Ei-
  senhower
  Earl Warren [4]: Eisenhower; Kenne-
  dy; L. B. Johnson (1965); Nixon
  *Administered oath of office to two presi-
  dents in one year* (3): Chase (Lincoln,
  A. Johnson); Waite (Garfield, Arthur);
  Stone (F. D. Roosevelt, Truman)
  *Oath administered by former President
  Taft* [2]: Coolidge (1925); Hoover
Administered by officials other than chief
justices [7] (8): Washington (twice), Tyler,
Fillmore, Arthur, T. Roosevelt (1901), Coo-
lidge (1923), L. B. Johnson (1963)

Oath administered by:
  Associate Justice William Cushing:
  Washington (1793)
  *Chief Justice of U. S. Circuit Court of
  District of Columbia William Cranch*
  [2]: Tyler, Fillmore
  *U. S. District Judge John R. Hazel, New
  York:* T. Roosevelt (1901)
  *U. S. District Judge Sarah T. Hughes,
  Texas (only female who administered
  oath):* L. B. Johnson (1963)
  *Chancellor of State of New York Robert
  R. Livingston:* Washington (1789)
  *Justice of New York Supreme Court
  John R. Brady:* Arthur (first ceremony)
  *Justice of the Peace John Calvin Coo-
  lidge (only father of president who ad-
  ministered oath):* Coolidge (1923)

LAWYERS

See OCCUPATIONS OF PRESIDENTS

LINEAGE

See FAMILY RELATIONSHIPS

MARRIAGE

See FAMILY RELATIONSHIPS; FIRST LA-
DIES; WIVES OF PRESIDENTS

MILITARY SERVICE

U. S. Army: [18]: Washington, Monroe, Jack-
son, W. H. Harrison, Tyler, Taylor, Pierce,
Lincoln, A. Johnson, Grant, Hayes, Gar-
field, Arthur, B. Harrison, McKinley, T.
Roosevelt, Truman, Eisenhower
U. S. Navy [3]: Kennedy, L. B. Johnson,
Nixon
Generals [12]: Washington, Jackson, W. H.
Harrison, Taylor, Pierce, A. Johnson,
Grant, Hayes, Garfield, Arthur, B. Harri-
son, Eisenhower
Professional soldiers [4]: W. H. Harrison,
Taylor, Grant, Eisenhower
Served during wartime [21]: Washington,
Monroe, Jackson, W. H. Harrison, Tyler,
Taylor, Pierce, Lincoln, A. Johnson, Grant,
Hayes, Garfield, Arthur, B. Harrison,

McKinley, T. Roosevelt, Truman, Eisenhower, Kennedy, L. B. Johnson, Nixon
Wars served in:
   Revolution [3]: Washington, Monroe, Jackson
   War of 1812 [4]: Jackson, W. H. Harrison, Tyler, Taylor
   Revolution and War of 1812: Jackson
   Black Hawk War [2]: Taylor, Lincoln
   Mexican War [3]: Taylor, Pierce, Grant
   War of 1812, Black Hawk War and Mexican War: Taylor
   Civil War [7]: A. Johnson, Grant, Hayes, Garfield, Arthur, B. Harrison, McKinley
   Mexican War and Civil War: Grant
   Spanish-American War: T. Roosevelt
   World War I [2]: Eisenhower, Truman
   World War II [4]: Eisenhower, Kennedy, L. B. Johnson, Nixon
   World War I and World War II: Eisenhower
Wounded or injured in action [4]: Monroe, Jackson, Hayes, Kennedy
Prisoner-of-war: Jackson

See also FORMER PRESIDENTS

NOBEL PRIZE

See PRIZES

OATH OF OFFICE

See INAUGURATIONS

OCCUPATIONS OF PRESIDENTS

Lawyers [23]: J. Adams, Jefferson, Monroe, J. Q. Adams, Jackson, Van Buren, Tyler, Polk, Fillmore, Pierce, Buchanan, Lincoln, Hayes, Garfield, Arthur, Cleveland, B. Harrison, McKinley, Taft, Wilson, Coolidge, F. D. Roosevelt, Nixon
Law professor: Taft
Newspapermen [3]: Taft, Harding, Kennedy
Presidents of colleges or universities [2]: Wilson, Eisenhower
Publisher: Harding
Schoolteachers [7]: J. Adams, Fillmore, Garfield, Arthur, McKinley, Harding, L. B. Johnson

Surveyors [3]: Washington, J. Adams, Lincoln

See also POLITICAL EXPERIENCE PRIOR TO OFFICE; FORMER PRESIDENTS

PHI BETA KAPPA

See EDUCATION

POCKET VETOES

See VETOES

POLITICAL CONVENTIONS

See CONVENTIONS

POLITICAL EXPERIENCE PRIOR TO OFFICE

PRESIDENTS:

Cabinet:

See ADMINISTRATIONS, CABINET MEMBERS

Congress:

Elected to and served in House of Representatives [17]: Madison, Jackson, W. H. Harrison, Tyler, Buchanan, Polk, J. Q. Adams, Fillmore, Pierce, A. Johnson, Lincoln, Garfield, Hayes, McKinley, L. B. Johnson, Kennedy, Nixon
   Speaker of the House: Polk
Elected to Senate [16]: Monroe, Jackson, J. Q. Adams, Van Buren, W. H. Harrison, Tyler, Buchanan, Pierce, A. Johnson, Garfield (did not serve), B. Harrison, Harding, Truman, L. B. Johnson, Kennedy, Nixon
Elected to House of Representatives and Senate [11]: Jackson, W. H. Harrison, Tyler, J. Q. Adams, Buchanan, Pierce, A. Johnson, Garfield (did not serve), L. B. Johnson, Kennedy, Nixon

Departments of State, Treasury and Post Office:

Department of State [7]: J. Adams, Jefferson, Monroe, J. Q. Adams, Van Buren, W. H. Harrison, Buchanan

Minister to Colombia: W. H. Harrison
Minister to France [2]: Jefferson, Monroe
Minister to Great Britain [5]: J. Adams, Monroe, J. Q. Adams, Van Buren, Buchanan
Minister to The Netherlands [2]: J. Adams, J. Q. Adams
Minister to Prussia: J. Q. Adams
Minister to Russia [2]: J. Q. Adams, Buchanan
Minister to Spain: Monroe
Department of the Treasury [2]:
Collector of Port of New York: Arthur
Internal Revenue Service: Taft
Post Office Department [2]:
Postmasters: Lincoln, Truman

Governors:

Governor-general of Philippines: Taft
Military governors [2]: Jackson, A. Johnson
Provisional governor of Cuba: Taft
State governors [13]: Jefferson, Monroe, Van Buren, Tyler, Polk, A. Johnson, Hayes, Cleveland, McKinley, T. Roosevelt, Wilson, Coolidge, F. D. Roosevelt
Massachusetts: Coolidge
New Jersey: Wilson
New York [4]: Van Buren, Cleveland, T. Roosevelt, F. D. Roosevelt
Ohio [2]: Hayes, McKinley
Tennessee [2]: Polk, A. Johnson
Virginia [3]: Jefferson, Monroe, Tyler
Territorial governor: W. H. Harrison

VICE PRESIDENTS:

Cabinet:

Served before term (4): Jefferson (J. Adams); Calhoun (J. Q. Adams); Van Buren (Jackson); Wallace (F. D. Roosevelt)

Congress:

Served in House of Representatives (21): Gerry (Madison); Tompkins (Monroe); R. M. Johnson (Van Buren); Calhoun (J. Q. Adams); King (Pierce); Tyler (W. H. Harrison); Fillmore (Taylor); Hamlin (Lincoln); A. Johnson (Lincoln); Breckinridge (Buchanan); Hendricks (Cleveland); Colfax (Grant); Wheeler (Hayes); Stevenson (Cleveland); Morton (B. Harrison); Sherman (Taft); Curtis (Hoover); Garner (F. D. Roosevelt); Barkley (Truman); L. B. Johnson (Kennedy); Nixon (Eisenhower)
Served in Senate (17): Burr (Jefferson); R. M. Johnson (Van Buren); King (Pierce); Van Buren (Jackson); Tyler (W. H. Harrison); Dallas (Polk); Hamlin (Lincoln); Wilson (Grant); A. Johnson (Lincoln); Hendricks (Cleveland); Fairbanks (T. Roosevelt); Curtis (Hoover); Barkley (Truman); L. B. Johnson (Kennedy); Humphrey (L. B. Johnson); Nixon (Eisenhower)
Served both in House of Representatives and Senate (10): R. M. Johnson, (Van Buren); King (Pierce); Tyler (W. H. Harrison); Hamlin (Lincoln); A. Johnson (Lincoln); Hendricks (Cleveland); Curtis (Hoover); Barkley (Truman); L. B. Johnson (Kennedy); Nixon (Eisenhower)

Governors:

Served as state governors (13): Jefferson (J. Adams); Clinton (Jefferson); Gerry (Madison); Tompkins (Monroe); Van Buren (Jackson); Tyler (W. H. Harrison); Hamlin (Lincoln); A. Johnson (Lincoln); Hendricks (Cleveland); T. Roosevelt (McKinley); Marshall (Wilson); Coolidge (Harding); Agnew (Nixon)

POLITICAL EXPERIENCE AFTER OFFICE

See **FORMER PRESIDENTS; FORMER VICE PRESIDENTS**

POLITICAL PARTIES

See **ADMINISTRATIONS,** POLITICAL PARTY AFFILIATIONS; **CONVENTIONS**

POPES

Met with Popes [5] (7):
Vatican City [5] (6): Wilson, Eisenhower, Kennedy, L. B. Johnson, Nixon (twice)
New York City: L. B. Johnson
Met with Popes on two occasions [2]: L. B. Johnson, Nixon

Former presidents who met with Popes (3): Van Buren, Pierce, Grant

Former president who refused to meet with Pope: T. Roosevelt

POSTMASTERS

See **POLITICAL EXPERIENCE PRIOR TO OFFICE**

PRESIDENT-VICE PRESIDENT TEAMS

See **ADMINISTRATIONS**

PRIZES

PRESIDENTS:

Received Nobel Prize [2]: T. Roosevelt, Wilson

Received Pulitzer Prize: Kennedy

VICE PRESIDENTS:

Received Nobel Prize (2): T. Roosevelt (McKinley); Dawes (Coolidge)

PULITZER PRIZE

See **PRIZES**

RELIGION

See **FAMILY RELATIONSHIPS**

SCHOOLTEACHERS

See **OCCUPATIONS OF PRESIDENTS**

SENATE

See **ADMINISTRATIONS; POLITICAL EXPERIENCE PRIOR TO OFFICE; FORMER PRESIDENTS**

SIBLINGS

See **FAMILY RELATIONSHIPS**

SLAVEOWNERS

Owned slaves [9]: Washington, Jefferson, Madison, Monroe, Jackson, Tyler, Polk, Taylor, A. Johnson

STATE DEPARTMENT

See **ADMINISTRATIONS, CABINETS; POLITICAL EXPERIENCE PRIOR TO OFFICE**

STATE OF THE UNION MESSAGES

Did not send or deliver [2]: W. H. Harrison, Garfield

STATES REPRESENTED

PRESIDENTS:

California: Hoover
Illinois [2]: Lincoln, Grant
Indiana: B. Harrison
Louisiana: Taylor
Massachusetts [4]: J. Adams, J. Q. Adams, Coolidge, Kennedy
Missouri: Truman
New Hampshire: Pierce
New Jersey: Wilson
New York [8]: Van Buren, Fillmore, Arthur, Cleveland, T. Roosevelt, F. D. Roosevelt, Eisenhower, Nixon
Ohio [6]: W. H. Harrison, Hayes, Garfield, McKinley, Taft, Harding
Pennsylvania: Buchanan
Tennessee [3]: Jackson, Polk, A. Johnson
Texas: L. B. Johnson
Virginia [5]: Washington, Jefferson, Madison, Monroe, Tyler
  "Virginia Regime" [4]: Washington, Jefferson, Madison, Monroe
Represented states that were not their native states [15]: Jackson, W. H. Harrison, Polk, Taylor, Lincoln, A. Johnson, Grant, Arthur, Cleveland, B. Harrison, Wilson, Coolidge, Hoover, Eisenhower, Nixon
Succeeded presidents who represented same state [4]: Madison, Monroe, Garfield, Cleveland
Defeated major candidates who represented same state [4]: Lincoln, T. Roosevelt, Harding, F. D. Roosevelt

VICE PRESIDENTS:

TERMS OF OFFICE

Alabama: King (Pierce)
California: Nixon (Eisenhower)
Illinois (2): Stevenson (Cleveland); Dawes (Coolidge)
Indiana (4): Colfax (Grant); Hendricks (Cleveland); Fairbanks (T. Roosevelt); Marshall (Wilson)
Iowa: Wallace (F. D. Roosevelt)
Kansas: Curtis (Hoover)
Kentucky (3): R. H. Johnson (Van Buren); Breckinridge (Buchanan); Barkley (Truman)
Maine: Hamlin (Lincoln)
Maryland: Agnew (Nixon)
Massachusetts (4): J. Adams (Washington); Gerry (Madison); Wilson (Grant); Coolidge (Harding)
Minnesota: Humphrey (L. B. Johnson)
Missouri: Truman (F. D. Roosevelt)
New Jersey: Hobart (McKinley)
New York (10): Burr (Jefferson); Clinton (Jefferson); Tompkins (Monroe); Van Buren (Jackson); Fillmore (Taylor); Wheeler (Hayes); Arthur (Garfield); Morton (B. Harrison); T. Roosevelt (McKinley); Sherman (Taft)
Pennsylvania: Dallas (Polk)
South Carolina: Calhoun (J. Q. Adams)
Tennessee: A. Johnson (Lincoln)
Texas (2): Garner (F. D. Roosevelt); L. B. Johnson (Kennedy)
Virginia (2): Jefferson (J. Adams); Tyler (W. H. Harrison)
Represented states other than their native states (13): Burr (Jefferson); King (Pierce); A. Johnson (Lincoln); Colfax (Grant); H. Wilson (Grant); Arthur (Garfield); Hendricks (Cleveland); Morton (B. Harrison); Stevenson (Cleveland); Fairbanks (T. Roosevelt); Coolidge (Harding); Dawes (Coolidge); Humphrey (L. B. Johnson)

SUPREME COURT

Chief justice who administered oath of office to successor (Burger): Warren
Associate justice who resigned under pressure of public opinion: Fortas

See also **ADMINISTRATIONS,** SUPREME COURT

PRESIDENTS:

Served shortest term: W. H. Harrison
Served second shortest term: Garfield
Served less than one term [9]: W. H. Harrison, Tyler, Taylor, Fillmore, A. Johnson, Garfield, Arthur, Harding, Kennedy
Served one four-year term [10]: J. Adams, J. Q. Adams, Van Buren, Polk, Pierce, Buchanan, Hayes, B. Harrison, Taft, Hoover
Served one term or less than one term [19]: J. Adams, J. Q. Adams, Van Buren, W. H. Harrison, Tyler, Polk, Taylor, Fillmore, Pierce, Buchanan, A. Johnson, Hayes, Garfield, Arthur, B. Harrison, Taft, Harding, Hoover, Kennedy
  In succession, served one term or less [8]: Van Buren, W. H. Harrison, Tyler, Polk, Taylor, Fillmore, Pierce, Buchanan
Served more than one term [16]: Washington, Jefferson, Madison, Monroe, Jackson, Lincoln, Grant, Cleveland, McKinley, T. Roosevelt, Wilson, Coolidge, F. D. Roosevelt, Truman, Eisenhower, L. B. Johnson
Elected to second terms [12]: Washington, Jefferson, Madison, Monroe, Jackson, Lincoln, Grant, Cleveland, McKinley, Wilson, F. D. Roosevelt, Eisenhower
Served two terms [9]: Washington, Jefferson, Madison, Monroe, Jackson, Grant, Cleveland, Wilson, Eisenhower
Served for eight years [8]: Jefferson, Madison, Monroe, Jackson, Grant, Cleveland (non-consecutive), Wilson, Eisenhower
Served more than two terms: F. D. Roosevelt
Elected to third term: F. D. Roosevelt
Served three terms: F. D. Roosevelt
Served more than three terms: F. D. Roosevelt
Elected to fourth term: F. D. Roosevelt
Served longest term: F. D. Roosevelt
Served non-consecutive terms: Cleveland
Had served as vice presidents [12]: J. Adams, Jefferson, Van Buren, Tyler, Fillmore, A. Johnson, Arthur, T. Roosevelt, Coolidge, Truman, L. B. Johnson, Nixon
Served after completion of vice-presidential terms [4]: J. Adams, Jefferson, Van Buren, Nixon
  Served directly upon completion of vice-presidential terms [3]: J. Adams, Jefferson, Van Buren

Served upon completion of two-term vice-presidential term: J. Adams

Served two terms upon completion of vice-presidential term: Jefferson

Served after, but not upon completion of two-term vice-presidential term: Nixon

Did not complete vice-presidential terms because of death of predecessors [8]: Tyler, Fillmore, A. Johnson, Arthur, T. Roosevelt, Coolidge, Truman, L. B. Johnson

Served only unexpired terms of predecessors [4]: Tyler, Fillmore, A. Johnson, Arthur

Served longest unexpired term of predecessor: Tyler

Elected to and served terms after having served unexpired terms of predecessors [4]: T. Roosevelt, Coolidge, Truman, L. B. Johnson

Served last presidential term that ended Mar. 4: Hoover

Served first presidential term that ended Jan. 20: F. D. Roosevelt

First term served under provisions of 22nd Amendment: Eisenhower

VICE PRESIDENTS:

Served shortest term: King (Pierce)

Served second shortest term: Tyler (W. H. Harrison)

Served less than one year (7): Tyler (W. H. Harrison); King (Pierce); A. Johnson (Lincoln); Arthur (Garfield); Hendricks (Cleveland); T. Roosevelt (McKinley); Truman (F. D. Roosevelt)

Served less than one term (14): Gerry (Madison); Tyler (W. H. Harrison); Fillmore (Taylor); King (Pierce); A. Johnson (Lincoln); Wilson (Grant); Arthur (Garfield); Hendricks (Cleveland); Hobart (McKinley); T. Roosevelt (McKinley); Sherman (Taft); Coolidge (Harding); Truman (F. D. Roosevelt); L. B. Johnson (Kennedy)

Did not perform any duties of office: King (Pierce)

Served four years (17): Jefferson (J. Adams); Burr (Jefferson); Van Buren (Jackson); R. M. Johnson (Van Buren); Dallas (Polk); Breckinridge (Buchanan); Hamlin (Lincoln); Colfax (Grant); Wheeler (Hayes); Morton (B. Harrison); Stevenson (Cleveland, second term); Fairbanks (T. Roosevelt); Dawes (Coolidge); Curtis (Hoover);

Wallace (F. D. Roosevelt); Barkley (Truman); Humphrey (L. B. Johnson)

Elected to two terms (7): J. Adams (Washington); Clinton (Madison); Tompkins (Monroe); Calhoun (Jackson); Marshall (Wilson); Garner (F. D. Roosevelt); Nixon (Eisenhower)

Served two terms (5): J. Adams (Washington); Tompkins (Monroe); Marshall (Wilson); Garner (F. D. Roosevelt); Nixon (Eisenhower)

Served more than seven years (4): J. Adams (Washington); Clinton (Jefferson and Madison); Calhoun (J. Q. Adams and Jackson); Garner (F. D. Roosevelt)

Served eight years (3): Tompkins (Monroe); Marshall (Wilson); Nixon (Eisenhower)

Served under two presidents (2): Clinton (Jefferson and Madison); Calhoun (J. Q. Adams and Jackson)

TRAVEL BY PRESIDENTS

Traveled outside U. S. [11]: T. Roosevelt, Taft, Wilson, Harding, Coolidge, F. D. Roosevelt, Truman, Eisenhower, Kennedy, L. B. Johnson, Nixon

During wartime [3]: F. D. Roosevelt, L. B. Johnson, Nixon

Most often while in office: F. D. Roosevelt

Traveled to most foreign countries while in office: Eisenhower

Only president since McKinley who didn't visit a foreign country while in office: Hoover

Traveled through Panama Canal while in office: F. D. Roosevelt

Continents visited:

Africa [2]: F. D. Roosevelt, Eisenhower

Asia [4]: F. D. Roosevelt, Eisenhower, L. B. Johnson, Nixon

Australia: L. B. Johnson

Europe [7]: Wilson, F. D. Roosevelt, Truman, Eisenhower, Kennedy, L. B. Johnson, Nixon

South America [5]: F. D. Roosevelt, Truman, Eisenhower, Kennedy, L. B. Johnson

Visited four foreign continents while in office [3]: F. D. Roosevelt, Eisenhower, L. B. Johnson

Foreign countries visited:
  Afghanistan: Eisenhower
  Algeria: F. D. Roosevelt
  Argentina [2]: F. D. Roosevelt, Eisenhower
  Austria: Kennedy
  Azores: L. B. Johnson, Nixon
  Bahamas [2]: Kennedy, Nixon
  Belgium [3]: Wilson, Truman, Nixon
  Bermuda [4]: Truman, Eisenhower, Kennedy, Nixon
  Brazil [3]: F. D. Roosevelt, Truman, Eisenhower
  Canada [7]: Harding, F. D. Roosevelt, Truman, Eisenhower, Kennedy, L. B. Johnson, Nixon
  Chile: Eisenhower
  China (Formosa): Eisenhower
  Colombia [2]: F. D. Roosevelt, Kennedy
  Costa Rica [2]: Kennedy, L. B. Johnson
  Cuba [2]: Coolidge, Truman
  El Salvador: L. B. Johnson
  Egypt: F. D. Roosevelt
  England [5]: Wilson, Truman, Eisenhower, Kennedy, Nixon
  Formosa: (*See* China)
  France [4]: Wilson, Eisenhower, Kennedy, Nixon
  Gambia: F. D. Roosevelt
  Germany [5]: Truman, Eisenhower, Kennedy, L. B. Johnson, Nixon
  Greece: Eisenhower
  Guatamala: L. B. Johnson
  Haiti: F. D. Roosevelt
  Honduras: L. B. Johnson
  India [2]: Eisenhower, Nixon
  Indonesia: Nixon
  Iran [2]: F. D. Roosevelt, Eisenhower
  Ireland [2]: Kennedy, Nixon
  Italy [6]: Wilson, F. D. Roosevelt, Eisenhower, Kennedy, L. B. Johnson, Nixon
  Korea [2]: Eisenhower, L. B. Johnson
  Liberia: F. D. Roosevelt
  Malaysia: L. B. Johnson
  Malta: F. D. Roosevelt
  Mexico [7]: Taft, F. D. Roosevelt, Truman, Eisenhower, Kennedy, L. B. Johnson, Nixon
  Morocco [2]: F. D. Roosevelt, Eisenhower
  New Zealand: L. B. Johnson
  Nicaragua: L. B. Johnson
  Okinawa: Eisenhower

  Pakistan [3]: Eisenhower, L. B. Johnson, Nixon
  Panama [4]: T. Roosevelt, Taft, F. D. Roosevelt, Eisenhower
  Philippines [3]: Eisenhower, L. B. Johnson, Nixon
  Portugal [3]: Eisenhower, L. B. Johnson, Nixon
  Rumania: Nixon
  Russia: (*See* U. S. S. R.)
  Scotland: Eisenhower
  Sicily: F. D. Roosevelt
  South Vietnam [2]: L. B. Johnson, Nixon
  Spain [2]: Eisenhower, Nixon
  Surinam: L. B. Johnson
  Switzerland: Eisenhower
  Thailand [2]: L. B. Johnson, Nixon
  Trinidad [2]: F. D. Roosevelt, Truman
  Tunisia [2]: F. D. Roosevelt, Eisenhower
  Turkey: Eisenhower
  Uruguay [3]: F. D. Roosevelt, Eisenhower, L. B. Johnson
  U.S.S.R.: F. D. Roosevelt
  Vatican City [5]: Wilson, Eisenhower, Kennedy, L. B. Johnson, Nixon
  Venezuela: Kennedy
  Vietnam: (*See* South Vietnam)
  West Germany: (*See* Germany)
  Yugoslavia: Nixon

U. S. possessions or territories visited:
  Alaska [5]: Harding, F. D. Roosevelt, Eisenhower, L. B. Johnson, Nixon
    After statehood [3]: Eisenhower, L. B. Johnson, Nixon
  American Samoa: L. B. Johnson
  Guam [2]: L. B. Johnson, Nixon
  Hawaii [5]: F. D. Roosevelt, Truman, Eisenhower, L. B. Johnson, Nixon
    After statehood [3]: Eisenhower, L. B. Johnson, Nixon
  Johnston Island: Nixon
  Midway Island: Nixon
  Puerto Rico [7]: T. Roosevelt, Hoover, F. D. Roosevelt, Truman, Eisenhower, Kennedy, L. B. Johnson
    Commonwealth of Puerto Rico [3]: Eisenhower, Kennedy, L. B. Johnson
  Virgin Islands [4]: Hoover, F. D. Roosevelt, Truman, Nixon
  Wake Island [2]: Truman, Eisenhower
First to travel by airplane: F. D. Roosevelt
Flew airplane while in office: Eisenhower

First to travel by helicopter: Eisenhower
Submerged in submarines [3]: T. Roosevelt, Truman, Eisenhower
Traveled by submarine [2]: Truman, Eisenhower

TREASURY DEPARTMENT

See ADMINISTRATIONS, CABINETS; POLITICAL EXPERIENCE PRIOR TO OFFICE

VETOES

Did not exercise veto [7]: J. Adams, Jefferson, J. Q. Adams, W. H. Harrison, Taylor, Fillmore, Garfield
Exercised regular veto but not pocket veto [3]: Washington, Monroe, Pierce
Exercised pocket veto but not regular veto: Van Buren

Regular Veto:

Exercised [29]: Washington, Madison, Monroe, Jackson, Tyler, Polk, Pierce, Buchanan, Lincoln, A. Johnson, Grant, Hayes, Arthur, Cleveland, B. Harrison, Cleveland, McKinley, T. Roosevelt, Taft, Wilson, Harding, Coolidge, Hoover, F. D. Roosevelt, Truman, Eisenhower, Kennedy, L. B. Johnson, Nixon
Not exercised [8]: J. Adams, Jefferson, J. Q. Adams, Van Buren, W. H. Harrison, Taylor, Fillmore, Garfield
First to exercise regular veto: Washington
Largest number of vetoes exercised: F. D. Roosevelt
    Second largest number exercised: Cleveland
First veto message delivered in person: F. D. Roosevelt
First veto message delivered on television: Nixon
Vetoes overridden:
    Largest number: A. Johnson
    Second largest number: Truman
    Majority of vetoes overridden [2]: Pierce, A. Johnson
    No veto overridden [11]: Washington, Madison, Monroe, Jackson, Polk, Buchanan, Lincoln, McKinley, Harding, Kennedy, L. B. Johnson

Pocket Veto:

Exercised [27]: Madison, Jackson, Van Buren, Tyler, Polk, Buchanan, Lincoln, A. Johnson, Grant, Hayes, Arthur, Cleveland, B. Harrison, Cleveland, McKinley, T. Roosevelt, Taft, Wilson, Harding, Coolidge, Hoover, F. D. Roosevelt, Truman, Eisenhower, Kennedy, L. B. Johnson, Nixon
Not exercised [10]: Washington, J. Adams, Jefferson, Monroe, J. Q. Adams, W. H. Harrison, Taylor, Fillmore, Pierce, Garfield
First to exercise pocket veto: Madison
Largest number of pocket vetoes exercised: F. D. Roosevelt
    Second largest number: Cleveland

VICE PRESIDENTS

EDUCATION:

College:

Did not attend college (11): Clinton, Van Buren, Fillmore, Hamlin, A. Johnson, Colfax, H. Wilson, Morton, Curtis, Garner, Truman
Attended college (28): J. Adams, Jefferson, Burr, Gerry, Tompkins, Calhoun, R. M. Johnson, Tyler, Dallas, King, Breckinridge, Wheeler, Arthur, Hendricks, Stevenson, Hobart, T. Roosevelt, Fairbanks, Sherman, Marshall, Coolidge, Dawes, Wallace, Barkley, Nixon, L. B. Johnson, Humphrey, Agnew
Graduated (24): J. Adams, Burr, Gerry, Tompkins, Calhoun, R. M. Johnson, Dallas, King, Breckinridge, Arthur, Hendricks, Hobart, T. Roosevelt, Fairbanks, Sherman, Marshall, Coolidge, Dawes, Wallace, Barkley, Nixon, L. B. Johnson, Humphrey, Agnew
Attended but were not graduated (4): Jefferson, Tyler, Wheeler, Stevenson
Colleges attended:
    Amherst: Coolidge
    Centre (2): Breckinridge, Stevenson
    Columbia: Tompkins
    Hamilton: Sherman
    Hanover: Hendricks
    Harvard (3): J. Adams, Gerry, T. Roosevelt
    Iowa: Wallace
    Johns Hopkins: Agnew

Marietta: Dawes
Marvin: Barkley
Minnesota: Humphrey
New Jersey: See Princeton
North Carolina: King
Ohio Wesleyan: Fairbanks
Princeton (2): Burr, Dallas
Rutgers: Hendricks
Southwest Texas State Teachers: L. B.
Johnson
Transylvania: R. M. Johnson
Union: Arthur
Vermont: Wheeler
Wabash: Marshall
Whittier: Nixon
William and Mary (2): Jefferson, Tyler
Yale: Calhoun

NAMES:

Changed name: Wilson (Grant)
Had same initials as previous vice president
(Coolidge): Curtis
Vice presidents named Johnson (3): R. M.
Johnson (Van Buren); A. Johnson (Lincoln);
L. B. Johnson (Kennedy)

OATH OF OFFICE:

Oath administered abroad: King (Pierce)

RELIGION:

Baptist (2): R. M. Johnson (Van Buren); Tru-
man (F. D. Roosevelt)
Congregationalist (4): H. Wilson (Grant);
Coolidge (Harding); Dawes (Coolidge);
Humphrey (L. B. Johnson)
Disciples of Christ: L. B. Johnson (Kennedy)
Dutch Reformed (4): Van Buren (Jackson);
Colfax (Grant); T. Roosevelt (McKinley);
Sherman (Taft)
Episcopalian (8): Gerry (Madison); Tyler (W.
H. Harrison); Arthur (Garfield); Hendricks
(Cleveland); Morton (B. Harrison); Curtis
(Hoover); Wallace (F. D. Roosevelt); Ag-
new (Nixon)
Methodist (3): Fairbanks (T. Roosevelt); Gar-
ner (F. D. Roosevelt); Barkley (Truman)
Presbyterian (11): Burr (Jefferson); Clin-
ton (Jefferson); Tompkins (Monroe); Cal-
houn (J. Q. Adams); Dallas (Polk); King
(Pierce); Breckinridge (Buchanan); Whee-
ler (Hayes); Stevenson (Cleveland); Ho-
bart (McKinley); Marshall (Wilson)

Society of Friends (Quakers): Nixon (Eisen-
hower)
Unitarian (3): J. Adams (Washington); Fill-
more (Taylor); Hamlin (Lincoln)
Same denomination as president (7): Gerry
(Madison); Tyler (W. H. Harrison); Breckin-
ridge (Buchanan); Stevenson (Cleveland);
Marshall (Wilson); Dawes (Coolidge); Wal-
lace (F. D. Roosevelt)
No specific denomination (2): Jefferson (J.
Adams); A. Johnson (Lincoln)

See also **ADMINISTRATIONS,** POLITICAL
PARTY AFFILIATIONS; **STATES REPRESEN-
TED; TERMS OF OFFICE; VITAL STATISTICS**

VITAL STATISTICS

PRESIDENTS:

Age:

Reached age of 90 [2]: J. Adams, Hoover
Reached age of 85 [4]: J. Adams, Madison,
Hoover, Truman
Reached age of 80 [6]: J. Adams, Jefferson,
Madison, J. Q. Adams, Hoover, Truman
Reached age of 75 [10]: J. Adams, Jefferson,
Madison, J. Q. Adams, Jackson, Van Buren,
Buchanan, Hoover, Truman, Eisenhower
Reached age of 70 [16]: J. Adams, Jefferson,
Madison, Monroe, J. Q. Adams, Jackson,
Van Buren, Tyler, Fillmore, Buchanan,
Hayes, Cleveland, Taft, Hoover, Truman,
Eisenhower
Lived to most advanced age: J. Adams
Younger than vice president [21]: Jefferson,
Madison, Madison (second term), Van
Buren, Polk, Pierce, Lincoln, Grant, Hayes,
Garfield, Cleveland, B. Harrison, Cleve-
land, T. Roosevelt, Taft, Wilson, Coolidge,
Hoover, F. D. Roosevelt (third term), Tru-
man, Kennedy
Younger than both vice presidents [2]: Madi-
son, Cleveland
Age upon leaving office:
Youngest: T. Roosevelt
Oldest: Eisenhower

Birth dates:

January [4]: Fillmore, McKinley, F. D.
Roosevelt, Nixon

February [3]: Washington, W. H. Harrison, Lincoln

March [4]: Madison, Jackson, Tyler, Cleveland

April [4]: Jefferson, Monroe, Buchanan, Grant

May [2]: Truman, Kennedy

July [2]: J. Q. Adams, Coolidge

August [3]: B. Harrison, Hoover, L. B. Johnson

September: Taft

October [5]: J. Adams, Hayes, Arthur, T. Roosevelt, Eisenhower

November [5]: Polk, Taylor, Pierce, Garfield, Harding

December [3]: Van Buren, A. Johnson, Wilson

Born after fathers' deaths [2]: Jackson, Hayes

Born on same day of the year [2]: Polk and Harding

Born while Julian calendar in use [4]: Washington, J. Adams, Jefferson, Madison

Born on July 4: Coolidge

Last born in eighteenth century: Fillmore

First born in nineteenth century: Pierce

Last born in nineteenth century: Eisenhower

First born in twentieth century: Kennedy

Birthplaces:

California: Nixon

Iowa: Hoover

Kentucky: Lincoln

Massachusetts [3]: J. Adams, J. Q. Adams, Kennedy

    Braintree [2]: J. Adams, J. Q. Adams

Missouri: Truman

New Hampshire: Pierce

New Jersey: Cleveland

New York [4]: Van Buren, Fillmore, T. Roosevelt, F. D. Roosevelt

    New York City: T. Roosevelt

North Carolina [2]: Polk, A. Johnson

Ohio [7]: Grant, Hayes, Garfield, B. Harrison, McKinley, Taft, Harding

    Consecutive presidents born in Ohio [3]: Grant, Hayes, Garfield

Pennsylvania: Buchanan

South Carolina: Jackson

Texas [2]: Eisenhower, L. B. Johnson

Vermont [2]: Arthur, Coolidge

Virginia [8]: Washington, Jefferson, Madison, Monroe, W. H. Harrison, Tyler, Taylor, Wilson

    Charles City County [2]: W. H. Harrison, Tyler

    Westmoreland County [2]: Washington, Monroe

    Consecutive presidents born in Virginia [3]: Jefferson, Madison, Monroe

First born in United States: Van Buren

First born in state that was not one of original 13: Lincoln

First born west of the Mississippi: Hoover

Born in same county as predecessor: Tyler

Born in same county as vice president: W. H. Harrison

Born in log cabins [7]: Jackson, Taylor, Fillmore, Pierce, Buchanan, Lincoln, Garfield

Height and Weight:

Tallest: Lincoln (6'4")

Shortest: Madison (5'4")

Six feet or over [14]: Washington, Jefferson, Monroe, Jackson, Tyler, Buchanan, Lincoln, Garfield, Arthur, Taft, Harding, F. D. Roosevelt, Kennedy, L. B. Johnson

Heaviest: Taft (332 lbs.)

Slightest: Madison (about 100 lbs.)

Death:

Age at death:
    Oldest: J. Adams
    Youngest: Kennedy

Died in office [8]: W. H. Harrison, Taylor, Lincoln, Garfield, McKinley, Harding, F. D. Roosevelt, Kennedy

    By assassination [4]: Lincoln, Garfield, McKinley, Kennedy

    From natural causes [4]: W. H. Harrison, Taylor, Harding, F. D. Roosevelt

    Died during first term [5]: W. H. Harrison, Taylor, Garfield, Harding, Kennedy

    Died during second term [2]: Lincoln, McKinley

    Died during fourth term: F. D. Roosevelt

Died on Fourth of July [3]: J. Adams, Jefferson, Monroe

Died on same day: J. Adams and Jefferson

Lived longest period after term: Hoover

Lived shortest period after term: Polk
During term, was only living president [4]:
J. Adams, Grant, T. Roosevelt, Hoover
Lay in state in Capitol Rotunda [8]: Lincoln,
Garfield, McKinley, Harding, Taft, Hoover,
Kennedy, Eisenhower
Lay in state in White House [6]: W. H. Harrison, Taylor, Lincoln, Harding, F. D. Roosevelt, Kennedy

Places of death:

California: Harding
Georgia: F. D. Roosevelt
Indiana: B. Harrison
Massachusetts [2]: J. Adams, Coolidge
New Hampshire: Pierce
New Jersey [2]: Garfield, Cleveland
New York [8]: Monroe, Van Buren, Fillmore, Grant, Arthur, McKinley, T. Roosevelt, Hoover
New York City [3]: Monroe, Arthur, Hoover
Ohio: Hayes
Pennsylvania: Buchanan
Tennessee [3]: Jackson, Polk, A. Johnson
Texas: Kennedy
Virginia [4]: Washington, Jefferson, Madison, Tyler
Washington, D. C. [7]: J. Q. Adams, W. H. Harrison, Taylor, Lincoln, Wilson, Taft, Eisenhower
White House [2]: W. H. Harrison, Taylor

Burial sites:

Illinois: Lincoln
Indiana: B. Harrison
Iowa: Hoover
Kansas: Eisenhower
Kentucky: Taylor
Massachusetts [2]: J. Adams, J. Q. Adams
New Hampshire: Pierce
New Jersey: Cleveland
New York [6]: Van Buren, Fillmore, Grant, Arthur, T. Roosevelt, F. D. Roosevelt
New York City: Grant
Ohio [5]: W. H. Harrison, Hayes, Garfield, McKinley, Harding
Pennsylvania: Buchanan
Tennessee [3]: Jackson, Polk, A. Johnson
Vermont: Coolidge
Virginia [7]: Washington, Jefferson, Madison, Monroe, Tyler, Taft, Kennedy

Arlington National Cemetery: [2]: Taft, Kennedy
Washington, D. C.: Wilson

VICE PRESIDENTS:

Age:

Youngest vice president who succeeded to presidency: T. Roosevelt
Oldest vice president who succeeded to presidency: Truman
Age at inauguration:
Youngest: Breckinridge (Buchanan)
Oldest: Barkley (Truman)

Birth dates:

Last in eighteenth century: Fillmore (Taylor)
First in nineteenth century: A. Johnson (Lincoln)
Last in nineteenth century: Barkley (Truman)
First in twentieth century: Nixon (Eisenhower)
First vice president who was not a British subject at birth: Calhoun (J. Q. Adams)

Birthplaces:

California: Nixon (Eisenhower)
Indiana: Marshall (Wilson)
Iowa: Wallace (F. D. Roosevelt)
Kansas: Curtis (Hoover)
Kentucky (4): R. M. Johnson (Van Buren); Breckinridge (Buchanan); Stevenson (Cleveland, second term); Barkley (Truman)
Maine: Hamlin (Lincoln)
Maryland: Agnew (Nixon)
Massachusetts (2): J. Adams (Washington); Gerry (Madison)
Missouri: Truman (F. D. Roosevelt)
New Hampshire: H. Wilson (Grant)
New Jersey (2): Burr (Jefferson); Hobart (McKinley)
New York (8): Clinton (Jefferson-Madison); Tompkins (Monroe); Van Buren (Jackson); Fillmore (Taylor); Colfax (Grant); Wheeler (Hayes); T. Roosevelt (McKinley); Sherman (Taft)
New York City (2): Colfax (Grant); T. Roosevelt (McKinley)
North Carolina (2): King (Pierce); A. Johnson (Lincoln)

Ohio (3): Hendrick (Cleveland); Fairbanks (T. Roosevelt); Dawes (Coolidge)
Pennsylvania: Dallas (Polk)
South Carolina: Calhoun (J. Q. Adams- Jackson)
South Dakota: Humphrey (L. B. Johnson)
Texas (2): Garner (F. D. Roosevelt); L. B. Johnson (Kennedy)
Vermont (3): Arthur (Garfield); Morton (B. Harrison); Coolidge (Harding)
Virginia (2): Jefferson (J. Adams); Tyler (W. H. Harrison)

Death:

Died in office (7):
   In first term (6): Gerry (Madison); King (Pierce); H. Wilson (Grant); Hendricks (Cleveland); Hobart (McKinley); Sherman (Taft)
   In second term: Clinton (Madison)
   After renomination: Sherman (Taft)
Died on birthday: Morton (B. Harrison)
Died on July 4th (3): Jefferson (J. Adams); J. Adams (Washington); Hamlin (Lincoln)

Places of death:

Alabama: King (Pierce)
Connecticut: Wallace (F. D. Roosevelt)
Illinois (2): Stevenson (Cleveland); Dawes (Coolidge)
Indiana (2): Hendricks (Cleveland); Fairbanks (T. Roosevelt)
Kentucky (2): R. M. Johnson (Van Buren); Breckinridge (Buchanan)
Maine: Hamlin (Lincoln)
Massachusetts (2): J. Adams (Washington); Coolidge (Harding)
Minnesota: Colfax (Grant)
New Jersey: Hobart (McKinley)
New York (9): Burr (Jefferson); Tompkins (Monroe); Van Buren (Jackson); Fillmore (Taylor); Wheeler (Hayes); Arthur (Garfield); Morton (B. Harrison); T. Roosevelt (McKinley); Sherman (Taft)
   New York City: Arthur (Garfield)
   Staten Island (2): Burr (Jefferson); Tompkins (Monroe)
Pennsylvania: Dallas (Polk)
Tennessee: A. Johnson (Lincoln)
Texas: Garner (F. D. Roosevelt)
Virginia (3): Jefferson (J. Adams); Tyler (W. H. Harrison); Barkley (Truman)
Washington, D. C. (6): Clinton (Jefferson-Madison); Gerry (Madison); Calhoun (J. Q.

Adams-Jackson); H. Wilson (Grant); Marshall (Wilson); Curtis (Hoover)

Burial sites:

Alabama: King (Pierce)
Illinois (2): Stevenson (Cleveland); Dawes (Coolidge)
Indiana (4): Colfax (Grant); Hendricks (Cleveland); Fairbanks (T. Roosevelt); Marshall (Wilson)
Iowa: Wallace (F. D. Roosevelt)
Kansas: Curtis (Hoover)
Kentucky (3): R. M. Johnson (Van Buren); Breckinridge (Buchanan); Barkley (Truman)
Maine: Hamlin (Lincoln)
Massachusetts (2): J. Adams (Washington); H. Wilson (Grant)
New Jersey (2): Burr (Jefferson); Hobart (McKinley)
New York (9): Clinton (Jefferson-Madison); Tompkins (Monroe); Van Buren (Jackson); Fillmore (Taylor); Wheeler (Hayes); Arthur (Garfield); Morton (B. Harrison); T. Roosevelt (McKinley); Sherman (Taft)
   New York City: Tompkins (Monroe)
Pennsylvania: Dallas (Polk)
South Carolina: Calhoun (J. Q. Adams-Jackson)
Tennessee: A. Johnson (Lincoln)
Texas: Garner (F. D. Roosevelt)
Vermont: Coolidge (Harding)
Virginia (2): Jefferson (J. Adams); Tyler (W. H. Harrison)
Washington, D. C.: Gerry (Madison)
   Lay in state in Capitol Rotunda: H. Wilson (Grant)

WAR MESSAGES

Gave war messages [7]: J. Adams, Madison, Polk, Lincoln, McKinley, Wilson, F. D. Roosevelt

WIVES OF PRESIDENTS

MARITAL DATA:

Age at marriage:
   Youngest: Eliza Johnson
   Teens (5): Abigail Adams, Elizabeth Monroe, Eliza Johnson, Alice Roosevelt, Marie (Mamie) Eisenhower

Twenties (30): Martha Washington, Martha Jefferson, Dorothea (Dolley) Madison, Louisa Adams, Rachel Jackson, Hannah Van Buren, Anna Harrison, Letitia Tyler, Julia Tyler, Sarah Polk, Margaret Taylor, Abigail Fillmore, Jane Pierce, Mary Lincoln, Julia Grant, Lucy Hayes, Lucretia Garfield, Ellen Arthur, Frances Cleveland, Caroline Harrison, Ida McKinley, Edith Roosevelt, Helen Taft, Ellen Wilson, Grace Coolidge, Lou Hoover, Anna Eleanor Roosevelt, Jacqueline Kennedy, Claudia (Lady Bird) Johnson, Thelma (Pat) Nixon

Thirties (3): Mary Harrison, Florence Harding, Elizabeth (Bess) Truman

Forties (2): Caroline Fillmore, Edith Wilson

Older than husbands (6): Martha Washington, Abigail Fillmore, Caroline Harrison, Florence Harding, Lou Hoover, Thelma (Pat) Nixon

Most senior to husband: Florence Harding

Wives of presidents who were not first ladies (7): Martha Jefferson, Rachel Jackson, Hannah Van Buren, Caroline Fillmore, Ellen Arthur, Mary Harrison, Alice Roosevelt

Widows at marriage (6): Martha Washington, Martha Jefferson, Dorothea (Dolley) Madison, Caroline Fillmore (second wife), Mary Harrison (second wife), Edith Wilson (second wife)

Survived husbands (23): Martha Washington, Dorothea (Dolley) Madison, Louisa Adams, Anna Harrison, Julia Tyler, Sarah Polk, Margaret Taylor, Caroline Fillmore, Mary Lincoln, Eliza Johnson, Julia Grant, Lucretia Garfield, Frances Cleveland, Mary Harrison, Ida McKinley, Edith Roosevelt, Helen Taft, Edith Wilson, Florence Harding, Grace Coolidge, Anna Eleanor Roosevelt, Marie (Mamie) Eisenhower, Jacqueline Kennedy

Remarried (2): Frances Cleveland, Jacqueline Kennedy

Survived by husbands (14): Abigail Adams, Martha Jefferson, Elizabeth Monroe, Rachel Jackson, Hannah Van Buren, Letitia Tyler, Abigail Fillmore, Jane Pierce, Lucy Hayes, Ellen Arthur, Caroline Harrison, Alice Roosevelt, Ellen Wilson, Lou Hoover

VITAL STATISTICS:

Age:

Lived to most advanced age: Mary Harrison

Reached age of 70 (17): Martha Washington, Abigail Adams, Dorothea (Dolley) Madison, Louisa Adams, Anna Harrison, Sarah Polk, Julia Grant, Lucretia Garfield, Frances Cleveland, Mary Harrison, Edith Roosevelt, Helen Taft, Edith Wilson, Grace Coolidge, Anna Eleanor Roosevelt, Elizabeth (Bess) Truman, Marie (Mamie) Eisenhower

Reached age of 75 (15): Dorothea (Dolley) Madison, Louisa Adams, Anna Harrison, Sarah Polk, Julia Grant, Lucretia Garfield, Frances Cleveland, Mary Harrison, Edith Roosevelt, Helen Taft, Edith Wilson, Grace Coolidge, Anna Eleanor Roosevelt, Elizabeth (Bess) Truman, Marie (Mamie) Eisenhower

Reached age of 80 (10): Dorothea (Dolley) Madison, Anna Harrison, Sarah Polk, Lucretia Garfield, Frances Cleveland, Mary Harrison, Edith Roosevelt, Helen Taft, Edith Wilson, Elizabeth (Bess) Truman

Reached age of 85 (7): Anna Harrison, Sarah Polk, Lucretia Garfield, Mary Harrison, Edith Roosevelt, Edith Wilson, Elizabeth (Bess) Truman

Dates of birth:

January (2): Julia Grant, Grace Coolidge

February (2): Louisa Adams, Elizabeth (Bess) Truman

March (5): Hannah Van Buren, Abigail Fillmore, Jane Pierce, Lou Hoover, Thelma (Pat) Nixon

April (2): Lucretia Garfield, Mary Harrison

May (3): Dorothea (Dolley) Madison, Julia Tyler, Ellen Wilson

June (5): Martha Washington, Elizabeth Monroe, Rachel Jackson, Ida McKinley, Helen Taft

July (4): Anna Harrison, Frances Cleveland, Alice Roosevelt, Jacqueline Kennedy

August (4): Lucy Hayes, Ellen Arthur, Edith Roosevelt, Florence Harding

September (2): Sarah Polk, Margaret Taylor

October (6): Martha Jefferson, Caroline Fillmore, Eliza Johnson, Caroline Harrison, Edith Wilson, Anna Eleanor Roosevelt

November (3): Abigail Adams, Letitia Tyler, Marie (Mamie) Eisenhower

December (2): Mary Lincoln, Claudia (Lady Bird) Johnson

Places of birth:

Abroad (London, England): Louisa Adams
Connecticut: Edith Roosevelt
Georgia: Ellen Wilson
Iowa (2): Lou Hoover, Marie (Mamie) Eisenhower
Kentucky: Mary Lincoln
Maryland: Margaret Taylor
Massachusetts (2): Abigail Adams, Alice Roosevelt
Missouri (2): Julia Grant, Elizabeth (Bess) Truman
Nevada: Thelma (Pat) Nixon
New Hampshire: Jane Pierce
New Jersey (Morristown) (2): Anna Harrison, Caroline Fillmore
New York (7): Elizabeth Monroe, Hannah Van Buren, Julia Tyler, Abigail Fillmore, Frances Cleveland, Anna Eleanor Roosevelt, Jacqueline Kennedy
 New York City (2): Elizabeth Monroe, Anna Eleanor Roosevelt
North Carolina: Dorothea (Dolley) Madison
Ohio (6): Lucy Hayes, Lucretia Garfield, Caroline Harrison, Ida McKinley, Helen Taft, Florence Harding
Pennsylvania: Mary Harrison
Tennessee (2): Sarah Polk, Eliza Johnson
Texas: Claudia (Lady Bird) Johnson
Vermont: Grace Coolidge
Virginia (6): Martha Washington, Martha Jefferson, Rachel Jackson, Letitia Tyler, Ellen Arthur, Edith Wilson

Dates of death:

On husband's birthday: Edith Wilson
Before husband's election (4): Martha Jefferson, Hannah Van Buren, Ellen Arthur, Alice Roosevelt
After election, before inauguration: Rachel Jackson
Before husband's inauguration (5): Martha Jefferson, Rachel Jackson, Hannah Van Buren, Ellen Arthur, Alice Roosevelt

Places of death:

California: Lucretia Garfield
Illinois: Mary Lincoln
Maryland: Frances Cleveland

Massachusetts (3): Abigail Adams, Jane Pierce, Grace Coolidge
Mississippi: Margaret Taylor
New York (8): Hannah Van Buren, Caroline Fillmore, Ellen Arthur, Mary Harrison, Alice Roosevelt, Edith Roosevelt, Lou Hoover, Anna Eleanor Roosevelt
 New York City (5): Ellen Arthur, Mary Harrison, Alice Roosevelt, Lou Hoover, Anna Eleanor Roosevelt
Ohio (4): Anna Harrison, Lucy Hayes, Ida McKinley, Florence Harding
Tennessee (3): Rachel Jackson, Sarah Polk, Eliza Johnson
Virginia (4): Martha Jefferson, Martha Washington, Elizabeth Monroe, Julia Tyler
Washington, D. C. (9): Dorothea (Dolley) Madison, Louisa Adams, Letitia Tyler, Abigail Fillmore, Julia Grant, Caroline Harrison, Helen Taft, Ellen Wilson, Edith Wilson
 White House (3): Letitia Tyler, Caroline Harrison, Ellen Wilson

Places of burial:

California: Lou Hoover
Georgia: Ellen Wilson
Illinois: Mary Lincoln
Indiana (2): Caroline Harrison, Mary Harrison
Iowa: Lou Hoover (reinterred, 1964)
Kentucky: Margaret Taylor
Massachusetts (3): Abigail Adams, Louisa Adams, Alice Roosevelt
New Hampshire: Jane Pierce
New York (7): Hannah Van Buren, Abigail Fillmore, Caroline Fillmore, Julia Grant, Ellen Arthur, Edith Roosevelt, Anna Eleanor Roosevelt
 New York City: Julia Grant
Ohio (5): Anna Harrison, Lucy Hayes, Lucretia Garfield, Ida McKinley, Florence Harding
Tennessee (3): Rachel Jackson, Sarah Polk, Eliza Johnson
Vermont: Grace Coolidge
Virginia (7): Martha Jefferson, Martha Washington, Dorothea (Dolley) Madison, Elizabeth Monroe, Letitia Tyler, Julia Tyler, Helen Taft
 Arlington National Cemetery: Helen Taft
Washington, D. C.: Edith Wilson

See also **FAMILY RELATIONSHIPS,** MARRIAGE, CHILDREN; **FIRST LADIES**

INDEX OF NAMES